NDER THE SUN

SCIENCE & TECHNOLOGY • BUILDINGS & STRUCTURES

INMENT • HUMAN WORLD • HUMAN ACHIEVEMENTS

RLD • HUMAN BEING • SCIENCE & TECHNOLOGY

WORLD • ARTS & ENTERTAINMENT • HUMAN WORLD

RTH & SPACE • LIVING WORLD • HUMAN BEING

RANSPORT • BUSINESS WORLD • ARTS & ENTERTAINMENT

TS & GAMES • EARTH & SPACE • LIVING WORLD

GS & STRUCTURES • TRANSPORT • BUSINESS WORLD

ACHIEVEMENTS • SPORTS & GAMES • EARTH & SPACE

NOLOGY • BUILDINGS & STRUCTURES • TRANSPORT

WORLD • HUMAN ACHIEVEMENTS • SPORTS & GAMES

The New Guinness Book of Records 1995

Editor
Peter Matthews

Founding Editor
Norris D. McWhirter

GUINNESS PUBLISHING

Copyright

British Library Cataloguing in Publication Data
A catalogue record for this book is available from the British Library

ISBN 0-85112-736-3. Australian Edition 0-85112-737-1.
'Guinness' is a registered trade mark of Guinness Publishing Ltd.

Printed and bound in Spain by Printer Industria Gráfica S.A., Barcelona

Contents

Features shown in italics

Introduction

Every day new records are set all around the world. Some occur through natural growth, some where existing records need updating, some from exciting new discoveries in science and technology. Most, however, come from the striving by men and women to set new standards.

Such achievements may come in areas of widespread interest, while others can only be fully appreciated by those with similar specialist skills.

Our collection of extremes, in, on and beyond the Earth has, we know, considerable appeal to peoples of all nations, and, of course, our book appears in many languages. Records in all categories can be fascinating, inspiring a variety of emotions, including incredulity, wonder and sorrow, but our aim is to inform and educate and to settle arguments which develop when people discuss facts.

The very existence of *The Guinness Book of Records* stimulates some into record-breaking endeavours. While some records can only be attained by people who have dedicated their lives to acquiring expertise, we are also very keen to include records to which people of no particular brilliance can contribute and I would mention in this context mass participation activities. Records such as the most people to collect litter in one city in one day, or to plant the most trees can be of benefit to society. While others such as the largest unsupported circle or the biggest teddy bears' picnic can simply be fun activities in which to be involved. Such categories present problems of logistics to the organisers but can also be of great benefit by providing fund-raising opportunities for charity.

The extent of change in *The Guinness Book of Records* each year is considerable. Not only are records continually being broken, but we are regularly changing the contents and introducing new items of widespread appeal, although they must be measurable and comparable—our basic criteria for inclusion as a record. This year we have also made extensive changes in modernising the design, incorporating many more

**Peter Matthews
with the editorial team. From left to right:
Amanda Brooks, Nicholas Heath-Brown, Peter Matthews,
Sarah Llewellyn-Jones, Stewart Newport and Debbie Collings.**

illustrations as well as features concentrating on the stories behind the records, interviews with record-breakers and quiz questions. Our aim is to make the enormous amount of information contained in the book as accessible as possible to all our readers.

Peter Matthews

Peter Matthews, Editor

GUINNESS PUBLISHING LTD, 33 LONDON ROAD, ENFIELD, MIDDLESEX, EN2 6DJ, ENGLAND

The story of the Guinness Book

The Guinness Book of Records was first produced to assist in resolving arguments that might take place on matters of fact.

The genesis of the idea came in 1951 when the then managing director of Guinness, Sir Hugh Beaver (1890–1967), was out shooting on the North Slob, by the River Slaney in County Wexford in the south-east of Ireland. Some golden plover were missed by the party, and later he discovered that reference books in the library of his host at Castlebridge House could not confirm whether that bird was Europe's fastest game bird.

Sir Hugh's experience led him to the view that there must be numerous such questions regarding superlatives debated nightly in the 81,400 pubs in Britain and in Ireland in which Guinness beer was on sale. On 12 September 1954 Norris and Ross McWhirter, then running a fact finding agency in London, were invited to the Guinness Brewery at Park Royal in north-west London to discuss the proposition that a collection of records should be published, and they so impressed the Guinness Board that they were immediately commissioned to follow it through.

An office was set up at 107 Fleet Street and intense work began. Less than a year later the inaugural edition, containing 198 pages, was produced, with the first copy bound on 27 August 1955. Well before Christmas the Guinness Book was No. 1 on the best-sellers list, and every edition since has been similarly represented.

The first US edition was published in New York in 1956, followed by editions in French (1962) and German (1963). In 1967 there were first editions in Danish, Japanese, Norwegian and Spanish, and the following year editions were published in Finnish, Italian and Swedish. In the 1970s there followed Czech, Dutch, Hebrew, Icelandic, Portuguese and Serb; in the 1980s translations into Arabic, Chinese, Greek, Hindi, Hungarian, Indonesian, Malay, Slovene and Turkish followed. Most recently, in the 1990s, editions have been published in Bulgarian, Korean, Macedonian, Malayalam, Polish, Romanian and Russian.

Our hope remains that, as for the first edition, so this new edition can assist in resolving inquiries on facts, and may turn the heat of argument into the light of knowledge.

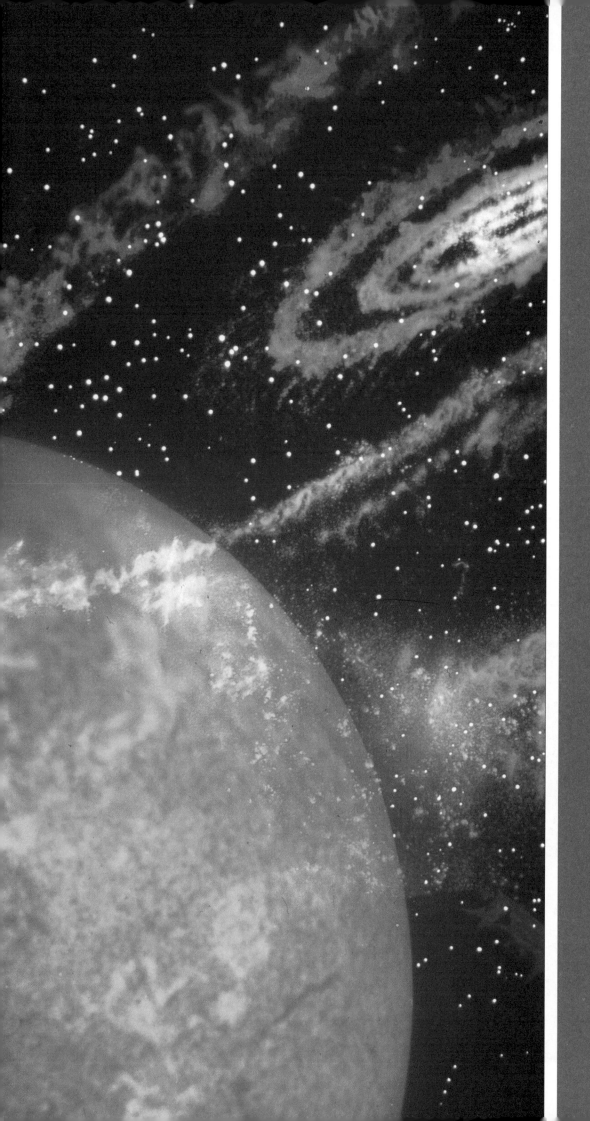

Earth & Space

The Universe

LIGHT YEAR—the distance travelled by light, the speed of which is 299,792.458 km/sec *186,282.397 miles/sec*, in one tropical year (365.24219878 mean solar days at January 0.12 hours Ephemeris time in AD 1900). It is equivalent to 9,460,528,405,000 km *5,878,499,814,000 miles*.

Largest structure in the Universe In November 1989 Margaret Geller and John Huchra (USA) announced the discovery of a 'Great Wall' in space. This is a concentration of galaxies in the form of a 'crumpled membrane' with a minimum extent of 280×800 million light years (2.6×10^{21} km $\times$ 7.5×10^{21} km *1.6×10^{21} miles $\times$ 4.7×10^{21} miles*) and a depth of up to 23 million light years (2.2×10^{20} km *1.4×10^{20} miles*).

Galaxies The largest is the central galaxy of the Abell 2029 galaxy cluster, 1070 million light years (1.01×10^{22} km *6.3×10^{21} miles*) distant in Virgo. Its discovery was announced in July 1990 by Juan M. Uson, Stephen P. Boughn and Jeffrey R. Kuhn (USA). It has a major diameter of 5,600,000 light years (5.3×10^{19} km *3.3×10^{19} miles*), which is eighty times the diameter of our own Milky Way galaxy, and has a light output equivalent to 2 trillion (2×10^{12}) Suns.

Our own galaxy is only one of 10 billion galaxies. It has a visible diameter of 75,000 light years (7.1×10^{17} km *4.4×10^{17} miles*) but is detectable up to at least three times this value. It has a mass 4×10^{11} times that of the Sun which is currently 26,100 light years (2.5×10^{17} km *1.5×10^{17} miles*) from the centre. It is part of the so-called 'Local Group', which is being gravitationally attracted towards the centre of the 'Local Supercluster', which is dominated by the Virgo Cluster of galaxies.

The brightest galaxy (or galaxy in the process of forming) is IRAS F10214+4724, which was detected as a faint source by IRAS (Infra Red Astronomy Satellite) in 1983 but was shown in February 1991 to have a far-infrared luminosity 3×10^{14} times greater than that of the Sun. It has a red shift of 2.286, equivalent to a distance of 11,600 million light years (1.10×10^{23} km *6.8×10^{22} miles*), but the remotest galaxy is the radio source 4C41.17, determined by K. Chambers, G. Miley and W. Van Bruegel in January 1990 to have a red shift of 3.800, equivalent to a distance of 12,800 million light years (1.21×10^{23} km *7.5×10^{22} miles*).

Age of the Universe For the age of the Universe a consensus value of 14±3 aeons or gigayears (an aeon or gigayear being 1000 million years) is obtained from various cosmological techniques. The equivalent value of the Hubble constant—named after Edwin Hubble (1889–1953) who first measured galactic distances in the 1920s—is 70±15 km per sec per megaparsec.

It was announced on 23 Apr 1992 that the COBE (Cosmic Background Explorer) satellite, launched by NASA on 18 Nov 1989, had detected minute fluctuations from the cosmic microwave background temperature of −270.424°C *−454.763°F*. This has been interpreted as evidence for the initial formation of galaxies within the Universe only a million years after the Big Bang (⇨ Stars, oldest).

Remotest object The interpretation of the red shifts of quasars in terms of distance is limited by a lack of knowledge of the Universal constants. The record red shift is 4.897 for the quasar PC 1247+3406 as determined by Donald P. Schneider, Maarten Schmidt and James E. Gunn and announced in May 1991, following spectroscopic and photometric observations made in February and April of the same year using the Hale Telescope at Palomar Observatory, California, USA. If it is assumed that there is an 'observable horizon', where the speed of recession is equal to the speed of light, i.e. at 14,000 million light years or 1.32×10^{23} km *8.23×10^{22} miles*, then a simple interpretation would place this quasar at 94.4 per cent of this value or 13,200 million light years (1.25×10^{23} km *7.8×10^{22} miles*).

Farthest visible object The remotest heavenly body visible with the naked eye is the Great Galaxy in Andromeda (mag. 3.47), known as Messier 31. It was first noted from Germany by Simon Marius (1570–1624). It is a rotating nebula in spiral form at a distance from the Earth of about 2,309,000 light years, or 2.18×10^{19} km *1.36×10^{19} miles*, and our Galaxy is moving towards it. Under good conditions for observations, Messier 33, the Spiral in Triangulum (mag. 5.79), can be glimpsed by the naked eye at a distance of 2,509,000 light years.

Quasars Quasi-stellar radio sources (quasars or QSOs) are believed to be the active centres of distant galaxies and appear as highly luminous point-like sources. Over 7200 are known and include the most luminous object in the sky, the quasar HS 1946+7658, which is at least 1.5×10^{15} times more luminous than the Sun. Its discovery was announced in July 1991 following the Hamburg Survey of northern quasars. This quasar has a red shift of 3.02 and is therefore at a distance of 12,400 million light years (1.17×10^{23} km *7.3×10^{22} miles*).

The most violent outburst observed in a quasar was recorded on 13 Nov 1989 by a joint US-Japanese team who noted that the energy output of the quasar PKS 0558−504 (which is about 2000 million light years distant) increased by two thirds in three minutes, equivalent to all the energy released by the Sun in 340,000 years.

Stars

MAGNITUDE—a measure of stellar brightness such that the light of a star of any magnitude bears a ratio of 2.511886 to that of a star of the next magnitude. Thus a fifth magnitude star is 2.511886 times brighter than a sixth magnitude star whilst a first magnitude star is 100 (or 2.511886^5) times brighter. Magnitude is expressed as a negative quantity for exceptionally bright bodies such as the Sun (apparent magnitude −26.78).

Nearest Excepting the special case of our own Sun, the nearest star is the very faint Proxima Centauri, discovered in 1915, which is 4.225 light years (4.00×10^{13} km *2.48×10^{13} miles*) away.

The nearest 'star' visible to the naked eye is the southern hemisphere binary Alpha Centauri, or Rigel Kentaurus (4.35 light years distant), with an apparent magnitude of −0.29. By AD 29,700 this binary will reach a minimum distance from the Earth of 2.84 light years and should then be the second brightest 'star', with an apparent magnitude of −1.20.

Largest The largest star is the M-class supergiant Betelgeux (Alpha Orionis—the top left star of Orion) which is 310 light years distant. It has a diameter of 700 million km *400 million miles*,

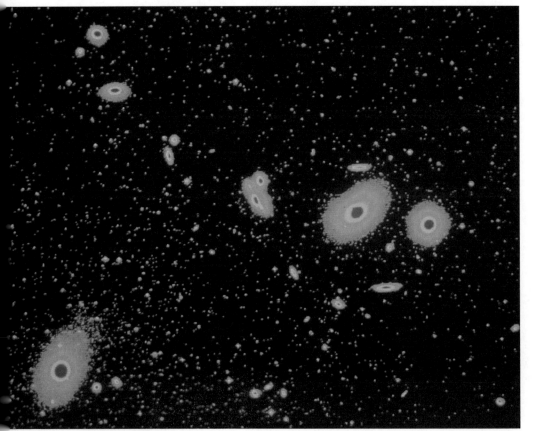

The Virgo Cluster of galaxies is the nearest major cluster of galaxies to our own 'Local Group'. We are approaching it at a speed of 720,000 km/h *450,000 mph*.

(Photo: Science Photo Library/Royal Observatory)

which is about 500 times greater than that of the Sun. It is surrounded by a dust 'shell' and also by an outer tenuous gas halo up to 8.5×10^{11} km *5.3 × 10¹¹ miles* in diameter.

Heaviest The heaviest star is the variable Eta Carinae, 9100 light years distant in the Carinae Nebula, with a mass 200 times greater than our own Sun.

Most luminous If all the stars could be viewed at the same distance, Eta Carinae would also be the most luminous star, with a total luminosity 6,500,000 times that of the Sun. However, the *visually* brightest star is the hypergiant Cygnus OB2 No. 12, which is 5900 light years distant. It has an absolute visual magnitude of −9.9 and is therefore visually 810,000 times brighter than the Sun. This brightness may be matched by the supergiant IV b 59 in the nearby galaxy Messier 101. During 1843 the absolute luminosity and absolute visual brightness of Eta Carinae temporarily increased to values 60 and 70 million times the corresponding values for the Sun.

Smallest Neutron stars, which may weigh up to three times the mass of the Sun, only have diameters of 10–30 km *6–19 miles*. Although black holes are point-like sources, their distortion of local space-time means that they appear as black stars, with a diameter of 59 km *37 miles* for one weighing ten times the mass of the Sun.

Lightest The white dwarf companion to the millisecond pulsar PSR 1957+20, the discovery of which was announced by A.S. Fruchter, D.R. Stinebring and J.H. Taylor in April 1988, has a mass only 0.02 that of the Sun and is being evaporated away by the fast-spinning neutron star. Brown dwarves such as the candidate GD 165B (⇨ below) are expected to have a mass 0.05 that of the Sun whilst normal stars (those undergoing continuous fusion of hydrogen) cannot have a mass less than 0.08 that of the Sun.

Dimmest GD 165B, the brown dwarf candidate companion to the white dwarf GD 165A which is 117 light years distant, is the dimmest star. It has a luminosity ten thousand times less than that of the Sun and a visual brightness eight million times less. Its discovery was announced by E.E. Becklin and B. Zuckerman in September 1988.

Brightest (As seen from earth) Sirius A (Alpha Canis Majoris), 8.64 light years distant, is the brightest star in the sky with an apparent magnitude of −1.46 at present, but this will rise to a maximum of −1.67 by AD 61,000. It has a diameter of 2.33 million km *1.45 million miles*, a mass 2.14 times greater than that of the Sun, and is visually 24 times brighter.

Youngest The youngest stars appear to be two protostars known collectively as IRAS−4 buried deep in dust clouds in the nebula NGC 1333, which is 1100 light years (1.04×10^{16} km *6.5 × 10¹⁵ miles*) distant. Announced in May 1991 by a combined British, German and American team, these protostars will not blaze forth as fully fledged stars for at least another 100,000 years.

Oldest The oldest stars in the Galaxy have been detected in the halo, high above the disc of the Milky Way, by a group, led by Timothy Beers (USA), which discovered 70 such stars by January

A star which has undergone complete gravitational collapse is known as a black hole. This artist's impression is of a binary star system consisting of a black hole and a normal orange-red star, with gas being pulled from the atmosphere of the normal star by the immense gravitational field of its companion.
(Photo: Science Photo Library/Dr Seth Shostak)

1991 but eventually expect to detect 500. Such stars would have been formed *c.*1 billion years after the Big Bang (⇨ Age of the Universe).

Pulsars For pulsars whose spin rates have been accurately measured, the fastest spinning is PSR B1937+214, which was discovered by a group led by Donald C. Backer in November 1982. It is in the minor constellation Vulpecula (the Little Fox), 16,000 light years (1.51×10^{17} km *9.4 × 10¹⁶ miles*) distant, and has a pulse period of 1.5578064883 millisec, which is equivalent to a spin rate of 641.9282546 revolutions per sec. However, the pulsar which has the slowest spin down rate, and is therefore the most accurate stellar clock, is PSR B1855+09 (discovered in December 1985) at only 2.1×10^{-20} sec per sec.

Brightest supernova The brightest ever seen by historic man is believed to be SN 1006, noted in April 1006 near Beta Lupi, which flared for two years and attained a magnitude of −9 to −10. The remnant is believed to be the radio source G 327.6+14.5, nearly 3000 light years distant. Others have occurred in 1054, 1604, 1885, and most recently on 23 Feb 1987, when Ian Shelton sighted that designated −69° 202 in the Large Magellanic Cloud 170,000 light years distant. This supernova was visible to the naked eye when at its brightest in May 1987.

Black Holes This term for a star that has undergone complete gravitational collapse was first used by Prof. John Archibald Wheeler at an Institute for Space Studies meeting in New York City, USA on 29 Dec 1967.

The best black hole candidate is the central star of the binary (or triple) star system V404 which is 5000 light years (4.7×10^{16} km *2.9 × 10¹⁶ miles*) distant in the constellation Cygnus and which first showed a possible black hole signature as the transient X-ray source GS 2023+338, discovered by the Ginga satellite in May 1989. In September 1991 J. Casares, P.A. Charles and T. Naylor firmly established the mass as being greater than six times that of the Sun (and more likely eight to fifteen times).

Constellations The largest of the 88 constellations is Hydra (the Sea Serpent), which covers 1302.844 deg² or 3.16 per cent of the whole sky and contains at least 68 stars visible to the naked eye (to 5.5 mag). The constellation Centaurus (Centaur), ranking ninth in area, however, embraces at least 94 such stars.

The smallest constellation is Crux Australis (Southern Cross), with an area of only 0.16 per cent of the whole sky, viz. 68.477 deg² compared with the 41,252.96 deg² of the whole sky.

The Sun

ASTRONOMICAL UNIT—the mean distance from the centre of the Earth to the centre of the Sun as defined in 1938, equivalent to 149,597,871 km *92,955,807 miles.*

Distance extremes The true distance of the Earth from the Sun is 1.00000102 astronomical units or 149,598,023 km *92,955,902 miles.* Our orbit being elliptical, the distance of the Sun varies between a minimum (perihelion) of 147,098,100 km *91,402,500 miles* and a maximum (aphelion) of 152,097,900 km *94,509,300 miles.* Based on an orbital circumference of 939,886,500 km *584,018,400 miles* and an orbital period (sidereal year) of 365.256366 days, the average orbital velocity is 107,220 km/h *66,620 mph*, but this varies between a minimum of 105,450 km/h *65,520 mph* at aphelion and a maximum of 109,030 km/h *67,750 mph* at perihelion.

Temperature and dimensions The Sun has a stellar classification of a *yellow dwarf* type G2, although its mass at 1.9889×10^{27} tonnes is 332,946.04 times that of the Earth and represents over 99 per cent of the total mass of the Solar System. The solar diameter at 1,392,140 km *865,040 miles* leads to a density of 1.408 times that of water or a quarter that of the Earth.

The Sun has a central temperature of about 15,400,000 K and a core pressure of 25.4 PPa *1650 million tons/in².* It uses up about 4 million tonnes of hydrogen per sec, equal to an energy output of 3.85×10^{26} watts, although it will have taken 10,000 million years to exhaust its energy supply (about 5000 million years from the present). The luminous intensity of the Sun is 2.7×10^{27} candela, which is equal to a luminance of 4.5×10^{8} candela/m² *290,000 candela/in²* (⇨ also Sunspots).

Sunspots To be visible to the *protected* naked eye, a sunspot must cover about one two-thousandth part of the Sun's disc and thus have an area of about 1300 million km² *500 million miles².*

The largest sunspot ever noted was in the Sun's southern hemisphere on 8 Apr 1947. Its area was about 18,000 million km² *7000 million miles²*, with an extreme longitude of 300,000 km *187,000 miles* and an extreme latitude of 145,000 km *90,000 miles.* Sunspots appear darker because they are more than 1500°C *2700°F* cooler than the rest of the Sun's surface temperature of 5507°C *9945°F.*

In October 1957 a smoothed sunspot count showed 263, the highest recorded index since records started in 1755 (cf. the previous record of 239 in May 1778). In 1943 one sunspot lasted for 200 days, from June to December.

Planets

Largest The nine major planets (including Earth) are bodies within the Solar System and revolve round the Sun in definite orbits.

Jupiter, with an equatorial diameter of 142,984 km *88,846 miles* and a polar diameter of 133,708 km *83,082 miles*, is the largest of the nine major planets, with a mass 317.828 times, and a volume 1323.3 times, that of the Earth. It also has the shortest period of rotation, resulting in a Jovian day of only 9 hr 50 min 30.003 sec in the equatorial zone.

Smallest and coldest The discovery of Pluto by Clyde William Tombaugh (US) at the Lowell Observatory, Flagstaff, Arizona, USA was announced on 13 Mar 1930. The planet has a diameter of 2280 km *1417 miles* and a mass 0.0021 that of the Earth. The discovery of Pluto's moon Charon was announced on 22 Jun 1978 from the US Naval Observatory, Flagstaff, Arizona. Although the surface temperature of Pluto is only approximately known, its surface composition suggests that it must be similar to the value of −235°C *−391°F* measured for Neptune's moon

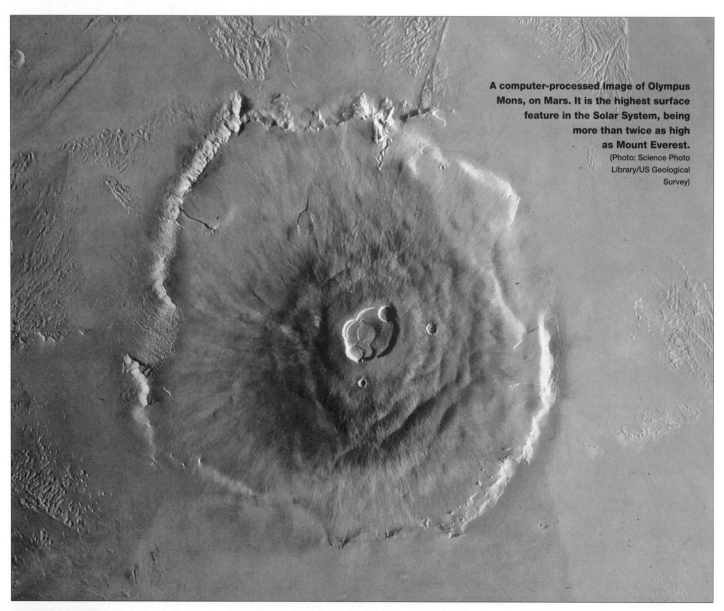

A computer-processed image of Olympus Mons, on Mars. It is the highest surface feature in the Solar System, being more than twice as high as Mount Everest.
(Photo: Science Photo Library/US Geological Survey)

The largest scale model of the solar system was developed by the Lakeview Museum of Arts and Sciences in Peoria, Illinois, USA. All of the planets were made to scale and were at the appropriate distance from the museum. The photograph below shows Mars and information on the Community Solar System. Sheldon Schafer, the museum's Science Director, is seen on the right with Jupiter.
(Photos: Lakeview Museum, USA)

The Lakeview Museum scale model was first displayed in April 1992. The Sun, with a diameter of 11 m *36 ft*, was painted on the exterior of the museum's planetarium, and the planets (spheres ranging in diameter from 2.5 cm *1 in* in the case of Pluto up to 1.1 m *3 ft 9 in* for Jupiter) were situated in appropriate locations in accordance with their distance from the Sun. This meant that the Earth was 1.2 km *¾ mile* away, with Pluto being in the town of Kewanee, some 64 km *40 miles* from the museum.

A smaller model of the solar system was created by Lars Broman and inaugurated by the Futures' Museum, Borlänge, Sweden on 29 Nov 1986. Its Sun had a diameter of 1.5 m *5 ft* and the planets ranged from 3.5 mm *⅛ in* to 140 mm *5½ in* in diameter, with the closest to the Sun being 60 m *200 ft* away and the furthest 6 km *3¾ miles* away. However, unlike the American model it also included the nearest star to the Sun, Proxima Centauri, which was sited to scale in the Museum of Victoria, Melbourne, Australia.

GUESS WHAT?
Q Which is the brightest star?
A See Page 7

Triton, the lowest observed surface temperature of any natural body in the Solar System.

Outermost The Pluto–Charon system orbits at a mean distance from the Sun of 5914 million km *3674 million miles* in a period of 248.54 years. The aphelion distance of 7395 million km *4595 million miles* is the greatest distance travelled by any non-cometary planetary bodies (this will next occur in AD 2113). Because of their large orbital eccentricities they are closer to the Sun than Neptune between 23 Jan 1979 and 15 Mar 1999. However, the mean distance of Pluto is less than that of the Kuiper belt object 1992 QB$_1$—the discovery of which was announced by David Jewitt (UK) and Jane Luu (USA) on 14 Sep 1992—which orbits at 6557 million km *4074 million miles*, although tentative evidence suggests that a second object 1993 FW, discovered by Luu and Jewitt on 28 Mar 1993, may be even further out. Based on the definition that the remotest Solar System object is that with the largest perihelion, this would be 1993 FW, which does not appear to approach the Sun closer than a distance of 6305 million km *3918 million miles*.

Fastest Mercury, which orbits the Sun at an average distance of 57,909,200 km *35,983,100 miles*, has a period of revolution of 87.9686 days, so giving the highest average speed in orbit of 172,248 km/h *107,030 mph*.

Hottest For Venus a surface temperature of 462°C *864°F* has been estimated from measurements made from the Soviet *Venera* and American *Pioneer* surface probes.

Nearest The fellow planet closest to the Earth is Venus, which is, at times, only 41,360,000 km *25,700,000 miles* inside the Earth's orbit, compared with Mars' closest approach of

55,680,000 km *34,600,000 miles* outside the Earth's orbit.

Brightest and faintest Viewed from the Earth, by far the brightest of the five planets visible to the naked eye is Venus, with a maximum magnitude of −4.4. Uranus, the first to be discovered by telescope when it was sighted by Sir William Herschel from his garden at 19 New King St, Bath on 13 Mar 1781, is only marginally visible, with a magnitude of 5.5. The faintest planet is Pluto, with a magnitude of 15.0.

Densest and least dense Earth is the densest planet, with an average density of 5.515 times that of water, while Saturn has an average density only about one-eighth of this value or 0.685 times that of water.

Surface features By far the highest and most spectacular surface feature on any planet is the volcano Olympus Mons (formerly Nix Olympica) in the Tharsis region of Mars. It has a diameter of 500–600 km *310–370 miles* and a height of 26 ± 3 km *75,450–95,150 ft* above the surrounding plain.

Conjunctions The most dramatic recorded conjunction of the seven principal members of the Solar System besides the Earth (Sun, Moon, Mercury, Venus, Mars, Jupiter and Saturn) occurred on 5 Feb 1962, when 16° covered all seven during an eclipse in the Pacific area. It is possible that the seven-fold conjunction of September 1186 spanned only 12°. The next notable conjunction will take place on 5 May 2000.

Satellites

Most and least The Solar System has a total of 61 satellites, with Saturn having the most at 18

whilst Earth and Pluto only have one satellite each and Mercury and Venus none. The most recently discovered, announced on 16 Jul 1990 by Mark R. Showalter (USA), is the Saturnian satellite Pan (Saturn XVIII) which was found on eleven *Voyager 2* photographs taken during the close approach in August 1981. It has a diameter of only about 20 km *12 miles* and orbits within the 322 km *200 mile* Encke gap in the A ring.

Distance extremes The distance of satellites from their parent planets varies from the 9377 km *5827 miles* of Phobos from the centre of Mars to the 23,700,000 km *14,700,000 miles* of Jupiter's outer satellite Sinope (Jupiter IX).

Largest and smallest The largest and heaviest satellite is Ganymede (Jupiter III), which is 2.017 times heavier than the Earth's Moon and has a diameter of 5268 km *3273 miles*. Of satellites whose diameters have been measured the smallest is Deimos, the outermost moon of Mars. Although irregularly shaped it has an average diameter of 12.5 km *7.8 miles*.

Asteroids

Number and distance extremes There are an estimated 45,000 asteroids but the orbits of only about 6100 have been computed. Whilst most orbit between Mars and Jupiter, distances from the Sun vary between 20,890,000 km *12,980,000 miles* for the Apollo asteroid 3200 Phaethon (discovered 11 Oct 1983) at perihelion and 7131 million km *4431 million miles* for the Kuiper belt object 1992 QB$_1$ at aphelion (⇨ Planets, outermost).

Largest and smallest The largest asteroid is 1 Ceres (the first discovered, by G. Piazzi at Palermo, Sicily on 1 Jan 1801) with an equatorial diameter of 959 km *596 miles* and a polar diameter of 907 km *563 miles*. The smallest asteroid is 1993 KA$_2$, with a diameter of *c.* 5 m *16 ft*.

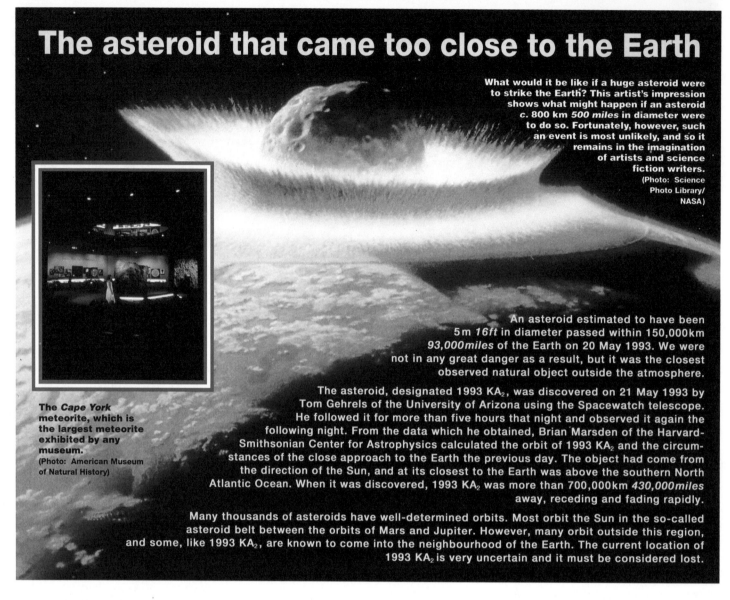

The asteroid that came too close to the Earth

What would it be like if a huge asteroid were to strike the Earth? This artist's impression shows what might happen if an asteroid *c.* 800 km *500 miles* in diameter were to do so. Fortunately, however, such an event is most unlikely, and so it remains in the imagination of artists and science fiction writers. (Photo: Science Photo Library/ NASA)

The *Cape York* meteorite, which is the largest meteorite exhibited by any museum. (Photo: American Museum of Natural History)

An asteroid estimated to have been 5 m *16 ft* in diameter passed within 150,000 km *93,000 miles* of the Earth on 20 May 1993. We were not in any great danger as a result, but it was the closest observed natural object outside the atmosphere.

The asteroid, designated 1993 KA$_2$, was discovered on 21 May 1993 by Tom Gehrels of the University of Arizona using the Spacewatch telescope. He followed it for more than five hours that night and observed it again the following night. From the data which he obtained, Brian Marsden of the Harvard-Smithsonian Center for Astrophysics calculated the orbit of 1993 KA$_2$ and the circumstances of the close approach to the Earth the previous day. The object had come from the direction of the Sun, and at its closest to the Earth was above the southern North Atlantic Ocean. When it was discovered, 1993 KA$_2$ was more than 700,000 km *430,000 miles* away, receding and fading rapidly.

Many thousands of asteroids have well-determined orbits. Most orbit the Sun in the so-called asteroid belt between the orbits of Mars and Jupiter. However, many orbit outside this region, and some, like 1993 KA$_2$, are known to come into the neighbourhood of the Earth. The current location of 1993 KA$_2$ is very uncertain and it must be considered lost.

Brightest and dimmest The brightest asteroid is 4 Vesta (discovered on 29 Mar 1807) with an absolute magnitude of 3.16. It is the only asteroid visible to the naked eye and attains a maximum apparent magnitude of 5.0 as viewed from the Earth. The dimmest asteroid is 1993KA$_2$ (⇨ above) whose absolute magnitude of 29 makes it the faintest object ever detected.

The Moon

The Earth's closest neighbour in space and its only natural satellite is the Moon, which has an average diameter of 3475.1 km *2159.3 miles* and a mass of 7.348×10^{19} tonnes, or 0.0123 Earth masses, so that its density is 3.344 times that of water.

The Moon orbits at a mean distance of 384,399.1 km *238,854.5 miles* centre-to-centre. In the present century the closest approach (smallest perigee) was 356,375 km *221,441 miles* centre-to-centre on 4 Jan 1912 and the farthest distance (largest apogee) was 406,711 km *252,718 miles* on 2 Mar 1984. The orbital period (sidereal month) is 27.321661 days, giving an average orbital velocity of 3683 km/h *2289 mph.*

Craters Only 59 per cent of the Moon's surface is directly visible from the Earth because it is in 'captured rotation', i.e. the period of rotation is equal to the period of orbit. The largest wholly visible crater is the walled plain Bailly, towards the Moon's South Pole, which is 295 km *183 miles* across, with walls rising to 4250 m *14,000 ft.* The

Orientale Basin, partly on the averted side, measures more than 960 km *600 miles* in diameter.

The deepest crater is the Newton Crater, with a floor estimated to be between 7000–8850 m *23,000–29,000 ft* below its rim and 4250 m *14,000 ft* below the level of the plain outside. The brightest (most reflective) directly visible spot on the Moon is Aristarchus.

Highest mountains In the absence of a sea level, lunar altitudes are measured relative to an adopted reference sphere of radius 1738.000 km *1079.943 miles.* Thus the greatest elevation attained on this basis by any of the US astronauts has been 7830 m *25,688 ft* on the Descartes Highlands by Capt. John Watts Young (USN) and Major Charles M. Duke, Jr on 27 Apr 1972.

Temperature extremes When the Sun is overhead the temperature on the lunar equator reaches 117°C *243°F* (17 deg C *31 deg F* above the boiling point of water). By sunset the temperature is 14°C *58°F,* but after nightfall it sinks to −163°C *−261°F.*

Eclipses

Earliest recorded Although computer programs can predict eclipses way back into history, there now appears to be no real evidence for ancient descriptions of eclipses prior to the partial eclipse observed in Ninevah in Assyria on 15 Jun 763 BC. The first definite evidence for a total eclipse stems from Chu-fu, China, observed on 17 Jul 709 BC.

The first description of a solar eclipse in Britain is that of 15 Feb 538, described in the Anglo-Saxon Chronicles with the Sun being two-thirds eclipsed in London. No centre of path of totality for a solar eclipse crossed London for the 837 years from 2 Nov 878 to 3 May 1715. On 14 Jun 2151 an eclipse will be 99 per cent total in London but total for a path stretching from Dover, Kent to Belfast. The next total eclipse in London will not occur until 5 May 2600. The most recent occasion when a line of totality of a solar eclipse crossed Great Britain was on 29 Jun 1927 but totality lasted only for 40 seconds and most of the track over north Wales and northern England was covered by cloud. The next instance of such an eclipse will clip the coast of Cornwall at St. Just at 10:10 a.m. on 11 Aug 1999 with totality there lasting 2 min 2 sec.

Longest duration The maximum *possible* duration of an eclipse of the Sun is 7 min 31 sec. The longest of recent date was on 20 Jun 1955 (7 min 8 sec), west of the Philippines, although it was clouded out along most of its track. An eclipse of 7 min 29 sec should occur in the mid-Atlantic Ocean on 16 Jul 2186.

The longest possible eclipse in the British Isles is 5 min 30 sec. In recent times that of 3 May 1715 was 4 min 4 sec but that of 22 Jul 2381, which will be observed in the Borders area, will last 5 min 10 sec.

The longest totality of any lunar eclipse is 104 minutes and has occurred many times.

Longest!

Although normally the longest possible duration of an eclipse of the Sun is 7 min 31 sec, durations can be extended when observers are airborne. The totality of the Sun was extended to 74 min for observers aboard a Concorde which took off from Toulouse, France and stayed in the shadow of the Moon from 10:51 to 12:05 GMT on 30 Jun 1973 over the Atlantic before landing in Chad.

Most and least frequent The highest number of eclipses possible in a year is seven, as in 1935, when there were five solar and two lunar eclipses. In 1982 there were four solar and three lunar eclipses. The lowest possible number in a year is two, both of which must be solar, as in 1944 and 1969. The only recent example of three total solar eclipses occurring at a single location was at a point 44°N, 67°E in Kazakhstan, east of the Aral Sea. These took place on 21 Sep 1941, 9 Jul 1945 and 25 Feb 1952.

Comets

Earliest recorded Records date from the 7th century BC. The successive appearances of Halley's Comet can be traced back to 240 BC. The first prediction of its return by Edmund Halley (1656–1742) proved true on Christmas Day 1758, 16 years after his death.

Largest The tail of the brilliant Great Comet of 1843 trailed for 330,000,000 km *205,000,000 miles*. The bow shock wave of Holmes Comet of 1892 once measured 2,400,000 km *1,500,000 miles* in diameter.

Brightest The brightest comets are held to be either the Cruls Comet of 1862 or the Ikeya-Seki Comet of 1965.

Shortest period The periodical comet which returns most frequently is the increasingly faint Encke's Comet, first identified in 1786 and only missed on 8 of its 63 returns. It has an orbital period of 1206 days (3.3 years) and has the closest approach to the Sun at 51 million km *32 million miles*, at which time its speed is 250,000 km/h *155,000 mph*. The most frequently observed comets are Schwassmann-Wachmann I, Kopff and Oterma, which can all be observed every year between Mars and Jupiter.

Longest period The longest period determined for a comet is 958 years, in the case of Comet 1894 Gale, equivalent to a mean distance of 14.5 billion km *9 billion miles*.

Closest approach On 1 Jul 1770, Lexell's Comet, travelling at 138,600 km/h *86,100 mph* (relative to the Sun), came to within 1,200,000 km *745,000 miles* of the Earth. However, more recently the Earth is believed to have passed through the tail of Halley's Comet on 19 May 1910.

Meteorites

When a *meteoroid* (consisting of broken fragments of cometary or asteroidal origin and ranging in size from fine dust to bodies several kilometres in diameter) penetrates to the Earth's surface, the remnant, which could be either aerolite (stony) or siderite (metallic), is described as a *meteorite*. Such events occur about 150 times per year over the whole land surface of the Earth.

In historic times the only recorded person injured by a meteorite was Ann Hodges of Sylacauga, Alabama, USA. On 30 Nov 1954 a 4 kg *9 lb* stone, some 18 cm *7 in* in length, crashed through the roof of her home, hitting Mrs Hodges on the arm and bruising her hip.

Oldest A revision by T. Kirsten in 1981 of the age estimates of meteorites which have remained essentially undisturbed after their formation suggests that the oldest which has been accurately dated is the Krähenberg meteorite at 4600 ± 20 million years, which is just within the initial period of Solar System formation. It was reported in August 1978 that dust grains in the Murchison meteorite which fell in Australia in September 1969 may be older than the Solar System.

Largest The largest known meteorite was found in 1920 at Hoba West, near Grootfontein in Namibia and is a block 2.7 m *9 ft* long by 2.4 m *8 ft* broad, estimated to weigh 59 tonnes. The largest meteorite exhibited by any museum is the *Cape York* meteorite, weighing 30,883 kg *68,085 lb*, found in 1897 near Cape York, on the west coast of Greenland, by the expedition of Commander (later Rear-Admiral) Robert Edwin Peary (1856–1920). It is now exhibited in the Hayden Planetarium in New York City, USA. The largest piece of stony meteorite recovered is a piece weighing 1770 kg *3902 lb*, part of a 4 tonne shower which struck Jilin (formerly Kirin), China on 8 Mar 1976.

Greatest!

The greatest meteor shower on record occurred on the night of 16–17 Nov 1966, when the Leonid meteors (which recur every 33¼ years) were visible between western North America and eastern Russia (then USSR). It was calculated that meteors passed over Arizona, USA at a rate of 2300 per min for a period of 20 min from 5 a.m. on 17 Nov 1966.

Greatest explosion The mysterious explosion of 10–15 megatons high explosive equivalent which occurred over the basin of the Podkamennaya Tunguska River on 30 Jun 1908 resulted in the devastation of an area of 3900 km² *1500 miles²* with the shock wave being felt up to 1000 km *625 miles* away. The cause has most recently been ascribed to the energy released following the total disintegration at an altitude of 10 km *33,000 ft* of a 30 m *98 ft* diameter common type stony meteoroid travelling at hypersonic velocity at an incoming angle of 45 degrees.

Lunar Twelve known meteorites are believed to be of lunar origin, as distinguished by characteristic element and isotopic ratios. The first eleven were found in Antarctica but the most recently discovered, which is only 3 cm *1 in* in diameter and weighs 19 g *0.67 oz*, was found at Calcalong Creek on the Nullarbor Plain to the north of the Great Australian Bight by D.H. Hill, W.V. Boynton and R.A. Haag (USA) with the discovery being announced in January 1991.

Craters It has been estimated that some 2000 asteroid Earth collisions have occurred in the last 600 million years. One hundred and two collision sites or astroblemes have been identified. A crater 240 km *150 miles* in diameter and 800 m *½ mile* deep was attributed to a meteorite in 1962 in Wilkes Land, Antarctica. Such a crater could have been caused by a meteorite weighing 13 billion tonnes striking at 70,800 km/h *44,000 mph*.

Soviet scientists reported in December 1970 an astrobleme with a diameter of 95 km *60 miles* and a maximum depth of 400 m *1300 ft* in the basin of the River Popigai. There is a crater-like formation or astrobleme 442 km *275 miles* in diameter on the eastern shore of the Hudson Bay, Canada, where the Nastapoka Islands are just off the coast. The largest and best-preserved crater which was definitely formed by a meteorite is the Coon Butte or Barringer Crater, discovered

GUESS WHAT?

Q Where is the largest volcano crater?

A See Page 20

---

24 Dec 1990

THE GUINNESS NEWS REVIEW

THE AMAZING CHRISTMAS PRESENT

Sleepy village hit 25 years ago today

In today's review we look back at the extraordinary events of Christmas Eve 1965, when the Leicestershire village of Barwell was hit by the largest meteorite ever to strike Britain. It was around 4.15 p.m. that there was a loud swishing noise and a man who was walking home took cover as he heard 5 or 6 thuds. A meteorite had landed!

The damage

Windows started to shatter, a factory roof was smashed, and the main street suddenly had a smoking crater in it. Joe Grewcock tried to pick up a piece of rock, and dropped it immediately he discovered how hot it was.

The figures

It is estimated that the total weight of the meteorite was 46 kg (102 lb). The largest single fragment, which was found by George Potterton, weighed 7.88 kg (17 lb 6 oz). It brought him a reward of £139 from the British Museum—not at all bad in those days.

in 1891, near Winslow, Arizona, USA. It is 1265m *4150ft* in diameter and now about 175m *575ft* deep, with a parapet rising 40–48m *130–155ft* above the surrounding plain. It has been estimated that an iron-nickel mass of some 2 million tonnes and a diameter of 61–79m *200–260ft* gouged this crater in *c.* 25,000 BC.

Brightest!

The brightest fireball ever photographically recorded was by Dr Zdeněk Ceplecha over Šumava, Czechoslovakia (now Czech Republic) on 4 Dec 1974. It had a momentary magnitude of –22 or around 10,000 times brighter than a full Moon.

The Earth

The Earth is approximately 4540 million years old. It is not a true sphere, but flattened at the poles and hence an oblate spheroid. The equatorial diameter (12,756.2726km *7926.3803 miles*) is 42.7694km *26.5757 miles* larger than the polar diameter of 12,713.5032km *7899.8046 miles*. The Earth has a pear-shaped asymmetry with the north pole radius being 45m *148ft* longer than the south pole radius. There is also a slight ellipticity of the equator with its major diameter at 14.95°W being 139m *456ft* longer than its minor axis. The greatest departures from the reference ellipsoid are a protuberance of 73m *240ft* in the area of Papua New Guinea and a depression of 105m *344ft* south of Sri Lanka, in the Indian Ocean.

The greatest circumference of the Earth, at the equator, is 40,075.012km *24,901.458 miles*, compared with 40,007.858km *24,859.731 miles* for the meridian. The area of the surface is estimated to be 510,065,500 km² *196,937,400 miles²* and the volume 1,083,207,000,000km³ *259,875,300,000 miles³*.

The mass of the Earth, which was first assessed by Dr Nevil Maskelyne (1732–1811) in Perthshire in 1774, is 5.974×10²¹tonnes and the density is 5.515 times that of water. The Earth picks up about 40,000 tonnes of cosmic dust a year. The true rotation period of the Earth, i.e. the mean sidereal day increased by 0.0084 sec to account for precession, is 23hr 56min 4.0989 sec mean solar time.

Structure and Dimensions

Oceans

The area of the Earth covered by oceans and seas (the hydrosphere) is estimated to be 362,033,000km² *139,782,000 miles²* or 70.98 per cent of the total surface. The mean depth of the hydrosphere is 3729m *12,234ft* and the volume 1,349,930,000km³ *323,870,000 miles³*, compared to 35,000,000km³ *8,400,000 miles³* of fresh water. The total weight of the water is 1.41 × 10¹⁸ tonnes, or 0.024 per cent of the Earth's weight.

Largest The largest ocean in the world is the Pacific. Excluding adjacent seas, it represents 45.9 per cent of the world's oceans and covers 166,241,700km² *64,186,300 miles²* in area. The average depth is 3940m *12,925ft*. The shortest

navigable trans-Pacific distance — between Guayaquil, Ecuador and Bangkok, Thailand — is 17,550 km *10,905 miles*.

Smallest The smallest ocean is the Arctic, which has an area of 13,223,700km² *5,105,700 miles²*. It has an average depth of 1038m *3407ft*.

Deepest The deepest part of the ocean was first pinpointed in 1951 by HM Survey Ship *Challenger* in the Marianas Trench in the Pacific Ocean. On 23 Jan 1960 the US Navy bathyscaphe *Trieste* descended to the bottom at 10,916m *35,813ft*. A more recent visit produced a figure of 10,924m± 10m *35,839ft±33ft*, from data obtained by the survey vessel *Takuyo* of the Hydrographic Department, Japan Maritime Safety Agency in 1984, using a narrow multi-beam echo sounder.

The deepest point in the territorial waters of the UK is an area 316m *1037ft* deep, 6 cables (*1100m*) off the island of Raasay, near Skye, in the Inner Sound at Lat. 57° 30′33″N, Long. 5°57′27″W.

Remotest!

The world's most distant point from land is a spot in the South Pacific, 48°30′S, 125°30′W, which is 2670km *1660miles* from the nearest points of land, namely Pitcairn Island, Ducie Island and Cape Dart, Antarctica. Centred on this spot is a circle of water with an area of 22,421,500 km² *8,657,000 miles²* — more than 5,000,000 km² *2,000,000 miles²* larger than Russia, the world's largest country.

Largest sea The largest of the world's seas is the South China Sea, with an area of 2,974,600km² *1,148,500 miles²*.

Largest bay The largest bay in the world measured by shoreline length is Hudson Bay, Canada, with a shoreline of 12,268km *7623 miles* and an area of 1,233,000km² *476,000 miles²*. Measured by area, the Bay of Bengal, in the Indian Ocean, is larger, at 2,172,000 km² *839,000 miles²*.

Great Britain Great Britain's largest bay is Cardigan Bay, which has a shoreline 225km *140 miles* long and measures 116km *72 miles* across from the Lleyn Peninsula, Gwynedd to St David's Head, Dyfed.

Largest gulf The largest gulf in the world is the Gulf of Mexico, with an area of 1,544,000km² *596,000 miles²* and a shoreline of 5000km *3100 miles* from Cape Sable, Florida, USA, to Cabo Catoche, Mexico.

Longest fjord The world's longest fjord is the Nordvest Fjord arm of the Scoresby Sund in eastern Greenland, which extends inland 313km *195 miles* from the sea. The longest Norwegian fjord is the Sognefjord, which extends 204km *127 miles* inland from the island of Sogneoksen to the head of the Lusterfjord arm at Skjolden. Its width ranges from 2.4km *1½ miles* at its narrowest up to 5.1km *3¼ miles* at its widest. It has a deepest point of 1308m *4291ft*.

Longest sea loch Loch Fyne, Scotland, extends 60.5km *37.6 miles* inland into Strathclyde.

Highest seamount The highest known submarine mountain, or seamount, is one discovered in 1953 near the Tonga Trench, between Samoa and New Zealand. It rises 8700m *28,500ft* from the sea bed, with its summit 365m *1200ft* below the surface.

Most southerly The most southerly part of the oceans is located at 85°34′S, 154°W, at the snout of the Robert Scott Glacier, 490km *305 miles* from the South Pole.

Sea temperature The temperature of the water at the surface of the sea varies greatly. It is as low as –2°C *28°F* in the White Sea and as high as 36°C *96°F* in the shallow areas of the Persian Gulf in summer. The highest temperature recorded in the ocean is 404°C *759°F*, for a hot spring measured by an American research submarine some 480km *300 miles* off the American west coast in 1985.

Clearest The Weddell Sea, 71°S, 15°W off Antarctica, has the clearest water of any sea. A 'Secchi' disc 30cm *1ft* in diameter was visible to a depth of 80m *262ft* on 13 Oct 1986, as measured by Dutch researchers at the German Alfred-Wegener Institute. Such clarity corresponds to what is attainable in distilled water.

Straits

Longest The longest straits in the world are the Tatarskiy Proliv or Tartar Straits between Sakhalin Island and the Russian mainland, running from the Sea of Japan to Sakhalinsky Zaliv — 800km *500 miles*, thus marginally longer than the Malacca Straits, between Malaysia and Sumatra.

Broadest The broadest *named* straits in the world are the Davis Straits between Greenland and Baffin Island, Canada, with a minimum width of 338km *210 miles*. The Drake Passage between the Diego Ramirez Islands, Chile and the South Shetland Islands is 1140km *710 miles* across.

Narrowest The narrowest navigable straits are those between the Aegean island of Euboea and the mainland of Greece. The gap is only 40m *45yd* wide at Khalkis.

The Seil Sound, Inner Hebrides, Scotland narrows to a point only 6m *20ft* wide where the Clachan bridge joins the island of Seil to the mainland, and has thus been said to span the Atlantic.

Waves

Highest The highest officially recorded sea wave was calculated at 34m *112ft* from trough to crest; it was measured by Lt Frederic Margraff, USN from the USS *Ramapo* proceeding from Manila, Philippines to San Diego, California, USA on the night of 6–7 Feb 1933, during a 126km/h *68knot* hurricane. The highest instrumentally measured wave was one 26m *86ft* high, recorded by the British ship *Weather Reporter*, in the North Atlantic on 30 Dec 1972 in Lat. 59°N, Long. 19°W.

On 9 Jul 1958 a landslip caused a 160km/h *100mph* wave to wash 524m *1720ft* high along the fjord-like Lituya Bay in Alaska, USA.

Highest seismic The highest reported *tsunami* (often wrongly called a tidal wave) was one triggered by an underwater landslide which struck the island of Lanai in Hawaii *c.*105,000 years ago and deposited sediment up to an altitude of approximately 375m *1230ft*. The highest known in modern times appeared off Ishigaki Island, Ryukyu island chain on 24 Apr 1771. It was possibly as high as 85m *278ft*, and tossed a 750-tonne block of coral more than 2.5km *1.3 miles* inland.

Currents

Greatest The greatest current in the oceans is the Antarctic Circumpolar Current or West Wind Drift Current. On the basis of four measurements taken in 1982 in the Drake Passage, between South America and Antarctica, it was found to be flowing at a rate of 130,000,000m³ *4.3billionft³* per sec. Results from computer modelling in 1990 estimate a higher figure of 195,000,000 m³ *6.9 billion ft³* per sec.

Strongest The world's strongest currents are the Nakwakto Rapids, Slingsby Channel, British Columbia, Canada (Lat. 51° 05′ N, Long. 127° 30′ W), where the flow rate may reach 30 km/h *16 knots*.

Great Britain The fastest current in British territorial waters is 19.8 km/h *10.7 knots* in the Pentland Firth between the Orkney Islands and the Scottish mainland.

Tides

The greatest tides occur in the Bay of Fundy, which divides the peninsula of Nova Scotia, Canada from the United States' north-easternmost state of Maine and the Canadian province of New Brunswick. Burncoat Head in the Minas Basin, Nova Scotia, has the greatest mean spring range, with 14.5 m *47 ft 6 in*. A range of 16.6 m *54 ft 6 in* was recorded at springs in Leaf Basin, in Ungava Bay, Québec, Canada in 1953. Tahiti, in the mid-Pacific Ocean, experiences virtually no tide.

Great Britain The place with the greatest mean spring range in Great Britain is Beachley, on the Severn, with a range of 12.40 m *40 ft 8½ in*, compared with the British Isles' average of 4.6 m *15 ft*. Prior to 1933, tides as high as 8.80 m *28 ft 11 in* above and 6.80 m *22 ft 3½ in* below datum (total range 15.60 m *51 ft 2½ in*) were recorded at Avonmouth, though an extreme range of 15.90 m *52 ft 2½ in* for Beachley was officially accepted. In 1883 a freak tide of greater range was reported from Chepstow, Gwent.

Icebergs

Largest and tallest The largest iceberg on record was an antarctic tabular iceberg of over 31,000 km² *12,000 miles²*, 335 km *208 miles* long and 97 km *60 miles* wide (and thus larger than Belgium), sighted 240 km *150 miles* west of Scott Island, in the South Pacific Ocean, by the USS *Glacier* on 12 Nov 1956. The 60 m *200 ft* thick arctic ice island T.1 (360 km² *140 miles²*), discovered in 1946, was tracked for 17 years.

The tallest iceberg measured was one of 167 m *550 ft* reported off western Greenland by the US icebreaker *East Wind* in 1958.

Most southerly arctic The most southerly arctic iceberg was sighted in the Atlantic by a USN weather patrol in Lat. 28° 44′ N, Long. 48° 42′ W, in April 1935. The southernmost iceberg reported in British home waters was sighted 96 km *60 miles* from Smith's Knoll, on the Dogger Bank, in the North Sea.

Most northerly antarctic The most northerly antarctic iceberg was a remnant sighted in the Atlantic by the ship *Dochra* in Lat. 26° 30′ S, Long. 25° 40′ W, on 30 Apr 1894.

Land

There is strong evidence that about 300 million years ago the Earth's land surface comprised a single primeval continent of 1.5×10^8 km² *60 million miles²*, now termed Pangaea, and even prior to its existence it is possible that there had been other super-continents. Pangaea is believed to have split about 190 million years ago, during the Jurassic Period, into two super-continents. These are termed Laurasia (Eurasia, Greenland and North America) and Gondwana (Africa, Arabia, India, South America, Oceania and Antarctica).

Rocks

The age of the Earth is generally considered to be within the range of 4540 ± 40 million years. However, no rocks of this great age have yet been found on the Earth, since geological processes have presumably destroyed them.

Oldest The greatest reported age for any scientifically dated rock is 3962 million years in the case of Acasta Gneisses found in May 1984. The rocks were discovered approximately 320 km *200 miles* north of Yellowknife, Northwest Territories, Canada by Dr Samuel Bowring (USA) as part of an ongoing Canadian geology survey mapping project.

Older minerals which are not rocks have also been identified. Some zircon crystals discovered

Furthest!

The point of land furthest from the sea is at Lat. 46° 16.8′ N, Long. 86° 40.2′ E in the Dzungarian Basin, which is in the Sinkiang Uighur Autonomous Region (Xinjiang Uygur Zizhiqu), China's most north-westerly province. It is at a straight-line distance of 2648 km *1645 miles* **from the nearest open sea—Baydaratskaya Guba to the north (Arctic Ocean), Feni Point to the south (Indian Ocean) and Bohai Wan to the east (Yellow Sea).**

The point remotest from the sea in Great Britain is near Meriden, W Mids, 117 km *72½ miles* **equidistant from the Severn bridge, the Dee estuary and the Welland estuary in the Wash. The equivalent point in Scotland is in the Forest of Atholl, north-west Tayside, 65 km** *40½ miles* **equidistant from the head of Loch Leven, Inverness Firth and the Firth of Tay. The geographical centre of the island of Great Britain is at national grid reference SD 718376, near Calderstones Hospital, 4 km** *2½ miles* **south-west of Clitheroe, Lancs.**

by Bob Pidgeon and Simon Wilde in the Jack Hills, 700 km *430 miles* north of Perth, Western Australia in August 1984 were found to be 4276 million years old. These are the oldest fragments of the Earth's crust discovered so far.

Great Britain The oldest rocks in Great Britain were originally sediments and basic igneous rocks probably formed c. 2900 million years ago. They, and granitic rocks intruded into them, were metamorphosed c. 2700 million years ago to form the gneisses of the Scourian Complex of the north-west Highlands and the Western Isles of Scotland.

Largest The largest exposed monolith in the world is Ayers Rock, known to Aborigines as *Uluru*, which rises 348 m *1143 ft* above the surrounding desert plain in Northern Territory, Australia. It is 2.5 km *1.5 miles* long and 1.6 km *1 mile* wide.

It was estimated in 1940 that La Gran Piedra, a volcanic plug located in the Sierra Maestra, Cuba, weighs 61,355 tonnes.

Continents

Largest Of the Earth's surface 41.25 per cent, or 210,400,000 km² *81,200,000 miles²*, is covered by continental masses, of which only 148,021,000 km² *57,151,000 miles²* (about two-thirds, or 29.02 per cent of the Earth's surface), is land above water, with a mean height of 756 m *2480 ft* above sea level. The Eurasian land mass is the largest, with

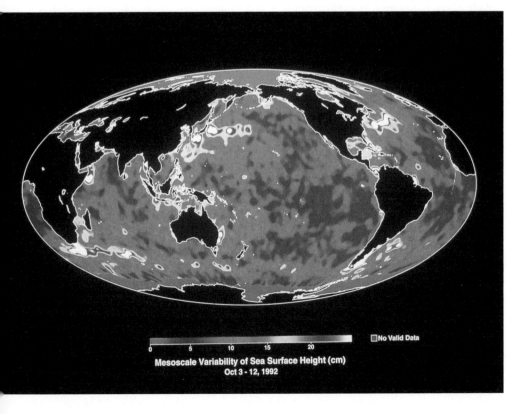

0   5   10   15   20   ☐ No Valid Data

Mesoscale Variability of Sea Surface Height (cm)
Oct 3 - 12, 1992

Ocean currents are the horizontal and vertical circulation system of water in the oceans. The greatest current is the Antarctic Circumpolar Current or West Wind Drift Current, which flows from west to east around Antarctica at a rate of 195,000,000 m³ *6·9 billion ft³* **per sec. This map shows the variability in sea level heights around the world—with dark blue being the most stable and white the least—and as a result highlights some of the world's major ocean currents (white, red and yellow).**
(Photo: Science Photo Library/NASA)

THE GUINNESS TIMES

15 April 1988

NEW ISLAND EMERGES FROM SEA

Surprise for fishermen

The world's newest island, named 'Pulau Batu Hairan', or Surprise Rock island, has emerged mysteriously from the sea. Three fishermen sighted it around 11 a.m. yesterday some 65 kilo-metres (40 miles) to the north-east of Kudat, in Malaysian waters.

It had not been there two days ago and one of the men said that the night before last they had heard some low rumbling sounds, probably the noise of the land mass as it was rising.

At the moment the island, possibly a remnant of a once bigger island, is only some 1.5 metres (5 feet) high, but it will quite probably continue to rise over the next week or so.

Some superstitious locals have expressed fears that a huge octopus may be lurking in the deep and the island might have been stirred up by its furious power!

---

an area (including islands) of 53,698,000 km² *20,733,000 miles²*. The Afro-Eurasian land mass, separated artificially only by the Suez Canal, covers an area of 84,702,000 km² *32,704,000 miles²* or 57.2 per cent of the Earth's land mass.

Smallest The smallest continent is the Australian mainland, with an area of 7,614,500 km² *2,939,960 miles²*, which, together with Tasmania, New Zealand, Papua New Guinea and the Pacific Islands, is sometimes described as Oceania.

Peninsula The world's largest peninsula is Arabia, with an area of about 3,250,000 km² *1,250,000 miles²*.

Islands

Largest Discounting Australia, which is usually regarded as a continental land mass, the largest island in the world is Greenland, with an area of about 2,175,000 km² *840,000 miles²*. The largest sand island in the world is Fraser Island, Queensland, Australia with a sand dune 120km *75 miles* long.

The largest island surrounded mostly by fresh water (48,000 km² *18,500 miles²*) is the Ilha de Marajó in the mouth of the River Amazon, Brazil. The world's largest inland island (i.e. land surrounded by rivers) is Ilha do Bananal, Brazil (20,000 km² *7700 miles²*). The largest island in a lake is Manitoulin Island (2766 km² *1068 miles²*) in the Canadian section of Lake Huron.

Great Britain The mainland of Great Britain is the eighth largest island in the world, with

an area of 229,979 km² *88,795 miles²*. It stretches 971 km *603½ miles* from Dunnet Head in the north to Lizard Point in the south and 463 km *287½ miles* across from Porthaflod, Dyfed to Lowestoft, Suffolk.

The largest lake island in Great Britain is Inchmurrin, in Loch Lomond, Strathclyde/Central with an area of 115 ha *284 acres*.

Remotest The most remote island in the world is Bouvet Island (Bouvetøya), discovered in the South Atlantic by J. B. C. Bouvet de Lozier on 1 Jan 1739 and first landed on by Capt. George Morris on 16 Dec 1825. Its position is 54° 26′ S, 3° 24′ E. This uninhabited Norwegian dependency is *c*. 1700 km *1050 miles* from the nearest land—the uninhabited Queen Maud Land coast of eastern Antarctica.

The remotest inhabited island in the world is Tristan da Cunha, discovered in the South Atlantic by Tristão da Cunha, a Portuguese admiral, in March 1506. It has an area of 98 km² *38 miles²*. After evacuation in 1961 (due to volcanic activity), 198 islanders returned in November 1963. The nearest inhabited land to the group is the island of St Helena, 2435 km *1315 nautical miles* to the north-east.

British Isles The remotest of the British islets is Rockall, 307 km *191 miles* west of St Kilda, Western Isles. This rock, measuring 21 m *70 ft* high and 25 m *83 ft* across, was not formally annexed until 18 Sep 1955.

The remotest British island which has ever been inhabited is North Rona, which is 71 km *44 miles* from the next nearest land at Cape Wrath and the Butt of Lewis. It was evacuated *c*. 1844. Currently the most remote inhabited British island is Fair Isle, 38.5 km *24 miles* to the south-west of Sumburgh Head, Shetland. It has a population of some 80 people.

Greatest archipelago The world's greatest archipelago is the crescent of more than 17,000 islands, 5600 km *3500 miles* long, which forms Indonesia.

Highest rock pinnacle The world's highest rock pinnacle is Ball's Pyramid near Lord Howe Island in the Pacific, which is 561 m *1843 ft* high, but has a base axis of only 200 m *220 yd*. It was first scaled in 1965.

Northernmost land On 26 Jul 1978 Uffe Petersen of the Danish Geodetic Institute observed the islet of Odaaq Ø, 30 m *100 ft* across, 1.36 km *1478 yd* north of Kaffeklubben Ø off Pearyland, Greenland in Lat. 83° 40′ 32.5″N, Long.

30° 40′ 10.1″W. It is 706.4 km *438.9 miles* from the North Pole.

Southernmost land The South Pole, unlike the North Pole, is on land. The Amundsen–Scott South Polar station was built there at an altitude of 2855 m *9370 ft* in 1957. The station is drifting bodily with the ice cap 8–9 m *27–30 ft* per annum in the direction 43°W and was replaced by a new structure in 1975.

Largest atoll The largest atoll in the world is Kwajalein in the Marshall Islands, in the central Pacific Ocean. Its slender coral reef 283 km *176 miles* long encloses a lagoon of 2850 km² *1100 miles²*.

The atoll with the largest land area is Christmas Atoll, in the Line Islands in the central Pacific Ocean. It has an area of 649 km² *251 miles²*, of which 321 km² *124 miles²* is land.

> There are four settlements on Christmas Atoll. The main one is London, which is 4 km *2½ miles* from Paris!

Longest reef The Great Barrier Reef off Queensland, north-eastern Australia is 2027 km *1260 miles* in length. It is not actually a single reef, but consists of thousands of separate reefs. Between 1959 and 1971, and again between 1979 and 1991, corals on large areas of the central section of the reef—approximately between Cooktown and Proserpine—were devastated by the crown-of-thorns starfish (*Acanthaster planci*).

Depressions

Deepest The deepest depression so far discovered is the bedrock of the Bentley sub-glacial trench, Antarctica at 2538 m *8326 ft* below sea level.

The greatest submarine depression is an area of the north-west Pacific floor which has an average depth of 4600 m *15,000 ft*.

The deepest exposed depression on land is the shore surrounding the Dead Sea, now 400 m *1310 ft* below sea level. The deepest point on the bed of this saltiest of all lakes is 728 m *2388 ft* below sea level. The rate of fall in the lake surface since 1948 has been 350 mm *13¾ in* per annum. The deepest part of the bed of Lake Baikal in Russia is 1181 m *3875 ft* below sea level.

Great Britain The lowest-lying area in Great Britain is in the Holme Fen area of the Great Ouse, in Cambridgeshire, at 2.7 m *9 ft* below sea level. The deepest depression in England is the bed of part of Lake Windermere, 28.6 m *94 ft* below sea level, and in Scotland the bed of Loch Morar, Highland, 300.8 m *987 ft* below sea level.

Largest The largest exposed depression in the world is the Caspian Sea basin in Azerbaijan, Russia, Kazakhstan, Turkmenistan and Iran. It is more than 518,000 km² *200,000 miles²*, of which 371,800 km² *143,550 miles²* is lake area. The preponderant land area of the depression is the Prikaspiyskaya Nizmennost, lying around the northern third of the lake and stretching inland for a distance of up to 450 km *280 miles*.

Caves

Longest The most extensive cave system in the world is that under the Mammoth Cave National Park, Kentucky, USA. Explorations by many groups of cavers have revealed that interconnected cave passages beneath the Flint, Mammoth Cave and Toohey Ridges make up a system with a total mapped length which is now 560 km *348 miles*.

Great Britain The longest cave system in Great Britain is the Ease Gill system, W Yorks which now has 70km *44 miles* of explored passage.

Largest The world's largest cave chamber is the Sarawak Chamber, Lubang Nasib Bagus, in the Gunung Mulu National Park, Sarawak, discovered and surveyed by the 1980 British–Malaysian Mulu Expedition. Its length is 700m *2300ft*, its average width is 300m *980ft* and it is nowhere less than 70m *230ft* high. It is large enough to span the West End of London, reaching from Trafalgar Square to beyond Piccadilly Circus and Leicester Square.

Underwater cave The longest explored underwater cave is the Nohoch Na Chich cave system in Quintana Roo, Mexico, with 23,744m *77,900ft* of mapped passages. Exploration of the system, which began in November 1987, has been carried out by the CEDAM Cave Diving Team under the leadership of Mike Madden (USA).

The longest dive into a single flooded cave passage is one of 4055m *13,300ft* into the Doux de Coly, Dordogne, France by Olivier Issler (Switzerland) on 4 Apr 1991.

Greatest descent The world depth record was set by the Groupe Vulcain in the Gouffre Jean Bernard, France at 1602m *5256ft* in 1989. However, this cave, explored via multiple entrances, has never been entirely descended, so the 'sporting' record for the greatest descent into a cave is recognized as 1508m *4947ft* in the Shakta Pantjukhina in the Caucasus Mountains of Georgia by a team of Ukrainian cavers in 1988.

Longest stalactite The longest known stalactite in the world is a wall-supported column extending 59m *195ft* from roof to floor in the Cueva de Nerja, near Málaga, in Spain. The longest free-hanging stalactites in the world are believed to be some *c.* 10m *33ft* long in the Gruta do Janelão, in Minas Gerais, Brazil.

Tallest stalagmite The tallest known stalagmite in the world is one in the Krásnohorská cave, near Rožňava, Slovakia, which is generally accepted as being about 32m *105ft* tall. The tallest cave column is considered to be the Flying

Deepest Caves by Countries

Depth			
m	ft	Location	
1602	5256	Réseau Jean Bernard	France
1508	4947	Shakta Pantjukhina	Georgia
1485	4872	Lamprechtsofen	Austria
1441	4728	Sistema del Trave	Spain
1415	4642	Boj Bulok	Uzbekistan
1386	4547	Cueva Cheve	Mexico
1370	4495	Ceki 2	Slovenia
1355	4445	Lukina Jama	Croatia
1284	4213	Siebenhengstehohlensystem	Switzerland
1210	3970	Abisso Olivifer	Italy
1195	3920	Cukurpinar Dudeni	Turkey
1170	3838	Anou Ifflis	Algeria
308	1010	Ogof Ffynnon Ddu	Wales
214	702	Giant's Hole System	England
181	594	Poll na Gceim	Republic of Ireland
179	587	Reyfad Pot	Northern Ireland
76	249	Cnoc nan Uamh	Scotland

Dragon Pillar, 39m *128ft* high, in Daji Dong, Guizhou, China.

Mountains

Highest An eastern Himalayan peak known as Peak XV on the Tibet–Nepal border was discovered to be the world's highest mountain in 1856 by the Survey Department of the Government of India, from theodolite readings taken in 1849 and 1850. Its height was calculated to be 8840m *29,002ft*. It was named Mt Everest after Col. Sir George Everest (1790–1866), formerly Surveyor-General of India, who pronounced his name 'Eve-rest'. There have been a number of surveys since then, with 8848m *29,029ft* now being the most widely accepted height. (For details of ascents of Everest ⇨ Mountaineering)

The mountain whose summit is farthest from the Earth's centre is the Andean peak of Chimborazo (6267m *20,561ft*), 158km *98 miles* south of the equator in Ecuador. Its summit is 2150m *7057ft* further from the Earth's centre than the summit of Mt Everest.

The highest mountain on the equator is Volcán Cayambe (5790m *18,996ft*), Ecuador, at Long. 77°58'W. A mountaineer on the summit would be moving at 1671km/h *1038mph* relative to the Earth's centre, due to the Earth's rotation.

The highest insular mountain in the world is Puncak Jaya in Irian Jaya, Indonesia. A survey by the Australian Universities' Expedition in 1973 yielded a height of 4884m *16,023ft*. Ngga Pulu (also in Irian Jaya), which is now 4861m *15,950ft*, was in 1936 possibly *c.* 4910m *16,110ft* before the melting of its snow cap.

United Kingdom The highest mountain in the UK is Ben Nevis (1343.6m *4408ft 1in* above sea level excluding the 3.65m *12ft* cairn), 6.85km *4¼ miles* south-east of Fort William, Argyll, Highland. It was climbed before 1720, but though acclaimed the highest in 1790, was not officially recognized to be higher than Ben Macdhui (1310m *4300ft*) until 1870. In 1834 Ben Macdhui and Ben Nevis (Gaelic, *Beinn Nibheis*) (first reference, 1778)

The longest cave system in the world is Mammoth Cave, in Kentucky, USA. People began venturing into the cave some 4000 years ago, and it is now a major attraction. The Frozen Niagara is just one of many spectacular sights.
(Photo: National Park Service)

were respectively quoted as 4570ft *1393m* and 4370ft *1332m*.

Unclimbed The highest unclimbed mountain is Kankar Pünsum (7541m *24,741ft*), on the Bhutan/Tibet border. It is the 67th named mountain peak in order of height. The highest unclimbed summit is Lhotse Middle (8414m *27,605ft*), one of the peaks of Lhotse, in the Khumbu district of the Nepal Himalaya. It is the tenth highest individually recognized summit in the world, Lhotse being the fourth highest mountain.

Tallest The world's tallest mountain measured from its submarine base (6000m *3280 fathoms*) in the Hawaiian Trough to its peak is Mauna Kea (White Mountain) on the island of Hawaii, with a combined height of 10,205m *33,480ft,* of which 4205m *13,796ft* are above sea level.

Greatest ranges The greatest of all mountain ranges is the submarine Mid-Ocean Ridge, which extends 65,000km *40,000 miles* from the Arctic Ocean to the Atlantic Ocean, around Africa, Asia and Australia, and under the Pacific Ocean to the west coast of North America. It has a greatest height of 4200m *13,800ft* above the base ocean depth.

The world's greatest land mountain range is the Himalaya-Karakoram, which contains 96 of the world's 109 peaks of over 24,000ft *7315m*. The longest range is the Andes of South America, which is approximately 7600km *4700 miles* in length.

Longest lines of sight Vatnajökull (2118m *6952 ft*), Iceland has been seen by refracted light from the Faeroe Islands 550km *340 miles* away. In Alaska, Mt McKinley (6193m *20,320ft*) has been sighted from Mt Sanford (4949m *16,237ft*)—a distance of 370km *230 miles*.

Greatest plateau The most extensive high plateau in the world is the Tibetan Plateau in Central Asia. The average altitude is 4900m *16,000ft* and the area is 1,850,000 km² *715,000 miles²*.

Sheerest wall Mt Rakaposhi (7788m *25,550ft*) rises 5.99 vertical kilometres *3.72 miles* from the

GUESS WHAT?
Q Why would you see stars on Mauna Kea?
A See Page 80

The dramatic Khône Falls on the Mekong River in Laos is the widest waterfall in the world.
(Photo: Explorer/P. Gontier)

Hunza Valley, Pakistan in 10 horizontal kilometres *6.2 miles* with an overall gradient of 31°.

The 975 m *3200 ft* wide north-west face of Half Dome, Yosemite, California, USA is 670 m *2200 ft* high but nowhere departs more than 7° from the vertical.

Highest halites Along the northern shores of the Gulf of Mexico for 1160 km *725 miles* there exist 330 subterranean 'mountains' of salt, some of which rise more than 18,300 m *60,000 ft* from bedrock and appear as the low salt domes first discovered in 1862.

Waterfalls

Highest The highest waterfall (as opposed to vaporized 'Bridal Veil') in the world is the Salto Angel in Venezuela, on a branch of the River Carrao, an upper tributary of the Caroní, with a total drop of 979 m *3212 ft*— the longest single drop being 807 m *2648 ft*. The 'Angel Falls' were named after the American pilot Jimmie Angel (died 8 Dec 1956), who recorded them in his log book on 16 Nov 1933. The falls, known by the Indians as Churun-Meru, had been reported by Ernesto Sánchez la Cruz in 1910.

The highest waterfall in the UK is Eas a'Chùal Aluinn, from Glas Bheinn (774 m *2541 ft*), Highland, with a drop of 201 m *658 ft*. The greatest single drop is one of 107 m *350 ft* in the case

of An Steall Ban (Steall), near Glen Nevis, Highland.

Greatest On the basis of the average annual flow, the greatest waterfall in the world is the Boyoma Falls in Zaïre with 17,000 m³/sec *600,000 cusec*. The flow of the Guaíra (Salto das Sete Quedas) on the Alto Paraná River between Brazil and Paraguay did on occasions in the past attain a rate of 50,000 m³/sec *1,750,000 cusec*. However, the closing of the Itaipú dam gates in 1982 ended this claim to fame.

Widest The widest waterfall in the world is the Khône Falls (15–21 m *50–70 ft* high) in Laos, with a width of 10.8 km *6.7 miles* and a flood flow of 42,500 m³/sec *1,500,000 cusec*.

Rivers

Longest The two longest rivers in the world are the Nile, flowing into the Mediterranean, and the Amazon, flowing into the South Atlantic. Which is the longer is more a matter of definition than simple measurement.

Not until 1971 was the true source of the Amazon discovered, by Loren McIntyre (USA) in the snow-covered Andes of southern Peru. The Amazon begins with snowbound lakes and brooks—the actual source has been named Laguna McIntyre—which converge to form the Apurimac. This joins other streams to become the Ene, the Tambo and then the Ucayali. From the confluence of the Ucayali and the Marañón the river is called the Amazon for the final 3700 km *2300 miles* as it flows through Brazil into the Atlantic Ocean. The Amazon has several mouths which widen towards the sea, so that the exact point where the river ends is uncertain. If the Pará estuary

(the most distant mouth) is counted, its length is approximately 6750 km *4195 miles*.

The length of the Nile watercourse, as surveyed by M. Devroey (Belgium) before the loss of a few miles of meanders due to the formation of Lake Nasser, behind the Aswan High Dam, was 6670 km *4145 miles*. This course is unitary from a hydrological standpoint and runs from the source in Burundi of the Luvironza branch of the Kagera feeder of the Victoria Nyanza via the White Nile to the delta in the Mediterranean.

Great Britain The longest river in Great Britain is the Severn, which empties into the Bristol Channel and is 354 km *220 miles* long. Its basin extends over 11,419 km² *4409 miles²*. It rises in north-western Powys, Wales, and flows through Shropshire, Hereford and Worcester, Gloucestershire and Avon. With 17 tributaries, it has more than any other British river.

Shortest As with the longest river, two rivers could also be considered to be the shortest river with a name. The Roe River, near Great Falls, Montana, USA, has two forks fed by a large fresh

GUESS WHAT?

Q What is the difference between the Salto Angel waterfall in Venezuela and the spectacular waterfall in Detroit?

A See Page 104

Longest!

The longest trans-continental waterway is 10,682 km *6637 miles* in length, and links the Beaufort Sea in northern Canada with the Gulf of Mexico in the south of the USA. It starts in the north at Tuktoyaktuk on the Mackenzie River, ending at Port Eads at the delta of the Mississippi. The final link was formed in 1976 with the completion of the South Bay Diversion Channel in Manitoba, Canada, joining the Churchill River system and the Nelson River system.

water spring. These relatively constant forks measure 61 m *201ft* (East Fork Roe River) and 17.7 m *58ft* (North Fork Roe River) respectively. The Roe River flows into the larger Missouri River. The D River, located at Lincoln City, Oregon, USA, connects Devil's Lake to the Pacific Ocean. Its length is officially quoted as 37 ± 1.5 m *120± 5ft*.

Longest!

The longest submarine river is one discovered in 1952, known as the Cromwell current. It is 300 km *190 miles* wide and flows eastward below the surface of the Pacific for 6500 km *4000 miles* along the equator. In places it flows at depths of up to 400 m *1300 ft*. Its volume is 1000 times that of the Mississippi.

Subterranean river **In August 1958 a concealed river, tracked by radio isotopes, was discovered flowing under the Nile with six times its mean annual flow, or 500,000 million m³ *20 trillion ft³*.**

Greatest flow The greatest flow of any river in the world is that of the Amazon, which discharges an average of 120,000 m³/sec *4,200,000 cusec* into the Atlantic Ocean, increasing to more than 200,000 m³/sec *7,000,000 cusec* in full flood. The lower 1450 km *900 miles* average 17 m *55 ft* in depth, but the river has a maximum depth of 124 m *407ft*.

Although the lengths of the rivers Amazon and Nile are similar, the flow of the Amazon is an amazing 60 times greater than that of the Nile.

Largest basin The largest river basin in the world is that drained by the Amazon, which covers about 7,045,000 km² *2,720,000 miles²*. It has countless tributaries and sub-tributaries, including the Madeira, which at 3380 km *2100 miles* is the longest tributary in the world, being surpassed by only 17 other rivers.

Longest estuary The world's longest estuary is that of the Ob', in the north of Russia, at 885 km *550 miles*. It is up to 80 km *50 miles* wide, and is also the widest river which freezes solid.

Largest delta The world's largest delta is that created by the Ganges and Brahmaputra in Bangladesh and West Bengal, India. It covers an area of 75,000 km² *30,000 miles²*.

Largest swamp The world's largest tract of swamp is the Gran Pantanal of Mato Grosso state in Brazil. It is about 109,000 km² *42,000 miles²* in area.

River Bores

The bore (abrupt rise of tidal water) on the Qiantong Jiang (Hangzhou He) in eastern China is the most remarkable of the 60 in the world. At spring tides the wave attains a height of up to 7.5 m *25ft* and a speed of 24–27 km/h *13–15 knots*. It is heard advancing at a range of 22 km *14 miles*. The annual downstream flood wave on the Mekong, in south-east Asia,

Lake Baikal in Russia is the deepest lake in the world, having a greatest depth of 1637 m *5371ft*. It lies in a deep structural hollow surrounded by mountains, and not far from its shore are remains of extinct volcanoes.
(Photo: Science Photo Library/Novosti Press Agency)

sometimes reaches a height of 14 m *46ft*. The greatest volume of any tidal bore is that of the Furo do Guajarú, a shallow channel which splits Ilha Caviana in the mouth of the Amazon.

The most notable of the eight river bores in the UK is that on the Severn, which attained a measured height of 2.8 m *9ft 3in* on 15 Oct 1966 downstream of Stonebench, and a speed of 20 km/h *13 mph*. It travels from Framilode towards Gloucester.

Lakes and Inland Seas

Largest The largest inland sea or lake in the world is the Caspian Sea (in Azerbaijan, Russia, Kazakhstan, Turkmenistan and Iran). It is 1225 km *760 miles* long and its area is 371,800 km² *143,550 miles²*. Of the total area, some 143,200 km² *55,280 miles²* (38.5 per cent) are in Iran, where it is called Darya-ye-Khazar. Its maximum depth is 1025 m *3360 ft* and the surface is 28.5 m *93ft* below sea level. Its estimated volume is 89,600 km³ *21,500 miles³* of saline water (⇨ also Depressions).

Deepest The deepest lake in the world is Lake Baikal in the southern part of eastern Siberia, Russia. It is 620 km *385 miles* long and between 32–74 km *20–46 miles* wide. In 1974 the lake's Olkhon Crevice was measured by the Hydrographic Service of the Soviet Pacific Navy and found to be 1637 m *5371ft* deep, of which 1181 m *3875ft* is below sea level (⇨ also Depressions).

The deepest lake in Great Britain is the 16.57 km *10.30 mile* long Loch Morar, Highland. Its surface is 9 m *30 ft* above sea level and its extreme depth 310 m *1017ft*. The lake with the greatest mean depth is Loch Ness, with 130 m *427ft*.

Highest The highest navigable lake in the world is Lake Titicaca (maximum depth 370 m *1214ft*, with an area of about 8290 km² *3200 miles²*) in South America (4790 km² *1850 miles²* in Peru and 3495 km² *1350 miles²* in Bolivia). It is 160 km *100 miles* long and is 3811 m *12,506ft* above sea level.

There are higher lakes in the Himalayas, but most are glacial and of a temporary nature only. A survey of the area carried out in 1984 showed a lake at a height of 5414 m *17,762ft*, named Panch Pokhri, which was 1.6 km *1 mile* long.

The highest lake in the UK is the 0.76 ha *1.9 acre* Lochan Buidhe at 1100 m *3600ft* above sea level in the Cairngorms, Grampian.

Freshwater The freshwater lake with the greatest surface area is Lake Superior, one of the Great Lakes of North America. The total area is 82,350 km² *31,800 miles²*, of which 53,600 km² *20,700 miles²* are in Minnesota, Wisconsin and Michigan, USA and 27,750 km² *11,100 miles²* in Ontario, Canada. It is 180 m *600ft* above sea level. The freshwater lake with the greatest volume is Lake Baikal in Siberia, Russia, with an estimated volume of 23,000 km³ *5500 miles³*.

The largest lake in the UK is Lough Neagh (14.6 m *48ft* above sea level) in Northern Ireland. It is 29 km *18 miles* long and 17.7 km *11 miles* wide, and has an area of 381.73 km² *147.39 miles²*. Its extreme depth is 31 m *102ft*.

Largest!

The largest lake in a lake is Manitou Lake (106.42 km² *41.09 miles²*) on the world's largest lake island, Manitoulin Island (2766 km² *1068 miles²*), in the Canadian part of Lake Huron. The lake itself contains a number of islands.

Underground lake **The world's largest underground lake is believed to be that in the Drachenhauchloch cave near Grootfontein, Namibia, discovered in 1986. When surveyed in April 1991 the surface area was found to be 2.61 ha *6.45 acres*. The surface of the lake is some 66 m *217ft* underground, and its depth 84 m *276ft*.**

Freshwater loch The largest lake in Great Britain, and the largest inland loch in Scotland, is Loch Lomond, which is situated in the Strathclyde and Central regions at a height of 7 m *23ft* above sea level. It is 36.44 km *22.64 miles* long and has a surface area of 70.04 km² *27.45 miles²*. Its greatest depth is 190 m *623ft*. The lake or loch with the greatest volume is, however, Loch Ness, with 7,443,000,000 m³ *262,845,000,000ft³*. The longest lake or loch is Loch Ness, which measures 38.99 km *24.23 miles*, although the three arms of the Y-shaped Loch Awe, Strathclyde aggregate 40.99 km *25.47 miles*.

Largest lagoon Lagoa dos Patos, located near the seashore in Rio Grande do Sul, southernmost Brazil, is 280km *174 miles* long and extends over 9850km² *3803 miles²*, separated from the Atlantic Ocean by long sand strips. It has a maximum width of 70km *44 miles*.

Other Features

Desert Nearly an eighth of the world's land surface is arid, with a rainfall of less than 25cm *10 in* per annum. The Sahara in North Africa is the largest desert in the world. At its greatest length it is 5150km *3200 miles* from east to west. From north to south it is between 1280 and 2250km *800 and 1400 miles*. The area covered by the desert is about 9,269,000 km² *3,579,000 miles²*.

Sand dunes The world's highest measured sand dunes are those in the Saharan sand sea of Isaouane-N-Tifernine of east central Algeria in Lat. 26°42'N, Long. 6°43'E. They have a wavelength of 5km *3 miles* and attain a height of 465m *1525ft*.

Largest!

The largest mirage on record was that sighted in the Arctic at 83°N, 103°W by Donald B. MacMillan in 1913. This type of mirage, known as the Fata Morgana, appeared as the same 'hills, valleys, snow-capped peaks extending through at least 120 degrees of the horizon' that Peary had misidentified as Crocker Land six years earlier. On 17 Jul 1939 a mirage of Snaefellsjökull (1446 m *4744 ft*) on Iceland was seen from the sea at a distance of 540–560 km *335–350 miles*.

Largest gorge The largest land gorge in the world is the Grand Canyon on the Colorado River in north-central Arizona, USA. It extends from Marble Gorge to the Grand Wash Cliffs, over a distance of 446km *277 miles*. It averages 16km *10 miles* in width and 1.6km *1 mile* in depth. The submarine Labrador Basin canyon, between Greenland and Labrador, Canada, is 3440km *2140 miles* long.

Deepest canyon A canyon or gorge is generally regarded as a valley with steep rock walls and a considerable depth in relation to its width. The Grand Canyon (⇨ above) has the characteristic vertical sections of wall, but is much wider than its depth. The Vicos Gorge in the Pindus mountains of north-west Greece is 900m *2950ft* deep and only 1100m *3600ft* between its rims. Gorges in many countries have a higher depth/width ratio, but none is as deep.

The often cited Colca canyon in Peru has the cross-profile of a valley, but is neither as deep nor as steep-sided as the Yarlung Zangbo valley (⇨ below). The deepest submarine canyon yet discovered is one 40 km *25 miles* south of Esperance, Western Australia which is 1800m *6000ft* deep and 32km *20 miles* wide.

Deepest valley The Yarlung Zangbo valley is 5075m *16,650ft* deep where it turns through the Himalayas in eastern Tibet, before the river changes its name to the Brahmaputra. The peaks of Namche Barwa (7753m *25,436ft*) and Jala Peri (7282m *23,891ft*) are just 21km *13 miles*

apart with the Yarlung Zangbo River in between, at an elevation of 2440m *8000ft*.

Cliffs The highest known sea cliffs in the world are those on the north coast of east Moloka'i, Hawaii near Umilehi Point, which descend 1010m *3300ft* to the sea at an average gradient of more than 55°.

The highest cliffs in the UK are the 400m *1300ft* Conachair cliffs on St Kilda, Western Isles (425m *1397ft*). The highest sheer sea cliffs on the mainland of Great Britain are at Clo Mor, 5km *3 miles* south-east of Cape Wrath, Sutherland which drop 281m *921ft*.

Natural arches The longest natural arch in the world is the Landscape Arch in the Arches National Park, 40km *25 miles* north of Moab in Utah, USA. This natural sandstone arch spans 88m *291ft* and is set about 30m *100ft* above the canyon floor. In one place erosion has narrowed its section to 1.8m *6ft*. Larger, however, is the Rainbow Bridge, Utah, USA, discovered on 14 Aug 1909, which although only 82.3m *270ft* long, is more than 6.7m *22ft* wide and rises to a height of 88.4m *290ft*.

Longest glaciers It is estimated that 13,600,000 km² *5,250,000 miles²*, or 9.7 per cent of the Earth's land surface, is permanently covered by glacier ice. The Antarctic ice sheet accounts for 86 per cent of this.

The world's longest glacier is the Lambert Glacier, discovered in Australian Antarctic Territory in 1956/7. Draining about a fifth of the East Antarctic ice sheet, it is up to 64km *40 miles* wide and, with its seaward extension (the Amery Ice Shelf) it measures at least 700km *440 miles* in length. The fastest-moving major glacier is the Jakobshavn Isbrae in Greenland, flowing at an average of 19m *62ft* per day.

Thickest ice The greatest recorded thickness of ice is 4.78km *2.97 miles* measured by radio echo soundings from a US Antarctic research aircraft at 69°9'38"S, 135°20'25"E, 400km *250 miles* from the coast in Wilkes Land, Antarctica on 4 Jan 1975.

Deepest permafrost The deepest recorded permafrost is more than 1370m *4500ft*, reported from the upper reaches of the Viluy River, Siberia, Russia in February 1982.

Natural Phenomena

Avalanches

Greatest The greatest natural avalanches occur in the Himalayas but no estimates of their volume have been published. It was estimated that 3,500,000m³ *120,000,000ft³* of snow fell in an avalanche in the Italian Alps in 1885. The 400km/h *250 mph* avalanche triggered by the Mount St Helens eruption on 18 May 1980 was estimated to measure 2800 million m³ *96,000 million ft³* (⇨ Accidents and Disasters).

Earthquakes

(Seismologists record all dates with the year *first*, based not on local time but on Universal Time/Greenwich Mean Time).

Greatest It is estimated that each year there are some 500,000 detectable seismic or micro-seismic

disturbances, of which 100,000 can be felt and 1000 cause damage. The deepest recorded hypocentres are of 720km *447 miles* in Indonesia in 1933, 1934 and 1943.

The most commonly used measure of the size (energy release) of an earthquake is its surface-wave magnitude (M_s), based on amplitudes of surface waves, usually at a period of 20 sec. This scale was developed by the American seismologists Benno Gutenberg and Dr Charles Richter (1949). The largest reported magnitudes on this scale are about 8.9, but the scale does not properly represent the size of the very largest earthquakes (those having an M_s of more than about 8), for which it is better to use the concept of seismic moment, M_O, developed by Kei Aki in 1966. Moment can be used to derive a 'moment magnitude', M_w, first used by Hiroo Kanamori in 1977. The largest recorded earthquake on the M_w scale is the Chilean shock of 22 May 1960, which had $M_w = 9.5$, but measured only 8.3 on the M_s scale.

GUESS WHAT?

Q What's the link between the Sahara and the saguaro?

A See Page 45

The 400 km/h *250 mph* avalanche triggered by the Mount St Helens eruption in Washington State, USA on 18 May 1980 was estimated to measure 2800 million m³ *96,000 million ft³*. This view is of the giant ash cloud formed by the further eruption more than two months later.
(Photo: Science Photo Library/David Weintraub)

Worst death toll The greatest estimate for a death toll is the 830,000 fatalities in a prolonged earthquake (*dizhen*) in the Shaanxi, Shanxi and Henan provinces of China, of 2 Feb 1556 (new style) (23 Jan old style).

The highest death toll in modern times has been in the Tangshan earthquake (Mag. $M_s = 7.9$) in eastern China on 27 Jul 1976 (local time was 3 a.m. 28 July). The first figure published on 4 Jan 1977 revealed 655,237 killed, later adjusted to 750,000. On 22 Nov 1979 the New China News Agency inexplicably reduced the death toll to 242,000.

The figure of 1,100,000 sometimes attributed to the eastern Mediterranean earthquake of 20 May 1202 is a gross exaggeration since it includes those dying in a famine the following year. A more plausible death toll is *c.* 30,000.

Material damage The greatest physical devastation was in the earthquake on the Kanto plain, Japan, of 1 Sep 1923 (Mag. $M_s = 8.2$, epicentre in Lat. 35° 15′ N, Long. 139° 30′ E). In Tokyo and Yokohama 575,000 dwellings were destroyed. The official total of persons killed and missing in this *Shinsai* or great 'quake and the resultant fires was 142,807.

Great Britain The highest instrumentally measured Magnitude is 5.5 for the Dogger Bank event of 7 Jun 1931. The highest measured on land was 4.8 for the Swansea earthquake of 27 Jun 1906 and also for the Lleyn earthquake of 19 Jul 1984.

The record undisputed death toll for Great Britain is two—an apprentice, Thomas Grey, struck by falling masonry from Christ's Hospital Church, near Newgate, London at 6 p.m. on 6 Apr 1580, and another young person, Mabel Everet, who

World's Strongest Earthquakes

Progressive list of instrumentally recorded earthquakes

Kanamori Scale Magnitudes M_W	Richter Scale Magnitude M_S	Location	Date
8.8	8.6	Ecuador	31 Jan 1906
9.0	8¼	Kamchatka, Russia (then USSR)	4 Nov 1952
9.1	7¾	Andreanof Islands, Aleutian Islands, USA	9 Mar 1957
9.5	8.3	Chile	22 May 1960

log E = 1.5M + 4.8 (joules)

died of injuries four days later. The shock was centred in the Straits of Dover.

The East Anglian or Colchester earthquake of 22 Apr 1884 (9:18a.m) (epicentre Lat. 51°49′N, Long. 0°54′E) caused damage to 1250 buildings estimated at more than £12,000. Langenhoe Church was wrecked. Windows and doors were rattled over an area of 137,000 km² *53,000 miles²* and the shock was felt in Exeter, Devon and Ostend, Belgium. It is estimated to be Mag. 4.4 on the Richter scale.

Unlucky!

Thomas Grey and Mabel Everet share the unfortunate distinction of being the only people to have been killed as a result of an earthquake which hit Britain. The earthquake, which occurred in 1580, was such a major event that it has even been suggested that Shakespeare is referring to it in *Romeo and Juliet*, when The Nurse says "Tis since the earthquake now eleven years'.

Volcanoes

The total number of volcanoes in the world which might be described as active (believed to have erupted in the past 10,000 years) is 1343, of which many are submarine. The name volcano derives from the now dormant Vulcano Island (from the god of fire Vulcanus) in the Mediterranean.

Greatest explosion The greatest explosion in historic times (possibly since Santoriní in the Aegean Sea, 95km *60 miles* north of Crete, in 1628 BC) occurred at *c.* 10a.m. (local time), or 3.00a.m. GMT, on 27 Aug 1883, with an eruption of Krakatoa, an island (then 47km² *18 miles²*) in the Sunda Strait, between Sumatra and Java, in Indonesia. One hundred and sixty-three villages were wiped out, and 36,380 people killed by the wave it caused. Pumice was thrown 55 km *34 miles* high and dust fell 5330 km *3313 miles* away 10 days later. The explosion was recorded four hours later on the island of Rodrigues, 4776km *2968 miles* away, as 'the roar of heavy guns', and was heard over one thirteenth of the surface of the globe. This explosion, estimated to have had about 26 times the power of the greatest H-bomb test (by the USSR), was still only a third of the Santoriní cataclysm.

Greatest eruption The total volume of matter discharged in the eruption of Tambora, a volcano on the Indonesian island of Sumbawa, from 5–10 Apr 1815, was 150–180km³ *36–43 miles³*. This compares with a probable 60–65km³ *14–16 miles³* ejected by Santoriní (⇨ above) and 20km³ *5 miles³* ejected by Krakatoa (⇨ above). The energy of the Tambora eruption, which lowered the height of the island by 1250m *4100ft* from 4100m *13,450ft* to 2850m *9350ft*, was 8.4×10¹⁹ joules. A crater 8km *5 miles* in diameter was formed. More than 90,000 were killed, or died as a result of the subsequent famine.

The ejecta in the Taupo eruption in New Zealand *c.* AD 130 has been estimated at 30,000 million tonnes of pumice moving at one time at 700km/h *400mph*. It flattened 16,000km² *6200 miles²*. Less than 20 per cent of the 14×10⁹ tonnes of pumice carried up into the air in this most violent of all documented volcanic events fell within 200km *125 miles* of the vent.

Longest lava flow The longest lava flow in historic times is a mixture of *pahoehoe* ropey lava (twisted cord-like solidifications) and *aa* blocky lava, resulting from the eruption of Laki in 1783 in south-east Iceland, which flowed 65–70km *40½–43½ miles*.

The largest known prehistoric flow is the Roza basalt flow in North America *c.* 15 million years ago, which had an unsurpassed length (300 km *190 miles*), area (40,000km² *15,400 miles²*)

and volume (1250km³ *300 miles³*).

Largest active Mauna Loa, on Hawaii, has the shape of a broad gentle dome 120km *75 miles* long and 50 km *31 miles* wide (above sea level), with lava flows which occupy more than 5125 km² *1980 miles²* of the island. It has a total volume of 42,500 km³ *10,200 miles³*, of which 84.2 per cent is below sea level. Its caldera, Mokuaweoweo, has an area of 10.5km² *4 miles²* and is 150–180m *500–600ft* deep. Mauna Loa rises 4170m *13,680ft* and has averaged one eruption every 4½ years since 1843, although none since 1984.

Highest active The highest volcano regarded as active is Ojos del Salado (which has fumaroles), at a height of 6887m *22,595ft*, on the frontier between Chile and Argentina.

Northernmost and southernmost The northernmost volcano is Beeren Berg (2276m *7470ft*) on the island of Jan Mayen (71°05′N) in the Greenland Sea. It erupted on 20 Sep 1970 and the island's 39 inhabitants (all male) had to be evacuated. The Ostenso seamount (1775 m *5825ft*), 556km *346 miles* from the North Pole in Lat. 85°10′N, Long. 133°W, was volcanic.

The most southerly known active volcano is Mt Erebus (3794 m *12,447 ft*), on Ross Island (77°35′S) in Antarctica.

Largest crater The world's largest caldera or volcano crater is that of Toba, north-central Sumatra, Indonesia, covering 1775km² *685 miles²*.

Geysers

Tallest The Waimangu (Maori 'black water') geyser, in New Zealand, erupted to a height in excess of 460m *1500ft* in 1903, when it was erupting every 30–36 hours, but has not been active since late 1904. In August 1903 four people were killed during one of its violent eruptions.

Currently the world's tallest active geyser is Steamboat Geyser in Yellowstone National Park, Wyoming, USA. During the 1980s it erupted at intervals ranging from 19 days to more than four years, although there were occasions in the 1960s when it erupted as frequently as every 4–10 days. The maximum height ranges from 60–115m *195–380ft*. The greatest measured water discharge was an estimated 28,000–38,000 hl *616,000–836,000gal* by the Giant Geyser, also in Yellowstone National Park. However, this estimate, made in the 1950s, was only a rough calculation.

Weather

The meteorological records given below relate largely to the last 150–170 years, since data before that time are both sparse and often unreliable. Reliable registering thermometers were introduced as recently as *c.* 1820. The longest period of observations have been maintained at the Radcliffe Observatory, Oxford since 1767, and on a daily basis since 1814, though discontinuous records have enabled the Chinese to assert that 903 BC was a very bad winter.

Palaeo-entomological evidence is that there was a southern European climate in England

c. 90,000 BC, while in *c.* 6000 BC the mean summer temperature reached 19°C *67°F*, or 3 degC *6 degF* higher than the present. It is believed that 1.2 million years ago the world's air temperature averaged 35°C *95°F*.

Ozone levels Ozone levels reached a record low on 12 Oct 1993 over the South Pole in Antarctica, when a figure of 91 Dobson units (DU) was recorded. This compares to 300 DU as a figure considered adequate to shield the Earth from solar ultra-violet radiation and sustain biological systems as we know them. The largest ozone depletion takes place in spring in Antarctica (August and September), and as late as 23 Aug 1993 a figure of 276 DU had been measured, indicating a loss of about ⅔ of the ozone in under two months. The ozone hole was discovered in 1985, and a hole the size of North America was created as a result of the events of the spring of 1993.

Most equable temperature The location with the most equable recorded temperature over a short period is Garapan, on Saipan in the Mariana Islands, Pacific Ocean. During the nine years from 1927–35, inclusive, the lowest temperature recorded was 19.6°C *67.3°F* on 30 Jan 1934 and the highest was 31.4°C *88.5°F* on 9 Sep 1931, giving an extreme range of 11.8degC *21.2degF*. Between 1911 and 1990 the Brazilian off-shore island of Fernando de Noronha had a minimum temperature of 17.7°C *63.9°F* on 27 Feb 1980 and a maximum of 32.2°C *90.0°F* on 3 Mar 1968, 25 Dec 1972 and 17 Apr 1973, giving an extreme range of 14.5degC *26.1degF*.

Greatest temperature ranges The greatest recorded temperature ranges in the world are around the Siberian 'cold pole' in the east of Russia. Temperatures in Verkhoyansk (67°33′N, 133°23′E) have ranged 105degC *188degF*, from −68°C *−90°F* to 37°C *98°F*. The greatest temperature variation recorded in a day is 56degC *100degF* (a fall from 7°C *44°F* to −49°C *−56°F*) at Browning, Montana, USA on 23–24 Jan 1916. The most freakish rise was 27degC *49degF* in 2 min at Spearfish, South Dakota, USA, from −20°C *−4°F* at 7:30a.m. to 7°C *45°F* at 7:32a.m. on 22 Jan 1943.

The British record is 29degC *52.2degF* (−7°C *19.4°F* to 22°C *71.6°F*) at Tummel Bridge, Tayside on 9 May 1978.

Highest shade temperature The highest ever recorded shade temperature is 58°C *136°F* at Al'Azīzīyah, Libya (alt. 111m *367ft*) on 13 Sep 1922.

The highest in Britain is 37.1°C *98.8°F* at Cheltenham (Glos) on 3 Aug 1990. The 38°C *100°F* which was once reported from Tonbridge (Kent) was a non-standard exposure and is estimated to be equivalent to 36–37°C *97–98°F*.

Hottest place On an annual mean basis, with readings taken over a six-year period from 1960 to 1966, the temperature at Dallol, in Ethiopia, was 34°C *94°F*. At Marble Bar, Western Australia (maximum 121°F *49°C*), 162 consecutive days with maximum temperatures of over 100°F *38°C* were recorded between 30 Oct 1923 and 8 Apr 1924. At Wyndham, also in Western Australia, the temperature reached 90°F *32°C* or more on 333 days in 1946.

In the appropriately-named Death Valley, California, USA, maximum temperatures of over 120°F *49°C* were recorded on 43 consecutive days, between 6 Jul and 17 Aug 1917.

The tallest geyser
— *Waimangu*

Imagine a fountain of boiling water higher than the Empire State Building, and you can picture the tallest geyser on record.

◆

A geyser is a spouting hot spring which discharges water and steam, so naturally the sight of one in action as it erupts presents one of the most spectacular phenomenon in nature. The greatest height to which a geyser has ever erupted is some 460m *1500ft*, in the case of Waimangu, near Rotorua in New Zealand, at the beginning of the 20th century. It was discovered on 30 Jan 1901 by Dr Humphrey Haines, who was investigating reports of huge steam clouds in the area. Its heyday was in 1903 when eruptions were occurring every 30–36 hours, with huge boulders and black water being ejected.

◆

Waimangu soon became a popular attraction, but its fame and reputation increased dramatically when four people were killed there in August 1903. They had been standing some 27m *90ft* away from the geyser when it displayed, but owing to the force of the eruption their bodies were found up to 800m *½mile* away. One was jammed between two rocks, one in a hole in the ground, one suspended in a tree and the fourth on flat ground.

◆

In late 1904 it ceased activity, and although the surrounding area erupted in 1917, the geyser itself did not. The ground in the area is still hot, but the dramatic sight of Waimangu erupting is now history.

Geyser basin

Point where the four people were standing

In Britain, annual mean temperatures of 11.5°C *52.7°F* were recorded both at Penzance, in Cornwall, and the Isles of Scilly in the period 1931 to 1960.

Driest place The annual mean rainfall on the Pacific coast of Chile between Arica and Antofagasta is less than 0.1mm *0.004in.*

In Britain, the lowest annual mean rainfall on record is at Lee Wick Farm, St Osyth, Essex, with 513mm *20.2in*, based on the period 1964 to 1982. The lowest rainfall recorded in a single year was 236mm *9.3in* at one station in Margate, Kent in 1921.

Longest drought Desierto de Atacama, in Chile, has virtually no rain, although several times a century a squall may strike a small area of it.

Britain's longest drought lasted 73 days, from 4 Mar to 15 May 1893, at Mile End, Greater London.

Most sunshine The annual average at Yuma, Arizona, USA is 90 per cent (over 4000 hr). St Petersburg, Florida, USA recorded 768 consecutive sunny days from 9 Feb 1967 to 17 Mar 1969.

The best in Britain was 78.3 per cent of the maximum possible in one month (382 hours out of 488) at Pendennis Castle, Cornwall in June 1925.

Least sunshine At the South Pole there is nil sunshine for 182 days every year and at the North Pole the same applies for 176 days.

From 18 November to 8 February each winter the south-eastern end of the village of Lochranza, Isle of Arran, Strathclyde is in shadow of mountains, and for the whole of December 1890, a figure of nil was registered at Westminster, London.

Best and worst British summers According to Prof. Gordon Manley's survey over the period 1728–1978 the best (i.e. driest and hottest) British summer was that of 1976 and the worst (i.e. wettest and coldest) that of 1879. Temperatures of more than 32°C *90°F* were recorded on 13 consecutive days (25 Jun–7 Jul 1976) within Great Britain, peaking at 35.9°C *96.6°F* in Cheltenham on 3 July. In 1983 there were 40 days with temperatures above 80°F *27°C* in Britain between 3 July–31 August, including 17 consecutively (3–19 July).

Lowest screen temperature A record low of −89.2°C *−128.6°F* was registered at Vostok, Antarctica (alt. 3419m *11,220ft*) on 21 Jul 1983. The coldest permanently inhabited place is the Siberian village of Oymyakon (pop. 4000), 63°16'N, 143°15'E (700m *2300ft*), in Russia where the temperature reached −68°C *−90°F* in 1933, and an unofficial −72°C *−98°F* has been published more recently.

Britain's lowest was −27°C *−17°F* on 11 Feb 1895 and again on 10 Jan 1982, both times at Braemar, Grampian. The −31°C *−23°F* at Blackadder, Borders, on 4 Dec 1879, and the −29°C *−20°F* at Grantown-on-Spey on 24 Feb 1955, were not standard exposures. The lowest maximum temperature for a day was −19.1°C *−2.4°F* at Braemar, again on 10 Jan 1982.

Coldest place Polus Nedostupnosti (Pole of Inaccessibility), Antarctica at 78°S, 96°E, is the coldest place in the world, with an extrapolated annual mean of −58°C *−72°F*. The coldest measured mean is −57°C *−70°F*, at Plateau Station, Antarctica.

For Britain, the coldest mean temperature is 6.3°C *43.4°F*, at Braemar, Grampian, based on readings taken between 1952 and 1981.

Longest freeze The longest recorded unremitting freeze in the British Isles was one of 40 days at the Great Dun Fell radio station, Appleby, Cumbria, from 23 Jan to 3 Mar 1986. Less rigorous early data include a frost from 5 Dec 1607 to 14 Feb 1608 and a 91-day frost on Dartmoor, Devon in 1854–5.

Wettest place By average annual rainfall, the wettest place in the world is Mawsynram, in Meghalaya State, India, with 11,873mm *467½in* per annum.

Styhead Tarn (487m *1600ft*), in Cumbria, with 4391mm *173in*, is Britain's wettest place.

Most rainy days Mt Wai-'ale-'ale (1569m *5148ft*), Kauai, Hawaii has up to 350 rainy days per annum.

The place in the British Isles which has had the most rainy days in a calendar year is Ballynahinch, in Co. Galway, Republic of Ireland, with 309 in 1923.

Most intense rainfall Difficulties attend rainfall readings for very short periods, but the figure of 38.1mm *1½in* in one min at Barst, Guadeloupe, in the Caribbean on 26 Nov 1970 is regarded as the most intense recorded in modern times.

The cloudburst of 'near 2ft *600mm* in less than a quarter of half an hour' at Oxford on the afternoon of 31 May (old style) 1682 is regarded as unacademically recorded. The most intense

Mawsynram in India is the wettest place in the world, with ten times more rain every year than New York and twenty times more than London.

A survey carried out by researchers from the Indian Meteorological Department between 1941 and 1979 showed that Mawsynram had on average 11,873mm *467½ in* rain per annum. Most of it falls in the monsoon season from June to September, and on average only 147 days each year have any rain. The weather station is located on the crest of the southern range of the Khasi Hills in Meghalaya, some 200km *125 miles* to the north-east of Dhaka, the capital of Bangladesh. Cherrapunji, which holds records for the greatest recorded rainfall in a month and also in a year, is only 16km *10 miles* away.

To appreciate just how much rain Mawsynram has, it is interesting to compare the figures with those for major cities around the world.

It's Raining *Again!*

Mawsynram has on average 11,873mm *467½ in* rain every year

Beijing has 1828mm *72 in*

Tokyo has 1565mm *61 ½ in*

Sydney has 1181mm *46 ½ in*

New York has 1100mm *43 ¼ in*

Rio de Janeiro has 1082mm *42 ½ in*

Toronto has 773mm *30 ½ in*

Mexico City has 709mm *28 in*

Paris has 619mm *24 ½ in*

Berlin has 603mm *23 ¾ in*

London has 593mm *23 ¼ in*

Although Mawsynram has so much rain, Sydney, Paris, Berlin and London actually have rain on *more* days — 152, 162, 167 and 153 respectively. At the other extreme it only rains in Beijing on 64 days.

= 500mm of rain

rainfall in Britain recorded to modern standards has been 51mm *2in* in 12min at Wisbech, Cambs on 27 Jun 1970.

Greatest rainfall

A record 1870mm *73.62in* of rain fell in the space of 24 hours in Cilaos (alt. 1200m *3940 ft*), La Réunion, Indian Ocean on 15 and 16 Mar 1952. This is equal to 7554tonnes of rain per acre. For a calendar month the record is 9300mm *366in* at Cherrapunji, Meghalaya, India in July 1861, and the 12-month record was also set at Cherrapunji, with 26,461mm *1041¾in* between 1 Aug 1860 and 31 Jul 1861.

In Great Britain, the 24-hour record is 279mm *11in* at Martinstown, Dorset on 18 and 19 Jul 1955. At Llyn Llydau, Snowdon, Gwynedd 1436mm *56½in* fell in October 1909, and over a 12-month period, 6527mm *257in* fell at Sprinkling Tarn, Cumbria, in 1954.

Falsest!

Falsest St Swithin's Days The legend that the weather on St Swithin's Day, celebrated on 15 July (old and new style) since AD 912, determines the rainfall for the next 40 days is one which has long persisted. There was a brilliant 13½hr of sunshine in London on 15 Jul 1924, but 30 of the next 40 days were wet. On 15 Jul 1913 there was a downpour lasting 15hr, yet it rained on only nine of the subsequent 40 days in London.

Longest!

The longest-lasting rainbow was one which was visible for over three hours, reported from the coastal border of Gwynedd and Clwyd on 14 Aug 1979.

Greatest flood Scientists reported the discovery of the largest fresh water flood in history in January 1993. It occurred *c.* 18,000 years ago when an ancient ice dammed-lake in the Altay Mountains of Siberia, Russia broke, allowing the water to pour out. The lake was estimated to be 120km *75miles* long and 760m *2500ft* deep. The main flow of water was reported to be 490m *1600ft* deep and travelling at 160km/h *100mph*.

Windiest place Commonwealth Bay, George V Coast, Antarctica, where gales reach 320km/h *200mph*, is the world's windiest place.

In Britain, an average reading of 33.1km/h *20.6mph* was registered at Fair Isle in the period 1974–8.

Highest surface wind-speed A surface wind-speed of 371km/h *231mph* was recorded at Mt Washington (1916m *6288ft*), New Hampshire, USA on 12 Apr 1934. The highest speed at a low altitude was registered on 8 Mar 1972 at the USAF base at Thule (44m *145ft*), in Greenland, when a peak speed of 333km/h *207mph* was recorded. The highest speed measured to date in a tornado is 450km/h *280mph* at Wichita Falls, Texas, USA on 2 Apr 1958.

The record high surface wind-speed for Britain is 150 knots (278km/h *172mph*), on Cairn Gorm Summit (1245m *4084ft*), on 20 Mar 1986. A figure of 285.2km/h *177.2mph*, at RAF Saxa Vord, Unst, in the Shetlands on 16 Feb 1962, was not recorded with standard equipment. British tornadoes may reach 290km/h *180mph*.

Tornadoes (⇨ *also Accidents and Disasters*) Britain's strongest tornado was at Southsea, Portsmouth, Hants on 14 Dec 1810 (Force 8 on the Meaden-TORRO scale). On 23 Nov 1981, 58 tornadoes were reported in one day from Anglesey to eastern England.

Highest waterspout The highest waterspout of which there is a reliable record was one observed on 16 May 1898 off Eden, New South Wales, Australia. A theodolite reading from the shore gave its height as 1528m *5014ft*. It was about 3m *10ft* in diameter.

The Spithead waterspout off Ryde, Isle of Wight on 21 Aug 1878 was measured by sextant to be 1600m or *'about a mile'* in height. A more realistic estimate of a waterspout was one which developed off Yarmouth, Isle of Wight on 6 Aug 1987. It was some 760m *2500ft* in height.

Greatest snowfall Over a 12-month period from 19 Feb 1971 to 18 Feb 1972, 31,102mm *1224½in* of snow fell at Paradise, Mt Rainier, in Washington State, USA. The record for a single snowstorm is 4800mm *189in* at Mt Shasta Ski Bowl, California, USA from 13–19 Feb 1959 and for a 24-hr period it is 1930mm *76in* at Silver Lake, Colorado, USA on 14–15 Apr 1921. The greatest depth of snow on the ground was 1146cm *37ft 7in* at Tamarac, California, USA in March 1911.

Britain's 12-month record is the 1524mm *60in* which fell in Upper Teesdale and also in the Denbighshire Hills, Clwyd, in 1947. London's earliest recorded snow was on 25 Sep 1885, and the latest on 2 Jun 1975. Less reliable reports suggest snow on 12 Sep 1658 (old style) and on 12 Jun 1791.

White Christmases London has experienced eight 'white' or snowing Christmas Days since 1900. These have been 1906, 1917 (slight), 1923 (slight), 1927, 1938, 1956 (slight), 1970 and 1981. These were more frequent in the 19th century and even more so before the change of the calendar which by removing 3–13 September brought forward all dates subsequent to 2 Sep 1752 by 11 days.

Heaviest hailstones The heaviest hailstones on record, weighing up to 1kg *2¼lb*, are reported to have killed 92 people in the Gopalganj district of Bangladesh on 14 Apr 1986.

The heaviest hailstones in Britain fell on 5 Sep 1958 at Horsham, W Sussex, and weighed 142g *5oz*. Much heavier ones are sometimes reported, but usually these are coalesced rather than single stones.

The crew of the US Air Weather Service aircraft, safely back on land after recording the lowest ever sea-level barometric pressure, over the Pacific Ocean in Typhoon Tip.
(Photo: USAF)

Barometric pressure The highest barometric pressure ever recorded was 1083.8mb *32in* at Agata, Siberia, Russia (alt. 262m *862ft*) on 31 Dec 1968. The highest in Britain was 1054.7mb *31.15in*, in Aberdeen on 31 Jan 1902.

The lowest sea-level pressure was 870mb *25.69in* in Typhoon Tip, 480km *300miles* west of Guam, Pacific Ocean, in Lat. 16°44′N, Long. 137°46′E, on 12 Oct 1979. Britain's lowest was 925.5mb *27.33in*, at Ochtertyre, near Crieff, Tayside on 26 Jan 1884.

Cloud extremes The highest standard cloud form is cirrus, averaging 8200m *27,000ft* and higher, but the rare nacreous or mother-of-pearl formation may reach nearly 24,500m *80,000ft*. The lowest is stratus, below 460m *1500ft*. The cloud form with the greatest vertical range is cumulonimbus, which has been observed to reach a height of nearly 20,000m *68,000ft* in the tropics.

Upper atmosphere Rocket-borne experiments indicate atmospheric temperatures as low as *c.* −173°C *−279°F* at an altitude of about 90km *56miles*. This is in the region of noctilucent cloud formation in the mesosphere.

Lightning!

The only man in the world to be struck by lightning seven times is ex-park ranger Roy C. Sullivan (US), the human lightning conductor of Virginia, USA. His attraction for lightning began in 1942 (lost big toe nail), and was resumed in July 1969 (lost eyebrows), in July 1970 (left shoulder seared), on 16 Apr 1972 (hair set on fire), on 7 Aug 1973 (new hair re-fired and legs seared), on 5 Jun 1976 (ankle injured), and he was sent to Waynesboro Hospital with chest and stomach burns on 25 Jun 1977 after being struck while fishing. In September 1983 he died by his own hand, reportedly rejected in love.

Thunder-days In Tororo, Uganda an average of 251 days of thunder per annum was recorded for the 10-year period 1967–76.

The record number of thunder-days recorded in a specific place in a calendar year in Britain is 38, twice. The first time was in 1912, at Stonyhurst, in Lancashire, and the second was in 1967, at Huddersfield, in W Yorks.

Longest sea-level fogs Sea-level fogs—with visibility less than 900 m *1000 yd*—persist for weeks on the Grand Banks, Newfoundland, Canada, with the average being more than 120 days per year.

The duration record for Britain is 4 days 18 hours, twice, in both cases in London. The first time was from 26 Nov to 1 Dec 1948 and the second from 5 to 9 Dec 1952. Lower visibilities occur at higher altitudes. Ben Nevis is reputedly in cloud 300 days per year.

Gems, Jewels and Precious Stones

Diamond

Largest 3106 carats. This was found on 26 Jan 1905 at the Premier Diamond Mine, near Pretoria, South Africa. It was named *The Cullinan* and was cut into 106 polished diamonds. It produced the largest cut fine quality colourless diamond, which weighs 530.2 carats. Several large pieces of low quality diamonds have been found including a carbonado of 3167 carats discovered in Brazil in 1905. Currently the largest known single piece of rough diamond still in existence weighs 1462 carats and is retained by De Beers in London.

Largest cut 545.67 carats, known as the *Unnamed Brown*. This was fashioned from a 755.50 carat rough into a fire rose cushion cut and acted as the forerunner to the *Centenary Diamond*, the world's largest flawless top colour modern fancy cut diamond at 273.85 carats.

Smallest brilliant cut 0.000102 carats, polished by D. Drukker & Zn NV of Amsterdam, Netherlands in 1985. The stone was polished with all 57 facets and has a diameter of 0.22 mm *0.009 in.*

Highest priced $12,760,000 for a pear-shaped mixed cut diamond of 101.84 carats. The stone was bought at Sotheby's, Geneva, Switzerland on 14 Nov 1990. The highest price known to be paid for a rough diamond was £5.8 million for a 255.10 carat stone from Guinea, by the William Goldberg Diamond Corporation in partnership with the Chow Tai Fook Jewellery Co. Ltd of Hong Kong, in March 1989. *Many polished diamond sales are considered private transactions and the prices paid are not disclosed.* The record per carat is $926,315.79, for a 0.95 carat fancy purplish red stone sold at Christie's, New York, USA on 28 Apr 1987.

Ruby

Largest star 6465 carats. The *Eminent Star* ruby, believed to be of Indian origin, is owned by Kailash Rawat of Eminent Gems Inc. of New York, USA. It is an oval cabochon with a six ray star, and measures 109 × 90.5 × 58 mm *4¼ × 3⅝ × 2¼ in.*

Highest priced $4,620,000. A ruby and diamond ring made by Chaumet in Paris, France, weighing 32.08 carats, was sold at Sotheby's, New York, USA on 26 Oct 1989. The record per

The largest star ruby is the *Eminent Star*, which weighs 6465 carats. The original rough from which it was cut weighed more than 30,000 carats.
(Photo: Eminent Gems Inc.)

carat is $227,300 for a ruby ring with a stone weighing 15.97 carats, which was sold at Sotheby's, New York, USA on 18 Oct 1988.

Emerald

Largest cut 86,136 carats. A natural beryl was found in Carnaiba, Brazil in August 1974. It was carved by Richard Chan in Hong Kong and valued at £718,000 in 1982.

Largest single crystal 7025 carats. The largest single emerald crystal of gem quality was found in 1969 at the Cruces Mine, near Gachala, Colombia, and is owned by a private mining concern.

Highest priced $3,080,000 (Single lot of emeralds). An emerald and diamond necklace made by Cartier, London in 1937 (a total of 12 stones weighing 108.74 carats) was sold at Sotheby's, New York, USA on 26 Oct 1989. The highest price for a single emerald is $2,126,646, for a 19.77 carat emerald and diamond ring made by Cartier in 1958, which was sold at Sotheby's, Geneva, Switzerland on 2 Apr 1987. This also represented the record price per carat for an emerald, at $107,569.

Sapphire

Largest star 9719.50 carats. A stone, cut in London in November 1989, has been named *The Lone Star* and is owned by Harold Roper.

Highest priced $2,791,723. A step-cut stone of 62.02 carats was sold as a sapphire and diamond ring at Sotheby's, St Moritz, Switzerland on 20 Feb 1988.

Opal

Largest 26,350 carats. The largest single piece of gem quality white opal was found in July 1989 at the Jupiter Field at Coober Pedy in South Australia. It has been named *Jupiter-Five* and is in private ownership.

Largest black opal 1520 carats. A stone found on 4 Feb 1972 at Lightning Ridge, New South Wales, Australia produced this finished gem, called the *Empress of Glengarry*. It measures 121 × 80 × 15 mm *4¾ × 3⅛ × ⅝ in*, and is owned by Peter Gray.

Largest rough black opal 2020 carats. The largest gem quality uncut black opal was also found at Lightning Ridge, on 3 Nov 1986. After cleaning it measures 100 × 66 × 63 mm *4 × 2⅝ × 2½ in*. It has been named *Halley's Comet* and is owned by a team of opal miners known as The Lunatic Hill Syndicate.

Pearl

Largest 6.37 kg *14 lb 1 oz*. The *Pearl of Lao-tze* (also known as the *Pearl of Allah*) was found at Palawan, Philippines on 7 May 1934 in the shell of a giant clam. It is 24 cm *9½ in* long and 14 cm *5½ in* in diameter.

Largest abalone pearl 469.13 carats. A baroque abalone pearl measuring 7 × 5 × 2.8 cm *2¾ × 2 × 1⅛ in* was found at Salt Point State Park, California, USA in May 1990. It is owned by Wesley Rankin and is called the *Big Pink*.

Largest cultured pearl 138.25 carats. A 40 mm *1½ in* round cultured pearl weighing 27.65 g *1 oz* was found near Samui Island, off Thailand, in January 1988. The stone is owned by the Mikimoto Pearl Island Company, Japan.

Highest priced $864,280. *La Régente*, an egg-shaped pearl weighing 15.13 g *302.68 grains* and formerly part of the French Crown Jewels, was sold at Christie's, Geneva, Switzerland on 12 May 1988.

Jade

Largest 577 tonnes. A single lens of nephrite jade was found in the Yukon Territory of Canada by Max Rosequist in July 1992. It is owned by Yukon Jade Ltd.

Max Rosequist, who discovered the world's largest piece of jade, enthused about his find, saying:– 'This massive piece of jade will become a source of wonderment and pleasure for thousands of people, bridging the gap from the present to the far distant future, and will be one of the few survivors from our generation. This immortal stone will be for art and jewellery lovers throughout all time.'

Amber

Largest 15.25 kg *33 lb 10 oz*. The 'Burma Amber' is located in the Natural History Museum, London.

Gold

Largest mass of gold 214.32 kg *7560 oz*. The *Holtermann Nugget*, found on 19 Oct 1872 in the Beyers & Holtermann Star of Hope mine, Hill End, New South Wales, Australia, contained some 99.8 kg *220 lb* of gold in a 285.7 kg *630 lb* slab of slate.

Largest pure nugget 69.92 kg *2248 troy oz*. The *Welcome Stranger*, found at Moliagul, Victoria, Australia in 1869, yielded 69.92 kg *2248 troy oz* of pure gold from 70.92 kg *2280¼ oz*.

Platinum

Largest 9635 g *340 oz*. The largest platinum nugget ever found was discovered in the Ural Mountains in Russia in 1843, but was melted down shortly after its discovery.

Largest existing 7860 g *277 oz*. The largest surviving platinum nugget is known as the *Ural Giant* and is currently in the custody of the Diamond Foundation in the Kremlin, Moscow, Russia.

Animal Kingdom

Unless otherwise stated, all measurements refer to adult specimens.

General Records

Oldest!

Animals moved from the sea to the land 414 million years ago, according to discoveries made in 1990 near Ludlow, Shrops. The world's first land animals include two kinds of centipede and a tiny spider found among plant debris. This suggests that life moved on to land much earlier than previously thought.

Loudest animal sound The low-frequency pulses made by blue whales when communicating with each other have been measured at up to 188 decibels, making them the loudest sounds emitted by any living source. They have been detected 850km *530 miles* away.

Most fertile It has been calculated that with unlimited food, a single cabbage aphid (*Brevicoryne brassicae*) could theoretically give rise in a year to a mass of descendants weighing 822 million tonnes, or more than three times the total weight of the world's human population.

Strongest In proportion to their size, the strongest animals are the larger beetles of the family Scarabaeidae, which are found mainly in the tropics. In tests carried out on a rhinoceros beetle of the family Dynastinae, it was found to support 850 times its own weight on the back. As a comparison, in a trestle lift a human can support 17 times his own body weight.

Strongest bite Experiments carried out with a 'Snodgrass gnathodynamometer' (shark-bite meter) at the Lerner Marine Laboratory in Bimini, Bahamas revealed that a 2m *6 ft 6¾ in* long dusky shark (*Carcharhinus obscurus*) could exert a force of 60kg *132 lb* between its jaws. This is equivalent to a pressure of 3 tonnes/cm² or *19.6 tons/in²* at the tips of the teeth.

Most acute sense of smell The most acute sense of smell exhibited in nature is that of the male emperor moth (*Eudia pavonia*), which, according to German experiments in 1961, can detect the sex attractant of the virgin female at the almost unbelievable range of 11km *6.8 miles* upwind. This scent has been identified as one of the higher alcohols ($C_{16}H_{29}OH$), of which the female carries less than 0.0001 mg.

Suspended animation In 1846 two specimens of the desert snail *Eremina desertorum* were pre-

Largest!

The largest structure ever built by living creatures is the 2027-km *1260-mile*-long Great Barrier Reef, off Queensland, Australia, covering an area of 207,000 km² *80,000 miles²*. It consists of countless millions of dead and living stony corals (order Madreporaria or Scleractinia). Over 350 species of coral are currently found there, and its accretion is estimated to have taken 600 million years.

Over 350 species of coral are currently found at the Great Barrier Reef in Australia, the largest coral structure.
(⇨ General Records, Largest animal-made structure)
(Photo: Planet Earth Pictures/ K Amsler)

Next time a dog's bark rattles your nerves, think of the howler monkeys *(Alouatta)* of Central and South America, whose fearsome screeches have been described as a cross between the bark of a dog and the bray of an ass increased a thousandfold! The males have an enlarged bony structure at the top of the windpipe which enables the sound to reverberate; once in full voice they can be heard clearly up to 16km *10 miles* away. They are the noisiest animals in the world.
(Photo: Jacana/J-P Varin)

sented to the British Museum (Natural History) as dead exhibits. They were glued on a small tablet and placed on display. Four years later, in March 1850, the Museum staff, suspecting that one of the snails was still alive, removed it from the tablet and placed it in tepid water. The snail moved and later began to feed. This hardy little creature lived for a further two years before it fell into a torpor and died.

Regeneration The sponges (*Porifera*) have the most remarkable powers of regeneration of lost parts of any animal, as they can regrow from a tiny fragment of themselves. If a sponge is forced through a fine-meshed silk gauze, the separate fragments can re-form into a full-size sponge.

Most dangerous The malarial parasites of the genus *Plasmodium* carried by mosquitoes of the genus *Anopheles*, have, excluding wars and accidents, probably been responsible for half of all human deaths since the Stone Age. According to 1993 World Health Organisation estimates, between 1.4 million and 2.8 million people die from malaria each year in sub-Saharan Africa alone.

Largest colonies The black-tailed prairie dog (*Cynomys ludovicianus*), a rodent of the family Sciuridae found in the western USA and northern Mexico, builds large colonies. One single 'town'

The mighty African bush elephant (*Loxodonta africana*) is the largest living land mammal. The average bull stands 3.2 m *10 ft 6 in* at the shoulder and weighs 5.7 tonnes.
(Photo: Planet Earth Pictures/J Downer)

GUESS WHAT?

Q How long is the shortest snake in the world?

A See Page 36

discovered in 1901 contained about 400 million individuals and was estimated to cover 61,440 km² *24,000 miles²*.

Greatest concentration A huge swarm of Rocky Mountain locusts (*Melanoplus spretus*) in Nebraska, USA on 15–25 Aug 1875 covered an area estimated at 514,374 km² *198,600 miles²* as they flew over the state. This swarm of locusts contained 12.5 trillion (12.5×10¹²) insects, weighing 25 million tonnes.

Greediest animal
The larva of the polyphemus moth (*Antheraea polyphemus*) of North America consumes an amount equal to 86,000 times its own birthweight in the first 56 days of its life. In human terms, this would be equivalent to a 3.17 kg *7 lb* baby taking in 273 tonnes of nourishment.

Greatest weight loss During the 7-month lactation period, a 120-tonne female blue whale (*Balaenoptera musculus*) can lose up to 25 per cent of her bodyweight nursing her calf.

Most valuable The most valuable animals are racehorses. The most paid for a yearling is $13.1 million on 23 Jul 1985 at Keeneland, Kentucky, USA by Robert Sangster and partners for *Seattle Dancer*. (⇨ Horse Racing)

Gender difference The most striking difference in size is in the marine worm *Bonellia viridis*.

Weighing just 1.5–2.5 g *0.05–0.09 oz*, Savi's white-toothed pygmy shrew, also called the Etruscan shrew (*Suncus etruscus*), has a head and body length of 36–52 mm *1.32–2.04 in* (at most about a quarter of the width of this page), and a tail length of 24–29 mm *0.94–1.14 in*. It is found along the Mediterranean coast and southwards to Cape Province, South Africa, and is the smallest land mammal./(Photo: Jacana/Mammifrance)

The females are 10–100 cm *4–40 in* long compared with 1–3 mm *0.04–0.12 in* for the male, thus making the females millions of times heavier than the males.

Slowest growth The slowest growth rate in the Animal Kingdom is that of the deep-sea clam *Tindaria callistisormis*, which takes about 100 years to reach a length of 8 mm *⅓ in*. It is found in the North Atlantic.

Largest eye The Atlantic giant squid has the largest eye of any animal—living or extinct. It has been estimated that the record example from Thimble Tickle Bay had eyes measuring 400 mm *15¾ in* in diameter, almost the width of this open book. (⇨ Largest squid)

Mammals

Largest The largest animal ever recorded is the blue or sulphur-bottom whale (*Balaenoptera musculus*), also called Sibbald's rorqual. Newborn calves are 6.5–8.6 m *21¼ ft–28½ ft* long and weigh up to 3 tonnes. The barely visible ovum of the blue-whale calf weighing a fraction of a milligram grows to a weight of *c.* 26 tonnes in 22¾ months, made up of 10¾ months' gestation and the first 12 months of life. This is equivalent to an increase of 3×10¹⁰. (⇨ General records)

Heaviest A female weighing 190 tonnes and measuring 27.6 m *90 ft 6 in* in length was caught in the Southern Ocean on 20 Mar 1947.

Longest The longest specimen ever recorded was a female measuring 33.58 m *110 ft 2½ in* landed in 1909 at Grytviken, South Georgia in the South Atlantic. A blue whale nicknamed 'Queen Victoria' sighted in the Bering Sea several times since 1987 is estimated to measure at least 45 m *148 ft*, but this was not authenticated.

Deepest dive On 25 Aug 1969 a bull sperm whale (*Physeter catadon*) was killed 160 m *100 miles* south of Durban, South Africa after it had surfaced from a dive lasting 1 hr 52 min, and inside its stomach were two small sharks which had been swallowed about an hour earlier. These were Scymnodon, a type found only on the sea floor. The water there exceeds a depth of 3193 m *9876 ft* for a radius of 48–64 km *30–40 miles*, which suggests that the sperm whale sometimes descends to over 3000 m *9840 ft* when seeking food and is limited by pressure of time rather than by pressure of pressure.

Largest on land The largest specimen of the African bush elephant was a bull shot in Mucusso, Angola on 7 Nov 1974. Lying on its side this elephant measured 4.16 m *13 ft 8 in* in a projected line from the highest point of the shoulder to the base of the forefoot, indicating a

The Kodiak bear of Kodiak Island and the adjacent Afognak and Shuyak Islands in the Gulf of Alaska, going fishing (*main picture*) and adopting a more intimidating pose (*above*). The average male has a nose-to-tail length of 2.4 m *8 ft*. They weigh 476–533 kg *1050–1175 lb*, and are the largest carnivores in the world. (⇨ Carnivores)

(Photo: Images Colour Library)

standing height of about 3.96 m *13 ft*. It weighed over 12 tonnes.

Tallest on land   The tallest elephants are those of the endangered desert species from Damaraland, Namibia because they have proportionately longer legs than other elephants. The tallest recorded example was a bull shot near Sesfontein, Damaraland on 4 Apr 1978 after it had allegedly killed 11 people and caused widespread crop damage. Lying on its side, this mountain of flesh measured 4.42 m *14½ ft* in a projected line from the shoulder to the base of the forefoot, indicating a standing height of about 4.21 m *13 ft 10 in*. It weighed an estimated 8 tonnes.

Largest marine   The largest toothed mammal is the sperm whale or cachalot (*Physeter catodon*). The 5 m *16 ft 5 in* long lower jaw of a sperm whale exhibited in the British Museum (Natural History) belonged to a bull measuring nearly 25.6 m *84 ft*.

Sleepiest!

Some armadillos (Dasypodidae), opossums (Didelphidae) and sloths (Bradypodidae) spend up to 80 per cent of their lives sleeping or dozing.

Tallest   The tallest living animal is the giraffe (*Giraffa camelopardalis*), found in the dry savannah and semi-desert areas of Africa south of the Sahara. The tallest specimen ever recorded was a Masai bull (*G. c. tippelskirchi*) named George, received at Chester Zoo on 8 Jan 1959 from Kenya. His 'horns' *almost* grazed the roof of the 6.09 m *20 ft* high Giraffe House when he was nine years old. George died on 22 Jul 1969.

Smallest marine   In terms of weight, the smallest totally marine mammal is Commerson's dolphin (*Cephalorhynchus commersonii*), also known as Le Jacobite, which is found off the tip of South America. The weights of a group of six specimens ranged from 23 kg *50.7 lb* to 35 kg *77.1 lb*.

Fastest on land   Over a short distance (i.e. up to 550 m *600 yd*) the cheetah or hunting leopard (*Acinonyx jubatus*) of the open plains of east Africa, Iran, Turkmenistan and Afghanistan has a probable maximum speed of about 100 km/h *60 mph* on level ground.

The pronghorn antelope (*Antilocapra americana*) of the western United States has been observed to travel at 56 km/h *35 mph* for 6 km *4 miles*, at 67 km/h *42 mph* for 1.6 km *1 mile* and 88.5 km/h *55 mph* for 0.8 km *½ mile*.

GUESS WHAT?

Q   What is the vegetable least likely to make you fat?

A   See Page 46

UK Over a sustained distance the roe deer (*Capreolus capreolus*) can cruise at 40–48 km/h *25–30 mph* for more than 32 km *20 miles*, with occasional bursts of up to 64 km/h *40 mph*. On 19 Oct 1970 a frightened runaway red deer (*Cervus elaphus*) charging through a street in Stalybridge, Greater Manchester registered 67.5 km/h *42 mph* on a police radar speed trap.

Fastest marine   On 12 Oct 1958 a bull killer whale (*Orcinus orca*) measuring an estimated 6.1–7.6 m *20–25 ft* in length was timed at 55.5 km/h *34.5 mph* in the east Pacific. Similar speeds have also been reported for Dall's porpoise (*Phocoenoides dalli*) in short bursts. (⇨ also Most wakeful)

Slowest   The ai or three-toed sloth of tropical South America (*Bradypus tridactylus*) has an average ground speed of 1.8–2.4 m *6–8 ft* per minute (0.1–0.16 km/h *0.07–0.1 mph*), but in the trees it can accelerate to 4.6 m *15 ft* per minute (0.27 km/h *0.17 mph*).

Most wakeful   It is claimed that Dall's porpoise (*Phocoenoides dalli*) never sleeps at all. (⇨ also Fastest marine)

Oldest   No other mammal can match the age attained by Man (*Homo sapiens*) (⇨ Human Being), but the Asiatic elephant (*Elephas maximus*) probably comes closest. Rajah, Sri Lanka's bull elephant who led the annual Perahera procession through Kandi carrying the Sacred Tooth of the Buddha from 1931, died on 16 Jul 1988 allegedly aged 81 years. The greatest verified age is 78 years for a cow named Modoc, who died at Santa Clara, California, USA on 17 Jul 1975.

Highest The yak (*Bos grunniens*) of Tibet and the Sichuanese Alps, China climbs to an altitude of 6100m *20,000ft* when foraging.

Largest herds The largest herds on record were those of the springbok (*Antidorcas marsupialis*) during migration across the plains of the western parts of southern Africa in the 19th century. In 1849 John (later Sir John) Fraser observed a *trekbokken* that took three days to pass through the settlement of Beaufort West, Cape Province.

Longest gestation period The Asiatic elephant (*Elephas maximus*) has an average gestation period of 609 days (over 20 months) and a maximum of 760 days—more than two and a half times that of humans.

Shortest gestation period The gestation periods of the American opossum (*Didelphis marsupialis*), also called the Virginian opossum and the rare water opossum or yapok (*Chironectes minimus*) of central and northern South America are all normally 12–13 days but can be as short as eight days.

Largest litter The greatest number of young born to a *wild* mammal at a single birth is 31 (30 of which survived) in the case of the tailless tenrec (*Tenrec ecaudatus*), found in Madagascar and the Comoro Islands. The normal litter size is 12–15, although females can suckle up to 24.

Youngest breeder The female True Lemming (*Lemmus lemmus*) of Scandinavia can become pregnant after 14 days. The gestation period is 16 to 23 days, and litter size varies from 1 to 13. They are also prolific animals: one pair of lemmings was reported to have produced eight litters in 167 days, after which the male died.

Carnivores

Largest on land In 1894 a weight of 751kg *1656lb* was recorded for a male Kodiak bear (*Ursus arctos middendorffi*) shot at English Bay, Kodiak Island, whose *stretched* skin measured 4.11m *13½ft* from nose to tail.

Heaviest In 1960 a polar bear allegedly weighing 1002kg *2210lb* was shot at the polar entrance to Kotzebue Sound, Alaska, USA. The average male weighs 386–408 kg *850–900 lb* and measures 2.4 m *8ft* from nose to tail.

Smallest The Siberian least weasel (*Mustela rixosa*) has an overall length of 177–207mm *6.96–8.14in* and a weight of 35–70g *1¼–2½oz*.

Largest feline The male long-furred Siberian tiger (*Panthera tigris altaica*), averages 3.15m *10ft 4in* in length from the nose to the tip of the extended tail, stands

99–107cm *39–42in* at the shoulder and weighs about 265kg *585lb*.

Lions The average African lion (*Pantheus leo*) measures 2.7 m *9ft* overall and weighs 181–181 kg *400–410 lb*. The heaviest wild African lion on record weighed 313kg *690lb* and was shot near Hectorspruit, Transvaal, South Africa in 1936.

Smallest feline Average males of the rusty-spotted cat (*Felis rubiginosa*) of southern India and Sri Lanka are 64–71cm *25–28in* long overall (the tail measures 23–25cm *9–10in*) and weigh about 1.35kg *3lb*.

Gorillas, Monkeys and other Primates

Largest The male eastern lowland gorilla (*Gorilla gorilla graueri*) of eastern Zaïre and south-western Uganda is 175cm *5ft 9in* tall and weighs 165kg *360lb*.

Tallest The greatest height (top of crest to heel) recorded for a gorilla in the wild is 1.88m *6ft 2in* for a mountain bull shot in the eastern Congo (Zaïre) *c.* 1920.

Heaviest The heaviest gorilla ever kept in captivity was a male of the mountain race named

N'gagi, who died in San Diego Zoo, California, USA on 12 Jan 1944 at the age of 18. He weighed 310kg *683lb* at his heaviest in 1943. He was 1.72m *5ft 7¾in* tall and boasted a record chest measurement of 198cm *78in*.

Smallest The rare pen-tailed tree shrew (*Ptilocercus lowii*) of Malaysia has a total length of 230–330mm *9–13in* (head

Gamma the oldest chimpanzee, who died of natural causes at the advanced age of 59.

(Photo: Yerkes Regional Primate Research Center)

and body 100–140mm *4–5½in*; tail 130–190mm *5–7½in*) and weighs 35–50g *1.23–1.76oz*.

Oldest The greatest age recorded for a non-human primate is 59 years 5 months for a chimpanzee (*Pan troglodytes*) named Gamma, who died at the Yerkes Primate Research Center in Atlanta, Georgia, USA on 19 Feb 1992. Gamma was born at the Florida branch of the Yerkes Center in September 1932.

Monkey The world's oldest monkey, a male white-throated capuchin (*Cebus capucinus*) called Bobo, died on 10 Jul 1988 aged 53 years.

Fastest!

The highest swimming speed recorded for a pinniped is a short spurt of 40km/h *25mph* by a Californian sea-lion (*Zalophus californianus*).

Fastest on land The fastest pinniped on land is the crabeater seal (*Lobodon carcinophagus*), which has been timed at 19km/h *12mph*.

The world's largest seal, the southern elephant seal *(Mirounga leonina)* of the sub-Antarctic islands, pictured here in tuneful repose. Bulls average 5m *16½ft* in length, have a maximum girth of 3.7m *12ft* and weigh about 2268kg *5000lb*.

(Photo: Jacana/Parer-Parer, Cook/Aus)

Seals, Sea-lions, Walruses

Live The largest reported live specimen is a bull nicknamed 'Stalin' from South Georgia at 2662kg *5869lb* and 5.10m *16ft 9in*, recorded by members of the British Antarctic Survey on 14 Oct 1989.

Smallest The smallest pinnipeds are the ringed seal (*Phoca hispida*) of the Arctic, the closely related Baikal seal (*P. sibirica*) of Lake Baikal and the Caspian seal (*P. caspica*) of the Caspian Sea. Males are up to 1.67m *5½ft* long and can weigh up to 127kg *280lb*.

Oldest A female grey seal (*Halichoerus grypus*) shot at Shunni Wick, Shetland on 23 Apr 1969 was believed to be 'at least 46 years old' based on a count of dentine rings.

Deepest dive In about May 1988 scientists from the University of California at Santa Cruz, USA tested the diving abilities of the northern elephant seal (*Mirounga angustirostris*) off Ano Nuevo Point, California. One female reached a record depth of 1257 m *4135 ft*, and another remained submerged for 48 minutes.

Bats

Largest The only flying mammals are bats (order Chiroptera), of which there are about 950 species. The largest in terms of wingspan is the Bismarck flying fox (*Pteropus neohibernicus*) of the Bismarck Archipelago and New Guinea. A specimen in the American Museum of Natural History has a wing spread of 165 cm *5 ft 5 in*

UK The very rare, large mouse-eared bat (*Myotis myotis*) has a wingspan of 355–450 mm *14–17¾ in* and weighs up to 45 g *1.6 oz* in the case of females.

Smallest The smallest bat in the world is Kitti's hog-nosed bat at 160 mm *6.29 in* and 1.75–2 g *0.062–0.071 oz*.

Oldest The greatest age reliably reported for a bat is 32 years for a banded female little brown bat (*Myotis lucifugus*) in the United States in 1987.

Largest colonies The largest concentration of bats found living anywhere in the world today is that of the Mexican free-tailed bat (*Tadarida brasiliensis*) in Bracken Cave, San Antonio, Texas, USA, where up to 20 million animals assemble after migration.

Sharpest!

Because of their ultrasonic echolocation, bats have the most acute hearing of any terrestrial animal. Vampire bats (family Desmodontidae) and fruit bats (Pteropodidae) can hear frequencies as high as 120–210 kHz, compared with 20 kHz for the human limit and 280 kHz for the common dolphin (*Delphinus delphis*).

Deepest The little brown bat (*Myotis lucifugus*) has been recorded at a depth of 1160 m *3805 ft* in a zinc mine in New York, USA. The mine serves as winter quarters for 1000 members of this species.

Rodents

Largest The capybara (*Hydrochaerus hydrochaeris*), also called the carpincho or water hog, of tropical South America, has a head and body length of 1.0–1.4 m *3¼–4½ ft* and can weigh up to 113 kg *250 lb*.

Smallest The northern pygmy mouse (*Baiomys taylori*) of Mexico and Arizona and Texas, USA is up to 109 mm *4.3 in* in total length and weighs 7–8 g *0.24–0.28 oz*.

Oldest The greatest reliable age reported for a rodent is 27 years 3 months for a Sumatran

Hibernation!

The barrow ground squirrel (*Spermophilus parryi barrowensis*) of Point Barrow, Alaska, USA hibernates for nine months of the year, the longest of any animal.

crested porcupine (*Hystrix brachyura*) which died in the National Zoological Park, Washington, DC, USA on 12 Jan 1965.

Fastest breeder The female meadow vole (*Microtus agrestis*), found in Britain, can reproduce from the age of 25 days and can have up to 17 litters of 6–8 young in a year.

Antelopes

Largest The rare giant eland (*Taurotragus derbianus*) of western and central Africa can attain a height of 1.83 m *6 ft* at the shoulder and weigh over 907 kg *2000 lb*.

Smallest The royal antelope (*Neotragus pygmaeus*) of western Africa stands 25–31 cm *10–12 in* tall at the shoulder and weighs 3–3.6 kg *7–8 lb*, the size of an average hare (*Lepus europaeus*).

Deer

Largest The largest deer is the Alaskan moose (*Alces alces gigas*). A bull standing 2.34 m *7 ft 8 in* between pegs and weighing an estimated 816 kg *1800 lb* was shot in the Yukon Territory of Canada in September 1897.

UK The largest British deer is the red deer, which is usually about 1.11 m *3 ft 8 in* tall and weighs 113 kg *250 lb*.

Smallest The smallest true deer (family Cervidae) is the northern pudu (*Pudu mephistopheles*), which is 33–35 cm *13–14 in* tall at the shoulder and weighs 7.2–8.1 kg *16–18 lb*. It is found in Ecuador and Colombia.

Oldest The world's oldest recorded deer is a red deer (*Cervus elaphus scoticus*) named Bambi (b. 8 Jun 1963), owned by the Fraser family of Kiltarlity, Beauly, Highland.

Kangaroos

Largest The male red kangaroo (*Megaleia rufa* or *Macropus rufus*) of central, southern and eastern Australia stands up to 213 cm *7 ft* tall, measures up to 245 cm *8 ft ½ in* in total length and weighs up to 85 kg *187 lb*.

Fastest The highest speed recorded for a marsupial is 64 km/h *40 mph* for a mature female eastern grey kangaroo (*Macropus giganteus* or *M. canguru*). The highest sustained speed is 56 km/h *35 mph* recorded for a large male

red kangaroo which died from its exertions after being paced for 1.6 km *1 mile*.

Highest jump A captive eastern grey kangaroo once cleared a 2.44 m *8 ft* fence when a car backfired, and there is also a record of a hunted red kangaroo clearing a stack of timber 3.1 m *10 ft* high.

Longest jump During a chase in New South Wales, Australia in January 1951, a female red kangaroo made a series of bounds which included one of 12.8 m *42 ft*.

Tusks

Longest The longest tusks (excluding prehistoric examples) are a pair from an elephant taken from Zaire and kept in the New York Zoological Society in Bronx Park, New York City, USA. The right tusk measures 3.49 m *11 ft 5½ in* along the outside curve, the left 3.35 m *11 ft* and their combined weight is 133 kg *293 lb*.

Heaviest A pair of elephant tusks in the British Museum (Natural History) from a bull shot in Kenya in 1897 weighed 109 kg *240 lb* (length 3.11 m *10 ft 2½ in*) and 102 kg *225 lb* (length 3.18 m *10 ft 5½ in*), giving a total weight of 211 kg *465 lb*.

Horns

Longest The longest horns of any living animal are those of the water buffalo (*Bubalus arnee=B. bubalis*) of India. One bull shot in 1955 had horns measuring 4.24 m *13 ft 11 in* from tip to tip along the outside curve across the forehead.

A record spread of 3.2 m *10 ft 6 in* was recorded for a Texas longhorn steer on exhibition at the Heritage Museum, Big Springs, Texas, USA.

Longest rhinoceros horn The longest recorded anterior horn for a rhinoceros is one of 62¼ in *158 cm* found on a female southern race White rhinoceros (*Ceratotherium simum simum*) shot in South Africa in *c*. 1848. The interior horn measured 22¼ in *57 cm*. There is also an unconfirmed record of an anterior horn measuring 81 in *206 cm*.

The so-called wild pony (*Equus caballus*) can weigh up to 320 kg *700 lb*, earning it the title of heaviest land mammal in the UK. This one grazes on the Isle of Ruhm, Scotland
(Photo: Planet Earth Pictures/ N Garbutt)

Largest antlers The record antler spread or 'rack' is 1.99 m *6 ft 6½ in* from a moose killed near the Stewart River, Yukon, Canada in October 1897 and now on display in the Field Museum, Chicago, Illinois, USA.

Horses and Ponies

(⇨ Agriculture for record prices)

Earliest domestication Evidence from the Ukraine indicates that horses may have been ridden earlier than 4000 BC. (⇨ Agriculture)

Largest The tallest and heaviest documented horse was the shire gelding Sampson (later renamed Mammoth), bred by Thomas Cleaver of Toddington Mills, Beds. This horse (foaled 1846) measured 21.2½ hands (2.19 m *7 ft 2½ in*) in 1850 and was later said to have weighed 1524 kg *3360 lb*.

Smallest The smallest recorded horse was the stallion Little Pumpkin (foaled 15 Apr 1973), which stood 35.5 cm *14 in* and weighed 9 kg *20 lb* on 30 Nov 1975. It was owned by J.C. Williams Jr of Della Terra Mini Horse Farm, Inman, South Carolina, USA.

The smallest breed of horse is the Falabella of Argentina, developed by Julio Falabella of Recco de Roca. The smallest example was a mare which was 38 cm *15 in* tall and weighed 11.9 kg *26¼ lb*.

Oldest The greatest age reliably recorded for a horse is 62 years for Old Billy (foaled 1760), bred by Edward Robinson of Woolston, Lancs. Old Billy died on 27 Nov 1822.

Thoroughbred The oldest recorded thoroughbred racehorse was the 42-year-old chestnut gelding Tango Duke (foaled 1935), owned by Carmen J. Koper of Barongarook, Victoria, Australia. The horse died on 25 Jan 1978.

Oldest pony The greatest age reliably recorded for a pony is 54 years for a stallion (*fl.* 1919) owned by a farmer in central France.

UK A moorland pony called Joey, owned by June and Rosie Osborne of the Glebe Equestrian Centre, Wickham Bishop, Essex, died in May 1988 at the age of 44.

Mules The largest mules on record are Apollo (foaled 1977) and Anak (foaled 1976), owned by Herbert L. Mueller of Columbia, Illinois, USA. Apollo stands 19.1 hands (1.96 m *6 ft 5 in*) tall and weighs 998 kg *2200 lb*, with Anak at 18.3 hands (1.91 m *6 ft 3 in*) and 952.2 kg *2100 lb*. Both are the hybrid offspring of Belgian mares and mammoth jacks.

Dogs

Largest The heaviest (and longest) dog ever recorded is Aicama Zorba of La-Susa (whelped 26 Sep 1981), an Old English mastiff owned by Chris Eraclides of London. 'Zorba' stands 94 cm *37 in* at the shoulder and weighed a peak 155.58 kg *343 lb* in November 1989.

Tallest The tallest dog ever recorded was Shamgret Danzas (whelped 1975), a great Dane owned by Wendy and Keith Comley of Milton Keynes, Bucks. This dog stood 105.4 cm *41½ in* tall

Tracking!

In 1925 a Dobermann pinscher named Sauer, trained by Detective-Sergeant Herbert Kruger, tracked a stock-thief 160 km *100 miles* across the Great Karroo, South Africa by scent alone.

The beautiful St Bernard, which, along with the Old English Mastiff, is the heaviest breed of domestic dog (*Canis familiaris*). Males of both species regularly weigh 77–91 kg *170–200 lb*.

(Photo: Spectrum Colour Library)

(106.6 cm *42 in* with hackles raised) and weighed up to 108 kg *238 lb*. He died on 16 Oct 1984.

Smallest The smallest dog on record was a matchbox-sized Yorkshire terrier owned by Arthur Marples of Blackburn, Lancs, a former editor of *Our Dogs*. This tiny atom, which died in 1945 aged nearly two, stood 6.3 cm *2½ in* at the shoulder and measured 9.5 cm *3¾ in* from the tip of its nose to the root of its tail. It weighed just 113 g *4 oz*.

The smallest living dog is Summerann Thumberlina, a Yorkshire terrier measuring 14 cm *5½ in* at the shoulder, 20.3 cm *8 in* long and weighing 567 g *20 oz*. Born on 5 Jan 1992, she is owned by Maureen Howes of Stourport-on-Severn, Hereford & Worcester.

Oldest Most dogs live for 8–15 years, and authentic records of dogs living over 20 years are rare and generally involve the smaller breeds. The greatest reliable age recorded for a dog is 29 years 5 months for an Australian cattle-dog named Bluey, owned by Les Hall of Rochester, Victoria, Australia. Bluey was obtained as a puppy in 1910 and worked among cattle and sheep for nearly 20 years before being put to sleep on 14 Nov 1939.

UK A Welsh collie named Taffy, owned by Evelyn Brown of Forge Farm, West Bromwich, W

Ratting!

During the period 1820–24 an 11.8-kg *26-lb* 'bull and terrier' dog named 'Billy' dispatched 4000 rats in 17 hr, a remarkable feat considering that he was blind in one eye. His most notable feat was the killing of 100 rats in 5 min 30 sec at the Cockpit in Tufton Street, Westminster, London on 23 Apr 1825. He died on 23 Feb 1829 at the age of 13. James Searle's famous 'bull and terrier' bitch 'Jenny Lind' was another outstanding ratter. On 12 Jul 1853 she was backed to kill 500 rats in under 3 hr at The Beehive in Old Crosshall Street, Liverpool, and completed the job in 1 hr 36 min.

Mids, lived for 27 years and 313 days. He was whelped on 2 Apr 1952 and died on 9 Feb 1980.

Most prolific The greatest ever sire was the champion greyhound *Low Pressure*, nicknamed Timmy (whelped September 1957), owned by Bruna Amhurst of Regent's Park, London. From December 1961 until his death on 27 Nov 1969 he fathered over 3000 offspring.

Most valuable The largest legacy devoted to a dog was £15 million bequeathed by Ella Wendel

This abundant litter of St Bernard pups was born on the 16 Oct 1993 to Monterosa Lady Beloved, owned by Carl Montgomery of Taunton, Somerset. There are fifteen in all, making the litter the largest to survive in the UK. /(Photo: C. Montgomery)

The greatest number of seizures by dogs is 969 (worth $182 million) in 1988 alone by Rocky and Barco, a pair of malinoises patrolling the Rio Grande Valley ('Cocaine Alley') along the Texas border, where the pair were so proficient that Mexican drug smugglers put a $30,000 price on their heads. The dogs hold the rank of honorary Sergeant Major and always wear their stripes on duty.

UK In October 1988 a German shepherd owned by the Essex Police sniffed out 2 tonnes of cannabis worth £6 million when sent into a remote cottage on the outskirts of Harlow, Essex.

Largest Pet Litters

Animal/Breed	No.	Owner	Date
CAT *Burmese/Siamese*	19[1]	V. Gane, Church Westcote, Kingham, Oxon	7 Aug 1970
DOG *American foxhound*	23	W. Ely, Ambler, Pennsylvania, USA	19 Jun 1944
St Bernard	23[2]	R. and A. Rodden, Lebanon, Missouri, USA	6–7 Feb 1975
Great Dane	23[3]	M. Harris, Little Hall, Essex	June 1987
FERRET *Domestic*	15	J. Cliff, Denstone, Uttoxeter, Staffs	1981
GERBIL *Mongolian*	14[4]	S. Kirkman, Bulwell, Notts	May 1983
GUINEA PIG	12	Laboratory specimen	1972
HAMSTER *Golden*	26[5]	L. and S. Miller, Baton Rouge, Louisiana, USA	28 Feb 1974
MOUSE *House*	34[6]	M. Ogilvie, Blackpool, Lancs	12 Feb 1982
RABBIT *New Zealand white*	24	J. Filek, Cape Breton, Nova Scotia, Canada	1978

[1] Four stillborn. [2] 14 survived. [3] 16 survived. [4] Litter of 15 recorded in 1960s by George Meares, geneticist-owner of gerbil-breeding farm in St Petersburg, Florida, USA using special food formula. [5] 18 killed by mother. [6] 33 survived.

of New York, USA to her standard poodle Toby in 1931.

Guide dog The longest period of *active service* reported for a guide dog is 14 years 8 months (August 1972–March 1987) in the case of a Labrador-retriever bitch named Cindy-Cleo (whelped 20 Jan 1971), owned by Aron Barr of Tel Aviv, Israel. The dog died on 10 Apr 1987.

Largest show The centenary of the annual Crufts show, held outside London for the first time at the National Exhibition Centre, Birmingham, W Mids on 9–12 Jan 1991, attracted a record 22993 entries.

GUESS WHAT?

Q Which animal has the largest eye?

A See Page 27

Highest jump The canine high jump record for a leap and scramble over a smooth wooden wall (without ribs or other aids) is 3.72m *12ft 2½in* achieved by an 18-month-old lurcher dog named Stag, at the annual Cotswold Country Fair in Cirencester, Glos, on 27 Sep 1993. The dog is owned by Mr and Mrs P.R.Matthews of Redruth, Cornwall.

Duke, a three-year-old German shepherd dog handled by Corporal Graham Urry of RAF Newton, Notts, scaled a ribbed wall with regulation shallow slats to a height of 3.58m *11ft 9in* on the BBC *Record Breakers* programme on 11 Nov 1986.

Longest jump A greyhound named 'Bang' jumped 9.14m *30ft* while hare coursing at Brecon Lodge, Glos in 1849. He cleared a 1.4m 4ft 6in gate and landed on a road, damaging his pastern bone.

Top show dogs The greatest number of Challenge Certificates (CC) won by a dog is 78 by the chow chow Ch. U'Kwong King Solomon (whelped 21 Jun 1968). Owned and bred by Joan Egerton of Bramhall, Cheshire, 'Solly' won his first CC at the Cheshire Agricultural Society Championship Show on 4 Jun 1969, and his 78th CC was awarded at the City of Birmingham Championship Show on 4 Sep 1976. He died on 3 Apr 1978.

The greatest number of 'Best-in-Show' awards won by any dog in all-breed shows is 203 by the Scottish terrier bitch Ch. Braeburn's Close Encounter (whelped 22 Oct 1978) by 10 Mar 1985. She is owned by Sonnie Novick of Plantation Acres, Florida, USA.

Drug sniffing Snag, a US customs labrador retriever trained and partnered by Jeff Weitzmann, has made 118 drug seizures worth a canine record $810 million (£580 million).

Cats

Largest The heaviest reliably recorded domestic cat was a neutered male tabby named 'Himmy', which weighed 21.3kg *46lb 15¼oz* (neck 38.1cm *15in*, waist 83.8cm *33in* and length 96.5cm *38in*) at the time of his death from respiratory failure on 12 Mar 1986 at the age of 10years 4months. Himmy was owned by Thomas Vyse of Redlynch, Cairns, Queensland, Australia.

UK An 11-year-old male tabby called Poppa, owned by Gwladys Cooper of Newport, Gwent, weighed 20.19kg *44½lb* in November 1984. It died on 25 Jun 1985.

Mousing champion A female tortoiseshell cat named Towser (b. 21 Apr 1963), owned by Glenturret Distillery Ltd near Crieff, Tayside, notched up an estimated lifetime score of 28,899. She averaged three mice per day until her death on 20 Mar 1987.

Smallest Tinker Toy, a male blue point Himalayan-Persian cat owned by Katrina and Scott Forbes of Taylorville, Illinois, USA, is just 7cm *2¾in* tall and 19cm *7½in* long.

Oldest The oldest reliably recorded cat was the female tabby Ma, which was put to sleep on 5 Nov 1957 at the age of 34. Her owner was Alice St George Moore of Drewsteignton, Devon.

Most prolific A tabby named Dusty (b. 1935) of Bonham, Texas, USA produced 420

The Oldest Caged Pets

Animal/Species	Name, Owner, etc.	Years	Months
BIRD *Parrot*	*Prudle* captured 1958, I. Frost, East Sussex	35	—
Budgerigar	*Charlie* April 1948–20 Jun 1977, J. Dinsey, Stonebridge, London	29	2
RABBIT *Wild*	*Flopsy* caught 6 Aug 1964, died 29 Jun 1983, L.B. Walker, Longford, Tasmania, Australia	18	10¾
GUINEA PIG	*Snowball* died 14 Feb 1979, M. A. Wall, Bingham, Notts	14	10½
GERBIL *Mongolian*	*Sahara* May 1973–4 Oct 1981, Aaron Milstone, Lathrup Village, Michigan, USA	8	4½
MOUSE *House*	*Fritzy* 11 Sep 1977–24 April 1985, Bridget Beard West House School, Edgbaston, Birmingham, W Mids	7	7
RAT *Common*	*Rodney* January 1983–25 May 1990, Rodney Mitchell, Tulsa, Oklahoma, USA	7	4

kittens during her breeding life. She gave birth to her last litter (a single kitten) on 12 Jun 1952.

Oldest feline mother In May 1987 Kitty, owned by George Johnstone of Croxton, Staffs, produced two kittens at the age of 30 years, making her the oldest feline mother on record. She died in June 1989, just short of her 32nd birthday, having given birth to a known total of 218 kittens.

Best climber On 6 Sep 1950 a four-month-old kitten belonging to Josephine Aufdenblatten of Geneva, Switzerland followed a group of climbers to the top of the 4478m *14,691ft* Matterhorn in the Alps.

Rabbits and Hares

Largest In April 1980 a five-month-old French lop doe weighing 12kg *26lb 7oz* was exhibited at the Reus Fair in north-east Spain.

Smallest Both the Netherland dwarf and the Polish have a weight range of 0.9–1.13kg *2–2½lb*. In 1975 Jacques Bouloc of Coulommière, France announced a new hybrid of these weighing 396g *14oz*.

Most prolific The most prolific domestic breeds produce 5–6 litters a year, each containing 8–12 kittens during their breeding life, compared with five litters and 3–7 young for the wild rabbit.

Longest ears Sweet Majestic Star, a champion black English lop owned and bred by Therese and Cheryl Seward of Exeter, Devon, had ears measuring 72.4cm *28½in* long and 18.4cm *7¼in* wide. He died on 6 Oct 1992. The ears of his grandson Sweet Regal Magic are also this length.

Largest hare In November 1956 a brown hare weighing 6.83kg *15lb 1oz* was shot near Welford, Northants. The average weight is 3.62kg *8lb*.

Birds

Largest The largest living bird is the North African ostrich (*Struthio c. camelus*). Male examples (hens are smaller) of this flightless (ratite) sub-species have been recorded up to 2.74m *9ft* tall and weighing 156.5kg *345lb*.

Heaviest flying The world's heaviest flying (carinate) birds are the Kori bustard or paauw (*Ardeotis kori*) of north-east and southern Africa

The fastest-flying birds *in level flight*: these are found among the duck and geese families (*Anatidae*). Some powerful species are the red-breasted merganser (*Mergus serrator*) and the spur-winged goose (*Plectropterus gambiensis*). Pictured here is another, the green-winged teal (*Anas crecca*) in full flight.
(Photo: Planet Earth Pictures/J Downer)

Heaviest!

The heaviest bird of prey is the Andean condor (*Vultur gryphus*), males of which average 9–11kg *20–25lb*. A weight of 14.1kg *31lb* has been claimed for a male California condor (*Gymnogyps californianus*) now preserved in the California Academy of Sciences at Los Angeles, USA, but this species is generally much smaller than the Andean condor and rarely exceeds 10.4kg *23lb*.

and the great bustard (*Otis tarda*) of Europe and Asia. Weights of 19kg *42lb* have been reported for the former. The heaviest reliably recorded great bustard weighed 18kg *39lb 11oz*, although there is an unconfirmed record of 21kg *46lb 4oz* for a male great bustard shot in Manchuria which was too heavy to fly.

The mute swan (*Cygnus olor*), which is resident in Britain, can reach 18.14kg *40lb* on very rare occasions, and there is a record from Poland of a cob (male) weighing 22.5kg *49lb 10oz* which had temporarily lost the power of flight. The largest nesting colony in Britain is the Abbotsbury Swannery at Chesil Beach, Dorset.

'Best talking bird' A female African grey parrot (*Psittacus erythacus*) named Prudle, formerly owned by Lyn Logue (died January 1988) and now in the care of Iris Frost of Seaford, E Sussex, won the 'Best talking parrot-like bird' title at the National Cage and Aviary Bird Show in London each December for 12 consecutive years (1965–76). Prudle, who has a vocabulary of nearly 800 words, was taken from a nest at Jinja, Uganda in 1958. She retired undefeated.

Largest vocabulary Puck, a budgerigar owned by Camille Jordan of Petaluma, California, USA had a vocabulary estimated at 1728 words as of 31 Jan 1993.

Highest flying birds Most migrating birds fly at relatively low altitudes (i.e. below 90m *300ft*), with only a few dozen species flying higher than 900m *3000ft*.

The highest confirmed altitude recorded for a bird is 11,277m *37,000ft* for a Ruppell's vulture (*Gyps rueppellii*), which collided with a commercial aircraft over Abidjan, Ivory Coast on 29 Nov 1973. The impact damaged one of the aircraft's engines, causing it to shut down, but the plane landed safely without further incident. Sufficient feather remains of the bird were recovered to

The American woodcock (*Crus leucogeranus*) Spot this camouflaged slow-flier—pictured here bound to the ground—which has been timed flying at just 8km/h *5mph* without stalling.
(Photo: Planet Earth Pictures/F Blackburn)

Oldest An unconfirmed age of about 82 years was reported for a male Siberian white crane (*Grus leucogeranus*) named Wolf at the International Crane Foundation, Baraboo, Wisconsin, USA. 'Wolf' died in late 1988 after breaking his bill while repelling a visitor near his pen.

The greatest irrefutable age reported for any bird is over 80 years for a male sulphur-crested cockatoo (*Cacatua galerita*) named Cocky, who died at London Zoo in 1982.

Domestic Excluding the ostrich, which has been known to live up to 68 years, the longest-lived domesticated bird is the goose (*Anser a. domesticus*), which has a normal life-span of about 25 years. On 16 Dec 1976 a gander named George, owned by Florence Hull of Thornton, Lancs, died aged 49 years 8 months. He was hatched in April 1927.

Longest flights The greatest distance covered by a ringed bird is 22,530km *14,000 miles* by an Arctic tern (*Sterna paradisea*), banded as a nestling on 5 Jul 1955 in the Kandalaksha Sanctuary on the White Sea coast of Russia and captured alive by a fisherman 13 km *8 miles* south of Fremantle, Western Australia on 16 May 1956. The bird had flown south via the Atlantic Ocean and then circled Africa before crossing the Indian Ocean. It did not survive to make the return journey.

Most airborne The most aerial of all birds is the sooty tern (*Sterna fuscata*), which, after leaving the nesting grounds, remains aloft continuously for 3–10 years whilst maturing before returning to land to breed as an adult.

The most aerial land bird is the common swift (*Apus apus*), which remains airborne for 2–3 years, during which time it sleeps, drinks, eats and even mates on the wing.

Fastest swimmer The gentoo penguin (*Pygoscelis papua*) has a maximum burst of speed of about 27km/h *17mph*.

Deepest dive In 1969 a depth of 265 m *870 ft* was recorded for a small group of 10 emperor penguins (*Aptenodytes forsteri*) at Cape Crozier, Antarctica by a team of US scientists. One bird remained submerged for 18 minutes.

Keenest vision It has been calculated that a large bird of prey can detect a target object at a distance 3–8 times greater than that achieved by humans, and thus a peregrine falcon (*Falco peregrinus*) can spot a pigeon at a range of over 8km *5 miles* under ideal conditions.

The woodcock (family Scolopacidae) has eyes set so far back on its head that it has a 360° field of vision, enabling it to see all round and even over the top of its head.

Shortest bill The shortest bill is that of the glossy swiftlet (*Collocalia esculenta*), whose bill is almost non-existent.

Longest feathers The longest feathers grown by any bird are those of the Phoenix fowl or onagadori (a strain of red junglefowl *Gallus gallus*), which has been bred in south-western Japan since the mid-17th century. In 1972 a tail covert measuring 10.6m *34ft 9½ in* was reported for a

---

allow the US Museum of Natural History to make a positive identification of this high-flier, which is rarely seen above 6000m *20,000ft*.

On 9 Dec 1967 about 30 whooper swans (*Cygnus cygnus*) were recorded at an altitude of just over 8230m *27,000ft* flying in from Iceland to winter at Loch Foyle bordering Northern Ireland and the Republic of Ireland. They were spotted by an airline pilot over the Outer Hebrides, and the height was also confirmed on radar by air traffic control.

Fastest bird The fastest bird on land is the ostrich, which, despite its bulk, can run at up to 65km/h *40mph* when necessary.

Tallest bird The tallest of the flying birds are cranes, tall waders of the family Gruidae, some of which can stand almost 2m *6ft 6in* high.

Largest wingspan The wandering albatross (*Diomedea exulans*) of the southern oceans has the largest wingspan of any living bird. The largest was a very old male with a wingspan of 3.63m *11ft 11in*, caught by members of the Antarctic research ship USNS *Eltanin* in the Tasman Sea on 18 Sep 1965.

Smallest The smallest is the bee hummingbird (*Mellisuga helenae*) of Cuba and the Isle of Pines. Males measure 57mm *2¼ in* in total length, half of which is taken up by the bill and tail, and weigh 1.6g *0.056oz* (females are slightly larger). (⇨ Smallest nest)

UK The smallest regularly breeding British bird is the goldcrest or golden crested wren (*Regulus regulus*), which is 90mm *3½ in* long and weighs

3.8–4.5g *0.13–0.16 oz*, half the weight of the common wren (*Troglodytes troglodytes*).

Bird of prey The smallest bird of prey is the 35g *1.23oz*, 140–152mm *5½–6 in* long, white-fronted falconet (*Microhierax latifrons*) of north-western Borneo.

Commonest The commonest of all the wild bird species found in Britain—more than 520 have been recorded this century—is now the blackbird (*Turdus merula*), with a breeding population of 5 million pairs. It is followed by the robin (*Erithicius rubecula*) and the blue tit (*Parus caeruleus*) with 4 million pairs each.

Most abundant The red-billed quelea (*Quelea quelea*), a seed-eatingweaver of the drier parts of Africa south of the Sahara, has an estimated adult breeding population of 1.5 billion, and at least 1 billion of these 'feathered locusts' are slaughtered annually without having any impact on the population figure.

Fastest flying Probably at least 50 per cent of the world's flying birds cannot exceed 64km/h *40mph* in level flight. The fastest living creature, however, is the peregrine falcon (*Falco peregrinus*) when stooping from great heights during territorial displays. In one series of German experiments, a velocity of 270 km/h *168mph* was recorded at a 30° angle of stoop, rising to a maximum of 350km/h *217mph* at an angle of 45°. The brown-throated spine-tail swift *Hirundapus giganteus* of Asia is also capable of 250–300km/h *155–186 mph*.

The fastest fliers in level flight are found among the ducks and geese (Anatidae). Some powerful species such as the red-breasted merganser (*Mergus serrator*), the eider (*Somateria mollissima*), the canvasback (*Aythya valisineria*) and the spur-winged goose) *Plectropterus gambiensis*) can probably exceed 104 km/h *65mph*.

Slowest flying The slowest-flying birds are the American woodcock (*Scolopax minor*) and the Eurasian woodcock (*S. rusticola*), which have been timed at 8km/h *5mph* without stalling.

> The fastest wing beat of any insect is that of the horned sungem (*Heliactin cornuta*) of tropical South America at 90 beats/sec.

g force!

American experiments have shown that the beak of the red-headed woodpecker (*Melanerpes erythrocephalus*) hits the bark of a tree with an impact velocity of 20.9km/h *13mph*, subjecting the brain to a deceleration of about 10*g* when the head snaps back.

rooster owned by Masasha Kubota of Kochi, Shikoku, Japan.

Largest egg The egg of an ostrich (*Struthio camelus*) normally measures 15–20cm *6–8in* long, 10–15cm *4–6in* in diameter and weighs 1.65–1.78kg *3.6–3.9lb* (around two dozen hens' eggs in volume). The egg requires about 40min for boiling and the shell, although only 1.5mm *0.06in* thick, can support the weight of a 127-kg *20-st* person. The largest egg on record weighed 2.3kg *5.1lb* and was laid on 28 Jun 1988 by a 2-year-old northern/southern hybrid (*Struthio c. camelus × S. c. australis*) at the Kibbutz Ha'on collective farm, Israel.

UK The largest egg laid by any bird on the British list is that of the mute swan (*Cygnus olor*) at 109–124mm *4.3–4.9in* long, 71–78.5mm *2.8–3.1in* in diameter and weighing 340–370g *12–13oz*.

Longest!

The bill of the Australian pelican (*Pelicanus conspicillatus*) is 34–47cm *13–18½in* long, and is the world's longest. The longest beak in relation to overall body length is that of the sword-billed hummingbird (*Ensifera ensifera*) of the Andes from Venezuela to Bolivia. It measures 10.2cm *4in* making it longer than the bird's actual body if the tail is excluded.

Smallest egg Eggs emitted from the oviduct before maturity, known as 'sports', are not considered to be of significance. The smallest egg laid by any bird is that of the vervain hummingbird (*Mellisuga minima*) of Jamaica. Two specimens measuring less than 10mm *0.39in* in length weighed 0.365g *0.0128oz* and 0.375g *0.0132oz*. (⇨ Smallest nest)

UK The smallest egg laid by a bird on the British list is that of the goldcrest (*Regulus regulus*), which measures 12.2–14.5mm *0.48–0.57in* long, 9.4–9.9mm *0.37–0.39in* in diameter and weighs 0.6g *0.021oz*.

Longest incubation The longest normal incubation period is 75–82 days for the wandering albatross (*Diomedea exulans*). There is an isolated case of an egg of the mallee fowl (*Leipoa ocellata*) of Australia taking 90 days to hatch, compared with its normal 62 days.

Shortest incubation The shortest incubation period is 10 days in the case of the great spotted woodpecker (*Dendrocopus major*) and the black-billed cuckoo (*Coccyzus erythropthalmus*).

The idlest of cock birds include hummingbirds (family Trochilidae), the eider duck (*Somateria mollissima*) and the golden pheasant (*Chrysolophus pictus*), whose breeding partners are responsible for 100 per cent of incubation duties. In contrast, the female common kiwi (*Apteryx australis*) leaves the male in charge for 75–80 days.

Largest nest The incubation mounds built by the mallee fowl (*Leipoa ocellata*) of Australia measure up to 4.57m *15ft* in height and 10.6m *35ft* across, and it has been calculated that a nest site may involve the mounding of 229m³ *8100ft³* of material weighing 300tonnes.

A nest measuring 2.9m *9½ft* wide and 6m *20ft* deep was built by a pair of bald eagles (*Haliaeetus leucocephalus*), and possibly their successors, near St Petersburg, Florida, USA. It was examined in 1963 and was estimated to weigh more than 2tonnes. The golden eagle (*Aquila chrysaetos*) also constructs huge nests, and one measuring 4.57m *15 ft* deep was reported from Scotland in 1954.

Smallest nest The smallest nests are built by Hummingbirds. That of the vervain hummingbird (*Mellisuga minima*) is about half the size of a walnut, while the deeper one of the bee hummingbird (*M. helenae*) is thimble-sized. (⇨ Smallest bird, Smallest egg)

Bird-spotters The world's leading bird-spotter or 'twitcher' is Phoebe Snetsinger of Webster Groves, Missouri, USA, who has logged 7530 out of the 9700 known species since 1965, representing over 74 per cent of the available total.

UK The British life list record is 485 by Ron Johns (b. 1941) of Slough, Bucks, who started spotting in 1952. The British year list record is 359 by Lee Evans (b. 1960) of Little Chalfont, Bucks, who established it in 1990 after travelling over 123,916km *77,000 miles*, compared with his average yearly total of 96,000km *60,000miles*.

24 hours The greatest number of species spotted in a 24-hour period is 342 by Kenyans Terry Stevenson, John Fanshawe and Andy Roberts on day two of the Bridwatch Kenya '86 event held on 29–30 November.

Reptiles

Crocodiles

Largest The largest reptile in the world is the estuarine or saltwater crocodile (*Crocodylus porosus*) of south-east Asia, the Malay Archipelago, Indonesia, northern Australia, Papua New Guinea, Vietnam and the Philippines. The Bhitarkanika Wildlife Sanctuary in Orissa State, India houses four protected estuarine crocodiles measuring more than 6m *19ft 8in* in length, the largest being over 7m *23ft* long.

The greatest authenticated age for a crocodilian is 66 years for a female American alligator (*Alligator mississipiensis*) which arrived at Adelaide Zoo, South Australia on 5 Jun 1914 as a 2-year-old, and died there on 26 Sep 1978.

Smallest Osborn's dwarf crocodile (*Osteolaemus osborni*), found in the upper region of the Congo River, west Africa, rarely exceeds 1.2m *3ft 11in* in length.

Lizards

Largest The largest lizard is the Komodo monitor or ora (*Varanus komodoensis*), found on the Indonesian islands of Komodo, Rintja, Padar and Flores. Males average 2.25m *7ft 5in* in length and weigh about 59kg *130lb*. The largest accurately measured specimen was a 3.05m *10ft 1in* long male presented to an American zoologist in 1928 by the Sultan of Bima. In 1937 it was put on display in St Louis Zoological Gardens, Missouri, USA for a short period, by which time it was 3.10m *10ft 2in* in long and weighed 166kg *365lb*.

Longest The slender Salvadori monitor (*Varanus salvadori*) of Papua New Guinea has been reliably measured at up to 4.75m *15ft 7in* in length, but nearly 70 per cent of its total length is taken up by the tail.

Oldest The greatest age recorded for a lizard is over 54years for a male slow worm (*Anguis fragilis*) kept in the Zoological Museum in Copenhagen, Denmark from 1892 until 1946.

Smallest *Sphaerodactylus parthenopion*, a tiny gecko indigenous to the island of Virgin Gorda, one of the British Virgin Islands, is the world's smallest lizard. It is known only from 15 specimens, including some pregnant females found between 10 and 16 Aug 1964. The three largest females measured 18mm *0.70in* from snout to vent, with a tail of approximately the same length.

Fastest The highest speed measured for any reptile on land is 29km/h *18mph* for a six-lined race runner (*Cnemidophorus sexlineatus*) near McCormick, South Carolina, USA in 1941.

Tortoises and Turtles

Largest The largest living chelonian is the widely distributed leatherback turtle (*Dermochelys coriacea*), which averages 1.83–2.13m *6–7ft* from the tip of the beak to the end of the tail (carapace 1.52–1.67m *5–5½ft*), about 2.13m *7ft* across the front flippers and weighs up to 450kg *1000lb*.

GUESS WHAT?

Q How many birds did Lee Evans spot in one year?

A See Page 35

In May 1987 it was reported by Dr Scott Eckert that a leatherback turtle (*Dermochelys coriacea*) fitted with a pressure-sensitive recording device had reached a depth of 1200m *3973ft* off the Virgin Islands in the West Indies, the deepest dive ever recorded by a turtle.
(Photo: Planet Earth Pictures/D. Perrine)

The largest leatherback turtle ever recorded is a male found dead on the beach at Harlech, Gwynedd on 23 Sep 1988. It measured 2.91 m *9 ft 5½ in* in total length over the carapace (nose to tail), 2.77 m *9 ft* across the front flippers and weighed 961.1 kg *2120 lb*. Although most museums refuse to exhibit large turtles because they can drip oil for up to 50 years, this specimen was put on display at the National Museum of Wales, Cardiff on 16 Feb 1990.

Largest tortoise The largest living tortoise is the Aldabra giant tortoise (*Geochelone gigantea*) of the Indian Ocean islands of Aldabra, Mauritius and the Seychelles (introduced 1874). A male named Esmerelda, a long-time resident on Bird Island, Seychelles, weighed 304 kg *670 lb* in November 1992.

Smallest The smallest marine turtle in the world is the Atlantic ridley (*Lepidochelys kempii*), which has a shell length of 50–70 cm *19.7–27.6 in* and a maximum weight of 36 kg *80 lb*.

Oldest The greatest authentic age recorded for a chelonian is over 152 years for a male Marion's tortoise (*Testudo sumeirii*) brought from the Seychelles to Mauritius in 1766 by the Chevalier de Fresne, who presented it to the Port Louis army garrison. This specimen, which went blind in 1908, was accidentally killed in 1918.

Fastest The highest speed claimed for any reptile in water is 35 km/h *22 mph* by a frightened Pacific leatherback turtle.

Snakes, General

Longest The reticulated python (*Python reticulatus*) of south-east Asia, Indonesia and the Philippines regularly exceeds 6.25 m *20 ft 6 in*, and the record length is 10 m *32 ft 9½ in* for a specimen shot in Celebes, Indonesia in 1912.

Shortest The world's shortest snake is the very rare thread snake (*Leptotyphlops bilineata*), known only from Martinique, Barbados and St Lucia. The longest examples measured 108 mm *4¼ in*.

UK The smallest native British snake is the smooth snake (*Coronella austriaca*), which averages up to 0.5 m *2 in in length*.

Heaviest The most massive snake is the anaconda (*Eunectes murinus*) of tropical South America and Trinidad. The average length is 5.5–6.1 m *18–20 ft*. A female shot in Brazil *c.* 1960 was not weighed, but as it was 8.45 m *27 ft 9 in* long with a girth of 111 cm *44 in*, it must have weighed nearly 227 kg *500 lb*.

Poisonous Snakes

Longest The longest venomous snake is the king cobra (*Ophiophagus hannah*), also called the hamadryad, which averages 3.65–4.5 m *12–15 ft* in length and is found in south-east Asia and the Philippines. A 5.54 m *18 ft 2 in* specimen captured alive near Fort Dickson in the state of Negri Sembilan, Malaya in April 1937 later grew to 5.71 m *18 ft 9 in* in London Zoo. It was destroyed at the outbreak of war in 1939.

Shortest The namaqua dwarf adder (*Bitis schneider*) of Namibia, has an average length of 200 mm *8 in*.

Heaviest The heaviest venomous snake is probably the eastern diamondback rattlesnake (*Crotalus adamanteus*) of the south-eastern United States, which averages 5.5–6.8 kg *12–15 lb* (1.52–1.83 m *5–6 ft* in length). The

Looks could kill

Most animals–even the poisonous species—do not pose any real threat to human wellbeing. Animal weaponry is largely designed for debilitating prey, or is used by the possessor in reflexive acts of defence. Nevertheless, the exceptional few, on the rare occasions that they make human contact, are lethal. The world's most venomous ones are pictured here; all of them exotic, strikingly beautiful, and very dangerous.

Poison-arrow frog *Dendrobates tinctorius* Photo: Planet Earth Pictures

Killing 50 men with one frog

These small, brightly coloured creatures—*Dendrobatus* and *Phyllobates*—secrete some of the most deadly biological toxins known to man. They come in varying colours; red, bright green, pink, orange or gold, and may be adorned with darker spots or stripes. In the Kokoi poison-arrow of Colombia, one ten-thousandth of a gram of its poison is enough to kill a man of average build. The native Indians of the rain forests can poison as many as fifty arrows with the fluids of one tiny specimen.

Habitat: the floor of the rain forest in South and Central America

Poison-arrow frog *Dendrobates auratus*/Photo: Planet Earth Pictures

Southern blue-ringed octopus *Hapalochlaena Maculosa* Photo: Planet Earth Pictures

Blue-ringed and terror-tinged

The deadly bite of this deceptively pretty octopus can kill in a matter of minutes. With a radial spread of just 100–150 mm *4–6 in*, the two main closely-related species *Hapalochlaena masculosa* and *H. lunulata*, contain a neurotoxic venom so potent that an antivenin can only rarely be used in time to save the victim.

Habitat: the coasts of Australia

Poison-arrow frog *Dendrobates pumilio*/Photo: Planet Earth Pictures

heaviest on record weighed 15 kg *34 lb* and was 2.36 m *7 ft 9 in* long.

Most venomous The most venomous land snake is the 2 m *6 ft 6¾ in* long smooth-scaled snake (*Parademansia microlepidotus*) of the Diamantina River and Cooper's Creek drainage basins in Channel County, Queensland and western New South Wales, Australia, whose venom is nine times as toxic as that of the tiger snake (*Notechis scutatus*) of South Australia and Tasmania. One specimen yielded 110 mg *0.00385 oz* of venom after milking—enough to kill 125,000 mice—but so far no human fatalities have been reported.

Snakebites More people die of snakebites in Sri Lanka than any comparable area in the world. An average of 800 people are killed annually on the island by snakes, with over 95 per cent of the fatalities caused by the common krait (*Bungarus caeruleus*), the Sri Lankan cobra (*Naja n. naja*) and Russell's viper (*Vipera russelli pulchella*).

The saw-scaled or carpet viper (*Echis carinatus*), which ranges from West Africa to India, bites and kills more people in the world than any other species.

UK The only venomous snake in Britain is the adder, or viper, (*Vipera berus*), whose bite has caused ten human deaths since 1890, including six children. The most recent recorded death was on 1 Jul 1975 when a 5-year-old was bitten

A fine pair of fangs:
A 6-ft gaboon viper can sport fangs
of around 50 mm *1.96 in*, and looks
considerably more docile with his
mouth shut.
(Photo: Jacana/M Liquet)

at Callander, Perthshire and died 44 hours later. (⇨ Longest venomous)

Longest fangs The longest fangs of any snake are those of the highly venomous gaboon viper (*Bitis gabonica*) of tropical Africa. On 12 Feb 1963 a gaboon viper under severe stress sank its fangs into its own back at Philadelphia

Illustration: Matthew Hillier.© Guinness Publishing

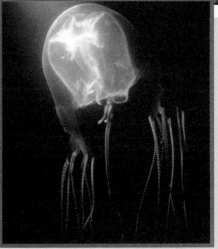

Australian box jellyfish
Cubomedusae Chironex Fleckeri

Sea snake
Hydrophis belcheri
Photo: Planet Earth Pictures

A sting in the tail

When approached by potential prey, the Australian box jellyfish suddenly releases a collagenous, stinging thread, which uncoils and turns inside out in the process, sometimes exposing lateral barbs. Some of the threads are hollow, and contain a cardiotoxic venom which can enter the body of the prey. The cubomedusan sea wasps—particularly the genera *Chironex* and *Chiopsalmus*—are especially dangerous. A sting can cause paralysis and death in a human within 3 minutes of contact.
Habitat: the coasts of Australia, especially Queensland, as far north as Malaya

Deadliest snake

All sea snakes are poisonous, though they cause few accidents due to their habitat. The *Hydrophis belcheri* has a myotoxic venom a hundred times as toxic as that of the Australian taipan (*Oxyuranus scutellatus*), whose bite can kill a man in minutes.
Habitat: Ashmore Reef in the Timor Sea, off north-west Australia

Monstrous Mollusc

There are some 400–500 species of cone shell, all of which can deliver a poisonous neurotoxin. The geographer cone (*Conus geographus*) and the court cone (*C. aulicus*), are considered to be the most deadly. The venom is injected by a unique fleshy, harpoon-like proboscis and symptoms include impaired vision, dizziness and nausea; it also causes paralysis and death.
Habitat: Polynesia to East Africa

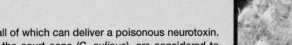

Cone shell *Conus marmoreus*/Photo: Planet Earth Pictures

The killer catch

The most poisonous fish in the world are the stonefish (Synanceidae), and in particular *Synanceja horrida*, which has the largest venom glands of any known fish. Direct contact with the spines of its fins, which contain a strong neurotoxic poison, often proves fatal.
Habitat: the tropical waters of the Indo-Pacific

Stonefish
Synanceia verrucosa
Photo: Planet Earth Pictures

A bird in the hand

Birds were believed to be almost entirely harmless until just three years ago, when a graduate student at the University of Chicago felt numbness and burning in his mouth when he licked his hands after handling a hooded pitohui bird. The poison turned out to be identical to that of the poison-arrow frog, though in a far less potent form.
Country of origin: New Guinea

Hooded pitohui nestlings *Pitohui dichrous*
Photo: NHPA/B.Beehler

Zoo, Pennsylvania, USA and died from traumatic injury to a vital organ. It did not, as was widely reported, succumb to its own venom.

Oldest The greatest reliable age recorded for a snake is 40 years 3 months 14 days for a male common boa (*Boa constrictor constrictor*) named 'Popeye', who died at Philadelphia Zoo, Pennsylvania, USA on 15 Apr 1977.

Fastest The fastest land snake is probably the slender black mamba (*Dendroaspis polylepis*) of the eastern part of tropical Africa. Top speeds of 16–19 km/h *10–12 mph* may be possible in short bursts over level ground, and it is said to chase people aggressively.

Frogs

Largest The largest known frog is the goliath frog (*Conraua goliath*). A specimen captured in April 1989 on the Sanaga River, Cameroon by Andy Koffman of Seattle, Washington, USA had a snout-to-vent length of 36.83 cm *14½ in* (87.63 cm *34½ in* overall with legs extended) and weighed 3.66 kg *8 lb 1 oz* on 30 Oct 1989.

Smallest!

The world's smallest frog is *Sminthillus limbatus* of Cuba.

Toad The world's smallest toad is the sub-species *Bufo taitanus beiranus*, originally of Mozambique, the largest specimen of which measured 24 mm *1 in* in length.

Largest toad The largest known toad is the marine toad (*Bufo marinus*) of tropical South America and Queensland, Australia (introduced). An average specimen weighs 450 g *1 lb* and the largest ever recorded was a male named *Prinsen* (The Prince), owned by Håkan Forsberg of Åkers Styckebruk, Sweden. It weighed 2.65 kg *5 lb 13½ oz* and measured 38 cm *15 in* snout-to-vent (53.9 cm *21¹/₅ in* when extended) in March 1991.

UK The largest toad and heaviest amphibian found in Britain is the common toad (*Bufo bufo*).

Longest jump (*Competition frog jumps are invariably the aggregate of three consecutive leaps.*)

The greatest distance covered by a frog in a triple jump is 10.3 m *33 ft 5½ in* by a South African sharp-nosed frog (*Ptychadena oxyrhynchus*) named Santjie at a frog Derby held at Lurula Natal Spa, Paulpietersburg, Natal, South Africa on 21 May 1977.

Fish

(⇨ also Angling)

General Records

Largest The world's largest fish is the rare plankton-feeding whale shark (*Rhineodon typus*), which is found in the warmer areas of the Atlantic, Pacific and Indian Oceans. The largest scientifically-recorded example was 12.65 m *41½ ft* long, measured 7 m *23 ft* round the thickest part of the body and weighed an estimated 15 tonnes. It was captured off Baba Island, near Karachi, Pakistan on 11 Nov 1949.

British Isles The largest fish recorded in British waters was a basking shark (*Cetorhinus maximus*) measuring 11.12 m *36 ft 6 in* and weighing an estimated 8 tonnes, washed ashore at Brighton, E Sussex in 1806.

Carnivorous The largest carnivorous fish is the rare great white shark (*Carcharodon carcharias*). The largest example accurately measured was 6.2 m *20 ft 4 in* long and weighed 2268 kg *5000 lb*. It was harpooned and landed in the harbour of San Miguel, Azores in June 1978. (⇨ Angling)

Smallest The shortest recorded marine fish—and the shortest known vertebrate—is the dwarf goby (*Trimmatom nanus*) of the Chagos Archipelago in the Indian Ocean. Average lengths recorded for a series of specimens collected by the 1978–79 Joint Services Chagos Research Expedition of the British Armed Forces were 8.6 mm *0.34 in* for males and 8.9 mm *0.35 in* for females.

Lightest The lightest of all vertebrates and the smallest catch possible is the dwarf goby (*Schindleria praematurus*) which weighs only 2 mg (equivalent to 14,184 to the ounce) and is 12–19 mm *¼–¾ in* long. It is found in Samoa.

Fastest The maximum swimming speed of a fish is dependent on its length and temperature. The cosmopolitan sailfish (*Istiophorus platypterus*) is considered to be the fastest species of fish over short distances, although practical difficulties make measurements extremely difficult to secure. In a series of speed trials carried out at the Long Key Fishing Camp, Florida, USA, one sailfish took out 91 m *300 ft* of line in 3 sec, which is equivalent to a velocity of 109 km/h *68 mph* (cf. 96 km/h *60 mph* for the cheetah).

Oldest In 1948 the death was reported of an 88-year-old female European eel (*Anguilla anguilla*) named 'Putte' in the aquarium at Hälsingborg Museum, Sweden. She was allegedly born in 1860 in the Sargasso Sea, North Atlantic, and was caught in a river as a 3-year-old elver.

Most abundant fish The most abundant species of fish is probably the 76 mm *3 in* long deep-sea bristlemouth (*Cyclothone elongata*), which has a worldwide distribution. It would take about 500 of them to weight 0.45 kg *1 lb*.

Oldest goldfish Goldfish (*Carassius auratus*) have been reported to live for over 50 years in China.

A goldfish named Fred, owned by A.R. Wilson of Worthing, W Sussex, died on 1 Aug 1980 aged 41 years.

Deepest Brotulids of the genus *Bassogigas* are generally regarded as the deepest-living vertebrates. The greatest depth from which a fish has been recovered is 8300 m *27,230 ft* in the Puerto Rico Trench (8366 m *27,488 ft*) in the Atlantic by Dr Gilbert L. Voss of the US research vessel *John Elliott*, who captured a 16.5 cm *6½ in* long *Bassogigas profundissimus* in April 1970. It was only the fifth such brotulid ever caught.

Most eggs The ocean sunfish (*Mola mola*) produces up to 30 million eggs, each measuring about 1.3 mm *0.05 in* in diameter, at a single spawning.

GUESS WHAT?

Q Which animal can lose the greatest weight in the fastest time?

A See Page 27

Fewest eggs The mouth-brooding cichlid *Tropheus moorii* of Lake Tanganyika, east Africa produces seven eggs or fewer during normal reproduction.

Most valuable The world's most valuable fish is the Russian sturgeon (*Huso huso*). One 1227-kg *2706-lb* female caught in the Tikhaya Sosna River in 1924 yielded 245 kg *541 lb* of best-quality caviar, which would be worth £189,350 on today's market.

The 76-cm *30-in* long ginrin showa koi, which won supreme championship in nationwide Japanese koi shows in 1976, 1977, 1979 and 1980, was sold two years later for 17 million yen (about £50,000). In March 1986 this ornamental carp was acquired by Derry Evans, owner of the Kent Koi Centre near Sevenoaks, Kent for an undisclosed sum, but the 15-year-old fish died five months later. It has since been stuffed and mounted to preserve its beauty.

Most electric The most powerful electric fish is the electric eel (*Electrophorus electricus*) from the rivers of Brazil, Colombia, Venezuela and Peru. An average-sized specimen can discharge 1 amp at 400 volts, but measurements up to 650 volts have been recorded.

Ferocious!

The razor-toothed piranhas of the genera *Serrasalmus*, *Pygocentrus* and *Pygopristis* are the most ferocious freshwater fish in the world. They live in the sluggish waters of the large rivers of South America, and will attack any creature, regardless of size, if it is injured or making a commotion in the water. On 19 Sep 1981 more than 300 people were reportedly killed and eaten when an overloaded passenger-cargo boat capsized and sank as it was docking at the Brazilian port of Obidos. According to one official, only 178 of the estimated number of people aboard the boat survived.

Freshwater

Largest The largest fish which spends its whole life in fresh or brackish water is the rare pla beuk (*Pangasianodon gigas*), found only in the Mekong River and its major tributaries in China, Laos, Cambodia and Thailand. The largest specimen, captured in the River Ban Mee Noi, Thailand, was reportedly 3 m *9 ft 10¼ in* long and weighed 242 kg *533½ lb*. This was exceeded by the European catfish or wels (*Silurus glanis*) in earlier times (in the 19th century lengths of 4.6 m *15 ft* and weights of 336 kg *720 lb* were reported for Russian specimens), but today anything over 1.83 m *6 ft* and 90 kg *200 lb* is considered large.

The most short-lived fish are probably certain species of the sub-order Cyprinodontei (Killifish), found in Africa and South America, which normally live for about eight months.

British Isles The largest fish ever caught in a British river was a common sturgeon (*Acipenser sturio*) weighing 230 kg *507½ lb* and measuring 2.74 m *9 ft*, which was accidentally

Crabs, lobster and other crustaceans

The heaviest crustacean, and the largest species of lobster, is the American or North Atlantic lobster *(Homarus americanus)*. On 11 Feb 1977 a specimen weighing 20.14 kg *44 lb 6 oz* and measuring 1.06 m *3 ft 6 in* from the end of the tail-fan to the tip of the largest claw was caught off Nova Scotia, Canada and later sold to a New York restaurant owner.

(Photo: Planet Earth Pictures/ G van Ryckevorsel)

Largest marine The largest of all crustaceans (although not the heaviest) is the taka-ashi-gani or giant spider crab *(Macrocheira kaempferi)*. A specimen with a claw-span of 3.7 m *12 ft 1½ in* weighed 18.6 kg *41 lb*. The heaviest is the American or North Atlantic lobster.

Largest freshwater The largest freshwater crustacean is the crayfish or crawfish *(Astacopsis gouldi)*, found in the streams of Tasmania, Australia. It has been measured up to 61 cm *2 ft* in length and may weigh as much as 4 kg *9 lb*. In 1934 an unconfirmed weight of 6.35 kg *14 lb* (total length 73.6 cm *29 in*) was reported for one caught at Bridport.

Largest concentration The largest single concentration of crustaceans ever recorded was a swarm of krill *(Euphausia superba)* estimated to weigh 10 million tonnes which was tracked by US scientists off Antarctica in March 1981.

netted in the Severn at Lydney, Glos on 1 Jun 1937. Larger specimens have been taken at sea—notably one weighing 317 kg *700 lb* and 3.18 m *10 ft 5 in* in length netted by the trawler *Ben Urie* off Orkney and landed on 18 Oct 1956.

Smallest freshwater The shortest and lightest freshwater fish is the dwarf pygmy goby *(Pandaka pygmaea)*, a colourless and nearly transparent species found in the streams and lakes of Luzon in the Philippines. Males are only 7.5–9.9 mm *0.28–0.38 in* long and weigh 4–5 mg *0.00014–0.00018 oz*.

Commercial The world's smallest commercial fish is the now endangered sinarapan *(Mistichthys luzonensis)*, a goby found only in Lake Buhi, Luzon, Philippines. Males are 10–13 mm *0.39–0.51 in* long, and a dried 454-g *1-lb* fish cake would contain about 70,000 of them.

Starfish

Largest A specimen collected by the Texas A&M University research vessel *Alaminos* in the Gulf of Mexico in 1968 measured 1.38 m *4½ ft* from tip to tip, but its disc was only 26 mm *1.02 in* in diameter.

Smallest The smallest known starfish is the asterinid sea star *Patiriella parvivipara* discovered by Wolfgang Zeidler on the west coast of the Eyre peninsula, South Australia in 1975. It has a maximum radius of only 4.7 mm *0.18 in* and a diameter of less than 9 mm *0.35 in*.

Deepest The greatest depth from which a starfish has been recovered is 7584 m *24,881 ft* for a specimen of *Porcellanaster ivanovi* collected by the Soviet research ship *Vityaz* in the Marianas Trench, west Pacific *c.* 1962.

Spiders

Largest The world's largest known spider is the goliath bird-eating spider *(Theraphosa leblondi)* of the coastal rainforests of Surinam, Guyana and French Guiana, but isolated specimens have also been reported from Venezuela and Brazil. A male collected by members of the Pablo San Martin Expedition at Rio Cavro, Venezuela in April 1965 had a record leg-span of 280 mm *11.02 in*.

UK Of the 617 known species of British spider covering an estimated population of over 500 billion, the cardinal spider *(Tegenaria gigantea)* of southern England has the greatest average leg-span. In October 1985 Lyndsay Jarrett of Marston Meysey, Wilts collected a female in her home with a leg-span of 139 mm *5½ in*. The well-known 'daddy longlegs' spider *(Pholcus phalangioides)* rarely exceeds 114 mm *4½ in* in leg-span, but one specimen collected in England measured 15.2 cm *6 in* across.

Heaviest Female bird-eating spiders are more heavily built than males and in February 1985

Oldest!

The longest-lived of all spiders are the primitive *Mygalomorphae* (tarantulas and allied species). One female theraphosid collected in Mexico in 1935 lived for an estimated 26–28 years.

UK The longest-lived British spider is probably the purse web spider *(Atypus affinis)*, one specimen of which was kept in a greenhouse for nine years.

Charles J. Seiderman of New York City, USA captured a female example near Paramaribo, Surinam which weighed a record peak 122.2 g *4.3 oz* before its death from moulting problems in January 1986. Other measurements included a maximum leg-span of 267 mm *10½ in*, a total body length of 102 mm *4 in* and 25 mm *1 in* long fangs.

UK The heaviest spider found in Britain is the orb weaver *(Araneus quadratus)*. On 10 Sep 1979 a female weighing 2.25 g *0.08 oz* was collected at Lavington, W Sussex by J. R. Parker.

Smallest The smallest known spider is *Patu marplesi* (family Symphytognathidae) of Western Samoa. The type specimen (male) found in moss at *c.* 600 m *2000 ft* in Madolelei, Upolu in January 1965 measured 0.43 mm *0.017 in* overall—about the size of a full-stop on this page.

UK The extremely rare money spider *Glyphesis cottonae* is found only in a swamp near Beaulieu Road Station, Hants and on Thursley Common, Surrey. Both sexes have a body length of 1 mm *0.04 in*.

Most venomous The world's most venomous spiders are the Brazilian wandering spiders of the genus *Phoneutria*, and particularly *P. fera*, which has the most active neurotoxic venom of any living spider. These large and highly aggressive creatures often enter human dwellings and hide in clothing or shoes. When disturbed they bite furiously several times, and hundreds of accidents involving these species are reported annually. Fortunately, however, an effective antivenin is available, and when deaths do occur they are usually of children under the age of seven.

Scorpions

Largest The largest of the 800 or so species of scorpion is the tropical 'emperor' *Pandinus imperator* of Guinea, males of which can have a body length of 18 cm *7 in* or more.

COVERED IN BEES–A HONEY OF A TIME

Jed Shaner, talking about his forthcoming attempt on the mantle of bees record, said:– 'It's not as bad as you'd think. It does draw attention. People say you're crazy, but everyone's crazy in their own way. There are things that other people do that I might think were crazy'.

When all the preparations were complete he was asked if he was afraid.

Still enthusiastic he replied 'So far, so good. Let's do it. We're going to have a honey of a time'.

The day after the successful attempt and showing no fear, Shaner said 'Records are made to be broken. We can always do it again.'

As *The News-Virginian* put it, 'Jed Shaner had a BEEautiful time'!

Smallest The world's smallest scorpion is *Microbothus pusillus*, which measures about 13mm *½ in* in total length and is found on the Red Sea coast.

Most venomous The most venomous scorpion in the world is the Palestine yellow scorpion (*Leiurus quinquestriatus*), which ranges from the eastern part of North Africa through the Middle East to the Red Sea. Fortunately, the amount of venom it delivers is very small (0.255 mg *0.000009 oz*) and adult lives are seldom endangered, but it has been responsible for a number of fatalities among children under the age of five.

Insects

It is estimated that there may be as many as 30 million species of insect—more specimens than all other animals put together—but thousands are known only from a single type specimen.

Heaviest The heaviest insects are the Goliath beetles (family Scarabaeidae) of Equatorial Africa. The largest are *Goliathus regius*, *G. goliathus* (=*G. giganteus*) and *G. druryi* and in measurements of one series of males (females are smaller) the lengths from the tips of the small frontal horns to the end of the abdomen were up to 110mm *4.33 in*, with weights of 70–100g *2½–3½ oz*.

UK The heaviest insect found in Britain is the stag beetle (*Lucanus cervus*) which is widely distributed over southern England. The largest specimen on record was a male which was 77.4mm

Loudest!

At 7400 pulses/min the tymbal organs of the male cicada (family Cicadidae) produce a noise (officially described by the US Department of Agriculture as 'Tsh-ee-EEEE-e-ou') detectable more than 400m *¼ mile* away. The only British species is the very rare mountain cicada (*Cicadetta montana*), which is confined to the New Forest area in Hampshire.

3.04 in long (body plus mandibles) and probably weighed over 6g *0.21 oz* when alive. It was collected at Sheerness, Kent in 1871 and is now in the British Museum (Natural History), London.

Longest The longest recorded insect in the world is *Pharnacia kirbyi*, a stick insect from the rainforests of Borneo. The longest-known specimen is in the British Natural History Museum in London, UK; it has a body length of 328mm *12.9 in* and a total length, including the legs, of over half a metre *20 in*. In the wild this species is often found with some legs missing because they are so long and easily trapped when the insect sheds its skin.

Smallest The smallest recorded insects are the 'feather-winged' beetles of the family Ptiliidae (=Trichopterygidae) and the battledore-wing fairy flies (parasitic wasps) of the family Mymaridae, which are smaller than some species of protozoa (single-celled animals).

Lightest The male bloodsucking banded louse (*Enderleinellus zonatus*) and the parasitic wasp *Caraphractus cinctus* may each weigh as little as 0.005 mg, or *5,670,000 to an oz*. Eggs of the latter each weigh 0.0002 mg (*141,750,000 to an oz*).

Largest grasshopper The largest grasshopper possibly in the world, is an unidentified species from the border of Malaysia and Thailand measuring 25.4cm *10 in* in length and capable of leaping 4.6m *15 ft*.

Fastest flying Acceptable modern experiments have established that the highest maintainable airspeed of any insect, including the deer botfly, hawk moths (Sphingidae), horse flies (*Tabanus bovinus*) and some tropical butterflies (Hesperiidae), is 39 km/h *24 mph*, rising to a maximum of 58 km/h *36 mph* for the Australian dragonfly *Austrophlebia costalis* for short bursts.

Fastest moving The fastest insects on land are certain large tropical cockroaches and the record is 5.4 km/h *3.36 mph*, or 50 body lengths per second, registered by *Periplaneta americana* at the University of California at Berkeley, USA in 1991.

Highest g force The click beetle (*Athous haemorrhoidalis*) averages *400 g* when 'jack-knifing' into the air to escape predators. One example measuring 12mm *½ in* in length and weighing 40 mg *0.00014 oz* which jumped to a height of 30cm *11¾ in* was calculated to have endured a

peak brain deceleration of *2300 g* by the end of the movement.

Oldest The longest-lived insects are the splendour beetles (Buprestidae). On 27 May 1983 a specimen of *Buprestis aurulenta* appeared from the staircase timber in the home of Mr W. Euston of Prittlewell, Southend-on-Sea, Essex after 47 years as a larva.

Fastest wing beat The fastest wing-beat of any insect under natural conditions is 62,760 per min by a tiny midge of the genus *Forcipomyia*. The muscular contraction–expansion cycle in 0.00045 sec further represents the fastest muscle movement ever measured.

Slowest wing beat The slowest wing beat of any insect is 300 per min by the swallowtail butterfly (*Papilio machaon*).

Largest cockroach The world's largest cockroach is *Megaloblatta longipennis* of Colombia. A preserved female in the collection of Akira Yokokura of Yamagata, Japan measures 97mm *3.81 in* in length and 45mm *1.77 in* across.

Dragonflies

Largest *Megaloprepus caeruleata* of Central and South America has been measured up to 191 mm *7.52 in* across the wings and 120 mm *4.72 in* in body length.

Smallest The world's smallest dragonfly is *Agriocnemis naia* of Myanmar (Burma). A specimen in the British Museum (Natural History) had a wing spread of 17.6mm *0.69 in* and a body length of 18mm *0.71 in*.

Fleas

Largest Siphonapterologists recognise 1830 varieties, of which the largest known is *Hystrichopsylla schefferi*, which was described from a single specimen taken from the nest of a mountain beaver (*Aplodontia rufa*) at Puyallup, Washington, USA in 1913. Females are up to 8mm *0.3 in* long.

Jumper!

The common flea (*Pulex irritans*) is the champion jumper among fleas. In one American experiment carried out in 1910 a specimen allowed to leap at will performed a long jump of 330mm *13 in* and a high jump of 197 mm *7¾ in*. In jumping 130 times its own height a flea subjects itself to a force of *200 g*.

Butterflies

Largest The largest known butterfly is the Queen Alexandra's birdwing (*Ornithoptera alexandrae*) of Papua New Guinea. Females may have a wingspan exceeding 280 mm *11 in* and weigh over 25g *0.9 oz*.

UK The largest butterfly found in Britain is the monarch butterfly (*Danaus plexippus*), also called the milkweed or black-veined brown butterfly, a rare vagrant which breeds in the southern United States and Central America. It has a wingspan of up to 127mm *5 in* and weighs about 1g *0.04 oz*. (⇨ Migration)

Smallest The smallest of the 140,000 known species of Lepidoptera is *Stigmella ridiculosa*, which has a wingspan of 2mm *0.079 in* with a similar body length and is found in the Canary Islands.

Migration A tagged female monarch butterfly (*Danaus plexippus*) released by Donald Davis at Presqu'ile Provincial Park near Brighton, Ontario, Canada on 6 Sep 1986 was recaptured 3432 km *2133 miles* away, on a mountain near Angangueo, Mexico, on 15 Jan 1987. This distance was obtained by measuring a line from the release site to the recapture site, but the actual distance travelled could be up to double this figure. (⇨ Largest butterfly)

Largest butterfly farm The Stratford-upon-Avon Butterfly Farm, Warks can accommodate 2000 exotic butterflies in authentic rainforest conditions. The total capacity of all flight areas at the farm, which opened on 15 Jul 1985, is over 4000 m³ *141,259 ft³*. The complex also comprises insect and plant houses and educational facilities.

Worms

Longest The longest known species of earthworm is *Microchaetus rappi* (=*M. microchaetus*) of South Africa. In *c.* 1937 a giant measuring 6.7 m *22 ft* in length when naturally extended and 20 mm *0.8 in* in diameter was collected in the Transvaal.

UK The longest earthworm found in Britain is *Lumbricus terrestris*. Its normal range is 90–300 mm *3½–12 in* but this species has been reliably measured up to 350 mm *13¾ in* when naturally extended. Measurements of up to 508 mm *20 in* have been claimed, but in each case the body was probably first macerated or mistaken for the intestinal tract of some small buried mammal.

Shortest *Chaetogaster annandalei* measures less than 0.5 mm *0.02 in* in length.

Molluscs

Oldest The longest-lived mollusc is the ocean quahog (*Arctica islandica*), a thick-shelled clam found in the mid-Atlantic. A specimen with 220 annual growth rings was collected in 1982.

Largest clam The largest of all existing bivalve shells is that of the marine giant clam *Tridacna gigas*, found on the Indo-Pacific coral reefs. One specimen measuring 115 cm *45¹/₅ in* in length and weighing 333 kg *734 lb* was collected off Ishigaki Island, Okinawa, Japan in 1956 but was not sci-entifically examined until August 1984. It probably weighed just over 340 kg *750 lb* when alive (the soft parts weigh up to 9.1 kg *20 lb*).

Winkling Sheila Bance picked 50 shells (with a straight pin) in 1 min 30.55 sec at the European Food and Drink Fair at Rochester, Kent on 7 May 1993.

> The record for opening oysters is 100 in 2 min 20.07 sec, by Mike Racz in Invercargill, New Zealand on 16 Jul 1990.

Largest snail (gastropod) The largest known gastropod is the trumpet or baler conch (*Syrinx aruanus*) of Australia. One specimen collected off Western Australia in 1979 and now owned by Don Pisor of San Diego, California had a shell 77.2 cm *30.4 in* long with a maximum girth of 101 cm *39¾ in*. It weighed nearly 18 kg *40 lb* when alive.

The largest known land gastropod is the African giant snail *Achatina achatina*, the largest recorded specimen of which measured 39.3 cm *15½ in* snout-to-tail when fully extended (shell length 27.3 cm *10¾ in*) in December 1978 and weighed exactly 900 g *2 lb*.

Charming the worms
from the ground

Visit the most charming of school fetes each summer at the Willaston County Primary School in Nantwich, Cheshire, and you will stumble across a vast expanse of three-metre square plots, each peopled with focused, intent individuals staring or poking gently at the ground. They might be brandishing a garden fork, a spade, or a radio. They are the contestants of the World Worm Charming Championship, inaugurated 1980, and they have 30 minutes to entice the worms from the comfort of their earthly dwellings.

Anyone can enter; the Championship, which is a burgeoning fund-raiser, attracts interest from all over the world. In 1993 there were 150 teams competing for the coveted Golden Rampant Worm trophy: local competition is fierce, however, and the trophy has never left the village of Willaston. There are two basic rules: no refreshment, stimulation or drugs, and no digging. The idea is to lure out the worms by vibration.

The world record was set in 1980, when Tom Shufflebotham raised an astonishing 511 worms from a 3-yard plot in the allowed time. His method was 'twanging'—a traditional technique in which a four-pronged pitchfork is placed in the ground and wiggled by the handle back and forth, causing the vibrations which persuade the worms to emerge.

Above, contestants at Willaston County Primary School encouraging the worms' advances.
(Photo: Mr & Mrs G D Farr)

> Worms, which depend on moisture to survive, normally burrow down into the top few feet of the ground. Continuous vibrations, from their underground perpective, are caused only by the sound of rain and their penchant for soaking up the maximum amount of moisture draws them to the surface.

A charmer at work
(Photo: Liverpool Daily Post and Echo)

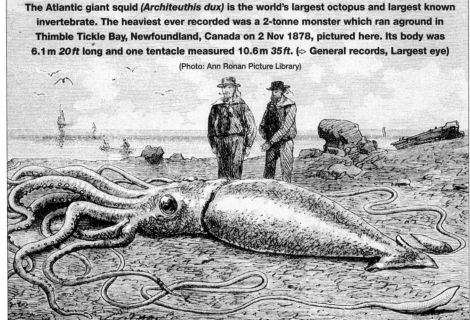

The Atlantic giant squid (*Architeuthis dux*) is the world's largest octopus and largest known invertebrate. The heaviest ever recorded was a 2-tonne monster which ran aground in Thimble Tickle Bay, Newfoundland, Canada on 2 Nov 1878, pictured here. Its body was 6.1m *20ft* long and one tentacle measured 10.6m *35ft*. (▷ General records, Largest eye)

(Photo: Ann Ronan Picture Library)

Named Gee Geronimo, this snail was owned by Christopher Hudson (1955–79) of Hove, E Sussex and was collected in Sierra Leone in June 1976.

UK The largest land snail found in Britain is the Roman or edible snail (*Helix pomatia*), with a body length of up to 10 cm *4 in* when fully extended and a shell length of 5 cm *2 in*. It weighs up to 85g *3oz*.

Snail racing On 20 Feb 1990 a garden snail named Verne, owned by Sally DeRoo of Canton, Michigan, USA completed a 31cm *12.2in* course at West Middle School in Plymouth, Michigan, in a record 2min 13sec at 0.233cm/sec.

The British record was set on 20–21 Jul 1991 when a garden snail named Streaker reportedly completed the 33cm *13in* course at the World Snail Racing Championships in Congham, Norfolk in 2min 22sec. Life on a gastropod breeding farm awaited the winner.

Jellyfish

Largest An Arctic giant (*Cyanea capillata arctica*) of the north-western Atlantic washed up in Massachusetts Bay, USA had a bell diameter of 2.28 m *7 ft 6 in* and tentacles stretching 36.5m *120ft*.

British Isles The largest cnidarian found in British waters is the rare lion's mane jellyfish (*Cyanea capillata*), also known as the common sea blub-

The Chinese alligator: the world's most endangered reptile. The total wild population of the protected Chinese alligator (*Alligator sinensis*) of the lower Yangzi River in the Anhui, Zhejiang and Jiangsu provinces of China is currently estimated at no more than a few hundred. Although captive breeding programmes are proving successful, the alligator cannot be reintroduced into the wild because of the destruction of its habitats and its extinction outside captivity is ecpected before the end of the century, if not sooner.

(Photo: Jacana/T Konig)

ber. One specimen measured at St Andrew's Marine Laboratory, Fife had a bell diameter of 91cm *35.8 in* and tentacles stretching over 13.7m *45ft*.

Sponges

Largest The largest known sponge is the barrel-shaped loggerhead sponge (*Spheciospongia vesparium*), measuring up to 105 cm *3 ft 6 in* in height and 91 cm *3ft* in diameter. It is found in the West Indies and in the waters off Florida, USA.

Heaviest In 1909 a wool sponge (*Hippospongia canaliculatta*) measuring 183 cm *6 ft* in circumference was collected off the Bahamas. It initially weighed 36–41 kg *80–90lb* but this fell to 5.44kg *12lb* after it had been dried and relieved of all excrescences. It is now preserved in the US National Museum, Washington, DC, USA.

Smallest The widely distributed *Leucosolenia blanca* is just 3mm *0.11in* tall when fully grown.

Deepest Sponges have been recovered from depths of 5637m *18,500ft*.

Endangered Species

Land Mammals

A number of mammals are known only from a single or type specimen.

General The Javan rhinoceros (*Rhinoceros sondaicus*), a solitary, single-horned species is considered to be the world's rarest large mammal. It is up to 1.7m *5½ft* tall at the shoulder and weighs 1400kg *3086 lb*. Once widely distributed, its population has declined to just 50–70 wild specimens, mainly as a result of illegal hunting of its horns for use in traditional Oriental medicines and the destruction of its habitats. There are none held in captivity.

Marine Mammals

Cetaceans Sightings of the vaquita or Gulf porpoise (*Phocoena sinus*) in the Gulf of California in 1986 (the first since 1980) suggest an estimated population of just 30, making this the rarest cetacean.

The population of the once common Mediterranean monk seal (*M. monachus*) is believed to have fallen to less than 300, mainly because of over-hunting and pollution.

The kakapo (*Stigops habrotilus*), a flightless bird from New Zealand, is the rarest bird in the world. In 1990 there were 43 known survivors but, as the kakapo breeds somewhat sporadically (only once in 4 or 5 years), and as several attempts to relocate it to increasingly inaccessible islands have failed, it may go the way of the dodo, the only bird with which is apparently shares any features.

(Photo: Jacana/G Moon/Aus)

Fish

Marine A coelacanth, a large, deepwater fish formerly known only from fossilized remains dating from 400–65 million years old, was landed at East London, South Africa on 22 Dec 1938 and only later identified as such and named *Latimeria chalumnae*. It is claimed to have filled in the 'missing link' between man and fish. Since this discovery, living coelacanths have been observed in their natural habitat 200 m *656 ft* below the waters off the Comoros in the Indian Ocean in the late 1980s.

Prehistoric Animals

Dinosaurs

Part of the reptile order, dinosaurs are undoubtably the best known group of extinct animals. The first dinosaur to be described scientifically was *Megalosaurus bucklandi* ('great fossil lizard') in 1824. Remains of this bipedal flesh-eater were found by workmen before 1818 in a slate quarry near Woodstock, Oxon and later placed in the University Museum at Oxford. The first fossil bone of *Megalosaurus* was actually illustrated in 1677, but its true nature was not realized until much later. It was not until 1842 that the name Dinosauria ('terrible lizards') was given to these newly-discovered giants.

Earliest The most primitive dinosaur is *Eoraptor lunensis* ('dawn stealer'), named in 1993 from a skeleton found in the foothills of the Andes in Argentina in rocks dated as 230 million years old. This dinosaur was 1 m *39 in* long and is classified as a theropod, a member of the group of meat-eating dinosaurs. It is the most primitive of the group since it lacks the dual-hinged jaw present in all other members.

Largest The largest ever land animals were sauropod dinosaurs, a group of long-necked, long-tailed, four-legged plant-eaters that lumbered around most of the world during the Jurassic and Cretaceous periods 208–65 million years ago.

Heaviest The largest known sauropods appear to have weighed around 50–100 tonnes, but this does not necessarily represent the ultimate weight limit for a land vertebrate. Theoretical calculations suggest that some dinosaurs approached the maximum body weight possible for a terrestrial animal, namely 120 tonnes. At weights greater than this, such massive legs would have been needed for that the dinosaur could not have moved.

The main contenders for the heaviest dinosaur are probably the titanosaurid *Antarctosaurus giganteus* ('Antarctic lizard') from Argentina and India, at 40–80 tonnes; the brachiosaurid *Brachiosaurus altithorax* (45–55 tonnes); the diplodocids *Seismosaurus halli* ('earthquake lizard') and *Supersaurus vivianae* (both over 50 tonnes).

UK Britain's heaviest known dinosaur was the diplodocid *Cetiosaurus oxoniensis* ('whale lizard'), from southern England about 170 million years ago at about 45 tonnes based on estimates on part of a femur found in Clifton Regnes, Olney, Bucks.

Longest Based on the evidence of footprints, the brachiosaurid *Breviparopus* attained a length of 48 m *157 ft*, which would make it the longest vertebrate on record. However, a diplodocid from

Tallest!

The tallest and largest dinosaur species known from a complete skeleton is *Brachiosaurus brancai* ('arm lizard') from the Tendaguru site in Tanzania, dated as Late Jurassic (150 million years ago). The site was excavated by German expeditions during the period 1909–11 and the bones prepared and assembled at the Humboldt Museum für Naturkunde in Berlin. A complete skeleton was constructed from the remains of several individuals and put on display in 1937. It is the world's largest and tallest mounted dinosaur skeleton, measuring 22.2 m *72 ft 9½ in* in overall length (height at shoulder 6 m *19 ft 8 in*) and has a raised head height of 14 m *46 ft*. A weight of 30–40 tonnes is likely. However, larger sizes are suggested by an isolated fibula from another *Brachiosaurus* in the same museum.

New Mexico, USA named *Seismosaurus halli* was estimated in 1991 to be 39–52 m *128–170 ft* long based on comparisons of individual bones.

Complete The longest dinosaur known from a complete skeleton is the diplodocid *Diplodocus carnegii* ('double beam'), assembled at the Carnegie Museum in Pittsburgh, Pennsylvania, USA from remains found in Wyoming in 1899. *Diplodocus* was 26.6 m *87½ ft* long, with much of that length made up by an extremely long whip-like tail, and probably weighed 5.8–18.5 tonnes, the higher estimates being the most likely. The mounted skeleton was so spectacular that casts were requested by other museums, and copies may be seen in London, La Plata, Washington, Frankfurt and Paris.

UK On the evidence of a haemal arch (the bone running beneath the vertebrae of the tail) found on the Isle of Wight, the brachiosaur *Pelorosaurus* ('monstrous lizard') may have reached 24 m *80 ft* in length. A more complete brachiosaurid was found on the island in 1993 and the jumbled bones, including much of the hips, ribs, shoulders and arms, indicated a 12 m *40 ft* long animal.

Smallest The chicken-sized *Compsognathus* ('pretty jaw') of southern Germany and south-east

Predator!

The largest flesh-eating dinosaur recorded so far is *Tyrannosaurus rex* ('king tyrant lizard'), which, 70 million years ago, reigned over parts of the USA and the provinces of Alberta and Saskatchewan, Canada. The largest and heaviest example, as suggested by a discovery in South Dakota, USA in 1991, was 5.9 m *19½ ft* tall, had a total length of 11.1 m *36½ ft* and weighed an estimated 6–7.4 tonnes.

A composite skeleton of a slightly smaller specimen of this nightmarish beast can be seen in the American Museum of Natural History, New York, USA.

France, and an undescribed plant-eating fabrosaurid from Colorado, USA measured 75 cm *29½ in* from the snout to the tip of the tail and weighed about 6.8 kg *15 lb*.

Fastest Trackways can be used to estimate dinosaur speeds, and one from the Late Morrison of Texas, USA discovered in 1981 indicated that a carnivorous dinosaur had been moving at 40 km/h *25 mph*. Some ornithomimids were even faster, and the large-brained, 100 kg *220 lb* *Dromiceiomimus* ('emu mimic lizard') of the Late Cretaceous of Alberta, Canada could probably outsprint an ostrich, which has a top speed of 65 km/h *40 mph*.

Largest footprints In 1932 the gigantic footprints of a large bipedal hadrosaurid ('duckbill') measuring 1.36 m *53½ in* in length and 81 cm *32 in* wide were discovered in Salt Lake City, Utah, USA, and other reports from Colorado and Utah refer to footprints 95–100 cm *37–40 in* wide. Footprints attributed to the largest brachiosaurids also range up to 100 cm *40 in* wide for the hind feet.

Most brainless *Stegosaurus* ('plated lizard'), which roamed across Colorado, Oklahoma, Utah and Wyoming, USA about 150 million years ago, measured up to 9 m *30 ft* in total length but had a walnut-sized brain weighing only 70 g *2½ oz*. This represented 0.004 of 1 per cent of its computed bodyweight of 1.75 tonnes (cf. 0.074 of 1 per cent for an elephant and 1.88 per cent for a human).

Largest skull The skulls of the long-frilled ceratopsids were the largest of all known land animals and culminated in the long-frilled *Torosaurus sp.* ('piercing lizard'). This herbivore, which measured about 7.6 m *25 ft* in total length and weighed up to 8 tonnes, had a skull measuring up to 3 m *9 ft 10 in* in length (including fringe) and weighing up to 2 tonnes. It ranged from Montana to Texas, USA.

Largest claws The therizinosaurids ('scythe lizards') from the Late Cretaceous of the Nemegt Basin, Mongolia had the largest claws of any known animal. In the case of *Therizinosaurus cheloniformis* they measured up to 91 cm *36 in* along the outer curve (cf. 20.3 cm *8 in* for *Tyrannosaurus rex*). It has been suggested that these talons were designed for grasping and tearing apart large victims, but this creature had a feeble skull partially or entirely lacking teeth and probably lived on termites.

UK In January 1983 a claw-bone measuring 30 cm *11.8 in* in length was found by amateur fossil collector William Walker near Dorking, Surrey. The claw was later identified as possibly belonging to a spinosaur measuring more than 9 m *29 ft 6 in* overall (estimated weight 2 tonnes), with a bipedal height of 3–4 m *9–13 ft*. It was also distinguished from other theropods by having 128 teeth instead of the usual 64. This enigma, said to be the most important dinosaur fossil found in Europe this century, was subsequently named *Baryonyx walkeri* ('heavy claw').

Largest eggs The largest known dinosaur eggs are those of *Hypselosaurus priscus* ('high ridge lizard'), a 12 m *40 ft* long titanosaurid which lived about 80 million years ago. Examples found in the Durance valley near Aix-en-Provence, France in October 1961 would have had, uncrushed, a length of 300mm *12in* (about the height of this page) and a diameter of 255mm *10in* (capacity 3.3litres *5.8pt*).

Other Reptiles

Earliest fossil reptile The oldest reptile fossil, nicknamed 'Lizzie the Lizard', was found on a site in Scotland by palaeontologist Stan Wood in March 1988. The 20.3cm *8in* long reptile is estimated to be about 340 million years old, 40 million years older than previously discovered reptiles. 'Lizzie' was officially named *Westlothiana lizziae* in 1991.

Largest predator The largest ever land predator may have been an alligator found on the banks of the Amazon in rocks dated as 8 million years old. Estimates from a skull 1.5m *5ft* long (complete with 10cm *4in* long teeth) indicate a length of 12m *40ft* and a weight of about 18 tonnes, making it larger than the fearsome *Tyrannosaurus rex*. It was subsequently identified as a giant example of *Purussaurus brasiliensis*, a species named in 1892 on the basis of smaller specimens.

Longest snake The longest prehistoric snake was the python-like *Gigantophis garstini*, which inhabited what is now Egypt about 38 million years ago. Parts of a spinal column and a small piece of jaw discovered at Fayum in the Western Desert indicate a length of about 11m *37ft*.

Mammals

Earliest In 1991 a partial skull of a mammal named *Adelobasileus cromptoni* was reported from 225 million year-old rocks in New Mexico, USA. The first true mammals, as represented by odd teeth, appeared about 220 million years ago during the Late Triassic. Modern mammals (therians) arose in the Mid-Cretaceous period, and the earliest representatives of modern orders, such as *Purgatorius*, the first primate, by the end of the Cretaceous period, 65 million years ago. This creature was similar in appearance to modern tree shrews of the order Scandentia.

Largest The largest land mammal ever recorded was *Indricotherium* (=*Baluchitherium* or *Paraceratherium*), a long-necked, hornless rhinocerotid which roamed across western Asia and Europe about 35 million years ago and first known from bones discovered in the Bugti Hills of Baluchistan, Pakistan in 1907–8. A restoration in the American Museum of Natural History, New York City, USA measures 5.41m *17ft 9in* to the top of the shoulder hump and 11.27m *37ft* in total length. The most likely maximum weight of this browser was revised in 1993 to 15–20tonnes from earlier estimates of 34 tonnes.

Antlers The prehistoric giant deer (*Megaloceros giganteus*), found in northern Europe and northern Asia as recently as 8000BC, had the longest horns of any known animal. One specimen recovered from an Irish bog had greatly palmated antlers measuring 4.3m *14ft* across, which corresponds to a shoulder height of 1.83m *6ft* and a weight of 500kg *1100lb*.

Birds

Earliest The earliest fossil bird is known from two partial skeletons found in Texas, USA in rocks dating from 220 million years ago. Named *Protoavis texensis* in 1991, this pheasant-sized creature has caused much controversy by pushing the age of birds back 45 million years from the previous record, that of the more familiar *Archeopteryx lithographica* from Germany.

Largest The largest prehistoric bird was the flightless *Dromornis stirtoni*, a huge emu-like creature which lived in central Australia 11 million years ago. Fossil leg bones found near Alice Springs in 1974 indicate that the bird must have stood *c.*3m *10ft* tall and weighed about 500kg *1100lb*.

The giant moa *Dinornis maximus* of New Zealand may have been even taller, attaining a height of 3.6m *12ft*, though 2.5m *8ft* is the maximum accepted by most experts. It weighed about 227kg *500lb*.

Flying bird The largest known flying bird was the giant teratorn (Argentavis magnificens), which lived in Argentina about 6 million years ago. Fossil remains discovered at a site 160km *100 miles* west of Buenos Aires, Argentina in 1979 indicate that this gigantic vulture had a wingspan of over 6m *19ft 8in* (possibly up to 7.6m *25ft*) and weighed 100–120kg *220–265lb*.

Fish

Largest No prehistoric fish larger than living species has yet been discovered. Modern estimates suggest that the great shark *Carcharodon megalodon* which abounded in Miocene seas some 15 million years ago did not exceed 13.1m *43ft* in length, far less than the 24m *80ft*

claimed in early, erroneous estimates based on ratios from fossil teeth.

Insects

Largest The largest prehistoric insect was the dragonfly *Meganeura monyi*, which lived about 300 million years ago. Fossil remains (impressions of wings) discovered at Commentry, France indicate a wingspan of up to 70cm *27½in*.

Plant Kingdom

General Records

Oldest 'King Clone', the oldest known clone of the creosote plant (*Larrea tridentata*), of California, USA, was estimated in February 1980 by Prof. Frank C. Vasek to be 11,700 years old.

Most massive The most massive organism was reported in December 1992 to be a network of quaking aspen trees (*Populus tremuloides*) growing in the Wasatch Mountains, Utah, USA from a single root system, covering 43ha *106 acres* and weighing an estimated 6000 tonnes. The clonal system is genetically uniform and acts as a single organism, with all the component trees, part of the willow family, changing colour or shedding leaves in unison. This particular network was first described in 1975.

Northernmost The yellow poppy (*Papaver radicatum*) and the Arctic willow (*Salix arctica*) survive, the latter in an extremely stunted form, on the most northerly land at Lat. 83°N.

Tallest Flowering Plants

All plants should, where possible, be entered in official international, national or local garden and/or horticultural contests.

WORLD RECORDS

Type	Size		Grower	Location	Year
ASPIDISTRA	1.42m	4ft 8in	C. Evans	Kiora, New South Wales, Australia	1989
CACTUS	10.7m	35ft 1in	A. Kashi	Mysore, India	1992
CHRYSANTHEMUM	2.7m	8ft 10in	M. Comer	Desford, Leics	1993
DAHLIA	7.8m	25ft 7in	R. Blythe	Nannup, Western Australia	1990
PETUNIA	4.19m	13ft 9in	B. Lavery	Llanharry, Mid Glam	1993
PHILODENDRON *Climbing*	339.55m	1114ft	F. Francis	University of Massachusetts, USA	1984
SUNFLOWER[1]	7.76m tall	25ft 5½ in	M. Heijms	Oirschot, Netherlands	1986

UK NATIONAL RECORDS

Type	Size		Grower	Location	Year
AMARYLLIS	1.32m	4ft 4in	Rev. and Mrs Miles	West Malling, Kent	1993
ASPIDISTRA	1.27m	4ft 2in	G. James	Staveley, Chesterfield, Derbys	1979
DAFFODIL	1.55m	5ft 1in	M. Lowe	Chessell, Isle of Wight	1979
DAHLIA	3.3m	10ft 10in	R. Lond	Diss, Norfolk	1989
GLADIOLUS	2.55m	8ft 4½in	A. Breed	Melrose, Borders	1981
LUPIN	1.9m	6ft 3in	K. Barnes	Guildford, Surrey	1988
PETUNIA	2.53m	8ft 4in	G. Warner	Dunfermline, Fife	1978
PHILODENDRON *Climbing*	224m	735ft	M.J. Linhart	Thornton, Leics	1990
Tree	11.7m	38½ ft	B. Lavery	Llanharry, Mid Glam	1992
SUNFLOWER[1]	7.17m	23ft 6½in	F. Kelland	Exeter, Devon	1976
UMBRELLA PLANT	6.4m	20ft 11in	B. Lavery	Llanharry, Mid Glam	1992

[1] *A sunflower with a head diameter of 82cm 32¼ in was grown by Emily Martin of Maple Ridge, British Columbia, Canada in Sep 1983. A fully mature sunflower measuring just 56mm 2⅛in was grown by Michael Lenke of Lake Oswego, Oregon, USA in 1985 using a patented bonsai technique.*

Southernmost Lichens resembling *Rhinodina frigida* have been found in Moraine Canyon at Lat. 86°09′S, Long. 157°30′W in 1971 and in the Horlick Mountain area of Antarctica at Lat. 86°09′S, Long. 131°14′W in 1965.

The southernmost recorded flowering plant was the Antarctic hair grass (*Deschampsia antarctica*) found in Lat. 68°21′S on Refuge Island, Antarctica on 11 Mar 1981.

Highest The greatest certain altitude at which any flowering plants have been found is 6400 m *21,000 ft* on Mt Kamet (7756 m *25,447 ft*) in the Himalayas by N.D. Jayal in 1955. They were *Ermania himalayensis* and *Ranunculus lobatus*.

Deepest The greatest depth at which plant life has been found is 269 m *884 ft* for algae found by Mark and Diane Littler off San Salvadore Island, Bahamas in October 1984. These maroon-coloured plants survived although 99.9995 per cent of sunlight was filtered out.

Roots The greatest reported depth to which roots have penetrated is a calculated 120 m *400 ft* for a wild fig tree at Echo Caves, near Ohrigstad, Transvaal, South Africa. A single winter rye plant (*Secale cereale*) has been shown to produce 622.8 km *387 miles* of roots in 0.051 m³ *1.83 ft³* of earth.

UK An elm tree root at least 110 m *360 ft* long was reported from Auchencraig, Largs, Strathclyde in about 1950.

Fastest growing Some species of the 45 genera of bamboo have been found to grow at up to 91 cm *3 ft* per day (0.00003 km/h *0.00002 mph*).

Flowers

Earliest flower A flower believed to be 120 million years old was identified in 1989 by Drs Leo Hickey and David Taylor of Yale University, Connecticut, USA from a fossil discovered near Melbourne, Victoria, Australia. The flowering angiosperm, which resembles a modern black pepper plant, had two leaves and one flower and is known as the Koonwarra plant.

Largest *UK* The largest bloom of any native British plant is that of the wild white water lily (*Nymphaea alba*), at 15 cm *6 in* across.

Inflorescence The largest known inflorescence (as distinct from bloom) is that of *Puya raimondii*, a rare Bolivian monocarpic member of the Bromeliaceae family. Its erect panicle (diameter 2.4 m *8 ft*) emerges to a height of 10.7 m *35 ft* and each of these bears up to 8000 white blooms. (⇨ Slowest flowering plant)

Smelliest!

The largest of all blooms are those of the parasitic stinking° corpse lily (*Rafflesia arnoldii*), which can grow to 91 cm *3 ft* wide, 1.9 cm *¾ in* thick and weigh up to 7 kg *15 lb*. The plants attach themselves to cissus vines in the jungles of south-east Asia and, true to name, have an extremely offensive scent.

Smallest flowering and fruiting The floating, flowering aquatic duckweed (*Wolffia angusta*) of Australia, described in 1980, is only 0.6 mm *0.0236 in* long and 0.33 mm *0.0129 in* wide. It weighs about 0.00015 g *5.2×10⁻⁶ oz* and its fruit, which resembles a minuscule fig, weighs 0.00007 g *2.4×10⁻⁶ oz*.

The most jack-o'-lanterns in one place at one time was 4,817, on 29 Oct 1993. The pumpkins were carved by the citizens of Keene, New Hampshire, USA for their annual Harvest Festival.
(Photo: T M McCarthy)

UK The smallest land plant regularly flowering in Britain is the chaffweed (*Cetunculus minimus*), a single seed of which weighs 0.00003 g *1×10⁻⁷ oz*.

Fastest growing It was reported from Tresco Abbey, Isles of Scilly in July 1978 that a *Hesperoyucca whipplei* of the Liliaceae family had grown 3.65 m *12 ft* in 14 days, a rate of about 254 mm *10 in* per day.

Slowest flowering The slowest flowering plant is the rare *Puyaraimondii*, the largest of all herbs, discovered at 3960 m *13 000 ft* in Bolivia in 1870. The panicle emerges after about 80–150 years of the plant's life. It then dies. One planted near sea level at the University of California's Botanical Garden, Berkeley, USA in 1958 grew to 7.6 m *25 ft* and bloomed as early as August 1986 after only 28 years. (⇨ Largest blooms)

Orchids *Tallest* The tallest of all orchids is *Grammatophyllum speciosum* from Malaysia, specimens of which have been recorded up to 7.6 m *25 ft* tall.

A height of 15 m *49 ft* has been recorded for *Galeola foliata*, a saprophyte of the vanilla

The longest daisy chain measured 2.12 km *6980 ft 7 in* and was made in 7 hr by villagers of Good Easter, Chelmsford, Essex on 27 May 1985. The team is limited to 16.

family. It grows in the decaying rain forests of Queensland, Australia, but is not free-standing.

Largest flower The largest orchid flower is that of *Paphiopedilum sanderianum*, whose petals are reported to grow up to 90 cm *3 ft* long in the wild. It was discovered in 1886 in the Malay Archipelago. A plant of this variety grown in Somerset in 1991 had three flowers averaging 61 cm *2 ft* from the top of the dorsal sepal to the bottom of the ribbon petals, giving a record stretched length of 122 cm *4 ft*.

Largest cactus The largest of all cacti is the saguaro (*Cereus giganteus* or *Carnegiea gigantea*), found in Arizona and California, USA and Mexico. The green fluted column is surmounted by candelabra-like branches rising to a height of 17.67 m *57 ft 11 ¾ in* in a specimen discovered in the Maricopa Mountains, near Gila Bend, Arizona on 17 Jan 1988.

An armless 24-m *78-ft*-tall cactus was measured in April 1978 by Hube Yates in Cave Creek, Arizona, USA. It was toppled in a windstorm in July 1986 at an estimated age of 150 years. (⇨ Table)

Largest rhododendron Examples of the scarlet *Rhododendron arboreum* reach a height of 20 m *65 ft* on Mt Japfu, Nagaland, India.

The crosssection of a trunk of *Rhododendron giganteum* with a reputed height of 27.5 m *90 ft* from Yunnan, China is preserved at Inverewe Gardens, Highland.

British Isles The largest rhododendron in Britain is a specimen 7.6 m *25 ft* tall and 82.9 m *272 ft* in circumference at Government House, Hillsborough, Co. Down. Another example 13 m *42 ft 8 in* high and 1.8 m *6 ft* in circumference has been measured at Fernhill, Dublin, Republic of Ireland.

Largest rose tree A 'Lady Banks' rose tree at Tombstone, Arizona, USA has a trunk 101 cm *40 in* thick, stands 2.74 m *9 ft* high and covers an area of 499 m² *5380 ft²*. It is supported by 68 posts and several thousand feet of piping, which enables 150 people to be seated under the arbour. The cutting came from Scotland in 1884.

Hanging basket A giant hanging basket measuring 6.1 m *20 ft* in diameter and containing about 600 plants was created by Rogers of Exeter Garden Centre in 1987. Its volume was approximately 118 m³ *4167 ft³* and it weighed an estimated 4 tonnes. Another example from France with the same diameter but more conical in shape was smaller in terms of volume.

Fruits and Vegetables

Most nutritive An analysis of 38 fruits commonly eaten raw (as opposed to dried) shows that the avocado (*Persea americana*) has the highest caloric value, with 163 kilocalories per edible 100 g *741 kilocal/lb*; it also contains vitamins A, C and E and 2.2 per cent protein. Avocados originated in Central America.

Largest Fruits and Vegetables

In the interests of fairness and to minimize the risk of mistakes being made, all plants should, where possible, be entered in official international, national or local garden contests. Only produce grown primarily for human consumption will be considered for publication. The assistance of Garden News and the World Pumpkin Confederation is gratefully acknowledged.

WORLD RECORDS

Type	Size		Grower	Location	Year
APPLE	1.43 kg	*3 lb 2 oz*	Miklovic family	Caro, Michigan, USA	1992
BEETROOT	17.46 kg	*38 lb 8 oz*	G. Wheeler	Holbury, Hants	1992
BROCCOLI	15.87 kg	*35 lb*	J & M Evans	Palmer, Alaska, USA	1993
CABBAGE	56.24 kg	*124 lb*	B. Lavery	Llanharry, Mid Glam	1989
CARROT[1]	7 kg	*15 lb 7 oz*	I. Scott	Nelson, New Zealand	1978
CELERY	20.89 kg	*46 lb 1 oz*	B. Lavery	Llanharry, Mid Glam	1990
COURGETTE	29.25 kg	*64 lb 8 oz*	B. Lavery	Llanharry, Mid Glam	1990
CUCUMBER[2]	9.1 kg	*20 lb 1 oz*	B. Lavery	Llanharry, Mid Glam	1991
GARLIC	1.19 kg	*2 lb 10 oz*	R. Kirkpatrick	Eureka, California, USA	1985
GRAPEFRUIT	2.97 kg	*6 lb 8½ oz*	J. and A. Sosnow	Tucson, Arizona, USA	1984
GRAPES (bunch)	9.4 kg	*20 lb 11½ oz*	Bozzolo y Perut Ltda	Santiago, Chile	1984
GREEN BEAN	109 cm	*43 in*	F. Etheridge	North Carolina, USA	1993
LEEK (pot)	5.5 kg	*12 lb 2 oz*	P. Harrigan	Linton, Northumberland	1987
LEMON	3.88 kg	*8 lb 8 oz*	C. and D. Knutzen	Whittier, California, USA	1983
MARROW	49.04 kg	*108 lb 2 oz*	B. Lavery	Llanharry, Mid Glam	1990
MELON (cantaloupe)	28.12 kg	*62 lb*	G. Daughtridge	Rocky Mount, North Carolina, USA	1991
ONION	5.05 kg	*11 lb 2 oz*	R. Holland	Cumnock, Strathclyde	1992
PARSNIP	4.36 m	*171 ¾ in*	B. Lavery	Llanharry, Mid Glam	1990
PINEAPPLE	7.96 kg	*17 lb 8 oz*	Dole Philippines Inc.	South Cotabato, Philippines	1984
POTATO[3]	3.2 kg	*7 lb 1 oz*	J. East	Spalding, Lincs	1963
	3.2 kg	*7 lb 1 oz*	J. Busby	Atherstone, Warks	1982
PUMPKIN	379.2 kg	*836 lb*	N. Craven	Stouffville, Ontario, Canada	1993
RADISH	17.2 kg	*37 lb 15 oz*	Litterini family	Tanunda, South Australia	1992
RHUBARB	2.67 kg	*5 lb 14 oz*	E. Stone	East Woodyates, Wilts	1985
SQUASH	250.24 kg	*821 lb*	L. Stellpflug	Rush, New York, USA	1990
STRAWBERRY	231 g	*8.17 oz*	G. Anderson	Folkestone, Kent	1983
SWEDE	24.27 kg	*53 lb 8 oz*	P. Lillie	Uxbridge, Ontario, Canada	1993
TOMATO	3.51 kg	*7 lb 12 oz*	G. Graham	Edmond, Oklahoma, USA	1986
TOMATO PLANT	16.3 m	*53 ft 6 in*	G. Graham	Edmond, Oklahoma, USA	1985
WATERMELON	118.84 kg	*262 lb*	B. Carson	Arrington, Tennessee, USA	1990

UK NATIONAL RECORDS

Type	Size		Grower	Location	Year
CARROT	5.2 kg	*11 lb 7½ oz*	B. Lavery	Llanharry, Mid Glam	1993
GOOSEBERRY	61.04 g	*2.18 oz*	K. Archer	Scholar Green, Cheshire	1993
GRAPEFRUIT	1.67 kg	*3 lb 11 oz*	Willington G.C.	Willington, Beds	1986
LEMON	2.13 kg	*4 lb 11 oz*	Pershore College	Pershore, Hereford & Worcester	1986
MELON (cantaloupe)	8.33 kg	*18 lb 5¾ oz*	B. Lavery	Llanharry, Mid Glam	1991
PEACH	411 g	*14½ oz*	J. Bird	London	1984
PUMPKIN	322 kg	*710 lb*	B. Lavery	Llanharry, Mid Glam	1989
SQUASH	228.61 kg	*504 lb*	B. Lavery	Llanharry, Mid Glam	1991
TOMATO	2.54 kg	*5 lb 9½ oz*	R. Burrows	Huddersfield, W Yorks	1985
TOMATO PLANT	13.96 m	*45 ft 9½ in*	Chosen Hill School	Gloucester	1981
WATERMELON	16.33 kg	*36 lb*	B. Lavery	Llanharry, Mid Glam	1990

[1] A 5.14 m 16 ft 10 ½ in long carrot was grown by Bernard Lavery of Llanharry, Mid Glam in 1991.

[2] A Vietnamese variety 1.83 m 6 ft long was reported by L. Szabó of Debrecen, Hungary in September 1976. A.C. Rayment of Chelmsford, Essex grew one measuring 1.10 m 43 ½ in in 1984–6.

[3] One weighing 8.275 kg 18 lb 4 oz reported dug up by Thomas Siddal in his garden in Chester on 17 Feb 1795. A yield of 233.5 kg 515 lb was achieved from a 1.1 kg 2 ½ lb parent seed by Bowcock planted in April 1977.

ON THE RECORD

The potato peelers in action during their successful attempt on the record in 1992.

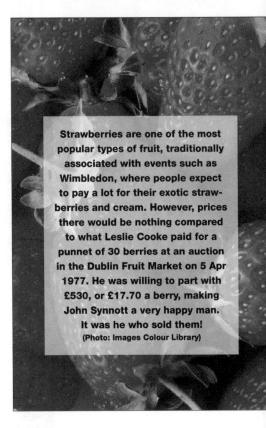

Strawberries are one of the most popular types of fruit, traditionally associated with events such as Wimbledon, where people expect to pay a lot for their exotic strawberries and cream. However, prices there would be nothing compared to what Leslie Cooke paid for a punnet of 30 berries at an auction in the Dublin Fruit Market on 5 Apr 1977. He was willing to part with £530, or £17.70 a berry, making John Synnott a very happy man. It was he who sold them!
(Photo: Images Colour Library)

Least nutritive The fruit with the lowest calorific value is the cucumber (*Cucumis sativus*), with 16 kilocal/100 g 73 kilocal/lb.

Most expensive fruit Anthony Baskeyfield purchased a grape for £700 from David Cinavas at the Helpston Garden Centre, Cambs on 28 Mar 1993. The sale was made in order to circumvent the Sunday Trading laws which apply in Great Britain, and a statue of Apollo (which was valued at £700) was given away with the grape.

Potato peeling The greatest quantity of potatoes peeled by five people to an institutional cookery standard with standard kitchen knives in 45 min is 482.8 kg *1064 lb 6 oz* (net) by Marj Killian, Terry Anderson, Barbara Pearson, Marilyn Small and Janene Utkin at the 64th Annual Idaho Spud Day celebration, held at Shelley, Idaho, USA on 19 Sep 1992.

Apple peeling The longest single unbroken apple peel on record is one of 52.51 m *172 ft 4 in,*

Potato peeling What do you do with the potatoes after you've beaten the record for peeling the greatest quantity in 45 minutes? One member of the team who set the record at Shelley kept a supply in her bath for weeks

"('In water, with salt. They'll keep').

One made doughnuts — 'They call them spudnuts'.

One even made ice-cream. Potato ice-cream?

'It's made from potatoes, isn't it? You can bet it's good!' said Marj Killian, who showed her dedication to the cause by adding that she'd never met a potato she didn't like."

peeled by Kathy Wafler of Wolcott, New York, USA in 11 hr 30 min at Long Ridge Mall, Rochester, New York on 16 Oct 1976. The apple weighed 567 g *20 oz*.

Apple picking The greatest recorded performance is 7180.3 kg *15,830 lb* picked in 8 hr by George Adrian of Indianapolis, Indiana, USA on 23 Sep 1980.

Cucumber slicing Norman Johnson of Blackpool College, Lancs set a record of 13.4 sec for slicing a 30.5 cm *12 in* cucumber, 3.8 cm *1½ in* in diameter, at 22 slices to the inch (total 264 slices) at the studios of West Deutscher Rundfunk in Cologne, Germany on 3 Apr 1983.

Vineyards

Largest The world's largest vineyard extends over the Mediterranean slopes between the Pyrénées and the Rhône in the *départements* Gard, Hérault, Aude and Pyrénées-Orientales. It covers an area of 840,000 ha *2,075,685 acres*, 52.3 per cent of which is *monoculture viticole*.

UK The largest vineyard in the UK is Denbies Wine Estate in Dorking, Surrey, covering 101 ha *250 acres*. Planting began in 1986 and the 276,000 vines planted so far have a projected annual production capacity of 500,000 bottles.

Most northerly The most northerly commercial vineyard in Britain and probably in the world is at Whitworth Hall, owned by Derek Parnaby at Sherrymoor, County Durham on Lat. 54°42′N.

Most southerly The most southerly commercial vineyards are found in central Otago, South Island, New Zealand south of Lat. 45°S.

Largest vine This was planted in 1842 at Carpinteria, California, USA. By 1900 it was yielding more than 9 tonnes of grapes in some years, and averaged 7 tonnes per year until it died in 1920.

UK Britain's largest vine is the Great Vine at Hampton Court, Greater London, planted in 1768. It has a circumference of 2.16 m *7 ft 1 in*, branches up to 34.7 m *114 ft* long and produces an average yield of 318.8 kg *703 lb*.

In 1990 Leslie Stringer of Dartford, Kent obtained a yield of over 2300 kg *5071 lb* from the Dartford Wondervine, planted in 1979. The plant was grown from a cutting taken from a vine planted in Banstead, Surrey in 1962.

Leaves

Largest The largest leaves of any plant are those of the raffia palm (*Raphia farinifera = R. ruffia*) of the Mascarene Islands in the Indian Ocean, and the Amazonian bamboo palm (*R. taedigera*) of South America and Africa, whose leaf blades may be up to 20 m *65½ ft* long with petioles measuring 3.96 m *13 ft*.

UK The largest leaves found on outdoor plants in Great Britain are those of *Gunnera manicata* from Columbia, with rhubarb-like leaves measuring up to 3 m *10 ft* in diameter on prickly stems up to 2.5 m *8 ft* tall.

Undivided The largest undivided leaf is that of *Alocasia macrorrhiza*, from Sabah, Malaysia. A specimen found in 1966 was 3.02 m *9 ft 11 in* long, 1.92 m *6 ft 3½ in* wide, and had a surface area of 3.17 m² *34.12 ft²*. A specimen of the water lily *Victoria amazonica* (Longwood hybrid) in the grounds of the Stratford-upon-Avon Butterfly Farm, Warks was 2.4 m *8 ft* in diameter on 2 Oct 1989.

Clovers A fourteen-leafed white clover (*Trifolium repens*) was found by Randy Farland near Sioux Falls, South Dakota, USA on 16 Jun 1975. A fourteen-leafed red clover (*Trifolium pratense*) was reported by Paul Haizlip at Bellevue, Washington, USA on 22 Jun 1987.

Seeds

Largest The largest seed in the world is that of the giant fan palm *Lodoicea maldivica* (= *L. callipyge*, *L. sechellarum*), commonly known as the double coconut or coco de mer, found wild only in the Seychelles. The single-seeded fruit weighs up to 20 kg *44 lb* and can take 10 years to develop.

Smallest The smallest seeds are those of epiphytic (non-parasitic plants growing on others) orchids, at 992.25 million seeds/g *35 million/oz* (cf. grass pollens at up to 170.1 billion grains/g *6 billion grains/oz*).

Most conquering conker The most victorious untreated conker — the fruit of the common horse-

Bernard Lavery and his prize produce

Bernard Lavery, who has been growing giant flowers & vegetables for 20 years, currently holds 15 world records and several UK national ones.

" Although by profession I am a seed and plant breeder, growing giant flowers and vegetables is my hobby. I derive an enormous amount of pleasure from stretching nature to its limits. And when it comes to culinary use, giant vegetables are exactly the same as 'normal' sized ones; when they are freshly harvested and before they become over-mature, they taste truly magnificent.

If you use seed which has the genetic capabilities to grow giant vegetables, then all you need to be a World Champion is some fertile ground, a little love and care, and Lady Luck sitting on your shoulder throughout the growing season.

America has traditionally been the home of big vegetables but the enthusiasm for growing 'giants' now stretches to Canada, Europe, Africa, Asia and Australasia. Growing giant vegetables has really taken off in a big way. It's great fun; it's easy, and anyone can do it — some 'giants' such as pumpkins, squash, and marrows, will increase in size by two or three inches a day and will seem to grow even as you are looking at them. "

Bernard Lavery and his prize produce
(Photos: B Lavery)

Weeds

Largest The largest weed is the giant hogweed (*Heracleum mantegazzianum*), originally from the Caucasus. It reaches 3.65m *12ft* tall and has leaves 91cm *3ft* long.

Most damaging The virulence of weeds tends to be measured by the number of crops they affect and the number of countries in which they occur. On this basis the worst would appear to be the purple nut sedge, nutgrass or nutsedge (*Cyperus rotundus*), a land weed native to India but which attacks 52 crops in 92 countries.

UK The most damaging and widespread cereal weeds in Britain are the wild oats *Avena fatua* and *A. ludoviciana*. Their seeds can withstand temperatures of 115.6°C *240°F* for 15 min and

remain viable, and up to 50 per cent losses have been recorded in crops affected by them.

Most spreading The greatest area covered by a single clonal growth is that of the wild box huckleberry (*Gaylussacia brachycera*), a mat-forming evergreen shrub first reported in 1796. A colony covering about 40ha *100 acres* was found on 18 Jul 1920 near the Juniata River, Pennsylvania, USA. It has been estimated that this colony began 13000 years ago.

Aquatic weeds The worst aquatic weed of the tropics and subtropics is the water hyacinth (*Eichhornia crassipes*), a native of the Amazon Basin, but which extends from Lat. 40°N to 45°S. The intransigence of aquatic plants in man-made lakes is illustrated by the mat-forming water weed *Salvinia auriculata*, found in Africa. It was

detected when Lake Kariba, which straddles the border of Zimbabwe and Zambia, was filled in May 1959 and within 13 months it had choked an area of 518km² *200 miles²*, rising to 1002km² *387 miles²* by 1963.

Seaweed

Longest The longest species of seaweed is the Pacific giant kelp (*Macrocystis pyrifera*), which, although it does not exceed 60m *196ft* in length, can grow 45cm *18in* in a day.

UK The longest of the 700 species of British seaweed is the brown seaweed (*Chorda filum*), which grows to a length of 6.10m *20ft*. The Japanese species *Sargassum muticum*, introduced into Britain *c.* 1970, can reach 9.0m *30ft*.

---

chestnut (*Aesculus hippocastanum*)—was a 'five thousander plus', which won the BBC Conker Conquest in 1954. However, a professor of botany believes that this heroic specimen might well have been a 'ringer', probably an ivory or tagua nut (*Phytelephas macrocarpa*). *The Guinness Book of Records* will not publish any category for the largest collection of conkers for fear that trees might suffer wholesale damage.

Trees

Earliest The earliest surviving species of tree is the maidenhair (*Ginkgo biloba*) of Zhejiang, China, which first appeared about 160 million years ago during the Jurassic era. It was 'rediscovered' by Kaempfer (Netherlands) in 1690 and reached England *c.* 1754. It has been grown in Japan since *c.* 1100, where it was known as *ginkyō* ('silver apricot') and is now known as *icho*.

Oldest Dendrochronologists estimate the *potential* life span of a bristlecone pine (*Pinus longaeva*) to be nearly 5500 years, and that of a giant sequoia (*Sequoiadendron giganteum*) at perhaps 6000 years, although no single cell lives more than 30 years. The oldest recorded tree was a bristlecone pine designated WPN-114 and found to be 5100 years old. It grew at 3275m *10,750ft* above sea level on the north-east face of Mt Wheeler, Nevada, USA.

Living The oldest recorded living tree is another bristlecone pine named 'Methuselah', growing at 3050m *10,000ft* on the California side of the White Mountains, USA and confirmed as 4700

The green in this picture is not an expanse of grass, but an expanse of water hyacinth—a weed so dense that it entirely conceals the water it grows upon. It is also the most wide-spread aquatic weed in the world.

(Photo: Jacana/R Konig)

years old. In March 1974 it was reported to have produced 48 live seedlings.

UK The longest-lived British tree is the yew (*Taxus baccata*), for which a maximum age of well over 1000 years is usually conceded. The

Massive!

The world's most massive single tree is 'General Sherman' the giant sequoia (*Sequoiadendron giganteum*) growing in the Sequoia National Park, California, USA. It stands 83.82m *275ft* tall, has a diameter of 11.1m *36.5ft* and a girth of 31.3m *102.6ft*. This tree is estimated to contain the equivalent of 606,100 board feet of timber, enough to make 5 billion matches, and its red-brown bark may be up to 61cm *24in* thick in parts. Its weight, including the root system, is estimated at 2000 tonnes.

oldest known is the Fortingall yew near Aberfeldy, Tayside, part of which still grows. In 1777 this tree was over 15m *50ft* in girth and it is estimated to be some 1500 years old.

The oldest dated coppice is a patch of 60 small-leaved lime trees at Silk Wood near Tetbury, Glos, estimated by DNA analysis to have derived from a tree living 2000 years ago.

Greatest spread The tree canopy covering the greatest area is that of the great banyan (*Ficus benghalensis*) in the Indian Botanical Garden, Calcutta, with 1775 prop or supporting roots and a circumference of 412m *1350ft*. It covers some 1.2ha *3 acres* and dates from before 1787.

UK The greatest spread in Britain is a canopy circumference of 198m *649 ft* for an oriental plane at Corsham Court, Wiltshire.

Greatest girth A circumference of 57.9m *190ft* was recorded for the pollarded (trimmed to encourage a more bushy growth) European chestnut (*Castanea sativa*) known as the 'Tree of the Hundred Horses' (*Castagno di Cento Cavalli*) on Mt Etna, Sicily, Italy in 1770 and 1780. It is now in three parts, widely separated.

'El Arbol del Tule' in Oaxaca state, Mexico is a 41m *135ft* tall Montezuma cypress (*Taxodium mucronatum*) with a girth in 1982 of 35.8m *117½ft*, measured 1.52m *5ft* above the ground. Generally speaking, however, the largest girths are attributed to African baobab trees (*Adansonia digitata*), with measurements of 43.0m *141ft* recorded.

Plant Kingdom

UK A sweet (Spanish) chestnut (*Castanea sativa*) in the grounds of Canford School, near Poole, Dorset has a trunk with a circumference of 13.33m *43ft 9in.*

Tallest A *Eucalyptus regnans* at Mt Baw Baw, Victoria, Australia is believed to have measured 143 m *470ft* in 1885. According to the researches of Dr A.C. Carder, the tallest tree ever measured was another Australian eucalyptus at Watts River, Victoria, Australia, reported in 1872 by forester William Ferguson. It was 132.6m *435ft* tall and almost certainly measured over 150m *500ft* originally. However, the Dyerville Giant, which fell in March 1991, was proven to be 113.38m *372ft* high, not counting the 1.5 m *5ft* of buried base. It grew in Humboldt Redwoods State Park, California, and was the tallest tree of modern times.

Living The tallest tree currently standing is the 'National Geographic Society' coast redwood (*Sequoia sempervirens*) in the Redwood National Park, California, USA. Its latest measurement was 111.56m *366ft* in May 1993, according to Ron Hildebrant of California.

British Isles The best two claimants for Britain's tallest tree are two Douglas firs (*Pseudotsuga menziesii*), both standing 64.5m *212ft* in 1993: one at the Forestry Commission property at The Hermitage, Perthshire; and the other at the National Trust for Scotland property at Dunans in Strathclyde. (⇨ Table)

UK A 26.3m *86ft 5in* tall Norway spruce (*Picea abies*) was grown on Viscount Weymouth's Longleat estate in Wiltshire and given to the King's College, Cambridge Choir School Development Appeal for Christmas 1989.

Fastest growing Discounting bamboo, which is classified as a woody grass, the fastest recorded rate of growth is 10.74m *35ft 3in* in 13 months (about 28mm *1¹/₁₀in* per day) by an *Albizzia falcata* planted on 17 Jun 1974 in Sabah, Malaysia.

Slowest growing Excluding *bonsai*—the 14th century Oriental art of cultivating miniature trees—the extreme in slow growth is represented by the *Dioon edule* (Cycadaceae) measured in Mexico between 1981 and 1986 by Dr Charles M. Peters, who found the average annual growth rate to be 0.76mm *0.03in*; a 120-year-old specimen was just 10cm *4in* tall.

Most leaves Little work has been done on the laborious task of establishing which species has the most leaves. A large oak has perhaps 250,000, but a cypress may have some 45–50 million leaf scales.

Remotest The most remote tree is believed to be a solitary Norwegian spruce on Campbell Island, Antarctica, whose nearest companion would be over 222km *120 nautical miles* away on the Auckland Islands.

Largest forest The largest afforested areas in the world are the vast coniferous forests of northern Russia, lying between Lat. 55°N and the

> The world's tallest cut Christmas tree was a 67.36m *221ft* Douglas fir (*Pseudotsuga menziesii*) erected at Northgate Shopping Center, Seattle, Washington, USA in December 1950.

Background: the sweet chestnut (*Castanea sativa*) holds both world and UK records for greatest girths. /(Photo: Jacana/H Berthoule)

Tallest Trees in the British Isles

Species	Location	m	ft
ALDER (Italian)	Westonbirt, Glos	34	111
ASH	Old Roar Ghyll, St. Leonards, E Sussex	38	124
BEECH	Hallyburton House, Tayside	46	150
BIRCH (Silver)	Ballogie, Grampian	30	98
CEDAR (of Lebanon)	Leaton Knolls, Shrops	43	141
CHESTNUT (Horse)	Ashford Chase, Petersfield, Hants	36	118
CHESTNUT (Sweet)	Reigate Park, Surrey	39	128
CYPRESS (Lawson)	Strone House, Strathclyde	42	138
EUCALYPTUS (Blue gum)	Glencormack, Co. Wicklow	44	144
FIR (Douglas)	The Hermitage, Perth, Tayside	64.5	212
	Dunans, Argyll	64.5	212
FIR (Grand)	Strone, Strathclyde	63	206
GINKGO	Sezincote, Glos	26	98
GINKGO	Bitton, Glos	26	85
HEMLOCK (Western)	Benmore, Argyll, Strathclyde	51	167
HOLLY	Hallyburton, Tayside	75	23
LARCH (European)	Glenlee, Dumfries & Galloway	46	150
LIME	Duncombe Park, Helmsley, N Yorks	44	144
METSEQUOIA	Leonardslee, Sussex	28	92
MONKEY PUZZLE	Bicton, Devon	30	98
OAK (Turkey)	Knightshayes, Tiverton, Devon	44	144
OAK (Common)[1]	Abbotsbury, Dorset	40	132
PINE (Corsican)	Adhurst St. Mary, Petersfield, Hants	46	150
PLANE	Bryanston School, Blandford, Dorset	48	156
POPLAR (Black Italian)	Lincoln Arboretum, Lincoln	44	144
SEQUOIA (Wellingtonia)[2]	Castle Leod, Strathpeffer, Highland	53	174
SPRUCE (Sitka)	Strathearn, Tayside	61	200
SYCAMORE	Lennoxlove, Haddington, Lothian	40	132
WALNUT (Black)	Much Hadham Rectory, Herts	36	118
WILLOW (Weeping)	Radnor Gardens, London	25	82
YEW[3]	Belvoir Castle, Leics	29	95

[1] The largest English Oaks are both 384 cm *12.6 ft* in diameter at Bowthorpe in Lincs and Fredville in Kent.
[2] The largest Sequoia (Wellingtonia) is 345 cm *11.3 ft* in diameter and is at Clunie Gardens, Tayside.
[3] The largest Yew is 334 cm *10.9 ft* in diameter at Ulcombe Church, Kent

Industrious tree-planters dig in to set the record for the most trees planted in a week: between 25 Nov and 5 Dec 1993, during National Tree Week, 300 schoolchildren and adults from the Walsall area planted 1774 trees in 17hr 20min (over six days). (Photo: Walsall Countryside Services)

Arctic Circle. The total wooded area covers 1.1 billion ha *2.7 billion acres*. In comparison, the largest area of forest in the tropics is the Amazon basin, covering some 330 million ha *815 million acres*.

UK The largest forest in Britain is the Kielder Forest District in Northumberland, covering 39380 ha *97309 acres*.

Largest hedges The world's tallest and longest hedge is the Meikleour beech hedge in Perthshire, planted in 1746 by Jean Mercer and her husband Robert Murray Nairne. Its tapered height when trimmed now varies from 24.4 m *80 ft* to 36.6 m *120 ft* along its length of 550 m *1804 ft*. Trimming takes place every 10 years or so and was last completed in six weeks in 1988.

A yew hedge planted in 1720 in Earl Bathurst's Park, Cirencester, Glos runs for 155.5 m *510 ft*, reaches 11 m *36 ft* in height and is 4.5 m *15 ft* thick at its base. The hedge takes about 20 days to trim.

The tallest box hedge is 12 m *40 ft* high and dates from the 18th century at Birr Castle, Co. Offaly, Republic of Ireland.

Hedge laying John Williams of Sennybridge and David James of Llanwern, Brecon, hedged by the 'stake and pleach' method a total of 241.4 m *264 yd* in 11 hr 24 min on 28 Apr 1986.

Longest avenue The world's longest avenue is the Nikko Cryptomeria Avenue comprising three parts converging on Imaichi City in the Tochigi Prefecture of Japan, with a total length of 35.41 km *22 miles*. Planted in 1628–48, over 13,500 of its original 200,000 Japanese cedar (*Cryptomeria japonica*) trees survive, at an average height of 27 m *88½ ft*.

UK The longest avenue of trees in Great Britain is the privately-owned stretch of 1750 beeches measuring 5.8 km *3.6 miles* in Savernake Forest, near Marlborough, Wilts.

Tree sitting The duration record for staying in a tree is more than 23 years, by Bungkas, who went up a palm tree in the Indonesian village of Bengkes in 1970 and has been there ever since. He lives in a nest which he made from branches and leaves. Repeated efforts have been made to persuade him to come down, but without success.

Tree climbing The fastest time up a 30.5 m *100 ft* fir spar pole and back down to the ground is 24.82 sec, by Guy German of Sitka, Alaska, USA on 3 Jul 1988 at the World Championship Timber Carnival in Albany, Oregon, USA. The fastest time up a 9 m *29 ft 6 in* coconut tree barefoot is 4.88 sec, by Fuatai Solo, 17, in Sukuna Park, Fiji on 22 Aug 1980.

Tree topping Guy German climbed a 30.5 m *100 ft* spar pole and sawed off the top (circumference of 100 cm *40 in*) in a record time of 53.35 sec at Albany, Oregon, USA on 3 Jul 1989.

Wood cutting The first recorded lumberjack sports competition was held in 1572 in the Basque region of Spain.

The following records were set at the Lumberjack World Championships at Hayward, Wisconsin, USA (founded 1960):

Power saw (three slices of a 51 cm *20 in* diameter white-pine log with a single-engine saw from dead start)—8.03 sec by Rick Halvorson (US) in 1993.

Bucking (one slice from a 51 cm *20 in* diameter white-pine log with a crosscut saw)—one-man, 17.14 sec by David Hocquard (New Zealand) in 1992; two-man, 6.77 sec by Gilles Levesques and Gaston Duperre (both Canada) in 1992.

Standing block chop (chopping through a vertical 35.5 cm *14 in* diameter white-pine log 76 cm *30 in* in length)—22.05 sec by Melvin Lentz (US) in 1988.

Underhand block chop (chopping through a horizontal 35.5 cm *14 in* diameter white-pine log 76 cm *30 in* in length)—17.84 sec by Laurence O'Toole (Australia) in 1985.

Springboard chopping (scaling a 2.7 m *9 ft* spar pole on springboards and chopping a 35.5 cm *14 in* diameter white-pine log)—1 min 18.45 sec by Bill Youd (Australia) in 1985.

Parks, Zoos, Oceanaria, Aquaria

Parks

Largest The world's largest national park is the National Park of North-Eastern Greenland, covering 972,000 km² *375,289 miles²* and stretching from Liverpool Land in the south to the northernmost island, Odaaq Ø, off Pearyland. Established in 1974 and enlarged in 1988, much of the park is covered by ice and is home to a variety of protected flora and fauna, including polar bears, musk ox and birds of prey.

UK The largest park in the United Kingdom is the Lake District National Park (designated as such in 1951), which covers 2292 km² *885 miles²* and lies wholly in Cumbria. The largest private park is Woburn Park (1200 ha *3000 acres*), near Woburn Abbey, the seat of the Dukes of Bedford.

Largest game reserve The world's largest zoological reserve is the Etosha National Park in Namibia. Established in 1907, it now covers 99,525 km² *38,427 miles²*.

Zoos

Oldest The earliest known collection of animals was established by Shulgi, a 3rd-dynasty ruler of Ur from 2097–2094 BC at Puzurish, Iraq. The oldest known zoo is at Schönbrunn, Vienna, Austria, built in 1752 by the Holy Roman Emperor Franz I for his wife Maria Theresa.

The oldest existing public zoological collection founded for the scientific study of animals is that of the Zoological Society of London, founded in 1826 by Sir Stamford Raffles (1781–1826). In January 1993 the collection comprised 18,128 specimens housed in Regent's Park, London (14.5 ha *36 acres*) and at Whipsnade Park, Beds (219 ha *541 acres*, opened 23 May 1931), representing the most comprehensive in the United Kingdom. The record annual attendances are 3,031,571 in 1950 for Regent's Park and 756,758 in 1961 for Whipsnade.

Without bars The earliest zoo without bars was at Stellingen, near Hamburg, Germany. It was founded in 1907 by Carl Hagenbeck (1844–1913), who used deep pits and large pens instead of cages to separate the exhibits from the visitors.

National Park Visits

Charles Shields, 76, and his wife Eloise, 75, have been enchanted by America's national parks for over 45 years. When the National Parks Service introduced a parks passport in 1985 the Shields had the book stamped at every park they visited. In 1991 a new Passport Book was issued and the Shields decided to visit as many national parks as possible.

“ We thought it would be fun to see all the parks and this got us into new areas we never would have gone to, learning about heroes of our country, our heritage, wonderful scenery and exciting experiences we had never dreamed of before.

Our main goal in doing this was to inspire others to visit parks and discover a whole new world of fun and entertainment, and see the broad scope of our country's past and

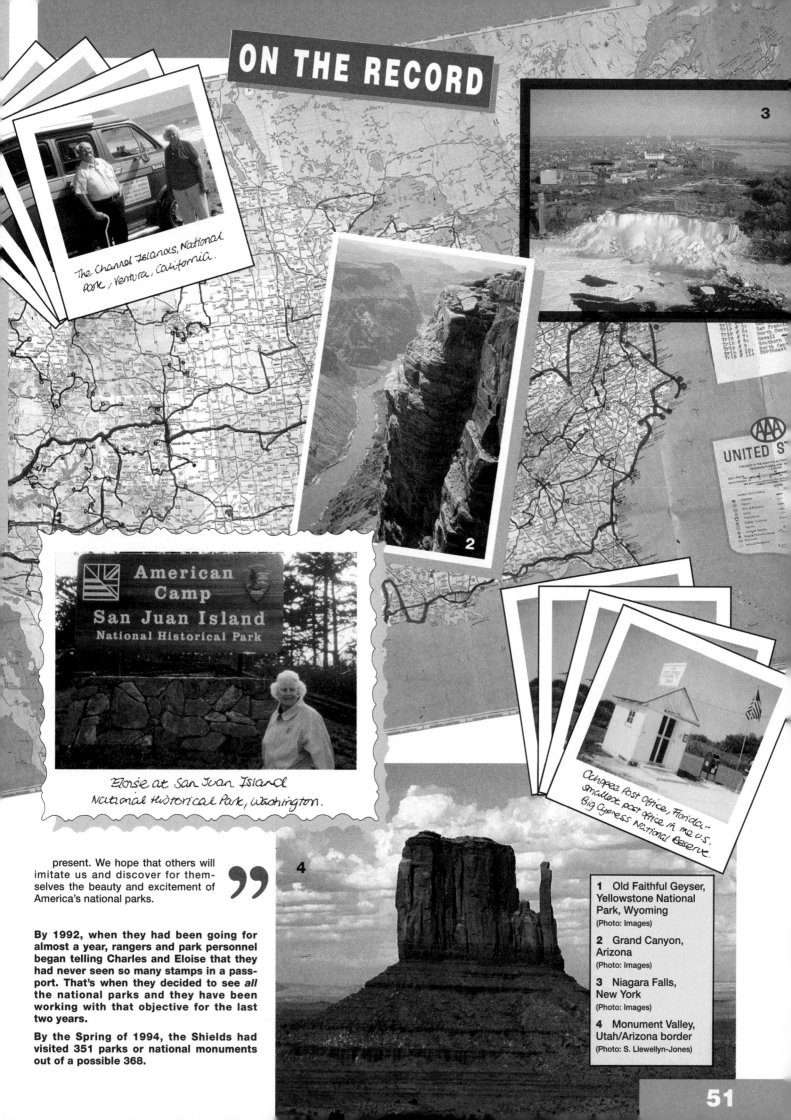

3

The Channel Islands, National Park, Ventura, California.

Eloise at San Juan Island National Historical Park, Washington.

American Camp San Juan Island National Historical Park

2

UNITED S

AAA

Ochopee Post Office, Florida— smallest post office in the U.S. Big Cypress National Reserve.

present. We hope that others will imitate us and discover for themselves the beauty and excitement of America's national parks.

4

By 1992, when they had been going for almost a year, rangers and park personnel began telling Charles and Eloise that they had never seen so many stamps in a passport. That's when they decided to see *all* the national parks and they have been working with that objective for the last two years.

By the Spring of 1994, the Shields had visited 351 parks or national monuments out of a possible 368.

1 Old Faithful Geyser, Yellowstone National Park, Wyoming
(Photo: Images)

2 Grand Canyon, Arizona
(Photo: Images)

3 Niagara Falls, New York
(Photo: Images)

4 Monument Valley, Utah/Arizona border
(Photo: S. Llewellyn-Jones)

Oceanaria

Earliest The world's first oceanarium was Marineland of Florida, opened in 1938 at a site 29km *18 miles* south of St Augustine, Florida, USA. Up to 26.3 million litres *5,800,000gal* of sea-water are pumped daily through two major tanks, one rectangular (30.48m *100ft* long by 12.19m *40ft* wide by 5.48m *18ft* deep) containing 1.7 million litres *375,000gal*, and one circular (71m *233ft* in circumference and 3.65m *12ft* deep) containing 1.5 million litres *330,000gal*. The tanks are seascaped and include coral reefs and even a shipwreck.

Aquaria

Largest In terms of the volume of water held, the Living Seas Aquarium, opened in 1986 at the EPCOT Center, Florida, USA, is the world's largest, with a total capacity of 23.66 million litres *6.25 million gal*. It contains over 3000 fish representing 65 species.

The largest in terms of marine-life is the Monterey Bay Aquarium opened on 20 Oct 1984 in California, USA, which houses 6500 specimens (525 species) of flora and fauna in its 95 tanks. The volume of water held is 3,375,000 litres *750,000gal*.

Microbes

Discovered in 1676 by microscopist Antony van Leeuwenhoek of Delft, Netherlands (1632–1723), protista are single-celled or acellular organisms with characteristics common to both plants and animals. The more plant-like are termed Protophyta (protophytes), including unicellular algae, and the more animal-like are placed in the phylum Protozoa (protozoans), including amoeba and flagellates.

Largest The largest known protozoans in terms of volume were calcareous foraminifera (*Foramini-*

ferida) of the genus Nummulites, one species of which, known from Middle Eocene rocks of Turkey, attained a diameter of 22cm *8½in*.

The largest existing protozoan, a species of the fan-shaped *Stannophyllum* (Xenophyophorida), can exceed this in length (25cm *9¾in* has been recorded) but not in volume.

Smallest protophyte The marine microflagellate alga Micromonas pusilla has a diameter of less than 2μm 0.00008in.

Fastest The protozoan *Monas stigmatica* has been found to move a distance equivalent to 40 times its own length in a second. No human can cover even seven times his own length in a second.

Fastest reproduction The protozoan *Glaucoma*, which reproduces by binary fission, divides as frequently as every three hours. Thus in the course of a day it could become a great-great-great-great-great-great grandparent and the progenitor of 512 descendants.

Bacteria

Antony van Leeuwenhoek (1632–1723) was the first to observe bacteria, in 1675.

Oldest Viable bacteria were reported in 1991 to have been recovered from sediments 3–4 million years old from the sea of Japan.

Living In 1991 it was reported that live bacteria were found in the carcass of a mastodon (an ancestor of the elephant) from Ohio, USA which died 12,000 years earlier and which, on the evidence of spear marks found in the ribs, repre-

sented the first proof of humans killing a prehistoric animal. The bacteria gave the flesh 'a bad smell' even after such a long time.

Largest The largest bacterium is *Epulopiscium fishelsoni*, described in 1993 as a symbiont inhabiting the intestinal tract of the brown surgeonfish (*Acanthurus nigrofuscus*) from the Red Sea and the Great Barrier Reef. Measuring 80 × 600 μm or more and therefore visible to the naked eye, this mega-micro-organism, first discovered by Israeli researchers in 1985, is so big it was originally thought to be a protozoan. At 1 million times larger than the human gut organism *Escherichia coli*, it is a reminder of the strange new life-forms we have yet to discover.

Smallest free-living entity The smallest of all free-living organisms are pleuro-pneumonia-like organisms (PPLO) of the *Mycoplasma*. One of these, *Mycoplasma laidlawii*, first discovered in sewage in 1936, has a diameter during its early existence of only 10^{-7}m. Examples of the strain known as H.39 have a maximum diameter of 3×10^{-7}m and weigh an estimated 10^{-16}g. Thus a 190-tonne blue whale would weigh 1.9×10^{24} times as much.

Highest In April 1967 the US National Aeronautics and Space Administration (NASA) reported that bacteria had been discovered at an altitude of 41.13km *25½ miles*.

Fastest By means of a polar flagellum rotating 100 times/sec, the rod-shaped *bacillus Bdellovibrio bacteriovorus* can travel 50 times its own length of 2μm per sec. This would be the equivalent of a human sprinter reaching 320km/h *200mph* or a swimmer crossing the English Channel in 6min.

Fungi

Fungi were once classified in the subkingdom Protophyta of the kingdom Protista.

Largest The world's largest fungus is a single living clonal growth of the underground fungus *Armillaria ostoyae*, reported in May 1992 as covering some 600ha *1500 acres* in the forests of Washington state, USA. Estimates based on its size suggest that the fungus is 500–1000 years old, but no attempts have been made to estimate its weight. Also known as the

A single living clonal growth of the fungus *Armillaria bulbosa*, reported on 2 Apr 1992 to be covering about 15ha *37 acres* of forest in Michigan, USA, was calculated to weigh over 100 tonnes, which is comparable to the weight of a blue whale. The organisam is thought to have originated from a single fertilized spore at least 1500 years ago. (Photo: Planet Earth Pictures/F C Millington)

honey or shoestring fungus, it fruits above ground as edible gilled mushrooms.

Largest edible A giant puffball (*Calvatia gigantea*) measuring 2.64m *8ft 8in* in circumference and weighing 22kg *48½lb* was found by Jean-Guy Richard of Montreal, Canada in 1987.

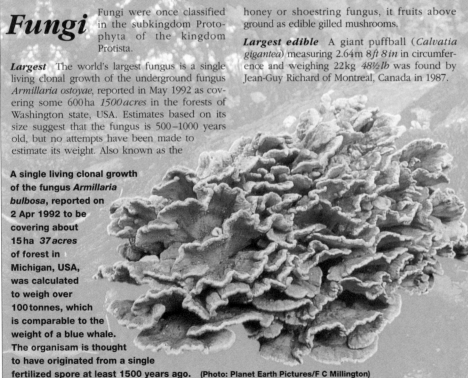

Heaviest An example of the edible chicken of the woods mushroom (*Laetiporus sulphureus*) weighing 45.4kg *100lb* was found in the New Forest, Hants by Giovanni Paba of Broadstone, Dorset on 15 Oct 1990.

The largest recorded tree fungus is the bracket fungus *Rigidoporus ulmarius* growing from dead elm wood in the grounds of the International Mycological Institute at Kew, Surrey. It measured 150×144cm *59×56¾in* with a circumference of 454cm *178¾in*. In 1992 it was growing at a rate of 22.5cm *9in* per year but this has now slowed.

Most poisonous The yellowish-olive death cap (*Amanita phalloides*), which can be found in Britain, is the world's most poisonous fungus, responsible for 90 per cent of fatal poisonings caused by fungi. Its total toxin content is 7–9mg dry weight, whereas the estimated lethal amount of amatoxins for humans, depending on bodyweight, is only 5–7mg— equivalent to less than 50g *1¾oz* of a fresh fungus. From 6–15 hours after eating, the effects are vomiting, delirium, collapse and death. Among its victims was Cardinal Giulio de' Medici, Pope Clement VII (b. 1478) on 25 Sep 1534.

Aeroflora The highest recorded total fungal spore count was 161,037/m³ *5,686,861/ft³* near Cardiff, S Glam on 21 Jul 1971. The lowest counts of airborne allergens are nil.

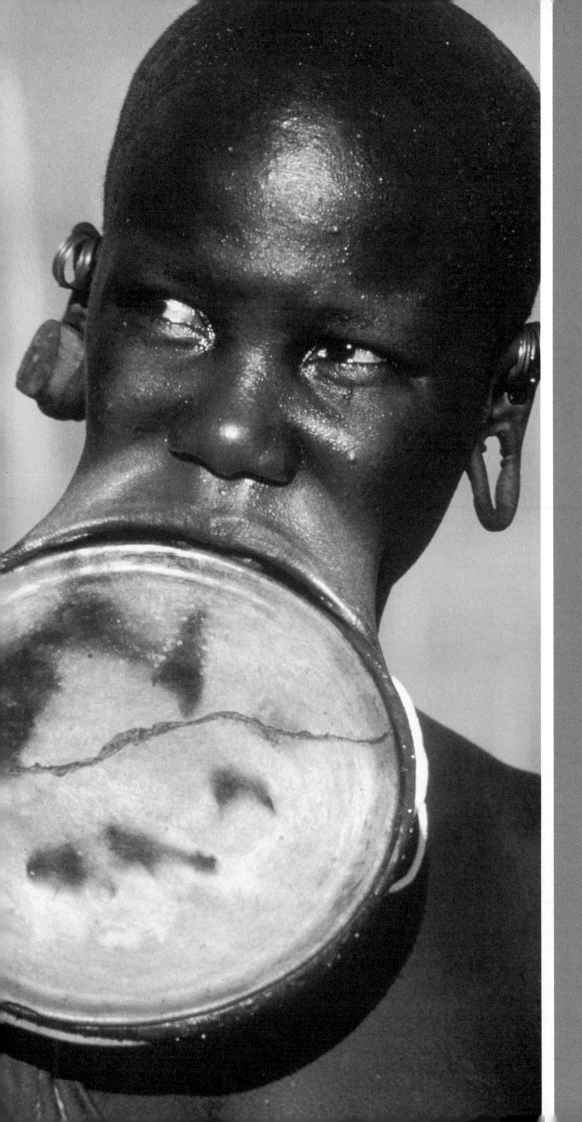

Human *Being*

Origins

Earliest Man

If the age of the Earth-Moon system (latest estimate 4540 ± 40 million years) is likened to a single year, hominids appeared on the scene at about 3:35 p.m. on 31 December. Britain's earliest traceable inhabitants arrived at about 10:50 p.m. and the life span of a 120-year-old person would be 0.83 seconds.

Man (*Homo sapiens*) is a species in the sub-family Homininae of the family Hominidae of the super-family Hominoidea of the sub-order Simiae (or Anthropoidea) of the order Primates of the infra-class Eutheria of the sub-class Theria of the class Mammalia of the sub-phylum Vertebrata (Craniata) of the phylum Chordata of the sub-kingdom Metazoa of the animal kingdom.

Earliest Primates These appeared in the late Cretaceous epoch about 65 million years ago. The earliest members of the sub-order Anthropoidea are known from both Africa and South America in the early Oligocene, 30–34 million years ago. Finds from Faiyûm, Egypt represent primates from the early Oligocene period, 37 million years.

Earliest hominoid The earliest hominoid fossil is a jaw-bone with three molars found in the Otavi Hills, Namibia on 4 Jun 1991. It had been provisionally dated at 10–15 million years old but later refined to 12–13 million years and named *Otavi pithecus namibiensis*.

Earliest hominid The earliest hominid relic is an Australopithecine jaw-bone, with two molars 5 cm *2 in* long, found near Lake Baringo, Kenya in February 1984. It has been dated to four million years ago by associated fossils and to 5.4–5.6 million years ago through rock correlation by potassium-argon dating.

Earliest genus Homo The earliest species of this genus is *Homo habilis*, or 'Handy Man', from Olduvai Gorge, Tanzania, named by Louis Leakey, Philip Tobias and John Napier in 1964 after a suggestion from Prof. Raymond Arthur Dart

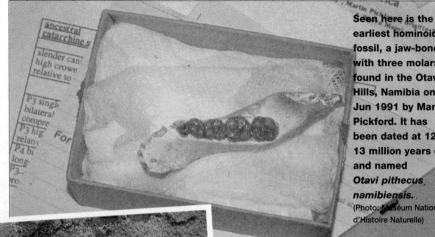

Seen here is the earliest hominoid fossil, a jaw-bone with three molars found in the Otavi Hills, Namibia on 4 Jun 1991 by Martin Pickford. It has been dated at 12–13 million years old and named *Otavi pithecus namibiensis*.
(Photo: Muséum National d'Histoire Naturelle)

Parallel tracks of hominid footprints extending over 24 m *80 ft* were discovered by Paul Abell and Dr Mary Leakey at Laetoli, Tanzania in 1978, in volcanic ash dating to 3·6 million years ago. The footprints show a well developed arch and no divergence of the big toe.
(Photo: Science Photo Library/John Reader)

(1893–1988). The greatest age attributed to fossils of this genus is about 2.4 million years for a piece of cranium found in western Kenya in 1965.

> **Oldest mummy**
> Mummification dates from 2600 BC or the 4th dynasty of the Egyptian pharaohs. The oldest complete mummy is of Wati, a court musician of c. 2400 BC from the tomb of Nefer in Saqqâra, Egypt, found in 1944.

Earliest Homo erectus This species (upright man), the direct ancestor of *Homo sapiens*, was discovered by Eugène Dubois (Netherlands) (1858–1940) at Trinil, Java in 1891. Javan *H. erectus* were redated to 1.8 million years in 1994.

septic blister on his right ankle, caused by a poorly fitting brace.

He was last measured on 27 Jun 1940 and was found to be 8 ft 11.1 in *272 cm* tall (arm-span 9 ft 5¾ in *288 cm*). Wadlow was still growing during his terminal illness and would probably have ultimately reached or just exceeded 9 ft *274 cm* in height if he had survived for another year.

His greatest recorded weight was 35 st 1 lb *222.7 kg* on his 21st birthday and when he died he weighed 31 st 5 lb *199 kg*. His shoes were size 37AA (18½ in *47 cm*) and his hands measured 12¾ in *32.4 cm* from the wrist to the tip of the middle finger.

The world's tallest recorded 'true' (non-pathological) giant was Angus Macaskill (1823–63), born on the island of Berneray in the Sound of Harris, Western Isles. He stood 7 ft 9 in *236 cm* and died in St Ann's, Cape Breton Island, Nova Scotia, Canada. His grandfather, Angus, was also a giant.

Earliest!

The oldest actual human remains ever found in Britain are pieces of a brain case from a specimen of *Homo sapiens*, recovered in June 1935 and March 1936 from the Boyn Hill Terrace in the Barnfield Pit, near Swanscombe, Kent. The remains were associated with a Middle Acheulian tool culture and probably date from either the Hoxnian or an earlier Interglacial Stage. Amino-acid dates for the Swanscombe deposits suggest an age of 400,000 years.

However, Lower Palaeolithic hand-axes from the Waverley Wood Farm site, Warwicks and the hand-axe factory and occupation site at Boxgrove, W Sussex may date from an age earlier than 600,000 years. Sites such as these with an Acheulian culture represent the earliest evidence of a human presence in Britain.

Dimensions

Giants

Growth of the body is determined by growth hormone. This is produced by the pituitary gland set deep in the brain. Over production in childhood produces abnormal growth and true gigantism is the result. The true height of human giants is frequently obscured by exaggeration and commercial dishonesty. The only admissible evidence on the actual height of giants is that collected since 1870 under impartial medical supervision.

Giants exhibited in circuses and exhibitions are routinely under contract not to be measured and are, almost traditionally, billed by their promoters at heights up to 46 cm *18 in* in excess of their true heights.

Tallest Men

The tallest man in medical history of whom there is irrefutable evidence is Robert Pershing Wadlow, born at 6:30 a.m. on 22 Feb 1918 in Alton, Illinois, USA and who died at 1:30 a.m. on 15 Jul 1940 in a hotel in Manistee, Michigan, as a result of a

Robert Wadlow

Weighing 3·85 kg *8½ lb* at birth, the abnormal growth of Robert Wadlow started at the age of 2 following a double hernia operation. His height progressed as follows:

Age	Height			Weight	
	cm	ft	in	kg	lb
5	163	5	4	48	105
8	183	6	0	77	169
9	189	6	2¼	82	180
10	196	6	5	95	210
11	200	6	7	–	–
12	210	6	10½	–	–
13	218	7	1¾	116	255
14	226	7	5	137	301
15	234	7	8	161	355
16	240	7	10¼	170	374
17	245	8	0½	143*	315
18	253	8	3½	–	–
19	258	8	5½	218	480
20	261	8	6¾	–	–
21	265	8	8¼	223	491
22.4**	272	8	11¹⁄₁₀	199	439

* Following severe influenza and infection of the foot.
** Still growing during his terminal illness.

GB William Bradley (1787–1820), born in Market Weighton, East Riding, now Humberside, stood 7ft 9in *236cm*.

John Middleton (1578–1623), the famous Childe of Hale, from near Liverpool, was credited with a height of 9ft 3in *282cm*

Patrick Cotter (O'Brien) (1760–1806), born in Kinsale, Co. Cork, was 8ft 1in *246cm* tall. He died at Hotwells, Bristol. Here he is seen with the Polish Dwarf, Joseph Borowlaski (3ft 3in *99cm*), who was patronized by George IV and who died in Durham in 1837.
(Photo: Ann Ronan Picture Library)

ton, now preserved in the Anatomical Museum in the Medical School at Birmingham University, has a height of 7ft 4in *223.5cm*. Her abnormal growth started at the age of 11 following a head injury, and on her 13th birthday she measured 6ft 6in *198cm*. Shortly before her death on 1 Apr 1922 she stood 7ft 7in *231cm* tall, but she had severe kyphoscoliosis and would have measured at least 7ft 11in *241cm* if she had been able to stand fully erect.

Kentucky, USA, who stood 7ft 2½in *220cm*, making them the tallest married couple on record.

Most dissimilar couple Fabien Pretou (b. 15 Jun 1968) (188.5cm *6ft 2in*) married Natalie Lucius (b. 19 Jan 1966) (94cm *3ft 1in*) at Seyssinet-Pariset, France on 14 Apr 1990.

Tallest twins *World* The world's tallest identical twins are Michael and James Lanier (b. 27 Nov 1969) from Troy, Michigan, USA. They measured 7ft 1in *216cm* at the age of 14 years and both now stand 7ft 4in *223.5cm*. Their sister Jennifer is 5ft 2in *157cm* tall.

but a life-size impression of his right hand (length 11½in *29.2cm*, cf. Wadlow's 12¾in *32.4cm*) painted on a panel in Brasenose College, Oxford indicates his true stature was nearer 7ft 9in *236cm*.

Living Claims for the tallest person in the world can be disputed by Haji Mohammad Alam Channa (b. 1956) of Bachal Channa, Sehwan Sharif, Pakistan and the world's tallest living woman, Sandy Allen (USA) (b. 18 Jun 1955) (⇨Tallest women), both are around 7ft 7¼in *231.7cm* tall.

UK The tallest man living in the UK is Christopher Paul Greener (b. New Brighton, Merseyside, 21 Nov 1943) of Hayes, Kent, who measures 7ft 6¼in *229cm* (weight 26st *165kg*).

Tallest Women

The tallest woman in medical history was the giantess Zeng Jinlian (b. 26 Jun 1964) of Yujiang village in the Bright Moon Commune, Hunan Province, central China, who measured 8ft 1¾in *248cm* when she died on 13 Feb 1982. This figure represented her height with assumed normal spinal curvature because she suffered from severe scoliosis (curvature of the spine) and could not stand up straight. She began to grow abnormally from the age of four months and stood 5ft 1½in *156cm* before her fourth birthday and 7ft 1½in *217cm* when she was 13. Her hands measured 10in *25cm* and her feet 14in *35.5cm* in length. Both her parents and her brother were of normal size.

GB The tallest woman in British medical history was Jane ('Ginny') Bunford, (b. 26 Jul 1895) of Bartley Green, Northfield, Birmingham. Her skele-

Living The world's tallest woman is Sandy Allen, (b. 18 Jun 1955) of Chicago, Illinois, USA. A 6½lb *2.95kg* baby, her abnormal growth began soon after birth. At 10 years of age she stood 6ft 3in *190.5cm*, and measured 7ft 1in *216cm* when she was 16. On 14 Jul 1977 this giantess underwent a pituitary gland operation, which inhibited further growth at 7ft 7¼in *231.7cm*. She now weighs 33st *209.5kg* and takes a size 16 EEE American shoe (14½ UK).

Married couple Anna Hanen Swan (1846–88) of Nova Scotia, Canada was said to be 8ft 1in *246cm* but actually measured 7ft 5½in *227cm*. At the church of St Martin-in-the-Fields, London on 17 Jun 1871 she married Martin van Buren Bates (1845–1919) of Whitesburg, Letcher County,

Sandy Allen, seen here at the launch of the 1994 edition of *The Guinness Book of Records* with champion bed-maker Nurse Michelle Benkel.
(Photo: K. Herschell for Guinness Publishing)

The world's tallest female identical twins are Heather and Heidi Burge (b. 11 Nov 1971) from Palos Verdes, California, USA; they are both 6ft 4¾in *195cm* tall.

UK The tallest identical male twins recorded in Britain were the Knipe brothers (b. 1761) of Magherafelt, near Londonderry, who both measured 7ft 2in *218cm*.

The tallest living male twins are Andrew and Timothy Hull (b. 23 and 24 Oct 1968 respectively) of Redditch, Worcs, who are 6ft 9.3in *206.5cm* and 6ft 10.3in *209cm* respectively.

The tallest identical female twins are Daphne Turner and Evelyn Staniford (*née* Gould) (b. 28 Apr 1931) who both measure 6ft ½in *184cm*. Each has a son who is over 6ft 5in *195.5cm*.

Dwarfs

The strictures that apply to giants apply equally to dwarfs, insofar that exaggeration gives way to understatement. In the same way as 9ft *274cm* is the limit towards which the tallest giants tend, so 22in *56cm* is the limit towards which the shortest adult dwarfs or midgets tend (cf. the average length of new-born babies is 18–20in *46–50cm*).

Shortest person The shortest mature human of whom there is independent evidence is Gul Mohammed (b. 15 Feb 1957) of New Delhi, India. On 19 Jul 1990 he was examined at Ram Manohar Hospital, New Delhi, and found to measure 22½in *57cm* in height (weight 17kg *37½lb*). The other members of his immediate family are of normal height.

The shortest ever female has been Pauline Musters ('Princess Pauline'), a Dutch dwarf. She was born at Ossendrecht on 26 Feb 1876 and measured 12in *30cm* at birth. At nine years of age she was 55cm *21.65in* tall and weighed only 1.5kg *3lb 5oz*. She died of pneumonia with meningitis on 1 Mar 1895 in New York City, USA at the age of 19. A post mortem examination showed her to be exactly 24in *61cm* (there was some elongation after death). Her mature weight varied from 7½–9lb *3.4–4kg* and her 'vital statistics' were 18½–19–17in *47–48–43cm*, which suggest she was overweight.

British Isles The shortest mature human ever recorded in Britain was Joyce Carpenter (1929–73), of Charford, now Hereford & Worcester, who stood 29in *74cm* tall and weighed 30lb *13.6kg*. She suffered from Morquio's disease which causes deformities of the spine and shortening of the neck and trunk.

Hopkins Hopkins (1737–54) of Llantrisant, Mid-Glamorgan, who suffered from progeria, was 31in *79cm* tall. He weighed 19lb 8.6kg at the age of 7 and 13lb *6kg* at the time of his death.

Shortest living *Female* Madge Bester (b. 26 Apr 1963) of Johannesburg, South Africa, is only 65cm *25.5in* tall. However, she suffers from Osteogenesis imperfecta (characterized by brittle bones and other deformities of the skeleton) and is confined to a wheelchair. Her mother Winnie is not much taller, measuring 70cm *27½in*, and is also confined to a wheelchair.

UK The shortest adult living is Michael Henbury-Ballan (b. 26 Nov 1958) of Bassett, Southampton, Hants who is 94cm *37in* tall and weighs 35kg *5½st*. A 2.66kg *5lb 14oz* baby, he stopped growing at the age of 13. His twin brother Malcolm is of normal height.

Patrick Scanlan (b. 1966) of Maida Vale, London stands 91cm *36in* tall and weighs only 19kg *42lb*, but he suffers from MPS, an enzyme disease that causes severe bone abnormalities, including curvature of the spine, and cannot stand erect. He stopped growing at the age of 4 years.

Twins The shortest twins ever recorded were the dwarfs Matjus and Bela Matina (b. 1903–fl.1935) of Budapest, Hungary, who later became naturalized American citizens. They both measured 76cm *30in*.

Living The world's shortest living identical twins are John and Greg Rice (b. 3 Dec 1951) of West Palm Beach, Florida, USA, who both measure 86.3cm *34in*.

The shortest identical twin sisters are Dorene Williams of Oakdale and Darlene McGregor of Almeda, California, USA (b. 1949), who each stand 124.4cm *4ft 1in*.

GUESS WHAT?

Q Which country did the oldest ever human being come from?

A See Page 59

Oldest!

There are only two centenarian dwarfs on record. The older was Hungarian-born Susanna Bokoyni (b. 6 Apr 1879), alias 'Princess Susanna', of Newton, New Jersey, USA, who died aged 105 years on 24 Aug 1984. She was 3ft 4in *101.5cm* tall.

The other was Miss Anne Clowes of Matlock, Derbys, who died on 5 Aug 1784 aged 103 years. She was 3ft 9in *114cm* tall.

Weight

Heaviest male The heaviest human in medical history was Jon Brower Minnoch (1941–83) of Bainbridge Island, Washington State, USA, who had suffered from obesity since childhood. The 6ft 1in *185cm* tall former taxi-driver was 28st *178kg* in 1963, 50st *317kg* in 1966 and 69st 9lb *442kg* in September 1976.

In March 1978, Minnoch was rushed to University Hospital, Seattle, saturated with fluid and suffering from heart and respiratory failure. It took a dozen firemen and an improvized stretcher to move him from his home to a ferry-boat. When he arrived at the hospital he was put in two beds lashed together. It took 13 people just to roll him over. Consultant endocrinologist Dr Robert Schwartz calculated that Minnoch must have weighed more than 100st *635kg* when he was admitted, a great deal of which was water accumulation due to his congestive heart failure. After nearly two years on a 1200-calories-a-day diet he was discharged at 34st *216kg*. In October 1981 he had to be readmitted, after putting on over 14st *89kg*. When he died on 10 Sep 1983 he weighed more than 57st *362kg*.

UK Peter Yarnall of East Ham, London weighed 58st *368kg* and was 5ft 10in *178cm* tall. The former docker began putting on weight at a rapid rate in 1978 and for the last two years of his life he was bedridden. He died on 30 Mar 1984 aged 34 years and it took ten firemen five hours to demolish the wall of his bedroom and winch his body down to street level. His coffin measured 7ft 4in *223cm* in length, 4ft *122cm* across and had a depth of 2ft 9in *84cm*.

Republic of Ireland The heaviest is reputed to have been Roger Byrne, who was buried in Rosenallis, Co. Laoighis (Leix), on 14 Mar 1804. He died in his 54th year, and his coffin and its contents weighed 52st *330kg*.

Living The heaviest living man is T. J. Albert Jackson (b. 1941 as Kent Nicholson), also known as 'Fat Albert', of Canton, Mississippi, USA. He has weighed 63st 9lb *404kg*. He has a 120in *305cm* chest, a 116in *294cm* waist, 70in *178cm* thighs and a 29½in *75cm* neck.

UK The professional wrestler Martin Ruane, alias Luke McMasters ('Giant Haystacks'), who was born in Camberwell, London in 1946 once claimed to be 50st *317kg*. His weight fluctuates between 45st *286kg* and 46st *292kg* and he is 6ft 11in *211cm* tall.

Heaviest female The heaviest female ever recorded was Rosalie Bradford (USA) (b. 27 Aug 1943), who it is claimed registered a peak weight of 75st *476kg* in January 1987. In August of that year she developed congestive heart failure and was rushed to hospital. She was consequently put on a carefully controlled diet and by February 1994 weighed 20st 3lb *128kg* (⇨Weight loss). Her target weight is 10st 10lb *68kg*.

UK The heaviest woman ever recorded was Mrs Muriel Hopkins (b. 1931) of Tipton, W Mids, who weighed 43st 11lb *278kg* (height 5ft 11in *180cm*) in 1978. Shortly before her death on 22 Apr 1979 she reportedly weighed 52st *330kg*, but this proved to be an over-estimate, and her actual weight was found to be 47st 7lb *301kg*. Her coffin measured 6ft 3in *190cm* in length, 4ft 5in *134cm* in width and was 3ft 9in *114cm* deep.

Weight loss *Dieting* The greatest recorded slimming feat by a male was that of Jon Brower Minnoch (⇨ Heaviest male) who had reduced to 34st *216kg* by July 1979, thus indicating a weight loss of at least 66st *419kg* in 16 months.

Female Rosalie Bradford (⇨ Heaviest female) went from a weight of 1050lb *476kg* in January 1987 to 283lb *128kg* in Febraury 1994, a loss of a record 767lb *348kg*.

The female champion in Britain is Mrs Dolly Wager (b. 1933) of Charlton, London, who, between September 1971 and 22 May 1973 reduced her weight from 31st 7lb *200kg* to 11st 70kg, so losing 20st 7lb *130kg* with Weight Watchers.

Sweating Ron Allen (b. 1947) sweated off 21½lb *9.7kg* of his weight of 17st 1lb *113kg* in Nashville, Tennessee, USA in 24 hours in August 1984.

Weight gain The reported record for weight gain is held by Jon Brower Minnoch (⇨ Heaviest male) at 14st *89kg* in 7 days in October 1981 before readmittance to University of Washington

Heaviest!

Billy Leon (1946–79) and Benny Loyd (b. 7 Dec 1946) McCrary, alias McGuire, of Hendersonville, North Carolina, USA were normal in size until the age of six when they both contracted German measles. In November 1978 they weighed 53st 1lb *337kg* (Billy) and 51st 9lb *328kg* (Benny) and had 84in *213cm* waists. As professional tag wrestling performers they were billed at weights up to 55st *349kg*. Billy died at Niagara Falls, Ontario, Canada on 13 Jul 1979.

Hospital, Seattle, USA. Arthur Knorr (USA) (1916–60) gained 21st *133kg* in the last six months of his life.

Miss Doris James of San Francisco, California, USA is alleged to have gained 23st 3lb *147kg* in the 12 months before her death in August 1965, aged 38, at a weight of 48st 3lb *306kg*. She was only 5ft 2in *157cm* tall.

Lightest The lightest adult on record was Lucia Xarate (1863–89) of San Carlos, Mexico, an emaciated ateleiotic dwarf of 26½in *67cm*, who weighed 2.13kg *4.7lb* at the age of 17. She 'fattened up' to 13lb *5.9kg* by her 20th birthday. At birth she weighed 2½lb *1.1kg*.

British Isles The lightest adult was Hopkins Hopkins (⇔ Dwarfs).

Robert Thorn (b. 1842) of March, Cambs weighed 49lb *22kg* at the age of 32. He was 4ft 6in *137cm* tall and had a 27in *68cm* chest (expanded), 4½in *11cm* biceps, and a 3in *8cm* wrist. A doctor who examined him said he had practically no muscular development, 'although he could run along the road'.

Greatest differential in weight The greatest weight difference recorded for a married couple is c. 589kg *92st 12lb* in the case of Jon Brower Minnoch (⇔ Heaviest male) and his 50kg *7st 12lb* wife Jeannette in March 1978.

The UK record is held by the wrestler Martin Ruane, alias Luke McMasters ('Giant Haystacks') and his 48kg *7½st* wife Rita, where their weight differential at one time may have been 270kg *42½st*.

ON THE RECORD

> After losing well over 750 pounds, what do you do for an encore? "I've got over 100 pounds to go," says Rosalie Bradford.
>
> Always chubby as a child, Bradford reached obesity around the time of her marriage. Her weight escalated after the birth of her first child and just kept on increasing as a combination of health and weight-related complaints forced her to stay in bed. Then a neighbour who visited often, wrote a letter to American TV diet guru Richard Simmons.
>
> "He called me up and said two things: 'God doesn't make junk' and 'You're worth the effort.' Well, I took what he said to heart. He sent me a diet package and I couldn't open it for months. Opening it meant I was committed to try, and then I might fail again. At first I couldn't plan my meals for the day. I had to lose 500 pounds before I could even stand up." Bradford had been in bed for eight years, and returning to her feet meant physiotherapy as well as more dieting.
>
> "It's amazing," she agrees. "I used to ask God to come down one night when He wasn't feeling too lousy, wave His magic wand and dump all that fat on the floor. It didn't work that way, and now I've learned what it means to take slow, little steps towards doing the right thing. It's going to be a lifelong effort. And now? Now I'm just waiting for the movie!

Reproductivity

Motherhood

Most children The greatest officially recorded number of children born to one mother is 69, by the wife of Feodor Vassilyev (b. 1707–*fl.*1782), a peasant from Shuya, 240km *150miles* east of Moscow, Russia. In 27 confinements she gave birth to 16 pairs of twins, seven sets of triplets and four sets of quadruplets. The case was reported to Moscow by the Monastery of Nikolskiy on 27 Feb 1782. Only two of these, who were born in the period c. 1725–65, failed to survive their infancy.

The world's most prolific mother is currently Leontina Albina (*née* Espinosa) (b. 1925) of San Antonio, Chile, who in 1981 produced her 55th and last child. Her husband Gerardo Secunda Albina (variously Alvina) (b. 1921) states that they were married in Argentina in 1943 and had 5 sets of triplets (all boys) before coming to Chile. Only 40 (24 boys and 16 girls) survive.

UK Elizabeth, wife of John Mott whom she married in 1676, of Monks Kirby, Warks, produced 42 live-born children. She died in 1720.

Today's champion mothers are believed to be Mrs Margaret McNaught (b. 1923), of Balsall Heath, Birmingham, 12 boys and 10 girls, all single births – two boys died in infancy and Mrs Mabel Constable (b. 1920), of Long Itchington, Warwicks, who also has had 22 children, including a set of triplets and two sets of twins.

Ireland Mrs Kathleen Scott (b. 4 Jul 1914) of Dublin gave birth to her 24th child on 9 Aug 1958.

Oldest mother It was reported in December 1993 that an Italian woman (b. February 1931) was expecting a baby in Febraury 1994. Menopause is the end of a women's reproductive life and occurs in the majority of women between the ages of 45 and 55 years. Recent hormonal techniques, however, have led to post-menopausal women becoming pregnant. It is therefore now feasible for a women of *any* age to give birth.

Babies

Heaviest single birth Big babies (i.e. over 10lb *4.5kg*) are usually born to mothers who are large, overweight or have a medical problem such as

Human Being

diabetes. The heaviest baby of a healthy mother was a boy weighing 10.2kg *22lb 8oz* who was born to Sig. Carmelina Fedele of Aversa, Italy in September 1955.

Mrs Anna Bates (*née* Swan) (1846–88), the 7ft 5½ in *227cm* Canadian giantess, gave birth to a boy weighing 23lb 12oz *10.8kg* (length 30in *76cm*) at her home in Seville, Ohio, USA on 19 Jan 1879, but the baby died 11 hours later.

UK It was reported in a letter to the *British Medical Journal* (1 Feb 1879) from a doctor in Torpoint, Cornwall that a child born on Christmas Day 1852 weighed 21lb *9.5kg*.

The only other reported birthweight in excess of 20lb *9kg* is 20lb 2oz *9.13kg* for a boy with a 14½in *37cm* chest born to a 33-year-old schoolmistress in Crewe, Cheshire on 12 Nov 1884.

Guy Warwick Carr was born on 9 Mar 1992, the eighth child of Andrew and Nicola Carr (5ft 2in *157cm* tall) of Kirkby-in-Furness, Cumbria, weighing 15lb 8oz *7kg*. He was 25in *63cm* in length and midwives at the Maternity Unit had to raid the Children's Ward for nappies and clothes large enough to fit him.

Twins The world's heaviest twins, weighing 27lb 12oz *12.6kg*, were born to Mrs J.P. Haskin, Fort Smith, Arkansas, USA on 20 Feb 1924.

Triplets *UK* The heaviest triplets in the UK, weighing 24lb *10.9kg*, were born to Mrs Mary McDermott of Bearpark, Co Durham on 18 Nov 1914.

> **Quadruplets** The world's heaviest quadruplets (2 girls, 2 boys), weighing 10.426 kg *22 lb 15¾oz*, were born to Mrs Tina Saunders at the St Peter's Hospital, Chertsey, Surrey on 7 Feb 1989.

Quintuplets Two cases have been recorded for heaviest quintuplets, with both recording a weight of 25lb *11.35kg*: on 7 Jun 1953 to Mrs Liu Saulian of Zhejiang, China; and on 30 Dec 1956 to Mrs Kamalammal of Pondicherry, India.

Lightest single births A premature baby girl weighing 280g *9.9oz* was reported to have been born on 27 Jun 1989 at the Loyola University Medical Center, Illinois, USA.

UK The lowest birthweight recorded for a surviving infant, of which there is definite evidence, is 10oz *283g* in the case of Mrs Marian Taggart (*née* Chapman) (1938–83). This baby was born six weeks premature in South Shields, Tyne & Wear. She was born unattended (length 12in *30cm*) and was nursed by Dr D.A. Shearer, who fed her hourly for the first 30 hours with brandy, glucose and water through a fountain-pen filler. At three weeks she weighed 1lb 13oz *821g* and by her first birthday 13lb 14oz *6.3kg*. Her weight on her 21st birthday was 7st 8lb *48kg*.

Lightest twins Mary, 16oz *453g*, and Margaret, 19oz *538g*, were born on 16 Aug 1931 to Mrs Florence Stimson, Old Fletton, Peterborough, Cambs.

Longest separated twins Through the help of New Zealand's television programme *Missing* on 27 Apr 1989, Iris (*née* Haughie) Johns and Aro (*née* Haughie) Campbell (b. 13 Jan 1914) were reunited after 75 years' separation.

Fastest triplet birth Bradley, Christopher and Carmon were born naturally to Mrs James E. Duck of Memphis, Tennessee, USA in two minutes on 21 Mar 1977.

Most premature babies James Elgin Gill was born to Brenda and James Gill, on 20 May 1987 in Ottawa, Ontario, Canada 128 days premature, and weighing 624g *1lb 6oz*.

UK Rukaya Bailey was born to Joanne Bailey 122 days premature on 26 Jun 1989 at Salford, Greater Manchester, and weighed 600g *1lb 3oz*.

Waiting!

Mrs Danny Petrungaro (*née* Berg) (b. 1953) of Rome, Italy, who had been on hormone treatment after suffering four miscarriages, gave birth normally to a baby girl, Diana, on 22 Dec 1987, but she was not delivered of the other twin, Monica, by Caesarean section, until 27 Jan 1988, 36 days later.

Twins Joshua and Evan Ernsteen were born on 18 Aug 1992 at Evanston Hospital, Illinois, USA 112 days premature.

Quadruplets Tina Piper of St Leonards-on-Sea, E Sussex, was delivered of quadruplets on 10 Apr 1988, at exactly 26 weeks' term. Oliver 2lb 9oz *1.16kg*, (died February 1989), Francesca 2lb 2oz *0.96kg*, Charlotte 2lb 4½oz *1.03kg* and Georgina 2lb 5oz *1.05kg* were all born at the Royal Sussex County Hospital, Brighton, Sussex.

Multiple Births

'Siamese' twins Conjoined twins derive the name 'Siamese' from the celebrated Chang and Eng Bunker ('Left' and 'Right' in Thai) born at Meklong on 11 May 1811 of Chinese parents. They were joined by a cartilaginous band at the chest. They married (in April 1843) the Misses Sarah and Adelaide Yates of Wilkes County, North Carolina, USA, and fathered 10 and 12 children respectively. They died within three hours of each other on 17 Jan 1874, aged 62.

Rarest The most extreme form of conjoined twins is dicephales tetrabrachius dipus (two heads, four arms and two legs). The only fully reported example is Masha and Dasha Krivoshlyapovy, born in the USSR on 4 Jan 1950.

Earliest successful separation The earliest successful separation of Siamese twins was performed on xiphopagus (joined at the sternum) girls at Mount Sinai Hospital, Cleveland, Ohio, USA by Dr Jac S. Geller on 14 Dec 1952.

Quindecaplets It was announced by Dr Gennaro Montanino of Rome that he had removed by hysterotomy after four months of the pregnancy the foetuses of ten girls and five boys from the womb of a 35-year-old housewife on 22 Jul 1971. A fertility drug was responsible for this unique instance of quindecaplets.

Highest number at a single birth Ten children (decaplets) (two males, eight females) were reported to have been born at Bacacay, Brazil on 22 Apr 1946. Reports were also received from Spain in 1924 and China on 12 May 1936.

The highest number medically recorded is nine (nonuplets) born to Mrs. Geraldine Brodrick at Royal Hospital for Women, Sydney, Australia on 13 Jun 1971. None of the five boys

GUESS WHAT?

Q What is the body's heaviest organ?

A See Page 64

(two stillborn) and four girls lived for more than 6 days. The birth of nine children has also been reported on at least two other occasions; Philadelphia, Pennsylvania, USA, 29 May 1971, and Bagerhat, Bangladesh, c. 11 May 1977, and in both cases none survived.

In Britain, the greatest number recorded is seven (septuplets) (four boys, three girls) born to Mrs Susan Halton (b. 1960) at Liverpool Maternity Hospital on 15 Aug 1987, none survived.

Most sets of multiple births in a family **Quintuplets** There is no recorded case of more than single set.

Quadruplets Four sets to Mde Feodor Vassilyev, Shuya, Russia (died *ante* 1770) (⇨ Motherhood).

Triplets 15 sets to Maddalena Granata, Italy (b. 1839–*fl.* 1886).

Twins 16 sets to Mde Vassilyev (⇨ above). Mrs Barbara Zulu of Barberton, South Africa bore 3 sets of girls and 3 mixed sets in seven years (1967–73). Mrs Anna Steynvaait of Johannesburg, South Africa produced 2 sets within 10 months in 1960.

UK–Twins 15 sets to Mrs Mary Jonas of Chester (died 4 Sep 1899), all sets were mixed.

Descendents

In polygamous countries, the number of a person's descendants can become incalculable. The last Sharifian Emperor of Morocco, Moulay Ismail (1672–1727), known as 'The Bloodthirsty', was reputed to have fathered a total of 525 sons and 342 daughters by 1703 and achieved a 700th son in 1721.

At the time of his death on 15 Oct 1992, Samuel S. Mast, aged 96, of Fryburg, Pennsylvania, USA, had 824 living descendants. The roll call comprised 11 children, 97 grandchildren, 634 great-grandchildren and 82 great-great-grandchildren.

Mrs Sarah Crawshaw (died 25 Dec 1844) left 397 descendants according to her gravestone in Stones Church, Ripponden, Halifax, W Yorks.

Great-great-great grandmother Harriet Holmes of Newfoundland, Canada (b. 17 Jan 1899) became the youngest living great-great-great-grandmother on 8 Mar 1987 at the age of 88 years 50 days.

Most living ascendants Megan Sue Austin of Bar Harbor, Maine, USA had a full set of grandparents and great-grandparents and five great-great-grandparents, making 19 direct ascendants when born on 16 May 1982.

Family tree The lineage of K'ung Ch'iu or Confucius (551–479 BC) can be traced back further than that of any other family. His four greats grandfather K'ung Chia is known from the 8th century BC. This man's 85th lineal descendants, Wei-yi (b. 1939) and Wei-ning (b. 1947), live today in Taiwan.

Greatest!

Augusta Bunge (*née* Pagel) (b. 13 Oct 1879) of Wisconsin, USA, learned that she had become a great-great-great-great-grandmother when her great-great-great-granddaughter gave birth to a son, Christopher John Bollig, on 21 Jan 1989.

GUESS WHAT?

Q Who are more likely to be colour blind, men or women?

A See Page 61

Longevity

No single subject is more obscured by vanity, deceit, falsehood and deliberate fraud than human longevity.

Centenarians surviving beyond their 113th year are extremely rare and the present absolute proven limit of human longevity does not yet admit of anyone living to celebrate their 121st birthday.

Data on documented centenarians has shown that only one 115-year life can be expected in 2.1 billion lives (cf. world population which was estimated to be c.5620 million by the end of 1993).

In the USA as of 1 Jul 1990 the figure was 36,306. The number of UK centenarians announced on 23 Dec 1992 comprised a total of 263 men and 2090 women.

Oldest authentic centenarian The greatest *authenticated* age to which any human has ever lived is 120 years 237 days in the case of Shigechiyo Izumi of Asan on Tokunoshima, an island 1320km *820 miles* south-west of Tokyo, Japan. He was born at Asan on 29 Jun 1865, and recorded as a 6-year-old in Japan's first census of 1871. He died in his double-glazed bungalow at 12:15 GMT on 21 Feb 1986 after developing pneumonia. He worked until 105. His wife died aged only 90. He drank *sho-chu* (firewater, distilled from sugar) and took up smoking when aged 0. He attributed his long life to 'God, Buddha and the Sun'.

Oldest living The oldest living person in the world whose date of birth can be authenticated is Jeanne Louise Calment who was born in France on 21 Feb 1875. She now lives in a nursing home in Arles, southern France where she celebrated her 119th birthday. (⇨ Arts & Entertainment)

UK The oldest living person in Britain is Rebecca Hewison (b. 29 Oct 1881), who lives in Grimsby, Humberside. The oldest living man is William Proctor (b. 29 Jun 1885), who lives in Wirral, Merseyside.

Family centenarians The first recorded case in the UK of four siblings being centenarians occurred on 2 Apr 1984 when Mrs Lily Beatrice Parsons (*née* Andrews) reached her 100th birthday. Her three sisters were Mrs Florence Eliza White (1874–1979), Mrs Maud Annie Spencer (1876–1978), Mrs Eleanor Newton Webber (1880–1983). The family came from Teignmouth, Devon.

Oldest twins Eli Shadrack and John Meshak Phipps were born on 14 Feb 1803 at Affington, Virginia, USA. Eli died at Hennessey, Oklahoma on 23 Feb 1911 at the age of 108 years 9 days, on which day John was still living in Shenandoah, Iowa.

On 17 Jun 1984, identical twin sisters Mildred Widman Philippi and Mary Widman Franzini of St Louis, Missouri, USA celebrated their 104th birthday. Mildred died on 4 May 1985, 44 days short of the twins' 105th birthday.

UK Identical twin spinsters, Alice Maria and Emily Edith Weller were born within 15 minutes of each other on 20 Apr 1888 in Epsom, Surrey. Alice died on 21 Feb 1991 when aged 102.

Authentic National Longevity Records

Country	Years days		Name	Born			Died	
Japan	120	237	Shigechiyo Izumi	29 Jun	1865		21 Feb	1986
France	119	40	Jeanne Louise Calment	21 Feb	1875		*fl.* April	1994
United States	116	88	Carrie White (Mrs) (*née* Joyner)	18 Nov	1874		14 Feb	1991
United Kingdom	115	229	Charlotte Hughes (Mrs) (*née* Milburn)	1 Aug	1877		17 Mar	1993
Canada	113	124	Pierre Joubert	15 Jul	1701		16 Nov	1814
Australia	112	330	Caroline Maud Mockridge	11 Dec	1874		6 Nov	1987
Wales	112	292	John Evans	19 Aug	1877		10 Jun	1990
Spain	112	228	Josefa Salas Mateo	14 Jul	1860		27 Feb	1973
Norway	112	61	Maren Bolette Torp	21 Dec	1876		20 Feb	1989
Morocco	112	+	El Hadj Mohammed el Mokri (Grand Vizier)	1844			16 Sep	1957
Poland	112	+	Roswlia Mielczarak (Mrs)	1868			7 Jan	1981
Netherlands	111	354	Thomas Peters	6 Apr	1745		26 Mar	1857
Ireland	111	327	The Hon. Katherine Plunket	22 Nov	1820		4 Oct	1932
Scotland	111	238	Kate Begbie (Mrs)	9 Jan	1877		5 Sep	1988
South Africa	111	151	Johanna Booyson	17 Jan	1857		16 Jun	1968
Sweden	111	350	Hulda Johansson	24 Feb	1882		*fl.* February	1994
Italy	111	12	Domenico Minervino	10 May	1880		22 May	1991
Czechoslovakia	111	+	Marie Bernatková	22 Oct	1857		*fl.* October	1968
Germany	111	+	Maria Corba	15 Aug	1878		*fl.* March	1990
Finland	111	+	Fanny Matilda Nystrom	30 Sep	1878			1989
Channel Islands	110	321	Margaret Ann Neve (*née* Harvey)	18 May	1792		4 Apr	1903
Northern Ireland	110	234	Elizabeth Watkins (Mrs)	10 Mar	1863		31 Oct	1973
Yugoslavia	110	+	Demitrius Philipovitch	9 Mar	1818		*fl.* August	1928
Greece	110	+	Lambrini Tsiatoura (Mrs)	1870			19 Feb	1981
USSR	110	+	Khasako Dzugayev	7 Aug	1860		*fl.* August	1970
Superior claims but insufficient authentication								
Brazil	123	30	Maria do Carmo	6 Mar	1871		*fl.* April	1994
United States	121	+	Mark Thrash	December	1822		17 Dec	1943
Spain	114	335	Benita Medrana	29 Dec	1864		28 Jan	1979
South Africa	114	+	Susan Johanna Deporter	1840			4 Aug	1954

Note: *fl.* is the abbreviation for the Latin = *floruit,* he or she was living (at the relevant date).

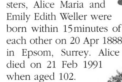

Oldest!

The longest-lived triplets recorded in Great Britain were Faith Alice, Hope Fanny and Charity Sarah Stockdale of Cracoe, near Skipton, N Yorks, born on 28–29 Dec 1857. Charity was the first to die, on 30 Jul 1944, aged 86 years 213 days.

The Ottman quads of Munich, Germany, Adolf, Anne-Marie, Emma and Elisabeth, were born on 5 May 1912. Adolf was the first to die, on 17 Mar 1992, aged 79 years 316 days.

Anatomy and Physiology

Of the 24 elements which constitute the human body, the commonest is hydrogen which accounts for 63 per cent.

Hands, Feet and Hair

Touch The extreme sensitivity of the fingers is such that a vibration with a movement of 0.02 of a micron can be detected.

Longest fingernails Fingernails grow about 0.05cm *0.02in* a week—four times faster than toenails. The aggregate measurement of those of Shridhar Chillal (b. 1937) of Pune, Maharashtra, India, on 7 Mar 1994 was 216in *549cm* for the five nails on his left hand (thumb 50in *127cm*, first

Shigechiyo Izumi, the oldest fully authenticated centenarian, with a statue of himself dedicated to his longevity.

The longest documented length of hair belongs to yogini Mata Jagdamba (b. 1917) of Ujjain, India which measures 13ft 10½in *4.23m*. Her hair had been longer but mishandling and a poor choice of shampoo sadly led to a reduction in length.

(Photo: Guinness Rishi)

GUESS WHAT?

Q Which is the loudest noise; a scream, shout or whistle?

A See Page 62

Expensive!

On 18 Feb 1988 a bookseller from Cirencester, Glos, paid £5575 for a lock of hair belonging to Vice Admiral Lord Nelson (1758–1805) at an auction held at Crewkerne, Somerset.

In 1816 a tooth belonging to Sir Isaac Newton (1642–1727) was sold in London for £730. It was purchased by a nobleman who had it set in a ring, which he wore constantly.

Standing The longest period on record that anyone has stood continuously is more than 17 years in the case of Swami Maujgiri Maharaj when performing the *Tapasya* or penance from 1955 to 1973 in Shahjahanpur, Uttar Pradesh, India. When sleeping he would lean against a plank. He died in September 1980 at the age of 85.

Longest hair Human hair grows at the rate of about 0.5in *1.2cm* in a month. If left uncut it will usually grow to a maximum of 2–3ft *61–91cm*.

The longest documented length of hair belongs to Mata Jagdamba (b. 1917) of Ujjain, India which measured 13ft 10½in *4.23m* on 21 Feb 1994.

Hair splitting The greatest reported achievement in hair splitting has been that of Alfred West (GB) (1901–85), who succeeded in splitting a human hair 17 times into 18 parts on eight occasions.

Longest beard The beard of Hans N. Langseth (b. 1846 near Eidsroll, Norway) measured 533cm *17½ft* at the time of his burial at Kensett, Iowa in 1927 after 15 years' residence in the United States. It was presented to the Smithsonian Institution, Washington, DC, in 1967.

The beard of the 'bearded lady' Janice Deveree (b. 1842) of Bracken County, Kentucky, USA was measured at 14in *36cm* in 1884.

Longest moustache The moustache of Kalyan Ramji Sain of Sundargarth, India grown since 1976, reached a span of 339cm *133½in* (right side 172cm *67·¾in* and left side 167cm *65·¾in*) in July 1993.

The longest moustache in Great Britain was that of John Roy (1910–88), of Weeley, near Clacton, Essex. It attained a peak span of 6ft 2½in *189cm* on 2 Apr 1976 (began growing in 1939). He accidentally sat on it in the bath in 1984 and lost 16½in *42cm*. He then took off the same amount from the other side to even the moustache.

The current UK champion is Ted Sedman of St Albans, Herts whose handlebar moustache measures 63in *160cm*.

Shaving The fastest barbers on record are Denny Rowe and Tom Rodden. Denny Rowe shaved 1994 men in 60min with a retractor safety razor in Herne Bay, Kent on 19 Jun 1988, taking on average 1.8sec per volunteer, and drawing blood four times. Tom Rodden of Chatham, Kent shaved 278 even braver volunteers in 60 min with a cut-throat razor on 10 Nov 1993 for the BBC *Record Breakers* programme, averaging 12.9sec per face. He drew blood seven times.

---

finger 38in *97cm*, second finger 41in *104cm*, third finger 44in *112cm*, and the fourth 43in *110cm*). He last cut his nails in 1952.

Most fingers and toes (polydactylism) At an inquest held on a baby boy at Shoreditch in the East End of London on 16 Sep 1921 it was reported that he had 14 fingers and 15 toes.

Least toes The two-toed syndrome exhibited by some members of the Wadomo tribe of the Zambezi Valley, Zimbabwe and the Kalanga tribe of the eastern Kalahari Desert, Botswana is hereditary via a single mutated gene. These 'ostrich people', as they are known, are not handicapped by their deformity, and can walk great distances without discomfort.

Largest feet If cases of elephantiasis are excluded, then the biggest feet currently known are those of Matthew McGrory (b. 17 May 1973) of Pennsylvania, USA, who wears size 23 US (22½ UK) shoes.

The owner of Britain's largest feet is John Thrupp (b. 1964) of Stratford-upon-Avon, Warks, who wears a size 21 shoe. He is 2.11m *6ft 11in* tall.

Motionlessness António Gomes dos Santos of Zare, Portugal continuously stood motionless for 15hr 2min 55sec on 30 Jul 1988 at the Amoreiras Shopping Centre, Lisbon.

Balancing on one foot

The longest recorded duration for balancing on one foot is 55hr 35min by Girish Sharma at Deori, India from 2–4 Oct 1992. The disengaged foot may not be rested on the standing foot nor may any object be used for support or balance.

Dentition

Earliest Tooth enamel is the only part of the human body which basically remains unchanged throughout life. It is also the hardest substance in the body, with a Knoop number of over 300. The first deciduous or milk teeth normally appear in infants at 5–8 months, these being the upper and lower jaw first incisors. There are many recorded examples of children born with teeth. Sean Keaney of Newbury, Berks was born on 10 Apr 1990 with 12 teeth. They were, however, extracted to prevent possible feeding problems. Molars usually appear at 24 months, but in Pindborg's case published in Denmark in 1970, a six-week premature baby was documented with eight teeth at birth, of which four were in the molar region.

Most set of teeth Cases of the growth in late life of a third set of teeth have been recorded several times. A reference to a case in France of a *fourth* dentition, known as Lison's case, was published in 1896.

Lifting and pulling with teeth Walter Arfeuille of Ieper-Vlamertinge, Belgium lifted weights totalling 281.5 kg *621lb* a distance of 17 cm *6¾in* off the ground with his teeth in Paris, France on 31 Mar 1990.

Earliest false teeth From discoveries made in Etruscan tombs, partial dentures of bridge-work type were being worn in what is now Tuscany, Italy as early as 700 BC. Some were permanently attached to existing teeth and others were removable.

Optics

Highest hyperacuity The human eye is capable of judging relative position with remarkable accuracy, reaching limits of between 3 and 5 seconds of arc.

In April 1984 Dr Dennis M. Levi of the College of Optometry, University of Houston, Texas, USA, repeatedly identified the relative position of a thin bright green line within 0.85 sec of arc. This is equivalent to a displacement of some ¼ in *6 mm* at a distance of 1 mile *1.6 km*.

Light sensitivity Working in Chicago, Illinois, USA in 1942, Maurice H. Pirenne detected a flash of blue light of 500nm in total darkness, when as few as five quanta or photons of light were available to be absorbed by the rod photoreceptors of the retina.

Bones

Longest Excluding a variable number of sesamoids (small rounded bones), there are 206 bones in the adult human body, compared with 300 for children (as they grow, some bones fuse together). The thigh bone or femur is the longest. It constitutes usually 27.5 per cent of a person's stature, and may be expected to be 19¾in *50cm*

long in a 6ft *183cm* tall man. The longest recorded bone was the 76cm *29.9in* femur of the German giant Constantine, who died in Mons, Belgium on 30 Mar 1902, aged 30. The femur of Robert Wadlow, the tallest man ever recorded, measured an estimated 29½in *75cm* (⇨ Tallest men).

Dedicated!

Brother Giovanni Battista Orsenigo of the Ospedale Fatebenefratelli, Rome, a monk who was also a dentist, conserved all the teeth he extracted in three enormous cases during the time he exercised his profession from 1868 to 1904. In 1903 the number was counted and found to be 2,000,744 teeth, indicating an average of 185 teeth, or nearly six total extractions a day.

Smallest The stapes or stirrup bone, one of the three auditory ossicles in the middle ear, measures 2.6–3.4 mm *0.10–0.13 in* in length and weighs from 2.0 to 4.3 mg *0.03–0.066 grains.*

Waists

Largest The largest waist ever recorded was that of Walter Hudson (1944–91) of New York, USA, which measured 119in *302cm* at his peak weight of 85st 7lb *545kg.*

Smallest The smallest waist of normal stature was that of Mrs Ethel Granger (1905–82) of Peterborough, Cambs, reduced from a natural 22in *56cm* to 13in *33cm* over the period 1929–39. A measurement of 13in *33cm* was also claimed for the French actress Mlle Polaire (real name Emile Marie Bouchand) (1881–1939).

Necks

Longest The maximum measured extension of the neck by the successive fitting of copper coils, as practised by the women of the Padaung or Kareni tribe of Myanmar (Burma), is 40cm *15¾in.* When the rings are removed, the muscles supporting the head and neck shrink to their normal length.

What number do you see? This shows a part of the standard test for colour blindness. Approximately one person in thirty is affected by red-green colour blindness and it is far more likely to occur in men. The condition is untreatable. The number you should see is 97.
(Photo: Science Photo Library/Adam Hart Davis)

THE GUINNESS TIMES 22 July 1992

If the train won't go, use your teeth

NEW RECORD SET BY ARMENIAN STRONGMAN

Robert Galstyan, 33, of Masis, Armenia set a new record yesterday for the greatest weight pulled with teeth.

He managed to pull two coupled railway wagons weighing a total of just over 219 tonnes a distance of 7 metres (23 feet).

He achieved this amazing feat using a steel cable attached to the first wagon on a railway track at the research training centre at Shcherbinka, Moscow. The centre had been chosen as the venue to ensure that the attempt would take place on flat ground. It was witnessed by a large crowd including the director of the research testing centre of the Russian Railway Ministry and a camera team who had come from Thailand specifically to see the record being set.

It might be frustrating to have to wait for a train when the driver hasn't turned up, but most commuters would prefer to wait than pull it all the way home!

Muscles

Largest Muscles normally account for 40 per cent of human bodyweight—and bulkiest of the 639 named muscles in the human body is usually the *gluteus maximus* or buttock muscle, which extends the thigh. However, in pregnancy the uterus or womb can increase its weight from about 30g *1oz* to over 1kg *2.2lb.*

Smallest The stapedius, which controls the stapes (⇨ above), is less than 0.127cm *0.05in* long.

Longest The longest muscle in the human body is the *sartorius* which is a narrow ribbon-like muscle which runs from the pelvis and across the front of the thigh to the top of the tibia below the knee.

Strongest The strongest muscle in the human body is the masseter (one on each side of the mouth) which is responsible for the action of biting. In August 1986, Richard Hofmann (b. 1949) of Lake City, Florida, USA, achieved a bite strength of 975lb *442kg* for approximately 2 seconds in a research test using a gnathodynamometer at the College of Dentistry, University of Florida, USA. This figure is more than six times the normal biting strength.

Most active It has been estimated that the eye muscles move more than 100,000 times a day. Many of these eye movements take place during the dreaming phase of sleep. (⇨ Longest and shortest dreams)

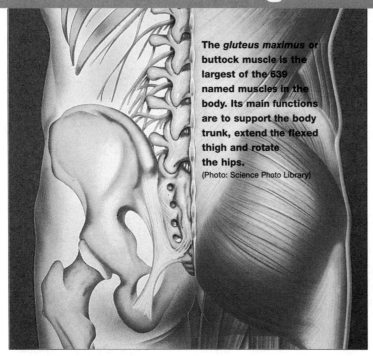

The *gluteus maximus* or buttock muscle is the largest of the 639 named muscles in the body. Its main functions are to support the body trunk, extend the flexed thigh and rotate the hips.

(Photo: Science Photo Library)

Largest chest measurements In the extreme case of Robert Earl Hughes (USA) (1926–58), his chest measured 124in *315cm*, and T. J. Albert Jackson, currently the heaviest living man (⇔ Heaviest men) has a chest measurement of 120in *305cm*.

The largest chest ever recorded in Britain was that of William Campbell (⇔ Heaviest men) which measured 96in *244cm*. Among muscular subjects (mesomorphs) of normal height, *expanded* chest measurements above 56in *142cm* are extremely rare.

The largest muscular chest measurement is that of Isaac Nesser of Greensburg, Pennsylvania, USA at 74¹/₁₆in *188cm*.

Jamie Reeves (b. 1962) of Sheffield, S Yorks, has a chest measurement of 152.4cm *60in*. At a height of 193cm *6ft 4in* he weighs 146kg *23st*.

Largest and smallest biceps Isaac Nesser (⇔ above) has biceps 29in *73cm* cold (not pumped).

The biceps of Robert Thorn (⇔ Lightest adult) measured 4¼in *10.8cm* when pumped up.

Brains

Lightest The lightest 'normal' or non-atrophied brain on record was one weighing 1096g *2lb 6.7oz* reported by Dr P. Davis and Prof. E. Wright of King's College Hospital, London in 1977. It belonged to a 31-year-old woman.

Most expensive skull The skull of Emanuel Swedenborg (1688–1772), the Swedish philosopher and theologian, was bought in London by the Royal Swedish Academy of Sciences for £5500 on 6 Mar 1978.

Computation Mrs Shakuntala Devi of India demonstrated the multiplication of two 13-digit numbers 7,686,369,774,870 × 2,465,099,745,779 which were randomly selected by the Computer Department of Imperial College, London on 18 Jun 1980, in 28seconds. Her correct answer was 18,947,668,177,995,426,462,773,730. Some experts on prodigies in calculation refuse to give credence to Mrs Devi on the grounds that her achievements are so vastly superior to the calculating feats of any other invigilated prodigy that the invigilation must have been defective.

Memory Bhanddanta Vicittabi Vumsa (1911–93) recited 16,000 pages of Buddhist canonical texts in Yangon (Rangoon), Myanmar (Burma) in May 1974.

Gon Yangling, 26, has memorized more than 15,000 telephone numbers in Harbin, China according to the Xinhua News Agency.

Card memorizing Dominic O'Brien (GB) memorized a random sequence of 40 separate packs of cards (2080) (with one error) all of which had been shuffled together on a single sighting, at the BBC Studios, Elstree, Herts on 26 Nov 1993. He also memorised a single pack of shuffled cards in a time of 43.59 seconds at the Guinness World of Records exhibition, London on 25 Mar 1994.

The greatest number of places of π Hideaki Tomoyori (b. 30 Sep 1932) of Yokohama, Japan recited 'pi' from memory to 40,000 places in 17hr 21min, including breaks totalling 4hr 15min, on 9–10 Mar 1987 at the Tsukuba University Club House.

The British record is 20,013 by Creighton Herbert James Carvello (b. 19 Nov 1944) on 27 Jun 1980 in 9hr 10min at Saltscar Comprehensive School, Redcar, Cleveland.

Voice

Greatest range The normal intelligible outdoor range of the male human voice in still air is 180m *200yd*. The *silbo*, the whistled language of the Spanish-speaking Canary Island of La Gomera, is intelligible across the valleys, under ideal conditions, at 8km *5miles*. There is a recorded case, under optimal acoustic conditions, of the human voice being detectable at a distance of 17km *10½ miles* across still water at night.

Screaming The highest scientifically measured emission has been one of 128dBA at 2½m *8ft 2in* by the screaming of Simon Robinson of McLaren Vale, South Australia at 'The Guinness Challenge' at Adelaide, Australia on 11 Nov 1988.

Whistling Roy Lomas achieved 122.5 dbA at 2½m *8ft 2in* in the Deadroom at the BBC studios in Manchester on 19 Dec 1983.

Shouting Annalisa Wray (b. 21 Apr 1974) of Comber, Co. Down, Northern Ireland achieved 119.4 dbA in shouting at the 7th International Rally Arura held in Coleraine Academical Institution, Coleraine, Londonderry, Northern Ireland on 11 Aug 1992.

Donald H. Burns of St George's, Bermuda achieved 119 dbA in shouting when he appeared on the Fuji TV film of *Narvhodo the World* at Liberty State Park, New Jersey, USA on 18 Jan 1989.

Town crier The greatest number of wins in the national Town Criers' Contest is 11 (between 1939–73) by Ben Johnson of Fowey, Cornwall.

Yodelling The most rapid recorded is 22 tones (15 falsetto) in 1second, by Peter Hinnen of Zürich, Switzerland on 9 Feb 1992.

Fastest talker Few people are able to speak *articulately* at a sustained speed above 300 words per minute.

Steve Woodmore of Orpington, Kent spoke 595 words in a time of 56.01 sec or 637.4 words per minute on the ITV Programme *Motor Mouth* on 22 Sep 1990.

Hamlet's soliloquy Sean Shannon a Canadian residing in Oxford recited Hamlet's soliloquy 'To be or not to be' (260 words) in a time of 24 sec (650 words per min) on BBC Radio Oxford on 26 Oct 1990.41/95 Sep Correction

Backwards talking Steve Briers of Kilgetty, Dyfed recited the entire lyrics of Queen's album *A Night at the Opera* at BBC North-West Radio 4's 'Cat's Whiskers' on 6 Feb 1990 in a time of 9min 58.44sec.

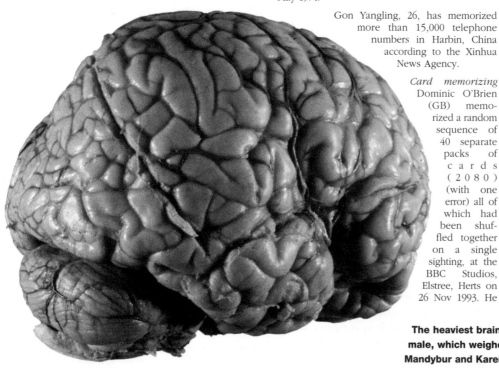

The heaviest brain ever recorded (left) was that of a 30-year-old male, which weighed 2300g *5lb 1.1oz* and was reported by Dr T. Mandybur and Karen Carey of the Department of Pathology and Laboratory Medicine at the University of Cincinnati, Ohio in December 1992. The average brain weighs 1400g *3lb*.

(Photo: Jay Card/University of Cincinatti)

In the ABO system for blood groups, O occurs in nearly half of the world population.
(Photo: The Image Bank/Ben Mitchell)

Blood

Groups On a world basis Group O is the most common (46 per cent), but in some areas, for example Norway, Group A predominates.

The full description of the commonest sub-group in Britain is O MsNs, P+, Rr, Lu(a−), K−, Le(a−b+), Fy (a+b+), Jk(a+b+), which occurs in one in every 270 people.

The rarest blood group of the ABO system, one of 14 systems, is AB, which occurs in less than 3 per cent of persons in the British Isles.

The rarest type in the world is a type of Bombay blood (sub-type h-h) found so far only in a Czechoslovak nurse in 1961, and in a brother (Rh positive) and sister (Rh negative) named Jalbert in Massachusetts, USA, reported in February 1968.

Recipient A 50-year-old haemophiliac, Warren C. Jyrich, required 2400 donor units of blood equivalent to 1080 litres, of blood when undergoing open-heart surgery at the Michael Reese Hospital, Chicago, Illinois, USA in December 1970.

Largest vein The largest is the inferior vena cava, which returns the blood from the lower half of the body to the heart.

Largest artery The largest is the *aorta*,

which is 3 cm *1.18 in* in diameter where it leaves the heart. By the time it ends at the level of the fourth lumbar vertebra it is about 1.75 cm *0.68 in* in diameter.

Cells

Largest The largest is the megakaryocyte, a blood cell, measuring 200 microns. It spends its life in the bone marrow rarely venturing out in the main stream of the blood itself. In the marrow it produces the 'stickiest' particles in the body — the platelets, which play an important role in stopping bleeding.

Smallest Some of the smallest cells are brain cells in the cerebellum and measure about 0.005 mm.

Longest The longest cells are neurons of the nervous system. Motor neurons some 1.3 m *4.26 ft* long have cell bodies (grey matter) in the lower spinal cord with axons (white matter) that carry nerve impulses from the spinal cord down to the big toe. Even longer are the cell systems which carry certain sensations (vibration and positional sense) back from the big toe to the brain. Their uninterrupted length, from the toe, and up the posterior part of the spinal cord to the medulla of the brain, is about equal to the height of the body.

Fastest turnover of body cells The body cells with the shortest life are in the lining of the alimentary tract (gut) where the cells are shed every 3 days.

Longest life Those with the longest life are brain cells which last for life. They may be three times as old as bone cells which may live to 25–30 years.

Longest memory The lymphocyte (type of white blood cell) has the longest memory of any cell in

the body. As successful generations of these cells, which are part of the body's immune defence system, are produced during one's life, they never forget an enemy.

Body Temperature

Highest Willie Jones, 52, was admitted to Grady Memorial Hospital, Atlanta, Georgia, USA on 10 Jul 1980 with heatstroke on a day when the temperature reached 32.2°C *90°F* with 44 per cent humidity. His temperature was found to be 46.5°C *115.7°F*. After 24 days he was discharged 'at prior baseline status'.

Lowest!

People may die of hypothermia with body temperatures of 35°C 95°F. The lowest authenticated body temperature is 14.2°C 57.5°F (rectal temperature) for Karlee Kosolofski, aged two, of Regina, Saskatchewan, Canada on 23 Feb 1994. She had accidentally been locked outside her home for six hours in a temperature of −22°C −8°F. Despite severe frostbite which meant the amputation of her left leg above the knee, she has made a full recovery.

Illness and Disease

Commonest *Non-contagious* The commonest non-contagious diseases are periodontal diseases, such as gingivitis (inflammation of the gums). In their lifetime few people used to escape the effects of tooth decay but the 1981 level of 93% among UK schoolchildren had fallen by 1992 to 55%.

Contagious The commonest contagious disease in the world is coryza (acute nasopharyngitis), or the common cold.

Highest mortality There are number of diseases which are generally considered to be universally fatal of which AIDS (Acquired Immune Deficiency Syndrome) and Rabies encephalitis, a virus infection of the central nervous system, are well known examples. The *disease* rabies, however, should not be confused with being bitten by a rabid animal. With immediate treatment the virus can be prevented from entering the nervous system and chances of survival are high.

Historically, the pneumonic form of plague (bacterial infection), as evidenced by the Black Death of 1347–51, killed everyone who caught it—a quarter of the then population of Europe and some 75 million worldwide.

Leading cause of death In industrialized countries diseases of the heart and of blood vessels account for more than 50 per cent of deaths. The commonest of these are heart attacks, strokes and gangrene of the lower limbs, commonly due to atheroma (degeneration of the arterial walls) obstructing the flow of blood. Deaths from these dieases of the circulatory system totalled 261,834 in England and Wales in 1991.

Alcoholic!

The California University Medical School, Los Angeles, USA reported in December 1982 the case of a confused but conscious 24-year-old female, who was shown to have a blood alcohol level of 1510 mg per 100 ml—nearly 19 times the UK driving limit (80 mg of alcohol per 100 ml of blood) and triple the normally lethal limit. After two days she discharged herself.

Tommy Johns of Brisbane, Queensland, Australia died in April 1988 from a brain tumour at the age of 66 years, after having been arrested nearly 3000 times for being drunk and disorderly in a public place.

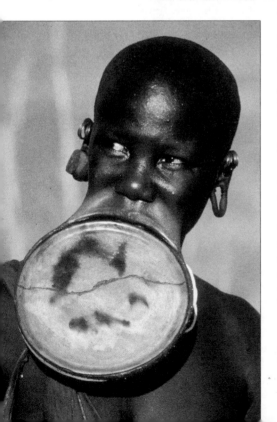

The world's largest lip plate? Normally worn for decoration, for the Surma people of Ethiopia the significance is a financial one. The process of inserting these plates (made by the women themselves from local clay, which are then coloured with ochre and charcoal, and fire-baked) begins approximately a year before marriage and the final size indicates the number of cattle required by the girl's family from her future husband for her hand. The example shown here required a payment of 50 cattle.
(Photo: Robert Estall Photographs/A. Fisher & C. Beckwith)

GUESS WHAT?

Q Which was successfully transplanted first, a heart or kidney?

A see Page 65

David Purley (1945–85) seen in action during the 1977 Race of Champions in his LEC CRP1 Formula 1 car. On 13 July that year he was to survive a crash during practice for the British Grand Prix at Silverstone, Northants on 13 Jul 1977 which involved a force of 179.8 g.
(Photo: Allsport)

Medical Extremes

Cardiac arrest The longest is four hours in the case of a Norwegian fisherman, Jan Egil Refsdahl (b. 1936), who fell overboard in the icy waters off Bergen on 7 Dec 1987. He was rushed to nearby Haukeland Hospital after his body temperature fell to 24°C 75°F and his heart stopped beating, but he made a full recovery after he was connected to a heart-lung machine normally used for heart surgery.

Cardiopulmonary resuscitation Brent Shelton and John Ash completed a CPR marathon (cardiopulmonary resuscitation—15 compressions alternating with two breaths) of 130hr from 28 Oct–2 Nov 1991 at Regina, Saskatchewan, Canada.

Longest coma Elaine Esposito (b. 3 Dec 1934) of Tarpon Springs, Florida, USA, never stirred after an appendectomy on 6 Aug 1941, when aged 6. She died on 25 Nov 1978 aged 43 years 357 days, having been in a coma for 37 years 111 days.

Longest and shortest dreams Dreaming sleep is characterized by rapid eye movements known as REM. The longest recorded period of REM is one of 2hr 23min on 15 Feb 1967 at the Department of Psychology, University of Illinois, Chicago by Bill Carskadon. In July 1984 the Sleep Research Centre, Haifa, Israel recorded nil REM in a 33-year-old male who had a shrapnel brain injury. (⇨ Muscles, most active)

g forces Racing driver David Purley (1945–85) survived a deceleration from 173km/h 108mph to zero in 66cm 26in in a crash at Silverstone, Northants on 13 Jul 1977 which involved a force of 179.8g. He suffered 29 fractures, three dislocations and six heart stoppages.

The highest g value voluntarily endured is 82.6g for 0.04 sec by Eli L. Beeding Jr on a water-braked rocket sled at Holloman Air Force Base, New Mexico, USA on 16 May 1958. He was subsequently hospitalized for three days.

Hospital stay The longest stay in a hospital was by Miss Martha Nelson who was admitted to the Columbus State Institute for the Feeble-Minded in Ohio, USA in 1875. She died in January 1975 at the age of 103 years 6 months in the Orient State Institution, Ohio after spending more than 99 years in hospitals.

Human salamanders The highest dry-air temperature endured by naked men in US Air Force experiments in 1960 was 205°C 400°F, and for heavily clothed men 260°C 500°F. Steaks require only 162°C 325°F to cook. Temperatures of 140°C 284°F have been found quite bearable in saunas.

Most injections Samuel L. Davidson (b. 30 Jul 1912) of Glasgow, has had at a conservative estimate 77,200 insulin injections since 1923.

Longest in 'iron lung' John Prestwich (b. 24 Nov 1938) of Kings Langley, Herts has been dependent on a negative pressure respirator since 24 Nov 1955.

Heaviest organ The skin is medically considered to be an organ and it weighs around 2.7kg 5.9lb in an average adult. The heaviest internal organ is the liver at 1.5kg 3.3lb. This is four times heavier than the heart.

Pill-taking The highest recorded total of pills swallowed by a patient is 565,939 between 9 Jun 1967 and 19 Jun 1988 by C.H.A. Kilner (1926–88) of Bindura, Zimbabwe.

Hiccoughing!

Charles Osborne (1894–1991) of Anthon, Iowa, USA started hiccoughing in 1922 while attempting to weigh a hog before slaughtering it. He was unable to find a cure, but led a reasonably normal life in which he had two wives and fathered eight children. He continued until a morning in February 1990. He died on 1 May 1991.

Post mortem birth The longest gestation interval in a post mortem birth was one of 84 days in the case of a baby girl born on 5 Jul 1983 to a brain-dead woman in Roanoke, Virginia, USA who had been kept on a life support machine since April.

Sleeplessness Research indicates that on the Circadian (Latin: circa = around; dies = a day) cycle for the majority peak efficiency is attained between 8 and 9 p.m. and the low point comes at 4 a.m. Victims of the very rare condition chronic colestites (total insomnia) have been known to go without definable sleep for many years.

Sneezing The longest lasting fit ever recorded is that of Donna Griffiths (b. 1969) of Pershore, Hereford & Worcester. She started sneezing on 13 Jan 1981, sneezed an estimated million times in the first 365 days and achieved her first sneeze-free day on 16 Sep 1983—the 978th day.

The highest speed at which expelled particles have ever been measured to travel is 167km/h 103.6 mph.

Snoring Kåre Walkert (b. 14 May 1949) of Kumla, Sweden, who suffers from the breathing disorder apnea, recorded peak levels of 93 dBA whilst sleeping at the Örebro Regional Hospital, Sweden on 24 May 1993.

Swallowing The worst reported case of compulsive swallowing involved an insane female, Mrs H. aged 42, who complained of a 'slight abdominal pain'. She proved to have 2533 objects, including 947 bent pins, in her stomach. These were removed by Drs Chalk and Foucar in June 1927 at the Ontario Hospital, Canada.

The heaviest object extracted from a human stomach has been a 2.53kg 5lb 3oz ball of hair from a 20-year-old female compulsive swallower in the South Devon and East Cornwall Hospital on 30 Mar 1895.

Underwater submergence In 1986 two-year-old Michelle Funk of Salt Lake City, Utah, USA, made a full recovery after spending 66 minutes underwater having falling into a swollen creek.

Eating!

Michel Lotito (b. 15 Jun 1950) of Grenoble, France, known as Monsieur Mangetout, has been eating metal and glass since 1959. Gastroenterologists have X-rayed his stomach and have described his ability to consume 900g 2lb of metal per day as unique. His diet since 1966 has included 18 bicycles, 15 supermarket trolleys, 7 TV sets, 6 chandeliers, 2 beds, a pair of skis, a low-calorie Cessna light aircraft and a computer. He is said to have provided the only example in history of a coffin (handles and all) ending up inside a man.

Lung power The inflation of a standard 1000g 35oz meteorological balloon to a diameter of 2.44m 8ft against time was achieved by Nicholas Mason of Cheadle, Greater Manchester in 45min 7sec for the Tarm Pai Du television programme in Thailand on 6 Nov 1992.

Longest without food and water The longest recorded case of survival without food and water is 18 days by Andreas Mihavecz, then 18, of Bregenz, Austria, who was put into a holding cell on 1 Apr 1979 in a local government building in Höchst, but totally forgotten by the police. On 18 Apr 1979 he was discovered close to death. He had been a passenger in a crashed car.

Most tattoos The ultimate in being tattooed is represented by Tom Leppard of Isle of Skye. He has gone for a leopard skin design, with all the skin between the dark spots tattooed saffron yellow. The area of his body covered is approximately 99.2 per cent.

Bernard Moeller of Pennsylvania, USA has 14,010 individual tattoos up to February 1994.

The world's most decorated woman is strip artiste 'Krystyne Kolorful' (b. 5 Dec 1952, Alberta, Canada). Her 95 per cent body suit took 10 years to complete.

GUESS WHAT?
Q Who was born in Alton, Illinois, USA in February 1918?
A See Page 54

Transplants

Body parts (some are tissues not organs) which can be transplanted successfully from one person to another are called allografts. Rejection of the donor tissue by the host's immune system is often a problem leading to failure (except for the cornea), although, immunosuppressive drugs such as corticosteriods can be given to combat this. The main problem with transplants is not the possibility of rejection or even the 'plumbing in', but that demand far outstrips supply. The feature illustrates those body parts which have 'successfully' been transplanted.

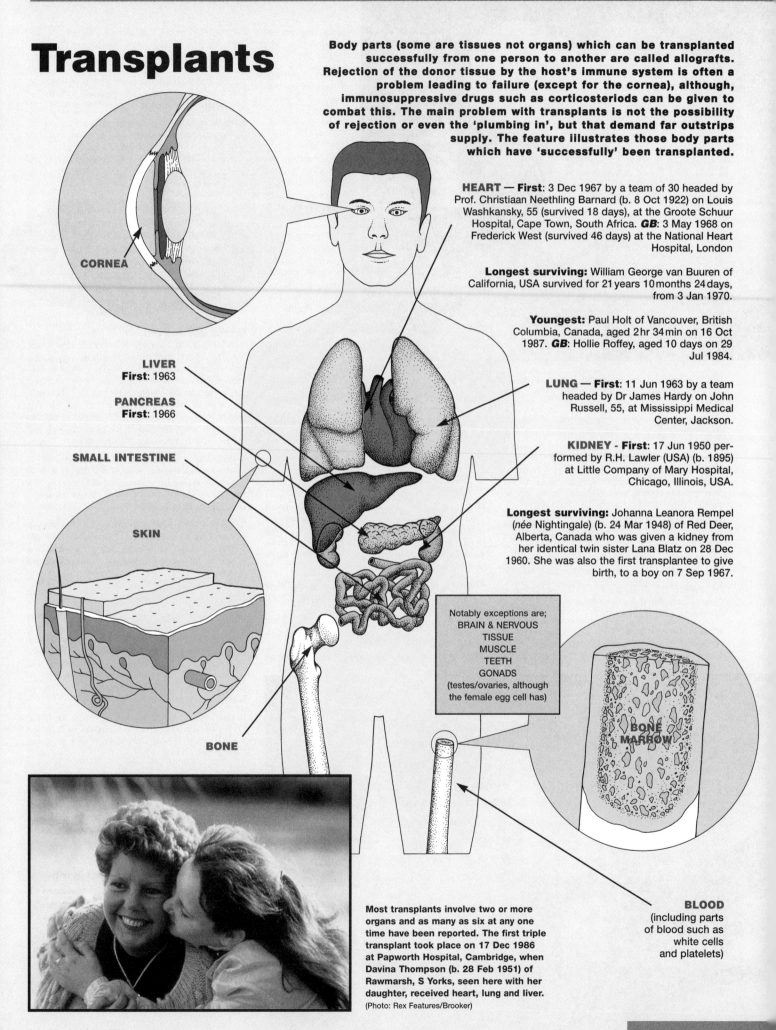

CORNEA

HEART — First: 3 Dec 1967 by a team of 30 headed by Prof. Christiaan Neethling Barnard (b. 8 Oct 1922) on Louis Washkansky, 55 (survived 18 days), at the Groote Schuur Hospital, Cape Town, South Africa. **GB**: 3 May 1968 on Frederick West (survived 46 days) at the National Heart Hospital, London

Longest surviving: William George van Buuren of California, USA survived for 21 years 10 months 24 days, from 3 Jan 1970.

Youngest: Paul Holt of Vancouver, British Columbia, Canada, aged 2 hr 34 min on 16 Oct 1987. **GB**: Hollie Roffey, aged 10 days on 29 Jul 1984.

LUNG — First: 11 Jun 1963 by a team headed by Dr James Hardy on John Russell, 55, at Mississippi Medical Center, Jackson.

KIDNEY - First: 17 Jun 1950 performed by R.H. Lawler (USA) (b. 1895) at Little Company of Mary Hospital, Chicago, Illinois, USA.

Longest surviving: Johanna Leanora Rempel (*née* Nightingale) (b. 24 Mar 1948) of Red Deer, Alberta, Canada who was given a kidney from her identical twin sister Lana Blatz on 28 Dec 1960. She was also the first transplantee to give birth, to a boy on 7 Sep 1967.

LIVER
First: 1963

PANCREAS
First: 1966

SMALL INTESTINE

SKIN

Notably exceptions are;
BRAIN & NERVOUS
TISSUE
MUSCLE
TEETH
GONADS
(testes/ovaries, although
the female egg cell has)

BONE

BONE MARROW

Most transplants involve two or more organs and as many as six at any one time have been reported. The first triple transplant took place on 17 Dec 1986 at Papworth Hospital, Cambridge, when Davina Thompson (b. 28 Feb 1951) of Rawmarsh, S Yorks, seen here with her daughter, received heart, lung and liver.
(Photo: Rex Features/Brooker)

BLOOD
(including parts of blood such as white cells and platelets)

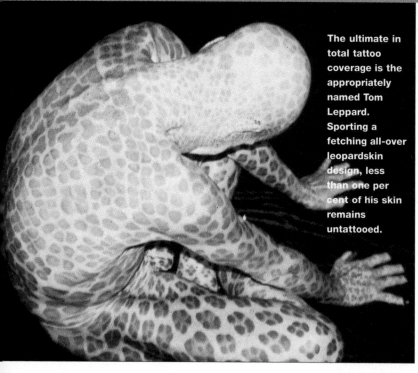

Britain's most decorated woman is Rusty Field (b. 1944) of Norfolk, who has reached 85 per cent of totality.

Operations

Longest The most protracted reported operation has been one of 96 hours performed from 4–8 Feb 1951 in Chicago, Illinois, USA on Mrs Gertrude Levandowski for the removal of an ovarian cyst. During the operation her weight fell 280 kg *44 st* to 140 kg *22 st*.

Most performed Dr M.C. Modi, a pioneer of mass eye surgery in India since 1943, has performed as many as 833 cataract operations in one day, visited 46,120 villages and 12,118,630 patients, performing a total of 610,564 operations to February 1993.

Dr Robert B. McClure (b. 1901) of Toronto, Canada performed a career total of 20,423 major operations from 1924 to 1978.

Most endured Since 22 Jul 1954 Charles Jensen of Chester, South Dakota, USA has had 934 operations to remove the tumours associated with basal cell naevus syndrome to the end of 1993.

Oldest patient The greatest recorded age at which anyone has undergone an operation is 111 years 105 days for a hip operation on James Henry Brett, Jr (1849–1961) of Houston, Texas, USA on 7 Nov 1960.

The greatest age in Britain for an operation was in the case of Miss Mary Wright (b. 28 Feb 1862) who died during a thigh operation at Boston, Lincs on 22 Apr 1971 aged 109 years 53 days.

Earliest general anaesthesia The earliest recorded operation under general anaesthesia was for the removal of a cyst from the neck of James Venable by Dr Crawford Williamson Long (1815–78), using diethyl ether $(C_2H_5)_2O$, in Jefferson, Georgia, USA on 30 Mar 1842.

Tracheostomy Winifred Campbell (1902–92) of Wanstead, London breathed through a silver tube in her throat for 88 years.

Haemodialysis patient Raymond Jones (1929–91) of Slough, Berks, suffered from kidney failure from the age of 34, and received continuous haemodialysis for 28 years. He averaged three visits per week to the Royal Free Hospital, Hampstead, London.

Munchausen's syndrome The most extreme recorded case of the rare and incurable condition known as 'Munchausen's syndrome' (a continual desire to have medical treatment) was William McIlroy (b. 1906), who cost the National Health Service an estimated £2.5 million during his 50-year career as a hospital patient. During that time he had 400 major and minor operations, and stayed at 100 different hospitals using 22 aliases. The longest period he was ever out of hospital was six months. In 1979 he hung up his bedpan for the last time, saying he was sick of hospitals, and retired to an old people's home in Birmingham, W Mids where he died in 1983.

Largest tumour The largest tumour ever reported was Dr Arthur Spohn's case of an ovarian cyst estimated to weigh 148.7 kg *23 st 6 lb* which was drained during the week prior to surgical removal of the cyst shell, in Texas, USA in 1905. She made a full recovery.

Fastest amputation The shortest time recorded for a leg amputation in the pre-anaesthetic era was 13–15 seconds by Napoleon's chief surgeon, Dominique Larrey. There could have been no ligation of blood vessels.

Largest gall bladder On 15 Mar 1989 at the National Naval Medical Center in Bethesda, Maryland, USA, Prof. Bimal C. Ghosh removed a gall bladder which weighed 10.4 kg *23 lb* from a 69-year-old woman. The patient had been complaining of increasing swelling around the abdomen, and after taking away this enlarged gall bladder, which weighed more than three times the average new born baby, the patient felt perfectly well and left hospital 10 days after the operation.

Gallstones The largest gallstone reported in medical literature was one of 6.29 kg *13 lb 14 oz* removed from an 80-year-old woman by Dr Humphrey Arthure at Charing Cross Hospital, London on 29 Dec 1952.

In August 1987 it was reported that 23,530 gallstones had been removed from an 85-year-old woman by Mr K. Whittle Martin at Worthing Hospital, W Sussex, after she complained of severe abdominal pain.

Artificial heart On 1–2 Dec 1982 at the Utah Medical Center, Salt Lake City, Utah, USA Dr Barney B. Clark, 61, of Des Moines, Washington, was the first recipient of an artificial heart. The surgeon was Dr William C. DeVries. The heart was a Jarvik 7 designed by Dr Robert K. Jarvik (b. 11 May 1946). Dr Clark died on 23 Mar 1983, 112 days later. William J. Schroeder survived for 620 days in Louisville, Kentucky from 25 Nov 1984 to 7 Aug 1986.

Britain's first artificial heart patient was Raymond Cook of Hucknall, Notts who temporarily received a Jarvik 7 on 2 Nov 1986 at Papworth Hospital, Cambridge, Cambs.

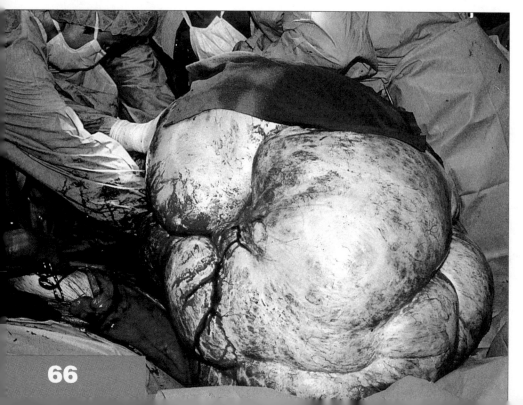

The largest tumour ever removed *intact* was a multicystic mass of the right ovary weighing 137.6 kg *303 lb*. The operation, which took over six hours, was performed by Professor Katherine O'Hanlan of Stanford University Medical Center, California, USA. The one metre diameter growth was removed in its entirety in October 1991 from the abdomen of an unnamed 34-year-old woman. The patient, who weighed 95 kg *210 lb* after the operation and has made a full recovery, left the operating theatre on one stretcher and the mass on another. Here, Professor O'Hanlan frees the last of the adhesions to the abdominal wall before rolling the mass onto a gurney.
(Photo: Professor K. O'Hanlan)

Science & Technology

Elements

Of the 109 known elements the first 94 exist naturally. At room temperature the elements consist of 2 liquids, 11 gases and 85 known solids (if they could be obtained in a coherent form elements 85, 87 and 101 to 109 would also prove to be solid at this temperature).

Sub-Atomic Particles

Electron volt (eV)—mass-energy unit equivalent to $1.7826627 \times 10^{-36}$ kg.

Quarks and Leptons There are three tiers or 'families' of quarks and leptons with two of each in each family. The lightest quark is the up quark with a short-range mass of 6MeV whilst the heaviest is the as-yet unobserved top quark, with a predicted mass of 150 GeV. The three neutrino leptons are predicted to have zero mass (the electron neutrino mass has been experimentally proved to be less than 10eV), whilst the heaviest lepton is the tau (discovered 1975) with a mass of 1.784GeV.

Quanta The photon (and the theoretically predicted graviton) are both expected to have zero mass with current cosmological models placing upper limits on these values of 3×10^{-27} eV and 4.3×10^{-34} eV respectively.

Heaviest known The heaviest gauge boson and the heaviest particle known is the Z° (discovered 1983) of mass 91.17GeV. It also has the shortest lifetime of any particle at 2.65×10^{-25} sec.

Hadrons Lightest and heaviest Of the 254 particles (and an equal number of anti-particles) predicted by the accepted existence of 78 meson multiplets and 61 baryon multiplets, the lightest is the neutral pion meson (discovered 1949) of mass 134.974Mev and the heaviest the upsilon (11020) meson (discovered 1984) of mass 11.02GeV.

Most and least stable The least stable hadron is the N (2600) baryon (discovered 1978–9) of lifetime 1.0×10^{-24} sec and the most stable is the proton, with a lifetime of at least 10^{25} years.

GUESS WHAT?

Q How many digits has the largest prime number?

A See Page 72

Isotopes

Most and least There are at least 2550 isotopes, and caesium (Cs) has the most at 37 whilst tin (Sn) has the most stable isotopes at 10. Hydrogen (H) has the least number of accepted isotopes at only three.

Lightest and heaviest The lightest nuclide is hydrogen 1 (H 1) or protium (discovered 1920) whilst the heaviest is meitnerium 266 (Mt 266; discovered 1982)—meitnerium being the proposed name for element 109.

Most and least stable As far as it is known the most stable radioactive isotope is the double beta decaying tellurium 128 (Te-128; discovered 1924 and radioactivity proved 1968), with a half-life of 1.5×10^{24} years. The least stable nuclide is lithium 5 (Li 5; discovered 1950) with a lifetime of 4.4×10^{-22} sec.

A microscopic image: the gold atoms here are yellow, red and brown on a graphite substrate. The graphite (carbon) atoms are shown as green.
(Photo: Science Photo Library/Philippe Plailly)

The 109 Elements

Rarest Only 0.16g *0.0056 oz* of astatine (At) is present in the Earth's crust, of which the isotope astatine 215 (At 215; discovered 1943) accounts for only 4.5 nanograms 1.6×10^{-10} oz. Radon (Rn) is the rarest element in the atmosphere at only 6×10^{-18} parts by volume (equivalent to only 2.4kg *5.3 lb* overall).

Commonest!

Hydrogen is the commonest element in both the Universe (over 90%) and the Solar System (70.68%). Iron is the commonest element in the earth, accounting for 36% of the mass, whilst molecular nitrogen (N_2) is the commonest in the atmosphere at 78.08% by volume or 75.52% by mass.

Newest Element 108, proposed name hassium (Hs) after the Latin name for the German state of Hessen, was discovered on only a three-atom basis at the Gesellschaft für Schwerionenforschung, Darmstadt, Germany, and announced in April 1984.

Density—Solid At room temperature the least dense metal is lithium (Li) at 0.5334g/dm³ and the densest is osmium (Os), at 22.59g/cm³ *0.8161lb/in³*.

Density—Gas At NTP (normal temperature and pressure 0°C and one atmosphere), the lightest gas is hydrogen (H) at 0.00008989g/cm³ *0.005612lb/ft³* whilst the densest is radon (Rn) at 0.01005g/cm³ *0.6274lb/ft³*.

Melting and Boiling Points *Highest* Metallic tungsten or wolfram (W) melts at 3420°C *6188°F*. The graphite form of carbon sublimes directly to vapour at 3704°C *6699°F* and can only be obtained as a liquid from above a temperature of 4730°C *8546°F* and a pressure of 10MPa 100 atmospheres.

Lowest Helium (He) cannot be obtained as a solid at atmospheric pressure, the minimum pressure being 2.532MPa *24.985 atmospheres* at a temperature of −272.375°C *−458.275°F*. Helium also has the lowest boiling point at −268.928°C *−458.275°F*. For metallic elements mercury (Hg) has the lowest melting and boiling points, at −38.829°C *−37.892°F* and 356.62°C *673.92°F* respectively.

Purest In April 1978 P.V.E. McClintock of the University of Lancaster reported success in obtaining the isotope helium 4 (He-4) with impurity levels at less than two parts in 10^{15}.

Hardest The carbon (C) allotrope diamond has a Knoop value of 8400.

Thermal expansion Caesium (Cs) has the highest thermal expansion of a metallic element, at 9.4×10^{-5} per deg C, while the diamond allotrope of carbon (C) has the lowest expansion at 1×10^{-6} per deg C.

One gram of gold (Au)—the most ductile of the 109 elements—can be drawn to 2·4 km, or 1 oz to 43 miles. The picture shows a thin sheet of hammered gold.
(Photo: Science Photo Library/Erich Schrempp)

View of the Tokamak Fusion Test Reactor (TFTR) at the Princeton University Plasma Physics Laboratory, New Jersey, USA, where the world's highest temperatures have been produced. (⇨ Highest temperature)
(Photo: US Department of Energy/Science Photo Library)

Highest tensile strength The strongest element is boron (B), with a tensile strength of 5.7 GPa *8.3×10⁵ lb/in².*

Liquid range Based on the differences between melting and boiling points, the element with the shortest liquid range (on the Celsius scale) is the inert gas neon (Ne) at only 2.542 degrees (from −248.594 to −246.052°C *−415.469 to −410.894°F*). The radioactive element neptunium (Np) has the longest range, at 3453 degrees (from 637 to 4090°C *1179 to 7394°F*).

Toxicity The severest restriction placed on any element in the form of a radioactive isotope is 2.4×10^{-16} g/m³ in air for thorium 228 (Th 228) or radiothorium, while for non-radioactive elements it is beryllium (Be), with a threshold limit in air of only 2×10^{-6} g/m³.

Scientists check the interior of the TFTR prior to a test run (left).
(Photo: Roger Ressmeyer, Starlight/Science Photo Library)

Chemical Extremes

Smelliest substance The most evil of the 17,000 smells so far classified is obviously a matter of opinion, but ethyl mercaptan (C_2H_5SH) and butyl seleno-mercaptan (C_4H_9SeH) are pungent claimants, each with a smell reminiscent of a combination of rotting cabbage, garlic, onions, burnt toast and sewer gas.

Most powerful nerve gas Ethyl S-2-diisopropylaminoethylmethyl phosphonothiolate, or VX, developed at the Chemical Defence Experimental Establishment, Porton Down, Wilts in 1952, is 300 times more powerful than the phosgene ($COCl_2$) used in World War I and has a lethal dosage is 10 mg-minute/m³ airborne, or 0.3 mg orally.

Most lethal man-made chemical The compound 2, 3, 7, 8-tetrachlorodibenzo-p-dioxin), or TCDD, is the most deadly of the 75 known dioxins, is admitted to be 150,000 times more deadly than cyanide, at 3.1×10^{-9} moles/kg.

Strongest acid and alkaline solutions Normal solutions of strong acids and alkalis tend towards pH values of 0 and 14 respectively, but this scale is inadequate for describing the 'superacids'—the strongest of which is an 80% solution of antimony pentafluoride in hydrofluoric acid (fluoro-antimonic acid HF: SbF_5). The H_0 acidity function of this solution has not been measured, but even a weaker 50% solution is 10^{18} times stronger than concentrated sulphuric acid.

Sweetest!

Talin obtained from arils (appendages found on certain seeds) of the katemfe plant (*Thaumatococcus daniellii*) discovered in West Africa is 6150 times as sweet as a one per cent sucrose solution.

Bitterest substance The bitterest-tasting substances are based on the denatonium cation and have been produced commercially as benzoate and saccharide. Taste detection levels are as low as one part in 500 million, and a dilution of one part in 100 million will leave a lingering taste.

Most absorbent substance The US Department of Agriculture Research Service announced on 18 Aug 1974 that 'H-span' or Super Slurper composed of one half starch derivative and one quarter each of acrylamide and acrylic acid can, when treated with iron, retain water at 1300 times its own weight.

Most refractory substance The most refractory compound is tantalum carbide $TaC_{0.88}$ which melts at 3990°C *7214°F.*

Most heat-resistant substance The existence of a complex material known as NFAARr or Ultra Hightech Starlite was announced in April 1993. Invented by Maurice Ward (GB; b. 1932), it is apparent that it can temporarily resist plasma temperatures (10,000°C *18,032°F*).

Least dense solid The solid substances with the lowest density are silica aerogels in which tiny spheres of bonded silicon and oxygen atoms are joined into long strands separated by pockets of air. The lightest of these aerogels, with a density of only 0.005 g/cm³ *5oz/ft³* was produced at the Lawrence Livermore Laboratory, California, USA. The main use will be in space to collect micrometeoroids and the debris present in comets' tails.

Highest superconducting temperature In May 1991 bulk superconductivity with a maximum transition temperature of −140.7°C *−221.3°F* was achieved at the Laboratorium für Festkörperphysik, Zurich, Switzerland, in a mixture of oxides of mercury, barium, calcium and

GUESS WHAT?

Q Where was the world's biggest blackout?

A See Page 74

copper, $HgBa_2Ca_2Cu_3O_{1+x}$ and $HgBa_2CaCu_2O_{6+x}$. Claims to have obtained higher temperatures have not been substantiated.

Most magnetic substance The most magnetic substance is neodymium iron boride $Nd_2Fe_{14}B$, with a maximum energy product (the highest energy that a magnet can supply when operating at a particular operating point) of up to 280 kJ/m³.

Most expensive perfume Retail prices tend to be fixed with an eye to public relations rather than the market cost of ingredients and packaging. From March 1984 Jõvan, based in Chicago, Illinois, USA, marketed a cologne called Andron, containing a trace of the attractant pheromone androstenol, at a cost of $2750 per oz.

Physical Extremes

Highest temperature The highest temperatures are produced at the centres of thermonuclear fusion explosions, namely of the order of 400,000,000°C. This temperature was attained in 1990 under controlled conditions in the Tokamak Fusion Test Reactor at the Princeton Plasma Physics Laboratory, New Jersey, USA by deuterium injection into a deuterium plasma.

Lowest temperature The absolute zero of temperature, 0 K on the Kelvin scale, corresponds to −273.15°C *−459.67°F.* The lowest temperature reached is 28×10^{-10} K, achieved in a nuclear demagnetization device at the Low Temperature Laboratory of the Helsinki University of Technology, Finland and announced in April 1993.

Highest pressures A sustained laboratory pressure of 170 GPa *11,000 tons force/in²* was reported from the giant hydraulic diamond-faced press at

A lotta
bottle!

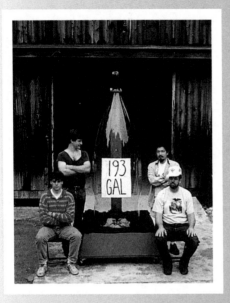

193 GAL

Above: the photo from the original endeavour. Left: the members of the glassblowing team with their bottle. Standing, Steve Tobin (left); Daisuke Shintani. Sitting, Dale Leader (left); Donald Friel of Wheaton Village.
All Photos: Wheaton Village

108 GAL

In the early 1900s a rivalry developed between glassblowers at the Whitall Tatum Company in Millville, New Jersey, USA and the Illinois Glass Company of Alton, Illinois, USA to see which firm could make the largest bottle. The culmination of this competition took place in late 1903 at Whitall Tatum, when a four-man crew set the record for the largest bottle ever blown—one of capacity 108 gal *408.8 lit.* It stood 5 ft 4 in *1.62m* tall and was 31 in *80cm* wide.

Sadly, the bottle was broken on its return from St. Louis, where it was being exhibited, to Millville, leaving virtually no material evidence of the event having taken place. The only surviving proof was a photograph showing the bottle towering over the team of brawny men who created it.

On 26 and 27 Sep 1992 a team of glassblowers decided to attempt to beat the record at the Wheaton Glass Factory in Wheaton Village, Millville, as part of the 'South Jersey Glass Blast', a celebration of the local glassmaking heritage. They practised for months to perfect the process they used to create the Big Bottle. Here's how they did it.

1. The end of a 4-ft *1.22-m* hollow pipe was turned in a 2200ºF *1204ºC* oven, and as much molten glass as possible was gathered onto it (see right).

2. Tobin, head of the team, blew down the pipe, creating a small bubble of air in the gather of glass.

3. The pipe was returned to the furnace to gather more glass a total of six times. By the time enough had been accumulated, the gather weighed around 90 lb *40.8 kg*. The heat was so intense that the blowers' face shields were distorted (see below right). A crossbar was attached to the blowpipe to support it.

4. The pipe and glass was transported to the mould—a steel drum lined with wooden slats,

specially constructed for the purpose. Shintani sat on a set of steps and blew compressed air into the glass through a hosepipe attached to the neck of the blowpipe.

5. As steam rose around them, the glass grew and sagged and the steps were raised by means of a forklift truck, suspending Shintani

high above the factory floor (see below, left-hand corner). The heat of the glass burnt the sides of the mould. Meanwhile, Tobin and Lewin kept reheating it with torches to prevent it from cooling and shattering as the air was blown in.

6. The bottle rose out of the mould and the neck was formed (see below). It had then reached its full height.

7. A fire-resistant sling made of fabric was used to carry the bottle to the huge custom-made annealing oven. It took four members of the team to move it, and two more to open the oven doors. The procedure was accomplished in a matter of seconds, to prevent the glass cooling down.

8. Once in the oven, the blowpipe had to be broken off, and then the bottle was left in the oven for 20 hours to anneal. After that it was removed and hoisted into the upright position.

The bottle stood 7ft 8in *2.3m* tall, with a calculated capacity of about 712 litres *188 gal*.

The finished product is on permanent exhibition at the Museum of American Glass at Wheaton Village in Millville, New Jersey.

The Raw Materials
The primary ingredient used in making glass is **silica**. This requires very intense heat for melting and the costs of sustaining these temperatures would be very high. To counteract this, **fluxes** are used—usually sodium oxide (soda ash) or calcium oxide (lime). These are placed in a furnace, along with **cullet**—recycled glass or rejected during the process of production—and melted at around 1500ºC *3020ºF.*

the Carnegie Institution's Geophysical Laboratory, Washington, DC, USA in June 1978.

Momentary pressures of 7000 GPa *498,000 tonnes/in²* were reported from the United States in 1958 using dynamic methods and impact speeds of up to 29,000 km/h *18,000 mph*.

Lowest friction The lowest coefficient of static and dynamic friction of any solid is about 0.04 for polytetrafluoroethene, or PTFE, ($[-C_2F_4-]_n$), which is equivalent to wet ice on wet ice. First mass-produced by E.I. du Pont de Nemours & Co. Inc. in 1943, it is marketed from the USA under the trade name Teflon.

In the centrifuge at the University of Virginia, USA a 13.6-kg *30-lb* rotor magnetically supported has been spun at 1000 rev/sec in a vacuum of 10^{-6} mm of mercury pressure. It loses only one revolution per second per day, thus spinning for years.

Powerful!

If fired simultaneously, the 4032 capacitors comprising the Zeus capacitor at the Los Alamos Scientific Laboratory, New Mexico, USA would produce, for a few microseconds, double the current generated elsewhere on Earth.

Highest velocity The highest velocity at which any solid object has been projected is 150 km/sec *93 miles/sec* reported in August 1980 for a plastic disc at the Naval Research Laboratory, Washington, DC, USA.

Hottest flame The hottest flame is produced by carbon subnitride (C_4N_2) which, at one atmosphere pressure, can generate a flame calculated to reach 4988°C *9010°F*.

Highest frequency The highest frequency measured *directly* is a visible yellow-green light at 520.2068085 terahertz for the o-component of the 17–1 P (62) transition line of iodine-127.

The highest measured frequency determined by precision metrology is a green light at 582.491703 terahertz for the b_{21} component of the R (15) 43–0 transition line of iodine-127.

Smallest hole Holes corresponding to a diameter of 3.16 Å (3.16×10^{-10} m) were produced on the surface of molybdenum disulphide by Dr Wolfgang Heckl (University of Munich) and Dr John Maddocks (University of Sheffield) using a chemical method involving a mercury drill. The holes were drilled on 17 Jul 1992 at the University of Munich, Germany.

Brightest light The brightest artificial sources are laser pulses generated at the Los Alamos National Laboratory, New Mexico, USA announced in March 1987. An ultraviolet flash lasting 1 picosecond (1×10^{-12} sec) is intensified to a power of 5×10^{15} W.

The most powerful searchlight ever was produced during World War II by The General Electric Company Ltd at the Hirst Research Centre, Wembley, London. It had a consumption of 600 kW and gave an arc luminance of 46,500 candelas/cm² *300,000 candelas/in²* and a maximum beam intensity of *2.7 billion candelas* from its parabolic mirror of 3.04 m *10 ft* diameter.

GUESS WHAT?

Q Which is the world's biggest computer company?

A See Page 73

Of continuously burning light sources, the most powerful is a 313kW high-pressure argon arc lamp of 1,200,000 candles, completed by Vortek Industries Ltd of Vancouver, British Columbia, Canada in March 1984.

Magnetic fields The strongest continuous field strength achieved was a total of 35.3±0.3 teslas at the Francis Bitter National Magnet Laboratory, Massachusetts Institute of Technology, USA on 26 May 1988 by a hybrid magnet with holmium pole pieces. These had the effect of enhancing the central magnetic field of 31.8 teslas generated by the hybrid magnet.

The weakest magnetic field measured is one of 8×10^{-15} teslas in the heavily shielded room at the same laboratory. It is used for research into the very weak magnetic fields generated in the heart and brain.

Highest vacuum In January 1991 K. Odaka and S. Ueda of Japan reported having obtained a vacuum of 7×10^{-11} Pa 7×10^{-16} atmospheres in a stainless steel chamber.

Highest voltage The highest-ever potential difference obtained in a laboratory has been 32±1.5 MV by the National Electrostatics Corporation at Oak Ridge, Tennessee, USA on 17 May 1979.

Scientific Instruments

Largest The largest scientific instrument (and arguably the world's largest machine) is the Large Electron Positron (LEP) storage ring at CERN, Geneva, Switzerland which is 3.8 m *12½ ft* in diameter and 27 km *17 miles* in circumference. Over 60,000 tonnes of technical equipment have been installed in the tunnel and its eight underground working zones. (⇨ Heaviest particle)

Finest balance The Sartorius Microbalance Model 4108, manufactured in Göttingen, Germany, can weigh objects of up to 0.5 g *0.018 oz* to an accuracy of 0.01 μg, or 1×10^{-8} g *3.5×10^{-10} oz*, which is equivalent to little more than one sixtieth of the weight of the ink on this full stop.

Largest bubble chamber The $7 million installation at Fermi National Accelerator Laboratory (Fermilab), Batavia, Illinois, USA was 4.57 m *15 ft* in diameter, contained 33,000 litres *7259 gal* of liquid hydrogen at a temperature of −247°C *−413°F*, and had a superconducting magnet of 3 tesla. Experimental results were obtained between 28 Sep 1973 and 1 Feb 1988.

Fastest centrifuge Ultracentrifuges were invented by the Swedish Nobel prize-winning chemist Theodor Svedberg (1884–1971) in 1923.

The highest man-made rotary speed ever achieved is 7250 km/h *4500 mph* by a tapered 15.2-cm *6-in* carbon fibre rod rotating in a vacuum at Birmingham University, reported on 24 Jan 1975.

Most powerful laser Albert Einstein (1879–1955) formulated the principle of light amplification by stimulated emissions of radiation in 1917. However, the first practical device was a gas maser (microwave amplification by stimulated emissions of radiation) produced in 1954 by J. Gordon, H. Zeiger and C. Townes.

The longest echo produced in any building is 15 sec following the closing of the door of the Chapel of the Mausoleum in Hamilton, Strathclyde, built 1840–55.

The first laser (a term coined by Richard Gould) was constructed in 1960 by Theodore Maiman of the Hughes Research Laboratory in California, USA, with similar devices developed independently by Soviet physicists N. Bassov and A. Prokhorov.

The most powerful laser is the 'Nova' at the Lawrence Livermore National Laboratory, California, USA. Its ten arms produce laser pulses capable of generating 100×10^{12} W of power, much of which is delivered to a target the size of a grain of sand in 1×10^{-9} sec. For this brief instance, that power is 200 times greater than the combined output of all the electrical generating plants in the US. Fitted with two target chambers, the laser itself is 91 m *300 ft* long and about three storeys high.

Heaviest magnet The heaviest magnet is in the Joint Institute for Nuclear Research at Dubna, near Moscow, Russia for the 10 GeV synchrophasotron. It weighs 36,000 tonnes and is 60 m *196 ft* in diameter.

Largest electromagnet The world's largest electromagnet is part of the L3 detector experiment at LEP (⇨Largest Scientific Instrument). The octagonal magnet consists of 6400 tonnes of low carbon steel yoke and 1100 tons of aluminium coil and 30,000 amperes of current flowing through the aluminium coil is used to create a uniform magnet field of 5 kilogauss. The magnet is higher than a four-storey building of about 1728 m³ *59,320 ft³* volume. Its total weight, including the frame, coil and inner support tube, is 7810 tons and it is composed of more metal than the Eiffel Tower.

Microscope!

The scanning tunnelling microscope (STM) invented at the IBM Zürich, Switzerland research laboratory in 1981 has a magnification ability of 100 million and a resolving power down to one hundredth the diameter of an atom (3×10^{-10} m), making it the world's most powerful microscope.

Most powerful particle accelerator The world's highest energy 'atomsmasher' is the 2-km *1.25-mile* diameter proton synchroton 'Tevatron' at Fermilab near Batavia, Illinois, USA. On 3 Jan 1987 a centre of mass energy of 1.8 TeV (1.8×10^{12} eV) was achieved by colliding beams of protons and antiprotons.

Plans by the US Department of Energy to build a superconducting supercollider (SSC) which uses two TeV proton colliding beams, was cancelled in October 1993.

Thinnest glass Type D263 glass, made by Deutsche Spezialglas AG of Grünenplan,

Scientific!

The highest auction price paid for a scientific instrument is £7,701,500 for a 21.5 cm *8½ in* diameter 19th century German gilt and lacquered brass mechanical calculator made by Johann Christoph Schuster. It was sold at Christie's, London on 19 May 1993 by telephone to Edgar Mannheim of Switzerland.

Germany for use in electronic and medical equipment, has a minimum thickness of 0.025 mm *0.00098 in* and a maximum thickness of 0.035 mm *0.00137 in*.

Finest cut The $13 million Large Optics Diamond turning Machine at the Lawrence Livermore National Laboratory in California, USA was reported in June 1983 to be able to sever a human hair 3000 times lengthways.

Smallest microphone A microphone with a frequency response of 10 Hz–10 kHz and measuring 1.5×0.76 mm *0.06×0.03 in* was developed in 1967 by Prof. Ibrahim Kavrak of Bogazici University, Istanbul, Turkey as a new technique in measuring pressure in fluid flow.

Smallest!

Dr Frederich Sachs, a biophysicist at the State University of New York at Buffalo, USA, has developed an ultra-microthermometer for measuring the temperature of single living cells. The tip is one micrometer in diameter, about $1/50$ the diameter of a human hair.

Largest barometer An oil-filled barometer, of overall height 13 m *42 ft*, was constructed by Allan Mills and John Pritchard of the Department of Physics and Astronomy, University of Leicester in 1991. It attained a *standard* height of 12.20 m *40 ft* (at which pressure mercury would stand at 0.76 m *2½ ft*).

Smallest prism A glass prism with sides measuring 0.004 mm *0.001 in*, barely visible to the naked eye, was created at the National Institute of Standards and Technology in Boulder, Colorado, USA in 1989.

Sharpest objects and smallest tubes The sharpest manufactured objects are glass micropipette tubes whose bevelled tips have outer and inner diameters of 0.02 μm and 0.01 μm respectively, the latter being 6500 times thinner than a human hair. They are used in intracellular work on living cells in techniques developed in 1977.

Slowest!

A nuclear environmental machine for testing stress corrosion that can be controlled at a speed as slow as one million millionth of a millimetre per minute (1 m *3.3 ft* in about 2000 million years) has been developed by Nene Instruments of Wellingborough, Northants.

Mathematics

In dealing with large numbers, the notation of ten raised to various powers is used to eliminate a profusion of noughts. For example, 19,160,000,000,000 km would be expressed as $1.916×10^{13}$ km. Similarly, a very small number, for example 0.0000154324 g, would be written as a negative power, i.e $1.54324×10^{-5}$. Of the prefixes used with numbers, the smallest is 'yocto' (y), of power 10^{-24} and the largest is 'yotta' (Y), of power 10^{24}. Both are based on the Greek octo, eight (for the eighth power of 10^3).

Largest number The largest lexicographically accepted named number in the system of successive powers of ten is

the centillion, first recorded in 1852. It is the hundredth power of a million, or 1 followed by 600 noughts (although only in the UK and Germany).

Prime numbers A prime number is any positive integer (excluding unity 1) having no integral factors other than itself and unity, e.g. 2, 3, 5, 7 or 11. The lowest prime number is thus 2.

The highest *known* prime number was discovered by computer scientists David Slowinski and Paul Gage at Cray Research, Inc on Minnesota, USA in January 1994, while they were conducting tests on a CRAY C90 series supercomputer (⇨ Most powerful computer). The new prime number has 258,716 digits, enough to fill over 21 pages of *The Guinness Book of Records*. In mathematical notation it is expressed as $2^{859433}-1$, which denotes two, multiplied by itself 859,433 times, minus one. Numbers expressed in this form are known as 'Mersenne' prime numbers, named after Father Marin Mersenne, a French monk (1588–1648) who spent years searching for prime numbers of this type (⇨ Perfect numbers)

The largest known twin primes are $1,706,595 × 2^{11235} -1$ and $1,706,595 × 2^{11235} +1$, found on 6 Aug 1989 by a team in Santa Clara, California, USA using an Amdahl 1200 supercomputer.

Composite numbers The lowest of the non-prime, or composite, numbers (excluding 1) is 4.

Perfect numbers A number is said to be perfect if it is equal to the sum of all divisors of the number other than itself, for example $1+2+4+7+14=28$. The lowest perfect number is 6, as in $1+2+3$.

All perfect numbers have a direct relationship to Mersenne primes. The highest known perfect number and the 33rd so far discovered is thus $(2^{859433}-1)×2^{859433}$. It has a total of 517,430 digits (enough to fill over 41 pages of *The Guinness Book of Records*) and it is derived from the largest known Mersenne prime. (⇨ Prime numbers)

Newest mathematical constant The study of turbulent water, the weather and other chaotic phenomena has revealed the existence of a new universal constant, the Feigenbaum number, first calculated by Mitchell J. Feigenbaum of the US. It is approximately equal to 4.669201609102990.

Most-proved theorem A book published in 1940 and entitled *The Pythagorean Proposition* contained 370 different proofs of Pythagoras'

GUESS WHAT?
Q who is the world's largest oil producer?
A See Page 77

Problems!

Fermat's last theorem has precipitated the most number of incorrect proofs than have been published for any other theorem. Pierre de Fermat inspired the centuries of hopeless searching when he recorded the deceptively simple theorem in the margin of a notebook, adding, 'I have found an admirable proof of this theorem, but the margin is too narrow to contain it'. Andrew J. Wiles of Princeton University, USA announced that he had found a proof of the theorem in June 1993, but in December he issued a statement saying he was still working on a 'calculation' that was 'not yet complete'. Many await anxiously the results of his investigations.

Largest mathematical prize Dr Paul Wolfskell left prize money in his will for the first person to solve the last theorem of Pierre Fermat (1601–65). This prize was worth 100,000 deutschmarks in 1908.

Longest computer computation for a yes–no answer The 20th Fermat number, $2^{2^{20}}+1$, was tested on a CRAY-2 supercomputer in 1986 to see if it was a prime number. After 10 days of calculation the answer was no.

theorem, including one by American President James Garfield (1831–81).

Longest proof The proof of the classification of all finite simple groups is spread over more than 14,000 pages in nearly 500 papers in mathematical journals, contributed by more than 100 mathematicians over a period of more than 35 years.

GUESS WHAT?

Q How thin is the thinnest glass?

A see Page 71

Oldest mathematical puzzle 'As I was going to St Ives, I met a man with seven wives. Every wife had seven sacks, and every sack had seven cats. Every cat had seven kits. Kits, cats, sacks and wives, how many were going to St Ives?

Apart from slight differences in wording, this is identical to a puzzle found in the Rhind papyrus, an Egyptian scroll bearing mathematical tables and problems, copied by the scribe A'h-mosè *c.* 1650BC.

Least numerate The Nambiquara people of the north-west Matto Grosso in Brazil lack any system of numbers. They do, however, have a verb which means 'they are alike'.

Most accurate version of 'pi' The most decimal places to which *pi* (π) has been calculated is 2,260,321,336 by brothers Gregory Volfovich and David Volfovich Chudnovsky, on their home-made supercomputer m zero in New York, New York, USA in Summer 1991.

Robot!

The world's smallest robot is the 'Monsieur' microbot, developed by the Seiko Epson Corporation of Japan in 1992. The light-sensitive robot measures less than 1 cm³ *0.06 in³*, weighs 1.5 g *0.05 oz* and is made of 97 separate watch parts (equivalent to two ordinary watches). Capable of speeds of 11.3 mm/sec *0.4 in/sec* for about 5 min when charged, the 'Monsieur' has earned a design award at the International Contest for Hill-Climbing Micromechanisms.

Most inaccurate In 1897 the General Assembly of Indiana, USA enacted in Bill No. 246 stating that *pi* was *de jure* 4, when even the Bible manages to imply that *pi* equals 3.

Earliest measures The earliest known measure of weight is the *beqa* of the Amratian period of Egyptian civilization *c.*3800BC, found at Naqada, Egypt. The weights are cylindrical, with rounded ends and weigh from 188.7–211.2 g *6.65–7.45 oz*.

The unit of length used by the megalithic tomb-builders in north-western Europe *c.* 3500BC, and generally known as the megalithic yard, was deduced by Prof. Alexander Thom (1894–1985) in 1966 to have been 82.90 ± 0.09 cm *2.72 ± 0.003 ft.*

Time measure The longest measure of time is the *para* in Hindu chronology. It is equivalent to the length of the complete life of Brahma, and is equivalent to 311,040,000,000,000 years (this is 68,500 times longer than the estimated age of the Earth). In astronomy a cosmic year is the period of rotation of the Sun around the centre of the Milky Way galaxy, i.e. 223 million years, assuming a circular orbit. In the Late Cretaceous Period of *c.* 85 million years ago the Earth rotated faster, resulting in 370.3 days per year, while in Cambrian times *c.* 600 million years ago there is evidence that the year comprised 425 days.

Computers

Earliest The earliest programmable electronic computer was the 1500-valve Colossus formulated by Prof. Max H.A. Newman (1897–1985) and built by T.H. Flowers. It was run in December 1943 at Bletchley Park, Bucks to break the German coding machine Enigma. It arose from a concept published in 1936 by Dr Alan Mathison Turing (1912–54) in his paper *On Computable Numbers with an Application to the* Entscheidungsproblem. Colossus was not declassified until 25 Oct 1975.

The world's first stored-programme computer was the Manchester University Mark I, which incorporated the Williams storage cathode ray tube (patented 11 Dec 1946). It ran its first program, by Prof. Tom Kilburn (b. 11 Aug 1921), for 52 min on 21 Jun 1948.

Computers were greatly advanced by the invention of the point-contact transistor by John Bardeen and Walter Brattain (announced in July 1948), and the junction transistor by R.L. Wallace, Morgan Sparks and Dr William Bradford Shockley (1910–89) in early 1951.

The concept of the integrated circuit, which has enabled micro-miniaturisation, was first published on 7 May 1952 by Geoffrey W.A. Dummer (GB; b. 1909) in Washington, DC, USA.

The invention of the microcomputer was attributed to a team led by M.E. Hoff, Jr of Intel Corporation with the production of the microprocessor chip '4004' in 1969–71. On 17 Jul 1990, however, priority was accorded to Gilbert Hyatt (b. 1938), who devised a single chip microcomputer at Micro Computer Inc. of Van Nuys, Los Angeles in 1968–71 with the award of US Patent No. 4942516.

Fastest The fastest general-purpose vector-parallel computer is the Cray Y-MP C90 supercomputer, with 2 gigabytes (gigabytes = one billion bytes) of central memory and with 16 CPUs (central processing units) giving a combined peak performance of 16 gigaflops (gigaflops = one billion flops/floating point operations/per second).

Several suppliers now market 'massively parallel' computers which, with enough processors, have a theoretical aggregate performance exceeding that of a C-90, though the performance on real-life applications can often be less. This is because it may be harder to harness effectively the power of a large number of small processors than a small number of large ones.

Fastest chip In March 1992 it was reported that DEC of Maynard, Massachusetts, USA had developed an all-purpose, 64-bit processor known as Alpha, which could run at speeds of up to 200 MHz (compared to 66 MHz for many modern personal computers). One Alpha chip is claimed to have about the same processing power as a CRAY-1, which went on sale in 1976 as the Cray company's first supercomputer at a cost of $7.5 million.

Fastest transistor A transistor capable of switching 230 billion times per second was announced by the University of Illinois at Urbana-Champaign in October 1986. The devices were made of indium, gallium arsenide and aluminium gallium arsenide and developed in collaboration with General Electric Company.

Computer company The world's largest computer firm is International Business Machines (IBM) Corporation of Armonk, New York, USA.

In April 1994, it had assets of $81.113 billion, gross revenues of $62.716 billion but net losses of $8.101 billion—the highest ever. The company has 267,196 employees worldwide (compared with a peak of 407,000 in 1986).

Power

Steam Engines *Oldest* The oldest steam engine in working order is the Smethwick Engine dating from 1779. Designed by James Watt (1736–1819) and built by the Birmingham Canal Company at a cost of £2000, the pump—originally a 60-cm *24-in* bore with a stroke of 2.4 m *8 ft*—worked on the canal locks at Smethwick, W Mids until 1891. The engine was presented to the Birmingham Museum of Science and Industry in 1960 and is regularly steamed for the public.

The oldest engine working as such and on its original site is the 1812 Boulton & Watt 26-hp, 1066-mm *42-in* bore beam engine on the Kennet and Avon Canal at Great Bedwyn, Wilts. It was restored by the Crofton Society in 1971 and still runs periodically.

Largest The largest-ever single-cylinder steam engine was designed by Matthew Loam of Cornwall and built by the Hayle Foundry Co. in 1849 for land draining at Haarlem, Netherlands. The cylinder was 3.65 m *12 ft* in diameter and each stroke, also of 3.65 m *12 ft*, lifted 61,096 litres *13,440 gal* of water.

Largest power plant The most powerful installed power station is the Itaipu hydro-electric plant on the Paraná River near the Brazil-Paraguay border. Opened in 1984, the station has now attained its ultimate rated capacity of 13,320 MW.

UK The power station with the greatest installed capacity in Great Britain is the Drax installation in North Yorkshire, with six 660 MW sets yielding 4000 MW.

Nuclear power stations The world's largest nuclear power station, consisting of 10 reactors giving a net output of 8814 MW, is in Fukushima, Japan.

Nuclear reactors Work began on the 1455 MW planned net capacity CHOOZ-B1 reactor in France in July 1982, and the first reactor became operational in 1991. The USA has the

most nuclear reactors (109), generating 98,729 megawatt hours or 29.8% of the world total.

UK The largest capacity AGR (advanced gas-cooled reactor) in the UK is Tooness, near Dunbar, Lothian which has a net capacity of 625 MW.

Boilers The world's largest boilers had a capacity of 1330 MW involving the evaporation of 4,232,000 kg *9,330,000 lb* of steam per hour. They were ordered in the United States from Babcock & Wilcox Ltd of London.

Generators The largest operational is a turbo-generator of 1450 MW (net) under installation at the Ignalina atomic power station in Lithuania.

Solar Power In terms of nominal capacity the largest solar electric power facility in the world is the Harper Lake Site (LSP 8 & 9) in the Mojave Desert, operated by UC Operating Services. These two solar electric generating stations (SEGS) have a nominal capacity of 160 MW (80 MW each). The station site covers 1280 acres.

Transformers The world's largest single-phase transformers are rated at 1,500,000 kVA. Of the eight service with the American Electric Power Service Corporation, five step down from 765 to 345 kV. Britain's largest transformers are rated at 1,000,000 kVA. Commissioned for the CEGB (Central Electric Generating Board) in October 1968, they were built by Hackbridge & Hewittic of Walton-on-Thames, Surrey.

Transmission lines The longest span of any power line between pylons is 5376 m *17,638 ft* across the Ameralik Fjord near Nuuk, Greenland. The span is part of the 132 Kv line built by A/S Betonmast of Oslo, Norway in 1991–2. The line serves the 2 × 15 MW Buksefjorden Hydro Power Station. It consists of four 900-mm² steel conductors weighing 43 tonnes each (the fourth is spare) and the conductor weight is 7.22 kg/m.

The longest in Britain are the 1618-m *5310-ft* lines built by J.L. Eve across the Severn, with main towers each 148 m *488 ft* high.

Highest The world's highest power lines span 3627 m *11,900 ft* across the Straits of Messina, Italy from towers at heights of 205 m *675 ft* (Sicily side) and 224 m *735 ft* (Calabria).

The highest lines in Britain are suspended from towers 192 m *630 ft* tall at a minimum height of 76 m *250 ft* across the Thames estuary. They are 1371 m *4500 ft* apart, have a breaking load of 130 tonnes and were made by BICC at West Thurrock, Essex.

Highest voltages The most powerful lines carry 1330 kV for 1970 km *1224 miles* on the DC Pacific Inter-tie in the USA. The Ekibastuz DC transmission lines in Kazakhstan were planned 2400 km *1490 miles* long with a 1.5 MV capacity.

GUESS WHAT?

Q There are 109 elements. Which is the 'Newest'?

A See Page 68

Turbines The largest hydraulic turbines are rated at 815 MW. They are 9.7 m *32 ft* in diameter, have a 407-tonne runner, a 317.5-tonne shaft and were installed by Allis-Chalmers at the Grand Coulee Third Powerplant, Washington, USA.

Smallest A self-sustaining gas turbine with compressor and turbine wheels measuring just 5 cm *2 in* with an operating speed of 50,000 rev/min

was built by Geoff Knights of London. The engine was completed and first ran on 4 Feb 1989.

Wind generators The $14.2 million GEC MOD-5A installation on the north shore of Oahu, Hawaii, USA produces 7.3 MW when the wind reaches 51.5 km/h *32 mph* through its 122-m *400-ft* rotors.

UK The 3 MW aerogenerator LS-1, with 60-m *196-ft-10-in* blades on a 37-m *121-ft*-tall tower on Burgar Hill, Evie, Orkney, was switched on in a gale on 10 Nov 1987. Built by the Wind Energy Group consortium of Taylor Woodrow, British Aerospace and GEC at a cost of £12 million, it can generate about 9 million kWh per year, enough for 2000 average houses.

Water mill The oldest water mill in continuous commercial use is Priston Mill near Bath, Avon, first mentioned in AD 931 in a charter of King Athelstan (reigned 924/5–939). It is driven by the Conygre Brook.

Windmills *Earliest* Although usually associated with the Netherlands, the earliest recorded windmills were used for grinding corn in Iran in the 7th century AD. The oldest Dutch mill is the tower-mill at Zeddam, Gelderland, built c.1450.

Most durable battery The zinc foil and sulfur dry-pile batteries made by Watlin and Hill of London in 1840 have powered ceaseless tintinnabulation inside a bell jar at the Clarendon Laboratory, Oxford since that year.

UK The earliest authenticated windmills in England date back to the last quarter of the 12th century: 1185 at Amberley, Sussex, and 1185–1190 at Weedley near Hull. A windmill at Wigston Parva, Leics, is claimed to date from 1137 but this has not been proven.

The oldest remains of a windmill in England is the stump, wrongly known as 'The Beacon', at Burton Dasset, Warks, which dates from the 14th century. The only windmill to remain in full commercial use since its construction in 1813 is the Subscription Mill at North Leverton, Notts.

Largest The tallest windmill in the world is the St Patrick's Distillery Mill in Dublin, now without sails. It is 150 ft *45.72 m* tall. The tallest working windmill in Europe is de Noord Molen at

Black-out!

The greatest power failure in history struck seven north-eastern US states and Ontario, Canada on 9–10 Nov 1965. About 30 million people over an area of 207,200 km² *80,000 miles²* were plunged into darkness; only two were killed.

Schiedam, Netherlands, at 109 ft 4 in *33.33 m*, though there are other disused Dutch windmills that are taller.

The UK's tallest working windmill is the five-sailed Maud Foster windmill at Boston, Lincs, built in 1819, which is 80 ft *24.38 m* high.

Largest battery The 10 MW lead-acid battery at Chino, California, USA has a design capacity of 40 MWh and will be used at an electrical sub-station for levelling peak demand loads. This $13 million project is a co-operative effort by Southern California Edison Co. Electric Power Research Institute and International Lead Zinc Research Organization Inc.

Engineering

Oldest machinery The earliest mechanism still in use is the *dâlu*—a water-raising instrument known to have been in use in the Sumerian civilization, which originated c. 3500 BC in lower Iraq.

Smallest man-made object By using field ion microscopy the tips of probes of scanning tunnelling microscopes have been shaped to end in a single atom—the last three layers constituting the world's smallest man-made pyramid, consisting of 7, 3 and 1 atoms. Since the announcement in

The largest-ever solar power plant in the Mojave Desert, California, viewed from the air. The plant in its entirety was operated by LUZ Engineering Co until the company went bankrupt in late 1992: their nine SEGS were then split between 3 other companies.

The installation had an array of 650,000 computer-controlled parabolic mirrors which track the sun across the sky (inset, far left), focusing its light onto tubes containing a synthetic oil. The oil, which is thus superheated to 391°C, is used to boil water for steam turbine generators in one of five power plants. Pictured left is a close-up of one of the power plants. (⬦ Solar power)
(Photos: Hank Morgan/Science Photo Library)

GUESS WHAT?

Q Which element has the highest boiling point?

A See Page 68

January 1990 that D.M. Eigler and E.K. Schweizer of the IBM Almaden Research Center, San Jose, California, USA had used an STM to move and reposition single atoms of xenon on a nickel surface in order to spell out the initials 'IBM', other laboratories around the world have used similar techniques on single atoms of other elements.

Steel production The world's largest producer of steel is the Nippon Steel Corporation of Japan, which produced 27.687 million tonnes of crude steel in the year ending March 1992, compared with 28.993 million tonnes in 1991. It now employs 37,388 staff, compared with 51,441 in 1988.

Blast furnace The world's largest blast furnace, with a volume of 5500m³, is the no. 5 furnace at the Cherepovets works in Russia.

Catalytic cracker The world's largest catalytic cracker is Exxon's Bayway Refinery plant at Linden, New Jersey, USA, with a fresh feed rate of 19 million litres *4.2 million gal* per day.

Conveyor belts The world's longest single-flight conveyor belt stretches across 29km *18 miles* in Western Australia and was installed by Cable Belt Ltd of Camberley, Surrey. Great Britain's longest, also installed by Cable Belt, runs for 8.9 km *5½ miles* underground at Longannet power station, Fife.

Most powerful gantry crane The 28.14-m *92.3-ft* wide Rahco (R.A. Hanson Disc Ltd) gantry crane at the Grand Coulee Dam, Washington, USA Third Powerplant was tested in 1975 to lift a load weighing 2232 tonnes. It lowered a 1789-tonne generator rotor with an accuracy of 0.8mm *¹/₃₂ in*.

Tallest mobile crane The 810-tonne Rosenkranz K10001, with a lifting capacity of 1000 tonnes and a combined boom and jib height of 202m *663ft*, is carried on 10 trucks each limited to a length of 23.06m *75ft 8in* and an axle weight of 118 tonnes. The crane can lift 30 tonnes to a height of 160m *525ft*.

Greatest load raised The heaviest operation in engineering history was the raising of the entire 1.6-km *1-mile* long offshore Ekofisk complex in the North Sea on 17–18 Aug 1987 because of subsidence of the sea bed. The complex, consisting of eight platforms weighing some 40,000 tonnes, was raised 6.5m *21ft 4in* by 122 hydraulic jacks run by computer-controlled hydraulic system.

Fork lift truck In 1991 Kalmar LMV of Lidhult, Sweden manufactured three counterbalanced fork lift trucks capable of lifting loads up to 90 tonnes at a load centre of 2400mm *90.5in*. They were built to handle the great man-made river project comprising two separate pipelines, one 998km

Largest!

The largest nuts ever made have an outer diameter of 132 cm *52 in*, a 63.5 cm *25 in* thread and weigh 4.74 tonnes. Known as 'Pilgrim Nuts', they are manufactured by Pilgrim Moorside Ltd of Oldham, Lancs for use on the columns of large forging presses.

620 miles long running from Sarir to the Gulf of Sirte and the other 897 km *557 miles* from Tazirbu to Benghazi, Libya.

Most powerful diesel engines Five 12RTA84 type diesel engines each with a 12-cylinder power unit giving a maximum continuous output of 41,920 kW *57,000 bhp* at 95 rev/min were constructed by Sulzer Brothers of Winterthur, Switzerland for container ships built for the American President Lines. The first of these ships, the *President Truman*, was delivered in April 1988.

Dragline The world's largest walking dragline is 'Big Muskie', the Bucyrus-Erie 4250W, with a weight of 12,000 tonnes and a bucket capacity of 168m³ *220yd³* on a 94.4-m *310-ft* boom. This is the largest mobile land machine and is now operating on the Central Ohio Coal Co. Muskingum site in Ohio, USA.

Escalators The earliest 'Inclined Escalator' was installed by Jesse W. Reno (USA; 1861–1947) on

Earthmover!

The giant-wheeled loader developed for open-air coal mining in Australia by SMEC, a consortium of 11 manufacturers in Tokyo, Japan, is 16.8m *55ft* long, weighs 180 tonnes, has a bucket capacity of 19 m³ *671 ft³* and is fitted with rubber tyres 3.5 m *11½ ft* in diameter.

The 70-storey, 296-m *971-ft-* tall Yokohama Landmark Tower in Yokohama, Japan, which houses the world's fastest domestic passenger lifts. It was opened to the public on 16 Jul 1993.

(Photo: Mitsubishi Electric Corp)

The express lifts were designed and built by Mitsubishi Electric Corporation of Tokyo, and operate at 45 km/h *28 mph*, taking passengers from the second floor to the 69th floor observatory in 40 sec.

(Photo: Mitsubishi Electric Corporation)

the pier at Coney Island, New York, USA in 1896, but the term was not registered in the USA until 28 May 1900.

The longest escalators in Britain are three flights at the Angel underground station, London, each measuring 60 m *197 ft*. Built by French engineers and installed as part of a £70 million facelift at the station, they caused great embarrassment to the management but no real surprise to London's commuters by breaking down three days after being put into operation on 12 Aug 1992.

The world's longest *ride* is on the four-section outdoor escalator at Ocean Park, Hong Kong, which

A snow-plough with a blade 15.3 m *50.25 ft* long, 1.24 m *4 ft* high and with a clearing capacity of 30.6 m³ *1080 ft³* in one pass was made by Aero Snow Removal Corporation of New York, USA in 1992 for operation at JFK International Airport.

(Photo: V Dejana)

has an overall length of 227 m *745 ft* and a total vertical rise of 115 m *377 ft*.

Moving walkways The world's longest moving walkways (also known as 'Travelators') are those installed in 1970 in the Neue Messe Centre, Düsseldorf, Germany, which measure 225 m *738 ft* between comb plates. The ultimate in pampering to weary shoppers is the moving walkway at *Okadaya More's* Shopping Mall at Kawasaki-shi, Japan, which has a vertical height of 83.4 cm *32.83 in*. It was installed by Hitachi Ltd.

Forging The largest forging on record was a generator shaft weighing 204.4 tonnes *450,600 lb*, and measuring 16.76 m *55 ft* long for Japan, forged by the Bethlehem Steel Corporation of Pennsylvania, USA in October 1973.

Lathe The largest is the 38.4 m *126 ft* long 416.2-tonne lathe built by Waldrich Siegen of Germany in 1973 for the South African Electricity Supply Commission at Rosherville.

Top spinning The duration record for spinning a clock-balance wheel by unaided hand is 5 min 26.8 sec, by Philip Ashley, 16, of Leigh, Lancs on 20 May 1968.

The record using 91.4 cm *36 in* of string with a 205.5 g *7¼ oz* top is 58 min 20 sec, by Peter Hodgson at Southend-on-Sea, Essex on 4 Feb 1985.

A team of 25 from the Mizushima Plant of Kawasaki Steel Works in Okayama, Japan spun a giant top 2 m *6 ft 6¾ in* tall and 2.6 m *8 ft 6¼ in* in diameter, weighing 360 kg *793.6 lb*, for 1 hr 21 min 35 sec on 3 Nov 1986.

Lifts The world's fastest domestic passenger lifts are those in the Yokohama Landmark Tower in Yokohama, Japan.

Much higher speeds are achieved in the winding cages of mine shafts. A hoisting shaft 2072 m *6800 ft* deep, owned by Western Deep Levels Ltd in South Africa, winds at speeds of up to 65 km/h *41 mph*. Otitis media (popping of the ears) presents problems above even 16 km/h *10 mph*.

Longest incarceration in a lift Graham Coates of Brighton, East Sussex established an involuntary duration record when trapped in a lift for 62 hr in Brighton on 24–28 May 1986.

Pipelines *Oil* The world's longest crude oil pipeline is the Interprovincial Pipe Line Co. installation from Edmonton, Alberta, Canada to Buffalo, New York, USA, a distance of 2856 km

David Beattie and Adrian Simons in action as they make their successful attempt on the escalator riding record.

Riding!

The record distance travelled on a pair of 'up' and 'down' escalators is 214.34 km *133.18 miles*, by David Beattie and Adrian Simons at Top Shop, Oxford Street, London from 17–21 Jul 1989. They each completed 7032 circuits.

1775 miles. A series of 13 pumping stations maintain a flow of 31,367,145 litres *6,900,000 gal* of oil per day along the pipe.

Gas The longest natural gas pipeline in the world is the Trans-Canada pipeline, which by 1974 had 9099 km *5654 miles* of pipe up to 106.6 cm *42 in* in diameter.

Most expensive The world's most expensive pipeline is the Alaska pipeline running 1287 km *800 miles* from Prudhoe Bay to Valdez. The pipe is 1.21 m *4 ft* in diameter and its capacity is now 2.1 million barrels per day.

Press The world's two most powerful production machines are forging presses in the USA. The Loewy closed-die forging press, in a plant leased from the US Air Force by the Wyman-Gordon Company at North Grafton, Massachusetts, weighs 9469 tonnes and stands 34.79 m *114 ft 2 in* high, of which 20.1 m *66 ft* is sunk below the operating floor. It has a rated capacity of 44,600 tonnes and became operational in October 1955. The second press is at the plant of the Aluminum Company of America in Cleveland, Ohio, USA.

The greatest press force of any sheet metal forming press is 106,000 tonnes for a QUINTUS fluid cell press delivered by ASEA to BMW AG in Munich, Germany in January 1986.

Worlds Largest Snow Plow ...
AERO SNOW REMOVAL CORP

Printer The world's fastest printer was the Radiation Inc. electro-sensitive system at the Lawrence Livermore Radiation Laboratory in Livermore, California, USA. High-speed recording of up to 36,000 lines per minute, each containing 120 alphanumeric characters, was attained by controlling electronic pulses through chemically-impregnated recording paper moving rapidly under closely-spaced fixed styluses. Thus the Bible (up to 773,746 words) could be printed in 65 seconds; 3048 times as fast as the peak rate of the world's fastest typist. (⇔ Fastest Typist)

Radar installation The largest of the three installations in the US Ballistic Missile Early Warning System (BMEWS) is that near Thule, Kalaallit Nunaat (Greenland), 1498 km *931 miles* from the North Pole. It was completed in 1960 at a cost of $500 million.

GUESS WHAT?

Q where is the largest windmill?

A See Page 74

Ropes The largest rope ever made was a coir fibre launching rope with a diameter of 119 cm *47 in* made in 1858 for the British liner *Great Eastern* by John and Edwin Wright of Birmingham, W Mids. It consisted of four strands, each of 3780 yarns.

Wire ropes The world's longest wire ropes are four made at British Ropes Ltd, Wallsend, Tyne & Wear, each measuring 24 km *15 miles*. The ropes are 35 mm *1.3 in* in diameter, weigh 108.5 tonnes each and were ordered by the CEGB for use in the construction of the 2000 MW cross-Channel power cable.

The suspension cables on the Seto Grand Bridge, Japan, completed in 1988, are 104 cm *41 in* in diameter.

A 56-cm *22-in* diameter cable-laid rope with a calculated breaking strength of 11,000 tonnes was manufactured for demonstration purposes only by Franklin Offshore Supply & Engineering PTE LTD of Singapore in 1992.

Shovel The Marion 6360 has a reach of 72.16 m *236.75 ft*, a dumping height of 46.63 m *153 ft* and a bucket capacity of 138 m³ *4860 ft³*. It is operated for open-cast coal mining near Percy in Illinois, USA by the Arch Mineral Corporation.

Wind tunnel The world's largest wind tunnel is at the NASA Ames Research Center in Mountain View, Palo Alto, California, USA. The largest test section measures 36 × 24 m *118 × 79 ft* and is powered by six 17,000 kW motors, giving a top speed of 200 km/h *124 mph*.

Mining and Drilling

Deepest Man's deepest penetration into the Earth's crust is a geological exploratory borehole near Zapolarny in the Kola peninsula of Arctic Russia, begun on 24 May 1970 and reported in April 1992 to have surpassed a depth of 12,262 m *40,230 ft*. The eventual target of 15,000 m *49,212 ft* is expected in 1995.

Coal cutting The individual coal cutting record is 45.4 tonnes per person in one shift (six hours) by five Soviet miners under the leadership of Aleksey Stakhanov at the Tsentralnaya-Irmino mine, Donetsk region, Ukraine (then USSR) on 19 Sep 1935.

Using machinery the British record output for a single colliery in a year is 3,045,986 tonnes, from Riccall Mine in the Selby Complex, N Yorks between April 1993 and March 1994. The record output in a week is 173,156 tonnes, produced at Wistow, also in the Selby Complex, in the week ending 16 Jan 1993.

Coal shovelling The record for filling a ½-ton *508-kg* hopper with coal is 26.83 sec, by Brian McArdle at the Fingal Valley Festival in Fingal, Tasmania, Australia on 5 Mar 1994.

The record by a team of two is 15.01 sec, by Brian McArdle and Rodney Spark, both of Middlemount, Queensland, Australia on the same occasion.

Ocean drilling The deepest recorded drilling into the sea bed is 2000 m *6563 ft* by the Ocean Drilling Program's vessel *JOIDES Resolution*, in

Drilling!

The deepest borehole in ice was reported in July 1993 to have reached the bottom of the Greenland ice sheet at a depth of 3053.51 m *10,018 ft* after five years' drilling by American researchers.

Fastest The most footage drilled in one month is 10,477 m *34,574 ft* in June 1988 by Harkins & Company Rig Number 13 during the drilling of four wells in McMullen County, Texas, USA.

the eastern equatorial Pacific in 1991. The deepest site in which drilling has been conducted is 7034 m *23,077 ft* below the surface on the western wall of the Marianas Trench, Pacific Ocean, by the Deep Sea Drilling Project's vessel *Glomar Challenger*.

Oil

Production The world's largest oil producer is Saudi Arabia, with production in 1993 of 8.198 million barrels per day (b/d).

Consumption The largest consumer is the USA with 781,000 thousand tonnes in 1992, 25 percent of the world's total. The UK consumed 82,400 thousand tonnes in 1992, 100 thousand tonnes less than in the peak year of consumption, 1991.

Background: copper mining, Arizona, USA
(Photo: Don Green Photography, Inc./Magma Copper Company)

Cable Car!

The highest and longest passenger-carrying aerial ropeway in the world is the Teleférico Mérida in Venezuela, from Mérida City (1639.5 m *5379 ft*) to the summit of Pico Espejo (4763.7 m *15,629 ft*), a rise of 3124 m *10,250 ft*. The ropeway is in four sections, involving three car changes in the 12.8-km *8-mile* ascent in one hour. The fourth span is 3069 m *10,070 ft* in length. The cars have a maximum capacity of 45 people and travel at 5 km/h *3 mph*.

Mine Records

Earliest
World 100,000 BC—CHERT (silica) Nazlet Sabaha Garb, Egypt.
UK 3390 BC±150—FLINT, Church Hill, Findon, W. Sussex
Deepest
World[1] 3581 m *11,749 ft*—GOLD, Western Deep Levels, Carletonville, South Africa.
UK 1315 m *4314 ft*—COAL, Plodder Seam, Bickershaw Colliery, Leigh, Lancs.
Coal
Oldest (UK) c. 1822, Wearmouth, Tyne and Wear.
Deepest (exploratory shaft) 2042 m *6700 ft*, Donbas field, Ukraine.
(open cast, lignite) 325 m *1066 ft*, near Bergheim, Germany.
Copper
Deepest (open pit) 800 m *2625 ft*, Bingham Canyon, near Salt Lake City, Utah, USA.
Longest (underground) 1600 km *994 miles*, Division El Teniente, Codelco, Chile.
Gold
Largest (world)[2] 4900 ha *12,107 acres*, East Rand Proprietary Mines Ltd, Boksburg, Transvaal, South Africa.
Richest 49.4 million fine oz (all-time yield), Crown Mines, Transvaal, South Africa.
UK 120,000 fine oz (1854–1914), Clogau, St David's (discovered 1836), Gwynedd.

Iron
Largest 20,300 million tonnes (45–65% ore), Lebedinsky, Kursk region, Russia.
Lead
Largest >10 per cent of world output, Viburnum Trend, Missouri, USA.
Platinum
Largest 28 tonnes per year, Rustenburg Platinum Mines Group, Transvaal, South Africa.
Quarry
Largest (world) 7.21 km² *2.81 miles²*, 3355 million tonnes (extracted), Bingham Canyon, Utah, USA.
UK 150 m *500 ft* deep, 2.6 km *1.6 miles* circumference, Old Delabole Slate Quarry (from c. 1570), Cornwall.
Spoil Dump
Largest (world) 7.4 billion ft³ *210 million m³*, New Cornelia Tailings, Ten Mile Wash, Arizona, USA.
UK 141 ha *348 acres*, Allerton Tip, near Castleford, W Yorks.
Tungsten
Largest 2000 tonnes per day, Union Carbide Mount Morgan mine, near Bishop, California, USA.
Uranium
Largest (in terms of world prod) 5380 tonnes uranium per year, Cameco's Lake mine in Saskatchewan, Canada, 15.5% of world production.

[1] Sinking began in Jul 1957 and 4267 m *14,000 ft* is regarded as the limit. Its No. 3 vertical ventilation shaft is the world's deepest shaft, at 2949 m *9675 ft*. This mine requires 128,050 tonnes of air per day and equivalent refrigeration energy for making 33,600 tonnes of ice. An underground shift comprises 11,150 men.
[2] It has been estimated that South Africa has produced in 96 years (1886–1982) more than 31 per cent of all gold mined since 3900 BC. Over 51 per cent of the world's output is produced at the 38 mines of the Witwatersrand fields, South Africa, first discovered in 1886.

Fields The world's largest oil field is the Ghawar field in Saudi Arabia, developed by Aramco, and measuring 240×35 km *150×22 miles*.

Refineries The world's largest oil refinery is the Petroleos de Venezuela S.A. refinery in Judibana, Falcón, Venezuela. It is operated by the Lagoven subsidiary of Petroleos and now processes 530,000 barrels of crude per day, compared with 571,000 in 1990.

UK The largest oil refinery in the UK is the Esso Refinery at Fawley, near Southampton, Hants. Opened in 1921 and much expanded in 1951, it has a capacity of 15.6 million tonnes per year.

Platforms *Heaviest* The world's heaviest oil platform is the *Pampo* platform in the Campos Basin off Rio de Janeiro, Brazil, built and operated by the Petrobrás company. Opened in the 1970s, the platform weighs 24,100 tonnes, covers 3000 m² *32,292 ft²* and produces 30,000 b/d. It operates at a height of 115 m *377 ft* from the sea bed.

Tallest In December 1993 the 'Auger' tension leg platform was installed in the Gulf of Mexico. Designed and engineered by the Shell Oil Company, it sets a new water-depth record for a drilling and production platform, extending 872 m *2860 ft* from seabed to surface.

Flare!

The greatest gas fire burnt at Gassi Touil in the Algerian Sahara from noon on 13 Nov 1961 to 9:30 a.m. on 28 Apr 1962. The pillar of flame rose 137 m *450 ft* and the smoke 182 m *600 ft*. It was eventually extinguished by Paul Neal ('Red') Adair (b. 1915) of Houston, Texas, USA, using 245 kg *540 lb* of dynamite, for a fee of about $1 million plus expenses.

Time Pieces

Most accurate The most accurate time-keeping device is a commercially-available atomic clock manufactured by Hewlett-Packard of Palo Alto, California, USA, unveiled in December 1991. Designated the HP 5071A primary frequency standard with caesium-2 technology, the device, costing $54,000 and about the size of a desktop computer, is accurate to one second in 1.6 million years.

Clocks

Oldest The world's oldest surviving working clock is the faceless clock dating from 1386, or possibly earlier, at Salisbury Cathedral, Wilts. It was restored in 1956, having struck the hours for 498 years and ticked more than 500 million times.

Largest The world's largest clock is the astronomical clock in the Cathedral of St Pierre, Beauvais, France, constructed between 1865 and 1868. It consists of 90,000 parts and is 12.1 m *40 ft* high, 6.09 m *20 ft* wide and 2.7 m *9 ft* deep.

Largest clock faces The world's largest clock face is that of the floral clock, which is 31 m *101 ft* in diameter. It was installed on 18 Jun 1991 at Matsubara Park, Toi, Japan.

Highest The world's highest two-sided clock is 177 m *580 ft* above street level on top of the Morton International Building, Chicago, Illinois, USA.

Largest sundial The world's largest sundial has a base diameter of 37.2 m *122 ft* and is 36.6 m *120 ft* high with a gnomon (projecting arm) of the same length. Designed by Arata Isozaki of Tokyo, Japan as the centrepiece of the Walt Disney World Co. headquarters in Orlando, Florida, USA, it was unveiled on 1 Mar 1991.

A sundial with a surface area of 3877.86 m² *41,741 ft²*, designed by Shin Minohara of the Tadashi Minohara Design Studio, was built at the Keihanna Interaction Plaza, Kyoto, Japan in 1991.

Most expensive The highest price paid for any clock is £905,882 at Christie's, New York, USA on 24 Apr 1991 by a private bidder for a rare 'Egyptian Revival' clock made by Cartier in 1927. Designed as an ancient Egyptian temple gate, with figures and hieroglyphs, the clock is made of mother-of-pearl, coral and lapis lazuli.

Watches

Largest The largest watch was a 'Swatch' 162 m *531 ft 6 in* long and 20 m *65 ft 7½ in* in diameter, made by D. Tomas Feliu, which was displayed on the Bank of Bilbao building, Madrid, Spain from 7–12 Dec 1985.

Heaviest The Eta 'watch' on the Swiss pavilion at Expo '86 in Vancouver, British Columbia, Canada from May to October weighed 35 tonnes and was 24.3 m *80 ft* high.

Smallest The smallest watches, measuring just over 12 mm *½ in* long and 4.76 cm *⁴⁄₁₆ in* wide, are produced by Jaeger le Coultre of Switzerland. They are equipped with a 15-jewelled movement and the movement and case weigh under 7 g *0.25 oz*.

Longest stoppage of 'Big Ben' The longest stoppage of the clock in the House of Commons clock tower, London since the first tick on 31 May 1859 has been 13 days, from noon on 4 April to noon on 17 Apr 1977. In 1945 a host of starlings slowed the minute hand by five minutes.

Astronomical clock The entirely mechanical 'Planetarium Copernicus', made by Ulysse Nardin of Switzerland, is the only wristwatch that indicates the time of day, the date, the phases of the Moon and the astronomical position of the Sun, Earth, Moon and the planets as known in Copernicus' day. It also represents the Ptolemaic universe showing the astrological 'aspects' at any given time.

Pendulum The world's longest pendulum measures 22.5 m *73 ft 9 ¾ in* and is part of the water-mill clock installed by the Hattori Tokeiten Co. in the Shinjuku NS building in Tokyo, Japan in 1983.

The record price paid for a watch is SwFr4.95 million (£1,864,304) at Habsburg Feldman, Geneva, Switzerland on 9 Apr 1989 for a Patek Philippe 'Calibre '89' with 1728 separate parts.
(Photo: Patek Philippe)

Spills The world's worst oil spill occurred as a result of a marine blow-out beneath the drilling rig *Ixtoc I* in the Gulf of Campeche, Gulf of Mexico, on 3 Jun 1979. The slick reached 640 km *400 miles* by 5 Aug 1979. It was eventually capped on 24 Mar 1980 after an estimated loss of up to 500,000 tonnes.

The worst single assault ever made upon the ecosystem was released on 19 Jan 1991 by the Iraqi President Saddam Hussein, who ordered the pumping of Gulf crude from the Sea Island terminal, Kuwait, and from seven large tankers. Provisional estimates put the loss at 816,000 tonnes.

British Isles The worst spill in British waters was from the 118,285 dwt *Torrey Canyon* which struck the Pollard Rock off Land's End on 18 Mar 1967, resulting in the loss of up to 120,000 tonnes of oil.

Oil tanks The largest oil tanks ever constructed are the five Aramco 1½-million-barrel storage tanks at Ju'aymah, Saudi Arabia. They are 21.94 m *72 ft* tall with a diameter of 117.6 m *386 ft* and were completed in March 1980.

Oil gusher The greatest wildcat ever recorded blew at Alborz No.5 well, near Qum, Iran on 26 Aug 1956. The uncontrolled oil gushed to a height of 52 m *170 ft* at 120,000 b/d at a pressure of 62,055 kPa *9000 lb/in²*. It was closed after 90 days' work by B. Mostofi and Myron Kinley of Texas, USA.

Natural Gas

Production The world's largest producer of natural gas was the former USSR with 811,565 million m³ in 1991, followed by the USA (526,356 million m³ *18,588,088 million ft³*). The UK produced 55,331 million m³ *1,953,996 million ft³*. The USA was the highest consumer, with 523,454 million m³ *18,485,605 million ft³* (33.4 percent residential and 66.6 percent non-residential).

Deposits The largest gas deposit in the world is at Urengoi, Russia, with an eventual production of 200,000 million m³ *261,600 million yd³* per year through six pipelines from proved reserves of 7,000,000 million m³ *9,155,600 million yd³*. The trillionth (10^{12}) cubic metre was produced on 23 Apr 1986.

Water wells The world's deepest water bore is the Stensvad Water Well 11-W1 of 2231 m *7320 ft* drilled by the Great Northern Drilling Co. Inc. in Rosebud County, Montana, USA in October–November 1961. The Thermal Power Co. geothermal steam well begun in Sonoma County, California, USA in 1955 is down to 2752 m *9029 ft*.

UK The deepest well in Great Britain is a water-table well 866 m *2842 ft* deep in the Staffordshire coal at Smestow, near Wolverhampton, W Mids.

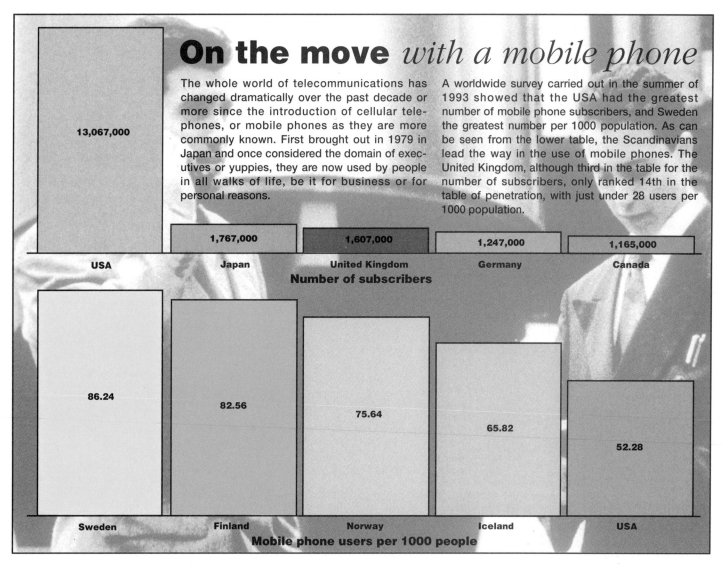

On the move *with a mobile phone*

The whole world of telecommunications has changed dramatically over the past decade or more since the introduction of cellular telephones, or mobile phones as they are more commonly known. First brought out in 1979 in Japan and once considered the domain of executives or yuppies, they are now used by people in all walks of life, be it for business or for personal reasons.

A worldwide survey carried out in the summer of 1993 showed that the USA had the greatest number of mobile phone subscribers, and Sweden the greatest number per 1000 population. As can be seen from the lower table, the Scandinavians lead the way in the use of mobile phones. The United Kingdom, although third in the table for the number of subscribers, only ranked 14th in the table of penetration, with just under 28 users per 1000 population.

Number of subscribers

USA	Japan	United Kingdom	Germany	Canada
13,067,000	1,767,000	1,607,000	1,247,000	1,165,000

Mobile phone users per 1000 people

Sweden	Finland	Norway	Iceland	USA
86.24	82.56	75.64	65.82	52.28

Telephones and Facsimiles

Telephones It has been estimated by the International Telecommunication Union that there were approximately 575 million telephone subscribers in the world by the end of 1992. The country with the greatest number was the United States, with 144,056,700. This compares with the United Kingdom figure of 26,084,000 (March 1993), or 450 per 1000 people. Monaco has the most per head of population, with 1004 per 1000. The greatest number of calls made in any country is in the United States, with 502.85 billion per annum.

Busiest routes The busiest international telephone route is between the USA and Canada. In 1992 there were some 3.7 billion minutes of two-way traffic between the two countries. The country with which Britain has most telephone contact is also the USA, with 1.2 billion minutes of two-way traffic in 1992.

Longest telephone cable The world's longest submarine telephone cable is ANZCAN, which runs for 15,151 km *9415 miles* (8181 nautical miles) from Port Alberni, Canada to Auckland, New Zealand and Sydney, Australia via Fiji and Norfolk Island. It cost some US$379 million and was inaugurated by HM Queen Elizabeth II in November 1984.

Largest and smallest telephones The world's largest operational telephone was exhibited at a festival on 16 Sep 1988 to celebrate the 80th birthday of Centraal Beheer, an insurance company based in Apeldoorn, Netherlands. It was 2.47 m *8ft 1in* high and 6.06 m *19ft 11in* long, and weighed 3.5 tonnes. The handset, being 7.14 m *23ft 5in* long, had to be lifted by crane in order to make a call.

The smallest operational telephone was created by Zbigniew Rózanek of Pleszew, Poland in September 1992. It measured just 6.7 × 1.9 × 2.8 cm *2⅝ × ¾ × 1⅛ in.*

> The first plastic telephone cards issued were those in Rome in January 1976. The highest price paid for a phone card is believed to be for the first card issued in Japan, which changed hands in January 1992 for £28,000.

Busiest telephone exchange GPT (GEC Plessey Telecommunications Ltd) demonstrated the ability of the 'System X' telephone exchange to handle 1,558,000 calls in an hour through one exchange at Beeston, Nottingham on 27 Jun 1989.

Largest switchboard The world's biggest switchboard is that in the Pentagon, Washington, DC, USA, with 34,500 lines handling nearly 1 million calls per day through 322,000 km *200,000 miles* of telephone cable.

Largest and smallest fax machines The largest facsimile machine is manufactured by WideCom Group Inc of Ontario, Canada. 'WIDEfax 36' is able to transmit, print and copy documents up to 91 cm *36 in* in width.

The smallest is the Real Time Strategies Inc. hand-held device Pagentry, which combines various functions including the transmission of messages to facsimile machines. It measures just 7.6 × 12.7 × 1.9 cm *3 × 5 × ¾ in* and weighs 141.75 g *5 oz.*

Optical fibre The longest distance at which signals have been transmitted without repeaters is 251.6 km *156.3 miles* at BT Laboratories at Martlesham Heath, Suffolk in February 1985. The laser wavelength was 1525 nm and the rate was 35 megabits/sec. The longest unspliced ducted optical fibre link, with a capacity of 8000 telephone lines, was installed by BT in February 1991. The optical fibres, made by Optical Fibres of Deeside, are 13.6 km *8.45 miles* long and link Gloucester and Painswick exchanges.

Morse code The highest recorded speed at which anyone has received Morse code is 75.2 words per minute. This was achieved by Ted R. McElroy of the USA in a tournament at Asheville, North Carolina, USA on 2 Jul 1939.

The highest speed recorded for hand key transmitting is 175 symbols a minute (equivalent to 35 wpm) by Harry A. Turner of the US Army Signal Corps at Camp Crowder, Missouri, USA on 9 Nov 1942.

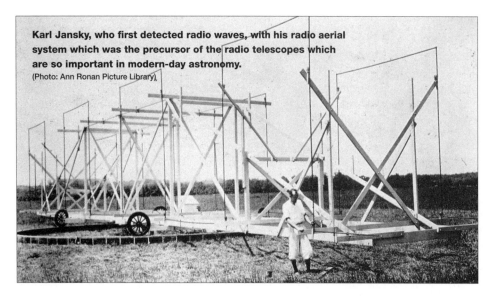

Karl Jansky, who first detected radio waves, with his radio aerial system which was the precursor of the radio telescopes which are so important in modern-day astronomy.
(Photo: Ann Ronan Picture Library)

Thomas Morris, a GPO operator, is reputed to have been able to send at 39–40wpm *c.* 1919, but this has not been verifiable.

Telescopes

Earliest In October 1608 three Dutch spectacle-makers stated that they had each invented a telescope and actually produced refracting telescopes. Credit is usually given to one of these, Hans Lippershey (*c.* 1570–1619), but Galileo (1564–1642) brought the invention to the notice of the scientific world, first constructing and using telescopes in 1609. However, recent examination of evidence for the claims by Thomas Digges (*c.* 1547–95) that his father Leonard Digges (*c.* 1520–59) had invented both a refractor and, it seems, a reflector as well, strongly indicates that a refractor at least existed in Elizabethan times. The first successful reflector to be made was that by Sir Isaac Newton (1642–1727), constructed in 1668 or 1669. He presented it, or a copy of it, to the Royal Society in 1671.

Largest telescope The Keck telescope on Mauna Kea, Hawaii, USA has a 1000cm *394in* mirror, made up of 36 segments fitted together to produce the correct curve. The first image of the spiral galaxy NGC1232 was obtained on 24 Nov 1990, when nine of the segments were in place. A twin Keck telescope is to be set up close to the first. When completed, Keck I and Keck II will be able to work together as an interferometer. Theoretically they would be able to see a car's headlights separately from a distance of 25,000km *15,500 miles.*

Largest reflector The largest single-mirror telescope now in use is the 6m *19ft 8in* reflector sited on Mount Semirodriki, near Zelenchukskaya in the Caucasus Mountains, Russia. It is at an alti-

tude of 2080m *6830ft* and was completed in 1976. It has never come up to expectations, partly because it is not set up on a really good observing site. The largest satisfactory single-mirror telescope is the 508cm *200in* Hale reflector at Mount Palomar, California, USA.

The largest British reflector is the 420cm *165in* William Herschel completed in 1987, which is set up at the Los Muchachos Observatory on La Palma, Canary Isles. Also at La Palma is the 256cm *101in* Isaac Newton telescope, transferred there from its old site at Herstmonceux in Sussex.

Metal-mirror A 183cm *72in* reflector was made by the third Earl of Rosse, and set up at Birr Castle, Republic of Ireland in 1845. The mirror was of speculum metal (an alloy of copper and tin). With it, Lord Rosse discovered the spiral forms of the galaxies. It was last used in 1909.

Largest planned The largest telescope of the century should be the VLT (Very Large Telescope) being planned by the European Southern Observatory. It will be at Paranal, northern Chile, and will consist of four 8m *26ft 3in* telescopes working together,

> Andy Perala, spokesman for the Keck Observatory, explained why the Keck telescope is so important, saying:– "If you hold your thumb at arm's length, the patch of sky your thumbnail hides holds 50,000 galaxies. There are billions out there".

providing a light-grasp equal to a single 16m *52ft 6in* mirror. It is hoped to have the first units working by 1995, and the complete telescope by 2000.

Infrared The largest infrared telescope is the UKIRT (United Kingdom Infrared Telescope) on Mauna Kea, Hawaii, USA, which has a 374cm *147 in* mirror. It is, however, so good that it can be used for visual work as well as infrared.

Southern The largest southern hemisphere telescope is the 401cm *157⅞in* reflector at Cerro Tololo in the Atacama Desert, northern Chile. The Anglo-Australian Telescope (AAT) at Siding Spring in New South Wales has a 389cm *153⅛in* mirror.

Sub-millimetre The James Clerk Maxwell telescope on Mauna Kea, Hawaii, USA has a 15m *49ft 3in* paraboloid primary, and is used for studies of the sub-millimetre part of the electromagnetic spectrum (0.3–1.0mm *0.01– 0.03in*). It does not produce a visual image.

Solar The McMath solar telescope at Kitt Peak, Arizona, USA has a 2.1m *6ft 11in* primary mirror; the light is sent to it via a 32° inclined tunnel from a coelostat (rotatable mirror) at the top end. Extensive modifications to it are now being planned.

Largest refractor An 18.9m *62ft* long 101.6cm *40in* refractor completed in 1897 is situated at the Yerkes Observatory, Williams Bay, Wisconsin, USA and belongs to the University of Chicago, Illinois. Although nearly 100 years old, it is still in full use on clear nights. A larger refractor measuring 150cm *59in* was built in France and shown at the Paris Exhibition in 1900. It was a failure and was never used for scientific work.

Britain's largest refractor is the 71.1cm *28in* Great Equatorial Telescope of 1893 installed in the Old Royal Observatory, Greenwich, southeast London.

Largest radio dish Radio waves from the Milky Way were first detected by Karl Jansky of Bell Telephone Laboratories, Holmdel, New Jersey, USA in 1931 when he was investigating 'static' with an improvised 30.5m *100ft* aerial. The only purpose-built radio telescope built before the outbreak of the war in 1939 was made by an amateur, Grote Reber, who detected radio emissions from the Sun. The diameter of the dish was 9.5m *31ft 2in.*

The pioneer large 'dish' was the 76m *250ft* telescope at Jodrell Bank, Cheshire, now known as

Radio astronomy is a young but important science, having really only developed since the war. The largest array is the VLA or Very Large Array radio telescope interferometer, which consists of 27 identical and movable radio antennae, some of which are visible in this photograph.
(Photo: Science Photo Library/R Ressmeyer, Starlight)

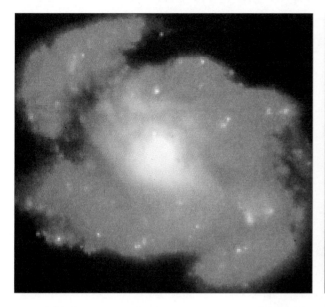

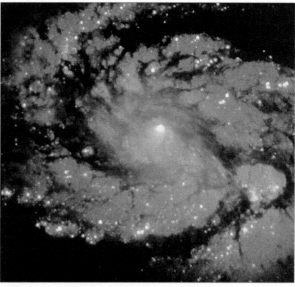

The Hubble Space Telescope is the largest space telescope. It proved necessary to carry out a servicing mission in December 1993, which fortunately proved to be highly successful, as can be seen from the before and after photographs of spiral galaxy M100.
(Photos: Science Photo Library/Space Telescope Science Inst./NASA)

the Lovell Telescope, completed in 1957. It is part of the MERLIN network, which includes other dishes in various parts of Britain.

The world's largest dish radio telescope is the partially-steerable ionospheric assembly built over a natural bowl at Arecibo, Puerto Rico, completed in November 1963. The dish has a diameter of 305m *1000ft* and covers 7.48ha *18½ acres*.

The world's largest fully-steerable dish is the 100m *328ft* diameter assembly at the Max Planck Institute for Radio Astronomy of Bonn in the Effelsberger Valley, Germany. It was completed in 1971 and weighs 3048tonnes.

Largest radio installation The largest radio installation is the Australia Telescope which includes dishes at Parkes (64m *210ft* in diameter), Siding Spring (22m *72ft*) and Culgoora (also 22m *72ft*). There are also links with tracking stations at Usuada and Kashima, Japan, and with the TDRS (Tracking and Data Relay Satellite), which is in a geosynchronous orbit. This is equivalent to a radio telescope with an effective diameter of 2.16 Earth diameters, or 27,523km *17,102 miles*.

The VLA (Very Large Array) of the US National Science Foundation is Y-shaped, with each arm 20.9km *13 miles* long and with 27 mobile antennae (each of 25m *82ft* diameter) on rails. It is 80km *50 miles* west of Socorro in the Plains of San Augustin, New Mexico, USA and was completed on 10 Oct 1980.

Largest Schmidt telescope A Schmidt telescope uses a spherical mirror with a correcting plate and can cover a very wide field with a single exposure. It is consequently invaluable in astronomy. The largest is the 2m *6ft 6¾in* instrument at the Karl Schwarzschild Observatory at Tautenberg, Germany. It has a clear aperture of 134cm *52¾in* with a 200cm *78¾in* mirror and a focal length of 4m *13ft*. It was brought into use in 1960.

Space telescope *Largest* The largest is the $2.1billion (£1.4billion) NASA Edwin P. Hubble Space Telescope of 11tonnes and 13.1m *43ft* in overall length, with a 240cm *94½in* reflector. It was placed in orbit at 613km *381miles* altitude aboard a US space shuttle on 24 April 1990.

Planeraria The ancestor of the modern planetarium is the rotatable Gottorp Globe, built by Andreas Busch in Denmark about 1660. It was 10.54m *34ft 7in* in circumference, weighed nearly 3½tonnes and is now preserved in St Petersburg, Russia. The stars were painted on the inside. The first modern planetarium was opened in 1923 at Jena, Germany; it was designed by Walther Bauersfelt of the Carl Zeiss company.

Observatory *Oldest* The oldest building extant is the 'Tower of the Winds', used by Andronichus of Cyrrhus in Athens, Greece *c.*100BC and equipped with sundials and clepsydras (water clocks).

Highest The high-altitude observatory at Denver, Colorado, USA is at 4300m *14,100ft* and was opened in 1973. The main instrument is a 61cm *24in* reflector. It is slightly higher than the observatory at the summit of Mauna Kea, in Hawaii at 4194m *13,760ft*.

Lowest The lowest 'observatory' is at Homestake Mine, South Dakota, USA, where the 'Telescope' is a tank of cleaning fluid (perchloroethylene), which contains chlorine, and can trap neutrinos from the Sun. The installation is 1.7km *1.1miles* below ground level, in the shaft of a gold-mine.

Rocketry

Earliest uses War 'flying fireworks', propelled by gunpowder (charcoal-saltpetre-sulfur), were described by Zeng Gongliang of China in 1042. War rockets originated in 1245 near Hangzhou, China.

The pioneer of military rocketry in Britain was Col. Sir William Congreve (1772–1828), Comptroller of the Royal Laboratory, Woolwich, London and Inspector of Military Machines. His 6lb rocket' was developed to a range of 1800m *2000yd* by 1805 and first used by the Royal Navy against Boulogne, France on 8 Oct 1806.

The first launch of a liquid-fuelled rocket (patented 14 Jul 1914) was by Dr Robert Hutchings Goddard (1882–1945) of the USA, at Auburn, Massachusetts, USA on 16 Mar 1926, when his rocket reached an altitude of 12.5m *41ft* and travelled a distance of 56m *184ft*.

The earliest Soviet rocket was the semi-liquid-fuelled GIRD–R1 (object 09), begun in 1931 and tested on 17 Aug 1933. Their first fully liquid-fuelled rocket, GIRD–X, was launched on 25 Nov 1933.

Highest velocity The first space vehicle to achieve the Third Cosmic velocity sufficient to break out of the Solar System was *Pioneer 10*. The Atlas SLV–3C launcher with a modified Centaur D second stage and a Thiokol TE–364–4 third stage left the Earth at an unprecedented 51,682km/h *32,114mph* on 3 Mar 1972.

However, the fastest escape velocity from Earth was 54,614km/h *34,134mph*, achieved by the ESA *Ulysses* spacecraft, powered by an IUS–PAM upper stage after deployment from the Space Shuttle *Discovery* on 7 Oct 1990, en route on orbit around the poles of the Sun via a fly-by of Jupiter.

Mariner 10 reached a recorded speed of 211,126km/h *131,954mph* as it passed Mercury in September 1974, but the highest speed of approximately 252,800km/h *158,000mph* is recorded by the NASA–German *Helios A* and *B* solar probes each time they reach the perihelion of their solar orbits (⇨ Closest approach to the Sun by a rocket).

Most powerful rocket The NI booster of the former USSR (also known as the G–1 in the west), first launched from the Baikonur Cosmodrome at Tyuratam, Kazakhstan on 21 Feb 1969, had a thrust of 4620 tonnes, but exploded at takeoff + 70 secs. Three other launch attempts also failed.

Rocket engine The most powerful rocket engine was built in the former USSR by the Scientific Industrial Corporation of Power Engineering in 1980. The RD–170 has a thrust of 806tonnes in open space and 740tonnes at the Earth's surface. It also has a turbopump rated at 190MW, and burns liquid oxygen and kerosene. The RD–170 powered the four strap-on boosters of the *Energiya* booster, launched in 1987 but now grounded by budget cuts.

Closest approach to the Sun by a rocket The research spacecraft *Helios B* approached within 43.5 million km *27 million miles* of the Sun, carrying both US and West German instrumentation, on 16 Apr 1976 (⇨ Highest velocity).

Remotest man-made object *Pioneer 10*, launched from Cape Canaveral, Florida, USA, crossed the mean orbit of Pluto on 17 Oct 1986, being then at a distance of 5.91 billion km *3.67 billion miles*. In AD 34,593 it will make its nearest approach to the star Ross 248, 10.3 light years distant. *Voyager 1*, travelling faster, will have surpassed *Pioneer 10* in remoteness from the Earth by the end of the century. *Pioneer 11* and *Voyager 2* are also leaving the solar system.

Progressive Rocket Altitude Records

Height		Rocket	Place	Launch Date
Miles	Km			
0.71	1.14	A 7.62 cm 3in rocket	Hackney, London, England	April 1750
1.25	2	Reinhold Tiling[1] (Germany) solid fuel rocket	Osnabrück, Germany	April 1931
1.9	3.1	'07' with liquid fuel engine '02' (USSR)	Nakhabino, Moscow region,USSR (now Russia)	16 Jul 1935
52.46	84.42	A4 rocket (Germany)[2]	Peenemünde, Germany	3 Oct 1942
c.85	c.136	A4 rocket (Germany)	Heidelager, Poland	early 1944
118	190	A4 rocket (Germany)	Heidelager, Poland	mid 1944
244	393	V2/WAC Corporal (2-stage) Bumper No. 5 (USA)	White Sands, New Mexico, USA[3]	24 Feb 1949
682	1097	Jupiter C (USA)	Cape Canaveral, Florida, USA	20 Sep 1956
>800	>1300	ICBM test flight R-7 (USSR)	Tyuratam, USSR (now Kazakhstan)	21 Aug 1957
>2700	>4345	Farside No. 5 (4-stage) (USA)	Eniwetok Atoll	20 Oct 1957
70,700	113,770	Pioneer 1-B Lunar Probe (USA)	Cape Canaveral, Florida, USA	11 Oct 1958
215,300,000*	346,480,000	Luna 1 or Mechtá (USSR)	Tyuratam, USSR (now Kazakhstan)	2 Jan 1959
242,000,000*	389,450,000	Mars 1 (USSR)	Tyuratam, USSR (now Kazakhstan)	1 Nov 1962
3,666,000,000[4]	5,900,000,000	Pioneer 10 (USA)	Cape Canaveral, Florida, USA	2 Mar 1972

*Apogee in solar orbit.

[1] There is some evidence that Tiling may shortly afterwards have reached 9.5 km 5.9 miles with a solid-fuel rocket at Wangerooge, East Friesian Islands, Germany.
[2] The A4 was latterly referred to as the V2 rocket, an acronym for second revenge weapon (Vergeltungswaffe) following upon the V1 'flying bomb'.
[3] The V2/WAC height may have been exceeded during the period 1950–6 to the time of the Jupiter C flight, as the Soviets reported in 1954 that a rocket had reached 386 km 240 miles at an unspecified date.
[4] Distance on crossing Pluto's orbit on 17 Oct 1986. Pioneer 11, Voyager 1 and Voyager 2 are also leaving the solar system.

On the Moon!

Lunar records The first direct hit on the Moon was achieved at 2 min 24 sec after midnight (Moscow time) on 14 Sep 1959, by the Soviet space probe *Lunar II* near the Mare Serenitatis. The first photographic images of the hidden side of the Moon were collected by the Soviet *Lunar III* from 6:30 a.m. on 7 Oct 1959 from a range of up to 70,400 km 43,750 miles, and transmitted to the Earth from a distance of 470,000 km 292,000 miles.

Space Flight

The physical laws controlling the flight of artificial satellites were first propounded by Sir Isaac Newton (1642–1727) in his *Philosophiae Naturalis Principia Mathematica* ('Mathematical Principles of Natural Philosophy'), begun in March 1686 and first published in July 1687.

The first artificial satellite was successfully put into orbit by an inter-continental ballistic missile from the Baikonur Cosmodrome at Tyuratam, Kazakhstan, 275 km 170 miles east of the Aral Sea and 250 km 155 miles south of the town of Baikonur, on the night of 4 Oct 1957. It reached an altitude of between 228.5 km (perigee or nearest point to Earth) and 946 km (apogee or furthest point from Earth) 142 miles and 588 miles, and a velocity of more than 28,565 km/h 17,750 mph. This spherical satellite *Sputnik 1* ('Fellow Traveller'), officially designated 'Satellite 1957 Alpha 2', weighed 83.6 kg 184.3 lb, with a diameter of 58 cm 22¾ in. Its lifetime is believed to have been 92 days, ending on 4 Jan 1958.

Helen Sharman, the first Briton in space, with Musa Manarov, one of the two cosmonauts who hold the space flight duration record, during her flight in May 1991. We think the picture's the right way up!
(Photo: NASA)

The 29.17 m 95 ft 8 in tall SL–1 launcher was designed under the direction of former Gulag prisoner Dr Sergey Pavlovich Korolyov (1907–66).

Earliest manned satellite The earliest manned space flight ratified by the world governing body, the Fédération Aéronautique Internationale (FAI, founded 1905), was by Cosmonaut Flight Major (later Col.) Yuri Alekseyevich Gagarin (1934–68) in *Vostok 1* on 12 Apr 1961. The take-off was from the Baikonur Cosmodrome, Kazakhstan at 6:07 a.m. GMT and the landing near Smelovka, near Engels, in the Saratov region of Russia, 115 minutes later. Col. Gagarin landed separately from his spacecraft 118 minutes after the launch, by parachute after ejecting 108 minutes into the flight as planned.

The maximum altitude during the 40,868.6 km 25,394½ mile flight of *Vostok 1* was listed at 327 km 203 miles, with a maximum speed of 28,260 km/h 17,560 mph. Col. Gagarin, invested a Hero of the Soviet Union and awarded the Order of Lenin and the Gold Star Medal, was killed in a jet plane crash near Moscow on 27 Mar 1968.

There had been 169 manned spaceflights to 18 Apr 1994, of which 92 were American and 77 Soviet or former Soviet Union, including 5 Russian.

First woman in space The first woman to orbit the Earth was Junior Lt (now Lt-Col. Eng.) Valentina Vladimirovna Tereshkova (b. 6 Mar 1937). She was launched in *Vostok 6* from the Baikonur Cosmodrome, Kazakhstan at 9:30 a.m. GMT on 16 Jun 1963. *Vostok 6* landed at 8:20 a.m. on 19 June, after a flight of 2 days 22 hr 50 min and 48 orbits (1,971,000 km 1,225,000 miles). It passed momentarily to within 5 km 3 miles of *Vostok 5*. Like Gagarin, Tereshkova ejected, after 2 days 22 hr 40 min and landed six minutes later. As at 18 Apr 1994 a total of 24 women had flown into space—20 Americans, two Soviets, one from the UK (⇔ below) and one Canadian—out of the total of 307 people who have been into space.

First Briton in space Helen Sharman (b. 30 May 1963) became the first Briton in space, in *Soyuz TM12* on 18 May 1991. She was the 15th woman in space, and the first non-Soviet, non-US woman. Britain became the 21st 'space nation' as a result.

Astronaut *Oldest* The oldest astronaut of the 307 people in space (to 18 Apr 1994) was Vance DeVoe Brand (USA) (b. 9 May 1931), aged 59, on 2 Dec 1990 while on the space shuttle mission aboard the STS 35 *Columbia*. The oldest woman was Shannon Lucid (USA), aged 50 years, on space shuttle mission STS 58 *Columbia* in

The Russian space station *Mir* was the home for Vladimir Titov and Musa Manarov during their year-long space flight.
(Photo: Science Photo Library/Novosti Press Agency)

October 1993. She is also the first woman to make four spaceflights.

Youngest The youngest has been Major (later Lt-Gen.) Gherman Stepanovich Titov (b. 11 Sep 1935), who was aged 25 years 329 days when launched in *Vostok 2* on 6 Aug 1961. The youngest woman in space was Valentina Tereshkova, who was 26 (⇨ First woman in space).

Longest and shortest manned space flight
The longest manned flight was by Col. Vladimir Georgeyevich Titov (b. 1 Jan 1947) and Flight Engineer Musa Khiramanovich Manarov (b. 22 Mar 1951), who were launched to the *Mir* space station aboard *Soyuz TM4* on 21 Dec 1987 and landed, in *Soyuz TM6* (with French cosmonaut Jean-Loup Chretien), at a secondary recovery site near Dzhezkazgan, Kazakhstan on 21 Dec 1988, after a space flight lasting 365 days 22hr 39min 47sec. This will be exceeded on 9 Jan 1995 by Dr Valeriy Poliyakov (⇨ below), who was launched to *Mir* on 8 Jan 1994 and who is scheduled to make a flight of about 430 days. The shortest manned flight was made by Cdr Alan Bartlett Shepard (b. 18 Nov 1923), USN aboard *Mercury Redstone 3* on 5 May 1961. His sub-orbital mission lasted 15min 28sec.

Although not spaceflights, the space shuttle *Challenger* flew for 73sec before being destroyed on 28 Jan 1986, while the launch escape system of *Soyuz T10A* took Vladimir Titov and Gennady Strekalov on a 17g ride lasting 5min 30sec after the *Soyuz* booster caught fire and eventually exploded before lift-off on 27 Sep 1983.

The most experienced space traveller is the Soviet (now Azerbaijani) flight engineer Musa Manarov who has clocked up 541 days 31min 10sec on two spaceflights in 1987–8 and 1990–1. This will be exceeded on about 4 Nov 1994 by Dr Valeriy Poliyakov (⇨ above), who has 240 days space experience from a previous flight in 1988–9.

The longest US manned spaceflight, 84 days 1hr 15min 31sec, was completed by *Skylab 4* astronauts Gerry Carr, Edward Gibson and Bill Pogue, in 1973–4. They are the most experienced US astronauts. The most experienced space shuttle flier is Story Musgrave, with 35days 18hr 5min on five flights.

Most journeys Capt. John Watts Young (b. 24 Sep 1930) (USN ret.) completed his sixth space flight on 8 Dec 1983, when he relinquished command of *Columbia* STS9/Spacelab after a space career of 34 days 19hr 41min 53sec. Young flew *Gemini 3, Gemini 10, Apollo 10, Apollo 16*, STS 1 and STS 9. The greatest number of flights by a Soviet cosmonaut is five by Vladimir Dzhanibekov (between 1978 and 1985). The most by a woman is four, by Shannon Lucid (STS 51G, 34, 43 and 58). Lucid is also the woman with most space experience, at 34 days 22hr 52min.

Largest crew The most crew on a single space mission is eight. This included one female and was launched on space shuttle STS 61A *Challenger* on 30 Oct 1985, carrying the West German Spacelab D1 laboratory. The flight (the 22nd shuttle mission) was commanded by Henry Warren 'Hank' Hartsfield and lasted 7days 44min 51sec. The most women in a space crew is three (of seven) during STS 40 *Columbia* in June 1991.

Most in space The greatest number of people in space at any one time has been 12, on three occasions. Seven Americans were aboard the space shuttle STS 35 *Columbia*, two Soviet cosmonauts aboard the *Mir* space station, and two cosmonauts and a Japanese journalist aboard *Soyuz TM11* on 2 Dec 1990. On 23–24 Mar 1992 six Americans and one Belgian were on space shuttle *Atlantis*, two cosmonauts from the Commonwealth of Independent States (CIS) on *Mir* and two CIS cosmonauts and a German on *Soyuz TM14*, and most recently on 31 Jul 1992 four CIS cosmonauts and one Frenchman were aboard *Mir* at the same time as five US astronauts, one Swiss and one Italian were on STS46 *Atlantis*.

A record five countries had astronauts or cosmonauts in space at the same time on 31 Jul 1992—CIS, France, Italy, Switzerland and USA (⇨ above).

Lunar conquest Neil Alden Armstrong (b. Wapakoneta, Ohio, USA of Scottish [via Ireland] and German ancestry, on 5 Aug 1930), command pilot of the *Apollo 11* mission, became the first man to set foot on the Moon, on the Sea of Tranquillity, at 02:56 and 15sec GMT on 21 Jul 1969. He was followed out of the lunar module *Eagle* by Col. Edwin Eugene 'Buzz' Aldrin, Jr, USAF (b. Montclair, New Jersey, USA of Swedish, Dutch and British ancestry, on 20 Jan 1930), while the command module *Columbia* piloted by Lt-Col. Michael Collins, USAF (b. Rome, Italy, of Irish and pre-Revolutionary American ancestry, on 31 Oct 1930) orbited above.

Eagle landed at 20:17 and 42sec GMT on 20 July and lifted off at 17:54 GMT on 21 July, after a stay of 21hr 36min. *Apollo 11* had blasted off from Cape Canaveral, Florida, USA at 13:32 GMT on 16 July and was a culmination of the US space programme which at its peak employed 376,600 people and in 1966–7 attained a record budget of $5.9 billion.

There were six lunar landings altogether, and twelve people made a total of 14 EVAs on the moon totalling 79hr 35min between July 1969 and December 1972.

ON THE RECORD

" At the age of 5, Shannon Lucid decided to become a pilot. She dreamed of exploring space before the word astronaut existed in the English language. Nowadays her dream is a trip to Mars. NASA has tested Lucid (along with other astronauts) to gauge the effect of long-term space travel on the human body. If her dream is realized, Lucid would have just one regret: "My two weeks in space was the longest time of my entire life without a book to read. Now that's a record!"

"There's no limit to the length of time I could spend in space," says Lucid. But space does take some getting used to. "It's never routine." Lucid can feel her heart calming while she's in orbit — and feels the strain it goes through getting up to normal rate back on the ground. "I couldn't go for a hike up a mountain right after returning to Earth," she says. "I'd really feel it. Also, in space body-fluid redistributes throughout the body. It doesn't bother me." She explains, "My face gets fuller, but my legs and waist get smaller." She laughs: "Some people have the kind of figure that looks better in space." "

Shannon Lucid (USA), who with four space flights has been on more than any other woman.
(Photo: NASA)

Astronauts Eugene Cernan and Harrison Schmitt of *Apollo 17* hold the record for the longest time spent on the Moon. The two photographs show Harrison Schmitt next to the US flag at the landing site and by a huge boulder—he was a professional geologist.
(Photos: Science Photo Library/NASA)

Suits for extra-vehicular activity worn by Space Shuttle crews from 1982 cost $3.4 million each—you could probably buy more than 15,000 suits on Earth for the cost of one spacesuit.

1935), who became the 12th man on the Moon. The crew were on the lunar surface for 74 hr 59 min during this longest of lunar missions, which took 12 days 13 hr 51 min on 7–19 Dec 1972.

Spacewalks Lt-Col. (now Maj. Gen.) Aleksey Arkhipovich Leonov (b. 20 May 1934) from *Voskhod 2* was the first person to engage in EVA 'extra-vehicular activity', on 18 Mar 1965. Capt. Bruce McCandless II, USN (b. 8 Jun 1937), from the space shuttle *Challenger*, was the first to engage in untethered EVA, at an altitude of 264 km *164 miles* above Hawaii, on 7 Feb 1984. His MMU (Manned Manoeuvering Unit) back-pack cost $15 million to develop. There had been 115 spacewalks to 18 Apr 1994, involving 87 people.

The first woman to perform an EVA was Svetlana Savitskaya (b. 8 Aug 1948) from *Soyuz T12/ Salyut 7* on 25 Jul 1984. The greatest number of space-walks is ten, by Russian cosmonaut Aleksandr Serebrov (b. 15 Feb 1944) during two missions in 1990 and 1993.

The longest spacewalk ever undertaken was one of 8 hr 29 min, by Pierre Thuot, Rick Hieb and Tom Akers of STS 49 *Endeavour* on 13 May 1992. Anatoly Solovyov and Aleksandr Balandin of *Soyuz TM9* made a 7 hr 16 min EVA outside the Mir space station on 1 Jul 1990, which was the longest by Soviet cosmonauts. The longest spacewalk by a woman lasted 7 hr 49 min and was made by Kathryn Thornton (USA) of STS 49 *Endeavour* on 14 May 1992.

Space fatalities The greatest published number to perish in any of the 170 attempted manned space flights to 18 Apr 1994 is seven (five men and two women) aboard the *Challenger* 51L on 28 Jan 1986, when an explosion occurred 73 sec after lift-off from the Kennedy Space Centre, Florida, at a height of 14,020 m *46,000 ft. Challenger* broke apart under extreme aerodynamic overpressure. Four people, all Soviet, have been killed during actual space-flight—Vladimir Komarov of *Soyuz 1* which crashed on landing on 24 Apr 1967, and the un-spacesuited Georgi Dobrovolsky, Viktor Patsayev and Vladislav Volkov who died when their *Soyuz 11* spacecraft depressurized during the re-entry on 29 Jun 1971.

First extra-terrestrial vehicle The first wheeled vehicle landed on the Moon was the unmanned *Lunokhod 1* which began its Earth-controlled travels on 17 Nov 1970. It moved a total of 10.54 km *6.54 miles* on gradients up to 30° in the Mare Imbrium and did not become non-functioning until 4 Oct 1971.

The lunar speed and distance record was set by the manned *Apollo 16* Rover, driven by John Young, with 18 km/h *11.2 mph* downhill and 33.8 km *22.4 miles*.

Heaviest and largest space objects The heaviest object orbited is the Saturn V third stage with *Apollo 15* (spacecraft), which, prior to trans-lunar injection into parking orbit on 26 Jul 1971, weighed 140.53 tonnes. The 200 kg *440 lb* US RAE (Radio Astronomy Explorer) B, or *Explorer 49*, launched on 10 Jun 1973, was larger, with antennae 450 m *1500 ft* from tip to tip.

Most expensive projects The total cost of the US manned space programme by the spring of 1994 is estimated to have exceeded $80 billion. The cost of the NASA shuttle programme has been more than $45 billion.

Altitude The greatest altitude attained by man was when the crew of the *Apollo 13* were at apocynthion (i.e. their furthest point) 254 km *158 miles* from the lunar surface, and 400,171 km *248,655 miles* above the Earth's surface, at 1:21 a.m. BST on 15 Apr 1970. The crew were Capt. James Arthur Lovell, Jr, USN (b. 25 Mar 1928), Fred Wallace Haise, Jr (b. 14 Nov 1933) and John L. Swigert (1931–82).

The greatest altitude attained by a woman is 600 km *375 miles*, by Kathryn Thornton (USA) (b. 17 Aug 1952) after an orbital engine burn on 10 Dec 1993 during the space shuttle STS 61 *Endeavour* mission.

Speed The fastest speed at which humans have travelled is 39,897 km/h *24,791 mph*. The command module of *Apollo 10*, carrying Col. (now Brig. Gen.) Thomas Patten Stafford, USAF (b. 17 Sep 1930), Cdr (now Capt.) Eugene Andrew Cernan (b. 14 Mar 1934) and Cdr (now Capt.) John Watts Young, USN (b. 24 Sep 1930), reached this maximum value at the 121.9 km *75.7 mile* altitude interface on its trans-Earth return flight on 26 May 1969.

The highest speed recorded by a woman is 28,582 km/h *17,864 mph*, by Kathryn Sullivan at the start of re-entry at the end of the STS 31 *Discovery* shuttle mission on 29 Apr 1990, although this may have been exceeded by Kathryn Thornton at the end of the STS 61 *Endeavour* mission on 13 Dec 1993. The highest recorded by a Soviet space traveller was 28,115 km/h *17,470 mph*, by Valentina Tereshkova of the USSR (⇨ First woman in space) in *Vostok 6* on 19 Jun 1963. However, because orbital injection of Soyuz spacecraft occurs at marginally lower altitude, it is probable that Tereshkova's speed was exceeded twice by Svetlana Savitskaya aboard *Soyuz T7* and *Soyuz T12* on 27 Aug 1982 and 28 Jul 1984, and also by Helen Sharman aboard *Soyuz TM12* on 18 May 1991.

Thomas Stafford, Eugene Cernan and John Young were travelling at an incredible 11.08 km/sec *6.88 miles/sec* when they set the all-time speed record.

Duration record on the Moon The crew of *Apollo 17* collected a record 114.8 kg *253 lb* of rock and soil during their three EVAs of 22 hr 5 min. They were Capt. Eugene Cernan (⇨ Speed) and Dr Harrison Hagen 'Jack' Schmitt (b. 3 Jul

Buildings&Structures

Origins

The remains of a stone tower 6m *20ft* high originally built into the walls of Jericho have been excavated and are dated to 5000BC. The foundations of the walls themselves have been dated to as early as 8350BC.

Earliest!

The earliest known human structure is a rough circle of loosely piled lava blocks found on the lowest cultural level at the Lower Palaeolithic site at Olduvai Gorge, Tanzania, and revealed by Dr Mary Leakey in January 1960. The structure was associated with artifacts and bones on a work-floor, dating from c. 1,750,000BC.

The earliest known evidence of a habitational structure is that of 21 huts with hearths or pebble-lined pits and delimited by stake-holes found in October 1965 at the Terra Amata site in Nice, France and thought to belong to the Acheulian culture of c. 400,000 years ago. Excavation in 1966 revealed one hut with palisaded walls with axes of 15 m *49ft* and 6 m *20ft*.

The oldest free-standing structures in the world are now believed to be the megalithic temples at Mgarr and Skorba in Malta. With those at Ggantija in Gozo, they date from c. 3250BC, some 3½ centuries earlier than the earliest Egyptian pyramid. (⇨ Specialized structures)

UK Twelve small stone clusters, associated with broken bones and charcoal in stratum C of the early Palaeolithic site at Hoxne, near Eye, Suffolk may be regarded as Britain's earliest structural remains, dated c. 250,000BC.

Remains of the earliest dated stone habitation structures and cooking pits were discovered at Culverwell, Isle of Portland, Dorset. They date to 5200 ±135BC and belong to the pre-Neolithic and Mesolithic period.

Wooden structures The world's oldest extant wooden buildings comprise the Pagoda, Chumanar Gate and Temple of Horyu (Horyu-ji) at Nara, Japan, dating from c. AD670 and completed in 715.

What is believed to be the oldest complete wooden building in England, a burial chamber of the Neolithic period c. 3000 BC measuring 8×2m *26×6½ft*, was discovered in December 1986 in the Fenlands, Cambridgeshire.

Buildings for Living

Habitations

Northernmost The Danish scientific station set up in 1952 in Pearyland, northern Greenland is over 1450km *900miles* north of the Arctic Circle and is manned every summer.

The most northerly continuously inhabited place is the Canadian Department of National Defence outpost at Alert on Ellesmere Island, Northwest Territories (Lat. 82°30′N, Long. 62°W), set up in 1950.

Southernmost The most southerly permanent human habitation is the United States' Amundsen – Scott South Polar Station, completed in 1957 and replaced in 1975.

GUESS WHAT?

Q where was the world's first shopping centre?

A See Page 93

Highest!

The highest inhabited buildings in the world are those in the Indo-Tibetan border fort of Bāsisi by the Māna Pass (Lat. 31°04′N, Long. 79°24′E) at c. 5990 m *19,700ft*.

In April 1961, a three-room dwelling believed to date from the late pre-Columbian period c. 1480 was discovered at 6600 m *21,650ft* on Cerro Llullaillaco (6723 m *22,057ft*), on the Argentine–Chile border.

Castles

Earliest The castle at Gomdan, Yemen dates from before AD100 and originally had 20 storeys.

Oldest The oldest stone castle in Great Britain is Chepstow Castle, Gwent, built c. 1067 on the west bank of the River Wye by William fitz Osbern.

Largest The largest ancient castle in the world is Hradčany Castle in Prague, Czech Republic, originating in the 9th century. It is an oblong-shaped irregular polygon with an axis of 570m *1870ft* and an average tranverse diameter of 128m *420ft*, giving a surface area of 7.28ha *18acres*.

The world's largest inhabited castle is the royal residence of Windsor Castle at Windsor, Berks. Originally of 12th century construction, it is in the form of a waisted parallelogram measuring 576×164m *1890×540ft*.

Largest moat From plans drawn by French sources it appears that the moats surrounding the Imperial Palace in Beijing, China are 49m *149.3 ft* wide and have a total length of 3290m *10,028 ft*. In all, the city's moats total 38 km *23½ miles*. (⇨ Palaces)

Forts Fort George in Ardersier, Highland, built in 1748–69, is 640m *2100ft* long and has an average width of 189m *620ft* on a site covering a total of 17.2ha *42½ acres*.

Sand castle The longest sand castle was 8.37km *5.2miles* long, made by staff and pupils of Ellon Academy, near Aberdeen, Grampian on 24 Mar 1988.

Palaces

Largest The Palace of Versailles, 23km *14 miles* south-west of Paris, is 580 m *1902ft* long and has a façade with 375 windows. The building, completed in 1682 for Louis XIV, occupied over 30,000 workmen under Jules Hardouin-Mansart (1646–1708).

Residential The palace (Istana Nurul Iman) of HM the Sultan of Brunei in the capital Bandar Seri Begawan was completed in January 1984 at a reported cost of £300 million. It is the largest residence in the world, with 1788 rooms and 257 lavatories. The underground garage accommodates the Sultan's 110 cars.

UK The largest-ever royal palace is Hampton Court, Greater London, acquired by Henry VIII from Cardinal Wolsey in 1525 and greatly enlarged by him and later by William III, Queen Anne and George I, whose son George II was its last resident monarch. It covers 1.6ha *4 acres* of a 271ha *669acre* site.

The largest palace in the United Kingdom in royal use is Buckingham Palace, London, so named after its site, bought in 1703 by John Sheffield, the 1st Duke of Buckingham and

The Temple of Mnadjra in Malta, one of the oldest free-standing structures in the world. (Photo: Spectrum Colour Library)

GUESS WHAT?

Q where can you fall 140 feet, turn upside-down seven times and survive?

A See Page 93

Largest!

The Imperial Palace (Gugong) in the centre of Beijing, China covers a rectangle measuring 960 × 750 m *3150 × 2460 ft* over an area of 72 ha *178 acres*. The outline survives from the construction of the third Ming Emperor, Yongle (1402–24), but due to constant reconstruction work most of the intra-mural buildings (five halls and 17 palaces) are from the 18th century.

Normanby (1648–1721). Buckingham House was reconstructed in the Palladian style between 1825 and 1836, following the design of John Nash (1752–1835). The 186-m *610-ft*-long East Front was built in 1846 and refaced in 1912. The Palace, which stands in 15.8ha *39 acres* of garden, has 600 rooms including a 34-m *111-ft* ballroom used for investitures.

Camping out The silent Indian *fakir* Mastram Bapu ('contented father') remained on the same spot by the roadside in the village of Chitra for 22 years, from 1960 through to 1982.

Housing

Earliest Eastry Court near Sandwich, Kent includes part of a Saxon building said to have been built in AD 603 by King Ethelbert, possibly as a palace. The present building is, however, in a much altered form.

Oldest inhabited Barton Manor in Pagham, W Sussex includes structures dating from Saxon times *c*. AD 800.

> **Most visited stately home**
> Warwick Castle near Stratford-on-Avon, Warks received 750,000 visitors in 1993. Built by the Beauchamp family, it dates from the 14th century.

England's oldest inhabited house is reputed to be Little Dean Hall, Forest of Dean, Glos, dating from AD 1080. A Roman temple was found in its grounds in 1982.

Largest residence The largest non-palatial residence is St Emmeram Castle in Regensburg, Germany. It has 517 rooms and a floor area of 21,460 m² *231,000 ft²*. It was owned by the late Prince Johannes von Thurn und Taxis, whose family use only 95 of the rooms. The castle is valued at more than 336 million DM (£122 million).

UK The main part of Wentworth Woodhouse, near Rotherham, S Yorks, built over 300 years ago, has more than 240 rooms and its principal façade is 183m *600ft* long. Formerly the seat of the Earls Fitzwilliam, the house is now privately owned by Wensley Haydon-Baillie.

The house with the most rooms is Knole, near Sevenoaks, Kent, believed to have had 365 rooms, one for each day of the year. Built around seven courtyards, its total depth from front to back is about 120m *400ft*. Building was begun in 1456 by Thomas Bourchier, Archbishop of Canterbury (1454–86), and the house was extended by Thomas Sackville, 1st Earl of Dorset, *c*. 1603–8. Knole is now administered by the National Trust. The royal residence of Sandringham House, Norfolk was reported to have had 365 rooms before the demolition of 73 surplus rooms in 1975.

The largest house in the Republic of Ireland is Castletown in Co. Kildare, owned and run by the Castletown Foundation, an independent charitable foundation set up by the Hon. Desmond Guinness.

Building began in 1722 and the house is approximately 121 m *400 ft* in length (including two wings) and has about 100 rooms.

Smallest house Britain's smallest house is the 19th-century fisherman's cottage at The Quay, Conwy, Gwynedd. Consisting of two tiny rooms and a staircase, it has a 182-cm *72-in* frontage, is 309 cm *122 in* high and measures 254 cm *100 in* from front to back.

THE GUINNESS TIMES   27th Sept 1993

Sand Castle Record Smashed

Higher than a two-storey house

A massive sand castle 21 feet 6 inches (6.56 metres) tall was built yesterday in Harrison Hot Springs on Canada's west coast, knocking 2 feet, or just over 60 centimetres, off the previous record.

Photo: Loretta MacMahon/Harrison Hot Springs

A team led by experienced sand sculptors Joe Maize, George Pennock and Ted Siebert spent 86½ man-hours meticulously constructing 'The Christmas Tree', as they called their work of art. It was made to look even more authentic by the addition of gifts.

The castle was made without any mechanical equipment— only the traditional tools of hands, buckets and shovels. Joe Maize had a particular problem, with a fear of heights, but he was still able to help as the sand castle neared completion. His obvious concern led one onlooker to suggest that the team should be named 'Jelly-legs Joe and the Acrophobiacs'.

The world's largest gingerbread house, 52ft *15.85 m* high and 32ft *9.75 m* square, was built by Chef David Sunken and Roger A. Pelcher of the Bohemian Club of Des Moines, Iowa, USA and 100 volunteers on 2 Dec 1988. They used 2000 sheets of gingerbread and 1650 lb *748.43 kg* of icing.

(Photo: Club Corporation of America)

The narrowest known house frontage is 119cm *47 in* for 50 Stuart Street, Millport, on the island of Great Cumbrae, Strathclyde.

Most expensive The most expensive private house ever built is the Hearst Ranch at San Simeon, California, USA. It was built between 1922 and 1939 for William Randolph Hearst (1863–1951), at a total cost of more than $30 million. It has more than 100 rooms, a 32-m *104-ft* long heated swimming pool, a 25-m *83-ft* long assembly hall and a garage for 25 limousines. The house required 60 servants to maintain it.

The highest price for any house on the 1993 UK residental property market was £25 million for The Rectory, King's Road, Chelsea, London, which was auctioned on 1 Nov 1993. Built in 1727 it has London's largest garden apart from Buckingham Palace, covering 2.5 acres *1.01 ha*.

Bricklaying Tony Gregory of Horndon on the Hill, Essex laid 747 bricks, each weighing 2 kg *4 lb 7 oz*, in 60 min at Grays, Essex on 18 Apr 1987. This was achieved in accordance with the rules of the Brick Development Association and the Guild of Bricklayers.

Barracks Great Britain's oldest purpose-built barracks are those at Berwick-on-Tweed, Northumberland, dating from 1719 and still in part-time use. The oldest building to be converted into barracks is New Town Fort, Gravesend, Kent which dates from 1322.

Buildings demolished by explosives The largest has been the 21-storey Traymore Hotel, Atlantic City, New Jersey, USA on 26 May 1972 by

Controlled Demolition Inc. of Towson, Maryland. This 600-room hotel had a cubic capacity of 181,340m³ *6,403,926ft³*.

The tallest chimney ever demolished by explosives was the Matla Power Station chimney, Kriel, South Africa, on 19 Jul 1981. It stood 275m *902ft* and was brought down in a joint project between the Santon (Steeplejack) Co. Ltd of Greater Manchester and Dykon, Inc. of Tulsa, Oklahoma, USA.

> **Fifteen members of the Black Leopard Karate Club demolished a seven-room wooden farmhouse west of Elnora, Alberta, Canada in 3hr 18min by foot and empty hand on 13 Jun 1982.**

In Great Britain Controlled Demolition Group Ltd of Leeds successfully demolished eight blocks of high rise flats at Kersal Vale, Salford, Manchester on 14 Oct 1990. The total cubic capacity of the tower blocks was 155,000 m³ *5,474,000ft³*.

Largest estate The UK's largest housing estate is the 675ha *1667acres* Becontree Estate on a site covering 1214ha *3000acres* in Barking and Redbridge, London, built between 1921 and 1929. It contains a total of 26,822 homes, with an estimated population of nearly 90,000.

Flats

Tallest The 343.5-m *1127-ft* John Hancock Center in Chicago, Illinois, USA, is 100 storeys high; floors 44–92 are residential.

The tallest purely residential block of flats is the 195-m *639-ft*, 70-storey Lake Point Tower in Chicago, Illinois, USA which has 879 apartments.

UK The tallest residential block in Great Britain is Shakespeare Tower, Barbican, City of London. The 44-storey block, topped out on 24 Mar 1969, is 127.77m *419ft 2½in* high and contains 116 flats.

GUESS WHAT?

Q How many slot machines are there in the world's largest casino?

A See Page 89

Largest complex The largest aggregation of private blocks are those forming the Barbican Estate, designed by architects Chamberlain, Powell and Son, in the City of London. The site occupies 16ha *40acres* and includes 2011 flats and parking for 2000 cars.

Pole sitting Modern records do not compare with that of St Simeon the Younger (*c.* AD 521– 97), called Stylites, a monk who spent his last 45 years up a stone pillar on the Hill of Wonders, near Antioch, Syria. His achievement is the longest-standing record chronicled in the *Guinness Book of Records*.

The 'standards of living' at the top of poles can vary widely. Mellissa Sanders lived in a shack measuring 1.8×2.1m *6×7ft* at the top of a pole in Indianapolis, Indiana, USA from 26 Oct

Rifling *with the spirits*

Winchester House in San Jose, California, USA was under construction for 38 years. The original house was an eight-room farmhouse with separate barn on the 161-acre estate of Oliver Winchester, the son of the manufacturer of the Winchester Repeating rifle—the most famous rifle used in conquering the West. After his death his wife Sarah Winchester, widowed in 1886, consulted a psychic in Boston, who told her that the spirits of those who had been killed by her family's rifles had placed a curse on her and would haunt her forever. She could apparently escape the curse by moving west, buying a house and continually rebuilding it under the direction of the spirits. By this means only could she escape the curse, and perhaps even find the key to eternal life.

Mrs. Winchester moved to California, whereupon she used her $1000-a-day private income to transform the farmhouse into a mansion, which now has 13 bathrooms, 52 skylights, 47 fireplaces, 10,000 windows, 40 staircases, 2000 doorways and three $10,000 elevators. She built steadily, 24 hours a day, until her death in 1922. Much of the renovation and rebuilding of the house was intended to confuse the resident ghosts: closets opening onto blank walls, secret passageways, trapdoors, and hundreds of pillars and posts that are upside down.

Above: One of several staircases leading to nowhere.

Main picture: An aerial view of the sprawling mansion. Some of the servants needed maps just to find their way around.

Above and below: Two more of the Winchester House rooms.

Far left: The Grand Ballroom, whose glass window contain unexplained Shakespearean quotations

1986–24 Mar 1988, a total of 516 days.

Rob Colley stayed in a barrel (maximum capacity 150 gal *682 litres*) at the top of a pole 43 ft *13.1 m* high at Dartmoor Wildlife Park, near Plymouth, Devon for 42 days 35 min from 13 Aug–24 Sep 1992.

Hotels

Oldest The Hōshi Ryokan at the village of Awazu in Japan, dates back to A.D. 717, when Garyo Hōshi built an inn near a hot water spring which was said to have miraculous healing powers. The waters are still celebrated for their recuperative effects and the Ryokan now has 100 bedrooms. (⇨ Oldest family business)

Largest The MGM Grand Hotel/Casino/ Theme Park in Las Vegas, Nevada, USA consists of four 30-storey towers on a 45.3 ha *112 acres* site. The hotel has 5009 rooms, with suites of up to 557 m² *6000 ft²*. The complex also includes a 15,200-seater arena, a 13.3 ha *33 acres* theme park and the world's largest casino.

It was started in 1991, topped out in February 1993 and opened officially in December 1993 at a cost of $1 billion. (⇨ also Largest casino)

UK Britain's largest hotel is the Grosvenor House Hotel in Park Lane, London, opened in 1929. It is eight storeys high, covers 1 ha *2½ acres* and caters for over 100,000 visitors per year in 470 rooms. The Great Room is the largest single hotel room measuring 55 × 40 m *181 × 131 ft* with a height of 7 m *23 ft*. Banquets for 1500 can readily be held there.

The London Forum Hotel in Cromwell Road is Britain's most capacious, accommodating 1856 guests in 910 bedrooms. It employs 330 staff and was opened in 1973. (⇨ Tallest)

Largest casino The casino at the MGM Grand Hotel in Las Vegas, Nevada, USA covers 15,932 m² *171,500 ft²* and comprises four gaming areas including 3500 slot machines, 165 games tables, plus several lounges and bars. (⇨ Largest hotel)

GUESS WHAT?

Q What is the most common pub name in Britain?

A See Page 95

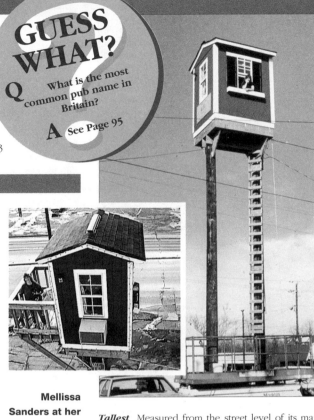

Mellissa Sanders at her tiny home where she spent nearly 1½ years from late 1986 to early 1988.

(Photos: Glen Burton and Mauri Rose Sanders)

Tallest Measured from the street level of its main entrance, the 73-storey Westin Stamford in Raffles City, Singapore was topped out in March 1985 at 226.1 m *742 ft*. The $235 million hotel is operated by Westin Hotel Co. and owned jointly by DBS Land and Overseas Chinese Banking Corporation. During 1990/1 it received a £54 million facelift.

Measured from its rear entrance level, the Westin Stamford Detroit Plaza, USA is 227.9 m *748 ft* tall.

Britain's tallest hotel is the 27-storey, 132-m *380-ft-tall* London Forum Hotel. (⇨ Largest)

Lock, stock and barrel

The three-storey brick Hotel Fairmount (built 1906) in San Antonio, Texas, USA, which weighed 1451 tonnes, was moved on 36 dollies with pneumatic tyres over city streets for approximately five blocks. It was also transported over a bridge, which had to be reinforced for the purpose. The move by Emmert International of Portland took six days, 30 Mar–4 Apr 1985, and cost $650,000.

The hotel originally stood behind the area now known as the Plaza del Rio Mall in San Antonio. When the mall was being planned, the city had to decide to keep the hotel as it was, to refurbish it, or to move it. 'Its a landmark, a part of history, and it was worthwhile saving it', says Terry Emmert of Emmert Construction, Portland, Oregon, USA. 'Sure, it was a complicated job, an interesting project. It's something we'd like to do every day, if we could.'

With the Hotel Fairmount, the challenge was keeping it together. Before moving, the hotel's structure was reinforced inside and out. Then it was wrapped in a steel cage of beams and cables. Hydraulic jacks raised the building at 34 points in its foundation,

Most expensive room The Galactic Fantasy Suite in the Crystal Tower of the Crystal Palace Resort and Casino in Nassau, Bahamas costs $25,000 (£17,360) per night, but the casino's big spenders are likely to be accommodated on a complimentary basis. Facilities include 'Ursula', the personal robot servant, a rotating sofa and bed, a thunder and lightning sound and light show and pulsating light columns activated by body heat.

Cards!

The greatest number of storeys achieved in building free-standing houses of standard playing cards is 75, to a height of 4.42 m *14 ft 6 in*, built by Bryan Berg of Spirit Lake, Iowa, USA on 18–20 Apr 1992. No adhesives are allowed in such houses.

UK The Presidential Suite of the Hotel Hyatt Carlton Tower, London costs £2000 plus VAT (£2,350 inc VAT).

Most remote The Garvault Hotel in Kinbrace, Highland is claimed to be the most isolated hotel in mainland Britain, being some 26 km *16 miles* from its nearest competitor at Forsinard, also in Highland.

Largest hotel lobby The lobby at the Hyatt Regency in San Francisco, California, USA is 107 m *350 ft* long, 49 m *160 ft* wide, and at 52 m *170 ft* tall is the height of a 17-storey building.

Hoteliers In terms of both worldwide distribution and number of hotels, the largest hotelier in the world is the Best Western International consortium (Head office in

ON THE RECORD

and hoisted it 2.6 m high. The hotel hung over the sidewalks on both sides of the street, requiring the removal of light poles, traffic lights and parking meters.

(Photo: Emmert International)

The world's most capacious building is The Boeing Company's main assembly plant in Everett, Washington, USA, at 5,564,200 m³ *196,476,000 ft³* on completion in 1968. Subsequent expansion programmmes have increased the volume to 13.4 million m³ *472 million ft³*, a further increase in volume of 50 per cent, completed in 1993 in preparation for production of the new 777 airliner. The site covers some 410 ha *1025 acres*.

(Photo: Boeing Commercial Airline Group)

UK The largest building in Britain is the Ford Parts Centre at Daventry, Northants, covering an area of 142,674 m² *1.5 million ft²*. It was opened on 6 Sep 1972 at a cost of nearly £8 million and employs 1300 people.

Administrative The largest ground area covered by any office building is that of the Pentagon, in Arlington, Virginia, USA. Built to house the US Defense Department's offices, it was completed on 15 Jan 1943 and cost an estimated $83 million. Each of the outermost sides is 281 m *921 ft* long and the perimeter of the building is about 1405 m *4610 ft*. Its five storeys enclose a floor area of 604,000 m² *149.2 acres*, the corridors total 27 km *17 miles* in length and there are 7748 windows to be cleaned. There are 29,000 people working in the building. (⇨ Telephones and Facsimiles)

Building contractor The largest construction group in the United Kingdom is Tarmac. The company had sales of £2.7 billion in 1993, and employs 24,814 staff. Peak sales turnover was £3.7 billion in 1990.

Brickworks The largest in the world is the London Brick Co. Ltd plant at Stewartby, Beds. Established in 1898, the site now covers 90 ha *221 acres* and has a weekly production capacity of 6 million bricks and brick equivalent.

Phoenix, Arizona, USA), which owns approximately 3500 hotels in 52 countries. In the UK alone Best Western Hotels have nearly 10,000 bedrooms in around 200 hotels.

GUESS WHAT?

Q Where is the UK's largest housing estate?

A See Page 88

tainer trucks and the building has 26.84 km *16.67 miles* of roadway and 2609 container truck parking spaces.

Commercial In terms of floor area, the world's largest commercial building under one roof is the flower auction building of the Co-operative VBA (Verenigde Bloemenveilingen Aalsmeer) in Aalsmeer, Netherlands. The building now measures 776 × 631 m *2546 × 2070 ft*, giving an area of 689,656 m² *5.27 million ft²* compared with an original area of 343,277 m² *3.7 million ft²*.

Buildings for Working

Construction project The largest public works project of modern times is the Madinat Al-Jubail Al-Sinaiyah project in Saudi Arabia, started in 1976 for the industrial city covering 1,014,600,000 m² *250,705 acres*. At the peak of construction, nearly 52,000 workers were employed, representing 62 nationalities, and a total volume of 270 million m³ *9535 million ft³* of earth has been dredged and moved, enough to construct a 1-m *3-ft-3-in*-high belt around the Earth at the equator seven times.

Urban development The world's largest urban regeneration project is London Docklands, which covers 22 km² *8½ miles²*. Over 2.5 million m² *27 million ft²* of commercial development space and over 17,000 new homes have been completed or are under construction, and £3.5 billion is being invested in new public transport. By 1992 £8 billion had been invested by the private sector, together with a further £1.1 billion by the London Docklands Development Corporation, with more than 40,000 jobs created since 1981. The London Docklands Canary Wharf development is also the world's largest commercial development. (⇨ also Tallest offices)

Industrial The largest multi-level industrial building that is one discrete structure is the container freight station of Asia Terminals Ltd at Hong Kong's Kwai Chung container port. The 15-level building was completed in 1994 and has a total area of 865,937 m² *9,320,867 ft²*. Building measurements of 276 × 292 m *906 × 958 ft* and a height of 109½ m *359.25 ft* will give a volume of 5,853,092 m³ *206,699,993 ft³*. The entire area in each floor of the building is directly accessible by 14 m *46 ft* con-

GUESS WHAT?

Q In what country is the world's longest moat?

A See Page 86

Offices

Largest The largest rentable office complex is the World Trade Center in New York City, USA, with a total of 1,114,800 m² *12 million ft²* of rentable space available in the seven buildings, including 406,000 m² *4.37 million ft²* in each of the twin towers. There are 99 lifts in each tower and 43,600 windows comprising 182,880 m² *600,000 ft²* of glass.

Largest!

Between 1942 and 1943 sixteen Navy airship wooden blimp hangars were built at various locations throughout the USA. They are 317 m *1040 ft* long, 51.91 m *170 ft 4 in* high at the crown and 90.37 m *296 ft 6 in* wide at the base. There are only eight remaining, one at Tillamook, Oregon and Elizabeth City, North Carolina; and two at Moffett Field and Santa Ana, California, and Lakehurst, New Jersey.

Sears Tower in Chicago, Illinois, USA, which, at 520 m *1707 ft*, is the tallest office building in the world.

(Photo: Spectrum Colour Library)

There are 50,000 people working in the complex, which attracts 90,000 visitors daily.

UK The largest single open-plan office in the United Kingdom is that of British Gas West Midlands at Solihull, Warks, built by Spooners (Hull) Ltd in 1962. It now measures 230 × 49 m *753 × 160 ft*, and can accommodate 2125 staff.

> In January 1994 it was announced that Russia was prepared to rent the Baikonur space centre—launch site for several satellites—for $115 million (£76.9 million) a year for 20 years.

Tallest The tallest office building in the world is the Sears Tower, national headquarters of Sears, Roebuck & Co. in Wacker Drive, Chicago, Illinois, USA, with 110 storeys rising to 443 m *1454 ft*. Its total height is 520 m *1707 ft* following the addition of two TV antennae. Construction began in August 1970 and the building was topped out on 4 May 1973, having surpassed the height of the World Trade Center in New York City at 2:35 p.m. on 6 Mar 1973 with the first steel column reaching to the 104th storey. The gross area of the tower is 418,050 m² *4.5 million ft²* and it is served by 104 lifts and 18 escalators. It has 16,100 windows.

UK The tallest office building in Britain is the Canary Wharf tower in London Docklands, at 243.8 m *800 ft*. The tallest of three towers at the development, the 50-storey building, resembling an obelisk, was designed by US architect Cesar Pelli and consists of nearly 16,000 pieces of steel. It overtook the National Westminster tower block by 61 m *200 ft* when it was topped out in November 1990.

The largest covered stadium is the Aztec Stadium in Mexico City (see below), opened in 1968, which has a capacity of 107,000 for football, although a record attendance of 132,274 was achieved for boxing on 20 Feb 1993. Nearly all seats are under cover. (▷ Boxing)

Lego tower The world's tallest Lego tower was 21.36 m *70 ft* high and built by Lego Belgium n.v./s.a. in Brussels on 26–27 Jun 1993.

The tallest Lego tower in Britain measured 20.86 m *68 ft 5 in* and was built by Lego UK Ltd at Earl's Court, London in March 1993 during the Daily Mail Ideal Home Exhibition.

Most expensive According to *World Rental Levels* by Richard Ellis of London, the highest rents in the world for prime offices are in Tokyo, Japan at £100.26 ($148.81) per ft² per annum (December 1993), compared with a peak of £127.20 ($206.68) in June 1991. Added service charges and rates raised the price to £113.06 ($167.81) per ft² (December 1993) and £137.35 ($225.34) at June 1991.

The UK equivalent for the same period was £40 per ft² per annum for offices in London's West End, rising to £68.34 with service charges included.

UK The largest embassy in Great Britain is that of the United States in Grosvenor Square, London. The Chancery Building alone, completed in 1960, has a usable floor area of 22,008 m² *236,895 ft²*, 600 rooms on seven floors and can accommodate 700 staff.

Largest exhibition centre The International Exposition Center in Cleveland, Ohio, USA is situated on a 76-ha *188-acre* site adjacent to Cleveland Hopkins International Airport in a building measuring 232,250 m² *2.5 million ft²*. An indoor terminal provides direct rail access and parking for 10,000 cars.

UK The National Exhibition Centre, Birmingham, W Mids, which opened in February 1976, consists of 15 halls covering 158,000 m² *1.7 million ft²*, a 12,000-seater arena, 2 hotels, car parking for 18,000, plus numerous restaurants and a lake on the 250-ha *618-acre* site.

The transparent acrylic glass 'tent' roof over the Munich Olympic Stadium, Germany measures 85,000 m² *914,940 ft²* in area and rests on a steel net supported by masts.

(Photo: Images)

Buildings for Leisure

Stadia

Largest The open Strahov Stadium in Prague, Czech Republic, completed in 1934, could accommodate 240,000 spectators for mass displays of up to 40,000 Sokol gymnasts.

Football The Maracaña Municipal Stadium in Rio de Janeiro, Brazil, has a normal capacity for 205,000, of whom 155,000 can be seated. A crowd of 199,854 was accommodated for the World Cup final between Brazil and Uruguay on 16 Jul 1950. A dry moat, 2.13 m *7 ft* wide and more than 1.5 m *5 ft* deep, protects players from spectators and vice versa.

Britain's most capacious football stadium was Hampden Park, Glasgow, Strathclyde, home of Queen's Park Football Club, opened on 31 Oct 1903. Its record attendance was 149,547 on 17 Apr 1937, but the current Ground Safety Certificate limits the capacity to 38,335 all-seated.

Covered The largest covered stadium in Great Britain is the Empire Stadium, Wembley, Middx, opened on 23 Apr 1923 and scene of the 1948 Olympic Games and the final of the 1966 World Cup. In 1962–3 the capacity under cover was increased to 100,000, with 45,000 seated and the original cost was

£1,250,000. Following a refurbishment programme and new safety guidelines the capacity has been reduced to 81,500 all seated.

Indoor The $173-million, 83.2-m *273-ft* tall Superdome in New Orleans, Louisiana, USA covering 5.26 ha *13 acres*, was completed in May 1975. Its maximum seating capacity is 97,365 for conventions and 76,791 for football. A gondola with six 8-m *26-ft* TV screens produces instant replays.

Largest roof The longest roof span in the world is 240m *787ft 4in* for the major axis of the elliptical Texas Stadium, completed in 1971 at Irving, Texas, USA.

Retractable roof The world's largest retractable roof covers the SkyDome, home of the Toronto Blue Jays baseball team, near the CN Tower in Toronto, Canada, completed in June 1989. The roof covers 3.2 ha *8 acres*, spans 209 m *674 ft* at its widest point and rises to 86m *282ft*. The stadium itself has a capacity of 67,000 for concerts, 53,000 for American football and 50,600 for baseball. (⇨ Baseball)

Largest air-supported building The octagonal Pontiac Silverdome Stadium in Detroit, Michigan, USA is 220 m *722ft* long, 159 m *522 ft* wide and has a capacity for 80,638. The air pressure is 34.4kPa *5lb/ft²* supporting the 4ha *10acre* translucent 'Fiberglas' roofing. The main floor measures 123×73m *402×240ft* and the roof is 62m *202ft* high. The structural engineers were Geiger-Berger Associates of New York City, USA.

The largest standard size airhall is 262m *860ft* long, 42.6m *140ft* wide and 19.8m *65ft* high, first sited at Lima, Ohio, USA and made by Irvin Industries of Stamford, Connecticut, USA.

Resorts

Largest amusement resort Disney World is set in 11,332 ha *28,000 acres* of Orange and Osceola counties, 32km *20 miles* south-west of Orlando, Florida, USA. It was opened on 1 Oct 1971 after a $400 million investment.

Most attended Disneyland at Anaheim, California, USA (opened 1955) received its 250-millionth visitor on 24 Aug 1985 at 9:52a.m and its 300-millionth visitor in 1989.

Largest pleasure beach Virginia Beach, Virginia, USA has 45km *28 miles* of beach front on the Atlantic and 16km *10miles* of estuary frontage. The area covers 803km² *310miles²* with 157 hotels and motels and 2230 campsites.

The most visited pleasure beach in Britain is at Blackpool, Lancs, attracting 17 million visitors annually.

Pleasure piers Earliest The earliest date attributed to a seaside 'jetty' is 1560 at Great Yarmouth, Norfolk; it was replaced by a new structure in 1808 which was washed away in 1953. The first 'proper' piers were constructed at Weymouth, Dorset in 1812, and Ryde, Isle of Wight in 1813–14. There is some doubt over the Weymouth date, though records show that a new reinforced concrete pier (pleasure/commercial) replaced an old 274m 900ft wooden pier in 1933. They both remain in situ today although greatly altered over the years.

Longest The longest pleasure pier in the world is Southend Pier, Southend-on-Sea, Essex. The original wooden pier was opened in 1830 and extended in 1846. The present iron pier is 2.15km *1.34 miles* long and was opened on 8 Jul 1889. In 1949–50 the pier had a peak 5.75 million visitors. The pier has been breached by 14 vessels since 1830 and there have been 3 major fires.

Most The resort with the most piers was Atlantic City, New Jersey, USA with eight, though currently only five remain, dating from 1883 to 1912. Of British resorts, Blackpool, Lancs now has three piers, the North, Central and South.

Naturist resorts The largest naturist site is Domaine de Lambeyran, near Lodève in southern France, at 340 ha *840 acres*. The centre Helio Marin at Cap d'Agde,

(Photos: WKVL Amusement Research Library)

Big Wheel!

The original Ferris wheel, named after its constructor George W. Ferris (1859–96), was erected in 1893 at the Midway, Chicago, Illinois, USA at a cost of $385,000. It was 76m *250ft* in diameter, 240 m *790 ft* in circumference, weighed 1087 tonnes and had 36 cars each carrying 40 seated and 20 standing passengers, giving a record capacity of 2160. The structure was removed in 1904 to St Louis, Missouri, USA and was eventually sold as scrap for $1800.

also in southern France, is visited by around 250,000 people per annum. The largest naturist site in Great Britain is that of the Naturist Foundation in Orpington, Kent, at 20ha *50acres*.

Fairs

Earliest The earliest major international fair was the Great Exhibition of 1851 in the Crystal Palace, Hyde Park, London, which in 141 days attracted 6,039,195 admissions.

Largest The site of the Louisiana Purchase Exposition at St Louis, Missouri, USA in 1904 covered 514.66ha *1271.76 acres* and there was an attendance of 19,694,855. Events of the 1904 Olympic Games were staged in conjunction with it. In 1897 a Ferris wheel with a diameter of 86.5m *284ft* was erected for the Earl's Court Exhibition, London. It had ten 1st class and 30 2nd class cars each carrying 30 people.

The largest diameter wheel now operating is the Cosmoclock 21 at Yokohama City, Japan. It is 105m *344½ft* high and 100m *328ft* in diameter, with 60 gondolas each with eight seats. There are such features as illumination by laser beams and acoustic effects by sound synthesizers. Sixty arms hold the gondolas, each serving as a second hand for the 13-m *42.65-ft* long electric clock mounted at the hub.

Britain's largest is that of 61m *200ft* diameter with a capacity for 240 people at Margate, Kent.

Roller Coasters

The maximum speeds and dimensions claimed for gravity based amusement devices have long been exaggerated for commercial reasons.

Left: the oldest operating roller coaster in Britain is the Scenic Railway at Dreamland Amusement Park, Margate, Kent. This traditional wooden coaster has continued to operate since it opened to the public on 3 Jul 1920.

GUESS WHAT?

Q What was the world's most expensive house sold in 1993?

A See Page 87

Oldest operating The *Rutschbahnen* (Scenic Railway) Mk.2 was constructed at the Tivoli Gardens, Copenhagen, Denmark in 1913. This coaster opened to the public in 1914, and has remained open ever since.

Longest The longest roller coaster in the world is *The Ultimate* at Lightwater Valley Theme Park in Ripon, N Yorks. The tubular steel track measures is 2.29km *1.42 miles*.

Greatest drop and fastest The *Steel Phantom* at Kennywood Amusement Park, West Mifflin, Pennsylvania, USA, has a vertical drop of 68.55m *225 ft* into a natural ravine, with a design speed of 128km/h *80 mph*.

Sharing the record in 1995 for the greatest drop will be the *Desperado*, a new steel roller coaster at Buffalo Bill's Resort and Casino, Primadonna Resorts Complex, Jean, Nevada, USA. The ride incorporates design features for an 'above ground' vertical drop of 68.55m 225ft.

Tallest The tallest above ground superstructure is *Pepsi Max—The Big One* at Blackpool Pleasure Beach, Lancs. This non-looping coaster has a design height of 71.6m *235 ft* above *Ordnance Datum* (a fixed national survey point). The ride design also features a first vertical drop of 63.7m *209 ft* above ground, with a speed of 128km/h *80 mph*.

Highest loop The first loop of the *Viper* at Six Flags Magic Mountain, Valencia, California, USA is 42.7m *140 ft* above the ground. Riders are turned upside-down seven times over the 1167m *3830 ft* track.

Greatest number The most roller coasters at any amusement park is 11 at Cedar Point Amusement Park/Resort in Sandusky, Ohio, USA. There is a choice of 2 wood and 9 steel track coasters.

Shopping Centres

The world's first shopping centre was built in 1896 at Roland Park, Baltimore, Maryland, USA.

The world's largest centre is the $1.1 billion West Edmonton Mall in Alberta, Canada, which was opened on 15 Sep 1981 and completed four years later. It covers 483,080m² *5.2 million ft²* on a 49-ha *121-acre* site and encompasses over 800 stores and services, as well as 11 major department stores. Parking is provided for 20,000 vehicles for more than 500,000 shoppers per week. (▷ Car parks)

The world's largest wholesale merchandise mart is the Dallas Market Center on Stemmons Freeway, Dallas, Texas, USA, covering nearly 864,000m²

The *Ultimate* at Lightwater Valley Theme Park in N Yorks—not for the faint-hearted—will give you the world's longest ride on a roller coaster.

(Photo: WKVL Amusement Research Library)

9.3 million ft² in six buildings. Together with two further buildings under separate management, the whole complex covers 70ha *175 acres* and houses some 2580 permanent showrooms displaying the merchandise of more than 30,000 manufacturers. The Center attracts 760,000 buyers each year to its 107 annual markets and trade shows.

UK The largest shopping complex in Britain and Europe is the MetroCentre in Gateshead, Tyne & Wear. The site covers an area of 54.63ha *135 acres* housing 340 retail units (including the largest single-storey branch of Marks and Spencer at 17,279m² *186,000 ft²*), giving a gross selling

area of 204,380m² *2.2 million ft²*. The complex also includes a leisure centre, a ten-screen cinema, a 28-lane bowling alley, parking for 12,000 cars and its own purpose-built British Rail station.

Britain's largest covered city centre shopping complex is Manchester's Arndale Centre, which has a floor area of 209,000m² *2,246,200 ft²* (gross retail area of 110,270m² *1,187,000 ft²*) including a car park for 1800 cars. The centre was completed in 1979 after three years' work and was the first such centre in Europe with its own radio station, called 'Centre Sound' Radio.

Longest mall The world's longest shopping mall measures 650m *2133 ft* and is part of the £40 million shopping centre at Milton Keynes, Bucks.

Nightclubs and Restaurants

Nightclubs The earliest nightclub (*boîte de nuit*) was 'Le Bal des Anglais' at 6 rue des Anglais, Paris, France. Established in 1843, it closed c.1960.

Largest 'Gilley's Club' (formerly 'Shelly's'), built in 1955, was extended in 1971 on Spencer Highway, Houston, Texas, USA, with a seating capacity of 6000 under one roof covering 1.6ha *4 acres*.

In the more classical sense the largest nightclub in the world is 'The Mikado' in the Akasaka district of Tokyo, Japan, with a seating capacity of 2000. Binoculars can be essential to an appreciation of the floor show.

Lowest The 'Minus 206' in Tiberias, Israel, on the shores of the Sea of Galilee is 206m *676 ft* below sea level. An alternative candidate has been the oft-raided 'Outer Limits', opposite the Cow Palace, San Francisco, California, USA. It has

been called 'The Most Busted Joint' and 'The Slowest to Get the Message'.

Restaurants *Earliest* The Casa Botin was opened in 1725 in Calle de Cuchilleros 17, Madrid, Spain.

Largest The Royal Dragon (Mang Gorn Luang) restaurant in Bangkok, Thailand, opened in October 1991, can seat 5000 customers served by 1200 staff.

Highest The highest restaurant in the world is at the Chacaltaya ski resort, Bolivia, at 5340m *17,519 ft*.

The Royal Dragon restaurant in Bangkok, Thailand. Because of the large service area (3.37ha *8.35 acres*), the staff wear roller skates not only to get from place to place but also to speed the service.

The highest in Great Britain is the Ptarmigan Observation Restaurant at 1112m *3650 ft* above sea level on Cairngorm, (1244m *4084 ft*) near Aviemore, Highland.

Restaurateurs The world's largest restaurant chain is operated by McDonald's Corporation of Oak Brook, Illinois, USA founded in 1955 by Ray A. Kroc (1902–84) after buying out the brothers Dick and 'Mac' McDonald, pioneers of the fast-food drive-in. By December 1992 McDonald's licensed and owned 13,093 restaurants in 60 countries. Worldwide sales in 1992 were $21.9 billion.

Their most capacious outlet is the 700-seat, 28,000-ft² restaurant in Beijing, China which opened on 23 Apr 1992. It employs a staff of 1,000.

'The Smiths Arms' in Godmanstone, Dorset, here viewed from both inside and out, has external dimensions of 12.04 × 3.5 m *39½ × 11½ ft* and is 3.65 m *12 ft* in height, making it one of the smallest pubs in the world.

(Photos: Gamma—S Morgan/Spooner)

Largest The largest beer-selling establishment in the world is the 'Mathäser', Bayerstrasse 5, Munich, Germany, where the daily sale reaches 48,000 litres *84,470 pints*. It was established in 1829, demolished in World War II and rebuilt by 1955. It now seats 5500 people.

UK The largest public house in Great Britain is the 'Downham Tavern', Downham Way, Bromley, Kent, built in 1930. Two large bars (counter length 13.7 m *45 ft*) accommodate 1000 customers and the pub employs 18–20 staff.

Tallest bar Humperdink's Seafood and Steakhouse Bar at Dallas, Texas, USA is 7.69 m *25 ft 3 in* high with two levels of shelving containing over 1000 bottles. The lower level has four rows of shelves approximately 12 m *40 ft* across and can be reached from floor level. If an order has to be met from the upper level, which has five rows of shelves, it is reached by climbing a ladder.

Longest The world's longest permanent continuous bar is the 123.7 m *405 ft 10 in* long counter in the 'Beer Barrel Saloon' at Put-in-Bay, South Bass Island, Ohio, USA opened in 1989. The bar is fitted with 56 beer taps and surrounded by 160 bar stools. The 'Bar at Erickson's', on Burnside Street, Portland, Oregon, USA in its heyday (1883–1920) possessed a bar measuring 208 m *684 ft*. The chief bouncer, Edward 'Spider' Johnson, had an assistant named 'Jumbo' Reilly who weighed 23st *322 lb* and was said to resemble 'an ill-natured orang-utan'. Beer was five cents for 16 fluid ounces. Longer temporary bars have been erected, notably for beer festivals.

The longest bar in Great Britain with beer pumps is the Long Bar at the Cornwall Coliseum Auditorium at Carlyon Bay, St Austell, Cornwall. It measures 31.8 m *104¼ ft* and has 34 dispensers. The Grandstand Bar at Galway Racecourse, Republic of Ireland, completed in 1955, measures 64 m *210 ft*.

The longest pub bar is the 31.7 m *104⅓ ft* counter at 'The Horse Shoe', Drury Street, Glasgow, Scotland.

Smallest The ground floor of 'The Nutshell' in Bury St. Edmunds, Suffolk is 4.82 × 2.28 m *15 ft 10 in × 7 ft 6 in*. It was granted a licence personally by a thirsty King Charles II (1630–1685) when passing by. The 'Lakeside Inn', at The Promenade, Southport, Merseyside has a floor area of 6.7 × 4.87 m *22 × 16 ft* and is 4.57 m *15 ft* in height.

The pub with the smallest bar room is the 'Dove Inn', Upper Mall, Chiswick, London measuring 127 × 239 cm *4 ft 2 in × 7 ft 10 in*.

Bars and Public Houses

Oldest There are various claimants to the title of Great Britain's oldest inn. A foremost claimant is 'The Fighting Cocks', at St Albans, Herts, an 11th-century structure on an eighth-century site. The timber frame of the Royalist Hotel, Digbeth Street, Stow-on-the-Wold, Glos has been dated to even earlier, it was 'The Eagle and the Child' in the 13th century and known to exist in AD947. An origin as early as AD560 has been claimed for 'Ye Olde Ferry Boat Inn' at Holywell, Cambs. There is some evidence that it antedates the local church, built in 980, but no documentation is available earlier than AD1100. The 'Bingley Arms', Bardsey, near Leeds, W Yorks, restored and extended in 1738, existed as the 'Priest's Inn', according to Bardsey Church records of AD905.

ON THE RECORD

'To beer or not to beer...'

Bruce Masters of Flitwick, Beds has visited a staggering 26,756 pubs and a further 1209 other drinking establishments since 1960, partaking of the local brew in each case where available. There are a total of 77,000 pubs nationwide.

" The idea came to me when I was sitting in the 'White Horse' at Chilgrove, near Chichester on 28 Jul 1971. I used to drive to my parents' house at Selsey from where I lived at that time, near Basingstoke, about once a fortnight. I would like to break the journey with a pint, and on the day in question it occurred to me that it would be fun to visit a different pub each time I made the journey. At the same time I thought that it would be fun to do a similar thing when I was changing trains in Reading. From the start of 1972 onwards visiting pubs grew into a keenly pursued hobby, aided by the fact that I was a bachelor, and I was able to travel as a result of my job. It was something I did to pass the time, and to come to a reasonably informed opinion as to whether or not I like British beer after all. On this point, I feel that further research is still necessary, and hope to carry it on for a good few years yet. You will therefore gather that, like Christopher Columbus, I arrived at where I finished up without actually setting out with the intention of doing so.

It would be impossible to say which is the best pint (or half-pint) I have ever had. Beer is inevitably a mood drink with varying preferences according to such factors as the time of year, apart from how well it is kept and served. I tend to prefer the middle strength 'real ales' and there are now many in the country, and the number is increasing all the time. Among some of the names that spring to mind are Owd Roger, Willie Warmer, Sinful Stout and Old Fart.

My accession to the Guinness Book of Records was followed by some media publicity in local and national newspapers both here and abroad, as well as local television. There was a little slip at the Canary Wharf launch, where it was announced that I had had a pint in each place rather than a half. A German national paper converted this to litres and did a lengthy article quantifying all aspects, including daily amounts consumed, and number of places visited to three places of decimals. The paper concerned also included a Shakespearian quotation 'To beer or not to beer, that is the question'. Whilst I know the answer, I can't help thinking that Hamlet would more probably have said that: you know what the Danes are like. "

Most remote The Old Forge public house at Inverie, Knoydart, Inverness-shire is 32 km *20 miles* by ferry and 38.6 km *24 miles* 'as the crow flies' from its nearest contender; there are no roads into or out of Knoydart.

Longest pub name 'The Old Thirteenth Cheshire Astley Volunteer Rifleman Corps Inn' in Astley Street, Stalybridge, Manchester has 55 letters. A very contrived name consisting of 12,822 letters and 1487 words was added to Bugsy's Amazin' Downtown Diner/Bar at King's Stables Road, Edinburgh, Scotland.

Highest!

The 'Snowdon Summit' licensed bar and cafeteria is the highest, at 1085 m *3560 ft*. It is only open in summer due to the prevailing weather conditions. In Great Britain the 'Tan Hill Inn' (licensee Margaret Baines) is 528 m *1732 ft* above sea level. It is just in N Yorks on the moorland road between Reeth, N Yorks and Brough, Cumbria.

Shortest name In Great Britain the shortest name was the 'X' at Westcott, Cullompton, Devon, but in October 1983 the name was changed to the 'Merry Harriers'.

Commonest name There are probably about 630 pubs in Britain called the 'Red Lion'. Arthur Amos of Bury St Edmunds, Suffolk, recorded 21,516 pub names from 1938 to his death in June 1986. His son John took over the collection, which now numbers 25,202.

Towers and Masts

Tallest Structures

The all-time height record for any structure is the guyed Warszawa Radio mast at Konstantynow, 96 km *60 miles* north-west of the capital of Poland. Prior to its fall during renovation work on 10 Aug 1991 it was 646.38 m *2120 ft 8 in* tall or more than four tenths of a mile. It was completed on 18 Jul 1974 and put into operation on 22 Jul 1974. It was designed by Jan Polak and weighed 550 tonnes.

After the collapse of the world's tallest tower in Poland in 1991 the local people laid claim to a new record—the world's longest tower!

Currently the tallest structure is a stayed television transmitting tower 629 m *2063 ft* tall, between Fargo and Blanchard, North Dakota, USA. It was built for Channel 11 of KTHI-TV in 30 days (2 Oct to 1 Nov 1963) by 11 men of Hamilton Erection, Inc. of York, South Carolina, USA. From then until the completion of the mast at Konstantynow it was the tallest structure in the world, and remained the second tallest between 1974 and 1991.

Great Britain The tallest structure in Britain is NTL's Belmont mast, north of Horncastle, Lincs, completed in 1965 to a height of 385.5 m *1265 ft* with 2.13 m *7 ft* added by meteorological equipment installed in September 1967. It serves Yorkshire TV and weighs 210 tonnes.

Tallest Towers

The tallest free-standing structure (as opposed to a guyed wire) in the world is the $63 million CN Tower in Toronto, Canada, which rises to 553.34 m *1815 ft 5 in*. Excavation began on 12 Feb 1973 for the erection of the 130,000-tonne reinforced, post-tensioned concrete structure,

THEN & NOW

200 years of tallest structures

The height of the world's tallest building has quadrupled in the past 200 years.

Plans are announced from time to time to construct a new structure or office building which would take on the status of the world's tallest structure, but these are not always actually built, as previously unforeseen problems can arise.

The tallest structure today is the KTHI-TV Mast in North Dakota, USA at 629 m (2063 ft), but 200 years ago the tallest was the Minster of Notre Dame in Strasbourg, France at just 142 m (466 ft). These illustrations show how the record has progressed over the last couple of centuries.

Artwork: Peter Harper

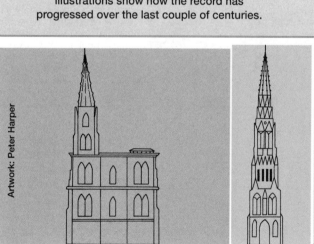

200 years ago	175 years ago	150 years ago	125 years ago	100 years ago	75 years ago	50 years ago	25 years ago	Now
142 m (466 ft) Minster of Notre Dame, Strasbourg, France. Completed in 1439. *Sandstone*	142 m (466 ft) Minster of Notre Dame, Strasbourg, France. Completed in 1439. *Sandstone*	142 m (466 ft) Minster of Notre Dame, Strasbourg, France. Completed in 1439. *Sandstone*	145 m (476 ft) St Nicholas Church, Hamburg, Germany. Completed in 1847. *Stone and iron*	300.5 m (985.9 ft) Eiffel Tower, Paris, France. Completed in 1889. *Iron*	300.5 m (985.9 ft) Eiffel Tower, Paris, France. Completed in 1889. *Iron*	381 m (1250 ft) Empire State Building, New York City, USA. Completed in 1930. *Steel and concrete*	629 m (2063 ft) KTHI-TV Mast, Fargo, North Dakota, USA. Completed in 1963. *Steel*	629 m (2063 ft) KTHI-TV Mast, Fargo, North Dakota, USA. Completed in 1963. *Steel*

which was 'topped out' on 2 Apr 1975. The 416-seat restaurant revolves in the Sky Pod at 351 m *1150 ft*, from which the visibility can extend to hills 120 km *74½ miles* distant.

Great Britain The tallest self-supported tower in Britain is the 330.5 m *1084 ft* tall NTL transmitter at Emley Moor, W Yorks, completed in September 1971. The structure, which cost £900,000, has an enclosed room at the 264 m *865 ft* level and weighs with its foundations more than 15,000 tonnes.

Bridges

Oldest Arch construction was understood by the Sumerians as early as 3200 BC and a reference exists to the bridging of the Nile in 2650 BC.

The oldest datable bridge in the world still in use is the slab stone single-arch bridge over the River Meles in Izmir (formerly Smyrna) Turkey, which dates from *c.* 850 BC. Remnants of Mycenaean bridges dated *c.* 1600 BC exist in the neighbourhood of Mycenae, Greece over the River Havos.

The clapper bridges of Dartmoor and Exmoor (e.g. the Tarr Steps over the River Barle, Exmoor, Somerset) are thought to be of prehistoric types although none of the existing examples can be certainly dated. They are made of large slabs of stone placed over boulders.

The Romans built stone bridges in England and remains of these have been found at Corbridge, Northumberland, dating to the 2nd century AD, and at Chesters, Northumberland and Willowford, Cumbria. Remains of a very early wooden bridge have been found at Aldwinkle, Northants.

Longest *Cable suspension* The world's longest bridge span is the main span of the Humber Estuary Bridge, Humberside, at 1410 m *4626 ft*. Work began on 27 Jul 1972, after a decision announced on 22 Jan 1966. The towers are 162.5 m *533 ft 1⅜ in* tall from datum and are 36 mm *1⅜ in* out of parallel to allow for the curvature of the Earth. Including the Hessle and the Barton side spans, the bridge stretches 2220 m or *1.37 miles*. It was structurally completed on 18 Jul 1980 at a cost of £96 million and was opened by HM the Queen on 17 Jul 1981.

The Akashi-Kaikyo road bridge linking Honshu and Shikoku, Japan was started in 1988 and completion is planned for 1998. The main span will be 1990 m *6528 ft* in length with an overall suspended length with side spans totalling 3910 m *12,828 ft*. Two towers will rise 297 m *974 ft 5 in* above water level, and the two main supporting cables will be 1100 mm *43¼ in* in diameter, making both tower height and cable diameter world records.

The Seto-Ohashi double-deck road and rail bridge linking Kojima, Honshu with Sakaide, Shikoku, Japan opened on 10 Apr 1988 at a cost of £4.9 billion and 17 lives. The tolls for cars are £33 each way. The overall length of the Seto-Ohashi Bridge is 12,306 m *43,374 ft*, making it the longest combined road/railway bridge in the

world. The Tsing Ma Bridge in Hong Kong, when completed, will have a main span of 1377 m *4518 ft*, making it the longest suspension bridge span for combined road/railway traffic.

Cable-stayed The longest cable-stayed bridge span in the world is the 530 m *1739 ft* Skarnsundet Bridge over the Trondheim Fjord in Norway, completed in 1991.

The Humber Estuary Bridge, the main span of which is 1410 m *4626 ft* long.
(Photo: Spectrum Colour Library)

The Pont de Normandie, in Le Havre, France, when completed, will have a cable-stayed main span of 856 m *2808 ft*.

Currently the longest cable-stayed bridge in the UK is the £86 million Queen Elizabeth II Bridge on the M25 motorway over the river Thames at Dartford, Kent with a span of 450 m *1476 ft* and opened to traffic in 1991.

The United Kingdom's longest-span cable-stayed bridge will be the second Severn Bridge, due for completion in 1996, with a main span of 456 m *1496 ft*. The overall length of the crossing structure will be 5168 m *16,955 ft*, making it the longest bridge in Britain. The bridge will join Avon with Gwent.

Cantilever The Quebec Bridge (Pont de Québec) over the St Lawrence River in Canada has the longest cantilever truss span of any in the world, measuring 549 m *1800 ft* between the piers and 987 m *3239 ft* overall. It carries a railway track and two carriageways. Work started in 1899, and

it was finally opened to traffic on 3 Dec 1917 at a cost of $Can22.5 million and 87 lives.

Great Britain's longest cantilever bridge is the Forth Bridge. Its two main spans are 521 m *1710 ft* long. It carries a double railway track over the Firth of Forth 47.5 m *156 ft* above the water level. Work began in November 1882 and the first test trains crossed on 22 Jan 1890 after an expenditure of £3 million. It was officially opened on 4 Mar 1890.

Floating The longest floating bridge is the Second Lake Washington Bridge, Evergreen, Seattle, Washington State, USA. Its total length is 3839 m *12,596 ft* and its floating section measures 2291 m *7518 ft*. It was built at a total cost of $15 million and completed in August 1963.

Covered The longest covered bridge is that at Hartland, New Brunswick, Canada, measuring 390.8 m *1282 ft* overall, completed in 1899.

Railway The world's longest rail/road bridge is the Seto-Ohashi Bridge (⇨ Cable suspension, above).

Britain's longest is the second Tay Bridge 3552 m *11,653 ft*, across the Firth of Tay at Dundee, Scotland, opened on 20 Jun 1887. It has 85 spans, of which 74—with a length of 3136 m *10,289 ft*—are over the waterway.

The 878 brick arches of the former London–Greenwich Railway viaduct between London Bridge and Deptford Creek, built in 1836, extend for 6 km *3¾ miles*.

Steel arch bridge The longest steel arch bridge is the New River Gorge bridge, near Fayetteville, West Virginia, USA, completed in 1977, with a span of 518 m *1700 ft*.

The longest in Great Britain is the Runcorn–Widnes bridge,

GUESS WHAT?

Q Which British river has a record-beaking tunnel and will have a record-breaking bridge?

A *See Page 98*

Cheshire opened on 21 Jul 1961, with a span of 329.8m *1082ft*.

Stone arch bridge The longest stone arch bridge is the 1161m *3810ft* long Rockville Bridge north of Harrisburg, Pennsylvania, USA, with 48 spans containing 196,000 tonnes of stone. It was completed in 1901.

The longest stone arch span is the Planen Bridge in Germany at 89.9m *295ft*.

The longest in the United Kingdom is the Grosvenor Bridge at Chester, Cheshire (61m *200ft*) completed in 1830. At the time of its construction this was the longest such span in the world.

Longest bridging The Second Lake Pontchartrain Causeway was completed on 23 Mar 1969, joining Mandeville and Metairie, Louisiana, USA. It has a length of 38,422m *126,055ft*. It cost $29.9 million and is 69m *228ft* longer than the adjoining First Causeway completed in 1956.

Widest The widest long-span bridge is the 503m *1650ft* Sydney Harbour Bridge, Australia, (48.8m *160ft* wide). It carries two electric overhead railway tracks, eight lanes of roadway and a cycle track and footway. It was officially opened on 19 Mar 1932.

The River Roch is bridged for a distance of 445m *1460ft* where the culvert passes through the centre of Rochdale, Greater Manchester and this is sometimes claimed to be a breadth.

Highest The highest bridge in the world is over the Royal Gorge of the Arkansas River in Colorado, USA, at 321m *1053ft* above the water level. It is a suspension bridge with a main span of 268m *880ft* and was constructed in six months, ending on 6 Dec 1929.

The tallest multispan cantilever construction viaduct in the United Kingdom is over the Dee on the A483 Newbridge Bypass, Clwyd. It is 57.3m *188ft* high. The Crumlin viaduct (61m *200ft*) held the United Kingdom record between 1857 until its demolition in 1966.

Highest!

The road bridge at the highest altitude in the world, 5602m *18,380ft*, is the 30m *98.4ft* long Bailey Bridge designed and constructed by Lt Col. S.G. Vombatkere and an Indian Army team in August 1982 near Khardung-La, in Ladakh, India.

Railway The highest railway bridge in the world is the Mala Rijeka viaduct of Yugoslav Railways at Kolasin on the Belgrade–Bar line. It is 198m *650ft* high and was opened on 1 Jun 1976. It consists of steel spans mounted on concrete piers.

The highest railway bridge in Great Britain is the Ballochmyle viaduct over the river Ayr, Strathclyde, built 51.5m *169ft* over the river bed in 1846–8. At that time it had the world's longest masonry railway arch span of 55.2m *181ft*.

Tallest The tallest bridge towers in the world are those of the Golden Gate Bridge, which connects San Francisco and Marin County, California, USA. The towers of this suspension bridge extend 227m *745ft* above the water. Completed in 1937, the bridge has an overall length of 2733m *8966ft*.

The Golden Gate Bridge will lose its status in 1998 to the Akashi-Kaikyo towers (⇨ Cable suspension bridges, longest).

Speedy!

Bridge building A team of British soldiers from 21 Engineer Regiment based at Nienburg, Germany constructed a bridge across a 8m *26ft* gap using a five-bay single-storey MGB (medium girder bridge) in a time of 7min 12sec at Hameln, Germany on 3 Nov 1992.

Lowest Britain's lowest bridge over a public road is just 1.61m *5ft 3½in* high. It is under a railway line and next to a level crossing at Hoddesdon, Herts.

Cycleway bridge The longest cycleway bridge is over the 17 railway tracks of Cambridge Station, Cambs. It has a tower 35m *115ft* high and two 50m *164ft* long approach ramps, and is 237.6m *779ft 6in* in length.

Viaducts

The longest railway viaduct in the world is the rock-filled Great Salt Lake Railroad Trestle, carrying the Southern Pacific Railroad 19km *11.85 miles* across the Great Salt Lake, Utah, USA. It was opened as a pile and trestle bridge on 8 Mar 1904, but converted to rock fill in 1955–60.

Aqueducts

Longest ancient The greatest of ancient aqueducts was that of Carthage in Tunisia, which ran 141km *87.6 miles* from the springs of Zaghouan to Djebel Djougar. It was built by the Romans during the reign of Publius Aelius Hadrianus (AD 117–138). In 1895, 344 arches still survived. Its original capacity has been calculated at 31.8 million litres *7 million gal* per day.

Tallest The tallest of the 14 arches of the Aguas Livres aqueduct, built in Lisbon, Portugal in 1784, is 65m *213ft*.

Longest modern The world's longest aqueduct, in the non-classical sense of water conduit, excluding irrigation canals, is the California State Water Project aqueduct, with a length of 1329km *826 miles*, of which 619km *385 miles* is canalized. It was completed in 1974.

The longest bridged aqueduct in Great Britain is the Pont Cysylltau in Clwyd on the Frankton to Llantisilio branch of the Shropshire Union Canal, generally known as the Llangollen or Welsh Canal. It is 307m *1007ft* long, and has 19 arches up to 36m *118ft* high above low water on the Dee. Designed by Thomas Telford (1757–1834), it was opened in 1805. It is still in use today by pleasure craft.

Canals

Earliest Relics of the oldest canals in the world, dated by archaeologists c. 4000 BC, were discovered near Mandali, Iraq early in 1968.

The earliest canals in Britain were first cut by the Romans. In the Midlands the 17km *11 mile* long Fossdyke Canal between Lincoln and the River Trent at Torksey, Lincs was built c. AD 65 and was scoured in 1122. It is still in use today.

Though the Exeter Canal was cut as early as 1564–6, the first wholly artificial major navigation canal in the United Kingdom was the 29.7km *18½ mile* long canal with 14 locks from Whitecoat Point to Newry, Northern Ireland, opened on 28 Mar 1742.

Longest The longest canal in the ancient world was the Grand Canal of China from Beijing to Hangzhou. It was begun in 540 BC and not completed until 1327, by which time it extended (including canalized river sections) for 1781km *1107 miles*. Having been allowed by 1950 to silt up to the point that it was nowhere more than 1.8m *6ft* deep, it is now, however, plied by vessels of up to 2000 tonnes.

The Beloye More (White Sea) Baltic Canal from Belomorsk to Povenets, Russia is 227km *141 miles* long and has 19 locks. It was completed with the use of forced labour in 1933 but cannot accommodate ships of more than 5m *16ft* in draught.

The world's longest big-ship canal is the Suez Canal linking the Red and Mediterranean Seas, opened on 16 Nov 1869. It took 10 years to build the canal, with a workforce of 1.5 million people, of whom 120,000 perished during the construction. It is 161.9km *100.6 miles* in length from Port Said lighthouse to Suez Roads, has a minimum width of 280m *919ft* and a maximum width of 345m *1132ft*.

The largest vessel to transit the Suez Canal has been *Hellas Fos*, of 555,051 dwt (length 414.23m *1359ft 0in*; beam 63.3m *207ft 8in*). It first transited the canal on 26 May 1986. The USS *Shreveport* transited southbound on 15–16 Aug 1984 in a record 7hr 45min. There are nearly 17,000 transits annually or some 47 per day.

Great Britain Canals and river navigations in Great Britain amount to approximately 5630km *3500 miles* with a further 290km *180 miles* being restored. Of these, 4000km *2500 miles* are interlinked.

Busiest The busiest ship canal is the Kiel Canal linking the North Sea with the Baltic Sea in Germany. Over 40,000 transits are recorded annually. The busiest in terms of tonnage of shipping is the Suez Canal, with 444,583,000 grt in the fiscal year 1992/3.

Largest canal system The seawater cooling system associated with the Madinat Al-Jubail Al-Sinaiyah construction project in Saudi Arabia is believed to be the world's largest canal system. It brings 10 million m³ *353 million ft³* of seawater per day to cool the industrial establishments (⇨ Construction project).

Longest artificial seaway The St Lawrence Seaway is 304km *189 miles* in length along the New York State–Ontario border from Montreal to Lake Ontario. It enables ships up to 222m *728ft* long and 8m *26.2ft* draught (some of which are of 26,400 tonnes) to sail 3769km *2342 miles* from the North Atlantic up the St Lawrence estuary and across the Great Lakes to Duluth, Minnesota, USA. The project, begun in 1954, cost $470 million and was opened on 25 Apr 1959.

Longest irrigation The Karakumsky Canal stretches 1200km *745 miles* from Haun-Khan to Ashkhabad, Turkmenistan. The 'navigable' length in 1993 was 800km *500 miles*.

Locks

Largest The Berendrecht lock, which links the River Scheldt with docks of Antwerp, Belgium, is the largest sea lock in the world. First locked in April 1989, it has a length of 500m *1640ft*, a width of 68m *223ft* and a sill level of 13.5m *44ft*. Each of its four sliding lock gates weighs 1500 tonnes.

GUESS WHAT?

Q Where is the longest canal-tunnel?

A See Page 99

Buildings and Structures

The largest and deepest lock in the United Kingdom is the Royal Portbury Lock, Bristol, opened in 1977, which measures 366.7 × 43 m *1199.8 × 140 ft* and has a depth of 20.2 m *66 ft*.

Highest rise and longest flight The world's highest lock elevator overcomes a head of 68.6 m *225 ft* at Ronquières on the Charleroi–Brussels Canal, Belgium. Two 236-wheeled caissons are each able to carry 1370 tonnes, and take 22 minutes to cover the 1432 m *4698 ft* long inclined plane.

The longest flight of locks in the United Kingdom is on the Worcester and Birmingham Canal at Tardebigge, Hereford & Worcester, where in a 4 km *2½ mile* stretch there are the Tardebigge (30 locks) and Stoke (six locks) flights which together drop the canal 78.9 m *259 ft*.

> In the 11.6 km *7¼ mile* stretch from Huddersfield to Marsden, W Yorks on the Huddersfield Narrow Canal (closed in 1944), there were a total of 42 locks.

Largest cut The Corinth Canal, Greece, opened in 1893, is 6.33 km *3.93 miles* long, 8 m *26 ft* deep, 24.6 m *81 ft* wide at the surface, and has an extreme depth of cutting of 79 m *259 ft*. It is still in use today. The Gaillard Cut (known as 'the Ditch') on the Panama Canal is 82 m *270 ft* deep between Gold Hill and Contractor's Hill with a bottom width of 152 m *500 ft*.

Dams

Most massive Measured by volume, the largest dam is New Cornelia Tailings on Ten Mile Wash, in Arizona, USA, with a volume of 209.5 million m³ *274.5 million yd³*. When completed, the Syncrude Tailings dam near Fort McMurray, in Alberta, Canada will be the largest, with a planned volume of 540 million m³ *706.3 million yd³*. Both are earthfill dams.

The most massive dam in Britain is the Northumbrian Water Authority's Kielder dam, a 52 m *170 ft* high earth embankment measuring 1140 m *3740 ft* in length and 5,300,000 m³ *6,932,000 yd³* in volume.

Highest The highest dam is currently the 300 m *984 ft* high Nurek dam on the River Vakhsh, Tajikistan, but this should be surpassed by the Rogunskaya dam, at 335 m *1098 ft*, also across the River Vakhsh. However, the break-up of the former Soviet Union has delayed its completion.

The rock-fill Llyn Brianne dam, Dyfed is Great Britain's highest dam, reaching 91 m *298½ ft* in November 1971. It became operational on 20 Jul 1972.

Longest The Kiev dam across the Dniepr, Ukraine, completed in 1964, has a crest length of 41.2 km *25.6 miles*.

The Yacyretá dam across the River Paraná on the Argentinian/Paraguayan border, due for completion in 1998, should be 69.6 km *43.2 miles* long.

Strongest Completed, but not operational, is the 245 m *803 ft* high Sayano-Shushenskaya dam on the River Yenisey, Russia, which is designed to bear a load of 18 million tonnes from a fully-filled reservoir of 31,300 million m³ *41,000 million yd³* capacity.

Largest concrete The Grand Coulee dam on the Columbia River, Washington State, USA was begun in 1933 and became operational on 22 Mar 1941. It was finally completed in 1942 at a cost of $56 million. It has a crest length of 1272 m *4173 ft* and is 167 m *550 ft* high. The volume of concrete poured was 8,092,000 m³ *10,585,000 yd³* to a weight of 19,595,000 tonnes.

Highest concrete The highest concrete dam is Grande Dixence, on the River Dixence in Switzerland, built between 1953 and 1961 to a height of 285 m *935 ft* with a crest length of 700 m *2297 ft*, using 5,960,000 m³ *7,800,000 yd³* of concrete.

Reservoirs

Largest The most voluminous man-made reservoir is the Kakhovskaya reservoir, on the River Dniepr in Ukraine, with a volume of 182.0 km³ *43.6 miles³* and an area of 2160 km² *834 miles²*. It was completed in 1955.

The world's largest artificial lake measured by surface area is Lake Volta, Ghana, formed by the Akosombo dam, completed in 1965. By 1969 the lake had filled to an area of 8482 km² *3275 miles²*, with a shoreline 7250 km *4500 miles* in length.

The completion in 1954 of the Owen Falls Dam near Jinja, Uganda, across the northern exit of the White Nile from the Victoria Nyanza marginally raised the level of that *natural* lake by adding 204.8 km³ *49.1 miles³*, and technically turned it into a reservoir with a surface area of 69,484 km² *26,828 miles²* and a capacity of 2.7 × 10¹² m³ *3.5 × 10¹² yd³*.

UK The most capacious reservoir in Britain is Kielder Water in the North Tyne Valley, Northumberland, which filled to 200 billion litres *44 billion gal* from 15 Dec 1980 to mid-1982, and which acquired a surface area of 1086 ha *2684 acres* and a perimeter of 43.4 km *27 miles* to become England's second largest lake.

Rutland Water has a lesser capacity, with 124.1 billion litres *27.3 billion gal*, and a lesser perimeter (38.6 km *24 miles*) but a greater surface area of 1254 ha *3100 acres*.

Largest polder (reclaimed land) Of the five great polders in the old Zuider Zee, Netherlands, the largest will be the Markerwaard, if it is completed, at 60,000 ha *148,250 acres* (603 km² *231 miles²*). However, for the time being the project has been abandoned. Work on the 106 km *65 mile* long surrounding dyke began in 1957. The water area remaining after the erection of the dam (32 km *20 miles* in length), built between 1927–32, is called IJsselmeer, which is due to have a final area of 1262.6 km² *487½ miles²*.

Largest levees The most massive ever built were the Mississippi levees, begun in 1717 but vastly augmented by the US Federal Government after the disastrous floods of 1927. These extended for 2787 km *1732 miles* along the main river from Cape Girardeau, Missouri, USA to the Gulf of Mexico and comprised more than 765 million m³ *1000 million yd³* of earthworks. Levees on the tributaries comprised an additional 3200 km *2000 miles*. Much of the area suffered from extensive flooding in the summer of 1993 resulting in widespread damage to the levees.

> The Grand Coulee Dam became even more well-known in 1958 when Lonnie Donegan had a top 10 hit in Britain with a song about it. Record-breaking dams are not normally the subject of successful pop songs!

Tunnels

Longest

Water-supply tunnel The longest tunnel of any kind is the New York City West Delaware water-supply tunnel, begun in 1937 and completed in 1944. It has a diameter of 4.1 m *13½ ft* and runs for 169 km *105 miles* from the Rondout reservoir into the Hillview reservoir, on the border of Yonkers and New York City, USA.

Longest!

The United Kingdom's longest is the London Water Ring Main, construction of which started in March 1986 and was completed in February 1993. When fully operational, the 80 km *50 mile* long Ring Main will carry 1300 million litres *285 million gal* of drinking water a day—half of London's requirements.

Rail The 53.85 km *33.46 mile* long Seikan rail tunnel was bored to 240 m *787 ft* beneath sea level and 100 m *328 ft* below the sea bed of the Tsugaru Strait between Tappi Saki, Honshū, and Fukushima, Hokkaidō, Japan. Tests started on the sub-aqueous section (23.3 km *14½ miles*) in 1964 and construction in June 1972. It was holed through on 27 Jan 1983 after a loss of 66 lives. The first test run took place on 13 Mar 1988.

Proposals for a Gotthard base tunnel between Erstfeld and Bodio, both in Switzerland, envisage a rail tunnel 57 km *35½ miles* long.

Construction of the world's longest undersea tunnel—the £10 billion Channel Tunnel under the English Channel between Folkestone, Kent and Calais, France—began on 1 Dec 1987 and was open for road traffic using the Shuttle and through passenger and freight trains in 1994. A land link was created between Great Britain and France when the service tunnel drives met under the channel on 1 Dec 1990. The length of each twin rail tunnel is 49.94 km *31.03 miles* and the diameter 7.6 m *24 ft 11 in*.

Great Britain's longest main-line railway tunnel is the Severn Tunnel 7 km *4 miles*, linking Avon and Gwent, constructed with 76,400,000 bricks between 1873 and 1886.

Continuous subway The Moscow metro Kaluzhskaya underground railway line from Medvedkovo to Bittsevsky Park is *c.* 37.9 km *23.5 miles* long and was completed in early 1990.

Road tunnel *Longest* The 16.32 km *10.14 mile* long two-lane St Gotthard road tunnel from Göschenen to Airolo, Switzerland opened to traffic on 5 Sep 1980. Nineteen lives were lost during its construction, begun in autumn 1969, at a cost of 690 million Swiss francs (then £175 million).

The longest road tunnel in the United Kingdom is the Mersey (Queensway) Tunnel, joining Liverpool and Birkenhead, Merseyside. It is 3.43 km *2.13 miles* long, or 4.62 km *2.87 miles* including branch tunnels. Work commenced in December 1925 and it was opened by HM King George V on 18 Jul 1934. The 11 m *36 ft* wide four-lane roadway carries nearly 7½ million vehicles a year. The first tube of the second Mersey (Kingsway) Tunnel was opened on 24 Jun 1971, with the breakthrough of the second in 1972.

Largest The largest diameter road tunnel in the world is that blasted through Yerba Buena Island, San Francisco, California, USA. It is 24 m *77 ft 10 in* wide, 17 m *56 ft* high and 165 m *540 ft* long. Around 250,000 vehicles pass through on its two decks every day.

Hydro-electric irrigation The 82.9 km *51½ mile* long Orange–Fish Rivers tunnel, South Africa, was bored between 1967 and 1973 at an estimated cost of £60 million. The lining to a minimum thickness of 23 cm *9 in* gave a completed diameter of 5.33 m *17 ft 6 in*. The Lesotho Highlands Water Project, when completed, will consist of several connected sections with a total length of 84 km *52¼ miles*.

The Majes dam project in Peru involves 98 km *60.9 miles* of tunnels for hydro-electric and water-supply purposes. The dam is at an altitude of 4200 m *13,780 ft*.

Longest and largest canal-tunnel The Rove tunnel on the Canal de Marseille au Rhône in the south of France was completed in 1927 and is 7120 m *23,359 ft* long, 22 m *72 ft* wide and 11.4 m *37 ft* high. Built to be navigated by sea-going ships, it was closed in 1963 following a collapse of the structure and has not been re-opened.

Great Britain The longest canal tunnel is the Standedge (more properly Stanedge) Tunnel in W Yorks on the Huddersfield Narrow Canal, built from 1794 to 4 Apr 1811. It measures 5.1 km *3 miles* in length and was closed on 21 Dec 1944. However, it is currently undergoing restoration.

The British canal system contained 84 tunnels exceeding 30 yd *27.4 m*, of which 49 are open today. The longest of these is the 2.88 km *1.79 mile* long Dudley Tunnel on the Birmingham & Black Country canals, although navigation is restricted.

Oldest navigable The Malpas tunnel on the Canal du Midi in south-west France was completed in 1681 and is 161 m *528 ft* long. Its completion enabled vessels to navigate from the Atlantic Ocean to the Mediterranean Sea via the river Garonne to Toulouse and the Canal du Midi to Sète.

Tunnelling The longest unsupported example of a machine-bored tunnel is the Three Rivers water tunnel, 9.37 km *5.82 miles* long with a 3.2 m *10 ft 6 in* diameter, constructed for the city of Atlanta, Georgia, USA from April 1980 to February 1982.

Sewerage The Chicago TARP (Tunnels and Reservoir Plan) in Illinois, USA when complete will involve 211 km *131 miles* of sewerage tunnelling. Phase I will comprise 177 km *110 miles* when complete. As of March 1994, 103 km *64 miles* are operational, 33.8 km *21 miles* are under construction, and the remaining 40.2 km *25 miles* are unfunded. The system will provide pollution control to the area and will service 3.9 million people in 52 communities over a 971 km² *375 miles²* area. The estimated cost for the project is $3.6 billion ($2.4 billion for Phase I, $1.2 billion for Phase II).

The Henriksdal plant in Stockholm, Sweden was the world's first major waste-water plant to be built underground. It was built between 1941 and 1971, and involved the excavation of nearly 1 million m³ *35,300,000 ft³* of rock. It is now being enlarged, with the extension due for completion in 1997.

Bridge-tunnel The Chesapeake Bay bridge-tunnel, opened to traffic on 15 Apr 1964, extends 28.40 km *17.65 miles* from Eastern Shore, Virginia Peninsula to Virginia Beach, Virginia, USA. The longest bridged section is Trestle C (7.34 km *4.56 miles* long) and the longest tunnel is the Thimble Shoal Channel Tunnel (1.75 km *1.09 miles*).

Specialized Structures

Advertising signs The highest is the logo 'I' at the top of the First Interstate World Centre building, Los Angeles, California, USA, a 73-storey building 310 m *1017 ft* high.

The largest and tallest free-standing advertising sign is at the Hilton Hotel and Casino in Las Vegas, Nevada, USA, and was completed in December 1993. Its two faces have a total area of 7648.5 m² *82,328 ft²* and it is 110.3 m *362 ft* high. It was constructed by John Renton Young Lighting and Sign of Las Vegas.

The most conspicuous sign ever erected was the electric Citroën sign on the Eiffel Tower, Paris. It was switched on on 4 Jul 1925, and could be seen 38 km *24 miles* away. It was in six colours with 250,000 lamps and 90 km *56 miles* of electric cables. The letter 'N' which terminated the name 'Citroën' between the second and third levels measured 20.8 m *68 ft 5 in* in height. The whole apparatus was taken down in 1936.

The largest advertisement on a building measured 3879 m² *41,756 ft²* and was erected to promote Emirates, the international airline of the United Arab Emirates. It was located by the M4 motorway, near Chiswick, London and was displayed from November 1992 to January 1993.

The UK's largest permanent advertising sign is 86.61 × 24.99 m *284 ft 2 in × 82 ft*, promoting South Cleveland Garages. It is sited on the roof of one of the stands at Ayresome Park, the home ground of Middlesbrough Football Club, in Cleveland.

Hoarding The world's largest hoarding is that of the Bassat Ogilvy Promotional Campaign for Ford España, measuring 145 m *475 ft 9 in* in length and 15 m *49 ft 3 in* in height. It is sited at Plaza de Toros Monumental de Barcelona, Barcelona, Spain and was installed on 27 Apr 1989.

In the Air!

Reebok International Ltd of Massachusetts, USA flew a banner from a single seater plane which read 'Reebok Totally Beachin'. The banner measured 15 m *50 ft* in height and 30 m *100 ft* in length, and was flown from 13–16 and 20–23 Mar 1990 for four hours each day.

Illuminated The world's largest illuminated sign is that at the Hilton Hotel and Casino in Las Vegas, Nevada, USA (⇨ above).

The UK's longest illuminated sign is that shared by P & O European Ferries and Stena Sealink at Dover Eastern Docks, Kent. It is 82 m *269 ft* long and 65 cm *25½ in* deep, and was installed by Dover Sign Co. in August 1993.

Neon The longest neon sign is the letter 'M' installed on the Great Mississippi River Bridge in Memphis, Tennessee, USA. It is 550 m *1800 ft* long and comprises 200 high-intensity lamps.

The largest measures 111.4 × 19.05 m *365 ft 6 in × 62 ft 6 in* and was built to promote

The background picture shows cleaning of the London Water Ring Main, which is the UK's longest water-supply tunnel.

(Photo: Thames Water plc)

999, a traditional Chinese medicine from the Nanfang Pharmaceutical Factory in China. It was erected between November 1992 and April 1993 on Hong Kong Island and contains 13.14 km *8.16 miles* of neon tubing.

Barn The largest barn in Great Britain is one at Frindsbury, Kent. Its length is 66.7 m *219 ft* and it is still wholly roofed.

The longest tithe barn in Britain is one measuring 81 m *268 ft* long at Wyke Farm, near Sherborne, Dorset.

The Ipsden Barn, Oxon, is 117 m *385½ ft* long but 9 m *30 ft* wide (1074 m² *11,565 ft²*).

Bonfire The largest bonfire was constructed at Workington, Cumbria by inhabitants of the town and off-duty firefighters. It was 37.33 m *122 ft 6 in* high, with an overall volume of 7100 m³ *250,700 ft³*, and was lit on 5 Nov 1993.

> The record-breaking bonfire built in Workington in 1993 beat the British record for the largest bonfire which had stood for 91 years!

Breakwater The world's longest breakwater is that which protects the Port of Galveston, Texas, USA. The granite South Breakwater is 10.85 km *6.74 miles* in length.

Great Britain's longest is the North Breakwater at Holyhead, Anglesey, which is 2.395 km *1.488 miles* in length and was completed in 1873.

Cemeteries *Largest* Ohlsdorf Cemetery in Hamburg, Germany is the largest cemetery, covering an area of 400 ha *990 acres*, with 967,774 burials and 397,966 cremations as at 31 Dec 1993. It has been in continuous use since 1877.

The tallest cemetery is the permanently illuminated Memorial Necrópole Ecumênica, in Santos, near São Paulo, Brazil, which is 10 storeys high, occupying an area of 1.8 ha *4.4 acres*. Its construction started in March 1983 and the first burial was on 28 Jul 1984.

(Photo: Acervo Memorial)

Great Britain's largest cemetery is Brookwood Cemetery, Brookwood, Surrey, owned by Mr Ramadan Güney. It is 200 ha *500 acres* in extent and has more than 231,000 interments.

Chimneys *Tallest* The coal power-plant No. 2 stack at Ekibastuz, Kazakhstan, completed in 1987, is 420 m *1377 ft* tall. The diameter tapers from 44 m *144 ft* at the base to 14.2 m *46 ft 7 in* at the top and it weighs 60,000 tonnes.

The tallest chimney in Great Britain is one of 259 m *850 ft* at Drax Power Station, N Yorks, completed in 1969. It has an untapered diameter of 26 m *85 ft* and also has the greatest capacity of any British chimney.

Most massive The world's most massive chimney in terms of internal volume was built by M.W. Kellog Co. for Empresa Nacional de Electricidad S.A at Puentes de García Rodríguez, Spain. The chimney is 350 m *1148 ft* tall, contains 15,750 m³ *20,600 yd³* of concrete and 1315 tonnes of steel and has an internal volume of 189,720 m³ *248,100 yd³*.

Columns The tallest columns are the thirty-six 27.5 m *90 ft* tall fluted pillars of Vermont marble in the colonnade of the Education Building, Albany, New York State, USA. Their base diameter is 1.98 m *6 ft 6 in*.

The tallest load-bearing stone columns in the world are those measuring 21 m *69 ft* in the Hall of Columns of the Temple of Amun at Karnak, opposite Thebes on the Nile, the ancient capital of Upper Egypt. They were built in the 19th dynasty in the reign of Rameses II *c.*1270 BC.

Cooling towers The largest cooling tower is 180 m *590 ft* tall and is adjacent to the nuclear power plant at Uentrop, Germany. It was completed in 1976.

UK The largest in the United Kingdom are at Drax Power Station, N Yorks. They are 115 m *377 ft* tall and 92.68 m *304 ft* in diameter at the base.

Crematorium The largest crematorium in the world is at the Nikolo-Arkhangelskiy Crematorium, east Moscow, Russia with seven twin cremators of British design, completed in March 1972. It covers an area of 210 ha *519 acres* and has six Halls of Farewell for atheists.

The oldest crematorium in Great Britain was built in 1879 at Woking, Surrey. The first cremation took place there on 26 Mar 1885.

Domes The largest is the Louisiana Superdome, New Orleans, USA, which has a diameter of 207.26 m *680 ft*.

Britain's largest is that of the Bell Sports Centre, Perth, Tayside with a diameter of 67 m *222 ft*. It was designed by D.B. Cockburn and constructed in Baltic whitewood by Muirhead & Sons Ltd of Grangemouth, Central.

Doors *Largest* The four doors in the Vehicle Assembly Building near Cape Canaveral, Florida, USA have a height of 140 m *460 ft*.

Great Britain's largest are those of the Britannia Assembly Hall, at Filton airfield, Avon. The doors are 315 m *1035 ft* in length and 20 m *67 ft* high, divided into three bays each 105 m *345 ft* across.

The largest simple hinged door in Great Britain is that of Ye Old Bull's Head, Beaumaris, Anglesey, which is 3.35 m *11 ft* wide and 3.96 m *13 ft* high.

Oldest Great Britain's oldest are those of Hadstock Church, near Saffron Walden, Essex, which date from *c.*1040 AD and exhibit evidence of Danish workmanship.

Heavy!

The heaviest door is that of the laser target room at Lawrence Livermore National Laboratory, California, USA. It weighs 326.5 tonnes, is up to 2.43 m *8 ft* thick and was installed by Overly Manufacturing Company.

Earthworks The largest earthworks prior to the mechanical era were the Linear Earth Boundaries of the Benin Empire (*c.*1300) in the Edo state (formerly Bendel) of Nigeria. In March 1993 it was estimated by Dr Patrick Darling that the total length of the earthworks was probably around 16,000 km *10,000 miles*, with the amount of earth moved estimated at 75 million m³ *100 million yd³*.

The greatest prehistoric earthwork in Britain is Wansdyke, originally Wodensdic, which ran 138 km *86 miles* from Portishead, Avon to Inkpen Beacon and Ludgershall, south of Hungerford,

Amazing mazes:

Featuring Cornelius the stegosaurus

The world's largest maze ever constructed was in the shape of a stegosaurus, made in a cornfield at Lebanon Valley College, Pennsylvania, USA. It was 152 m *500 ft* long and covered an area of 11,700 m² *126,000 ft²*, and was in existence for two months between September and November 1993.

The stegosaurus, called Cornelius, was the brainchild of Adrian Fisher of Minotaur Designs in St Albans, Herts, who has designed over 100 mazes worldwide. He explains how this particular challenge arose.

" It was one of those wonderful occasions when everything came together at once. Former student Don Frantz wanted Lebanon Valley College to help the Red Cross Appeal for Flood Victims of the Midwest, where millions of cornfields had been devastated. How about using a cornfield to raise funds and give everyone a great time? The biggest maze in the world would certainly generate media interest! We brainstormed the idea, and thus the Amazing Maize Maze was born.

All summer, paths were cut through 6 ft high rows of maize. Together with Chase Senge, we created a total maze experience with an intense level of staffing, horsedrawn haywagon rides, an all-day barbecue, a sound and music system throughout the maze, a quiz trail, portable Colour Mazes, a free soda fountain within the hedges, and a portaloo half-way round ("it's such a big maze, you might need it!"). As performance art, a traditional English village green "Robin Hood's Race" Turf Maze was dug in 24 hours, and much enjoyed.

The record size and giant image from the sky attracted TV, radio and press coverage coast-to-coast throughout the USA and worldwide. Over a sunny weekend, 6,000 visitors raised over $32,000 for the Red Cross Appeal. It was one of the happiest maze events I have known. "

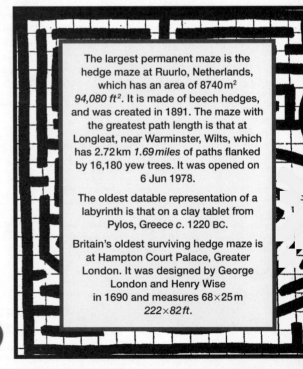

The largest permanent maze is the hedge maze at Ruurlo, Netherlands, which has an area of 8740 m² *94,080 ft²*. It is made of beech hedges, and was created in 1891. The maze with the greatest path length is that at Longleat, near Warminster, Wilts, which has 2.72 km *1.69 miles* of paths flanked by 16,180 yew trees. It was opened on 6 Jun 1978.

The oldest datable representation of a labyrinth is that on a clay tablet from Pylos, Greece *c.* 1220 BC.

Britain's oldest surviving hedge maze is at Hampton Court Palace, Greater London. It was designed by George London and Henry Wise in 1690 and measures 68×25 m *222×82 ft*.

Berks. It was built by the Belgae (*c.*150 BC) as their northern boundary.

Fences *Longest* The dingo-proof wire fence enclosing the main sheep areas of Australia is 1.8m *6ft* high, plus 30cm *1ft* underground and stretches for 5531km *3437miles*. The Queensland state government discontinued full maintenance in 1982.

Flagpoles The tallest flagpole was erected outside the Oregon Building at the 1915 Panama-Pacific International Exposition in San Francisco, California, USA. Trimmed from a Douglas fir, it stood 91.3m *299ft 7in* in height and weighed 47tonnes.

The tallest unsupported flagpole in the world is the 86m *282ft* tall steel pole weighing 54,400kg *120,000lb*, which was erected on 22 Aug 1985 at the Canadian Expo 86 exhibition in Vancouver, British Columbia. This supports a gigantic ice hockey stick 62.5m *205ft* in length.

Great Britain's tallest flagpole is a 68m *225ft* tall Douglas fir staff at Kew, Richmond-upon-Thames, Surrey. Cut in Canada, it was shipped across the Atlantic and towed up the river Thames on 7 May 1958, to replace the old 65m *214ft* tall staff erected in 1919.

Fountains The tallest is the fountain at Fountain Hills, Arizona, USA, built at a cost of $1.5 million for McCulloch Properties Inc. When all three pumps are on, it can reach 190m *625ft*, if conditions are right (for example, no wind).

Britain's tallest is the Emperor Fountain at Chatsworth, Bakewell, Derbyshire. When first tested on 1 Jun 1844, it attained the then unprecedented height of 79m *260ft*. In recent years it has not been played to more than 76m *250ft* and rarely beyond 55m *180ft*.

Fumigation The largest fumigation carried out was during the restoration of the Mission Inn complex in Riverside, California, USA on 28 Jun–1 Jul 1987 to rid the buildings of termites. Over 350 tarpaulins were used, each weighing up to 160kg *350lb*, and the operation involved completely covering the 6500m² *70,000ft²* site and buildings—domes, minarets, chimneys and balconies, some of which exceeded 30m *100ft* in height.

Garbage dump Reclamation Plant No. 1, on Staten Island, New York, USA, which opened in March 1947, is the world's largest sanitary landfill. It covers 1200ha *3000 acres* and is estimated to contain 100,000 tonnes of rubbish, including 14,000 tonnes processed in 1993.

Gasholders The largest gasholders are at Fontaine L'Evêque, Belgium, where disused mines have been adapted to store up to 500 million m³ *17,650million ft³* of gas at ordinary pressure.

The largest known remaining conventional gasholder is that at Simmering, Vienna, Austria, completed in 1968, with a height of 84m *275ft* and a capacity of 300,000m³ *10.6 million ft³*.

Great Britain's largest was at the East Greenwich Gas Works. The No. 2 holder was built in 1891 with an original capacity for 346,000m³ *12,200,000ft³*. It was later reconstructed with a capacity of 252,000m³ *8.9 million ft³*, a water tank 92m *303ft* in diameter and a full inflated height of 45m *148ft*. However, it has been demolished in the meantime and the record is now held by the No. 1 holder, built in 1885, also at Greenwich. It has a capacity of 229,000m³ *8.1 million ft³* and a height of 61m *200ft*.

Globe The largest revolving globe is a sphere 10m *33ft* in diameter, weighing 30tonnes. It is called 'Globe of Peace' and was built between 1982 and 1987 by Orfeo Bartolucci from Apecchio, Pesaro, Italy.

Jetty The longest deep-water jetty is the Quai Hermann du Pasquier at Le Havre, France, with a length of 1520m *5000ft*. It is part of an enclosed basin and has a constant depth of water of 9.8m *32ft* on both sides.

Kitchen An Indian government field kitchen set up in April 1973 at Ahmadnagar, Maharashtra, then a famine area, daily provided 1.2million subsistence meals.

Lamp-post The tallest lighting columns are the four made by Petitjean & Cie of Troyes, France and installed by Taylor Woodrow at Sultan Qaboos Sports Complex, Muscat, Oman. They stand 63.5m *208ft 4in* high.

Lighthouses *Tallest* The steel tower near Yamashita Park in Yokohama, Japan is 106m *348ft* high. It has a power of 600,000 candelas and a visibility range of 32km *20 miles*.

The tallest lighthouse in Great Britain is the 49m *160ft 9in* tall Bishop Rock Lighthouse, 6.4km *4 miles* west of the Isles of Scilly.

Most powerful The lighthouse in Great Britain with the most powerful light is Strumble Head Lighthouse on Ynysmeicl (St Michael's Island), 4.8km *3 miles* west of Fishguard, Dyfed, Wales. Its intensity is 6,000,000 candela and its range is 39km *24 miles*, characterized by four white flashes every 15 seconds.

Greatest range The lights with the greatest range are those 332m *1089ft* above the ground on the Empire State Building, New York City, USA. Each of the four-arc mercury bulbs has a rated candlepower of 450,000,000, visible 130km *80 miles* away on the ground and 490km *300 miles* away from aircraft.

Marquees *Largest* A marquee covering an area of 17,500m² *188,350ft²* (1.7ha *4.32acres*) was erected by the firm of Deuter from Augsburg, Germany for the 1958 'Welcome Expo' in Brussels, Belgium.

Britain's largest marquee was one made by Piggot Brothers in 1951 and used by the Royal Horticultural Society at their annual show in the grounds of the Royal Hospital in Chelsea, London. It measured 94×146m *310×480ft* and consisted of 30km *18¾ miles* of 91cm *36in* wide canvas covering a ground area of 13,820m² *148,800ft²*.

The largest single-unit tent in Britain covers a ground area of *c.* 12,000m² *130,000ft²* and was

Tallest!

The world's tallest fences are security screens 20m *65ft* high erected by Harrop-Allin of Pretoria, South Africa in November 1981 to protect fuel depots and refineries at Sasolburg from terrorist rocket attack.

GUESS WHAT?

Q Which country is the largest producer of gas?

A See Page 78

ON THE RECORD

THE AMAZING MAIZE MAZE

(Photo: Dwayne Arehart)

manufactured by Clyde Canvas Ltd of Edinburgh, Lothian.

Maypole The tallest maypole erected in Britain was one of Sitka spruce 32.12m *105ft 7in* tall, put up in Pelynt, Cornwall on 1 May 1974.

Menhir The tallest known menhir is the Grand Menhir Brisé at Locmariaquer, Brittany, France, which was originally 18m *59ft* high and weighed over 300tonnes, but is now in four pieces.

Monuments *Tallest* The tallest monument is the stainless-steel Gateway to the West arch in St Louis, Missouri, USA, completed on 28 Oct 1965 to commemorate the westward expansion after the Louisiana Purchase of 1803. It is a sweeping arch spanning 192m *630ft* and rising to the same height. It cost $29 million and was designed in 1947 by the Finnish-American architect Eero Saarinen (1910–61).

The tallest monumental column is that commemorating the Battle of San Jacinto (21 Apr 1836), on the bank of the San Jacinto River near Houston, Texas, USA. Constructed from 1936–9, the tapering column is 173m *570ft* tall, 14m *47ft* square at the base, and 9m *30ft* square at the observation tower, which is surmounted by a star weighing 199.6tonnes.

Great Britain's largest megalithic prehistoric monument and largest existing henge are the 11.5ha *28½ acre* earthworks and stone circles of Avebury, Wilts, 'rediscovered' in 1646. The earliest calibrated date in the area of this Neolithic site is *c*.4200BC. The work is 365m *1200ft* in diameter with a 12m *40ft* ditch around the perimeter.

The henge of Durrington Walls, Wilts, obliterated by road building, had a diameter of 472m *1550ft*. It was built *c*.2500BC and required some 900,000 man-hours.

The largest trilithons exist at Stonehenge, to the south of Salisbury Plain, Wilts, with single sarsen blocks weighing over 45tonnes and requiring over 550 men to drag them up a 9 degree gradient. The earliest stage of the construction of the ditch has been dated to 2800BC.

Oldest The oldest scheduled ancient monument is Kent's Cavern, near Torquay, Devon, which is a cave site containing deposits more than 300,000 years old dating from the Lower Palaeolithic period.

Newest The newest scheduled ancient monument is a hexagonal pillbox and 48 concrete tank-traps near Christchurch, Dorset, built in World War II and protected since 1973.

Mound The largest artificial mound is the gravel mound built as a memorial to the Seleucid King Antiochus I (reigned 69–34BC), which stands on the summit of Nemrud Dagi (2494m *8182ft*), south-east of Malatya, eastern

The unfinished obelisk, probably commissioned by Queen Hatshepsut *c*.1490BC and *in situ* at Aswan, Egypt, is 41.75m *136ft 10in* long and weighs 1168tonnes.

(Photo: Spectrum Colour Library)

Turkey. It is 59.8m *197ft* tall and covers 3ha *7.5acres*.

The largest in Great Britain is Silbury Hill, 9.7km *6 miles* west of Marlborough, Wilts, which involved the moving of an estimated 680,000tonnes of chalk, at a cost of 18 million man-hours to make a cone 39m *130ft* high with a base of 2ha *5½ acres*. Prof. Richard Atkinson, who was in charge of the 1968 excavations, showed that it is based on an innermost central mound, similar to contemporary round barrows, and it is now dated to 2745±185BC.

Obelisk (monolithic) *Largest* The 'skewer' or 'spit' (from the Greek *obeliskos*) of Tuthmosis III brought from Aswan, Egypt by Emperor Constantius in the spring of AD 357 was repositioned in the Piazza San Giovanni in Laterane, Rome on 3 Aug 1588. Once 36m *118ft 1in* tall, it now stands 32.81m *107ft 7in* and weighs 455tonnes.

The longest time a raised obelisk has remained *in situ* is that still at Heliopolis, near Cairo, erected by Senusret I *c*.1750BC.

Tallest The world's tallest obelisk is the Washington Monument in Washington, DC, USA. Situated in a 43ha *106 acre* site and standing 169.3m *555ft 5⅛in* high, it was built to honour

The memorial to King Antiochus I in Turkey is the world's largest artificial mound.

(Photo: Spectrum Colour Library)

Seven Wonders of the World

The Seven Wonders of the World were first designated by Antipater of Sidon in the 2nd century BC. They were:– the Pyramids of Giza, the Hanging Gardens of Babylon, the Statue of Zeus at Olympia, the Temple of Artemis at Ephesus, the Tomb of King Mausolus, the Colossus of Rhodes and the Pharos of Alexandria.

Only the Pyramids of Giza still exist substantially today. They are to be found near El Giza (El Gizeh), south-west of El Qâhira (Cairo) in Egypt. They were built by three Fourth Dynasty Egyptian Pharaohs: Khwfw (Khufu or Cheops), Kha-f-Ra (Khafre, Khefren or Chepren) and Menkaure (Mycerinus). The great pyramid (The 'Horizon of Khufu') was finished under Rededef c.2580 BC. Its original height was 146.7m *481ft 3in* (now, since the loss of its topmost stones and the pyramidion, reduced to 137.5m *451ft 1in*) with a base line of 230m *756ft*, thus covering slightly more than 5ha *13acres*. It has been estimated that a permanent work force of 100,000 required 30 years to manoeuvre into position the 2,300,000 limestone blocks averaging 2½ tonnes each, totalling about 5,840,000 tonnes and a volume of 2,595,000 m³ *91,640,000ft³*.

Of the other six wonders only fragments remain of the Temple of Artemis (Diana) of the Ephesians, built c.350BC at Ephesus, Turkey (destroyed by the Goths in AD 262), and of the Tomb of King Mausolus of Caria, built at Halicarnassus, now Bodrum, Turkey, c.325BC.

No trace remains of:– the Hanging Gardens of Semiramis, at Babylon, Iraq c.600BC; the statue of Zeus (Jupiter), by Phidias (5th century BC) at Olympia, Greece (lost in a fire at Istanbul) in marble, gold and ivory and 12m *40ft* tall; the figure of the god Helios (Apollo), a 35m *117ft* tall statue sculptured 292–280BC, by Chares of Lindus (destroyed by an earthquake in 224BC); and the world's earliest lighthouse, 122m *400ft* tall built by Sostratus of Cnidus (c.270BC) as a pyramid shaped tower of white marble, on the island of Pharos (Greek, *pharos*=lighthouse), off the coast of El Iskandariya (Alexandria), Egypt (destroyed by earthquake in AD1375).

George Washington (1732–99), the first President of the United States.

The United Kingdom's tallest is Cleopatra's Needle on the Embankment, London, which at 20.88 m *68ft 5in* is the world's 11th tallest. Weighing 189.35tonnes, it was towed up the Thames from Egypt on 21 Jan 1878 and positioned on 13 September.

Piers The Dammam Pier, Saudi Arabia, on the Persian Gulf, is the longest in the world with an overall length of 10.93km *6.79 miles*. It was begun in July 1948 and completed on 15 Mar 1950. The area was subsequently developed by 1980 into the King Abdul Aziz Port, with 39 deepwater berths. The original causeway, much widened, and the port extends to 12.8 km *7.95 miles* including other port structures.

Great Britain's longest is the Bee Ness Jetty, completed in 1930, which stretches 2500m *8200ft* along the west bank of the river Medway, 8.8km *5½ miles* below Rochester, at Kingsnorth, Kent.

Promenade The longest covered promenade is the Long Corridor in the Summer Palace in Beijing, China, running for 728m *2388ft*. It is built entirely of wood and divided by crossbeams into 273 sections.

Pyramids *Largest* The largest pyramid, and the largest monument ever constructed, is the

Quetzalcóatl at Cholula de Rivadabia, 101km *63miles* south-east of Mexico City. It is 54m *177ft* tall and its base covers an area of nearly 18.2ha *45acres*. Its total volume has been estimated at 3.3million m³ *4.3million yd³* compared with the current volume of 2.4million m³ *3.1million yd³* for the Pyramid of Khufu or Cheops (⇨ Seven Wonders of the World).

Oldest The Djoser Step Pyramid at Saqqâra, Egypt, was constructed by Imhotep to a height of 62m *204ft*, and originally had a Tura limestone casing dating from c.2900BC.

Scaffolding The tallest scaffolding was erected by Regional Scaffolding & Hoisting Co., Inc. of Bronx, New York, USA around the New York City Municipal Building, and was in place from 1988–92. Its total height was 198m *650ft* and its volume 135,900 m³ *4,800,000ft³*. The work required 12,000 scaffold frames.

Scarecrow The tallest scarecrow was 'Stretch II', constructed by the Speers family of Paris, Ontario, Canada and a crew of 15 at the Paris Fall Fair on 2 Sep 1989. It was 31.56m *103ft 6¾in* in height.

Sewage works The Stickney Water Reclamation Plant, at Stickney, in the suburbs of Chicago, Illinois, USA, serves an area containing nearly 2,200,000 people. A total of 656 staff are employed at the plant, which treated an average of 3126 million litres *688 million gal* of waste per day in 1993.

UK The largest full treatment works in Britain and Europe is the Beckton Works, east London, which serves a population equivalent of 2,980,000 and handles an estimated daily flow of 955 million litres *210 million gal*. The total capacity of the tanks is 773,000 m³ *27,300,000ft³*.

The gigantic statue of Buddha in Tokyo is quite a sight now, but three little visitors decided that they couldn't wait for it to be completed and climbed on to one of its huge toes before the foot was attached to the rest of the statue.

(Photos: Gamma— Kaku Kurita and Torin Boyd)

Snow and ice constructions A snow palace 26.5m *87ft* high, one of four structures which together spanned 214.2m *702ft 8in*, was unveiled on 7 Feb 1987 at Asahikawa City, Hokkaidō, Japan.

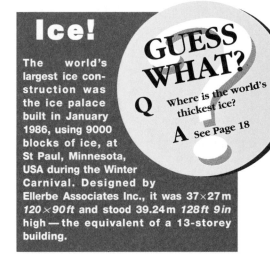

Ice!

The world's largest ice construction was the ice palace built in January 1986, using 9000 blocks of ice, at St Paul, Minnesota, USA during the Winter Carnival. Designed by Ellerbe Associates Inc., it was 37×27m *120×90ft* and stood 39.24m *128ft 9in* high—the equivalent of a 13-storey building.

GUESS WHAT?

Q Where is the world's thickest ice?

A See Page 18

Snowman The tallest was 27.47m *90ft 1in* high and was made by a team of eight local residents at Saas-Fee, Switzerland. It took 21 days to build the snowman, which was completed on 6 Nov 1993.

Stairway The longest service staircase is for the Niesenbahn funicular near Spiez, Switzerland, which rises to 2365m *7759ft*. It has 11,674 steps and a bannister.

The longest stairs in Great Britain are those from the transformer gallery to the surface, 324m *1065ft*, in the Cruachan Power Station, Argyll. They have 1420 steps and the plant's work-study unit allows 27min 41.4sec for the ascent.

Spiral The tallest spiral staircase is on the outside of the chimney Bobila Almirall located in Terrassa, Barcelona, Spain. Built by Mariano Masana i Ribas in 1956, it is 63.2m *207ft* high and has 217 steps.

The longest spiral staircase is one 336m *1103ft* deep with 1520 steps installed in the Mapco-White County Coal Mine, Carmi, Illinois, USA by Systems Control Inc. in May 1981.

Statues *Tallest* A bronze statue of Buddha 120m *394ft* high was completed in Tokyo, Japan in January 1993. It is 35m *115ft* wide and weighs 1000 tonnes. The statue took seven years to make, and was a joint Japanese–Taiwanese project.

The statue of Maitreya, which stands 26m *85ft* high, is carved out of a single piece of white sandalwood tree. It is located at the Lama Temple (Yonghegong), in the north-east of Beijing. The Imperial Court allowed two years for the carving of the statue and finished the project in 1750.

Longest Near Bamiyan, Afghanistan there are the remains of the recumbent Sakya Buddha, built of plastered rubble, which was 'about 305m' *1000ft* long and is believed to date from the 3rd or 4th century AD.

Swing A glider swing 9.1m *30ft* high was constructed by Kenneth R. Mack, Langenburg, Saskatchewan, Canada for Uncle Herb's Amusements in 1986. The swing is capable of taking its four riders to a height of 7.6m *25ft* off the ground.

Tidal river barrier The largest tidal river barrier is the Oosterscheldedam, a storm-surge barrier in the south-western corner of the Netherlands. It has 65 concrete piers and 62 steel gates, and covers a total length of 9km *5½ miles*. It was opened by HM Queen Beatrix on 4 Oct 1986.

is 19.65m *64½ ft* in height and 23m *75½ ft* in diameter, with a capacity of 7.41 million litres *1.63 million gal.*

Oldest The world's oldest known vat is still in use at Hugel et Fils (founded 1639) in Riquewihr, Haut-Rhin, France. Twelve generations of the family have used it since 1715.

Walls *Longest* The Great Wall of China is the longest in the world and has a main-line length of 3460km *2150 miles*—nearly three times the length of Britain. Completed during the reign of Qin Shi Huangdi (221–210 BC), it also has 3530km *2195 miles* of branches and spurs. Its height varies from 4.5–12m *15–39ft* and it is up to 9.8m *32ft* thick. It runs from Shanhaiguan, on the Gulf of Bohai, to Yumenguan and Yangguan, and was kept in repair up to the 16th century.

Thickest Urnammu's city walls at Ur (now Muqayyar, Iraq), destroyed by the Elamites in 2006 BC, were 27m *88ft* thick and made of mud brick.

The walls of the Great Tower or Donjon of Flint Castle, Clwyd, built in 1277–80, are 7m *23ft* thick.

Indoor waterfall The tallest indoor waterfall measures 34.75m *114ft* in height and is backed by 840m² *9000ft²* of marble. It is situated in the lobby of Greektown's International Center Building, Detroit, Michigan, USA.

Water tower The Waterspheroid at Edmond, Oklahoma, USA, built in 1986, rises to a height of 66.5m *218ft*, and has a capacity of 1,893,000 litres *416,000 gal.* The tower was manufactured by Chicago Bridge and Iron.

Waterwheel The Mohammadieh Noria wheel at Hamah, Syria has a diameter of 40m *131ft* and dates from Roman times.

The largest waterwheel in the British Isles is the Lady Isabella at Laxey, Isle of Man with a diameter of 22m *72ft 2in* and an axle weighing 10 tonnes. It was completed on 24 Sep 1854 for draining the local lead mine but has not been used commercially since 1929, although it is still in working order for tourists.

Windows The largest sheet of glass ever manufactured was one of 50m² *540ft²*, or 20×2.5m *65ft 7in × 8ft 2¼ in*, exhibited by the Saint Gobin Co. in France at the *Journées Internationales de Miroiterie* in March 1958.

The largest single windows in the world are those in the Palace of Industry and Technology at Rondpoint de la Défense, Paris, France, with an extreme width of 218m *715ft* and a maximum height of 50m *164ft*.

The United Kingdom record was a sheet made by Pilkington of St Helens, Merseyside for the Festival of Britain in 1951, measuring 2.5×15.2m *8ft 2¼ in × 49ft 10½ in*.

Stained glass The tallest piece of stained glass is the 41.14m *135ft* high back-lit glass mural installed in 1979 in the atrium of the Ramada Hotel, Dubai (⬦ Religions, Stained glass).

The largest single stained-glass window in the UK is one with an area of 746.9m² *8039ft²*, designed by Brian Clarke and installed at the Victoria Quarter, Leeds, W Yorks in 1990 (⬦ Religions, Stained glass).

Ziggurat The largest ziggurat ever built was that of the Elamite King Untas, *c*.1250 BC, known as the Ziggurat of Choga Zambil, 30km *18.6 miles* from Haft Tepe, Iran. The outer base was 105 ×105m *344×344ft* and the fifth 'box' 28×28m *92×92ft*, nearly 50m *164ft* above.

The largest partially surviving ziggurat is the Ziggurat of Ur (now Muqayyar, Iraq) with a base 61 × 45.7m *200 ×150ft*, built to three storeys and surmounted by a summit temple. The first and part of the second storeys now survive to a height of 18m *60ft*. It was built in the reign of Ur-nammu (*c*. 2113–2096 BC).

Record-breaking windows at the Palace of Industry and Technology in Paris.
(Photo: Gamma)

Tombs The Mount Li tomb, the burial place of Qin Shi Huangdi, the 1st Emperor of Qin, dates to 221 BC and is situated 40km *25 miles* east of Xianyang, China. The two walls surrounding the grave measure 2173×974m *7129 × 3195ft* and 685×578m *2247 × 1896ft*. Several pits in the tomb contained a vast army of an estimated 8000 life-size terracotta soldiers.

A tomb housing 180,000 World War II dead on Okinawa, Japan was enlarged in 1985 to accommodate another 9000 bodies thought to be buried on the island.

Totem pole A 52.73m *173ft* tall pole was raised on 6 Jun 1973 at Alert Bay, British Columbia, Canada. It tells the story of the Kwakiutl and took 36 man-weeks to carve.

Vats *Largest* 'Strongbow', which is used by H.P. Bulmer Ltd, the English cider-makers of Hereford,

It was reported in October 1990 that after two years of exertion Lin Youdian had become the first person to walk the entire length of the Great Wall of China.

Some 51.5km *32 miles* of the wall have been destroyed since 1966 and part of the wall was blown up to make way for a dam in July 1979.

The longest of the Roman walls in Britain was the 4.5–6m *15– 20ft* tall Hadrian's Wall, built AD 122–26. It crossed the Tyne-Solway isthmus for 118km *73½ miles* from Bowness-on-Solway, Cumbria, to Wallsend-on-Tyne, Tyne & Wear, and was abandoned in AD 383.

Transport

Ships

Earliest

Oldest active The screw propeller was invented and patented by a Kent farmer, Sir Francis Pettit Smith (1808–71), on 31 May 1836 (British Patent No. 7104).

Ocean-going The world's oldest active ocean-going ship is the *MV Doulos* (Greek for 'servant'), built in 1914 in the USA and first named *Medina*. She is currently operating as an international Educational and Christian service vessel with approximately 300 crew, staff and passengers on board from 30 different nations.

UK The oldest British vessel afloat is the *Foudroyant*, built of teak in Bombay in 1817 as HMS *Trincomalee*, and for many years a familiar sight moored in Portsmouth Harbour, Hants. Used as a training ship since 1897, the *Foudroyant* was moved from Portsmouth to Hartlepool, Cleveland in 1987 for repairs and restoration as a typical naval frigate of the Nelson era before eventually being displayed in a specially constructed dry-dock at Hartlepool.

Earliest powered vessels Marine propulsion by steam engine was first achieved in 1783 when the Marquis Jouffroy d'Abbans (1751–1832) ascended a reach of the river Saône near Lyon, France, in the 180-tonne paddle steamer *Pyroscaphe*.

The first successful power-driven vessel was the tug *Charlotte Dundas*, a stern paddle-wheel steamer built for the Forth and Clyde Canal in 1801–2 by William Symington (1763–1831), using a double-acting condensing engine constructed by James Watt (1736–1819).

Earliest turbine ship The *Turbinia* was designed by the Hon. Sir Charles Parsons (1854–1931) and built in 1894 at Wallsend-on-Tyne, Tyne & Wear. She was 30m *100ft* long, had a displacement of 45.2tonnes and was powered by three steam turbines totalling about 2000 shaft

GUESS WHAT?

Q What is the longest time between drop and pick-up of a message in a bottle?

A *See Page 108*

horsepower (shp). First publicly demonstrated in 1897, when a speed of 34.5knots *64km/h* was achieved, the ship is now preserved at Newcastle-upon-Tyne.

Wooden ships Heaviest The 8662-tonne, 101.7-m *333⅔-ft*-long *Richelieu* was launched in Toulon, France on 3 Dec 1873.

Longest The longest wooden ship ever constructed was the 115-m *377-ft-4-in Rochambeau* formerly the *Dunderberg*, built in New York (1867–72). By comparison, the biblical length of Noah's Ark was 300cubits or, at 45.7cm *18in* to a cubit, 137m *450ft*.

Shipwrecks

Oldest The oldest shipwreck ever found at sea is one off Ulu Buren, near Kas, southern Turkey, which is dated to the 14th Century BC. It is not yet clear whether artefacts excavated from the sea off the isle of Dhókós, near the Greek island of Hydra and dated to 2450 BC ± 250, came from a wreck.

The largest wreck removal was carried out in 1979 by Smit Tak International, who removed the remains of the 120,000-ton French tanker *Betelgeuse* from Bantry Bay, Republic of Ireland within 20 months.

Warships

Largest battleships The largest battleships ever commissioned were the Japanese vessels *Yamato* (completed on 16 Dec 1941 and sunk south-west of Kyūshū, Japan by US planes on 7 Apr 1945) and *Musashi* (sunk in the Philippine Sea by 11 bombs

Wreck!

The 321,186-tonne deadweight VLCC (very large crude carrier) *Energy Determination* blew up and broke in two in the Strait of Hormuz, Persian Gulf on 12 Dec 1979. The ship was in ballast at the time but its hull value was $58 million.

Collision!

The closest approach to an irresistible force striking an immovable object occurred on 16 Dec 1977, 35 km *22 miles* off the coast of southern Africa, when the tanker *Venoil* (330,954 dwt) struck her sister ship *Venpet* (330,869 dwt).

The world's oldest active paddle steamer continuously operated as such is *Skibladner*, which has plied Lake Mjøsa, Norway since 1856. She was built in Motala, Sweden and has had two major refits.
(Photo: Quadrant Picture Library)

Battleships!

The last battleships in active service were the USS *Missouri* and USS *Wisconsin*, 270m *887ft* long and with a full load displacement of 58,000 tonnes. Both were first commissioned in 1944 and later recommissioned in 1986 and 1988 respectively following major refits. Armaments include nine 16-inch guns used in the Gulf War in 1991 and capable of firing 1225-kg *2700-lb* projectiles a distance of 39 km *23 miles*. Both ships, together with two others of the same class, USS *New Jersey* and USS *Iowa*, are now in reserve.

and 16 torpedoes on 24 Oct 1944). Both ships had a full load displacement of 69,988tons, an overall length of 263m *863ft*, a beam of 38.7m *127ft* and a full load draught of 10.8m *35½ft*. They were armed with nine 460-mm *18.1-in* guns in three triple turrets. Each gun weighed 164.6tonnes, was 22.8m *75ft* long and fired 1451-kg *3200-lb* projectiles.

UK Britain's largest and last battleship was HMS *Vanguard* (1944–60). She had a full load displacement of 52,245tonnes, was 248.1m *814ft* long overall and was armed with eight 15-in guns, which were originally mounted in the battlecruisers *Courageous* and *Glorious* in 1917. *Vanguard* was completed too late for service in World War II, and spent much of her time in the Home Fleet's Training Squadron before being broken up at Faslane, Strathclyde in 1960.

Fastest warship On 25 Jan 1980 a US Navy hovercraft—the 23.7-m *78-ft*-long, 100-tonne test vehicle SES-100B—achieved a speed of 91.9knots *170km/h*. (⇨ Hovercraft)

Fastest destroyer The highest speed attained by a destroyer was 45.25knots *83.42km/h* by the 2830-tonne French ship *Le Terrible* in 1935. Built in Blainville, France and powered by four Yarrow small tube boilers and two Rateau geared turbines, giving 100,000 shp, she was decommissioned at the end of 1957.

Largest aircraft carriers The warships with the largest full load displacement in the world are the Nimitz class US Navy aircraft carriers USS *Nimitz, Dwight D. Eisenhower, Carl Vinson, Theodore Roosevelt, Abraham Lincoln* and *George Washington*, the last two of which displace 102,000tons. They are 332.9m *1092ft* long, have 1.82ha *4½ acres* of flight deck and, driven by four nuclear-powered 260,000shp geared steam turbines, can reach speeds of well over 30knots *56km/h*. Their complement is 5986. Two more ships of this class, *John C. Stennis* and *United States* are under construction.

UK The Royal Navy's largest fighting ship is the aircraft carrier HMS *Ark Royal*, commissioned on 1 Nov 1985. She has a 167.6-m *550-ft*-long flight deck, is 209.3m *685.8ft* long overall and is powered by four Rolls-Royce Olympus TM3B gas turbines delivering 97,200 hp to give a top speed of 28knots *51.8km/h*.

Most landings The greatest number on an aircraft carrier in one day was 602, achieved by Marine Air Group 6 of the United States Pacific Fleet Air Force aboard the USS *Matanikau* on 25 May 1945 between 8a.m. and 5p.m.

Guns and armour The largest guns ever mounted in any of HM ships were the 18-in pieces in the light battlecruiser (later aircraft carrier) HMS *Furious* in 1917. In 1918 they were transferred to the monitors HMS *Lord Clive* and *General Wolfe*.

The thickest armour ever carried was in HMS *Inflexible* (completed 1881), measuring 60 cm *24 in* backed by teak up to a maximum thickness of 107 cm *42 in*.

Longest submarine patrol The longest submerged and unsupported patrol made public is 111 days (57,085 km *30,804 nautical miles*) by HM Submarine *Warspite* (Cdr J.G.F. Cooke RN) in the South Atlantic from 25 Nov 1982 to 15 Mar 1983.

The largest propeller ever is the 11-m *36-ft-1-in* diameter triple-bladed screw made by Kawasaki Heavy Industries of Japan and delivered on 17 Mar 1982 for the 208,739 dwt bulk carrier *Hoei Maru* (now *New Harvest*).

Submarines

Largest The world's largest submarines are of the Russian Typhoon class. The launch of the first at the secret covered shipyard at Severodvinsk in the White Sea was announced by NATO on 23 Sep 1980. The vessels are believed to have a dived displacement of 26,500 tonnes, to measure 170 m *558 ft* overall and to be armed with 20 multiple warhead SS-NX-20 missiles with a range of 8895 km *4800 nautical miles*. Six of the class are now in service.

Human Power!

The fastest speed attained by a human-powered propeller submarine is 5.94 ± 0.05 knots *3.06 m/sec* by *F.A. U-Boat*, designed and built by the Florida Atlantic University Ocean Engineering Department, Boca Raton, Florida, USA, using a two-blade high aspect ratio propeller propulsion system, on 8 Mar 1994. It was crewed by Charles Callaway and William Fay, with team leader Karl Heeb.

The record by a human-powered non-propeller submarine is 2.9 ± 0.1 knots *1.49 m/sec* by *SubDUDE*, designed by the Scripps Institution of Oceanography, University of California, San Diego, USA using a horizontal oscillating foil propulsion system on 21 Aug 1992. It was crewed by Kimball Millikan and Ed Trevino, with team leader Kevin Hardy.

UK The largest submarines ever built for the Royal Navy are the four nuclear-powered vessels of the Vanguard class, the first three of which, *Vanguard*, *Victorious* and *Vigilant* were laid down in 1986–91, with HMS *Vanguard* commissioned in 1993 at a cost of £600 million. They are 150 m *491 ft 8 in* long, have a beam of 12.8 m

42 ft, a draught of 12 m *39.4 ft* and have a dived displacement of about 16,000 tonnes.

Fastest The Russian Alpha class nuclear-powered submarines have a reported maximum speed of over 45 knots *83.4 km/h*. With use of titanium alloy, they are believed to be able to dive to 762 m *2500 ft*. A US spy satellite over the naval yard in Leningrad

GUESS WHAT?
Q How old was David Sandeman when he sailed across the Atlantic?
A See Page 110

GUESS WHAT?
Q What was the 'terrible turtle'?
A See Page 111

The largest liner under the British Flag is MV *Queen Elizabeth 2* of 69,053 grt and an overall length of 293 m *963 ft*. Her maiden voyage for the Cunard Line was on 2 May 1969 and she set a 'turn round' record of 3 hr 18 min at New York City, USA on 14 Dec 1993. She was built by John Brown & Co (Clydebank) Ltd, Scotland and refitted by Lloyd Werft, Bremerhaven, Germany with diesel electric engines in 1986–7 to give a maximum speed of 32½ knots. She is the last passenger liner to be regularly employed on transatlantic service between Southampton, Hants and New York, USA and can accommodate 1929 passengers and 1007 crew.
(Photo: Quadrant Picture Library/Matthews)

Deepest dive The 30-ton US Navy deep submergence vessel *Sea Cliff* (DSV 4), commissioned in 1973, reached a depth of 6000 m *20,000 ft* in March 1985.

(now St. Petersburg) on 8 Jun 1983 showed they were being lengthened and they are now 81.5 m *267.4 ft* long.

Passenger Ships

Largest liners The RMS *Queen Elizabeth* (finally 82,998 but formerly 83,673 gross tons), of the Cunard fleet, was the largest passenger vessel ever built and had the largest displacement of any liner in the world. She had an overall length of 314 m *1031 ft*, was 36 m *118 ft 7 in* in breadth and was powered by steam turbines which developed 168,000 hp. Her last passenger voyage ended on 15 Nov 1968. In 1970 she was removed to Hong Kong to serve as a floating marine university and renamed *Seawise University*. She was burnt out on 9 Jan 1972 when three simultaneous outbreaks of fire strongly pointed to arson. The gutted hull had been cut up and removed by 1978. *Seawise* was a pun on the owner's initials, C.Y. Tung (1911–82).

The largest in current use and the longest ever is the *Norway* of 76,049 gross register tons 315.53 m *1035 ft 7½ in* in overall length, with a passenger capacity of 2022 and 900 crew. She was built as the SS *France* in 1960 and renamed after purchase in June 1979 by Knut Kloster of Norway. She is normally employed on cruises in the Caribbean and based at Miami, USA. Work undertaken during an extensive refit during the autumn of 1990 increased the number of passenger decks to 11. She draws 10.5 m *34½ ft*, has a beam of 33.5 m *110 ft* and cruises at 18 knots for the Royal Viking Line.

The largest-ever cruise liners are to be built by the Fincantieri Yard in Italy for P&O, and are planned for completion in 1997. The 100,000-ton liners will carry 2600 passengers and will cost £263 million.

Yachts *Largest* The largest yacht is the Saudi Arabian royal yacht *Abdul Aziz*, which is 147 m *482 ft* long. Built in Denmark and completed on 22 Jun 1984 at Vospers Yard, Southampton, Hants, she was estimated in September 1987 to be worth over $100 million.

Private The largest private (non-Royal) yacht is the 122 m *400 ft* former ferry *Alexander*, converted in 1986.

Hydrofoils The largest passenger hydrofoils are three 165-ton Supramar PTS 150 Mk IIIs, which carry 250 passengers at 40 knots *74 km/h* across the Öre Sound between Malmö, Sweden and Copenhagen, Denmark. They were built by Westermoen Hydrofoil Ltd of Mandal, Norway.

Canoe!

The kauri wood Maori war canoe *Nga Toki Matawhaorua* weighed 20.3 tonnes and was 35.7 m *117 ft* long. It was shaped with adzes at Kerikeri Inlet, New Zealand in 1940. The crew numbered 70 or more.

The 'Snake Boat' *Nadubhagóm* from Kerala, southern India has a crew of 109 rowers and nine 'encouragers'. It is 41.1 m *135 ft* long.

GUINNESS NEWS

7 June 1983

Bottle found after 73 years

Message safely received!

A bottle evidently thrown overboard from a ship nearly 73 years ago has been found washed up on Moreton Island, off Australia's Gold Coast.

Damp

It was spotted by Vicki Keller and Alan Mills from Brisbane as they were cycling through the foothills of sand dunes on the south side of the island. Although the message was damp and difficult to make out, it is just possible to decipher 'Put overboard SS Arawatta coming down the coast from Cairns to Brisbane 9.6.1910'. There is also a reference to 'Linabury, Mayor Murwillumbah', and a Mr Linabury did indeed take office as mayor of Murwillumbah in 1909.

Imprint

The bottle is made of clear glass and is about 10cm (4 inches) long. The imprint is still clearly visible and says 'tricopheros for the skin and hair'—an advertiser's dream!

Cargo Vessels

Largest The world's largest ship of any kind is the oil tanker *Jahre Viking* (formerly the *Happy Giant* and *Seawise Giant*), at 564,650 tonnes deadweight. The tanker is 458.45m *1504ft* long overall, has a beam of 68.8m *226 ft* and a draught of 24.61m *80ft 9in*. Declared a total loss after being disabled by severe bombardment in 1987–8 during the Iran-Iraq war, the tanker underwent extensive renovation in Singapore and Dubai, United Arab Emirates costing some $60 million and was relaunched under its new name in November 1991.

The largest ship carrying dry cargo is the ore carrier *Berge Stahl* of 364,767 tonnes deadweight,

built in South Korea for its Norwegian owner Sig Bergesen. The vessel is 343m *1125ft* long, has a beam of 63.5m *208ft* and was launched on 5 Nov 1986.

Car ferries The world's largest car and passenger ferry in terms of tonnage is *Silja Europa* which entered service in 1993 between Stockholm, Sweden and Helsinki, Finland. Operated by the Silja Line, she is of 59,914 grt, with a length of 201.8m *662ft*, and a beam of 32.6m *107ft*. She can carry 3000 passengers, 350 cars and 60 lorries.

Fastest The fastest car ferries are the twin-hulled, wave-piercing Sea Cats constructed of aluminium alloy by International Catamarans of Hobart, Tasmania which have a cruising speed of 35 knots and are capable of 42 knots. They are 74m *242ft 9in* overall with a beam of 26m *85ft 3½ in*. The first was launched in 1990 with the name *Christopher Columbus*, but has since been renamed *Hoverspeed Great Britain*. Each can carry 432 passengers and 80 cars.

In 1995 a five times larger and even faster vessel is due to enter service with Stena Line between Holyhead, Wales and Dun Laoghaire, Ireland. Stena AB of Sweden have ordered two HSS (Highspeed Sea Service) catamarans from a Finnish builder. Service speed will be 40 knots.

Container ships *Earliest* Shipborne containerization began in 1955 when the tanker *Ideal X* was converted by Malcolm McLean of the United States to carry containers on deck only.

Largest American President Lines has built five ships in Germany—*President Adams*, *President Jackson*, *President Kennedy*, *President Polk* and *President Truman*—which are termed post-Panamax, being the first container vessels too large for transit of the Panama Canal. They are 275.14m *902.69ft* in length and 39.41m *129.29ft* in beam; the maximum beam for the Panama transit is 32.3m *106 ft*. These vessels have a

The world's largest RoRo (roll-on, roll-off) ships are five 730-ft *222.5-m*-long barges operated by Crowley American Transport of Jacksonville, Florida, USA.
(Photo: Aero-pic Jacksonville)

quoted capacity of 4300 TEU (standard length Twenty foot (i.e. 6.096m) Equivalent Unit containers); they have, however, carried more than this in normal service.

Longest Although of smaller registered tonnage, *Dresden Express*, built in South Korea in 1991 for the German Hapag-Lloyd company, is longer, at 294m *964ft* and with a quoted capacity of 4422 TEU.

Most powerful dredger The *Prins der Nederlanden* of 10,586 grt can dredge 20,000 tonnes of sand from a depth of 35m *115ft* via two suction tubes in less than an hour. She is 142.7m *468.4ft* long

Largest hydrofoil The *Plainview* (314 tonnes full load) naval hydrofoil, 64.6m *212ft* long, was launched by the Lockheed Shipbuilding and Construction Co. at Seattle, Washington, USA on 28 Jun 1965. She has a service speed of 92km/h *57.2 mph*.

Most powerful icebreakers The most powerful purpose-built icebreakers are the *Rossiya* and her sister ships *Sovetskiy Soyuz* and *Oktyabryskaya Revolutsiya*. Built in Leningrad (now St. Petersburg), Russia and completed in 1985, *Rossiya* is of 23,460 tonnes, is 148m *485ft* long and is powered by 55.95kW *75,000hp* nuclear engines.

The largest *converted* icebreaker was the 306.9-m *1007-ft*-long SS *Manhattan* (43,000 shp), which was converted into a 152,407-tonne icebreaker by the Humble Oil Co. She made a double voyage through the North-

GUESS WHAT?

Q How many people travelled in the world's longest canoe?

A See Page 107

Largest whale factory
The Russian *Sovetskaya Ukraina* (32,034 gross tons) with a summer deadweight of 46,738 tonnes was completed in October 1959. She is 217.8m *714½ft* in length and 25.8m *84ft 7in* in the beam.

GUESS WHAT?

Q Why is John Moir's record so riveting?

A See Page 110

West Passage in arctic Canada from 24 August to 12 November 1969.

The North-West Passage was first navigated by Roald Engebereth Gravning Amundsen of Norway (1872–1928) in the sealing sloop *Gjøa* in 1906.

Light vessels The earliest station still marked by a light vessel is the Sunk in the North Sea, off Harwich, Essex, established in 1802. A Nore light vessel was first placed in the Thames estuary in 1732.

Note: By 1989 all Trinity House manned light vessels around the coasts of England and Wales had been withdrawn and replaced by automatic vessels or LANBYs (Large Automatic Navigation Buoys).

Oldest active The oldest active square-rigged sailing vessel in the world is the restored SV *Maria Asumpta*, (formerly the *Ciudad de Inca*), built near Barcelona, Spain in 1858. She is 29.8 m *98 ft* overall of 127 gross registered tonnage. She was restored in 1981–2 and is used for film work, promotional appearances at regattas and sail training. She is operated by The Friends of *Maria Asumpta* of Lenham, Maidstone, Kent.

Largest The largest vessel ever built in the era of sail was the *France II* (5806 gross tons), launched at Bordeaux, France in 1911. This was a steel-hulled, five-masted barque (square-rigged on four masts and fore and aft rigged on the aftermost mast). Her hull measured 127.4 m *418 ft* overall. Although principally designed as a sailing vessel with a stump top gallant rig, she was also fitted with two auxiliary engines; however these were removed in 1919 and she became a pure sailing vessel. She was wrecked off New Caledonia on 12 Jul 1922.

The only seven-masted sailing schooner ever built was the 114.4-m *375.6-ft*-long *Thomas W. Lawson* (5218 gross tons), built at Quincy, Massachusetts, USA in 1902 and wrecked off the Isles of Scilly, Cornwall on 15 Dec 1907. (⇨ Largest junks)

Largest in service The world's only surviving First Rate Ship-of-the-Line is the Royal Navy's 104-gun battleship HMS *Victory*, laid down at Chatham, Kent on 23 Jul 1759 and constructed from the wood of some 2200 oak trees. She bore the body of Admiral Nelson from Gibraltar to Portsmouth, Hants arriving 44 days after serving as his victorious flagship at the Battle of Trafalgar on 21 Oct 1805. In 1922 she was moved to No. 2 dock at Portsmouth—site of the world's oldest graving dock.

Longest The longest sailing ship is the 187-m *613-ft* French-built *Club Med 1*, with five aluminium masts and 2800 m² *30,139 ft²* of computer-controlled polyester sails. Operated as a Caribbean cruise vessel for 425 passengers for Club Med, with the small sail area and powerful engines she is really a motor-sailer. A sister-ship *Club Med II* has been commissioned.

Junks A river junk 110 m *361 ft* long, with treadmill-operated paddle-wheels, was recorded in AD 1161.

The largest on record was the sea-going *Zheng He*, flagship of Admiral Zheng He's 62 treasure ships of *c.* 1420, with a displacement of

Tugs!

The largest and most powerful tugs are the *Nikolay Chiker* (SB 131) and *Fotiy Krylov* (SB 135), commissioned in 1989 and built by Hollming Ltd of Finland for the former USSR. Of 25,000 bhp and with a bollard pull in excess of 291 tons, they are 98.8 m *324 ft* long and 19.45 m *64 ft* wide. SB 135 is reported to have been acquired by the Tsavliris Group of Companies of Piraeus, Greece, and to have been renamed *Tsavliris Giant*.

Model Boats!

Members of the Lowestoft Model Boat Club crewed a radio controlled scale model boat on 17–18 Aug 1991 at Dome Leisure Park, Doncaster to a 24-hr distance record of 178.92 km *111.18 miles*.

David and Peter Holland of Doncaster, S. Yorks, members of the Conisbrough and District Modelling Association, crewed a scale model boat of the Bridlington trawler *Margaret H* 41.1 m *135 ft* long continuously on one battery for 24 hours for a distance of 53.83 km *33.45 miles* at the Dome Leisure Complex, Doncaster on 15–16 Aug 1992.

3150 tonnes and a length variously estimated up to 164 m *538 ft*. She is believed to have had nine masts. In *c.* AD 280 a floating fortress 183 m *600 ft* square, built by Wang Jun on the Yangzi river, took part in the Jin-Wu river war. Present-day junks do not, even in the case of the Jiangsu traders, exceed 52 m *170 ft* in length.

Largest sails Sails are known to have been used for marine propulsion since 3500 BC. The largest spars ever carried were those in HM Battleship *Temeraire*, completed at Chatham, Kent, on 31 Aug 1877. She was broken up in 1921. The fore and main yards measured 35 m *115 ft* in length. The foresail contained 1555 m *5100 ft* of canvas weighing 2.03 tonnes, and the total sail area was 2322 m² *25,000 ft²*.

Tallest mast The *Velsheda*, a J-class sailing vessel, is the tallest known single masted yacht in the world, at 51.6 m *169 ¼ ft* measured from heel fitting to mast truck. Built in 1933, the second of the four British J-class yachts, she is unusual in being the only one ever built that was not intended for the America's Cup race. With a displacement of 145 tonnes, she supports a sail area of 696.75 m² *7500 ft²*.

The largest sailing ship now in service is the *Sedov* at 109 m *357 ft* long, built in 1921 at Kiel, Germany and used for training by the Russians. She is 14.6 m *48 ft* in width, with a displacement of 6300 tonnes, 3556 grt and a sail area of 4192 m² *45,123 ft²*.

(Photo: Quadrant Picture Library/A.R. Dalton)

Rail ferries The largest international rail ferries are the *Klaipeda*, *Vilnius*, *Mukran* and *Greifswald*, operating in the Baltic sea between Klaipeda, Lithuania and Mukran, Germany. Built in Wismar, Germany, each ferry is 11,700 tons deadweight and has two decks measuring 190.5 m *625 ft* in length and 91.86 m *301.4 ft* wide. Each vessel can lift 103 standard 14.83 m *48.65 ft*, 84-ton railcars and cover 506 km *273 nautical miles* in 17 hr.

Merchant Shipping

Total The world total of merchant shipping, excluding vessels of less than 100 grt, non-propelled craft, naval auxiliaries, the US Reserve Fleet, and ships restricted to harbour or river/canal service, was 80,655 ships of 457,914,808 grt at 31 Dec 1993.

Shipbuilding Worldwide production of ships completed in 1993, with the same exclusions as above, was 20 million grt. The figures for Russia,

Sailing Ships

Ukraine and the People's Republic of China are incomplete.

Japan completed 9.1 million grt (45 per cent of the world total) in 1993 and UK completions totalled 18 ships of 229,474 grt.

The world's leading shipbuilder in 1993 was Daewoo Shipbuilding & Heavy Machinery Ltd of South Korea, which completed 13 ships of 1.55 million gross tons.

Shipbuilding!

The fastest times in which complete ships of more than 10,000 tons were ever built were achieved at Kaiser's Yard, Portland, Oregon, USA during the wartime programme for building 2742 Liberty ships in 18 shipyards from 27 Sep 1941. In 1942 No. 440, named *Robert E. Peary*, had her keel laid on 8 November, was launched on 12 November and was operational after 4 days 15½ hr on 15 November. She was broken up in 1963.

Biggest owner The largest ship owners are the Japanese NYK Group, whose fleet of owned vessels totalled 11,096,170 tons gross at 1 Feb 1994.

Largest fleet The largest merchant fleet in the world at the end of 1993 was that under the flag of Panama, totalling 57,618,623 tons gross. The equivalent UK figure was 1532 ships of 4,116,868 tons gross.

Riveting The world record for riveting is 11,209 in 9 hr, by John Moir at the Workman Clark Ltd shipyard, Belfast in June 1918. His peak hour was his 7th, with 1409 rivets, an average of nearly 23½ per min.

Hovercraft

Earliest The ACV (air-cushion vehicle) was first made a practical proposition by Sir Christopher Sydney Cockerell (b. 4 Jun 1910), a British engineer who had the idea in 1954, published his Ripplecraft report 1/55 on 25 Oct 1955 and patented it on 12 Dec 1955.

The earliest patent relating to air-cushioned craft was applied for in 1877 by Sir John I. Thornycroft (1843–1928) of London, and the idea was developed by Toivo Kaario of Finland in 1935.

The first flight by a hovercraft was made by the 4-tonne Saunders-Roe SRN1 at Cowes, Isle of Wight on 30 May 1959. With a 680-kg *1500-lb* thrust Viper turbojet engine, this craft reached 68 knots *126 km/h* in June 1961.

The first hovercraft public service was run across the Dee estuary between Rhyl, Clwyd and Wallasey, Merseyside by the 60-knot *111-km/h*, 24-passenger Vickers-Armstrong VA-3 between July and September 1962.

Largest The SRN4 Mk III, a British-built civil hovercraft, weighs 305 tons and can accommodate 418 passengers and 60 cars. She is 56.38 m *185 ft* in length, and is powered by four Bristol Siddeley Marine Proteus engines, giving a maximum speed in

excess of the scheduled permitted cross-Channel operating speed of 65 knots.

Cross-Channel The fastest scheduled crossing of the Channel by hovercraft was achieved by an SRN 4 Mark II Mountbatten class hovercraft operated by Hoverspeed, on 1 Sep 1984, when *The Swift* completed the Dover–Calais run in 24 min 8.4 sec to average more than 54½ knots.

Highest The highest altitude reached by a hovercraft was on 11 Jun 1990 when *Neste Enterprise* and her crew of ten reached the navigable source of the Yangzi river, China at 4983 m *16,050 ft*.

The greatest altitude at which a hovercraft is operating is on Lake Titicaca, Peru, where since 1975 an HM2 Hoverferry has been hovering 3811 m *12,506 ft* above sea level.

Ocean Crossings

Earliest Atlantic The earliest crossing of the Atlantic by a power vessel, as opposed to an auxiliary-engined sailing ship, was a 22-day voyage begun in April 1827, from Rotterdam, Netherlands, to the West Indies, by the *Curaçao*. She was a 38.7-m *127-ft* wooden paddle boat of 438 tons, built as the *Calpe* in Dover, Kent in 1826 and purchased by the Dutch Government for a West Indian mail service.

The earliest Atlantic crossing entirely under steam (with intervals for desalting the boilers) was by HMS *Rhadamanthus*, from Plymouth, Devon to Barbados, West Indies in 1832.

The earliest crossing under continuous steam power was by the condenser-fitted packet ship *Sirius*, 714 tonnes from Queenstown (now Cóbh), Republic of Ireland to Sandy Hook, New Jersey, USA, in 18 days 10 hr from 4–22 Apr 1838.

Fastest Atlantic The fastest crossing of the Atlantic was by the 68-m *222-ft* powerboat *Destriero*, 6–9 Aug 1992. The crossing lasted 2 days 10 hr 34 min 47 sec (45.7 knots smg), and the skipper was Cesare Fiorio (Italy).

The fastest regular commercial crossing and therefore winner of the Hales Trophy or 'Blue Riband' is by the liner *United States* (then 51,988, now 38,216 gross tons), former flagship of the United States Lines. On her maiden voyage between 3–7 Jul 1952 from New York, USA to Le Havre, France and Southampton, Hants, she averaged 35.39 knots, *65.95 km/h* for 3 days 10 hr 40 min (6:36 p.m. GMT, 3 July to 5:16 a.m., 7 July) on a route of 5465 km *2949 nautical miles* from the Ambrose light vessel to the Bishop Rock lighthouse, Isles of Scilly, Cornwall. During this run, on 6–7 July, she steamed the greatest distance ever covered by any ship in a day's run (24 hr) — 1609 km *868 nautical miles*, averaging 36.17 knots *67.02 km/h*. The maximum speed attained from her 240,000-shaft horsepower engines was 38.32 knots *71.01 km/h* in trials on 9–10 Jun 1952.

Fastest Pacific The fastest crossing from

Warship!

The world's fastest warship is the 100-tonne US Navy test hovercraft SES-100B—it is 23.7 m *78 ft* long. She attained a world record 91.9 knots *170 km/h* on 25 Jan 1980 on the Chesapeake Bay Test Range, Maryland, USA. As a result of the success of this test craft, a 3000-tonne US Navy Large Surface Effect Ship (LSES) was built by Bell Aerospace under contract from the Department of Defense in 1977–81. (⊳ Warships)

Oldest & Youngest!

Solo transatlantic crossings

**Youngest sailing: 17 yr 176 days
David Sandeman (GB) 43 days, 1976**

**Oldest sailing: 76 yr 165 days
Stefan Szwarnowski (GB) 72 days, 1989**

**Youngest rowing: 25 yr 306 days
Sean Crowley (GB) 95 days 22 hr, 1988**

**Oldest rowing: 51 yr
Sidney Genders (GB) 160 days 8 hr, 1970**

Yokohama, Japan to Long Beach, California, USA (4840 nautical miles *8960 km*) took 6 days 1 hr 27 min (30 Jun–6 Jul 1973) by the container ship *Sea-Land Commerce* 50,315 tons, at an average speed of 33.27 knots *61.65 km/h*.

Fastest Channel crossing The SeaCat catamaran ferry *Hoverspeed France* sailed from Dover to Calais in 34 min 23 sec on 15 Oct 1991, at an average speed of 37.87 knots *70 km/h*.

Speeds on Water

The highest speed ever achieved on water is an estimated 300 knots *555 km/h* by Kenneth Peter Warby (b. 9 May 1939) on the Blowering Dam Lake, New South Wales, Australia on 20 Nov 1977 in his unlimited hydroplane *Spirit of Australia*.

The official world water speed record is 275.8 knots *511.11 km/h* set on 8 Oct 1978 by Warby on Blowering Dam Lake.

Mary Rife of Flint, Texas, USA set a women's unofficial record of 332.6 km/h *206.72 mph* in her blown fuel hydro *Proud Mary* in Tulsa, Oklahoma, USA on 23 Jul 1977. Her official record is 317 km/h *197 mph*.

Ports

Largest The Port of New York and New Jersey, USA is the world's largest, with a navigable waterfront of 1215 km *755 miles* (474 km *295 miles* in New Jersey) stretching over 238 km² *92 miles²*. A total of 261 general cargo berths and 130 other piers gives a berthing capacity of 391 ships at any one time and the total warehousing floor space is 170.9 ha *422.4 acres*.

The largest British port by tonnage is London (including Tilbury), which handles some 55 million tonnes each year. The largest container port is Felixstowe, Suffolk which handled 1,137,947 actual containers, 1,638,644 TEUs and 16,037,610 tonnes of cargo in 1993.

Busiest The world's busiest port and largest artificial harbour is Rotterdam, Netherlands, covering 100 km² *38 miles²*, with 122.3 km *76 miles* of quays.

Busiest!

Britain's busiest port in terms of ship movements is Dover, Kent which handled 25,951 ship arrivals in 1993. It also handled 18.47 million passengers, 3 million accompanies vehicles, 148,000 coaches and 1.1 million road haulage vehicles.

GUESS WHAT?

Q What is the 24-hour distance record for a model boat?

A See Page 109

Longest hovercraft journey

The extraordinary Trans-African hovercraft Expedition led by David Smithers FRGS, took place between 15 Oct 1969 and 3 Jan 1970 and covered 8047 km *5000 miles* in 83 days. It was the longest hovercraft journey ever undertaken before or since. The Winchester class SR.N6 and its international crew travelled through eleven countries of West and Central Africa, starting at Dakar, Senegal then continuing up to St Louis and along the Senegal River, ending in Kinshasa, capital of the Congo. It crossed remote, inaccessible and even totally unexplored territories on its way.

The expedition was only partly an exploratory adventure: it was also a means of attempting to prove the hovercraft's worth as a vehicle for negotiating areas that had previously seemed impenetrable. And there were tremendous scientific gains from the journey. During the course of the expedition, which crossed areas with a very high incidence of disease, studies were carried out on medical and expedition survival, navigability, tropical disease, irrigation, anthropology, zoology, and wildlife preservation.

Below: Great crowds of amazed people crowded around the Hovercraft whenever stops were made at pre-arranged fuel dumps. As the turbine suddenly roared and the craft rose up on its inflating skirts panic would ensue amidst the instant sandstorm.

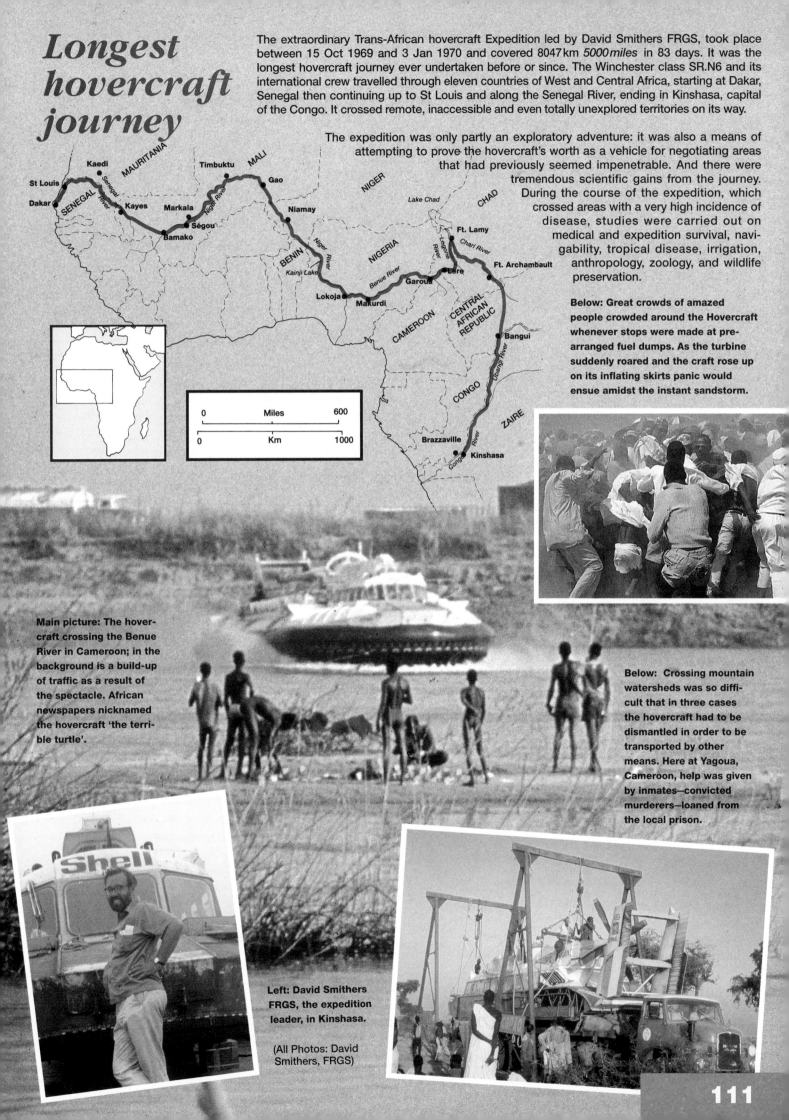

Main picture: The hovercraft crossing the Benue River in Cameroon; in the background is a build-up of traffic as a result of the spectacle. African newspapers nicknamed the hovercraft 'the terrible turtle'.

Below: Crossing mountain watersheds was so difficult that in three cases the hovercraft had to be dismantled in order to be transported by other means. Here at Yagoua, Cameroon, help was given by inmates—convicted murderers—loaned from the local prison.

Left: David Smithers FRGS, the expedition leader, in Kinshasa.

(All Photos: David Smithers, FRGS)

Transatlantic Rowing and Sailing Records

(More detailed marine tables compiled from information supplied by Nobby Clarke and Richard Boehmer can be found in earlier editions)

Category	Vessel	Skipper/Crew	Start	Finish	Duration
FIRST SOLO SAILING E–W	15 ton gaff sloop	Josiah Shackford (US)	Bordeaux, France 1786	Surinam (Guiana)	35 days
FIRST ROWING	Ship's boat *c.* 6.1m *20ft*	John Brown and five British deserters from garrison	St Helena 10 Jun 1799	Belmonte, Brazil (fastest-ever row)	28 days (83 mpd)
FIRST SOLO SAILING W–E	*Centennial* 6.1m *20ft*	Alfred Johnson (US)	Shag Harbor, Maine, USA 1876	Wales	46 days
FIRST SOLO ROWING E–W	*Britannia* 6.7m *22ft*	John Fairfax (GB)	Las Palmas, Canary Island 20 Jan 1969	Ft Lauderdale, Florida, USA, 19 Jul 1969	180 days
FIRST SOLO ROWING W–E	*Super Silver* 6.1m *20ft*	Tom McClean (Ireland)	St John's, Newfoundland, Canada 1969	Black Sod Bay, Republic of Ireland 27 Jul 1969	70.7 days
FIRST ROW *Both directions*	*QE III* 6.05m *19ft 10in*	Don Allum (GB)	Canary Islands 1986 St John's, Canada	Nevis, West Indies Ireland 1987	114 days 77 days
FASTEST SAIL W–E *Non-solo*	*Jet Services 5* 22.9m *75ft* catamaran sloop	Serge Madec (France)	Ambrose Light Tower, USA 2 Jun 1990	Lizard Point, Cornwall 9 Jun 1990	6 days 13hr 3min *32 sec* (18.4 knots smg)
FASTEST SAIL W–E *Solo*	*Pierre 1er* 18.3m *60ft* trimaran sloop	Florence Arthaud (France)	Ambrose Light Tower, USA 24 Jul 1990	Lizard Point, Cornwall 3 Aug 1990	9 days 21hr 42min (12.2 knots smg)
FASTEST SAIL E–W *Solo (beats non-solo)*	*Fleury Michon (IX)* 18.3m *60ft* trimaran	Philippe Poupon (France)	Plymouth, Devon (STAR) 5 Jun 1988	Newport, Rhode Island 15 Jun 1988	10 days 9hr (11.6 knots smg)

Transpacific Records

Category	Vessel	Skipper/Crew	Start	Finish	Duration
FIRST ROWING	*Britannia II* 10.7m *35ft*	John Fairfax (GB) Sylvia Cook (GB)	San Francisco, USA 26 Apr 1971	Hayman Island, Australia 22 Apr 1972	362 days
FIRST SOLO ROWING E–W	*Hele-on-Britannia* 9.75m *32ft*	Peter Bird (GB)	San Francisco, USA 23 Aug 1982	Gt Barrier Reef, Australia 14 Jun 1983	294 days 14 480 km *9000 miles*
FIRST SOLO ROWING W–E	*Sector* 8m *26ft*	Gérard d'Aboville (France)	Choshi, Japan 11 Jul 1991	Ilwaco, Washington, USA, 21 Nov 1991	133 days 10150 km *6300 miles*
FASTEST SAIL *California–Japan*	*Aotea* 12.2 m *40 ft* trimaran	Peter Hogg (New Zealand)	San Francisco, USA 13 Apr 1992	Tokyo, Japan 18 May 1992	34 days 6 hr 26 min (4.66 knots smg)

N.B. The earliest single-handed Pacific crossings were achieved East–West by Bernard Gilboy (US) in 1882 in the 5.48-m 18-ft double-ender Pacific to Australia, and West–East by Fred Rebel (Latvia) in the 5.48 m 18ft Elaine (from Australia) and Edward Miles (US) in the 11.2 m 36¾ ft Sturdy II (from Japan), both in 1932, the latter via Hawaii. smg = speed made good.

Marine Circumnavigation Records

(More detailed marine tables compiled from information supplied by Nobby Clarke and Richard Boehmer can be found in earlier editions)
Strictly speaking, a circumnavigation involves passing through a pair of antipodal points and all the records listed below are known to have met this requirement unless marked with an asterisk. A non-stop circumnavigation is entirely self-maintained; no water supplies, provisions, equipment or replacements of any sort may be taken aboard en route. Vessels may anchor, but no physical help may be accepted apart from passing mail or messages. All distances refer to nautical miles.

Category	Vessel	Skipper	Start	Finish
FIRST	*Vittoria* Expedition of Fernão de Magalhães (Ferdinand Magellan)	Juan Sebastián de Elcano or del Cano (d. 1526) and 17 crew	Seville, Spain 20 Sep 1519	San Lucar, Italy 6 Sep 1522 30,700 miles *93,573.6 km*
FIRST SOLO	*Spray* 11.2m *36ft 9in* gaff yawl	Capt Joshua Slocum (US) (a non-swimmer)	Newport, RI, USA via Magellan Straits, Chile 24 Apr 1895	3 Jul 1898 46,000 miles *140,028 km*
FIRST NON-STOP SOLO W–E	*Suhaili* 9.87m *32ft 4in* Bermudan ketch	Robin Knox-Johnston (GB)	Falmouth, Cornwall 14 Jun 1968	22 Apr 1969 (312 days)
FIRST NON-STOP SOLO E–W	*British Steel* 18m *59ft* ketch	Chay Blyth (GB)	Hamble River, Hants 18 Oct 1970	6 Aug 1971 (292 days)
FASTEST NON-STOP *Any vessel*	*Enza* 28.0 m *92 ft* catamaran	Peter Blake (NZ) and Robin Knox-Johnston (GB)	Ushant, France 16 Jan 1994	Ushant, France 1 Apr 1994 Holder Jules Verne Trophy 74 days 22 hr 17 min
FASTEST SOLO *Under sail*	*Ecureil d'Aquitaine II* 18.3 m *60 ft* monohull	Titouan Lamazou (France)	Les Sables d'Olonne Nov 1989	Les Sables d'Olonne March 1990 109 days, 8 hr, 48 m

Eduard Roditi, author of Magellan of the Pacific, advances the view that Magellan's slave, Enrique, was the first circumnavigator. He had been purchased in Malacca and it was shown that he already understood the Filipino dialect Vizayan, when he reached the Philippines from the east. He 'tied the knot' off Limasawa on 28 Mar 1521.

British Isles Records

Category	Vessel	Skipper	Start	Finish	Duration
AROUND MAINLAND BRITAIN *Fastest power*	*Drambuie Tantalus* 15.3 m *50 ft* monohull	Dag Pike (GB)	Ramsgate 9 Jul 1992	Ramsgate 11 Jul 1992	1 day 20 hr 3 min (36.6 knots smg)
AROUND BRITISH ISLES *Fastest sailing multihull*	*Saab Turbo* 22.9 m *75 ft* catamaran	François Boucher (France)	Plymouth, Devon (RB & I) 18 Jun 1989	Plymouth (4 stops) 3 Jul 1989	7 days 7 hr 30 min (+ 8 days in port)
ENGLISH CHANNEL *both ways* *Fastest sailing multihull*	*Fleury Michon VIII* 22.9 m *75 ft* trimaran	Philippe Poupon (France)	Calais, France Dec 1986	Calais via Dover, Kent Dec 1986	2 hr 21 min 57 sec (18.6 knots smg)

ULDB = Ultra-light displacement boat. RB & I = Round Britain & Ireland Race. smg = speed made good. All mileages are nautical miles.

Other Marine Records

(More detailed marine tables compiled from information supplied by Richard Boehmer can be found in earlier editions) For speed records ⇨Yachting.

Category	Vessel	Skipper	Start	Finish	Duration
DURATION AND DISTANCE *Non-stop by sail*	*Parry Endeavour* 13.9 m *44 ft* Bermudan sloop	Jon Sanders (Australia)	Fremantle, W Australia 25 May 1986	Fremantle 13 Mar 1988	71 000 miles in 658 days (av. speed 4.5 knots)
BEST DAY'S RUN* *Under sail*	*Lyonnaise des Eaux-Dumez* 80 ft *24.4 m* trimaran	Olivier de Kersauson (France)	48° 39'S 33° 28'E 0625 GMT 10 Feb 1994	49°21'S 47°03'E 07:09 GMT 11 Feb 1994	524.6 miles in 24 hours (21.9 knots smg)
BEST DAY'S RUN *Solo*	*Laiterie Mont St Michel* 18.3 m *60 ft* trimaran	Olivier Moussy (France)	50°13'N, 11°30'W 18:18 GMT 6 Jun 1988	48°18'N, 23°30'W 21:17 GMT 7 Jun 1988	430.8 miles (GCD)/24 hr (18.0 knots smg)
BEST DAY'S RUN *Sailboard*	*Fanatic board* Gaastra sail	Françoise Canetos (France)	Sète, France 13 Jul 1988	14 Jul 1988	227 miles/24 hr (9.46 knots smg)

*Best day's run for any vessel under sail. GCD = Great circle distance. smg = speed made good. All mileages are nautical miles.

It handled 292 million tonnes of sea-going cargo in 1991.

Although the port of Hong Kong handles less tonnage in total seaborne cargo than Rotterdam, it is the world's leading container port, handling a record 7.97 million TEUs in 1992.

Dry dock With a maximum shipbuilding capacity of 1,200,000 tons dwt, the Daewoo Okpo No. 1 Dry Dock, Koje Island, South Korea is 530 m *1740 ft* long and 131 m *430 ft* wide and was completed in 1979. The dock gates, 14 m *46 ft* high and 10 m *33 ft* thick at the base, are the world's most massive.

Britain's largest dry dock is the Harland & Wolff building dock, Queen's Island, Belfast. It was excavated by George Wimpey Ltd to a length of 556 m *1825 ft* and a width of 93 m *305 ft* and can accommodate tankers of 1 million tons dwt. Work was begun on 26 Jan 1968 and completed on 30 Nov 1969; this involved the excavation of 306,000 m³ *400,000 yd³* of soil.

Coaching

Before the widespread use of tarred road surfaces from 1845, coaching was slow and hazardous. The zenith was reached on 13 Jul 1888 when James William Selby drove the *Old Times* coach 108 miles *173 km* from London to Brighton and back with eight teams and 14 changes in 7 hr 50 min, to average 13.8 mph *22.2 km/h*. A four-horse carriage could maintain a speed of 21⅓ mph *34 km/h* for nearly an hour.

Carriage!

Carriage driving The only man to drive 48 horses in a single hitch is Dick Sparrow of Zearing, Iowa, USA, between 1972 and 1977. The lead horses were on reins 41 m *135 ft* long.

Floyd Zopfi of Stratford, Wisconsin, USA has driven 52 llamas in a hitch on several occasions since 1990, with the lead llamas (four abreast) on reins 46 m *150 ft* long.

The *Border Union* stagecoach, built *c.* 1825, ran four in hand from Edinburgh to London (393 miles *632 km*). When it ceased in 1845, due to competition from railways, the allowed schedule was 42 hr 23 min to average better than 9¼ mph *14.9 km/h*.

The record for changing a team of four horses by 12 ostlers is 21.32 sec, set by the Norwich Union Charity Mail Coach team led by driver John Parker, at Donington Race Circuit, Leics on 9 Aug 1990.

The longest horse-drawn procession was a cavalcade of 68 carriages, which measured 920 m *1006 yd* 'nose to tail', organized by the Spies Travelling Company of Denmark on 7 May 1986. It carried 810 people through the woods around Copenhagen.

The 52 llamas which helped Floyd Zopfi to set a new carriage driving record.

(Photo: Satinwood Photography/© Floyd Zopfi)

Bicycles

Earliest The earliest machine propelled by cranks and pedals with connecting rods and which was actually built, was in 1839–40 by Kirkpatrick Macmillan (1810–78) of Dumfries, Scotland. A copy of the machine is now in the Science Museum, Kensington, London.

The continuous history of cycling began with the *vélocipède* built in March 1861 by Pierre Michaux and his son Ernest of Rue de Verneuil, Paris, France.

In 1870, James Starley of Coventry, W. Midlands constructed the first penny-farthing or Ordinary bicycle. It had wire-spoked wheels for lightness and was later available with an optional-speed gear.

GUESS WHAT?

Q Where is the longest cycleway bridge?

A See Page 97

Penny Farthing!

The record for riding an Ordinary bicycle (penny-farthing) from Land's End to John o' Groats is 5 days 1 hr 45 min by G. P. Mills of Anfield Bicycle Club, riding a 53 inch-Humber a distance of 861 miles, 4–9 Jul 1886.

Smallest The world's smallest wheeled rideable bicycle is one with wheels of 1.9 cm *0.76 in* in diameter which was ridden by its constructor Neville Patten of Gladstone, Queensland, Australia for a distance of 4.1 m *13 ft 5½ in* on 25 Mar 1988.

Largest The largest bicycle, as measured by the wheel diameter, is 'Frankencycle', built by Dave Moore of Rosemead, California, USA and first ridden by Steve Gordon of Moorpark, California, on 4 Jun 1989. The wheel diameter is 3.05 m *10 ft* and it is 3.35 m *11 ft 2 in* high.

Longest The longest true bicycle ever built (i.e. without a third stabilizing wheel) is one designed and built by Terry Thessman of Pahiatua, New Zealand. It measures 22.24 m *72.96 ft* in length and weighs 340 kg *750 lb*. It was ridden by four riders a distance of 246 m *807 ft* on 27 Feb 1988. Cornering remains a problem.

Wheelie A duration record for a bicycle wheelie is 5 hr 12 min 33 sec set by David Robilliard at the Beau Sejour Leisure Centre, St Peter Port, Guernsey, Channel Islands on 28 May 1990.

Human-powered vehicles (HPVs) *Fastest land* The world speed records for human-powered vehicles (HPVs) over a 200 m flying start are: 105.36 km/h *65.48 mph* (single rider) by Fred Markham at Mono Lake, California, USA on 11 May 1986; and 101.3 km/h *62.92 mph* (multiple riders) by Dave Grylls and Leigh Barczewski at the Ontario Speedway, California on 4 May 1980. The one-hour standing start (single rider) record is held by Pat Kinch, riding *Kingcycle Bean*, averaging a speed of 75.57 km/h *46.96 mph* on 8 Sep 1990 at Millbrook Proving Ground, Bedford.

Water cycle The men's 2000 m record (single rider) is 20.66 km/h *12.84 mph* by Steve Hegg on *Flying Fish* at Long Beach, California, USA on 20 Jul 1987.

Unicycles

Tallest The tallest unicycle ever mastered is one 31.01 m *101 ft 9 in* tall ridden by Steve McPeak (with a safety wire suspended by an overhead crane) for a distance of 114.6 m *376 ft* in Las Vegas, USA in October 1980. The freestyle riding (i.e. without any safety harness) of ever taller unicycles must inevitably lead to serious injury or fatality.

Smallest Peter Rosendahl (Sweden) rode an 8 in *20 cm* high unicycle with a wheel diameter of 1 in *2.5 cm*, with no attachments or extensions fitted, a distance of 12 ft *3.6 m* at Las Vegas, Nevada, USA on 25 Mar 1994.

Fastest sprint Peter Rosendahl set a sprint record for 100 m from a standing start of 12.11 secs (29.72 km/h *18.47 mph*) at Las Vegas on 25 Mar 1994.

100 miles Takayuki Koike of Kanagawa, Japan set a record for 100 miles *160.9 km* of 6 hr 44 min 21.84 sec on 9 Aug 1987 (average speed 23.87 km/h *14.83 mph*).

Endurance Akira Matsushima (Japan) unicycled 5248 km *3260 miles* from Newport, Oregon to Washington DC, USA from 10 Jul–22 Aug 1992.

Land's End to John o' Groats Mike Day (b. 13 Mar 1965) of Southgate, London and Michel Arets (b. 9 Sep 1959) of Brussels, Belgium rode 1450 km *901 miles* from Land's End, Cornwall to John o' Groats, Highland, in 14 days 12 hr 41 min, 27 Aug–10 Sep 1986.

Backwards Peter Rosendahl rode backwards for a distance of 74.75 km *46.7 miles* in 9 hr 25 min on 19 May 1990.

Jacques Puyoou of Pau, Pyrénées-Atlantiques, France with his wife on the world's smallest rideable tandem (36 cm *14 in* long wheel to wheel).
(Photo: J.L. Cachou/Galerie Commerciale Baratnau)

Motorcycles

Earliest The earliest internal combustion-engined motorized bicycle was a wooden-framed machine built at Bad Cannstadt, Germany between October–November 1885 by Gottlieb Daimler (1834–1900) and first ridden by Wilhelm Maybach (1846–1929). It had a top speed of 19 km/h *12 mph* and developed one-half of one horsepower from its single-cylinder 264cc four-stroke engine at 700 rpm. Known as the 'Einspur', it was lost in a fire in 1903.

The first motorcycles of entirely British production were the 1046cc Holden flat-four and the 2¾ hp Clyde single both produced in 1898.

The earliest factory which made motorcycles in large numbers was opened in 1894 by Heinrich and Wilhelm Hildebrand and Alois Wolfmüller at Munich, Germany. In its first two years this factory produced over 1000 machines, each having a water-cooled 1488cc twin-cylinder four-stroke engine developing about 2.5 bhp at 600 rpm—the highest capacity motorcycle engine ever put into production.

GUESS WHAT?

Q How long is the longest car?

A See Page 116

The Dillon Colossal Tricycle being ridden by its designer Arthur Dillon and his son Christopher. The back wheels are 11 ft *3.35 m* high, constructed by David Moore, and the front is 5 ft 10 in *1.77 m* in diameter.
(Photo: Sidney Cooper)

Fastest production road machine The 151hp 1-litre Tu Atara YB6 EI has a road-tested top speed of 300km/h *186 mph*.

Fastest racing machine There is no satisfactory answer to the identity of the fastest track machine other than to say that the current machines have all been geared to attain speeds marginally in excess of 300km/h *186 mph* under race conditions.

Highest speeds Official world speed records must be set with two runs over a measured distance made in opposite directions within a time limit of 1hr for FIM records and of 2hr for AMA records.

Dave Campos (USA), riding a 23ft *7 m* long streamliner named *Easyriders*, powered by two 91 in³ Ruxton Harley-Davidson engines, set AMA and FIM absolute records with an overall average of 322.150 mph *518.450km/h* and completed the faster run at an average of 322.870 mph *519.609 km/h*, at Bonneville Salt Flats, Utah, USA on 14 Jul 1990.

The highest speed achieved over two runs in the UK is 332.30km/h *200.9 mph* by Michel Booys riding a streamliner motorcycle, built by Alexander Macfadzean and powered by a turbo-charged 588cc Norton rotary engine, at Bruntingthorpe Proving Ground, Leics on 24 Aug 1991.

The fastest time for a single run over 440yd from a standing start is 7.08sec by Bo O'Brechta (USA) riding a supercharged 1200cc Kawasaki-based machine at Ontario, California, USA in 1980.

The highest terminal velocity recorded at the end of a 440yd run from a standing start is 321.14km/h *199.55mph* by Russ Collins (USA) at Ontario, California, USA on 7 Oct 1978.

Longest *World* Gregg Reid of Atlanta, Georgia, USA designed and built a 4.57m *15ft 6 in* long 250cc motorbike weighing 235kg *520lb*. It is street legal.

UK Les Nash of Coventry, W Mids constructed a 'self made' 3500cc machine with a Rover V-8 engine. It measures 3.81 × 1.22m *12ft 6 in × 4ft* and weighs more than 220lb *500lb*.

Smallest Simon Timperley and Clive Williams of Progressive Engineering Ltd, Ashton-under-Lyne, Greater Manchester designed and constructed a motorcycle with a wheel-base of 10.79cm *4.25in*, a seat height of 4.9cm *3.75in* and with a wheel diameter of 1.9cm *0.75in* for the front and 2.41cm *0.95in* for the back. The bike was ridden a distance of 1m *3.2ft*.

Magnor Mydland of Norway has constructed a motorcycle with a wheelbase of 12cm *4.72in*, a seat height of 148mm *5.82in* and with wheels 38mm *1.49in* for the front and 49mm *3.39in* for the back in diameter. He rode a distance of 570m *1870ft* reaching a speed of 11.6km/h *7.2mph*.

Duration The longest time a motor scooter, a Kinetic Honda DX 100cc, has been kept in non-stop motion is 1001hr when ridden by Har Parkash Rishi, Amarjeet Singh and Navjot Chadha of India. The team covered a distance of 30,965km *19,241 miles* at Traffic Park, Pune, Maharashtra, India between 22 April and 3 Jun 1990.

Longest ride Jari Saarelainen (b. 4 Apr 1959) of Finland riding his Honda Gold Wing 1500cc

The first woman to circumnavigate the world solo on a motorcycle was Brazillian Moniika Vega, seen here with her trusty 125cc Honda in Japan during her 444 day journey.
(Photo: Moniika Vega)

motorcycle travelled a distance of 108,000km *67,109 miles* through 43 countries. He set off from Helsinki, Finland on 1 Dec 1989 and returned 742 days later on 12 Dec 1991.

The first woman to circumnavigate the world solo was Moniika Vega (b. 9 May 1962) of Rio de Janeiro, Brazil riding her Honda 125cc motorcycle. Her journey commenced at Milan, Italy on 7 Mar 1990 and she returned to Italy on 24 May 1991 having covered a distance of 83,500km *51,885 miles* and visited 53 countries.

Jim Rogers and Tabitha Eastabrook of New York, USA travelled a distance of 91,766 km *57,022 miles* on their motorcycles covering six continents. They set off from New York, USA in March 1990 and returned in November 1991.

> **Ramp jumping**
> The longest distance ever achieved for motorcycle long-jumping is 76.5m *251ft*, by Doug Danger on a 1991 Honda CR500 at Loudon, New Hampshire, USA on 22 Jun 1991.

Pyramid The Dare Devils of the Corp of Signals, Indian Army, established a world record with a pyramid of 81 men on nine motorcycles. The pyramid which was held together by muscle and determination only, with no straps, harnesses or any other aids, travelled a distance of 300m *328yd* at Shivchhatrapati Stadium, Pune, India on 25 Jan 1994.

Wheelie *Distance* Yasuyuki Kudō covered 331km *205.7 miles* non-stop on the rear wheel of his Honda TLM220R motorcycle at the Japan Automobile Research Institute proving ground, Tsukuba, near Tsuchiura, Japan on 5 May 1991.

Wall of Death!

The greatest endurance feat on a 'wall of death' was 7 hr 0 min 13 sec, by Martin Blume at Berlin, Germany on 16 Apr 1983. He rode over 12,000 laps on the 10 m *33 ft* diameter wall on a Yamaha XS 400, averaging 45 km/h *30 mph* for the 292 km *181½ miles*.

Speed The highest speed attained on a back wheel of a motorcycle is 254.07 km/h *157.87 mph* by Jacky Vranken (Belgium) on a Suzuki GSXR 1100 at St Truiden military airfield, Belgium on 8 Nov 1992.

Most on one machine The record for the most people on a single machine is all 46 members of the Illawarra Mini Bike Training Club, New South Wales, Australia. They rode on a 1000cc motorcycle and travelled a distance of 1mile *1.609km* on 11 Oct 1987.

Oldest motorcyclist Arthur Merrick Cook (b. 13 Jun 1895) of Exeter, Devon still regularly rides his Suzuki 125 GS Special motorcycle every day.

Motorcars

Earliest

Model The earliest automobile of which there is a record is a two-foot-long steam-powered model constructed by Ferdinand Verbiest (died 1687), a Belgian Jesuit priest, and described in his *Astronomia Europaea*. His model of 1668 was possibly inspired either by Giovanni Branca's description of a steam turbine, published in his *La Macchina* in 1629, or even by Nan Huairen (writings on 'fire carts') in the Chu kingdom (*c*. 800 BC).

Passenger-carrying The earliest full-scale automobile was the first of two military steam tractors, completed at the Paris Arsenal in October 1769 by Nicolas-Joseph Cugnot (1725–1804). This reached 3.6km/h *2¼ mph*. Cugnot's second, larger tractor, completed in May 1771, today survives in the Conservatoire Nationale des Arts et Métiers in Paris.

The world's first passenger-carrying automobile was a steam-powered road vehicle carrying eight passengers and built by Richard Trevithick (1771–1833). It first ran at Camborne, Cornwall on 24 Dec 1801.

Internal combustion Isaac de Rivaz (Switzerland) (died 1828) built a carriage powered by his 'explosion engine' in 1805. The first practical internal-combustion engined vehicle was that built by the Londoner Samuel Brown (Brit. Pat. No. 5350, 25 Apr 1826), whose 4 hp two-cylinder 88 litre-engined carriage climbed Shooters Hill, Blackheath, Kent in May 1826.

> **GUESS WHAT?**
> Q Where is the oldest steam engine still in working order?
> A See Page 73

The first successful petrol-driven car, the Motorwagen, built by Karl-Friedrich Benz (1844–1929) of Karlsruhe, Germany, ran at Mannheim, in late 1885. The three-wheeler weighed 254kg *5cwt* and could reach a speed of 13–16km/h *8–10mph*. Its single-cylinder engine (bore 91.4mm *3.6 in*, stroke 160mm *6.3 in*) delivered 0.85hp at 400rpm. It was patented on 29 Jan 1886. Its first 1km *0.6 mile* road test was reported in the local newspaper, the *Neue Badische Landeszeitung*, of 4 Jun 1886, under the heading 'Miscellaneous'.

Britain's continuous motoring history started in November 1894 when Henry Hewetson drove his imported Benz Velo in the south-eastern suburbs of London.

This Lego Technic Super-Car (below) is an exact replica of Lego's largest model ever. The larger Super-Car contains approximately 650,000 pieces and took a staggering 5850 hours to design and build, whereas the commercially available version has a mere 1346 parts and hopefully should not take as long to construct.
(Photo: Lego System A/S)

Arrow 6−66 Raceabout of 1912−18, the US Peerless 6−60 of 1912−14 and the Fageol of 1918.

Most powerful The most powerful current production car is the McLaren F1 which develops 627 bhp.

Heaviest The heaviest car recently in production (up to twenty-five were made annually) appears to be the Soviet-built Zil−41047 limousine with a 3.88m *12.72 ft* wheel-base. It weighs 3335 kg *7352 lb*. A 'stretched' Zil (two to three made annually) was used by former President Mikhail Gorbachev until December 1991. It weighed 6 tonnes and used 75mm *3 in* armour-plated steel for protection in key areas. The eight-cylinder, 7-litre engine guzzled fuel at the rate of 9.6km *6 miles* to the gallon.

Lightest Louis Borsi of London has built and driven a 9.5kg *21 lb* car with a 2.5cc engine. It is capable of 25km/h *15 mph*.

Most expensive *Standard* The most expensive list-price British standard car is the McLaren F1 quoted at £540,000 plus tax.

Used The greatest confirmed price paid is $15 million for the 1931 Bugatti Type 41 Royale Sports Coupé by Kellner, sold by Nicholas Harley to the Meitec Corporation of Japan, completed on 12 Apr 1990.

Most inexpensive The cheapest car of all time was the 1922 Red Bug Buckboard, built by the Briggs & Stratton Co. of Milwaukee, Wisconsin, USA, listed at $125−150. It had a 1.57m *62 in* wheel-base and weighed 111kg *245 lb*. Early

Registrations!

Licence plate No. 9 was sold at a Hong Kong government auction for HK$13 million on 19 Mar 1994 to Albert Yeung Sau-shing. 'Nine' sounds like the word 'dog' in Chinese and is considered lucky because 1994 is the Year of The Dog. The highest price paid for a British registration plate is £203,500 by an undisclosed buyer for K1NGS at Christie's, London on 10 Dec 1993.

Production

The number of vehicles constructed world-wide in 1992 was a record 47,955,000, of which 34,838,000 were motorcars. The peak year for motorcars only was 1990 when 35,277,986 were produced.

The UK production figure for 1993 was 1,568,991 vehicles of which 1,375,524 were cars. The peak year for production was 1964 when 2,332,376 vehicles (1,867,640 cars) were manufactured.

The world's largest manufacturer of motor vehicles and parts (and the largest manufacturing company) is General Motors Corporation of Detroit, Michigan, USA. The company has on average 710,800 employees. A peak figure of 948,000 vehicles were produced in 1978 and the Company's highest yearly income was $138.2 billion in 1989.

The largest manufacturer in Britain is the Rover Group plc, which produced 426,744 vehicles in 1993. The company produced almost three out of every ten cars built in Britain and accounted for nearly one-third of the number of cars exported from the UK.

Largest car plant The largest single automobile plant in the world is the Volkswagenwerk at Wolfsburg, Germany, with approx 60,000 employees and a facility for producing 4000 vehicles every day. The factory buildings cover an area of 150 ha *371 acres* and the whole plant covers 760 ha *1878 acres*, with 74km *46 miles* of rail sidings.

Longest in production The Morgan 4/4 celebrated its 58th birthday on 27 Dec 1993. Built by the Morgan Motor Car Co. of Malvern, Hereford & Worcester (founded 1910), there is still a six to eight-year waiting list for delivery.

The 21 millionth Volkswagen 'Beetle' rolled off the last remaining production line, at Puebla, Mexico in December 1991.

Britain's champion seller has been the Mini (5.28 million produced), designed by Sir Alec Issigonis (1906−88), which originally sold for £496 19s 2d in August 1959.

Largest Of cars produced for private use, the largest was the Bugatti 'Royale' type 41, known in Britain as the 'Golden Bugatti', of which only six were assembled at Molsheim, France by the Italian Ettore Bugatti (1882−1947). First built in 1927, this machine has an eight-cylinder engine of 12.7 litres capacity, and measures over 22ft *6.7 m* in length. The bonnet is over 7ft *2.25 m* long.

Largest engines The greatest engine capacity of a production car was 13.5 litres, for the US Pierce-

Longest!

A 30.5 m *100 ft* long 26-wheeled limo was designed by Jay Ohrberg of Burbank, California, USA. It has many features, including a swimming pool, a king-sized water bed and a helicopter landing pad. It is designed to drive as one piece or it can be changed to bend in the middle. Its main purpose is for use in films and exhibitions.

models of the King Midget cars were sold in kit form for self-assembly for as little as $100 in 1948.

In March 1994 the cheapest listed new car in Britain was the Lada Riva 1.5E at £3995.

Fastest

Land speed
The *official* one-mile land-speed record is 1019.467 km/h *633.468 mph*, set by Richard Noble (b. 6 Mar 1946) on 4 Oct 1983 over the Black Rock Desert, Nevada, USA in his 17,000lb thrust Rolls-Royce Avon 302 jet-powered *Thrust 2*, designed by John Ackroyd.

The highest speed attained in Britain is 444km/h *276 mph* by Poutiaiten Risto (Finland) in a Top Fuel dragster on 27 May 1991 at the Santa Pod County Raceway, Beds.

Rocket-engined The highest speed attained is 1016.086km/h *631.367 mph* over the first measured kilometre by *The Blue Flame*, a rocket powered four-wheeled vehicle driven by Gary Gabelich (b. 23 Aug 1940) (USA) on the Bonneville Salt Flats, Utah, USA on 23 Oct 1970. Momentarily Gabelich exceeded 1046 km/h *650 mph*. The car was powered by a liquid natural gas/hydrogen peroxide rocket engine which could develop thrust up to 22,000lb.

The highest reputed land speed figure in one direction is 1190.377 km/h *739.666 mph* or Mach 1.0106 by Stan Barrett (USA) in the *Budweiser Rocket*, a rocket-engined three-wheeled car, at Edwards Air Force Base, California, USA on 17 Dec 1979. *This published speed of Mach 1.0106 is* not *officially sanctioned by the USAF as the Digital Instrument Radar was not calibrated or certified. The radar information was not generated by the vehicle directly but by an operator aiming a dish by means of a TV screen.*

The highest land speed recorded by a woman is 843.323 km/h *524.016 mph* by Mrs Kitty Hambleton (*née* O'Neil) (USA) in the rocket-powered three-wheeled SM1 *Motivator* over the Alvard Desert, Oregon, USA on 6 Dec 1976. Her official two-way record was 825.126 km/h *512.710 mph* and she probably touched 965 km/h *600 mph* momentarily.

Piston-engined The highest speed measured for a wheel-driven car is 696.331km/h *432.692mph* by Al Teague (USA) in *Speed-O-Motive/Spirit of 76* on Bonneville Salt Flats, Utah, USA on 21 Aug 1991 over the final 132ft of a mile run (425.230 mph for the whole mile).

Diesel-engined The prototype 3litre Mercedes C 111/3 attained 327.3 km/h *203.3 mph* in tests on the Nardo Circuit, southern Italy on 5–15 Oct 1978, and in April 1978 averaged 314.5km/h *195.4 mph* for 12 hours, so covering a world record 3773.5km *2344.7 miles*.

Electric car *UK Land speed* On 22 Jun 1991 Max Rink (18) of Oundle School, Peterborough achieved a speed of 111.37km/h *69.21mph* over a one km flying start, at Bruntingthorpe Proving

Ground, Leics. Over the two runs the average speed achieved was 106.43km/h *66.14mph*. The vehicle weighed only 60kg *132lb* and was built in 1986 by four 14-year-old pupils from Oundle School.

Parade of Rolls-Royce cars
A line of 147 Rolls-Royces, organized by the Rolls-Royce Owners' Club of Australia, drove around Lake Wendouree, Ballarat, Victoria on 19 Sep 1992.

Steam car On 19 Aug 1985 Robert E. Barber broke the 79-year-old record for a steam car when *Steamin' Demon*, built by the Barber-Nichols Engineering Co., reached 234.33km/h *145.607mph* at Bonneville Salt Flats, Utah, USA.

Road cars Various de-tuned track cars have been licensed for road use but are not normal production models.

The highest speed ever attained by a standard production car is 349.21km/h *217.1mph* for a Jaguar XJ220, driven by Martin Brundle at the Nardo test track, Italy on 21 Jun 1992.

The highest road-tested acceleration reported for a standard production car is 0–60 mph in 3.275sec for a Ford RS200 Evolution, driven by Graham Hathaway at the Boreham Proving Ground, Essex on 28 Apr 1993.

The fastest lap on a UK circuit by a production car was achieved in a Ferrari 512TR at an average speed of 282.2km/h *175.4 mph*, with a peak speed over ½ mile of 285.2km/h *177.3 mph* by Andrew Frankel of *Autocar & Motor* magazine at Millbrook, Beds on 10 Jun 1992.

Driving

Highest mileage
The highest recorded mileage for a car is 1,512,755 miles *2,434,575 km* up to 25 Jan 1994 for a 1963 Volkswagen 'Beetle' owned by Albert Klein of Pasadena, California, USA.

Six continents The fastest drive taking in the six continents, with a total distance of more than an equator's length (40,075km *24,901 miles*), is one of 39days 7hr 55min by Navin Kapila, Man Bahadur and Vijay Raman driving a Contessa Classic. They left New Delhi, India on 22 Nov 1992 and returned to the same place on 31 Dec 1992.

Amphibious circumnavigation
The only circumnavigation by an amphibious vehicle was by Ben Carlin (Australia) (died 7 Mar 1981) in the amphibious jeep, *Half-Safe*. He completed the last leg of the Atlantic crossing (the English Channel) on 24 Aug 1951. He arrived back in Montreal, Canada on 8 May 1958, having completed a circumnavigation of 39,000miles *62,765 km* over land and 9600miles *15,450km* by sea and river. He was accompanied on the transatlantic stage by his ex-wife Elinore (USA) and on the long trans-Pacific stage (Tokyo to Anchorage, Alaska) by Broye Lafayette De-Mente (USA) (b. 1928).

The Blue Flame, the fastest ever rocket-powered vehicle.
(Photo: Quadrant Picture Library)

One-year duration record The greatest distance ever covered in one year is 573,029km *354,257 miles* by two Opel Rekord, both of which covered this distance between 18 May 1988 and the same date in 1989 without any major mechanical breakdowns. The vehicles were manufactured by the Delta Motor Corporation, Port Elizabeth, South Africa, and were driven on tar and gravel roads in the Northern Cape by a team of company drivers from Delta.

Trans-Americas Garry Sowerby (Canada), with Tim Cahill (USA) as co-driver and navigator, drove a 1988 GMC Sierra K3500 from Ushuaia, Tierra del Fuego, Argentina to Prudhoe Bay, Alaska, USA, a distance of 23,720km *14,739 miles*, in a total elapsed time of 23days 22hr 43min from 29 September to 22 Oct 1987. The vehicle and team were surface freighted from Cartagena, Colombia to Balboa, Panama so as to by-pass the Darién Gap.

Cape to London The record time for the 18,787 km *11,674 mile* road route from Cape Town, South Africa to London is 14days 19hr 26min, set by husband and wife team Brig. John and Dr Lucy Hemsley from 8–22 Jan 1983 in a Range Rover. Apart from the Channel crossing they were the first to drive entirely overland from Cape Town to London.

British counties Nigel Seaward, Emma Vowles, Adrian Tudway and Corrine Roe of the Metropolitan Police completed a tour of the 73 counties of the United Kingdom, covering a distance of 5410.4km *3362miles* in a time of 96hr 6min between 17–21 Sep 1993.

Around Ireland Larry Mooney (driver), Paul Gleeson and Alan Park (navigators), all of Northern Ireland drove around the 32 counties of Ireland in a time of 12hr 19min between 21–22 Jun 1991, covering a distance of 917.7km *570.2 miles* an average speed of 74 km/h *46 mph*.

Round Britain economy A Daihatsu Charade 1.0 turbo diesel driven by Helen Horwood, Joanne Swift and John Taylor around a 5827km *3621 mile* course from 7–14 Oct 1991 returned a fuel consumption of 103.01mpg.

The record for a petrol engined car is 85.96mpg for a Honda Civic ETi driven by Team Mad Scientist & Crazy Guys + Naughty Ladies, led by Dr. Shigeru Miyano, from 18–25 Sep 1993.

Skid Marks!

The longest recorded on a public road were 290m *950ft* long left by a Jaguar car involved in an accident on the M1 near Luton, Beds on 30 Jun 1960. Evidence given in the subsequent High Court case *Hurlock* v. *Inglis et al.* indicated a speed 'in excess of 100 mph before the application of the brakes'.

The skid marks made by the jet-powered *Spirit of America*, driven by Norman Craig Breedlove, after the car went out of control at Bonneville Salt Flats, Utah, USA on 15 Oct 1964, were nearly 6 miles *9.6 km* long.

GUESS WHAT?
Q What connects the fastest car ferry and the discovery of America?
A See Page 108

Petrol consumption *Most economical* Amongst production cars available in the United Kingdom the Citroen AX 14DTR could make this claim. The Department of Transport figures are 62.8mpg (urban cycle), 85.6 mpg (steady 56mph), 58.9mpg (steady 75mph).

On 9 Aug 1989 motoring writer Stuart Bladon drove a Citroen AX 14DTR a distance of 180.26km *112.01miles* using one gallon of fuel driving on the M11 Motorway in a test run arranged by Lucas Diesel Systems.

Longest fuel range The greatest distance driven without refuelling in a standard vehicle is 2724km *1691.6 miles* by a 1991 Toyota LandCruiser diesel station wagon (factory optional twin fuel tanks, capacity 174litres *38.2gal*). The Toyota was driven by Ewan Kennedy with Ian Lee (observer) from Nyngan, New South Wales, Australia to Winton, Queensland and back between 18–21 May 1992. The average speed was 60km/h *37mph*.

The greatest distance travelled by a vehicle on the contents of a standard fuel tank is 2153.4km *1338.1miles* by an Audi 100 TDI diesel car (capacity 17.62gal *80.1litres*). Stuart Bladon, with RAC observer Robert Proctor, drove from John o' Groats to Land's End and returned to Scotland between 26–28 Jul 1992.

Driving in reverse Charles Creighton (1908–70) and James Hargis of Maplewood, Missouri, USA drove their Model A Ford 1929 roadster in reverse from New York, USA 5375km *3340 miles* to Los Angeles, California, from 26 Jul–13 Aug 1930 without once stopping the engine. They arrived back in New York in reverse on 5 September, so completing 11,555km *7180 miles* in 42 days.

Brian 'Cub' Keene and James 'Wilbur' Wright drove their Chevrolet Blazer 14,533 km *9031 miles* in 37 days (1 August–6 Sep 1984) in reverse through 15 US states and Canada. Though it was prominently named 'Stuck in Reverse', law enforcement officers in Oklahoma refused to believe it and insisted they drove in reverse, i.e. forwards, out of the state.

The highest average speed attained in any non-stop reverse drive exceeding 800km *500 miles* was achieved by Gerald Hoagland, who drove a 1969 Chevrolet Impala 806.2km *501miles* in 17hr 38min at Chemung Speed Drome, New York, USA on 9–10 Jul 1976, to average 45.72km/h *28.41mph*.

Battery-powered vehicle David Turner and Tim Pickhard of Turners of Boscastle Ltd, Cornwall, travelled 1408km *875miles* from Land's End to John o' Groats in 63hr in a Freight Rover Leyland Sherpa powered by a Lucas electric motor from 21–23 Dec 1985.

Two-side-wheel driving *Car* Bengt Norberg (b. 23 Oct 1951) of Äppelbo, Sweden drove a Mitsubishi Colt GTi-16V on two side wheels non-stop for a distance of 310.391km *192.873miles* in a time of 7hr 15min 50sec. He also achieved a distance of 44.808km *27.842 miles* in 1hour at Rattvik Horse Track, Sweden on 24 May 1989.

Sven-Erik Söderman (Sweden) (b. 26 Sep 1960) achieved a speed of 164.38km/h *102.14mph* over

The successful team of students from Lycée St Joseph la Joliverie, St Sébastien sur Loire, France with their 'car' which achieved a performance of 7591 mpg in the Shell Mileage Marathon at Silverstone, Northants on 17 Jul 1992.
(Photo: Gamma/A. Le Bot)

a 100m flying start on the two wheels of an Opel Kadett at Mora Siljan airport, Mora, Sweden on 2 Aug 1990. Söderman achieved a record speed for the flying kilometre of 152.96km/h *95.04mph* at the same venue on 24 Aug 1990.

Truck Sven-Erik Söderman drove a Daf 2800 7.5 ton truck on two wheels for a distance of 10.83km *6.73miles* at Mora Siljan airport on 19 May 1991.

Bus Bobby Ore (b. Jan 1949) drove a double-decker bus a distance of 246m *810ft* on two-wheels at North Weald airfield, Essex on 21 May 1988.

Most durable driver Goodyear Tire and Rubber Co. test driver Weldon C. Kocich drove 5,056,472km *3,141,946 miles* from 5 Feb 1953 to 28 Feb 1986, so averaging 153,226 km *95,210miles* per year.

Oldest driver Roy M. Rawlins (b. 10 Jul 1870) of Stockton, California, USA was warned for driving at 95mph *152km/h* in a 55mph *88.5km/h* zone in June 1974. On 25 Aug 1974 he was awarded a California State licence valid until 1978, but Mr Rawlins died on 9 Jul 1975, one day short of his 105th birthday.

Mrs Maude Tull of Inglewood, California, USA, who took to driving aged 91 after her husband died, was issued a renewal on 5 Feb 1976 when aged 104.

Britain's oldest known drivers have been Benjamin Kagan (1878–1988) of Leeds and Rev. Albert Thomas Humphrey (1886–1988) from Pawlett, near Bridgwater, Somerset; both drove up to the age of 102.

The greatest age at which an individual has first passed the Department of Transport driving test has been 90 years 229 days by Mrs Gerty Edwards Land (b. 9 Sep 1897) on 27 Apr 1988 in Colne, Lancs. The oldest man to pass was David Coupar (b. 9 Feb 1898) on 4 Mar 1987 in Perth, Perthshire. He was aged 89 years 2 months.

Youngest driver Stephen Andrew Blackbourn of Lincoln having passed his driving test on his 17th

Ramp Jumping!

The longest ramp jump in a car, with the car landing on its wheels and being driven on, is 70.73m *232 ft*, by Jacqueline De Creed (*née* Creedy) in a 1967 Ford Mustang at Santa Pod Raceway, Beds on 3 Apr 1983.

birthday, went on to pass the advanced test less than five hours later on 20 Feb 1989. His brother Mark previously held the record.

Driving tests The record for persistence in taking the Department of Transport's driving test is held by Mrs Git Kaur Randhawa (b. 7 Feb 1937) of Hayes, Middlesex, who triumphed at her 48th attempt, after more than 330 lessons, on 19 Jun 1987.

The world's easiest tests have been those in Egypt, in which the ability to drive 6m *19.6ft* forward and the same in reverse has been deemed sufficient. In 1979 it was reported that accurate reversing between two rubber traffic cones had been added. 'High cone attrition' soon led to the substitution of white lines.

Worst!

It was reported that a 75-year-old male driver received ten traffic tickets, drove on the wrong side of the road four times, committed four hit-and-run offences and caused six accidents, all within 20 minutes, in McKinney, Texas, USA on 15 Oct 1966.

Specialized Vehicles

Largest The most massive automotive land vehicle is 'Big Muskie' built by Bucyrus Erie. (⇨ Engineering, dragline)

Longest The Arctic Snow Train has 54 wheels and is 174.3m *572ft* long. It was built by R.G. Le Tourneau Inc. of Longview, Texas, USA for the US Army. Its gross train weight is 400tons, with a top speed of 32km/h *20mph*, and it was driven by a crew of six when used as an 'overland train' for the military. It generates 4680shaft horsepower and has a fuel capacity of 29,648litres *6522gal*. It is owned by the world-famous wirewalker Steve McPeak (USA) who makes all repairs, including every punctured wheel, single-handed in often sub-zero temperatures in Alaska.

Ambulance The world's largest ambulances are the 18m *59ft* long articulated Alligator Jumbulances Marks VI, VII, VIII and IX, operated by the ACROSS Trust to convey the sick and handicapped on holidays and pilgrimages across Europe. They are built by Van Hool of Belgium with Fiat engines at a cost £200,000 and carry 44 patients and staff.

Buses *Earliest* The first municipal motor omnibus service in the world was inaugurated on 12 Apr 1903 and ran between Eastbourne railway station and Meads, E Sussex.

Longest The longest are the articulated DAF Super CityTrain buses of Zaïre, with 110 passenger seats and room for 140 'strap-hangers' in the first trailer and 60 seated and 40 'strap-hangers' in the

GUESS WHAT?
Q where would you find the world's most durable battery?
A *See Page 74*

second, making a total of 350. Designed by the President of the Republic of Zaïre, Citoyen Mobutu Sese Seko Kuku Ngbendu wa za Banga (b. 14 Oct 1930), they are 32.20m *105.64ft* long and weigh 28 tonnes unladen.

The longest rigid single bus is 14.96m *49ft* long, carries 69 passengers and is built by Van Hool of Belgium.

Largest fleet The 6580 single-decker buses in Rio de Janeiro, Brazil make up the world's largest bus fleet.

The largest fleet in the UK is operated by London Buses. At 25 Feb 1994, 5034 buses and coaches were operated of which 3519 were double deckers (including 754 of the familiar Routemasters, in service since 1958), 227 were single deckers and coaches and 1288 were mini/midibuses.

Longest route The longest regularly scheduled bus route is operated by Expreso Internacional Ormeño S.A. of Lima, Peru which runs a regular scheduled service between Caracas, Venezuela and Buenos Aires, Argentina. The route is 9660km *6003 miles* long and takes 214 hours which includes a 12-hour stop in Santiago, Chile and 24-hour stop in Lima.

The longest route in Britain is route 806 between Penzance, Cornwall and Dundee, Tayside at 1102km *685 miles*, operated by Western National Ltd and Tayside Travel Services Ltd, each company allocating coaches on alternate days.

Caravans *Largest* The largest two-wheeled five-storey caravan was built in 1990 for H.E Sheik Hamad Bin Hamdan Al Nahyan of Abu Dhabi, United Arab Emirates. It is 20m *66ft* long, 12m *39ft* wide and weighs 120tons. There are eight bedrooms and bathrooms, four garages and water storage for 24,000litres *5279gal.*

Longest journey The continuous motor caravan journey of 231,288km *143,716 miles* by Harry B. Coleman and Peggy Larson in a Volkswagen Camper from 20 Aug 1976 to 20 Apr 1978 took them through 113 countries.

Fastest The world speed record for a caravan tow is 204.02km/h *126.77mph* for a Roadstar caravan towed by a 1990 Ford EA Falcon saloon and driven by 'Charlie' Kovacs, at Mangalore Airfield, Seymour, Victoria, Australia on 18 Apr 1991.

Crawler The largest is the Marion eight-caterpillar crawler used originally for conveying Saturn V rockets, but now Shuttles, to their launch pads at Cape Canaveral, Florida, USA. The two built cost $12.3 million, each measuring 131ft 4in × 114ft *40 × 34.7m.* The loaded train weight is 8165 tonnes. The windscreen wiper blades are 106cm *42in* long and are the world's largest.

Dumper truck The world's largest is the Terex Titan 33–19 manufactured by General Motors Corporation and now in operation at Westar Mine, British Columbia, Canada. It has a loaded weight of 548.6tonnes and a capacity of 317.5tonnes. When tipping its height is 17m *56ft.* The 16-cylinder engine delivers 3300hp. The fuel tank holds 5910litres *1300gal.*

Fire engines The fire appliance with the greatest pumping capacity is the 860hp eight-wheel Oshkosh firetruck (manufactured by Oshkosh Truck Corporation, Oshkosh, Wisconsin, USA), weighing 60 tonnes and used for aircraft and runway fires. It can discharge 189,000 litres *41,600gal* of foam through two turrets in just 150 seconds.

Fastest The fastest on record is the Jaguar XJ12 'Chubb Firefighter', which on 2 Nov 1982 atttained a speed of 210.13 km/h *130.57 mph* in tests when servicing the *Thrust 2* land speed record trials. (⬦ Fastest cars, land speed)

> **Fire pumping** The greatest volume of water stirrup-pumped by a team of eight in 80 hours is 143,459 litres *31,557gal*, by firefighters based at Knaresborough Fire Station, N Yorks, from 25–28 Jun 1992.

Go-Karting The highest mileage recorded in 24 hours on a outdoor circuit by a four-man team is 1638km *1018 miles* on a one-mile track at the Erbsville Kartway, Waterloo, Ontario, Canada. The 5hp 140cc Honda engined kart was driven by Owen Nimmo, Gary Ruddock, Jim Timmins and Danny Upshaw on 4–5 Sep 1983.

The highest mileage recorded in 24 hours on an indoor track by a four-man team driving 160cc karts is 1422.6km *883.9 miles* at the Welsh Karting Centre, Cardiff, Gwent. The drivers were Ian O'Sullivan, Paul Marram, Richard Jenkins and Michael Watts on 26 Nov 1993.

Lawn mowers The widest gang mower in the world is the 5ton 60ft *18m* wide 27-unit 'Big Green Machine' used by the turf farmer Jay Edgar Frick of Monroe, Ohio, USA. It mows an acre in 60 seconds.

A 12-hour run-behind record of 169.1km *105.1 miles* was set at Wisborough Green, W Sussex on 28–29 Jul 1990 by the 'Doctor's Flyers' team.

The greatest distance covered in the annual 12-hour Lawn Mower Race (under the rules of the British Lawn Mower Racing Association) is 468km *291 miles* by John Gill, Robert Jones and Steve Richardson of Team Gilliams at Wisborough Green, W Sussex on 1 and 2 Aug 1992.

Pedal car The record for John o' Groats, Highland to Land's End, Cornwall is 59hr 21min by a team of five from the Lea Manor High School and Community College, Luton on 30 May–1 June 1993.

Snowmobiles John Outzen, Andre, Carl and Denis Boucher drove snowmobiles a distance of 16,499.5km *10,252.3 miles* in 56 riding days from Anchorage, Alaska, USA to Dartmouth, Nova Scotia, Canada from 2 Jan–3 Mar 1992.

> **GUESS WHAT?**
> Q What is the world's fastest growing grass?
> A See Page 45

Tony Lenzini of Duluth, Minnesota, USA drove his 1986 Arctic Cat Cougar snowmobile a total of 11,604.6km *7211 miles* in 60 riding days between 28 Dec 1985 and 20 Mar 1986.

Solar powered The highest speed attained by a solely solar-powered land vehicle is 78.39km/h *48.71mph* by Molly Brennan driving the General Motors *Sunraycer* at Mesa, Arizona, USA on 24 Jun 1988. The highest speed of 135km/h *83.88 mph* using solar/battery power was achieved by Star Micronics solar car *Solar Star* driven by Manfred Hermann on 5 Jan 1991 at Richmond RAAF Base, Richmond, NSW, Australia.

Taxis The largest taxi fleet is that in Mexico City, with 60,000 'normal' taxis, *pesaros* (communal fixed route taxis) and *settas* (airport taxis).

John Outzen, Andre, Carl and Denis Boucher at the finish in Dartmouth, Nova Scotia, with the snowmobiles which carried them across a continent.
(Photo: John Outzen)

Currently there are 16,565 taxis and 20,220 taxi-drivers in London.

The longest fare on record is one of 23,196km *14,413 miles* at a cost of 70,000 Finnmarks (approximately £9000). Mika Lehtonen and Juhani Saramies left Nokia, Finland on 2 May 1991 and travelled through Scandinavia down to Spain and arrived back in Nokia on 17 May 1991.

Charles Kerslake (b. 27 Jun 1895) held a London Metropolitan cab licence from February 1922 until his retirement in May 1988 aged 92 years 11 months.

Trams *Longest journey* The longest now possible is from Krefeld St Tönis to Witten Annen Nord, Germany. With luck at the eight inter-connections, the 105.5km *65.5 mile* trip can be achieved in 5½ hours.

The longest drive on a lawn mower was a distance of 4882km *3034 miles*, when Ian Ireland of Harlow, Essex drove an Iseki SG15 between Harlow, and Southend Pier, Essex from 13 Aug to 7 Sep 1989. He was assisted by members of 158 Round Table, Luton, Beds and raised over £15,000 in aid of the Leukaemia Research Fund.

Transport

Les Shockley's jet truck *ShockWave* the world's most powerful truck.
(Photo: Les Shockley)

The city of St Petersburg, Russia has the most extensive tramway system with 690.6km *429.1miles* of track and 2402 cars on 64 routes.

Oldest The oldest trams in revenue service in the world are motorcars 1 and 2 of the Manx Electric Railway, dating from 1893. These run regularly on the 28.5 km *17¾ miles* railway between Douglas and Ramsey, Isle of Man.

Trolleybuses The last trolleybus in Britain, owned by Bradford Corporation, ran in 1972. Plans have been made to reintroduce trolleybuses by both West and South Yorks Passenger Transport Executives.

Truck Les Shockley of Galena, Kansas, USA drove his Jet Truck *ShockWave* powered by three Pratt & Whitney jet engines developing 36,000 hp to a record speed of 412km/h *256 mph* in 6.36 sec over a quarter-mile standing start on 4 Jun 1989 at Autodrome de Monterrey, Monterrey, Mexico. He set a further record for the standing mile at 605km/h *376 mph* at Paine Field, Everett, Washington, USA on 18 Aug 1991.

Wrecker The world's most powerful wrecker is the Twin City Garage and Body Shop's 20.6 tonnes, 11 m *36 ft* long International M6-23 'Hulk' 1969 stationed at Scott City, Missouri, USA. It can lift in excess of 295 tonnes on its short boom.

GUESS WHAT?
Q Where would you find the tallest chimney ever to be demolished?
A See Page 88

Services

Car parks The world's largest is the West Edmonton Mall, Edmonton, Alberta, Canada, which can hold 20,000 vehicles. There are overflow facilities on an adjoining lot for 10,000 more cars.

The largest parking area in Great Britain is that for 15,000 cars and 200 coaches at the National Exhibition Centre, Birmingham, West Midlands (⇔ Buildings for Working, exhibition centres).

Parking meters The earliest were installed in the business district of Oklahoma City, Oklahoma, USA on 19 Jul 1935. They were invented by Carl C.

Magee (USA) and reached London in 1958.

Traffic lights Semaphore-type traffic *signals* were set up in Parliament Square, London in 1868 with red and green gas lamps for night use. It was not an offence to disobey traffic signals until assent was given to the 1930 Road Traffic Act. Traffic *lights* were introduced in Great Britain with a one-day trial in Wolverhampton on 11 Feb 1928. They were first permanently operated in Leeds, W Yorks on 16 Mar 1928 and in Edinburgh, Scotland on 19 Mar 1928.

The first vehicle-actuated lights were installed by Plessey at the Cornhill–Gracechurch junction, City of London in April 1932.

Filling stations The largest concentration of pumps are 204—96 of them Tokheim Unistar (electronic) and 108 Tokheim Explorer (mechanical)—in Jeddah, Saudi Arabia.

The highest filling station in the world is at Leh, Ladakh, India, at 3658 m *12,001 ft*, operated by the Indian Oil Corporation.

Garage The largest private garage is one of two storeys built outside Bombay for the private collection of 176 cars owned by Pranlal Bhogilal (b. 1939).

The KMB Overhaul Centre, operated by the Kowloon Motor Bus Co. (1933) Ltd, Hong Kong, is the world's largest multi-storey service centre. Purpose built for double decker buses, its four floors occupy in excess of 47,000m² *11.6 acres*.

Car wrecking In a career lasting 25 years from 1968 to 1993 Dick Sheppard of Gloucester wrecked a total of 2003 cars.

Tow The longest on record is one of 8038km *4995 miles* from Ascot, Berks to Widmerpool, Notts conducted by the Automobile Association from 4–12 May 1993. They used a LandRover which towed a replica Model T Ford van.

Tyres *Largest* The world's largest ever manufactured were by the Goodyear Tire & Rubber Co. for giant dumper trucks. They measure 12ft *3.65 m* in diameter, weigh 12,500lb *5670 kg* and cost $74,000. A tyre 17ft *5.2 m* in diameter is believed to be the limitation of what is practical.

Tyres!

The greatest number of motor tyres supported in a free-standing 'lift' is 96, by Gary Windebank of Romsey, Hants in February 1984. The total weight was 653 kg *1440 lb*. The tyres used were Michelin XZX 155 × 13.

Loads

Heaviest load On 14–15 Jul 1984 John Brown Engineers & Contractors BV moved the Conoco Kotter Field production deck with a roll-out weight of 3805 tonnes for the Continental Netherlands Oil Co. of Leidsenhage, Netherlands.

The heaviest road load moved in the United Kingdom has been the 2045 tonnes, 79 m *259 ft*

GUESS WHAT?
Q Where would you find the world's tallest lamp-posts?
A See Page 101

long Ingst motorway bridge on the M4 near Bristol. redundant after 26 years of use. The operation closed the Motorway from late on 28 Feb to 3 Mar 1992 and was conducted by Edmund Nuttall civil engineering firm and Econfreight, contractors.

Longest The longest item moved by road was a high-pressure steel gas storage vessel 83.8m *275 ft* long and weighing 233 tonnes transported to a new site at Beckton gasworks in east London on 10 Jul 1985. The overall train length was 99m *325 ft*.

This motorized scale model car, created by Nippondenso of Kariya, Japan, and seen on a US one cent coin, is of Toyota's first passenger car, the 1936 Model AA Sedan. It is one-thousandth the size of the actual car and only 4.785mm long, 1.730mm wide and 1.736mm high. The bumper for example is only 50 microns thick (cf. hair at 80 microns). The motor (the coil of which is only 1mm in diameter) drives the front wheels with the power being delivered from an external source through the copper wire seen entering via the roof. The car has a top speed of 0.018km/h *0.011 mph*.
(Photo: Nippondenso Co. Ltd)

Model Cars

Non-stop duration A Scalextric Jaguar XJ8 ran non-stop for 866hr 44min 54sec and covered a distance of 2850.39km *1771.2 miles* from 2 May to 7 Jun 1989. The event was organized by the Rev. Bryan G. Apps, and church members of Southbourne, Bournemouth, Dorset.

Distance (24 hours) On 5–6 Jul 1986 the North London Society of Model Engineers team at the ARRA club in Southport, Merseyside achieved a 24-hour distance record for a 1:32 scale car of 492.364km *305.949 miles*, 11,815 laps of the track driving a Rondeau M482C Group C Sports car, built by Ian Fisher. This was under the rules of the B.S.C.R.A (British Slot Car Racing Association). A team of eight set a new distance record of 271.126km *168.56 miles* for the H: scale 24-hour Le Mans Slot Car Race driving a Mercedes at the Welfare Sports Centre, Derby on 20–21 Jun 1992.

The longest slot car track measures 292m *958 ft* and was built at Mallory Park Circuit, Leicester on 22 Nov 1991 using pieces collected from enthusiasts and one lap was successfully completed by a car.

Roads

Trackway *Oldest* The oldest known trackway in England is the Sweet Track in the Somerset Levels near Shapwick. Dendrochronologists in 1990 indicated that the road was built from trees felled in the winter of 3807–3806 BC.

The oldest in the Republic of Ireland are at Corlea and Derryoghil bogs near Lanesborough, Co. Roscommon, where prehistoric tracks made of oak and ash logs, radiocarbon dated to *c.* 2500–2300 BC, have been discovered.

Road mileages The country with the greatest length of road is the United States (all 50 states), with 6,244,497 km *3,880,151 miles* of graded roads.

Great Britain has 386,471 km *240,142 miles* of road, including 3209 km *1994 miles* of motorway.

Longest motorable road The Pan-American Highway, from north-west Alaska, USA to Santiago, Chile, thence eastward to Buenos Aires, Argentina and terminating in Brasilia, Brazil is over 24,140 km *15,000 miles* in length. There is, however, a small incomplete section in Panama and Colombia known as the Darién Gap.

Great Britain The longest designated road in Great Britain is the A1 from London to Edinburgh, of 648 km *403 miles.*

The longest Roman roads were Watling Street, from Dubrae (Dover), 346 km *215 miles* through Londinium (London) to Viroconium (Wroxeter), and Fosse Way, which ran 350 km *218 miles* from Lindum (Lincoln) through Aquae Sulis (Bath) to Isca Dumnoniorum (Exeter), although a 16 km *10 mile* section near Ilchester remains indistinct.

Longest and shortest gaps The greatest error a motorway driver can make when missing an exit is travelling southbound on the M11 in Hertfordshire. The gap between junctions 10 (Duxford) and 8 (Bishop's Stortford) is 28.6 km *17.8 miles.* Junction 9 is open only to northbound drivers. The shortest gap between two exits is less than 160 m *174 yd*, between junctions 19 (Clydebank) and 18 (Charing Cross), on the eastbound M8 in central Glasgow.

Highest The highest trail in the world is a 13 km *8 mile* stretch of the Gangdise, Tibet between Khaleb and Xinjifu, Tibet, which in two places exceeds 6080 m *20,000 ft.*

The highest road in the world is in Khardungla pass at an altitude of 5682 m *18,640 ft.* This is one of the three passes of the Leh–Manali road completed in 1976 by the Border Roads Organization, New Delhi, India; motor vehicles have been able to use it from 1988.

Europe The highest motor road is the Pico de Veleta in the Sierra Nevada, southern Spain. The shadeless climb of 36 km *22.4 miles* brings the motorist to 3469 m *11,384 ft* above sea level and became, on completion of a road on its southern side in 1974, arguably Europe's highest 'pass'.

Great Britain The highest unclassified road in the United Kingdom is the A6293 tarmaced private extension at Great Dun Fell, Cumbria (847 m *2780 ft*), leading to a Ministry of Defence and Air Traffic Control installation. A permit is required to use it.

The highest classified road in Britain is the A93 road over the Grampians through Cairnwell, a pass between Blairgowrie, Tayside and Braemar, Grampian, which reaches a height of 670 m *2199 ft.* An estate track exists to the summit of Ben a'Bhuird 1176 m *3860 ft* in Grampian.

Lowest The lowest road is along the Israeli shores of the Dead Sea at 393 m *1290 ft* below sea level.

The lowest surface roads in Great Britain are in the Holme Fen area of Cambridgeshire 2.75 m *9 ft* below sea level.

Widest The widest road in the world is the Monumental Axis, running for 2.4 km *1½ miles* from the Municipal Plaza to the Plaza of the Three Powers in Brasilia, the capital of Brazil. The six-lane boulevard was opened in April 1960 and is 250 m *820.2 ft* wide.

The San Francisco–Oakland Bay Bridge Toll Plaza has 23 lanes (17 westbound) serving the bridge in Oakland, California, USA.

The only instance of 17 carriageway lanes side by side in Britain occurs on the M61 at Linnyshaw Moss, Worsley, Greater Manchester.

Traffic volume The most heavily travelled stretch of road is Interstate 405 (San Diego Freeway), in Orange County, California, USA, which has a peak-hour volume of 25,500 vehicles. This volume occurs on a 0.9 mile stretch between Garden Grove Freeway and Seal Beach Boulevard.

The greatest at any one point in Great Britain is at Hyde Park Corner, London. The peak flow (including the underpass) for 24 hours in 1990 was 240,000 vehicles.

Motorway Britain's busiest and most heavily travelled motorway is the M25; with the section between Junctions 13 (Staines) and 14 (Heathrow) having an average traffic flow of 168,000 vehicles over a 24 hour period.

Traffic density The territory with the highest traffic density in the world is Hong Kong. In 1992 there were 418 vehicles per mile of serviceable roads, i.e. a density of 3.84 m *4.21 yd* per vehicle. The comparative figure for Great Britain was 15.5 m *17 yd* per vehicle in 1992.

Most complex interchange The most complex interchange on the British road system is that at Gravelly Hill, north of Birmingham on the Midland Link Motorway section of the M6, opened on 24 May 1972. Popularly known as 'Spaghetti Junction', it includes 18 routes on six levels (together with a diverted canal and river). Its construction consumed 26,000 tonnes of steel, 250,000 tonnes of concrete and 300,000 tonnes of earth, and cost £8.2 million.

Longest ring-road Work on the M25 six lane London Orbital Motorway, 195.5 km *121½ miles* long commenced in 1972 and was completed on 29 Oct 1986 at an estimated cost of £909 million, or £7.5 million per mile.

Longest viaduct The longest elevated viaduct on the British road system is the 4.78 km *2.97 mile* Gravelly Hill to Castle Bromwich section of the M6 in the West Midlands. It was completed in May 1972. (⇨ Most complex interchange)

Streets *Longest* The longest designated street in the world is Yonge Street, running north and west from Toronto, Canada. The first stretch, completed on 16 Feb 1796, ran 55 km *34 miles.* Its official length, now extended to Rainy River on the Ontario–Minnesota border, is 1896.3 km *1178.3 miles.*

Narrowest The world's narrowest street is in the village of Ripatransone in the Marche region of Italy. It is called Vicolo della Virilita ('Virility Alley') and is 43 cm *16.9 in* wide.

Shortest The title of 'The Shortest Street in the World' is claimed by the town of Bacup in Lancashire, where Elgin Street, situated by the old market ground, measures just 17 ft *5.2 m.*

Steepest The steepest street in the world is Baldwin Street, Dunedin, New Zealand, which has a maximum gradient of 1 in 1.266.

GUESS WHAT?

Q Where is the world's longest road tunnel?

A See Page 98

Jams!

Traffic jams The longest ever reported was that which stretched 176 km *109 miles* northwards from Lyon towards Paris, France on 16 Feb 1980. A record traffic jam was reported of 1½ million cars crawling bumper-to-bumper over the East-West German border on 12 Apr 1990.

The longest in Britain were two of 40 miles *64.3 km*: on the M1 from Junction 13 (Milton Keynes) to Junction 18 (Rugby) on 5 Apr 1985; and on the M6 between Charnock Richard and Carnforth, Lancs on 17 Apr 1987 involving 200,000 people and a tailback of 50,000 cars and coaches.

Norris McWhirter, founder editor of *The Guinness Book Of Records*, one small step from completing an ascent of the steepest street in the world, Baldwin Street in Dunedin, New Zealand.
(Photo: Tessa McWhirter)

Britain's steepest motorable road is the unclassified Chimney Bank at Rosedale Abbey, N Yorks which is signposted '1 in 3'. The county surveyor states it is 'not quite' a 33 per cent gradient. Unclassified road No. 149 at Ffordd Penllech, Harlech which is narrow and twisting, is at its steepest gradient 1 in 2.91.

Milestone Britain's oldest milestone *in situ* is a Roman stone dating from AD 150 on the Stanegate, at Chesterholme, near Bardon Mill, Northumberland.

> **Longest ford** The longest on any classified road in England is in Violet's Lane, north of Furneux Pelham, Herts, measuring 903 m *987½ yd* in length.

Squares *Largest* Tiananmen 'Gate of Heavenly Peace' Square in Beijing, described as the navel of China, covers 39.6 ha *98 acres*.

Great Britain The largest square in Great Britain is the 2.82 ha *6.99 acre* Ladbroke Square (open to residents only), constructed in 1842–5, while Lincoln's Inn Fields covers 2.76 ha *6.84 acres*.

Railways

Trains

Earliest Wagons running on wooden rails were used for mining as early as 1550 at Leberthal, Alsace, and in Britain for conveying coal from Strelley to Wollaton near Nottingham from 1604–15 and at Broseley Colliery, Shrops in October 1605.

Richard Trevithick built his first steam locomotive for the 914 mm *3 ft* gauge iron plateway at Coalbrookdale, Shrops in 1803, but there is no evidence that it ran. His second locomotive drew wagons in which men rode on a demonstration run at Penydarren, Mid Glamorgan on 22 Feb 1804, but it broke the plate rails.

The first permanent public railway to use steam traction was the Stockton & Darlington, from its opening on 27 Sep 1825 from Shildon to Stockton via Darlington, in Cleveland. The 7-tonne *Locomotion* could pull 48 tonnes at a speed of 24 km/h *15 mph*. It was designed and at times driven by George Stephenson (1781–1848).

The first regular steam passenger service was inaugurated over a one-mile section (between Bogshole Farm and South Street in Whitstable, Kent) on the 10.05 km *6¼ mile* Canterbury & Whitstable Railway on 3 May 1830, hauled by the engine *Invicta*.

Fastest The highest speed attained by a railed vehicle is 9851 km/h *6121 mph*, or Mach 8, by an unmanned rocket sled over the 15.2 km *9½ mile* long rail track at White Sands Missile Range, New Mexico, USA on 5 Oct 1982.

The highest speed recorded on any national rail system is 515.3 km/h *320.2 mph* by the French SNCF high-speed train TGV (Train à Grande Vitesse) Atlantique between Courtalain

The Train à Grande Vitesse zooms through the French countryside as it achieves the record speed of 515.3 km/h *320.2 mph*.
(Photo: Sipa Press/Chamussy)

and Tours on 18 May 1990. The TGV Sud-Est was brought into service on 27 Sep 1981. By September 1983 it had reduced its scheduled time for the Paris–Lyon run of 425 km *264 miles* to two hours exactly, so averaging 212.5 km/h *132 mph*.

The highest speed ever ratified for a steam locomotive was 201 km/h *125 mph* over 402 m *440 yd* by the LNER 4–6–2 No. 4468 *Mallard* (later numbered 60022), which hauled seven coaches weighing 243 tonnes gross down Stoke Bank, near Essendine, between Grantham, Lincs, and Peterborough, Cambs, on 3 Jul 1938. Driver Joseph Duddington was at the controls with Fireman Thomas Bray. The engine suffered damage to the middle big-end bearing.

Great Britain British Rail inaugurated their HST (High Speed Train) daily services between London–Bristol and South Wales on 4 Oct 1976. The electric British Rail APT-P (Advanced Passenger Train-Prototype) attained 261 km/h *162 mph* between Glasgow and Carlisle on its first revenue-earning run on 7 Dec 1981. It covered the 644 km *400 miles* from Glasgow to London in 4¼ hr, but was subsequently withdrawn from service because of technical problems.

The fastest scheduled train in Britain is the Edinburgh–London *Flying Scotsman*, which covers the 633.2 km *393.5 miles* in 249 minutes, at an average speed of 152.6 km/h *94.8 mph* including two stops. This train is powered by the fastest locomotives in service, the Class 91 25 kV electric type, one of which reached 261 km/h *162 mph* between Grantham and Peterborough on 18 Sep 1989.

Longest non-stop run The longest journey without any scheduled stop is the *Newcastle Pullman*, which covers the 374.1 km *232.5 miles* between Darlington and London in 2 hr 22 min.

Most powerful The world's most powerful steam locomotive, measured by tractive effort, was No. 700, a triple-articulated or triplex six-cylinder 2–8–8–8–4 engine built by the Baldwin Locomotive Works in 1916 for the Virginian Railway, USA. It had a tractive force of 75,434 kg *166,300 lb* when working compound and 90,520 kg *199,560 lb* when working simple.

The heaviest train ever hauled by a single engine is believed to be one of 15,545 tonnes made up of 250 freight cars stretching 2.5 km *1.6 miles* by the *Matt H.*

GUESS WHAT?
Q What is the connection between Robert Galstyan and trains?
A See Page 61

Shay (No. 5014), a 2–8–8–8–2 engine, which ran on the Erie Railroad from May 1914 until 1929.

On 19 Jun 1990 a single locomotive hauled a 5226-tonne train with 50 wagons carrying limestone from Merehead Quarry, Somerset to Acton, Greater London—the heaviest on record in Britain (⇨ Freight trains).

Largest steam locomotive The largest operating steam locomotive is the Union Pacific RR *Challenger* type 4–6–6–4 No. 3985, built by the American Locomotive Co. in 1943. In working order, with tender, it weighs 485 tonnes. It is used on enthusiasts' specials in the USA.

Greatest load The world's strongest rail carrier, with a capacity of 807 tonnes, is the 336-tonne 36-axle 'Schnabel'. It is 92 m *301 ft 10 in* long and was built for a US railway by Krupp, Germany in March 1981.

> # Moving!
>
> The heaviest load ever moved on rails is the 10,860-tonne Church of the Virgin Mary (built in 1548 in Most, now Czech Republic), in October–November 1975, because it was in the way of coal workings. It was moved 730 m *800 yd* at 0.002 km/h *0.0013 mph* over four weeks, at a cost of £9 million.

The heaviest load carried in Britain was a boiler drum weighing 279 tonnes and 37.1 m *122 ft* long which was carried from Immingham Dock to Killingholme, Humberside in September 1968.

Freight trains The world's longest and heaviest freight train on record, with the largest number of wagons recorded, made a run on the 1065 mm *3 ft 6 in* gauge Sishen–Saldanha railway in South Africa on 26–27 Aug 1989. The train consisted of 660 wagons each loaded to 105 tons gross, a tank car and a caboose, moved by nine 50 kV electric and seven diesel-electric locomotives distributed along the train. The train was 7.3 km *4½ miles* long and weighed 69,393 tons excluding locomotives. It travelled a distance of 861 km *535 miles* in 22 hr 40 min.

Britain's heaviest freight train runs from Merehead Quarry, Somerset to Acton, Greater London, usually with 5100 tonnes of limestone in 50 wagons. The train is hauled by a single 'Class 59' Co-Co diesel-electric locomotive (⇨ Most powerful above).

The longest regular freight train journey in Britain is the twice-weekly china clay train from Burngullow, Cornwall to Irvine, Scotland, a round trip of 1834 km *1140 miles*, hauled by the same pair of diesel locomotives throughout.

Longest passenger train The longest passenger train measured 1732.73 m *1895 yd*. Its 70 coaches were pulled by one electric locomotive, and the total weight was 2786 tonnes. This train of the National Belgian Railway Company took

1hr 11min 5sec to complete the 62km *38.5 mile* journey from Ghent to Ostend on 27 Apr 1991.

Tracks

Longest The world's longest run is one of 9438km *5864½ miles* on the Trans-Siberian line in Russia, from Moscow to Nakhodka on the Sea of Japan. There are 97 stops on the journey, which is scheduled to take 8days 4hr 25min.

The longest and newest cross-country railway in the world is the 3145km *1954 mile* Baikal–Amur Mainline (BAM), begun in 1938, restarted in 1974 and put into service on 27 Oct 1984. It runs from Ust-Kut, Eastern Siberia to Komsomolsk on the Amur River in Russia.

Spiked!

In the World Championship Professional Spike Driving Competition held at the Golden Spike National Historic Site in Utah, USA, Dale C. Jones, 49, of Lehi, Utah, USA drove six 17.8cm *7 in* railroad spikes in a time of 26.4sec on 11 Aug 1984. He incurred no penalty points under the official rules.

Longest straight The Australian National Railways Trans-Australian line over the Nullarbor Plain, from Mile 496 between Nurina and Loongana, Western Australia to Mile 793 between Ooldea and Watson, South Australia, is 478km *297 miles* dead straight, although not level.

The longest straight in Britain is the 29km *18 miles* between Barlby Junction and Brough, N Yorks on the 'down' line from Selby to Kingston-upon-Hull, Humberside.

Widest and narrowest gauge The widest in standard use is 1.676m *5ft 6 in*, as used in Spain, Portugal, India, Pakistan, Bangladesh, Sri Lanka, Argentina and Chile.

The narrowest gauge on which public services are operated is 260mm *10¼ in* on the Wells Harbour (1.12km *0.7 mile*) and the Wells Walsingham Railways (6.5km *4 miles*) in Norfolk.

Highest line At 4818m *15,806 ft* above sea level, the standard gauge (1435mm *4ft 8½ in*) track on the Morococha branch of the Peruvian State Railways at La Cima is the highest in the world.

The highest railway in Britain is the Snowdon Mountain Railway, which rises from Llanberis, Gwynedd to 1064m *3493 ft* above sea-level, just below the summit of Snowdon (*Yr Wyddfa*). It has a gauge of 800mm *2ft 7½ in*.

Lowest line The world's lowest line is in the Seikan Tunnel which crosses the Tsugaro Strait between Honshu and Hokkaido, Japan. It reaches a depth of 240m *786 ft* below sea level. The tunnel was opened on 13 Mar 1988 and is 53.8km *33½ miles* long.

Trains stop in the middle of the Seikan Tunnel for two minutes so that passengers can take pictures through the windows of panels on the walls of the tunnel.

The lowest in Europe is the Channel Tunnel, where the rails are 127m *417 ft* below mean sea level.

In Britain, the Severn Tunnel descends to 43.8m *144 ft* below sea level.

Steepest railway The world's steepest railway is the Katoomba Scenic Railway in the Blue Mountains of NSW, Australia. It is 310m *1020 ft* long with a gradient of 1 in 0.82. A 220hp electric winding machine hauls the car by twin steel cables 22mm diameter. The ride takes about 1min 40sec and carries around 420,000 passengers a year.

Steepest gradient The world's steepest gradient worked by adhesion is 1:11, between Chedde and Servoz on the metre-gauge SNCF Chamonix line, France.

The steepest sustained adhesion-worked gradient on a main line in the United Kingdom is the 3.2km *2 mile* Lickey incline of 1:37.7, just south-west of Birmingham, W Mids.

Busiest system The railway carrying the largest number of passengers is the East Japan Railway Co., which in 1992 carried 16,306,000 daily, providing it with a revenue of $18.8 billion.

Greatest length of railway The country with the greatest length of railway is the United States with 273,048 km *169,664 miles* of track.

Stations

Largest The world's largest station is Grand Central Terminal, Park Avenue and 42nd Street, New York City, USA, built from 1903–13. It covers 19ha *48 acres* on two levels with 41 tracks on the upper level and 26 on the lower. On average more than 550 trains and 200,000 people per day use it.

The largest railway station in Britain is Waterloo, London (11.4ha *28¼ acres*). Following completion of five new platforms in 1993 for international trains using the Channel Tunnel, its 24 platforms have a total length of 6194m *20,321 ft*.

Oldest Liverpool Road Station, Greater Manchester was first used on 15 Sep 1830. Part of the original station is now a museum.

Busiest The busiest railway junction in the world is Clapham Junction, London, with an average of 2200 trains passing through each 24hours. All trains from Waterloo and all the Brighton line trains from Victoria pass through.

Highest Condor station in Bolivia at 4786m *15,705 ft* on the metre gauge Rio Mulato to Potosi line is the highest in the world.

The highest passenger station on the British main-line rail network is Corrour, Highland at an altitude of 410.5m *1347 ft* above sea level.

Waiting rooms The world's largest waiting rooms are the four in Beijing Station, Chang'an Boulevard, Beijing, China, opened in September 1959, with a total standing capacity of 14,000.

Platforms The longest railway platform in the world is the Kharagpur platform, West Bengal,

An aerial shot of the massive Bailey Yard goods yard at North Platte, Nebraska, USA.
(Photo: Union Pacific Railroad)

Bill Curtis of Clacton-on-Sea, Essex is acknowledged as the world champion train spotter—or 'gricer' (after Richard Grice, the first champion). His totals include some 60,000 locomotives, 11,200 electric units and 8300 diesel units, clocked up over a period of 40 years in a number of different countries.

India, which measures 833m *2733 ft* in length.

The State Street Center subway platform on 'The Loop' in Chicago, Illinois, USA is 1066m *3500 ft* in length.

The longest in Britain is the 602.7m *1977 ft 4 in* long platform at Gloucester.

Goods yard The largest goods yard is Bailey Yard at North Platte, Nebraska, USA, which covers 2850 acres *1153 ha* and has 418km *260 miles* of track. It handles an average of 108 trains and some 8500 wagons every day.

Underground Railways

Busiest The world's busiest ever metro system has been the Greater Moscow Metro (opened 1935) in Russia. At its peak there were 3.3 billion passenger journeys in a year, although by 1991 the figure had declined to 2.5 billion. It has 3500 railcars and a workforce of 25,000. There are 141 stations (18 of which have more than one name, being transfer stations) and 226.7km *140 miles* of track.

Most extensive The subway with most stations in the world is the New York City Metropolitan Transportation Authority subway, USA (first section opened on 27 Oct 1904). There are 469 stations (277 of which are underground) in a network which covers 383km *238 miles*. It serves an estimated 5 million underground passengers per day.

The most extensive underground or rapid transit railway system in the world is the London Underground, with 408km *254 miles* of route, of which 135km *85 miles* is bored tunnel and 32km *20 miles* is 'cut and cover'. The whole system is operated by a staff of 17,000 serving 273 stations.

Enthusiastic!

The record time for doing a tour of the London Underground taking in all of the 273 stations is 18 hr 41 min 41 sec by a team of five—Robert A. Robinson, Peter D. Robinson, Timothy J. Robinson, Timothy J. Clark and Richard J. Harris—on 30 Jul 1986.

The 4134 cars forming a fleet of 570 trains carried 728 million passengers in 1992–3.

Rail Travel

Calling all stations Alan M. Witton of Chorlton, Manchester visited every open British Rail station (2362) in a continuous tour for charity of 26,703 km *16,593 miles* in 452 hr 16 min from 13 Jul–28 Aug 1980.

Colin M. Mulvany and Seth N. Vafiadis of west London visited every open British Rail station (2378) embracing also the Tyne & Wear, Glasgow and London underground systems (333 stations) for charity in 31 days 5 hr 8 min 58 sec. They travelled over 24,989 km *15,528 miles* to average 61.2 km/h *38.1 mph* from 4 Jun–5 Jul 1984.

Four points of the compass Tony Davies of Stafford visited the northernmost, southernmost, westernmost and easternmost stations in Great Britain in a time of 37 hr 34 min from 14–15 Apr 1993. These are Thurso, Scotland (north), Lowestoft, Suffolk (east), Penzance, Cornwall (south) and Arisaig, Scotland (west).

> Tony Davies, who set the record for travelling by rail to the four points of the compass, said:– 'Every train I travelled on was either on time or early. I was amazed'.

Most miles in 7 days Andrew Kingsmell and Sean Andrews of Bromley, Kent together with Graham Bardouleau of Crawley, W Sussex travelled 21,090 km *13,105 miles* on the French national railway system in 6 days 22 hr 38 min from 28 Nov–5 Dec 1992.

Most miles in 24 hours The greatest distance travelled in Britain in 24 hours (without duplicating any part of the journey) is 2842.5 km *1766¼ miles* by Norma and Jonathan Carter, 15, from 3–4 Sep 1992.

Longest journey In the course of some 73 years commuting by British Rail from Kent to London, Ralph Ransome of Birchington travelled an equivalent of an estimated 39 times round the world. He retired at the age of 93 on 5 Feb 1986.

The peak year for rail travel in Britain was 1957, when 1101 million journeys were made. The number of journeys made in the 12 months to 31 Mar 1993 was 744.8 million.

Suggestion boxes The most prolific example on record of the use of any suggestion box scheme is that of John Drayton (1907–87) of Newport, Gwent, who plied the British rail system with a total of 31,400 suggestions from 1924 to August 1987. More than one in seven were adopted and 100 were accepted by London Transport.

Most countries travelled through in 24 hours The record number of countries travelled through entirely by train in 24 hours is eleven, by Alison Bailey, Ian Bailey, John English and David Kellie on 1–2 May 1993. Their journey started in Hungary and continued through Slovakia, the Czech Republic, Austria, Germany, back into Austria, Liechtenstein, Switzerland, France, Luxembourg, Belgium and the Netherlands, where they arrived 22 hr 10 min after setting off.

Model railway A standard 'Life-Like' BL2 HO scale electric train pulled six eight-wheel coaches for 1207½ hr from 4 Aug–23 Sep 1990 covering a distance of 1463.65 km *909½ miles*. The event was organized by Ike Cottingham and Mark Hamrick of Mainline Modelers of Akron, Ohio, USA.

Longest!

A rail ticket measuring 34 m *111 ft 10½ in* was issued to Ronald, Norma and Jonathan Carter for a series of journeys throughout England between 15–23 Feb 1992.

The longest recorded run by a model *steam* locomotive is 231.7 km *144 miles* in 27 hr 18 min by the 18.4 cm *7¼ in* gauge 'Winifred', built in 1974 by Wilf Grove at Thames Ditton, Surrey, from 7–9 Sep 1979. 'Winifred' works on 5.6 kg/cm² *80 lb/in²* pressure and is coal-fired, with cylinders 54 mm *2⅛ in* in diameter and 79 mm *3⅛ in* stroke.

The most miniature model railway ever built is one of 1:1400 scale by Bob Henderson of Gravenhurst, Ontario, Canada. The engine measures 5 mm *³⁄₁₆ in* overall.

Aviation

Earliest Flights

The first controlled and sustained power-driven flight occurred near the Kill Devil Hill, Kitty Hawk, North Carolina, USA at 10:35 a.m. on 17 Dec 1903, when Orville Wright (1871–1948) flew the 9 kW *12-hp* chain-driven *Flyer I* for a distance of 36.5 m *120 ft* at an airspeed of 48 km/h *30 mph*, a ground speed of 10.9 km/h *6.8 mph* and an altitude of 2.5–3.5 m *8–12 ft* for about 12 seconds, watched by his brother Wilbur (1867–1912), four men and a boy. The *Flyer I* was first exhibited in the National Air and Space Museum at the Smithsonian Institution, Washington DC, USA on 17 Dec 1948.

The first hop by a man-carrying aeroplane entirely under its own power was made when Clément Ader (1841–1925) of France flew in his *Éole* for about 50 m *164 ft* at Armainvilliers, France on 9 Oct 1890. It was powered by a lightweight steam engine of his own design, which developed about 15 kW *20-hp*, but the flight was neither sustained nor controlled.

Great Britain The first officially recognized flight in the British Isles was made by the US (later British) citizen Samuel Franklin Cody (1861–1913) who flew 423 m *1390 ft* in the British Army Aeroplane No. 1 at Farnborough, Hants on 16 Oct 1908.

Horatio Frederick Phillips (1845–1924) almost certainly covered 152 m *500 ft* in his *Multiplane* 'Venetian blind' aeroplane at Streatham, London in 1907.

The first Briton to fly was George Pearson Dickin (1881–1909), a journalist from Southport, Lancs as a passenger to Wilbur Wright at Auvours, France on 3 Oct 1908.

The first resident British citizen to fly in Britain was J.T.C. Moore-Brabazon (later Lord Brabazon of Tara) (1884–1964), with three short but sustained flights from 30 Apr–2 May 1909.

Jet-engined Proposals for jet propulsion date back to Capt. Marconnet of France in 1909.

The earliest tested run was that of British Power Jets' experimental WU1 (Whittle Unit No. 1) at Rugby on 12 Apr 1937, invented by Flying Officer (later Air Commodore Sir) Frank Whittle (b. 1 Jun 1907), who had applied for a patent on jet propulsion in 1930.

The first flight by an aeroplane powered by a turbojet engine was made by the Heinkel He 178, piloted by Flugkapitän Erich Warsitz, at Marienehe, Germany on 27 Aug 1939. It was powered by a Heinkel He S3b engine weighing 378 kg *834 lb* (as installed with long tailpipe) designed by Dr Hans Pabst von Ohain.

The first British jet flight, of 17 minutes, was made by Flt Lt P.E.G. 'Jerry' Sayer (killed 1942) in the Gloster-Whittle E.28/39 (wing span 8.84 m *29 ft*, length 7.70 m *25 ft 3 in*) fitted with an 0.39 tonne *860 lb* thrust Whittle W-1 engine at Cranwell, Lincs on 15 May 1941. Maximum speed was *c.* 560 km/h *350 mph*. It is now in the Science Museum, London.

Supersonic flight The first was achieved on 14 Oct 1947 by Capt. (later Brig. Gen.) Charles ('Chuck') Elwood Yeager (b. 13 Feb 1923), over Lake Muroc, California, USA in a Bell X-1 rocket plane at Mach 1.015 (1078 km/h *670 mph*) at an altitude of 12,800 m *42,000 ft*. The XS-1 is in the Smithsonian Institution, Washington, DC, USA.

Pumping!

A five-man team (one pusher, four pumpers) achieved a speed of 33.12 km/h *20.58 mph* in moving a hand-pumped railcar over a 300 m *984 ft* course at Rolvenden, Kent on 21 Aug 1989, recording a time of 32.61 sec.

Speed!

The use of the Mach scale for aircraft speeds was introduced by Prof. Ackeret of Zürich, Switzerland. The Mach number is the ratio of the velocity of a moving body to the local velocity of sound. This ratio was first employed by Dr Ernst Mach (1838–1916) of Vienna, Austria in 1887. Thus Mach 1.0 equals 1224.67 km/h *760.98 mph* at sea level at 15° C *59° F*, and is assumed, for convenience, to fall to a constant 1061.81 km/h *659.78 mph* in the stratosphere, i.e. above 11,000 m *36,089 ft*.

The former Soviet Tupolev Tu-144, first flown on 31 Dec 1968 and therefore the first supersonic airliner to fly, entered service initially carrying cargo only.

Cross-Channel The earliest crossing of the English channel was made on 25 Jul 1909 when Louis Blériot (1872–1936) of France flew his Blériot XI monoplane, powered by a 17.25 kw *23-hp* Anzani engine, 41.8 km *26 miles* from Les Barraques, France to Northfall Meadow, near Dover Castle, Kent in 36½ minutes, after taking off at 4:41 a.m.

Off to Paris!

The fastest time to travel the 344 km *214 miles* from central Paris, France, to central London (BBC TV centre) is 38 min 58 sec by David Boyce of Stewart Wrightson (Aviation) Ltd on 24 Sep 1983. He travelled by motorcycle and helicopter to Le Bourget; Hawker Hunter jet (piloted by the late Michael Carlton) to Biggin Hill, Kent; and by helicopter to the TV centre car park.

Trans-Atlantic The first crossing of the North Atlantic by air was made by Lt Cdr. (later Rear Admiral) Albert Cushion Read (1887–1967) and his crew (Stone, Hinton, Rodd, Rhoads and Breese) in the 84-knot *155km/h* US Navy/Curtiss flying-boat NC-4 from Trepassey Harbor, Newfoundland, Canada via the Azores, to Lisbon, Portugal from 16–27 May 1919. The whole flight of 7591km *4717miles*, originating from Rockaway Air Station, Long Island, New York, USA on 8 May, required 53 hr 58 min, terminating at Plymouth, Devon on 31 May.

Non-stop The first non-stop transatlantic flight was achieved 18 days later. The pilot, Capt. John Williams Alcock (1892–1919), and navigator, Lt Arthur Whitton Brown (1886–1948) left Lester's Field, St John's, Newfoundland, Canada at 4:13p.m. GMT on 14 Jun 1919, and landed at Derrygimla bog near Clifden, Co. Galway, Republic of Ireland at 8:40a.m. GMT, 15 June, having covered 3154km *1960 miles* in their Vickers Vimy, powered by two 300kW *360-hp* Rolls-Royce Eagle VIII engines.

Solo The first solo trans-Atlantic flight was achieved by Capt. (later Brigadier Gen.) Charles Augustus Lindbergh (1902–74) who took off in his 165kW *220-hp* Ryan monoplane *Spirit of St Louis* at 12:52p.m. GMT on 20 May 1927 from Roosevelt Field, Long Island, New York, USA. He landed at 10:21p.m. GMT on 21 May 1927 at Le Bourget Airfield, Paris, France. His flight of 5810km *3610miles* lasted 33hr 29½ min so winning a prize of $25,000. It is in the Smithsonian Institution, Washington, DC, USA.

Trans-Pacific The first non-stop flight was by Major Clyde Pangborn and Hugh Herndon in the Bellanca cabin monoplane *Miss Veedol.* They took off from Sabishiro Beach, Japan and covered the distance of 7335km *4558miles* to Wenatchee, Washington State, USA in 41hr 13min from 3–5 Oct 1931.

Circumnavigational flights
Strict circumnavigation of the globe requires the aircraft to pass through two antipodal points, thus covering a minimum distance of 40,007.86 km *24,859.73 miles.*

Earliest The earliest such flight, of 42,398km *26,345 miles,* was by two US Army Douglas DWC seaplanes in 57 'hops' between 6 April and 28 Sep 1924, beginning and ending at Seattle, Washington State, USA. The *Chicago* was piloted by Lt Lowell H. Smith and Lt Leslie P. Arnold, and the *New Orleans* by Lt Erik H. Nelson and Lt John Harding. Their flying time was 371hr 11min.

Fastest The fastest flight under the FAI (Fédération Aéronautique Internationale) rules,

which permit flights that exceed the length of the Tropic of Cancer or Capricorn (36,787.6 km *22,858.8 miles*), was that of 32hr 49min by an Air France Concorde (Capts. Claude Delorme and Jean Boyé) westabout from Lisbon, Portugal via Santo Domingo, Acapulco, Honolulu, Guam, Bangkok and Bahrain on 12–13 Oct 1992. Flight AF 1492 was undertaken to celebrate the 500th anniversary of Christopher Columbus' discovery of the New World.

First without refuelling
Richard G. 'Dick' Rutan and Jeana Yeager, in their specially constructed aircraft *Voyager*, designed by Dick's brother Burt Rutan, flew from Edwards Air Force Base, California, USA between 14–23 Dec 1986. Their flight took 9days 3min 44sec and they covered a distance of 40,212km *24,987 miles* averaging 186.11 km/h *115.65 mph*. The plane, with a wing span of 33.77m *110 ft 10 in*, was capable of carrying 5636litres *1240 gal* of fuel weighing 4052 kg *8934lb*. The pilot flew in a cockpit measuring 1.71 × 0.55m *5ft 7in × 1ft 10in* and the off-duty crew member occupied a cabin 2.29 × 0.61m *7ft 6 in × 2 ft.* *Voyager* is in the Smithsonian Institution, Washington, DC, USA.

First circum-polar Capt. Elgen M. Long, 44, achieved the first circum-polar flight in a Piper PA-31 Navajo from 5 Nov–3 Dec 1971. He covered 62,597km *38,896 miles* in 215 flying hours.

Aircraft

Largest wing span The aircraft with the largest wing span ever constructed is the $40-million Hughes H4 Hercules flying-boat, usually referred to as *Spruce Goose.* The eight-engined 193-tonne aircraft has a wing span of 97.51m *319 ft 11in* and a length of 66.64m *218ft 8in*. It was raised 70ft *21.3m* into the air in a test run of 1000 yd *914 m*, piloted by Howard Hughes (1905–76), off Long Beach Harbor, California, USA on 2 Nov 1947, but never flew again.

Among current aircraft, the Ukrainian Antonov An-124 has a wing span of 73.3m *240 ft 5¾ in,* and the Boeing 747-400 one of 64.92m *213 ft.*

A modified six-engine version of the An-124, known as An-225 which was built to carry the former Soviet space shuttle *Buran*, has a wing span of 88.4m *290 ft* (⇨ Heaviest below).

The $34-million Piasecki Heli-Stat, comprising a framework of light-alloy and composite materials, to mount four Sikorsky SH-34J helicopters and the envelope of a Goodyear ZPG-2 patrol airship, was exhibited on 26 Jan 1984 at

Lakehurst, New Jersey, USA. Designed for US Forest Service use and designated Model 94-37J Logger, it had an overall length of 104.55m *343ft* and was intended to carry a payload of 21.4tons. It crashed on 1 Jul 1986.

Heaviest The aircraft with the highest standard maximum take-off weight is the Antonov An-225 *Mriya* (Dream) of 600tonnes *1,322,750lb*. Such an aircraft lifted a payload of 156,300 kg *344,579lb* to a height of 12,410m *40,715 ft* on 22 Mar 1989. The flight was made by Capt. Alexander Galunenko with his crew of seven pilots and covered a distance of 2100km *1305 miles* in 3 hr 47 min (⇨ Most capacious).

Ultralight On 3 Aug 1985 Anthony A. Cafaro (b. 30 Nov 1951) flew an ultralight aircraft (maximum weight 111kg *245lb*, maximum speed 104.6km/h *65mph*, fuel capacity 19litres *4¼ gal*) single-seater Gypsy Skycycle for 7hr 31min at

> **Roy Castle, host of the BBC TV *Record Breakers* programme, flew on the wing of a Boeing Stearman biplane for 3 hr 23 min on 2 Aug 1990, taking off from Gatwick, W Sussex and landing at Le Bourget, near Paris, France.**

> **GUESS WHAT?**
> Q Who completed the first trans-pacific row?
> A See Page 112

Plane Pulling!

David Huxley single-handedly pulled a Boeing 767 weighing 105 tonnes a distance of 62.14m *203ft 10in* across the tarmac at the Qantas jet base at Sydney, Australia on 9 Mar 1994.

A team of 59 Qantas personnel pulled a Boeing 747 weighing 205 tonnes a distance of 100 metres in 62.1 sec at Perth airport, Australia on 22 Oct 1988.

The team of 59 Qantas employees during their successful plane pulling record attempt (above right) and feeling the after-effects moments later (right).
(Photos: Ian Cugley)

1088 people *in one aircraft*

An astounding record was set on 24 May 1991 when 1086 Ethiopian Jews were evacuated to Israel in one plane. This was more than double the normal capacity of a passenger jumbo jet, and not surprisingly never before had so many people flown in a commercial airliner. Two babies were born en route bringing the total who landed in Israel to 1088.

The flight was just one of 40 which were put on to evacuate a total of 14,200 Jews to their promised land from Addis Ababa, the besieged capital of Ethiopia, all in the space of 24 hours. The exercise, code-named Operation Solomon, had been planned over several weeks with US diplomatic assistance, and President Bush personally helped with the request to the Ethiopian government for permission to be granted to carry out the airlift. The Jewish Agency for Israel and El Al, the Israeli national airline, helped co-ordinate the whole operation.

Following the collapse of the Marxist regime in Ethiopia and the instal-lation of an interim government, Addis Ababa was under siege by rebels support-ing the former president. With the rebels being Arab-backed and felt to be anti-Jewish, it became increasingly evident that the airlift had to be carried out as quickly as possible, hence the packed conditions on the planes. On the record-breaking flight some of the rows of ten seats had as many as eighteen people jammed into them, with no toilets as the aim was simply to bring as the greatest possible number of people to Israel. The flights were operated by El Al and the Israel Air Force, with one Ethiopian plane also being used.

A number of the evacuees had never been close to a plane, let alone actually flown on one. Conditions were unbearable, even if there was great anticipation over the new life that was about to begin. Four babies were born during the flights, and the happi-ness continued as the planes flew into Israeli airspace, with announcements in the local language of the immigrants causing spontaneous singing and celebration. The culmination of each flight was of course a safe landing in Israel, with some of the arrivals having to be carried down the gangways. Many arrivals kneeled to kiss the ground in gratitude upon their arrival.

(Photos: Rex Features/Sipa Press)

The record time for refuelling an aeroplane (with 390 litres *85 gal* of 100 octane avgas) is 3 min 24 sec, for a 1975 Cessna 310 (N92HH), by the Sky Harbor Air Service line crew. It had landed at Cheyenne airport, Wyoming, USA on 5 Jul 1992 during an around the world air race.

Dart Field, Mayville, New York, USA. Nine fuel 'pick-ups' were completed during the flight.

Smallest The smallest biplane ever flown was *Bumble Bee Two*, designed and built by Robert H. Starr of Arizona, USA. It was 2.64m *8 ft 10 in* long, with a wing span of 1.68m *5 ft 6 in*, and weighed 179.6kg *396 lb* empty. The highest speed attained was 306 km/h *190 mph*. On 8 May 1988 after flying to a height of 120m *400 ft* it crashed, and was totally destroyed.

The smallest monoplane ever flown is the *Baby Bird*, designed and built by Donald R. Stits. It is 3.35m *11 ft* long, with a wing span of 1.91m *6 ft 3 in* and weighs 114.3kg *252 lb* empty. It is powered by a 41.25kW *55-hp* two-cylinder Hirth engine, giving a top speed of 177 km/h *110 mph*. It was first flown by Harold Nemer on 4 Aug 1984 at Camarillo, California, USA.

The smallest twin-engined aircraft is believed to be the Colomban MGI5 Cricri (first flown 19 Jul 1973), which has a wing span of 4.9m *16 ft* and measures 3.91m *12 ft 10 in* long overall. It is pow-ered by two 11kW *15 hp* JPX PUL engines.

Bombers *Heaviest* The former Soviet four-jet Tupolev Tu-160 has a maximum take-off weight of 275 tonnes *606,270 lb*.

Fastest The world's fastest operational bombers include the French Dassault Mirage IV, which can fly at Mach 2.2 (2333 km/h *1450 mph*) at 11,000m *36,000 ft*.

The American variable-geometry or 'swing-wing' General Dynamics FB-111A has a maximum speed of Mach 2.5, and the former Soviet swing-wing Tupolev Tu-22M, known to NATO as 'Backfire', has an estimated over-target speed of Mach 2.0 but could be as fast as Mach 2.5.

Largest airliner The highest capacity jet airliner is the Boeing 747-400, which entered service with Northwest Airlines on 26 Jan 1989; it has a wing span of 64.4m *211 ft 5 in*, a range exceeding 12,500 km *8000 miles* and can carry up to 567 passengers. The original Boeing 747 'Jumbo Jet' was first flown on 9 Feb 1969. It can carry from 385 to more than 560 passengers and has a maxi-mum speed of 969 km/h *602 mph*. Its wing span is 59.6m *195 ft 8 in* and its length 70.7m *231 ft 10 in*. It entered service on 22 Jan 1970.

The largest-span British aircraft was the Bristol Type 167 Brabazon, which had a maximum take-off weight of 131.4 tonnes, a wing span of 70.10m *230 ft* and a length of 53.94m *177 ft*. This eight-engined transport first flew on 4 Sep 1949 but did not enter series production. The largest production aircraft was the four-jet Super VC10, the last design constructed by Vickers, which weighed 149.5 tons and had a wing span of 44.55 m *146 ft 10 in*.

Fastest airliner The Tupolev Tu-14, first flown on 31 Dec 1988, was reported to have reached Mach 2.4 (2587 km/h *1600 mph*), but normal cruising speed was Mach 2.2. It flew at Mach 1 for the first time on 5 Jun 1969 and exceeded Mach 2 on 26 May 1970, the first commercial transport to do so. Scheduled services began on 26 Dec 1975, flying freight and mail.

The BAC/Aérospatiale Concorde, first flown on 2 Mar 1969, cruises at up to Mach 2.2 (2333 km/h *1450 mph*) and became the first supersonic air-liner used on passenger services on 21 Jan 1976. The New York–London record is 2 hr 54 min 30 sec, set on 14 Apr 1990.

Most capacious The Aero Spacelines Super Guppy has a cargo hold with a usable volume of 1410 m³ *49,790 ft³* and a maximum take-off weight of 79.38 tonnes. Its wing span is 47.62m *156 ft 3 in* and its length 43.05m *141 ft 3 in*. Its cargo compartment is 33.17m *108 ft 10 in* long with a cylindrical section 7.62m *25 ft* in diameter.

The Ukrainian Antonov An-124 *Ruslan* has a cargo hold with a usable volume of 1014 m³ *35,800 ft³* and a maximum take-off weight of 405 tonnes. A special-purpose heavy-lift version of the An-124, known as An-225 *Mriya* (Dream), has been devel-oped with a stretched fuselage providing as much as 1190 m³ *42,000 ft³* usable volume. Its cargo compartment includes an unobstructed 43m *141 ft* hold length, with maximum width and height of 6.4m *21 ft* and 4.4m *14 ft 5 in* respec-tively (⇔ Heaviest, above).

Largest propeller The largest plane propeller ever used was the 6.9m *22 ft 7½ in* diameter Garuda propeller, fitted to the Linke-Hofmann R II built in Breslau, Germany (now Wroclaw,

Poland) which flew in 1919. It was driven by four 193 kW *260-hp* Mercedes engines and turned at only 545 rpm.

Heaviest commercial cargo movement
The Ukrainian aircraft designer Antonov and the British charter company Air Foyle carried out the heaviest commercial air cargo movement, by taking three transformers weighing 43 tonnes each and other equipment from Barcelona, Spain to Nouméa, New Caledonia (Pacific) between 10–14 Jan 1991. The total weight carried in the An-124 *Ruslan* (⟳ Most capacious) was 140 tonnes.

Air Foyle and Antonov also hold the record for carrying the heaviest single piece of cargo, by flying a 124-tonne power plant generator from Düsseldorf, Germany to New Delhi, India on 22 Sep 1993. Again the aircraft used was the Ukrainian An-124 *Ruslan*. Owing to the huge weight carried, it was necessary to make six refuelling stops during the 9000 km *5600 mile* flight.

Most flights by propeller-driven airliner
General Dynamics (formerly Convair) reported in March 1994 that some of its CV-580 turboprop airliners had logged over 150,000 flights, many typically averaging no more than 20 minutes in short-haul operations.

Most flights by a jet airliner
A survey of ageing airliners or so-called 'geriatric jets' published in April 1994 in the weekly *Flight International* magazine reported a McDonnell Douglas DC-9 still in service which had logged 95,939 flights in under 28 years.

The most hours recorded by a jet airliner still in service is the 94,804 hours in under 25 years reported for a Boeing 747 in the same issue of *Flight International* (⟳ above).

Oldest jet airliner
According to the London-based aviation information and consultancy company Airclaims, a first-generation airliner built in January 1959—a Douglas DC-8—was still in service in May 1994 as a flying operating theatre.

Scheduled flights
Longest The longest non-stop scheduled flight is currently one of 12,825 km *7969 miles*, by joint operation between South African Airways and American Airlines for their

flight from New York, USA to Johannesburg, South Africa. In terms of time taken, the longest is 15 hr 35 min, for Taipei, Taiwan to Paris, France with Air France.

The longest non-stop flight by a commercial airliner was one of 18,545 km *10,008 nautical miles* from Auckland, New Zealand to Le Bourget, Paris, France in 21 hr 46 min on 17–18 Jun 1993 by the Airbus Industrie A340-200. It was the return leg of a flight which had started at Le Bourget the previous day.

A Boeing 767-200ER flight from Seattle, Washington, USA to Nairobi, Kenya on 8–9 Jun 1990 set a new speed and endurance record for the longest delivery flight by a twin-engined commercial jet. The Royal Brunei Airlines Boeing 767 flew 14,890 km *8040 nautical miles* great-circle distance in 18 hr 29 min, consuming 75.4 tonnes of fuel.

Shortest!

The shortest scheduled flight is by Loganair between the Orkney Islands of Westray and Papa Westray which has been flown with Britten-Norman BN-2 Islander twin-engined 10-seat transports since September 1967. Though scheduled for 2 minutes, in favourable wind conditions it was once accomplished in 58 sec by Capt. Andrew D. Alsop. The check-in time for the flight is 20 minutes.

Round the world
The fastest time for a circumnavigation under FAI regulations using scheduled flights is 44 hr 6 min by David J. Springbett (b. 2 May 1938) of Taplow, Bucks. His route took him from Los Angeles, California, USA east-about via London, Bahrain, Singapore, Bangkok, Manila, Tokyo and Honolulu from 8–10 Jan 1980 over a course of 37,124 km *23,068 miles*.

Longest air ticket
A 12 m *39 ft 4½ in* single air ticket was issued to Bruno Leunen of Brussels, Belgium in December 1984 for a 85,623 km *53,203 mile* round trip on 80 airlines with 109 stopovers.

Brother Michael Bartlett of London used a monthly Skypass issued by the Belgian national airline Sabena to fly between London and Brussels 128 times between 18 Oct and 17 Nov 1993. He stapled the individual tickets together to form a 25.3 m *83 ft* long ticket, and covered a total of 41,771 km *25,956 miles* during the month.

John o' Groats–Land's End
The record time for an 'End to End' flight over Great Britain where supersonic overflying is banned is 46 min 44 sec by a McDonnell F-4K Phantom (Wing Cdr John Brady and Flt Lt Mike Pugh) on 24 Feb 1988.

Highest Speed

Official record
The airspeed record is 3529.56 km/h *2193.17 mph*, by Capt. Eldon W. Joersz and Major George T. Morgan, Jr, in a Lockheed SR-71A 'Blackbird' near Beale Air Force Base, California, USA over a 25 km *15½ mile* course on 28 Jul 1976.

Air-launched records
The fastest fixed-wing aircraft was the US North American Aviation X-15A-2, which flew for the first time (after modification from the X-15A) on 25 Jun 1964, powered by a liquid oxygen and ammonia rocket propulsion system. The landing speed was 389.1 km/h *242 mph*. The highest speed attained was

Pierre Baud, captain of the Airbus Industrie A340-200 which flew non-stop from Auckland, New Zealand to Le Bourget, near Paris, France.
(Photo: Airbus Industrie)

7274 km/h *4520 mph* (Mach 6.7) when piloted by Major William J. Knight, USAF (b. 1930), on 3 Oct 1967. An earlier version piloted by Joseph A. Walker (1920–66) reached 107,960 m *354,200 ft* over Edwards Air Force Base, California, USA on 22 Aug 1963.

United States NASA Rockwell International space shuttle orbiter *Columbia*, commanded by Capt. John W. Young, USN, and piloted by Capt. Robert L. Crippen, USN was launched from the Kennedy Space Center, Cape Canaveral, Florida, USA on 12 Apr 1981. *Columbia* broke all records in space by a fixed-wing craft, with 26,715 km/h *16,600 mph*

ON THE RECORD

Round the world— antipodal points
Brother Michael Bartlett of Balham, London, an 'Eccentric Globetrotter', travelled round the world on scheduled flights, taking in exact antipodal points, in a time of 67 hr 4 min from 10–13 Jun 1993. Leaving from London he flew via Tokyo, Japan and Auckland, New Zealand to Palmerston, also in New Zealand, and then by car to Ti Tree Point, on Highway 52. He later changed planes at Madrid airport, Spain (the point exactly opposite Ti Tree Point on the other side of the world). His journey took him a total distance of 41,619 km *25,861 miles*.

ECCENTRIC GLOBETROTTER
BROTHER MICHAEL O.G.S

ROUND THE WORLD ANTIPODAL IV TRIP 1993

Thurs 10.6.93	London Heathrow/Tokyo 19.45 > 15.30 JL 402
Fri 11.6.93	Tokyo/Auckland 18.00 > 07.15 JL 773
Sat 12.6.93	Auckland/Palmerston 09.00 > 09.50 NZ 673
	Car to Ti Tree Point (Hertz)
Sat 12.6.93	Palmerston/Auckland 15.00 > 16.00 NZ 676
Sat 12.6.93	Auckland/Los Angeles 18.15 > 11.10 UA 842
Sat 12.6.93	Los Angeles/London Heathrow 12.40 > 06.55 UA 934
Sun 13.6.93	London Heathrow/Madrid 09.00 12.15 BA 458
Sun 13.6.93	Madrid/London Heathrow 13.50 > 15.00 BA 459

Total = 67 Hours 15 Minutes Block Time
Total Mileage 25,841 (subject to confirmation)

Brother Michael Bartlett, who holds a number of flying records, says:–

"My original intention to gain entry into the Guinness Book of Records was met with ridicule! Now holder of ten certificates, the planning, research, fund raising and preparation for another trip is part of my daily life! When travelling, fun is to be found around the corner. The problems expected are rarely the difficulties experienced. The reward of adventure is a record!"

at main engine cut-off. After re-entry from 122km *400,000ft* she glided home weighing 97tonnes, and with a landing speed of 347km/h *216mph*, on Rogers Dry Lake, California, USA on 14 Apr 1981. The fastest space shuttle landing speed was 407km/h *253mph* by STS 3 *Columbia* on 30 Mar 1982.

Under the FAI (Fédération Aéronautique Internationale) regulations for Category P for aerospacecraft, *Columbia* is holder of the current absolute world record for duration—14 days 0 hr 13 min to main gear touchdown when launched on its 15th mission, STS 58, with seven crewmen on 18 Oct 1993.

Fastest jet The USAF Lockheed SR-71, a reconnaissance aircraft, has been the world's fastest jet (⇔ official record, above). First flown in its definitive form on 22 Dec 1964, it was reportedly capable of attaining an altitude of close to 100,000ft *30,000m*. It had a wing span of 16.94m *55ft 7in* and a length of 32.73m *107ft 5in* and weighed 77.1tonnes *170,000lb* at take-off. Its reported range at Mach 3 was 4800km *3000miles* at 24,000m *79,000ft*.

Fastest combat jet The fastest combat jet is the former Soviet Mikoyan MiG-25 fighter (NATO code name 'Foxbat'). The single-seat 'Foxbat-A' has a wing span of 13.95m *45ft 9in*, is 23.82m *78ft 2in* long and has an estimated maximum take-off weight of 37.4tonnes *82,500lb*. The reconnaissance 'Foxbat-B' has been tracked by radar at about Mach 3.2 (3395km/h *2110mph*).

Fastest biplane The fastest was the Italian Fiat CR42B, with a 753kW *1010hp* Daimler-Benz DB601A engine, which attained 520km/h *323mph* in 1941. Only one was built.

Fastest piston-engined aircraft On 21 Aug 1989, in Las Vegas, Nevada, USA, the *Rare Bear*, a modified Grumman F8F Bearcat piloted by Lyle Shelton, set the FAI approved world record for a 3km *1⅞ mile* course of 850.24km/h *528.33mph*.

Fastest propeller-driven aircraft The fastest propeller-driven aircraft in use is the former Soviet Tu-95/142 (NATO code-name *Bear*) with four 14,795hp *11,033kW* engines driving eight-blade contra-rotating propellers with a maximum level speed of Mach 0.82 or 925km/h *575mph*.

The turboprop-powered Republic XF-84H experimental US fighter which flew on 22 Jul 1955 had a top *design* speed of 1078km/h *670mph*, but was abandoned.

Fastest transatlantic flight The flight record is 1hr 54min 56.4sec by Major James V. Sullivan, 37, and Major Noel F. Widdifield, 33, flying a Lockheed SR-71A 'Blackbird' eastwards on 1 Sep 1974. The average speed, slowed by refuelling from a Boeing KC-135 tanker aircraft, for the New York–London stage of 5570.80km *3461.53 miles* was 2908.3km/h *1806.96mph*.

The solo record (Gander, Newfoundland, Canada to Gatwick, W Sussex) is 8hr 47min 32sec, an average speed of 426.7km/h *265.1mph*, by Capt. John J.A. Smith in a Rockwell Commander 685 twin-turboprop on 12 Mar 1978.

---

24 Hours!

Brother Michael Bartlett of London made 42 scheduled passenger flights with Heli Transport of Nice, southern France between Nice, Sophia Antipolis, Monaco and Cannes in 13hr 33min on 13 Jun 1990.

Duration The duration record is 64days 22hr 19min 5sec, set by Robert Timm and John Cook in the Cessna 172 *Hacienda*. They took off from McCarran Airfield, Las Vegas, Nevada, USA just before 3:53p.m. local time on 4 Dec 1958 and landed at the same airfield just before 2:12p.m. on 7 Feb 1959. They covered a distance equivalent to six times round the world, being refuelled without any landings.

Visiting 12 EC countries by scheduled flights David Beaumont of Wimbledon, London visited the 12 European community countries as a passenger on 12 different scheduled flights in a time of 27hr 14min on 21–22 Nov 1993.

Touchdown in the 12 EC countries On 13 Jun 1989 pilots Michael Hamlin and Robert Noortman of Hamlin Jet Ltd flew a Cessna Citation *Biz Jet One* a distance of 5950km *3700miles*. They touched down at 12 different landing strips of the 12 EC countries in a time of 18hr 55min.

Airports

Largest The £2.1 billion King Khalid international airport outside Riyadh, Saudi Arabia covers an area of 225km² *55,040acres*. It was opened on 14 Nov 1983. It also has the world's tallest control tower, 81m *265ft* in height.

The Hajj Terminal at the £2.8 billion King Abdul-Aziz airport near Jeddah, Saudi Arabia is the world's largest roofed structure, covering 1.5km² *370acres*.

The world's largest airport terminal is at Hartsfield International Airport, Atlanta, Georgia, USA, opened on 21 Sep 1980, with floor space covering 23.3ha *57½ acres* and still expanding. In 1993 the terminal handled 47,751,000 passengers using 145 gates, although it has a capacity for 75 million. A new section of the terminal is scheduled to open soon which will increase the number of gates to 179.

UK Over 90 airline companies from 85 countries operate scheduled services into Heathrow airport, London (1197ha *2958acres*). Between 1 Jan–31 Dec 1993 there were 394,100 air transport movements, handled by a staff of 53,000 employed by the various companies, government departments and Heathrow Airport Limited, a subsidiary of BAA plc. The total number of passengers, both incoming and outgoing, was 47,600,000 including transit passengers (⇔ also Busiest, below).

One day records at Heathrow were set on 6 Jul 1990 with 1232 flights handled and on 31 Jul 1993 with 160,733 passengers. The airport's busiest single hour of two-way passenger flow was recorded on 18 Aug 1990 when 12,434 passengers travelled through the four terminals.

To New York!

The record from central London to downtown New York City, New York, USA—by helicopter and Concorde—is 3hr 59min 44sec and the return 3hr 40min 40sec, set by David J. Springbett and David Boyce on 8–9 Feb 1982.

Busiest The Chicago international airport, O'Hare Field, Illinois, USA, had a total of 65,091,168 passengers and 859,208 aircraft movements in the year 1993. This represents a take-off or landing every 37sec around the clock.

Heathrow Airport, London, handles more international traffic than any other, with 40,788,000 international passengers in 1993.

> The busiest landing area ever has been Bien Hoa Air Base, South Vietnam, which handled approximately 1,000,000 take-offs and landings in 1970.

Helipad The heliport at Morgan City, Louisiana, USA, one of many used for energy-related offshore operations into the Gulf of Mexico, has pads for 46 helicopters. The world's largest heliport has been An Khe, South Vietnam, during the Vietnam War, with an area of 2×3km *1¼ × 1¾ miles* and could accommodate 434 helicopters.

Landing fields *Highest* The highest is La Sa (Lhasa) airport, Tibet, People's Republic of China, at 4363m *14,315ft*.

Lowest The lowest landing field is El Lisan on the east shore of the Dead Sea, 360m *1180ft* below sea level, but during World War II BOAC Short C-class flying boats operated from the surface of the Dead Sea at 394m *1292ft* below sea level.

The lowest international airport is Schiphol, Amsterdam, Netherlands at 4.5m *15ft* below sea level.

Longest runways The longest runway is at Edwards Air Force Base on the west side of Rogers dry lakebed at Muroc, California, USA, and is 11.92km *7.41miles* in length. The *Voyager* aircraft, taking off for its round-the-world unrefuelled flight (⇔ Circumnavigational flights), used 4.3km *14,200ft* of the 4.6km *15,000ft* long main base concrete runway.

The world's longest civil airport runway is one of 4.89km *3.04miles* at Pierre van Ryneveld airport, Upington, South Africa, built between August 1975 and January 1976.

A paved runway 6.24km *3.88miles* long appears on maps of Jordan at Abu Husayn.

The longest runway normally available to civil aircraft in the United Kingdom is the Northern Runway, or 09L/27R, at Heathrow Airport, London, measuring 3.90km *2.42miles*.

The most southerly major runway (1.6km *1mile* in length) in the world is at Ushuaia, Argentina (Lat 54°48′S), which has scheduled flights the whole year round to four other places in Argentina including the capital city, Buenos Aires.

Largest hangars Hangar 375 ('Big Texas') at Kelly Air Force Base, San Antonio, Texas, USA, completed on 15 Feb 1956, has four doors each 76m *250ft* wide, 18.3m *60ft* high, and weighing 608tonnes. The high bay is 610 × 90 × 27.5m *2000 × 300 × 90ft* in area and is surrounded by a 17.8ha *44acre* concrete apron. It is the largest free-standing hangar in the world.

Delta Air Lines' jet base on a 56.6ha *175acre* site at Hartsfield International Airport, Atlanta, Georgia, USA has 14.5ha *36acres* roof area. A recent addition to the hangar gives it a high-bay area of 317 × 74 × 27m *1041 × 242 × 90ft*.

GUESS WHAT?
Q Chicago is to airports as Rotterdam is to what?
A See Page 110

UK The largest hangar building in the United Kingdom is that at the former Bristol Aeroplane Company's works at Filton, Avon, now part of British Aerospace. It was built for the Brabazon project (⇨ Largest airliner) and subsequently used for assembly of the Britannia turboprop airliner. It has a floor area of 3 ha *7½ acres* and a capacity of 934,000 m³ *33,000,000 ft³*. The two airship hangars at Cardington, Beds have a smaller floor area (2.1 ha *5⅛ acres*) but each have a larger overall capacity, at 1,138,000 m³ *40,194,000 ft³* (⇨ also Largest doors).

Airlines

Busiest The country with the busiest airlines system is the United States, where the total number of passengers for air carriers in scheduled domestic operations exceeded 450 million in 1993.

On 31 Dec 1993 British Airways operated a fleet of 250 aircraft. It employed an average of 49,584 staff, and 28,100,000 passengers were carried in 1992–3 on 599,000 km *372,000 miles* of unduplicated routes.

Busiest international route The city-pair with the highest international scheduled passenger traffic is London/Paris. More than 3.4 million passengers flew between the two cities in 1991/2, or nearly 4700 each way each day (although London-bound traffic is higher than that bound for Paris). The busiest intercontinental route is London/New York, with 2.25 million passengers flying between the two cities in 1991/2.

Largest The former Soviet Union's state airline Aeroflot, so named since 1932, was instituted on 9 Feb 1923 and has been the largest airline of all-time. In its last complete year of formal existence (1990) it employed 600,000 (more than the top 18 US airlines put together) and flew 139 million passengers with 20,000 pilots along 1,000,000 km *620,000 miles* of domestic routes across 11 time zones.

Following the break-up of the Soviet Union, the company which now carries the greatest number of passengers is American Airlines, with 86,007,000 in 1992. The airline with the longest route network is the German airline Lufthansa, which covers 942,000 km *585,000 miles*.

Oldest Aircraft Transport & Travel was founded in 1916 and began regular scheduled flights from London to Paris on 25 Aug 1919, although it was swallowed up with several other airlines in 1924 to form Imperial Airways, the forerunner of British Overseas Airways Corporation, which with British European Airways later became British Airways. Of current airlines the oldest is Koninklijke-Luchtvaart-Maatschappij NV (KLM), the national airline of the Netherlands. It was established in October 1919 and opened its first scheduled service (Amsterdam–London) on 17 May 1920.

Delag (Deutsche Luftschiffahrt AG) was founded at Frankfurt am Main, Germany on 16 Nov 1909 and started a scheduled airship service on 17 Jun 1910.

Chalk's International Airline has flown amphibious planes from Miami, Florida, USA to the Bahamas since July 1919. Albert 'Pappy' Chalk flew from 1911–75.

Aerospace company The world's largest aerospace company is Boeing of Seattle, Washington, USA, with 1993 sales of $25.3 billion and a workforce of 134,400 world-wide. Cessna Aircraft Company of Wichita, Kansas, USA has been the most productive, manufacturing more than 178,000 aircraft since 1911.

Personal Aviation Records

Oldest and youngest passengers Airborne births are reported every year.

The oldest person to fly has been Mrs Jessica S. Swift (b. Anna Stewart, 17 Sep 1871), aged 110 years 3 months, from Vermont to Florida, USA in Dec 1981.

The oldest Briton to fly is Charlotte Hughes of Redcar, Cleveland (b. 1 Aug 1877). She was given a flight on Concorde from London to New York as a 110th birthday present on 4 Aug 1987, returning four days later.

Most experienced passenger Edwin A. Shackleton of Bristol, Avon has flown as a passenger in 502 different types of aircraft. His first flight was in March 1943 in D.H. Dominie R9548; other aircraft have included helicopters, gliders, microlights, gas and hot air ballons.

Pilots *Oldest* Stanley Wood (1896–1994) of Shoreham-by-Sea, W Sussex, was still taking the controls of aircraft at the age of 96, the last occasion being when he flew a Warrior plane on 7 Jun 1993. His first solo flight had been an unofficial one during World War I, which means that his flying career spanned more than 80 per cent of the history of aviation.

Mrs Peggy Follis (b. 7 Aug 1913) of London qualified as a pilot on 8 Aug 1991 when aged 78 years.

Longest serving military pilot Squadron Leader N.E. Rose, AFC and bar, AMN (RAF Retd) (b. 30 May 1924) flew military aircraft without a break in service for 47 years from 1942 to 1989 achieving 11,539 hours of flying in 54 different categories of aircraft. He learnt to fly in a Tiger Moth in Southern Rhodesia, and then flew Hurricanes in World War II.

Most flying hours *Pilot* John Edward Long (b. 10 Nov 1915) (USA) logged a total of 59,300 hr of flying as a pilot between 1 May 1933 and 1 May 1994—cumulatively nearly seven years airborne.

Passenger The record as a supersonic passenger is held by Fred Finn, who made his 706th Atlantic crossing in Concorde on 22 Oct 1993. He commutes regularly from New Jersey, USA to London and has flown a total distance of 17,637,301 km *10,959,311 miles*.

Most planes flown James B. Taylor, Jr (1897–1942) flew 461 different types of powered aircraft during his 25 years as an active experimental and demonstration pilot for the US Navy and a number of American aircraft companies. He was one of the few pilots of the 1920s and 1930s qualified to perform terminal-velocity dives.

> Up to her retirement in 1988 Maisie Muir of Orkney, Scotland flew over 8400 times with Loganair in connection with business duties for the Royal Bank of Scotland.

Most Trans-Atlantic flights Between March 1948 and his retirement on 1 Sep 1984 Charles M. Schimpf, a flight service manager with Trans World Airlines, logged a total of 2880 Atlantic crossings—a rate of 6.4 per month.

Helicopters

Earliest Leonardo da Vinci (1452–1519) proposed the idea of a helicopter-type craft, although the Chinese had built helicopter-like toys as early as the 4th century BC.

A craft resembling to a helicopter was built in France by Paul Cornu and flown for 20 sec on 13 Nov 1907, but it was not until 1935 that the French Breguet-Dorand Laboratory Gyroplane became the first helicopter to be fully controllable and fly successfully.

Largest The Russian Mil Mi-12 was powered by four 6500 hp *4847 kW* turboshaft engines and had a rotor diameter of 67 m *219 ft 10 in*, with a length of 37 m *121 ft 4½ in* and a weight of 103.3 tonnes. It was demonstrated in prototype form at the Paris Air Show in 1971 but never entered service.

John Edward Long, who has been flying planes for 61 years. His first attempt to fly was when he was a young boy—he took his mother's ironing board, strapped it on his shoulders, got on his bicycle and went down a hill as fast as he could get the bicycle to go! (Photo: Paul Robertson Photography)

The largest rotorcraft was the Piasecki Heli-Stat, which used four Sikorsky S-58 airframes attached to a surplus Goodyear ZPG-2 airship. Powered by four 1525 hp piston engines and 104.5 m *343 ft* long, 33.8 m *111 ft* high, and 45.4 m *149 ft* wide, it first flew in October 1985 at Lakehurst, New Jersey, USA but was destroyed in a crash on 1 Jul 1986.

Smallest The single-seat Seremet WS-8 ultralight helicopter was built in Denmark in 1976 with a 35 hp engine and an empty weight of 53 kg *117 lb*. The rotor diameter was 4.5 m *14 ft 9 in*.

Fastest!

Under FAI rules, the world's speed record for helicopters was set by John Trevor Eggington with co-pilot Derek J. Clews, who averaged 400.87 km/h *249.09 mph* over Glastonbury, Somerset on 11 Aug 1986 in a Westland Lynx demonstrator.

Longest flight Under FAI rules the world record for the longest unrefuelled non-stop flight was held by Robert Ferry, flying a Hughes YOH-6A over a distance of 3561.6 km *2213.1 miles* from Culver City, California to Ormond Beach, Florida, USA on 6 Apr 1966.

Highest altitude The record for helicopters is 12,442 m *40,820 ft* by an Aérospatiale SA315B Lama, flown by Jean Boulet over Istres, France on 21 Jun 1972. The highest recorded landing has

GUESS WHAT?

Q Apart from being the oldest British citizen to fly, what other record does Charlotte Hughes hold?

A See Page 59

Transport

been at 7500 m *24,600 ft* during SA315B demonstrations in the Himalayas in 1969.

Flying-Boat

Fastest The fastest flying-boat ever built was the Martin XP6M-1 SeaMaster, the US Navy four-jet-engined minelayer flown in 1955–9, with a top speed of 1040 km/h *646 mph*. In September 1948 the Martin JRM-2 Mars flying-boat set a payload record of 30,992 kg *68,327 lb*.

The flying-boat speed record is 911.98 km/h *566.69 mph*, set up by Nikolay Andreyevskiy and crew of two in a Soviet Beriev M-10, powered by two AL-7 turbojets, over a 15–25 km *9.3–15½ mile* course at Joukovsky-Petrovskoye, USSR on 7 Aug 1961.

Airships

Earliest The earliest flight in an airship was by Henri Giffard from Paris to Trappes in his steam-powered coal-gas airship 2500 m³ *88,300 ft³* in volume and 43.8 m *144 ft* long, on 24 Sep 1852.

The earliest British airship was a 566 m³ *20,000 ft³* craft, 22.8 m *75 ft* long built by Stanley Spencer and first flown from Crystal Palace, London on 22 Sep 1902.

Largest The largest was the 213.9-tonne German *Graf Zeppelin II* (LZ 130), with a length of 245 m *804 ft* and a capacity of 200,000 m³ *7,062,100 ft³*. She made her maiden flight on 14 Sep 1938 and was dismantled in April 1940. Her sister ship *Hindenburg* was 1.70 m *5 ft 7 in* longer.

The largest airship currently certificated for the public transport of passengers is the Sentinel 1000, which has a length of 67.5 m *221 ft 5 in* and a capacity of 10,000 m³ *353,100 ft³*. It was built by Westinghouse Airships, Inc. of Elizabeth City, North Carolina, USA and made its maiden flight on 26 Jun 1991.

The largest British airship was the R101 built by the Royal Airship Works, Cardington, Beds, which first flew on 14 Oct 1929. She was 237 m *777 ft* in length and had a capacity of 155,995 m³ *5,508,800 ft³*. She crashed near Beauvais, France, killing all but six of the 54 aboard, on 5 Oct 1930.

Greatest passenger load The most people ever carried in an airship was 207, in the US Navy *Akron* in 1931. The transatlantic record is 117, by the German *Hindenburg* in 1937. She exploded at Lakehurst, New Jersey, USA on 6 May 1937.

Distance records The FAI accredited straight-line distance record for airships is 6384.5 km *3967.1 miles*, set up by the German *Graf Zeppelin*, captained by Dr Hugo Eckener, between 29 Oct–1 Nov 1928.

Doug Daigle, Brian Watts and Dave Meyer of Tridair Helicopters, and Rod Anderson of Helistream, Inc. of California, USA maintained a continuous hover in a 1947 Bell 47B model for 50 hr 50 sec during 13–15 Dec 1989.

From 21–25 Nov 1917 the German Zeppelin L59 flew from Yambol, Bulgaria to south of Khartoum, Sudan, and returned to cover a minimum of 7250 km *4500 miles*.

Duration record The longest recorded flight by a non-rigid airship (without refuelling) is 264 hr 12 min by a US Navy Goodyear-built ZPG-2 class ship (Commander J.R. Hunt, USN) from South Weymouth Naval Air Station, Massachusetts, USA from 4–15 Mar 1957, landing back at Key West, Florida, USA after having flown 15,205 km *9448 miles*.

Autogyros

Speed, altitude and distance records Wing Cdr Kenneth H. Wallis (GB) holds the straight-line distance record of 874.32 km *543.27 miles* set in his WA-116/F on 28 Sep 1975 with a non-stop flight from Lydd, Kent to Wick, Highland.

On 20 Jul 1982, flying from Boscombe Down, Wilts, he set a new altitude record of 5643.7 m *18,516 ft* in his WA-121/Mc.

Wing Cdr. Wallis flew his WA-116/F/S, with a 45 kW *60-hp* Franklin aero-engine, to a record speed of 193.6 km/h *120.3 mph* over a 3 km *1⅞ mile* straight course at Marham, Norfolk on 18 Sep 1986.

Wing Cdr Kenneth Wallis in one of his autogyros. His most famous autogyro was probably *Little Nellie*, which appeared in the James Bond film *You Only Live Twice*.

Ballooning

Earliest The earliest recorded ascent was by a model hot-air balloon invented by Father Bartolomeu de Gusmão (né Lourenço) (1685–1724), which was flown indoors at the Casa da India, Terreiro do Paço, Portugal on 8 Aug 1709.

Distance record The record distance travelled by a balloon is 8382.54 km *5208.68 miles*, by the Raven experimental helium-filled balloon *Double Eagle V* (capacity 11,300 m³ *399,100 ft³*) from 9–12 Nov 1981. The journey started from Nagashima, Japan and ended at Covello, California, USA. The crew for this first manned balloon crossing of the Pacific Ocean were Ben L. Abruzzo, 51, Rocky Aoki, 43 (Japan), Ron Clark, 41, and Larry M. Newman, 34.

Duration record Richard Abruzzo, 29, together with Troy Bradley, 28, set a duration record of 144 hr 16 min in *Team USA* in crossing the Atlantic Ocean from Bangor, Maine, USA to Ben Slimane, Morocco on 16–22 Sep 1992.

Atlantic crossing Col. Joe Kittinger, USAF (⇨ Parachuting) became the first man to complete a solo trans-atlantic crossing by balloon. In the 2850 m³ *101,000 ft³* helium-filled balloon *Rosie O'Grady*, Kittinger lifted off from Caribou, Maine, USA on 14 Sep

Human power!

Kanellos Kanellopoulos (b. 25 Apr 1957) averaged 30.3 km/h *18.8 mph* in his 34.1 m *112 ft* wing span machine flying from Crete to the island of Santoríni on 23 Apr 1988, covering 119 km *74 miles* in 3 hr 56 min.

1984 and completed a distance of 5701 km *3543 miles* before landing at Montenotte, near Savona, Italy 86 hours later on 18 Sep 1984.

Highest *Unmanned* The highest altitude attained by an unmanned balloon was 51,800 m *170,000 ft* by a Winzen balloon of 1.35 million m³ *47.8 million ft³* launched at Chico, California, USA in 1972.

Manned The greatest altitude reached in a manned balloon is an unofficial 37,750 m *123,800 ft* by Nicholas Piantanida (1933–66) of Bricktown, New Jersey, USA, from Sioux Falls, South Dakota on 1 Feb 1966. He landed in Iowa but did not survive.

The official record (closed gondola) is 34,668 m *113,740 ft* by Commander Malcolm D. Ross, USNR and the late Lt Cdr. Victor A. Prother, USN in an ascent from USS *Antietam* over the Gulf of Mexico on 4 May 1961 in a 339,800 m³ *12 million ft³* balloon.

Owing to an oversight, Harold Froelich and Keith Lang, scientists from Minneapolis, USA, ascended in an open gondola and without the protection of pressure suits to an altitude of 12,840 m *42,126 ft*, on 26 Sep 1956. During their 6½-hour flight, at maximum altitude and without goggles, they observed the Earth and measured a temperature of −58°C *−72°F*.

Largest The largest balloon ever built, by Winzen Research Inc. of South St Paul, Minnesota, USA, (now Winzen International Inc.), had an inflatable volume of 2 million m³ *70 million ft³* and was 300 m *1000 ft* in height. It was made in 1975 and was unmanned.

Hot-air This form of ballooning was revived in the USA in 1961, and the first World Championships were held in Albuquerque, New Mexico, USA on 10–17 Feb 1973.

Altitude Per Lindstrand achieved the altitude record of 19,811 m *64,997 ft* in a Colt 600 hot-air balloon over Laredo, Texas, USA on 6 Jun 1988.

Atlantic crossing Richard Branson (GB) with his pilot Per Lindstrand (GB) were the first to cross the Atlantic in a hot-air balloon, from 2–3 Jul 1987. They ascended from Sugarloaf, Maine, USA and covered the distance of 4947 km *3075 miles*, to Limavady, Co. Londonderry, Northern Ireland in 31 hr 41 min.

Pacific crossing Richard Branson and Per Lindstrand crossed the Pacific in the *Virgin Otsuka Pacific Flyer* from the southern tip of Japan to Lac la Matre, Yukon, north-western Canada on 15–17 Jan 1991 in a 73,600 m³ *2.6 million ft³* hot-air balloon (the largest ever flown) to set FAI records for duration (46 hr 15 min) and distance (great circle 7671.9 km *4768 miles*).

Mount Everest Two balloons achieved the first overflight of the summit of Mount Everest at the same time on 21 Oct 1991. They were *Star Flyer 1*, piloted by Chris Dewhirst (Australia) with cameraman Leo Dickinson, and *Star Flyer 2*, piloted by Andy Elson and cameraman Eric Jones (all British). The two 6800 m³ *240,000 ft³* balloons set hot-air balloon records for the highest launch at 4735 m *15,536 ft* and touch-down at 4940 m *16,200 ft*.

Most passengers in a balloon A balloon of 73,600 m³ *2.6 million ft³* capacity named *Super Maine* was built by Tom Handcock of Portland, Maine, USA.

Tethered, it rose to a height of 12.25 m *50 ft* with 61 passengers on board on 19 Feb 1988.

The Dutch balloonist Henk Brink made an untethered flight of 200 m *656 ft* in the 24,000 m³ *850,000 ft³* balloon *Nashua Number One* carrying a total of 50 passengers and crew. The flight, on 17 Aug 1988, lasted 25 min, commenced from Lelystad airport, Netherlands, and reached an altitude of 100 m *328 ft*.

Ballooning mass ascent The greatest mass ascent from a single site took place when 128 hot-air balloons took off within 1 hour at the Ninth Bristol International Balloon Festival at Ashton Court, Bristol, Avon on 15 Aug 1987.

Most to jump from a balloon On 12 Sep 1992 a record fifteen people (a group of Royal Marines plus friends) all parachuted from a hot air balloon over the Somerset/Devon county boundary.

Ballooning
the Abruzzo way

Ben Abruzzo

Richard Abruzzo

PRESQUE ISLE
USA MAINE
BANGOR
MAINE

MISEREY
FRANCE

BEN SLIMANE
MOROCCO

The close-up, right, shows just how cramped it was inside.

The picture above shows *Team USA* during its successful flight. Ben and Richard celebrate Ben's trans-pacific flight in 1981 below. This set a new distance record (but not duration), and still stands.

(Photos: Garth Sonnenberg, Team USA and TransPac)

When Richard Abruzzo set a new ballooning duration record of 144 hr 16 min in September 1992 he beat a record which had stood for fourteen years. What was particularly noteworthy, however, and very rare in the field of record-breaking, was the fact that the previous record had been held by his father, Ben Abruzzo.

On 12 Aug 1978 Ben Abruzzo, 48, along with Maxie Anderson and Larry Newman, set off from Presque Isle, in Maine, USA with the aim of achieving the first ever crossing of the north Atlantic in their helium-filled balloon *Double Eagle II*. After a journey lasting 137 hr 6 min they landed at Miserey, in northern France, on 17 August after a flight in which they had experienced icy winds. Although they had hoped to travel as far as Le Bourget airport, just outside Paris, unfavourable winds made them abandon their plan and they came down in a field where crowds rushed to welcome them as heroes. Richard was an admiring teenager at the time, but when his parents were tragically killed in a

plane crash in 1985, he was already dreaming of making a transoceanic fight. An ideal opportunity arose to test his abilities against the best when an international transatlantic race was organized in 1992 with participants from a number of different countries. Richard, 29, and his flying partner Troy Bradley set off from Bangor, in Maine, on 16 Sep 1992 in their helium and hot-air balloon *Team USA*. They were not the first to reach Europe, but they were able to keep aloft for a sufficient time to surpass the previous duration record.

Helped by winds which took them in a south-easterly direction, they eventually landed in a third continent, Africa, at Ben Slimane, not far from Casablanca, Morocco on 22 September after an exhausting flight. As with his father's record flight, they were met by a throng of curious onlookers who came to see them as they landed. Naturally Richard was a very proud man as he said 'That we were able to break one of his records made this achievement special'.

(Illustration: Frances Button.© Guinness Publishing)

The same group made a similar ascent on 1 Oct 1992 and this time a record ten people jumped *simultaneously*, from a height of 1800 m *6000 ft*.

Model Aircraft

Altitude Maynard L. Hill (USA), flying a radio-controlled model, established the world record for altitude, reaching a height of 8208 m *26,922 ft* on 6 Sep 1970.

Distance Gianmaria Aghem (Italy) holds the closed-circuit distance record, with 1239 km *769.9 miles*, set on 26 Jul 1986.

Speed The speed record is 390.92 km/h *242.92 mph*, set by Walter Sitar (Austria) on 10 Jun 1977.

Duration The record duration is 33 hr 39 min 15 sec by Maynard Hill (⇔ above), with a powered model on 1–2 Oct 1992. An indoor model with a wound rubber motor designed by James Richmond (USA) set a duration record of 52 min 14 sec on 31 Aug 1979. Jean-Pierre Schiltknecht flew a solar driven model airplane for a duration record of 10 hr 43 min 51 sec at Wetzlar, Germany on 10 Jul 1991.

Largest model glider In January 1990 *Eagle III*, a radio controlled glider weighing 6.5 kg *14 lb 8 oz* with a wing span of 9.80 m *32 ft 6 in*, was designed and constructed by Carlos René Tschen and Carlos René Tschen Jr of Colonia San Lázaro, Guatemala.

Smallest The smallest to fly is one weighing 0.1 g *0.004 oz* powered by an attached horsefly and designed by insectonaut Don Emmick of Seattle, Washington State, USA. On 24 Jul 1977 it flew for 5 minutes at Kirkland, Washington State, USA.

One of the most spectacular parachuting records is the free fall formation record, when parachutists link up in mid-air. Precision timing is needed, but the result is stunning if it succeeds, as this attempt on the record did when 200 people held the formation for more than 6 seconds.
(Photo: Gamma/P Passe)

Paper Aircraft

Duration The level flight duration record for a hand-launched paper aircraft is 17.20 sec by Ken Blackburn at Milwaukee, Wisconsin, USA on 28 Jul 1987.

Distance An indoor distance of 58.82 m *193 ft* was recorded by Tony Felch at the La Crosse Center, Wisconsin, USA on 21 May 1985. A paper plane was seen to fly 2 km *1¼ miles* by 'Chick' C.O. Reinhart from a tenth-storey office window at 60 Beaver Street, New York City, USA across the East River to Brooklyn in August 1933, helped by a thermal from a coffee-roasting plant.

Largest The largest flying paper aeroplane, with a wing span of 9.15 m *30 ft 6 in*, was constructed by pupils from various schools in Hampton, Virginia, USA and flown on 25 Mar 1992. It was launched indoors from a 3 m *10 ft* high platform and flown for a distance of 35 m *114 ft 9 in*.

Parachuting Records

It is estimated that the human body reaches 99 per cent of its low-level terminal velocity after falling 573 m 1880 ft, which takes 13–14 sec. This is 188–201 km/h 117–125 mph at normal atmospheric pressure in a random posture, but up to 298 km/h 185 mph in a head-down position.

FIRST Tower [1] Louis-Sébastien Lenormand (1757–1839), quasi-parachute, Montpellier, France, 1783.
Balloon André-Jacques Garnerin (1769–1823), 680 m *2230 ft* Monceau Park, Paris, France, 22 Oct 1797.
Aircraft *Man:* 'Captain' Albert Berry, an aerial exhibitionist, St Louis, Missouri, USA, 1 Mar 1912. *Woman:* Mrs Georgia 'Tiny' Broadwick (b. 1893), Griffith Park, Los Angeles, USA, 21 Jun 1913.

LONGEST DURATION FALL Lt Col. Wm H. Rankin, USMC, 40 min due to thermals, North Carolina, USA, 26 Jul 1956.

LONGEST DELAYED DROP World *Man:* Capt. Joseph W. Kittinger [2], 25,820 m *84,700 ft* or *16.04 miles*, from balloon at 31,330 m *102,800 ft*, Tularosa, New Mexico, USA, 16 Aug 1960. *Woman:* E. Fomitcheva (USSR) 14,800 m *48,556 ft*, over Odessa, USSR, 26 Oct 1977.
Over UK *Man (Civilian):* M. Child, R. McCarthy, 10,180 m *33,400 ft* from balloon at 10,850 m *35,600 ft*, Kings Lynn, Norfolk, 18 Sep 1986. *Woman (Civilian):* Francesca Gannon and Valerie Slattery, 6520 m *21,391 ft* from aircraft at 7600 m *24,900 ft*, Netheravon, Wilts, 11 Mar 1987. *Group:* S/Ldr J. Thirtle, Fl. Sgt A.K. Kidd, Sgts L. Hicks (died 1971), P.P. Keane, K.J. Teesdale, 11,943 m *39,183 ft* from aircraft at 12,613 m *41,383 ft*, Boscombe Down, Wilts, 16 Jun 1967.

BASE JUMP Highest Nicholas Feteris and Dr Glenn Singleman from a ledge (the 'Great Trango Tower') at 5880 m *19,300 ft* in the Karakoram, Pakistan, 26 Aug 1992. *Jumps from buildings and claims for lowest base jumps will not be accepted.*

MID-AIR RESCUE Earliest Miss Dolly Shepherd (1886–1983) brought down Miss Louie May on her single 'chute from balloon at 3350 m *11,000 ft*, Longton, Staffs, 9 Jun 1908.
Lowest Andy Peckett saved Maurizio Brambilla (unconscious), who had been injured when jumping out of aircraft at 4600 m *15,000 ft*. He pulled his ripcord at 610 m *2000 ft*—7 sec from impact, Vichy, France, 11 Aug 1993.

HIGHEST LANDING Ten USSR parachutists (four were killed), 7133 m *23,405 ft*, Lenina Peak, USSR May 1969.

HIGHEST ESCAPE Flt Lt J. de Salis, RAF and Fg Off. P. Lowe, RAF, 17,100 m *56,000 ft*, Monyash, Derby, 9 Apr 1958.
Lowest S/Ldr Terence Spencer, RAF, 9–12 m *30–40 ft*, Wismar Bay, Baltic, 19 Apr 1945.

TOTAL SPORT PARACHUTING DESCENTS *Man:* Don Kellner (USA), 20,000, various locations in the USA up to 14 Nov 1993. *Woman:* Valentina Zakoretskaya (USSR), 8000, over USSR, 1964–80.

24-HOUR TOTAL *Man:* Dale Nelson (USA), 301 (in accordance with United States Parachute Association rules), Pennsylvania, USA, 26–27 May 1988. *Woman:* Cheryl Stearns (USA), 255 at Lodi, California, USA 26–27 Nov 1987.

HIGHEST STACK 38, by a team of American parachutists at Richland, Washington, USA; held for 10.3 sec on 10 Oct 1992.

LARGEST FREE FALL FORMATION 200, from 10 countries held for 6.47 sec, from 5030 m *16,500 ft*, over Myrtle Beach, California, USA, 23 Oct 1992. *Women:* 100, from 20 countries held for 5.97 sec, from 5200 m *17,000 ft*, Aéreodrome du Cannet des Maures, France, 14 Aug 1992.
UK 60, held for 4 sec, from 4600 m *15,000 ft*, Peterborough, Cambs, 8 Jun 1989.

OLDEST *Man:* Edwin C. Townsend (died 7 Nov 1987), 89 years, Vermillion Bay, Louisiana, USA, 5 Feb 1986. *Woman:* Sylvia Brett (GB), 80 years 166 days, Cranfield, Beds, 23 Aug 1986.
Tandem, *Man:* Frank Blazek (USA), 91 years 312 days, Westhampton Beach, New York, USA, 21 Jul 1992. *Woman:* Corena Leslie (USA), 89 years 326 days, Buckeye airport, Arizona, USA, 8 Jun 1992.

SURVIVAL FROM LONGEST FALL WITHOUT PARACHUTE World Vesna Vulovic (Yugoslavia), air hostess in DC-9 which blew up at 10,160 m *33,330 ft* over Srbská Kamenice, Czechoslovakia (now Czech Republic), 26 Jan 1972.
UK Flt-Sgt Nicholas Stephen Alkemade (died 22 Jun 1987), from blazing RAF Lancaster bomber, at 5500 m *18,000 ft* over Germany (near Oberkürchen), 23 Mar 1944.

[1] *In 1687 the king of Ayutthaya, Siam was reported to have been diverted by an ingenious athlete parachuting with two large umbrellas. Faustus Verancsis is reputed to have descended in Hungary with a framed canopy in 1617.*
[2] *Maximum speed in rarefied air was 1006 km/h 625¼ mph at 90,000 ft 27,400 m—hence marginally supersonic.*

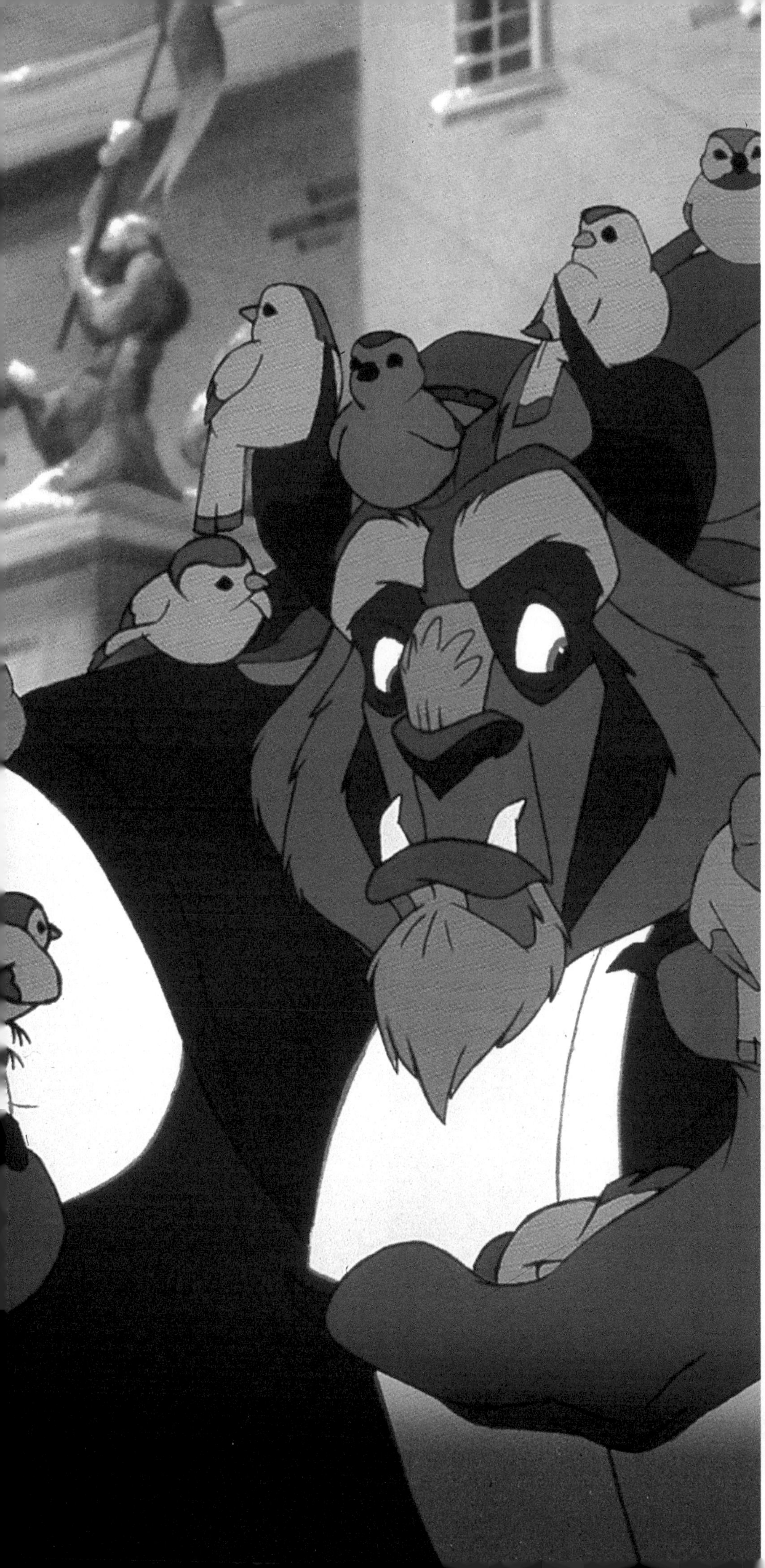

Arts & Entertainment

Pablo Diego José Francisco de Paula Juan Nepomuceno Crispin Crispiano de la Santisima Trinidad Ruiz y Picasso (1881–1973) of Spain was the most prolific painter in a career which lasted 78 years. It has been estimated that Picasso produced about 13,500 paintings or designs, 100,000 prints or engravings, 34,000 book illustrations and 300 sculptures or ceramics. His lifetime *oeuvre* has been valued at £500 million.

(Photo: Gamma)

Highest Prices

Sales were at auction unless stated otherwise and include the buyer's premium.

Item	Sold by	Price m denotes millions
Painting *Portrait of Dr Gachet*, Vincent van Gogh (1853–90)[1]	Christie's, New York, 15 May 1990	$82.5m (£49.1m)
UK Turner's *Van Tromp Going About to Please His Masters*	The University of London, Feb 1993 (private sale)	£11m
20th-century Picasso's *Les Noces de Pierette*	Binoche et Godeau, Paris, 30 Nov 1989	FF 315m (£51.895m)
Living artist *Interchange*, Willem de Kooning (USA; b. Rotterdam, 1904)	Sotheby's, New York, 8 Nov 1989	$20.68m (£13m)
UK *Triptych May–June*, Francis Bacon (1909–92)[2]	Sotheby's, New York, 2 May 1989	$6.27m (£3.71m)
Print 1655 etching *Christ Presented to the People*, Rembrandt (1606–69)	Christie's, London, Dec 1985	£561,600
Drawing *Jardin de Fleurs (1888)*, Vincent Van Gogh	Christie's, New York, 14 Nov 1990	$8.36m (£4.27m)
Poster by Charles R Mackintosh (1868–1928)	Christie's, London, Feb 1993	£68,200
Sculpture *The Dancing Faun*, by Adrien de Vries (1545/6–1626)[3]	Sotheby's, London, 7 Dec 1989	£6.82 m
Living Sculptor 190.5-cm 75-in-long elmwood *Reclining figure*, Henry Moore (1898–1986)	Sotheby's, New York, 21 May 1982	$1.265m

[1] The painting depicts Van Gogh's physician and was completed only weeks before the artist's suicide in 1890. It was sold within three minutes. [2] An advertisement for the 1895 exhibition of contemporary art at the Glasgow Institute of Fine Arts. [3] London dealer Cyril Humpris bought the figure from an unnamed Brighton, W Sussex couple who had paid £100 for it in the 1950s and in whose garden it had stood unremarked upon for 40 years.

Painting

Largest The largest painting in the world measures 6727.56m² *72,437ft²* after allowing for shrinkage of the canvas. It is made up of brightly coloured squares superimposed by a 'Smiley' face and was painted by students of Robb College at Armidale, New South Wales, Australia, aided by local schoolchildren and students from neighbouring colleges. The canvas was completed by its designer, Australian artist Ken Done, and unveiled at the University of New England at Armidale on 10 May 1990.

UK The oval painting *Triumph of Peace and Liberty* by Sir James Thornhill (1676–1734) on the ceiling of the Painted Hall in the Royal Naval College, Greenwich measures 32.3×15.4m *106 × 51ft* and took 20 years (1707–27) to complete.

GUESS WHAT?

Q In which country did the highest response to a radio quiz take place?

A See Page 158

Auction The largest painting ever auctioned was Carl Larsson's *Midvinterblot*, painted in Stockholm, Sweden from 1911 to 1915 and sold at Sotheby's, London on 25 Mar 1987 for £880,000 to the Umeda Gallery of Japan. The painting measured 13.4×2.7m *44×9ft*.

Most valuable The 'Mona Lisa' (*La Gioconda*) by Leonardo da Vinci (1452–1519) in the Louvre, Paris, France was assessed for insurance purposes at $100 million for its move to Washington, DC,

USA and New York City for exhibition from 14 Dec 1962 to 12 Mar 1963. However, insurance was not concluded because the cost of the closest security precautions was less than that of the premiums. It was painted *c.* 1503–07 and measures 77×53cm *30.5×20.9in.* It is believed to portray either Mona (short for Madonna) Lisa Gherardini, the wife of Francesco del Giocondo of Florence, or Constanza d'Avalos, coincidentally nicknamed La Gioconda, mistress of Giuliano de Medici. King Francis I of France bought the painting for his bathroom in 1517 for 4000 gold florins, or 13.94kg *30.75lb* of gold. The equivalent today (April 1994) would be £121,500.

Oldest RA The oldest ever Royal Academician was (Thomas) Sidney Cooper, who died on 8 Feb 1902 aged 98yr 136days having exhibited 266 paintings over the record span of 69 consecutive years (1833–1902).

Youngest RA Mary Moser (later Mrs Hugh Lloyd, 1744–1819) was elected on the foundation of the Royal Academy in 1768 when aged 24.

Largest galleries The world's largest art gallery is the Winter Palace and the neighbouring Hermitage in St Petersburg, USSR. A visitor has to walk 24km *15 miles* to see each of the 322 galleries, which house nearly 3 million works of art and objects of archaeological interest.

A poster measuring 21,936m² *236,119 ft²* was made by the Community Youth Club of Hong Kong on 26 Oct 1993. The poster was designed along the theme of the international year of the family, and was laid at Victoria Park, Hong Kong.

(Photo: East Asia Pro Photo Lab)

The youngest exhibitor at the Royal Academy of Arts Annual Summer Exhibition was Lewis Melville 'Gino' Lyons (b. 30 Apr 1962). His *Trees and Monkeys* was painted on 4 Jun 1965, submitted on 17 Mar 1967 and exhibited on 29 Apr 1967, the day before his fifth birthday.

Planet Ocean, by the artist Wyland, is the largest mural in the world, measuring 105 ft *32 m* high and 1220 ft *78.8 m* long. It is painted on the Long Beach Arena in California, USA and was completed on 4 May 1992.

(Photos: Gamma/Giboux)

Most heavily endowed The J. Paul Getty Museum in Malibu, California, USA was established with an initial £700 million budget in January 1974 and now has an annual budget of £104 million for acquisitions to stock its 38 galleries.

Finest paint brush The finest standard brush sold is the 000 in Series 7 by Winsor and Newton known as a 'triple goose'. It is made of 150–200 Kolinsky sable hairs weighing 15 mg *0.00053 oz.*

Murals

Largest Britain's largest mural covers 1709 m^2 *18,396 ft^2* and is painted on the Stage V wall of BBC Television Centre, London. Commissioned as the result of a competition run by the *Going Live* programme, the mural was painted in September 1991 by the Scenic Set company to a design by Vicky Askew.

Mosaics

Largest The world's largest mosaic is on the walls of the central library of the Universidad Nacional Autónoma de Mexico in Mexico City. Of the four walls, the two largest measure 1203 m^2 *12,949 ft^2*, and the scenes on each represent the pre-Hispanic past.

UK The largest Roman mosaic in Britain is the Woodchester Pavement in Gloucester of *c.* AD 325. It measures 14.3 m^2 *47 ft^2* and comprises 1.6 million tesserae (tiles). Excavated in 1793 and now re-covered with protective earth, a total reconstruction was carried out by Robert and John Woodward of Stroud, Glos and completed in June 1987.

Sculpture

Hill figures In August 1968 a 100-m *330-ft*-tall figure was found on a hill above Tarapacá, Chile.

UK The largest human hill carving in Britain is the 'Long Man' of Wilmington, E Sussex, at 68 m *226 ft* long.

The oldest of Britain's 'White Horses' is the Uffington horse in Oxfordshire, dating from the late Iron Age (*c.* 150 BC) and measuring 114 m *374 ft* from nose to tail and 36 m *120 ft* high.

Largest The mounted figures of Jefferson Davis (1808–89), Gen. Robert Edward Lee (1807–70) and Gen. Thomas Jonathan (Stonewall) Jackson (1824–63) are 27.4 m *90 ft* high and cover 0.5 ha *1.33 acres* on the face of Stone Mountain, near Atlanta, Georgia, USA. Roy Faulkner was on the mountain face for 8 years 174 days with a thermo-jet torch, working with the sculptor

Sand!

The longest sand sculpture ever made was the 26,375.9 m *86,535 ft* long sculpture named 'The GTE Directories Ultimate Sand Castle', built by more than 10,000 volunteers at Myrtle Beach, South Carolina, USA on 31 May 1991.

The tallest was the 'Invitation to Fairyland', which was 17.12 m *56 ft 2 in* high, and was built by 2000 local volunteers at Kaseda, Japan on 26 Jul 1989 under the supervision of Gerry Kirk of Sand Sculptors International of San Diego and Shogo Tashiro of Sand Sculptors International of Japan.

Walker Kirtland Hancock and other helpers, from 12 Sep 1963 to 3 Mar 1972.

Scrap-metal The largest scrap-metal sculpture was built by Sudhir Deshpande of Nashik, India and unveiled in February 1990. Named *Powerful*, the colossus weighs 27 tonnes and stands 17 m *55¾ ft* tall.

Antiques

All prices quoted are inclusive of the buyer's premium and all records were set at public auction unless stated otherwise.

Auctioneers The oldest firm of art auctioneers in the world is the Stockholms Auktionsverk of Sweden, which was established on 27 Feb 1647. Christie's of London held their first art auction in 1766. The largest firm is the Sotheby Group of London and New York, founded in 1744 although trading until 1778 was primarily in books. Sotheby's turnover in 1989 was a record $2.9 billion (£1.7 billion) and their New York sales set a single series record of $360.4 million (£201.9 million) in May 1990.

Carpets The most valued carpet ever made was the Spring carpet of Khusraw made for the audience hall of the Sassanian palace at Ctesiphon, Iraq. It consisted of about 650 m^2 *7000 ft^2* of silk and gold thread encrusted with emeralds. It was cut up as booty by looters in AD 635 and, from the known realization value of the pieces, must have had an original value of some £100 million.

In 1946 the Metropolitan Museum in New York City, USA privately paid $1 million for the 8.07 × 4.14 m *26.5 × 13.6 ft* Anhalt Medallion carpet made in Tabriz or Kashan, Persia (now Iran) *c.* 1590.

The highest price paid at auction is £441,500 for a 17th-century Persian rug at Christie's, London on 29 Apr 1993.

Ceramic The highest price paid for any ceramic is £3.74 million for a Chinese Tang dynasty (AD 618–906) horse sold by the British Rail Pension Fund and bought by a Japanese dealer at Sotheby's, London on 12 Dec 1989. The horse was stolen from a warehouse in Hong Kong on 14 November, but was recovered on 2 December in time for the sale.

Furniture The highest price ever paid for a single piece of furniture is £8.58 million ($15.1 million) at Christie's, London on 5 Jul 1990 for the 18th-century Italian 'Badminton Cabinet' owned by the Duke of Beaufort. It was bought by Barbara Piasecka Johnson of Princeton, New Jersey, USA.

Jewellery The world's largest jewellery auction, which included a Van Cleef and Arpels 1939 ruby and diamond

The largest and most elaborate jewelled egg stands 70 cm *2 ft* tall and was fashioned from 16·8 kg *37 lb* of gold studded with 20,000 pink diamonds. Designed by London jeweller Paul Kutchinsky, the Argyle Library Egg took six British craftsmen 7000 man-hours to create and has a price tag of £7 million. It was unveiled on 30 Apr 1990 before going on display at the Victoria and Albert Museum, London.

(Photos: Gamma\Wada)

necklace, realized £31,380,197 when the collection belonging to the Duchess of Windsor (1896–1986) was sold at Sotheby's, Geneva, Switzerland on 3 Apr 1987.

The record for individual items of jewellery is £3.1 million for two pear-shaped diamond drop earrings of 58.6 and 61.8 carats bought and sold anonymously at Sotheby's, Geneva on 14 Nov 1980.

Playing cards The highest price for a deck of playing cards is $143,352 (£99,000) paid by the Metropolitan Museum of Art, New York City, USA at Sotheby's, London on 6 Dec 1983.

The highest price paid for a single card was £5000 for a card used as currency in Canada dated 1717. It was sold by the dealer Yasha Beresiner to Lars Karlson (Sweden) in October 1990.

Thimble The record for a thimble is £18,000 at Phillips' Midland branch on 13 Dec 1992 for a late 16th century gold jewelled thimble reputed to have belonged to Queen Elizabeth I. It was bought by Asprey's on behalf of a client.

Toys!

The most expensive antique toy was sold for $231,000 (£128,333) by the trustees in bankruptcy of London dealers Mint & Boxed to a telephone bidder at Christie's, New York City, USA on 14 Dec 1991. The work is a hand-painted tin plate replica of the 'Charles' hose reel, a piece of firefighting equipment, measuring 381 × 584mm *15 × 23in* and built *c.* 1870 by George Brown & Co. of Forestville, Connecticut, USA. Claims that this toy had been sold privately for $1 million in 1990 were subsequently refuted.

The highest price paid for a single toy soldier is £3375 for a uniformed scale figure of Hitler's deputy, Rudolf Hess, made by the Lineol company of Brandenburg, Germany. The figure was among several sold by the Danish auction house Boyes in London on 23 Apr 1991.

Language

Commonest language The most common first language is Chinese, spoken by more than 1000 million people. The so-called 'common speech' (*puŝtōnghuà*) is the standard form of Chinese, with a pronunciation based on that of Beijing. The equivalent in Taiwan is known as *guóyuŝ* ('national speech') and in the West as Mandarin.

The most widespread and the second most commonly spoken language is English, with a conservative estimate of 800 million speakers, rising to a liberal 1500 million. Of these, some 350 million are native speakers, mainly in the US (about 220 million), the UK (55 million), Canada (17 million) and Australia (15 million).

Most languages About 845 of the world's languages and dialects are spoken in India. Owing to its many isolated valleys, the former Australian ter-

ritory of Papua New Guinea has the greatest concentration of separate languages in the world, with an estimated 869, i.e. each language has about 4000 speakers.

Most complex The following extremes of complexity have been noted: the Amele language of Papua New Guinea has the most verb forms, with over 69,000 finite forms and 860 infinitive forms of the verb; Haida, the North American Indian language, has the most prefixes (70); Tabassaran, a language of southeast Daghestan, uses the most noun cases (48); the Eskimo language used by the Inuit has 63 forms of the present tense and simple nouns have as many as 252 inflections.

Least irregular verbs The artificial language Esperanto was first published by its inventor Dr Ludwig Zamenhof (1859–1917) of Warsaw in 1887 without irregular verbs. It is now estimated (by text book sales) to have a million speakers. The even earlier interlanguage Volapük, invented by Johann Martin Schleyer (1831–1912), also has absolutely regular configuration.

Most irregular verbs According to *The Morphology and Syntax of Present-day English* by Prof. Olu Tomori, English has 283 irregular verbs, 30 of which are merely formed with prefixes.

Rarest sounds The rarest speech sound is probably that written 'ř' in Czech and termed a 'rolled post-alveolar fricative'. It occurs in very few languages and is the last sound mastered by Czech children. In the southern Bushman language *!xo* there is a click articulated with both lips, which is written ʘ. This character is usually referred to as a 'bull's eye' and the sound, essentially a kiss, is termed a 'velaric ingressive bilabial stop'. In some contexts the 'l' sound in the Arabic word *Allah* is pronounced uniquely in that language.

Debating Students of St Andrews Presbyterian College in Laurinburg, North Carolina, USA, together with staff and friends, debated the motion 'There's No Place Like Home' for 517hr 45min from 4–26 Apr 1992. The aim of the debate was to increase awareness of the problems of being homeless.

Most synonyms The condition of being inebriated has more synonyms than any other condition or object. Paul Dickson of Garrett Park, Maryland, USA has compiled a list of 2660 words and phrases in his book *Word Treasury*.

Greatest linguist If the yardstick of ability to speak with fluency and reasonable accuracy is maintained, it is doubtful whether any human being could maintain fluency in more than 20–25 languages concurrently or achieve fluency in more than 40 in a lifetime.

A contender for the title of the world's greatest linguist was Dr Harold Williams of New Zealand (1876–1928), a journalist and one-time foreign editor of *The Times*. He was reputed to speak 58 languages and many dialects fluently.

Self-taught in Latin, Greek, Hebrew and many of the European and Pacific island languages as a boy, Harold Williams reputedly spoke 58 languages and many dialects fluently. He was the only person to attend the League of Nations in Geneva, Switzerland and converse with every delegate in their own language.

The greatest living linguist is Ziad Fazah (b. 10 Jul 1954), originally from Liberia but now a naturalized Brazilian citizen, who speaks and writes 58 languages. He was tested in a live interview in Athens, Greece on 30 Jul 1991, when he surprised members of the audience by talking to them in their various native tongues. He is currently a private language teacher.

Alphabets

Oldest letter The letter 'O' is unchanged in shape since its adoption in the Phoenician alphabet *c.* 1300BC.

Newest letters Until about 1600 there was no clear distinction in the English alphabet between the letters 'i' and 'j' or 'u' and 'v'. After 1600 'i' and 'u' came to represent vowels only, while 'j' and 'v' became consonants. Even as recently as the 19th century some dictionaries did not distinguish between 'i' and 'j' and in Alexander Cruden's *Concordance to the Holy Scriptures* (1815), the next word after *I* is *Jacinth*, while *Joyous* is followed by *Iron*. There are 65 alphabets now in use worldwide.

Longest The language with the most letters is Khmer (Cambodian), with 74 (including some without any current use).

Shortest Rotokas of central Bougainville Island, Papua New Guinea has the least letters of any alphabet, with 11 (a, b, e, g, i, k, o, p, ř, t and u).

Most and least consonants The language with most distinct consonantal sounds was that of the Ubykhs in the Caucasus, with 80–85. Ubykh speakers migrated from the Caucasus to Turkey in the nineteenth century and the last fully competent speaker, Tevfik Esenç, died in October 1992. The language with the least consonants is Rotokas, which has only six. (⇨ Shortest)

Most and least vowels The language with the most vowels is Sedang, a central Vietnamese language with 55 distinguishable vowel sounds, and that with the least is the Caucasian language Abkhazian with two.

Words

Longest Lengthy concatenations and some compound or agglutinative words or nonce words can be written in the closed-up style of a single word. The longest known example is a compound 'word' of 195 Sanskrit characters (transliterating to 428 letters in the Roman alphabet) describing the region near Kanci, Tamil Nadu, India, which appears in a

Succint!

The most challenging word for any lexicographer to define briefly is the Fuegian (southernmost Argentina and Chile) word *mamihlapinatapai*, meaning 'looking at each other hoping that either will offer to do something which both parties desire but are unwilling to do'.

Longest acronym The longest acronym is NIIOMTPLABOPARMBETZHELBETRAB-SBOMONIMONKONOTDTEKHSTROMONT with 56 letters (54 in Cyrillic) in the *Concise Dictionary of Soviet Terminology, Institutions and Abbreviations* (1969), meaning: the laboratory for shuttering, reinforcement, concrete and ferroconcrete operations, for composite-monolithic and monolithic constructions, of the Department of the Technology of Building-assembly operations, of the Scientific Research Institute of the Organization for mechanization and

16th-century work by Tirumalāmbā, Queen of Vijayanagara.

English The longest word in the *Oxford English Dictionary* is *pneumonoultramicroscopicsilicovolcanoconiosis (-koniosis)*, which has 45 letters and describes 'a lung disease caused by the inhalation of very fine silica dust'. It is described as 'factitious' by the editors of the dictionary. Chemical names, if spelt out as opposed to being listed by their formulae, may run to thousands of letters.

Longest scientific name The systematic name for *deoxyribonucleic acid* (DNA) of the human mitochondria contains 16,569 nucleotide residues and is thus *c.* 207,000 letters long. It was published in key form in *Nature* on 9 Apr 1981.

Longest palindromes The longest known palindromic word is *saippuakivikauppias* (19 letters), which is Finnish for 'a dealer in lye' (caustic soda or potash). The longest in English is *tattarrattat* (12 letters), a nonce-word meaning rat-a-tat appearing in the *Oxford English Dictionary*.

Some baptismal fonts in Greece and Turkey bear the circular 25-letter inscription NIΨON ANOMHMATA MH MONAN OΨIN, meaning 'wash (my) sins not only (my) face'. This appears at St Mary's Church, Nottingham, St Paul's, Woldingham, Surrey and other churches.

Longest anagrams The longest non-scientific English words which can form anagrams are the 17-letter transpositions *representationism* and *misrepresentation*. The longest scientific transposals are *hydroxydesoxycorticosterone* and *hydroxydeoxycorticosterones*, with 27 letters.

Abbreviations *Longest* The longest known abbreviation is S.K.O.M.K.H.P.K.J.C.D.P.W.B., the initials of the Syarikat Kerjasama Orang-orang Melayu Kerajaan Hilir Perak Kerana Jimat Cermat Dan Pinjam-meminjam Wang Berhad. This is the Malay name for The Cooperative Company of the Lower State of Perak Government's Malay People for Money Savings and Loans Ltd, in Teluk Anson, Perak, West Malaysia (formerly Malaya). The abbreviation for this abbreviation is Skomk.

Shortest The 55-letter full name of Los Angeles (El Pueblo de Nuestra Señora la Reina de los Angeles de Porciúncula) is abbreviated to L.A., or 3.63 per cent of its full length.

Longest Words

JAPANESE[1]	Chi-n-chi-ku-ri-n (12 letters) *a very short person (slang)*
SPANISH	Superextraordinarisimo (22) *extraordinary*
FRENCH	Anticonstitutionnellement (25) *anticonstitutionally*
ITALIAN	Precipitevolissimevolmente (26) *as fast as possible*
PORTUGUESE	Inconstitucionalissimamente (27) *with the highest degree of unconstitutionality*
ICELANDIC	Haecstaréttarmálaflutningsmaður (29) *supreme court barrister*
RUSSIAN	Ryentgyenoelyektrokardiografichyeskogo (33 Cyrillic letters, transliterating as 38) *of the X-ray electrocardiographic*
HUNGARIAN	Megszentségtelenithetetlenségeskedéseitekért (44) *for your unprofanable actions*
DUTCH	Kindercarnavalsoptochtvoorbereidingswerkzaamheden (49) *preparation activities for a children's carnival procession*
DANISH	Speciallægepraksisplanlægningsstabiliseringsperiode (51) *the stabilization period of the planning of medical specialist's practices*
FINNISH	Lentokonesuihkuturbiinimoottoriapumekaanikkoaliupseerioppilas (61) *apprentice corporal, working as assistant mechanic in charge of aeroplane turbine engines*
GERMAN[2,3]	Donaudampfschiffahrtselektrizitaetenhauptbetriebswerkbau-unterbeamtengesellschaft (80) *the club for subordinate officials of the head office management of the Danube steamboat electrical services (name of a pre-war club in Vienna)*
SWEDISH[3]	Nordöstersjökustartilleriflygspaningssimulatoranläggning-smaterielunderhållsuppföljningssystemdiskussionsinläggsför-beredelsearbeten (130) *preparatory work on the contribution to the discussion on the maintaining system of support of the material of the aviation survey simulator device within the north-east part of the coast artillery of the Baltic*

[1] *Patent applications sometimes harbour long compound 'words'. An extreme example is one of 13 kana (Japanese syllabary) which transliterates to the 40-letter Kyukitsurohekimenfuchakunenryosekisanryo meaning 'the accumulated amount of fuel condensed on the wall face of the air intake passage'.*
[2] *The longest dictionary word in everyday usage is Rechtsschutzversicherungsgesellschaften (39) meaning 'insurance companies which provide legal protection'.*
[3] *Agglutinative words are limited only by imagination and are not found in standard dictionaries. The first 100-letter such word was published in 1975 in Afrikaans.*

GUESS WHAT?

Q What is the language most commonly spoken?

A See Page 136

See Page 136

Personal Names

Longest pedigree It is claimed on behalf of the Clan Mackay that their clan can be traced to Loarn, the Irish invader of south-west Pictland, now Argyll, *c.* AD 501. The only non-royal English pedigree that can show with certainty a clear pre-Conquest descent is that of the Arden family, which includes Mary Arden, Shakespeare's mother.

Longest personal name The longest name appearing on a birth certificate is that of Rhoshandiatellyneshiaunneveshenk Koyaanfsquatsiuty Williams, born to Mr and Mrs James Williams in Beaumont, Texas, USA on 12 Sep 1984. On 5 Oct 1984 the father filed an amendment which expanded his daughter's first name to 1019 letters and the middle name to 36 letters.

Most first names Laurence Watkins (b. 9 Jun 1965) of Auckland, New Zealand claims a total of 2310 Christian names, added by deed poll in 1991 after official opposition by the Registrar and a prolonged court battle. The great-great-grandson of Carlos III of Spain, Don Alfonso de Borbón y Borbón (1866–1934), had 94 Christian names, several of which were lengthened by hyphenation.

UK John and Margaret Nelson of Chesterfield, Derbys gave their daughter Tracy (b. 13 Dec 1985) a total of 139 other Christian names. In November 1986 the names were recorded on a document separate from the birth certificate.

Shortest surnames The commonest single-letter surname is 'O', prevalent in Korea but with 52 examples in US telephone books (1973–81) and 12 in Belgium.

British Isles On the Department of Social Security index there are six examples of a one-letter surname—'A', 'B', 'J', 'N', 'O' and 'X'. The Christian name 'A' has been used for five generations in the Lincoln Taber family of Fingringhoe, Essex.

Commonest first names In 1993 the most popular names in Britain were Daniel for boys and Rebecca for girls. For more facts on first names, surnames and nicknames dip into the updated, revised and expanded sixth edition of *The Guinness Book of Names*.

technical aid to building of the Academy of Building and Architecture of the USSR.

Commonest words and letters The most frequently used words in written English are, in descending order of frequency: *the, of, and, to, a, in, that, is, I, it, for* and *as*. The most commonly used in conversation is 'I'. The commonest letter is 'e'. More words begin with the letter 's' than any other, but the most commonly *used* initial letter is 't' as in 'the', 'to', 'that' or 'there'.

The most overworked word in English is 'set', which Dr Charles Onions (1873–1965) of Oxford University Press gave 58 noun uses, 126 verbal uses and ten as a participial adjective.

Smith!

The commonest surname in the English-speaking world is Smith. The most recent published count showed 659,050 nationally insured Smiths in Great Britain, of whom 10,102 were plain John Smith and another 19,502 were John (plus one or more names) Smith. Including uninsured persons there were over 800,000 Smiths in England and Wales alone, of whom 81,493 were called A. Smith.

Longest Place-Names

In its most scholarly transliteration, Krungthep Mahanakhon, the 167-letter official name for Bangkok, the capital of Thailand, has 175 letters.

The official short version (without capital letters which are not used in Thai) is included below.

World

krungthephphramahanakhon bowonratanakosin mahintharayuthaya mahadilokphiphobnovpharad radchataniburirom udomsantisug (111 letters)

Longest in use

Taumatawhakatangihangakoauauotamateaturipukakapikimaungahoronukupokaiwhenuakitanatahu (85 letters, Southern Hawke's Bay, New Zealand)[1]

British Isles

Gorsafawddachaidraigddanheddogleddollônpenrhynareurdraethceredigion (67 letters, Fairbourne Steam Railway, near Barmouth, Gwynedd)[2]

Llanfairpwllgwyngyllgogerychwyrndrobwllllantysiliogogogoch (58 letters, Anglesea, Gwynedd)[3]

[1] Unofficial name of a hill, the Maori translation meaning 'The place where Tamatea, the man with the big knees, who slid, climbed and swallowed mountains, known as landeater, played his flute to his loved one'. [2] Commercially-motivated creation on a station board 19.5m 64ft long. [3] Concocted version of a name translated as 'St Mary's Church by the pool of the white hazel trees, near the rapid whirlpool, by the red cave of the Church of St Tysilio'. This is the name used for the reopened (April 1973) village railway station in Anglesey, Gwynedd and was coined by a local bard, Y Bardd Cocos (John Evans, 1827–95) as a hoax. The official name consists of the first 20 letters.

Surnames!

A six-barrelled surname was borne by Major L.S.D.O.F. (Leone Sextus Denys Oswolf Fraudatifilius) Tollemache-Tollemache de Orellana-Plantagenet-Tollemache-Tollemache (1884–1917). At school he was known as Tolly. Of non-repetitious surnames, the last example of a five-barrelled one was that of the Lady Caroline Jemima Temple-Nugent-Chandos-Brydges-Grenville (1858–1946).

The longest single English surname is Featherstonehaugh (17 letters), variously pronounced Featherstonehaw or Festonhaw or Fessonhay or Freestonhugh or Feerstonhaw or Fanshaw. In Scotland the surname Nin (feminine of Mac) Achinmacdholica-chinskerray (29 letters) was recorded in an 18th-century parish register.

Place-Names

Earliest The world's earliest known place-names are pre-Sumerian, e.g. Kish, Ur and the now lost Attara, and therefore earlier than *c.* 3600 BC.

British Isles The earliest recorded British place-name is Belerion, the Penwith peninsula of Cornwall, referred to as such by Pytheas of Massilia *c.* 308 BC. The name Salakee (meaning 'tin island') on St Mary's, Isles of Scilly is, however, arguably of a pre-Indo-European substrate.

Shortest The shortest place-names consist of just single letters and examples can be found in various countries around the world, and include the villages of Y, France, Å in Denmark, Norway and Sweden and the River E, Highland.

Most spellings The spelling of the Dutch town of Leeuwarden has been recorded in 225 versions since AD 1046. Bromsberrow, Glos is recorded in 161 spellings since the 10th century, as reported by local historian Lester Steynor.

Most common The most common place-name in Great Britain is Newton, meaning 'new settlement', occurring 467 times (151 in its simple form and 316 in compound names). Of the basic form, 90 are found in Scotland, and 40 of these are in the Grampian region alone.

Literature

Oldest book The oldest handwritten book, still intact, is a Coptic Psalter dated to about 1600 years ago, found in 1984 at Beni Suef, Egypt.

UK The earliest known manuscript written in Britain is a bifolium of Eusebius' *Historia Ecclesiastica* from *c.* AD 625, possibly from the Jarrow library. Fragments of Roman wooden writing tablets found in the 1970s at Vindolanda (Chesterholme), Northumberland have been shown to make up the earliest known substantial written records in British history. These contain letters and a quotation from the Roman poet Virgil (70–19 BC) and are dated to *c.* AD 100.

Oldest mechanically printed It is widely accepted that the earliest mechanically printed full-length book was the Gutenberg Bible, printed in Mainz, Germany, *c.*1454 by Johann Henne zum Gensfleisch zur Laden, called 'zu Gutenberg' (*c.* 1398–1468).

Largest publications The largest publication ever compiled was the *Yongle Dadian* (the great thesaurus of the Yongle reign) of 22,937 manuscript chapters (370 still survive) in 11,095 volumes. It was written by 2000 Chinese scholars in 1403–08. The entire Buddhist scriptures are inscribed on 729 marble slabs measuring 1.5×1m 5×3½ft housed in 729 stupas in the Kuthodaw Pagoda, south of Mandalay, Myanmar (Burma). They were incised in 1860–68.

UK The 1112-volume set of *British Parliamentary Papers* was published by the Irish University Press in 1968–72. A complete set weighs 3.3 tonnes, costs £50,000 and would take six years to read at ten hours per day. The production involved the skins of 34,000 Indian goats and the use of £15,000 worth of gold ingots. The total print is 500 sets and the price per set in 1987 was £49,500.

CD-ROM In 1990 The British Library published its *General Catalogue of Printed Books to 1975* on a set of three CD-ROMs, priced at £9000. Alternatively, readers can spend six months scanning 178,000 catalogue pages in 360 volumes.

Dictionaries Deutsches Wörterbuch, started by Jacob and Wilhelm Grimm in 1854, was completed in 1971 and consists of 34,519 pages and 33 volumes costing DM5425 in 1988. (⇨Longest literary gestation)

Gestation!

The standard German dictionary *Deutsches Wörterbuch* was begun by the brothers Grimm (Jacob and Wilhelm, 1785–1863 and 1786–1859 respectively) in 1854 and finished in 1971. *Acta Sanctorum*, begun by Jean Bolland in 1643, arranged according to saints' days, reached the month of November in 1925 and an introduction for December was published in 1940.

Smallest!

The smallest marketed, bound and printed book is one printed on 22 gsm paper measuring 1mm×1mm 1/25 × 1/25 in, comprising the children's story *Old King Cole!*. Eighty-five copies were published in March 1985 by The Gleniffer Press of Paisley, Strathclyde. The pages can be turned (with care) only by the use of a needle.

The largest English-language dictionary is the 20-volume *Oxford English Dictionary*, with 21,728 pages. The longest entry is that for the verb *set*, with over 75,000 words of text. The greatest outside contributor has been Marghanita Laski (1915–88), with a reputed 250,000 quotations from 1958 until her death.

Fiction The novel *Tokuga-Wa Ieyasu* by Sohachi Yamaoka has been serialized in Japanese daily newspapers since 1951, requiring nearly 40 volumes. The longest published novel of note is *Les hommes de bonne volonté* by Louis Henri Jean Farigoule (1885–1972), alias Jules Romains, of France, in 27 volumes in 1932–46.

Oxford University Press received back their proofs of *Constable's Presentments* from the Dugdale Society in December 1984. They had been sent out for correction 35 years earlier in December 1949.

Maps

Oldest A clay tablet depicting the river Euphrates flowing through northern Mesopotamia, Iraq dates to *c.* 2250 BC. The earliest printed map in the world is one of western China dated to AD 1115.

Largest The largest permanent, two-dimensional atlas measures

A map dating from 1486 based on Ptolemy Geography. (⇨Most expensive)
(Photo: e.t.archive/British Library)

4552 m² *49,000 ft²* and was painted by students of O'Hara Park School, Oakley, California, USA in the summer of 1992.

The Challenger relief map of British Columbia, Canada, measuring 575 m² *6080 ft²*, was designed and built in the period 1945–52 by the late George Challenger and his son Robert. It is now on display at the Pacific National Exhibition in Vancouver, British Columbia.

Most expensive The highest price paid for an atlas is $1,925,000 for a copy of Ptolemy's *Cosmographia* at Sotheby's, New York City, USA on 31 Jan 1990.

Who's Who!

Who's Who, founded in 1848 and first published in 1849, was the first biographical reference book in which all the entries were compiled by the biographees themselves, and were therefore *autobiographical*.

The longest entry in Who's Who was that of the Rt Hon. Sir Winston Leonard Spencer Churchill (1874–1965), who appeared in 67 editions from 1899 (18 lines) and had 211 lines by the 1965 edition. The longest entry in the book's current wider format is that of Dame Barbara Cartland, who is allocated 199 lines in the 1993 edition (⇨ Most prolific author). Apart from those who qualify for inclusion by hereditary title, the youngest entrant has been (Lord) Yehudi Menuhin OM KBE (b. New York City, USA, 22 Apr 1916), the concert violinist, who first appeared in the 1932 edition at the age of 15.

Highest Prices

Books The highest price paid for any book is £8.14 million for the 226-leaf manuscript *The Gospel Book of Henry the Lion, Duke of Saxony* at Sotheby's, London on 6 Dec 1983. The book, which measures 4.3 × 25.4 cm *13½ × 10 in*, was illuminated *c.* 1170 by the monk Herimann at Helmershansen Abbey, Germany with 41 full-page illustrations and was bought by Hans Kraus for the Hermann Abs consortium.

The record for a *printed* book is $5.39 million (£3.28 million) for an Old Testament (Genesis to Psalms) of the Gutenberg Bible printed in 1455 in Mainz, Germany. It was bought by Tokyo booksellers Maruzen Co. Ltd at Christie's, New York, USA on 22 Oct 1987.

Broadsheet The highest price ever paid for a printed page was $2,420,000 (£1,367,700) for one of the 24 known copies of *The Declaration of Independence*, printed by John Dunlap in Philadelphia, Pennsylvania, USA in 1776. It was sold by Samuel T. Freeman & Co. to Donald Scheer of Atlanta, Georgia on 13 Jun 1991.

Musical manuscript The auction record for a musical manuscript is £2,585,000 paid by London dealer James Kirkman at Sotheby's, London on 22 May 1987 for a 508-page, 21.6 × 16.5-cm *8½ × 6½-in* bound volume of nine complete symphonies in Mozart's hand. The record for a single musical manuscript is £1.1 million paid at Sotheby's, London on 6 Dec 1991 for the autograph copy of the Piano Sonata in E minor, opus 90 by Ludwig van Beethoven (1770–1827).

Most expensive The highest price ever paid on the open market for a single signed autograph letter was $748,000 (£422,000) on 5 Dec 1991 at Christie's, New York, USA for a letter written by Abraham Lincoln on 8 Jan 1863 defending criticism of the Emancipation Proclamation. It was sold to Profiles in History of Beverly Hills, CA.

The highest price paid for an autograph letter signed by a living person is $12,500 (*c.* £5,380) at the Hamilton Galleries on 22 Jan 1981 for a letter from President Ronald Reagan praising Frank Sinatra.

Diaries and Letters

Longest kept diary Col. Ernest Loftus of Harare, Zimbabwe began his daily diary on 4 May 1896 at the age of 12 and continued it until his death on 7 Jul 1987 aged 103 years 178 days, a total of 91 years.

UK T.C. Baskerville of Chorlton-cum-Hardy, Manchester, has written an entry in his diary of international and home affairs every day for 54 years from 1939. It now comprises an estimated

Victor Marie Hugo (1802–85), who holds the record for producing the shortest correspondence. This was between Hugo and his publisher, Hurst and Blackett, in 1862. The author was on holiday and anxious to know how his new novel *Les Misérables* was selling. He wrote '?' and received the reply '!'.
(Photo: Archiv für Kunst und Geschichte, Berlin)

7 million words in 40,608 pages. It includes signatures of all the Prime Ministers from Sir Winston Churchill to John Major.

Longest letter to an editor The *Upper Dauphin Sentinel* of Pennsylvania, USA published a letter of 25,513 words over eight issues from August to November 1979, written by John Sultzbaugh of Lykens, Pennsylvania.

Most letters to an editor David Green, author and solicitor of Castle Morris, Dyfed, had had 134 letters published in the main correspondence columns of *The Times* on 10 May 1994, the most for any correspondent. His record year was 1972 with 12; his shortest was 'Sir, "Yes".' on 31 May 1993.

Shortest letter to The Times The shortest letter to *The Times* comprised the single abbreviated symbol 'Dr ²?' in the interrogative from R. S. Cookson of London NW11 on 30 Jul 1984 in a correspondence on the correct form of recording a plurality of academic doctorates. On 8 Jan 1986 a letter was sent to *The Times* by a seven-year-old girl from the Isle of Man. It read 'Sir, Yours faithfully Caroline Sophia Kerenhappuch Parkes'. The brief epistle was intended to inform readers of her unusual name, Kerenhappuch, mentioned in a letter the previous week from Rev. John Ticehurst on the subject of uncommon 19th-century names.

Most letters Uichi Noda, former Vice Minister of Treasury and Minister of Construction in Japan, wrote 1307 letters amounting to 5 million characters to his bedridden wife Mitsu during his overseas trips from July 1961 until her death in March 1985. These letters have been published in 25 volumes totalling 12,404 pages.

GUESS WHAT?

Q What is the longest place-name in use?

A See Page 138

Bill in Italy in 1944.

Helen in 1942, a year after they met.

Bill Cook & Helen Appleton met in the summer of 1941 when Bill was a 27-year-old Army chaplain and Helen was a student, aged 21, living with her father at the time in Diss, Norfolk. It was love at first sight. After a courtship lasting two months, and shortly before Bill was due to take up an overseas post, they became engaged.

Separated by war, they had no idea when they would actually be able to marry. They began exchanging love letters, and by the end of their 4½-year separation they had sent a record 6000 to each other!

Helen and Bill celebrated their forty-eighth wedding anniversary on 23 Aug 1993.

Helen and Bill Cook with their love letters.

Christmas cards The earliest known Christmas card was sent out by Sir Henry Cole (1808–82) in 1843 but this practice did not become an annual ritual until 1862.

The greatest number of personal Christmas cards sent out is believed to be 62,824 by Werner Erhard of San Francisco, California, USA in December 1975. Many must have been to unilateral acquaintances.

Christmas card exchange Frank Rose of Burnaby, British Columbia, Canada and Gordon Loutet of Lake Cowichan, British Columbia have deliberately exchanged the same Christmas card every year since 1929.

Pen pals The longest sustained correspondence on record is one of 75 years from 11 Nov 1904 between Mrs Ida McDougall of Tasmania, Australia and Miss R. Norton of Sevenoaks, Kent until Mrs McDougall's death on 24 Dec 1979.

Rarest and most valuable signature Only one example of the signature of Christopher Marlowe (1564–93) is known. It is in the Kent County Archives on a will of 1583.

Authors

Most prolific A lifetime output of 72–75 million words has been calculated for Charles Harold St John Hamilton, alias Frank Richards (1876–1961), the creator of Billy Bunter. In his peak years (1915–26) he wrote up to 80,000 words a week for the boys' school weeklies *Gem* (1907–39), *Magnet* (1908–40) and *Boys' Friend*.

Most prolific novelist The greatest number of novels published is 904 by Kathleen Lindsay (Mrs Mary Faulkner) (1903–73) of Somerset West, Cape Province, South Africa. She wrote under two other married names and eight pen names. Baboorao Arnalkar (b. 9 Jun 1907) of Maharashtra State,

India published 1092 short mystery stories in book form and several non-fiction books between 1936 and 1984.

UK The most prolific author is currently Dame Barbara Cartland, with 602 titles published in 30 languages to date. She has averaged 23 titles per year for the last 20 years and was made a Dame of the Order of the British Empire by HM The Queen in the 1991 New Year's Honours List for services to literature and the community.

Although it is difficult to put precise figures to the output of Enid Mary Blyton (1897–1968) (Mrs Darrell Waters) she is thought to have completed no less than 600 books in all; some sources believe her complete works to be in excess of 700. Her books have been translated into 165 languages.

Text books Britain's most successful writer of text books is ex-schoolmaster Ronald Ridout (b. 23 Jul 1916) who has had 515 titles published since 1958, with sales of 91.35 million. His *The First English Workbook* has sold 5.6 million copies.

Pseudonyms!

The writer with the greatest number of pseudonyms is the Russian humorist Konstantin Arsenievich Mikhailov (b. 1868), whose 325 pen names are listed in the *Dictionary of Pseudonyms* by I.F. Masanov, published in Moscow in 1960. The names, ranging from Ab. to Z, were mostly abbreviations of his real name.

Greatest advance The greatest advance for a single book is $14 million (£7.3 million), reported in August 1992 to have been paid by Berkeley Putnam for the North American rights to *Without Remorse* by Tom Clancy. On 9 Feb 1989 the American horror writer Stephen King (b. 21 Sep 1947) was reported to have scooped a £26 million advance for his next four books.

On 6 May 1992 the British journalist and author Barbara Taylor Bradford (b. 10 May 1933) concluded a deal with Harper Collins for £17 million (over some five years) for three novels.

Top-selling authors The world's top-selling fiction writer is Dame Agatha Christie (*née* Miller, later Lady Mallowan, 1890–1976), whose 78 crime novels have sold an estimated 2 billion copies in 44 languages. Agatha Christie also wrote 19 plays and six romantic novels under the pseudonym Mary Westmacott. Royalty earnings are estimated to be worth £2.5 million per year.

Biography!

Georges Simenon wrote 22 autobiographical books from 1972. The longest biography in publishing history is that of Sir Winston Churchill by his son Randolph (4832 pages) and Martin Gilbert (17,811 pages), to date comprising 22 volumes and 9,694,000 words.

GUESS WHAT?

Q What was the largest ever *Mastermind* score?

A See Page 159

Oldest!

The accolade for the world's slowest-selling book (known in US publishing as slooow sellers) probably belongs to David Wilkins' translation of the New Testament from Coptic into Latin, published by Oxford University Press (OUP) in 1716 in 500 copies. Selling an average of one each 20 weeks, it remained in print for 191 years.

Non-fiction It has been reported that 800 million copies of the red-covered booklet *Quotations from the Works of Mao Zedong* (*Tse-tung*) were sold or distributed between June 1966, when possession became virtually mandatory in China, and September 1971, when its promoter Marshal Lin Biao died in an air crash.

Oldest The oldest author in the world was Alice Pollock (*née* Wykeham-Martin, 1868–1971) of Haslemere, Surrey, whose first book *Portrait of My Victorian Youth* (Johnson Publications) was published in March 1971 when she was aged 102 years 8 months.

Longest poem The longest poem ever published has been the Kirghiz folk epic *Manas*, which appeared in printed form in 1958 but which has never been translated into English. According to the *Dictionary of Oriental Literatures*, this three-part epic runs to about 500,000 lines. Short translated passages appear in *The Elek Book of Oriental Verse*.

The longest poem in English is one on the life of King Alfred by John Fitchett (1766–1838) of Liverpool, Merseyside, which ran to 129,807 lines and took 40 years to write. His editor, Robert Riscoe, added the concluding 2585 lines.

Best-Selling Books

The world's best-selling and most widely distributed book is the Bible, with an estimated 2.5 billion copies sold between 1815 and 1975. Since 1976 combined global sales of Today's English

The top-selling living author is Dame Barbara Cartland, pictutred here with her DBE. Her 602 titles have enjoyed global sales of over 650 million. (⇨ Most prolific author)

(Photo: Rex Features/N. Jorgensen)

Version (*Good News*) New Testament and Bible (which is copyright of the Bible Societies) have exceeded 122 million copies. By the end of 1993, the whole bible had been translated into 337 languages; 2062 languages have at least one book of the bible in that language. The oldest publisher of bibles is the Cambridge University Press, which began with the Geneva version in 1591. (⇨ Oldest publisher)

Excluding versions of the Bible, the world's all-time best-selling book is *The Guinness Book of Records*, first published in October 1955 by Guinness Superlatives, a subsidiary of Arthur Guinness Son & Co. (Park Royal) Ltd, and edited by Norris Dewar McWhirter (b. 12 Aug 1925) and his twin brother Alan Ross McWhirter (killed 27 Nov 1975). Global sales in some 37 languages have reached 76 million to April 1994.

Fiction Due to a lack of audited figures, it is impossible to state with certainty which single work of fiction has the highest sales. Three novels have been credited with sales of around 30 million: *Valley of the Dolls* (1966) by Jacqueline Susann (1921–74), which sold 6.8 million copies in just the first six months, although it is now out of print; *To Kill a Mockingbird* (1960) by Harper Lee and *Gone With the Wind* by Margaret Mitchell.

Alistair Stuart MacLean (1922–87) wrote 30 books, 28 of which each sold over a million copies in the UK alone. His books have been translated into 28 languages and 13 have been filmed. It has been estimated that a 'MacLean' novel is purchased every 18 seconds.

Best-Sellers!

The longest duration on the *New York Times* best-seller list (founded 1935) has been for *The Road Less Traveled* by M. Scott Peck, which on 2 Oct 1988 had its 258th week on the lists.

UK A Brief History of Time (Transworld/Bantam Press) by Prof. Stephen Hawking (b. 8 Jan 1942) has appeared in *The Sunday Times* best-seller list (which excludes books published annually) for a record 234 weeks to 13 Feb 1994. *The Country Diary of an Edwardian Lady* (Michael Joseph, Webb & Bower) by Edith Holden (1871–1920) held the No. 1 position for 64 weeks.

Publishers and Printers

In 1993 the UK published a record 82,322 new titles and editions, an increase of 4.4 per cent on the 1992 total.

Oldest publisher Cambridge University Press has a continuous history of printing and publishing since 1584. The University received Royal Letters Patent to print and sell all manner of books on 20 Jul 1534.

In 1978 the Oxford University Press (OUP) celebrated the 500th anniversary of the printing of the first book in the City of Oxford in 1478. This was before OUP itself was in existence.

Most prolific publisher At its peak in 1989, Progress Publishers (founded in 1931 as the Publishing Association of Foreign Workers in the USSR) of Moscow, USSR printed over 750 titles in 50 languages annually.

Largest publisher The world's largest publisher is Matra-Hachette of Paris, France. Sales in 1992

totalled an equivalent of £6,957 million.

Largest printer The largest printers in the world are Dai Nippon Printing Co Ltd of Tokyo, Japan. Net sales as of 31 Mar 1994 were 1,192,109 million yen (£7,797.678 million) and current assets are 626,112 million yen (£4,095.45 million). The DNP group employees approximately 35,000 people.

Highest Printings

It is believed that in the USA, Van Antwerp Bragg and Co. printed some 60 million copies of the 1879 edition of *The McGuffey Reader*, compiled by Henry Vail in the pre-copyright era for distribution to public schools.

GUESS WHAT?

Q How bad was the world's worst singer?

A See Page 146

Oldest museum The world's oldest extant museum is the Ashmolean in Oxford, built between 1679 and 1683 and named after the collector Elias Ashmole (1617–92). Since 1924 it has housed an exhibition of historic scientific instruments.

Largest museum The Smithsonian Institution comprises 16 museums and the National Zoological Park in Washington, DC, USA. It contains over 140 million items and has over 6000 employees. (⇨Most popular)

The American Museum of Natural History in New York City, USA, founded in 1869, comprises 23 interconnected buildings. The buildings of the Museum and the Planetarium contain 11,148 m² *1.2 million ft²* of floor space, accommodating more than 30 million artifacts and specimens and the museum attracts over 3 million visitors each year.

UK The largest and most visited museum in the United Kingdom is the British Museum (founded in 1753), which was opened to the public in 1759. The main building in Bloomsbury, London was begun in 1823 and has a total floor area of 8.7 ha *21.5 acres*. In 1993, 6,208,960 people passed through its doors.

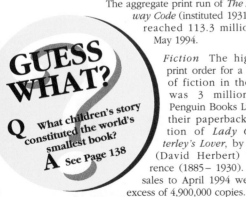

The United States Library of Congress (founded on 24 Apr 1800) in Washington, DC, USA is the world's largest, and contains 104,834,652 items, including manuscripts, computer tape cartridges (*see inset, top*), and, of course, books. There are 16,055,353 books in the classified collections and 88,779,299 items in non-classified. The library occupies about 265,000 m² *2.85 million ft²* of space in the Capitol Hill buildings, with additional offices and branches worldwide. On 30 Sep 1993 there were 856 km *532 miles* of shelving and 5033 employees.
(Photos: Library of Congress)

A view of the main building from the street.

Bookshops The bookshop with most titles and the longest shelving (48 km *30 miles*) in the world is W. & G. Foyle Ltd of London. Established in 1904 in a small shop in Islington, the company is now at 113–119 Charing Cross Road in premises measuring 7044 m² *75,825 ft²*. The most capacious individual bookstore in the world measured by square footage is the Barnes & Noble Bookstore at 105 Fifth Ave at 18th Street, New York City, USA. It covers 14,330 m² *154,250 ft²* and has 20.71 km *12.87 miles* of shelving.

Libraries and Museums

Largest library The United States Library of Congress (founded on 24 Apr 1800) in Washington, DC, USA contains 104,834,652 items.

UK The largest library in the United Kingdom is the British Library, comprising 19 buildings in London and a 24.3 ha *60 acre* site at Boston Spa, W Yorks, and with a total staff of some 2500. The Library contains over 18 million volumes. Stock increases involve over 12.8 km *8 miles* of new shelving annually. The Newspaper Library at Colindale, north London, opened in 1932, has 583,000 volumes and parcels comprising 70,000 different titles on 35.4 km *22 miles* of shelving. The Document Supply Centre in West Yorks (shelf capacity 157.7 km *98 miles*) runs the largest library inter-lending operation in the world; it handles annually over 3 million requests from other libraries (UK and overseas) for items they do not hold in stock. The National Sound Archive holds 1 million discs and 62,000 hours of recorded tape.

CD-ROM MicroPatent of East Haven, Connecticut, USA, the commercial publisher of patent information, has a collection of 1580 discs containing almost 20 million pages of every US utility patent. It is the largest CD-ROM library in the world.

The highest attendance for any museum is over 118,437 (with the doors temporarily closed) on 14 Apr 1984 at the Smithsonian's National Air and Space Museum, Washington, DC, USA, opened in July 1976.

Overdue!

The record for an unreturned and overdue library book was set when a book in German on the Archbishop of Bremen, published in 1609, was borrowed from Sidney Sussex College, Cambridge by Colonel Robert Walpole in 1667–68. It was found by Prof. Sir John Plumb in the library of the then Marquess of Cholmondeley at Houghton Hall, Norfolk and returned 288 years later. No fine was exacted.

Newspapers

Oldest A copy has survived of a news pamphlet published in Cologne, Germany in 1470. The oldest existing newspaper in the world is the Swedish official journal *Post och Inrikes Tidningar*, founded in 1645 and published by the Royal Swedish Academy of Letters.

Heaviest The most massive single issues of a newspaper have been of the *Sunday New York Times*, which by August 1987 had reached 6.35 kg *14 lb*.

Largest *UK* The *Worcestershire Chronicle* was the largest British newspaper, and a surviving issue of 16 Feb 1859 measures 82 × 57 cm *32¼ × 22½ in*.

Smallest The smallest original page size was 7.6 × 9.5 cm *3 × 3¾ in* for the *Daily Banner* (25 cents per month) of Roseberg, Oregon, USA. Issues dated 1 and 2 Feb 1876 survive.

Longest editorship The longest editorship of any UK national newspaper was 57 years by C.P. (Charles Prestwich) Scott (1846–1932) of the *Manchester Guardian* (the *Guardian* from 1959),

The initial print order for the new postcode directory produced by Deutsche Bundespost for United Germany was 42,300,000 copies. Issued on 1 Jul 1993, the print run took 59,220 tons of paper and 2,480 trucks to transport. The publications were distributed to 36,300,000 homes and businesses.

The aggregate print run of *The Highway Code* (instituted 1931) has reached 113.3 million to May 1994.

Fiction The highest print order for a work of fiction in the UK was 3 million by Penguin Books Ltd for their paperback edition of *Lady Chatterley's Lover*, by D.H. (David Herbert) Lawrence (1885–1930). Total sales to April 1994 were in excess of 4,900,000 copies.

GUESS WHAT?

Q What children's story constituted the world's smallest book?

A See Page 138

By the book

ZIMBABWE INTERNATIONAL BOOK FAIR 1993

The cover of the book.

A page from the finished product.

On 5th Aug 1993, the record for the fastest publishing of a book was broken resoundingly at the annual Zimbabwe Book Fair. The book was an anthology of Zimbabwean poetry and prose on the importance of reading and learning. The final production was more than twice as fast as the previous world record.

Before the record attempt began, and in full view of the visitors at the book fair, authors, editors, sub-editors, proof-readers, illustrators and typesetters worked together to produce the required copy on computer by the evening of Thursday 5 August. They completed their work within one day. Then the record-breaker really began: the printers were standing by to print the book against the clock; starting at 4:04 p.m., they completed it in less than five and a half hours. By the end of the evening they had exceeded even their own target, printing a total of 2000 copies of the publication.

To improve their record even further, the book was also produced in four other formats on the same day: Braille (8 hours 19 min), Large Print (8 hours 18 min), CD-ROM and audio-tape (11 hours 26 min).

THE CHALLENGE

To print 1000 books of 100 pages in less than 12 hours 0 minutes.

Text: Printed 1 colour throughout with about 8 line drawings, from disk to ready copy

Binding: sections of text folded and thread-sewn into covers

Cover: Printed two colours on one side only from copy

Number of books to be printed: 1000

The first half-hour: touching up the film (above and right).

Between 6.33 pm and 8.54 pm: binding.

The first half-hour: typesetting the pages.

9.27 pm: Mission accomplished!

4:04 P.M.
Printed out supplied disk.
'Paginated' the book: separated and laid out the pages in correct order to produce film.
Processed film.
Prepared plates for printing machines.

4:35 P.M.
Printed cover in 2 colours on one side only.
Printed various sections that will constitute book: 3 sections of 32 pages, 1 section of 4 pages, totalling 100 pages.

6:33 P.M.
Folded all sections and collated into book units.
Sewed all units and combined with covers.
Trimmed and Finished.

8:54 P.M.
1000 copies were printed—the previous record was broken.

9:27 P.M.
A further 1000 beyond the target were printed. Time taken: 5 hours 23 minutes.

Sir Etienne Dupuch (1899–91) of Nassau, Bahamas was editor-in-chief of *Tribune* from 1 Apr 1919 to 1972, and contributing editor until his death on 23 Aug 1991, a total of 72 years.
(Photo: R Chapman for Guinness Publishing)

The largest issue of a newspaper ever produced and circulated was the 14 Jun 1993 edition of the daily newspaper 'Het Volk', which was published in Gent, Belgium with a page size of 142 × 99.5 cm 55.9 × 39.2 in. It sold 50,000 copies.
(Photo: Gamma/Lebrun/Photo News)

who occupied the post from the age of 26 in 1872 until his retirement in 1929.

Most durable feature Mary MacArthur of Port Appin, Strathclyde has contributed a regular feature to *The Oban Times and West Highland Times* since 1926.

Most durable advertiser The Jos Neel Co., a clothing store in Macon, Georgia, USA (founded 1880) has run an 'ad' in the *Macon Telegraph* every day in the upper left corner of page 2 since 22 Feb 1889, a total of 37,325 times to March 1992.

Most advertising pages The greatest number of pages of advertisements sold in a single issue of a periodical is 829.54 by the October 1989 edition of *Business Week*.

Most syndicated columnist Ann Landers (*née* Eppie Lederer, b. 4 Jul 1918) appears in over 1200 newspapers with an estimated readership of 90 million. Her only serious rival is 'Dear Abby' (Mrs Pauline Phillips), her identical twin sister based in Beverly Hills, California, USA.

Circulation

Highest The highest circulation for any newspaper in the world was that for *Komsomolskaya Pravda* (founded 1925), the youth paper of the former Soviet Communist Party, which reached a peak daily circulation of 21,975,000 copies in May 1990. The eight-page weekly newspaper *Argumenty i Fakty* (founded 1978) of Moscow, USSR attained a figure of 33,431,100 copies in May 1990, when it had a estimated readership of over 100 million.

The highest circulation for any *currently* published newspaper is that of *The Yomiuri Shimbun*, founded 1874, which publishes morning and evening editions, and had a combined daily circulation of 14.552 million as of January 1994. The implication of these figures is that 1 out of every 4.3 households in Japan reads *The Yomiuri Shimbun*.

UK The *News of the World* (founded 1 Oct 1843) attained peak sales of 8,480,878 copies in April 1951 and had an estimated readership of over 19 million. The latest sales figure is 4.7 million copies per issue, with an estimated readership of 12.5 million. The highest net sale of any daily newspaper in the UK is 4.0 million, with an estimated readership of 10.0 million at March 1994 for *The Sun*.

Periodicals

Oldest The oldest continuing periodical in the world is *Philosophical Transactions of the Royal Society*, published in London, which first appeared on 6 Mar 1665. Britain's oldest weekly periodical is *The Lancet*, first published in 1823.

Annual The most durable annual is *Old Moore's Almanack*, published since 1697, when it

appeared as a broadsheet produced by Dr Francis Moore (1657–1715) of Southwark, London to advertise his 'physiks'. Published by W. Foulsham & Co. Ltd of Slough, Berks, its aggregate sales to date is over 113 million.

Largest circulations Total sales through non-commercial channels by Jehovah's Witnesses of *The Truth that Leads to Eternal Life*, published by the Watchtower Bible and Tract Society of New York City, USA on 8 May 1968, reached 107,619,787 in 117 languages by April 1994.

The peak circulation of any weekly periodical was achieved by the US *TV Guide* which, in 1974, became the first magazine to sell a billion copies in a year. In its 45 basic international editions, *Reader's Digest* (established February 1922) circulates 28 million copies monthly in 17 languages, including a US edition of more than 16.72 million copies and a UK edition (established 1939) of over 1.6 million copies 1990). Readership in the UK alone was estimated at 6,418,000 between April and September 1993.

Parade, the US syndicated colour magazine, has been distributed with 352 newspapers every Sunday since 18 Jul 1993, giving a peak circulation of 36.73 million.

UK Before deregulation of the listings market in March 1991, the highest circulation of any periodical in Britain was that of the *Radio Times* (instituted on 28 Sep 1923). The highest sales figure for any issue was 11,037,139 copies for the 1989 Christmas edition.

Largest The bulkiest consumer magazine ever published was the 10 Jan 1990 issue of *Shukan Jutaku Joho* (Weekly Housing Information), running to 1940 pages. Published in Japan by the Recruit Company Ltd, it retailed for 350 yen.

Comic Strip!

The earliest cartoon is 'The Yellow Kid', which first appeared in the *New York Journal* on 18 Oct 1896.

The longest-lived newspaper comic strip is the 'Katzenjammer Kids' (Hans and Fritz), created by Rudolph Dirks and first published in the *New York Journal* on 12 Dec 1897.

The most syndicated strip is 'Peanuts' by Charles Schulz of Santa Rosa, California, USA. First published in October 1950, it currently appears in 2300 newspapers in 68 countries and 26 languages. In 1990 Schulz's income was estimated at $5 million per month.

In July 1982 Robert Turcot of Québec, Canada compiled a crossword comprising 82,951 squares. It contained 12,489 clues across, 13,125 down and covered 3.55 m² 38.28 ft².

Fastest!

Dr John Sykes (1929–93) won The Times/ Collins Dictionaries championship 10 times between 1972 and 1990, when he solved each of the four puzzles in an average time of 8 min and beat the field by a record margin of 9½ min on 8 Sep at the Hilton hotel, London. He set a championship best time of 4 min 28 sec in 1989.

ON THE RECORD

C R O S S W O R D S

C	**O M P I L I N G**		**S**
O			**O**
			L
			V
			I
			N
			G

Compiling the Crosswords...

Roger F Squires of Ironbridge, Shrops compiles 38 puzzles single-handedly each week. His total output to September 1994 was over 44,000 crosswords and his millionth clue was published in The Daily Telegraph on 6 Sep 1989.

" I joined the Royal Navy as a boy seaman straight from Wolverhampton Grammar School at the age of 15. By the age of 22 I was a Lieutenant flying in the Fleet Air Arm. In between periods at sea, our squadron was based near Helston and we suffered many 'Cornish Clamps' when heavy sea mist and rain rolled in calling a halt to any flying. I was a keen amateur magician and one of my favourite tricks was to deal myself 13 spades from a shuffled pack. When flying was held up I used to fill in the time by solving crosswords, until I was completing 12 a day. When we returned to sea in an aircraft-carrier there were long stretches without newspapers and I began compiling puzzles. Eventually I sold my first one, to the *Radio Times*.

I have always treated crosswords as an extension of being a magician—I try to mystify, but primarily, to entertain. I am one of only three compilers that have had puzzles published in all the 'quality' newspapers: *The Times*, *The Daily Telegraph*, *The Financial Times*, *The Guardian* and *The Independent*, as well as a high number of national newspapers and periodicals. Since I began, I have filed every clue with signs indicating in which outlet it appeared. This means I do not repeat a clue in the same newspaper, a good clue may appear over the years in different outlets and the 90,000 clues currently on file can give me ideas when trying to think of a new one. A 'quality' paper crossword can take me a whole day, but some quick puzzles can take 20 minutes.

My favourite clue, because of its inherent simplicity, is 'A Stiff examination' for 'Post Mortem'. "

...and solving them

Roy Dean of Bromley, Kent holds the record for the fastest recorded time for completing The Times crossword—3 min 45 sec in the BBC Today radio studio on 19 Dec 1970. On average it takes him 10 minutes to complete *The Times* crossword every day.

" In 1976 I was on the Foreign Office desk dealing with our economic relations with the Indian subcontinent. We had become concerned that our two-way trade with India was not flourishing as well as it should, and following talks with Indian officials it was agreed that trade relations would benefit from the formal framework of a bilateral economic cooperation agreement. The terms were drawn up, and I travelled to Delhi with Peter Shore, the Secretary of State for Trade, for the official signing of the agreement.

We were cordially received and entertained by our Indian counterparts. Naturally Mr Shore wished to call on Mrs Indira Gandhi. But it became clear that wheras the Indian Prime Minister would have been glad to meet her British opposite number officially, in accordance with strict protocol she would not be able to see a mere trade minister.

I discussed the problem with her private secretary. He had mentioned to Mrs Gandhi that I was a crossword champion. She herself liked to relax from the cares of office with a puzzle at the end of the day, and she expressed an interest in meeting me. Thus it came about that I was ushered into her sanctum for a chat about our shared enthusiasm, with my Minister waiting in the wings. I was privileged to enjoy an informal conversation with Mrs Gandhi for ten minutes. Once the ice was broken, the Minister was invited to pay a courtesy call on her and conduct his official business, which he did very successfully. Of such is the stuff of diplomacy. "

Music

Madeleine Marie Robin (1918–60), the French operatic coloratura, could produce and sustain the B above high C in the mad scene in Donizetti's *Lucia di Lammermoor*. Since 1950 singers have achieved high and low notes far beyond the hitherto accepted extremes. However, notes at the bass and treble extremities of the register tend to lack harmonics and are of little musical value. Dan Britton of Branson, Missouri, USA can produce the note E-0 (18.84Hz).

The highest note put into song is Giv first occurring in Mozart's *Popoli di Tessaglia*.

The lowest vocal note in the classical repertoire is in Mozart's *Die Entführung aus dem Serail* in

Ivan Rebroff, the German bass, singing in a shower. Rebroff has a voice extending easily over four octaves from low F to high F, 1¼ octaves above C. This is one of the greatest voice ranges possessed by any living singer.
(Photo: Gamma/A Skopelos)

Osmin's aria which calls for a low D (73.4Hz).

Songs

Oldest The *shaduf* chant has been sung since time immemorial by irrigation workers on the man-powered, pivoted-rod bucket raisers of the Nile water mills (or *saqiyas*) in Egypt. An Assyrian love song, from *c.* 1800 BC to an Ugaritic god from a tablet of notation and lyric was reconstructed for an 11-string lyre at the University of California, Berkeley, USA on 6 Mar 1974.

The oldest known harmonized music performed today is the English song *Sumer is icumen in*, which dates from *c.* 1240.

National anthems The oldest national anthem is the *Kimigayo* of Japan, the words of which date from the 9th century, whilst the oldest music belongs to the anthem of the Netherlands. The

GUESS WHAT?

Q What country has the most TV sets?

A See Page 159

shortest anthems are those of Japan, Jordan and San Marino, each with only four lines. Of the 11 wordless national anthems, the oldest is that of Spain, dating from 1770.

Longest rendering of national anthem 'God Save the King' was played non-stop 16 or 17 times by a German military band on the platform of Rathenau railway station, Brandenburg, Germany on the morning of 9 Feb 1909. The reason was that King Edward VII was struggling inside the train with the uniform of a German field-marshal before he could emerge.

Worst!

While no agreement exists as to the identity of history's greatest singer, there is unanimity on the worst. The excursions of the soprano Florence Foster Jenkins (1868–1944) into lieder and even high coloratura culminated on 25 Oct 1944 in her sell-out concert at the Carnegie Hall, New York City, USA. The diva's (already high) high F was said to have been made higher in 1943 by a crash in a taxi. It is one of the tragedies of musicology that Madame Jenkins' *Clavelitos*, accompanied by Cosmo McMoon, was never recorded for posterity.

Top songs The most frequently sung songs in English are *Happy Birthday to You* (based on the original *Good Morning to All*), by Kentucky Sunday School teachers Mildred Hill and Patty Smith Hill of New York, USA (written in 1893 and under copyright from 1935 to 2010); *For He's a Jolly Good Fellow* (originally the French *Malbrouk*), known at least as early as 1781, and *Auld Lang Syne* (originally the Strathspey *I Fee'd a Lad at Michaelmass*), some words of which were written by Robert Burns (1759–96).

Songwriters!

The most successful songwriters in terms of number one singles are John Lennon (1940–80) and Paul McCartney (b. 18 Jun 1942). McCartney is credited as writer on 32 number one hits in the US to Lennon's 26 (with 23 co-written), whereas Lennon authored 29 UK number ones to McCartney's 28 (25 co-written).

Singer's pulling power In 1850, up to $653 was paid for a single seat at the US concerts of Johanna ('Jenny') Maria Lind (1820–87), the 'Swedish nightingale'. She had a vocal range from g to e[111].

Earliest hymn There are more than 950,000 Christian hymns in existence. The music and parts of the text of a hymn in the *Oxyrhynchus Papyri* from the 2nd century are the earliest known hymnody. The earliest exactly datable hymn is the *Heyr Himna Smíóur* (*Hear, the Maker of Heaven*) from 1208 by the Icelandic bard and chieftain Kolbeinn Tumason (1173–1208).

Longest hymn The *Hora novissima tempora pessima sunt; vigilemus* by Bernard of Cluny (mid 12th century) runs to 2966 lines. The longest in English is *The Sands of Time are Sinking* by Anne Ross Cousin (*née* Cundell, 1824–1906), which has 152 lines, though only 32 lines appear in the Methodist Hymn Book.

Most prolific hymnists Frances (Fanny) Jane van Alstyne (1820–1915) of the US wrote 8500 hymns, and is reputed to have finished one hymn in 15 minutes. Charles Wesley (1707–88) wrote about 6000 hymns.

Bells

Oldest The world's oldest bell is the tintinnabulum found in the Babylonian Palace of Nimrod in 1849 by Austen (later Sir) Henry Layard (1817–94), dating from *c.* 1100 BC. The oldest known tower bell is one in St Benedict Church, Rome, Italy dated 'anno domini millesimo sexagesimo IX' (1069).

UK The fragile hand bell known as the Black or Iron Bell of St Patrick is dated *c.* AD 450. The oldest tower bell in Great Britain is one of 50 kg *1 cwt* at St Botolph, Hardham, Sussex, still in use and dated *ante* 1100.

Heaviest The Tsar Kolokol, cast by Russian brothers I.F. and M.I. Motorin on 25 Nov 1735 in Moscow, weighs 202 tonnes and measures 6.6 m *22 ft* in diameter, 6.14 m *20 ft* high and 60 cm *24 in* at its thickest point. The bell was cracked in a fire in 1737 and a fragment, weighing about 11.5 tonnes, was broken off. The bell has stood, unrung, on a platform in the Kremlin in Moscow since 1836 with the broken section alongside.

The heaviest bell still in use is the Mingun bell, weighing 92 tonnes with a diameter of 5.09 m *16 ft 8½ in* at the lip, in Mandalay, Myanmar (Burma). The bell is struck by a teak boom from the outside. It was cast at Mingun late in the reign of King Bodawpaya (1782–1819).

UK The heaviest bell hung in Great Britain is 'Great Paul' in the south-west tower of St Paul's Cathedral, London. Cast in 1881, it weighs 17 tonnes, has a diameter of 2.9 m *9 ft 6½ in* and sounds the note E-flat.

Most broadcast bell 'Big Ben', the hour bell in the clock tower of the House of Commons, was cast in 1858 and weighs 13.8 tonnes. It plays the note E natural.

Bell ringing Eight bells have been rung to their full 'extent' (40,320 unrepeated changes of Plain Bob Major) only once without relays. This took place in a bell foundry at Loughborough, Leics, beginning at 6:52 a.m. on 27 Jul 1963 and ending at 12:50 a.m. on 28 July, after 17 hr 58 min. The peal was composed by Kenneth Lewis of Altrincham, Manchester and the eight ringers were conducted by Robert B. Smith of Marple, Manchester. Theoretically it would take 37 years 355 days to ring 12 bells (maximus) to their full extent of 479,001,600 changes.

Oldest!

George Symonds (1875–1974) of Ipswich, Suffolk was a regular bell-ringer for 89 years. He conducted a peal at the age of 97 and rang his last peal in 1973 at the age of 98. He is thus the oldest ringer ever to have conducted and rung a peal, and also the longest-serving ringer.

The youngest was Jonathan Carpenter of Warfield, Berks, who rang his first peal at Warfield Church on 19 Jun 1982 at the age of 7 years and 299 days.

> The grandest grand piano was one of 1.25 tonnes and 3.55 m *11 ft 8 in* in length made by Chas H. Challen & Son Ltd of London in 1935. The longest bass string measured 3.02 m *9 ft 11 in*, with a tensile strength of 30 tonnes.

Most peals rung The greatest number of peals (minimum of 5000 changes, all in tower bells) rung in a year is 303, by Colin Turner of Abingdon, Oxon in 1989.

As of 1 Jan 1994 both John Mayne of St Albans, Herts and Peter Border of Barford, Warks had rung in more than 3000 peals.

Instruments

Most expensive piano The highest price ever paid for a piano was $390,000 (£167,800) at Sotheby Parke Bernet, New York, USA on 26 Mar 1980 for a Steinway grand of *c.* 1888 sold by the Martin Beck Theater. It was bought by a non-pianist.

Largest organ The largest and loudest musical instrument ever constructed is the now only partially functional Auditorium Organ in Atlantic City, New Jersey, USA. Completed in 1930, this heroic instrument had two consoles (one with seven manuals and another movable one with five), 1477 stop controls and 33,112 pipes, ranging in tone from 4.7 mm *⅛ in* to the 19.5-m *64-ft* tone. It had the volume of 25 brass bands, with a range of seven octaves.

Fully-functional The world's largest fully functional organ is the six manual 30,067 pipe Grand Court Organ installed in the Wanamaker Store, Philadelphia, Pennsylvania, USA in 1911 and enlarged between then and 1930. It has a 19.5-m *64-ft* tone gravissima pipe.

UK The largest organ in Great Britain is that completed in Liverpool Anglican Cathedral on 18 Oct 1926,

A drum kit consisting of 112 pieces—88 drums, 18 cymbals, 4 hi-hats, 1 gong, 1 cowbell and various other assorted accessories—was constructed by Jeffrey Carlo of Brentwood, New York, USA in 1990.

The world's largest acoustic guitar props up the workforce that produced it: Christopher Challen (current project designer), Anthony Dale (current education co-ordinator), Jem Le Livre, Lucy Coad, Ian Blythe and Julian Thompson. It is 8.66 m *28 ft 5 in* long and 0.972 m *3 ft 2 in* deep and is exhibited at the Stradivarium exhibition in The Exploratory, Bristol. The dimensions were enlarged from the proportions of the classical guitar made by Antonius Stradivarius in the Ashmolean Museum, Oxford, and when played the five strings resonate very impressively.

(Photo: The Stradivarium)

Largest guitar The largest (and possibly the loudest) playable guitar in the world is 11.63 m *38 ft 2 in* tall, 4.87 m *16 ft* wide and weighs 446 kg *1865 lb*. Modelled on the Gibson 'Flying V', it was made by students of Shakamak High School in Jasonville, Indiana, USA. The instrument was unveiled on 17 May 1991 when, powered by six amplifiers, it was played simultaneously by six members of the school.

Most expensive guitar A Fender Stratocaster belonging to Jimi Hendrix (1942–70) was sold by his former drummer 'Mitch' Mitchell for £198,000 at Sotheby's, London on 25 Apr 1990.

Most valuable violin The highest price paid at auction for

> **Four hundred separate drums were played in 20.50 sec by Carl Williams at the Alexander Stadium, Birmingham, W Mids on 4 Oct 1992.**

with two five-manual consoles and 9704 speaking pipes (originally 10,936) ranging from 1.9 cm *¾ in* to 9.75 m *32 ft*.

Loudest organ stop The Ophicleide stop of the Grand Great in the Solo Organ in the Atlantic City Auditorium (see above) is operated by a pressure of water 24 kPa *3½ lb/in²* and has a pure trumpet note of ear-splitting volume, more than six times the volume of the loudest locomotive whistles.

Largest brass instrument The largest recorded brass instrument is a contrabass tuba standing 2.28 m *7½ ft* tall, with 11.8 m *39 ft* of tubing and a bell 1 m *3 ft 4 in* across. This tuba was constructed for a world tour by the band of American composer John Philip Sousa (1854–1932), c. 1896–98. It is now owned by a circus promoter in South Africa.

Largest stringed instrument The largest movable stringed instrument ever constructed was a pantaleon with 270 strings stretched over 4.6 m² *50 ft²* used by George Noel in 1767. The

> **On 14 Dec 1991 the 2000-piece 'Young People's Orchestra and Chorus of Mexico', consisting of 53 youth orchestras from Mexico plus musicians from Venezuela and the former USSR, gave a full classical concert conducted by Fernando Lozano and others at the Magdalena Mixhiuca Sports Centre, Mexico City.**

greatest number of musicians required to operate a single instrument was the six required to play the gigantic orchestrion, known as the Apollonican, built in 1816 and played until 1840.

Largest double bass A double bass measuring 4.26 m *14 ft* tall was built in 1924 in Ironia, New Jersey, USA by Arthur K. Ferris, allegedly on orders from the Archangel Gabriel. It weighed 590 kg *1301 lb* with a sound box 2.43 m *8 ft* across, and had leathern strings totalling 31.7 m *104 ft*. Its low notes could be felt rather than heard.

Sixteen musicians played a double bass simultaneously (five fingering and eleven bowing) in a rendition of Strauss' *Perpetuum Mobile* at Blandford Town Hall on 6 Jun 1989.

Durable!

The Romanian pianist Cella Delavrancea (1887–1991) gave her last public recital, receiving six encores, at the age of 103. Yiannis Pipis (b. 25 Nov 1889) of Nicosia, Cyprus has been a professional Folkloric violinist since 1912.

The world's oldest active musician is Jennie Newhouse (b. 12 Jul 1889) of High Bentham, N Yorks, who has been the regular organist at the church of St Boniface in Bentham since 1920.

---

a violin, or any instrument, is £902,000 ($1.7 million) for the 1720 'Mendelssohn' Stradivarius, named after the German banking family who were descendants of the composer. It was sold to a mystery buyer at Christie's, London on 21 Nov 1990.

Most valuable 'cello The highest ever auction price for a violoncello is £682,000 paid at Sotheby's, London on 22 Jun 1988 for a Stradivarius known as 'The Cholmondeley', which was made in Cremona, Italy c. 1698.

Largest drum A drum with a 3.96 m *13 ft* diameter was built by the Supreme Drum Co., London and played at the Royal Festival Hall, London on 31 May 1987.

Orchestras

Oldest The first modern symphony orchestra—basically four sections consisting of woodwind, brass, percussion and bowed string instruments—was founded at the court of Duke Karl Theodor

Arts and Entertainment

The Austrian Herbert von Karajan (1908–89), principal conductor of the Berlin Philharmonic Orchestra for 35 years, was the most prolific conductor ever, having made over 800 recordings covering all the major works. Von Karajan also conducted the Philharmonia Orchestra of London, the Vienna State Opera and La Scala Opera of Milan; he founded the Salzburg Easter Festival in 1967.
(Photo: Deutsche Grammophon/Image Select)

men at the Ullevaal Stadium, Oslo, Norway from Norges Musikkorps Forbund bands on 28 Jun 1964.

Excluding 'sing alongs' by stadium crowds, the greatest choir is one of 60,000, which sang in unison as a finale of a choral contest among 160,000 participants in Breslau, Germany on 2 Aug 1937.

One-man Rory Blackwell, aided by his double left-footed perpendicular percussion-pounder, plus his three-tier right-footed horizontal 22-pronged differential beater, and his 12-outlet bellow-powered horn-blower, played 108 different instruments (19 melody and 89 percussion) simultaneously in Dawlish, Devon on 29 May 1989. He also played 314 instruments in a single rendition in 1 min 23.07 sec, again at Dawlish, on 27 May 1985.

Most Grammy awards An all-time record 31 awards to an individual (including a special Trustees' award presented in 1967) have been won since 1958 by the British conductor, Sir Georg Solti (b. Budapest, Hungary, 21 Oct 1912).

The Chicago Symphony Orchestra, whose principal conductor is Sir Georg Solti, has won 46 awards.

Bottle!

In an extraordinary display of oral campanology, the Brighton Bottle Orchestra—Terry Garoghan and Peter Miller—performed a musical medley on 444 miniature Gordon's gin bottles at the Brighton International Festival, E Sussex on 21 May 1991. It took 18 hours to tune the bottles, and about 10 times the normal rate of puff (90 breaths/min) to play them. Apparently there is no risk of intoxication, as the bottles are filled with water.

at Mannheim, Germany in 1743. The oldest existing symphony orchestra, the Gewandhaus Orchestra of Leipzig, Germany, was also established in 1743. Originally known as the Grosses Concert and later as the Musikübende Gesellshaft, its current name dates from 1781.

Largest On 17 Jun 1872, Johann Strauss the younger (1825–99) conducted an orchestra of 987 pieces supported by a choir of 20,000 at the World Peace Jubilee in Boston, Massachusetts, USA. The number of first violinists was 400.

Largest band The most massive band ever assembled was one of 20,100 bands

The largest marching band was one of 6017 players—including 927 majorettes and standard-bearers—on 27 Jun 1993. They marched for 940 m *3084 ft* at Stafsberg Airport in Hamar, Norway, under the direction of Odd Aspli, Chairman of Hamar County Council.
(Photo: Brox Reklamefoto)

GUESS WHAT?

Q How late was the world's most overdue book?

A See Page 142

The greatest number won in a year is eight by Michael Jackson in 1984.

Concert Attendances

Estimating the size of audiences at open-air events where no admission is paid is often left to the police, media reporters, promoters and publicity agents. Estimates therefore vary widely and it is very difficult to check the accuracy of claims.

Rock/pop festival The best claim is believed to be 725,000 for Steve Wozniak's 1983 US Festival in San Bernardino, California. The Woodstock Music and Art Fair held on 15–17 Aug 1969 at Bethel, New York, USA is thought to have attracted an audience of 300–500,000. The attendance at the 3rd Pop Festival at East Afton Farm, Freshwater, Isle of Wight on 30 Aug 1970 was claimed by its promoters, Fiery Creations, to be 400,000.

An estimated record 800,000 attended a free open-air concert by the New York Philharmonic conducted by Zubin Mehta, on the Great Lawn of Central Park, New York, USA on 5 Jul 1986, as part of the Statue of Liberty Weekend.

Solo performer The largest *paying* audience ever attracted by a solo performer was an estimated 180–184,000 in the Maracaña Stadium, Rio de Janeiro, Brazil to hear Paul McCartney (b. 1942) on 21 Apr 1990. A figure of 180,000 has also been quoted for the attendance of Tina Turner's (b. Natbush, Tennessee, USA; 26 Nov 1938) concert there in 1988.

Jean-Michel Jarre, the *son et lumière* specialist, entertained an estimated audience of 2 million in Paris, France at a free concert on Bastille day (14 July) 1990.

Most successful tour The Rolling Stones 1989 'Steel Wheels' North American tour earned an estimated £185 million ($310 million) and was attended by 3.2 million people in 30 cities.

The longest single aria, in the sense of an operatic solo, is Brünnhilde's immolation scene in Wagner's Götter-dämmerung, a well-known recording of which has been timed at 14 min 46 sec precisely.

Wembley Stadium Michael Jackson sold out seven nights at Wembley Stadium, performing to a total audience of 504,000 on 14, 15, 16, 22, 23 Jul and 26, 27 Aug 1988.

Largest concert On 21 Jul 1990 Potsdamer Platz, straddling East and West Berlin, was the site of the largest single rock concert in terms of participants and organisation ever staged. Roger Waters' production of Pink Floyd's *The Wall* involved 600 people performing on a stage measuring 168×25m *551×82ft* at its highest point. An estimated 200,000 people gathered for the building and demolition of a wall made of 2500 styrofoam blocks symbolising the demise of the Berlin Wall.

Composers

Most prolific The most prolific composer was Georg Philipp Telemann (1681–1767) of Germany. He wrote 12 complete sets of services (one cantata every Sunday) for a year, 78 services for special occasions, 40 operas, 600 to 700 orchestral suites, 44 passions, as well as concertos, sonatas and other chamber music. The most prolific symphonist was Johann Melchior Molter (*c.* 1695–1765) of Germany with over 170. Franz Joseph Haydn (1732–1809) of Austria wrote 108 numbered symphonies, many of which are regularly played today.

Longest symphony The symphony *Victory at Sea*, written by Richard Rodgers for the documentary film of the same name and arranged by Robert Russell Bennett for NBC TV in 1952, lasted 13 hours.

Opera

Longest The longest of commonly performed operas is *Die Meistersinger von Nürnberg* by Wilhelm Richard Wagner (1813–83) of Germany. A normal uncut version as performed by the Sadler's Wells company between 24 Aug and 19 Sep 1968 entailed 5hr 15min of music.

Shortest The shortest opera published is *The Sands of Time* by Simon Rees and Peter Reynolds, first performed by Rhian Owen and Dominic Burns on 27 Mar 1993 at The Hayes, Cardiff, S Glam and lasting for 4 min 9 sec. A shorter performance, lasting only 3 min 34 sec, was then achieved under the direction of Peter Reynolds at BBC Television Centre, London, on 14 Sep 1993.

Longest operatic encore The longest encore listed in the *Concise Oxford Dictionary of Opera*, was of the entire opera Cimarosa's *Il Matrimonio Segreto* at its première in 1792. This was at the command of the Austro-Hungarian Emperor Leopold II (reigned 1790–92).

Youngest opera singers Ginetta Gloria La Bianca, born in Buffalo, New York, USA on 12 May 1934, sang Rosina in *The Barber of Seville* at the Teatro dell'Opera, Rome, Italy on 8 May 1950 aged 15 years 361 days, having appeared as Gilda in *Rigoletto* at Velletri 45 days earlier on 24 March.

Oldest opera singers The tenor Giovanni Martinelli sang the part of Emperor Altoum in *Turandot* in Seattle, Washington, USA on 4 Feb 1967 when aged 81.

Longest career Danshi Toyotake (b. Yoshie Yokota, 1891–1989) of Hyogo, Japan sang *Musume Gidayu* (traditional Japanese narrative) for 91 years from the age of seven. Her professional career spanned 81 years.

Largest opera houses The Metropolitan Opera House at the Lincoln Center, New York City, USA, completed in September 1966 at a cost of $45.7 million, has a seating and standing room capacity of 4065, with seating for 3800 in the 137m *451ft* deep auditorium. The stage is 70m *230ft* wide and 45m *148ft* deep.

Applause!

On 24 Feb 1988 Luciano Pavarotti (b. 12 Oct 1935) received 165 curtain calls and was applauded for 1hr 7min after singing the part of Nemorino in Gaetano Donizetti's *L'elisir d'amore* at the Deutsche Oper in Berlin, Germany.

The greatest recorded number of curtain calls ever received at a ballet is 89 by Dame Margot Fonteyn de Arias (née Margaret Evelyn Hookham (1919–91) and Rudolf Hametovich Nureyev (1938–93) after a performance of *Swan Lake* at the Vienna Staatsoper, Austria in October 1964.

Placido Domingo (b. 21 Jan 1941) was applauded for 1hr 20min through 101 curtain calls after a performance of *Othello* at the Vienna Staatsoper on 30 Jul 1991.

Ballet

Fastest 'entrechat douze' In the *entrechat* (a vertical spring from the fifth position with the legs extended criss-crossing at the lower calf), the starting and finishing position each count as one, such that in an *entrechat douze* there are 5 crossings and uncrossings. This was performed by Wayne Sleep (b. 17 Jul 1948) for the BBC *Record Breakers* programme on 7 Jan 1973. He was in the air for 0.71 sec.

Grands jetés On 28 Nov 1988 Wayne Sleep completed 158 *grands jetés* along the length of Dunston Staiths, Gateshead, Tyne & Wear in 2 min.

Most turns The greatest number of spins called for in classical ballet choreography is 32 *fouettés rond de jambe en tournant* in *Swan Lake* by Pyotr Ilyich Chaykovskiy (Tchaikovsky) (1840–93). Delia Gray (b. 30 Oct 1975) of Bishop's Stortford, Herts achieved 166 such turns during the Harlow Ballet School's summer workshop at The Playhouse, Harlow, Essex on 2 Jun 1991.

The largest number of ballet dancers used in a production in Britain has been 2000 in the London Coster Ballet of 1962, directed by Lillian Rowley, at the Royal Albert Hall, London.

Recorded Sound

Smallest cassette The NT digital cassette made by the Sony Corporation of Japan for use in dictating machines measures just 30×21×5mm *1¹/₅ × ⁴/₅ × ¹/₅ in.*

Smallest functional record Six titles of 33.3mm *1⁵/₁₆ in* diameter were recorded by HMV's studio at Hayes, Middx on 26 Jan 1923 for Queen Mary's Dolls' House. Some 92,000 of these miniature records were pressed including 35,000 of *God Save The King* (Bb 2439).

Most successful solo recording artist Both Elvis Aron Presley (1935–77) Harry Lillis (alias

Silence!

The longest interval between the known composition of a major composer and its performance in the manner intended is from 3 Mar 1791 until 9 Oct 1982 (over 191 years), in the case of Mozart's *Organ Piece for a Clock*, a fugue fantasy in F minor (K 608), arranged by the organ builders Wm Hill & Son and Norman & Beard Ltd at Glyndebourne, E Sussex.

Successful!

Kylie Minogue (b. 28 May 1968), whose debut album *Kylie* topped the chart in July 1988, holds the record for the best-ever start to a singles chart career, with her first 10 singles reaching the Top 5.

Bing) Crosby Jr (1904–77) could be considered for this title. Elvis Presley has had over 170 major hit singles and over 80 top-selling albums since 1956. He holds the record for the most number one hits, with 17, and his music has spent a record total of 1145 weeks on the chart.

Bing Crosby made more recordings than Presley, with 2600 singles and 125 albums cut in his lifetime. On 9 Jun 1960 the Hollywood Chamber of Commerce presented him with a platinum disc to commemorate the sale of 200 million records; on 15 Sep 1970 he received a second platinum disc when Decca claimed sales of 300,650,000 discs.

Most recordings In the largest ever recording project, 180 compact discs containing the complete set of authenticated works by Mozart were released by Philips Classics in 1990–91 to commemorate the bicentenary of the composer's death. The complete set comprises over 200 hours of music and would occupy 2m *6½ft* of shelving.

Earliest golden discs The first actual piece eventually to aggregate a total sale of a million copies was of performances by Enrico Caruso (b. Naples, Italy, 1873, d. 2 Aug 1921) of the aria *'Vesti la giubba'* ('On with the Motley') from the opera *I Pagliacci* by Ruggiero Leoncavallo (1858–1919), the earliest version of which was recorded with piano on 12 Nov 1902. The first single recording to surpass the million mark was Alma Gluck's *Carry Me Back to Old Virginny* on the Red Seal Victor label on the 12-in *30.48-cm* single faced (later backed) record No. 74420.

Most golden discs The only *audited* measure of gold, platinum and multi-platinum singles and albums within the United States is certification by the Recording Industry Association of America (RIAA), introduced on 14 Mar 1958.

The Rolling Stones have 55, made up of 34 gold, 15 platinum and 6 multiplatinum (for sales of 2 million or more), the most for any group. The group with the most multiplatinum albums is the Beatles with 11.

In August 1992, following new audit figures, the estate of Elvis Presley was presented with 110 gold and platinum records, making him the most certified recording artist ever. The female solo artist to receive the most awards is Barbra Streisand, with 56 (7 gold singles, 30 gold albums and 19 platinum albums). (⇨Most Number Ones—US Albums)

The first platinum album was awarded to the Eagles for *Greatest Hits, 1971–75* in 1976. The group Chicago holds the record for most platinum albums, with 17. Barbra Streisand holds the record for a solo artist, with 19, and the record for most multiplatinum, with seven. Paul McCartney holds the record for a male solo artist, with 12, while Billy Joel holds the record for the most multi-platinum albums for an individual, with eight.

Most successful group The Beatles have amassed the greatest sales for any group. The band, from Liverpool, Merseyside, comprised George Harrison (b. 25 Feb 1943), John Ono (formerly John Winston) Lennon (b. 9 Oct 1940–killed 8 Dec 1980), James Paul McCartney (b. 18 Jun 1942) and Richard Starkey, *alias* Ringo Starr (b. 7 Jul 1940). All-time sales have been estimated by EMI at over 1 billion discs and tapes. All four ex-Beatles sold many million further records as solo artists.

Biggest sellers (Singles) The biggest-selling record to date is *White Christmas* written by Irving Berlin (b. Israel Bailin, 1888–1989) and recorded by Bing Crosby on 29 May 1942. It was announced on Christmas Eve 1987 that North American sales alone reached 170,884,207 copies by 30 Jun 1987. (⇨Most weeks on chart—US singles) The highest claim for any 'pop' record is an unaudited 25 million for *Rock Around the Clock*, copyright in 1953 by James E. Myers under the name Jimmy DeKnight and the late Max C. Freedmann and recorded on 12 Apr 1954 by Bill Haley (1927–1981) and his Comets.

UK The top-selling British single is *I Want to Hold Your Hand* by The Beatles, released in 1963, with world sales of over 13 million. The top-selling single in the UK is *Do They Know It's Christmas*,

GUESS WHAT?

Q Where is a hi-hat found?

A See Page 146

Most charted artist Elvis Presley's records spent a cumulative total of 1145 weeks on on the charts. (⇨ Most successful recording artist)

written and produced by Bob Geldof and Midge Ure and recorded by Band Aid in 1984, with sales of 3.6 million by May 1987 and a further 8.1 million worldwide. The profits went to the Ethiopian Famine Relief Fund.

Biggest sellers (Albums) The best-selling album of all time is *Thriller* by Michael Jackson (b. 29 Aug 1958), with global sales of over 47 million copies to date. The best-selling album by a group is Fleetwood Mac's *Rumours* with over 21 million sales to May 1990. (⇨Most weeks on chart—UK albums)

Most No.1's!

The Beatles and Elvis Presley hold the record for the most No. 1 hits with 17 each, with Presley also having an overall record 109 hits in the UK singles chart from May 1956 to date and the longest time on the charts, at 1145 weeks.

The best selling album by a British group is *Dark Side of the Moon* by Pink Floyd with sales audited at 19.5 million to December 1986. The best-selling album in Britain is *Sgt Pepper's Lonely Hearts Club Band* by The Beatles, with an 'official' figure of 4.25 million sales since its release in June 1967.

Whitney Houston by Whitney Houston, released in 1985 and with sales of over 14 million copies (including over 9 million in the US, 1 million in the UK and a further million in Canada), is the best-selling debut album of all time.

Soundtrack The best-selling movie soundtrack is *Saturday Night Fever*, with sales of over 26.5 million to May 1987.

Fastest-selling The fastest-selling non-pop record of all time is *John Fitzgerald Kennedy—A Memorial Album* (Premium Albums), recorded on 22 Nov 1963, the day of President Kennedy's assassination, which sold 4 million at 99 cents in six days (7–12 Dec 1963). The fastest-selling British record is the Beatles' double album *The Beatles* (Apple) with 'nearly 2 million' sold in its first week in November 1968.

Best-selling classical album The best-selling classical album is *In Concert*, with global sales of 5 million copies to date. It was recorded by José Carreras, Placido Domingo and Luciano Pavarotti at the 1990 World Cup Finals in Rome, Italy.

Phonographic identification Dr Arthur B. Lintgen (b. 1932) of Rydal, Pennsylvania, USA, has a proven and as yet unique ability to identify the music on phonograph records purely by visual inspection without hearing a note.

Fastest rapper Rebel X.D. of Chicago, Illinois, USA rapped 674 syllables in 54.9 sec at the Hair Bear Recording Studio, Alsip, Illinois on 27 Aug 1992. This represents 12.2 syllables per sec.

Advance sales The greatest advance sale for a single worldwide is 2.1 million for *Can't Buy Me Love* by the Beatles, released on 21 Mar 1964. The UK record for advance sales of an album is 1.1 million for *Welcome to the Pleasure Dome*, the debut album by Frankie Goes To Hollywood, released in 1984.

Largest contract The largest recording contract ever was that agreed between Michael Jackson and Sony in March 1991. It was for $890 million; prospective earnings of $1 billion were reported.

The first actual golden disc was one sprayed by RCA Victor for the US trombonist and band-leader Alton 'Glenn' Miller (1904–44) for his *Chattanooga Choo Choo* on 10 Feb 1942.
(Photo: Hulton-Deutsch Collection)

TOP 10 TEN

The Top Ten Singles in the UK and the US, judged by the total number of weeks at number one.

UK

	Title & Artist	Year	Wks at No. 1
1	**I Believe** Frankie Laine	1953	18
2	**(Everything I Do) I Do it For You** Bryan Adams	1991	16
3	**Bohemian Rhapsody** Queen	1975/6 & 1991/2	14
4	**Rose Marie** Slim Whitman	1955	11
5	**Cara Mia** David Whitfield	1954	10
6	**Here in my Heart** Al Martino	1952/3	9
6	**Oh Mein Papa** Eddie Calvert	1954	9
6	**Secret Love** Doris Day	1954	9
6	**Diana** Paul Ankas	1957	9
6	**Mull of Kintyre/Girls' School** Wings	1977/8	9
6	**You're the One that I Want** John Travolta & Olivia Newton-John	1978	9
6	**Two Tribes** Frankie Goes to Hollywood	1984	9

US

	Title & Artist	Year	Wks at No. 1
1	**I Will Always Love You** Whitney Houston	1992	14
2	**End of the Road** Boyz II Men	1992	13
3	**Physical** Olivia Newton-John	1981	10
3	**You Light Up My Life** Debby Boone	1977	10
5	**Endless Love** Diana Ross & Lionel Richie	1981	9
5	**Singing the Blues** Guy Mitchell	1956	9
5	**Mack the Knife** Bobby Darin	1959	9
5	**Bette Davis Eyes** Kim Carnes	1981	9
5	**Theme from 'A Summer Place'** Percy Faith	1960	9
5	**Hey Jude** Beatles	1968	9

US figures © 1955–1993 by Billboard Publications

1. John Travolta & Olivia Newton-John/(Photo: Brad Elterman/London Features International Ltd)

2. Frankie Goes to Hollywood/(Photo: M Prior/LFI)

3. Whitney Houston/(Photo: LFI)

4. Queen/(Photo: LFI)

5. Bryan Adams/(Photo: Phil Loftus/LFI)

6. Doris Day/(Photo: Gabi Rona)

7. Boyz II Men/(Photo: LFI)

The Guinness Book of Number One Hits reveals the who, why, when and where of each chart-topper, including information on the songwriters and producers, as well as the date each reached the pinnacle and the length of its duration there.

Presley also had the most hit albums (94 from 1956 to April 1989). The best-selling female singer of all time, with the most No. 1 albums (6), and most hit albums (40 between 1963 and April 1989), is Barbra Streisand. (⇔ Most golden discs)

GUESS WHAT?

Q What brand of bottles did the world's largest bottle orchestra use?

A See Page 148

Most song titles—DJ challenge Disc-jockey John Murray of Kirkcaldy, Fife played 37 song titles from two decks in two minutes on the BBC *Record Breakers* programme broadcast on 16 Nov 1990.

The charts (UK Singles)

Most weeks on chart The longest stay is 122 weeks for *My Way* by Francis Albert Sinatra (b. 12 Dec 1915) in nine separate runs from 2 Apr 1969 to 1 Jan 1972. The record for most consecutive weeks on the chart is 56 weeks for Engelbert Humperdinck's *Release Me*, from 26 Jan 1967.

Most hit singles Cliff Richard (b. 14 Oct 1940) holds the record for the most hit singles, with 110 to November 1992.

The charts (UK Albums)

First and longest number one The first No. 1 LP was the film soundtrack *South Pacific*, which held the position for a record 70 consecutive weeks, eventually totalling a record 115 weeks at No. 1.

Most weeks on chart The album with the most total weeks on chart is *Rumours* by Fleetwood Mac with 433 weeks by December 1991.

The recording of Vivaldi's *Four Seasons* by the English Chamber Orchestra directed by Nigel Kennedy had topped the classical chart for over one year since its release on 25 Sep 1989.

Most number ones The Beatles have had the most No.1 albums with 12, and Elvis Presley the most hit albums, a total of 91.

The charts (US Singles)

Most number ones The Beatles have had the most No. 1 hits, with 20. Elvis Presley has had the most hit singles on *Billboard* Hot 100, namely

149 from 1956 to May 1990.

Most weeks on chart Bing Crosby's *White Christmas* spent a total of 72 weeks in the chart between 1942 and 1962, while *Tainted Love* by Soft Cell stayed on the chart for 43 *consecutive* weeks from January 1982.

The charts (US Albums)

Most weeks at number one The soundtrack *South Pacific* was No. 1 for 69 weeks (non-consecutive) from May 1949.

Most weeks on chart *Dark Side of the Moon* by Pink Floyd enjoyed 730 weeks on the *Billboard* charts to April 1989.

Most number ones The Beatles had the most No. 1s (15), Elvis Presley was the most successful soloist, with nine No. 1 albums. Elvis

Dancing

Marathon dancing must be distinguished from dancing mania, or tarantism, which is a pathological condition. The worst outbreak of the latter was at Aachen, Germany in July 1374, when hordes of men and women broke into a frenzied and compulsive choreomania in the streets. It lasted for many hours until injury or complete exhaustion ensued.

Largest and longest dances An estimated 30,000 people took part in a Madison/Electric Slide line dance held during the 1991 Comin' Home African American Holiday Celebration in Columbus, Ohio, USA on 12 Jul 1991.

The fastest flamenco dancer ever measured is Solero de Jerez, aged 17, who in Brisbane, Australia in September 1967 attained 16 heel taps per second, in an electrifying routine.

Just some of the 6196 people who set the record for the greatest assemblage of tap dancers, in New York in August 1993. The three minute routine was choreographed to the musical selection 'The Stray Cat Strut'.

(Photo: © Macy's Northeast, Inc. All Rights Reserved)

The most taxing marathon dance staged as a public spectacle was one by Mike Ritof and Edith Boudreaux, who logged 5148hr 28½min to win $2000 at Chicago's Merry Garden Ballroom, Belmont and Sheffield, Illinois, USA from 29 Aug 1930 to 1 Apr 1931. Rest periods were progressively cut from 20 to 10 to 5 to nil minutes per hour, with 10-inch steps and a maximum of 15 seconds for closure of eyes.

Cathy McConochie led an ensemble of 18 dancers through the streets of Sacramento, California, USA on 30 May 1992 during the Sacramento Children's Festival in a choreographed routine, covering a distance of 14.2km *8.8miles*.

Ballroom The world's most successful professional ballroom dancing champions have been Bill and Bobbie Irvine, who won 13 world titles between 1960 and 1968.

Limbo!

The lowest height for a bar (flaming) under which a limbo dancer has passed is 15.25cm *6in* off the floor, by Dennis Walston, alias King Limbo, at Kent, Washington State, USA on 2 Mar 1991.

The record for a performer on roller skates is 11.94cm *4⁷/₁₀ in*, achieved by Syamala Gowri (b. 31 Oct 1988), at Hyderabad, Andhra Pradesh, India on 10 May 1993.

Conga The longest recorded conga was the Miami Super Conga, held in conjunction with Calle Ocho—a party to which Cuban-Americans invite the rest of Miami for a celebration of life together. Held on 13 Mar 1988, the conga consisted of 119,986 people.

The longest conga in Britain comprised a 'snake' of 8659 people from the South-Eastern Region of the Camping and Caravanning Club of Great Britain and Ireland. It took place on 4 Sep 1982 at Brands Hatch, Kent.

Country dancing The largest genuine Scottish country dance ever staged was a 512-some reel, held in Toronto, Canada on 17 Aug 1991 and organized by the Toronto branch of the Royal Scottish Country Dance Society.

Tap The fastest *rate* ever measured for tap dancing is 32 taps per second by Stephen Gare of Sutton Coldfield, W Mids, at the Grand Hotel, Birmingham, W Mids on 28 Mar 1990.

Roy Castle, host of the BBC TV *Record Breakers* programme, achieved one million taps in 23hr 44min at the Guinness World of Records exhibition, London on 31 Oct–1 Nov 1985.

The greatest-ever assemblage of tap dancers in a single routine numbered 6196 outside Macy's Store in New York City, USA on 22 Aug 1993.

Dancing dragon The longest dancing dragon measured 1483.83m *4868ft 2in* from the end of its nose to the tip of its tail. A total of 1019 people brought the dragon to life, making it dance for 1 minute at the Volksfeest Havelte, a festival held at Havelte, Netherlands on 4 Sep 1993.

The greatest recorded number of theatrical, film and television roles is 3385 since 1951 by Jan Leighton of New York City, USA. Here he portrays Satan and Louis XIV.
(Photo: Jan Leighton)

Theatre

Oldest indoor theatre The oldest indoor theatre in the world is the Teatro Olimpico in Vicenza, Italy. Designed in the Roman style by Andrea di Pietro, alias Palladio (1508–80), it was begun three months before his death and finished by his pupil Vicenzo Scamozzi (1552–1616) in 1583. It is preserved today in its original form.

UK The oldest theatre still in use in Great Britain is The Royal in Bristol, Avon. The foundation stone was laid on 30 Nov 1764, and the theatre was opened on 30 May 1766 with a 'Concert of Musick and a Specimen of Rhetorick'. The City Varieties Music Hall in Leeds, W Yorks was a singing room in 1762 and so claims to outdate the Theatre Royal. Actors had the legal status of rogues and vagabonds until the passing of the Vagrancy Act in 1824.

Largest The world's largest building used for theatre is the National People's Congress Building (*Ren min da hui tang*) on the west side of Tiananmen Square, Beijing, China. It was completed in 1959 and covers an area of 5.2ha *12.9 acres*. The theatre seats 10,000 and is occasionally used as such, as in 1964 for the play *The East is Red*. The most capacious purpose-built theatre is the Perth Entertainment Centre, Western Australia, with 8500 seats and a main stage area measuring 21.3 × 13.7m *70 × 45ft*. It was opened on 26 Dec 1974.

Smallest The world's smallest regularly operated professional theatre is the Piccolo in Juliusstrasse, Hamburg, Germany. It was founded in 1970 and has a maximum capacity of 30 seats.

Largest amphitheatre The Flavian amphitheatre or Colosseum of Rome, Italy, completed in AD 80, covers 2ha *5 acres* and has a capacity of 87,000. It has a maximum length of 187m *612ft* and a maximum width of 175m *515ft*.

Longest runs The longest continuous run of any show in the world

The ultimate in low attendances was achieved on 24 Nov 1983, when the comedy Bag, written by Bryony Lavery and directed by Michele Frankel, opened to a nil attendance at Grantham Leisure Centre, Lincs.

is *The Mousetrap* by Dame Agatha Christie (1890–1976), which opened on 25 Nov 1952 at the Ambassadors Theatre, London (capacity 453) and moved after 8862 performances to the St Martin's Theatre next door on 25 Mar 1974. The 17,256th performance was on 9 May 1994, and the box office has grossed £20 million from more than 9 million attenders.

Revue The greatest number of performances of any theatrical presentation is 47,250 (to April 1986) for *The Golden Horseshoe Revue*, a show staged at Disneyland Park, Anaheim, California, USA from 16 Jul 1955 to 12 Oct 1986. It was seen by 16 million people.

Musical shows The off-Broadway musical show *The Fantasticks* by Tom Jones and Harvey Schmidt opened on 3 May 1960, and the total number of performances to 26 Apr 1992 is 13,270 at the Sullivan Street Playhouse, Greenwich Village, New York, USA.

UK The longest-running musical show performed in Britain was *The Black and White Minstrel Show*, later *Magic of the Minstrels*. The aggregate but discontinuous number of performances was 6464 with a total attendance of 7,794,552. The show opened at the Victoria Palace, London on 25 May 1962 and closed on 4 Nov 1972. It reopened for a season in June 1973 at the New Victoria and finally closed on 8 Dec 1973.

The longest running West End musical is *Cats* which has been playing at the New

Stage!

The world's largest stage is in the Ziegfeld Room in Reno, Nevada, USA with a 53.6m *176ft* passerelle, three main lifts each capable of raising 1200 show girls (65.3 tonnes), two 19.1m *62½ft* circumference turntables and 800 spotlights.

Comedy!

The longest-running comedy in Britain was *No Sex Please We're British*, written by Anthony Marriott and Alistair Foot and presented by John Gale. It opened at the Strand Theatre on 3 Jun 1971, transferred to the Duchess Theatre on 2 Aug 1986 and finally ended on 5 Sep 1987 after 16¼ years and 6761 performances. It was directed by Allan Davis throughout its run.

Shakespeare!

The longest of the 37 plays written by William Shakespeare (1564–1616) is *Hamlet* (1604), comprising 4042 lines and 29,551 words. Of Shakespeare's 1277 speaking parts, the longest is that of Hamlet, at 1569 lines and 11,610 words.

London Theatre, Drury Lane since 12 May 1981. The aggregate box office gross is estimated at over £250 million.

Shortest runs The shortest theatrical run on record was of *The Intimate Revue* at the Duchess Theatre, London, on 11 Mar 1930. Anything which could go wrong did. With scene changes taking up to 20 min apiece, the management scrapped seven scenes to get the finale on before midnight. The run was described as 'half a performance'.

Greatest loss The largest loss sustained by a theatrical show was borne by the American producers of the Royal Shakespeare Company's musical *Carrie*, which closed after five performances on Broadway on 17 May 1988 at a cost of $7 million (£3 million).

One-man shows The longest run of one-man shows is 849, by Victor Borge (b. Copenhagen, 3 Jan 1909) in *Comedy in Music* from 2 Oct 1953 to 21 Jan 1956 at the Golden Theater, Broadway, New York City, USA.

The world aggregate record for one-man shows is 1700 performances of *Brief Lives* by Roy Dotrice (b. Guernsey, 26 May 1923), including 400 straight at the Mayfair Theatre, London ending on 20 Jul 1974. He was on stage for more than 2½ hr per performance of this 17th-century monologue and required 3 hr for make-up and 1 hr for removal of make-up, so aggregating 40 weeks in the chair.

Most ardent theatre-goers Dr H. Howard Hughes (b. 1902), Prof. Emeritus of Texas Wesleyan College, Fort Worth, Texas, USA attended 6136 shows in the period 1956–87.

Britain's leading 'first nighter' Edward Sutro (1900–78) saw 3000 first-night productions from 1916–56 and possibly more than 5000 shows in his 60 years of theatre-going. The highest precisely recorded number of theatre attendances in Britain is 3687 shows in 33 years from 28 Mar 1953 until his death on 10 Sep 1986 by John Iles of Salisbury, Wilts.

Most durable performers Kanmi Fujiyama (b. 1929) played the lead role in 10,288 performances by the comedy company Sochiku Shikigeki from November 1966 to June 1983.

UK David Raven played Major Metcalfe in *The Mousetrap* on 4575 occasions between 22 Jul 1957 and 23 Nov 1968.

Jack Howarth (1896–1984) was an actor on the stage and later in television for 76 years from 1907 until his last appearance after 23 years as Albert Tatlock in *Coronation Street* on 25 Jan 1984 (⇨ Most durable television shows). Frances Etheridge has played Lizzie, the housekeeper, in

Gold in the Hills more than 660 times over a span of 47 years since 1936. (⇨ Longest runs)

Most durable understudy On 12 Mar 1994 Nancy Seabrooke, 79, retired from the Company of *The Mousetrap* after having understudied the part of 'Mrs Boyle' for 15 years and 6240 performances.

Advance sales The musical *Miss Saigon*, produced by Cameron Mackintosh and starring Jonathan Pryce and Lea Salonga, opened on Broadway in April 1991 after generating record advance sales of $36 million.

Longest chorus line The longest chorus line in performing history numbered up to 120 in some of the early Ziegfeld's Follies. In the finale of *A Chorus Line* on the night of 29 Sep 1983, when it broke the record as the longest-running Broadway show ever, 332 top-hatted 'strutters' performed on stage.

On 28 Mar 1992 at the Swan Centre, Eastleigh 543 members of the cast of *Showtime News*, a major production by Hampshire West Guides, performed a routine choreographed by professional dancer Sally Horsley.

Arts festival The world's largest arts festival is the annual Edinburgh Festival Fringe (instituted in 1947). In 1993, its record year, 582 groups gave 14,108 performances of 1643 shows between 15 August and 4 September. Prof. Gerald Berkowitz of Northern Illinois University attended a record 145 separate performances at the 1979 Festival between 15 August and 8 September.

Fashion shows The greatest distance covered by a model on a catwalk is 133.7 km *83.1 miles* by Eddie Warke at Parke's Hotel, Dublin, Republic of Ireland from 19–21 Sep 1983. The record by female models is 114.4 km *71.1 miles*, by Roberta Brown and Lorraine McCourt on the same occasion. The compère was Marty Whelan of Radio 2.

Circus

The oldest permanent circus building is Cirque d'Hiver (originally Cirque Napoléon), which opened in Paris, France on 11 Dec 1852. The largest travelling circus tent was that of Ringling Bros and Barnum & Bailey, which they used on USA tours from 1921 to 1924. It covered 8492 m² *2.10 acres*, consisting of a round top 61 m *200 ft* in diameter with five middle sections 18 m *60 ft* wide.

The largest audience for a circus was 52,385 for Ringling Bros and Barnum & Bailey, at the Superdome, New Orleans, Louisiana, USA on 14 Sep 1975, and the largest in a tent was 16,702 (15,686 paid), also for Ringling Bros and Barnum & Bailey, at Concordia, Kansas, USA on 13 Sep 1924.

Flexible pole The first and only publicly performed quadruple back somersault on the flexible pole was accomplished by Maxim Dobrovitsky (USSR) of the Yegorov Troupe at the International Circus Festival of Monte Carlo in

Monaco on 4 Feb 1989. Corina Colonelu Mosoianu (Romania) is the only person to have performed a triple full twisting somersault, on 17 Apr 1984 at Madison Square Garden, New York City, USA.

Risley A back somersault feet to feet was first performed by Richard Risley Carlisle and son (USA) at the Theatre Royal, Edinburgh in February 1844.

Teeter board The Shanghai Acrobats achieved a six-person high unaided column (with only one person on each level) at Shanghai, China in 1993.

Trampoline Marco Canestrelli (USA) performed a septuple twisting back somersault to bed at Ringling Bros and Barnum & Bailey Circus, St Petersburg, Florida, USA on 5 Jan 1979. He also achieved a quintuple twisting back somersault to a two high column, to Belmonte Canestrelli at Ringling Bros and Barnum & Bailey Circus, New York City, USA on 28 Mar 1979. Richard Tison (France) achieved a triple twisting triple back somersault at Berchtesgaden, Germany on 30 Jun 1981.

Stilt-walking Even with a safety or Kirby wire, very high stilts are *extremely* dangerous—25 steps are deemed to constitute 'mastery'. The tallest stilts ever mastered measured 12.36 m *40 ft 9½ in* from ground to ankle. Eddy Wolf ('Steady Eddy') of Loyal, Wisconsin, USA walked a distance of 25 steps without touching his safety handrail wires on 3 Aug 1988 using aluminium stilts of this length.

The heaviest stilts ever mastered weighed 25.9 kg *57 lb* each, and were the ones used by Eddy Wolf in his successful attempt on the height record (⇨ above).

Photography

Earliest photographs The earliest known surviving photograph, also by Niépce, was taken in 1827 using a camera obscura and shows the view from the window of his home. Rediscovered by Helmut Gernsheim in 1952, it is now in the Gernsheim Collection at the University of Texas, Austin, USA.

UK The oldest surviving photograph taken in England is as negative image of a window in Lacock Abbey, Wilts, taken in August 1835 by William Henry Fox Talbot (1800–77), inventor of the negative-positive process. Donated to the Science Museum, London, it is now at the National Museum of Photography, Film and Television, Bradford, W Yorks.

Cameras

Largest The largest and most expensive industrial camera ever built is the 27-tonne Rolls-Royce camera commissioned in 1956 and now owned

> Ian Ashpole, having performed a trapeze act at 5005 m *16,420 ft*, said:– 'Apart from the cold and oxygen problems, it was no different to doing it at 20 feet.'

> **GUESS WHAT?**
> Q Which opera singer was applauded for 1 hr 20 min after his performance in *Othello*?
> A See Page 149

> The greatest number of plates spun simultaneously is 108, by Dave Spathaky of London for the *Tarm Pai Du* television programme in Thailand on 23 Nov 1992.

> A photograph by Alfred Stieglitz of the hands of his wife, Georgia O'Keeffe, called *Georgia O'Keeffe—A Portrait with Symbol*, was sold at Christie's, New York, on 8 Oct 1993 for a record $398,500 £260,458.

Roll Up!

For the record-breaking circus

A visit to the circus has excited young and old alike over the years, and millions of people have been in awe of the amazing feats which are performed there. The high wire, flying trapeze and human cannonballs are just some of the spectacular activities shown in this imaginary circus.

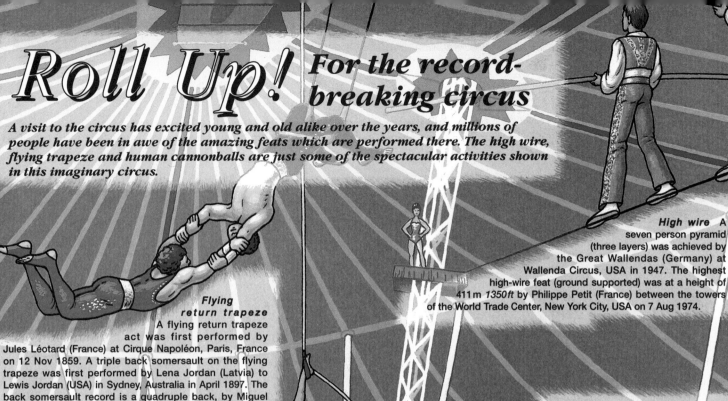

High wire A seven person pyramid (three layers) was achieved by the Great Wallendas (Germany) at Wallenda Circus, USA in 1947. The highest high-wire feat (ground supported) was at a height of 411 m *1350 ft* by Philippe Petit (France) between the towers of the World Trade Center, New York City, USA on 7 Aug 1974.

Flying return trapeze A flying return trapeze act was first performed by Jules Léotard (France) at Cirque Napoléon, Paris, France on 12 Nov 1859. A triple back somersault on the flying trapeze was first performed by Lena Jordan (Latvia) to Lewis Jordan (USA) in Sydney, Australia in April 1897. The back somersault record is a quadruple back, by Miguel Vasquez (Mexico) to Juan Vasquez at Ringling Bros and Barnum & Bailey Circus, Tucson, Arizona, USA on 10 Jul 1982. The greatest number of consecutive triple back somersaults successfully carried out is 135, by Jamie Ibarra (Mexico) to Alejandro Ibarra, between 23 July–12 Oct 1989, at various locations in the USA.

Wild animal presentations Willy Hagenbeck (Germany) worked with 70 polar bears in a presentation at the Paul Busch Circus, Berlin, Germany in 1904. The greatest number of lions mastered and fed in a cage by an unaided lion-tamer was 40, by 'Captain' Alfred Schneider in 1925. Clyde Raymond Beatty (USA) handled 43 'cats' (lions and tigers) simultaneously in 1938. Beatty was the featured attraction at every show he appeared in for more than 40 years. He insisted upon being called a lion-trainer.

Aerial acts The highest trapeze act was performed by Ian Ashpole (Great Britain) at a height of 5005 m *16,420 ft*, suspended from a hot-air balloon between St. Neots, Cambs and Newmarket, Suffolk on 16 May 1986. Janet May Klemke (USA) performed a record 305 one arm planges at Medina Shrine Circus, Chicago, Illinois, USA on 21 Jan 1938. A single-heel hang on a swinging bar was first performed by Angela Revelle in Australia in 1977.

Human pyramid The weight record is 771 kg *1700 lbs*, when Tahar Douis supported twelve members of the Hassani Troupe (three levels in height) at the BBC TV studios, Birmingham, W Mids on 17 Dec 1979. The height record is 12 m *39 ft*, when Josep-Joan Martinez Lozano of the Colla Vella dels Xiquets mounted a nine-high pyramid at Valls, Spain on 25 Oct 1981.

Human cannonball The first human cannonball was Eddie Rivers (USA) billed as 'Lulu', from a Farini cannon at Royal Cremorne Music Hall, London in 1871. The record distance a human has been fired from a cannon is 53.4 m *175 ft* in the case of Emanuel Zacchini (Italy) in the USA in 1940.

Horseback riding The record for consecutive somersaults on horseback is 23, by James Robinson (USA) at Spalding & Rogers Circus, Pittsburgh, Pennsylvania, USA in 1856. Willy, Beby and Rene Fredianis (Italy) performed a three high column at Nouveau Cirque, Paris, France in 1908, a feat not since emulated. 'Poodles' Hanneford (Ireland) (b. England) holds the record for running leaps on and off, with 26 at Barnum & Bailey Circus, New York, USA in 1915.

Illustration: Frances Button.© Guinness Publishing

by BPCC Graphics Ltd of Derby. It is 2.69m *8ft 10in* high, 2.51m *8¼ft* wide and 14.02m *46ft* long. The lens is a 160-cm *63-in* f16 Cooke Apochromatic and the bellows were made by Camera Bellows Ltd of Birmingham, W Mids.

A pinhole camera was created from a Portakabin unit measuring 10.4×2.9× 2.64m *34×9½×9ft* by photographers John Kippen and Chris Wainwright at the National Museum of Photography, Film and Television in Bradford, W Yorks on 25 Mar 1990. The unit produced a direct positive measuring 10.2×1.8m *33×6ft*.

Largest lens The National Museum of Photography, Film and Television in Bradford, W Yorks has the largest lens on display, made by Pilkington Special Glass Ltd of St Asaph, Clwyd. Its dimensions are: focal length 8.45m *333in*, diameter 1.372m *54in*, weight 215kg *474lb*. Its focal length enables handwriting on the museum's walls to be read from a distance of 12.19m *40ft*.

Smallest Excluding those built for intra-cardiac surgery and espionage, the smallest marketed camera has been the circular Japanese 'Petal' camera, with a diameter of 2.9cm *1.14in* and a thickness of 1.65cm *0.65in*. It has a focal length of 12mm *0.47in*.

Fastest!

A camera built for research into high-power lasers by The Blackett Laboratory of Imperial College of Science and Technology, London registered images at a rate of 33 billion frames per sec. The fastest production camera is currently the Imacon 675, made by Hadland Photonics Ltd of Bovington, Herts, operating at up to 600 million frames per sec.

Most expensive The most expensive camera equipment in the world is that of Nikon Corporation of Tokyo, Japan, whose complete range of 29 cameras, 90 lenses and 659 accessories cost £155,361.49 excluding VAT in May 1992.

The highest auction price for any camera is £39,600, at Christie's, London on 25 Nov 1993. The camera was custom-made for the Sultan Abdel Aziz of Morocco in 1901, when each of its metal components was removed by the manufacturer and replaced with parts of gold. The sultan originally paid £2,100 for this piece of renovation; in trade magazines of the time it was condemned as 'wanton squandering'.

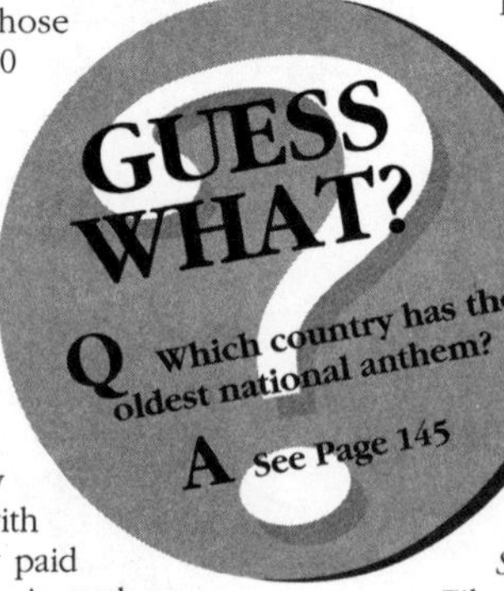

Negative!

On 6 May 1992 Thomas Bleich of Austin, Texas, USA produced a negative measuring 712.47 × 25.4 cm *23ft 4½ ×10½in* using a 26.67 cm *10½in* focal length Turner-Reich lens and Kodak No. 10 Cirkut Camera. The photograph was a portrait of about 3500 attendants at a concert in Austin.

Cinema

Films

The earliest motion pictures were made by Louis Aimé Augustin Le Prince (1842–90). The earliest surviving film (sensitized 53.9mm *2⅛in* wide paper roll) is from his camera, patented in Britain on 16 Nov 1888, taken in early October 1888 of the garden of his father-in-law, Joseph Whitley, in Roundhay, Leeds, W Yorks at 10–12 frames/ sec.

The first commercial presentation of motion pictures was at Holland Bros' Kinetoscope Parlor at 1155 Broadway, New York City, USA on 14 Apr 1894. Viewers could see five films for 25 cents or 10 for 50 cents from a double row of Kinetoscopes developed by William Kennedy Laurie Dickson (1860– 1935), assistant to Thomas Edison (1847– 1931), in 1889–91.

Earliest feature film The world's first full-length feature film was *The Story of the Kelly Gang*, made in Melbourne, Victoria, Australia in 1906. Produced on a budget of £450, this biopic of the notorious armoured bushranger Ned Kelly (1855–80) ran for 60–70min and opened at the Melbourne Town Hall on 26 Dec 1906. It was produced by the local theatrical company J. and N. Tait.

Earliest 'talkie' The earliest sound-on-film motion picture was achieved by Eugene Augustin Lauste (1857–1935), who patented his process on 11 Aug 1906 and produced a workable system using a string galvanometer in 1910 at Benedict Road, Stockwell, London. The earliest public presentation of sound-on-film was by the Tri-Ergon process at the Alhambra cinema, Berlin, Germany on 17 Sep 1922.

Largest output India's production of feature-length films was a record 948 in 1990, and its annual output has exceeded 700 every year since 1979.

Least expensive full-length feature film The total cost of production for the 1927 Australian film *The Shattered Illusion*, by Victorian Film Productions, was £300. It took 12 months to complete and included spectacular scenes of a ship being overwhelmed by a storm.

Most expensive film rights The highest price ever paid for film rights was $9.5 million announced on 20 Jan 1978 by Columbia for *Annie*, the Broadway musical by Charles Strouse starring Andrea McCardle, Dorothy Loudon and Reid Shelton. The highest fee for a commissioned script was negotiated between Columbia and Joe Eszterhas in April 1993 for a film about the downfall of Gambino Family head John Gotti. The deal will be worth a reported $3.4 million to Eszterhas if the film goes into production and if he is the sole scriptwriter.

Fastest film production The feature film Mohabbat Ka-Mashiba was filmed by a 90-strong

Expensive!

At the time of its release in July 1991, *Terminator 2: Judgement Day*, was reported to have cost Carolco Pictures $95 million (revised from earlier reports of $104), plus print and advertising costs of about $20 million. Its star, Arnold Schwarzenegger, was believed to have received a fee of $15 million for the film.

In terms of real costs adjusted for inflation, the most expensive film ever made was Cleopatra (USA, 1963), whose $44 million budget would be equivalent to over $200 million in 1993.

GUESS WHAT?
Q Which country has the oldest national anthem?
A See Page 145

production team in 48 hours in 1990. It was written, produced and directed by M.Maroof of Lucknow, India.

Highest box office gross The film with the highest earnings was Universal's *Jurassic Park* (US 93), which had earned $868,132,005 by the end of 1993 ($337,832, 005 in North America; $530,300,000 elsewhere).

UK The highest-ever grossing film in the UK is *Jurassic Park*, with box office takings of £46,439,567 to November 1993.

Largest loss Inchon!, a film starring Lord Olivier OM (1907–89) about UN landings in Inchon Bay during the Korean War, was given limited release in south-west USA and then withdrawn four days later after having earned less than $5000. The film had cost in excess of $102 million to make.

Highest earnings Jack Nicholson stood to receive up to $60 million for playing 'The Joker' in Warner Brothers' $50 million *Batman*, through a percentage of the film's receipts in lieu of salary.

The highest paid child performer is Macaulay Culkin (b. 26 Aug 1980), who, at the age of 11, was paid $1 million for *My Girl* (1991). This was followed by a contract for $5 million (plus 5 per cent of gross) for *Home Alone II: Lost in New York* (1992), the sequel to his 1990 box-office hit.

Most durable series The longest series of films is the 101 features made in Hong Kong about the 19th century martial arts hero Huang Fei-Hong, starting with *The True Story of Huang Fei-Hong* (1949) and continuing with *Once Upon a Time in China 2* (1992). The most durable continuing series with the same star is Shockiku Studios of Japan's 46 *Tora-San* comedy films, featuring Kiyoshi Atsumi (b. 1929) in a 'Chaplinesque' rôle from August 1969 to December 1992.

Largest studios The largest film studio complex in the world is that at Universal City, Los Angeles, California, USA. The Back Lot, comprising 561 buildings, includes 34 sound stages on the 170-ha *420-acre* site. The largest studio in Britain is Pinewood Studios in Iver, Bucks, covering 36.8ha *91acres*. Built in 1936, it includes 75 buildings and 18 stages.

Largest!

The largest-ever film set, measuring 400 × 230 m *1312 ×754 ft*, was the Roman Forum, designed by Veniero Colosanti and John Moore for Samuel Bronston's production of *The Fall of the Roman Empire* (1964). It was built on a 22.25-ha *55-acre* site outside Madrid, Spain. 1100 workmen spent seven months laying the surface of the Forum with 170,000 cement blocks, erecting 6705m *22,000ft* of concrete stairways, 601 colums and 350 statues, and constructing 27 full-size buildings.

Character!

The character most frequently recurring on the screen is Sherlock Holmes, created by Sir Arthur Conan Doyle (1859–1930). The Baker Street sleuth has been portrayed by some 75 actors in over 211 films since 1900.

Most film extras It is believed that over 300,000 extras appeared in the funeral scene of *Gandhi*, the 1982 epic directed by Lord Richard Attenborough CBE (b.29 Aug 1923).

Most expensive prop The highest price paid at auction for a film prop is $275,000 at Sotheby's, New York City, USA on 28 Jun 1986 for James Bond's Aston Martin DB5 from *Goldfinger* (UK, 1964).

In horror films the character most often portrayed is Count Dracula, created by the Irish writer Bram Stoker (1847–1912). Representations of the Count or his immediate descendants outnumber those of his closest rival, Frankenstein's creation, by 160 to 115.

Longest directorial career The directorial career of King Vidor (1894–1982) lasted for 67 years, beginning with the actuality *Hurricane in Galvaston* (1913) and culminating in another short, a documentary called *The Metaphor* (1980).

Oldest director The Dutch director Joris Ivens (1898–1989) directed the Franco-Italian co-production *Une Histoire de Vent* in 1988 at the age of 89. He made his directorial debut with the Dutch film *De Brug* in 1928. Hollywood's oldest director was George Cukor (1899–1983), who made his 50th and final film, MGM's *Rich and Famous*, in 1981 at the age of 81.

Youngest director *Lex the Wonderdog*, a thriller of canine detection, was written, produced, and directed by Sydney Ling (b. 1959) when he was 13 years old. He was the youngest-ever director of a professionally-made, feature-length film.

Oldest performers The oldest screen performer in a speaking rôle was Jeanne Louise Calment (b. 1875–*fl.* May 1994), who portrayed herself at the age of 114 in the 1990 Canadian film *Vincent and Me*—a modern-day fantasy about a young girl who travels through time to the 19th Century to meet Van Gogh. Ms Calment is the last living person to have known Vincent van Gogh. (⇨ Human Being)

UK The oldest British film performer was Dame Gwen Ffrancon-Davies (1891–1992), who appeared in the Sherlock Holmes TV movie *The Master Blackmailer* (GB; 1991) at the age of 100. She died one month after the film was screened.

Most durable performers The record for the longest screen career is 80 years by German actor Curt Bois (1900–91), who made his debut in *Der Fidele Bauer* (1908) at the age of eight and whose last film was *Wings of Desire* (1988). The most enduring star of the big screen was Lillian Gish (1893–1993; although her birthdate was previously given as 14 Dec 1896). She made her debut in *An Unseen Enemy* (1912) and her last film in a career spanning 75 years was *The Whales of August* (1987).

Most generations of screen actors in a family There are four generations of screen actors in the Redgrave family.

Roy Redgrave (1872–1922) made his screen debut in 1911 and continued to appear in Australian films until 1920. Sir Michael Redgrave married actress Rachel Kempson and their two daughters Vanessa and Lynn and son Corin are all actors. Vanessa's two daughters Joely and Natasha and Corin's daughter Jemma are already successful actresses with films such as *Wetherby*, *A Month in the Country* and *The Dream Demon* to their respective credit.

Most costume changes Elizabeth Taylor changed costume 65 times in *Cleopatra* (1963).

Steven Spielberg (USA; b. 18 Dec 1947) at the 1994 Oscar ceremony, where two of his films, *Jurassic Park* and *Schindler's List*, won 10 Oscars between them. He is the wealthiest and most successful film-maker ever, with seven movies in the all-time top ten. Collectively, his films have grossed an all-time total of more than $2.17 billion.
(Photo: Gamma/B King/Liaison)

Jaws, which grossed $260 million in 1975.
(Photo: Kobal Collection Universal)

ET: The Extra Terrestrial (1982), which held the title of top grossing film ever until it was overtaken by Jurassic Park.
(Photo: Kobal Collection)

The Color Purple (1985).
(Photo: Kobal Collection/Warner Brothers)

Jurassic Park (⇨Highest box office gross)
(Photo: Kobal Collection)

GUESS WHAT?

Q Which English word has the most uses?

A See Page 137

The largest number of costumes used for any one film was 32,000 for the 1951 film *Quo Vadis*.

The costumes were designed by Irene Sharaff and cost $130,000.

Oscar winners Walter (Walt) Elias Disney (1901–66) has won more 'Oscars'—the awards of the United States Academy of Motion Picture Arts and Sciences, instituted on 16 May 1929 and named after Oscar Pierce of Texas, USA—than any other person. The count comprises 20 statuettes and 12 other plaques and certificates, including posthumous awards.

The only person to win four Oscars in a starring role is Katharine Hepburn (b. USA, 12 May 1907) for *Morning Glory* (1932–3), *Guess Who's Coming to Dinner* (1967), *The Lion in Winter* (1968) and *On Golden Pond* (1981). The awards were made in 1934, 1968, 1969 and 1982 respectively. She has been nominated 12 times. Edith Head (1907–81) won eight individual awards for costume design.

The film with most awards is *Ben Hur* (1959) with 11. The film receiving the highest number of nominations is *All About Eve* (1950) with 14.

Youngest winners The youngest winner in competition is Tatum O'Neal (b. 5 Nov 1963), who was aged 10 when she received the award in 1974 for Best Supporting Actress in *Paper Moon* (1973). Shirley Temple (b. 23 Apr 1928) was awarded an honorary Oscar at the age of five for achievements in 1934.

Oldest winners The oldest recipients, George Burns (b. 20 Jan 1896), Best Supporting actor for *The Sunshine Boys* in 1976, and Jessica Tandy (b. 7 Jun 1909), Best Actress for *Driving Miss Daisy* in 1990, were both 80 at the time of their presentation, although Miss Tandy was the elder by five months.

Versatile!

The only three performers to have won Oscar, Emmy, Tony and Grammy awards have been actress Helen Hayes (b. 1900) in 1932–1976; composer Richard Rodgers (1902–1979) and actress/-singer/dancer Rita Moreno (b. 1931) in 1961–1977. Barbra Streisand received Oscar, Grammy and Emmy awards in addition to a special 'Star of the Decade' Tony award.

Cinemas

Largest The largest cinema in the world is the Radio City Music Hall, New York City, USA, opened on 27 Dec 1932 with 5945 (now 5874) seats. Kinepolis, the first eight screens of which opened in Brussels, Belgium in 1988, is the world's largest cinema complex. It has 24 screens and a total seating capacity of 7000. The Odeon, Leicester Square, London has 1983 seats.

Highest cinema-going The largest cinema audience is that of China, with a peak 21.8 billion in 1988. The year with the highest cinema attendance in the UK was 1946 with a weekly average of 31.4 million viewers.

Biggest screen The largest permanently installed cinema screen measures 33.3 × 24.7 m

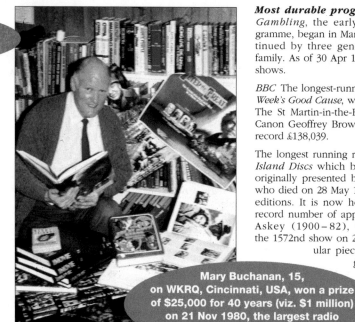

Mary Buchanan, 15, on WKRQ, Cincinnati, USA, won a prize of $25,000 for 40 years (viz. $1 million) on 21 Nov 1980, the largest radio prize ever.

Gwilym Hughes of Dolgellau, Gwynedd had seen 21,625 films by May 1994. He saw his first film in 1953 whilst in hospital.
(Photo: Mr G A Hughes)

109.25 × 81.04 ft and is in the Ssangyong Earthscape Pavilion in the Science Park, Taejon, Korea. A temporary screen measuring 90.5×10 m *297×33 ft* was used at the 1937 Paris Exposition.

Radio

The earliest patent for telegraphy without wires (wireless) was received by Dr Mahlon Loomis (USA) (1826–86). It was entitled 'Improvement in Telegraphy' and was dated 20 Jul 1872 (US Pat. No. 129,971). He in fact demonstrated only potential differences on a galvanometer between two kites 22 km *14 miles* apart in Loudoun County, Virginia, USA in October 1866.

Earliest patent A public demonstration of wireless transmission of speech was given in the town square of Murray, Kentucky, USA in 1892 by Nathan B. Stubblefield, who died destitute on 28 Mar 1928. The first patent for a system of communication by means of electro-magnetic waves, numbered No. 12039, was granted on 2 Jun 1896 to the Italian-Irish Marchese Guglielmo Marconi (1874–1937). The first permanent wireless installation was constructed at The Needles on the Isle of Wight, Hants by Marconi's Wireless Telegraph Co. Ltd in November 1897.

Earliest broadcast The world's first advertised broadcast was made on 24 Dec 1906 by the Canadian-born Prof. Reginald Aubrey Fessenden (1868–1932) from the 128-m *420-ft* mast of the National Electric Signalling Company at Brant Rock, Massachusetts, USA. The transmission included Handel's *Largo*. Fessenden had achieved the broadcast of speech as early as November 1900 but this was highly distorted.

UK The first experimental broadcasting transmitter in Great Britain was set up at the Marconi Works in Chelmsford, Essex in December 1919, and broadcast a news service in February 1920. The earliest regular broadcast was made from the Marconi transmitter '2MT' at Writtle, Essex on 14 Feb 1922.

Most durable programmes *Rambling with Gambling*, the early morning WOR-NY programme, began in March 1925 and has been continued by three generations of the Gambling family. As of 30 Apr 1993, there had been 21,281 shows.

BBC The longest-running BBC radio series is *The Week's Good Cause*, which began on 24 Jan 1926. The St Martin-in-the-Fields Christmas appeal by Canon Geoffrey Brown on 14 Dec 1986 raised a record £138,039.

The longest running record programme is *Desert Island Discs* which began on 29 Jan 1942 and originally presented by its creator Roy Plomley, who died on 28 May 1985 having presented 1791 editions. It is now hosted by Sue Lawley. The record number of appearances is four by Arthur Askey (1900–82), the last time being on the 1572nd show on 20 Dec 1980; the most popular piece of music chosen by the guests is Beethoven's 'O Freunde, nicht diese tone' (Ode to Joy), which has been requested 60 times.

The longest-running solo radio feature is *Letter from America* by (Alfred) Alistair Cooke (b. 20 Nov 1908), first broadcast on 24 Mar 1946. The original broadcaster of the series was Raymond Gram Swing. The longest-running radio serial is *The Archers*, created by Godfrey Baseley and first broadcast on 1 Jan 1951. The only role played without interruption from the start is that of Philip Archer by Norman Painting (b. 23 Apr 1924).

The country with the greatest number of radio broadcasting stations is the United States, where there were 11,608 authorized stations at 31 Mar 1994.

Highest listening Surveys carried out in 90 countries showed that, in 1993, the global estimated audience for the BBC World Service, broadcast in 39 languages, was 130 million regular listeners—greater than the combined listenership of Voice of America, Radio Moscow and *Deutsche Welle*. This represents an increase of 10 million on the 1992 figure; it is still a conservative estimate, however, as listenership for several countries, such as China, Cuba, Myanmar (Burma), Iran, and Vietnam is not yet available.

The peak recorded listenership on BBC Radio was 30 million on 6 Jun 1950 for the boxing match between Lee Savold (US) and Bruce Woodcock (GB) (b. 1921).

Highest response The highest recorded response to a radio show occurred on 21–27 Jun 1993, during which FM Osaka 85.1 in Osaka, Japan received a total of 8,091,309 calls in

Quiz!

The youngest person to become 'Brain of Britain' on BBC radio was Anthony Carr of Anglesey, Gwynedd in 1956 at the age of 16. The oldest contestant has been the author and translator Hugh Merrick (1898–1980) in his 80th year in August 1977.

response to a phone-in lottery. The prize was 100,000 yen (around £920), and a chance of winning it was offered for a twenty-minute period every hour, for 10 hours each day. The maximum call-count in one day of phone-ins (3 hours 20 minutes) was 1,540,793, on 23 Jun 1993.

The record score is 35 by the 1981 winner Peter Barlow of Richmond, Surrey and Peter Bates of Taunton, Somerset who won the title in 1984.

Television

Earliest service John Logie Baird launched his first television 'service' via a BBC transmitter on 30 Sep 1929 and marketed the first sets, Baird Televisors, at 26 guineas (£27.30) in May 1930. The world's first high-definition (i.e. 405 lines) television broadcasting service was opened from Alexandra Palace, London on 2 Nov 1936, when there were about 100 sets in the United Kingdom.

Most durable shows The world's most durable TV show is NBC's *Meet the Press*, first transmitted on 6 Nov 1947 and then shown weekly from 12 Sep 1948. The programme was originated by Lawrence E. Spivak, who appeared weekly as either moderator or panel member until 1975. As of 23 May 1993, 2294 shows had been aired. Tim Russert is now the host.

UK Britain's most durable surviving television programme is the seasonal ballroom dancing show *Come Dancing*, first transmitted on 29 Sep 1950. The children's programme *Sooty* was first presented on the BBC by its deviser Harry Corbett (1918–89) in 1952. In 1968, *Sooty* moved to Thames Television and when Harry retired in 1975, the show was continued by his son Matthew (b. 28 Mar 1948), who still handles the puppets today.

The *BBC News* was inaugurated in vision on 5 Jul 1954. Richard Baker read the news from 1954 to Christmas 1982. Of current affairs programmes BBC's weekly *Panorama* was first transmitted on 11 Nov 1953 but has summer breaks. The monthly *Sky at Night* has been presented by Patrick Moore CBE without a break or a miss since 24 Apr 1957.

Serial The longest-running domestic drama serial is Granada's *Coronation Street* which ran twice weekly from 9 Dec 1960 until 20 Oct 1989, after which viewers were treated to a third weekly episode. William Roache has played Ken Barlow without a break since the outset.

Quizzes The greatest number of participants was 80,799 in the All-Japan High School Quiz Championship televised by NTV on 31 Dec 1983.

Most takes The highest number of 'takes' for a TV commercial is 28 by comedienne Pat Coombs in 1973. Her explanation was 'Every time we came to the punch line I just could not remember the name of the product'.

Most expensive television rights In November 1991 it was reported that a group of US and European investors, led by CBS, had paid $8 million for the television rights to *Scarlett*, the sequel to Margaret Mitchell's *Gone With the Wind*, written by Alexandra Ripley.

Most sets The global total of homes with television surpassed 500 million in 1987, led by the USA with 89.13 million. The USA had, by January 1993, 93.1 million TV households, with 57.21 million on cable TV.

Greatest audience The highest ever audience for a single programme was 133.4 million viewers watching the NBC transmission of Super Bowl XXVII on 31 Jan 1993. The *Muppet Show* has been the most widely viewed programme in the world, with an estimated audience of 235 million in 106 countries at August 1989.

UK The biggest audience for a single broadcast on British television is 25.21 million for the England v. West Germany World Cup semi-final match on 4 Jul 1990. An aggregate audience of 39 million was estimated to have watched the wedding of TRH the Prince and Princess of Wales in London on 29 Jul 1981.

Most expensive production *The Winds of War*, a seven-part Paramount World War II saga aired by ABC, was the most expensive ever TV production costing $42 million over 14 months' shooting. The final episode on 13 Feb 1983 attracted a rating of 41 per cent of the total number of viewers, and a 56 per cent share of sets were tuned in.

Largest contracts Oprah Winfrey (b. Kosclusko, Mississippi, USA; 29 Jun 1954) reportedly signed a contract with the King World Corporation through her own company Harpo in mid-March 1994 which guarantees Harpo £300 million by 31 Dec 2000, or £46,150,000 per annum for 6½ years.

UK The largest contract in British television was one of a reported £9 million, inclusive of production expenses, signed by Tom Jones (b. Thomas Jones Woodward, 7 Jun 1940) of Treforest, Mid Glam in June 1968 with ABC-TV of the United States and ATV in London for 17 one-hour shows per annum from January 1969 to January 1974.

Matthew Corbett with his father Harry, who first presented *Sooty* in 1952. Sooty brandishes the infamous water pistol.
(Photo: Barry Gomer)

Sooty and friends with Matthew Corbett, the team who make up the UK's most durable children's television programme.
(Photo: Matthew Corbett Ltd)

SOOTY

second 'Red Nose Day' hosted by comedians Lenny Henry and Griff Rhys-Jones, raised a UK record £26,660,145.

Biggest sale The greatest number of episodes of any TV programme ever sold was 1144 episodes of *Coronation Street* by Granada Television to CBKST Saskatoon, Saskatchewan, Canada on 31 May 1971. This constituted 20 days 15 hr 44 min continuous viewing. A further 728 episodes (Jan 1974–Jan 1981) were sold to CBC in August 1982.

Largest sets The Sony Jumbo Tron colour TV screen at the Tsukuba International Exposition '85 near Tokyo, Japan in March 1985 measured 24.3 × 45.7 m *80 × 150 ft*. The largest cathode ray tubes for colour sets are 94 cm *37 in* models manufactured by Mitsubishi Electric of Japan.

Smallest sets The Seiko TV-Wrist Watch, launched on 23 Dec 1982 in Japan, has a 30.5-mm *1.2-in* screen and weighs only 80 g *2.8 oz*. Together with the receiver unit and headphones, the entire black and white system, costing 108,000 yen, weighs only 320 g *11.3 oz*.

The smallest single-piece set is the Casio-Keisanki TV-10 weighing 338 g *11.9 oz* with a 6.85-cm *2.7-in* screen, launched in Tokyo in July 1983.

The smallest and lightest colour set, measuring 60 × 24 × 91 mm *2.4 × 0.9 × 3.6 in* and weighing 168.5 g *6 oz* with battery, is the Casio CV-1, launched by the Casio Computer Co. Ltd of Japan in July 1992. It has a screen size of 35 mm *1.4 in* and retails in Japan for 40,000 yen (about £200).

GUESS WHAT?

Q What was the world's slowest-selling book?

A See Page 141

The highest paid television performer is the comedian Bill Cosby, who was reported in October 1991 to have an estimated income of $115 million for 1990 and 1991.

As of April 1994, *Beauty and the Beast* had sold 21 million units in the US and 12 million in the rest of the world. It was released in September 1993 in the UK, where it has sold 2½ million copies to date. *The Jungle Book* is the biggest-seller ever in the UK, with 5 million units, although it has sold only about 19 million in the US. Finally, *Aladdin* has sold 25 million in the US, and will be released in the UK in August, when it is likely to overtake *Beauty and the Beast* as the world's best-selling video.

(Photo: Walt Disney Co)

Most successful telethon The world record for a telethon is $78,438,573 in pledges in 21½ hours by the 1989 Jerry Lewis Labor Day Telethon on 4 Sep. *The Comic Relief '89 Appeal*, the

It was reported in March 1988 that Pepsi Cola had paid Michael Jackson £7 million to do four TV commercials for them.

Advertisements

Highest rates The highest TV advertising rate is $1,700,000 per minute for NBC network prime-time during the transmission of Super Bowl XXVI on 26 Jan 1992, watched by over 120 million viewers.

Fastest A TV advertisement for Reebok's InstaPUMP shoes was created, filmed, and aired during SuperBowl XXVII at the Atlanta Georgia Dome, USA. Filming continued up until the beginning of the fourth quarter of play; editing began in the middle of the third quarter and the finished product was aired during the advertisement break at the two-minute warning of the fourth quarter. It starred Emmitt Smith of the Dallas Cowboys and lasted 30 seconds.

Longest The longest advertisement broadcast on British television was 7 min 10 sec by Great Universal Stores on TV-AM's *Good Morning Britain* on 20 Jan 1985, at a cost of £100,000.

Shortest *UK* An advertisement for the 1993 Guinness Book of Records lasting just 3 sec was devised by agency Leo Burnett and broadcast on UK satellite stations up to Christmas 1992.

An advertisement lasting only four frames (there are 30 frames in a second) was aired on KING-TV's 'Evening Magazine' on 29 Nov 1993 in Seattle, Washington, USA. The ad was for Bon Marche's Frango candies, and cost $3,780.

Prolific!

The most prolific television writer in the world was the Rt Hon. Lord Willis (1918–92). From 1949 he created 41 series, including the first seven years and 2.25 million words of *Dixon of Dock Green*, which ran on BBC television from 1955 to 1976, 37 stage plays and 39 feature films. He had 29 plays produced and his total output since 1942 is estimated to be 20 million words.

FRANGO

FRANGO

MINT CHOCOLATES

Business World

Commerce

Oldest industry The oldest known industry is flint knapping, involving the production of chopping tools and hand axes, dating from 2.5 million years ago in Ethiopia. The earliest evidence of trading in exotic stone and amber dates from *c.* 28,000 BC in Europe.

Oldest company Although not strictly a company, the Royal Mint has origins dating back to AD 287. It is now based in Llantrisant, Pontyclun, Mid-Glamorgan.

The oldest existing documented company is Stora Kopparbergs Bergslags of Falun, which has been in continuous operation since the 11th century. It is first mentioned in historical records in the year 1288, when a Swedish bishop bartered an eighth share in the enterprise, and it was granted a charter in 1347.

Oldest!

The Hōshi Ryokan in the village of Awaza, Japan dates back to A.D. 717 and is a family business spanning 46 generations. (⇨ Hotels, Oldest)

The oldest family business in the UK is John Brooke & Sons Holdings Ltd, spinners and clothiers of Huddersfield, W Yorks, which was founded in 1541. The present directors, brothers E.L.M. and M.R.H. Brooke, are of the 16th generation.

Largest companies The largest manufacturing company in the world in terms of assets, sales and employees is General Motors Corporation of Detroit, Michigan, USA, with operations throughout the world supporting a workforce of 710,800. Its assets in 1993 were $188,201 million, with sales totalling $138,220 million. The company announced a profit of $2.5 billion for the year.(⇨ Greatest sales, Greatest loss)

UK The net assets of Shell Transport and Trading Co. plc at 31 Dec 1992 were £13.64 billion, mainly comprising its 40 per cent share in the net assets of the Royal Dutch Shell Group of companies which stood at £34.11 billion. Group companies employ some 127,000 staff.

Company director-ships The all-time record for directorships was set by Hugh T. Nicholson (1914–85), formerly senior partner of Harmood Banner & Sons of London, who, as a liquidating chartered accountant, became director of all 451 companies of the Jasper group in 1961 and had seven other directorships. The director with the most listings in the 1994 *Directory of Directors* is Peter Michael George, with 212.

Smallest company equity Britain's smallest ever company was Frank Davies Ltd, incorporated on 22 Aug 1924 with a ½d share capital divided into two ¼d shares. Having converted to decimal coinage (£0.002 divided into two shares of £0.001), it was finally dissolved in 1978 without ever having increased its share capital.

Largest employer The world's largest commercial or utility employer is Indian Railways, with 1,654,066 staff in 1992. The largest employer in the UK is the National Health Service, with 1,238,000 staff (excluding general practitioners) at 30 Sep 1993.

Greatest sales The *Fortune* 500 List of leading industrial corporations of April 1994 is headed by General Motors Corporation of Detroit, Michigan, USA (⇨ Largest companies, Greatest loss). The first company to surpass the $1 billion mark in annual sales was the United States Steel (now USX) Corporation of Pittsburgh, Pennsylvania in 1917.

Greatest profit The greatest net profit ever made by a corporation in 12 months is $7.6 billion by American Telephone and Telegraph Co. (AT&T) from 1 Oct 1981 to 30 Sep 1982.

Jumble sale The Cleveland Convention Center, Ohio, USA White Elephant Sale (instituted 1933) on 18–19 Oct 1983 raised $427,935.21. The great-

GUESS WHAT?

Q Which country is the largest crop producer in the world?

A See Page 172

Faux pas!

If measured by financial consequence, the greatest *faux pas* on record was that of the young multi-millionaire James Gordon Bennett (1841–1918), committed on 1 Jan 1877 at the family mansion of his demure fiancée, one Caroline May, in Fifth Avenue, New York, USA. Bennett arrived in a two-horse cutter late and obviously in wine. By dint of intricate footwork, he gained the portals to enter the withdrawing room, where he was the cynosure of all eyes. He mistook the fireplace for a plumbing fixture more usually reserved for another purpose. The May family broke the engagement and Bennett was obliged to spend the rest of his foot-loose and fancy-free life based in Paris with the resultant non-collection of millions of dollars in tax by the US Treasury.

est amount of money raised at a one-day sale is $203,247.12 at the 61st one-day rummage sale organized by the Winnetka Congregational Church, Illinois, USA on 13 May 1993.

Britain's largest jumble sale was Jumbly '79, sponsored by *Woman's Own*, at Alexandra Palace, London from 5–7 May 1979 in aid of the Save the Children Fund. The attendance was 60,000 and the gross takings were in excess of £60,000.

Greatest loss The world's worst annual net trading loss is $23.5 billion (£15.5 billion) reported for 1992 by General Motors. The bulk of this figure was, however, due to a single charge of some $21 billion for employees' health costs and pensions and disclosed because of new US accountancy regulations.(⇨ also Largest companies)

UK The greatest annual loss made by a British company is £3.91 billion by the National Coal Board (now British Coal) in the year ending 31 Mar 1984.

Take-overs The highest bid in a corporate take-over was $21 billion for RJR Nabisco Inc., the tobacco, food and beverage company, by the Wall Street leveraged buyout firm Kohlberg Kravis Roberts, who offered $90 a share on 24 Oct 1988. By 1 Dec 1988 the bid, led by Henry Kravis, had reached $109 per share to aggregate $25 billion.

UK The largest bid ever made for a British company is £13 billion for BAT Industries on 11 Jul 1989 by Hoylake, led by Sir James Goldsmith, Jacob Rothschild and Kerry Packer. Hanson Trust won control of Consolidated Gold Fields (founded 1897) on 7 Aug 1989 with a bid of £3.5 billion.

The biggest barter in trading history was 36 million barrels of oil, valued at £900 million, exchanged for 10 Boeing 747s destined for the Royal Saudi Airline in July 1984.

Bankruptcies
Corporate The biggest corporate bankruptcy in terms of assets was $35.9 billion filed by Texaco in 1987.

Banks The world's largest multilateral development bank is the International Bank for Reconstruction and Development, founded on 27 Dec 1945 and known as the World Bank. Based in Washington, DC, USA, the bank had an authorized share capital of $167.8 billion at 30 Jun 1993, at which time the World Bank also had unallocated reserves of $14 billion and accumulated net income of $1.13 billion.

The world's biggest commercial bank by assets is the Dai-Ichi Kangyo Bank Ltd of Japan, with $427.1 billion at 31 Mar 1993. The bank with most branches is the State Bank of India, which had 12,704 outlets at 1 Apr 1994 and assets of $36 billion.

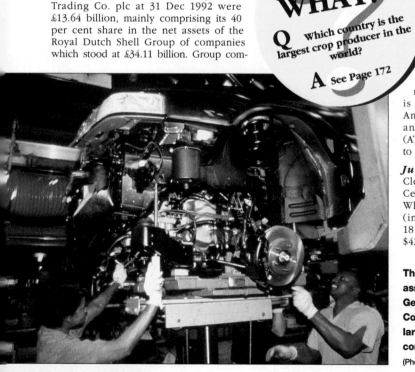

The automotive assembly plant of General Motors Corporation, the largest manufacturing company in the world.

(Photo:Gamma/Caputo/Liaison)

On 3 Sep 1992 Kevin Maxwell (b. 20 Feb 1959), son of the former press magnate Robert Maxwell (1923–91), became the world's biggest bankrupt with debts of £406·8 million./(Photo: Rex Features/Today Newspaper)

UK The bank with the largest network in the United Kingdom is the National Westminster, with consolidated total assets of £152.9 billion and 2533 branches in 1993.

Oldest The UK's oldest independent bank is C. Hoare & Co., founded in London in 1672 by goldsmith Richard Hoare. Child & Co. of Fleet St, although now part of the Royal Bank of Scotland, can trace its origins back to 1584 when its founder William Wheeler became formally apprenticed as a goldsmith.

Building lender The biggest lender in the world is the Japanese government-controlled House Loan Corporation.

Surveyors The world's largest firm of surveyors and real estate consultants is Jones, Lang Wootton of London, with more than 65 offices in 25 countries and a staff of 3500. Valuations completed in 1993 amounted to $121 billion, resulting in a worldwide fee income of $300 million.

Accountants The accounting company with the largest worldwide fee income is Arthur Anderson & Co SC, with $6.017 billion as of July 1993. The company has 66,478 employees and 324 offices. The largest accounting company for employees and office locations is KPMG Peat Marwick McLintock. It has 73,000 employees, and 837 offices in 124 countries. Their worldwide fee income was $6 billion as of July 1993.

Chemists The largest chain of chemist stores in the world is Rite Aid Corporation of Shiremanstown, Pennsylvania, USA which had 2439 branches throughout the US in 1993. The Walgreen Co. of Deerfield, Illinois, USA has fewer shops, but a larger volume of sales, totalling $8.3 billion in 1993.

UK Britain's largest chain of pharmacies is Boots The Chemists, which had 1123 retail stores at March 1994. The firm was founded by Jesse Boot (1850–1931), later the 1st Baron Trent.

Department stores The largest department store in the United Kingdom is Harrods Ltd of Knightsbridge, London, named after Henry Charles Harrod (1800–85), who opened a grocery in Knightsbridge in 1849. It now has a total selling floor space of 10.5ha *25 acres*, with 50 lifts and 36 flights of stairs and escalators, and employs 3500–4000 people depending on the time of year. It achieved record sales of over £395 million in the year ending 30 Jan 1994.

The record for one day of business is over £11 million in the January 1994 sale, with over £24 million taken in the first four days and over £55 million taken during the month.

Toyshop The world's biggest toyshop is Hamleys, founded in 1760 in Holborn, London and moved to Regent Street, London W1 in 1901. Its selling space covers 4180m² *45,000ft²* on six floors, and over 400 staff are employed during the Christmas season.

Retailers The world's largest retailing firm is Wal-Mart Inc of Bentonville, Arkansas, founded by Sam Walton (1920–92) in 1962, with unaudited sales and net income of $67.3 billion and $2.3 billion respectively at 31 Jan 1994. It has 2308 outlets.

Most outlets Woolworth Corporation now operates more than 8368 retail stores worldwide, giving the company revenues for 1993 of $9.6 billion. Frank Winfield Woolworth opened his first store, 'The Great Five Cent Store', in Utica, New York, USA on 22 Feb 1879.

> The largest-ever auction was of the Hughes Aircraft Co. for $5 billion by General Motors of Detroit, Michigan, USA on 5 Jun 1985.

Insurance

Largest insurance companies The world's largest single insurance association is the Blue Cross and Blue Shield Association, the hospital insurance organization, with 65.8 million members in 1993 and a total of $62 billion paid out in benefits.

The company with the highest volume of insurance in force in the world is the Metropolitan Life Insurance Co. of New York City, USA, with a record $1240.7 billion at year end 1993. The Prudential Insurance Company of America of Newark, New Jersey has the greatest volume of consolidated assets, totalling $218 billion in 1993.

UK The Prudential Corporation plc had total assets at 1 Jan 1994 of £64.8 billion.

Largest policy The largest life assurance policy ever issued was for $100 million, bought by a major US entertainment corporation on the life of a leading US entertainment industry figure. The policy was sold in July 1990 by Peter Rosengard of London and was placed by Shel Bachrach of Albert G. Ruben & Co. Inc. of Beverly Hills, California, USA and Richard Feldman of the Feldman Agency, East Liverpool, Ohio with nine insurance companies to spread the risk.

Marine insurance The largest ever marine insurance loss was $836 million for the Piper Alpha Oil Field in the North Sea. On 6 Jul 1988 a leak from a gas compression chamber underneath the living quarters ignited and triggered a series of explosions which blew Piper Alpha apart. Of the 232 people on board, only 65 survived.

Real Estate

The world's largest landowner is the United States Government, with a holding of 295 million ha *728 million acres*, which represents an area 12 times larger than the United Kingdom. It has been suggested that the former Soviet Government constitutionally owned all the land in the entire country, with the exception, perhaps, of that on which foreign embassies stand: a total of 22.4 million km² *8.6 million miles²*.

British Isles The largest landowner is the Forestry Commission (instituted 1919), with 1,127,594ha *2,786,285 acres* throughout England, Scotland and Wales. The largest private landowner is the National Trust in England, Wales and Northern Ireland, with 232,029ha *573,335 acres*.

The UK's greatest-ever private landowner, however, was George Granville Sutherland-Leveson-Gower, 3rd Duke of Sutherland (1828–92), who owned 550,000ha *1.4 million acres* in 1883. The individual with the largest acreage is currently the 9th Duke of Buccleuch (b. 28 Sep 1923), who owns 136,035ha *336,000 acres*.

The longest accepted land tenure is that held by St Paul's Cathedral, London of land at Tillingham, Essex, given by Aethelbert, King of Kent no later than AD616.

Smallest holding The Electricity Trust of South Australia are the proprietors of a registered and separately-delineated piece of land in Adelaide measuring just 25.4mm *1in* on all four sides, i.e. one square inch.

Prices The most expensive piece of property ever recorded, the land around the central Tokyo retail food store Mediya Building in the Ginza district, was quoted in October 1988 by the Japanese National Land Agency at a peak 33.3 million yen per m² (then equivalent to $248,000).

Employment

Working careers The longest working life has been that of 98 years by Mr Izumi (⇨ Oldest authentic centenarian) who began work goading draught animals at a sugar mill at Isen, Tokunoshima, Japan in 1872. He retired as a sugar cane farmer in 1970 aged 105.

UK The longest working career was that of Susan O'Hagan (1802– 1909) who was in domestic service with three generations of the Hall family of Lisburn, near Belfast, Co. Antrim for 97 years from the age of 10 to light duties at 107.

Longest working week A case of a working week of 142hours (with an average each day of 3hr 42min 51sec for sleep) was recorded in June 1980 by Dr Paul Ashton, 32, the anaesthetics registrar at Birkenhead General Hospital, Merseyside. He described the week in question as 'particularly bad but not untypical'. Some non-consultant doctors are contracted to work 110hours a week or be available for 148hours.

Unemployment *Highest* The highest recorded percentage unemployment in Great Britain was on 23 Jan 1933, when the total of unemployed persons on the Employment Exchange registers was 2,979,400, representing 23.0 per cent of the insured working population. The peak figure for the post-war period in the UK has been 12.3 per cent of the workforce (3,407,729 unemployed) on 9 Jan 1986.

Payout!

The highest payout on a single life was reported on 14 Nov 1970 to be some $18 million to Linda Mullendore, widow of an Oklahoma, USA rancher. Her murdered husband had paid $300,000 in premiums in 1969.

ON THE RECORD

Longest-serving company chairman

James H. Todd, who served as chairman of the wine merchant Findlater Mackie Todd & Co Ltd for 63 years.

(Photo: Findlater Mackie Todd & Co Ltd)

" Perhaps I might mention one thing which has remained stationary for the past thirty years—the salaries of both my brother and myself. We did put the matter before the shareholders one day and they decided that there should be no alteration, for, with the huge increases in duties and costs of the wine, etc., it was necessary to plough back any surplus profits into the business if we wanted to expand. I suppose we should have threatened to strike— "

From a speech made at a dinner in December 1954 in honour of James Todd and his brother Capt. William J. Todd, who had at that time served with the company for 70 and 60 years respectively.

Longest!

The longest recorded industrial career in one job in Britain was that of Miss Polly Gadsby, who started work with Archibald Turner & Co. of Leicester at the age of nine. In 1932, after 86 years' service, she was still at her bench wrapping elastic at the age of 95. Theodore C. Taylor (1850–1952) served 86 years with J.T. & J. Taylor of Batley, W Yorks including 56 years as chairman.

Edward William Beard (1878–1982), a builder from Swindon, Wilts retired in October 1981 after 85 years with the firm he had founded in 1896.

Lowest In December 1973 in Switzerland the total number of unemployed was reported to be 81 from a population of 6.6 million. The lowest recorded peacetime level of unemployment in Britain was 0.9 per cent on 11 Jul 1955, when 184,929 persons were registered. The peak figure for the employed labour force in the UK has been 26,917,000 in December 1989.

Employment agency The world's largest employment services group is Manpower, with worldwide sales of all their brand units of $4.26 billion for 1993.

Strikes Earliest The earliest recorded strike was one by an orchestra leader named Aristos from Greece, in Rome *c.* 309 BC. The dispute concerned meal breaks.

Largest The most serious single labour dispute in the UK was the General Strike of 4–12 May 1926, called by the Trades Union Congress in support of the Miners' Federation. During the nine days of the strike 1,580,000 people were involved and 14,220,000 working days were lost. In the year 1926 as a whole a total of 2,750,000 people were involved in 323 different labour disputes and the working days lost during the year amounted to 162,300,000, the highest figure ever recorded.

Longest strike The world's longest recorded strike ended on 4 Jan 1961, after 33 years. It concerned the employment of barbers' assistants in Copenhagen, Denmark. The strike that caused most disruption was that at the plumbing fixtures factory of the Kohler Co. in Sheboygan, Wisconsin, USA, between April 1954 and October 1962. The strike is alleged to have cost the United Automobile Workers' Union about $12 million to sustain.

UK Britain's most protracted national strike was called by the National Union of Mineworkers from 8 Mar 1984 to 5 Mar 1985. HM Treasury estimated the cost to be £2.625 billion or £118.93 per household.

Trade unions Largest The world's largest union is the National Education Association in the United States, with 2.1 million members as of January 1994.

The largest union in the UK is Unison, with 1.5 million members, formed on 1 Jul 1993 from the merger between Nalgo, Nupe and Cohse. This compares with a peak membership of 2,086,281 in 1979 for the Transport and General Workers' Union (TGWU).

Smallest The ultimate in small unions was the Jewelcase and Jewellery Display Makers Union (JJDMU), founded in 1894. It was dissolved on 31 Dec 1986 by its general secretary, Charles Evans. The motion was seconded by Fergus McCormack, its only surviving member. The smallest union is currently the 16-member Sheffield Wool Shear Workers.

Longest name The union with the longest name is the International Association of Marble, Slate and Stone Polishers, Rubbers and Sawyers, Tile and Marble Setters' Helpers and Marble Mosaic and Terrazzo Workers' Helpers, or the IAMSSPRSTMSHMMTWH of Washington, DC, USA.

Economics

National Economies

Richest country The richest country in the world, according to the UN Statistical Division, is Lichtenstein, which in 1992 had an average gross national product (GNP) per capita of $54,607.

Poorest country According to the 1993 *World Bank Atlas*, Mozambique had the lowest GNP per capita in 1992, with only $60, but figures were unavailable for several countries.

National debt The largest national debt of any country in the world is that of the United States. By the end of 1993 it had reached a $4351.2 billion, with net interest payments on the debt of a record $213 billion.

UK The national debt in Great Britain was less than £1 million during the reign of James II in 1687; in March 1992 it was £213,457 million.

Largest GNP The country with the largest gross national product is the United States, with a record $5904 billion for the year ending 31 Dec 1993.

UK The GNP of the UK in 1993 was $1024 billion.

Foreign aid The greatest donor of foreign aid has been the United States—the total net foreign aid given by its government between 1 Jul 1945 and 1 Jan 1991 was $312.7 billion. The country receiving most US aid in 1991 was Israel with $3.65 billion. US foreign aid began with $50,000 to Venezuela for earthquake relief in 1812.

Pension!

Miss Millicent Barclay was born on 10 Jul 1872, three months after the death of her father, Col. William Barclay, and became eligible for a Madras Military Fund pension to continue until her marriage. She died unmarried on 26 Oct 1969, having drawn the pension for every day of her life of 97 years 3 months.

Balance of payments The record deficit for any country for a calendar year was $167.3 billion reported by the US in 1987. The record surplus was Japan's $136.1 billion for 1992.

UK The most favourable yearly current balance of payments figure has been a surplus of £6748 million in 1981. The worst figure was a deficit of £21,726 million in 1989.

Worst inflation The world's worst inflation occurred in Hungary in June 1946, when the 1931 gold pengö was valued at 130 million trillion (1.3×10^{20}) paper pengös. Notes were issued for 'Egymillard billion' (one milliard billion or 10^{21}) pengös on 3 June and withdrawn on 11 Jul 1946. Vouchers for 1000 billion billion (10^{27}) pengös were issued for taxation payment only.

The most well-known and most frequently analysed hyperinflationary episode occured in Germany in 1923. The circulation of the Reichsbank mark on 6 Nov 1923 reached 400,338,326,350,700,000,000 and inflation was 755,700 millionfold on 1913 levels.

The country suffering the highest inflation in 1993 was Moldova, with 2707 per cent.

UK The worst rate in a year was for August 1974 to August 1975, when inflation ran at a rate of 26.9 per cent. The increase in the Tax and Price Index (allowing for tax reliefs) was 8.1 per cent for the 12 months to June 1990. The largest 12 month increase in the TPI (extrapolated) was 31.9 per cent, also recorded in August 1975.

Least inflation The country with the least inflation in 1993 was the Central African Republic, where prices fell by 4.2 per cent.

(Photos: Gamma/Y. Gellie (left); Gamma/K Arell/Spooner))

Largest budget The greatest governmental expenditure ever made by any country was $1.408 trillion by the US government for the fiscal year 1993. The highest-ever revenue figure was $1.154 trillion by the US in the same year. An expenditure budget of $1.518 trillion was sent to Congress on 7 February for the fiscal year of 1995, which starts on 1 Oct 1994.

The greatest fiscal surplus ever was $8,419,469,844 in the United States in 1947/48. The worst deficit was $290 billion in the US fiscal year 1992.

UK The greatest general UK government expenditure is £286.6 billion planned for the fiscal year 1993/4. The highest general government receipts are expected to be £223.1 billion for the same fiscal year. The public sector borrowing requirement was at a peak of £45 billion (excluding privatisation proceeds) in 1993/4 compared with a debt repayment of £7,588 million in 1988/89.

Highest taxation The country with the highest taxation is Norway, where the highest rate of income tax in 1992 was 65 per cent, although additional personal taxes made it possible to be charged in excess of 100 per cent. In January 1974 the 80 per cent limit was abolished there, and some 2000 citizens were then listed in the *Lignings Boka* as paying more than 100 per cent of their taxable income. The shipping magnate Hilmar Reksten (1897–1980) was assessed at 491 per cent.

Debt!

The country most heavily in overseas debt at year end 1992 was the United States, with $549.7 billion, although the size of its debt is small relative to its economic strength. Among developing countries, Brazil has the highest foreign debt, with $116.5 billion at the end of 1992.

The sovereign countries with the lowest income tax are Bahrain (left) and Qatar, (right) where the rate, regardless of income, is nil.

In Denmark the highest rate of income tax is 68 per cent, but a net wealth tax of 1 per cent can result in tax of over 100 per cent on income in extreme situations.

UK In the UK until 1979 the former top earned and unearned rates were 83 per cent and 98 per cent. The standard rate of tax was reduced to 25 per cent and the higher rate to 40 per cent in the 1988 Budget. The all-time record was set in 1967/68, when a 'special charge' of up to 9s. (45p) in the £ additional to surtax brought the top rate to 27s3d in the £ (or 136 per cent) on investment income.

Lowest rates of taxation (UK) Income tax was first introduced in Great Britain in 1799 for incomes above £60 per annum. It was discontinued in 1815, only to be reintroduced in 1842 at the rate of 7d (2.91p) in the £. It was at its lowest at 2d (0.83p) in the £ in 1875, gradually climbing to 1s3d (6.24p) by 1913. From April 1941 until 1946 the record peak of 10s (50p) in the £ was maintained to assist in the financing of the war effort.

Least taxed No tax is levied on the Sarkese (inhabitants of Sark) in the Channel Islands.

Minimum lending rate The highest-ever figure for the British bank rate (since 13 Oct 1972, the minimum lending rate) was 17 per cent from 15 Nov 1979 to 3 Jul 1980. The longest period without a change was the 12 years 13 days from 26 Oct 1939 to 7 Nov 1951, during which time the rate stayed at 2 per cent. This lowest-ever rate had been first attained on 22 Apr 1852.

Personal Wealth

The cosmetician Madame C.J. Walker (*née* Sarah Breedlove; 1857–1919) of Delta, Louisiana, USA is reputed to have become the first self-made millionairess. She was an uneducated Negro orphan whose fortune was founded on a hair straightener.

UK The richest woman in Britain is the shipping heiress Chryss Goulandris, worth £280 million in 1993.

Richest families It was tentatively estimated in 1974 that the combined value of the assets nominally controlled by the Du Pont family of some 1600 members may be of the order of $150,000 million. The family arrived in the USA from France on 1 Jan 1800. Capital from Pierre Du Pont (1730–1817) enabled his son Eleuthère Irénée Du Pont to start his explosives company in the United States.

A more conclusive estimate for an individual family is the Walton retailing family, worth an estimated $24 billion, compared with Britain's retailing giants, the Sainsbury family, with an estimated $5.2 billion.

Youngest millionaires The youngest person ever to accumulate a million dollars was the American child film actor Jackie Coogan (1914–84), co-star with Sir Charles Chaplin (1889–1977) in *The Kid*, made in 1921.

The youngest millionairess was Shirley Temple

The 10 million Pengö banknote, issued for a short time in April 1945 when Hungarian inflation was beginning to reach devastating proportions (⇨Worst inflation). Two of these notes bought one dollar on the Budapest black market, whereas on the pre-war rate of exchange one dollar had been worth less than 6 pengös. Whilst coffee cost 35–40 million pengös per pound, and flour was one million pengös a pound, the assistant to the photographer who took the picture earned just 15 million a week.

(Photo: Hulton Deutsch Collection)

Gold!

The world's greatest monetary gold reserves are those of the United States Treasury at 261.79 million fine oz at the end of 1993, equivalent to $93.036 billion at the current price of $355.10 per fine oz. The United States Bullion Depository at Fort Knox, 48km *30 miles* south-west of Louisville, Kentucky, USA, has been the principal federal depository of US gold since December 1936. Gold is stored in 446,000 standard mint bars of 12.4414kg *400 troy oz* measuring 17.7 × 9.2 × 4.1 cm *7 × 3⅝ × 1⅝ in*. Gold's peak price was $850 on 21 Jan 1980.

UK The UK's gold reserves totalled 18.45 million fine oz at September 1993.

(b. USA, 23 Apr 1928) now Mrs Charles Black, who accumulated wealth exceeding $1 million before she was 10 from a childhood acting career spanning 1934–9.

Highest incomes The largest incomes derive from the collection of royalties per barrel by rulers of oil-rich sheikhdoms who have not formally revoked personal entitlement. Shaikh Zayid ibn Sultan an-Nuhayan (b. 1918), Head of State of the United Arab Emirates, arguably has title to some $9 billion of the country's annual gross national product.

Highest personal tax demands The highest disclosed UK personal income tax demand raised is one for £5,371,220 for 1981 against merchant banker Nicholas van Hoogstraten.

Greatest wills The highest-valued will ever proved in the UK was worth £118,221,949 net, left by the 6th Marquess of Cholmondeley (1919–90). He was the former Lord Great Chamberlain, and as such was the figure who walked backwards in front of the Queen at the State Opening of Parliament.

On 29 Apr 1985 the estate of Sir Charles Clore (1904–79) was agreed by a court hearing at £123 million. The Inland Revenue initially claimed £84 million in duties, but settled for £67 million.

The largest fortune proved in the will of a woman in the UK was £92,814,057 net by Dorothy de Rothschild (1895–1988), matriarch of the leading family in world Jewry.

Greatest miser If meanness is measurable as a ratio between expendable assets and expenditure then Henrietta (Hetty) Howland Green (*née* Robinson) (1835–1916), who kept a balance of over $31,400,000 in one bank alone, was the all-time world champion. Her son had to have his leg amputated because of her delays in finding a *free* medical clinic. She herself ate cold porridge because she was too thrifty to heat it. Her estate proved to be worth $95 million (equivalent to $1725 million in 1993).

Greatest bequests The largest single bequest in the history of philanthropy was the $1 billion art collection of the American publisher Walter Annenberg, who, on 12 Mar 1991, announced his intention to leave the collection to the Metropolitan Museum of Art in New York City, USA.

The largest single cash bequest was the $500 million gift (equivalent in 1993 to $6 billion), announced on 12 Dec 1955, to 4157 educational and other institutions by the Ford Foundation (established 1936) of New York, USA.

UK The greatest benefactions of a British millionaire were those of William Richard Morris, later the Viscount Nuffield (1877–1963), which totalled more than £30 million between 1926 and his death on 22 Aug 1963.

Highest salary Fund manager George Soros earned $650 million in 1992, according to *Financial World's* list of the highest-paid individuals on Wall Street.

Golden handshake *Business Week* magazine reported in May 1989 that the largest golden handshake ever given was one of $53.8 million, to F. Ross Johnson, who left RJR Nabisco as chairman in February 1989.

In the UK, Dr Ernest Mario (b. 12 Jun 1938) was reported to have received a pay-off of at least £2.7 million after he resigned in March 1993 from his position as chief executive of Glaxo, following boardroom disagreements over future policy.

Stock Exchanges

Oldest The oldest of the world's Stock Exchanges is that of Amsterdam, Netherlands, founded in 1602 with dealings in printed shares of the United East India Company of the Netherlands in the Oude Zijds Kapel. The largest trading volume in 1992 was New York with £1161 billion, ahead of London with £1045 billion and the Federation of Germany Stock Exchanges with £891 billion.

London Stock Exchange *Most bargains* The highest number of equity bargains in one day was 114,973 on 22 Oct 1987. The record for a year is 13,557,455 bargains in 1987. There were 7367 securities listed at 31 Dec 1992 (cf. the 9749 peak in June 1973). Their total nominal value was £511.6 billion (gilt-edged £172 billion), with a market value of £2579.3 billion (gilt-edged £186.5 billion).

Trading volume The busiest session on the London market was on 28 Jan 1993, when 1.3 billion shares were traded.

FT-SE 100 share index *Closing prices* The FT-SE 100 index reached an all-time intraday peak of 3539.2 on 3 Feb 1994 and a closing high of 3520.3 on 2 Feb 1994. The lowest closing figure was 986.9 on 23 Jul 1984.

Greatest rise and fall The greatest rise in a day has been 142.2 points to 1943.8 on 21 Oct 1987, and the greatest fall in a day's trading was 250.7 points to 1801.6 on 20 Oct 1987.

New York Stock Exchange The market value of stocks listed on the New York Stock Exchange reached an all-time high of $3200 billion at the end of March 1991.

The record day's trading was 608,148,710 shares on 20 Oct 1987, compared with 16,410,030 shares traded on 29 Oct 1929, the 'Black Tuesday' of the famous 'crash', a record unsurpassed until April 1968.

The largest stock trade in the history of the NYSE took place on 10 Apr 1986, and involved a 48,788,800-share block of Navistar International Corporation stock traded at $10 in a transaction worth $487,888,000.

The highest price paid for a seat on the New York Stock Exchange was $1.15 million in 1987. The lowest 20th-century price was $17,000, set in 1942.

Closing prices The highest closing figure on the Dow Jones Industrial average (instituted 8 Oct 1896) of selected stocks was 3981.96 on 20 Jan 1994.

The Depression caused the Dow Jones average to plunge from 381.71 on 3 Sep 1929 to its lowest ever closing figure of 41.22 on 2 Jul 1932.

Greatest rise and fall The record daily rise is 186.84 points, to 2027.85, achieved on 21 Oct 1987. The largest decline in a day's trading was 508 points (22.6 per cent) on 19 Oct 1987 (Black Monday). The total lost in security values from 1 Sep 1929 to 30 Jun 1932 was $74 billion. The greatest paper loss in a year was $210 billion in 1974.

Company names *Longest* The longest company name on the Index registered under the Companies Acts is 'The Only Ordinary People Trying to Impress the Big Guys with Extraordinary Ideas, Sales, Management, Creative Thinking and Problem Solving Consultancy Company Ltd', company number 2660603.

Shortest The shortest names on the Index are D Ltd, E Ltd, H Ltd, Q Ltd, X Ltd and Y Ltd.

Largest flotation The flotation of British Gas plc had an equity offer which produced the record sum of £7.75 billion, to 4.5 million shareholders. Allotment letters were dispatched on 15 Dec 1986.

The record number of investors for a single issue is 5.9 million in the Mastergain '92 equity fund floated by the Unit Trust of India, Bombay in April and May 1992.

Rights issue The largest recorded rights issue in Britain was one of £1,350 million by ZENECA, announced on 1 Jun 1993.

Highest share value The highest denomination of any share quoted in the world was a single share in Moeara Enim Petroleum Corporation, worth £50,586 (165,000 Dutch florins) on 22 Apr 1992.

AGM attendance A world record total of 20,109 shareholders attended the AGM in April

GUESS WHAT?

Q How much does five minutes cost with the highest-paid investment consultant?

A See Page 168

Dowry!

The largest recorded dowry was that of Elena Patiño, daughter of Don Simón Iturbi Patiño (1861–1947), the Bolivian tin millionaire, who in 1929 bestowed £8 million (equivalent to £230 million in 1993) from a fortune at one time estimated to be worth £125 million.

Dr Ronald Dante was paid $3,080,000 for lecturing students on hypnotherapy at a two-day course held in Chicago, USA on 1–2 Jun 1986. He was teaching for 8 hours each day, and thus earned $192,500 per hour.

GUESS WHAT?

Q What is the highest number attributed to a house in Britain?

A See Page 170

'If you can count your millions, you are not a billionaire' *Jean Paul Getty*

'So how much money do you really have in the bank...?': Nubar Gulbenkian (left) and J. Paul Getty in earnest conversation at a Foyle's Literary Luncheon in London, in March 1965.
(Photo: George Hales/Hulton Deutsch Collection Limited)

The comparison and estimation of extreme personal wealth can rarely be totally accurate, and reports vary widely for certain individuals. Whilst vast fortunes are often attributed to the world's monarchs, much of their wealth represents national rather than personal assets. With private individuals, apart from the element of approximation that stems from any attempt to pin down the value of assets, the common restraint is that people simply do not like to discuss how much money they have!

Billion-dollar men & billion-dollar women The richest in the world is HM Sir Muda Hassanal Bolkiah Mu'izzaddin Waddaulah (b. 15 Jul 1946) of Brunei, self-appointed Prime Minister and Finance and Home Affairs Minister, who has a fortune estimated at $37 billion by *Fortune* magazine in 1993. On the 25th anniversary of his accession to the throne in 1992, he paraded through the streets in a chariot of gold drawn by 40 men.

David Sainsbury checking out some of the family produce./(Photo: Rex Features)

Britain's richest man is David Sainsbury of the famous retailing family. His fortune was estimated at $2.2 billion in 1993. HM the Queen is asserted by some to be the world's wealthiest **woman**, with a fortune estimated at £6.75 billion ($11.7 billion). An alternative estimate published by *The Economist* in January 1992 placed her personal wealth at much closer to £150 million; *BusinessAge* matched this estimate in Autumn 1993. If these views are accurate, the two strongest contenders for the richest woman in the world are Alice Walton of the richest family in the United States (⇨Richest families), and Liliane Bettencourt, daughter of Nestle's founder Eugene Schueller.

The **youngest** billionaire is William Gates, 38, who was co-founder of software house Microsoft of Seattle, Washington, USA. Gates was only 20 years old when he set up his company in 1976 and it took him 11 years to reach billionaire status. His fortune is now thought to be around $8 billion.

United States (⇨Richest families)

Coining the phrase

The term millionaire dates from c. 1740 and billionaire (in the original American sense of one thousand million) from 1861. The first billionaires were John Davison Rockefeller (1839–1937) and Andrew William Mellon (1855–1937), with Rockefeller believed to be the first to a billion dollars. In 1937, the last year in which all three were alive, a billion US dollars were worth £205 million, but that amount of sterling would today have a purchasing power exceeding £5 billion.

John D. Rockefeller in the 1880s. (Photo: Hulton Deutsch Collection Limited)

Liliane Bettencourt with her husband
(Photo: Gamma)

Bill Gates, the youngest of the billionaires.
(Photo: Rex Features)

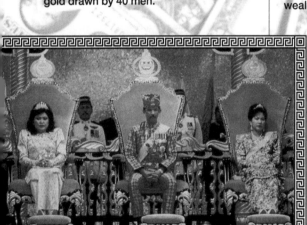

The Sultan of Brunei, the man who has it all (including a reported 153 cars). Here he is seated with his two wives: on his left is Princess Salaha and on his right, Mariam Bell, a former air hostess now known as Pengiram Isteri Hajjah Mariam.
(Photo: Gamma)

The country with the most dollar billionaires is the United States, with 108.

THE GUINNESS TIMES

8 April 1982

New York

All in a day's work

It's not every day that an envelope containing $37.1 million in negotiable bearer certificates is lost on the streets of New York.

But it was two days ago, when Jim Priceman, a $17,000-a-year assistant cashier at brokerage house Doft & Co. Inc, left his office in search of a tuna sandwich for lunch. There was a snowstorm in New York; the streets were filled with people rushing past him to reach the safety of their homes before the approaching hurricane took hold. An envelope full of money lay on the snowy street, having been blown from the pouch of a courier on route to A.B. Becker Inc. of Wall Street.

After first ignoring it, it struck Mr Priceman that the envelope might contain something important; he returned to the packet, opened it, and discovered its astonishing contents.

He did not consider keeping the money for a moment. 'I knew how hard it would have been for them to cover the money at the end of the day,' he recalled, 'It would have been a real pain in the neck.' And so Priceman picked up his lunch, went back to his office, handed the package to his boss and got on with his work.

1961 of the American Telephone and Telegraph Co. (AT&T).

Greatest personal loss The highest recorded personal paper losses on stock values were incurred by Ray A. Kroc (1902–84), former chairman of McDonald's Corporation, amounting to $65 million on 8 Jul 1974. (⇔ Restaurateurs)

Paper Money

Earliest Paper money was an invention of the Chinese, first tried in AD 812 and prevalent by AD 970. The world's earliest banknotes (*banco-sedler*) were issued in Stockholm, Sweden in July 1661, the oldest survivor being one of five dalers dated 6 Dec 1662. The oldest surviving printed Bank of England note is one for £555 to bearer, dated 19 Dec 1699, measuring 11.4 × 19.1cm *4½ × 7½ in.*

Largest The largest paper money ever issued was the one-guan note of the Chinese Ming Dynasty issue of 1368–99, which measured 22.8×33.0cm *9×13 in.* In October 1983 one sold for £340.

Highest values The highest-value notes in circulation are US Federal Reserve $10,000 banknotes, bearing the head of Salmon P. Chase (1808–73). It was announced in 1969 that no further notes higher than $100 would be issued, and only 345 $10,000 bills remain in circulation or unretired. The highest value ever issued by the US Federal Reserve System is a note for $100,000, bearing the head of Woodrow Wilson (1856–1924), which is only used for transactions between the Federal Reserve and the Treasury Department.

Two Bank of England notes for £1 million still exist, dated before 1812, but these were used only for internal accounting. There are also two Treasury £1 million notes dating from 1948 in existence, one of which was sold to dealer Brian Dawson for £23,100 at Christie's, London on 9 Oct 1990.

The highest-value notes in Great Britain which have been *issued* are £1000 notes, first printed in 1725, discontinued on 22 Apr 1943 and withdrawn on 30 Apr 1945. Just over 100 of these notes were still unretired up to April 1993.

Lowest values The lowest-value (and the lowest-denomination) legal tender banknote is the one-sen (or 1/100th of a rupiah) Indonesian

---

note. Its exchange value in early 1993 was 327,170 to the £.

The lowest-denomination Bank of England notes ever printed were the black on pale blue half-crown (now 12½p) notes in 1941, signed by the late Sir Kenneth Peppiatt. Very few examples survive and they are valued at not less than £1500.

> Chris Boyd of New Malden, Surrey has accumulated banknotes from 210 different countries since he started collecting in 1990.

Highest circulation The highest ever Bank of England note circulation in the UK was £19,059 million worth on 24 Dec 1992—equivalent to a pile 381km *237 miles* high in new £5 notes.

Smallest!

The smallest national note ever issued was the 10-bani note of the Ministry of Finance of Romania in 1917. It measured (printed area) 27.5 × 38 mm *1 1/16 × 1 1/2 in.* Of German *Notgeld*, the smallest were the 1–3 pfg notes of Passau (1920–21), measuring 18 × 18.5 mm *11/16 × 3/4 in.*

Most expensive The record price paid at auction for a single lot of banknotes was £240,350 (including buyer's premium) by Richard Lobel, on behalf of a consortium, at Phillips, London on 14 Feb 1991. The lot consisted of a cache of British military notes which were found in a vault in Berlin, Germany, and contained more than 17 million notes.

Cheques and Coins

Mohammad Irshadullah Hamidi, making sure that his pyramid of 870 horizontal coins on a single vertical coin is not going to topple over.

Most Valued!

The greatest aggregate market value of any corporation in March 1994 was £77.4 billion for Exxon of Irving, Texas, USA.

UK The largest wholly British company in terms of market capitalization is currently Shell Transport & Trading, valued at £23.403 billion at 6 Jun 1994.

Highest!

The highest-paid investment consultant in the world is Harry D. Schultz, who lives in Monte Carlo and Zurich, Switzerland. His standard consultation fee for 60 minutes is $2400 on weekdays and $3400 at weekends. Most popular are the five-minute phone consultations at $200 (i.e. $40 a minute). His 'International Harry Schultz Letter', instituted in 1964, sells at $50 per copy. A life subscription costs $2400.

More than a million coins were needed to set the record for the most valuable pile of coins. Not surprisingly excited faces could be seen all around!
(Photo: YWCA)

Largest The greatest amount paid by a single cheque in the history of banking was £1,420,000,000. Issued on 11 Jul 1989 and signed by D. Gareth Jones, Abbey National Building Society Treasurer and Assistant General Manager, and Jonathan C. Nicholls, Abbey National Building Society Assistant Treasurer, the cheque represented a payment from the expiring Abbey National Building Society in favour of the newly created Abbey National plc. A larger one, for $4,176,969,623.57, was drawn on 30 Jun 1954, although this was an internal US Treasury cheque.

Collection—record price The highest price ever paid for a coin collection was $25,235,360 for the Garrett family collection of US and colonial coins collected between 1860 and 1942, which had been donated to Johns Hopkins University, Baltimore, Maryland, USA. The sales were made at four auctions held on 28–29 Nov 1979 and 25–26 Mar 1981 at the Bowers & Ruddy Galleries in Wolfeboro, New Hampshire, USA.

Hoards The most valuable hoard of coins was one of about 80,000 aurei in Brescello near Modena, Italy in 1714, believed to have been deposited c. 37 BC. The largest deliberately buried hoard ever found was the Brussels hoard of 1908 containing c. 150,000 coins.

The largest hoard of English coins was the Tutbury (Staffs) hoard of 1831 containing over 20,000 silver coins, the majority of which were pence of Edward I (1271–1307).

Pile of Coins!

The most valuable pile of coins had a total value of $126,463.61 and consisted of 1,000,298 American coins of various denominations. It was constructed by the YWCA of Seattle-King County, Washington, USA at Redmond, Washington on 28 May 1992.

A giant gold one-thousand muhur, the largest-ever gold coin (this shot is of the reverse) dating back to the reign of Nur-ud-din Muhammad Jahangir (1605–1627), one of 'the Great Mughals' of India. Weighing 11.935 kg *32 troy pounds*, it was minted in 1613 in Agra and is an impressive 20.3 cm wide. The muhurs were Islamic coins of a special artistic quality, struck for ceremonial gifts; the 1000 muhurs were presented only to ambassadors.
(Photo: HABSBURG)

The Nepalese silver ¼ jawa c. 1740 (pictured with ruler), which weighs 0.002 g *14,000 to the oz.*
(Photo: The British Museum)

Swedish plate money (bottom right-hand corner), the heaviest known example of which is the 19.71-kg *43-lb 7¼-oz* Swedish 10-daler copper plate of 1644.
(Photo: Ashmolean Museum Oxford)

Edward VI gold ten shilling piece of 1548 (below).
(Photo: Ashmolean Museum Oxford)

Coins

Oldest
World: c. 630 BC electrum staters of King Gyges of Lydia, Turkey[1]. *British:* c. 90 BC Westerham-type gold stater[2].

Earliest Dated
World: Samian silver tetradrachm struck in Zankle (now Messina), Sicily, dated year 1, viz 494 BC— shown as 'A'. *Christian Era:* MCCXXXIIII (1234) Bishop of Roskilde coins, Denmark (6 known). *British:* 1539 James V of Scotland gold 'bonnet piece'. *Earliest English:* 1548 Edward VI gold ten shillings (MDXLVIII).

Heaviest
World: 19.71 kg *43 lb 7¼ oz* Swedish 10-daler copper plate 1644[3]. *British:* 121.1 g *4¼ oz* Shrewsbury silver pound of 1644, the heaviest of the Charles I silver pounds from the English Civil War[4].

Lightest
World: 0.002 g *14,000 to the oz* Nepalese silver ¼ jawa c. 1740. *British:* 2.66 grains *180 to the oz* Henry VIII 2nd coinage silver farthings (1526–42).

Most Expensive
World: $3190000 for the King of Siam Proof Set, a set of 1804 and 1834 US coins which had once been given to the King of Siam, purchased by Iraj Sayah and Terry Brand at Superior Galleries, Beverly Hills, California, USA on 28 May 1990. Included in the set of nine coins was the 1804 silver dollar, which had an estimated value of about $2,000,000. The record price paid for an individual coin is $1,500,000, for the US 1907 Double Eagle Ultra High Relief $20 gold coin, sold by MTB Banking Corporation of New York, USA to a private investor on 9 Jul 1990. *British:* £124,300 (including buyer's premium) bid for a Victoria gothic crown in gold (2 known), at a joint auction between Spink & Son, London and the Taisei Stamp and Coin Co., in Tokyo, Japan on 3 Jul 1988.

Footnotes
[1] *Chinese uninscribed 'spade' money of the Zhou Dynasty has been dated to c. 550 BC.*
[2] *Bellovaci-type gold staters, which were struck in northern France and not in Britain, circulated as early as c. 130 BC.*
[3] *The largest coin-like medallion was completed on 21 Mar 1986 for the World Exposition in Vancouver, British Columbia, Canada, Expo 86—a $1,000,000 gold piece. Its dimensions were 95.25 cm 37½ in diameter and 19.05 mm ¾ in thick, and it weighed 166 kg 365 lb 15 oz or 5337 oz (troy) of gold.*
[4] *The heaviest current British coin is the 39.94 g 1⅜ oz gold £5 piece.*

A giant pink piggy bank measuring 2.31 × 3.61 m *7½ × 12 ft* with a capacity of 7.2 m³ *254.25 ft³* was made by Mercian Housing Association Ltd in May 1990.

Coin

balancing Mohammad Irshadullah Hamidi of Muzaffarpur, India stacked a pyramid of 870 coins on the edge of a coin free-standing vertically on the base of a coin which was on a table on 16 Mar 1993.

The tallest single column of coins ever stacked on the edge of a coin was made up of 253 Indian one rupee pieces on top of a vertical five rupee coin, by Dipak Syal of Yamuna Nagar, India on 3 May 1991. He also balanced 10 one rupee coins and 10 ten paise coins alternately horizontally and vertically in a single column on 1 May 1991.

Coin snatching The greatest number of new 10p pieces clean-caught from being flipped from the back of a forearm into the same downward palm is 328, by Dean Gould of Felixstowe, Suffolk on 6 Apr 1993.

Mints *Largest* The largest mint in the world is that of the US Treasury. It was built from 1965–69 on Independence Mall, Philadelphia, Pennsylvania, covers 4.7 ha *11.5 acres* and has an annual production capacity of 12 billion coins (down from 15 billion). One new high-speed stamping machine called *Graebner Press* can produce coins at a rate of 42 000 per hour and the record production was 19.5 billion coins produced between the Philadelphia and Denver mints in 1982.

Smallest The smallest issuing mint in the world belongs to the Sovereign Military Order of Malta, in the City of Rome. Its single-press mint is housed in one small room and has issued proof coins since 1961. (⇨ Smallest countries)

Column of coins The most valuable column of coins was worth 39,458 Irish pounds (then £37,458) and was 1.88 m *6 ft 2 in* high. It was built by St Brigid's Family and Community Centre at Waterford, Republic of Ireland on 20 Nov 1993.

Line of coins The most valuable line of coins was made up of 1,724,000 US quarters to a value of $431,000. It was 41.68 km *25.9 miles* long and was laid at the Atlanta Marriott Marquis Hotel, Georgia, USA by members of the National Exchange Club on 25 Jul 1992. The most valuable line of coins in Britain was the 'Golden Mile' of £1 coins with a value of £71,652, laid at the Town Hall at Romford, Essex on 22 Apr 1990. The attempt was carried out under the supervision of Pauline Obee, assisted by volunteers from Havering-atte-Bower, Essex.

The longest line of coins on record had a total length of 48.89 km *30.38 miles* and was made using 1,886,975 2p coins. It was laid by the Friends of the Samaritans at the Great Park, Windsor, Berks on 16 Aug 1992.

Charity fund-raising The greatest recorded amount raised by a charity walk or run is $Can 24.7 million by Terry Fox (1958–81) of Canada who, with an artificial leg, ran from St John's, Newfoundland to Thunder Bay, Ontario in 143 days from 12 Apr–2 Sep 1980. He covered 5373 km *3339 miles*.

Charity credit cards The Leeds Permanent Building Society Visa affinity credit card has raised over £5 million since it launch in 1988. The main beneficiaries are the British Heart Foundation, Imperial Cancer Research Fund and Mencap.

Postal Services

Largest mail The country with the largest volume of mail in the world is the United States, whose population posted 171 billion letters and packages in the fiscal year ending 1993 (equivalent to 675 items per capita). At that time the US Postal Service employed 710,000 people and had the world's largest civilian vehicle fleet of 198,000 cars and trucks.

The UK total was 16,364 million letters and 183.6 million parcels in the year ending 31 Mar 1992. The most mail to have passed through the Post office on one day was 122.9 million items on 13 Dec 1993.

Oldest pillar boxes A cast iron posting box dating from *c.* 1690 was found at the White Hart coaching inn, Spilsby, Lincs in January 1988. The oldest pillar box still in service in the British Isles is one dating from 8 Feb 1853 in Union Street, St Peter Port, Guernsey, Channel Islands. Cast by John Vaudin in Jersey, it was restored to its original maroon livery in October 1981.

Post offices The country with the greatest number of post offices is India, with 144,829 in 1988. At 31 Mar 1993 there were 19,958 post offices in the UK, the oldest of which is at Sanquhar, Dumfries & Galloway, first referred to in 1763. The northernmost post office in the British Isles is at Haroldswick, Unst, Shetland Islands and the most southerly is at Samarès, Jersey, Channel Islands, although it is not run by the British Post Office.

The longest post office counter in Britain measured 56.4 m *185 ft* and had 33 positions when opened in 1962 at Trafalgar Square, London. The longest is currently one of 47.85 m *157 ft* with 17 positions at George Square, Glasgow, Strathclyde. The post office with the greatest number of positions is the Trafalgar Square post office, with 22 excluding two parcel hatches.

Most expensive postage stamp The record price paid at auction in the UK for a single stamp is £203,500 (including buyer's premium) for a Bermuda 1854 Perot Postmaster's stamp (1d red on bluish wove paper on an 1855 letter) sold by Christie's Robson Lowe, London on 13 Jun 1991.

Stamp licking John Kenmuir of Hamilton, Strathclyde licked and affixed 393 stamps in 4 min at the BBC TV studios on 26 Sep 1990, later shown on the *Record Breakers* programme.

The earliest usage of the earliest stamp: the penny black. Although the penny blacks were available from some of the main post offices of London from 1 May 1840, they were not in fact valid until 6 May. This letter from Andrew Smith of London to his wife Nancy was treated as unpaid and thus marked with an instruction that 2d was to be recovered from the recipient. (Photo: David Feldman SA (Geneva))

Postage Stamps

(Auction records unless stated otherwise and all prices include buyer's premium)

Highest Price (World)

Sw.Fr.5,750,000 (£2,590,090). Mauritius 'Bordeaux Cover'; an 1847 letter to winemerchants in Brodeaux, franked with the 1-penny and 2d first issues of Mauritius. It was bought by an anonymous buyer in less than a minute, at a sale at the Hotel International In Zurich on 3 Nov 1993.

Highest Price (UK)

£374,000. China 1878 5 candarins 'wide spacing' unique mint sheet of 25, sold at Sotheby's, London on 11 Sep 1991 and bought by a Hong Kong collector. *Single stamp*: The Swedish 3 skilling-banco was sold in May 1990 for S.Fr.1,877,500 (approx £850,000). (⇨Rarest)

Highest Total (World)

Sw.Fr. 15,000,000 (£6,756,756). The Mauritius auction of 3 Nov 1993, conducted by Geneva-based auctioneer David Feldman. The collection comprised 183 pages of the classic issues of Mauritius, owned by Japanese engineer-industrialist Hiroyuki Kanai.

Highest Total (UK)

£2,201,463. The Major James Starr collection of Chinese stamps on 11–13 Sep 1991, with all 993 lots sold.

Largest (Special Purpose)

247.7 × 69.8 mm *9¾ × 2¾ in*. China 1913. 10 cent letter stamp.

Largest (Standard Postage)

160 × 110 mm *6⁵⁄₁₆ × 4⁵⁄₁₆ in*. Marshall Islands 75 cents issued 30 Oct 1979.

Smallest

8 × 9.5 mm *⁵⁄₁₆ × ³⁄₈ in*. Colombian State of Bolivar, 1863–6. 10 cent and 1 peso value.

Highest Denomination

£100. Red and black, Kenya, Uganda and Tanganyika 1925.

Lowest Denomination

3000 pengö of Hungary. Issued 1946 when 150 million million pengö equalled 1p. (⇨ Worst inflation)

Rarest (World)

Unique examples include: British Guiana 1 cent black on magenta of 1856 (last on the market in 1980), and the Swedish 3 skilling-banco yellow colour error of 1855.

Addresses!

The practice of numbering houses began on the Pont Notre Dame, Paris, France in 1463. The highest-numbered house in Britain is No. 2679 Stratford Road, Hockley Heath, W Mids, owned since 1977 by Mr and Mrs Malcolm Aldridge.

Agriculture

Farms

Earliest The earliest mainland site in Britain is at Freshwater West, Dyfed, dated 5000–4680 BC.

Largest The largest farms in the world are *kolkhozy* collective farms in the former USSR. These were reduced in number from 235,500 in 1940 to 26,900 in 1988 and represented a total cultivated area of 169.2 million ha *417.6 million acres*. Units of over 25,000 ha *60,000 acres* were not uncommon.

British Isles The UK has about 18.5 million ha *45.7 million acres* of farmland on 241,400 holdings, the largest of which are the Scottish hill farms in the Grampians. The largest arable holding is farmed by the Earl of Iveagh at Elveden, Suffolk, where 4500 ha *11,000 acres* are farmed on an estate covering 9100 ha *22,500 acres*. Production in 1991 included 9613 tonnes of grain and 42,495 tonnes of sugar beet. Other vegetable crops, including potatoes, peas and carrots, produced a yield of over 25,186 tonnes. The livestock includes 1000 ewes and 6795 pigs.

Cattle station The world's largest cattle station is the Anna Creek station of South Australia owned by the Kidman family. It covers 30,000 km² *11,600 miles²*, or 23 per cent the size of England, with the biggest component being Strangway at 14,000 km² *5500 miles²*.

Chicken ranch The Agrigeneral Company L.P. in Ohio, USA has 4.8 million hens laying some 3.7 million eggs daily.

Community garden The largest such project is that operated by the City Beautiful Council and the Benjamin Wegerzyn Garden Center at Dayton, Ohio, USA. It comprises 1173 allotments, each measuring 74.5 m² *812 ft²*.

Piggery The world's largest piggery is the COMTIM unit near Timisoara, Romania. It has around 70,000 sows producing around 1,200,000 pigs per year.

Sheep station The largest sheep station in the world is Commonwealth Hill, in the north-west of South Australia. It grazes between 50,000 and 70,000 sheep, along with 24,000 uninvited kangaroos, in an area of 10,567 km² *4080 miles²* enclosed by 221 km *138 miles* of dog-proof fencing. The head count on Sir William Stevenson's 16,579 ha *40,970 acre* Lochinver station in New Zealand was 127,406 sheep on 1 Jan 1993.

Farming Records

Barley A yield of 12.2 tonnes/ha of winter barley was achieved on 2 Aug 1989 by Gordon Rennie of Edington Mains, Chirnside, Borders from 21.29 ha *52.6 acres*.

Potatoes Norfolk farmer Roger Southwell harvested 205.65 tonnes of potatoes in four hours from an area of 2.46 ha *6.07 acres* at Watermill Farm, Northwold, Norfolk on 1 Nov 1989. The machinery used was made by Standen Engineering Ltd of Ely, Cambs.

Wheat The largest single fenced field sown with wheat measured 14,160 ha *35,000 acres* and was sown in 1951 south-west of Lethbridge, Alberta, Canada. The British record yield is 13.99 tonnes/ha *111.4 cwt/acre* from 17.49 ha *43.24 acres* by Gordon Rennie of Clifton Mains, Newbridge, Lothian in 1981.

Field to loaf The fastest time for producing 13 loaves (a baker's dozen) from growing wheat is 12 min 11 sec, by representatives from the villages of Clapham and Patching in West Sussex on 23 Aug 1992. They used 13 microwaves to bake the loaves.

Using a traditional baker's oven actually bake to the bread, the record time is 19 min 14 sec, by a team led by John Haynes and Peter Rix at Alpheton, Suffolk on 22 Aug 1993.

Baling *Largest rick* A rick of 40,400 bales of straw was built between 22 Jul and 3 Sep 1982 by Nick and Tom Parsons with a gang of eight at Cuckoo Pen Barn Farm, Birdlip, Glos. The completed rick measured 45.7×9.1×18.2 m *150×30×60 ft* high and weighed some 711 tonnes. The team baled, hauled and ricked 24,200 bales in seven consecutive days from 22–29 July.

United Nations Food and Agricultural Organization figures for 1991 (the last year for which comparable data is available) showed the world's leading fishing nation to be China, with a total catch of 13.13 million tonnes. This was from a world total of 96.92 million tonnes for the year./(Photo: Gamma/Shinouvelle)

The pioneer farm owned by Laucidio Coelho near Campo Grande, Mato Grosso, Brazil c. 1901 covered 8700 km² *3358 miles²* and supported 250,000 head of cattle at the time of the owner's death in 1975.

The farms of Bernard Matthews plc produce 10 million turkeys per year and employ a staff of 2500. The largest farm, at North Pickenham, Norfolk, produces 1 million turkeys.
(Photo: Bernard Matthews Turkey Farm)

Fastest Svend Erik Klemmensen of Trustrup, Djursland, Denmark baled 200 tonnes of straw in 9 hr 54 min using a Hesston 4800 baling machine on 30 Aug 1989.

Bale rolling Michael Priestley and Marcus Stanley of Heckington Young Farmers Club rolled a 1.2 m *3 ft 11 in* wide cylindrical bale over a 50 m *164 ft* course in 18.06 sec at the Lincolnshire Federation of Young Farmers' Clubs annual sports day at Sleaford, Lincs on 25 Jun 1989.

Combine harvesting Philip Baker of West End Farm, Merton, Bicester, Oxon harvested 165.6 tonnes of wheat in eight hours using a Massey Ferguson MF 38 combine on 8 Aug 1989.

Ploughing The world championship (instituted 1953) has been staged in 18 countries and won by competitors from 12 nations. The United Kingdom has been the most successful country, winning 10 championships. The only person to take the title three times is Hugh B. Barr of Northern Ireland, in 1954–56.

The fastest recorded time for ploughing an acre *0.404 ha* to United Kingdom Society of Ploughmen rules is 9 min 49.88 sec by Joe

GUESS WHAT?

Q Where was Britain's largest jumble sale?

A See Page 162

Harvesters!

On 9 Aug 1990 an international team from CWS Agriculture, led by estate manager Ian Hanglin, harvested 358.09 tonnes of wheat in eight hours from 44 ha *108.72 acres* at Cockayne Hatley Estate, Sandy, Beds. The equipment consisted of a Claas Commandor 228 combine fitted with a Shelbourne Reynolds SR 6000 stripper head.

Langcake at Hornby Hall Farm, Brougham, Penrith, Cumbria on 21 Oct 1989. He used a case IH 7140 Magnum tractor and Kverneland four-furrow plough.

The greatest area ploughed with a six-furrow plough to a depth of 25cm *9in* in 24 hours is 91.37 ha *173 acres*. This was achieved by Matthias Robrahn of Germany, in a *John Deere* Type 4955 (228 PS) on 23-24 Sep 1992.

Livestock Prices

Some exceptionally high livestock auction prices are believed to result from collusion between buyer and seller to raise the ostensible price levels of the breed concerned. Others are marketing and publicity exercises with little relation to true market prices.

Cattle The highest price ever paid was $2.5 million for the beefalo named Joe's Pride (a ⅜ bison, ⅜ Charolais, ¼ Hereford), sold by D. C. Basalo of Burlingame, California to the Beefalo Cattle Co. of Calgary, Canada on 9 Sep 1974.

UK A 14-month-old Canadian Holstein bull called Pickland Elevation B. ET was bought by Premier Breeders of Stamfordham, Northumberland for £233,000 in September 1982.

The highest price paid for any farm animal at auction in the UK is 65,000 guineas (£68,250) for Grantchester Heather VIII, a Holstein Friesian cow sold to Brian Draper of Shrewsbury, Shrops by John Suenson-Taylor of Audlem, Cheshire at the Grantchester sale on 12 Aug 1992.

Cow The highest price paid for a cow is $1.3 million for a Holstein at auction in East Montpelier, Vermont, USA in 1985. The British record is £68,250, also for a Holstein Friesian. (⇨ above)

Goat On 25 Jan 1985 an Angora buck bred by Waitangi Angoras of Waitangi, New Zealand was

Mushroom!

The world's largest mushroom farm is owned by Moonlight Mushrooms Inc. and was founded in 1937 in a disused limestone mine near Worthington, Pennsylvania, USA. The farm employs 1106 people who work in a maze of underground galleries 251 km *156 miles* long, producing 24,500 tonnes of mushrooms per year. The French annual consumption is unrivalled at 3.17 kg *7 lb* per person.

sold to Elliott Brown Ltd of Waipu, New Zealand for NZ $140,000.

Horse The highest price paid for a draught horse is $47,000 by C.G. Good of Ogden, Iowa, USA for the seven-year-old Belgian stallion named Farceur at Cedar Falls, Iowa on 16 Oct 1917.

A Welsh mountain pony stallion named Coed Cock Bari was sold to an Australian bidder in Wales in September 1978 for 21,000 guineas (£22,050).

Sheep The highest price ever paid for a sheep is $A450,000 (£205,000) by Willogoleche Pty Ltd for the Collinsville stud JC&S43 at the 1989 Adelaide Ram Sales, South Australia. The British record is £32,000 for a Scottish Blackface lamb ram named Old Sandy, sold by Michael Scott at Lanark, Strathclyde on 14 Oct 1988.

Lowest price The lowest price ever realized for livestock was at a sale at Kuruman, Cape Province, South Africa in 1934, where donkeys were sold for less than 2p each.

Cattle

The country with the largest stock of cattle in 1993 is India, with an estimated 271.3 million head from a world total of 1.05 billion head. The leading producer of milk in 1993 was the US, with 68.7 million tonnes. (⇨Milk yields)

Largest The heaviest cattle on record was a Holstein–Durham cross named Mount Katahdin, which, from 1906 to 1910, frequently weighed 2267kg *5000 lb*. He stood 1.88m *6 ft 2 in* at the shoulder and had a girth measuring 3.96m *13 ft*. The cattle was exhibited by A.S. Rand of Maine, USA and died in a barn fire *c.*1923.

UK Britain's largest breed of cattle is the South Devon, bulls of which measure up to 1.55m *5 ft 1 in* at the withers and weigh about 1250 kg *2755 lb*. The heaviest example on record weighed 1678kg *3700 lb*.

The British record for any breed is 2032 kg *4480 lb* recorded for The Bradwell Ox, owned by William Spurgin of Orpland Farm, Bradwell-on-Sea, Essex. In 1830, when six years old, this bull measured 4.57m *15 ft* from nose to tail and had a maximum girth of 3.35m *11 ft*.

Smallest The smallest breed of domestic cattle is the Ovambo of Namibia, with bulls and cows averaging 225 kg *496 lb* and 160 kg *353 lb* respectively.

UK The smallest British breed is the miniature Dexter, bulls of which weigh 450kg *992 lb* and stand 1.1m *3 ft 3⅓ in* at the withers. In May 1984 a height of just 86.3cm *34 in* was reported for an adult Dexter cow named Mayberry, owned by R. Hillier of Church Farm, South Littleton, Evesham, Worcs.

Birthweights On 28 May 1986 a Holstein cow owned by

> The longest cow shed in Britain is that of the Yorkshire Agricultural Society at Harrogate, N Yorks. It is 139 m *456 ft* long and can cater for 686 cows. The National Agricultural Centre at Kenilworth, Warks, completed in 1967, can house 782 animals.

Largest crop producers

China is the largest overall crop producer, commanding 19% of world production

Crop	Producer	Amount in 1993 (million tons)
Maize	USA	165,145,008
Oats	Russian Federation	9,916,000*
Seed Cotton	China (Mainland)	11,340,000
Wheat	China (Mainland)	103,000,000
Rice, Paddy	China (Mainland)	180,000,000*
Barley	Russian Federation	23,500,000*

* Estimates by the Food and Agriculture Organization of the United Nations

Sherlene O'Brien of Simitar Farms, Henryetta, Oklahoma, USA gave birth to a perfectly formed stillborn calf weighing 122.4kg *270 lb*. The sire was an Aberdeen-Angus bull which had 'jumped the fence'. The heaviest recorded live birthweight for a calf is 102kg *225 lb* from a British Friesian cow at Rockhouse Farm, Bishopston, Swansea, W Glam in 1961.

Lightest The lowest live birthweight accurately recorded for a calf is 5.4kg *12 lb* for a healthy female born on 5 Mar 1992 on the farm of Pat and Eileen Dugan of Towner, North Dakota, USA. She was cross bred between a charlois heifer and a black angus bull.

A crossbred Angus calf owned by Leroy and Jo Seiner of Humansville, Missouri, USA weighed 7.6 kg *16 lb 12 oz* at two weeks old and an estimated 4kg *9 lb* at birth on 12 Sep 1991.

Most prolific On 25 Apr 1964 it was reported that a cow named Lyubik had given birth to seven calves in the former Soviet town of Mogilev. A case of five live calves at one birth was reported in 1928 by T.G. Yarwood of Manchester.

The lifetime breeding record is 39 in the case of Big Bertha. (⇨ Oldest)

Sires Soender Jylland's Jens, a Danish black-and-white bull, left 220,000 surviving progeny by artificial insemination when he was put down at the age of 11 in Copenhagen in September 1978. Bendalls Adema, a Friesian bull, died at the age of 14 in Clondalkin, Dublin, Republic of Ireland on 8 Nov 1978, having sired an estimated 212,000 progeny by artificial insemination.

> Big Bertha (b. 17 Mar 1944), a Dremon owned by Jerome O'Leary of Blackwatersbridge, Co. Kerry, Republic of Ireland, died less than three months short of her 49th birthday, on 31 Dec 1993. (⇨ also Most prolific)

Milk yields The highest recorded world lifetime yield of milk is 211,025kg *465,224 lb* to 1 May 1984 from the unglamorously named cow No. 289, owned by M.G. Maciel & Son of Hanford, California, USA. The greatest yield from any British cow was 165,000kg *363,759 lb* by Winton Pel Eva 2, owned by John Waring of Glebe House, Kilnwick, near Pocklington, Humberside.

The greatest recorded yield for one lactation (maximum 365 days) is 25,247kg *55,661 lb* in 1975 by the Holstein Beecher Arlinda Ellen, owned by Mr and Mrs Harold Beecher of Rochester, Indiana, USA.

British Isles Oriel Freda 10 (b. 21 Feb 1978), a Friesian owned by the Mellifont Abbey Trust of Collon, Co.

GUESS WHAT?

Q what is the longest time for which someone has drawn a pension?

A See Page 164

Louth, Republic of Ireland, produced 21,513 kg *47,427½ lb* in 305 days in 1986. The British lactation record (305 days) is 19,400 kg *42,769 lb*, produced in 1984–5 by Michaelwood Holm Emoselle 25 (b. 1 Aug 1973), a Friesian owned by Mr and Mrs M.T. Holder of Aylesmore Farm, Newent, Glos. (⇔ also Butterfat yields)

The highest reported milk yield in a day is 109.3 kg *241 lb* by Urbe Blanca in Cuba on or about 23 Jun 1982.

Cheese The world's biggest producer of cheese is the US with an estimated total in 1993 of 6.5 million lbs. The most popular cheese in Britain is Cheddar, accounting for about 60 per cent of total consumption.

Hand-milking of cow Joseph Love of Kilifi Plantations Ltd, Kenya milked 531 litres *117 gal* from 30 cows on 25 Aug 1992.

Butterfat yields The world record lifetime yield is 7425 kg *16,370 lb* by the US Holstein Breezewood Patsy Bar Pontiac in 3979 days. The British record butterfat yield in a lifetime is 5518 kg *12,166 lb* (from 123,865 kg *273,072 lb* at 4.45 per cent) by the Ayrshire cow Craighead Welma, owned by W. Watson Steele.

Expensive!

The highest price ever paid for a pig is $56,000 for a cross-bred barrow named Bud, owned by Jeffrey Roemisch of Hermleigh, Texas, USA and bought by E.A. Bud Olson and Phil Bonzio on 5 Mar 1983. The British record is 3300 guineas (£3465) paid by Malvern Farms for a Swedish Landrace gilt Bluegate Ally 33rd, owned by the Davidson Trust, in a draft sale at Reading, Berks on 2 Mar 1955.

Pig!

UK The British Gloucester Old Spot breed is known to have exceeded 635 kg *1400 lb* in weight. The heaviest on record was a boar bred by Joseph Lawton of Astbury, Cheshire (and possibly owned by Joseph Bradbury of Little Hay Wood, Staffs), which weighed 639.5 kg *1410 lb*, stood 1.43 m *4 ft 8¼ in* at the shoulder and was 2.94 m *9 ft 8 in* long.

Goats

Largest The largest goat ever recorded was a British Saanen named Mostyn Moorcock, owned by Pat Robinson of Ewyas Harold, Hereford & Worcester, which reached a weight of 181.4 kg *400 lb* (shoulder height 111.7 cm *44 in* and overall length of 167.6 cm *66 in*). He died in 1977 at the age of four.

Smallest Some pygmy goats weigh only 15–20 kg *33–44 lb*.

Oldest The oldest goat on record was a Golden Guernsey-Anglo Nubian cross named Naturemade Aphrodite (15 Jul 1975–23 Aug 1993), belonging to Katherine Whitwell of Moulton, Newmarket, Suffolk, who died aged 18 years and 1 month. 'Aphrodite' bred for ten consecutive years, during which time she reared 26 kids, including five sets of triplets and one set of quads.

Most prolific According to the British Goat Society, at least one or two cases of quintuplets are recorded annually out of the 10,000 goats registered, but some breeders only record the females born. On 14 Jan 1980 a nanny named Julie, owned by Galen Cowper of Nampah, Idaho, USA, gave birth to septuplets, but they all died, including the mother.

Milk yields The highest recorded milk yield for any goat is 3499 kg *7714 lb* in 365 days by Osory Snow-Goose, owned by Mr and Mrs G. Jameson of Leppington, New South Wales, Australia, in 1977.

Cynthia-Jean ('Baba'), owned by Carolyn Freund-Nelson of Northport, New York, USA, has lactated continuously since June 1980.

Pigs

China was the world's leading hog farming nation in 1993, with an estimated 384.2 million head from a worldwide total of 754.3 million head.

Largest The heaviest pig ever recorded was a Poland–China hog named Big Bill, weighing 1157.5 kg *2552 lb* just before being put down after accidently breaking a leg en route to the Chicago World Fair for exhibition in 1933. Other statistics included a height of 1.52 m *5 ft* at the shoulder and a length of 2.74 m *9 ft*.

Smallest The smallest breed of pig is the Mini Maialino, developed by Stefano Morini of St Golo d'Enza, Italy after 10 years' experimentation with Vietnamese pot-bellied pigs. The piglets weigh 400 g *14 oz* at birth and 9 kg *20 lb* at maturity.

Most prolific A Newsham Large White × Landrace sow from Meeting House Farm, Staintondale, near Scarborough, N Yorks farrowed 189 piglets (seven stillborn) in nine litters up to 22 Mar 1988. Between 6 May 1987 and 9 Feb 1988 she gave birth to 70 piglets.

Birthweights The heaviest weight for a piglet at weaning (eight weeks) is 36.7 kg *81 lb* for a boar, one of a litter of nine farrowed on 6 Jul 1962 by the Landrace gilt Manorport Ballerina 53rd ('Mary'), and sired by a Large White named Johnny at Kettle Lane Farm, West Ashton, Trowbridge, Wilts.

Poultry

Forecasts for 1993 show that the United States is the world's leading producer of chicken meat, or broiler, with a total of 15.02 million tons. The world's leading egg producer is China, where an estimated 215 billion were laid in 1993.

Largest chickens The largest recorded chicken is Big Snow, a rooster weighing 10.51 kg *23 lb 3 oz* on 12 Jun 1992, with a chest girth of 84 cm *2 ft 9 in* and standing 43.2 cm *1 ft 5 in* at the shoulder. Owned and bred by Ronald Alldridge of Deuchar, Queensland, Australia, Big Snow died of natural causes on 6 Sep 1992.

Most prolific The highest authenticated rate of egg-laying is 371 in 364 days by a White Leghorn (No. 2988) in an official test conducted by Prof. Harold V. Biellier ending on 29 Aug 1979 at the College of Agriculture, University of Missouri, USA. The British record is 353 eggs in 365 days in a national laying test at Milford, Surrey in 1957 by a Rhode

A world record litter of 37 piglets was born to Sow 570, A Meishan cross Large White-Duroc on 21 Sep 1993, at Mr and Mrs M.P Ford's Eastfield House Farm in Melbourne, York. Of the 36 piglets that were born alive, 33 survived.
(Photo: Phil Callaghan)

Island Red Wonderful Lady, owned by W. Lawson of Welham Grange, Retford, Notts.

The highest annual average per bird for a flock is 322.2 eggs in 52 weeks, from 1400 free-range ISA Brown layers, owned by Jim and Erica Short of Withybush Farm, near Cranleigh, Surrey.

Largest egg The heaviest egg reported is one of 454 g *16 oz*, with a double yolk and double shell, laid by a White Leghorn at Vineland, New Jersey, USA on 25 Feb 1956. The largest recorded egg measuring 31 cm *12¼ in* around the long axis, 22.8 cm *9 in* around the short and weighing 'nearly 12 oz', laid by a Black Minorca at Mr Stafford's Damsteads Farm, Mellor, Lancs in 1896.

Plucking!

Chicken and turkey plucking Ernest Hausen (1877–1955) of Fort Atkinson, Wisconsin, USA died undefeated after 33 years as champion. On 19 Jan 1939 he was timed at 4.4 sec for plucking a chicken.

Vincent Pilkington of Cootehill, Co. Cavan, Republic of Ireland killed and plucked 100 turkeys in 7hr 32min on 15 Dec 1978. His record for a single turkey is 1min 30sec, set on RTE Television in Dublin on 17 Nov 1980.

Most yolks The highest claim for the number of yolks in a hen's egg is nine, reported by Diane Hainsworth of Hainsworth Poultry Farms, Mount Morris, New York, USA in July 1971, and also from a hen in Kyrgyzstan in August 1977.

Flying Sheena, a barnyard bantam owned by Bill and Bob Knox, flew 192.07 m *630 ft 2 in* at Parkesburg, Pennsylvania, USA on 31 May 1985.

Wool!

The highest speed in which the manufacture of a three-piece suit has been executed from sheep to finished article is 1 hr 34 min 33.42 sec, by 65 members of the Melbourne College of Textiles, Pascoe Vale, Victoria, Australia on 24 Jun 1982. Catching and fleecing took 2 min 21 sec, and carding, spinning, weaving and tailoring occupied the remaining time.

The Exeter Spinners— Audrey Felton, Christine Heap, Eileen Lancaster, Marjorie Mellis, Ann Sandercock and Maria Scott—produced a jumper by hand from raw fleece in 1 hr 55 min 50.2 sec on 25 Sep 1983 at BBC Television Centre, London.

The longest thread of wool, hand-spun and plied to weigh 10 g *0.35 oz*, was one with a length of 553.03 m *1815 ft 3 in*, achieved by Julitha Barber of Bull Creek, Western Australia, Australia at the International Highland Spin-In, Bothwell, Tasmania on 1 Mar 1989.

Egg dropping The greatest height from which fresh eggs have been dropped (to earth) and remained intact is 198 m *650 ft*, by David S. Donoghue from a helicopter on 2 Oct 1979 on a golf course in Tokyo, Japan.

Egg shelling Two kitchen hands, Harold Witcomb and Gerald Harding, shelled 1050 dozen eggs in a 7¼ hr shift at Bowyers, Trowbridge, Wilts on 23 Apr 1971. Both men were blind.

Ducks *Most prolific* An Aylesbury duck belonging to Annette and Angela Butler of Princes Risborough, Bucks laid 457 eggs in 463 days, including an unbroken run of 375 in as many days. The duck died on 7 Feb 1986. Another duck of the same breed owned by Edmond Walsh of Gormanstown, Co. Kildare, Republic of Ireland laid eggs every year until her 25th birthday. She died on 3 Dec 1978 aged 28 yr 6 months.

Goose egg The heaviest goose egg weighed 680 g *24 oz*, measured 34 cm *13½ in* round the long axis and a maximum of 24 cm *9½ in* around the short axis. It was laid on 3 May 1977 by a white goose named Speckle, owned by Donny Brandenberg of Goshen, Ohio, USA. The average weight is 283–340 g *10–12 oz*.

Turkey The greatest dressed weight recorded for a turkey is 39.09 kg *86 lb* for a stag named Tyson reared by Philip Cook of Leacroft Turkeys Ltd, Peterborough, Cambs. It won the last annual 'heaviest turkey' competition, held in London on 12 Dec 1989, and was auctioned for charity for a record £4400.

Sheep

The world's leading producer of sheep is Australia, with an estimated total of 147.1 million head in 1993.

Largest The largest sheep ever recorded was a Suffolk ram named Stratford Whisper 23H, which weighed 247.2 kg *545 lb* and stood 1.09 m *43 in* tall in March 1991. It is owned by Joseph and Susan Schallberger of Boring, Oregon, USA.

Smallest The smallest breed of sheep is the Ouessant, from the Ile d'Ouessant, Brittany, France at 13–16 kg *29–35 lb* in weight and standing 45–50 cm *18–20 in* at the withers. The species was saved from extinction by breeding programmes.

Birthweights The highest recorded birthweight for a lamb is 17.2 kg *38 lb* at Clearwater, Sedgwick County, Kansas, USA in 1975, but neither lamb nor ewe survived. Another lamb of the same weight was born on 7 Apr 1975 on the Gerald Neises Farm, Howard, South Dakota, USA but died soon afterwards.

UK On 13 Apr 1990 it was reported that a Kent ewe had given birth to a live lamb weighing 12.7 kg *28 lb* on the Belton estate, near Grantham, Lincs, farmed by Les Baker. A crossbred Suffolk lamb of the same weight was delivered on 22 Jan 1992 at Stoupergate Farm, owned by D. and E. Brooke, in Hatfield, S Yorks.

Lightest The lowest live birthweight recorded for a lamb is 900 g *1 lb 15¾ oz* for a female Texel (one of twins), born on 28 Mar 1991 at the farm

> The highest price ever paid for wool is $A3008.5 per kg greasy for a bale of Tasmania superfine at the wool auction in Tasmania, Australia on 23 Feb 1989 by Fujii Keori Ltd of Osaka, Japan—top bidders since 1973.

A Merino wether from the K.P. & B.A. Reynolds Company's Willow Springs Station, South Australia in November 1990 produced 29.5 kg *65 lb* of wool from a fleece 63.5 cm *25 in* long, representing a 7-year growth.

The badger-faced Welsh mountain lamb named Lyle, born at Thorpe Park, Chertsey, Surrey, who equalled the world record for the lightest lamb at 900 g *1 lb 15¾ oz* on 8 Jun 1991. Here Lyle is far outweighed by a bag of sugar
(Photo: Leisure Sport Ltd/Thorpe Park)

owned by Verner and Esther Jensen in Rødekro, Denmark.

Oldest A crossbred sheep owned by Griffiths & Davies of Dolclettwr Hall, Taliesin, near Aberystwyth, Dyfed gave birth to a healthy lamb in 1988 at the age of 28, after lambing successfully more than 40 times. She died on 24 Jan 1989 just one week before her 29th birthday.

Shearing The highest speed for sheep shearing in a working day was recorded by Alan McDonald, who machine-sheared 805 lambs in nine hours (an average of 89.4 per hour) at Waitnaguru, New Zealand on 20 Dec 1990. Peter Casserly of Christchurch, New Zealand achieved a solo blade (i.e. hand-shearing) record of 353 lambs in nine hours on 13 Feb 1976. The women's record is 390 lambs in eight hours by Deanne Sarre of Pingrup at Yealering, Western Australia on 1 Oct 1989.

UK The British record set under National Shearing Competitions Committee rules is 1869 by the team of William Workman, Ian Matthews, Howell Havard and Philip Evans at Pant Farm, Merthyr Cynog, Powys on 30 Jun 1990. The solo record is 625 ewes by Nicky Beynon of Gower, W Glam on 10 Jul 1993 at Canon Farm, near Carno, Powys.

In a 24-hour shearing marathon, Alan MacDonald and Keith Wilson machine-sheared 2220 sheep at Warkworth, Auckland Province, New Zealand on 26 Jun 1988. Godfrey Bowen of New Zealand sheared a Cheviot ewe in 46 sec at the Royal Highland Show in Dundee, Tayside in June 1957.

Longest survival On 24 Mar 1978 Alex Maclennan found one ewe still alive after he had dug out 16 sheep buried in a snowdrift for 50 days near the River Skinsdale on Mrs Tyser's Gordonbush Estate in Sutherland, Highland after the great January blizzard. The sheep's hot breath creates air-holes in the snow, and the animals gnaw their own wool for protein.

Sheep to shoulder At the International Wool Secretariat Development Centre, Ilkley, W Yorks, a team of eight using commercial machinery produced a jumper—from shearing sheep to the finished article—in 2 hr 28 min 32 sec on 3 Sep 1986.

Human World

Human World

Political and Social

Countries

Largest The largest country is Russia, with a total area of 17,075,400 km² *6,592,800 miles²*. It is 70 times larger than the UK, but with a population in 1993 of 148.0 million has only 2.55 times more people than the UK.

The UK covers 244,100 km² *94,247 miles²* (including 3218 km² *1242 miles²* of inland water), or 0.16 per cent of the total land area of the world. Great Britain is the world's eighth largest island, with an area of 229,979 km² *88,795 miles²* and a coastline 7930 km *4928 miles* long, of which Scotland accounts for 4141 km *2573 miles*, England 3104 km *1929 miles* and Wales 685 km *426 miles*.

Smallest The smallest independent country in the world is the State of the Vatican City or Holy See (Stato della Città del Vaticano), which was made an enclave within the city of Rome, Italy on 11 Feb 1929. The enclave has an area of 44 ha *108.7 acres*. The world's smallest republic is Nauru, in the Pacific Ocean. It has an area of 2129 ha *5263 acres* and a population of 10,000 (latest estimate 1993).

The smallest colony in the world is Gibraltar (since 1969, the City of Gibraltar), with an area of 5.8 km² *1440 acres/2¼ miles²*. However, Pitcairn Island, the only inhabited island (55 people in late 1993) of a group of four (total area 4 km² *18½ miles²*), has an area of 388 ha *960 acres/1½ miles²*.

Flattest and most elevated The country with the lowest 'high point' is Maldives; it attains 2.4 m *8 ft*. The country with the highest 'low point' is Lesotho, where the Senqu (Orange) river-bed is 1381 m *4530 ft* above sea level where it flows out of the country.

Largest political division The Commonwealth, a free association of 51 independent states and their dependencies, covers an area of 30,554,762 km² *11,797,193 miles²* with a population estimated to be 1,547,303,000. Almost all member countries once belonged to the former British Empire. They believe in

Russia—the biggest country

The world's largest country is Russia, with a total area of 17,075,400 km² (6,592,800 miles²), or 11.5 per cent of the world's total land area. Even with the break-up of the former Soviet Union, which had an area of 22,402,200 km² (8,649,500 miles²), Russia is far larger than any other country. It is nearly twice the size of Canada (the second largest country), China and the United States of America and more than twice as large as Brazil. Australia would also fit into Russia twice,

France would 31 times, Germany 47 times and the United Kingdom nearly 70 times.

The distance from the easternmost point of Russia to its westernmost point is similar to that from London to Perth (in Australia), New York to New Delhi or Sydney to Istanbul. When flying abroad many people will experience jet lag on long journeys, but Russia has *eleven* time zones even within its borders.

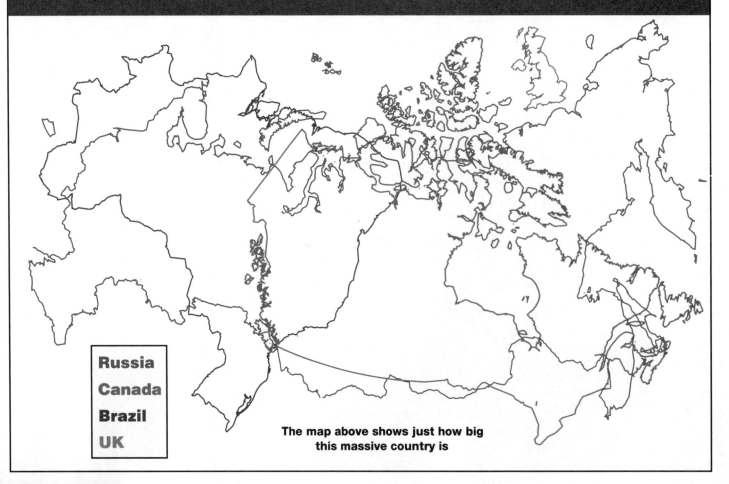

Russia
Canada
Brazil
UK

The map above shows just how big this massive country is

Very small countries apart, Bangladesh has the highest population density, with more than three times as many people per square mile or square kilometre than the UK. The threat of flooding is a constant worry, and well over a million people have died there as a result of cyclones and similar storms which have hit the extensive coastal lowland areas.
(Photo: Gamma/Bartholomew)

democracy and equal rights for all men and women regardless of race, colour, religion or politics. The Commonwealth promotes world peace, international understanding and an end to poverty and racism.

National boundaries There are 319 national land boundaries in the world. The continent with the greatest number is Africa, with 109. Of the estimated 420 maritime boundaries, only 140 have so far been ratified. The ratio of boundaries to area of land is greatest in Europe.

The frontier which is crossed most frequently is that between the United States and Mexico. It extends for 3110km *1933 miles* and in the year to 30 Sep 1993 there were 452,657,133 crossings.

Longest boundary The longest *continuous* boundary in the world is that between Canada and the United States, which (including the Great Lakes boundaries) extends for 6416km *3987 miles* (excluding the frontier of 2547km *1538 miles* with Alaska). If the Great Lakes boundary is excluded, the longest land boundary is that between Chile and Argentina, which is 5255km *3265 miles* in length.

The UK's boundary with the Republic of Ireland measures 358km *223 miles.*

Shortest boundary The 'frontier' of the Holy See in Rome measures 4.07km *2.53 miles.* The land frontier between Gibraltar and Spain at La Linea, closed between June 1969 and February 1985, measures 1.53km *1672 yd.*

In Africa, Zambia, Zimbabwe, Botswana and Namibia almost meet at a single point on the Zambezi river.

Most boundaries The country with the most land boundaries is China, with 16 — Mongolia, Russia, North Korea, Hong Kong, Macau, Vietnam, Laos, Myanmar (Burma), India, Bhutan, Nepal, Pakistan, Afghanistan, Tajikistan, Kyrgyzstan and Kazakhstan. These extend for 24,000km *14,900 miles.*

The country with the largest number of maritime boundaries is Indonesia, with 19. The longest maritime boundary is that between Greenland and Canada at 2697km *1676 miles.*

Coastlines Canada has the longest coastline of any country in the world, with 243,798km *151,489 miles* including islands.

GUESS WHAT?

Q In which country did the world's most devastating flood occur?

A See Page 179

The sovereign country with the shortest coastline is Monaco, with 5.61 km *3½ miles*, excluding piers and breakwaters.

Populations

World The current (1994) population of the world is estimated to be 5666 million. At the beginning of the century it was just 1633 milllion, and in the year 2000 it is expected to be 6228 million.

The all-time peak annual increase of 2.06 per cent in the period 1965–70 had declined to 1.74 per cent by 1985–90. In spite of the reduced percentage increase, world population is currently growing by more than 93 million people every year. Projections issued by the United nations have estimated that the population should stabilize at around 11,600 million c. 2150.

The average daily increase in the world's population is approximately 256,000 or an average of some 178 per minute.

Most populous country The most populated country is China, which in *pinyin* is written Zhongguo (meaning 'central kingdom'). It had an estimated population of 1,179,467,000 in mid-1993 and has a rate of natural increase of nearly 13.6 million per year or more than 37,000 a day. Its population is more than that of the whole world 150 years ago.

Least populous The independent state with the smallest population is the Vatican City or the Holy See (⇨ Smallest country above), with 1800 inhabitants in 1993.

Most densely populated The most densely populated territory in the world is the Portuguese province of Macau, on the southern coast of China. It has an estimated population

Capital!

The nearest capitals of two neighbouring countries are the Vatican City and Rome (Italy), as the Vatican is actually surrounded by Rome. The greatest distance between the capitals of countries which share a common border is 4200 km *2600 miles*, in the case of Moscow (Russia) and Pyongyang (Democratic People's Republic of Korea).

of 378,000 (1993) in an area of 18.0km² *6.9 miles²*, giving a density of 21,000/km² *54,783/mile².*

The principality of Monaco, on the south coast of France, has a population of 30,500 (1993) in an area of just 1.95km² *0.75 miles²*, a density equal to 15,641/km² *40,667/mile².*

Of territories with an area of more than 1000km², Hong Kong (1075km² *415 miles²*) contains an estimated 6,020,000 people (1993), giving the territory a density of 5600/km² *14,506/mile².* Hong Kong is the most populous of all colonies. The 1976 by-census showed that the West Area of the urban district of Mong Kok on the Kowloon Peninsula had a density of 252,090/km² *652,910/mile².*

Of countries over 2500 km² or *1000 miles²* the most densely populated is Bangladesh, with a population of 115,075,000 (1993) living in 148,383 km² *57,295 miles²* at a density of 776/km² *2008/mile².*

The Indonesian island of Java (with an area of 132,186 km² *51,037 miles²*) had a population of 112,159,200 in 1993, giving a density of 848/km² *2198/mile².*

United Kingdom The UK (241,752 km² *93,316 miles²*) had an estimated population of 58,245,000 in early 1994, giving a density of 241/km² *624/mile².* The 1993 population density for the Borough of Islington, London was 11,887/km² *30,783/mile².*

Most sparsely populated Antarctica became permanently occupied by relays of scientists from 1943. The population varies seasonally and reaches 2000 at times.

The least populated territory, apart from Antarctica, is Greenland, with a population of 55,700 (1993) in an area of 2,175,600 km² *840,000 miles²*, giving a density of one person to every 39.1km² *15.1 miles².*

United Kingdom The lowest population density for any administrative area in the UK is that of Highland, Scotland with 8.0/km² *20.8/mile².*

Emigration More people emigrate from Mexico than from any other country, mainly to the USA.

The Soviet invasion of Afghanistan in December 1979 caused an influx of 2.9 million Afghan refugees into Pakistan and a further 2.2 million into Iran.

A total of 133,000 British citizens emigrated from the UK in 1992. The largest number of emigrants from the British Isles in any one year was 360,000 in 1852, mainly from Ireland.

Immigration The country which regularly receives the most legal immigrants is the United States. It has been estimated that between 1820 and 1992 the USA received 59,795,158 *official* immigrants. One in 76 of the US population is, however, an *illegal* immigrant. In the fiscal year to September 1986, a record 1,615,854 people were arrested by US patrols on the Mexican border. In late 1993 there were some 28 million refugees worldwide. The country with the greatest number is Iran, with some 4.2 million, mostly from Afghanistan and Iraq.

The peak year for immigration into the UK was the 12 months from 1 Jul 1961 to 30 Jun 1962, when about 430,000 Commonwealth citizens arrived. The number of foreign immigrants in the year 1992 was 117,000.

Tourism The World Tourism Organization reports that the most popular destination is France, which in 1992 received 59,590,000 foreign tourists. The country with the greatest receipts from tourism is the United States, with $53.9 billion in 1992. The biggest spenders on foreign tourism are Americans, who in the same year spent $39.9 billion abroad.

GUESS WHAT?

Q Which is the most frequently crossed frontier?

A See Page 177

A record 19.3 million foreign tourists visited the United Kingdom in 1993. The highest level of expenditure was also in 1993, with £9.1 billion.

Birth rate *Highest and lowest* The crude birth rate—the number of births per 1000 population—for the whole world was estimated to be 27.0 per 1000 in 1985–90. The highest rate estimated by the United Nations for 1985–90 was 55.6 per 1000 for Malawi. Excluding the Vatican City, where the rate is negligible, the lowest recorded rate was 9.5 per 1000 for San Marino for the same period.

The crude birth rate for the UK was 13.5 registered live births per 1000 population in 1992. There were 781,000 live births altogether (on average 2140 per day or 89 per hour), of which 240,800 were outside marriage.

Death rate The crude death rate—the number of deaths per 1000 population of all ages—for the whole world was an estimated 9.7 per 1000 in 1985–90. East Timor had a rate of 45.0 per 1000 from 1975–80, although this had subsided to 21.5 in 1985–90. The highest estimated rate in the same period was 23.4 for Sierra Leone. The lowest estimated rate for 1985–90 was 3.5 deaths per 1000 for Bahrain.

The crude death rate for the UK was 11.0 in 1992. There were 634,200 deaths altogether (on average 1738 per day or 72 per hour).

Natural increase The rate of natural increase for the whole world was estimated to be 17.3

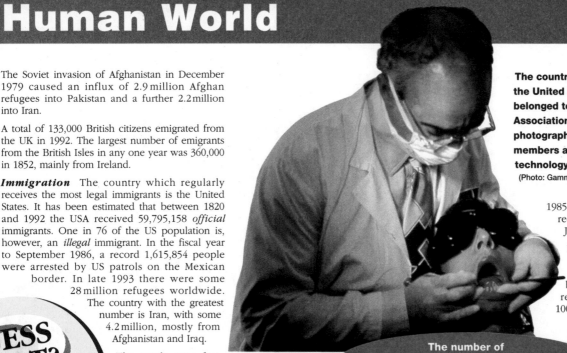

The country with the most dentists is the United States, where 139,404 belonged to the American Dental Association at the end of 1993. This photograph shows just one of their members at work using modern technology.
(Photo: Gamma/Hensey)

The number of dentists registered in the UK as at 1 Jan 1993 was 27,068.

(27.0 births less 9.7 deaths) per 1000 in 1985–90 compared with a peak 20.6 per 1000 in 1965–70. The highest of the latest available recorded rates was 37.4 (43.0 less 5.6) for Oman in 1985–90.

The 1992 rate for the UK was 2.5 (13.5 births less 11.0 deaths). In 1976 the population actually decreased, with a rate of 0.1 (12.1 births less 12.2 deaths).

Suicide The daily rate of suicides throughout the world is estimated to be more than 2700. The country with the highest rate is Sri Lanka, with 47 per 100,000 population in 1991. The country with the lowest recorded rate is Jordan, with just a single case in 1970 and hence a rate of 0.04 per 100,000.

In the United Kingdom there were 4628 suicides in 1992, giving a rate of 8.0 per 100,000 population.

Marriage and divorce The marriage rate for the Northern Mariana Islands, in the Pacific Ocean, is 31.2 per 1000 population. In the UK there were 349,739 marriages in 1991—a rate of 6.1 per 1000 population. The average (mean) age for first marriages in England and Wales in 1991 was 27.5 years (men) and 25.5 years (women).

The country with most divorces is the United States, with a total of 1,215,000 in 1992—a rate of 4.7 per thousand population. The all-time high rate was 5.4 per thousand in 1979. There were 173,700 divorces in 1991 in the UK.

Sex ratio There are estimated to be 1014 males in the world for every 1000 females. The country with the largest recorded shortage of women is the United Arab Emirates, which has an estimated 484 to every 1000 males. The country with the largest recorded shortage of males is Ukraine, with an estimated 1154 females to every 1000 males.

The sex ratio in the UK, which was 1069 females to every 1000 males in 1961, had become 1045 to every 1000 males by 1992, and is expected to be 1034 per 1000 by the turn of the century.

Infant mortality The world infant mortality rate—the number of deaths at ages under one year per 1000 live births—was 68 per 1000 for

1985–90. The lowest of the latest recorded rates is 5 per 1000 in Japan for the period 1985–90.

In Ethiopia the infant mortality rate was unofficially estimated to be nearly 550 per 1000 live births in 1969. The highest rate recently estimated is 172 per 1000 in Afghanistan (1985–90).

The rate of infant mortality for the UK was a record low of 6.6 in 1992.

Expectation of life at birth World expectation of life has risen from 46.4 years (1950–5) towards 63.3 years (1985–1990). There is evidence that expectation of life in Britain in the 5th century AD was 33 years for males and 27 years for females. In the decade 1890–1900 the expectation of life among the population of India was 23.7 years.

The highest average expectation of life at birth is in Japan, with 83.0 years for women and 76.3 years for men in 1992. The lowest estimated for the period 1985–90 is 39.4 years for males in Sierra Leone and 42.0 years for females in Afghanistan.

Going Down!

The lowest rate of natural increase in any independent country in recent times was in Hungary, which actually experienced a population decline in 1985–90, with a figure of –1.7 per 1000 (11.9 births and 13.6 deaths).

The latest available figures for the UK (1989–91) are 73.0 years for males and 78.5 years for females, putting it in 17th position in the world rankings. The British figures for 1901 were 45.5 years for males and 49.0 years for females.

Housing For comparison, dwelling units are defined as a structurally separated room or rooms occupied by private households of one or more people and having separate access or a common passageway to the street.

The country with the greatest number of dwelling units is China, with 276,947,962 in 1990.

Great Britain had an estimated stock of 23,301,000 dwellings at the end of 1992, of which 66.3 per cent were owner-occupied. The record number of permanent houses built in a year was 425,835 in 1968.

Hospitals The country with the greatest number of hospitals is China, with 63,101 in 1991. Nauru has the most hospital beds per person (250 for every 10,000 people), and Nepal the fewest (2 per 10,000).

Physicians The country with the greatest number of physicians is China, which had 1,808,000 in 1992, including those practising dentistry and those of traditional Chinese medicine.

Chad has the highest number of people per physician, with 47,640.

There were 155,585 doctors on the General Medical Council's Principal List, and therefore entitled to practise in the UK, as at 1 Jan 1994, giving one doctor to every 374 people.

Doctors!

The eight sons and two daughters of Dr William and Beryl Waldron of Knocknacarra, Co. Galway, Republic of Ireland all qualified as doctors from University College Galway between 1976 and 1990. The Barcia family from Valencia, Spain have had the same medical practice for seven generations since 1792.

Mental health The country with the most psychologists and psychiatrists is the United States. The registered membership of the American Psychological Association (instituted in 1892) was 124,000 in 1994, and the membership of the American Psychiatric Association (instituted in 1844) was 38,285.

Political Unrest

Saving of life The greatest number of people saved from extinction by one man is estimated to be nearly 100,000 Jews in Budapest, Hungary from July 1944 to January 1945 by the Swedish diplomat Raoul Wallenberg (b. 4 Aug 1912). After escaping an assassination attempt by the Nazis, he was imprisoned without trial in the Soviet Union. On 6 Feb 1957 Andrey Gromyko, Deputy Foreign Minister, said prisoner 'Walenberg' had died in a cell in Lubyanka Jail, Moscow on 16 Jul 1947. Sighting reports within the Gulag system persisted for years after his disappearance.

GUESS WHAT?

Q How many life-saving awards has Eric Deakin received?

A See Page 194

Mass killings *China* The greatest massacre ever imputed by the government of one sovereign nation against the government of another is that of 26.3 million Chinese between 1949 and May 1965,

Worst Disasters in the World

Disaster	Number killed	Location	Date
Pandemic	75,000,000	Eurasia: The Black Death (bubonic, pneumonic and septicaemic plague)	1347–51
Genocide	c. 35,000,000	Mongol extermination of Chinese peasantry	1311–40
Famine	c. 30,000,000[1]	Northern China	1959–61
Influenza	21,640,000	World-wide	1918–19
Circular Storm[2]	1,000,000	Ganges Delta Islands, Bangladesh	12–13 Nov 1970
Flood	900,000	Huang He River, China	Oct 1887
Earthquake	830,000	Shaanxi, Shanxi and Henan provinces, China	2 Feb 1556
Landslides (Triggered off by single earthquake)	180,000	Gansu Province, China	16 Dec 1920
Atomic Bomb	155,200	Hiroshima, Japan (including radiation deaths within a year)	6 Aug 1945
Conventional Bombing[3]	c. 140,000	Tokyo, Japan	10 Mar 1945
Volcanic Eruption	92,000	Tambora, Sumbawa, Indonesia	5–10 Apr 1815
Avalanches	c. 18,000[4]	Yungay, Huascarán, Peru	31 May 1970
Marine (Single ship)	c. 7700	*Wilhelm Gustloff* (25,484 tons) German liner torpedoed off Danzig by Soviet submarine S-13 (only 903 survivors)	30 Jan 1945
Dam Burst	c. 5000[5]	Machhu River Dam, Morvi, Gujarat, India	11 Aug 1979
Panic	c. 4000	Chongqing, China, air raid shelter	6 Jun 1941
Smog	3500–4000	London fog, England	4–9 Dec 1952
Industrial (Chemical)	3350	Union Carbide methylisocyanate plant, Bhopal, India	2–3 Dec 1984
Tunnelling (Silicosis)	c. 2500	Hawk's Nest hydroelectric tunnel, W. Virginia, USA	1931–35
Fire[6] (Single building)	1670	The Theatre, Guangdong (Canton), China	May 1845
Explosion	1635[7]	Halifax, Nova Scotia, Canada	6 Dec 1917
Mining[8]	1549	Honkeiko (Benxihu) Colliery, China (coal dust explosion)	26 Apr 1942
Riot	c. 1400	Riots following arrest of woman selling contraband cigarettes, Taiwan	March 1947
Tornado	c. 1300	Shaturia, Bangladesh	26 Apr 1989
Mass Suicide[9]	960	Jewish Zealots, Masada, Israel	73
Railway	>800	Bagmati River, Bihar, India	6 Jun 1981
Fireworks	>800	Dauphin's wedding, Seine, Paris, France	16 May 1770
Aircraft (Civil)[10]	583	KLM-Pan Am Boeing 747 ground crash, Tenerife	27 Mar 1977
Man-eating Animal	436	Champawat district, India, tigress shot by Col. Jim Corbett (1875–1955)	1902–7
Terrorism	329	Bomb aboard Air India Boeing 747, crashed into Atlantic south-west of Ireland. Sikh extremists suspected	23 Jun 1985
Hail	246	Moradabad, Uttar Pradesh, India	20 Apr 1888
Road[11]	176	Petrol tanker explosion inside Salang Tunnel, Afghanistan	3 Nov 1982
Offshore Oil Platform	167	Piper Alpha oil production platform, North Sea	6 Jul 1988
Submarine	130	*Le Surcouf* rammed by US merchantman *Thompson Lykes* in Caribbean	18 Feb 1942
Lightning	81	Boeing 707 jet airliner, struck by lightning near Elkton, Maryland, USA	8 Dec 1963
Helicopter	61	Russian military helicopter carrying refugees shot down near Lata, Georgia	14 Dec 1992
Mountaineering	43	Lenin Peak, Tajikistan/Kyrgyzstan border (then USSR)	13 Jul 1990
Ski Lift (Cable car)	42	Cavalese resort, northern Italy	9 Mar 1976
Nuclear Reactor	31[12]	Chernobyl No. 4, Ukraine (then USSR)	26 Apr 1986
Elevator (Lift)	31	Gold mine lift at Vaal Reefs, South Africa fell 1.9 km *1.2 miles*	27 Mar 1980
Yacht Racing	19	28th Fastnet Race—23 boats sank or abandoned in Force 11 gale	13–15 Aug 1979
Space Exploration	7[13]	US Challenger 51L Shuttle, Cape Canaveral, Florida, USA	28 Jan 1986
Nuclear Waste Accident	high but undisclosed[14]	Venting of plutonium extraction wastes, Kyshtym, Russia (then USSR)	c. Dec 1957

FOOTNOTES

[1] It has been estimated that more than 5 million died in the post-World War I famine of 1920–1 in the USSR. The Soviet government informed Mr (later President) Herbert Hoover in July 1923 that the ARA (American Relief Administration) had since August 1921 saved 20 million lives from famine and famine-related diseases.

[2] This figure published in 1972 for the Bangladeshi disaster was from Dr Afzal, Principal Scientific Officer of the Atomic Energy Authority Centre, Dacca. One report asserted that less than half of the population of the four islands of Bhola, Charjabbar, Hatia and Ramagati (1961 Census 1.4 million) survived. The most damaging hurricane recorded was Hurricane Andrew from 23–26 Aug 1992, which was estimated to have done c. $22 billion worth of damage.

[3] The number of civilians killed by the bombing of Germany has been put variously at 593,000 and 'over 635,000', including some 35,000 deaths in the raids on Dresden, Germany from 13–15 Feb 1945. Total Japanese fatalities were 600,000 (conventional) and 220,000 (nuclear).

[4] A total of 18,000 Austrian and Italian troops were reported to have been lost in the Dolomite valleys of northern Italy on 13 Dec 1916 in more than 100 snow avalanches. Some of the avalanches were triggered by gunfire.

[5] The dynamiting of a Yangzi Jiang dam at Huayuan Kou by Guomindang (GMD) forces in April 1938 during the Sino-Japanese war is reputed to have resulted in 890,000 deaths.

[6] >200,000 killed in the sack of Moscow, as a result of fires started by the invading Tatars in May 1571. Worst-ever hotel fire, 162 killed, Hotel Daeyungak, Seoul, South Korea 25 Dec 1971. Worst circus fire, 168 killed, Hartford, Connecticut, USA 6 Jul 1944.

[7] Some sources maintain that the final death toll was over 3000 on 6–7 December. Published estimates of the 11,000 killed at the BASF chemical plant explosion at Oppau, Germany on 21 Sep 1921 were exaggerated. The most reliable estimate is 561 killed.

[8] The worst gold-mining disaster in South Africa was when 182 were killed in Kinross gold mine on 16 Sep 1986.

[9] As reported by the historian Flavius Josephus (c. 37–100). In modern times, the greatest mass suicide was on 18 Nov 1978 when 913 members of the People's Temple cult died of mass cyanide poisoning near Port Kaituma, Guyana. Some 7000 Japanese committed suicide, many of them jumping off cliffs to their deaths, in July 1944 during the US Marines' assault of the island of Saipan.

[10] The crash of JAL's Boeing 747, flight 123, near Tokyo on 12 Aug 1985, in which 520 passengers and crew perished, was the worst single plane crash in aviation history.

[11] Western estimates gave the number of deaths at c. 1100. Latvia has the highest fatality rate in road accidents, with 34.7 deaths per 100,000 population, and Malta the lowest, with 1.6 per 100,000.

[12] Explosion at 0123 hrs local time. Thirty-one was the official Soviet total of immediate deaths. It is not known how many of the c. 200,000 people involved in the clean-up operation died in the five-year period following the disaster since no systematic records were kept. The senior scientific officer Vladimir Chernousenko, who gave himself two to four years to live owing to his exposure to radiation, put the death toll to be between 7000 and 10,000 in a statement on 13 Apr 1991.

[13] In the greatest space disaster on the ground 91 people were killed when an R-16 rocket exploded during fuelling at the Baikonur Space Center, Kazakhstan on 24 Oct 1960.

[14] More than 30 small communities in a 1200 km[2] 460 mile[2] area were eliminated from maps of the USSR in the years after the accident, with 17,000 people evacuated. It was possibly an ammonium nitrate-hexone explosion. A report released in 1992 indicated that 8015 people had died over a 32-year period of observation as a direct result of discharges from the complex.

GUESS WHAT?

Q In which famous event was Mao Zedong involved in the 1930s?

A See Page 198

Worst Disasters in the British Isles

Disaster	Number killed	Location	Date
Famine	1,500,000[1]	Ireland (famine and typhus)	1846–51
Pandemic (the Black Death)	800,000		1347–50
Influenza	225,000		Sep–Nov 1918
Circular Storm	c. 8000	'The Channel Storm'	26 Nov 1703
Smog	3500–4000	London fog	4–9 Dec 1952
Flood	c. 2000[2]	Severn Estuary	20 Jan 1606
Bombing	1436	London	10–11 May 1941
Marine (single ship)	c. 800[3]	HMS *Royal George* off Spithead, Hants	29 Aug 1782
Riot	565 (min)	London anti-Catholic Gordon riots	2–13 Jun 1780
Mining	439	Universal Colliery, Senghenydd, Mid Glam	14 Oct 1913
Terrorism (aircraft)	270[4]	Bomb aboard Pan Am Boeing 747, crashed over Lockerbie, Dumfries & Galloway	21 Dec 1988
Dam Burst	250	Bradfield Reservoir, Dale Dyke, near Sheffield, S Yorks (embankment burst)	12 Mar 1864
Railway	227[5]	Triple collision, Quintinshill, Dumfries & Galloway	22 May 1915
Fire (single building)	188[6]	Theatre Royal, Exeter	5 Sep 1887
Panic	183	Victoria Hall, Sunderland, Tyne and Wear	16 Jun 1883
Offshore Oil Platform	167	Piper Alpha oil production platform, North Sea	6 Jul 1988
Landslide	144	Pantglas coal tip No. 7, Aberfan, Mid Glam	21 Oct 1966
Explosion	134[7]	Chilwell, Notts (explosives factory)	1 Jul 1918
Nuclear Reactor	footnote[8]	Cancer deaths; Windscale (now Sellafield), Cumbria	10 Oct 1957
Submarine	99	HMS *Thetis*, during trials, Liverpool Bay	1 Jun 1939
Tornado	75	Tay Bridge collapsed under impact of 2 tornadic vortices	28 Dec 1879
Helicopter	45	Chinook, off Sumburgh, Shetland Islands	6 Nov 1986
Road	33[9]	Coach crash, River Dibb, near Grassington, N Yorks	27 May 1975

FOOTNOTES

[1] *Based on the net rate of natural increase between 1841 and 1851, a supportable case for a loss of population of 3 million can be made out if rates of under-enumeration of 25 per cent (1841) and 10 per cent (1851) are accepted. Potato rot (Phytophthora infestans) was first reported on 13 Sep 1845.*

[2] *Death tolls of 100,000 were reputed in England and Holland in the floods of 1099, 1421 and 1446.*

[3] *c. 4000 were lost on HM troopship Lancastria, 16,243 grt, off St Nazaire, France on 17 Jun 1940.*

[4] *The worst crash by a UK operated aircraft was that of a Dan-Air Boeing 727 from Manchester which crashed into a mountain on the Canary Islands on 25 Apr 1980, killing 146 people. There were no survivors.*

[5] *The 194.7m 213yd long troop train was telescoped to 61.2m 67yd. Signalmen Meakin and Tinsley were sentenced for manslaughter.*

Britain's worst underground train disaster was the Moorgate Tube disaster of 28 Feb 1975, when 43 persons were killed.

[6] *In July 1212, 3000 were killed in the crush, burned or drowned when London Bridge caught fire at both ends. Britain's most destructive fire was that leading to a £165 million loss at the Army Ordnance depot, Donnington, Shrops on 24 Jun 1983.*

[7] *HM armed cruiser Natal blew up off Invergordon, Highland on 30 Dec 1915, killing 428.*

[8] *There were no deaths as a direct result of the fire, but the number of cancer deaths that might be attributed to it was estimated by the National Radiological Protection Board in 1989 to be 100.*

[9] *The greatest pile-up on British roads was on the M6 near Lymm Interchange, near Thelwall, Cheshire on 13 Sep 1971. Two hundred vehicles were involved, with 10 dead and 61 injured. The worst year for road deaths in Great Britain was 1941, with 9161 deaths.*

Younger generations will be unable to recall the London 'pea-soupers' which were a feature of life before the Clean Air Act of 1956 took effect. Here a bus gingerly makes its way towards Kew Green in the world's worst smog, that of 1952.
(Photo: Hulton-Deutsch Collection)

during the regime of Mao Zedong (Mao Tse-tung, 1893–1976). This accusation was made by an agency of the Soviet government in a radio broadcast on 7 Apr 1969. The broadcast broke down the figure into four periods: 2.8 million (1949–52); 3.5 million (1953–7); 6.7 million (1958–60); and 13.3 million (1961–May 1965).

The Walker Report, published by the US Senate Committee of the Judiciary in July 1971, placed the parameters of the total death toll within China since 1949 between 32.25 and 61.7

Biggest demonstration
A figure of 2.7 million was reported from China for a demonstration against the USSR in Shanghai on 3–4 Mar 1969 following border clashes.

million.

An estimate of 63.7 million was published by Jean-Pierre Dujardin in *Figaro* magazine of 19–25 Nov 1978.

In the 13th–17th centuries there were three periods of wholesale massacre in China. The numbers of victims attributed to these events are assertions rather than reliable estimates. The figure put on the Mongolian invasions of northern China from 1210–19 and from 1311–40 are both of the order of 35 million, while the number of victims of the bandit leader Zhang Xianzhong (c. 1605–47), known as the 'Yellow Tiger', from 1643–7 in the Sichuan province has been put at 40 million.

USSR Scholarly estimates for the number of human casualties of Soviet communism focus on some 40 million, excluding those killed in the 'Great Patriotic War'. Larger figures are claimed in Moscow today but these are not necessarily more authoritative. Nobel prizewinner Aleksandr Solzhenitsyn (b. 11 Dec 1918) put the total as high as 66,700,000 for the period between October 1917 and December 1959.

Nazi Germany The most extreme extermination campaign against a people was the Holocaust or the genocidal 'Final Solution' (*Endlösung*) ordered by Adolf Hitler, before or at the latest by autumn 1941 and continuing into May 1945. Reliable estimates of the number of victims range from 5.1 to 6 million Jews.

Cambodia As a percentage of a nation's total population the worst genocide appears to have been that in Cambodia (formerly Kampuchea). According to the Khmer Rouge Foreign Minister, Ieng Sary, more than a third of the 8 million Khmers were killed between 17 Apr 1975, when the Khmer Rouge captured Phnom Penh, and January 1979, when they were overthrown. Under the rule of Saloth Sar, alias Pol Pot, a founder member of the CPK (Communist Party of Kampuchea, formed in September 1960), towns, money and property were abolished and economical execution by bayonet and club introduced. Deaths at the Tuol Sleng interrogation centre reached 582 in a day.

People were murdered in Cambodia in the late 1970s simply for being too well educated.

Towns and Cities

Oldest The oldest known walled town in the world is Arīhā (Jericho). The radiocarbon dating on specimens from the lowest levels reached by archaeologists indicates habitation there by perhaps 2700 people as early as 7800 BC. The settlement of Dolní Věstonice, Czech Republic has been dated to the Gravettian culture *c.* 27,000 BC. The oldest capital city in the world is Dimashq (Damascus), Syria. It has been continuously inhabited since *c.* 2500 BC.

Great Britain *Towns, villages and boroughs* The oldest town in Great Britain is often cited as Colchester, the old British Camulodunum, headquarters of Belgic chiefs in the first century BC. However, the name of the tin trading post Salakee, St Mary's, Isles of Scilly is derived from pre-Celtic roots and hence *ante* 550 BC.

> The most remote village on mainland Great Britain is Inverie, Highland, which is a walk of 43.5 km *27 miles* from Arnisdale, also in Highland, its nearest village.

The smallest place with a town council is Fordwich, in Kent (population 249). England's largest village is Lancing, W Sussex, with an estimated population of 18,100.

Most populous The most populous urban agglomeration in the world as listed in the United Nations' 1992 publication *World Urbanization Prospects* is Tokyo, with a population of 25,000,000 in 1990. By the end of the century this is expected to have increased to 28,000,000.

Great Britain The most populous conurbation in Britain is Greater London, with an estimated 6,809,000 people (1993); its peak figure was 8,615,050 in 1939. The residential population of the City of London (274 ha *677.3 acres* plus 24.9 ha *61.7 acres* foreshore) is 4000 (1993 estimate) compared with 129,000 in 1851. The daytime figure is 325,000.

Largest in area The world's largest city, in area, is Mount Isa, Queensland, Australia. The area administered by the City Council is 41,225 km² *15,917 miles²*. The largest conurbation in the UK is Greater London, with an area of 1579.5 km² *609.8 miles²*.

Highest The highest capital in the world, before the domination of Tibet by China, was Lhasa, at an elevation of 3684 m *12,087 ft* above sea level. La Paz, administrative and *de facto* capital of Bolivia, stands at an altitude of 3631 m *11,916 ft* above sea level. Its airport, El Alto, is at 4080 m *13,385 ft*. Sucre, the legal capital of Bolivia, stands at 2834 m *9301 ft* above sea level. Wenchuan, founded in 1955 on the Qinghai–Tibet road north of the Tangla range in China, is the highest town in the world at 5100 m *16,730 ft* above sea level. A settlement on the T'e-li-mo trail in southern Tibet is sited at an altitude of 6019 m *19,800 ft*.

Great Britain The highest village in Britain is Flash, Staffs, which is at 462.7 m *1518 ft* above sea level.

Lowest The Israeli settlement of Ein Bokek, which has a synagogue, on the shores of the Dead Sea is the lowest in the world, at 393.5 m *1291 ft* below sea level.

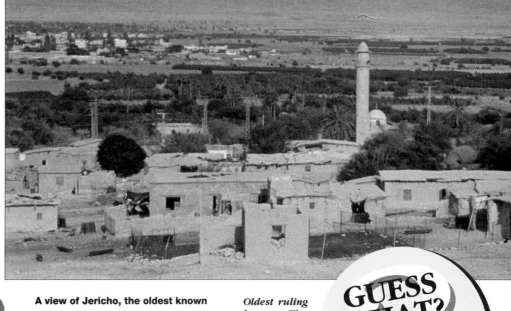

A view of Jericho, the oldest known walled town.

(Photo: Gamma/E. Baitel)

Northernmost The northernmost village is Ny-Ålesund (78° 55′ N), a coalmining settlement on King's Bay, Vest Spitsbergen, in the Norwegian territory of Svalbard. The northernmost capital is Reykjavík, Iceland (64° 08′ N). Its population was 100,850 in 1992.

Southernmost The world's southernmost village is Puerto Williams (population about 1000) on the north coast of Isla Navarino, in Tierra del Fuego, Chile, 1090 km *680 miles* north of Antarctica. Wellington, New Zealand, with a 1991 population of 325,700, is the southernmost capital city (41° 17′ S). The world's southernmost administrative centre is Port Stanley, Falkland Islands (51° 43′ S), with a population of 1643 in 1991.

Most remote from sea The large town most remote from the sea is Urumqi (Wu-lu-mu-ch'i) in Xinjiang, the capital of China's Xinjiang Uygur Autonomous Region, at a distance of about 2500 km *150 miles* from the nearest coastline. Its population was estimated to be 1,379,000 in late 1993.

New towns!

Of the 32 set up in Great Britain, that with the largest eventual planned population is Milton Keynes, Bucks, with a current population of 179,000 and a projected 210,000 people for the end of the century.

Royalty and Heads of State

World!

Of the world's 191 sovereign states, 145 are republics. The other 46 are headed by 1 emperor, 14 kings, 3 queens, 2 sultans, 1 grand duke, 2 princes, 3 amirs, an elected monarch, the Pope, a president chosen from and by 7 hereditary sheiks, a head of state currently similar to a constitutional monarch, and 2 nominal non-hereditary 'princes' in one country. Queen Elizabeth II is head of state of 15 Commonwealth countries in addition to the UK.

GUESS WHAT?

Q Who is presently the oldest king?

A See Page 182

Oldest ruling house The Emperor of Japan, Akihito (b. 23 Dec 1933), is the 125th in line from the first Emperor, Jimmu Tenno or Zinmu, whose reign was traditionally from 660 to 581 BC, but more probably dates from *c.* 40 BC to *c.* 10 BC.

Her Majesty Queen Elizabeth II (b. 21 Apr 1926) represents dynasties historically traceable back at least 54 generations to the 4th century AD in the case of Tegid, great grandfather of Cunedda, founder of the House of Gwynedd in Wales. If the historicity of some early Scoto-Irish and Pictish kings were acceptable, the lineage could be extended to about 70 generations.

Reigns *Longest all-time* The longest recorded reign of any monarch is that of Phiops II (also known as Pepi II), or Neferkare, a Sixth Dynasty pharaoh of ancient Egypt. His reign began *c.* 2281 BC, when he was 6 years of age, and is believed to have lasted *c.* 94 years. Minhti, King of Arakan, which is now part of Myanmar (Burma), is reputed to have reigned for 95 years between 1279 and 1374. Musoma Kanijo, chief of the Nzega district of western Tanganyika (now part of Tanzania), reputedly reigned for more than 98 years from 1864, when aged 8, until his death on 2 Feb 1963.

Longest current The King of Thailand, Bhumibol Adulyadej (Rama IX) (b. 5 Dec 1927), is currently the world's longest-reigning monarch, having succeeded to the throne following the death of his older brother on 9 Jun 1946. The most durable monarch is the King of Cambodia, Norodom Sihanouk (b. 31 Oct 1922), who first became King on 16 Apr 1941 but abdicated on 2 Mar 1955, and then returned to the throne on 24 Sep 1993. The longest-reigning queen is HM Queen Elizabeth II (⇨ above), who succeeded to the throne on 6 Feb 1952 on the death of her father.

Shortest The Crown Prince Luis Filipe of Portugal was mortally wounded at the same time that his father was killed by a bullet which severed his carotid artery, in the streets of Lisbon on 1 Feb 1908. He was thus technically King of Portugal (Dom Luis III) for about 20 minutes.

Highest post-nominal numbers The highest post-nominal number ever used to designate a member of a royal house was 75, briefly enjoyed

British Monarchy Records

Longest Reign or Tenure

Kings: 59 years 96 days[1] George III, from 1760–1820
Queens Regnant: 63 years 216 days Victoria, from 1837–1901
Queens Consort: 57 years 70 days Charlotte, from 1761–1818
(Consort of George III)

Shortest Reign or Tenure

Kings: 77 days[2] Edward V, in 1483
Queens Regnant: 13 days[3] Jane, from 6–19 Jul 1553
Queens Consort: 154 days Yoleta, from 1285–6
(Second Consort of Alexander III)

Longest Lived

Kings: 81 years 239 days[4] George III (1738–1820)
Queens Regnant: 81 years 243 days Victoria (1819–1901)
Queens Consort: 93 years Lady Elizabeth Bowes Lyon, Queen Elizabeth, the Queen Mother (b. 4 Aug 1900)

Oldest to Start Reign or Consortship

Kings: 64 years 10 months William IV (reigned 1830–7)
Queens Regnant: 37 years 5 months Mary I (reigned 1553–8)
Queens Consort: 56 years 53 days Alexandra (1844–1925)
(Consort of Edward VII, reigned 1901–10)

Youngest to Start Reign or Consortship

Kings: 269 days Henry VI in 1422
Queens Regnant: 6 or 7 days Mary, Queen of Scots in 1542
Queens Consort: 6 years 11 months Isabella (Second Consort of Richard II) in 1396

FOOTNOTES
[1] *James Francis Edward, the Old Pretender, known to his supporters as James III, styled his reign from 16 Sep 1701 until his death on 1 Jan 1766 (i.e. 64 years 109 days).*
[2] *There is a strong probability that in pre-Conquest times Sweyn 'Forkbeard', the Danish King of England, reigned for only 40 days in 1013–14.*
[3] *She accepted the allegiance of the Lords of the Council (9 July) and was proclaimed on 10 July so is often referred to as the 'Nine-day Queen'.*
[4] *Richard Cromwell (b. 4 Oct 1626), the 2nd Lord Protector from 3 Sep 1658 until his abdication on 24 May 1659, lived under the alias John Clarke until 12 Jul 1712, aged 85 years 9 months and was thus the longest-lived head of state.*

by Count Heinrich LXXV Reuss zu Schleiz (1800–1801). All male members of this branch of the German family are called Heinrich and are successively numbered from I upwards in three sequences. The first began in 1695 (and ended with Heinrich LXXV), the second began in 1803 (and ended with Heinrich XLVII) and the third began in 1910. These are purely *personal* numbers and should not be confused with *regnal* numbers.

Longest-lived 'royals' The longest life among the blood royal of Europe was that of the Princess Pauline Marie Madeleine of Croy (1887–1987), who celebrated her 100th birthday in her birthplace of Le Roeulx, Belgium on 11 Jan 1987.

HRH Princess Alice (b. 25 Feb 1883), a granddaughter of Queen Victoria, became the longest-lived British royal ever on 15 Jul 1977 and died aged 97 years 313 days on 3 Jan 1981. She fulfilled 20,000 engagements, including the funerals of five British monarchs.

Youngest king and queen The country with the youngest king is Swaziland, where King Mswati

Heaviest!

The world's heaviest monarch is the 1.90 m *6 ft 3 in* tall King Taufa'ahau of Tonga, who in September 1976 was weighed on the only adequate scales in the country, at the airport, recording 209.5 kg *33 st*. By 1985 he was reported to have slimmed down to 139.7 kg *22 st* and in early 1993 he was 127.0 kg *20 st*. The Tongan High Commissioner's embassy car in London has the number plate '1 TON', although this is an abbreviated reference to his status rather than any allusion to his monarch's weight.

III (⇨ below) was crowned on 25 Apr 1986 aged 18 years 6 days. He was born Makhosetive, the 67th son of King Subhusa II. The country with the youngest queen is Denmark, with Queen Margrethe II (b. 16 Apr 1940).

Most prolific The most prolific monogamous 'royal' was Prince Hartmann of Liechtenstein (1613–86), who had 24 children, of whom 21 were born live, by Countess Elisabeth zu Salm-Reifferscheidt (1623–88). HRH Duke Roberto I of Parma (1848–1907) also had 24 children, but by two wives.

Heads of State *Oldest and youngest* The oldest head of state in the world is Joaquín Balaguer, President of the Dominican Republic (b. 1 Sep 1907). The oldest monarch is King Taufa'ahau of Tonga (b. 4 Jul 1918), who is also the heaviest (⇨ above). The youngest is King Mswati III of Swaziland (b. 19 Apr 1968) (⇨ above).

Meeting The summit segment of the United Nations Conference on Environment and Development, on 12–13 Jun 1992, was attended by 92 heads of state and heads of government—the largest gathering of world leaders. The summit had 103 participants altogether and was one of the meetings at the 'Earth Summit', which was held in Rio de Janeiro, Brazil from 3–14 Jun 1992.

The highest-paid legislators are the Japanese, seen here in session. The Prime Minister has an annual salary of £232,000.
(Photo: Gamma/K. Kurita)

Legislatures

Parliaments—World

Earliest and oldest The earliest known legislative assembly or *ukkim* was a bicameral one in Erech, Iraq *c.*2800 BC. The oldest recorded legislative body is the Icelandic *Althing*, founded in AD 930. This body, which originally comprised 39 local chieftains at Thingvellir, was abolished in 1800, but restored by Denmark to a consultative status in 1843 and a legislative status in 1874. The legislative assembly with the oldest *continuous* history is the Isle of Man Tynwald which may have its origins in the late ninth century and hence possibly pre-date the *Althing*.

Largest The largest legislative assembly in the world is the National People's Congress of the People's Republic of China. The Eighth National People's Congress, the first session of which was convened in March 1993, is composed of 2978 deputies indirectly elected from 22 provinces, five autonomous regions and three municipalities directly under the Central Government, and from the Chinese People's Liberation Army, representing the Communist Party of China, eight democratic parties and people without any political affiliations. The Congress is elected for a term of five years.

Protest!

The greatest petition on record was signed by 13,078,935 people in South Korea between 11 Nov–23 Dec 1991. They were protesting against efforts by advanced agricultural exporting countries to open their country's rice market to foreign imports.

Greatest petitions In Great Britain the largest theoretically has been the Great Chartist Petition of 1848, but of the 5,706,000 'signatures' only 1,975,496 were valid. Otherwise the largest in Britain was in support of ambulance workers in their pay dispute, when a national petition containing 4,680,727 signatures was delivered to the House of Commons on 14 Dec 1989. Since 1974, the signatures on petitions which have been presented have not been counted at the House of Commons.

Highest-paid legislators The most highly paid of the world's legislators are the Japanese. The Prime Minister has an annual salary of 38,463,360 yen (£232,000) including monthly allowances and bonuses, whilst members of both the House of

(Photo: Gamma/T. Selwyn)

Shortest The parliament of Edward I, summoned to Westminster for 30 May 1306, lasted only 1 day. That of Charles II at Oxford lasted 7 days, from 21–28 Mar 1681. The shortest United Kingdom Parliament was that of George III, lasting from 15 Dec 1806 to 29 Apr 1807, a period of only 4 months and 14 days.

were being contested, out of an eligible electorate of 488,678,993. The elections were contested by 359 parties, and there were nearly 565,000 polling stations manned by 3 million staff. As a result of the election a new government was formed under the leadership of P. V. Narasimha Rao of the Congress (I) Party.

Closest The ultimate in close general elections occurred in Zanzibar (now part of Tanzania) on 18 Jan 1961, when the Afro-Shirazi Party won by a single seat, after the seat of Chake-Chake on Pemba Island had been gained by a single vote.

> The longest speech made was one by Chief Mangosuthu Buthelezi, the Zulu leader, when he gave an address to the KwaZulu legislative assembly between 12 and 29 Mar 1993. He spoke on 11 of the 18 days, averaging nearly 2½ hours on each of the 11 days.

The narrowest recorded percentage win in an election was for the office of Southern District Highway Commissioner in Mississippi, USA on 7 Aug 1979. Robert E. Joiner was declared the winner over W. H. Pyron, with 133,587 votes to 133,582. The loser thus obtained more than 49.999 per cent of the votes.

Representatives and the House of Councillors have annual salaries of 23,633,565 yen (£142,000) including bonuses.

Longest membership The longest span as a legislator was 83 years, by József Madarász (1814–1915). He first attended the Hungarian Parliament from 1832–86 as *oblegatus absentium* (i.e. on behalf of an absent deputy). He was a full member from 1848–50 and from 1861 until his death on 31 Jan 1915.

Longest speeches The longest speech made in the United Nations has been one of 4 hr 29 min on 26 Sep 1960 by President Fidel Castro Ruz (b. 13 Aug 1927) of Cuba.

Women's suffrage As far back as 1838 the Pitcairn Islands incorporated female suffrage in its constitution, although this was only de facto and not legally binding. The earliest legislature with female voters was the Territory of Wyoming, USA in 1869, followed by the Isle of Man in 1881. The attempted exercise of the franchise by Mrs Lily Maxwell in Manchester on 26 Nov 1867 was declared illegal on 9 Nov 1868.

> The earliest country to have universal female suffrage was New Zealand in 1893.

Longest sittings
The longest sitting in the House of Commons was one of 41½ hr from 4 p.m. on 31 Jan 1881 to 9:30 a.m. on 2 Feb 1881, on the question of better Protection of Person and Property in Ireland. The longest sitting of the Lords has been 19 hr 16 min from 2:30 p.m. on 29 Feb to 9:46 a.m. on 1 Mar 1968 on the Commonwealth Immigrants Bill (committee stage). The longest sitting of a standing committee was from 10:30 a.m. on 11 May to 12:08 p.m. on 13 May 1948, when Standing Committee D considered the Gas Bill through two nights for 49 hr 38 min.

Friends!

The oldest treaty still in force is the Anglo-Portuguese Treaty, which was signed in London over 621 years ago on 16 Jun 1373, making Portugal the UK's oldest ally. The text was confirmed 'with my usual flourish' by John de Banketre, Clerk.

Longest speeches The longest recorded continuous speech in the Chamber of the House of Commons was that of Rt Hon Henry Peter Brougham (1778–1868) on 7 Feb 1828, when he spoke for 6 hours on Law Reform. Brougham, created the 1st Lord Brougham and Vaux on 22 Nov 1830, then set the House of Lords record, also with 6 hours, on 7 Oct 1831, when speaking on the second reading of the Reform Bill, 'fortified by 3 tumblers of spiced wine'.

The longest back-bench speech under present, much stricter standing orders has been one of 4 hr 23 min by Sir Ivan Lawrence (b. 24 Dec 1936), Conservative Member for Burton, opposing the Water (Fluoridation) Bill on 6 Mar 1985. John Golding (b. 9 Mar 1931) (then Labour, Newcastle-under-Lyme) spoke for 11 hr 15 min in committee on small amendments to the British Telecommunications Bill on 8–9 Feb 1983.

Divisions The record number of divisions in a House of Commons day is 64 on 23–24 Mar 1971, including 57 in succession between midnight and noon. The greatest number of votes in a division was 660, with a majority of 40 (350–310) against the government of the Marquess of Salisbury on the vote of no confidence on 11 Aug 1892.

Elections—World

Largest The largest elections in the world were those beginning on 20 May 1991 for the Indian *Lok Sabha* (Lower House), which has 543 elective seats. A total of 315,439,908 people cast their votes in the 511 constituencies where the seats

Most decisive North Korea recorded a 100 per cent turn-out of electors and a 100 per cent vote for the Workers' Party of Korea in the general election of 8 Oct 1962. The next closest approach was in Albania on 14 Nov 1982, when a single voter spoiled national unanimity for the official (and only) Communist candidates, who consequently obtained 99.99993 per cent of the poll in a reported 100 per cent turn-out of 1,627,968.

Longest in power In Mongolia the Communists (Mongolian People's Revolutionary Party) have been in power since 1924, although only in the last three years within a multi-party system. In February 1992 the term 'People's Republic' was dropped from the name.

Cheat!

In the Liberian presidential election of 1927 President Charles D.B. King (1875–1961) was returned with a majority over his opponent, Thomas J.R. Faulkner of the People's Party, officially announced as 234,000. President King thereby claimed a 'majority' more than 15½ times greater than the entire electorate.

Highest personal majority The highest ever personal majority for any politician has been 4,726,112 in the case of Boris Yeltsin, the unofficial Moscow candidate, in the parliamentary elections held in the former Soviet Union on 26 Mar 1989. Yeltsin received 5,118,745 votes out of the 5,722,937 which were cast in the Moscow constituency, his closest rival obtaining 392,633 votes. Benazir Bhutto achieved 96.71 per cent of the poll in the Larkana-III constituency at the 1988 general election in Pakistan, with 82,229 votes. The next highest candidate obtained just 1979 votes.

Largest party The largest political party is the Chinese Communist Party, formed in 1920, which has an estimated membership of 50.3 million.

Largest ballot paper On 5 Mar 1985 in the State Assembly (*Vidhan Sabha*) elections in Karnataka, India there were 301 candidates for Belgaum City.

Political instability El Salvador has averaged one government every eighteen months since it obtained its independence in 1821, whilst Syria had 17 governments in the space of just 33 months between March 1949 and December 1951,

Parliaments—United Kingdom

Earliest The earliest known use of the term 'parliament' is in an official royal document, in the meaning of a summons to the King's (Henry III's) Council, dating from 19 Dec 1241. The Houses of Parliament of the United Kingdom in the Palace of Westminster, London had 1851 members (House of Lords 1200, of whom *c.* 650 are active; House of Commons 651) in April 1994.

Longest The longest English Parliament was the 'Pensioners' Parliament of Charles II, which lasted from 8 May 1661 to 24 Jan 1679, a period of 17 years 8 months and 16 days. The longest United Kingdom Parliament was that of George V, Edward VIII and George VI, lasting from 26 Nov 1935 to 15 Jun 1945, a span of 9 years 6 months and 20 days.

thus averaging a change every other month. Some statisticians contend that Bolivia, since it became a sovereign country in 1825, has had a record 191 attempted coups. Only 23 of these, however, have been successful.

Shake Hands!

The record number of hands shaken by a public figure at an official function was 8513 by President Theodore Roosevelt (1858–1919) at a New Year's Day White House presentation in Washington, DC, USA on 1 Jan 1907.

Kang Ho Dong, a Korean wrestler, shook hands with 28,233 different people in 8 hours during Expo 93 in Taejon, South Korea on 22 Aug 1993.

Prime Ministers and Statesmen

Oldest The longest-lived Prime Minister of any country was Naruhiko Higashikuni (Japan), who was born on 3 Dec 1887 and died on 20 Jan 1990, aged 102 years 48 days. He was his country's first Prime Minister after World War II, but held office for less than two months, resigning in October 1945.

The oldest age at *first* appointment has been 81, in the case of Morarji Ranchhodji Desai of India (b. 29 Feb 1896) in March 1977. Philippe Pétain (1856–1951), although not 'Prime Minister', became 'Chief of State' of the French State on 10 Jul 1940 at the age of 84.

Currently the oldest Prime Minister is Emile Jonassaint of Haiti, who having been chosen as President by the military regime was also proclaimed Prime Minister at the age of 81 in May 1994.

Longest term of office The longest-serving Prime Minister of a sovereign state is currently Khalifa bin Sulman al-Khalifa (b. 3 Jul 1933) of Bahrain, who has held office since Bahrain became independent in August 1971. By then he had already been in office for 1½ years.

Marshal Kim Il Sung (*né* Kim Sung Chu) (b. 15 Apr 1912) has been head of government or head of state of the Democratic People's Republic of Korea since 25 Aug 1948.

Andrey Andreyevich Gromyko (1909–89) had been Minister of Foreign Affairs of the USSR since 15 Feb 1957 (having been Deputy Foreign Minister since 1946), when he was elected President of the USSR in 2 Jul 1985, a position he held until 30 Sep 1988.

Pyotr Lomako (1904–90) served in the government of the former USSR as Minister for Non-Ferrous Metallurgy from 1940 to 1986. He was relieved of his post after 46 years on 1 Nov 1986, aged 82, having served on the Central Committee of the CPSU since 1952.

Women Indira Gandhi (1917–84) of India was Prime Minister for a record 15 years in two spells, from 1966 to 1977 and 1980 to 1984. Eugenia Charles (b. 15 May 1919) of Dominica is the current record-holder, having taken office when her Dominica Freedom Party won the elections in July 1980.

GUESS WHAT?

Q who is currently India's Prime Minister, having taken office in 1991?

A See Page 183

The greatest representation of women in a cabinet is in Norway, where following a reshuffle in January 1994 there are currently eight women ministers including the Prime Minister, Gro Harlem Brundtland.

European Parliament election records
Germany has most representatives in the 567-member parliament, with 99, and Luxembourg the fewest, with 6. The best turnout has been in Belgium in 1989, when 93 per cent of the electorate voted (although voting is compulsory there), and the lowest has been in the United Kingdom in 1984, when just 32.5 per cent of the electorate cast their votes.

Majorities—United Kingdom

Largest The largest majority, in 1931 by the coalition of Conservatives, Liberals and National Labour, was 491 seats and 60.5 per cent of the vote. The largest majority in the era before universal suffrage was 288 by a 'Liberal' alliance of Whigs, Radicals and Irish supporters of O'Connell in 1832.

Indira Gandhi holds the duration record for a female Prime Minister, having held office in India for a total of 15 years in two spells.

Smallest The narrowest majority was that of Labour in 1964, with four over the Conservatives and Liberals combined. In the two elections of 1910 the Liberals had a majority of two in February and there was a dead heat in December, but in both cases they had the support of the Irish Nationalists and Labour, which gave them in practice majorities of 122 and 126.

Division The largest majority on a division in the House of Commons was one of 547 (556 for and 9 against), on a procedural motion relating to the European Communities (Amendment) Bill on 15 Apr 1994.

House of Lords

Oldest member The oldest member ever was the Rt Hon. Lord Shinwell (1884–1986), who first sat in the Lower House in November 1922 and

El Hadji Muhammad el Mokri, Grand Vizier of Morocco, died on 16 Sep 1957 at a reputed age of 116 Muslim years, equivalent to 112½ Gregorian years (⇨ also Longevity—Authentic National Longevity Records table).

El Hadji Muhammad el Mokri, the Grand Vizier of Morocco (wearing the cape with the white pointed hood) with various other dignitaries outside the Sultan's palace in Rabat, Morocco. He held office—roughly equivalent to being a Prime Minister—until he was well past 100.
(Photo: Popperfoto)

Prime Minister
at the age of 28

Are you 28 and interested in running the country? Well in Liechtenstein, the tiny country between Switzerland and Austria, this is precisely what is happening at the moment. The principality with a population of 30,000—less than the Faeroe Islands but more than San Marino—has as its Prime Minister a 28-year-old by the name of Dr Mario Frick. He took office on 15 Dec 1993, having previously been Deputy Prime Minister, following general elections held on 24 October in which his party (the Fatherland Union, or *Vaterländische Union*) obtained just over 50 per cent of the votes cast.

Not surprisingly Dr Frick is currently the world's youngest Prime Minister. He has a legal background, and as part of his studies wrote a thesis on 'The Recognition and Enforcement of Foreign Judgements in the Principality of Liechtenstein in Consideration of Swiss, Austrian and German Law'. His government will no doubt be determined to maintain Liechtenstein as a nation with one of the highest standards of living in the world.

Photo: Fürstentum Liechtenstein Presse- und Informationsamt

The President of the European Parliament is directly elected by its members for a term of 2½ years. France is the only country to have had more than one President—Simone Veil, who was elected in 1979 (left), and Pierre Pflimlin, who was elected in 1984 (far left).
(Photos: Gamma/D. Simon)

lived to be 101 years 202 days (⇨ Peerage). The oldest peer to make a maiden speech was Lord Maenan (1854–1951) at the age of 94 years 123 days (⇨ Most durable judges).

Youngest member The youngest current member of the House of Lords to have taken his seat is the Earl of Hardwicke (b. 3 Feb 1971).

Political Office Holders

Party The longest period of party ascendancy in British political and parliamentary history is definitional. The Whig Ascendancy ran from 17 Mar 1715 to the death of King George II on 25 Oct 1760, and followed until the assuming of office of the Earl of Bute on 26 May 1762—47 years 2 months, in which time there were eight general elections. The Tory Ascendancy ran from the appointment of William Pitt (the Younger) on 19 Dec 1783, as confirmed by the general election of March–May 1784, until the fall of the Duke of Wellington's second administration on 21 Nov 1830—46 years 11 months, during which time there were seven general elections.

Prime Ministers The only Prime Minister to retain power for four successive general elections was Lord Liverpool, in 1812 (30 Sep–24 Nov), 1818 (11 Jun–4 Aug), 1820 (1 Mar–21 Apr) and 1826 (3 Jun–23 Jul). Since the reduction of the term of Parliaments from seven years to five years in 1911, the only Prime Minister to have been returned to power in three successive general elections is Margaret Thatcher (b. 13 Oct 1925), on 3 May 1979, 9 Jun 1983 and 11 Jun 1987. She is also the longest-serving Prime Minister this century, at 11 years 203 days, from 3 May 1979–22 Nov 1990.

MPs *Youngest* Henry Long (1420–90) was returned for an Old Sarum seat at the age of 15. His precise date of birth is unknown. Minors were debarred in law in 1695 and in fact in 1832.

The youngest ever woman MP has been Josephine Bernadette Devlin, now Mrs McAliskey (b. 23 Apr 1947), elected for Mid Ulster (Independent Unity) aged 21 years 359 days on 17 Apr 1969.

Up and Up!

In the line of duty, Brian Davis has mounted 334 of the 364 steps of the tower in the Houses of Parliament 4691 times in ten years to 31 Mar 1994—equivalent to 29 ascents of Mt Everest.

The current Father of the House—the MP with the longest unbroken service—is the Rt Hon. Sir Edward Heath, seen here enjoying one of the hobbies for which he is renowned.
(Photo: Gamma/T. Spooner)

The youngest current member is Matthew Taylor, MP (Liberal Democrat) for Truro (b. 3 Jan 1963).

Oldest Sir Francis Knollys (*c.* 1550–1648), 'the ancientest Parliament man in England', was re-elected for Reading in 1640 when apparently aged 90, and was probably 97 or 98 at the time of his death.

The oldest of 20th-century members has been Samuel Young (b. 14 Feb 1822), Nationalist MP for East Cavan (1892 to 1918), who died on 18 Apr 1918, aged 96 years 63 days.

Father of the House The title is nowadays bestowed on the Member who has the longest unbroken service in the Commons. The earliest occurrence of the phrase dates from 1816. The oldest Father was the Rt Hon. Charles Pelham Villiers (Wolverhampton South) when he died on 16 Jan 1898, aged 96 years 13 days. The current Father is the Rt Hon. Sir Edward Heath, MP (Old Bexley and Sidcup), who took the oath as MP on 2 Mar 1950.

The fastest election result was in the 1959 general election, when the result from Billericay, Essex was announced as early as 57 minutes after the polls closed, at 9:57 p.m.

Longest span Sir Francis Knollys (⇨ above) was elected for Oxford in 1575 and died a sitting member for Reading 73 years later in 1648.

The longest span of service of any 20th-century MP is 63 years 360 days (1 Oct 1900 to 25 Sep 1964) by the Rt Hon. Sir Winston Leonard Spencer Churchill (1874–1965), with breaks only in 1908 and from 1922–4. The record for a woman is 42 years 4 months (27 Oct 1931 to 28 Feb 1974) by Dame Irene Ward, who was MP for Wallsend from 1931 to 1945 and Tynemouth from 1950 to 1974.

The longest continuous span was that of C.P. Villiers (⇨ above), who was a member for 63 years 6 days, having been returned at 17 elections. The longest living of all parliamentarians was Theodore Cooke Taylor (1850–1952), Liberal MP for Batley from 1910–18.

Briefest span There are two 18th-century examples of posthumous elections. Capt. the Hon. Edward Legge, RN (1710–47) was returned unopposed for Portsmouth on 15 Dec 1747. News came later that he had died in the West Indies 87 days before polling. In 1780 John Kirkman, standing for the City of London, expired before polling had ended but was nonetheless duly returned. A.J. Dobbs (Lab, Smethwick), elected on 5 Jul 1945, was killed on the way to take his seat.

United Kingdom Electoral Records

Votes (electorate)
MOST: 33,610,399, general election 9 Apr 1992.
MOST (party): 14,094,116 (Con.), general election 9 Apr 1992.

Votes (individual)
MOST: 75,205, Sir Cooper Rawson (Con.), Brighton, Sussex, 1931.
LEAST: Nil, F.R. Lees (Temperance Chartist), Ripon, Yorks, Dec 1860.
LEAST SINCE UNIVERSAL FRANCHISE: 5, Lt. Cdr W. Boaks (Public Safety Democratic Monarchist White Resident), Glasgow, Hillhead, 25 Mar 1982; Dr Kailish Trivedi (Independent Janata), Kensington by-election, 14 Jul 1988.
LEAST SINCE UNIVERSAL FRANCHISE IN GENERAL ELECTION: 13, B.C. Wedmore (Belgrano), Finchley, 9 Jun 1983.

Majority
HIGHEST: *Man*: 62,253, Sir Cooper Rawson (Con.), Brighton, Sussex, 1931. *Woman*: 38,823, Countess of Iveagh (Con.), Southend, Essex, 1931.
HIGHEST (current): 36,230 by Rt Hon. John Major (Con., Huntingdon).
NARROWEST: 1 vote, Matthew Fowler (Lib.), Durham, 1895; 1 vote, H.E. Duke (Unionist), Exeter, Devon, Dec 1910. *Since Universal Franchise*: 2 votes, A.J. Flint (National Labour), Ilkeston, Derbyshire, 1931.
NARROWEST (current): 19 by Walter Sweeney (Con., Vale of Glamorgan).

Most Recounts
7: Brighton, Kemptown 1964 and Peterborough 1966.

General Election Poll
HIGHEST: 93.42%, Fermanagh & S Tyrone, 1951.
LOWEST: 29.7%, Kennington, London, 1918.

Largest Constituency by Area
Ross, Cromarty & Skye, 954,680 ha *2,472,260 acres*.

Largest Electorate
217,900, Hendon (Barnet), 1941.

Smallest Electorate
10,851, City of London, 1945.

Most Rotten Borough
(8 Electors for 2 unopposed members) 1821 Old Sarum, Wiltshire. No elections contested 1295–1831.

Most Parliamentary Contests
16 by Rt Hon. Tony Benn (formerly A.N. Wedgwood-Benn) (b. 3 Apr 1925) since November 1950.

Most By-Election Candidates
19: Newbury, 6 May 1993, won by David Rendel (Lib. Dem.).

Longest Gap Between By-Elections
There were no by-elections between those at Hemsworth, Kincardine & Deeside and Langbaurgh on 7 Nov 1991 and that at Newbury on 6 May 1993—1 year 181 days later.

The longest budget speech was that of the Rt Hon. David (later Earl) Lloyd George (1863–1945) on 29 Apr 1909, which lasted 4 hr 51 min, although with a 30 minute tea-break. He was later to be Prime Minister, from 7 Dec 1916 to 19 Oct 1922.

Prime Ministerial Records

LONGEST SERVING	20 years 315 days	1st	Sir Robert Walpole (1676–1745)	3 Apr 1721–11 Feb 1742
MOST MINISTRIES	5	40th	Earl Baldwin (1867–1947)	22 May 1923–28 May 1937
SHORTEST SERVICE IN OFFICE	120 days	21st	George Canning (1770–1827)	10 Apr–8 Aug 1827
YOUNGEST TO ASSUME OFFICE	24 years 205 days	16th	Hon. William Pitt (1759–1806)	19 Dec 1783 (declined when 23 years 275 days)
OLDEST FIRST TO ASSUME OFFICE	70 years 109 days	30th	Viscount Palmerston (1784–1865)	6 Feb 1855
GREATEST AGE IN OFFICE	84 years 64 days	32nd	William Gladstone (1809–98)	3 Mar 1894 (elected at 82 years 171 days)
SHORTEST MINISTRY	22 days	23rd	Duke of Wellington (1769–1852)	17 Nov–9 Dec 1834

Women The first woman to be elected to the House of Commons was Mme Constance Georgine Markievicz (*née* Gore Booth). She was elected as member (Sinn Fein) for St Patrick's Dublin on 28 Dec 1918. The first woman to take her seat was the Viscountess Astor (1879–1964) (*née* Nancy Witcher Langhorne at Danville, Virginia, USA; formerly Mrs Robert Gould Shaw), who was elected Unionist member for the Sutton division of Plymouth, Devon on 28 Nov 1919, and took her seat 3 days later.

Heaviest and tallest The heaviest MP of all time is believed to be Sir Cyril Smith, Liberal member for Rochdale from October 1972 to April 1992, when in January 1976 his peak reported weight was 189.6kg *29st 12lb*.

Sir Louis Gluckstein (1897–1979), Conservative member for East Nottingham (1931–45), was an unrivalled 2.02m *6ft 7½in*. Currently the tallest is the Hon. Archie Hamilton (b. 30 Dec 1941), Conservative member for Epsom and Ewell, at 1.98m *6ft 6in*.

Mayoralties The longest recorded mayoralty was that of Edmond Mathis (1852–1953), *maire* of Ehuns, Haute-Saône, France for 75 years (1878–1953). Anthony Jennings served as Mayor of Fordwich, Kent for 44 consecutive years from 1785–1829.

Local government service duration records The oldest local office was that of reeve, to supervise villeins. First mentioned in AD 787, it evolved to that of shire reeve, hence sheriff.

Major Sir Philip Barber (1876–1961) served as county councillor for Nottinghamshire for 63 years 41 days, from 8 Mar 1898 to 18 Apr 1961. Matthew Anderson was a member of the Borough Council of Abingdon, Oxon for 69 years 4 months, from April 1709 until August 1778.

> **Henry Winn (1816–1914) served as parish clerk for Fulletby, near Horncastle, Lincs for 76 years.**

Betty Boothroyd, the current Speaker, is the first woman to have been elected to this post in the history of the House of Commons.
(Photo: Central Office of Information)

Judicial

Legislation and Litigation

Statutes *Oldest* The earliest surviving judicial code was that of King Ur-Nammu during the third dynasty of Ur, Iraq, *c.* 2250 BC. The oldest English statute in the Statute Book is a section of the Statute of Marlborough of 18 Nov 1267, re-entitled in 1948 'The Distress Act 1267' and most recently cited in the High Court in 1986. Some statutes enacted by Henry II (died 1189) and earlier kings are even more durable as they have been assimilated into the Common Law.

> **GUESS WHAT?**
> Q How many volumes does 'British Parliamentary Papers' consist of?
> A See Page 138

Longest in the UK The weightiest piece of legislation ever written is the Income and Corporation Taxes Act 1988 of more than 1000 pages and weighing 2.5kg *5½lb*.

Shortest The shortest statute is the Parliament (Qualification of Women) Act 1918, which runs to 27 operative words: 'A woman shall not be disqualified by sex or marriage from being elected to or sitting or voting as a Member of the Commons House of Parliament.' Section 2 contains a further 14 words giving the short title.

Patents The earliest of all known English patents was that granted by Henry VI in 1449 to Flemish-born John of Utyman for making coloured glass for the windows of Eton College. The peak number of applications for patents filed in the UK in any one year was 63,614 in 1969. The shortest patent is one of 48 words filed on 14 May 1956 and concerned a harrow attachment. The longest, comprising 2290 pages of text and 495 sheets of drawings, was filed on 31 Mar 1965 by IBM to cover a computer.

Thomas Alva Edison (1847–1931) has had the most patents, with 1093 either on his own or jointly. They included the microphone, the motion-picture projector and the incandescent electric lamp.

Most protracted litigation A controversy over the claim of the Prior and Convent (now the Dean and Chapter) of Durham Cathedral to administer the spiritualities of the diocese during a vacancy in the See grew fierce in 1283. The dispute, with the Archbishop of York, flared up again in 1672 and 1890; an attempt in November 1975 to settle the issue, then 692 years old, was unsuccessful. Neither side admits the legitimacy of writs of appointment issued by the other even though identical persons are named.

Longest hearings The longest civil case heard before a jury is *Kemner* v. *Monsanto Co.*, which concerned an alleged toxic chemical spill in Sturgeon, Missouri, USA in 1979. The trial started on 6 Feb 1984, at St Clair County Court House, Belleville, Illinois, USA before Circuit Judge Richard P. Goldenhersh, and ended on 22 Oct 1987. The testimony lasted 657 days, following which the jury deliberated for two months. The residents of Sturgeon were awarded $1 million nominal compensatory damages and $16,280,000 punitive damages, but these awards were overturned by the Illinois Appellate Court on 11 Jun 1991 because the jury in the original trial had not found that any damage had resulted from the spill.

The Supreme Court of Sri Lanka spent a record 527 days hearing a challenge to the election of President Ranasinghe Premadasa as head of state in 1988. A total of 977 witnesses gave evidence over a three year period, from 19 Jun 1989 to 30 Jun 1992. The challenge, brought by the opposition leader Sirimavo Bandaranaike, was rejected by the court on 1 Sep 1992.

Guilty!

The greatest attendance at any trial was at that of Major Jesús Sosa Blanco, aged 51, for an alleged 108 murders. At one point in the 12½ hr trial (5:30 p.m. to 6 a.m., 22–23 Jan 1959), 17,000 people were present in the Havana Sports Palace, Cuba. He was executed on 18 Feb 1959.

Longest British hearings The longest trial in the annals of British justice was the Tichborne personation case. The civil trial began on 11 May 1871, lasted 103 days and collapsed on 6 Mar 1872. The criminal trial went on for 188 days, resulting in a sentence on 28 Feb 1874 for two counts of perjury (two 7-year consecutive terms of imprisonment with hard labour) on London-born Arthur Orton, alias Thomas Castro (1834–98), who claimed to be Roger Charles Tichborne (1829–54), the elder brother of Sir Alfred Joseph Doughty-Tichborne, 11th Bt (1839–66). The whole case thus spanned 1025 days. The jury were out for only 30 minutes.

The impeachment of Warren Hastings (1732–1818), which began in 1788, dragged on for 7 years until 23 Apr 1795, but the trial lasted only 149 days. Hastings was appointed a member of the Privy Council in 1814.

The longest single fraud trial was the Britannia Park trial, which began on 10 Sep 1990 and ended on 4 Feb 1992 after 252 working days. The case centred on the collapse of the Britannia theme park near Heanor, Derbys in 1985. The fraud case *R.* v. *Bouzaglo and Others* ended before Judge Brian Gibbens (1912–85) on 1 May 1981 having lasted 274 days, but with two separate trials. They appealed on 10 Dec 1981.

Murder The longest murder trial in Britain was that at the Old Bailey, London of Reginald Dudley, 51, and Robert Maynard, 38, in the Torso Murder of Billy Moseley and Micky Cornwall which ran before Mr Justice Swanwick from 11 Nov 1976 to 17 Jun 1977

Patience!

Gaddam Hanumantha Reddy, a civil servant, brought a series of legal actions against the Hyderabad state government and the Indian government covering a total period of 44 years 9 months and 8 days from April 1945 through to January 1990. The litigation outlasted the entire period of his employment in the Indian Administrative Service. He complained that his results in the entrance examination for the Hyderabad Civil Service entitled him to greater seniority and higher pay. After winning the legal battle he did indeed receive his promotion.

with 136 trial days. Both men were sentenced to life imprisonment (minimum 15 years).

The case of Stephen Miller, Yusef Abdullahi and Tony Paris lasted longer, but there were two hearings. They were accused of murdering Lynette White, a Cardiff prostitute, on 14 Feb 1988. The first hearing in 1989 lasted 82 days, but ended with the death of the judge, Mr Justice McNeill. The second one lasted 115 days, ending on 20 Nov 1990. The three men were found guilty and sentenced to life imprisonment, but were cleared by the Court of Appeal on 10 Dec 1992.

Highest bail The highest bail set by a British court was £10 million. Leonard Bartlett and Iain Mackintosh, both of London, were bailed on fraud charges by Bow Street Magistrates' Court on 24 Mar 1994 subject to the condition that they each provided sureties worth that sum. The figure was later reduced to £1 million on appeal.

The highest bail figure on which a defendant was released by a British court is £3.5 million, which was set for Asil Nadir, the chairman of Polly Peck International, on 17 Dec 1990. He had developed the company over 20 years from a small clothing concern into an international group, but it collapsed in September 1990 and he subsequently faced 18 charges of theft and false accounting amounting to £25 million. He jumped bail on 4 May 1993, fleeing to Cyprus.

Greatest damages
Civil damages The largest damages awarded in legal history were $11.12 billion to Pennzoil Co. against Texaco Inc. concerning the latter's allegedly unethical tactics in January 1984 to break up a merger between Pennzoil and Getty Oil Co., by Judge Solomon Casseb, Jr in Houston, Texas, USA on 10 Dec 1985. An out-of-court settlement of $5500 million was reached after a 48-hour negotiation on 19 Dec 1987.

The largest damages awarded against an individual were $2.1 billion. On 10 Jul 1992 Charles H Keating Jr, the former owner of Lincoln Savings and Loan of Los Angeles, California, USA, was ordered by a federal jury to pay this sum to 23,000 small investors who were defrauded by his company. The figure was subject to final approval by the judge.

Personal injury The greatest personal injury damages awarded to an individual were $163,882,660, awarded by a jury to Shiyamala Thirunayagam, aged 27, in the Supreme Court of the State of New York on 27 Jul 1993. She was almost completely paralysed after the car in which she was travelling hit a truck which had broken down in the fast lane of the New Jersey Turnpike on 4 Oct 1987. Because the defendants would have challenged the jury's verdict in a higher court Mrs Thirunagayam agreed to accept a lump sum of $8,230,000 for her pain and suffer-

ing, and a guarantee that the defendants would pay up to $55,000,000 for her future medical expenses.

The compensation for the disaster on 2–3 Dec 1984 at the Union Carbide Corporation plant in Bhopal, India was agreed at $470 million. The Supreme Court of India passed the order for payment on 14 Feb 1989 after a settlement between the corporation and the Indian government, which represented the interests of more than 500,000 claimants including the families of 3350 people who died.

> The shortest recorded British murder hearings were *R. v. Murray* on 28 Feb 1957 and *R. v. Cawley* at Winchester assizes on 14 Dec 1959. Proceedings occupied only 30 seconds on each occasion.

Defamation The record award in a libel case is $58 million, to Vic Feazell, a former district attorney, on 20 Apr 1991 at Waco, Texas, USA. He claimed that he had been libelled by a Dallas-based television station and one of its reporters in 1985, and that this had ruined his reputation. The parties reached a settlement on 29 Jun 1991, but neither side would disclose the amount.

The record damages for libel in Great Britain was the £1.5 million award to Lord Aldington, a former brigadier and former chairman of the Sun Alliance insurance company, against Count Nikolai Tolstoy, a historian, and Nigel Watts, a property developer. The award was made by a High Court jury on 30 Nov 1989 following accusations that Lord Aldington had been a war criminal. However, he did not actually receive this amount.

Greatest compensation for wrongful imprisonment Robert McLaughlin, 29, was awarded $1,935,000 in October 1989 for wrongful imprisonment as a result of a murder in New York City, USA in 1979 which he did not commit. He had been sentenced to 15 years in prison and actually served six years, from 1980 to 1986, when he was released after his foster father succeeded in showing the authorities that he had nothing to do with the crime.

Patent case Litton Industries Inc. was awarded $1.2 billion in Los Angeles, California, USA on 31 Aug 1993 in damages from Honeywell Inc. after a jury had decided that Honeywell had violated a Litton patent covering airline-navigation systems. Litton had filed a law suit in March 1990, which was followed by a counterclaim from Honeywell nine months later.

Largest suit The greatest amount of damages ever sought to date is $675,000,000,000,000 (then equivalent to 10

GUESS WHAT?

Q Who had a record 1093 patents?

A See Page 187

times the US national wealth) in a suit by Mr I. Walton Bader brought in the US District Court, New York City, USA on 14 Apr 1971 against General Motors and others for polluting all 50 states.

Highest costs The Blue Arrow trial, involving the illegal support of the company's shares during a rights issue in 1987, is estimated to have cost approximately £35 million. The trial at the Old Bailey, London lasted a year and ended on 14 Feb 1992 with four of the defendants being convicted. Although they received suspended prison sentences, they were later cleared on appeal.

> The shortest valid will in the world is 'Vše zene', the Czech for 'All to wife', written and dated 19 Jan 1967 by Herr Karl Tausch of Langen, Germany.

Wills The shortest will contested but subsequently admitted to probate in English law was the case of *Thorne* v. *Dickens* in 1906. It consisted of the three words 'All for mother' in which 'mother' was not his mother but his wife. The smallest will preserved by the Record Keeper is an identity disc 3.8 cm 1½ in in diameter belonging to A.B. William Skinner, killed aboard HMS *Indefatigable* at Jutland in 1916. It had 40 words engraved on it including the signatures of two witnesses and was proved on 24 Jun 1922.

The longest will on record was that of Mrs Frederica Evelyn Stilwell Cook (b. USA), proved at Somerset House, London on 2 Nov 1925. It consisted of four bound volumes containing 95,940 words, primarily concerning some $100,000 worth of property.

The oldest written will dates from 2061 BC, and is that of Nek'ure, the son of the Egyptian pharaoh Khafre. The will was carved onto the walls of his tomb, and indicated that he would bequeath 14 towns, 2 estates and other property to his wife, another woman and three children.

Most durable judges The oldest recorded active judge was Judge Albert R. Alexander (1859–1966) of Plattsburg, Missouri, USA. He was enrolled as a member of the Clinton County Bar in 1926, and was later the magistrate and probate judge of Clinton County until his retirement aged 105 years 8 months on 9 Jul 1965.

The greatest recorded age at which any British judge has sat on a bench was 93 years 9 months in the case of Sir William Francis Kyffin Taylor (later Lord Maenan), who was born on 9 Jul 1854 and retired as presiding judge of the Liverpool Court of Passage in April 1948, having held that position since 1903. Sir Salathiel Lovell (1619–1713) was still sitting when he died on 3 May 1713 in his 94th or 95th year.

Youngest judge John Payton was elected as a Justice of the Peace in Plano, Texas, USA and took office at the age of 18 years 11 months in January 1991. David Elmer Ward had to

Divorce!

The largest publicly declared settlement was that achieved in 1982 by the lawyers of Soraya Khashóggi from her husband Adnan — £500 million plus property. Mrs Anne Bass, former wife of Sid Bass of Texas, USA, was reported to have rejected $535 million as inadequate to live in the style to which she had been made accustomed.

The highest divorce award in Great Britain was one of £1,295,000 (£1,000,000 in cash plus a £295,000 maisonette), made to Yugoslavian-born Radojka Gojkovic against her former husband in the High Court Family Division on 17 Feb 1989. The settlement was upheld by the Court of Appeal on 12 Oct 1989.

Longest!

There is a lease concerning a plot for a sewage tank adjoining Columb Barracks, Mullingar, Co. Westmeath, Republic of Ireland, which was signed on 3 Dec 1868 for 10 million years. Leases in Ireland lasting 'for ever' are quite common.

await the legal age of 21 before taking office after nomination in 1932 as Judge of the County Court (a higher level) at Fort Myers, Florida, USA.

Muhammad Ilyas passed the examination enabling him to become a Civil Judge in July 1952 at the age of 20 years 9 months, although formalities such as medicals meant that it was not until eight months later that he started work as a Civil Judge in Lahore, Pakistan.

The youngest certain age at which any English judge has been appointed is 28, in the case of Sir Ernest Wild KC (1869–1934) who was appointed Judge of the Norwich Guildhall Court of Record in 1897 at that age.

Most judges Lord Balmerino was found guilty of treason by 137 of his peers on 28 Jul 1746. In the 20th century, 26 judges of the European Court of Human Rights in Strasbourg, France gave judgment in *Brannigan and McBride* v. *United Kingdom* on 26 May 1993. The court rejected the applicants' challenge to their detention in Northern Ireland under the Prevention of Terrorism Act.

Most successful lawyer Sir Lionel Luckhoo, senior partner of Luckhoo and Luckhoo of Georgetown, Guyana, succeeded in getting 245 successive murder charge acquittals between 1940 and 1985.

Most durable solicitors William George (1865–1967), brother of Prime Minister David Lloyd George, passed his preliminary law examination in May 1880 and was practising until December 1966 at the age of 101 years 9 months. The most durable firm is Pickering Kenyon of London, which was founded by William Umfreville in 1561.

Oldest lawyer Cornelius Van de Steeg (1889–1994) of Perry, Iowa, USA was still practising as a lawyer at the age of 101 years 11 months in April 1991.

Law firms The largest law firm is Baker & McKenzie, employing 1684 lawyers, 528 of whom are partners, in 32 countries at 28 Feb 1994. It also has the highest revenues, with $512 million in 1993. The firm was founded in Chicago, Illinois, USA in 1949.

Crime

Largest criminal organizations In terms of profit, the largest syndicate of organized crime is believed to be the Mafia, which has its origins in Sicily and dates from the 13th century, and which has infiltrated the executive, judiciary and legislature of the United States. It consists of some 3000 to 5000 individuals in 25 'families' federated under 'The Commission', with an annual turnover in vice, gambling, protection rackets, tobacco, bootlegging, hijacking, narcotics, loan-sharking and prostitution which was estimated by *US News & World Report* in December 1982 at $200 billion, with a profit estimated in March 1986 by the Attorney Rudolph Giuliani at $75 billion.

In terms of numbers, the Yamaguchi-gumi gang of the *yakuza* in Japan has 30,000 members. There are some 90,000 *yakuza* or gangsters altogether, in more than 3000 groups. They go about their business openly and even advertize for recruits. On 1 Mar 1992 new laws were brought in to combat their activities, which include drug trafficking, smuggling, prostitution and gambling.

Assassinations The most frequently assassinated heads of state in modern times have been the Tsars of Russia. In the two hundred years from 1718 to 1918 four Tsars and two heirs apparent were assassinated, and there were many other unsuccessful attempts.

The target of the highest number of *failed* assassination attempts on an individual head of state in modern times was Charles de Gaulle (1890–1970), President of France from 1958 to 1969. He was reputed to have survived no fewer than 31 plots against his life between 1944, when the shadow government which he had formed returned to Paris from Algeria, and 1966 (although some plots were foiled before culminating in actual physical attacks).

Most prolific murderers It was established at the trial of Behram, the Indian Thug, that he had strangled at least 931 victims with his yellow and white cloth strip or *ruhmal* in the Oudh district between 1790 and 1840. It has been estimated that at least 2,000,000 Indians were strangled by Thugs (*burtotes*) during the reign of the Thugee (pronounced tugee) cult from 1550 until its final suppression by the British raj in 1853.

20th century A total of 592 deaths was attributed to one Colombian bandit leader, Teófilo ('Sparks') Rojas, between 1948 and his death in an ambush near Armenia, Colombia on 22 Jan 1963. Some sources attribute 3500 slayings to him during *La Violencia* of 1945–62.

Cornelius Van de Steeg, who was still practising as a lawyer a month short of his 102nd birthday.
(Photo: Mr & Dr E. Van De Bittner)

In a drunken rampage lasting 8 hours on 26–27 Apr 1982, policeman Wou Bom-kon, 27, killed 57 people and wounded 35 with 176 rounds of rifle ammunition and hand grenades in the Kyong Sang-namdo province of South Korea. He blew himself up with a grenade.

There are believed to be more than 250,000 members of Chinese triad societies worldwide, but they are fragmented into many groups which often fight each other and compete in disputed areas. Hong Kong alone has some 100,000 triads.

The most profitable criminal organization is the Mafia. Often associated with the island of Sicily, these photographs show a trial at Palermo and demonstrate the measures which have to be taken to ensure security during such trials.
(Photos: P. Guerrin)

Human World

United Kingdom The biggest murder in the UK this century was committed by the unknown person or people who planted the bomb on Pan Am flight PA103, which crashed over Lockerbie, Dumfries and Galloway on 21 Dec 1988, killing a total of 270 people in the aeroplane and on the ground.

Mary Ann Cotton (*née* Robson) (b. 1832 at East Rainton, Co. Durham), hanged in Durham Jail on 24 Mar 1873, is believed to have poisoned 14, possibly 20, people.

Dennis Andrew Nilsen (b. 1948), then of 23 Cranley Gardens, Muswell Hill, north London, admitted to 15 one-at-a-time murders between December 1978 and February 1983. He was sentenced to life imprisonment, with a 25-year minimum, on 4 Nov 1983 at the Old Bailey by Mr Justice Croom-Johnson for six murders and two attempted murders.

Dominic McGlinchey (1955–94) admitted in a press interview in November 1983 to at least 30 killings in Northern Ireland. He was jailed for 10 years at Dublin's Special Criminal Court on 11 Mar 1986 for shooting with intent to resist arrest in Co. Clare, Republic of Ireland on 17 Mar 1984, but was released on 5 Mar 1993 having served just under seven years.

On 7 May 1981 John Thompson of Hackney, London was found guilty at the Old Bailey of the 'specimen' murder by arson of Archibald Campbell and jailed for life. There were 36 other victims at the Spanish Club, Denmark Street, London.

Lynching The worst year in the 20th century for lynchings in the United States was 1901, with 130, while the first year with no reported cases was 1952. The last lynching case recorded in Britain was that of *R. v. Caskie and Stevenson* on 29 Dec 1922. The accused were discharged after a verdict of not proven for murder by assault of Robert Alexander Stewart, 32, at Dalmarnock Bridge, Glasgow on 11 Sep 1922. Stewart was falsely thought by a tram conductor to be kidnapping Alistair John Sinclair, aged five, who gave evidence not under oath and standing on a seat.

Mass poisoning On 1 May 1981 an 8-year-old boy became the first of more than 600 victims of the Spanish cooking oil scandal. On 12 June it was discovered that his cause of death was the use of 'denatured' industrial colza from rape seed. The trial of 38 defendants, including the manufacturers Ramón and Elías Ferrero, lasted from 30 Mar 1987 to 28 Jun 1988. The 586 counts on which the prosecution demanded jail sentences totalled 60,000 years.

Robbery The greatest robbery on record was that of the Reichsbank following Germany's collapse in April–May 1945. The Pentagon in Washington described the event, first published

GUESS WHAT?

Q How many people died in the world's worst air disaster, in 1977?

A See Page 179

in *The Guinness Book of Records* in 1957, as 'an unverified allegation'. *Nazi Gold* by Ian Sayer and Douglas Botting, published in 1984, however, finally revealed full details and estimated that the total haul would have been equivalent to £2500 million at 1984 values.

The government of the Philippines announced on 23 Apr 1986 that it had succeeded in identifying $860.8 million 'salted' by the former President Ferdinand Edralin Marcos (1917–89) and his wife Imelda. The total national loss from November 1965 was believed to be $5–$10 billion.

Treasury Bills and certificates of deposit worth £292 million were stolen when a mugger attacked a money-broker's messenger in the City of London on 2 May 1990. As details of the documents stolen were quickly flashed on the City's market dealing screens and given to central banks worldwide, the chances of anyone being able to benefit from the theft were considered to be very remote.

The robbery in the Knightsbridge Safety Deposit Centre, London on 12 Jul 1987 was estimated at £30 million by the Metropolitan Police and has been said to be nearer to £60 million by the robbers themselves. Of the 126 boxes broken into, property was stolen from 113. The managing director Parvez Latif, 30, was among those charged on 17 Aug 1987 (⇔ below).

Art On 14 Apr 1991 twenty paintings, estimated to be worth $500 million, were stolen from the Van Gogh Museum in Amsterdam, Netherlands. However, only 35 minutes later they were found in an abandoned car not far from the museum. Just over a year earlier, on 18 Mar 1990, eleven paintings by Rembrandt, Vermeer, Degas, Manet and Flinck, plus a Chinese bronze beaker of about 1200 BC and a finial in the form of an eagle, worth in total an estimated $200 million, had been stolen from the Isabella Stewart Gardner Museum in Boston, Massachusetts, USA. Unlike the Van Gogh paintings, these have not been recovered in the meantime.

On 24 Dec 1985 a total of 140 'priceless' gold, jade and obsidian artifacts were stolen from the National Museum of Anthropology, Mexico City. The majority of the stolen objects were recovered in June 1989 from the Mexico City home of a man described by officials as the mastermind of the theft.

Bank During the extreme civil disorder prior to 22 Jan 1976 in Beirut, Lebanon, a guerrilla force blasted the vaults of the British Bank of the Middle East in Bab Idriss and cleared out safe deposit boxes with contents valued by Lucien Dahdah, former Finance Minister, at

$50 million and by another source at an 'absolute minimum' of $20 million.

Train The greatest recorded train robbery occurred between 3:03 a.m. and 3:27 a.m. on 8 Aug 1963, when a General Post Office mail train from Glasgow, Strathclyde was ambushed at Sears Crossing and robbed at Bridego Bridge near Mentmore, Bucks. The gang escaped with about 120 mailbags containing £2,631,784 worth of banknotes being taken to London for destruction. Only £343,448 was recovered.

Jewels The greatest recorded theft of jewels was from the Knightsbridge Safety Deposit Centre, London (⇔ above), when jewels with an estimated value of £25 million (then $40 million) were stolen as part of a larger robbery.

The largest robbery exclusively of jewels was from the bedroom of the 'well-guarded' villa of Prince Abdel Aziz bin Ahmed Al-Thani near Cannes, France on 24 Jul 1980. They were valued at $16 million (then £6.7 million).

Greatest kidnapping ransom The greatest ransom ever reported in modern times is 1500 million pesos ($60 million) for the release of the brothers Jorge Born, 40, and Juan Born, 39, of the family firm Bunge and Born, paid to the left-wing urban guerrilla group Montoneros in Buenos Aires, Argentina on 20 Jun 1975.

Kidnapped!

Historically the greatest ransom paid was that for Atahualpa by the Incas to Francisco Pizarro in 1532–3 at Cajamarca, Peru, which constituted a hall full of gold and silver, worth in modern money some $170 million.

Largest narcotics haul The greatest drug haul in terms of value was achieved on 28 Sep 1989, when cocaine with an estimated street value of $6–7 billion was seized in a raid on a warehouse in Los Angeles, California, USA. The haul of 20 tonnes was prompted by a tip-off from a local resident who had complained about heavy lorry traffic and people leaving the warehouse 'at odd hours and in a suspicious manner'.

The greatest haul in terms of weight was by the authorities in Bilo, Pakistan on 23 Oct 1991. The seizure comprised 38.9 tonnes *85,846 lb* of hashish and 3.23 tonnes *7128 lb* of heroin.

In Britain, cocaine with a value of £250 million and weighing 1.3 tonnes was seized at Birkenhead, Merseyside on 24 Jan 1994 after a Polish-American ship, the *Jurata*, arrived there on its way from Venezuela to Poland. The cocaine was hidden in a consignment of bitumen.

The largest quantity of drugs seized in one operation by weight was from the *Britannia Gazelle*, a British-registered oil rig support ship. The vessel had been boarded in the North Sea on 20 Nov 1992 and brought back to Hull, Humberside where more than 1000 sacks containing a total of 20 tonnes of cannabis were recovered the next day.

Largest narcotics operation The bulkiest drugs seizure was 2903 tonnes of Colombian marijuana in a 14-month-long project code-named 'Operation Tiburon', carried out by the Drug Enforcement Administration and Colombian authorities. The arrest of 495 people and the seizure of 95 vessels was announced on 5 Feb 1982.

Thief!

On a moonless night at dead calm high water on 5 Jun 1966, armed with only a sharp axe, N. William Kennedy slashed free the mooring lines of the 10,639-dwt SS *Orient Trader*, owned by Steel Factors Ltd of Ontario, at Wolfe's Cove, St Lawrence Seaway, Canada. The vessel drifted to a waiting blacked-out, tug thus evading a ban on any shipping movements during a violent wildcat waterfront strike. She then sailed for Spain.

Stolen!

It is arguable that the *Mona Lisa*, though never valued, is the most valuable object ever stolen. It disappeared from the Louvre, Paris on 21 Aug 1911. It was recovered in Italy in 1913, when Vincenzo Perugia was charged with its theft.

Fingerprints The first effective system of identification by fingerprints—the science of dactylography—was instituted in 1896 by Edward Henry, an inspector-general of police in British India, who eventually became Commissioner of Metropolitan Police in London.

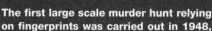

Crime prevention
A team of ten people, consisting of representatives from Lancashire Constabulary, a local cycle shop and local schools, succeeded in postcoding 841 bicycles in four hours at Beaumont College, Lancaster on 16 Apr 1994.

Caught!

The first large scale murder hunt relying on fingerprints was carried out in 1948, when more than 46,000 sets of prints—those of almost the entire adult male population of Blackburn, Lancs—were examined in tracing Peter Griffiths as the killer of 3-year-old June Devaney, whom he had abducted from Queen's Park Hospital after leaving his prints on a bottle beside the child's hospital cot.

Greatest banknote forgery The greatest forgery was the German Third Reich's forging operation, code name 'Operation Bernhard', run by Major Bernhard Krüger during World War II. It involved more than £130 million worth of British notes in denominations of £5, £10, £20 and £50. They were produced by 140 Jewish prisoners at Sachsenhausen concentration camp.

Biggest bank fraud The Banca Nazionale del Lavoro, Italy's leading bank, admitted on 6 Sep 1989 that it had been defrauded of a huge amount of funds, subsequently estimated to be in the region of $5 billion, with the disclosure that its branch in Atlanta, Georgia, USA had made unauthorized loan commitments to Iraq. Both the bank's chairman, Nerio Nesi, and its director general, Giacomo Pedde, resigned following the revelation.

GUESS WHAT?

Q What is the highest-value banknote currently in circulation?

A See Page 168

Capital Punishment

The discovery of Tollund man in a bog near Silkeborg, Denmark in 1950 showed that capital punishment dates at least from the Iron Age. The countries in which capital punishment is still prevalent include China, Iran, Iraq, Saudi Arabia, Malaysia, USA (36 states) and some of the independent countries which were formerly in the USSR. Capital punishment was first abolished *de facto* in 1798 in Liechtenstein.

Capital punishment in the British Isles had been widely practised up until the reign of William I (1066–87), but was virtually abolished by him. It was then brought back for murder and a growing number of other crimes by Henry I in the next century. It reached a peak in the reign of Edward VI (1547–53), when an average of 560 persons were executed annually at Tyburn (near the point where Marble Arch now stands, in London) alone. It has been estimated that as many as 50,000 people may have been done to death at Tyburn by the time the last execution took place there in 1783.

Largest hanging The most people hanged from one gallows were 38 Sioux Indians by William J. Duly outside Mankato, Minnesota, USA on 26 Dec 1862 for the murder of a number of unarmed citizens. The Nazi Feldkommandant simultaneously hanged 50 Greek resistance men as a reprisal measure in Athens on 22 Jul 1944.

Last hangings The last public execution in England took place outside Newgate Prison, London at 8a.m. on 26 May 1868, when Michael Barrett was hanged for his part in the Fenian bomb outrage on 13 Dec 1867, when 12 were killed outside the Clerkenwell House of Detention, London.

The last executions in the UK were those of Peter Anthony Allen (b. 4 Apr 1943), hanged at Walton Prison, Liverpool by Robert L. Stewart, and of John Robson Walby (b. 1 Apr 1940), alias Gwynne Owen Evans, by Harry B. Allen at Strangeways Gaol, Manchester, both on 13 Aug 1964. They had been found guilty of the capital murder of John Alan West on 7 April 1964.

The last public hanging in the United States occurred at Owensboro, Kentucky on 14 Aug 1936, when Rainey Bethea was executed in the presence of a crowd of more than 10,000. The following year a 'private' hanging was performed which was actually witnessed by some 500 people although the number of official witnesses was limited to just 12—Roscoe 'Red' Jackson was hanged on 21 May 1937 at Galena, Missouri.

Crowds look on with anticipation at the last public hanging in the USA. More than 10,000 people attended the execution, of 22-year-old Rainey Bethea, in Kentucky in 1936.
(Photo: Poperfoto)

Youngest The lowest reliably recorded age was of a girl aged seven, hanged at King's Lynn, Norfolk in 1808. In Britain the death penalty for persons under 16 was excluded in the Children Act of 1908, although no person under that age had been executed for many years prior to this.

Oldest The oldest person hanged in the UK this century was a man of 71 named Charles Frembd (*sic*) at Chelmsford Gaol on 4 Nov 1914, for the murder of his wife at Leytonstone, London.

The scene at the Los Angeles warehouse in 1989 after the discovery of cocaine with an estimated value of more than $6 billion, making it the most valuable drugs seizure on record.
(Photo: Gamma/Biggins)

In 1843 Allan Mair was executed at Stirling, Central for murder. He was 82, and was hanged sitting in a chair as he was incapable of standing up.

Hanging in chains The last recorded use of a gibbet occurred at Leicester in August 1832, when a local bookbinder, James Cook, was hanged for murder, and his corpse suspended in iron hoops, 10m *33ft* above the ground, with the head shaved and tarred.

Boiling to death In 1530, John Roose, a cook, became the first person to be executed in England under a new law of Henry VIII whereby

GUESS WHAT?

Q Paul Geidel is to prisons as Martha Nelson is to what?

A See Page 64

Burnt!

The last case of execution by burning in Britain occurred in March 1789, when a woman named Murphy was 'burnt with fire until she was dead'. This punishment, reserved for women convicted of coining or petit treason (murder of a husband), was abolished in the following year.

any person convicted of poisoning was to be judged guilty of high treason and executed in this cruel manner. Roose had killed two members of the Bishop of Rochester's household by poison.

Last death sentences The last person to be sentenced to death in the British Isles was Tony Teare, 22, who was convicted at Douglas, Isle of Man of murdering a 22-year-old woman, Corinne Bentley, and sentenced on 10 Jul 1992 to be hanged. The sentence was duly commuted to life imprisonment, and later that year the Manx parliament formally abolished the death penalty on the island, the last part of the British Isles to do so.

Last beheadings The last person to be publicly guillotined in France was the murderer Eugen Weidmann, before a large crowd at Versailles, near Paris at 4:50a.m. on 17 Jun 1939. The last use of the guillotine before abolition on 9 Sep 1981 was on 10 Sep 1977 at Baumettes Prison, Marseille, for torturer and murderer Hamida Djandoubi, aged 28.

The last man to be executed by beheading in Britain was Simon Fraser, Lord Lovat, who was beheaded in his eightieth year on Tower Hill, London in March 1747, for his part in the Jacobite rebellion.

Busiest prison The prison in which most death sentences have been carried out in Britain is Wandsworth, London. Between 1878, when Wandsworth became the hanging prison for London south of the Thames, and 1965, when the death penalty was abolished, 134 executions took place there.

Death Row The longest sojourn on Death Row was the 39 years of Sadamichi Hirasawa (1893–1987) in Sendai Jail, Japan. He was convicted in 1948 of poisoning 12 bank employees with potassium cyanide to effect a theft of £100, and died aged 94. On 31 Oct 1987 Liong Wie Tong, 52, and Tan Tian Tjoen, 62, were executed for robbery and murder by firing squad in Jakarta, Indonesia after 25 years on Death Row.

Executioners The Sanson family of France supplied executioners through several generations, from 1688 to 1847. Charles-Henri Sanson, known as *Monsieur de Paris*, despatched nearly 3000 victims in two years during the Terror, from 1793–4, including the king, Louis XVI, on 21 Jan 1793.

For 55 years from 1901 to the resignation of Albert Pierrepoint in February 1956, the Pierrepoint family largely monopolized the task of executing murderers in Britain. Henry Albert Pierrepoint officiated from 1901 to 1910. The longest-serving of the Pierrepoints was his elder brother Thomas, who was in action from 1906 to 1946. Albert (1905–92), son of Henry, himself

claimed to have officiated at the hanging of 550 men and women in several countries, including a record 27 war criminals in one day in Germany.

The longest period of office of a public executioner was that of William Calcraft (1800–79), who was in action from 1829 to 25 May 1874 and officiated at nearly every hanging outside and later inside Newgate Prison, London.

The oldest active executioner in British history was John Murdoch, who was already 64 when he was retained as an assistant hangman in Scotland in 1831.

> **John Murdoch** carried out his last execution in Glasgow in 1851, aged 84, and was able to mount the scaffold only with the aid of a staff.

Prison Sentences

Longest sentences Chamoy Thipyaso, a Thai woman known as the queen of underground investing, and seven of her associates were each jailed for 141,078 years by the Bangkok Criminal Court, Thailand on 27 Jul 1989 for swindling the public through a multi-million dollar deposit-taking business.

A sentence of 384,912 years was *demanded* at the prosecution of Gabriel March Grandos, 22, at Palma de Mallorca, Spain on 11 Mar 1972 for failing to deliver 42,768 letters, or 9 years per letter.

The longest sentence imposed on a mass murderer was 21 consecutive life sentences and 12 death sentences in the case of John Gacy, who killed 33 boys and young men between 1972 and 1978 in Illinois, USA. He was sentenced by a jury in Chicago, Illinois on 13 Mar 1980, and was eventually executed on 10 May 1994.

Witchcraft!

The last legal execution of a witch was that of Anna Göldi at Glarus, Switzerland on 18 Jun 1782. It is estimated that at least 200,000 witches were executed during the European witchcraze of the 16th and 17th centuries.

The last person executed in Britain for witchcraft was Jenny Horn, burned alive at Dornoch, Highland in 1722.

Kevin Mulgrew from the Ardoyne district of Belfast was sentenced on 5 Aug 1983 to life imprisonment for the murder of Sergeant Julian Connolley of the Ulster Defence Regiment. In addition he was given a further 963 years to be served concurrently on 84 other serious charges, including 13 conspiracies to murder and 8 attempted murders.

The longest single period served by a reprieved murderer in Great Britain this century is 41 years 9 months up to 30 Apr 1994, by John Thomas Straffen, who was convicted at Winchester on 25 Jul 1952 of the murder of Linda Bowyer, aged 5, and sentenced to death. Straffen had escaped from Broadmoor, and was reprieved on account of his mental abnormality, but was not judged insane, and has been in prison ever since.

Oldest Bill Wallace (1881–1989) was the oldest prisoner on record, spending the last 63 years of his life in Aradale Psychiatric Hospital, at Ararat, Victoria, Australia. He had shot and killed a man at a restaurant in Melbourne, Victoria in December 1925, and having been found unfit to plead, was transferred to the responsibility of the

Mental Health Department in February 1926. He remained at Aradale until his death on 17 Jul 1989, shortly before his 108th birthday.

Longest time served Paul Geidel (1894–1987) was convicted of second-degree murder on 5 Sep 1911 when a 17-year-old porter in a hotel in New York, USA. He was released from the Fishkill Correctional Facility, Beacon, New York aged 85 on 7 May 1980, having served 68 years, 8 months and 2 days—the longest recorded term in US history. He first refused parole in 1974.

Blasphemy The last person to be imprisoned for blasphemy in Great Britain was George Jacob Holyoake, who was sentenced to six months at Gloucester Assizes on 15 Aug 1842. He had been arrested after delivering a lecture at Cheltenham, Glos, in the course of which he had said that he did not believe 'there is such a thing as God'.

Most arrests A record for arrests was set by Tommy Johns (1922–88) in Brisbane, Queensland, Australia on 9 Sep 1982 when he faced his 2000th conviction for drunkenness since 1957. His total at the time of his last drink on 30 Apr 1988 was 'nearly 3000'.

Under arrest!

The greatest mass arrest reported in a democratic country was of 15,617 demonstrators on 11 Jul 1988, rounded up by South Korean police to ensure security in advance of the 1988 Olympic Games in Seoul.

The largest in the UK occurred on 17 Sep 1961, when 1314 demonstrators supporting unilateral nuclear disarmament were arrested for obstructing highways leading to Parliament Square, London by sitting down. As a consequence of the 1926 General Strike there were 3149 prosecutions, for incitement (1760) and violence (1389).

Fines

Heaviest The largest fine ever was one of $650 million, imposed on the US securities house Drexel Burnham Lambert in December 1988 for insider trading. This figure represented $300 million in direct fines, with the balance to be put into an account to satisfy claims of parties that could prove they were defrauded by Drexel's actions.

The record for an individual is $200 million, which Michael Milken agreed to pay on 24 Apr 1990. In addition, he agreed to settle civil charges filed by the Securities and Exchange Commission. The payments were in settlement of a criminal racketeering and securities fraud suit brought by the US government. He was released from a 10-year prison sentence in January 1993.

United Kingdom The heaviest fine ever imposed in the UK was £5 million on Gerald Ronson (b. 26 May 1939), the head of Heron International, announced on 28 Aug 1990

> **Bill Wallace spent** 63 years in prison and was still there at the age of 107. When asked why, he responded:– 'There was a man... Well, to tell you the truth, I don't know'.

at Southwark Crown Court, London. Ronson was one of four defendants in the Guinness case concerning the company's takeover bid for Distillers.

The highest fine ever imposed on a UK company was 32 million ECUs (equivalent to £24.3 million) on British Steel by the European Commission on 16 Feb 1994 for colluding in price-fixing in the 1980s.

Prisons

Largest The largest prison built in Britain, and the first to be built and run by the state instead of local authorities, was Millbank Penitentiary in London. Completed in 1821, it covered 3 ha *7 acres* of ground and had 5 km *3 miles* of passages. It was closed in 1890 as an expensive failure, and demolished in 1903. The site is now partly occupied by the Tate Gallery. The most capacious prison in Great Britain is Wandsworth, south London, with a certified normal accommodation of 965. A peak occupancy of 1556 was reached on 17 Aug 1990.

Highest population Some human rights organizations have estimated that there are 20 million prisoners in China, which would be equal to 1715 per 100,000 population, although this figure is not officially acknowledged. Among countries for which statistics are available, that with the highest per capita prison population is the USA, with 455 prisoners per 100,000 people.

Prison fatalities The largest number of prison fatalities in one incident occurred at Fort William, Calcutta, India, on the night of 20 Jun 1756, when 146 people — 145 men and 1 woman — were locked in a military prison cell measuring 5.5 m × 4.25 m *18 × 14 ft* by order of Surajah Dowlah, Nawab of Bengal. By 6 a.m. next morning, when the cell was opened, only 22 men and the woman were left alive, leaving 123 dead. Most of the victims died from suffocation or by being crushed to death.

E GUINNESS NEWS 16 Nov 1969

BACK TO PRISON AFTER 46 YEARS

77-year-old turned in by his son

Leonard T. Fristoe was in prison again in California last night after nearly 46 years at large. He had been serving a life sentence for killing two sheriff's deputies when he escaped on 15 December 1923, just 2½ years into his life term.

Since then it appears that he has had a busy life using the name of Claude R. Willis, having lived in Mexico, Canada, and various parts of the United States. He married a woman from New York in 1927, but she died in 1963 never having learnt about his dual identity. His 39-year-old son, Claude R. Willis Jr, only found out about his past very recently. Father and son had a major argument yesterday which became so heated that the police were called, and it was then that Claude Jr blurted out what he had learnt about his father's past.

Claude Sr, or Leonard T. Fristoe, revealed his true identity to police following his arrest. His story has been verified with prison records from the 1920s.

(Photo: Associated Press)

GUESS WHAT?

Q Around how many people died in the world's worst riots?

A See Page 179

Most expensive prison Spandau Prison, in Berlin, Germany originally built in 1887 for 600 prisoners, was used solely for the Nazi war criminal Rudolf Hess (1894–1987) for the last twenty years of his life. The cost of maintenance of the staff of 105 was estimated in 1976 to be $415,000 per annum. On 19 Aug 1987 it was announced that Hess had strangled himself two days earlier with a piece of electrical flex. In October 1987 the prison was demolished.

Most labour camp escapes A former Soviet citizen Tatiana Mikhailovna Russanova, now living in Haifa, Israel, escaped from various Stalin labour camps in the former Soviet Union on 15 occasions between 1943 and 1954, being recaptured and sentenced 14 times. All of the escapes are judicially recognized by independent Russian lawyers, although only nine are recognized by Soviet Supreme Court officials.

The rescue of the Americans from the Iranian prison (⇨ below) was arranged by their employer, H. Ross Perot. Over 10 years later he was to make the news again when he proposed standing for US president in 1992.

Greatest gaol break In February 1979 a retired US Army colonel, Arthur 'Bull' Simons, led a band of 14 to break into Gasre prison, Tehran, Iran to rescue two fellow Americans. Some 11,000 other prisoners took advantage of this and the Islamic revolution in what became history's largest ever gaol break.

In September 1971 Raúl Sendic and 105 other Tupamaro guerillas, plus five non-political prisoners, escaped from a Uruguayan prison through a tunnel 91 m *298 ft* long.

The greatest gaol break in the UK was that from the Maze Prison on 25 Sep 1983, when 38 IRA prisoners escaped from Block H-7.

Honours, Decorations and Awards

Oldest order The earliest honour known was the 'Gold of Honour' for extraordinary valour awarded in the 18th Dynasty *c*.1440–1400 BC. A statuette was found at Qan-el-Kebri, Egypt. The oldest true order was the Order of St John of Jerusalem (the direct descendant of which is the Sovereign Military Order of Malta), legitimized in 1113.

Victoria Cross *Double awards* The only three men ever to have been awarded a bar to the Victoria Cross (instituted 29 Jan 1856) are:

Surg.-Capt. (later Lt-Col.) Arthur Martin-Leake VC*, VD, RAMC (1874–1953) (1902 and bar 1914).

Capt. Noel Godfrey Chavasse VC*, MC, RAMC (1884–1917) (1916 and bar posthumously 1917).

Second-Lt. (later Capt.) Charles Hazlitt Upham VC*, NZMF (b. 21 Sep 1908) (1941 and bar 1942).

The most VCs awarded in a war were the 634 in World War I (1914–18). The greatest number of VCs gained exclusively in a single action was 11 at Rorke's Drift in the Zulu War on 22–23 Jan 1879.

Youngest The earliest established age for a VC is 15 years 100 days for hospital apprentice Andrew (wrongly gazetted as Arthur) Fitzgibbon (b. 13 May 1845 at Peteragurh, northern India) of the Indian Medical Services for bravery at the Taku Forts in northern China on 21 Aug 1860. The youngest living VC is Capt. Rambahadur Limbu (b. 1 Nov 1939 at Chyangthapu, Nepal) of the 10th Princess Mary's Own Gurkha Rifles. The award was for his courage as a lance-corporal while fighting in the Bau district of Sarawak, east Malaysia on 21 Nov 1965.

Oldest Capt. William Raynor was the oldest person to receive the medal. It was awarded when he was 62, for the part he played in blowing up an arms store besieged by insurgents on 11 May 1857, the second day of the Indian Mutiny.

Longest-lived The longest-lived of all the 1351 recipients of the Victoria Cross has been Lt-Col. Harcus Strachan. He was born in Bo'ness, West Lothian on 7 Nov 1884 and died in Vancouver, British Columbia, Canada on 1 May 1982 aged 97 years 175 days.

Record price The highest price ever paid for a Victoria Cross was £132,000 for the VC—and other medals—awarded to Major Edward 'Mick' Mannock (⇨ Top-scoring air aces) posthumously in 1919, in recognition of bravery of the first order in aerial combat. It was sold to a private collector at Billingshurst, W Sussex on 19 Sep 1992.

The record for a George Cross is £20,250 at Christie's on 14 Mar 1985, for that of Sgt Michael Willets (3rd Battalion Parachute Regiment), killed by an IRA bomb in Ulster in 1971.

Most highly decorated The four living persons to have been twice decorated with any of the UK's topmost decorations are Capt. C. H. Upham

The various medals awarded to 'Mick' Mannock, including the Victoria Cross (left), which were sold for a record £132,000 in September 1992.
(Photo: Sotheby's)

Most statues The world record for raising statues to oneself was set by Joseph Vissarionovich Dzhugashvili, alias Stalin (1879–1953), the leader of the Soviet Union from 1924–53. It is estimated that at the time of his death there were *c.* 6000 statues to him throughout the USSR and in many cities in eastern Europe. The country's highest mountain was named Pik Stalina (Stalin Peak), although it was renamed in 1962. In addition numerous enterprises, schools, institutes and theatres were named after him, as were 15 Soviet towns or cities. The last statue of Stalin was demolished in 1992 in Ulan Bator, the capital of Mongolia.

The man to whom most statues have been raised is Buddha. The 20th-century champion is Vladimir Ilyich Ulyanov, alias Lenin (1870–1924), busts of whom have been mass-produced, as also has been the case with Mao Zedong (Mao Tse-tung) (1893–1976) and Ho Chi Minh (1890–1969).

Most honorary degrees The greatest number of honorary degrees awarded to any individual is 129, given to Rev. Father Theodore M. Hesburgh (b. 25 May 1917), president of the University of Notre Dame, Indiana, USA. These have been accumulated since 1954.

VC and bar; HM the Queen Mother CI, GCVO, GBE, who is a Lady of the Garter and a Lady of the Thistle; HRH the Duke of Edinburgh KG, KT, OM, GBE and HRH Prince Charles KG, KT, GCB. Britain's most highly decorated woman is the World War II British agent Mrs Odette Hallowes GC, MBE, Légion d'Honneur, Ordre St George (Belge), who survived imprisonment and torture at the hands of the Gestapo from 1943–5.

Youngest awards Kristina Stragauskaite of Skirmantiskes, Lithuania was awarded a medal 'For Courage in Fire' when she was just 4years 252days old. She had saved the lives of her younger brother and sister when a fire had broken out on 7 April 1989 in the family's home while her parents were out. The award was decreed by the Presidium of the Lithuanian Soviet Socialist Republic.

The youngest age at which an official gallantry award has ever been won is eight years in the case of Anthony Farrer, who was given the Albert Medal on 23 Sep 1916 for fighting off a cougar at Cowichan Lake, Vancouver Island, Canada to save Doreen Ashburnham. She was also awarded the Albert Medal, which she exchanged in 1974 for the George Cross.

Most lifeboat medals Sir William Hillary (1771–1847), founder of the Royal National Lifeboat Institution in 1824, was personally and uniquely awarded four RNLI Gold Medals, in 1825, 1828 and 1830 (twice).

Most post-nominal letters HRH the Duke of Windsor (1894–1972) when Prince of Wales had 10 sets and was also a privy counsellor, viz. KG, PC, KT, KP, GCB, GCSI, GCMG, GCIE, GCVO, GBE, MC. He later appended the ISO but never did so in the cases of the OM, CH or DSO, of which orders he had also been sovereign.

Lord Roberts, who was also a privy counsellor, was the only non-royal holder of eight sets of *official* post-nominal letters.

Civilian gallantry Reginald H. Blanchford of Guernsey has received the following awards for life saving on land and at sea: MBE for gallantry in 1950; Queen's Commendation in 1957; Life Saving Medal of The Order of St John in Gold in 1957 with gold bar in 1963; George Medal in 1958; Carnegie Hero Fund's Bronze Medallion in 1959; OBE 1961. He was made a Knight of Grace of The Order of St John in 1970 and most recently received the American Biographical Institute's Silver Shield of Valor in 1992.

Order of Merit The Order of Merit (instituted on 23 Jun 1902) is limited to 24 members at any one time. The longest-lived of the 162 holders has been the Rt Hon. Bertrand Arthur William Russell, 3rd Earl Russell, who died on 2 Feb 1970 aged 97 years 260 days. The oldest recipient was Dame Ninette de Valois (b. 6 Jun 1898), who received the Order at the age of 94 years 179 days on 2 Dec 1992. The youngest recipient has been HRH the Duke of Edinburgh, who was appointed on his 47th birthday on 10 Jun 1968.

Money!

The most valuable annual prize is the Louis Jeantet Prize for Medicine, which in 1994 was worth SFr 2,100,000 (equivalent to approximately £953,000). It was first awarded in 1986 and is intended to 'provide substantial funds for the support of biomedical research projects'.

GUESS WHAT?

Q How old was Andrew Fitzgibbon when he was awarded the VC?

A See Page 193

Help!

The greatest rescue in Britain was on 17 Mar 1907, when four lifeboats lifted 456 shipwreck survivors to safety off the Lizard, Cornwall.

The greatest number of awards gained by a member of the Royal Life Saving Society is 221 by Eric Deakin of Hightown, Lancs since 1960.

Nobel Prizes

Earliest 1901 for Physics, Chemistry, Physiology or Medicine, Literature and Peace.

Most Prizes USA has won 215, outright or shared, including most for Physiology or Medicine (70); Physics (57); Chemistry (38); Peace (18); Economics (21). France has most for Literature (12). The United Kingdom total is 90, outright or shared, comprising Chemistry (23); Physiology or Medicine (23); Physics (20); Peace (10); Literature (8); Economics (6).

Oldest Laureate Professor Francis Peyton Rous (US) (1879–1970) in 1966 shared in the Physiology or Medicine prize at the age of 87.

Youngest Laureates *At time of award:* Professor Sir Lawrence Bragg (1890–1971) 1915 Physics prize at 25. *At time of work:* Bragg, and Theodore W. Richards (US) (1868–1928), 1914 Chemistry prize for work done when 23.

Most 3 Awards: International Committee of the Red Cross, Geneva (founded 1863) Peace 1917, 1944 and 1963 (shared); 2 Awards: Dr Linus Carl Pauling (US) (b. 28 Feb 1901) Chemistry 1954 and Peace 1962; Mme Marja Sklodowska Curie (Polish-French) (1867–1934) Physics 1903 (shared) and Chemistry 1911; Professor John Bardeen (US) (1908–91) Physics 1956 (shared) and 1972 (shared); Professor Frederick Sanger (b. 13 Aug 1918) Chemistry 1958 and 1980 (shared); Office of the United Nations' High Commissioner for Refugees, Geneva (founded 1951) Peace 1954 and 1981.

Highest Prize Swedish Krona 7,000,000 (for 1994), equivalent to £602,000.

Lowest Prize Swedish Krona 115,000 (for 1923), equivalent to £6620.

The Royal Society The longest term as a Fellow of the Royal Society (founded 1660) has been approximately 68 years in the case of Sir Hans Sloane (1660–1753), who was elected in 1685. The longest-lived Fellow was Sir Rickard Christophers (1873–1978), who died aged 104 years 84 days. The youngest Fellow is believed to have been Sir Joseph Hodges, who was born *c.* 1704 and elected on 5 Apr 1716 at about 12 years of age. The oldest person to have been elected as a Fellow was Sir Rupert Edward Cecil Lee Guinness, the 2nd Earl of Iveagh (1874–1967), who was elected in 1964 at the age of 90.

Erasmus Darwin was elected on 9 Apr 1761 and was followed by his son Robert (1788 to 1848), *his* son Charles (1839 to 1882), his sons Sir George (1879 to 1912), Francis (1882 to 1925) and Horace (1903 to 1928) and Sir George's son Sir Charles (1922 to 1962), so spanning over 200 years with five generations.

Peerage

Longest-lived peer The longest-lived peer ever recorded was the Rt Hon. Emanuel Shinwell (1884–1986), who was created a life baron in 1970 and died on 8 May 1986 aged 101 years 202 days. The oldest peeress recorded was the Countess Desmond, who was alleged to be 140 when she died in 1604. This claim is patently exaggerated but it is accepted that she may have been 104. Currently the oldest peer is the Rt Hon. Jeffery Amherst, 5th Earl Amherst (b. 13 Dec 1896).

Youngest peers Twelve Dukes of Cornwall became (in accordance with the grant by the Crown in Parliament) peers at birth as the eldest sons of a

GUESS WHAT?

Q As well as being the longest-lived peer, what other distinction does Emanuel Shinwell hold?

A See Page 184

sovereign; and the 9th Earl of Chichester inherited his earldom at his birth on 14 Apr 1944, 54 days after his father's death. The youngest age at which a person has had a peerage conferred on him is 7 days old in the case of the Earldom of Chester on HRH the Prince George (later George IV) on 19 Aug 1762.

Longest peerage The longest tenure of a peerage has been 87 years 10 days in the case of Charles St Clair, Lord Sinclair, born 30 Jul 1768, succeeded 16 Dec 1775 and died aged 94 years 243 days on 30 Mar 1863.

The shortest enjoyment of a peerage was the 'split second' by which the law assumes that the Hon. Wilfrid Carlyl Stamp (b. 28 Oct 1904), the 2nd Baron Stamp, survived his father, Sir Josiah Charles Stamp, the 1st Baron Stamp, when both were killed as a result of German bombing of London on 16 Apr 1941. Apart from this legal fiction, the shortest recorded peerage was one of 30 min in the case of Sir Charles Brandon, the 3rd Duke of Suffolk, who died aged 13 or 14 just after succeeding his brother Henry, when both were suffering a fatal illness, at Buckden, Cambs on 14 Jul 1551.

Knights *Youngest and oldest* The youngest age for the conferment of a knighthood is 29 days for HRH the Prince George (b. 12 Aug 1762) (later George IV) by virtue of his *ex officio* membership of the Order of the Garter consequent upon his creation as Prince of Wales on 17 or 19 Aug 1762. The greatest age for the conferment of a knighthood is on a 100th birthday, in the case of the Knight Bachelor Sir Robert Mayer (1879–1985), who was also made a KCVO by the Queen at the Royal Festival Hall, London on 5 Jun 1979.

Proud!

George and Elizabeth Coles of Australia had four sons knighted — Sir George (1885–1977); Sir Arthur (1892–1982); Sir Kenneth (1896–1985) and Sir Edgar (1899–1981). George re-married and had a fifth son who was also knighted — Sir Norman (1907–89).

The largest gathering of Nobel laureates took place in 1991, for the 90th anniversary jubilee of the Nobel prizes.
(Photo: Gamma/Presens Bild)

Military and Defence

War

Earliest conflict The oldest known offensive weapon is a broken wooden spear found in April 1911 at Clacton-on-Sea, Essex by S. Hazzledine Warren. This is much beyond the limit of radio-carbon dating but is estimated to have been fashioned before 200,000 BC.

Longest The longest war which could be described as continuous was the Thirty Years War, between various European countries from 1618 to 1648. As a result the map of Europe was radically changed. The so-called 'Hundred Years War' between England and France, which lasted from 1338 to 1453 (115 years), was in fact an irregular succession of wars rather than a single one. The *Reconquista*—the series of campaigns in the Iberian Peninsula to recover the region from the Islamic Moors—began in 718 and continued intermittently until 1492, when Granada, the last Moorish stronghold, was finally conquered.

War over!

The shortest war on record was that between the UK and Zanzibar (now part of Tanzania), which lasted from 9:02 to 9:40 a.m. on 27 Aug 1896. The UK battle fleet under Rear-Admiral (later Admiral Sir) Harry Rawson (1843–1910) delivered an ultimatum to the self-appointed Sultan Sa'īd Khalid to evacuate his palace and surrender. This was not forthcoming until after 38 minutes of bombardment. Admiral Rawson received the Brilliant Star of Zanzibar (first class) from Hamud ibn Muhammad, the new Sultan.

Bloodiest By far the most costly war in terms of human life was World War II (1939–45), in which the total number of fatalities, including battle deaths and civilians of all countries, is estimated to have been 54.8 million, assuming 25 million Soviet fatalities and 7.8 million Chinese civilians killed. The country which suffered most was Poland, with 6,028,000 or 17.2 per cent of its population of 35,100,000 killed.

In the Paraguayan war of 1864–70 against Brazil, Argentina and Uruguay, Paraguay's population was reduced from 1,400,000 to 220,000 survivors, of whom only 30,000 were adult males.

Survivors!

Dr William Brydon (1811–73) and two natives were the sole survivors of a seven-day retreat of 13,000 soldiers and camp-followers from Kabul, Afghanistan. Dr Brydon's horse died 2 days after his arrival at Jellalabad, some 115 km 70 miles to the east on the route to the Khyber Pass, on 13 Jan 1842.

Most costly The material cost of World War II far transcended that of the rest of history's wars put together and has been estimated at $1.5 trillion. The total cost to the Soviet Union was estimated in May 1959 at 2.5 trillion roubles, while a figure of $530 billion has been estimated for the USA.

In the case of the UK the cost of £34,423 million was over five times as great as that of World War I (£6700 million) and 158.6 times that of the Boer War of 1899–1902 (£217 million).

Bloodiest battle *Modern* It is difficult to compare the major battles of World Wars I and II because of the timescales. The 142-day long first battle of the Somme, France (1 Jul–19 Nov 1916) produced an estimated total number of casualties of over 1.22 million, of which 398,671 were British (57,470 on the first day) and more than 600,000 German. The losses of the German Army Group Centre on the Eastern Front between 22 Jun and 8 Jul 1944 (17 days) totalled 350,000. The greatest death toll in a battle has been estimated at *c.* 1,109,000 in the Battle of Stalingrad, USSR (now Volgograd, Russia), which ended with the German surrender on 31 Jan 1943 by Field Marshal Friedrich von Paulus (1890–1957). The Soviet army also lost *c.* 650,800 soldiers who were injured but survived. Additionally, only 1515 civilians from a pre-war population of more than 500,000 were found alive after the battle. The final drive on Berlin, Germany by the Soviet Army and the battle for the city which followed, from 16 Apr–2 May 1945, involved 3.5 million men, 52,000 guns and mortars, 7750 tanks and 11,000 aircraft on both sides.

Ancient Modern historians give no credence, on logistic grounds, to the casualty figures attached to ancient battles, such as the 250,000 reputedly killed at Plataea (Greeks *v.* Persians) in 479 BC or the 200,000 allegedly killed in a single day at Châlons-sur-Marne, France (Huns *v.* Romans) in AD 451. More reliably the Romans estimated the number of their own dead at the Battle of Cannae in 216 BC at 48,200, with the best estimate for the losses amongst the opposing forces under Hannibal being 5700.

British The bloodiest battle fought on British soil was the battle of Towton, near Tadcaster, N Yorks on 29 Mar 1461, when 36,000 Yorkists defeated 40,000 Lancastrians. The total loss has been estimated at between 28,000 and 38,000 killed. A figure of 80,000 British dead was attributed by Tacitus to the battle of AD 61 between Queen Boudicca (Boadicea) of the Iceni and the Roman Governor of Britain Suetonius Paulinus, for the reputed loss of only 400 Romans in an army of 10,000. The site of the battle is unknown but may possibly have been near Borough Hill, Daventry, Northants, or more probably near Hampstead Heath, London.

Greatest naval battle The greatest number of ships and aircraft ever involved in a sea–air action was 231 ships and 1996 aircraft in the Battle of Leyte Gulf, in the Philippines. It raged from 22–27 Oct 1944, with 166 Allied and 65 Japanese warships engaged, of which 26 Japanese and six US ships were sunk. In addition, 1280 US and 716 Japanese aircraft were engaged. The greatest purely naval battle of modern times was the Battle of Jutland on 31 May 1916, in which 151 Royal Navy warships were involved against 101 German warships. The Royal Navy lost 14 ships and 6097 men and the German fleet 11 ships and 2545 men. The greatest of ancient naval battles was the Battle of Salamis, Greece in September 480 BC. There were an estimated 800 vessels in the defeated Persian fleet and 380 in the victorious fleet of the Athenians and their allies, with a possible involvement of 200,000 men. The death toll at the Battle of Lepanto on 7 Oct 1571 has been estimated at 33,000.

GUESS WHAT?

Q Which country built the largest battleships?

A See Page 106

> **Military feast**
> It was estimated that some 30,000 guests attended a military feast given at Radewitz, Poland on 25 Jun 1730 by King August II (1709–33).

Airborne!

The largest airborne invasion was the Anglo-American assault of three divisions (34,000 men), with 2800 aircraft and 1600 gliders, near Arnhem, in the Netherlands, on 17 Sep 1944.

Last invasion of Great Britain The Irish-American adventurer General Tate landed at Carreg Wastad Point, Pembroke (now Dyfed) with 1400 French troops on 12 Feb 1797 They surrendered outside Fishguard, a few miles away, to Lord Cawdor's force of the Castlemartin Yeomanry and some local inhabitants armed with pitchforks.

Longest range attacks The longest range attacks in air history were those undertaken by seven B-52G bombers, which took off from Barksdale air force base, Louisiana, USA on 16 Jan 1991 to deliver air-launched cruise missiles against targets in Iraq shortly after the start of the Gulf War. Each flew a distance of 22,500 km *14,000 miles*, refuelling four times in flight, with the round-trip mission lasting some 35 hours.

Greatest *seaborne invasion*

The greatest invasion in military history was the Allied land, air and sea operation against the Normandy coasts of France on D-Day, 6 Jun 1944. On the first three days 38 convoys of 745 ships moved in, supported by 4066 landing craft, carrying 185,000 men, 20,000 vehicles and 347 minesweepers. The air assault comprised 18,000 paratroopers from 1087 aircraft. The 42 available divisions had air support from 13,175 aircraft. Within a month 1,100,000 troops, 200,000 vehicles and 750,000 tons of stores were landed.

The Normandy landings of 6 Jun 1944, generally referred to as D-Day, represent the greatest invasion in military history. The photograph above (top) shows the Allied commanders during one of their meetings to plan the operation. American jeeps are loaded onto the landing craft (left), and troops wade through the sea on arriving in France (above).
(Photos: Gamma Archives)

Largest civilian evacuation Following the Iraqi invasion of Kuwait in August 1990, Air India evacuated 111,711 of its nationals who were working in Kuwait. Beginning on 13 August, 488 flights took the ex-patriates back to India over a two-month period.

Worst sieges The worst siege in history was the 880-day siege of Leningrad, USSR (now St Petersburg, Russia), by the German Army from 30 Aug 1941 until 27 Jan 1944. The best estimate is that between 1.3 and 1.5 million defenders and citizens died. This included 641,000 people who died of hunger in the city and 17,000 civilians killed by shelling. More than 150,000 shells and 100,000 bombs were dropped on the city. The longest recorded siege was that of Azotus (now Ashdod), Israel which according to Herodotus was besieged by Psamtik I of Egypt for 29 years in the period 664–610BC.

Chemical warfare The greatest number of people killed through chemical warfare were the estimated 4000 Kurds who died at Halabja, Iraq in March 1988 when President Saddam Hussein used chemical weapons against Iraq's Kurdish minority for the support it had given to Iran in the Iran–Iraq war.

Defence Spending

In 1992 it was estimated that the world's spending on defence was running at an annual rate of some $1,213 billion. In 1993 there were 24,567,000 full-time armed forces regulars or conscripts plus 38,124,000 reservists, totalling 62,691,000. The budgeted expenditure on defence by the US government for the fiscal year 1993 was $258.87 billion. The defence budget of Russia was given as 8,950 billion roubles in 1993. The UK defence budget for 1993/4 is £23.76 billion.

Armed Forces

Largest China's People's Liberation Army's strength in 1993 was estimated to be 3,030,000 (comprising land, sea and air forces), with reductions continuing. Her reserves which can be mobilized number around 1.2 million plus many more for local militia duty. Numerically, the world's largest army is also that of the People's Republic of China, with a total strength of some 2.3 million in mid-1993.

Prior to its break-up, the USSR had the largest regular armed force in the world, with 3,400,000 personnel in 1991. The latest figure for the Russian armed forces is c. 2 million.

The UK's military manpower is 275,000 (1993), of which the army has the most, with 124,500. The maximum ever strength of the army was 3.8 million, in March 1918.

Armies *Oldest* The oldest army in the world is the 80–90 strong Pontifical Swiss Guard in the Vatican City, with a regular foundation dating back to 21 Jan 1506. Its origins, however, predate 1400. (For details of largest armies ⇨ above)

Navies *Largest* The largest navy in the world in terms of manpower is the United States Navy, with 510,600 plus 183,000 Marines in mid-1993.

The strength of the Royal Navy in mid-1993 was 59,300, including The Fleet Air Arm and Royal Marines (7250). In 1914 the Royal Navy had 542 warships including 72 capital ships with 16 building, making it the largest navy in the world at the time.

Air forces *Oldest* The earliest autonomous air force is the Royal Air Force, which can be traced back to 1878, when the War Office commissioned the building of a military balloon. Balloons had been used for military observation by both sides during the American Civil War (1861–5).

Largest The greatest air force of all time was the United States Army Air Corps (now the US Air Force), which had 79,908 aircraft in July 1944 and 2,411,294 personnel in March 1944. The US Air Force, including strategic missile forces, had 450,000 personnel and 5900 (plus more in store) aircraft in mid-1993.

The strength of the Royal Air Force in 1993 was 81,000, with 38 operational squadrons.

Oldest soldiers The oldest 'old soldier' of all time was probably John B. Salling of the army of the Confederate States of America and the last accepted survivor of the US Civil War (1861–5). He died in Kingsport, Tennessee, USA on 16 Mar 1959, aged 113 years 1 day.

The oldest Chelsea pensioner, based *only* on the evidence of his tombstone, was 111-year-old William Hiseland (6 Aug 1620–7 Feb 1732). George Ives (b. Brighton, E. Sussex, 17 Nov 1881, d. 12 Apr 1993) of the 1st Imperial Yeomanry fought in the Boer War, and also lived to the age of 111. After the war ended he emigrated to Canada, where he lived for some 90 years. The longest-serving British soldier has been Field Marshal Sir William Gomm (1784–1875), who was an ensign in 1794 and Constable of the Tower of London over 80 years later at his death aged 91.

Youngest soldiers Luís Alves de Lima e Silva, Marshal Duke of Caxias (25 Aug 1803–7 May 1880), Brazilian military hero and statesman, entered his infantry regiment at the age of five in 1808. He was promoted to Captain in 1824 and made Duke in 1869. Fernando Inchauste Montalvo (b. 18 Jun 1930), the son of a major in the Bolivian air force, went to the front with his father on his 5th birthday during the war between Bolivia and Paraguay (1932–5). He had received military training and was subject to military discipline.

The youngest enlistment in Britain in the 20th century is believed to be that of William Frederick Price (b. 1 Jun 1891), who was enlisted into the army at Aldershot on 23 May 1903, when aged 11 years 356 days.

Conscientious objector *Most obdurate* The only conscientious objector to be six times court-martialled in World War II was Gilbert Lane of Wallington, Surrey. He served 31 months' detention and 183 days' imprisonment.

Top jet ace The greatest number of kills claimed in jet-to-jet battles is 21, by Capt. Nikolai Vasilevich Sutyagin (USSR) in the Korean war (1950–3).

Anti-submarine successes The highest number of U-boat kills attributed to one ship in World War II was 15, to HMS *Starling* (Capt. Frederic John Walker DSO***, RN). Captain Walker was in command at the sinking of a total of 25 U-boats between 1941 and the time of his death on 9 Jul 1944. The US Destroyer Escort *England* sank six Japanese submarines in the Pacific between 18 and 30 May 1944.

Most successful submarine captains The most successful of all World War II

Evacuated!

The greatest evacuation in military history was that carried out by 1200 Allied naval and civil craft from the beach-head at Dunkerque (Dunkirk), France between 27 May and 4 Jun 1940. A total of 338,226 British and French troops were taken off.

Precision!

On 8–9 Jul 1987 a 90-man squad of the Queen's Colour Squadron, RAF performed a total of 2,722,662 drill movements (2,001,384 rifle and 721,278 foot) at RAF Uxbridge, Middx from memory and without a word of command in 23 hr 55 min.

TOP-SCORING AIR ACES (WORLD WARS I AND II)

The 'scores' of air aces in both wars are still disputed. The highest figures officially attributed are:

World War I
World: 80 Rittmeister Manfred Freiherr (Baron) von Richthofen (Germany)
UK: 57[1] Major James T.B. McCudden VC, DSO*, MC*, MM

World War II
World: 352[2] Major Erich Hartmann (Germany)
UK: 38[3] Group Capt. (now Air Vice-Marshal) James Edgar Johnson DSO**, DFC*

[1] 73 'victories' are frequently attributed to Major Edward Mannock VC, DSO**, MC*, although he actually claimed no more than 50 — the total stated in his VC citation. The figure of 73 is thought to be used so that he would appear to beat the 72 'victories' which were claimed by the Canadian pilot Lt-Col. William 'Billy' Bishop VC, although many of these are considered to be unsubstantiated.
[2] The highest total in one sortie is 13 in 17 min by Major Erich Rudorffer, on the Russian front on 6 Nov 1943.
[3] The greatest number of successes against flying bombs (V1s) was by Sqn Ldr Joseph Berry DFC** (b. Nottingham, 1920, killed 2 Oct 1944), who brought down 60 during the V1 campaign between 13 Jun and 1 Sep 1944, 57 of them at night. The most successful fighter pilot in the RAF was Sqn Ldr Marmaduke Thomas St John Pattle DFC*, of South Africa, with a known total of at least 40 enemy aircraft.

Youngest conscripts
President Francisco Macias Nguema of Equatorial Guinea (deposed in August 1979) decreed in March 1976 compulsory military service for all boys aged between seven and 14. The edict stated that any parent refusing to hand over his or her son 'will be imprisoned or shot'.

GUESS WHAT?

Q What is the greatest depth to which a submarine has descended?

A see Page 107

submarine commanders was Leutnant Otto Kretschmer, captain of the U.23 and U.99, who up to March 1941 sank one destroyer and 44 Allied merchantmen totalling 266,629 gross registered tons.

In World War I Kapitänleutnant (later Vizeadmiral) Lothar von Arnauld de la Perière, in the U.35 and U.139, sank 195 Allied ships totalling 458,856 gross registered tons.

Greatest mutiny In World War I, 56 French divisions comprising some 650,000 men and their officers, refused orders on the Western Front sector of General Robert Nivelle in April 1917 after the failure of his offensive.

Longest march The longest march in military history was the famous Long March by the Chinese Communists in 1934–5. In 368 days, of which 268 days were days of movement, from October to October, their force of some 100,000 covered 9700 km *6000 miles* from Ruijin, in Jiangxi, to Yan'an, in Shaanxi. They crossed 18 mountain ranges and 24 rivers, and eventually reached Yan'an with only about 8000 surviors following continual rearguard actions against nationalist Guomindang (GMD) forces.

The largest target ever sunk by a submarine was the Japanese aircraft carrier Shinano (59,994 tonnes) by USS Archerfish (Cdr Joseph F. Enright, USN) on 29 Nov 1944.

Bombs

Heaviest The heaviest conventional bomb ever used operationally was the Royal Air Force's *Grand Slam*, weighing 9980 kg *22,000 lb* and 7.74 m *25 ft 5 in* long, dropped on Bielefeld railway viaduct, Germany on 14 Mar 1945. In 1949 the United States Air Force tested a bomb weighing 19,050 kg *42,000 lb* at Muroc Dry Lake, California, USA.

The heaviest known nuclear bomb was the MK 17 carried by US B-36 bombers in the mid-1950s. It weighed 19,050 kg *42,000 lb* and was 7.47 m *24 ft 6 in* long.

Atomic The first atom bomb dropped on Hiroshima, Japan by the United States at 8:16 a.m. on 6 Aug 1945 had an explosive power equivalent to that of 12.5 kilotons of trinitrotoluene ($C_7H_5O_6N_3$), called TNT. Code-named *Little Boy*, it was 3.04 m *10 ft* long and weighed 4080 kg *9000 lb*. It burst 565 m *1850 ft* above the city centre. The most powerful thermonuclear device so far tested is one with a power equivalent to that of 57 megatons of TNT, detonated by the former USSR in the Novaya Zemlya area at 8:33 a.m. GMT on 30 Oct 1961. On 9 Aug 1961, Nikita Khrushchev, then the Chairman of the Council of Ministers of the USSR, declared that the Soviet Union was capable of constructing a 100-megaton bomb, and announced the possession of one during a visit to what was then East Berlin, East Germany on 16 Jan 1963.

Largest nuclear weapons The most powerful ICBM (inter-continental ballistic missile) is the former USSR's SS-18 (Model 5), officially called the RS-20, which is believed to be armed with 10 MIRVs (multiple independently targetable re-entry

vehicles), each of 750-kilotons. SS-18 ICBMs are located on the territories of both Russia and Kazakhstan, although the dismantlement of those in Kazakhstan has begun. Earlier models had a single 20-megaton warhead. START 2 (START = Strategic Arms Reduction Talks) requires all SS-18, and all other ICBMs with more than one warhead, to be eliminated. The US Titan II carrying a W-53 warhead was rated at 9 megatons but was withdrawn, leaving the 1.2 megaton W-56 as the most powerful US weapon.

Largest 'conventional' explosion The largest use of conventional explosives was by a team of Chinese army engineers who blew up a mountain to allow for the expansion of an airport in Zhuhai, an economic development zone near Macao. A total of nearly 11,300 tonnes of TNT were detonated on 28 Dec 1992 after 1000 technicians had spent several months preparing for the explosion.

Quick march!

A team of nine representing II Squadron RAF Regiment from RAF Hullavington, Wilts, each man carrying a pack weighing at least 40 lb *18.1 kg*, including a rifle, completed the London marathon in 4 hr 33 min 58 sec on 21 Apr 1991.

Flt Sgt Chris Chandler set an individual record in the RAF Swinderby Marathon at Swinderby, Lincs on 25 Sep 1992, with a pack weighing 40 lb *18.1 kg*. His time was 3 hr 56 min 10 sec.**mbs**

Tanks

Earliest The first tank was *No. 1 Lincoln*, modified to become *Little Willie*, built by William Foster & Co. Ltd of Lincoln. It first ran on 6 Sep 1915. Tanks first saw action with the Heavy Section, Machine Gun Corps, later the Tank Corps, at the Battle of Flers-Courcelette, France on 15 Sep 1916. The Mark I 'Male' tank, armed with a pair of 6-pounder guns and three machine guns, weighed 28.4 tonnes and was powered by a 105 hp motor, giving a maximum road speed of 4.8–6.4 km/h *3–4 mph*.

GUESS WHAT?

Q where is the world's largest nuclear power station?

A See Page 73

Heaviest The heaviest tank ever constructed was the German Panzer Kampfwagen Maus II, which weighed 192 tonnes. By 1945 it had reached only the experimental stage and was abandoned. The heaviest operational tank used by any army was the 75.2 tonne 13-man French Char de Rupture 2C bis of 1922. It carried a 155mm *6⅛ in* howitzer and was powered by two 250hp engines giving a maximum speed of 12km/h *8 mph*. The heaviest British tank was the Experimental Heavy Tank TOG 2 built in 1941. It weighed 80 tonnes, was 10.13m *33 ft 3 in* long, had a crew of six and a top speed of 13.7 km/h *8½ mph*. It is on permanent display at the Tank Museum, Bovington, Dorset. The heaviest British tank to enter service was *Conqueror*, at 66 tonnes.

The most heavily armed tank in recent times has been the Soviet T-72, with a 125mm *4⅞ in* high-velocity gun. The American Sheridan light tank mounts a 152mm *6 in* weapon which is both a gun and a missile launcher combined but this is not a long barrelled, high-velocity gun of the conventional type. The British AVRE *Centurion* had a 165mm *6½ in* low-velocity demolition gun.

Fastest The American experimental tank M1936 built by J. Walter Christie was clocked at 103.4 km/h *64.3 mph* during official trials in Britain in 1938.

Most prolific The greatest production of any tank was that of the Soviet T-54/55 series, of which more than 50,000 were built between

The fastest tracked armoured reconnaissance vehicle is the British *Scorpion*, which can touch 80 km/h *50 mph* with a 75 per cent payload.
(Photo: Gamma/Debay)

The shock-wave from the thermonuclear device detonated on 30 Oct 1961 circled the world three times, taking 36 hr 27 min for the first circuit.

1954 and 1980 in the USSR alone, with further production in the one-time Warsaw Pact countries and China.

Guns

Earliest Although it cannot be accepted as proven, it is believed that the earliest guns were constructed in both China and in north Africa in *c.* 1250. The earliest representation of an English gun is contained in an illustrated manuscript dated 1326, now at Oxford.

Largest The largest gun ever constructed was used by the Germans in the siege of Sevastopol, USSR (now Russia) in July 1942. It was of a calibre of 800mm *31in* with a barrel 28.87m *94ft 8½ in* long. Internally it was named *Schwerer Gustav*, and was one of three guns which were given the general name of *Dora*, although the other two were not finished and so were not used in action. It was built by Krupp, and its remains were discovered near Metzenhof, Bavaria in August 1945. The whole assembly of the gun was 42.9m *141ft* long and weighed 1344tonnes, with a crew of 1500. The range for an 8.1tonne projectile was 46.67km *29 miles.*

During World War I the British Army used a gun of 457mm *18in* calibre. The barrel alone weighed 127tonnes. In World War II the *Bochebuster*, a train-mounted howitzer with a calibre of 457mm *18in* firing a 1130kg *2500lb* shell to a maximum range of 20,850m *22,800yd*, was used from 1940 onwards as part of the Kent coast defences.

> **Three teams of eight members from 72 Ordnance Company (V) RAOC pulled a 25-pounder field gun over a distance of 177.98km *110.6 miles* in 24 hours at Donnington, Shrops on 2–3 Apr 1993.**

Greatest range The greatest range ever attained by a gun was achieved by the HARP (High Altitude Research Project) gun, consisting of two 420mm *16½ in* calibre barrels in tandem 36.4m *119ft 5in* long and weighing 150tonnes, at Yuma, Arizona, USA. On 19 Nov 1966 an 84kg *185lb* projectile was fired to an altitude of 180km *112 miles.*

The static V3 underground firing tubes built in 50° shafts during World War II near Mimoyècques, not far from Calais, France, to bombard London were never operative. This would have been a distance of some 150km *95 miles.*

The famous long-range gun which shelled Paris in World War I was the *Paris-Geschütz* (Paris Gun), with a calibre of 210mm *8¼ in*, a designed range of 127.9km *79½ miles* and an achieved range of 122km *76 miles* from the Forest of Crépy in March 1918.

Mortars The largest mortars ever constructed were Mallet's mortar (Woolwich Arsenal, London, 1857) and the *Little David* of World War II, made in the USA. Each had a calibre of 914mm *36 in*, but neither was ever used in action. The heaviest mortar employed was the tracked German 600mm *23½ in* siege piece *Karl*, of which there were seven such mortars built. Only six of these were actually used in action, although never all at the same time, at Sevastopol, USSR in 1942, at Warsaw, Poland in 1944, and at Budapest, Hungary, also in 1944.

Largest cannon The highest-calibre cannon ever constructed is the *Tsar Pushka* (*King of Cannons*), now housed in the Kremlin, Moscow, Russia. It was built in the 16th century with a

bore of 890mm *35 in* and a barrel 5.34m *17ft 6 in* long. It weighs 39.3tonnes or 2400 *poods* (sic). The Turks fired up to seven shots per day from a bombard 7.92m *26 ft* long, with an internal calibre of 1066mm *42 in*, against the walls of Constantinople (now Istanbul) from 12 Apr–29 May 1453. The cannon was dragged by 60 oxen and 200 men and fired a 540kg *1200lb* stone ball.

The heaviest cannon was built in 1868 at Perm, Russia and weighs 144.1tonnes, although it has a bore of only 508mm *20in* and a barrel 4.6m *15ft 1in* long. It fired 300 shots in tests, using iron balls weighing nearly ½tonne.

Education

University *Oldest* The Sumerians had scribal schools or *É-Dub-ba* soon after 3500BC. The oldest existing educational institution in the world is the University of Karueein, founded in AD859 in Fez, Morocco. The University of Bologna, the oldest in Europe, was founded in 1088.

The oldest university in the UK is the University of Oxford, which came into being *c.* 1167. The oldest of the existing colleges is probably University College (1249), though its foundation is less well documented than that of Merton in 1264.

> **Compulsory education was first introduced in 1819 in Prussia. It became compulsory in the UK in 1870.**

Greatest enrolment The university with the greatest enrolment in the world is the State University of New York, USA, which had 397,637 students at 64 campuses throughout the state in late 1993. The greatest enrolment at a university centred in one city is at the University of Rome (*La Sapienza*), in Italy, which had 184,000students in 1993. It was built in the 1920s as a single-site campus, and still is mainly based there although some faculties are now outside the campus.

Britain's largest university is the University of London, with 69,640 internal students and 23,100 external students (1992/3), totalling 92,740. The Open University at Walton Hall near Milton Keynes, Bucks was first called the University of the Air and was granted a Royal Charter on 30 May 1969. In 1993 it supported 96,487 undergraduate and associate registered students following undergraduate or diploma in education courses, 7473 postgraduate students and 21,332 student-course registrations for associate short-courses.

Largest The largest existing university building in the world is the M.V. Lomonosov State University on the Lenin Hills, south of Moscow, Russia. It stands 240m *787ft 5in* tall, and has 32 storeys and 40,000 rooms. It was constructed from 1949–53.

Higher education India has the greatest number of institutions, with 6600, whilst the USA has both the greatest number of students (13,711,000) and the highest ratio, at 5596 tertiary level students per 100,000 population.

Professor *Youngest* The youngest at which anybody has been elected to a chair in a university is 19 years in the case of Colin MacLaurin (1698–1746), who was elected to Marischal College, Aberdeen as Professor of Mathematics on 30 Sep 1717. In 1725 he was made Professor of Mathematics at Edinburgh University on the recommendation of Sir Isaac Newton (1642–1727), who was a professor at Cambridge at the age of 26. Henry Phillpotts (1778–1869) became

a don at Magdalen College, Oxford on 25 Jul 1795 aged 17 years 80 days.

Most durable Dr Joel Hildebrand (1881–1983), Professor Emeritus of Physical Chemistry at the University of California, Berkeley, USA, first became an assistant professor in 1913 and published his 275th research paper 68 years later in 1981. The longest period for which any professorship has been held in Britain is 63 years in the case of Thomas Martyn (1735–1825), Professor of Botany at Cambridge University from 1762 until his death. The last professor-for-life was the pathologist Prof. Henry Roy Dean (1879–1961) for his last 39 years at Cambridge.

Youngest undergraduate and graduate Michael Kearney (⇨ Youngest A level pass below) started studying for an Associate of Science degree at Santa Rosa Junior College, California, USA in September 1990 at the age of 6years 7months.

In Britain, the most extreme recorded cases of undergraduate juvenility were those of Alexander Hill (1785–1867), who entered St Andrews University at the age of 10 years 4 months in November 1795, and William Thomson (1824–1907), later Lord Kelvin, who entered Glasgow University also at the age of 10years 4months, in October 1834.

Adragon Eastwood De Mello (b. 5 Oct 1976) of Santa Cruz, California, USA obtained his BA in mathematics from the University of California in Santa Cruz on 11 Jun 1988 at the age of 11years 8months.

Ganesh Sittampalam (b. 11 Feb 1979) of Surbiton, Surrey became Britain's youngest undergraduate this century when he started a BSc mathematics degree course at the University of Surrey at the age of 11years 8months in October 1990. Less than two years later, in July 1992, he became Britain's youngest graduate this century, obtaining his degree at the age of 13years 5months.

> **Mr and Mrs Harold Erickson of Naples, Florida, USA saw all of their 14 children—11 sons and three daughters—obtain university or college degrees between 1962 and 1978.**

Youngest doctorate On 13 Apr 1814 the mathematician Carl Witte of Lochau was made a Doctor of Philosophy of the University of Giessen, Germany when aged 12.

School *Oldest* The title of the oldest existing school in Britain is contested. It is claimed that King's School in Canterbury, Kent was a foundation of St Augustine, some time between his arrival in Kent in AD597 and his death *c.* 604. Cor Tewdws (College of Theodosius) at Llantwit Major, South Glamorgan, reputedly burnt down in AD446, was refounded, after a lapse of 62 years, by St Illtyd in 508, and flourished into the 13th century. Winchester College was founded in 1382. Lanark Grammar School claims to have been referred to in a papal bull drawn up in 1183 by Lucius III.

Most expensive Excluding schools catering for specialist needs, the most expensive school in Great Britain is Carmel College, Wallingford, Oxon (headmaster P.D. Skelker). The maximum annual fee for boarders in 1993/4 is £12,450.

The most expensive school which is a member of the Girls' School Association is Roedean School, Brighton, East Sussex (headmistress Mrs A.R. Longley), with annual fees in 1993/4 of £11,985 for boarders.

In the academic year 1993/4 Bartholomews Tutorial College, Brighton, E Sussex (principal W. Duncombe) charges up to £15,837.75 for A level science students (including accommodation).

Internationally the most expensive schools in the world tend to be prestigious international finishing schools, such as those in Switzerland.

Largest In 1992/3 Rizal High School, Pasig, Manila, Philippines had an enrolment of 16,535 regular students, although numbers slightly declined for 1993/4.

The school with the most pupils in Great Britain was Banbury Comprehensive, Oxon with 2767 in the 1975 summer term. The highest enrolment in 1993/4 was 2364 at St Louise's Comprehensive College, Belfast.

Schools The country with the greatest number of primary schools is China, with 893,623 in 1991. San Marino has the lowest pupil to teacher ratio, with 5.5 children per teacher.

At general secondary level India has the most schools, with 219,595 in 1991, whilst San Marino has the best ratio—6.5 pupils per teacher.

Most O and A levels Since 1965 Dr Francis L. Thomason of Hammersmith, London has accumulated 70 O and O/A levels, 16 A levels and 1 S level, making a total of 87, of which 36 have been in the top grade. David Biggins of Sheffield, S Yorks has passed a total of 18 A levels since 1982.

The highest number of top-grade A levels attained at one sitting is seven, by Matthew James of Mortimer Wilson School, Alfreton, Derbys in June 1993, and by Stephen Murrell—who also obtained an eighth pass at grade B—of Crown Woods School, Eltham, London in June 1978. Robert Pidgeon (b. 7 Feb 1959) of St Peter's School, Bournemouth, Dorset secured 13 O level passes at grade A at one sitting in the summer of 1975, and subsequently passed three A levels at grade A and two S levels with firsts. Nicholas Barberis achieved a total of 27 top grades while at Eltham College, London, passing 20 O/AO levels and 7 A levels, all at grade A, between 1984 and 1988.

Youngest A level pass Ganesh Sittampalam (b. 11 Feb 1979) of Surbiton, Surrey is the youngest person to have passed an A level, achieving grade A in both Mathematics and Further Mathematics in June 1988, when aged 9 years 4 months.

Michael Kearney (b. 18 Jan 1984) of Mobile, Alabama, USA received his high school diploma—equivalent to A levels in the UK—in June 1990 at the age of 6 years 5 months.

Youngest GCSE pass Sonali Pandya (b. 9 Apr 1985) of Edgware, London obtained a grade E in her GCSE Computer Studies examination in June 1993 at the age of 8 years 2 months.

Youngest headmaster The youngest headmaster of a major public school in Great Britain was the Rev. G. S. Evans (b. 3 Jun 1802), who took up his duties as headmaster of Mill Hill School in January 1828 at the age of 25 years 6 months, but held office for less than a year.

Most durable teachers Medarda de Jesús León de Uzcátegui, alias La Maestra Chucha, has been teaching in Caracas, Venezuela for a total of 83 years. In 1911, at the age of 12, she and her two sisters set up a school there which they named *Modelo de Aplicación*. Since marrying in 1942, she has run her own school, which she calls the *Escuela Uzcátegui*, from her home in Caracas.

David Rhys Davies (1835–1928) taught as a pupil teacher and subsequently as a teacher and headmaster for a total of 76 years. Most of his teaching was done at Talybont-on-Usk School, near Brecon, Powys (1856–79) and at Dame Anna Child's School, Whitton, Powys. Elsie Marguerite Touzel (1889–1984) of Jersey, Channel Islands began her teaching career aged 16 in 1905 and taught at various schools in Jersey until her retirement 75 years later on 30 Sep 1980.

Highest endowment The greatest single gift in the history of education has been $500 million, to the US public education system by Walter Annenberg in December 1993. The gift was intended to help fight violence in American schools.

> **Which school?**
>
> The greatest documented number of schools attended by a pupil is 265, by Wilma Williams, now Mrs R.J. Horton, from 1933–43 when her parents were in show business in the USA.

> Walter Annenberg, who donated $500 million to public education, said:– 'I keep reading about so many youngsters with knives and revolvers and threatening the lives of teachers. I felt I had to drop a bomb to show the public what needs to be done'.

Religions

Oldest Human burial, which has religious connotations, is known from c. 60,000 BC among *Homo sapiens neanderthalensis* in the Shanidar cave, northern Iraq.

Largest Religious statistics are necessarily only tentative, since the test of adherence to a religion varies widely in rigour, while many individuals, particularly in the East, belong to two or more religions.

Christianity is the world's prevailing religion, with some 1.87 billion adherents in 1993, or 33.5 per cent of the world's population. There were 1.04 billion Roman Catholics in the same year. The largest non-Christian religion is Islam (Muslim), with some 1.01 billion followers in 1993.

In the UK the Roman Catholic population is 5,815,000, while the Anglicans have an actual membership (a different measure) of 1,855,000. They comprise members of the Established Church of England, the Dis-established Church in Wales, the Scottish Episcopal Church and the Church of Ireland. The Church of England has 2 provinces (Canterbury and York), 44 dioceses, 10,857 full-time diocesan clergy, including 744 women, and 13,082 parishes as at 31 Dec 1993. In Scotland the largest membership is that of the Church of Scotland (46 presbyteries), which had 732,963 members at the end of 1993.

> **Oldest A level pass**
> George Lush of Hatfield, Herts passed A level Italian in 1969, obtaining a grade D, just a few months before his 89th birthday.

Places of Worship

Earliest Many archaeologists are of the opinion that the decorated Upper Palaeolithic caves of Europe (c. 30,000–10,000 BC) were used as places of worship or religious ritual. The oldest surviving Christian church in the world is a converted house in Qal'at es Salihiye (formerly Douro-Europos) in eastern Syria, dating from AD 232.

Oldest *Great Britain* The oldest places of worship are the enigmatic stone circles or henges of the Neolithic period, for example Avebury, Wilts, dating from c. 3000–2800 BC. The earliest Christian church in the UK was at Colchester, Essex and was built c. AD 320. Its ruins can still be seen next to the modern police station. The oldest surviving ecclesiastical building in the UK is a 6th-century cell built by St Brendan in AD 542 on Eileachan Naoimh (pronounced 'Noo'), Garvelloch Islands, Strathclyde.

Largest temple The largest religious structure ever built is Angkor Wat ('City Temple'), enclosing 162.6 ha *402 acres* in Cambodia (formerly Kampuchea), south-east Asia. It was built to the Hindu god Vishnu by the Khmer King Suryavarman II in the period 1113–50. Its curtain wall measures 1280 × 1280 m *4199 × 4199 ft* and its population, before it was abandoned in 1432, was 80,000. The whole complex of 72 major monuments, begun c. AD 900, extends over 24 × 8 km *15 × 5 miles*.

The largest Buddhist temple in the world is Borobudur, near Jogjakarta, Indonesia, built in the 8th century. It is 31.5 m *103 ft* tall and 123 m *403 ft* square.

The largest Mormon temple is the Salt Lake Temple, Utah, USA, dedicated on 6 Apr 1893, with a floor area of 23,505 m² *253,015 ft²* or *5.8* acres.

Cathedrals *Largest* The world's largest cathedral is the cathedral church of the Diocese of New York, St John the Divine, with a floor area of 11,240 m² *121,000 ft²* and a volume of 476,350 m³ *16,822,000 ft³*. The nave is the longest in the world at 183.2 m *601 ft* in length, with a vaulting 37.8 m *124 ft* in height.

> The cornerstone of St John the Divine was laid on 27 Dec 1892, but work on the Gothic building was stopped in 1941. Although work restarted in earnest in July 1979, it has not yet been completed, and so is referred to in New York as 'St John the Unfinished'.

The cathedral covering the largest area is that of Santa Mariá de la Sede in Seville, Spain. It was built in Spanish Gothic style between 1402 and 1519, and is 126.2 m *414 ft* long, 82.6 m *271 ft* wide and 30.5 m *100 ft* high to the vault of the nave.

The largest cathedral in the British Isles is the Cathedral Church of Christ in Liverpool. It was built in modernized Gothic style, and work was begun on 18 Jul 1904; it was finally consecrated on 25 Oct 1978 after 74 years (cf. Exeter Cathedral, 95 years). The building encloses 9687 m² *104,275 ft²* and has an overall length of 193.9 m *636 ft*. The Vestey Tower is 100.9 m *331 ft* high. It contains the highest vaulting in the world—53.3m *175ft* maximum at undertower, and the highest Gothic arches ever built, being 32.6m *107ft* at apexes.

Smallest The smallest church in the world designated as a cathedral—the seat of a diocesan bishop—is that of the Christ Catholic Church, Highlandville, Missouri, USA. It was consecrated in July 1983. It measures 4.3×5.2m *14×17ft* and has seating for 18 people.

The smallest cathedral in use in the UK is Cumbrae Cathedral (the Cathedral of the diocese of the Isles) at Millport on the isle of Cumbrae, Strathclyde, which was built in 1849–51. The nave measures only 12.2×6.1m *40×20ft* and the total floor area is 197.3m² *2124ft²*.

Largest church The largest church in the world is the Basilica of Our Lady of Peace (Notre Dame de la Paix) at Yamoussoukro, Ivory Coast, completed in 1989 at a cost of £100million. It has a total area of 30,000m² *100,000ft²* with seating for 7000 people. Including its golden cross, it is 158m *519ft* high.

The elliptical basilica of St Pie X at Lourdes, France, completed in 1957 at a cost of £2million, has a capacity of 20,000 under its giant span arches and a length of 200m *660ft*.

The largest church in the UK is the Collegiate Church of St Peter in Westminster, usually referred to as Westminster Abbey, which was built between AD 1050–1745. Its maximum length is 161.5m *530ft*, the breadth across the transept 61.9m *203ft* and the internal height 30.98m *101ft 8in*. The largest parish church is the Parish Church of the Most Holy and Undivided Trinity at Kingston-upon-Hull, Humberside covering 2530 m² *27,235ft²* and with an external length and width of 87.7×37.7m *288×124ft*.

Tiny!

The world's smallest church is the chapel of Santa Isabel de Hungría, in Colomares, a monument to Christopher Columbus at Benalmádena, Málaga, Spain. It is an irregular shape and has a total floor area of 1.96m² *21⅛ft²*.

Longest The crypt of the underground Civil War Memorial Church in the Guadarrama Mountains, 45km *28miles* from Madrid, Spain, is 260m *853ft* in length. It took 21 years (1937–58) to build, at a reported cost of £140million, and is surmounted by a cross 150m *492ft* tall.

Largest synagogue The largest synagogue in the world is Temple Emanu-El on Fifth Avenue at 65th Street, New York City, USA. The temple, completed in September 1929, has a frontage of 45.7m *150ft* on Fifth Avenue and 77.1m *253ft* on 65th Street. The sanctuary proper can accommodate 2500 people, and the adjoining Beth-El Chapel seats 350. When all the facilities are in use, more than 6000 people can be accommodated.

The largest synagogue in Great Britain is the Edgware Synagogue, Barnet, London, completed in 1959, with seating for 1630. That with the highest registered membership is Ilford Synagogue, London with 2210 members.

Largest mosque The largest mosque is Shah Faisal Mosque, near Islamabad, Pakistan. The total area of the complex is 18.97ha *46.87acres*, with the covered area of the prayer hall being 0.48ha *1.19acres*. It can accommodate 100,000 worshippers in the prayer hall and the courtyard, and a further 200,000 people in the adjacent grounds.

Tallest minaret The tallest minaret in the world is that of the Great Hassan II Mosque, Casablanca, Morocco, measuring 200m *656ft*. The cost of construction of the mosque was 5 billion dirhams (£360 million). Of ancient minarets the tallest is the Qutb Minar, south of New Delhi, India, built in 1194 to a height of 72.54m *238ft*.

Tallest and oldest stupa The now largely ruined Jetavanarama dagoba in the ancient city of Anuradhapura, Sri Lanka, is some 120m *400ft* in height. The 99.3m *326ft* tall Shwedagon pagoda, in Yangon (Rangoon), Myanmar (Burma), is built on the site of a pagoda dating from 585BC which was 8.2m *27ft* tall.

Most expensive icon The record price for an icon is $150,000 paid at Christie's, New York, USA on 17 Apr 1980 for the *Last Judgement* (from the George R. Hann collection, Pittsburgh, Pennsylvania), made in Novgorod, Russia in the 16th century.

Tallest spire The tallest cathedral spire in the world is that of the Protestant Cathedral of Ulm in Germany. The building is early Gothic and was begun in 1377. The tower, in the centre of the west façade, was not finally completed until 1890

The spectacular Great Hassan II Mosque in Morocco, which was officially opened on 30 Aug 1993, with the tallest minaret in the world towering high above the surrounding area.
(Photo: Gamma/C. Vioujard)

Gold!

The sacred object with the highest intrinsic value is the 15th-century gold Buddha in Wat Trimitr Temple in Bangkok, Thailand. It is 3m *10ft* tall and weighs an estimated 5½ tonnes. At the May 1994 price of £257 per fine ounce, its intrinsic worth was £32.4 million. The gold under the plaster exterior was found only in 1954.

and is 160.9m *528ft* high. The world's tallest church spire is that of the Chicago Temple of the First Methodist Church on Clark Street, Chicago, Illinois, USA. The building consists of a 22-storey skyscraper (erected in 1924) surmounted by a parsonage at 100.5m *330ft*, a 'Sky Chapel' at 121.9m *400ft* and a steeple cross at 173.1m *568ft* above street level.

The highest spire in Great Britain is that of the church of St Mary, called Salisbury Cathedral, Wilts. The Lady Chapel was built in the years 1220–5 and the main fabric of the cathedral was finished and consecrated in 1258. The spire was added later, *ante* 1305, and reaches a height of 123.1m *404ft*. The central spire of Lincoln Cathedral, which was completed *c.* 1307 and fell in 1548, was 160m *525ft* tall.

Stained glass Oldest Pieces of stained glass dated before AD 850, some possibly even to the 7th century, excavated by Prof. Rosemary Cramp, were set into a window of that date in the nearby St Paul's Church, Jarrow, Co. Durham. The oldest complete stained glass in the world represents the Prophets in a window of the Cathedral of Augsburg, Germany, dating from the second half of the 11th century. The oldest datable stained glass in the UK is represented by a figure of St Michael in All Saints Church at Dalbury, near Derby, from the late 11th century.

GUESS WHAT?

Q Where is the tallest piece of stained glass?

A See Page 104

A small part of the 7430 m² 80,000 ft² of stained-glass windows at the Basilica of Our Lady of Peace, at Yamoussoukro in the Ivory Coast.
(Photo: Gamma/G. Bassignac)

Largest The largest stained-glass window is that of the Resurrection Mausoleum in Justice, Illinois, USA, measuring 2079 m² *22,381 ft²* in 2448 panels, completed in 1971. Although not one continuous window, the Basilica of Our Lady of Peace (Notre Dame de la Paix) at Yamoussoukro, Ivory Coast contains a number of stained-glass windows covering a total area of 7430 m² *80,000 ft²*.

The largest single ecclesiastical stained-glass window in Great Britain is the east window in Gloucester Cathedral measuring 21.9 × 11.6 m *72 × 38 ft*, set up to commemorate the Battle of Crécy (1346), while the largest area of stained glass comprises the 128 lights, totalling 2320 m² *25,000 ft²*, in York Minster (⇨ Largest window).

Brasses The world's oldest monumental brass is that commemorating Bishop Yso von Wölpe in the Andreaskirche, Verden, near Hanover, Germany, dating from 1231. An engraved coffin plate of St Ulrich (died 973), laid in 1187, was found buried in the Church of SS Ulrich and Afra, Augsburg, Germany in 1979.

The oldest brass in Great Britain is of Sir John D'Abernon (died 1277) at Stoke D'Abernon, near Leatherhead, Surrey, dating from c. 1320. A dedication brass dated 24 Apr 1241 in Ashbourne Church, Derbys has been cited as the earliest arabic writing extant in Britain.

Church Personnel

There are more than 2000 'registered' saints, of whom around two-thirds are either Italian or French. The first Christian martyr was St Stephen, executed c. AD 36. Britain's first was St Alban, executed c. AD 209.

Canonization The shortest interval that has elapsed between the death of a saint and his or her canonization was in the case of St Peter of Verona, Italy, who died on 6 Apr 1252 and was canonized 337 days later on 9 Mar 1253. The longest interval is 857 years, in the case of St Leo III, who died in 816 and was not canonized until 1673.

Bishops *Longest-serving* Bishop Louis François de la Baume de Suze (1603–90) was a bishop for a record 76 years 273 days from 6 Dec 1613.

The longest tenure of any Church of England bishopric is 57 years in the case of the Rt Rev. Thomas Wilson, who was consecrated Bishop of Sodar and Man on 16 Jan 1698 and died in office on 7 Mar 1755. Of English bishoprics, the longest tenures — if one excludes the unsubstantiated case of Aethelwulf, reputedly Bishop of Hereford from 937 to 1012 — are those of 47 years by Jocelin de Bohun of Salisbury (1142–89) and Nathaniel Crew or Crewe of Durham (1674–1721).

Oldest The oldest serving bishop (excluding suffragans and assistants) in the Church of England as at April 1994 was the Rt Rev. Eric Kemp, Bishop of Chichester, who was born on 27 Apr 1915.

The oldest Roman Catholic bishop in recent years has been Archbishop Edward Howard, formerly Archbishop of Portland-in-Oregon, USA (b. 5 Nov 1877), who died aged 105 years 58 days on 2 Jan 1983. He had celebrated mass about 27,800 times. Bishop Herbert Welch of the United Methodist Church, who was elected a Bishop for Japan and Korea in 1916, died on 4 Apr 1969 aged 106.

Youngest The youngest bishop of all time was HRH the Duke of York and Albany, the second son of George III, who was elected Bishop of Osnabrück, through his father's influence as Elector of Hanover, at the age of 196 days on 27 Feb 1764. He resigned 39 years later. The youngest serving bishop (excluding suffragans and assistants) in the Church of England is the Rt Rev. David Stancliffe, Bishop of Salisbury, who was born on 1 Oct 1942.

Oldest parish priest Father Alvaro Fernandez (8 Dec 1880 – 6 Jan 1988) served as a parish priest at Santiago de Abres, Spain from 1919 until he was 107 years old. The oldest Anglican clergyman, Rev. Clement Williams (b. 30 Oct 1879), died aged 106 years 3 months on 3 Feb 1986. He lined the route at Queen Victoria's funeral and was ordained in 1904.

Longest service The longest Church of England incumbency on record is one of 75 years 357 days, by Rev. Bartholomew Edwards, Rector of St Nicholas, Ashill, Norfolk from 1813 to 1889. There is some doubt as to whether Rev. Richard Sherinton was installed at Folkestone from 1524 or 1529 to 1601. If the former is correct it would surpass the Edwards record (⇨ above). The parish of Farrington, Hants had only two incumbents in a period of 122 years: Rev. J. Benn (28 Mar 1797 to 1857) and Rev. T.H. Massey (1857 to 5 Apr 1919). From 1675 to 1948 the incumbents of Rose Ash, Devon were from eight generations of the family of Southcomb.

Rev. K.M. Jacob (b. 10 Jul 1880) was made a deacon in the Marthoma Syrian Church of Malabar in Kerala, southern India in 1897. He served his church until his death on 28 Mar 1984, 87 years later.

Longest-serving chorister John Love Vokins (1890–1989) was a chorister for 92 years. He joined the choir of Christ Church, Heeley, Sheffield, S Yorks in 1895 and that of St Michael's, Hathersage, Derbys, 35 years later, and was still singing in 1987.

Oldest warden Having become a chorister in 1876 at the age of nine, Thomas Rogers was appointed vicar's warden in 1966 at Montacute, Somerset, aged 99.

Papal Records

Longest Papal Reign
Pius IX — Giovanni Maria Mastai-Ferretti (1846–78). 31 years 236 days

Shortest Papal Reign
Stephen II (died 752). 2 days

Longest-Lived Popes
St Agatho (died 681) (probably exaggerated)
? 106 years. Leo XIII — Gioacchino Pecci (1810–1903). 93 years 140 days

Youngest Elected Pope
John XII — Ottaviano (c. 937–64) in 955. 18 years old

The last British Pope was Adrian IV — Nicholas Breakspear (c. 1100–59). He was elected on 4 Dec 1154.

Sunday school F. Otto Brechel (1890–1990) of Mars, Pennsylvania, USA completed 88 years (4576 Sundays) of perfect attendance at church school at three different churches in Pennsylvania — the first from 1902 to 1931, the second from 1931 to 1954, and the third from 1954 onwards.

F. Otto Brechel, who holds the Sunday School attendance record, attributed his record to good health, saying:– 'I've never been sick in bed, and I can't even remember ever having a headache or bellyache. That's one part of it, but I believe God wants me to make this record'.

Oldest parish register The oldest part of any parish register surviving in England contains entries from the summer of 1538. There is a sheet from that of Alfriston, E Sussex recording a marriage on 10 Jul 1504, but it is thought that this is possibly a reference to 1544 as it is among entries from 1547. The original register for Great Bricett, Suffolk contained two burial entries dated 1525. A nineteenth century survey refers to Tonsor, Northants having register entries dated 1440.

Largest funerals The funeral of the charismatic C.N. Annadurai (died 3 Feb 1969), Madras Chief Minister, was attended by 15 million people, according to a police estimate. The queue at the grave of the Russian singer and guitarist Vladimir Visotsky (died 28 Jul 1980), stretched for 10 km *6 miles* (⇨ below). The longest funeral in Britain was probably that of Vice-Admiral Viscount Nelson on 9 Jan 1806. Ticket-holders were seated in St Paul's Cathedral by 8:30 a.m. Many were unable to leave until 9 p.m.

Millions!

The greatest recorded number of human beings assembled with a common purpose was an estimated 15 million at the Hindu festival of Kumbh mela, which was held at the confluence of the Yamuna (formerly the Jumna), the Ganges and the invisible 'Saraswathi' at Allahabad, Uttar Pradesh, India on 6 Feb 1989 (⇨ above).

Human Achievements

Endurance and Endeavour

Most travelled The world's most travelled man is John D. Clouse from Evansville, Indiana, USA, who has visited all of the sovereign countries and all but six of the non-sovereign or other territories which existed in early 1994 (⇨ Countries).

The most travelled couple are Dr Robert and Carmen Becker of East Northport, New York, USA, both of whom have visited all of the sovereign countries and all but nine of the non-sovereign or other territories.

The most travelled man in the horseback era was believed to be the Methodist preacher Bishop Francis Asbury (b. Handsworth, W Mids, 1745), who travelled 425,000km *264,000 miles* in North America between 1771 and 1815.

> On his travels through North America Francis Asbury preached some 16,000 sermons and ordained nearly 3000 ministers.

Longest walks The first person reputed to have 'walked round the world' is George Matthew Schilling (USA) from 3 Aug 1897 to 1904, but the first verified achievement was by David Kunst (b. 1939, USA) from 20 Jun 1970 to 5 Oct 1974.

Tomás Carlos Pereira (b. Argentina, 16 Nov 1942) spent 10 years, from 6 Apr 1968 to 8 Apr 1978, walking 48,000km *29,800 miles* around five continents. Steven Newman of Bethel, Ohio, USA spent four years, from 1 Apr 1983 to 1 Apr 1987, walking 36,200km *22,500 miles* around the world, covering 20 countries and five continents.

Courage!

Rick Hansen (b. Canada, 1957), who was paralysed from the waist down in 1973 as a result of a motor accident, wheeled his wheelchair 40,074.06km *24,901.55 miles* through four continents and 34 countries. He started his journey from Vancouver on 21 Mar 1985 and arrived back there on 22 May 1987.

George Meegan (b. 2 Oct 1952) from Rainham, Kent walked 30,431km *19,019 miles* from Ushuaia, the southern tip of South America, to Prudhoe Bay in northern Alaska, taking 2426 days from 26 Jan 1977 to 18 Sep 1983. He thus completed the first traverse of the Americas and the western hemisphere.

Sean Eugene McGuire (USA; b. 15 Sep 1956) walked 11,791km *7327 miles* from the Yukon River, north of Livengood, Alaska to Key West, Florida in 307 days, from 6 Jun 1978 to 9 Apr 1979. The trans-Canada (Halifax to Vancouver) record walk of 6057km *3764 miles* is 96 days by Clyde McRae, aged 23, from 1 May to 4 Aug 1973. John Lees (b. 23 Feb 1945) of Brighton, E Sussex walked 4628km *2876 miles* across the USA from City Hall, Los Angeles, California to City Hall, New York in 53 days 12hr 15min (averaging 86.49km *53.75 miles* a day) between 11 April and 3 Jun 1972.

British Isles The longest walk round the coast of the British Isles was one of 15,239km *9469 miles*

by John Westley of Cheshunt, Herts from 5 Aug 1990 to 20 Sep 1991. His walk began and ended at Tower Bridge, London. Vera Andrews set a record for the longest walk in mainland Britain, when she covered a total distance of 11,777 km *7318 miles* between 2 Jan and 24 Dec 1990, taking in all of the British Gas showrooms. She started and finished at her home town of Clacton-on-Sea, Essex.

North Pole conquest The claims of the two Arctic explorers Dr Frederick Albert Cook (1865–1940) and Cdr (later Rear-Ad.) Robert Edwin Peary (1856–1920), of the US Naval Civil Engineering branch, to have reached the North Pole lack irrefutable proof, and several recent surveys have produced conflicting conclusions. On excellent pack ice and modern sledges, Wally Herbert's 1968–9 expedition (⇨ Arctic crossing, below) attained a best day's route mileage of 37 km *23 miles* in 15hr. Cook (⇨ above) claimed 42km *26 miles* twice, while Peary claimed an average of 61km *38 miles* over eight consecutive days, which many glaciologists regard as quite unsustainable.

The first people indisputably to have reached the North Pole at ground level—the exact point Lat. 90° 00′ 00″ N (± 300 metres)—were Pavel Afanasyevich Geordiyenko, Pavel Kononovich Sen'ko, Mikhail Mikhaylovich Somov and Mikhail Yemel'yenovich Ostrekin (all of the former USSR), on 23 Apr 1948.

The earliest indisputable attainment of the North Pole by surface travel over the sea-ice took place at 3 p.m. (Central Standard Time) on 19 Apr 1968, when expedition leader Ralph Plaisted (USA), accompanied by Walter Pederson, Gerald Pitzl and Jean Luc Bombardier, reached the pole after a 42-day trek in four skidoos (snowmobiles).

Naomi Uemura (1941–84), the Japanese explorer and mountaineer, became the first person to reach the North Pole in a solo trek across the Arctic sea-ice at 4:45a.m. GMT on 1 May 1978. He had travelled 725km *450 miles*, setting out on 7 Mar from Cape Edward, Ellesmere Island in northern Canada.

The first people to ski to the North Pole were the seven members of a Soviet expedition, led by Dmitry Shparo. They reached the pole on 31 May 1979 after a trek of 1500km *900 miles* which took them 77 days.

South Pole conquest The first men to cross the Antarctic Circle (Lat.66°33′S) were the 193 crew members of the *Resolution* (462 tons) (Capt. James Cook, RN, 1728–79) and *Adventure* (336 tons) (Lt Tobias Furneaux, RN) on 17 Jan 1773 at 39°E. The first person known to have sighted the Antarctic ice shelf was Capt. Fabian Gottlieb Benjamin von Bellingshausen (Russia) (1778–1852) on 27 Jan 1820 from the vessel *Vostok* accompanied by *Mirnyy.*

The South Pole (alt. 2779m *9186ft* on ice and 102m *336ft* bedrock) was first reached at 11 a.m. on

> **GUESS WHAT?**
>
> **Q** Who completed the fastest walk from Land's End to John o' Groats?
>
> **A** See Page 231

14 Dec 1911 by a Norwegian party of five men led by Capt. Roald Engebereth Gravning Amundsen (1872–1928), after a 53-day march with dog sledges from the Bay of Whales, into which he had penetrated in the vessel *Fram.*

The longest unsupported trek in Antarctica was by team-leader Sir Ranulph Fiennes, 48, with Dr Michael Stroud, 37, who set off from Gould Bay on 9 Nov 1992, reached the South Pole on 16 Jan 1993 and finally abandoned their walk on the Ross ice shelf on 11 February. They covered a distance of 2170km *1350 miles* during their 94-day trek (⇨ Longest sledge journeys).

First to see both poles The first people to see both poles were Amundsen (⇨ above) and Oskar Wisting when they flew aboard the airship *Norge* over the North Pole on 12 May 1926, having previously been to the South Pole on 14 Dec 1911.

First to visit both poles Dr Albert Paddock Crary (USA) (1911–87) reached the North Pole in a Dakota aircraft on 3 May 1952. On 12 Feb 1961 he arrived at the South Pole by Sno Cat on a scientific traverse party from the McMurdo Station.

Pole to pole circumnavigation The first pole to pole circumnavigation was achieved by Sir Ranulph Fiennes Bt (b. 1944) and Charles Burton of the British Trans-Globe Expedition, who travelled south from Greenwich (2 Sep 1979), via the South Pole (15 Dec 1980) and the North Pole (10 Apr 1982), and back to Greenwich, arriving on 29 Aug 1982 after a 56,000km *35,000 mile* trek (⇨ Arctic crossing and Antarctic crossing).

> Dr Jean-Louis Etienne, (France, aged 39), was the first person to reach the North Pole solo and without dogs, on 11 May 1986 after 63 days.

First to walk to both poles The first man to walk to both the North and the South Pole was Robert Swan (b. 28 Jul 1956). He led the three-man Footsteps of Scott expedition, which reached the South Pole on 11 Jan 1986, and three years later headed the eight-man Icewalk expedition, which arrived at the North Pole on 14 May 1989.

Arctic crossing The first crossing of the Arctic sea-ice was achieved by the British Trans-Arctic Expedition, which left Point Barrow, Alaska on 21 Feb 1968 and arrived at the Seven Island archipelago north-east of Spitzbergen 464 days later, on 29 May 1969. This involved a haul of 4699km *2920 miles* with a drift of 1100km *700 miles*, compared with the straight-line distance of 2674km *1662 miles*. The team comprised Wally Herbert (leader), 34, Major Ken Hedges, RAMC, 34, Allan Gill, 38, and Dr Roy Koerner (glaciologist), 36, and 40 huskies.

The only crossing achieved in a single season was that by Fiennes and Burton (⇨ Pole to pole circumnavigation and Antarctic crossing) from Alert via the North Pole to the Greenland Sea in open snowmobiles.

Antarctic crossing The first surface crossing of the Antarctic continent was completed at 1:47p.m. on 2 Mar 1958, after a trek of 3473km *2158 miles* lasting 99 days from 24 Nov 1957, from Shackleton Base to Scott Base via the pole. The crossing party of 12 was led by Dr (now Sir) Vivian Ernest Fuchs (b. 11 Feb 1908).

The 4185km *2600 mile* trans-Antarctic leg from

Alone!

The first person to reach the South Pole solo and unsupported was Erling Kagge, aged 29 (Norway), on 7 Jan 1993 after a 50-day trek of 1400km *870 miles* from Berkner Island.

Sanae to Scott Base of the 1980–2 Trans-Globe Expedition was achieved in 67 days, from 28 Oct 1980 to 11 Jan 1981, having reached the South Pole on 15 Dec 1980. The three-man party on snowmobiles comprised Sir Ranulph Fiennes Bt, Oliver Shepard and Charles Burton (⇨ Pole to pole circumnavigation and Arctic crossing).

Longest sledge journeys

The longest polar sledge journey was that undertaken by the International Trans-Antarctica Expedition (six members), who sledged a distance of some 6040 km *3750 miles* in 220 days from 27 Jul 1989 (Seal Nunataks) to 3 Mar 1990 (Mirnyy). The expedition was accompanied by a team of 40 dogs, but a number of them were flown out from one of the staging posts for a period of rest before returning to the Antarctic. The expedition was supported by aircraft throughout its duration.

The longest *totally self-supporting* polar sledge journey ever made was one of 2170 km *1350 miles* from Gould Bay to the Ross ice shelf by Sir Ranulph Fiennes and Dr Michael Stroud (⇨ South Pole conquest).

Greatest ocean descent

The record ocean descent was achieved in the Challenger Deep of the Marianas Trench, 400 km *250 miles* south-west of Guam in the Pacific Ocean, when the Swiss-built US Navy bathyscaphe *Trieste*, manned by Dr Jacques Piccard (Switzerland) (b. 28 Jul 1922) and Lt Donald Walsh, USN reached a depth of 10,916 m *35,813 ft* at 1:10 p.m. on 23 Jan 1960 (⇨ Oceans deepest).

Deep-diving records

The official record depth for the *ill-advised* and dangerous activity of breath-held diving is 107 m *351 ft* by Angela Bandini (Italy) off Elba, Italy on 3 Oct 1989. She was under water for 2 min 46 sec.

The record dive with scuba (self-contained under-water breathing apparatus) is 133 m *437 ft* by John J. Gruener and R. Neal Watson (US) off Freeport, Grand Bahama on 14 Oct 1968.

The record dive utilizing gas mixtures was a simulated dive to a depth of 701 m *2300 ft* of sea-water by Théo Mavrostomos as part of the HYDRA 10 operation at the Hyperbaric Center of Comex in Marseilles, France on 20 Nov 1992, during a 43-day dive. He was breathing 'hydreliox' (hydrogen, oxygen and helium).

Théo Mavrostomos (left) reaching his record simulated dive to a depth of 701 m *2300 ft*, where he spent 2 hours, and with the colleagues who joined him on the Comex HYDRA 10 operation (below).
(Photos: Gamma)

Arnaud de Nechaud de Feral performed a saturation dive of 73 days from 9 Oct–21 Dec 1989 in a hyperbaric chamber simulating a depth of 300 m *985 ft*, as part of the HYDRA 9 operation carried out by Comex at Marseilles, France. He was breathing 'hydrox', a mixture of hydrogen and oxygen.

Richard Presley spent 69 days 19 min in a module underwater at a lagoon in Key Largo, Florida, USA from 6 May to 14 Jul 1992. The test was carried out as part of a mission entitled Project Atlantis which had as its aim to explore the human factors of living in an undersea environment.

High altitude diving

The record for high altitude diving is 5032 m *16,509 ft*, in a lake in the crater of Popocatépetl, a dormant volcano in Mexico. Roger Weihrauch (Germany) spent 20 minutes exploring the 5 m *16 ft* deep lake on 20 Nov 1983.

Submergence

The *continuous* duration record (i.e. no rest breaks) for scuba (i.e. self-contained underwater breathing apparatus, used without surface air hoses) is 212 hr 30 min, by Michael Stevens of Birmingham in a Royal Navy tank at the National Exhibition Centre, Birmingham from 14–23 Feb 1986.

Deepest salvage

The greatest depth at which salvage has been successfully carried out is 5258 m *17,251 ft*, in the case of a helicopter which had crashed into the Pacific Ocean in August 1991 with the loss of four lives. Crew of the USS *Salvor* and personnel from Eastport International managed to raise the wreckage to the surface on 27 Feb 1992 so that the authorities could try to determine the cause of the accident.

The deepest salvage operation ever achieved with divers was on the wreck of HM cruiser *Edinburgh*, sunk on 2 May 1942 in the Barents Sea off northern Norway, inside the Arctic Circle, in 245 m *803 ft* of water. Over 31 days (from 7 Sep–7 Oct 1981), 12 divers worked on the wreck in pairs. A total of 460 gold ingots (the only 100 per cent salvage to date) was recovered.

Deepest underwater escapes

The deepest underwater rescue ever achieved was of the *Pisces III*, in which Roger R. Chapman (28), and Roger Mallinson (35), were trapped for 76 hours when it sank to 480 m *1575 ft*, 240 km *150 miles* south-east of Cork, Republic of Ireland on 29 Aug 1973. It was hauled to the surface on 1 September by the cable ship *John Cabot* after work by *Pisces V*, *Pisces II* and the remote-control recovery vessel *Curv* (Controlled Underwater Recovery Vehicle).

> **The greatest depth from which an actual escape without any equipment has been made is 68.6 m *225 ft*, by Richard A. Slater from the rammed submersible *Nekton Beta* off Catalina Island, California, USA on 28 Sep 1970.**

The record for an escape with equipment was by Norman Cooke and Hamish Jones on 22 Jul 1987. During a naval exercise they escaped from a depth of 183 m *601 ft* from the submarine HMS *Otus* in Bjornefjorden, off Bergen, Norway. They were wearing standard suits with a built-in lifejacket, from which air expanding during the ascent passes into a hood over the escaper's head.

Greatest penetration into the earth

The deepest penetration made into the ground by human beings is in the Western Deep Levels Mine at Carletonville, Transvaal, South Africa, where a record depth of 3581 m *11,749 ft* was attained on 12 Jul 1977 (⇨ Borings and mines).

Marriage

Most marriages

The greatest number of marriages contracted by one person in the monogamous world is 27, by former Baptist minister Glynn 'Scotty' Wolfe (b. 1908) of Blythe, California, USA, who first married in 1927. He thought that he had a total of 41 children.

The greatest number of monogamous marriages by a woman is 22, by Linda Essex of Anderson, Indiana, USA. She has had 15 different husbands since 1957, her most recent marriage being in October 1991. However, that also ended in a divorce.

The record for bigamous marriages is 104, by Giovanni Vigliotto, one of many aliases used by either Fred Jipp (b. New York City, 3 Apr 1936) or Nikolai Peruskov (b. Siracusa,

---

Safe!

The longest recorded survival alone on a raft is 133 days (4½ months) by Second Steward Poon Lim (b. Hong Kong) of the UK Merchant Navy, whose ship, the SS *Ben Lomond*, was torpedoed in the Atlantic 910 km *565 miles* west of St Paul's Rocks in Lat. 00°30′N, Long. 38°45′W at 11:45 a.m. on 23 Nov 1942. He was picked up by a Brazilian fishing boat off Salinópolis, Brazil on 5 Apr 1943 and was able to walk ashore.

Tabwai Mikaie and Arenta Tebeitabu, two fishermen from the island of Nikunau in Kiribati, survived for 177 days adrift at sea in their fishing boat—a 4 m *13 ft* open dinghy. They were caught in a cyclone shortly after setting out on a trip on 17 Nov 1991 and were found washed ashore in Western Samoa, 1800 km *1100 miles* away, on 11 May 1992. A third man had left with them but died a few days before they reached Western Samoa.

GUESS WHAT?

Q What is the greatest number of times that anyone has been a best man?

A See Page 206

In 1988 the Olympic Stadium in Seoul had been packed with spectators watching the Olympic Games. Four years later it was to be the venue for an equally enthusiastic crowd of people, as the largest mass wedding ceremony took place, with 20,825 couples being married.
(Photo: Gamma)

Love!

Sicily, 3 Apr 1929) during 1949–81 in 27 US states and 14 other countries. On 28 Mar 1983 in Phoenix, Arizona, USA he received 28 years for fraud and six for bigamy, and was fined $336,000. He died in February 1991.

Richard and Carole Roble of South Hempstead, New York, USA have married each other 53 times, with their first wedding being in 1969. They have chosen a different location each time, including having ceremonies in all of the states of the USA.

In Britain, the only woman to contract eight legal marriages is Olive Joyce Wilson of Marston Green, Birmingham, W Mids. She has consecutively been Mrs John Bickley, Mrs Don Trethowan, Mrs George Hundley, Mrs Raymond Ward, Mrs Harry Latrobe, Mrs Leslie Harris, Mrs Ray Richards, and now Mrs John Grassick. All were divorced except Mr Hundley, who died.

Oldest bride and bridegroom The oldest recorded bridegroom has been Harry Stevens, aged 103, who married Thelma Lucas, 84, at the Caravilla Retirement Home, Wisconsin, USA on 3 Dec 1984. The oldest recorded bride is Minnie Munro, aged 102, who married Dudley Reid, 83, at Point Clare, New South Wales, Australia on 31 May 1991.

The British record was set by Sir Robert Mayer (1879–1985), who married Jacqueline Noble, 51, in London on 10 Nov 1980 when aged 101 years. Mrs Winifred Clark (b. 13 Nov 1871) became Britain's oldest recorded bride when she married Albert Smith, 80, at St Hugh's Church, Cantley, S Yorks the day before her 100th birthday.

Youngest married It was reported in 1986 that an 11-month-old boy was married to a 3-month-old girl in Bangladesh to end a 20-year feud between two families over a disputed farm.

Longest marriage The longest recorded marriages were both of 86 years. Sir Temulji Bhicaji Nariman and Lady Nariman, who were married from 1853 to 1940, were cousins and the marriage took place when both were aged five. Sir Temulji (b. 3 Sep 1848) died, aged 91 years 11 months, in August 1940 at Bombay, India. Lazarus Rowe (b. Greenland, New Hampshire, USA in 1725) and Molly Webber were recorded as marrying in 1743. He died first, in 1829, also after 86 years of marriage.

> The world champion 'best man' is Ting Ming Siong, from Sibu, Sarawak, in Malaysia, who officiated at a wedding for the 891st time since 1976 in March 1994.

At Last!

The longest engagement on record was between Octavio Guillen and Adriana Martinez. They finally took the plunge after 67 years in June 1969 in Mexico City. Both were then aged 82.

The British record is for a marriage of 82 years between James Frederick Burgess (b. 3 Mar 1861, died 27 Nov 1966) and his wife Sarah Ann, *née* Gregory (b. 11 Jul 1865, died 22 Jun 1965). They were married on 21 Jun 1883 at St James's, Bermondsey, London.

Golden weddings The greatest number of golden weddings in a family is 10, the six sons and four daughters of Joseph and Sophia Gresl of Manitowoc, Wisconsin, USA all celebrating golden weddings between April 1962 and September 1988, and the six sons and four daughters of George and Eleonora Hopkins of Patrick County, Virginia, USA all celebrating their golden weddings between November 1961 and October 1988.

The British record is seven, the three sons and four daughters of Mr and Mrs F. Stredwick of East Sussex all celebrating their golden weddings between May 1971 and April 1981.

Wedding ceremonies The largest mass wedding ceremony was one of 20,825 couples officiated over by Sun Myung Moon (b. 1920) of the Holy Spirit Association for the Unification of World Christianity in the Olympic Stadium in Seoul, South Korea on 25 Aug 1992. In addition a further 9800 couples around the world took part in the ceremony through a satellite link.

Most expensive The wedding of Mohammed, son of Shaik Rashid Bin Saeed Al Maktoum, to Princess Salama in Dubai in May 1981 lasted seven days and cost an estimated £22 million. It was held in a purpose-built stadium for 20,000 people.

Greatest attendance An estimated 30,000 guests from the Belz Hasidic community attended the wedding of Aharon Mordechai Rokeah and Sara Lea Lemberger in Jerusalem, Israel on 4 Aug 1993.

Feasts and Celebrations

Banquets The most lavish menu ever served was for the main banquet at the Imperial Iranian 2500th Anniversary gathering at Persepolis in October 1971. The feast comprised quails' eggs stuffed with Iranian caviar, a mousse of crayfish tails in Nantua sauce, stuffed rack of roast lamb, a main course of roast peacock stuffed with *foie gras*, fig rings and raspberry sweet champagne sherbet—and the very best wines.

The largest feast was attended by 150,000 guests on the occasion of the renunciation ceremony of Atul Dalpatlal Shah, when he became a monk, at Ahmedabad, India on 2 Jun 1991.

Dining out The world champion for eating out was Fred E. Magel of Chicago, Illinois, USA, who over a period of 50 years dined out 46,000 times in 60 countries as a restaurant grader. His favourite dishes were South African rock lobster and mousse of fresh English strawberries.

The greatest altitude at which a formal meal has been held is 6768 m *22,205 ft*, at the top of Mt Huascaran, Peru, when nine members of the Ansett Social Climbers from Sydney, Australia scaled the mountain on 28 Jun 1989 with a dining table, chairs, wine and three-course meal. At the summit they put on top hats, thermal black ties and ball-dresses for their dinner party, which was marred only by the fact that the wine turned to ice.

Party-giving The International Year of the Child children's party in Hyde Park, London on 30–31 May 1979 was attended by the royal family and 160,000 children.

The world's biggest birthday party was attended by 75,000 people at Buffalo, New York, USA on 4 Jul 1991 as part of the 1991 Friendship Festival, an annual event held every July to celebrate the national birthdays of the USA and Canada.

The largest Christmas party ever staged was that thrown by the Boeing Co. in the 65,000-seat Kingdome, Seattle, Washington State, USA. The party was held in two parts on 15 Dec 1979, and a total of 103,152 people attended.

On 1 Oct 1993 a total of 326,913 people attended 10,399 coffee mornings held simultaneously throughout Great Britain as part of the Macmillan Nurse Appeal, raising £750,000 in the process.

The largest teddy bears' picnic ever staged was attended by 16,837 bears together with their owners in Christchurch, New Zealand on 16 Jan 1994.

Miscellaneous Endeavours

We are excluding records in the 'Human Achievements' area where the duration of the event is the only criterion for inclusion in favour of records which include a greater skill element.

Balloon sculpture The largest balloon sculpture was a reproduction of Van Gogh's *Fishing Boats on the Beach of Les Saintes Maries*, made out of 25,344 coloured balloons on 28 Jun 1992. Students from Haarlem Business School created the picture at a harbour in Ouddorp in the Netherlands.

Barrel rolling The record for rolling a full 36 gal *1.64 hl* metal beer barrel over a measured mile is 8 min 7.2 sec, by Phillip Randle, Steve Hewitt, John Round, Trevor Bradley, Colin Barnes and Ray Glover of Haunchwood Collieries Institute and Social Club, Nuneaton, Warks on 15 Aug 1982. A team of 10 rolled a 63.5 kg *140 lb* barrel 241 km *150 miles* in 30 hr 31 min in Chlumčany, Czech Republic on 27–28 Oct 1982.

Barrow pushing The heaviest loaded one-wheeled barrow pushed for a minimum 200 level feet *61 level metres* was one loaded with bricks weighing a gross 3.753 tonnes *8275 lb*. It was pushed a distance of 74.1 m *243 ft* by John Sarich at London, Ontario, Canada on 19 Feb 1987.

Barrow racing The fastest time attained in a 1 mile *1.609 km* wheelbarrow race is 4 min 48.51 sec, by Piet Pitzer and Jaco Erasmus at the Transvalia High School, Vanderbijlpark, South Africa on 3 Oct 1987.

Bath tub racing The record for a 36 mile *57.9 km* bath tub race is 1 hr 22 min 27 sec, by Greg Mutton at the Grafton Jacaranda Festival, New South Wales, Australia on 8 Nov 1987. Tubs are limited to 75 in *1.90 m* and 6 hp *4.5 kW* motors. The greatest distance for paddling a hand-propelled bath tub in still water for

Party!

The largest birthday party in Britain was attended by an estimated 10,000 people on 5 Aug 1989 at Douglas, Isle of Man. The party was held to mark the 50th birthday of Trevor Baines, a well-known local businessman.

24 hr is 145.6 km *90½ miles*, by 13 members of Aldington Prison Officers Social Club, near Ashford, Kent on 28–29 May 1983.

Baton twirling The greatest number of complete spins done between tossing a baton into the air and catching it is 10 by Donald Garcia, on the BBC *Record Breakers* programme on 9 Dec 1986.

Bed making The pair record for making a bed with 1 blanket, 2 sheets, an undersheet, an uncased pillow, 1 counterpane and 'hospital' corners is 14.0 sec, by Sister Sharon Stringer and Nurse Michelle Benkel of the Royal Masonic Hospital, London at the launch of the 1994 edition of *The Guinness Book of Records*, held at Canary Wharf, London on 26 Nov 1993.

The record time for one person to make a bed is 28.2 sec, by Wendy Wall, 34, of Hebersham, Sydney, Australia on 30 Nov 1978.

Bed pushing The record distance is 5204 km *3233 miles 1150 yd*, in the case of a wheeled hospital bed by a team of nine employees of Bruntsfield Bedding Centre, Edinburgh from 21 Jun–26 Jul 1979.

Bed race The record time for the annual Knaresborough Bed Race (established 1966) in N Yorks is 12 min 9 sec for the 3.27 km *2 mile 63 yd* course crossing the River Nidd by the Vibroplant team on 9 Jun 1990.

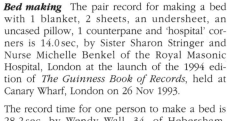

The largest beer tankard was made by the Selangor Pewter Co. (now known as Royal Selangor International Sdn Bhd) of Kuala Lumpur, Malaysia and unveiled on 30 Nov 1985. It measures 1.99 m *6 ft 6 in* in height and has a capacity of 2796 litres *615 gal*.

Beer mat flipping Dean Gould of Felixstowe, Suffolk flipped a pile of 111 mats (1.2 mm thick 490 gsm wood pulp board) through 180 degrees and caught them on 13 Jan 1993.

Beer stein carrying Duane Osborn covered a distance of 15 m *49 ft 2½ in* in 3.65 sec with five full steins in each hand in a contest at Cadillac, Michigan, USA on 10 Jul 1992.

Brick balancing John Evans of Marlpool, Derbys balanced 66 bricks (weighing a total of 134.4 kg *296 lb 4 oz*) on his head for 10 seconds at Cannock, Staffs on 12 Feb 1994.

Brick lifting Russell Bradley of Worcester lifted 31 bricks laid side by side off a table, raising them to chest height and holding them there for two seconds on 14 Jun 1992. The greatest weight of bricks lifted was by Fred Burton of Cheadle, Staffs, who held 20 far heavier bricks weighing a total of 88.45 kg *195 lb* for three seconds on 21 Jan 1994.

Bubble David Stein of New York City, USA created a 15.2 m *50 ft* long bubble on 6 Jun 1988. He made the bubble using a bubble wand, washing-up liquid and water.

Bubble-gum blowing The greatest reported diameter for a bubble-gum bubble under the

Bears are dominant at the largest teddy bears' picnic ever staged, at Christchurch in New Zealand. They were all accompanied by humans, who also enjoyed the day even if they were not the centre of attention.

(Photo: Christchurch Press Co. Ltd)

Beer keg *lifting*

ON THE RECORD

Carl Fentham set a beer keg lifting record by raising a keg weighing 62.5kg *137lb 13oz* above his head 676 times in the space of six hours at Dudley, W Mids on 12 Jun 1993. How did Carl come to achieve this amazing feat?

(G = Guinness Book of Records, CF = Carl Fentham)

G: You set the record in 1993. When did you first become interested in record-breaking?

CF: After a record had been set by the manager of the gymnasium where I train. Ralph Farquharson set the beer keg lifting record at 509 lifts in 1989 but unfortunately he didn't make the book as the record was broken again before it was published.

G: Had you heard of The Guinness Book of Records beforehand?

CF: Yes, I had the book as a Christmas present when I was a child.

G: Was it a case of just finding any record to beat, or were you particularly interested in the beer keg lifting record?

CF: I was particularly interested in the beer keg lift when Ralph failed to get into the book. I promised him I'd get the record back for Harborne gym.

G: How much training did you have to do before the attempt?

CF: I began beer keg lifting in March 1992 but as I was approaching peak condition around September I pulled a back muscle and was unable to train for three months. I started again in January 1993 and in addition to the beer kegs, brought weights, swimming and hill running into my programme.

G: So how did the attempt go. Were you confident?

CF: No, I wasn't very confident because I didn't really know how it would go, but by the time the day had come I wanted that record—bad!

G: Presumably you had supporters who were letting you know if you were on target throughout the six hours.

CF: Yes. Two of the support crew had been with me throughout every single practice session and they had worked out a programme which was accurate up to the second.

G: How did you feel when you knew that you had beaten the record? Excitement or relief?

CF: Both—the record had started off as a bit of a joke, but before long everyone was asking me when I was going to do it, and soon I had pressured myself into it.

G: And lastly it must have taken you quite a time to recover!

CF: Yes, for two weeks after the event I wasn't able to drive because I couldn't grip the hand-brake or gear lever. More than six months later I was still suffering with backache quite badly.

G: In spite of that, a record well deserved. Congratulations Carl!

Photos: Mick Williams

strict rules of this highly competitive activity is 55.8cm *22in*, by Susan Montgomery Williams of Fresno, California, USA in June 1985.

Bucket chain The longest fire service bucket chain stretched over 3496.4m *11,471ft*, with 2271 people passing 50 buckets along the complete course at the Centennial Parade and Muster held at Hudson, New York, USA on 11 Jul 1992.

Catapulting The greatest recorded distance for a catapult shot is 415m *1362ft* by James M. Pfotenhauer, using a patented 5.22m *17ft 1½in* Monarch IV Supershot and a 53-calibre lead musket ball on Ski Hill Road, Escanaba, Michigan, USA on 10 Sep 1977.

Cigar box balancing Terry Cole of Walthamstow, London balanced 220 unmodified cigar boxes on his chin for nine seconds on 24 Apr 1992.

Clapping The duration record for continuous clapping (sustaining an average of 160 claps per min, audible at 110m *120yd*) is 58hr 9min by V. Jeyaraman of Tamil Nadu, India from 12–15 Feb 1988.

Coal carrying In the greatest non-stop bag carrying feat, 1cwt *50.8kg* of household coal in an open bag was carried 54.7km *34 miles* by Neil Sullivan, 37, of Small Heath, Birmingham, in 12hr 45min on 24 May 1986.

David Jones of Huddersfield, W Yorks holds the record for the annual race at Gawthorpe, W Yorks, carrying a 50kg *110lb* bag over the 1012.5m *1107.2 yd* course in 4min 6sec on 1 Apr 1991.

Crate climbing Philip Bruce stacked 38 beer crates in a single column and climbed up them to a height of 9.65m *31ft 8in* at Sowerby Bridge, West Yorks on 26 Aug 1991.

Crawling The longest continuous voluntary crawl (progression with one or other knee in unbroken contact with the ground) is 50.6km *31½ miles*, by Peter McKinlay and John Murrie, who covered 115 laps of an athletics track at Falkirk, Central on 28–29 Mar 1992.

Egg and spoon racing Dale Lyons of Meriden, W Mids ran the London marathon (42.195km *26 miles 385yd*) while carrying a dessert spoon with a fresh egg on it in 3hr 47min on 23 Apr 1990.

Escapology Nick Janson of Benfleet, Essex has escaped from handcuffs locked on him by more than 1400 different police officers over the period since 1954.

Over a space of 15 months ending on 9 Mar 1985, Jagdish Chander, 32, crawled 1400km *870miles* from Aligarh to Jamma, India to appease his revered Hindu goddess, Mata.

Footbag The world record for keeping a footbag airborne is 51,155 consecutive kicks by Ted Martin (USA) at Mount Prospect, Illinois, USA on 29 May 1993. The doubles record is 100,001 consecutive kicks by Ted Martin and Andy Linder (both USA), also at Mount Prospect, Illinois on 9 Apr 1994. The greatest number of kicks in five minutes is 912 by Kenny Shults (USA) at Golden, Colorado on 30 Jul 1991.

French knitting Leon Milich of Epping, Victoria, Australia has produced a piece of French knitting 8.59km *5 miles 595 yd* long since he started work on it in 1970.

Glass balancing John Elliot succeeded in balancing 40 pint glasses on his chin for 10 seconds at Tidworth, Hants on 16 Dec 1993.

Gurning The only gurner to have won six national titles is Ron Looney of Egremont, Cumbria, from 1978–83.

High diving Col. Harry A. Froboess (Switzerland) jumped 120m *394 ft* into the Bodensee from the airship *Graf Hindenburg* on 22 Jun 1936.

The greatest height reported for a dive into an air bag is 99.4m *326 ft* by stuntman Dan Koko, who jumped from the top of Vegas World Hotel and Casino on to a 6.1×12.2×4.2m *20×40×14 ft* target on 13 Aug 1984. His impact speed was 141km/h *88 mph*.

Hitch-hiking The title of world champion hitch-hiker is claimed by Stephan Schlei of Ratingen, Germany, who since 1960 has obtained free rides totalling 695,597km *432,224 miles*.

Hod carrying Russell Bradley of Worcester carried bricks weighing 164kg *361 lb 9 oz* up a ladder of the minimum specified length of 12ft *3.65 m* on 28 Jan 1991 at Worcester City Football Club. The hod weighed 43kg *94 lb 13 oz* and he was thus carrying a total weight of 207kg *456 lb 6 oz*.

He also carried bricks weighing 264kg *582 lb* in a hod weighing 48kg *105 lb 13 oz* a distance of 5m *16 ft 5 in* on the flat, before ascending a runged ramp to a height of 2.49m *8 ft 2 in* at Worcester on 20 Nov 1993. This gave a total weight of 312kg *687 lb 13 oz*.

Human centipede The largest 'human centipede' to move 30m *98 ft 5 in* (with ankles firmly tied together) consisted of 1537 pupils from Great Barr School, Birmingham, W Mids on 11 Mar 1994. Nobody fell over in the course of the walk.

Human logos The largest human logo ever made was the Human US Shield, consisting of 30,000 officers and men at Camp Custer, Battlecreek, Michigan, USA on 10 Nov 1918.

Kissing Alfred A.E. Wolfram of New Brighton, Minnesota, USA kissed 8001 people in 8hr at the Minnesota Renaissance Festival on 15 Sep 1990— one every 3.6 seconds.

Ha! Ha!

What constitutes a joke? How much does the audience need to laugh, if at all? Unfortunately the more the audience laughs, the more difficult it is to tell jokes quickly—a comedian would not want to carry on if his audience cannot hear what he is saying. Working on the basis that a joke must have a beginning, a middle and an end, Felipe Carbonell of Lima, Peru told 345 jokes in one hour on 29 Jul 1993, whilst Mike Hessman of Columbus, Ohio, USA has claimed 12,682 in 24hr on 16–17 Nov 1992.

Kite flying The following records are all recognized by *Kite Lines* magazine:–

The longest kite flown was 1034.45m *3394 ft* in length. It was made and flown by Michel Trouillet and a team of helpers at Nîmes, France on 18 Nov 1990.

The largest kite flown was one of 553m² *5952 ft²*. It was first flown by a Dutch team on the beach at Scheveningen, Netherlands on 8 Aug 1981.

A record height of 9740m *31,955 ft* was reached by a train of eight kites over Lindenberg, Germany on 1 Aug 1919.

The altitude record for a single kite is 3801m *12,471 ft*, in the case of a kite flown by Henry Helm Clayton and A.E. Sweetland at the Blue Hill Weather Station, Milton, Massachusetts, USA on 28 Feb 1898.

The fastest speed attained by a kite was 193km/h *120 mph* flown by Pete DiGiacomo at Ocean City, Maryland, USA on 22 Sep 1989.

The greatest number of figure-of-eights achieved with a kite in an hour is 2911, by Stu Cohen at Ocean City, Maryland, USA on 25 Sep 1988.

The greatest number of kites flown on a single line is 11,284 by Sadao Harada and a team of helpers at Sakurajima, Kagoshima, Japan on 18 Oct 1990.

The longest recorded flight is one of 180hr 17min by the Edmonds Community College team at Long Beach, Washington State, USA from 21–29 Aug 1982. Managing the flight of this J-25 parafoil was Harry N. Osborne.

Knitting The world's fastest hand-knitter of all time has been Gwen Matthewman of Featherstone, W Yorks. She attained a speed of 111 stitches per min in a test at Phildar's Wool Shop, Central Street, Leeds, W Yorks on 29 Sep 1980.

Knot-tying The fastest recorded time for tying the six Boy Scout Handbook Knots (square knot, sheet bend, sheep shank, clove hitch, round turn and two half hitches, and bowline) on individual ropes is 8.1sec by Clinton R. Bailey, Sr, 52, of Pacific City, Oregon, USA on 13 Apr 1977.

Mrs Matthewman's knitting technique has been filmed by the world's only Professor of Knitting—a Japanese.

Ladder climbing A 10-man team from WR67 Derbyshire Fire & Rescue Service climbed a vertical height of 51.18km *31.80 miles* up a fire-service ladder in 24hours at Derby on 1–2 Apr 1994.

Land rowing The greatest distance covered by someone on a land rowing machine is 5278.5km *3280 miles*, by Rob Bryant of Fort Worth, Texas, USA, who 'rowed' across the USA. He left Los Angeles, California on 2 Apr 1990, reaching Washington, DC on 30 July.

Leap-frogging The greatest distance covered was 1603.2km *996.2 miles*, by 14 students from Stanford University, California, USA, who started leap-frogging on 16 May 1991 and stopped 244hr 43min later on 26 May.

Litter collection The greatest number of volunteers involved in collecting litter in one location on one day is 50,405, along the coastline of California, USA on 2 Oct 1993 in conjunction with the International Coastal Cleanup.

Log rolling The record number of International Championships won is 10, by Jubiel Wickheim of Shawnigan Lake, British Columbia, Canada, between 1956 and 1969.

Fastest magician Eldon D. Wigton, alias Dr Eldonie, performed 225 different tricks in 2 min at Kilbourne, Ohio, USA on 21 Apr 1991.

Milk crate balancing Terry Cole of Walthamstow, London managed to balance 29 crates on his chin for the minimum specified 10sec on 16 May 1994.

John Evans of Marlpool, Derbys balanced 90 crates (weighing a total of 129kg *284 lb*) on his head for 10 seconds on 27 Oct 1993 for the BBC *Record Breakers* programme.

Musical chairs The largest game on record was one starting with 8238 participants, ending with Xu Chong Wei on the last chair, which was held at the Anglo-Chinese School, Singapore on 5 Aug 1989.

Needle threading The record number of times that a strand of cotton has been threaded through a number 13 needle (eye 12.7×1.6mm *½×1⁄16 in*) in 2hr is 20,675, achieved by Om Prakash Singh of Allahabad, India on 25 Jul 1993.

Noodle making Mark Pi of Hilliard, Ohio, USA made 4096 noodle strings (i.e 2^{12}, in twelve movements) from a single piece of noodle dough in 41.34sec on the *Vicki* NBC television show on 15 Dec 1993. This is nearly 100 noodles per second.

Paper chain A paper chain 59.05km *36.69 miles* long was made by 60 students from University College Dublin as part of UCD Science Day in Dublin, Republic of Ireland on 11–12 Feb 1993. The chain consisted of nearly 400,000 links and was made over a period of 24 hours.

Pass the parcel The largest game of pass the parcel involved 3464 people who removed 2000 wrappers in two hours from a parcel measuring 1.5×0.9×0.9m *5×3×3 ft* at Alton Towers, Staffs on 8 Nov 1992. The event was organized by Parcelforce International and the final present was an electronic keyboard, won by Sylvia Wilshaw.

Pedal-boating Kenichi Horie of Kobe, Japan set a pedal-boating distance record of 7500km *4660 miles*, leaving Honolulu, Hawaii, USA on 30 Oct 1992 and arriving at Naha, Okinawa, Japan on 17 Feb 1993.

Pram pushing The greatest distance covered in pushing a pram in 24hr is 563.62km *350.23 miles* by 60 members of the Oost-Vlanderen branch of Amnesty International at Lede, Belgium on 15 Oct 1988.

A ten-man team from the Royal Marines School of Music, Deal, Kent, with an adult 'baby', covered a distance of 437.2km *271.7 miles* in 24hr from 22–23 Nov 1990.

Riding in armour The longest recorded ride in armour is one of 334.7km *208 miles* by Dick Brown, who left Edinburgh, Lothian on 10 Jun 1989 and arrived in his home town of Dumfries four days later. His total riding time was 35hr 25min.

GUESS WHAT?

Q What record did Santjie set in 1977?

A See Page 38

Human Achievements

Gary Stewart achieved a record 177,737 pogo-stick jumps at Huntington Beach, California, USA on 25–26 May 1990.
(Photo: S. Seal/K. Taylor)

Detroit, Michigan, USA on 26 Jun 1978 at 11 min 23.8 sec.

Brian McCauliff ran a vertical mile (ascending and descending eight times) on the stairs of the Westin Hotel, Detroit, Michigan, USA in 1 hr 38 min 5 sec on 2 Feb 1992.

Russell Gill climbed the 835 steps of the Rhodes State Office Tower in Columbus, Ohio, USA 53 times (a total of 44,255 steps and a vertical height of 8141.8 m *26,712 ft*) in 9 hr 16 min 24 sec on 20 Feb 1994. He went down by lift each time.

The record for the 1760 steps (vertical height 342 m *1122 ft*) in the world's tallest free-standing structure, Toronto's CN Tower, Canada, is 7 min 52 sec by Brendan Keenoy on 29 Oct 1989.

The record for the 1336 stairs of the world's tallest hotel, the Westin Stamford Hotel, Singapore, is 6 min 55 sec by Balvinder Singh, in their 3rd Annual Vertical Marathon on 4 Jun 1989.

Sunil Tamang of the 7th Gurkha Rifles climbed up the 50 storeys of Canary Wharf, Britain's tallest building, in a time of 7 min 3.44 sec on 22 Aug 1992.

Step-ups Gareth Morris of Perton, W Mids completed 1873 step-ups in an hour on 30 Jan 1993 using a 38 cm *15 in* high exercise bench.

Stilt-walking The fastest stilt-walker on record is Roy Luiking, who covered 100 m *328 ft* on 30.5 cm *1 ft* high stilts in 13.01 sec at Didam, Netherlands on 28 May 1992. Over a long distance, the fastest was M. Garisoain of Bayonne, France, who in 1892 walked the 8 km *4.97 miles* from Bayonne to Biarritz on stilts in 42 min, an average speed of 11.42 km/h *7.10 mph*.

The greatest distance ever walked on stilts is 4804 km *3008 miles*, from Los Angeles, California, USA to Bowen, Kentucky, USA by Joe Bowen from 20 Feb–26 Jul 1980. In 1891 Sylvain Dornon stilt-walked from Paris, France to Moscow, Russia in 50 stages, covering 2945 km *1830 miles*. Another source gives his time as 58 days. Either way, although Bowen covered a greater distance, Dornon walked at a much higher speed.

Stone skipping (Ducks and drakes) The video-verified stone skipping record is 38 skips, achieved by Jerdone at Wimberley, Texas, USA on 20 Oct 1991.

Stretcher bearing The longest distance a stretcher with a 63.5 kg *10 st* 'body' has been carried is 270.15 km *167.86 miles*, in 49 hr 2 min from 29 Apr–1 May 1993. This was achieved by two teams of four from CFB (Canadian Forces Base) Trenton in and around Trenton, Ontario, Canada.

String ball, largest The largest ball of string on record is one 4.03 m *13 ft 2½ in* in diameter and 12.65 m *41 ft 6 in* in circumference, amassed by J.C. Payne of Valley View, Texas, USA between 1989 and 1992.

Tightrope walking The world tightrope endurance record is 205 days, by Jorge Ojeda-Guzman of Orlando, Florida, USA, on a wire 11 m *36 ft* long, which was 10.7 m *35 ft* above the ground. He was there from 1 Jan–25 Jul 1993 and entertained the crowds by walking, balancing on a chair and dancing.

Ashley Brophy of Neilborough, Victoria, Australia walked 11.57 km *7.18 miles* on a wire 45 m *147 ft 8 in* long and 10 m *32 ft 10 in* above the ground at the Adelaide Grand Prix, Australia on 1 Nov 1985 in 3½ hr.

Steve McPeak (b. 21 Apr 1945) of Las Vegas, Nevada, USA ascended the 46.6 mm *1⅞ in* diameter Zugspitzbahn cable on the Zugspitze, Germany for a vertical height of 705 m *2313 ft* in three stints aggregating 5 hr 4 min on 24, 25 and 28 Jun 1981. The maximum gradient over the stretch of 2282 m *7485 ft* was more than 30 degrees.

The greatest drop over which anyone has walked on a tightrope is 3150 m *10,335 ft*, above the French countryside, by Michel Menin of Lons-le-Saunier, France, on 4 Aug 1989.

Typewriting The highest recorded speeds attained with a ten-word penalty per error on a manual machine are: five min—176 wpm net Mrs Carole Forristall Waldschlager Bechen at Dixon, Illinois, USA on 2 Apr 1959; and one hour—147 wpm net Albert Tangora (US) (Underwood Standard), 22 Oct 1923.

The official hour record on an electric typewriter is 9316 words (40 errors) on an IBM machine, giving a net rate of 149 words per min, by Margaret Hamma, now Mrs Dilmore (US), in Brooklyn, New York, USA on 20 Jun 1941. In an official test in 1946, Stella Pajunas, now Mrs Garnand, attained a rate of 216 words in a minute on an IBM machine.

Gregory Arakelian of Herndon, Virginia, USA set a speed record of 158 wpm, with two errors, on a personal computer in the Key Tronic World Invitational Type-Off, which attracted some 10,000 entrants worldwide. He recorded this speed in the semi-final, in a three-minute test, on 24 Sep 1991.

Mikhail Shestov set a numerical record by typing spaced *numbers* from 1 to 795 on a PC without any errors in 5 minutes at BBC Television Centre, London for the *Record Breakers* programme on 14 Oct 1993.

> The highest auction price paid for a suit of armour was £1,925,000, by B.H. Trupin (USA) on 5 May 1983 at Sotheby's, London for a suit made in Milan by Giovanni Negroli in 1545 for Henri II of France.

Rope slide
The greatest distance recorded in a rope slide is from near the top of Blackpool Tower, Lancs—at a height of 126.8 m *416 ft*—to a fixed point 343.8 m *1128 ft* from the base of the tower. Set up by the Royal Marines, the rope was descended on 8 Sep 1989 by Sgt Alan Heward and Cpl Mick Heap of the Royal Marines, John Herbert of Blackpool Tower, and Cheryl Baker and Roy Castle of the BBC *Record Breakers* programme. The total length descended was 366.4 m *1202 ft*.

Shorthand The highest recorded speeds ever attained under championship conditions are 300 words per min (99.64 per cent accuracy) for five minutes and 350 wpm (99.72 per cent accuracy, that is, two insignificant errors) for two minutes, by Nathan Behrin (US) in tests in New York in December 1922. Behrin (b. 1887) used the Pitman system, invented in 1837. Arnold Bradley achieved a speed of 309 wpm without error using the Sloan-Duployan system, with 1545 words in 5 minutes in a test in Walsall, W Mids on 9 Nov 1920.

Spitting The greatest recorded distance for a cherry stone is 26.96 m *88 ft 5½ in*, by Horst Ortmann at Langenthal, Germany on 29 Aug 1992. The record for projecting a water-melon seed is 20.96 m *68 ft 9⅛ in* by Lee Wheelis at Luling, Texas, USA on 24 Jun 1989.

> Randy Ober of Bentonville, Arkansas, USA spat a tobacco wad 14.50 m *47 ft 7 in* at the Calico 5th Annual Tobacco Chewing and Spitting Championships, held north of Barstow, California on 4 Apr 1982.

Stair climbing The 100-storey record for stair climbing was set by Dennis W. Martz in the Detroit Plaza Hotel,

Oldest!

The oldest tightrope-walker was 'Professor' William Ivy Baldwin (1866–1953), who crossed the South Boulder Canyon, Colorado, USA on a 97.5 m *320 ft* wire with a 38.1 m *125 ft* drop on his 82nd birthday on 31 Jul 1948.

WORLD'S LARGEST BALL OF STRING

J.C. Payne (wearing the red cap) with his huge ball of string—the sign says it all! In November 1993 he had a narrow escape when the ball toppled off a stand and started rolling towards him, but luckily he saw it and managed to get out of the way.
(Photo: Gamma)

> Les Stewart of Mudjimba Beach, Queensland, Australia has typed the numbers 1 to 820,000 in *words* on 16,290 quarto sheets as of 26 Mar 1994. His target is to become a 'millionaire'.

> I feel that the Guinness Book is a very positive source of inspiration for people to recognize their unlimited potential, and of course it has revolutionized my life!

Ashrita Furman
Eight world records

8

Who holds the milk bottle balancing record?
Who holds the hop-scotch record?
Who holds the somersaulting record?

The answer to these three questions, and to five other similar questions, is Ashrita Furman of Jamaica, New York State, USA. Since first beating the somersault record on 19 Nov 1980 he has become a dedicated record-breaker, using meditation and concentration to help him in his efforts.

Ashrita's impressive collection of currently-published records shows his ability to excel in a wide range of activities:–

1 **Brick carrying** He carried a 9lb *4.1kg* brick in one hand a record distance of 103km *64 miles* on 13–14 Jun 1993.

2 **Hop-scotch** He successfully completed a record 307 games of hop-scotch in 24 hours on 5–6 Apr 1991.

3 **Joggling (juggling and running at the same time)** He completed the marathon — 42.195km *26 miles 385yd* — in 3hr 22min 32.5sec on 4 Jul 1988.

4 **Joggling** He also holds the record over 50 miles *80.5km*, with a time of 8hr 52min 7sec on 12 Mar 1989.

5 **Milk bottle balancing** He covered a record distance of 113.76km *70.16 miles* balancing a milk bottle on his head on 1–2 Aug 1993. It took him 18hr 46min to complete the walk.

6 **Pogo stick jumping** He set a distance record of 24.125km *14.99 miles* on 25 May 1991.

7 **Somersaults** He performed a record 8341 consecutive forward rolls on 30 Apr 1986. It took him 10hr 30min and he covered 19.67km *12 miles 390yards*.

8 **Basketball dribbling** He dribbled a basketball a distance of 133.5km *83 miles* in 24 hours on 6–7 Jan 1994.

He has also been known to skip long distances at great speed and yodel for hours on end, and may soon be attempting a backwards unicycling or a roller skating record.

Photo: Ramaniya Zealey

Photo: I. A. Konopiaty

Photo: Ando Hixon

Photo: Ellen Elizabeth Smith

Photo: Prashphutito Greco

Photo: Kailash Beyer

(In action) (It's over)

Photos: Nikunja Ebner

Photo: Thomas Pliske

'Fast' Eddy McDonald, the yo-yo speed record-holder, demonstrating his skills. Tricks which he performs with a yo-yo include *Shoot the Moon* and *Monkey up the Tree*.

Unsupported circle The highest recorded number of people who have demonstrated the physical paradox of all being seated without a chair is an unsupported circle of 10,323 employees of the Nissan Motor Co. at Komazawa Stadium, Tokyo, Japan on 23 Oct 1982. The British record is 7402 participants at Goodwood Airfield, W Sussex on 25 May 1986, as part of a Sport Aid event.

Whip cracking The longest whip ever 'cracked' is one of 56.24 m *184 ft 6 in* (excluding the handle), wielded by Krist King of Pettisville, Ohio, USA on 17 Sep 1991.

Window cleaning Keith Witt of Amarillo, Texas, USA cleaned three standard 1079 × 1194 mm *42½ × 47 in* office windows with a 300 mm *11.8 in* long squeegee and 9 litres *2 gal* of water in 10.13 sec on 31 Jan 1992. The record was achieved at the International Window Cleaning Association convention at San Antonio, Texas, USA.

Writing, minuscule In 1926 an account was published of Alfred McEwen's pantograph record in which the 56-word version of the Lord's Prayer was written by diamond point on glass in the space of 0.04 × 0.02 mm *0.0016 × 0.0008 in*.

Surendra Apharya of Jaipur, India wrote 10,056 characters (speeches by Jawaharlal Nehru, the first Prime Minister of independent India) within the size of a definitive Indian postage stamp, measuring 19.69 × 17.82 mm *0.78 × 0.70 in*, in December 1990, and also wrote 1749 characters (names of various countries, towns and regions) on a single grain of rice on 19 May 1991. Chang Shi-Qi of Wuhan, China wrote 308 characters ('God bless you' 28 times) on a human hair 2 cm *8/10 in* long at the Guinness World of Records Exhibition, Singapore on 2 Jun 1992.

Yo-yo 'Fast' Eddy McDonald of Toronto, Canada completed 21,663 loops with a yo-yo in 3 hr on 14 Oct 1990 at Boston, Massachusetts, USA, having previously set a 1 hr speed record of 8437 loops at Cavendish, Prince Edward Island, Canada on 14 Jul 1990.

Juggling

12 rings (flashed) Albert Lucas (US), 1985; Anthony Gatto (US), 1993.

8 clubs (flashed) Anthony Gatto (US), 1989.

11 bean bags (flashed) Bruce Serafian (US), 1992.

10 balls (flashed) Enrico Rastelli (Italy), 1920s; Albert Lucas (US), 1984.

10 balls (bounce juggled) Tim Nolan (US), 10 balls, 1988.

8 plates (juggled) Enrico Rastelli (Italy), 1920s; Albert Lucas (US), 1984.

7 flaming torches (juggled) Anthony Gatto (US), 1989.

Basketball spinning Bruce Crevier (US), 16 basketballs (whole body), 1992.

Ball spinning (on one hand) François Chotard (France), 9 balls, 1990.

Duration: 5 clubs without a drop 45 min 2 sec, Anthony Gatto (US), 1989.

Duration: 3 objects without a drop Jas Angelo (GB), 8 hr 57 min 31 sec, 1989.

7 ping-pong balls with mouth (flashed) Tony Ferko (Czechoslovakia), 1987.

Pirouettes with 3 cigar boxes Kris Kremo (Switzerland) (quadruple turn with 3 boxes in mid-air), 1977.

5 balls inverted Bobby May (US), 1953.

3 objects while running (Joggling) Owen Morse (US), 100 m in 11.68 sec, 1989 and 400 m in 57.32 sec, 1990; Kirk Swenson (US), 1 mile *1.6 km* in 4 min 43 sec, 1986 and 5000 m *3.1 miles* in 16 min 55 sec, 1986; Michael Hout (US), 110 m hurdles in 18.9 sec, 1993; Albert Lucas (US), 400 m hurdles in 1 min 10.37 sec, 1989; Owen Morse, Albert Lucas, Tuey Wilson and John Wee (all US), 1 mile *1.6 km* relay in 3 min 57.38 sec, 1990.

5 objects while running (Joggling) Owen Morse (US), 100 m in 13.8 sec, 1988. Bill Gillen (US), 1 mile *1.6 km* in 7 min 41.01 sec, 1989 and 5000 m *3.1 miles* in 28 min 11 sec, 1989.

Food

Apple pie The largest apple pie ever baked was that made by ITV chef Glynn Christian in a 12 × 7 m *40 × 23 ft* dish at Hewitts Farm, Chelsfield, Kent from 25–27 Aug 1982. Over 600 bushels of apples were included in the pie, which weighed 13.66 tonnes *30,115 lb*.

Banana split The longest banana split ever created measured 7.32 km *4.55 miles* in length, and was made by residents of Selinsgrove, Pennsylvania, USA on 30 Apr 1988.

Food records—what they said

Beating the record for the largest banana split or cake, doughnut or ice-cream sundae is a huge undertaking. In many cases whole towns or cities are brought together, whether to help in the attempt or eat the resulting delicacy, producing quotes such as:—

'You just dive in, full force'—banana split

'Wow! I never expected it to be this big'—the largest cake

'It's a good community project. The fact that it's all for charity makes it worthwhile'—doughnut

'It's nice to get away from the everyday things you do and get a little wild and extravagant'—ice-cream sundae

Fun and fund-raising at its best

Barbecue The record attendance at a one-day barbecue was 44,158, at Warwick Farm Racecourse, Sydney, Australia on 10 Oct 1993. The greatest meat consumption ever recorded at a one-day barbecue was at the Iowa State Fairgrounds, Des Moines, Iowa, USA on 21 Jun 1988—9.13 tonnes *20,130 lb* of pork consumed in 5 hr. The greatest quantity of meat consumed at any barbecue was 9.58 tonnes *21,112 lb* of beef at the Sertoma Club Barbecue, New Port Richey, Florida, USA, from 7–9 Mar 1986.

Biscuit The largest biscuit ever made was a chocolate chip cookie with an area of 93 m²

François Chotard, the record-breaking ball-spinner from France.

821 jugglers kept 2463 objects in the air simultaneously, each person juggling at least three objects at Seattle, Washington, USA in 1990.

Philip Masters, who was in charge of the project to build the largest and tallest Easter egg, surveys his creation along with his admiring family.
(Photo: Bert Banner)

1001ft², made at Santa Anita Fashion Park in Arcadia, California, USA on 15 Oct 1993. It was 10.67 m × 8.72 m *35ft × 28ft 7in* and contained more than 3,000,000 chocolate chips.

Cakes The largest cake ever created weighed 58.08 tonnes *128,238 lb 8 oz*, including 7.35 tonnes *16,209 lb* of icing. It was made to celebrate the 100th birthday of Fort Payne, Alabama, USA, and was in the shape of Alabama. The cake was prepared by a local bakery, Earth-Grains, the first cut being made by 100-year old resident Ed Henderson on 18 Oct 1989.

The tallest cake was 30.85 m *101ft 2½ in* high, created by Beth Cornell Trevorrow and her team of helpers at the Shiawassee County Fairgrounds, Michigan, USA. It consisted of 100 tiers and was completed on 5 Aug 1990.

The Alimentarium, a museum of food in Vevey, Switzerland, has on display the world's oldest cake, which was sealed and 'vacuum-packed' in the grave of Pepionkh, who lived in Ancient Egypt around 2200 BC. The 11 cm *4.3 in* wide cake has sesame on it and honey inside, and was possibly made with milk.

Cheese The largest cheese ever created was a cheddar of 18.17 tonnes *40,060 lb*, made on 13–14 Mar 1988 at Simon's Specialty Cheese, Little Chute, Wisconsin, USA. It was subsequently taken on tour in a specially designed, refrigerated 'Cheesemobile'.

Cherry pie The largest cherry pie on record weighed 17.11 tonnes *37,740 lb 10 oz* and contained 16.69 tonnes *36,800 lb* of cherry filling. It measured 6.1 m *20ft* in diameter, and was baked by members of the Oliver Rotary Club at Oliver, British Columbia, Canada on 14 Jul 1990.

GUESS WHAT?

Q Which country is the largest producer of cheese?

A See Page 173

Chocolate model The largest chocolate model was one weighing 4 tonnes *8818 lb*, in the shape of a traditional Spanish sailing ship. It was made by Gremi Provincial de Pastisseria, Confitería i Bolería school, Barcelona, Spain in February 1991 and measured 13 × 8.5 × 2.5 m *42ft 8in × 27ft 10½ in × 8ft 2½ in.*

Success!

The world's leading food company is the Swiss-based Nestlé, with sales in 1993 totalling 57.5 billion Swiss francs (£26.3 billion). The biggest seller among their famous confectionery products is KitKat, 11.3 billion fingers of which were sold worldwide during the year. Every second 360 KitKat fingers are consumed throughout the world.

Christmas pudding The largest was one of 3.28 tonnes *7231 lb 1 oz*, made by the villagers of Aughton, Lancs and officially unveiled at the Famous Aughton Pudding Festival held on 11 Jul 1992. Work on the pudding had started on 3 July and it was ready the day before the festival.

Cocktail The largest cocktail on record was a margarita of 7574.6 litres *1666.2 gal*, made by Chi-Chi's in celebration of Cinco de Mayo (a Mexican festival) and the Kentucky Derby Festival at Louisville, Kentucky, USA on 5 May 1994. It consisted of water, Sauza tequila, sweet and sour concentrate and Cointreau orange liqueur.

Doughnut The largest ever made was an American-style jelly doughnut weighing 1.7 tonnes *3739 lb*, which was 4.9 m *16ft* in diameter and 40.6 cm *16 in* high in the centre. It was made by representatives from Hemstrought's Bakeries, Donato's Bakery and the radio station WKLL-FM at Utica, New York, USA on 21 Jan 1993.

Easter eggs The heaviest Easter egg on record, and also the tallest, was one weighing 4.76 tonnes *10,482 lb 14 oz*, 7.1 m *23ft 3 in* high, made by staff of Cadbury Red Tulip at their factory at Ringwood, Victoria, Australia. It was completed on 9 Apr 1992.

Haggis The largest haggis on record weighed 303.2 kg *668 lb 7 oz* and was made using 80 ox stomachs by the Troon Round Table, Burns Country Foods and a team of chefs at the Hilton Hotel in Glasgow, Strathclyde on 24 May 1993.

Hamburger The largest hamburger on record was one of 2.50 tonnes *5520 lb*, made at the Outagamie County Fairgrounds, Seymour, Wisconsin, USA on 5 Aug 1989.

Ice-cream sundae The largest ice-cream sundae was one weighing 24.91 tonnes *54,914 lb 13 oz*, made by Palm Dairies Ltd under the supervision of Mike Rogiani in Edmonton, Alberta, Canada on 24 Jul 1988. It consisted of 20.27 tonnes *44,689 lb 8 oz* of ice-cream, 4.39 tonnes *9688 lb 2 oz* of syrup and 243.7 kg *537 lb 3 oz* of topping.

Jelly The world's largest jelly, a 35,000 litre *7700 gal* water-melon flavoured pink jelly made by Paul Squires and Geoff Ross, was set at Roma Street Forum, Brisbane, Queensland, Australia on 5 Feb 1981 in a tank supplied by Pool Fab.

Kebab The longest kebab ever was one 630.0 m *2066 ft 11 in* long, made by the Namibian Children's Home at Windhoek, Namibia on 21 Sep 1991.

Lasagne The largest lasagne was one weighing 3.71 tonnes *8188 lb 8 oz* and measuring 21.33 × 2.13m *70 × 7ft*. It was made by the Food Bank for Monterey County at Salinas, California, USA on 14 Oct 1993.

Loaf The longest loaf on record was a Rosca de Reyes 1064 m *3491 ft 9 in* long, baked at the Hyatt Regency Hotel in Guadalajara, Mexico on 6 Jan 1991. If a consumer of a 'Rosca', or twisted loaf, finds the embedded doll, that person has to host the Rosca party (held annually at Epiphany) the following year.

The most expensive food is saffron powder, which is sold at Harrods in London for £1985.49p per 1 lb 454g.

The largest pan loaf ever baked, by staff of Sasko in Johannesburg, South Africa on 18 Mar 1988, weighed 1.43 tonnes *3163 lb 10 oz* and measured 3 × 1.25 × 1.1 m *9 ft 10 in × 4 ft 1 in × 3 ft 7 in.*

Lollipop The world's largest ice lolly was a sweet lemon and chocolate one of 6.36 tonnes *14,027 lb*, made by the Police Children's and Youth Club at Sisimiut, Greenland and completed

The combination of a haggis and a kilt must mean Scotland (right). The team, with tartan in background, can relax and celebrate knowing they've beaten the record for the largest haggis (below).
(Photos: Kenneth Ferguson)

on 21 Mar 1993. The ceremonies were attended by Father Christmas. The largest 'regular' lollipop was a peppermint-flavoured one weighing 1.37 tonnes *3011 lb 5 oz*, made by staff of BonBon at Holme Olstrup, Denmark on 22 Apr 1994.

Meat pie The largest meat pie on record weighed 9.03 tonnes *19,908 lb* and was the ninth in the series of Denby Dale, W Yorks pies. It was baked on 3 Sep 1988 to mark the bicentenary of Denby Dale pie-making, the first one in 1788 having been made to celebrate King George III's return to sanity.

> The fourth Denby Dale meat pie (Queen Victoria's Jubilee, 1887) went a bit 'off' and had to be buried.

Milk shake The largest milk shake was a chocolate one of 7160.8 litres *1575.2 gal*, made by the Smith Dairy Products Co. at Orrville, Ohio, USA on 20 Oct 1989.

Mince pie The largest mince pie recorded was one of 1.02 tonnes *2260 lb*, measuring 6.1 × 1.5 m *20 × 5 ft*, baked at Ashby-de-la-Zouch, Leics on 15 Oct 1932.

Paella The largest paella measured 20 m *65 ft 7 in* in diameter and was made by Juan Carlos Galbis and a team of helpers in Valencia, Spain on 8 Mar 1992. It was eaten by 100,000 people.

Pastry The longest pastry was a mille-feuille (cream puff pastry) 1037.25 m *3403 ft* in length, made by employees of Pidy, a company based in Ypres, Belgium on 4–5 Sep 1992.

Pizza The largest pizza ever baked was one measuring 37.4 m *122 ft 8 in* in diameter, made at Norwood Hypermarket, Norwood, South Africa on 8 Dec 1990.

An appropriate location for the largest ice lolly, and appropriate weather conditions too. A well-known gentleman in red with a white beard joined excited onlookers for the successful attempt on the record.
(Photo: Lind)

Popcorn The largest container full of popcorn was one with 169.33 m³ *5979.33 ft³* of popped corn. It was just over 6 m *19 ft 8 in* in diameter and 5.81 m *19 ft 1 in* in height. It took the staff from United Cinemas International in Derby three days to achieve the record, beginning their attempt on 23 Aug 1991 and completing it on 26 August.

Salami The longest salami on record was one 20.95 m *68 ft 9 in* long with a circumference of 63.4 cm *25 in*, weighing 676.9 kg *1492 lb 5 oz*, made by staff of A/S Svindlands Pølsefabrikk at Flekkefjord, Norway from 6–16 Jul 1992.

Sausage The longest continuous sausage on record was one of 21.12 km *13⅛ miles*, made at the premises of Keith Boxley at Wombourne, near Wolverhampton, W Mids in 15 hr 33 min on 18–19 Jun 1988.

Spice, most expensive Prices for wild ginseng (root of *Panax quinque-folium*) from the Chan Pak Mountain area of China, thought to have aphrodisiac qualities, were reported in November 1979 to be as high as $23,000 per ounce in Hong Kong.

Stick of rock The largest stick of rock was one weighing 413.6 kg *911 lb 13 oz*. It was 5.03 m *16 ft 6 in* long and 43.2 cm *17 in* thick, and was made by the Coronation Rock Company of Blackpool, Lancs on 20 Jul 1991.

Strawberry bowl The largest bowl of strawberries had a net weight of 2.39 tonnes *5266 lb*. The strawberries were picked at Joe Moss Farms near Embro, Ontario, Canada and the bowl was filled at the Kitchener-Waterloo Hospital, also in Ontario, on 29 Jun 1993.

Sweets The largest sweet on record was a marzipan chocolate weighing 1.85 tonnes *4078 lb 8 oz*, made at the Ven International Fresh Market, Diemen, Netherlands on 11–13 May 1990.

It needed a very large bottle-opener to open the largest bottle of beer, which contained 625·5 litres *137½ gal* of Kingfisher beer, the leading Indian lager.
(Photo: Barry Duffield Photography)

Trifle The largest sherry trifle on record was one weighing 3.13 tonnes *6896 lb*, including 91 litres *20 gal* of sherry, made on 26 Sep 1990 by students of Clarendon College of Further Education, Nottingham.

Yorkshire pudding The largest Yorkshire pudding was one with an area of 42.04 m² *452.2 ft²*, measuring 9.18 × 4.58 m *30 ft 1¼ in × 15 ft 0¼ in*. It was made by staff from the catering department of Rotherham Council at Rotherham, S Yorks on 1 Aug 1991 to celebrate Yorkshire Day.

Drink

Alcohol consumption Poland has the highest consumption of spirits per person, with 4.5 litres *7.9 pints* of pure alcohol per annum. Germany is the leading beer consumer, with 142.7 litres *251.1 pints* annually per person and France heads the list for wine, with 66.8 litres *117.6 pints* per person in a year. The UK ranks 22nd, 10th and 25th in the three lists.

Beer *Oldest* Written references to beer have been found dating from as far back as *c.* 5000 BC, as part of the daily wages of workers at the Temple of Erech in Mesopotamia. Physical evidence of beer dating from *c.* 3500 BC has been detected in remains of a jug found at Godin Tepe, Iran in 1973 during a Royal Ontario Museum expedition. It was only in 1991 that analysis of the remains was carried out, which established that residues in deep grooves in the jug were calcium oxalate, also known as beer-stone and still created in barley-based beers.

Strongest Uncle Igor's Famous Falling Over Water, brewed by the Ross Brewing Company and on sale at The Bristol Brewhouse, Bristol,

> ## GUESS WHAT?
>
> Q In which country is the world's largest beer-selling establishment?
>
> A see Page 94

Avon, has an alcohol volume of 21.0 per cent. It is only sold by the wine glass.

Bottles *Largest* A bottle 3.11 m *10 ft 2 in* tall and 3.5 m *11 ft 6 in* in circumference was filled with 2250 litres *495 gal* of Schweppes Lemonade in Melbourne, Victoria, Australia on 17 Mar 1994 to celebrate 200 years of Schweppes.

The largest bottle of beer was 2.54 m *8 ft 4 in* tall and 2.17 m *7 ft 1½ in* in circumference, and was unveiled at the Shepherd Neame Brewery at Faversham, Kent on 27 Jan 1993. It took 13 minutes to fill the bottle with Kingfisher beer.

Smallest The smallest bottles of liquor now sold are of White Horse Scotch Whisky, which stand just over 5 cm *2 in* high and contain 1.3 ml *22 minims*. A mini case of 12 bottles costs about £8.00, and measures 5.3 × 4.8 × 3.4 cm *2¹⁄₁₆ × 1⅞ × 1¹⁄₁₆ in*. The distributors are Cumbrae Supply Co., Linwood, Strathclyde.

Brewers The oldest brewery in the world is the Weihenstephan Brewery, Freising, near Munich, Germany, founded in AD 1040.

The largest single brewing organization in the world is Anheuser-Busch Inc. of St Louis, Missouri, USA, with 13 breweries in the United States. In 1993 the company sold 10.23 billion litres *2.25 billion gal*, the greatest annual volume ever produced by any brewing company in a year.

The largest brewery on a single site is that of the Coors Brewing Co. at Golden, Colorado, USA, where 2.25 billion litres *495.5 million gal* were produced in 1993. At the same location is the world's largest aluminium can manufacturing plant, with a capacity of more than 5 billion cans annually.

United Kingdom The UK's largest brewing company is Bass Brewers, the brewing company of Bass PLC. In 1993 it sold 8.38 million barrels of beer and had a 23.0 per cent share of the UK beer market. Its Carling Black Label is Britain's top-selling beer.

Distillers The world's most profitable spirits producer is United Distillers, the spirits company of Guinness plc, having made a profit of £701 million in 1993. The largest blender and bottler of Scotch whisky is also United Distillers, whose Shieldhall plant in Glasgow, Strathclyde has the capacity to fill an estimated 144 million bottles of Scotch a year. The world's best-selling brands of Scotch and gin, Johnnie Walker Red Label and Gordon's, are both products of the company.

Most alcoholic drinks When Estonia was independent between the two world wars, the Estonian Liquor Monopoly marketed 98 per cent alcohol distilled from potatoes (196 per cent US proof).

Spirits *Most expensive* A bottle of 50-year-old Glenfiddich whisky was sold for a record price of 99,999,999 lire (approx. £45,200) to an anonymous Italian businessman at a charity auction in Milan, Italy. The postal auction was held over a two-month period from October to December 1992. The most expensive spirit on sale is Springbank 1919 Malt Whisky, a bottle of which costs £6750 (including VAT) at Fortnum & Mason in London.

Vintners The world's oldest champagne firm is Ruinart Père et Fils, founded in 1729. The oldest cognac firm is Augier Frères & Cie, established in 1643.

Wine *Oldest* It is thought that Stone Age man may have been cultivating wine as early as *c.* 8000 BC. Physical evidence of wine dating from as far back as *c.* 3500 BC has been detected in remains of a Sumerian jar found at Godin Tepe, Iran in 1973 during a Royal Ontario Museum expedition. It was only in 1989 that analysis of the remains was carried out, which established that a large red stain showed the presence of tartaric acid, a chemical naturally abundant in grapes.

The oldest bottle of wine to have been sold at auction was a bottle of 1646 Imperial Tokay, which was bought by John A. Chunko of Princeton, New Jersey, USA and Jay Walker of Ridgefield, Connecticut, USA for SFr 1250 (including buyer's premium) at Sotheby's, Geneva, Switzerland on 16 Nov 1984. At the time the sum paid was equivalent to £405.

Most expensive £105,000 was paid for a bottle of 1787 Château Lafite claret, sold to Christopher Forbes (US) at Christie's, London on 5 Dec 1985. The bottle was engraved with the initials of Thomas Jefferson (1743–1826), 3rd President of the United States—'Th J'—a factor which greatly affected the bidding.

The record price for a glass of wine is FF8600 (£982), for the first glass of Beaujolais Nouveau 1993 released in Beaune (from Maison Jaffelin), in the wine region of Burgundy, France. It was bought by Robert Denby at Pickwick's, a British pub in Beaune, on 18 Nov 1993.

Tasting The largest ever reported was that sponsored by WQED, a San Francisco television station, in San Francisco, California, USA on 22 Nov 1986. Some 4000 tasters consumed 9360 bottles of wine.

Soft drinks Pepsico of Purchase, New York, USA topped the *Fortune 500* table for beverage companies in April 1994, with total sales for 1993 of $25.0 billion, compared with $14.0 billion for the Coca-Cola Company of Atlanta, Georgia. Coca-Cola is, however, the world's most popular soft drink, with sales in 1993 of 506 million drinks per day, representing an estimated 46 per cent of the world market.

Manufactured Articles

Basket The world's largest hand-woven basket measures 14.63 × 7.01 × 5.79 m *48 × 23 × 19 ft* and was made by the Longaberger Company of Dresden, Ohio, USA in 1990.

Beer cans William B. Christensen of Madison, new Jersey, USA has a collection of over 75,000 different beer cans from some 125 different countries, colonies and territories.

A Rosalie Pilsner can sold for $6000 in the USA in April 1981. A collection of 2502 unopened bottles and cans of beer from 103 countries was bought for $25,000 by the Downer Club ACT of Australia at the Australian Associated Press Financial Markets Annual Charity Golf Tournament on 23 Mar 1990.

Beer labels (Labology) Jan Solberg of Oslo, Norway has amassed 353,500 different beer labels from around the world to May 1992.

The greatest collection of different British beer labels is 34,429 by Keith Osborne, President of The Labologists' Society (founded by Guinness Exports Ltd in 1958). His oldest is one from Abbott and Son of the Bow Brewery, issued around 1850.

Beer mats (tegestology) The world's largest collection of beer mats is owned by Leo Pisker of Langenzersdorf, Austria, who has collected 140,180 different mats from 159 countries to date. The largest collection of British mats to date is 69,300, owned by Timothy Stannard of Birmingham, W Mids.

One of the brands produced by Anheuser-Busch, Budweiser, is the top-selling beer in the world, with 4.82 billion litres *1.06 billion gal* sold in 1993.

Peter Dowdeswell of Earls Barton, Northants drank a yard of ale (1.42 litres *2½ pints*) in 5.0 sec at RAF Upper Heyford, Oxon on 4 May 1975.

The longest bench in the world, called 'Big Benn', was made by Norimasa Yabuyamada of Toyama, Japan, between April and September 1991. It was 8.97m *29.43ft* long, 74cm *2.43ft* wide and 60cm *1.97ft* high.

Bottle caps Helge Friholm (b. 1909) of Søborg, Denmark has amassed 73,823 different bottle caps from 179 countries since 1950.

Pyramid A pyramid consisting of 362,194 bottle caps was constructed by a team of 11 led by Yevgeniy Lepechov at Chernigov, Kiev, Ukraine from 17–22 Nov 1990.

Can construction A 1:4 scale-model of the Basilica di Sant'Antonio di Padova was built from 3,245,000 empty beverage cans in Padova (Padua), Italy by the charities AMNIUP, AIDO, AVIS and GPDS. The model, measuring 29.15 × 23 × 17.05m *96 × 75 × 56ft*, was completed on 20 Dec 1992 after 20,000 hours.

Chandeliers The world's largest set of chandeliers was created by the Kookje Lighting Co. Ltd of Seoul, South Korea. It is 12m *39ft* high, weighs 10.67 tonnes and has 700 bulbs. Completed in November 1988, it occupies three floors of the Lotte Chamshil Department Store in Seoul.

Britain's largest chandelier measures 9.1m *30ft* and is in the Chinese Room at the Royal Pavilion, Brighton, E Sussex. It was made in 1818 and weighs a ton.

Christmas cracker The largest functional cracker ever constructed was 45.72m *150ft* long and 3.04m *10ft* in diameter. It was made by the international rugby league footballer, Ray Price for Markson Sparks! of New South Wales, Australia and pulled in the car park at Westfield Shopping Town, Chatswood, Sydney, Australia on 9 Nov 1991.

Cigarette cards The largest known cigarette card collection is that of Edward Wharton-Tigar (b. 1913) of London with over 1 million cigarette and trade cards in some 45,000 sets. This collection has been bequeathed to the British Museum, who have agreed to make it available for public study.

Cigarette lighters Frans Van der Heyden of Vlijmen, Netherlands has collected a total of 51,006 different lighters to date.

Credit cards The largest collection of valid credit cards is one of 1384 all different) by Walter Cavanagh (b. 1943) of Santa Clara, California, USA. The cost of acquisition to 'Mr Plastic Fantastic' was nil, but they are worth more than $1.6 million in credit. They are kept in the world's longest wallet—76.2m *250ft* in length and weighing 17.36kg *38lb 4oz*.

The world's longest wedding dress train measured 157m *515ft* and was made by the Hansel and Gretel bridal outfitters of Gunskirchen, Germany in 1992. Britain's longest wedding dress train measured 29.8m *97ft 7¾ in* and was made by Margaret Riley of Thurnby Lodge, Leics for the blessing of the marriage of Diane and Steven Reid in Thurmaston, Leics on 6 May 1990.

Fabrics The oldest surviving fabric, radiocarbon dated to *c.* 7000 BC, was reported in July 1993 to have been discovered in south-eastern Turkey. The semi-fossilized cloth, measuring roughly 76 × 38mm *3 × 1½ in* was believed to be linen.

The most expensive wool fabric is manufactured by Fujii Keori Ltd of Osaka, Japan from bales of Tasmanian Superfine, which retailed at 3 million yen per metre in January 1989.

Fan A hand-painted Spanish fan made of fabric and wood measuring 4.71m *15ft 5¼ in* when unfolded and 2.44m *8ft* high was completed by D. Juan Reolid González of Torrent, Valencia, Spain in June 1991.

Fireworks *Largest* The largest firework ever produced was *Universe I Part II*, exploded for the Lake Toya Festival, Hokkaido, Japan on 15 Jul 1988. The 700-kg *1543-lb* shell was 139cm *54.7in* in diameter and burst to a diameter of 1.2km *0.75 miles*.

Catherine Wheel A self-propelled horizontal firework wheel 14.4m *47ft 4in* wide and built by the Florida Pyrotechnic Arts Guild, was displayed at the Pyrotechnics Guild International Convention in Idaho Falls, Idaho, USA on 14 Aug 1992.

Bottles!

George E. Terren of Southboro, Massachusetts, USA had a collection of 31,804 bottles (miniatures) of distilled spirit and liquor at 31 May 1993.

The record for beer is 3803 unduplicated full bottles from 102 countries collected by Ted Shuler of Germantown, Tennessee, USA. Ron Werner of Bothell, Washington, USA has a collection of 4414 different bottles from 71 countries, but some 2000 are empty.

Claive Vidiz, President of the Brazilian Whisky Collector's Association has a collection of 2301 full original Whisky bottles. He houses them in a specially built museum in São Paulo, Brazil.

The world's physically largest cheque measured 21.36 × 9.58m *70 × 31ft*. It was presented by InterMortgage of Leeds, W Yorks to Yorkshire Television's 1992 Telethon Appeal on 4 Sep 1992 to the value of £10,000.

Dress
A wedding outfit created by Hélène Gainville with jewels by Alexander Reza is estimated to be worth $7,301,587. The dress is embroidered with diamonds mounted on platinum and was unveiled in Paris, France on 23 Mar 1989.

GUESS WHAT?
Q How many cigar boxes can Terry Cole balance on his chin?
A See Page 208

The Big Cover-Up

The world's largest blanket—weighing all of four tonnes and measuring a very comfortable 17,289.8 m² *168,107.8 ft²*—came spilling out of the aircraft hangar at Dishforth, North Yorkshire on Sunday 30 May 1993. Fifty members of the Knitting & Crochet Guild had spent the previous fifty hours stitching together thousands of the six-inch squares and individual blankets which constituted the record breaker; the contributing pieces had, in turn, been knitted by a huge variety of people from knitwear designers to Brownies. The blanket was reduced into manageable sections before being distributed throughout the world by charities.

The record attempt was the result of more than two years of planning and organisation by the Appeal Co-ordinator, Gloria Buckley, who was made a life member of the Knitting and Crochet Guild for her efforts.

Ten girls from Cedar Girls Secondary School in Singapore constructed a can pyramid of 3795 cans in 28 minutes and 53 seconds at Marina City Park, Singapore on 10 Nov 1993, at an event organised by Marina Jaycees of Singapore.

(Photos: Marina Jaycees)

It functioned for 3 min 45 sec. A vertical wheel at the same event, built by Essex Pyrotechnics Ltd of Saffron Walden, Essex, was 13.8 m *45½ ft* in diameter and functioned for 1 min 20 sec.

Flags The world's largest flag, measuring 154×78 m *505×255 ft* and weighing 1.36 tonnes, is the American 'Superflag' owned by 'Ski' Demski of Long Beach, California, USA. It was made by Humphrey's Flag Co. of Pottstown, Pennsylvania and unfurled on 14 Jun 1992.

The largest Union Flag (or Union Jack) measured 73.15×32.91 m *240×108 ft* and was displayed at the Royal Tournament, Earl's Court, London in July 1976. It weighed more than a ton and was made by Form 4Y of Bradley Rowe School, Exeter, Devon.

The largest flag flown from a flagstaff is a Brazilian national flag measuring 70×100 m *229 ft 8 in × 328 ft 1 in* in Brasília.

Garden gnome The earliest recorded garden gnome was one placed in the rockery at Lamport Hall, Northants in 1847 by Sir Charles Isham, Bt

Carol McFadden of Oil City, Pennsylvania, USA has collected 17,122 different pairs of earrings since 1951. She had her ears pierced just two years ago.

(1819–1903) who treated gnomes as if they were real people.

Jigsaw puzzles The earliest jigsaws were made as 'dissected maps' by John Spilsbury (1739–69) in Russell Court off Drury Lane, London c.1762. Enthusiasts call themselves dissectologists.

The world's largest jigsaw puzzle measured 4783 m² *51,484 ft²* and consisted of 43,924 pieces. Assembled on 8 Jul 1992, it was devised by Centre Socio-Culturel d'Endoume in Marseille, France and was designed on the theme of the environment.

A puzzle consisting of 204,484 pieces was made by BCF Holland b.v. of Almelo, Netherlands and assembled by students of the local Gravenvoorde

School on 25 May–1 June 1991. The completed puzzle measured 96.25 m² *1036 ft²*.

Custom-made Stave puzzles of 2640 pieces, created by Steve Richardson of Norwich, Vermont, USA, cost $8680 in June 1992.

Kettle The largest antique copper kettle was one standing 0.9 m *3 ft* high with a 1.8 m *6 ft* girth and a 90 litre *20 gal* capacity, built in Taunton, Somerset, for the hardware merchants Fisher and Son c. 1800.

Knife The penknife with the greatest number of blades is the Year Knife made by cutlers Joseph Rodgers & Sons, of Sheffield, S Yorks, whose trademark was granted in 1682. The knife was made in 1822 with 1822 blades and a blade was added every year until 1973 when there was no further space. It was acquired by Britain's largest hand tool manufacturers, Stanley Works (Great Britain) Ltd of Sheffield, S Yorks, in 1970.

Matchbox labels Teiichi Yoshizawa (b. 1904) of Chiba-Ken, Japan has amassed 743,512 different matchbox labels (including advertising labels) from over 130 countries since 1925. Phillumenist Robert Jones of Indianapolis, USA has a collection of some 280,000 (excluding advertising labels).

Matchstick model Joseph Sciberras of Malta constructed an exact replica, including the interior, of St. Publius Parish Church, Floriana, Malta consisting of over 3 million matchsticks. Made to scale, the model measures $2 \times 2 \times 1.5$ m *6½ × 6½ × 5 ft.*

Pens The most expensive writing pen is the 5003.002 Caran D'Ache 18-carat solid gold Madison slimline ballpoint pen incorporating white diamonds of 6.35 carats, exclusively distributed by Jakar International Ltd of London. Its recommended retail price in 1995 is £27,500 (incl. VAT).

A Japanese collector paid 1.3 million French francs in Feb 1988 for the 'Anémone' fountain pen made by Réden,

Litter Bin!

The world's largest bin was made by Natsales of Durban, South Africa for 'Keep Durban Beautiful Association Week' from 16–22 Sep 1991. Made of fibre glass, the bin is 6.01m *19 ft 9 in* tall and is a replica of the standard Natsales make with a capacity of 43,507 litres *9570 gal.*

France. It was encrusted with 600 precious stones, including emeralds, amethysts, rubies, sapphires and onyx, and took skilled craftsmen over a year to complete.

Pottery The largest thrown vase on record is one measuring 5.34m *17 ft 6 in* in height (including a 1.30-m *4-ft-3-in*-tall lid), weighing 600 kg *1322 lb 12 oz*. It was completed on 1 Jun 1991 by Faiarte Ceramics of Rustenberg, South Africa. The Chinese ceramic authority Chingwah Lee of San Francisco, California, USA was reported in August 1978 to have appraised a unique 99-cm *39-in* Kangxi four-sided vase at $60 million.

Quilt The world's largest quilt was made by 7000 citizens of North Dakota for the 1989 centennial of North Dakota. It measured 25.9 × 40.8 m *85 × 134 ft.*

The largest patchwork quilt made in the UK measured 15.24 × 28.3 m *50 ft × 92 ft 10 in* and was completed on 14 Aug 1990 by residents of Anchor Housing Association sheltered schemes throughout the country.

Scarf The longest scarf ever knitted measured 32 km *20 miles* long. It was made by residents of Abbeyfield Houses for the Abbeyfield Society of Potters Bar, Herts and was completed on 29 May 1988.

Shoes Emperor Field Marshal Jean Fedor Bokassa of the Central African Empire (now Republic) commissioned pearl-studded shoes at a cost of $85,000 from the House of Berluti, Paris, France for his self-coronation at Bangui on 4 Dec 1977.

Silver The largest single pieces of silver are a pair of water jugs of 242.7 kg *10,408 troy oz* (4.77 cwt) made by Gorind Narain in 1902 for the Maharaja of Jaipur (1861–1922). They are 1.6 m *5 ft 3 in* tall, 2.48 m *8 ft 1½ in* in circumference and have a

capacity of 8182 litres *1800 gal*. They are now in the City Palace, Jaipur, India.

Sofa The longest standard marketed sofa is the Augustus Rex, 3.74 m *12 ft 3 in* long, made by Dodge & Son of Sherborne, Dorset. The retail price in 1994 was £1850 plus 25 m *82 ft* of fabric of the customer's choice.

In April 1990 a jacquard fabric sofa 6.63 m *21 ft 9 in* long, with an estimated value of $8000 was specially manufactured by Mountain View Interiors of Collingwood, Ontario, Canada.

Table The longest table was set up in Pesaro, Italy on 20 Jun 1988 by the US Libertas Scavolini Basketball team. It was 3070 m *3357 yd* in length and was used to seat 12,000 people.

Tapestry and embroidery The largest tapestry ever woven is the *History of Iraq*, with an area of 1242.1 m² *13,370.7 ft²*. It was designed by the artist Frane Delale and produced by the Zivtex Regeneracija Workshop in Zabok, Yugoslavia. Completed in 1986, it now adorns the wall of an amphitheatre in Baghdad, Iraq.

Britain's largest single tapestry is *Christ in Glory* which measures 22.77 × 11.59 m *74 ft 8 × 38 ft* and weighs just over 1 tonne. It was designed by Graham Vivian Sutherland (1903–80) for an altar-hanging in Coventry Cathedral, W Midlands and made by 12 weavers at Pinton Frères of Felletin, France in two years. It cost £10,500 and was delivered on 1 Mar 1962 for the consecration of the cathedral on 25 May.

Longest scenic tapestry The famous Bayeux hanging *Telle du Conquest, dite tapisserie de la reine Mathilde*, depicting events of 1064–66 in 72 scenes is 70.40 m *231 ft* long, 49.5 cm *19½ in* wide and was probably worked in Canterbury, Kent, *c.* 1086. It was 'lost' for 2½ centuries from 1476 until 1724.

Longest stuffed toy
A stuffed snake measuring 312.1 m *1023.95 ft* was completed in October 1993 by parents, staff and children of Bucknell C.E. Primary School, Shrops.

Embroidery
An embroidery 20.3 cm *8 in* deep and 407.82 m *1338 ft* long depicting scenes from C.S. Lewis's *Narnia* children's stories was made by Margaret S. Pollard of Truro, Cornwall to the order of Michael Maine. Its total area is about 82 m² *937 ft²*.

Ties A collection of 10,453 ties accumulated by Bill McDaniel of Santa Maria, California, USA was sold to a museum in St Augustine, Florida in 1992.

Wallet The worst wallet to have had stolen is a platinum-cornered, diamond-studded crocodile creation made by Louis Quatorze of Paris and Mikimoto of Tokyo which sold in September 1984 for £56,000.

Yo-yo A yo-yo measuring 3.17 m *10 ft 4 in* in diameter and weighing 407 kg *897 lb* was devised by J.N. Nichols (Vimto) Ltd and made by engineering students at Stockport College. It was launched by crane from 57.5 m *187 ft* at Wythenshawe, Manchester on 1 Aug 1993 and yo-yoed about four times.

Zip-fastener The world's longest zip-fastener was laid around the centre of Sneek, Netherlands on 5 Sep 1989. The brass zipper, made by Yoshida (Netherlands) Ltd, is 2851 m *9353.56 ft* long and consists of 2,565,900 teeth.

ON THE RECORD

On 18 Oct 1994, I shall have been collecting ties for 67 years, and have enjoyed every minute of it. My last count was 7445. I get my ties from many sources: tie clubs or fan clubs, famous people I met in the forces overseas during the war, and many great artists I have met in the *Barton Arms*, after they had performed at the famous Aston Hippodrome. My proudest day was on 29 Sep 1993 when I was invited by the President of the British Tie Guild to receive the honorary title of 'Grabatologist', and also the award of a gold and silver-plated salver, fully engraved. The new-found title of 'Grabatologist', a word with Greek origins, was the first ever awarded, and it is now awaiting entry into the official Oxford Dictionary. I have many favourite ties, but I have always treasured a tie given to me by Dante the magician in 1935. It was made in 1920 by Maccalsfield of Lancs, and was known as the Maccalsfield Long Scarf. I suppose a tie connecting me to the great *Guinness Book of Records* would to me be the greatest tie of them all!

The UK's champion grabatologist, Tom Holmes of Walsall, W Mids, who has collected 7445 different ties since 1928.

(Photos: Rex Features/Nils Jorgensen)

Sports and Games

General Records

Fastest The fastest projectile speed in any moving ball game is *c.* 302km/h *188mph* in pelota. This compares with 273km/h *170mph* (electronically timed) for a driven golf ball.

Largest playing field For any ball game, the largest playing field is 12.4 acres *5ha* for polo, or a maximum length of 300yd *274m* and a width, without side boards, of 200yd *182m*. With boards the width is 160yd *146m*.

Twice a year in the Parish of St Columb Major, Cornwall, a game called hurling (not to be confused with the Irish game) is played on a 'pitch', which consists of the entire parish, approximately 25 square miles *64.7km²*.

World record breakers *Youngest* The youngest at which anybody has broken a non-mechanical world record is 12yr 298 days for Gertrude Caroline Ederle (USA) (b. 23 Oct 1906) with 13min 19.0sec for women's 880yd freestyle swimming at Indianapolis, USA on 17 Aug 1919.

Oldest Gerhard Weidner (West Germany) (b. 15 Mar 1933) set a 20-mile walk record on 25 May 1974, aged 41yr 71 days, the oldest to set an official world record, open to all ages, recognized by an international governing body.

Most prolific Between 24 Jan 1970 and 1 Nov 1977 Vasiliy Alekseyev (USSR) (b. 7 Jan 1942) broke 80 official world records in weightlifting.

Champion *Youngest* The youngest successful competitor in a world title event was a French boy, whose name is not recorded, who coxed the Netherlands' Olympic pair at Paris on 26 Aug 1900. He was not more than ten and may have been as young as seven.

Fu Mingxia (China) (b. 16 Aug 1978) won the women's world title for platform diving at Perth, Australia on 4 Jan 1991, at the age of 12yr 141 days.

The youngest individual Olympic winner was Marjorie Gestring (USA) (b. 18 Nov 1922), who took the springboard diving title at the age of 13yr 268 days at the Olympic Games in Berlin on 12 Aug 1936.

Oldest Fred Davis (b. 14 Feb 1913) won (and retained) the world professional billiards title in 1980, aged 67.

Oldest competitor at major games William Edward Pattimore (b. 1 Mar 1892) competed for Wales at bowls at the 1970 Commonwealth Games in Edinburgh at the age of 78, the oldest competitor at such an international event open to competitors of all ages.

Britain's oldest Olympian was Hilda Lorna Johnstone (1902–90) who was 70yr 5 days when she was placed twelfth in the Dressage competition at the 1972 Olympic Games.

Most versatile Charlotte 'Lottie' Dod (1871–1960) won the Wimbledon singles tennis title five times between 1887 and 1893, the British Ladies' Golf Championship in 1904, an Olympic silver medal for archery in 1908, and represented England at hockey in 1899. She also excelled at skating and tobogganing.

Mildred 'Babe' Zaharias (*née* Didrikson) (1914–56) (USA) won two gold medals (80m hurdles and javelin) and a silver (high jump) at the 1932 Olympic Games. She set world records at those three events in 1930–2. She was an All-American basketball player for three years and set the world record for throwing the baseball 90.22m *296ft*. Switching to golf she won the US Women's Amateur title in 1946 and the US Women's Open in 1948, 1950 and 1954. She also excelled at several other sports.

Charles Burgess Fry (GB) (1872–1956) was perhaps the most versatile male sportsman at the highest level. On 4 Mar 1893 he equalled the world long jump record of 7.17m *23ft 6½in.* He represented England *v.* Ireland at soccer (1901) and played first-class rugby for the Barbarians. His greatest achievements, however, were at cricket, where he headed the English batting averages in six seasons and captained England in 1912. He was also an excellent angler and tennis player.

Longest reign Jacques Edmond Barre (France) (1802–73) was a world champion for 33 years (1829–62) at real tennis. Although archer Alice Blanche Legh (1855–1948) did not compete every year, she was a British champion for a span of 41 years (1881–1922), during which she won 23 national titles, the last when she was aged 67.

Largest crowd The greatest number of live spectators for any sporting spectacle is the estimated 2,500,000 who have lined the route of the New York Marathon. However, spread over three weeks, it is estimated that more than 10,000,000 see the annual *Tour de France* cycling race.

Stadium A crowd of 199,854 attended the Brazil *v.* Uruguay soccer match, in the Maracaña Municipal Stadium, Rio de Janeiro, Brazil on 16 Jul 1950.

Most participants On 15 May 1988 an estimated 110,000 runners (including unregistered athletes) ran in the Examiner Bay to Breakers 12.2km *7.6 mile* race in San Francisco, California, USA.

The 1988 Women's International Bowling Congress Championship tournament attracted 77,735 bowlers for the 96-day event held 31 March–4 July at Reno/Carson City, Nevada, USA.

Worst disasters In recent history, the stands at the Hong Kong Jockey Club racecourse collapsed and caught fire on 26 Feb 1918, killing an estimated 604 people.

During the reign of Antoninus Pius (AD 138–161), 1112 spectators were quoted as being killed when the upper wooden tiers in the Circus Maximus, Rome collapsed during a gladiatorial combat.

Britain As a result of overcrowding just after the start of the FA Cup semi-final between Liverpool and Nottingham Forest at the Leppings Lane end of Hillsborough Stadium, Sheffield, S Yorks on 15 Apr 1989, 96 people were killed and 170 injured.

Aerobatics

World Championships Held biennially since 1960 (except 1974), scoring is based on a system originally devised by Col. José Aresti of Spain. The competition consists of a known and unknown compulsory and a free programme.

The men's team competition has been won a record six times by the USSR. Petr Jirmus (Czechoslovakia) is the only man to become world champion twice, in 1984 and 1986. Betty Stewart (USA) won the women's competition in 1980 and 1982.

Lyubov Nemkova (USSR) won a record five medals: first in 1986, second in 1982 and 1984 and third in 1976 and 1978. The oldest ever world champion has been Henry Haigh (USA) (b. 12 Dec 1924), aged 63 in 1988.

British The only medal achieved by Britain has been a bronze in the team event in 1976. The highest individual placing by a Briton is fourth by Neil Williams (1935–77) in 1976.

Inverted flight The duration record is 4hr 38min 10sec by Joann Osterud from Vancouver to Vanderhoof, Canada on 24 Jul 1991.

Loops Joann Osterud achieved 208 outside loops in a 'Supernova' Hyperbipe over North Bend, Oregon, USA on 13 Jul 1989. On 9 Aug 1986, David Childs performed 2368 inside loops in a Bellanca Decathlon over North Pole, Alaska.

Brian Lecomber completed 180 consecutive inside loops in a Jaguar Extra 230 on 29 Jul 1988 over Plymouth, Devon.

American Football

NFL Records

Championships The Green Bay Packers won a record 11 NFL titles, 1929–31, 1936, 1939, 1944, 1961–2, 1965–7.

Most consecutive wins The record is 18 by: the Chicago Bears (twice), 1933–4 and 1941–2; the Miami Dolphins, 1972–3; and the San Francisco 49ers, 1988–9. The most consecutive games without defeat is 25 by Canton (22 wins and 3 ties) in 1921–3.

Most games played George Blanda (b. 17 Sep 1927) played in a record 340 games in a record 26 seasons in the NFL (Chicago Bears 1949–58, Baltimore Colts 1950, Houston Oilers 1960–66

NFL Records

Most Points

Career	2002	George Blanda (Chicago Bears, Baltimore Colts, Houston Oilers, Oakland Raiders), 1949–75
Season	176	Paul Hornung (Green Bay Packers), 1960
Game	40	Ernie Nevers (Chicago Cardinals) v. Chicago Bears, 28 Nov 1929

Most Touchdowns

Career	126	Jim Brown (Cleveland Browns), 1957–65
Season	24	John Riggins (Washington Redskins), 1983
Game	6	Ernie Nevers (Chicago Cardinals) v. Chicago Bears, 28 Nov 1929
		William Jones (Cleveland Browns) v. Chicago Bears, 25 Nov 1951
		Gale Sayers (Chicago Bears) v. San Francisco 49ers, 12 Dec 1965

Most Yards Gained Rushing

Career	16,726	Walter Payton (Chicago Bears), 1975–88
Season	2105	Eric Dickerson (Los Angeles Rams), 1984
Game	275	Walter Payton (Chicago Bears) v. Minnesota Vikings, 20 Nov 1977

Most Yards Gained Receiving

Career	13,821	James Lofton (Breen Bay Packers, Los Angeles Raiders, Buffalo Bills), 1978–92
Season	1746	Charley Hennigan (Houston Oilers), 1961
Game	336	Willie Anderson (Los Angeles Rams), v. New Orleans Saints, 26 Nov 1989

Most Yards Gained Passing

Career	47,003	Fran Tarkenton (Minnesota Vikings, New York Giants), 1961–78
Season	5084	Dan Marino (Miami Dolphins), 1984
Game	554	Norm Van Brocklin (Los Angeles Rams) v. New York Yanks, 28 Sep 1951

Most Passes Completed

Career	3686	Fran Tarkenton (Minnesota Vikings, New York Giants), 1961–78
Season	404	Warren Moon (Houston Oilers), 1991
Game	42	Richard Todd (New York Jets) v. San Francisco 49ers, 21 Sep 1980

Pass Receptions

Career	847	Art Monk (Washington Redskins), 1980–92
Season	112	Sterling Sharp (Green Bay Packers), 1993
Game	18	Tom Fears (Los Angeles Rams) v. Green Bay Packers, 3 Dec 1950

Field Goals

Career	373	Jan Stenerud (Kansas City Chiefs, Green Bay Packers, Minnesota Vikings), 1967–85
Season	35	Ali Haji-Sheikh (New York Giants), 1983
Game	7	Jim Bakken (St Louis Cardinals), v. Pittsburgh Steelers, 24 Sep 1967
		Rich Karlis (Minnesota Vikings) v. Los Angeles Rams, 5 Nov 1989
Longest	63	Tom Dempsey (New Orleans Saints) v. Detroit Lions, 8 Nov 1970

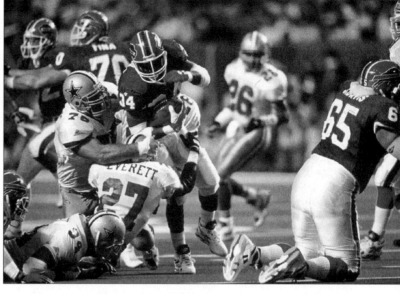

Despite losing in the Super Bowl for the third straight year, some Buffalo Bills players could take consolation from record breaking performances. The most notable of these was Thurman Thomas (No. 34) who scored a record-tying fourth career touchdown.
(Photo: Allsport/Stephen Dunn)

Longest pass completion A pass completion of 99yd has been achieved on six occasions and has always resulted in a touchdown. The most recent was a pass from Ron Jaworski (b. 23 Mar 1951) to Mike Quick (b. 14 May 1959) of the Philadelphia Eagles against the Atlanta Falcons on 10 Nov 1985.

Super Bowl

First held in 1967 between the winners of the NFL and the AFL. Since 1970 it has been contested by the winners of the National and American Conferences of the NFL.

The most wins is four by the Pittsburgh Steelers, 1975–6, 1979–80; the San Francisco 49ers, 1982, 1985, 1989–90 and the Dallas Cowboys, 1972, 1978, 1993–4.

The highest team score and record victory margin was when the San Francisco 49ers beat the Denver Broncos 55–10 at New Orleans, Louisiana on 28 Jan 1990. The highest aggregate score was in 1993 when the Dallas Cowboys beat the Buffalo Bills 52–17. In their 42–10 victory over the Denver Broncos on 31 Jan 1988, the Washington Redskins scored a record 35 points in the second quarter.

On 13 Nov 1993 Don Francis Shula (b. 4 Jan 1930) became the most successful coach in NFL history, as a win by the Miami Dolphins was his 325th, passing the previous mark set by George Halas. Shula had started with the Baltimore Colts in 1963 and moved to Miami in 1970.
(Photo: Allsport/Caryn Levy)

and Oakland Raiders 1967–75). The most consecutive games played is 282 by Jim Marshall (Cleveland Browns 1960 and Minnesota Vikings 1961–79).

Longest run from scrimmage Tony Dorsett (b. 7 Apr 1954) scored on a touchdown run of 99yd for the Dallas Cowboys v. the Minnesota Vikings on 3 Jan 1983.

Super Bowl Game & Career Records

POINTS	18	Roger Craig (San Francisco 49ers)	1985
		Jerry Rice (San Francisco 49ers)	1990
Career	24	Franco Harris (Pittsburgh Steelers)	1975–6, 1979–80
		Roger Craig	1985, 1989–90
		Jerry Rice	1989–90
		Thurman Thomas (Buffalo Bills)	1990–94
TOUCHDOWNS	3	Roger Craig	1985
		Jerry Rice	1990
Career	4	Franco Harris	1975–6, 1979–80
		Roger Craig	1985, 1990
		Jerry Rice	1989–90
		Thurman Thomas	1990–94
TOUCHDOWN PASSES	5	Joe Montana (San Francisco 49ers)	1990
Career	11	Joe Montana	1982, 1985, 1989–90
YDS GAINED PASSING	357	Joe Montana	1989
Career	1142	Joe Montana	1982, 1985, 1989–90
YDS GAINED RECEIVING	215	Jerry Rice	1989
Career	364	Lynn Swann (Pittsburgh Steelers)	1975–6, 1979–80
YDS GAINED RUSHING	204	Timmy Smith (Washington Redskins)	1988
Career	354	Franco Harris	1975–6, 1979–80
PASSES COMPLETED	31	Jim Kelly (Buffalo Bills)	1994
Career	83	Joe Montana	1982, 1985, 1989–90
PASS RECEPTIONS	11	Dan Ross (Cincinnati Bengals)	1982
		Jerry Rice	1989
Career	27	Andre Reed (Buffalo Bills)	1990–94
FIELD GOALS	4	Don Chandler (Green Bay Packers)	1968
		Ray Wersching (San Francisco 49ers)	1982
Career	5	Ray Wersching	1982, 1985
MOST VALUABLE PLAYER	3	Joe Montana	1982, 1985, 1990

Other Records

Highest team score Georgia Tech, Atlanta, Georgia scored 222 points, including a record 32 touchdowns, against Cumberland University, Lebanon, Tennessee (nil) on 7 Oct 1916.

Angling

Oldest existing club The Ellem fishing club was formed by a number of Edinburgh and Berwickshire gentlemen in Scotland in 1829. Its first annual general meeting was held on 29 Apr 1830.

Largest single catch The largest officially ratified fish ever caught on a rod was a man-eating great white shark

Fisheries!

The record for a single trawler is £278,798 from a 37,897-tonne catch by the Icelandic vessel *Videy* at Hull, Humberside on 11 Aug 1987. The greatest catch ever recorded from a single throw is 2471 tonnes by the purse seine-net boat M/S *Flømann* from Hareide, Norway in the Barents Sea on 28 Aug 1986. It was estimated that more than 120 million fish were caught in this shoal.

(Carcharodon carcharias) weighing 1208 kg *2664 lb* and measuring 5.13 m *16 ft 10 in* long, caught on a 59 kg *130 lb* test line by Alf Dean at Denial Bay, near Ceduna, South Australia on 21 Apr 1959. A great white shark weighing 1537 kg *3388 lb* was caught by Clive Green off Albany, Western Australia on 26 Apr 1976 but will remain unratified as whale meat was used as bait.

The biggest ever rod-caught fish by a British angler is a 620 kg *1366 lb* great white shark, by Vic Samson at The Pales, South Australia on 8 Apr 1989.

In June 1978 a great white shark measuring 6.2 m *20 ft 4 in* in length and weighing over 2268 kg *5000 lb* was harpooned and landed by fishermen in the harbour of San Miguel, Azores.

World Freshwater Championship The *Confédération Internationale de la Pêche Sportive* (CIPS) championships were inaugurated as European championships in 1953 and recognized as World championships in 1957.

France won the European title in 1956 and 12 world titles between 1959 and 1990. Robert Tesse (France) took the individual title a record three times, 1959–60, 1965.

The record weight (team) is 34.71 kg *76.52 lb* in 3 hr by West Germany on the Neckar at Mannheim, Germany on 21 Sep 1980. The individual record is 16.99 kg *37.45 lb* by Wolf-Rüdiger Kremkus (West Germany) at Mannheim on 20 Sep 1980. The most fish caught is 652 by Jacques Isenbaert (Belgium) at Danaújváros, Hungary on 27 Aug 1967.

Fly fishing World fly fishing championships were inaugurated by the CIPS in 1981. The most team titles is five by Italy, 1982–4, 1986, 1992. The most individual titles is two by Brian Leadbetter (GB), 1987 and 1991.

Casting The longest freshwater cast ratified under ICF (International Casting Federation) rules is 175.01 m *574 ft 2 in* by Walter Kummerow (West Germany), for the Bait Distance Double-Handed 30 g event held at Lenzerheide, Switzerland in the 1968 Championships. The British national record is 148.78 m *488 ft 1 in* by Andy Dickison on the same occasion.

At the currently contested weight of 17.7 g, known as 18 g Bait Distance, the longest Double-Handed cast is 139.31 m *457 ft ½ in* by Kevin Carriero (USA) at Toronto, Canada on 24 Jul 1984. The British national records are: Fixed spool reel, 138.79 m *455 ft 3 in* by Hugh Newton at Peterborough, Cambs on 21 Sep 1985; and Multiplier reel, 108.97 m *357 ft 6 in* by James Tomlinson at Torrington, Devon on 27 Apr 1985.

The longest Fly Distance Double-Handed cast is 97.28 m *319 ft 1 in* by Wolfgang Feige (West Germany) at Toronto, Canada on 23 Jul 1984. Hywel Morgan set a British national record of 91.22 m *299 ft 2 in* at Torrington, Devon on 27 Apr 1985.

The UK Surfcasting Federation record (150 g *5¼ oz* weight) is 257.32 m *844 ft 3 in* by Neil Mackellow at Peterborough, Cambs on 1 Sep 1985.

World Angling Records; Freshwater and Saltwater

A selection of All-Tackle records ratified by the International Game Fish Association as at January 1994

Species	lb	oz	kg	Name	Location	Date
Barracuda, Great	85	0	38.55	John W. Helfrich	Christmas Island, Kiribati	11 Apr 1992
Bass, Striped	78	8	35.60	Albert R. McReynolds	Atlantic City, New Jersey, USA	21 Sep 1982
Catfish, Flathead	91	4	41.39	Mike Rogers	Lake Lewisville, Texas, USA	28 Mar 1982
Cod, Atlantic	98	12	44.79	Alphonse J. Bielevich	Isle of Shoals, New Hampshire, USA	8 Jun 1969
Halibut, Pacific	368	0	166.92	Celia H. Dueitt	Gustavus, Alaska, USA	5 Jul 1991
Mackerel, King	90	0	40.82	Norton I. Thomton	Key West, Florida, USA	16 Feb 1976
Marlin, Black	1560	0	707.61	Alfred C. Glassell Jr	Cabo Blanco, Peru	4 Aug 1953
Pike, Northern	55	1	25.00	Lothar Louis	Lake of Grefeern, Germany	16 Oct 1986
Sailfish (Pacific)	221	0	100.24	C. W. Stewart	Santa Cruz Island, Ecuador	12 Feb 1947
Salmon, Atlantic	79	2	35.89	Henrik Henriksen	Tana River, Norway	1928
Shark, Hammerhead	991	0	449.50	Allen Ogle	Sarasota, Florida, USA	30 May 1982
Shark, Porbeagle	507	0	230.00	Christopher Bennett	Pentland Firth, Caithness	9 Mar 1993
Shark, Thresher	802	0	363.80	Dianne North	Tutukaka, New Zealand	8 Feb 1981
Shark, White	2664	0	1208.38	Alfred Dean	Ceduna, South Australia	21 Apr 1959
Snook	53	10	24.32	Gilbert Ponzi	Parasmina Ranch, Costa Rica	18 Oct 1978
Sturgeon, White	468	0	212.28	Joey Pallotta III	Benicia, California, USA	9 Jul 1983
Swordfish	1182	0	536.15	L. Marron	Iquique, Chile	17 May 1953
Trout, Brook	14	8	6.57	Dr W. J. Cook	Nipigon River, Ontario, Canada	July 1916
Trout, Brown	40	4	18.25	Howard L. Collins	Heber Springs, Arkansas, USA	9 May 1992
Trout, Lake	66	8	30.16	Rodney Harback	Great Bear Lake, NWT, Canada	19 Jul 1991
Trout, Rainbow	42	2	19.10	David Robert White	Bell Island, Alaska, USA	22 Jun 1970
Tuna, Bluefin	1496	0	679.00	Ken Fraser	Aulds Cove, Nova Scotia, Canada	26 Oct 1979
Tuna, Yellowfin	388	12	176.35	Curt Wiesenhutter	San Benedicto Island, Mexico	1 Apr 1977
Wahoo	155	8	70.53	William Bourne	San Salvador, Bahamas	3 Apr 1990

IGFA!

The International Game Fish Association (IGFA) recognizes world records for a large number of species of game fish (both freshwater and saltwater). Their thousands of categories include all-tackle, various line classes and tippet classes for fly fishing. New records recognized by the IGFA reached an annual peak of 1074 in 1984.

The heaviest freshwater category recognized is for the sturgeon—record weight of 212.28 kg *468 lb* caught by Joey Pallotta on 9 Jul 1983 off Benicia, California, USA.

British Angling Records

COARSE FISH: A selection of those fish recognized by the National Association of Specialist Anglers

Species	lb	oz	dr	kg	Name of Angler	Location	Date
Barbel	15	11	–	7.116	A. Harman	Southern river	1993
Bleak		4	4	0.120	B. Derrington	River Monnow, Wye Mouth	1982
Bream (Common, Bronze)	16	9	–	7.512	M. McKeown	Southern water	1991
Bream, Silver		15	–	0.425	D. E. Flack	Grime Spring, Lakenheath, Suffolk	1988
Carp	51	8	–	23.358	C. Yates	Redmire Pool, Herefordshire	1980
Carp, Grass	25	4	–	11.453	D. Buck	Honeycroft Fisheries, Canterbury, Kent	1993
Catfish (Wells)	49	14	–	22.623	S. Poyntz	Homersfield Lake, Norwich, Norfolk	1993
Chub	8	4	–	3.743	G. F. Smith	Royalty Fishery, Hampshire Avon	1913
Dace	1	4	4	0.574	J. L. Gasson	Little Ouse, Thetford, Norfolk	1960
Eel	11	2	–	5.046	S. Terry	Kingfisher Lake, Ringwood, Hants	1978
Gudgeon		5	–	0.141	D. Hall	River Nadder, Salisbury, Wilts	1990
Perch	5	9	–	2.523	J. Shayler	Private water, Kent	1985
Pike	46	13	–	21.236	R. Lewis	Llandefgfedd Reservoir, Pontypool, Gwent	1992
Roach	4	3	–	1.899	R. N. Clarke	Dorset Stour	1990
Tench	14	7	–	6.548	G. Bevan	Southern stillwater	1993
Zander (Pikeperch)	18	10	–	8.448	D. Litton	Cambridge stillwater	1988

FRESHWATER GAME FISH:

Species	lb	oz	dr	kg	Name of Angler	Location	Date
Salmon	64	–	–	29.03	Miss G. W. Ballantine	River Tay, Scotland	1922
Trout, American Brook	5	13	8	2.65	A. Pearson	Avington Fishery, Hants	1981
Trout, Brown	19	9	4	8.88	J. A. F. Jackson	Loch Quoich, Inverness	1978
Trout, Rainbow	24	2	13	10.96	J. Moore	Pennine Trout Fishery, Littleborough, Lancs	1990
Trout, Sea	22	8	–	10.20	S. Burgoyne	River Leven	1989

Archery

Oldest club The oldest archery body in the British Isles is the Society of Archers in Yorkshire, formed on 14 May 1673, though the Society of Kilwinning Archers, in Scotland, has contested the Pa-pingo Shoot since 1488.

World Championships The most titles won by a man is four by Hans Deutgen (Sweden) (1917–89) in 1947–50, and the most by a woman is seven by Janina Spychajowa-Kurkowska (Poland) (1901–79) in 1931–4, 1936, 1939 and 1947. The USA has a record 14 men's and 8 women's team titles.

Olympic Games Hubert van Innis (Belgium) (1866–1961) won six gold and three silver medals at the 1900 and 1920 Olympic Games.

British Championships The most titles is 12 by Horace Alfred Ford (1822–80) in 1849–59 and 1867, and 23 by Alice Blanche Legh (1855–1948) in 1881, 1886–92, 1895, 1898–1900, 1902–9, 1913 and 1921–2. Miss Legh was inhibited from winning from 1882 to 1885– because her mother was champion–and for four further years 1915–18 because there were no Championships during World War I.

British records York round–possible 1296 pts: Single round, 1190 Steven Hallard (b. 22 Feb 1965); Double round, 2284 Steven Hallard.

Hereford (Women)–possible 1296 pts: Single round, 1206 Pauline Edwards (b. 23 Apr 1949); Double round, 2380 Joanne Franks (later Edens) (b. 1 Oct 1967) at the British Target Championships on 8 Sep 1987.

FITA round (Men): Single round, 1314 Steven Hallard; Double round, 2616 Steven Hallard, both at Lausanne, Switzerland in July 1989.

FITA round (Women): Single round, 1323 Alison Williamson (b. 3 Nov 1971) at the Olympics at Barcelona, Spain in August 1992; Double round, 2591 Alison Williamson at Belgian FITA Star on 5 Jun 1989.

24 hours–target archery The highest recorded score over 24 hours by a pair of archers is 76,158 during 70 Portsmouth Rounds (60 arrows per round at 20yd at 60cm FITA targets) by Simon Tarplee and David Hathaway at Evesham, Worcs on 1 Apr 1991. During this attempt Simon Tarplee set an individual record of 38,500.

> Gary Sentman, of Roseberg, Oregon, USA drew a longbow weighing a record 79.83kg *176lb* to the maximum draw on the arrow of 72cm *28¼in* at Forksville, Pennsylvania, USA on 20 Sep 1975.

Athletics

Fastest speed An analysis of split times at each 10 metres in the 1988 Olympic Games 100m final in Seoul on 24 Sep 1988 won by Ben Johnson (Canada) in 9.79sec (average speed 36.77km/h *22.85mph* but later disallowed as a world record due to his positive drugs test for steroids) from Carl Lewis (USA) 9.92, showed that both Johnson

World Archery Records

MEN (Single FITA rounds)

Event	Pts	Poss	Name and Country	Year
FITA	1354	1440	Han Seung-hoon (South Korea)	1994
90m	330	360	Vladimir Yesheyev (USSR)	1990
70m	344	360	Hiroshi Yamamoto (Japan)	1990
50m	345	360	Richard McKinney (USA)	1982
30m	360	360	Han Seung-hoon (South Korea)	1994
Final	345	360	Vladimir Yesheyev (USSR)	1990
Team	3963	4320	USSR (Stanislav Zabrodskiy, Vadim Shikarev, Vladimir Yesheyev)	1989
Final	1005	1080	South Korea (Kim Sun-bin, Yang Chang-hoon, Park Jae-pyo)	1990

WOMEN (Single FITA rounds)

Event	Pts	Poss	Name and Country	Year
FITA	1375	1440	Cho Youn-jeong (South Korea)	1992
70m	*341	360	Kim Soo-nyung (South Korea)	1990
	338	360	Cho Youn-jeong (South Korea)	1992
60m	347	360	Kim Soo-nyung (South Korea)	1989
50m	340	360	Lim Jung (South Korea)	1994
30m	357	360	Joanne Edens (GB)	1990
Final	346	360	Kim Soo-nyung (South Korea)	1990
Team	4025	4320	South Korea (Kim Soo-nyung, Wang Hee-nyung, Kim Kyung-wook)	1989
Final	1030	1080	South Korea (Kim Soo-nyung, Lee Eun-kyung Lee Seon-hee)	1991

*unofficial

Indoor Double FITA rounds at 25m

Men	591	600	Erwin Verstegen (Holland)	1989
Women	592	600	Petra Ericsson (Sweden)	1991

Indoor FITA round at 18m

Men	591	600	Vladimir Yesheyev (USSR)	1989
Women	587	600	Denise Parker (USA)	1989

and Lewis reached a peak speed (40m–50m and 80m–90m respectively) of 0.83sec for 10m, i.e. 43.37 km/h *26.95mph*. In the women's final Florence Griffith-Joyner was timed at 0.91sec for each 10m from 60m to 90m, i.e. 39.56km/h *24.58mph*.

Highest jump above own head The greatest height cleared above an athlete's own head is 59cm *23¼in* by Franklin Jacobs (USA) (b. 31 Dec 1957), 1.73m *5ft 8in* tall, who jumped 2.32m *7ft 7¼in* at New York, USA, on 27 Jan 1978. The greatest height cleared by a woman above her own head is 32cm *12¾in* by Yolanda Henry (USA) (b. 2 Dec 1964), 1.68m *5ft 6in* tall, who jumped 2.00m *6ft 6¾in* at Seville, Spain on 30 May 1990.

Most Olympic titles The most Olympic gold medals won is ten (an absolute Olympic record) by Raymond Clarence Ewry (USA) (1873–1937) in the standing high, long and triple jumps in 1900, 1904, 1906 and 1908.

Women The most gold medals won by a woman is four shared by: Francina 'Fanny' Elsje Blankers-Koen (Netherlands) (b. 26 Apr 1918) 100m, 200m, 80m hurdles and 4×100m relay, 1948; Elizabeth 'Betty' Cuthbert (Australia) (b. 20 Apr 1938) 100m, 200m, 4×100m relay, 1956 and

400m, 1964; Bärbel Wöckel (*née* Eckert) (GDR) (b. 21 Mar 1955) 200m and 4×100m relay in 1976 and 1980; and Evelyn Ashford (USA) (b. 15 Apr 1957) 100m and 4×100m relay in 1984, 1988 and 1992.

Most wins at one Games The most gold medals at one celebration is five by Paavo Johannes Nurmi (Finland) (1897–1973) in 1924; 1500m, 5000m, 10,000m cross-country, 3000m team and cross-country team. The most at individual events is four by Alvin Christian Kraenzlein (USA) (1876–1928) in 1900: 60m, 110m hurdles, 200m hurdles and long jump.

Most Olympic medals The most medals won is 12 (nine gold and three silver) by Paavo Nurmi (Finland) in the Games of 1920, 1924 and 1928.

Women The most medals won by a woman athlete is seven by Shirley Barbara de la Hunty (*née* Strickland) (Australia) (b. 18 Jul 1925) with three gold, one silver and three bronze in the 1948, 1952 and 1956 Games. A re-read of the photo-finish indicates that she finished third, not fourth, in the 1948 200 metres event, thus unofficially increasing her medal haul to eight. Irena Szewinska (*née* Kirszenstein) (Poland) (b. 24 May 1946) won three gold, two silver and two bronze in

GUESS WHAT?

Q How high can a horse jump?

A See Page 250

(Photo: Allsport/Gray Mortimore)

> At the Bislett Games in Oslo in 1993, Yobes Ondieki became the first man to run 10,000m in under 27 minutes. Remarkably this was only the second track 10km of Ondieki's career, his previous effort being 28:25.44 in 1983.

World Records *Men*

World outdoor records for the men's events scheduled by the International Amateur Athletic Federation. Fully automatic electric timing is mandatory for events up to 400 metres.

Running	min:sec	Name and Country	Venue	Date
100 m	9.86*	Frederick Carleton 'Carl' Lewis (USA) (b. 1 Jul 1961)	Tokyo, Japan	25 Aug 1991
200 m	19.72A	Pietro Paolo Mennea (Italy) (b. 28 Jun 1952)	Mexico City, Mexico	12 Sep 1979
400 m	43.29	Harry Lee 'Butch' Reynolds Jr (USA) (b. 8 Aug 1964)	Zürich, Switzerland	17 Aug 1988
800 m	1:41.73	Sebastian Newbold Coe (GB) (b. 29 Sep 1956)	Florence, Italy	10 Jun 1981
1000 m	2:12.18	Sebastian Newbold Coe (GB)	Oslo, Norway	11 Jul 1981
1500 m	3:28.82	Noureddine Morceli (Algeria) (b. 20 Feb 1970)	Rieti, Itlay	6 Sep 1992
1 mile	3:44.39	Noureddine Morceli (Algeria)	Rieti, Italy	5 Sep 1993
2000 m	4:50.81	Said Aouita (Morocco) (b. 2 Nov 1959)	Paris, France	16 Jul 1987
3000 m	7:28.96	Moses Kiptanui (Kenya) (b. 1 Sep 1971)	Cologne, Germany	16 Aug 1992
5000 m	12:56.96	Haile Guebre Selassie (Ethiopia) (b. 18 Apr 1973)	Hengelo, Netherlands	4 Jun 1994
10,000 m	26:58.38	Yobes Ondieki (Kenya) (b. 21 Feb 1961)	Oslo, Norway	10 Jul 1993
20,000 m	56:55.6	Arturo Barrios (Mexico) (b. 12 Dec 1963)	La Flèche, France	30 Mar 1991
25,000 m	1hr 13:55.8	Toshihiko Seko (Japan) (b. 15 Jul 1956)	Christchurch, New Zealand	22 Mar 1981
30,000 m	1hr 29:18.8	Toshihiko Seko (Japan)	Christchurch, New Zealand	22 Mar 1981
1 hour	21,101m	Arturo Barrios (Mexico)	La Flèche, France	30 Mar 1991
110 m hurdles	12.91	Colin Ray Jackson (GB) (b. 18 Feb 1967)	Stuttgart, Germany	20 Aug 1993
400 m hurdles	46.78	Kevin Curtis Young (USA) (b. 6 Sep 1966)	Barcelona, Spain	6 Aug 1992
3000 m s'chase	8:02.08	Moses Kiptanui (Kenya)	Zürich, Switzerland	19 Aug 1992
4×100 m	37.40	USA	Barcelona, Spain	8 Aug 1992
		(Michael Marsh, Leroy Russell Burrell, Dennis A Mitchell, Carl Lewis)		
	37.40	USA	Stuttgart, Germany	21 Aug 1993
		(John A Drummond Jr, Andre Cason, Dennis A Mitchell, Leroy Burrell)		
4×200 m	1:18.68	Santa Monica Track Club (USA)	Walnut, California, USA	17 Apr 1994
		(Michael Marsh, Leroy Burrell, Floyd Wayne Heard, Carl Lewis)		
4×400 m	2:54.29	USA	Stuttgart, Germany	21 Aug 1993
		(Andrew Valmon, Quincy Watts, Harry Reynolds, Michael Duane Johnson)		
4×800 m	7:03.89	Great Britain	Crystal Palace, London	30 Aug 1982
		(Peter Elliott, Garry Peter Cook, Steven Cram, Sebastian Coe)		
4×1500 m	14:38.8	West Germany	Cologne, Germany	17 Aug 1977
		(Thomas Wessinghage, Harald Hudak, Michael Lederer, Karl Fleschen)		

* Ben Johnson (Canada) (b. 30 Dec 1961) ran 100 m in 9.79sec at Seoul, South Korea on 24 Sep 1988, but was subsequently disqualified on a positive drugs test for steroids. He later admitted to having taken drugs over many years, and this invalidated his ratified 9.83sec at Rome, Italy on 30 Aug 1987.
A This record was set at high altitude—Mexico City 2240m 7349ft. Best mark at low altitude: 200m: 19.73sec, Michael Lawrence Marsh (USA) (b. 4 Aug 1967), Barcelona, Spain, 5 Aug 1992.

Field Events	m	ft	in		Venue	Date
High Jump	2.45	8	0½	Javier Sotomayor (Cuba) (b. 13 Oct 1967)	Salamanca, Spain	27 Jul 1993
Pole Vault	6.13	20	1¼	Sergey Nazarovich Bubka (Ukraine) (b. 4 Dec 1963)	Tokyo, Japan	19 Sep 1992
Long Jump	8.95	29	4½	Michael Anthony 'Mike' Powell (USA) (b. 10 Nov 1963)	Tokyo, Japan	30 Aug 1991
Triple Jump	17.97	58	11½	William Augustus 'Willie' Banks (USA) (b. 11 Mar 1956)	Indianapolis, USA	16 Jun 1985
Shot	23.12	75	10¼	Eric Randolph 'Randy' Barnes (USA) (b. 16 Jun 1966)	Los Angeles, California, USA	20 May 1990
Discus	74.08	243	0	Jürgen Schult (GDR) (b. 11 May 1960)	Neubrandenburg, Germany	6 Jun 1986
Hammer	86.74	284	7	Yuriy Georgiyevich Sedykh (USSR) (b. 11 Jun 1955)	Stuttgart, Germany	30 Aug 1986
Javelin	95.66	318	10	Jan Zelezny (Czech Republic) (b. 16 Jun 1966)	Sheffield, S Yorks	29 Aug 1993

Decathlon	8891 points	Dan Dion O'Brien (USA) (b. 18 Jul 1966)	Talence, France	4-5 Sep 1992

Day 1: 100m 10.43sec, LJ 8.08m *26ft 6¼in*, SP 16.69m *54ft 9¼in*, HJ 2.07m *6ft 9½in*, 400m 48.51sec,
Day 2: 110m H 13.98sec, D 2.07m *159ft 4in*, PV 5.00m *16ft 4¼in*, J 62.58m *205ft 4in*, 1500m 4:42.10sec

---

only woman athlete to win a medal in four successive Games.

Most Olympic titles *British* The most gold medals won by a British athlete (excluding tug of war and walking, *q.v.*) is two by: Charles Bennett (1871–1949) (1500m and 5000m team, 1900); Alfred Edward Tysoe (1874–1901) (800m and 5000m team, 1900); John Thomas Rimmer (1879–1962) (4000m steeplechase and 5000m team, 1900); Albert George Hill (1889–1969) (800m and 1500m, 1920); Douglas Gordon Arthur Lowe (1902–81) (800m 1924 and 1928); Sebastian Newbold Coe (b. 29 Sep 1956) (1500m 1980 and 1984) and Francis Morgan 'Daley' Thompson (b. 30 Jul 1958) (decathlon 1980 and 1984). Daley Thompson was also world champion at the decathlon in 1983.

Most Olympic medals *British* The most medals won by a British athlete is four by Guy Montagu Butler (1899–1981) gold for the 4×400m relay and silver for 400m in 1920 and bronze for each of these events in 1924, and by Sebastian Coe, who also won silver medals at 800 m in 1980 and 1984. Three British women athletes have won three medals: Dorothy Hyman (b. 9 May 1941) with a silver (100m, 1960) and two bronze (200m, 1960 and 4 × 100m relay, 1964), Mary Denise Rand (*née* Bignal), (b. 10 Feb 1940) with a gold (long jump), a silver (pentathlon) and a bronze (4 × 100m relay), all in 1964 and Kathryn Jane Cook (*née* Smallwood) (b. 3 May 1960), all bronze–at 4 × 100m relay 1980 and 1984, and at 400m in 1984.

Olympic champions *Oldest and youngest* The oldest athlete to win an Olympic title was Irish-born Patrick Joseph 'Babe' McDonald (*né* McDonnell) (USA) (1878–1954) who was aged 42yr 26days when he won the 25.4kg 56lb weight throw at Antwerp, Belgium on 21 Aug 1920. The oldest female champion was Lia Manoliu (Romania) (b. 25 Apr 1932) aged 36yr 176days when she won the discus at Mexico City on 18 Oct 1968. The youngest gold medallist was Barbara Pearl Jones (USA) (b. 26 Mar 1937)

Merlene Ottey has won a record ten medals at the World Championships but it was not until 1993 that she won her first individual gold.
(Photo: Allsport/Mike Powell)

who at 15yr 123days was a member of the winning 4×100m relay team, at Helsinki, Finland on 27 Jul 1952. The youngest male champion was Robert Bruce Mathias (USA) (b. 17 Nov 1930) aged 17yr 263days when he won the decathlon at the London Games on 5–6 Aug 1948.

The oldest Olympic medallist was Tebbs Lloyd Johnson (GB) (1900–84), aged 48yr 115days when he was third in the 1948 50,000m walk. The oldest woman medallist was Dana Zátopková (Czechoslovakia) (b. 19 Sep 1922) aged 37yr 348days when she was second in the javelin in 1960.

World Championships World Championships, distinct from the Olympic Games, were inaugurated in 1983, when they were held in Helsinki, Finland. The most medals won is ten by Frederick Carleton 'Carl' Lewis (b. 1 Jul 1961), a record eight gold, 100m, long jump and 4×100m relay 1983; 100m, long jump and 4×100m relay 1987; 100m and 4×100m relay 1991; silver at long jump 1991 and bronze at 200m 1993. Lewis has also won eight Olympic golds, 1984–92. The most medals by a women is ten by Merlene Ottey (Jamaica) (b. 10 May 1960) two gold, two silver, six bronze, 1983–93. The most gold medals won by a woman is four by Jackie Joyner-Kersee (USA) (b. 3 Mar 1962) long jump 1987, 1991, heptathlon, 1987, 1993.

Indoor First held as the World Indoor Games in 1985, they are now staged biennially. The most individual titles is four by: Stefka Kostadinova (Bulgaria) (b. 25 Mar 1965) high jump 1985,

1987, 1989, 1993; and Mikhail Shchennikov (Russia) (b. 24 Dec 1967) 5000m walk 1987, 1989, 1991, 1993.

Most participants The most participants at a world championships is 11,475 (9328 men, 2147 women) for the 1993 World Veterans' Athletic Championships at Miyazaki, Japan.

World record breakers *Oldest and youngest* For the greatest age at which anyone has broken a world record under IAAF jurisdiction (⇨ General Records). The female record is 36yr 139days for Marina Styepanova (*née* Makeyeva) (USSR) (b. 1 May 1950) with 52.94 sec for the 400 m hurdles at Tashkent, USSR on 17 Sep 1986. The youngest individual record breaker is Wang

The six days of the Chinese National Games at Beijing in September 1993 were marked by the greatest displays of women's distance running ever seen. On the first day Wang Junxia (right) destroyed Ingrid Kristiasen's world 10,000m record of 30:13.74 by recording 29:31.78. Her last 3000m of this race was run in 8:17.47, well inside the 8:22.62 world record for the distance. That record was improved on day five of the Games, when Zhang Linli ran 8:22.06 and then Wang won her heat with 8:12.19. The next day Wang improved again to 8:06.11. In between these fantastic runs, Wang ran 1500m on the third day in 3:51.96, compared to the world record of 3:52.47 which Tatyana Kazanakina had run 13 years earlier; but Wang finished second to Qu Yunxia, who ran 3:50.46.
(Photo: Allsport/Gary M. Prior)

World Records *Women*

World outdoor records for the women's events scheduled by the International Amateur Athletic Federation plus the new events of pole vault and hammer. Fully automatic electric timing is mandatory for all events up to 400metres.

Running	min:sec	Name and Country	Venue	Date
100 m	10.49	Delorez Florence Griffith Joyner (USA) (b. 21 Dec 1959)	Indianapolis, Indiana, USA	16 Jul 1988
200 m	21.34	Delorez Florence Griffith Joyner (USA)	Seoul, South Korea	29 Sep 1988
400 m	47.60	Marita Koch (GDR) (b. 18 Feb 1957)	Canberra, Australia	6 Oct 1985
800 m	1:53.28	Jarmila Kratochvílová (Czechoslovakia) (b. 26 Jan 1951)	Münich, Germany	26 Jul 1983
1000 m	2:30.6	Tatyana Providokhina (USSR) (b. 26 Mar 1953)	Podolsk, USSR	20 Aug 1978
	2:30.67	Christine Wachtel (GDR) (b. 6 Jan 1965)	Berlin, Germany	17 Aug 1990
1500 m	3:50.46	Qu Yunxia (China) (b. 25 Dec 1972)	Beijing, China	11 Sep 1993
1 mile	4:15.61	Paula Ivan (Romania) (b. 20 Jul 1963)	Nice, France	10 Jul 1989
2000 m	5:28.69	Maricica Puică (Romania) (b. 29 Jul 1950)	Crystal Palace, London	11 Jul 1986
3000 m	8:06.11	Wang Junxia (China) (b. 9 Jan 1973)	Beijing, China	13 Sep 1993
5000 m	14:37.33	Ingrid Kristiansen (*née* Christensen) (Norway) (b. 21 Mar 1956)	Stockholm, Sweden	5 Aug 1986
10,000 m	29:31.78	Wang Junxia (China)	Beijing, China	8 Sep 1993
100 m hurdles	12.21	Yordanka Donkova (Bulgaria) (b. 28 Sep 1961)	Stara Zagora, Bulgaria	20 Aug 1988
400 m hurdles	52.74	Sally Jane Janet Gunnell (GB) (b. 29 Jul 1966)	Stuttgart, Germany	19 Aug 1993
4×100 m	41.37	GDR	Canberra, Australia	6 Oct 1985
		(Silke Gladisch (now Möller), Sabine Rieger (now Günther), Ingrid Auerswald (*née* Brestrich), Marlies Göhr (*née* Oelsner))		
4×200 m	1:28.15	GDR	Jena, Germany	9 Aug 1980
		(Marlies Göhr (*née* Oelsner), Romy Müller (*née* Schneider), Bärbel Wöckel (*née* Eckert), Marita Koch)		
4×400 m	3:15.17	USSR	Seoul, South Korea	1 Oct 1988
		(Tatyana Ledovskaya, Olga Nazarova (*née* Grigoryeva), Maria Pinigina (*née* Kulchunova), Olga Bryzgina (*née* Vladykina))		
4×800 m	7:50.17	USSR	Moscow, USSR	5 Aug 1984
		(Nadezhda Olizarenko (*née* Mushta), Lyubov Gurina, Lyudmila Borisova, Irina Podyalovskaya)		

Field Events	m	ft	in	Name and Country	Venue	Date
High Jump	2.09	6	10¼	Stefka Kostadinova (Bulgaria) (b. 25 Mar 1965)	Rome, Italy	30 Aug 1987
Pole Vault	4.11	13	5¾	Sun Caiyun (China) (b. 21 Jul 1973)	Guangzhou, China	21 Mar 1994
Long Jump	7.52	24	8¼	Galina Chistyakova (USSR) (b. 26 Jul 1962)	Leningrad, USSR	11 Jun 1988
Triple Jump	15.09	49	6	Ana Biryukova (Russia) (*née* Dereyankina) (b. 27 Sep 1967)	Stuttgart, Germany	21 Aug 1993
Shot	22.63	74	3	Natalya Venedictovna Lisovskaya (USSR) (b. 16 Jul 1962)	Moscow, USSR	7 Jun 1987
Discus	76.80	252	0	Gabriele Reinsch (GDR) (b. 23 Sep 1963)	Neubrandenburg, Germany	9 Jul 1988
Hammer	66.84	219	3	Olga Kuzenkova (Russia) (b. 4 Oct 1970)	Sochi, Russia	Feb 1994
Javelin	80.00	262	5	Petra Felke (now Meier) (GDR) (b. 30 Jul 1959)	Potsdam, Germany	9 Sep 1988

Heptathlon	7291 points	Jacqueline Joyner-Kersee (USA) (b. 3 Mar 1962)	Seoul, South Korea	23–24 Sep 1988

100m hurdles 12.69sec; High Jump 1.86m *6ft 1¼in*; Shot Put 15.80m *51ft 10in*; 200m 22.56sec; Long Jump 7.27m *23ft 10¼in*; Javelin 45.66m *149ft 10in*; 800m 2min 08.51sec

World Indoor Records

Track performances around a turn must be made on a track of circumference no longer than 200 metres.

MEN

Running	min:sec		Name and Country	Venue	Date
50 m	5.61*		Manfred Kokot (GDR) (b. 3 Jan 1948)	East Berlin, Germany	4 Feb 1973
	5.61*		James Sanford (USA) (b. 27 Dec 1957)	San Diego, CA, USA	20 Feb 1981
60 m	6.41*		Andre Cason (USA) (b. 13 Jan 1969)	Madrid, Spain	14 Feb 1992
200 m	20.36		Bruno Romal Marie-Rose (France) (b. 20 May 1965)	Liévin, France	22 Feb 1987
400 m	45.02		Danny Joe Everett (USA) (b. 1 Nov 1966)	Stuttgart, Germany	2 Feb 1992
800 m	1:44.84		Paul Ereng (Kenya) (b. 22 Aug 1967)	Budapest, Hungary	4 Mar 1989
1000 m	2:15.26		Noureddine Morceli (Algeria) (b. 20 Feb 1970)	Birmingham, W Mids	22 Feb 1992
1500 m	3:34.16		Noureddine Morceli (Algeria)	Seville, Spain	28 Feb 1991
1 mile	3:49.78		Eamonn Coghlan (Ireland) (b. 21 Nov 1952)	East Rutherford, NJ, USA	27 Feb 1983
3000 m	7:37.31		Moses Kiptanui (Kenya) (b. 1 Sep 1971)	Seville, Spain	20 Feb 1992
5000 m	13:20.4		Suleiman Nyambui (Tanzania) (b. 13 Feb 1953)	New York, USA	6 Feb 1983
50 m hurdles	6.25		Mark McKoy (Canada) (b. 10 Dec 1961)	Kobe, Japan	5 Mar 1986
60 m hurdles	7.30		Colin Jackson (GB) (b. 18 Feb 1967)	Sindelfingen, Germany	6 Mar 1994
4×200 m	1:22.11		United Kingdom	Glasgow, Strathclyde	3 Mar 1991
			(Linford Christie, Darren Braithwaite, Ade Mafe, John Regis)		
4×400 m	3:03.05		Germany	Seville, Spain	10 Mar 1991
			(Rico Lieder, Jens Carlowitz, Karsten Just, Thomas Schönlebe)		
5000 m walk	18:11.41u		Ronald Weigel (GDR) (b. 8 Aug 1959)	Vienna, Austria	13 Feb 1988
	18:15.25		Grigoriy Kornev (Russia) (b. 14 Mar 1961)	Moscow, Russia	7 Feb 1992

Ben Johnson (Canada) (b. 30 Dec 1961) ran 50m in 5.55sec at Ottawa, Cananda on 31 Jan 1987 and 60m in 6.41sec at Indianapolis, USA on 7 Mar 1987, but these were invalidated due to his admission of having taken drugs, following his disqualification at the 1988 Olympics.
u not officially recognised.

Field Events

	m	ft	in	Name and Country	Venue	Date
High Jump	2.43	7	11½	Javier Sotomayor (Cuba) (b. 13 Oct 1967)	Budapest, Hungary	4 Mar 1989
Pole Vault	6.15	20	2¼	Sergey Nazarovich Bubka (Ukraine) (b. 4 Dec 1963)	Donetsk, Ukraine	21 Feb 1993
Long Jump	8.79	28	10¼	Fredrick Carleton 'Carl' Lewis (USA) (b. 1 Jul 1961)	New York, USA	27 Jan 1984
Triple Jump	17.77	58	3½	Leonid Voloshin (Russia) (b. 30 Mar 1966)	Grenoble, France	6 Feb 1994
Shot	22.66	74	4¼	Eric Randolph 'Randy' Barnes (USA) (b. 16 Jun 1966)	Los Angeles, CA, USA	20 Jan 1989

Heptathlon

6476 points ....Dan Dion O'Brien (USA) (b. 18 Jul 1966) ....Toronto, Canada ....13–14 Mar 1993
(60m 6.67 sec; LJ, 7.84 m; SP, 16.02 m; HJ, 2.13 m; 60 m hurdles, 7.85 sec; PV, 5.20 m; 1000 m 2:57.96)

WOMEN

Running	min:sec		Name and Country	Venue	Date
50 m	6.00		Merlene Ottey (Jamaica) (b. 10 May 1960)	Moscow, Russia	4 Feb 1994
60 m	6.92		Irina Privalova (Russia) (b. 12 Nov 1968)	Madrid, Spain	11 Feb 1993
200 m	21.87		Merlene Ottey (Jamaica)	Liévin, France	13 Feb 1993
400 m	49.59		Jarmila Kratochvílová (Czechoslovakia) (b. 26 Jan 1951)	Milan, Italy	7 Mar 1982
800 m	1:56.40		Christine Wachtel (GDR) (b. 6 Jan 1965)	Vienna, Austria	13 Feb 1988
1000 m	2:33.93		Inna Yevseyeva (Ukraine) (b. 14 Aug 1964)	Moscow, Russia	7 Feb 1992
1500 m	4:00.27		Doina Melinte (Romania) (b. 27 Dec 1956)	East Rutherford, NJ, USA	9 Feb 1990
1 mile	4:17.14		Doina Melinte (Romania)	East Rutherford, NJ, USA	9 Feb 1990
3000 m	8:33.82		Elly van Hulst (Netherlands) (b. 9 Jun 1957)	Budapest, Hungary	4 Mar 1989
5000 m	15:03.17		Elizabeth McColgan (GB) (b. 24 May 1964)	Birmingham, W Mids	22 Feb 1992
50 m hurdles	6.58		Cornelia Oschkenat (GDR) (b. 29 Oct 1961)	Berlin, Germany	20 Feb 1988
60 m hurdles	7.69		Lyudmila Narozhilenko (Russia) (b. 21 Apr 1964)	Chelyabinsk, Russia	4 Feb 1993
4×200 m	1:32.55		S. C. Eintracht Hamm (West Germany)	Dortmund, Germany	19 Feb 1988
			(Helga Arendt, Silke-Beate Knoll, Mechthild Kluth, Gisela Kinzel)		
4×400 m	3:27.22		Germany	Seville, Spain	10 Mar 1991
			(Sandra Seuser, Katrin Schreiter, Annet Hesselbarth, Grit Breuer)		
3000 m walk	11:44.00		Alina Ivanova (Ukraine) (b. 25 Jun 1969)	Moscow, Russia	7 Feb 1992

Field Events

	m	ft	in	Name and Country	Venue	Date
High jump	2.07	6	9½	Heike Henkel (Germany) (b. 5 May 1964)	Karlsruhe, Germany	9 Feb 1992
Long jump	7.37	24	2¼	Heike Drechsler (GDR) (b. 16 Dec 1964)	Vienna, Austria	13 Feb 1988
Triple jump	14.90	48	10½	Inna Lasovskaya (Russia) (b. 17 Dec 1969)	Liévin, France	13 Feb 1994
Shot	22.50	73	10	Helena Fibingerová (Czechoslovakia) (b. 13 Jul 1959)	Jablonec, Czechoslovakia	19 Feb 1977

Pentathlon

4991 points ....Irina Belova (Russia) (b. 27 Mar 1968) ....Berlin, Germany ....14–15 Feb .1992
(60m hurdles 8.22 sec; HJ 1.93 m; SP 13.25 m; LJ 6.67 m; 800 m 2:10.26)

---

one relay title by Emmanuel McDonald Bailey (Trinidad) (b. 8 Dec 1920), between 1946 and 1953. The most won outdoors in a single event is 13 by Denis Horgan (Ireland) (1871–1922) in the shot put between 1893 and 1912. Thirteen senior AAA titles were also won by: Michael Anthony Bull (b. 11 Sep 1946) at pole vault, eight indoor and five out, and by Geoffrey Lewis Capes (b. 23 Aug 1949) at shot, six indoor and seven out.

The greatest number of WAAA outdoor titles won by one athlete is 14 by Suzanne Allday (*née* Farmer) (b. 26 Nov 1934) with seven each at shot and discus between 1952 and 1962. She also won two WAAA indoor shot titles.

Most international appearances The greatest number of international matches contested for any nation is 89 by shot-putter Bjørn Bang Andersen (b. 14 Nov 1937) for Norway, 1960–81.

The greatest number of full Great Britain international appearances (outdoors and indoors) is 73 by Verona Marolin Elder (*née* Bernard) (b. 5 Apr 1953), mostly at 400 m, from 1971 to 1983. The men's record is 67 by shot-putter Geoff Capes, 1969–80. At pole vault and decathlon Mike Bull had 66 full internationals or 69 including the European Indoor Games, before these were official internationals. The most outdoors is 61 by hammer thrower Andrew Howard Payne (b. South Africa, 17 Apr 1931) from 1960 to 1974.

Oldest and youngest internationals The oldest full Great Britain international was Donald James Thompson (b. 20 Jan 1933), aged 58 yr 89 days, at 200 km walk at Bazencourt, France on 20–21 Apr 1991. In the same race Edmund Harold Shillabeer (b. 2

Ana Biryukova in action during the 1993 World Championships where she became the first woman to triple jump over 15 metres.
(Photo: Allsport/Gray Mortimore)

Yan (China) (b. 9 Apr 1971) who set a women's 5000 m walk record at age 14 yr 334 m days with 21 min 33.8 sec at Jian, China on 9 Mar 1986. The youngest male is 17 yr 198 days Thomas Ray (GB) (1862–1904) when he pole-vaulted 3.42m *11ft 2¾in* on 19 Sep 1879 (prior to IAAF ratification).

Jesse Owens (USA) (1913–80) set six world records in 45 min at Ann Arbor, Michigan on 25 May 1935 with a 9.4 sec 100 yd at 3:15 p.m., a 8.13 m 26 ft 8¼ in long jump at 3:25 p.m., a 20.3 sec 220 yd (and 200 m) at 3:45 p.m. and a 22.6 sec 220 yd low hurdles (and 200 m) at 4 p.m.

Most national titles
Great Britain The most national senior titles won by an athlete is 31 by Judith Miriam Oakes (b. 14 Feb 1958) at the shot with 11 WAAA or AAA outdoor, 12 WAAA indoor and eight UK titles, 1977–94. The greatest number of senior AAA titles (excluding those in tug of war events) won by one athlete is 14 individual and

Aug 1939) became the oldest international débutant, aged 51 yr 260 days. The oldest woman was Christine Rosemary Payne (*née* Charters, now Chimes) (b. 19 May 1933) at discus in the Great Britain *v.* Finland match on 26 Sep 1974, aged 41 yr 130 days. The youngest man was high jumper Ross Hepburn (b. 14 Oct 1961) *v.* the USSR on 26 Aug 1977, aged 15 yr 316 days, and the youngest woman was Janis Walsh (now Cue) (b. 28 Mar 1960) *v.* Belgium (indoor) at 60 m and 4 × 200 m relay on 15 Feb 1975, aged 14 yr 324 days.

Longest winning sequence Iolanda Balas (Romania) (b. 12 Dec 1936) won a record 150 consecutive competitions at high jump from 1956 to 1967. The record at a track event is 122 at 400 metres hurdles by Edwin Corley Moses (USA) (b. 31 Jul 1955) between his loss to Harald Schmid (West Germany) (b. 29 Sep 1957) at Berlin, Germany on 26 Aug 1977 and that to Danny Lee Harris (USA) (b. 7 Sep 1965) at Madrid, Spain on 4 Jun 1987.

'End to end' The fastest confirmed run from John o' Groats to Land's End is 10 days 15 hr 27 min by Donald Alexander Ritchie (GB) (b. 6 Jul 1944) from 1–12 Apr 1989. A faster 10 days 3 hr 30 min was claimed by Fred Hicks (GB) for 1410 km *876 miles* on 20–30 May 1977. The fastest by a women is 13 days 17 hr 42 min by walker Ann Sayer (⟷ Walking). A relay team of 10 from Vauxhall Motors A.C. covered the distance in 76 hr 58 min 29 sec from 31 May–3 Jun 1990.

GUESS WHAT?
Q How many hurdles races did *Sir Ken* win in succession?
A See Page 266

Colin Jackson
(right) celebrates winning the 1993
World Championships, he took 100th of a
second off the world record with a time of
12.91 sec.
(Photo: Allsport/Gray Mortimore)

United Kingdom (National) Records *Men*

Running	min:sec	Name	Venue	Date
100 m	9.87	Linford Christie (b. 10 Apr 1960)	Stuttgart, Germany	15 Aug 1993
200 m	19.94	John Paul Lyndon Regis (b. 13 Oct 1966)	Stuttgart, Germany	20 Aug 1993
400 m	44.47	David Grindley (b. 3 Sep 1965)	Barcelona, Spain	3 Aug 1992
800 m	1:41.73	Sebastian Newbold Coe (b. 29 Sep 1956)	Florence, Italy	10 Jun 1981
1000 m	2:12.18	Sebastian Newbold Coe	Oslo, Norway	11 Jul 1981
1500 m	3:29.67	Stephen Cram (b. 14 Oct 1960)	Nice, France	16 Jul 1985
1 mile	3:46.32	Stephen Cram	Oslo, Norway	27 Jul 1985
2000 m	4:51.39	Stephen Cram	Budapest, Hungary	4 Aug 1985
3000 m	7:32.79	David Robert Moorcroft (b. 10 Apr 1953)	Crystal Palace, London	17 Jul 1982
5000 m	13:00.41	David Robert Moorcroft	Oslo, Norway	7 Jul 1982
10,000 m	27:23.06	Eamonn Thomas Martin (b. 9 Oct 1958)	Oslo, Norway	2 Jul 1988
20,000 m	57:28.7	Carl Edward Thackery (b. 14 Oct 1962)	La Flèche, France	31 Mar 1990
25,000 m	1 hr 15:22.6	Ronald Hill	Bolton, Lancashire	21 Jul 1965
30,000 m	1 hr 31:30.4	James Noel Carroll Alder (b. 10 Jun 1940)	Crystal Palace, London	5 Sep 1970
1 hour	20,855 m	Carl Edward Thackery	La Flèche, France	31 Mar 1990
110 m hurdles	12.91	Colin Ray Jackson (b. 18 Feb 1967)	Stuttgart, Germany	20 Aug 1993
400 m hurdles	47.82	Kriss Kezie Uche Chukwu Duru Akabusi (b. 28 Nov 1958)	Barcelona, Spain	6 Aug 1991
3000 m s'chase	8:07.96	Mark Robert Rowland (b. 7 Mar 1963)	Seoul, South Korea	30 Sep 1988
4×100 m	37.77	National Team: Colin Jackson, Anthony Alexander Jarrett, John Regis, Linford Christie	Stuttgart, Germany	22 Aug 1993
4×200 m	1:21.29	National Team: Marcus Adam, Adeoye Mafe, Linford Christie, John Regis	Birmingham	23 Jun 1989
4×400 m	2:57.53	National Team: Roger Anthony Black, Derek Redmond, John Regis, Kriss Akabusi	Tokyo, Japan	1 Sep 1991
4×800 m	7:03.89	National Team: Peter Elliott, Gary Peter Cook, Stephen Cram, Sebastien Coe	Crystal Palace, London	30 Aug 1982
4×1500 m	14:56.8	National Team: Alan David Mottershead, Geoffrey Michael Cooper, Stephen John Emson, Roy Wood	Bourges, France	24 Jun 1979

Field Events	m	ft	in	Name	Venue	Date
High Jump	2.37	7	9¼	Stephen James Smith (b. 29 Mar 1973)	Seoul, South Korea	20 Sep 1992
	2.37	7	9¼	Stephen James Smith	Stuttgart, Germany	22 Aug 1993
(indoors)	2.38	7	9¾	Stephen James Smith	Wuppertal, Germany	4 Feb 1994
Pole Vault	5.65	18	6½	Keith Frank Stock (b. 18 Mar 1957)	Stockholm, Sweden	7 Jul 1981
Long Jump	8.23	27	0	Lynn Davies (b. 20 May 1942)	Berne, Switzerland	30 Jun 1968
Triple Jump	17.57A	57	7¾	Keith Leroy Connor (b. 16 Sep 1957)	Provo, Utah, USA	5 Jun 1982
Shot	21.68	71	1½	Geoffrey Lewis Capes (b. 23 Aug 1949)	Cwmbran, Gwent	18 May 1980
Discus	64.32*	211	0	William Raymond Tancred (b. 6 Aug 1942)	Woodford, Essex	10 Aug 1974
Hammer	77.54	254	5	Martin Girvan (b. 17 Apr 1960)	Wolverhampton, W Mids	12 May 1984
Javelin	91.46	300	1	Stephen James Backley (GB) (b. 12 Feb 1969)	Auckland, New Zealand	25 Jan 1992

A Record set at high altitude, best at low altitude: 17.44 m 57 ft 2¾ in by Jonathon David Edwards (b. 10 May 1966) at Stuttgart, Germany on 16 Aug 1993.
* William Raymond Tancred threw 64.94 m 213 ft 1 in at Loughborough, Leicestershire on 21 Jul 1974 and Richard Charles Slaney (b. 16 May 1956) threw 65.16 m 213 ft 9 in at Eugene, Oregon, USA on 1 Jul 1985 but these were not ratified.

Decathlon 8847 points Francis Morgan 'Daley' Thompson (b. 30 Jul 1958) Los Angeles, USA 8–9 Aug 1984
1st day: 100 m 10.44 sec, LJ 8.01 m *26 ft 3½ in*, SP 15.72 m *51 ft 7 in*, HJ 2.03 m *6 ft 8 in*, 400 m 46.97 sec
2nd day: 110 m H 14.33 sec, D 46.56 m *152 ft 9 in*, PV 5.00 m *16 ft 4¾ in*, J 65.24 m *214 ft 0 in*, 1500 m 4:35.00 sec

United Kingdom (National) Records *Women*

Running	min:sec	Name	Venue	Date
100 m	11.10	Kathryn Jane Smallwood (now Cook) (b. 3 May 1960)	Rome, Italy	5 Sep 1981
200 m	22.10	Kathryn Jane Cook (*née* Smallwood)	Los Angeles, California, USA	9 Aug 1984
400 m	49.43	Kathryn Jane Cook (*née* Smallwood)	Los Angeles, California, USA	6 Aug 1984
800 m	1:57.42	Kirsty Margaret McDermott (now Wade) (b. 6 Aug 1962)	Belfast, Northern Ireland	24 Jun 1985
1000 m	2:33.70	Kirsty Margaret McDermott (now Wade)	Gateshead, Tyne and Wear	9 Aug 1985
1500 m	3:59.96	Zola Budd (now Pieterse) (b. 26 May 1966)	Brussels, Belgium	30 Aug 1985
1 mile	4:17.57	Zola Budd (now Pieterse)	Zürich, Switzerland	21 Aug 1985
2000 m	5:29.58	Yvonne Carol Grace Murray (b. 4 Oct 1964)	Crystal Palace, London	11 Jul 1986
3000 m	8:28.83	Zola Budd (now Pieterse)	Rome, Italy	7 Sep 1985
5000 m	14:48.07	Zola Budd (now Pieterse)	Crystal Palace, London	26 Aug 1985
10,000 m	30:57.07	Elizabeth McColgan (*née* Lynch) (b. 24 May 1964)	Hengelo, Netherlands	25 Jun 1991
100 m hurdles	12.82	Sally Jane Janet Gunnell (b. 29 Jul 1966)	Zürich, Switzerland	17 Aug 1988
400 m hurdles	52.74	Sally Jane Janet Gunnell	Stuttgart, Germany	19 Aug 1993
4×100 m	42.43	National Team: Heather Regina Hunte (now Oakes), Kathryn Jane Smallwood (now Cook), Beverley Lanita Goddard (now Callender), Sonia May Lannaman	Moscow, USSR	1 Aug 1980
4×200 m	1:31.57	National Team; Donna-Marie Louise Hartley (*née* Murray), Verona Marolin Elder (*née* Bernard), Sharon Colyear (now Danville), Sonia May Lannaman	Crystal Palace, London	20 Aug 1977
4×400 m	3:22.01	National Team: Phyllis Smith (*née* Watt), Lorraine I Hanson, Linda Keough, Sally Janet Jane Gunnell	Tokyo, Japan	1 Sep 1991
4×800 m	8:19.9	National Team: Ann Margaret Williams, Paula Tracy Fryer, Yvonne Murray, Diane Delores Edwards	Sheffield, S Yorks	5 Jun 1992

Field Events	m	ft	in	Name	Venue	Date
High Jump	1.95	6	4¾	Diana Clare Elliot (now Davies) (b. 7 May 1961)	Oslo, Norway	26 Jun 1982
Pole Vault	3.65	11	11¾	Katherine 'Kate' Staples (b. 2 Nov 1965)	Sheffield, S Yorks	11 Jun 1994
Long Jump	6.90	22	7¾	Beverly Kinch (b. 14 Jan 1964)	Helsinki, Finland	14 Aug 1983
Triple Jump	14.08	46	2¼	Michelle Amanda Griffith (b. 6 Oct 1971)	Sheffield, S Yorks	11 Jun 1994
Shot	19.36	63	6¼	Judith Miriam Oakes (b. 14 Feb 1958)	Gateshead, Tyne and Wear	14 Aug 1988
Hammer	59.94	196	8	Lorraine A. Shaw (b. 2 Apr 1968)	Colindale, London	2 Apr 1994
Discus	67.48	221	5	Margaret Elizabeth Ritchie (b. 6 Jul 1952)	Walnut, California, USA	26 Apr 1981
Javelin	77.44	254	1	Fatima Whitbread (b. 3 Mar 1961)	Stuttgart, Germany	28 Aug 1986

Heptathlon 6623 points — Judy Earline Veronica Simpson (*née* Livermore) (b. 14 Nov 1960) — Stuttgart, Germany — 29-30 Aug 1986

100 m hurdles 13.05 sec; High Jump 1.92 m *6 ft 3½ in*; Shot 14.75 m *48 ft 4 in*; 200 m 25.09 sec; Long Jump 6.56 m *21 ft 6¼ in*; Javelin 40.92 m *134 ft 3 in*; 800 m 2 min 11.70 sec

Sally Gunnell Olympic champion at 400 m hurdles in 1992 adding the World title in 1993 when she ran a world record time of 52.74, with Sandra Farmer-Patrick (USA), second in 52.79, also under the old world record.
(Photo: Allsport/Tony Duffy)

Longest running race The longest race ever staged was the 1929 trans-continental races from New York City to Los Angeles, California, USA of 5898 km *3665 miles*. The Finnish-born Johnny Salo (1893–1931) was the winner in 1929 in 79 days, from 31 March to 18 June. His elapsed time of 525 hr 57 min 20 sec (averaging 11.21 km/h *6.97 mph*) left him only 2 min 47 sec ahead of Englishman Pietro 'Peter' Gavuzzi (1905–81).

The longest race staged annually is the New York 1300 Mile race, held since 1987, at Flushing Meadow-Corona Park, Queens, New York. The fastest time to complete the race is 16 days 17 hr 36 min 14 sec by Istvan Sidos (Hungary) from 15 Sep–2 Oct 1993.

Longest runs Al Howie (GB) ran across Canada, from St Johns to Victoria, a distance of 7295.5 km *4533.2 miles*, in 72 days 10 hr 23 min, 21 Jun–1 Sep 1991. Robert J Sweetgall (USA) (b. 8 Dec 1947) ran 17,071 km *10,608 miles* around the perimeter of the USA starting and finishing in Washington, DC, 9 Oct 1982–15 Jul 1983. Ron Grant (Australia) (b. 15 Feb 1943) ran around Australia, 13,383 km *8316 miles* in 217 days 3 hr 45 min, 28 Mar–31 Oct 1983. Max Telford (New Zealand) (b. Hawick, 2 Feb 1955) ran 8224 km *5110 miles* from Anchorage, Alaska to Halifax, Nova Scotia, in 106 days 18 hr 45 min from 25 Jul to 9 Nov 1977.

The fastest time for the cross-America run is 46 days 8 hr 36 min by Frank Giannino Jr (USA) (b. 1952) for the 4989 km *3100 miles* from San Francisco to New York from 1 Sep–17 Oct 1980. The women's trans-America record is 69 days 2 hr 40 min by Mavis Hutchinson (South Africa) (b. 25 Nov 1942) from 12 Mar–21 May 1978.

Greatest mileage Douglas Alistair Gordon Pirie (GB) (1931–91), who set five world records in the 1950s, estimated that he had run a total distance of 347,600 km *216,000 miles* in 40 years to 1981.

Dr Ron Hill (b. 21 Sep 1938), the 1969 European and 1970 Commonwealth marathon champion, has not missed a day's training since 20 Dec 1964. His meticulously compiled training log shows a total of 206,039 km *126,027 miles* from 3 Sep 1956 to 19 May 1994. He has finished 114 marathons, all sub 2:52 and has raced in 55 nations.

The greatest competitive distance run in a year is 8855 km *5502 miles* by Malcolm Campbell (GB) (b. 17 Nov 1934) in 1985.

1000 hours Craig Rowe (Australia) ran 3.307 km within an hour, every hour, for 1000 consecutive hours at Manly Beach, Australia on 18 Jul–29 Aug 1993.

Top!

Ultra runner Hilary Walker (b. 9 Nov 1953) ran the length of the Friendship Highway from Lhasa, Tibet to Kathmandu, Nepal, a distance of 950 km *590 miles*, in 14 days 9 hrs 36 min from 18 Sep–2 Oct 1991. The run was made at an average altitude of 4200 m *13,780 ft* with a maximum height attained of 5220 m *17,126 ft* at Jia Tsuo La.

Mass relay records The record for 100 miles *160.9 km* by 100 runners from one club is 7 hr 53 min 52.1 sec by Baltimore Road Runners Club, Towson, Maryland, USA on 17 May 1981. The women's record is 10 hr 47 min 9.3 sec on 3 Apr 1977 by the San Francisco Dolphins Southend Running Club, USA. The record for 100 × 100 m is 19 min 14.19 sec by a team from Antwerp at Merksem, Belgium on 23 Sep 1989.

The longest relay ever run was 17,391 km *10,806 miles* by 23 runners of the Melbourne Fire Brigade, around Australia on Highway No. 1, in

GUESS WHAT?

Q what is the first event of a decathlon?

A See Page 224

50 days 43 min, 6 Aug–25 Sep 1991. The most participants is 6500, 260 teams of 25, for the Batavierenrace from Nijmegen to Enschede, Netherlands on 25 Apr 1992. The greatest distance covered in 24 hours by a team of ten is 450.978 km *280.224 miles* by Oxford Striders RC at East London, South Africa on 5–6 Oct 1990.

Marathon

Oldest The Boston marathon, the world's longest-lasting major marathon, was first held

Cosmas N'Deti celebrates winning the 1994 Boston Marthon in a time of 2 hr 7 min 14 sec. The field was one of the quickest ever with a record 11 runners completing the course in under 2 hr 10 min.
(Photo: Allsport)

Ultra Long Distance World Records

MEN

Track	hr:min:sec	Name	Venue	Date
50 km	2:48:06	Jeff Norman (GB)	Timperley, Manchester	7 Jun 1980
50 miles	4:51:49	Don Ritchie (GB)	Hendon, London	12 Mar 1983
100 km	6:10:20	Don Ritchie (GB)	Crystal Palace, London	28 Oct 1978
100 miles	11:30:51	Don Ritchie (GB)	Crystal Palace, London	15 Oct 1977
200 km	15:11:10**	Yiannis Kouros (Greece)	Montauban, France	15–16 Mar 1985
200 miles	27:48:35	Yiannis Kouros (Greece)	Montauban, France	15–16 Mar 1985
500 km	60:23:00	Yiannis Kouros (Greece)	Colac, Australia	26–29 Nov 1984
500 miles	105:42:09	Yiannis Kouros (Greece)	Colac, Australia	26–30 Nov 1984
1000 km	136:17:00	Yiannis Kouros (Greece)	Colac, Australia	26 Nov–1 Dec 1984

kilometres				
24 hours	283.600	Yiannis Kouros (Greece)	Montauban, France	15–16 Mar 1985
48 hours	452.270	Yiannis Kouros (Greece)	Montauban, France	15–17 Mar 1985
6 days	1023.200	Yiannis Kouros (Greece)	Colac, Australia	26 Nov–1 Dec 1984
(indoors)	1030.000	Jean-Gilles Boussiquet (France)	La Rochelle, France	16–23 Nov 1992

Road*	hr:min:sec			
50 km	2:43:38	Thompson Magawana (South Africa)	Claremont–Kirstenbosch	12 Apr 1988
50 miles	4:50:21	Bruce Fordyce (South Africa)	London–Brighton	25 Sep 1983
1000 miles	10d10:30:35	Yiannis Kouros (Greece)	New York, USA	21–30 May 1988

kilometres				
24 hours	286.463	Yiannis Kouros (Greece)	New York, USA	28–29 Sep 1985
6 days	1028.370	Yiannis Kouros (Greece)	New York, USA	21–26 May 1988

WOMEN

Track	hr:min:sec	Name	Venue	Date
15 km	49:44.0	Silvana Cruciata (Italy)	Rome, Italy	4 May 1981
20 km	1:06:48.8	Isumi Maki (Japan))	Amagasaki, Japan	20 Sep 1993
25 km	1:29:29.2	Karolina Szabo (Hungary)	Budapest, Hungary	23 Apr 1988
30 km	1:47:05.6	Karolina Szabo (Hungary)	Budapest, Hungary	23 Apr 1988
50 km	3:26:45	Carolyn Hunter-Rowe (GB)	Barry, S Glam	7 Mar 1993
50 miles	6:12:11	Hilary Walker (GB)	Tooting Bec, London	16 Oct 1993
100 km	7:50:09	Ann Trason (USA)	Hayward, California, USA	3–4 Aug 1991
100 miles	14:29:44	Ann Trason (USA)	Santa Rosa, California, USA	18–19 Mar 1989
200 km	19:28:48**	Eleanor Adams (GB)	Melbourne, Australia	19–20 Aug 1989
200 miles	39:09:03	Hilary Walker (GB)	Blackpool, Lancashire	5–6 Nov 1988
500 km	77:53:46	Eleanor Adams (GB)	Colac, Australia	13–15 Nov 1989
500 miles	130:59:58	Sandra Barwick (New Zealand)	Campbelltown, Australia	18–23 Nov 1990

kilometres				
1 hour	18.084	Silvana Cruciata (Italy)	Rome, Italy	4 May 1981
24 hours	240.169	Eleanor Adams (GB)	Melbourne, Australia	19–20 Aug 1989
48 hours	366.512	Hilary Walker (GB)	Blackpool, Lancashire	5–7 Nov 1988
6 days	883.631	Sandra Barwick (New Zealand)	Campbelltown, Australia	18–24 Nov 1990

Road*	hr:min:sec			
30 km	1:38:27	Ingrid Kristiansen (Norway)	London	10 May 1987
50 km	3:08:13	Frith van der Merwe (South Africa)	Claremont-Kirstenbosch	25 Mar 1989
50 miles	5:40:18	Ann Trason (USA)	Houston, Texas, USA	23 Feb 1991
100 km	7:09:44	Ann Trason (USA)	Amiens, France	27 Sep 1993
100 miles	13:47:41	Ann Trason (USA)	Queens, New York	4 May 1991
200 km	19:08:21	Sigrid Lomsky (Germany)	Basel, Switzerland	1–2 May 1993
(indoors)	19:00:31	Eleanor Adams (GB)	Milton Keynes	3–4 Feb 1990
1000 km	7d1:11:00	Sandra Barwick (New Zealand)	Queens, New York	16–23 Sep 1991
1000 miles	12d14:38:40	Sandra Barwick (New Zealand)	Queens, New York	16–29 Sep 1991

*Where superior to track bests and run on properly measured road courses. It should be noted that road times must be assessed with care as course conditions can vary considerably. ** No stopped time known.

on 19 Apr 1897 and covered 39 km *24 miles 1232 yd.*

Fastest It should be noted that courses may vary in severity. The following are the best times recorded, all on courses whose distance has been verified.

The world records are: (men) 2 hr 6 min 50 sec by Belayneh Dinsamo (Ethiopia) (b. 28 Jun 1965) at Rotterdam, Netherlands on 17 Apr 1988 and (women) 2 hr 21 min 6 sec by Ingrid Kristiansen (*née* Christensen) (Norway) (b. 21 Mar 1956) at London on 21 Apr 1985.

The British records are: (men) 2 hr 7 min 13 sec by Stephen Henry Jones (b. 4 Aug 1955) at Chicago, Illinois, USA on 20 Oct 1985 and (women) 2 hr 25 min 56 sec by Véronique Marot (b. 16 Sep 1955) at London on 23 Apr 1989.

Most competitors The record number of confirmed finishers in a marathon is 27,797 from 28,656 starters in the New York City on 1 Nov 1992. A record 105 men ran under 2 hr 20 min and 46 under 2 hr 15 min in the World Cup marathon at London on 21 Apr 1991, and a record 11 men ran under 2 hr 10 min at Boston on 18 Apr 1994, although the course is overall downhill and there was a strong following wind on the point-to-point course. A record 9 women ran under 2 hr 30 min in the first Olympic marathon for women at Los Angeles, USA on 5 Aug 1984.

Most run by an individual Sy Mah (Canada) (1926–88) ran 524 marathons of 26 miles 385 yd or longer from 1967 to his death in 1988. He paced himself to take 3½ hr each run.

John A. Kelley (USA) (b. 6 Sep 1907) has finished the Boston Marathon 61 times, winning in 1933 and 1945, to 1992.

Three in three days The fastest combined time for three marathons in three days is 8 hr 22 min 31 sec by Raymond Hubbard (Belfast 2 hr 45 min

New York v *London*
A comparison of two major marathons

Since the first London marathon in 1981, the marathons at New York and London have contested who is the largest in term of finishers. The New York marathon began with a very small number of entries in 1970 and steadily rose until there were 13,223 finishers in 1981, the year of the first London marathon. This first marathon had 6418 finishers but the following list shows how the record progressed from this point:

13,223	New York	1981
15,758	London	1982
15,776	London	1983
16,580	London	1984
18,175	London	1986
19,710	London	1987
21,141	New York	1987
22,244	New York	1988
22,587	London	1989
24,588	New York	1989
24,871	London	1990
25,797	New York	1991
27,797	New York	1992

(Photos: Allsport/Allsport USA)

Progessive time records

NEW YORK (since 1976)
MEN

2:10:10	Bill Rodgers (USA)	1976
2:09:41	Alberto Salazar (USA)	1980
2:08:13	Alberto Salazar (USA)	1981*
2:08:20	Steve Jones (GB)	1988
2:08:01	Juma Ikangaa (Japan)	1989

WOMEN

2:39:11	Miki Gorman (USA)	1976
2:32:30	Grete Waitz (Norway)	1978
2:27:33	Grete Waitz (Norway)	1979
2:25:42	Grete Waitz (Norway)	1980
2:25:29	Allison Roe (New Zealand)	1981*
2:25:30	Ingrid Kristiansen (Norway)	1989
2:24:40	Lisa Ondieki (Australia)	1992

* Course found to be 170yd short

LONDON
MEN

2:11:48	Dick Beardsley (USA) & Inge Simonsen (Norway)	1981
2:09:24	Hugh Jones (GB)	1982
2:08:16	Steve Jones (GB)	1985

WOMEN

2:29:57	Joyce Smith (GB)	1981
2:29:43	Joyce Smith (GB)	1982
2:25:29	Grete Waitz (Norway)	1983
2:24:26	Ingrid Kristiansen (Norway)	1984
2:21:06	Ingrid Kristiansen (Norway)	1985

THEN & NOW

55sec, London 2hr 48min 45sec and Boston 2hr 47min 51sec) on 16–18 Apr 1988.

Highest altitude The highest start to a marathon is for the biennially-held Everest Marathon, first run on 27 Nov 1987. It begins at Gorak Shep, 5212m *17,100ft* and ends at Namche Bazar, 3444m *11,300ft*. The fastest times to complete this race are, men 3hr 59min 4sec by Jack Maitland, and women 5hr 44min 32sec by Dawn Kenwright, both in 1989.

Oldest finishers The oldest man to complete a marathon was Dimitrion Yordanidis (Greece), aged 98, in Athens, Greece on 10 Oct 1976. He finished in 7 hr 33 min. Thelma Pitt-Turner (New Zealand) set the women's record in August 1985, completing the Hastings, New Zealand marathon in 7 hr 58 min at the age of 82.

Priscilla Margaret 'Tabby' Puzey, 38, pushed a pram while running the Abingdon half marathon on 13 Apr 1986 in 2hr 4min 9sec.

Half marathon The distance of a half the full marathon has become established in recent years as one of the most popular for road races. In 1992 the IAAF held the first official world championships at this distance.

The world best time on a properly measured course is 59min 47sec by Moses Tanui (Kenya) (b. 20 Aug 1965) at Milan, Italy on 3 Apr 1993. The British best is 60min 59sec by Steve Jones from Newcastle to South Shields, Tyneside on 8 Jun 1986.

Ingrid Kristiansen (Norway) ran 66min 40sec at Sandes, Norway on 5 Apr 1987, but the measurement of the course has not been confirmed. She holds the recognised best by a woman with 68min 32sec at New Bedford, USA on 19 Mar 1989. Liz McColgan ran 67min 11sec at Tokyo, Japan on 26 Jan 1992, but the course was 33m downhill, a little more than the allowable 1 in 1000 drop; she also ran a British best of 68min 42sec at Dundee, Tayside on 11 Oct 1992.

Backwards running Timothy 'Bud' Badyna (USA) ran the fastest marathon in 3hr 53min 17sec at Toledo, Ohio, USA on 24 Apr 1994. He also ran 10km in 45min 37sec at Toledo on 13 Jul 1991. Donald Davis (USA) (b. 10 Feb 1960) ran 1mile in 6min 7.1sec at the University of Hawaii on 21 Feb 1983. Ferdie Ato Adoboe (Ghana) ran 100yd in 12.7sec (100m in 13.6sec) at Smith's College, Northampton, Massachusetts, USA on 25 Jul 1991.

Arvind Pandya of India ran backwards across America, Los Angeles to New York, in 107 days, 18 Aug–3 Dec 1984. He also ran backwards from John o' Groats to Land's End in 26days 7hr, 6 Apr–2 May 1990.

GUESS WHAT?

Q Where is the oldest marathon held?

A See Page 229

Running Backwards

ON THE RECORD

" He walked at seven months and started jogging at eight years old. But Bud Badyna didn't take up the sport that would make him a record holder until he was 23. That's when he got what he calls the "screwball" idea to start running backwards. These days he's running marathons—and breaking his own record with each one he runs. "I finish in the top 40 or 50 percent every time," Badyna says. "So I'm beating more than half. Sure, I can run faster frontwards—but it's not as much fun."

Bud is a paramedic when he's not running around backwards. He got his nickname as a kid from his passion for Florida's Busch Gardens and his collection of Budweiser memorabilia. You've heard about the loneliness of the long-distance runner, but it doesn't apply to Bud. He gets attention wherever he goes. When you run backwards, it's not safe to run alone. "My younger brother Troy is my spotter. He rides his bicycle behind me, which means I'm facing him. He has to peek around me to see what's coming." Running backwards has its hazards. "I've only fallen half a dozen times; once over a person, once over a cone. The rest of the time I just tripped over my own feet."

His own feet are the biggest problem. "The balls of my feet under my toes really take a beating. I get tons of blood blisters, and my toenails fall off. They don't grow back for a year." "

(Photo: Davida Badyna)

GUESS WHAT?

Q Who is reputed to be the first person to walk round the world?

A See Page 204

Walking

Most Olympic medals The only walker to win three gold medals has been Ugo Frigerio (Italy) (1901–68) with the 3000 m in 1920, and 10,000 m in 1920 and 1924. He also holds the record of most medals with four (he won the bronze medal at 50,000 m in 1932), a total shared with Vladimir Stepanovich Golubnichiy (USSR) (b. 2 Jun 1936), who won gold medals for the 20 km in 1960 and 1968, the silver in 1972 and the bronze in 1964.

The best British performance has been two gold medals by George Edward Larner (1875–1949) for the 3500 m and the 10 miles in 1908, but Ernest James Webb (1872–1937) won three medals, being twice 'walker up' to Larner and finishing second in the 10,000 m in 1912.

Most titles Four-time Olympian, Ronald Owen Laird (b. 31 May 1938) of the New York AC, won a total of 65 US national titles from 1958 to 1976, plus four Canadian Championships.

The greatest number of UK national titles won by a British walker is 27 by Vincent Paul Nihill (b. 5 Sep 1939) from 1963 to 1975.

'End to end' The fastest Land's End to John o' Groats walk is 12 days 3 hr 45 min for 1426.4 km *886.3 miles* by WO2 Malcolm Barnish of the 19th Regiment, Royal Artillery from 9–21 Jun 1986. The women's record is 13 days 17 hr 42 min by Ann Sayer (b. 16 Oct 1936), 20 Sep–3 Oct 1980. The Irish 'end to end' record over the 644 km 400.2 miles from Malin Head, Donegal to Mizen Head, Cork is 5 days 22 hr 30 min, set by John 'Paddy' Dowling (b. 15 Jun 1929) on 18–24 Mar 1982.

24 hours The greatest distance walked is 226.432 km *140 miles 1229 yd* by Paul Forthomme (Belgium) on a road course at Woluwe, Belgium on 13–14 Oct 1984. The best by a woman is 211.25 km *131.27 miles* by Annie van der Meer-Timmermann (Netherlands) at Rouen, France on 10 Apr–11 May 1986.

Backwards walking The greatest ever exponent of reverse pedestrianism has been Plennie L. Wingo (b. 24 Jan 1895) then of Abilene, Texas, USA who completed his 12,875 km *8000 mile* trans-continental walk from Santa Monica, California, USA to Istanbul, Turkey from 15 Apr 1931 to 24 Oct 1932. The longest distance recorded for walking backwards in 24 hours is 153.52 km *95.40 miles* by Anthony Thornton (USA) in Minneapolis, Minnesota, USA on 31 Dec 1988–1 Jan 1989.

Walking

It should be noted that severity of road race courses and the accuracy of their measurement may vary, sometimes making comparisons of times unreliable.

WORLD BESTS

MEN

20 km: 1 hr 17 min 25.5 sec (track), Bernardo Segura (Mexico) (b. 11 Feb 1970) at Fana, Norway on 7 May 1994.

30 km: 2 hr 2 min 41 sec, Andrey Perlov (USSR) (b. 12 Dec 1961) at Sochi on 19 Feb 1989.

50 km: 3 hr 37 min 41 sec, Andrey Perlov (USSR) at Leningrad, USSR on 5 Aug 1989.

WOMEN

10 km: 41 min 30 sec, Kerry Ann Saxby (Australia) (b. 2 Jun 1961) at Canberra, Australia on 27 Aug 1988; and Ileana Salvador (Italy) (b. 16 Jan 1962) at Livorno, Italy on 10 Jul 1993.

20 km: 1 hr 29 min 40 sec, Kerry Saxby at Värnamo, Sweden on 13 May 1988.

50 km: 4 hr 50 min 28 sec, Kora Sommerfield (Australia) at Neuilly-sur-Marne, France on 26 Sep 1993.

BRITISH BESTS

MEN

20 km: 1 hr 22 min 03 sec, Ian Peter McCombie (b. 11 Jan 1961) at Seoul, South Korea on 23 Sep 1988.

30 km: 2 hr 7 min 56 sec, Ian Peter McCombie at Edinburgh, Lothian on 27 Apr 1986.

50 km: 3 hr 51 min 37 sec, Christopher Lloyd Maddocks (b. 28 Mar 1957) at Burrator, Devon on 28 Oct 1990.

WOMEN

10 km: 45 min 28 sec, Victoria Anne Lupton (b. 17 Apr 1972) at Livorno, Italy on 10 Jul 1993.

20 km: 1 hr 40 min 45 sec, Irene Bateman at Basildon, Essex on 9 Apr 1983.

50 km: 4 hr 50 min 51 sec, Sandra Brown (GB) (b. 1 Apr 1949) at Basildon, Essex on 13 Jul 1991.

Mark Kenny, the walking on hands sprint champion, likes to practice as soon as he gets out of the house—whatever the weather.
(Photo: David A. Breen)

Hand Walk!

The distance record for walking on hands is 1400 km *870 miles*, by Johann Hurlinger of Austria, who in 55 daily 10-hr stints walked from Vienna to Paris in 1900, averaging 2.54 km/h *1.58 mph*. Mark Kenny of Norwood, Massachusetts, USA completed a 50 m inverted sprint in 16.93 sec on 19 Feb 1994. A four-man relay team of David Lutterman, Brendan Price, Philip Savage and Danny Scannell covered 1 mile *1.6 km* in 24 min 48 sec on 15 Mar 1987 at Knoxville, Tennessee, USA.

Badminton

World championships *Individual (instituted 1977)* A record five titles have been won by Park Joo-bong (South Korea) (b. 5 Dec 1964), men's doubles 1985 and 1991 and mixed doubles 1985, 1989 and 1991. Three Chinese players have won two individual world titles: men's singles: Yang Yang (b. 8 Dec 1963) 1987 and 1989; women's singles: Li Lingwei 1983 and 1989; Han Aiping (b. 22 Apr 1962) 1985 and 1987.

Team The most wins at the men's World Team Badminton Championships for the Thomas Cup (instituted 1948) is nine by Indonesia (1958, 1961, 1964, 1970, 1973, 1976, 1979, 1984 and 1994). The most wins at the women's World Team Badminton Championships for the Uber Cup (instituted 1956) is five by: Japan (1966, 1969, 1972, 1978 and 1981); and China (1984, 1986, 1988, 1990 and 1992).

All-England Championships For long the most prestigious championships, they were institiued in 1899. A record eight men's singles were won by Rudy Hartono Kurniawan (Indonesia) (b. 18 Aug 1948), in 1968–74 and 1976. The greatest number of titles won (including doubles) is 21 by George Alan Thomas (1881–1972) between 1903 and 1928. The most by a woman is 17 by: Muriel Lucas (later Mrs King Adams), 1899–1910; and Judith Margaret 'Judy' Hashman (*née* Devlin) (USA) (b. 22 Oct 1935) including a record ten singles, 1954, 1957–8, 1960–4, 1966–7.

Shortest game Christine Magnusson (Sweden) beat Martine de Souza (Mauritius) 11–1, 11–0 in 8min 30 sec at the 1992 Olympics at Barcelona, Spain.

Longest rallies In the men's singles final of the 1987 All-England Championships between Morten Frost (Denmark) and Icuk Sugiarto (Indonesia) there were two successive rallies of over 90 strokes.

GUESS WHAT?

Q How fast is the fastest recorded pitcher in baseball?

A See Page 234

Baseball

Origins Played annually between the winners of the National League and the American League, the World Series was first staged unofficially in 1903, and officially from 1905. The most wins is 22 by the New York Yankees between 1923 and 1978 from a record 33 series appearances for winning the American League titles between 1921 and 1981. The most National League titles is 19 by the Dodgers—Brooklyn 1890–1957, Los Angeles 1958–88.

Most valuable player The only men to have won this award twice are: Sanford 'Sandy' Koufax (b. 30 Dec 1935) (Los Angeles, NL 1963, 1965), Robert 'Bob' Gibson (b. 9 Nov 1935) (St. Louis NL, 1964, 1967) and Reginald Martinez 'Reggie' Jackson (b. 18 May 1946) (Oakland AL 1973, New York AL, 1977).

Attendance The record attendance for a series is 420,784 for the six games when the Los Angeles Dodgers beat the Chicago White Sox 4–2 between 1 and 8 Oct 1959. The single game record is 92,706 for the fifth game of this series at the Memorial Coliseum, Los Angeles on 6 Oct 1959.

Major League

Most games played Peter Edward 'Pete' Rose (b. 14 Apr 1941) played in a record 3562 games with a record 14,053 at bats for Cincinnati NL 1963–78 and 1984–6, Philadelphia NL 1979–83, Montreal NL 1984. Henry Louis 'Lou' Gehrig (1903–41) played in 2130 successive games for the New York Yankees (AL) from 1 Jun 1925 to 30 Apr 1939.

Most home runs *Career* Henry Louis 'Hank' Aaron (b. 5 Feb 1934) holds the major league career record with 755 home runs; 733 for the Milwaukee (1954–65) and Atlanta (1966–74) Braves in the National League and 22 for the Milwaukee Brewers (AL) 1975–6. On 8 Apr 1974 he had bettered the previous record of 714 by George Herman 'Babe' Ruth (1895–1948). Ruth hit his home runs

Indonesian Susi Susanti, in action during the 1993 World Championships where she won the singles title. She has won a record four Grand Prix titles and was the winner of the first official Olympic title in 1992.
(Photo: Allsport/Mike Cooper)

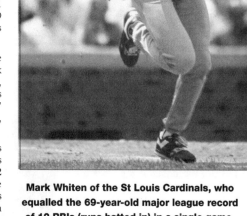

Mark Whiten of the St Louis Cardinals, who equalled the 69-year-old major league record of 12 RBIs (runs batted in) in a single game, against the Cincinnati Reds on 7 Sep 1993.
(Photo: Allsport USA)

from 8399 times at bat, the highest home run percentage of 8.5%. Joshua Gibson (1911–47) of Homestead Grays and Pittsburgh Crawfords, Negro League clubs, achieved a career total of nearly 800 homers including an unofficial record season's total of 75 in 1931.

Season The US major league record for home runs in a season is 61 by Roger Eugene Maris (1934–85) for New York Yankees in 162 games in 1961. 'Babe' Ruth hit 60 in 154 games in 1927 for the New York Yankees. The most official home runs in a minor league season is 72 by Joe Bauman of Roswell Rockets, New Mexico in 1954.

Game The most home runs in a major league game is four, first achieved by Robert Lincoln 'Bobby' Lowe (1868–1951) for Boston *v.* Cinncinnati on 30 May 1894. The feat had been achieved a further ten times since then.

Consecutive games The most consecutive games hitting home runs is eight by Richard Dale Long (b. 6 Feb 1926) for Pittsburgh (NL), 19–28 May 1956 and by Donald Arthur Mattingly (b. 21 Apr 1961) for New York (AL), July 1987.

Most games won by a pitcher Denton True 'Cy' Young (1867–1955) had a record 511 wins and a record 749 complete games from a total of 906 games and 815 starts in his career for Cleveland NL 1890–98, St Louis NL 1899–1900, Boston AL 1901–08, Cleveland AL 1909–11 and Boston NL 1911. He pitched a record total of

World Series Records

Most series played	14	Lawrence Peter 'Yogi' Berra (New York, AL)	1947–63
Most series played, pitcher	11	Edward Charles 'Whitey' Ford (New York, AL)	1950–64
Most home runs in a game	3	George Herman 'Babe' Ruth (New York, AL)	6 Oct 1926
	3	George Herman 'Babe' Ruth (New York, AL)	9 Oct 1928
	3	Reginald Martinez Jackson (New York, AL)	18 Oct 1977
Runs batted in	6	Robert C. Richardson (New York, AL)	8 Oct 1960
Strikeouts	17	Robert Gibson (St Louis, NL)	2 Oct 1968
Perfect game (9 innings)		Donald James Larson (New York, AL) v Brooklyn	8 Oct 1956

Note: AL - American League NL - National League

7357 innings. The career record of most games pitching is 1070 by James Hoyt Wilhelm (b. 26 Jul 1923) for a total of nine teams between 1952 and 1972; he set the career record with 143 wins by a relief pitcher. The season's record is 106 games pitched by Michael Grant Marshall (b. 15 Jan 1943) for Los Angeles (NL) in 1974.

Most consecutive games won by a pitcher Carl Owen Hubbell (1903–88) pitched the New York Giants to 24 consecutive wins, 16 in 1936 and 8 in 1937.

Most consecutive hits Michael Franklin 'Pinky' Higgins (1909–69) had 12 consecutive hits for Boston (AL) 19–21 Jun 1938. This was equalled by Walter 'Moose' Droppo (b. 30 Jan 1923) for Detroit (AL) 14–15 Jul 1952. Joseph Paul DiMaggio (b. 25 Nov 1914) hit in a record 56 consecutive games for New York in 1941; he was 223 times at bat, with 91 hits, scoring 16 doubles, 4 triples and 15 home runs.

Most consecutive scoreless games Orel Leonard Hershiser IV (b. 16 Sep 1958) pitched a record 59 consecutive shutout innings from 30 Aug to 28 Sep 1988.

Perfect game A perfect nine innings game, in which the pitcher allows the opposition no hits, no runs and does not allow a man to reach first base, was first achieved by John Lee Richmond (1857–1929) for Worcester against Cleveland in the NL on 12 Jun 1880. There have been 13 subsequent perfect games over nine innings, but no pitcher has achieved this feat more than once. On 26 May 1959 Harvey Haddix Jr. (b. 18 Sep 1925) for Pittsburgh pitched perfect game for 12 innings against Milwaukee in the National League, but lost in the 13th.

Cy Young award Awarded annually from 1956 to the outstanding pitcher on the major leagues, the most wins is four by Stephen Norman Carlton (b. 22 Dec 1944) (Philadelphia, NL) 1972, 1977, 1980, 1982.

US Major League Baseball Records

Batting

AVERAGE, Career, .366 Tyrus Raymond 'Ty' Cobb (Detroit AL, Philadelphia AL) 1905–28. **Season**, .440 Hugh Duffy (Boston NL) 1894.

RUNS, Career, 2245 Tyrus Raymond Cobb 1905–28. **Season**, 192 William Robert Hamilton (Phildelphia NL) 1894.

HOME RUNS, Career*[1], 755 Henry 'Hank' Aaron (Milwaukee NL, Atlanta NL, Milwaukee AL) 1954–76. **Season**, 61 Roger Eugene Maris (New York AL) 1961.

RUNS BATTED IN, Career, 2297 Henry 'Hank' Aaron 1954–76. **Season**, 190 Lewis Rober 'Hack' Wilson (Chicago NL) 1930. **Game**, 12 James LeRoy Bottomley (St Louis NL) 16 Sep 1924; Mark Whiten (St Louis NL) 7 Sep 1993. **Innings**, 7 Edward Cartwright (St Louis AL) 23 Sep 1890.

BASE HITS, Career, 4256 Peter Edward Rose (Cincinnati NL, Philadelphia NL, Montreal NL, Cincinnati NL) 1963–86. **Season**, 257 George Harold Sisler (St Louis AL) 1920.

TOTAL BASES, Career, 6856 Henry 'Hank' Aaron 1954–76. Season, 457 George Herman 'Babe' Ruth (New York AL) 1921.

HITS, Consecutive, 12 Michael Franklin 'Pinky' Higgins (Boston AL) 19–21 Jun 1938; Walter 'Moose' Dropo (Detroit AL) 14–15 Jul 1952.

CONSECUTIVE GAMES BATTED SAFELY, 56 Joseph Paul DiMaggio (New York AL) 15 May–16 Jul 1941.

STOLEN BASES, Career, 1095 Rickey Henley Henderson (Oakland AL, New York AL, Oakland AL, Toronto AL) 1979–93. **Season**, 130 Rickey Henderson 1982.

CONSECUTIVE GAMES PLAYED*[2], 2130 Henry Louis 'Lou' Gehrig (New York AL) 1 Jun 1925–30 Apr 1939.

Pitching

GAMES WON, Career, 511 Denton True 'Cy' Young (Cleveland NL, St Louis NL, Boston AL, Cleveland AL, Boston NL) 1890–1911. **Season**, 60 Charles Gardner Radbourn (Providence NL) 1884.

CONSECUTIVE GAMES WON, 24 Carl Owen Hubbell (New York NL) 1936–7.

SHUTOUTS, Career, 113 Walter Perry Johnson (Washington AL) 1907–27. **Season**, 16 George Washington Bradley (St Louis NL) 1876; Grover Cleveland Alexander (Philadelphia NL) 1916.

STRIKEOUTS, Career, 5714 Lynn Nolan Ryan (New York NL, California AL, Houston AL, Texas AL) 1966–93. **Season**, 383 Lynn Nolan Ryan (California AL) 1973. (513 Matthew Aloysius Kilroy (Baltimore AA) 1886). **Game** (9 innings), 20 Roger Clemens (Boston AL) v. Seattle 29 Apr 1986.

NO-HIT GAMES, Career, 7 Lynn Nolan Ryan 1973–91.

EARNED RUN AVERAGE, Season, 0.90 Ferdinand Schupp (140 inns) (New York NL) 1916; 0.96 Hubert 'Dutch' Leonard (222 inns) (Boston AL) 1914; 1.12 Robert Gibson (305 inns) (St Louis NL) 1968.

Note: AL - American League
NL - National League
* Japanese League records that are superior to those in the US major leagues;
[1]868 Sadaharu Oh (Yomiuri) 1959–80.
[2]2215 Sachio Kinugasa (Hiroshima) 1970–87.

Youngest player Frederick Joseph Chapman (1872–1957) pitched for Philadelphia in the American Association at 14 yr 239 days on 22 Jul 1887, but did not play again.

The youngest major league player of all time was the Cincinnati pitcher Joseph Henry Nuxhall (b. 30 Jul 1928), who played one game in June 1944, aged 15 yr 314 days. He did not play again in the NL until 1952. The youngest player to play in a minor league game was Joe Louis Reliford (b. 29 Nov 1939) who played for the Fitzgerald Pioneers against Statesboro Pilots in the Georgia State League, aged 12 yr 234 days on 19 Jul 1952.

Oldest player Leroy Robert 'Satchel' Paige (1906–82) pitched for Kansas City A's (AL) at 59 years 80 days on 25 Sep 1965.

Card!

The most valuable cigarette card is one of the six known baseball series cards of Honus Wagner, who was a non-smoker, which was sold at Sotheby's, New York, USA for $451,000 on 22 Mar 1991. The buyers were Bruce McNall, owner of the Los Angeles Kings ice hockey club, and famous team member Wayne Gretzky.

Record attendances The all-time season record for attendances for both leagues is 70,257,938 in 1993. The record for an individual league is 36,912,502 for the National League in 1991. The record for an individual team is 4,483,350 for the home games of the Colorado Rockies at Mile High Stadium, Denver in 1993.

An estimated 114,000 spectators watched a game between Australia and an American Services team in a demonstration event during the Olympic Games at Melbourne on 1 Dec 1956.

Longest home run The longest measured home run in a major league game is 634 ft by Mickey Mantle (b. 20 Oct 1931) for the New York Yankees against the Detroit Tigers at Briggs Stadium Detroit on 10 Sep 1960.

Longest throw Glen Edward Gorbous (b. Canada,

GUESS WHAT?
Q What is the largest attendance for a basketball match?
A See Page 235

Barry Bonds of the Pittsburgh Pirates making another spectacular play and showing why he was voted the National League's Most Valuable Player for a record-equalling third time in 1993.
(Photo: Allsport USA/Otto Gruele)

Another near full house at Denver's Mile High Stadium, home of the Colorado Rockies. During their first major league season, 1993, the Rockies had the highest ever aggregate attendance for their home games, 4,483,350.
(Photo: Allsport USA/Tim Defrisco)

8 Jul 1930) threw 135.88 m *445 ft 10 in* on 1 Aug 1957.

Women Mildred Ella 'Babe' Didrikson (later Mrs Zaharias) (USA) (1914–56) threw 90.2 m *296 ft* at Jersey City, New Jersey, USA on 25 Jul 1931.

Lynn Nolan Ryan (then of the California Angels) (b. 31 Jan 1947) was measured to pitch at 162.3 km/h *100.9 mph* at Anaheim Stadium, California, USA on 20 Aug 1974.

Fastest base runner The fastest time for circling bases is 13.3 sec by Ernest Evar Swanson (1902–73) at Columbus, Ohio, USA in 1932, at an average speed of 29.70 km/h *18.45 mph*.

Basketball

Most titles *Olympic* The USA has won ten men's Olympic titles. From the time the sport was introduced to the Games in 1936 to 1972, they won 63 consecutive matches until they lost 50–51 to the USSR in the disputed Final in Munich. Since then they have won a further 29 matches and had another loss to the USSR (in 1988).

The women's title has been won a record three times by the USSR in 1976, 1980 and 1992 (by the Unified team from the republics of the ex-USSR).

World The USSR has won most titles at both the men's World Championships (instituted 1950) with three (1967, 1974 and 1982) and women's

(instituted 1953) with six (1959, 1964, 1967, 1971, 1975 and 1983). Yugoslavia have also won three men's world titles: 1970, 1978 and 1990.

European The most wins in the European Championships for men is 14 by the USSR, and in the women's event 21 also by the USSR, winning all but the 1958 championship since 1950, in this biennial contest.

The most European Champions Cup (instituted 1957) wins is seven by Real Madrid, Spain 1964–5, 1967–8, 1974, 1978 and 1980.

The women's title has been won 18 times by Daugava, Riga, Latvia between 1960 and 1982.

English The most English National Championship titles (instituted 1936) have been won by London Central YMCA, with eight wins in 1957–8, 1960, 1962–4, 1967 and 1969.

The English National League title has been won seven times by Crystal Palace 1974, 1976–8, 1980 and 1982–3. In the 1989/90 season Kingston won all five domestic trophies; the National League and Championship play-offs, the National Cup, League Cup and WIBC. The English Women's Cup (instituted 1965) has been won a record eight times by the Tigers, 1972–3, 1976–80 and 1982.

Highest score In a senior international match Iraq scored 251 against Yemen (33) at New Delhi in November 1982 at the Asian Games.

The highest in a British Championship is 125 by England *v.* Wales (54) on 1 Sep 1978. England beat Gibraltar 130–45 on 31 Aug 1978.

US College The NCAA aggregate record is 399 when Troy State (258) beat De Vry Institute, Atlanta (141) at Troy, Alabama on 12 Jan 1992. Troy's total is the highest individual team score in a match.

United Kingdom The highest score recorded in a match is 250 by the Nottingham YMCA Falcons *v.* Mansfield Pirates at Nottingham on 18 Jun 1974. It was a handicap competition and Mansfield received 120 points towards their total of 145.

The highest score in a senior National League match is 174 by Chiltern Fast Break *v.* Swindon Rakers (40) on 13 Oct 1990.

The highest in the National Cup is 157 by Solent Stars *v.* Corby (57) on 6 Jan 1991.

Individual Mats Wermelin (Sweden), age 13, scored all 272 points in a 272–0 win in a regional boys' tournament in Stockholm, Sweden on 5 Feb 1974.

The record score by a woman is 156 points by Marie Boyd (now Eichler) of Central HS, Lonaconing, Maryland, USA in a 163–3 defeat of Ursaline Academy, Cumbria on 25 Feb 1924.

The highest score by a British player is 124 points by Paul Ogden for St Albans School, Oldham (226) *v.* South Chadderton (82) on 9 Mar 1982.

The highest individual score in a league match in Britain is 108 by Lewis Young for Forth Steel in his team 's 154–74 win over Stirling in the Scottish League Division One at Stirling on 2 Mar 1985.

The record in an English National League (Div. One) or Cup match is 73

GUESS WHAT?

Q Where was the world's largest basket made?

A See Page 215

points by Terry Crosby (USA) for Bolton in his team's 120–106 defeat by Manchester Giants at Altrincham, Cheshire on 26 Jan 1985; by Billy Hungrecker in a semi-final play-off for Worthing *v.* Plymouth at Worthing, W Sussex on 20 Mar 1988; and by Renaldo Lawrence for Stevenage in his team's 113–102 win against Gateshead on 30 Dec 1989.

GUESS WHAT?

Q How far did Ashrita Furman dribble a basketball in 24 hours?

A See Page 211

National Basketball Association

Most titles Boston Celtics have won a record 16 NBA titles, 1957, 1959–66, 1968–9, 1974, 1976, 1981, 1984, 1986.

Highest score The highest aggregate score in an NBA match is 370 when the Detroit Pistons (186) beat the Denver Nuggets (184) at Denver on 13 Dec 1983. Overtime was played after a 145–145 tie in regulation time. The record in regulation time is 320, when the Golden State Warriors beat Denver 162–158 at Denver on 2 Nov 1990. The most points in a half is 107 by the Phoenix Suns in the first half against Denver on 11 Nov 1990. The most points in a quarter is 58 (fourth) by Buffalo at Boston on 20 Oct 1972.

Individual scoring Wilton Norman 'Wilt' Chamberlain (b. 21 Aug 1936) set an NBA record with 100 points for Philadelphia *v* New York at Hershey, Pennsylvania on 2 Mar 1962. This included a record 36 field goals and 28 free throws (from 32 attempts) and a record 59 points in a half (the second). The free throws game record was equalled by Adrian Dantley (b. 28 Feb 1956) for Utah *v.* Houston at Las Vegas on 5 Jan 1984. The most points scored in an NBA game in one quarter is 33 (second) by George Gervin for San Antonio *v.* New Orleans on 9 Apr 1978.

Most games Kareem Abdul-Jabbar (formerly Ferdinand Lewis Alcindor) (b. 16 Apr 1947) took part in a record 1560 NBA regular season games over 20 seasons, totalling 57,446 minutes played, for the Milwaukee Bucks, 1969–75, and the Los Angeles Lakers, 1975–89. He also played a record 237 play-off games. The most successive games is 906 by Randy Smith for Buffalo, San Diego, Cleveland and New York from 18 Feb 1972 to 13 Mar 1983. The record for complete games played in one season is 79 by Wilt Chamberlain for Philadelphia in 1962, when he was on court for a record 3882 minutes. Chamberlain went through his entire career of 1045 games without fouling out.

Most points Kareem Abdul-Jabbar set NBA career records with 38,387 points (average 24.6 points per game), including 15,837 field goals in regular season games, and 5762 points, including 2356 field goals in play-off games. The previous record holder, Wilt Chamberlain, had an average of 30.1 points per game for his total of 31,419 for Philadelphia 1959–62, San Francisco 1962–5, Philadelphia 1964–8 and Los Angeles 1968–73. He scored 50 or more points in 118 games, including 45 in 1961/2 and 30 in 1962/3 to the next best career total of 17. He set season's records for points and scoring average with 4029 at 50.4 per game, and also for field goals, 1597, for Philadelphia in 1961/2. The highest career average for players exceeding 10,000 points is 32.3 by Michael Jordan (b. 17 Feb 1963), 21,541 points in 667 games for the Chicago Bulls, 1984–93. Jordan also holds the career scoring average record for play-offs at 34.7 for 3850

points in 111 games, 1984–93.

Winning margin The greatest winning margin in an NBA game is 68 points when the Cleveland Cavaliers beat the Miami Heat, 148–80 on 17 Dec 1991.

Winning streak Los Angeles Lakers won a record 33 NBA games in succession from 5 Nov 1971 to 7 Jan 1972, as during the 1971/2 season they won a record 69 games with 13 losses.

Youngest and oldest player The youngest NBA player has been Bill Willoughby (b. 20 May 1957), who made his début for Atlanta Hawks on 23 Oct 1975 at 18 yr 156 days. The oldest NBA regular player was Kareem Abdul-Jabbar, who made his last appearance for the Los Angeles Lakers at 42 yr 59 days in 1989.

Other records

Most points The records for the most points scored in a college career are (women): 4061, Pearl Moore of Francis Marion College, Florence, South Carolina, USA, 1975–9; (men): 4045 by Travis Grant for Kentucky State, USA in 1969–72.

In the English National League, Russ Saunders (b. 25 Nov 1957) has scored 5504 points, 1982–93, and the most apperances is 383 by Paul Philp (b. 23 Dec 1952), 1972–93.

Tallest players Suleiman 'Ali Nashnush (1943–91) was reputed to be 2.45 m *8 ft ¼ in* when he played for the Libyan team in 1962.

British Christopher Greener of London Latvians was 2.29 m *7 ft 6¼ in* and made his international début for England *v.* France on 17 Dec 1969.

The tallest in NBA history has been Manute Bol (Sudan) (b. 16 Oct 1962) of the Washington Bullets and Golden State Warriors at 7 ft 6¾ in 2.30 m. He made his pro début in 1985.

Shooting speed The greatest goal-shooting demonstration has been by Ted St Martin of Jacksonville, Florida, USA who, on 25 Jun 1977, scored 2036 consecutive free throws. On 11 Jun 1992 Jeff Liles scored 231 out of 240 attempts in 10 minutes at Southern Nazarene University, Bethany, Oklahoma, USA. He repeated this total of 231 (241 attempts) on 16 June. This speed record is achieved using one ball and one rebounder.

In 24 hours Fred Newman scored 20,371 free throws from a total of 22,049 taken (92.39 per cent) at Caltech, Pasadena, California, USA on 29–30 Sep 1990.

Steve Bontrager (USA) (b. 1 Mar 1959) of Polycell Kingston scored 21 points in a minute from seven positions in a demonstration for BBC TV's *Record Breakers* on 29 Oct 1986.

Dribbling!

Bob Nickerson of Gallitzin, Pennsylvania, Dave Davlin of Garland, Texas and Jeremy Kable of Highspire, Pennsylvania, all USA, have each successfully demonstrated the ability to dribble four basketballs simultaneously.

Longest goal Christopher Eddy (b. 13 Jul 1971) scored a field goal, measured at 27.49 m *90 ft 2¼ in,* for Fairview High School *v.* Iroquois High School at Erie, Pennsylvania, USA on 25 Feb 1989. The shot was made as time expired in overtime and it won the game for Fairview, 51–50.

British A distance of 23.10 m *75 ft 9½ in* is claimed by David Tarbatt (b. 23 Jan 1949) of Altofts Aces *v.* Harrogate Demons at Featherstone, W Yorks on 27 Jan 1980.

Largest attendance The largest crowd for a basketball match is 80,000 for the final of the European Cup Winners' Cup between AEK Athens (89) and Slavia Prague (82) at the Olympic stadium, Athens, Greece on 4 Apr 1968.

Billiards

Most titles *World* The greatest number of World Championships (instituted 1870) won by one player is eight by John Roberts Jr (GB) (1847–1919) in 1870 (twice), 1871, 1875 (twice), 1877 and 1885 (twice). The record for world amateur titles is four by Robert James Percival Marshall (Australia) (b. 10 Apr 1910) in 1936, 1938, 1951 and 1962.

Britain The greatest number of United Kingdom professional titles (instituted 1934) won is seven (1934–9 and 1947) by Joe Davis (1901–78), who also won four world titles (1928–30 and 1932). The greatest number of English Amateur Championships (instituted 1888) won is 15 by Norman Dagley (b. 27 Jun 1930) in 1965–6, 1970–5, 1978–84. The record number of women's titles is nine by Vera Selby (b. 13 Mar 1930), 1970–78. Uniquely, Norman Dagley has won the English Amateur Championships (as above), World Amateur Championships (1971, 1975), United Kingdom Professional Championship (1987) and World Professional Championship (1987).

Youngest champion The youngest winner of the world professional title is Mike Russell (b. 3 Jun 1969), aged 20 yr 49 days, when he won at Leura, Australia on 23 Jul 1989.

Highest breaks Tom Reece (1873–1953) made an unfinished break of 499,135, including 249,152 cradle cannons (two points each) in 85 hr 49 min against Joe Chapman at Burroughes' Hall, Soho Square, London between 3 Jun and 6 Jul 1907. This was not recognized because press and public were not continuously present.

The highest certified break made by the anchor cannon is 42,746 by William Cook (England) from 29 May to 7 Jun 1907.

Walter Lindrum made an unofficial 100 break in 27.5 sec in Australia on 10 Oct 1952. His official record is 100 in 46.0 sec set in Sydney, Australia in 1941.

The official world record under the then baulk-line rule is 1784 by Joe Davis in the United Kingdom Championship on 29 May 1936.

Walter Albert Lindrum (Australia) (1898–1960) made an official break of 4137 in 2 hr 55 min against Joe Davis at Thurston's on 19–20 Jan 1932, before the baulk-line rule was in force. Geet Sethi (India) made a break of 1276 in the World Professional Championship in Bombay, India on 1 Oct 1992.

The highest break recorded in amateur competition is 1149 by Michael Ferreira (India) at Calcutta, India on 15 Dec 1978. Under the more stringent 'two pot' rule, restored on 1 Jan 1983, the highest break is Ferreira's 962 unfinished in a tournament at Bombay, India on 29 Apr 1986.

3 Cushion

Most titles William F. Hoppe (USA) (1887–1959) won 51 billiards championships in all forms spanning the pre- and post-international era from 1906 to 1952.

UMB Raymond Ceulemans (Belgium) (b. 12 Jul 1935) has won 20 world three-cushion championships (1963–73, 1975–80, 1983, 1985, 1990).

Bar billiards Keith Sheard scored 28,530 in 19 min 5 sec in a league game at the Crown and Thistle, Headington, Oxford on 9 Jul 1984. Sheard scored 1500 points in a minute on BBC TV's *Record Breakers* on 23 Sep 1986.

The highest score in 24 hours by a team of five is 1,754,730 by Les Green, Ricard Powell, Kevin Clark, Mick Lingham and Curt Driver of The Shipwrights Arms, Chatham, Kent on 26–27 May 1990.

Board Games

Chess

World Championships World champions have been officially recognized since 1886. The longest undisputed tenure was 26 yr 337 days by Dr Emanuel Lasker (1868–1941) of Germany, from 1894 to 1921.

The women's world championship title was held by Vera Francevna Stevenson-Menchik (USSR, later GB) (1906–44) from 1927 until her death, and was successfully defended a record seven times.

Team The USSR has won the biennial men's team title (Olympiad) a record 18 times between 1952 and 1990, and the women's title 11 times from its introduction in 1957 to 1986.

Youngest Gary Kimovich Kasparov (USSR) (b. 13 Apr 1963) won the title on 9 Nov 1985 at 22 yr 210 days.

Maya Grigoryevna Chiburdanidze (USSR) (b. 17 Jan 1961) won the women's title in 1978 when only 17.

Oldest Wilhelm Steinitz (Austria, later USA) (1836–1900) was 58 yr 10 days when he lost his title to Lasker on 26 May 1894.

Most active Anatoliy Yevgenyevich Karpov (USSR) (b. 23 May 1951) in his tenure as champion, 1975–85, averaged 45.2 competitive games per year, played in 32 tournaments and finished first in 26.

Most British titles The most British titles have been won by Dr Jonathan Penrose (b. 7 Oct 1933) with ten titles in 1958–63, 1966–9. Rowena Mary Bruce (*née* Dew) (b. 15 May 1919) won 11 women's titles between 1937 and 1969.

Highest rating The highest rating ever attained on the officially adopted Elo System (devised by Arpad E. Elo (1903–92)) is 2805 by Gary

Kasparov (USSR) at the end of 1992. The highest-rated woman player is Judit Polgar (Hungary), who achieved a peak rating of 2630 at the end of 1993.

> **The oldest pieces identified as chess pieces were found at Nashipur, datable to c.AD 900.**

The top British player on the Elo list has been Nigel David Short (b. 1 Jun 1965) who reached a peak rating of 2685 at the end of 1991. The top British woman is Susan Kathryn Arkell (*née* Walker) (b. 28 Oct 1965) who reached a peak of 2355 on 1 Jul 1988.

Fewest games lost by a world champion José Raúl Capablanca (Cuba) (1888–1942) lost only 34 games (out of 571) in his adult career, 1909–39. He was unbeaten from 10 Feb 1916 to 21 Mar 1924 (63 games) and was world champion 1921–7.

Most opponents The record for most consecutive games played is 663 by Vlastimil Hort (Czechoslovakia, later Germany) (b. 12 Jan 1944) over 32½ hours at Porz, Germany on 5–6 Oct 1984. He played 60–120 opponents at a time, scoring over 80 per cent wins and averaging 30 moves per game. He also holds the record for most games simultaneously, 201 during 550 consecutive games of which he only lost ten, in Seltjarnes, Iceland on 23–24 Apr 1977.

Slowest moves The slowest reported moving (before time clocks were used) in an official event is reputed to have been by Louis Paulsen (Germany) (1833–91) against Paul Charles Morphy (USA) (1837–84) at the first American Chess Congress, New York on 29 Oct 1857. The game ended in a draw on move 56 after 15 hours of play of which Paulsen used c. 11 hours.

Grand Master Friedrich Sämisch (Germany) (1896–1975) ran out of the allotted time (2 hr 30 min for 45 moves) after only 12 moves, in Prague, Czechoslovakia, in 1938.

> **The shortest time taken to complete the game of solitaire is 10.0 sec by Stephen Twigge at Scissett Baths, W Yorks on 2 Aug 1991.**

The slowest move played, since time clocks were introduced, was at Vigo, Spain in 1980 when Francisco R. Torres Trois (b. 3 Sep 1946) took 2 hr 20 min for his seventh move *v.* Luis M. C. P. Santos (b. 30 Jun 1955).

The Master game with most moves on record was one of 269 moves, when Ivan Nikolic´ drew with Goran Arsovic´ in a Belgrade, Yugoslavia tournament, on 17 Feb 1989. It took a total of 20 hr 15 min.

Draughts

World champions Walter Hellman (USA) (1916–75) won a record eight world titles during his tenure as world champion 1948–75.

British titles The British Championship (biennial) was inaugurated in 1886 and has been won six times by Samuel Cohen (London) (1905–72), 1924, 1927, 1929, 1933, 1937 and 1939. John McGill (Kilbride) (b. 1936) won six Scottish titles between 1959 and 1974.

Youngest and oldest national champion Asa A. Long (b. 20 Aug 1904) became the youngest US national champion, aged 18 yr 64 days, when he won in Boston, Massachusetts, USA on 23 Oct 1922. He became the oldest, aged 79 yr 334 days, when he won his sixth title in Tupelo, Mississippi, USA on 21 Jul 1984. He was also world champion 1934–8.

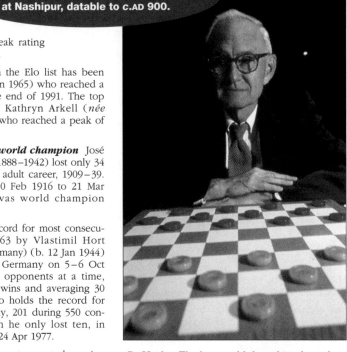

Dr Marion Tinsley, world draughts champion from 1975–91, who was internationally undefeated in matchplay from 1947.
(Photo: Gamma/A. Berg)

Most opponents Charles Walker played a record 296 games simultaneously, winning 294 and drawing the other two, at Kenosha, Wisconsin, USA on 6 Jun 1993.

The largest number of opponents played without a defeat or draw is 172 by Nate Cohen of Portland, Maine, USA at Portland on 26 Jul 1981. This was not a simultaneous attempt, but consecutive play over a period of four hours.

Scrabble (Crossword Game)

Highest scores The highest competitive game score is 1049 by Phil Appleby (b. 9 Dec 1957) in June 1989. His opponent scored 253 and the margin of victory, 796 points, is also a record.

His score included a single turn of 374 for the word 'OXIDIZERS'. The highest competitive single turn score recorded, however, is 392 by Dr Saladin Karl Khoshnaw (of Kurdish origin) in Manchester in April 1982. He laid down 'CAZIQUES', which means 'native chiefs of West Indian aborigines'.

Most titles British National Championships were instituted in 1971. Philip Nelkon (b. 21 Jul 1956) has won a record four times, 1978, 1981, 1990 and 1992.

Toppling!

The greatest number of dominoes set up single-handed and toppled is 281,581 out of 320,236 by Klaus Friedrich, 22, at Fürth, Germany on 27 Jan 1984. The dominoes fell within 12 min 57.3 sec, having taken 31 days (10 hr daily) to set up.

Thirty students at Delft, Eindhoven and Twente Technical Universities in the Netherlands set up 1,500,000 dominoes representing all of the European Community countries. Of these, 1,382,101 were toppled by one push on 2 Jan 1988.

Ralf Laue successfully stacked 296 dominoes on a single supporting domino on 11 Jul 1993 in Leipzig, Germany.

World Championship The first world championship was held in London in 1991 and was played in English. The winner was Peter Morris (USA) (b. 1962) who collected a first prize of $10,000.

Cresta Run The course is 1212 m *3977 ft* long with a drop of 157 m *514 ft* and the record is 50.41 sec (av. 86.56 km/h *53.79 mph*) by Christian Bertschinger (Switzerland) (b. 8 Feb 1964) on 23 Feb 1992. On 20 Jan 1991 he set a record from Junction (890 m *2920 ft*) of 41.45 sec.

The greatest number of wins in the Grand National (instituted 1885) is eight by the 1948 Olympic champion Nino Bibbia (Italy) (b. 15 Mar 1922) in 1960–64, 1966, 1968 and 1973; and by Franco Gassner (Switzerland) (b. 2 May 1945) in 1981, 1983–6, 1988–9 and 1991. The greatest number of wins in the Curzon Cup (instituted 1910) is eight by Bibbia in 1950, 1957–8, 1960, 1962–4, and 1969.

Margit Schumann (GDR) (b. 14 Sep 1952) has won five women's titles, 1973–5, 1976 (Olympic) and 1977. Steffi Walter (*née* Martin) (GDR) (b. 17 Sep 1962) became the first rider to win two Olympic single-seater luge titles, with victories at the women's event in 1984 and 1988.

The oldest person to have ridden the Cresta Run successfully is Robin Todhunter (GB) (b. 10 Mar 1903), aged 83 yr 329 days on 2 Feb 1987.

The appropriately-numbered two-man bob of Switzerland I, driven by Gustav Weder and crewed by Donat Acklin, winning their second Olympic gold (1992 and 1994) and a record fourth success for Switzerland.
(Photo: Allsport/Pascal Rondeau)

Bobsleigh and Tobogganing

Bobsledding

Most titles *World and Olympic* The world four-man bob title (instituted 1924) has been won 20 times by Switzerland (1924, 1936, 1939, 1947, 1954–7, 1971–3, 1975, 1982–3, 1986–90, 1993) including a record five Olympic victories (1924, 1936, 1956, 1972 and 1988).

Switzerland have won the two-man title 17 times (1935, 1947–50, 1953, 1955, 1977–80, 1982–3, 1987, 1990, 1992 and 1994) including a record four Olympic successes (1948, 1980, 1992 and 1994).

Eugenio Monti was a member of eleven world championship crews, eight two-man and three four-man in 1957–68.

The most Olympic gold medals won by an individual is three by Meinhard Nehmer (GDR) (b. 13 Jun 1941) and Bernhard Germeshausen (GDR) (b. 21 Aug 1951) in the 1976 two-man, 1976 and 1980 four-man events. The most medals won is six (two gold, two silver, two bronze) by Eugenio Monti (Italy) (b. 23 Jan 1928), 1956 to 1968.

The only British victory was at two-man bob in 1964 by the Hon. Thomas Robin Valerian Dixon (b. 21 Apr 1935) and Anthony James Dillon Nash (b. 18 Mar 1936).

Tobogganing

Oldest club The St Moritz Tobogganing Club, Switzerland, founded in 1887, is the oldest toboggan club in the world. It is notable for being the home of the Cresta Run, which dates from 1884.

Lugeing

Most titles The most successful riders in the World Championships (instituted 1953) have been Thomas Köhler (GDR) (b. 25 Jun 1940), who won the single-seater title in 1962, 1964 (Olympic) and 1967 and shared the two-seater title in 1965, 1967 and 1968 (Olympic). Georg Hackl (GDR/Germany) (b. 9 Sep 1966) has won four single-seater titles, 1989, 1990, 1992 (Olympic) and 1994 (Olympic).

The highest recorded, photo-timed speed is 137.4 km/h *85.38 mph* by Asle Strand (Norway) at Tandadalens Linbana, Sälen, Sweden on 1 May 1982.

German Georg Hackl won the single-seater luge Olympic title in 1994, a record fourth individual world or Olympic title.
(Photo: Allsport/Pascal Rondeau)

Bowling (Tenpin)

Highest scores The highest individual score for three sanctioned games (possible 900) is 899 by Thomas Jordan (USA) (b. 27 Oct 1966) at Union, New Jersey, USA on 7 Mar 1989. The record by a woman is 864 by Jeanne Maiden (b. 10 Nov 1957) of Tacoma, Washington at Solon, Ohio, USA on 23 Nov 1986. This series included a record 40 consecutive strikes.

The maximum 900 for a three-game series was achieved by Glenn Richard Allison (b. 22 May 1930) at the La Habra Bowl in Los Angeles, California, USA on 1 Jul 1982, but this was not recognized by the ABC due to the oiling patterns on the boards. It has been recorded five times in unsanctioned games–by Leon Bentley at Lorain, Ohio, USA on 26 Mar 1931; by Joe Sargent at Rochester, New York, USA in 1934; by Jim Murgie in Philadelphia, Pennsylvania, USA on 4 Feb 1937; by Bob Brown at Roseville Bowl, California, USA on 12 Apr 1980 and by John Strausbaugh at York, Pennsylvania, USA on 11 Jul 1987. Such series must have consisted of 36 consecutive strikes (i.e. all pins down with one ball).

The highest average for a season attained in sanctioned competition is 245.63 by Doug Vergouven of Harrisonville, Missouri, USA in 1989/90. The women's record is 232 by Patty Ann of Appleton, Wisconsin, USA in 1983/4.

Great Britain The British record for a three–game series is 847 by Lawrence William Ellis (b. 7 Dec 1950) at Airport Bowl, Hounslow, Greater London on 30 Aug 1992.

The three–game series record for a woman player is 740 by Elizabeth Cullen at the Astra Bowl, RAF Brize Norton, Oxon on 15 Mar 1983.

The maximum score for a single game of 300 has been achieved on several occasions. The first man to do so was Albert Kirkham (b. 1931) of Burslem, Staffs on 5 Dec 1965. The first woman was Georgina Wardle (b. 24 Jul 1948) at the Sheffield Bowl, S Yorks on 20 Jan 1985. The first person to achieve the feat twice is Patrick Duggan (b. 26 May 1944), in 1972 and 1986, both at Bexleyheath Bowl, Kent.

PBA records Earl Roderick Anthony (b. 27 Apr 1938) was the first to win $1 million and won a record 41 PBA titles in his career.

The season's record earnings is $298,237 by Mike Aulby (b. 25 Mar 1960) in 1989. The career record is $1,606,961 by Marshall Holman (b. 29 Sep 1954) to end of 1993.

Highest!

The greatest score in 24 hours by a team of six is 217,969 at Strykers Pleasure Bowl, Bushbury, Wolverhampton, W Mids on 15–16 Oct 1993. A member of the team, Dean Steeles, set an individual record of 48,969.

GUESS WHAT?

Q Who is the fastest recorded bowler in cricket?

A See Page 243

he has won six World Championship gold medals.

The Leonard Trophy has been won three times by Scotland, 1972, 1984 and 1992.

Elsie Wilke (New Zealand) won two women's singles titles, 1969 and 1974. Three women have won three gold medals: Merle Richardson (Australia) fours 1977, singles and pairs 1985; Dorothy Roche (Australia) triples 1985 and 1988, fours 1988; and Margaret Johnston (Ireland) singles 1992 and pairs 1988 and 1992.

English and British Championships The record number of English Bowls Association (founded 8 Jun 1903) championships is 16 won or shared by David Bryant, including six singles (1960, 1966, 1971–3, 1975), three pairs (1965, 1969, 1974), three triples (1966, 1977, 1985) and four fours championships (1957, 1968, 1969 and 1971). He has also won seven British Isles titles (four singles, one pairs, one triple, one fours) in the period 1957–86. 1987.

The youngest ever EBA singles champion was David A. Holt (b. 9 Sep 1966) at 20 yr 346 days in 1987.

Highest score In an international bowls match, Swaziland beat Japan by 63–1 during the World Championships at Melbourne, Australia on 16 Jan 1980.

Most eights Freda Ehlers and Linda Bertram uniquely scored three consecutive eights in the Southern Transvaal pairs event at Johannesburg, South Africa on 30 Jan 1978.

Indoor

World Championships (instituted 1979) The most singles titles is three by: David Bryant, 1979–81 and Richard Corsie (GB), 1989, 1991 and 1993. Bryant with Tony Allcock (b. 11 Jun 1955) has won the pairs (instituted 1986) six times, 1986–7, 1989–92.

English Nationals (instituted 1960) The EIBA Singles Championship has been won most often by David Bryant with nine wins between 1964 and 1983. The youngest EIBA singles champion, John Dunn (b. 6 Oct 1963), was 17 yr 117 days when he won in 1981.

Highest score The highest total in fours is 59 by Eastbourne & District Indoor Bowls Club against Egerton Park, at Eastbourne, E Sussex on 7 Feb 1989; and by Glebelands against Temple Fortune at Finchley, Greater London on 6 Jan 1994. The greatest 'whitewash' is 55–0 by C. Hammond and B. Funnell against A. Wise and C. Lock in the second round of the EIBA National Pairs Championships on 17 Oct 1983 at The Angel, Tonbridge, Kent.

Bowls

Outdoor

World Championships (instituted 1966) The only man to win two or more singles titles is David John Bryant (England) (b. 27 Oct 1931), who won in 1966, 1980 and 1988. With the triples 1980, and the Leonard Trophy 1980 and 1988,

Boxing

Longest fights The longest recorded fight with gloves was between Andy Bowen of New Orleans (1867–94) and Jack Burke at New Orleans, Louisiana, USA on 6–7 Apr 1893. It lasted 110 rounds, 7 hr 19 min (9:15 p.m.–4:34 a.m.), and was declared a no contest (later changed to a draw). Bowen won an 85-round bout on 31 May 1893.

The longest bare-knuckle fight was 6 hr 15 min between James Kelly and Jack Smith at Fiery Creek, Dalesford, Victoria, Australia on 3 Dec 1855.

The greatest number of rounds was 276 in 4 hr 30 min when Jack Jones beat Patsy Tunney in Cheshire in 1825.

Shortest fights There is a distinction between the quickest knock-out and the shortest fight. A knock-out in 10½ sec (including a 10 sec count) occurred on 23 Sep 1946, when Al Couture struck Ralph Walton while the latter was adjusting a gum shield in his corner at Lewiston, Maine, USA. If the time was accurately taken it is clear that Couture must have been more than half-way across the ring from his own corner at the opening bell.

The shortest fight on record appears to be one in a Golden Gloves tournament at Minneapolis, Minnesota, USA on 4 Nov 1947, when Mike Collins floored Pat Brownson with the first punch and the contest was stopped, without a count, 4 sec after the bell.

The shortest world title fight was 20 sec, when Gerald McClellan (USA) beat Jay Bell in an WBC middleweight bout at Puerto Rico on 7 Aug 1993.

The shortest ever heavyweight world title fight was the James J. Jeffries (1875–1953)–Jack Finnegan bout at Detroit, USA on 6 Apr 1900, won by Jeffries in 55 sec.

The shortest ever British title fight was one of 40 sec (including the count), when Dave Charnley knocked out David 'Darkie' Hughes in a lightweight championship defence in Nottingham on 20 Nov 1961.

Eugene Brown, on his professional debut, knocked out Ian Bockes of Hull at Leicester on 13 Mar 1989. The fight was officially stopped after '10 seconds of the first round'. Bockes got up after a count of six but the referee stopped the contest.

Most British titles The most defences of a British heavyweight title is 14 by 'Bombardier' Billy Wells (1889–1967) from 1911 to 1919.

The only British boxer to win three Lonsdale Belts outright was heavyweight Henry William Cooper (b. 3 May 1934). He retired after losing to Joe Bugner (b. Hungary, 13 Mar 1950), having held the British heavyweight title from 12 Jan 1959 to 28 May 1969 and from 24 Mar 1970 to 16 Mar 1971.

The fastest time to win a Lonsdale Belt, for three successive championship wins, is 160 days by Colin McMillan at feather-weight, 22 May–29 Oct 1991.

The longest time for winning a Lonsdale Belt outright is 8 yr 236 days by Kirkland Laing (b. 20 Jun 1954), 4 Apr 1979–26 Nov 1987.

Lennox Lewis is the only British boxer to win both a world professional title and an Olympic gold (although he represented Canada when he won the super-heavyweight title in 1988).

(Photo: Allsport/Simon Bruty)

GUESS WHAT?

Q How many golds have Canada won at the Olympics?

A See Page 277

Tallest The tallest boxer to fight professionally was Gogea Mitu (b. 1914) of Romania in 1935. He was 2.23 m *7 ft 4 in* and weighed 148 kg *327 lb*. John Rankin, who won a fight in New Orleans, Louisiana, USA in November 1967, was reputedly also 2.23 m *7 ft 4 in*. Jim Culley, 'The Tipperary Giant', who fought as a boxer and wrestled in the 1940s is also reputed to have been 2.23 m *7 ft 4 in*.

Most fights without loss Edward Henry (Harry) Greb (USA) (1894–1926) was unbeaten in a sequence of 178 bouts, but these included 117 'no decision', of which five were unofficial losses, in 1916–23.

Of boxers with complete records, Packey McFarland (USA) (1888–1936) had 97 fights (5 draws) in 1905–15 without a defeat.

Pedro Carrasco (Spain) (b. 7 Nov 1943) won 83 consecutive fights from 22 April 1964 to 3 Sep 1970, drew once and had a further nine wins before his loss to Armando Ramos in a WBC lightweight contest on 18 Feb 1972.

Attendances Highest The greatest paid attendance at any boxing match is 132,274 for four world title fights at the Aztec Stadium, Mexico City on 20 Feb 1993, headed by the successful WBC super lightweight defence by Julio César Chávez (Mexico) over Greg Haugen (USA).

The indoor record is 63,350 at the Ali *v.* Leon Spinks (b. 11 Jul 1953) fight in the Superdome, New Orleans, Louisiana, USA on 15 Sep 1978.

The British attendance record is 82,000 at the Len Harvey *v.* Jock McAvoy fight at White City, London on 10 Jul 1939.

The highest non-paying attendance is 135,132 at the Tony Zale *v.* Billy Pryor fight at Juneau Park, Milwaukee, Wisconsin, USA on 16 Aug 1941.

Lowest The smallest attendance at a world heavy-weight title fight was 2434, at the Cassius (Muhammad Ali) Clay *v* Sonny Liston fight at Lewiston, Maine, USA on 25 May 1965.

World Champions: Heavyweight

Reign Longest Joe Louis (USA) (b. Joseph Louis Barrow, 1914–81) was champion for 11 years 252 days, from 22 Jun 1937, when he knocked out James Joseph Braddock in the eighth round at Chicago, Illinois, USA, until announcing his retirement on 1 Mar 1949. During his reign Louis made a record 25 defences of his title.

Shortest Tony Tucker (USA) (b. 28 Dec 1958) was IBF champion for 64 days, 30 May–2 Aug 1987, the shortest duration for a title won and lost in the ring.

Most recaptures Muhammad Ali is the only man to regain the heavy-weight championship twice. Ali first won the title on 25 Feb 1964, defeating Sonny Liston. He defeated George Foreman on 30 Oct 1974, having been stripped of the title by the world boxing authorities on 28 Apr 1967. He won the WBA title from Leon Spinks on 15 Sep 1978, having previously lost to him on 15 Feb 1978.

Undefeated Rocky Marciano (USA) (b. Rocco Francis Marchegiano) (1923–69) is the only world champion at *any weight* to have won every fight of his entire completed professional career, from 17 Mar 1947–21 Sep 1955 (he announced his retirement on 27 Apr 1956); 43 of his 49 fights were by knock-outs or stoppages.

Heaviest Primo Carnera (Italy) (1906–7), the 'Ambling Alp', who won the title from Jack Sharkey in New York City, USA on 29 Jun 1933, scaled 118 kg *260 lb* for this fight but his peak weight was

Youngest!

Mike Tyson (USA) was 20 yr 144 days when he beat Trevor Berbick (USA) to win the WBC version at Las Vegas, Nevada, USA on 22 Nov 1986. He added the WBA title when he beat James 'Bonecrusher' Smith on 7 Mar 1987 at 20 yr 249 days. He became universal champion on 2 Aug 1987 when he beat Tony Tucker (USA) for the IBF title.

122 kg *269 lb*. He had an expanded chest measurement of 137 cm *54 in* and the longest reach at 217 cm *85½ in* (fingertip to fingertip).

Lightest Robert James 'Bob' Fitzsimmons (1863–1917), from Helston, Cornwall weighed 75 kg *165 lb*, when he won the title by knocking out James J. Corbett at Carson City, Nevada, USA on 17 Mar 1897.

Longest-lived Jack Sharkey (b. Joseph Paul Zukauskas, 26 Oct 1902), champion from 21 Jun 1932 to 29 Jun 1933, surpassed the previous record of 87 yr 341 days held by Jack Dempsey (1895–1983) on 3 Oct 1990.

World Champions: Any weight

Reign Longest The Joe Louis heavyweight duration record of 11 yr 252 days stands for all divisions.

Shortest Tony Canzoneri (USA) (1908–59) was world light-welterweight champion for 33 days, 21 May to 23 Jun 1933, the shortest period for a boxer to have won and lost the world title in the ring.

Youngest Wilfred Benitez (b. New York, 12 Sep 1958) of Puerto Rico, was 17 yr 176 days when he won the WBA light welterweight title in San Juan, Puerto Rico on 6 Mar 1976.

Oldest Archie Moore, who was recognized as a light heavyweight champion up to 10 Feb 1962 when his title was removed, was then believed to be between 45 and 48.

Longest career Bob Fitzsimmons had a career of over 31 years from 1883 to 1914. He had his last world title bout on 20 Dec 1905 at the age of 42 yr 208 days. Jack Johnson (USA) (1878–1946) also had a career of over 31 years, 1897–1928.

Longest fight The longest world title fight (under Queensberry Rules) was that between the lightweights Joe Gans (1874–1910), of the USA, and Oscar Matthew 'Battling' Nelson (1882–1954), the 'Durable Dane', at Goldfield, Nevada, USA on 3 Sep 1906. It was terminated in the 42nd round when Gans was declared the winner on a foul.

Most different weights The first boxer to have won world titles at four weight categories was Thomas Hearns (USA) (b. 18 Oct 1958), WBA welterweight in 1980, WBC super welterweight in 1982, WBC light heavy-weight in 1987 and WBC middleweight in 1987. He added a fifth weight division when he won the super mid-dleweight title recog-nized by the newly created World Boxing Organization (WBO) on 4 Nov 1988, and he won the WBA light heavyweight title on 3 Jun 1991.

Oldest!

Jersey Joe Walcott (USA) (b. Arnold Raymond Cream, 1914–94) was 37 yr 168 days, when he knocked out Ezzard Mack Charles (1921–75) on 18 Jul 1951 in Pittsburgh, Pennsylvania, USA. He was also the oldest holder at 38 yr 236 days, losing his title to Rocky Marciano on 23 Sep 1952.

Sugar Ray Leonard (USA) (b. 17 May 1956) has also claimed world titles in five weight categories. Having previously won the WBC welterweight in 1979 and 1980, WBA junior middleweight in 1981 and WBC middleweight in 1987, he beat Donny Lalonde (Canada) on 7 Nov 1988, for both the WBC light heavyweight and super middleweight titles. However, despite the fact that the WBC sanctioned the fight, it is contrary to their rules to contest two divisions in the one fight. Consequently, although Leonard won, he had to relinquish one of the titles.

GUESS WHAT?

Q Who was the lightest heavyweight world champion?

A See Page 239

The feat of holding world titles at three weights *simultaneously* was achieved by Henry 'Homicide Hank' Armstrong (USA) (1912–88), at featherweight, lightweight and welterweight from August to December 1938. It is argued, however, that Barney Ross (b. Barnet David Rosofsky, USA) (1909–67) held the lightweight, junior-welterweight and welterweight, simultaneously, from 28 May to 17 Sep 1934 (although there is some dispute as to when he relinquished his light-weight title).

In recent years there has been a proliferation of weight categories and governing bodies but Armstrong was undisputed world champion at widely differing weights which makes his achievement all the more remarkable.

Most recaptures The only boxer to win a world title five times at one weight is 'Sugar' Ray Robinson (USA) (b. Walker Smith Jr, 1921–89), who beat Carmen Basilio (USA) in the Chicago Stadium on 25 Mar 1958, to regain the world middleweight title for the fourth time.

Dennis Andries (b. Guyana, 5 Nov 1953) became the first British boxer to regain a world title twice. He had initially won the WBC light-heavyweight title on 30 Apr 1986 and first regained the title on 22 Feb 1989 after being beaten in 1987. He regained the title for a second time on 28 Jul 1990.

Most title bouts The record number of title bouts in a career is 37, of which 18 ended in 'no decision', by three-time world welterweight champion Jack Britton (USA) (1885–1962) in 1915–22. The record containing no 'no decision' contests is 27 (all heavyweight) by Joe Louis between 1937–50.

Greatest weight difference When Primo Carnera (Italy) 122 kg *269 lb* fought Tommy Loughran (USA) 83 kg *183 lb* for the world heavy-weight title at Miami, Florida, USA on 1 Mar 1934, there was a weight difference of 39 kg *86 lb* between the two fighters. Carnera won the fight on points.

Greatest 'tonnage' The greatest 'tonnage' recorded in any fight is 317 kg *699 lb* when Claude 'Humphrey' McBride (Oklahoma), 154 kg *339½ lb*, knocked out Jimmy Black (Houston), who

weighed 163 kg *359½ lb* in the third round at Oklahoma City on 1 Jun 1971.

The greatest 'tonnage' in a world title fight was 221.5 kg *488¼ lb*, when Carnera, then 117.5 kg *259 lb* fought Paolino Uzcudun (Spain) 104 kg *229¼ lb* in Rome, Italy on 22 Oct 1933.

Amateur

Most Olympic titles Only two boxers have won three Olympic gold medals: southpaw László Papp (Hungary) (b. 25 Mar 1926), middle-weight 1948, light-middleweight 1952 and 1956; and Teofilo Stevenson (Cuba) (b. 23 Mar 1952), heavyweight 1972, 1976 and 1980.

The only man to win two titles in one celebration was Oliver L. Kirk (USA), who won both bantam and featherweight titles in St Louis, Missouri, USA in 1904, but he needed only one bout in each class.

Another record that will stand forever is that of the youngest Olympic boxing champion: Jackie Fields (*né* Finkelstein) (USA) (b. 9 Feb 1908) who won the 1924 featherweight title at 16 years 162 days. The minimum age for Olympic boxing competitors is now 17.

Oldest gold medallist Richard Kenneth Gunn (GB) (1871– 1961) won the Olympic featherweight gold medal on 27 Oct 1908 in London aged 37 yr 254 days.

World Championships A record number of four world titles (instituted 1974) have been won by Félix Savon (Cuba) heavyweight 1986, 1989, 1991 and 91 kg 1993.

Most British titles The greatest number of ABA titles won by any boxer is eight by John Lyon (b. 9 Mar 1962) at light-flyweight 1981–4 and at fly-weight 1986–9.

Alex 'Bud' Watson (b. 27 May 1914) of Leith, Scotland won the Scottish heavyweight title in 1938, 1942–3, and the light-heavyweight championship 1937–9, 1943–5 and 1947, making ten in all. He also won the ABA light-heavyweight title in 1945 and 1947.

Longest span The greatest span of ABA title-winning performances is that of the heavyweight Hugh 'Pat' Floyd (b. 23 Aug 1910), who won in 1929 and gained his fourth title 17 years later in 1946.

Canoeing

Most titles *Olympic* Gert Fredriksson (Sweden) (b. 21 Nov 1919) won a record six Olympic gold medals, 1948–60. He added a silver and a bronze for a record eight medals.

The most by a woman is four by Birgit Schmidt (*née* Fischer) (GDR) (b. 25 Feb 1962), 1980–92.

The most gold medals at one Games is three by Vladimir Parfenovich (USSR) (b. 2 Dec 1958) in 1980 and by Ian Ferguson (New Zealand) (b. 20 Jul 1952) in 1984.

World Including the Olympic Games a record 25 titles have been won by Birgit Schmidt, 1978–93.

The men's record is 13 by Gert Fredriksson, 1948–60, Rüdiger Helm (GDR) (b. 6 Oct 1956), 1976–83, and Ivan Patzaichin (Romania) (b. 26 Nov 1949), 1968–84.

The most individual titles by a British canoeist is five by Richard Fox (b. 5 Jun 1960) at K1 slalom in 1981, 1983, 1985, 1989 and 1993. Fox also won five gold medals at K1 team, between 1981 and 1993.

Highest speed The German four-man kayak Olympic champions in 1992 at Barcelona, Spain covered 1000 m in 2 min 52.17 sec in a heat on 4 August. This represents an average speed of 20.90 km/h *12.98 mph*.

At the 1988 Olympics, the Norwegian four achieved a 250 m split of 42.08 sec between 500 m and 750 m in a heat, for a speed of 21.39 km/h *13.29 mph*.

Longest journey Father and son Dana and Donald Starkell paddled from Winnipeg, Manitoba, Canada by ocean and river to Belem, Brazil, a distance of 19,603 km *12,181 miles* from 1 Jun 1980 to 1 May 1982. All portages were human powered.

Without portages or aid of any kind the longest is one of 9820 km *6102 miles* by Richard H. Grant and Ernest 'Moose' Lassy circum-navigating the eastern USA via Chicago, New Orleans, Miami, New York and the Great Lakes from 22 Sep 1930 to 15 Aug 1931.

North Sea On 17–18 May 1989, Kevin Danforth and Franco Ferrero completed the Felixstowe to Zeebrugge route in 27 hr 10 min in a double sea kayak. The open crossing, over 177 km *110 miles*, was self-contained and unsupported.

River Rhine The fastest time, solo and unsupported, is 10 days 12 hr 9 min by Frank Palmer, 15–25 May 1988. The supported team record is 7 days 23 hr 31 sec by the RAF Laarbruch Canoe Club, led by Andy Goodsell, 17–24 May 1989. The 'Rhine Challenge', as organized by the International Long River Canoeists Club, begins from an official marker post in Chur, Switzerland and ends at Willemstad, Netherlands, a distance of 1149 km *714 miles*.

24 hours Zdzislaw Szubski paddled 252.9 km *157.1 miles* in a Jaguar K1 canoe on the Vistula River, Wloclawek to Gdansk, Poland on 11–12 Sep 1987.

Flat water Marinda Hartzenberg (South Africa) paddled, without benefit of current, 220.69 km *137.13 miles* on Loch Logan, Bloemfontein, South Africa on 31 Dec 1990–1 Jan 1991.

Open sea Randy Fine (USA) paddled 194.1 km *120.6 miles* along the Florida coast on 26–27 Jun 1986.

Greatest lifetime distance Fritz Lindner of Berlin, Germany, totalled 103,444 km *64,277 miles* from 1928 to 1987.

Eskimo rolls Ray Hudspith (b. 18 Apr 1960) achieved 1000 rolls in 34 min 43 sec at the Elswick Pool, Newcastle upon Tyne on 20 Mar 1987. He completed 100 rolls in 3 min 7.25 sec at Killingworth Leisure Centre, Tyne and Wear on 3

Longest!

The Canadian Government Centennial Voyageur Canoe Pageant and Race from Rocky Mountain House, Alberta to the Expo 67 site at Montreal, Quebec was 5283 km *3283 miles*. Ten canoes represented Canadian provinces and territories. The winner was the Province of Manitoba canoe *Radisson*, which took from 24 May to 4 Sep 1967.

Most!

Vic Toweel (South Africa) (b. 12 Jan 1929) knocked down Danny O'Sullivan of London 14 times in ten rounds in their world bantamweight fight at Johannesburg on 2 Dec 1950, before the latter retired.

Raft!

A raft of 568 kayaks and canoes, organized by the Notts County Scout Council with the assistance of scouts from Derbys, Leics and Lincs, was held together by hands only, while free floating for 30 seconds, on the River Trent, Nottingham on 30 Jun 1991.

Mar 1991. Randy Fine (USA) completed 1796 continuous rolls at Biscayne Bay, Florida, USA on 8 Jun 1991.

'Hand rolls' Colin Brian Hill (b. 16 Aug 1970) achieved 1000 rolls in 31 min 55.62 sec at Consett, Co. Durham on 12 Mar 1987. He also achieved 100 rolls in 2 min 39.2 sec at Crystal Palace, London on 22 Feb 1987. He completed 3700 continuous rolls at Durham City Swimming Baths, Co. Durham on 1 May 1989.

Card Games

Contract Bridge

Biggest tournament The Epson World Bridge Championship, held on 20–21 Jun 1992, was contested by more than 102,000 players playing the same hands, at over 2000 centres worldwide.

Most world titles The World Championship (Bermuda Bowl) has been won a record 13 times by Italy's Blue Team (*Squadra Azzura*), 1957–59, 1961–63, 1965–67, 1969, 1973–75 and by the USA, 1950–51, 1953–54, 1970–71, 1976–77, 1979, 1981, 1983, 1985, 1987. Italy also won the team Olympiad in 1964, 1968 and 1972. Giorgio Belladonna (b. 7 Jun 1923) was in all the Italian winning teams.

Big Deal!

The mathematical odds against dealing 13 cards of one suit are 158,753,389,899 to 1, while the odds against a named player receiving a 'perfect hand' consisting of all 13 spades are 635,013,559,599 to 1. The odds against each of the four players receiving a complete suit (a 'perfect deal') are 2,235,197, 406,895,366,368,301,599,999,999 to 1.

The USA have a record six wins in the women's world championship for the Venice Trophy: 1974, 1976, 1978, 1987, 1989 and 1991, and three women's wins at the World Team Olympiad: 1976, 1980 and 1984.

Most hands In the 1989 Bermuda Bowl in Perth, Australia, Marcel Branco (b. 1945) and Gabriel Chagas (b. 1944) (both Brazil) played a record 752 out of a possible 784 boards.

Cribbage

Rare hands Five maximum 29 point hands have been achieved Sean Daniels of Astoria, Oregon, USA,

Ralf Laue held 326 standard playing cards in a fan in one hand, so that the value and colour of each one was visible, at Leipzig, Germany on 18 Mar 1994.

Jim Karol of North Catasauqua, Pennsylvania, USA threw a standard playing card 61.26 m *201 ft 0 in* at Mount Ida College, Newton Centre, Massachusetts, USA on 18 Oct 1992.

1989–92. Paul Nault of Athol, Massachusetts, USA had two such hands within eight games in a tournament on 19 Mar 1977.

Most points in 24 hours The most points scored by a team of four, playing singles in two pairs, is 117,652 by John Graham, Colin Lee, Gabriel Le Roux and Nick Steynberg at Shelley Beach Shopping Centre, Natal, South Africa on 24–25 Jul 1992.

Cricket

Batting Records, Teams

Highest innings Victoria scored 1107 runs in 10 hr 30 min against New South Wales in an Australian Sheffield Shield match at Melbourne on 27–28 Dec 1926.

Test England scored 903 runs for seven wickets declared in 15 hr 17 min, *v.* Australia at The Oval, London on 20, 22 and 23 Aug 1938.

County Championship Yorkshire scored 887 in 10 hr 50 min, *v.* Warwickshire at Edgbaston, Birmingham on 7–8 May 1896.

Lowest innings The traditional first-class record is 12 by Oxford University (who batted a man short) *v.* the Marylebone Cricket Club (MCC) at Cowley Marsh, Oxford on 24 May 1877, and by Northamptonshire *v.* Gloucestershire at Gloucester on 11 Jun 1907. However, 'The Bs' scored 6 in their second innings *v.* England at Lord's, London on 12–14 Jun 1810 in one of the major matches of that era.

Test 26 by New Zealand *v.* England at Auckland on 28 Mar 1955.

Aggregate for two innings 34 (16 and 18) by Border *v.* Natal in the South African Currie Cup at East London on 19 and 21 Dec 1959.

Greatest victory A margin of an innings and 851 runs was recorded, when Pakistan Railways (910 for 6 wickets declared) beat Dera Ismail Khan (32 and 27) at Lahore on 2–4 Dec 1964.

In England England won by an innings and 579 runs (also the record for a Test)

During the Fifth Test in Antigua against England, West Indian Brain Lara scored a mammoth 375, the highest ever individual score in a Test match. Above, he celebrates having passed the previous record of 365 by Gary Sobers. Left, he hits one of his 45 fours.

This proved to be the start of the greatest run scoring spree in the history of cricket with the following successive scores for Warwickshire: 147, 106, 120 not out, 136, 26, 140 and 501 not out, the highest ever score in first-class cricket. This innings of 501 included 308 runs scored from strokes worth four or more.
(Photos: Allsport/Ben Radford)

against Australia at The Oval on 20–24 Aug 1938 when Australia scored 201 and 123 with two men short in both innings. The most one-sided county match was when Surrey (698) defeated Sussex (114 and 99) by an innings and 485 runs at The Oval on 9–11 Aug 1888.

Most runs in a day Australia scored 721 all out (ten wickets) in 5 hr 48 min against Essex at Southchurch Park, Southend-on-Sea on 15 May 1948.

Test 588 at Old Trafford, Manchester on 27 Jul 1936 when England added 398 and India were 190 for 0 in their second innings by the close.

Batting Records, Individuals

Highest innings Brian Charles Lara (b. 2 May 1969) scored 501 not out in 7 hr 54 min for Warwickshire *v.* Durham at Edgbaston on 3 and 6 Jun 1994. The highest by an English player is 424 in 7 hr 50 min by Archibald Campbell Maclaren (1871–1944) for Lancashire *v.* Somerset at Taunton, Somerset on 15–16 Jul 1895.

Test Brian Lara scored 375 in 12 hr 46 min for West Indies *v.* England at Recreation Ground, St John's, Antigua on 16–18 Apr 1994. The English Test record is 364 by Sir Leonard Hutton

Individual Cricket Records

FIRST-CLASS (FC) AND TEST CAREER

Batting			Name	Team	Date
Most runs	FC	61,237	Sir John Berry 'Jack' Hobbs (1882–1963) (av. 50.65)	Surrey/England	1905–34
	Test	11,174	Allan Robert Border (b. 27 Jul 1955) (av. 50.56)	Australia (156 Tests)	1978–94
Most centuries	FC	197	Sir Jack Hobbs (in 1315 innings)	Surrey/England	1905–34
	Test	34	Sunil Gavaskar (in 214 innings)	India	1971–87
Highest average	FC	95.14	Sir Donald George Bradman (b. 28 Aug 1908)	NSW/South Australia/Australia	1927–49
			(28 067 runs in 338 innings, including 43 not outs)		
	Test	99.94	Sir Donald Bradman (6996 runs in 80 innings)	Australia (52 Tests)	1928–4

Bowling					
Most wickets	FC	4187	Wilfred Rhodes (1877–1973) (av. 16.71)	Yorkshire/England	1898–1930
	Test	434	Kapil Dev Nikhanj (b. 6 Jan 1959)	India (131 Tests)	1978–94
Lowest average	Test	10.75	George Alfred Lohmann (1865–1901) (112 wkts)	England (18 Tests)	1886–96
(min 15 wkts)					

Wicket-Keeping					
Most dismissals	FC	649	Robert William Taylor (b. 17 Jul 1941)	Derbyshire/England	1960–88
	Test	355	Rodney William Marsh (b. 11 Nov 1947)	Australia (96 Tests)	1970–84
Most catches	FC	1473	Robert Taylor	Derbyshire/England	1960–88
	Test	343	Rodney Marsh	Australia	1970–84
Most stumpings	FC	418	Leslie Ethelbert George Ames (1905–90)	Kent/England	1926–51
	Test	52	William Albert Stanley Oldfield (1894–1976)	Australia (54 Tests)	1920–37

Fielding					
Most catches	FC	1018	Frank Edward Woolley (1887–1978)	Kent/England	1906–38
	Test	155	Allan Robert Border	Australia (156 Tests)	1978–94

IN A TEST SERIES

Batting		Name	Teams (No. of Tests)	Season
Most runs	974	Sir Donald Bradman (av. 139.14)	Australia v. England (5)	1930
Most centuries	5	Clyde Leopold Walcott (b. 17 Jan 1926)	West Indies v. Australia (5)	1954/5
Highest average	563.00	Walter Reginald Hammond	England v. New Zealand (2)	1932/3
		(563 runs, 2 inns, 1 not out)		

Bowling				
Most wickets	49	Sydney Francis Barnes (1873–1967) (av. 10.93)	England v. South Africa (4)	1913/14
Lowest average	5.80	George Alfred Lohmann (35 wkts)	England v. South Africa (3)	1895/6
(min 20 wkts)				

Wicket-Keeping				
Most dismissals	28	Rodney Marsh (all caught)	Australia v. England (5)	1982/3
Most stumpings	9	Percy William Sherwell (1880–1948)	South Africa v. Australia (5)	1910/11

Fielding				
Most catches	15	Jack Morrison Gregory (1895–1973)	Australia v. England (5)	1920/21

All-Round				
400 runs/30 wkts	475/34	George Giffen (1859–1927)	Australia v. England (5)	1894/5

IN A FIRST-CLASS SEASON IN ENGLAND

Batting		Name (Team)	Year
Most runs	3816	Denis Charles Scott Compton (b. 23 May 1918) (av. 90.85) (Middlesex & England)	1947
Most centuries	18	Denis Compton (in 50 innings with 8 not outs) (Middlesex & England)	1947
Highest average	115.66	Sir Donald Bradman (2429 runs, 26 innings, 5 not outs) (Australians)	1938

Bowling			
Most wickets	304	Alfred Percy 'Tich' Freeman (1888–1965) (1976.1 o, av. 18.05) (Kent & England)	1928
Lowest average	8.54	Alfred Shaw (1842–1907) (186 wkts) (Nottinghamshire & England)	1880
(min 100 wkts)			

Wicket-Keeping			
Most dismissals	128	Leslie Ames (79 caught, 49 stumped) (Kent & England)	1929
Most catches	96	James Graham Binks (b. 5 Oct 1935) (Yorkshire)	1960
Most stumpings	64	Leslie Ames (Kent)	1932

Fielding			
Most catches	78	Walter Reginald Hammond (1903–65) (Gloucestershire & England)	1928

on 20 Feb 1990, in a deliberate attempt to give away runs, Robert Howard Vance (b. 31 Mar 1955) bowled an over containing 22 balls, 17 of which were deliberate no-balls (the umpire losing count and declaring over one ball early!). From this over Lee Kenneth Germon (b. 4 Nov 1968) of Canterbury hit 70 runs, including eight sixes and five fours, Richard George Petrie (b. 23 Aug 1967) scored five runs including one four, and with two runs from no-balls off which no runs were hit, a total of 77 runs was conceded.

Most sixes in an innings John Richard Reid (b. 3 Jun 1928) hit 15 in an innings of 296, lasting 3 hr 40 min, for Wellington v. Northern Districts in a Plunket Shield match at Wellington, New Zealand on 14–15 Jan 1963.

Test Walter Hammond hit ten sixes in his 336 not out for England v. New Zealand at Auckland on 31 Mar and 1 Apr 1933.

Triple hundred and hundred The only batsman to have scored a triple hundred and a hundred in the same match is Graham Alan Gooch (b. 23 Jul 1953) for England v. India at Lord's in 1990. He scored 333 in the first innings on 26–27 July and 123 in the second on 30 July for a record Test aggregate 456 runs.

Double hundreds The only batsman to score double hundreds in both innings is Arthur Edward Fagg (1915–77), who made 244 and 202 not out for Kent v. Essex at Colchester, Essex from 13–15 Jul 1938. Sir Donald Bradman scored a career record 37 double hundreds, 1927–49.

Fastest scoring 100 The fastest against genuine bowling was completed in 35 min off between 40 and 46 balls by Percy George Herbert Fender (1892–1985), in his 113 not out for Surrey v. Northamptonshire at Northampton on 26 Aug 1920. Glen Chapple (b. 23 Jan 1974) completed a century in an estimated 21 min off 27 balls for

(1916–90) against Australia at The Oval on 20, 22 and 23 Aug 1938.

Longest innings Hanif Mohammad (Pakistan) (b. 21 Dec 1934) batted for 16 hr 10 min for 337 runs against the West Indies at Bridgetown, Barbados on 20–23 Jan 1958. The English record is 13 hr 17 min by Len Hutton in his record Test score of 364.

Most runs off an over The first batsman to score 36 runs off a six ball over was Sir Garfield St Aubrun Sobers (b. 28 Jul 1936) off Malcolm Andrew Nash (b. 9 May 1945) for Nottinghamshire v. Glamorgan at Swansea on 31 Aug 1968. His feat was emulated by Ravishankar Jayadritha Shastri (b. 27 May 1962) for Bombay v. Baroda at Bombay, India on 10 Jan 1985 off the bowling of Tilak Raj Sharma (b. 15 Jan 1960).

Playing in a Shell Trophy match for Wellington v. Canterbury at Christchurch

GUESS WHAT?

Q What is the greatest number of runs off a single ball?

A See Page 246

Graeme Hick is the youngest player to have scored 20,000 runs in first-class cricket, aged 27 yr 20 days.

(Photo: Allsport/Adrian Murrell)

Lancashire *v.* Glamorgan in contrived circumstances at Old Trafford on 19 Jul 1993.

The fastest hundred in a major one-day competition was by Graham David Rose (b. 12 Apr 1964) off 36 balls for Somerset against Devon in the NatWest Trophy first round at Torquay on 27 Jun 1990.

The fastest Test hundred was completed in 70 min off 67 balls by Jack Morrison Gregory (1895–1973), in his 119 for Australia *v.* South Africa at Johannesburg on 12 Nov 1921. The fastest in terms of fewest balls received was one off 56 balls by Isaac Vivian Alexander Richards (b. 7 Mar 1952) for the West Indies *v.* England at St John's, Antigua on 15 Apr 1986. His final score was 110 not out in 81 minutes.

Edwin Boaler Alletson (1884–1963) scored 189 runs in 90 min for Nottinghamshire *v.* Sussex at Hove on 20 May 1911. The most prolific scorer of hundreds in an hour or less was Gilbert Laird Jessop (1874–1955), with 14 between 1897 and 1913.

Fastest 200 Scored in 113 min by Ravi Shastri off 123 balls for Bombay *v.* Baroda at Bombay on 10 Jan 1985 (⇨ Most runs off an over). Clive Hubert Lloyd (b. 31 Aug 1944), for West Indians *v.* Glamorgan at Swansea on 9 Aug 1976, and Gilbert Jessop (286), for Gloucestershire *v.* Sussex at Hove on 1 Jun 1903, both scored 200 in 120 min. Lloyd received 121 balls, but the figure for Jessop is not known.

Fastest 300 Completed in 181 min by Denis Compton, who scored 300 for the MCC *v.* North-Eastern Transvaal at Benoni, South Africa on 3–4 Dec 1948.

Slowest scoring The longest time a batsman has ever taken to score his first run is 1 hr 37 min by Thomas Godfrey Evans (b. 18 Aug 1920), before he scored 10 not out for England *v.* Australia at Adelaide on 5–6 Feb 1947. The longest innings without scoring is 87 min by Vincent Richard Hogg (b. 3 Jul 1952) for Zimbabwe–Rhodesia 'B' *v.* Natal 'B' at Pietermaritzburg in the South African Castle Bowl competition on 20 Jan 1980.

The slowest hundred on record is by Mudassar Nazar (b. 6 Apr 1956) for Pakistan *v.* England at Lahore on 14–15 Dec 1977. He required 9 hr 51 min for 114, reaching the 100 in 9 hr 17 min. The slowest double hundred is one of 12 hr 57 min (548 balls) by Don Sardha Brendon Priyantha Kuruppu (b. 5 Jan 1962) during an innings of 201 not out for Sri Lanka *v.* New Zealand at Colombo on 16–19 Apr 1987.

Highest partnership For any wicket is the fourth-wicket stand of 577 by Gul Mahomed (1921–92), 319, and Vijay Samuel Hazare (b. 11 Mar 1915), 288, for Baroda *v.* Holkar at Baroda, India on 8–10 Mar 1947.

In England 555, for the first-wicket by Percy Holmes (1886–1971) (224 not out) and Herbert Sutcliffe (1894–1978) (313) for Yorkshire *v.* Essex at Leyton, Essex on 15–16 Jun 1932.

Test 467, for the third wicket by Martin David Crowe (b. 22 Sep 1962) (299) and Andrew Howard Jones (b. 9 May 1959) (186) for New Zealand *v.* Sri Lanka at Wellington on 3–4 Feb 1991.

Scored!

Cedric Ivan James 'Jim' Smith (1906–79) scored 50 in 11 minutes for Middlesex *v.* Gloucestershire at Bristol on 16 Jun 1938. He went on to score 66. A faster 50 was completed off 13 balls in 8 min (1:22 to 1:30 p.m.) in 11 scoring strokes by Clive Clay Inman (b. 29 Jan 1936) in an innings of 57 not out for Leicestershire *v.* Nottinghamshire at Trent Bridge, Nottingham on 20 Aug 1965 but full tosses were bowled to expedite a declaration.

Bowling

Most wickets *In an innings* Only one bowler has taken all ten wickets in an innings on three occasions—Alfred 'Tich' Freeman of Kent, 1929–31. The fewest runs scored off a bowler taking all ten wickets is ten, off Hedley Verity (1905–43) for Yorkshire *v.* Nottinghamshire at Leeds on 12 Jul 1932 though the full analyses for some early performances of the feat are unknown. The only bowler to bowl out all ten was John Wisden (1826–84) for North *v.* South at Lord's in 1850.

In a match James Charles 'Jim' Laker (1922–86) took 19 wickets for 90 runs (9–37 and 10–53) for England *v.* Australia at Old Trafford from 27–31 Jul 1956.

Most consecutive wickets No bowler in first-class cricket has yet achieved five wickets with five consecutive balls. The nearest approach was that of Charles Warrington Leonard Parker (1882–1959) (Gloucestershire) in his own benefit match against Yorkshire at Bristol on 10 Aug 1922, when he struck the stumps with five successive balls but the second was called as a no-ball. The only man to have taken four wickets with consecutive balls more than once is Robert James Crisp (1911–94) for Western Province *v.* Griqualand West at Johannesburg, South Africa on 24 Dec 1931 and against Natal at Durban, South Africa on 3 Mar 1934.

Patrick Ian Pocock (b. 24 Sep 1946) took five wickets in six balls, six in nine balls and seven in eleven balls for Surrey *v.* Sussex at Eastbourne, E Sussex on 15 Aug 1972. In his own benefit match at Lord's on 22 May 1907, Albert Edwin Trott

(1873–1914) of Middlesex took four Somerset wickets with four consecutive balls and then later in the same innings achieved a 'hat trick'.

Most consecutive maidens Hugh Joseph Tayfield (1929–94) bowled 16 consecutive eight-ball maiden overs (137 balls without conceding a run) for South Africa *v.* England at Durban on 25–26 Jan 1957. The greatest number of consecutive six-ball maiden overs bowled is 21 (131 balls) by Rameshchandra Gangaram 'Bapu' Nadkarni (b. 4 Apr 1932) for India *v.* England at Madras on 12 Jan 1964. Alfred Shaw (1842–1907) of Nottinghamshire bowled 23 consecutive 4-ball maiden overs (92 balls) for North *v.* South at Trent Bridge, Nottingham on 17 Jul 1876.

Most balls The most balls bowled in a match is 917 by Cottari Subbanna Nayudu (b. 18 Apr 1914), 6–153 and 5–275, for Holkar *v.* Bombay at Bombay on 4–9 Mar 1945. The most balls bowled in a Test match is 774 by Sonny Ramadhin (b. 1 May 1929) for the West Indies *v.* England, 7–49 and 2–179, at Edgbaston on 29 May–4 Jun 1957. In the second innings he bowled a world record 588 balls (98 overs).

Most expensive bowling The most runs conceded by a bowler in a match is 428 by Cottari Nayudu in the Holkar *v.* Bombay match above. The greatest number of runs hit off one bowler in an innings is 362, off Arthur Alfred Mailey (1886–1967) of New South Wales by Victoria at Melbourne on 24–28 Dec 1926. The most runs conceded in a Test innings is 298 by Leslie O'Brien 'Chuck' Fleetwood-Smith (1908–71) for Australia *v.* England at The Oval on 20–23 Aug 1938.

All-Rounders

The double The 'double' of 1000 runs and 100 wickets in the same season was performed a record number of 16 times by Wilfred Rhodes between 1903 and 1926. The greatest number of consecutive seasons in which a player has performed the 'double' is 11 (1903–13) by George Herbert Hirst (1871–1954), of Yorkshire and England. Hirst is also the only player to score 2000 runs (2385) and take 200 wickets (208) in the same season (1906).

> **The highest electronically measured speed for a ball bowled by any bowler is 160.45 km/h 99.7 mph by Jeffrey Robert Thomson (Australia) (b. 16 Aug 1950) against the West Indies in December 1975.**

Test cricket *Career* The best all-round record is Kapil Dev Nikhanj (India) (b. 6 Jan 1959) who has scored 5248 runs (av. 31.05), 434 wickets (av. 29.64) and 64 catches in 131 matches, 1978–94. England's best is Ian Terence Botham (England) (b. 24 Nov 1955) with 5200 runs (av. 33.54), 383 wickets (av. 28.40) and 120 catches in 102 matches, 1977–92.

Match and innings Botham is the only player to score a hundred and take eight wickets in an innings in the same Test, with 108 and 8–34 for

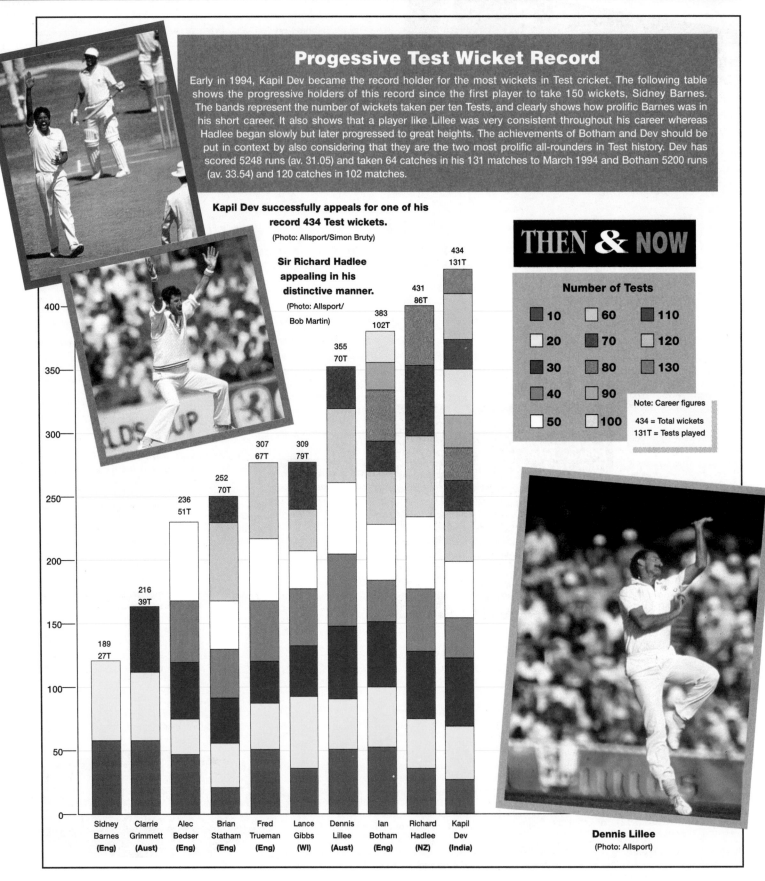

Progessive Test Wicket Record

Early in 1994, Kapil Dev became the record holder for the most wickets in Test cricket. The following table shows the progressive holders of this record since the first player to take 150 wickets, Sidney Barnes. The bands represent the number of wickets taken per ten Tests, and clearly shows how prolific Barnes was in his short career. It also shows that a player like Lillee was very consistent throughout his career whereas Hadlee began slowly but later progressed to great heights. The achievements of Botham and Dev should be put in context by also considering that they are the two most prolific all-rounders in Test history. Dev has scored 5248 runs (av. 31.05) and taken 64 catches in his 131 matches to March 1994 and Botham 5200 runs (av. 33.54) and 120 catches in 102 matches.

Kapil Dev successfully appeals for one of his record 434 Test wickets.
(Photo: Allsport/Simon Bruty)

Sir Richard Hadlee appealing in his distinctive manner.
(Photo: Allsport/ Bob Martin)

THEN & NOW

Number of Tests

10	60	110
20	70	120
30	80	130
40	90	
50	100	

Note: Career figures
434 = Total wickets
131T = Tests played

Chart values:
- Sidney Barnes (Eng): 189, 27T
- Clarrie Grimmett (Aust): 216, 39T
- Alec Bedser (Eng): 236, 51T
- Brian Statham (Eng): 252, 70T
- Fred Trueman (Eng): 307, 67T
- Lance Gibbs (WI): 309, 79T
- Dennis Lillee (Aust): 355, 70T
- Ian Botham (Eng): 383, 102T
- Richard Hadlee (NZ): 431, 86T
- Kapil Dev (India): 434, 131T

Dennis Lillee
(Photo: Allsport)

England v. Pakistan at Lord's on 15–19 Jun 1978. He scored a hundred (114) and took more than ten wickets (6–58 and 7–48) in a Test, for England v. India in the Golden Jubilee Test at Bombay on 15–19 Feb 1980. This feat was emulated by Imran Khan Niazi (b. 25 Nov 1952) with 117, 6–98 and 5–82 for Pakistan v. India at Faisalabad on 3–8 Jan 1983.

Century on début and wicket with first ball
Frederick William Stocks (b. 6 Nov 1918) of Nottinghamshire achieved the unique feat of scoring a century on his first-class début, v. Kent at Trent Bridge on 13 May 1946, and of taking a wicket with his first ball in first-class cricket, v. Lancashire at Old Trafford on 26 Jun 1946.

Wicket-Keeping

Most dismissals *Innings* The most dismissals is nine (eight catches and a stumping) by Tahir Rashid (b. 21 Nov 1960) for Habib Bank v.

Pakistan Automobile Corporation at Gujranwala, Pakistan on 29 Nov 1992. Three other players have taken eight catches in an innings: Arthur Theodore Wallace 'Wally' Grout (1927–68) for Queensland v. Western Australia at Brisbane on 15 Feb 1960; David Edward East (b. 27 Jul 1959) for Essex v. Somerset at Taunton on 27 Jul 1985; and Stephen Andrew Marsh (b. 27 Jan 1961) for Kent v. Middlesex on 31 May and 1 Jun 1991. The most stumpings in an innings is six by Henry

'Hugo' Yarnold (1917–74) for Worcestershire v. Scotland at Broughty Ferry, Tayside on 2 Jul 1951.

Match The most dismissals is 12 by: Edward Pooley (1838–1907), eight caught, four stumped, for Surrey v. Sussex at The Oval on 6–7 Jul 1868; nine caught, three stumped by both Donald Tallon (1916–84) for Queensland v. New South Wales at Sydney, Australia on 2–4 Jan 1939, and by Hedley Brian Taber (b. 29 Apr 1940) for New South Wales v. South Australia at Adelaide on 13–17 Dec 1968. The record for catches is 11 by: Arnold Long (b. 18 Dec 1940), for Surrey v. Sussex at Hove on 18 and 21 Jul 1964, by Rodney Marsh for Western Australia v. Victoria at Perth on 15–17 Nov 1975; by David Leslie Bairstow (b. 1 Sep 1951) for Yorkshire v. Derbyshire at Scarborough on 8–10 Sep 1982; by Warren Kevin Hegg (b. 23 Feb 1968) for Lancashire v. Derbyshire at Chesterfield on 9–11 Aug 1989; by Alec James Stewart (b. 8 Apr 1963) for Surrey v. Leicestershire at Leicester on 19–22 Aug 1989; and by Timothy John Neilsen (b. 5 May 1968) for South Australia v. Western Australia at Perth on 15–18 Mar 1991. The most stumpings in a match is nine by Frederick Henry Huish (1869–1957) for Kent v. Surrey at The Oval on 21–23 Aug 1911.

Most dismissals in Tests Innings The record is seven (all caught) by Wasim Bari (b. 23 Mar 1948) for Pakistan v. New Zealand at Auckland on 23 Feb 1979, by Bob Taylor for England v. India at Bombay on 15 Feb 1980, and by Ian David Stockley Smith (b. 28 Feb 1957) for New Zealand v. Sri Lanka at Hamilton on 23–24 Feb 1991.

Match The record is ten, all caught, by Bob Taylor for England v. India at Bombay, 15–19 Feb 1980.

Greatest!

The greatest number of victories since 1890, when the Championship was officially constituted, has been by Yorkshire with 29 outright wins (the last in 1968), and one shared (1949). The record number of consecutive title wins is seven by Surrey from 1952 to 1958. The greatest number of appearances in County Championship matches is 762 by Wilfred Rhodes for Yorkshire between 1898 and 1930, and the greatest number of consecutive appearances is 423 by Kenneth George Suttle (b. 25 Aug 1928) of Sussex between 1954 and 1969. James Graham 'Jimmy' Binks (b. 5 Oct 1935) played in all 412 County Championship matches for Yorkshire between his début in 1955 and his retirement in 1969.

Fielding

Most catches Innings The greatest number of catches in an innings is seven, by Michael James Stewart (b. 16 Sep 1932) for Surrey v. Northamptonshire at Northampton on 7 Jun 1957; and by Anthony Stephen Brown (b. 24 Jun 1936) for Gloucestershire v. Nottinghamshire at Trent Bridge on 26 Jul 1966.

Match Walter Hammond held ten catches (four in the first innings, six in the second) for Gloucestershire v. Surrey at Cheltenham on 16–17 Aug 1928.

The most catches in a Test match is seven by: Greg Chappell for Australia v. England at Perth on 13–17 Dec 1974; Yajurvindra Singh (b. 1 Aug 1952) for India v. England at Bangalore on 28 Jan–2 Feb 1977; and Hashan Prasantha Tillekeratne (b. 14 Jul 1967) for Sri Lanka v. New Zealand at Colombo on 7–9 Dec 1992.

Test Records

Test appearances The most Test matches played is 156 by Allan Robert Border (Australia) (b. 27 Jul 1955), 1979–94. Border's total includes a record 153 consecutive Tests and a record 93 as captain. The English record for most Tests is 117 by David Ivon Gower (b. 1 Apr 1957), 1978–92; and for consecutive Tests is 65 by Alan Philip Eric Knott (b. 9 Apr 1946), 1971–7 and Ian Botham, 1978–84.

Longest match The lengthiest recorded cricket match was the 'timeless' Test between England and South Africa at Durban on 3–14 Mar 1939. It was abandoned after ten days (eighth day rained off) because the ship taking the England team

home was due to leave. The total playing time was 43hr 16min and a record Test match aggregate of 1981 runs was scored.

Largest crowds The greatest attendance at a cricket match is about 394,000 for the Test between India and England at Eden Gardens, Calcutta on 1–6 Jan 1982. The record for a Test series is 933,513 for Australia v. England (five matches) in 1936/7. The greatest recorded attendance at a cricket match on one day was 90,800 on the second day of the Test between Australia and the West Indies at Melbourne on 11 Feb 1961. The English match record is 159,000 for England v. Australia at Headingley, Leeds on 22–27 Jul 1948, and the record for one day probably a capacity of 46,000 for Lancashire v. Yorkshire at Old Trafford on 2 Aug 1926. The English record for a Test series is 549,650 for the series against Australia in 1953. The highest attendance for a limited-overs game is an estimated 90,450 at Eden Gardens to see India play South Africa on the latter's return to official international cricket, on 10 Nov 1991.

Most successful Test captain Clive Hubert Lloyd (b. 31 Aug 1944) led the West Indies in 74 Test matches from 22 Nov 1974 to 2 Jan 1985. Of these, 36 were won, 12 lost and 26 were drawn. His team set records for most successive Test wins, 11 in 1984, and most Tests without defeat, 27, between losses to Australia in December 1981 and January 1985 (through injury Lloyd missed one of those matches, when the West Indies were captained by Vivian Richards).

> A cricket ball (155g 5oz) was reputedly thrown 128.6m 140 yd 2ft by Robert Percival, a left-hander, on Durham Sands racecourse on Easter Monday, 18 April 1882.

One-Day Internationals

World Cup The West Indies are the only double winners, in 1975 and 1979

One-day international records Team The highest innings score by a team is 363–7 (55 overs) by England v. Pakistan at Trent Bridge on 20 Aug 1992. The lowest completed innings total is 43 by Pakistan v. the West Indies at Newlands, Cape Town, South Africa on 25 Feb 1993. The largest victory margin is 232 runs by Australia v.

English One–Day Cricket Records

	NatWest Trophy (1981) (formerly Gillette Cup (1960–80))	Sunday League (1969)	Benson & Hedges (1972)
Total (highest)	413–4.Somerset v. Devon, Torquay, 1990	360–3 Somerset v. Glamorgan, Neath, 1990	388–7 Essex v. Scotland, Chelmsford, 1992
Total (lowest)	39.......Ireland v. Sussex, Hove, 1985	23 ......Middlesex v. Yorkshire, Headingley, 1974	50 ......Hampshire v. Yorkshire, Headingley, 1991
Highest innings	206.....Alvin Isaac Kallicharran (b. 21 Mar 1949), Warwickshire v. Oxon, Edgbaston, 1984	176.....Graham Alan Gooch (b. 23 Jul 1953), Essex v. Glamorgan, Southend, 1983	198* ...Graham Gooch,Essex v. Sussex, Hove, 1982
Best Bowling	8–21...Michael Anthony Holding (b. 16 Feb 1954), Derbyshire v. Sussex, Hove, 1988	8–26 ..Keith David Boyce (b. 11 Oct 1943), Essex v. Lancashire, Old Trafford, 1971**	7–12...Wayne Wendell Daniel (b. 16 Jan 1956), Middlesex v.Minor Counties (East), Ipswich, 1978
Most dismissals	6.........Robert William Taylor (b. 17 Jul 1941), Derbyshire v. Essex, Derby, 1981 6.........Terry Davies (b. 25 Oct 1960), Glamorgan v. Staffordshire, Stone, 1986 6.........Keith Brown Middlesex v. Minor Counties Wales, Northop Hall, 1994	7 ....Bob Taylor, Derbyshire v. Lancashire, Old Trafford, 1975	8 ....Derek John Somerset Taylor (b. 12 Nov 1942), Somerset v. Combined Universities, Taunton, 1982
Career - runs	2287...Graham Gooch, Essex 1973–93	7491...Graham Gooch, Essex 1973–93	4607 ..Graham Gooch, Essex 1973–94
- wickets	81.......Geoffrey Graham Arnold (b. 3 Sep 1944), Surrey, Sussex 1963–80	386 ....John Kenneth Lever (b. 24 Feb 1949), Essex 1969–89	149 ....John Lever, Essex 1972–89
- dismissals	66.......Bob Taylor, Derbyshire 1963–84	255 ....David Bairstow, Yorkshire 1970–90	122.....David Bairstow, Yorkshire 1972–90
Most wins	5.........Lancashire 1970–2, 1975, 1990	3 ....Kent 1972–3, 1976 3 ....Essex 1981, 1984–5 3 ....Lancashire 1969–70, 1989 3 ....Worcestershire 1971, 1987–8	3 ....Kent 1973, 1976, 1978 3 ....Leicestershire 1972, 1975, 1985

*Not out   ** Alan Ward (b. 10 Aug 1947) took 4 wickets in 4 balls, Derbyshire v. Sussex, Derby, 1970.

Extras!

Sri Lanka (323–2 to 91), at Adelaide, Australia on 28 Jan 1985.

Individual The highest individual score is 189 not out by Isaac Vivian Alexander Richards (b. 7 Mar 1952) for the West Indies *v.* England at Old Trafford on 31 May 1984. The best bowling analysis is 7–37 by Aqib Javed (b. 5 Aug 1972) for Pakistan *v.* India at Sharjah on 25 Oct 1991. The best partnership is 263 by Aamir Sohail (b. 14 Sep 1966) (134) and Inzamam-ul-Haq (b. 3 Mar 1970) (137 not out) for Pakistan *v.* New Zealand at Sharjah, UAE on 20 Apr 1994.

Career The most matches played is 273 by Allan Border (Australia), 1979–93. The most runs scored is 8649 (av. 41.38) by Desmond Leo Haynes (West Indies) (b. 15 Feb 1956) in 238 matches, 1977–94; this total includes a record 17 centuries. The most wickets taken is 251 (av. 27.22) by Kapil Dev (India) in 220 matches, 1978–94. The most dismissals is 204 (183 ct, 21 st) by Peter Jeffrey Leroy Dujon (West Indies) (b. 28 Mar 1956) in 169 matches, 1981–91. The most catches by a fielder is 127 by Border.

Oldest and Youngest

First-class The oldest player in first-class cricket was the Governor of Bombay, Raja Maharaj Singh (India) (1878–1959), aged 72yr 192days, when he batted, scoring 4, on the opening day of the match played on 25–27 Nov 1950 at Bombay for his XI *v.* Commonwealth XI. The youngest is reputed to be Esmail Ahmed Baporia (India) (b. 24 Apr 1939) for Gujarat *v.* Baroda at Ahmedabad, India on 10 Jan 1951, aged 11yr 261days. The oldest Englishman was Benjamin Aislabie (1774–1842) for MCC (of whom he was the secretary) *v.* Cambridge University at Lord's on 1 and 2 Jul 1841, when he was aged 67yr 169days. The youngest English first-class player was Charles Robertson Young (1852–?) for Hampshire *v.* Kent at Gravesend on 13 Jun 1867, aged 15yr 131days.

Test The oldest man to play in a Test match was Wilfred Rhodes, aged 52yr 165days, for England *v.* West Indies at Kingston, Jamaica on 12 April 1930. Rhodes made his Test début in the last Test of William Gilbert Grace (1848–1915), who at 50yr 320days at Nottingham on 3 Jun 1899 was the oldest ever Test captain. The youngest Test captain was the Nawab of Pataudi (later Mansur Ali Khan) at 21yr 77days on 23 Mar 1962 for India *v.* West Indies at Bridgetown, Barbados. The youngest Test player was Mushtaq Mohammad (b. 22 Nov 1943), aged 15yr 124days, for Pakistan *v.* West Indies at Lahore on 26 March 1959. England's youngest player was Dennis Brian Close (b. 24 Feb 1931) aged 18yr 149days *v.* New Zealand at Old Trafford on 23 Jul 1949.

Women's Cricket

Batting *Individual* The highest individual innings recorded is 224 not out by Mabel Bryant for Visitors *v.* Residents at Eastbourne, E Sussex in August 1901. The highest innings in a Test match is 193 by Denise Audrey Annetts (now Anderson) (b. 30 Jan 1964), in 381 minutes, for Australia *v.* England at Collingham, Notts on 23–24 Aug 1987 in a four-day Test. With Lindsay Reeler (b. 18 Mar 1961), 110 not out, she added 309 for the third wicket, the highest Test partnership. The highest in a three-day Test is 189 (in 222 minutes) by Elizabeth Alexandra 'Betty' Snowball (1907–88) for England *v.* New Zealand at Christchurch, New Zealand on 16 Feb 1935.

Rachael Flint (*née* Heyhoe) (b. 11 Jun 1939) has scored the most runs in Test cricket with 1814 (av. 49.02) in 25 matches from December 1960 to July 1979.

Team The highest innings score by any team is 567 by Tarana *v.* Rockley, at Rockley, New South Wales, Australia in 1896. The highest Test innings is 525 by Australia *v.* India at Ahmedabad on 4 Feb 1984. The highest score by England is 503 for five wickets declared by England *v.* New Zealand at Christchurch, New Zealand on 16 and 18 Feb 1935. The most in a Test in England is 426 by India at Stanley Park, Blackpool, Lancs on 3–7 Jul 1986.

The lowest innings in a Test is 35 by England *v.* Australia at St Kilda, Melbourne, Australia on 22 Feb 1958. The lowest in a Test in England is 63 by New Zealand at Worcester on 5 Jul 1954.

World Cup!

Bowling Mary Beatrice Duggan (England) (1925–73) took a record 77 wickets (av. 13.49) in 17 Tests from 1949 to 1963. She recorded the best Test analysis with seven wickets for six runs for England *v.* Australia at St Kilda, Melbourne on 22 Feb 1958.

Rubina Winifred Humphries (b. 19 Aug 1915), for Dalton Ladies *v.* Woodfield SC, at Huddersfield, W Yorks on 26 Jun 1931, took all ten wickets for no runs. (She also scored all her team's runs.) This bowling feat was equalled by Rosemary White (b. 22 Jan 1938) for Wallington LCC *v.* Beaconsfield LCC in July 1962.

All-round Elizabeth Rebecca 'Betty' Wilson (Australia) (b. 21 Nov 1921) was the first Test player, man or woman, to score a century and take ten wickets in a Test match. She took 7–7, including a hat-trick, and 4–9 and scored exactly 100 in the second innings against England at St Kilda on 21–24 Feb 1958. Enid Bakewell (b. 18 Dec 1940) was the first English Test player, man or woman, to achieve this Test Match double. Playing against the West Indies at Edgbaston on 1–3 Jul 1979, she scored 112 not out and had match figures of 10–75.

Wicketkeeping Lisa Nye (b. 24 Oct 1966) claimed a Test record eight dismissals (six caught, two stumpings) in an innings for England *v.* New Zealand at New Plymouth on 12–15 Feb 1992. Christina Matthews (Australia) (b. 1959) has taken a record 53 dismissals (43 catches, 10 stumpings) in 19 Tests.

Minor Cricket Records

Highest individual innings In a Junior House match between Clarke's House (now Poole's) and North Town, at Clifton College, Bristol, 22–23, 26–28 Jun 1899, Arthur Edward Jeune Collins (1885–1914) scored an unprecedented 628 not out in 6hr 50min, over five afternoons' batting, carrying his bat through the innings of 836. The scorer, E. W. Pegler, gave the score as '628–plus or minus 20, shall we say'.

Highest partnership During a Harris Shield match in 1988 at Sassanian Ground, Bombay, India, Vinod Kambli (b. 18 Jan 1972) (349 not out) and Sachin Tendulkar (b. 24 Apr 1973) (326 not out) put on an unbeaten partnership of 664 runs for the third wicket for Sharadashram Vidyamandir *v.* St Xavier's High School.

Fastest individual scoring Stanley Keppel 'Shunter' Coen (South Africa) (1902–67) scored 50 runs (11 fours and one six) in 7min for Gezira *v.* the RAF in 1942. The fastest hundred by a prominent player in a minor match was by Vivian Frank Shergold Crawford (1879–1922) in 19min at Cane Hill, Surrey on 16 Sep 1899. Lindsay Martin scored 100 off 20 deliveries (13 sixes, 5 fours and 2 singles) for Rosewater *v.* Warradale on 19 Dec 1987. David Michael Roberts Whatmore (b. 6 Apr 1949) scored 210 (including 25 sixes and 12 fours) off 61 balls for Alderney *v.* Sun Alliance at Alderney, Channel Islands on 19 Jun 1983. His first 100 came off 33 balls and his second off 25 balls.

Most runs off an over H. Morley scored 62, nine sixes and two fours, off an eight-ball over from R. Grubb which had four no-balls, in a Queensland country match in 1968/9.

Bowling Nine wickets with nine consecutive balls were taken by: Stephen Fleming, for Marlborough College 'A' XI *v.* Bohally Intermediate at Blenheim, New Zealand in December 1967; and by Paul Hugo for Smithfield School *v.* Aliwal North, South Africa in February 1931. In the Inter-Divisional Ships Shield at Purfleet, Essex on 17 May 1924, Joseph William Brockley (b. 9 Apr 1907) took all ten wickets, clean bowled, for two runs in 11 balls–including a triple hat trick. Jennings Tune took all ten wickets, all bowled, for 0 runs in five overs for Cliffe *v.* Eastrington in the Howden and District League at Cliffe, Yorkshire on 6 May 1922. Wynton Edwards of Queen's College took 10 for 0 (10 overs) against Selborne College at Queenstown, South Africa on 25 Mar 1950 and Errol Hall also took 10 for 0 (27 balls) for Australian *v.* Tannymorel at Warwick, Queensland on 2 Nov 1986.

In 1881 Frederick Robert Spofforth (1853–1926) at Bendemeer, New South Wales, Australia clean bowled all ten wickets in *both* innings (final

Most runs!

Robert Fulford, twice croquet world champion, in action at the Hurlingham Club, home of the World Championships.

(Photo: Allsport/Tom Hevezi)

figures 20 for 48). J. Bryant for Erskine *v.* Deaf Mutes in Melbourne on 15 and 22 Oct 1887, and Albert Rimmer for Linwood School *v.* Cathedral GS at Canterbury, New Zealand in December 1925, repeated the feat. In the 1910 season, H. Hopkinson, of Mildmay CC, London, took 99 wickets for 147 runs.

Longest throw A cricket ball (155g *5½oz*) was reputedly thrown 128.6m *140yd 2ft* by Robert Percival, a left-hander, on Durham Sands racecourse on Easter Monday, 18 Apr 1882.

Wicket-keeping Welihinda Badalge Bennett (b. 25 Jan 1933) caught four and stumped six batsmen in one innings, on 1 March 1953 for Mahinda College *v.* Galle CC, at the Galle Esplanade, Sri Lanka.

Fielding In a Wellington, New Zealand secondary schools 11-a-side match on 16 Mar 1974, Stephen Lane, 13, held 14 catches in the field (seven in each innings) for St Patrick's College, Silverstream *v.* St Bernard's College, Lower Hutt.

Sixes!

Cedric Ivan James Smith (1906–79) hit nine successive sixes for a Middlesex XI *v.* Harrow and District at Rayner's Lane, Harrow in 1935. This feat was repeated by Arthur Dudley Nourse (1910–81) in a South African XI *v.* Military Police match at Cairo, Egypt in 1942/3. Nourse's feat included six sixes in one over.

Croquet

Most championships The greatest number of victories in the Open Croquet Championships (instituted at Evesham, Worcestershire, 1867) is ten by John William Solomon (b. 22 Nov 1931) (1953, 1956, 1959, 1961, 1963–8). He also won ten Men's Championships (1951, 1953, 1958–60, 1962, 1964–5, 1971–2), ten Open Doubles (with Edmond Patrick Charles Cotter (b. 1904)) (1954–5, 1958–9, 1961–5 and 1969) and one Mixed

Doubles (with Freda Oddie) in 1954, making a total of 31 titles. Solomon has also won the President's Cup (instituted 1934, an invitation event for the best eight players) on nine occasions (1955, 1957–9, 1962–4, 1968 and 1971), and was Champion of Champions on all four occasions that that competition was run (1967–70).

George Nigel Aspinall (b. 29 Jul 1946) has won the President's Cup a record 11 times, 1969–70, 1973–6, 1978, 1980, 1982, 1984–5.

Dorothy Dyne Steel (1884–1965), fifteen times winner of the Women's Championship (1919–39), won the Open Croquet Championship four times (1925, 1933, 1935–6). She had also five Doubles and seven Mixed Doubles for a total of 31 titles.

World championships The first World Championships were held at the Hurlingham Club, London in 1989 and have been held annually since. The only double winner is Robert Fulford (GB) (b. 1970), 1990 and 1992.

International trophy The MacRobertson Shield (instituted 1925) has been won a record nine times by Great Britain, 1925, 1937, 1956, 1963, 1969, 1974, 1982, 1990 and 1993.

A record seven appearances have been made by John G. Prince (New Zealand) (b. 23 Jul 1945) in 1963, 1969, 1975, 1979, 1982, 1986 and 1990; on his debut he was the youngest ever international at 17yr 190days.

Cross-country Running

World Championships The inaugural International Cross-Country Championships took place at the Hamilton Park Racecourse, Scotland on 28 Mar 1903.

The greatest margin of victory is 56sec or 356m *390yd* by John 'Jack' Thomas Holden (England) (b. 13 Mar 1907) at Ayr Racecourse, Strathclyde on 24 Mar 1934.

Since 1973 the events have been official world championships under the auspices of the International Amateur Athletic Federation.

Most wins The greatest number of team victories has been by England with 45 for men, 11 for junior men and seven for women. The USA and USSR each has a record eight women's team victories. The greatest team domination was by Kenya at Auckland, New Zealand on 26 March 1988. Their senior men's team finished eight men in the first nine, with a low score of 23 (six to score) and their junior men's team set a record low score, 11 (four to score) with six in the first seven.

The greatest number of men's individual victories is five by John Ngugi (Kenya) (b. 10 May 1962), 1986–89 and 1992. The women's race has been won five times by: Doris Brown-Heritage (USA) (b. 17 Sep 1942), 1967–71; and by Grete Waitz

(*née* Andersen) (Norway) (b. 1 Oct 1953), 1978–81 and 1983.

Most appearances Marcel van de Wattyne (Belgium) (b. 7 Jul 1924) ran in a record 20 races, 1946–65. The women's record is 16 by Jean Lochhead (Wales) (b. 24 Dec 1946), 1967–79, 1981, 1983–84.

English Championship The National Cross-Country Championship was inaugurated at Roehampton, London in 1877.

The most individual titles won is four by Percy Haines Stenning (1854–92) (Thames Hare and Hounds) in 1877–80 and Alfred E. Shrubb (1878–1964) (South London Harriers) in 1901–4. The most successful club in the team race has been Birchfield Harriers from Birmingham with 28 wins and one tie between 1880 and 1988.

The most individual wins in the English women's championships is six by Lillian Styles, 1928–30, 1933–4 and 1937; the most successful team is Birchfield Harriers with 13 titles.

The largest field was the 2195 finishers in the senior race in 1990 at Leeds, W Yorks on 24 February. In this race, a record 250 clubs scored (by having six runners finish).

Largest field The largest recorded field in any cross-country race was 11,763 starters (10,810 finished) in the 30km *18.6 miles* Lidingöloppet, near Stockholm, Sweden on 3 Oct 1982.

Curling

Most titles Canada has won the men's World Championships (instituted 1959) 22 times, 1959–64, 1966, 1968–72, 1980, 1982–3, 1985–7, 1989–90, 1993–4.

The most Strathcona Cup (instituted 1903) wins is seven by Canada (1903, 1909, 1912, 1923, 1938, 1957, 1965) against Scotland.

The most women's World Championships (instituted 1979) is eight by Canada (1980, 1984–7, 1989, 1993–4).

Fastest game Eight curlers from the Burlington Golf and Country Club curled an eight-end game in 47min 24sec, with time penalties of 5min 30sec, at Burlington, Ontario, Canada on 4 Apr 1986, following rules agreed with the Ontario Curling Association. The time is taken from when the first rock crosses the near hogline until the game's last rock comes to a complete stop.

Largest bonspiel The largest bonspiel in the world is the Manitoba Curling Association Bonspiel held annually in Winnipeg, Canada. In 1988 there were 1424 teams of four men, a total of 5696 curlers, using 187 sheets of curling ice.

Largest rink The world's largest curling rink was the Big Four Curling Rink, Calgary, Alberta, Canada, opened in 1959 and closed in 1989. Ninety-six teams and 384 players were accommodated on two floors each with 24 sheets of ice.

Throw!

The longest throw of a curling stone was a distance of 175.66m *576ft 4in* by Eddie Kulbacki (Canada) at Park Lake, Neepawa, Manitoba, Canada on 29 Jan 1989. The attempt took place on a specially prepared sheet of curling ice on frozen Park Lake, a record 1200 ft *365.76m* long.

World Cycling Records

These records are those recognized by the Union Cycliste Internationale (UCI). *From 1 Jan 1993 their severely reduced list no longer distinguished between those set by professionals and amateurs, indoor and outdoor, or at altitude and sea level.*

MEN

Distance	min:sec	Name and Country	Venue	Date
Unpaced Standing Start				
1 km	1:02.091	Maic Malchow (GDR)	Colorado Springs, USA	28 Aug 1986
4 km	4:20.894	Graeme Obree (GB)	Hamar, Norway	19 Aug 1993
4 km team	4:03.822	Australia	Hamar, Norway	20 Aug 1993
1 hour (kms)	52.713	Graeme Obree (GB)	Bordeaux, France	27 Apr 1994
Unpaced Flying Start				
200 metres	10.099	Vladimir Adamashvili (USSR)	Moscow, USSR	6 Aug 1990
500 metres	26.649	Aleksandr Kirichenko (USSR)	Moscow, USSR	29 Oct 1988

WOMEN

Distance	min:sec	Name and Country	Venue	Date
Unpaced Standing Start				
500 m	33.438	Galina Yenyukhina (Russia)	Moscow, Russia	29 Apr 1993
3 km	3:37.347	Rebecca Twigg (USA)	Hamar, Norway	20 Aug 1993
1 hour (kms)	46.3527	Jeannie Longo (France)	Mexico City	1 Oct 1989
Unpaced Flying Start				
200 metres	10.831	Olga Slyusareva (Russia)	Moscow, Russia	6 Aug 1990
500 metres	29.655	Erika Salumäe (USSR)	Moscow, USSR	6 Aug 1987

Graeme Obree on his way to setting the world one-hour record at Bordeaux, using his distinctive skiing-style crouch on his homemade bike. The governing body have since banned such riding styles from any future record attempts.
(Photo: Vandystadt/Bruno Bade)

GUESS WHAT?

Q What is the highest speed achieved on a unicycle?

A See Page 114

Cycling

Highest speed The highest speed ever achieved on a bicycle is 245.077 km/h *152.284 mph* by John Howard (USA) behind a wind-shield at Bonneville Salt Flats, Utah, USA on 20 Jul 1985. It should be noted that considerable help was provided by the slipstreaming effect of the lead vehicle.

The British speed record is 158.05 km/h *98.21 mph* over 200 metres by David Le Grys (b. 10 Aug 1955) on a closed section of the M42 at Alvechurch, Warks on 28 Aug 1985.

The 24 hr record behind pace is 1958.196 km *1216.8 miles* by Michael Secrest at Phoenix International Raceway, Arizona on 26–27 Apr 1990.

Roller cycling James Baker (USA) achieved a record speed of 246.5 km/h *153.2 mph* at El Con Mall, Tucson, Arizona, USA on 28 Jan 1989.

Most titles *Olympic* The most gold medals won is three by Paul Masson (France) (1874–1945) in 1896, Francisco Verri (Italy) (1885–1945) in 1906 and Robert Charpentier (France) (1916–66) in 1936. Daniel Morelon (France) (b. 28 Jul 1944) won two in 1968 and a third in 1972; he also won a silver in 1976 and a bronze medal in 1964. In the 'unofficial' 1904 cycling programme, Marcus Latimer Hurley (USA) (1885–1941) won four events.

World World Championships are contested annually. They were first staged for amateurs in 1893 and for professionals in 1895.

The most wins at a particular event is ten by Koichi Nakano (Japan) (b. 14 Nov 1955), professional sprint 1977–86.

The most wins at a men's amateur event is seven by Daniel Morelon (France), sprint 1966–67, 1969–71, 1973, 1975; and Leon Meredith (GB) (1882–1930), 100 km motor paced 1904–5, 1907–9, 1911, 1913.

The most women's titles is eight by Jeannie Longo (France) (b. 31 Oct 1958), pursuit 1986 and 1988–9; road 1985–7 and 1989 and points 1989.

British Beryl Burton (b. 12 May 1937), 25 times British all-round time trial champion (1959–83), won 72 individual road TT titles, 14 track pursuit titles and 12 road race titles to 1986. Ian Hallam (b. 24 Nov 1948) won a record 25 men's titles, 1969–82.

Tour de France (instituted 1903) The greatest number of wins in the *Tour de France* is five by Jacques Anquetil (France) (1934–1987), 1957, 1961–4; Eddy Merckx (Belgium) (b. 17 Jun 1945), 1969–72 and 1974; and Bernard Hinault (France) (b. 14 Nov 1954), 1978–9, 1981–2 and 1985.

The closest race ever was in 1989 when after 3267 km *2030 miles* over 23 days (1–23 Jul) Greg LeMond (USA) (b. 26 Jun 1960), who completed the Tour in 87 hr 38 min 35 sec, beat Laurent Fignon (France) (b. 12 Aug 1960) in Paris by only 8 sec.

The fastest average speed was 39.504 km/h *24.547 mph* by Miguel Induráin (Spain) (b. 16 Jul 1964) in 1992.

Tour of Britain (Open) Four riders have won the Tour of Britain twice each—Bill Bradley (GB) (1959–60), Leslie George West (GB) (1965, 1967), Fedor den Hertog (Netherlands) (1969, 1971) and Yuriy Kashurin (USSR) (1979, 1982).

The closest race ever was in 1976 when after 1665.67 km *1035 miles* over 14 days (30 May–12 Jun) Bill Nickson (GB) (b. 30 Jan 1953) beat Joe Waugh (GB) by 5 sec.

The fastest average speed is 42.185 km/h *26.213 mph* by Joey McLoughlin (GB) (b. 3 Dec 1964) in the 1986 race (1714 km *1065 miles*).

The longest ever Tour was in 1953 (2624.84 km *1631 miles* starting and finishing in London).

Six-day races The most wins in six-day races is 88 out of 233 events by Patrick Sercu (b. 27 Jun 1944), of Belgium, 1964–83.

Longest one-day race The longest single-day 'massed start' road race is the 551–620 km *342–385 miles* Bordeaux–Paris, France event. Paced over all or part of the route, the highest average speed was in 1981 with 47.186 km/h *29.32 mph* by Herman van Springel (Belgium) (b. 14 Aug 1943) for 584.5 km *363.1 miles* in 13 hr 35 min 18 sec.

British Road Records

Type	Time (hr:min:sec)	Name	Date
100 Miles			
Men's bike	3:11:11	Ian Cammish (b. 1 Oct 1956)	10 Aug 1993
Men's trike	3:39:51	Dave Pitt (b. 3 Mar 1950)	18 Oct 1991
Women's bike	3:49:42	Pauline Strong (b. 19 Mar 1956)	18 Oct 1991
London to Brighton and Back			
Men's bike	4:15:08	Phil Griffiths (b. 18 Mar 1949)	20 Jul 1977
Men's trike	4:51:07	Dave Pitt	25 Jul 1979
Women's bike	4:55:28	Gill Clapton (b. 25 Sep 1942)	15 Jul 1972
London to Bath and Back			
Men's bike	9:03:07	John Woodburn (b. 22 Dec 1936)	13 Jun 1981
Men's trike	10:19:00	Ralph Dadswell (b. 28 Jul 1964)	22 Jun 1991
Women's bike	10:41:22	Eileen Sheridan (b. 18 Oct 1923)	22 Aug 1952
Land's End to John O' Groats			
Men's bike	1 day 21:02:18	Andy Wilkinson (b. 22 Aug 1963)	29 Sep–1 Oct 1990
Men's trike	2 days 5:29:01	Ralph Dadswell	10–12 Aug 1992
Women's bike	2 days 6:49:45	Pauline Strong	28–30 Jul 1990

Cross-America The trans-America solo records recognized by the Ultra-Marathon Cycling Association are: men, Paul Selon 8 days 8 hr 45 min; women, Susan Notorangelo 9 days 9 hr 9 min, both in the Race Across America, Costa Mesa, California to New York, 5000 km *3107 miles* in August 1989.

GUESS WHAT?

Q What is the fastest time to run across America?

A See Page 228

The trans-Canada record is 13 days 9 hr 6 min by Bill Narasnek of Lively, Ontario, 6037 km *3751 miles* from Vancouver, BC to Halifax, Nova Scotia on 5–18 Jul 1991.

Daniel Buettner, Bret Anderson, Martin Engel and Anne Knabe cycled the length of the Americas, from Prudhoe Bay, Alaska, USA to the Beagle Channel, Ushuaia, Argentina from 8 Aug 1986–13 Jun 1987. They cycled a total distance of 24,568 km *15,266 miles*.

Endurance Thomas Edward Godwin (GB) (1912–75) in the 365 days of 1939 covered 120,805 km *75,065 miles* or an average of 330.96 km *205.65 miles* per day. He then completed 160,934 km *100,000 miles* in 500 days to 14 May 1940.

Jay Aldous and Matt DeWaal cycled 22,997 km *14,290 miles* on a round-the-world trip from This is the Place Monument, Salt Lake City, Utah, USA in 106 days, 2 Apr–16 Jul 1984.

Tal Burt (Israel) circumnavigated the world (21,329 km *13,253 road miles*) from Place du Trocadero, Paris, France in 77 days 14 hr, from 1 Jun–17 Aug 1992.

Nick Sanders cycled 7728 km *4802 miles* around Britain in 22 days, 10 Jun–1 Jul 1984.

Cycle touring The greatest mileage amassed in a cycle tour was more than 646,960 km *402,000 miles* by the itinerant lecturer Walter Stolle (b. Sudetenland, 1926) from 24 Jan 1959 to 12 Dec 1976. He visited 159 countries starting from Romford, Essex. From 1922 to 25 Dec 1973 Tommy Chambers (1903–84) of Glasgow, rode a verified total of 1,286,517 km *799,405 miles*.

Visiting every continent, John W. Hathaway (b. England, 13 Jan 1925) of Vancouver, Canada covered 81,430 km *50,600 miles* from 10 Nov 1974 to 6 Oct 1976. Veronica and Colin Scargill, of Bedford, travelled 29,000 km *18,020 miles* around the world on a tandem, 25 Feb 1974–27 Aug 1975.

The most participants in a bicycle tour are 31,678 in the 90 km *56 miles* London to Brighton Bike Ride on 19 Jun 1988. However, it is estimated that 45,000 cyclists took part in the 75 km *46 miles* Tour de l'Ile de Montréal, Canada on 7 Jun 1992. The most participants in a tour in excess of 1000 km are 2037 (from 2157 starters) for the Australian Bicentennial Caltex Bike Ride from Melbourne to Sydney from 26 Nov–10 Dec 1988.

Cyclo-Cross

The greatest number of World Championships (instituted 1950) has been won by Eric de Vlaeminck (Belgium) (b. 23 Aug 1945) with the Amateur and Open in 1966 and six Professional titles in 1968–73.

British titles (instituted 1955) have been won most often by John Atkins (b. 7 Apr 1942) with five Amateur (1961–2, 1966–8), seven Professional (1969–75) and one Open title in 1977.

Three Peaks Stephen Poulton cycled from sea level at Caernarvon, Gwynedd, via the peaks of Snowdon, Scafell Pike and Ben Nevis, to sea level Fort William, Highland in 41 hr 51 min, from 1–2 Jul 1980.

Cycle Speedway

First mention of the sport is at Coventry in 1920 and it was first organized in 1945. The sport's governing body, the Cycle Speedway Council, was formed in 1973.

The most British Senior Team Championships (instituted 1950) is nine by Poole, Dorset (1982, 1984, 1987–93).

The most individual titles is four by Derek Garnett (b. 16 Jul 1937) (1963, 1965, 1968 and 1972); he also won the inaugural British Veterans' Championship in 1987.

Darts

Most titles Eric Bristow (b. 25 Apr 1957) has most wins in the World Masters Championship (instituted 1974) with five, 1977, 1979, 1981 and 1983–4, the World Professional Championship (instituted 1978) with five, 1980–81 and 1984–6, and the World Cup Singles (instituted 1977), four, 1983, 1985, 1987 and 1989.

John Lowe (b. 21 Jul 1945) is the only other man to have won each of the four major titles: World Masters, 1976 and 1980; World Professional, 1979, 1987 and 1993; World Cup Singles, 1981; and *News of the World*, 1981.

World Cup The first World Cup was held at the Wembley Conference Centre, London in 1977. England has a record seven wins at this biennial tournament. Eric Bristow and John Lowe played on all seven teams.

A biennial World Cup for women was instituted in 1983 and has been won three times by England.

Record prize John Lowe won £102,000 for achieving the first 501 scored with the minimum nine darts in a major event on 13 Oct 1984 at Slough in the quarter-finals of the World Match-play Championships. His darts were six successive treble 20s, treble 17, treble 18 and double 18.

Speed records The fastest time taken to complete three games of 301, finishing on doubles, is 1 min 38 sec by Ritchie Gardner on BBC TV's *Record Breakers* on 12 Sep 1989.

Darts Scoring Records

24-Hour

MEN (8 players) 1,722,249 by Broken Hill Darts Club at Broken Hill, New South Wales, Australia on 28–29 Sep 1985. **WOMEN** (8 players) 744,439 by a team from the Lord Clyde, Leyton, London on 13–14 Oct 1990. **INDIVIDUAL** 566,175 by Russell Locke at Hugglescote Wornking Mens Club, Leics on 17–18 Sep 1993. **BULLS AND 25s** (8 players) 510,625 by a team at the Kent and Canterbury Hospital Sports and Social Club, Canterbury on 20–21 Oct 1989.

10-Hour

MOST TREBLES 3056 (from 7992 darts) by Paul Taylor at the Woodhouse Tavern, Leytonstone, London on 19 Oct 1985. **MOST DOUBLES** 3265 (from 8451 darts) by Paul Taylor at the Lord Brooke, Walthamstow, London on 5 Sep 1987. **HIGHEST SCORE** (retrieving own darts) 465,919 by Jon Archer and Neil Rankin at the Royal Oak, Cossington, Leics on 17 Nov 1990. **BULLS** (individual) 1261 by Glenn Silva (USA) at Thee London Pub One, Margate, Florida, USA on 13 feb 1994.

6-Hour

MEN 210,172 by Russell Locke at the Hugglescote Working Mens Club, Coalville, Leics on 10 Sep 1989. **WOMEN** 99,725 by Karen Knightly at the Lord Clydeon 17 Mar 1991.

Million and One Up

MEN (8 players) 36,583 darts by a team at the Buzzy's Pub and Grub, Lynn, Massachusetts, USA on 19–20 Oct 1991. **WOMEN** (8 players) 70,019 darts by The Delinquents darts team at the Top George, Combe Martin, Devon on 11–13 Sep 1987.

Highest!

Canadians Bruce Bell, Philip Whelan and Suzanne MacFadyen cycled at an altitude of 6960 m *22,834 ft* on the peak of Mt Aconcagua, Argentina on 25 Jan 1991. This achievement was equalled by Mozart Hastenreiter Catão (Brazil) on 11 Mar 1993 and by Tim Sumner (GB) and Jonathon Green (GB) on 6 Jan 1994.

Least!

Roy Edwin Blowes (Canada) (b. 8 Oct 1930) was the first person to achieve a 501 in nine darts, 'double-on, double-off', at the Widgeons pub, Calgary, Canada at 9 Mar 1987. His scores were: bull, treble 20, treble 17, five treble 20s and a double 20 to finish.

The record time for going round the board clockwise in 'doubles' at arm's length is 9.2 sec by Dennis Gower at the Millers Arms, Hastings, E Sussex on 12 Oct 1975 and 14.5 sec in numerical order by Jim Pike (1903–60) at the Craven Club, Newmarket, Suffolk in March 1944.

The record for this feat at the 9 ft *2.7 m* throwing distance, retrieving own darts, is 2 min 13 sec by Bill Duddy (b. 29 Sep 1932) at The Plough, Haringey, London on 29 Oct 1972.

Least darts Scores of 201 in four darts, 301 in six darts, 401 in seven darts and 501 in nine darts, have been achieved on various occasions.

The lowest number of darts thrown for a score of 1001 is 19 by: Cliff Inglis (b. 27 May 1935) (160, 180, 140, 180, 121, 180, 40) at the Bromfield Men's Club, Devon on 11 Nov 1975 and Jocky Wilson (b. 22 Mar 1950) (140, 140, 180, 180, 180, 131, Bull) at The London Pride, Bletchley, Bucks on 23 Mar 1989. A score of 2001 in 52 darts was achieved by Alan Evans (b. 14 Jun 1949) at Ferndale, Mid Glam on 3 Sep 1976; 3001 in 73 darts was thrown by Tony Benson at the Plough Inn, Gorton, Manchester on 12 Jul 1986. Linda Batten (b. 26 Nov 1954) set a women's 3001 record of 117 darts at the Old Wheatsheaf, Enfield, London on 2 Apr 1986 and a total of 100,001 was achieved in 3579 darts by Chris Gray at the Dolphin, Cromer, Norfolk on 27 Apr 1993.

Equestrian Sports

Show Jumping

Olympic Games The most Olympic gold medals is five by Hans Günter Winkler (West Germany) (b. 24 Jul 1926), four team in 1956, 1960, 1964 and 1972 and the individual Grand Prix in 1956. He also won team silver in 1976 and team bronze in 1968 for a record seven medals overall.

The most team wins in the Prix des Nations is six by Germany in 1936, 1956, 1960, 1964 and as West Germany in 1972 and 1988.

The lowest score obtained by a winner is no faults by Frantisek Ventura (Czechoslovakia) (1895–1969) on *Eliot*, 1928; Alwin Schockemöhle (West Germany) (b. 29 May 1937) on *Warwick Rex*, 1976 and Ludger Beerbaum (Germany) (b. 25 Aug 1963) on *Classic Touch*, 1992.

Pierre Jonquères d'Oriola (France) (b. 1 Feb 1920) uniquely won the individual gold medal twice, 1952 and 1964.

World Championships The men's World Championships (instituted 1953) have been won twice by Hans Günter Winkler (West Germany) (1954–5) and Raimondo d'Inzeo (Italy) (b. 8 Feb 1925) (1956 and 1960).

The women's title (1965–74) was won twice by Jane 'Janou' Tissot (*née* Lefebvre) (France) (b. Saigon, 14 May 1945) on *Rocket* (1970 and 1974).

A team competition was introduced in 1978 and the most wins is two by France, 1982 and 1990.

President's Cup Instituted in 1965 for Nations Cup teams, it has been won a record 14 times by Great Britain, 1965, 1967, 1970, 1972–4, 1977–9, 1983, 1985–6, 1989, 1991. David Broome (b. 1 Mar 1940) has represented Great Britain 106 times in Nations Cup events, 1959–94.

World Cup Instituted in 1979, double winners have been Conrad Homfeld (USA) (b. 25 Dec 1951), 1980 and 1985; Ian Millar (Canada) (b. 6 Jan 1947), 1988–9; and John Whitaker (GB) (b. 5 Aug 1955), 1990–91.

King George V Gold Cup and Queen Elizabeth II Cup David Broome has won the King George V Gold Cup (first held 1911) a record six times, 1960 on *Sunsalve*, 1966 on *Mister Softee*, 1972 on *Sportsman*, 1977 on *Philco*, 1981 on *Mr Ross* and 1991 on *Lannegan*.

The Queen Elizabeth II Cup (first held 1949), for women, has been won five times by his sister Elizabeth Edgar (b. 28 Apr 1943), 1977 on *Everest Wallaby*, 1979 on *Forever*, 1981 and 1982 on *Everest Forever*, 1986 on *Everest Rapier*.

GUESS WHAT?
Q What is the longest running show on television?
A See Page 159

The only horse to win both these trophies is *Sunsalve* in 1957 (with Elisabeth Anderson) and 1960.

Three-Day Event

Olympic Games and World Championships Charles Ferdinand Pahud de Mortanges (Netherlands) (1896–1971) won a record four Olympic gold medals, team 1924 and 1928, individual (riding *Marcroix*) 1928 and 1932, when he also won a team silver medal.

Bruce Oram Davidson (USA) (b. 13 Dec 1949) is the only rider to have won two world titles (instituted 1966), on *Irish Cap* in 1974 and *Might Tango* in 1978.

Richard John Hannay Meade (GB) (b. 4 Dec 1938) is the only British rider to win three Olympic gold medals—as an individual in 1972 with team titles in 1968 and 1972.

Badminton The Badminton Three-Day Event (instituted 1949) has been won six times by Lucinda Jane Green (*née* Prior-Palmer) (b. 7 Nov 1953), in 1973 (on *Be Fair*), 1976 (*Wide Awake*), 1977 (*George*), 1979 (*Killaire*), 1983 (*Regal Realm*) and 1984 (*Beagle Bay*).

Dressage

Olympic Games and World Championships Germany (West Germany 1968–90) have won a record eight team gold medals, 1928, 1936, 1964, 1968, 1976, 1984, 1988 and 1992, and have most team wins, six, at the World Championships (instituted 1966). Dr Reiner Klimke (West Germany) (b. 14 Jan 1936) has won a record six Olympic golds (team 1964–88, individual, 1984). He also won individual bronze in 1976 for a record seven medals overall and is the only rider to win two world titles, on *Mehmed* in 1974 and *Ahlerich* in 1982. Henri St Cyr (Sweden) (1904–79) won a record two individual Olympic gold medals, 1952 and 1956. This was equalled by Nicole Uphoff (Germany) in 1992, having previously won in 1988.

World Cup Instituted in 1986, the only double winner is Christine Stückelberger (Switzerland) (b. 22 May 1947) on *Gauguin de Lully* in 1987–8.

Carriage driving

World Championships were first held in 1972. Three team titles have been won by: Great Britain, 1972, 1974 and 1980; Hungary, 1976, 1978 and 1984; and the Netherlands, 1982, 1986 and 1988.

Two individual titles have been won by: György Bárdos (Hungary), 1978 and 1980; Tjeerd Velstra (Netherlands), 1982 and 1986; and Ijsbrand Chardon (Netherlands), 1988 and 1992.

Jumping!

The official *Fédération Equestre Internationale* records are: high jump 2.47 m *8 ft 1¼ in* by *Huasó*, ridden by Capt. Alberto Larraguibel Morales (Chile) at Viña del Mar, Santiago, Chile on 5 Feb 1949; long jump over water 8.40 m *27 ft 6¾ in* by *Something*, ridden by André Ferreira (South Africa) at Johannesburg, South Africa on 25 Apr 1975.

The British high jump record is 2.32 m *7 ft 7¼ in* by the 16.2 hands *165 cm* grey gelding *Lastic* ridden by Nick Skelton (b. 30 Dec 1957) at Olympia, London on 16 Dec 1978.

On 25 Jun 1937, at Olympia, the Lady Wright (*née* Margery Avis Bullows) set the best recorded height for a British equestrienne on her liver chestnut *Jimmy Brown* at 2.23 m *7 ft 4 in*.

Fencing

Most titles *World* The greatest number of individual world titles won is five by Aleksandr Romankov (USSR) (b. 7 Nov 1953), at foil 1974, 1977, 1979, 1982 and 1983, but Christian d'Oriola (France) won four world foil titles, 1947, 1949, 1953–4 as well as two individual Olympic titles (1952 and 1956).

Four women foilists have won three world titles: Helene Mayer (Germany) (1910–53), 1929, 1931, 1937; Ilona Schacherer-Elek (Hungary) (1907–88), 1934–35, 1951; Ellen Müller–Preis (Austria) (b. 6 May 1912), 1947, 1949–50; and Cornelia Hanisch (West Germany) (b. 12 Jun 1952), 1979, 1981, 1985. Of these only Ilona Schacherer-Elek also won two individual Olympic titles (1936 and 1948). The longest span for winning an individual world or Olympic title is 20 years by Aladár Gerevich (Hungary) (b. 16 Mar 1910) at sabre, 1935–55.

Olympic The most individual Olympic gold medals won is three by Ramón Fonst (Cuba) (1883–1959) in 1900 and 1904 (two) and by Nedo Nadi (Italy) (1894–1952) in 1912 and 1920 (two). Nadi also won three team gold medals in 1920 making five gold medals at one celebration, the record for fencing and then a record for any sport. Aladár Gerevich (Hungary) won seven golds, one individual and six team, 1932–60; a span of 28 years, an Olympic record.

Edoardo Mangiarotti (Italy) (b. 7 Apr 1919) with six gold, five silver and two bronze, holds the record of 13 Olympic medals. He won them for foil and épée from 1936 to 1960.

The most gold medals by a woman is four (one individual, three team) by Yelena Dmitryevna Novikova (*née* Belova) (USSR) (b. 28 Jul 1947) from 1968 to 1976, and the record for all medals is seven (two gold, three silver, two bronze) by Ildikó Sági (formerly Ujlaki, *née* Retjö) (Hungary) (b. 11 May 1937) from 1960 to 1976.

British Three British fencers have won individual world titles: Gwen Neligan (1906–72) at foil in 1933; Henry William Furze 'Bill' Hoskyns (b. 19 Mar 1931) at épée in 1958; and Allan Louis Neville Jay (b. 30 Jun 1931) at foil in 1959, when he also won silver in épée. The only British fencer to win an Olympic gold medal is Gillian Mary Sheen (now Donaldson) (b. 21 Aug 1928) in the 1956 foil.

A record three Olympic medals were won by Edgar Isaac Seligman (1867–1958) with silver medals in the épée team event in 1906, 1908 and 1912.

Bill Hoskyns has competed most often for Great Britain with six Olympic appearances, 1956–76.

Amateur Fencing Association titles The most won at one weapon is ten at women's foil by Gillian Sheen, 1949, 1951–8, 1960. The men's records are: foil, 7 by John Emyrs Lloyd (1908–1987) 1928, 1930–3, 1937–8; épée, 6 by Edward Owen 'Teddy' Bourne (b. 30 Sep 1948) 1966, 1972, 1974, 1976–8 and William Ralph Johnson (b. 3 Jun 1948) 1968, 1982, 1984–5, 1987, 1990; and sabre, 6 by Dr Roger F. Tredgold (1912–75) 1937, 1939, 1947–9, 1955.

GUESS WHAT?
Q Where would you find the world's tallest fence?
A See Page 101

Field Sports

Hunting

Pack *Largest* The pack with the greatest number of hounds has been the Duke of Beaufort's hounds maintained at Badminton, Avon since 1786. At times hunting six days a week, this pack once had 120 couples of hounds. It now meets four days a week.

Longest mastership The 10th Duke of Beaufort (1900–84) was Master of Foxhounds from 1924 until his death in 1984 and hunted his hounds on 3895 days from 1920–67.

Longest hunt The longest recorded hunt was one held by Squire Sandys which ran from Holmbank, northern Lancs to Ulpha, Cumbria, a total of nearly 80 miles *128km* in reputedly only 6hr, in January or February 1743.

The longest duration hunt was one of 10hr 5min by Charlton Hunt of W Sussex, which ran from East Dean Wood at 7:45a.m. to a kill over 57¼ miles *92km* away at 5:50p.m. on 26 Jan 1738.

Most widespread hunting Between 1969 and 1992, John N. P. Watson (b. 18 Jun 1927), hunting correspondent to *Country Life*, hunted with 283 different packs of foxhounds, staghounds and harehounds in Britain, Ireland, USA and Europe.

Game Shooting

Largest tally to a single sportsman A record 556,813 head of game fell to the guns of the 2nd Marquess of Ripon (1852–1923) between 1867 and when he dropped dead on a grouse moor after shooting his 52nd bird on the morning of 22 Sep 1923. This figure included 241,234 pheasants, 124,193 partridge and 31,900 hares. (His game books are held by the gunmakers James Purdey and Sons.)

Thomas, 6th Baron Walsingham (1843–1919), bagged 1070 grouse, a one-day record for a single gun, in Yorkshire on 30 Aug 1888.

The longest mastership of a pack was by Jean Bethel 'Betty' McKeever (*née* Dawes) (1901–90), who was Master of the Blean Beagles in Kent from 1909 until her death. She was given her first pack by her father at the age of eight and remained the sole Master.

Fives

Eton Fives

Most titles One pair has won the amateur championship (Kinnaird Cup) ten times—Brian C. Matthews (b. 15 Aug 1957) and John P. Reynolds (b. 9 Aug 1961), 1981–90. John Reynolds won an eleventh title with Manuel de Souza-Girao (b. 20 Aug 1970) in 1991.

Rugby Fives

Most titles The greatest number of Amateur Singles Championships (instituted 1932) ever won is 20 by Wayne Enstone (b. 12 Jun 1951) in 1973–8 and 1980–93.

The record for the Amateur Doubles Championship (instituted 1925) is 10 by David

Football International Competition Records

Title (instituted)	Most Wins	Highest score (single game)
National level		
Olympic Games (1896)	3 Great Britain 1900, 08, 12	17–1 Denmark v. France 'A', 1908
(*unofficial until 1908*)	3 Hungary, 1952, 64, 68	
S. American Championships (1910)	15 Argentina, 1910, 21, 25, 27, 29,	12–0 Argentina v. Ecuador, 1942
(*Copa America since 1975*)	37, 41, 45–7, 55, 57, 59, 91, 93	
Asian Cup (1956)	3 Iran, 1968, 72, 76	10–1 China v. Brunei, 1976
African Cup of Nations (1957)	4 Ghana, 1963, 65, 78, 82	9–1 Ghana v. Niger, 1969
European Championships (1958)	2 West Germany, 1972, 80	12–1 Spain v. Malta, 1983
Club level		
World Club Championship (1960)	3 Peñarol (Uruguay), 1961, 66, 82	5–1 Real Madrid (Spain) v. Penarol, 1960
(*between winners of European*	3 Nacional (Uruguay), 1971, 80, 88	5–0 Peñarol v. Benfica (Portugal), 1961
Cup and Copa Libertadores)	3 Milan (Italy), 1969, 89, 90	
Europe		
UEFA Cup (1955)	3 Barcelona (Spain), 1958, 60, 66	14–0 Ajax (Netherlands) v. Red Boys (Luxembourg), 1984
European Cup (1956)	6 Real Madrid, 1956–60, 66	12–2 Feyenoord (Netherlands) v. KR Reykjavik (Iceland), 1969
Cup Winners Cup (1960)	3 Barcelona, 1979, 82, 89	16–1 Sporting Club Portugal v. Apoel Nicosia (Cyprus), 1963
South America		
Copa Libertadores (1960)	7 Independiente (Argentina), 1964–5, 72–5, 84	11–2 Peñarol v. Valencia (Venezuela), 1970
Africa		
Cup of Champion Clubs (1964)	3 Canon Yaoundé (Cameroon), 1971, 78, 80	9–0 Kambe Warriors (Zambia) v. Manjantja Maseru (Lesotho), 1972
	3 Hafia FC Conakry (Guinea), 1972, 75, 77	
	3 Zamalek (Eygpt), 1984, 86, 93	
Cup Winners Cup (1975)	4 Al Alhy Cairo (Eygpt), 1984–6, 93	12–1 SC Pamba (Tanzania) v. Anse Boileau (Seychelles), 1990

John Hebden (b. 30 Jun 1948) and Ian Paul Fuller (b. 25 May 1953) in 1980–85 and 1987–90.

Football (Association)

THE FIFA WORLD CUP

The *Fédération Internationale de Football Association* (FIFA), which was founded on 21 May 1904, instituted the first World Cup on 13 Jul 1930, in Montevideo, Uruguay. It is held quadrennially. See Stop Press for 1994 updates.

Team records

Most wins Three wins have been achieved by Brazil 1958, 1962 and 1970; Italy 1934, 1938 and 1982; and West Germany 1954, 1974 and 1990.

Appearances Brazil, uniquely, have taken part in all 15 finals tournaments. Only two other nations have entered all World Cup competitions, France and the USA although the USA withdrew in 1938 without playing.

Most goals *Game* This occurred in a qualifying match in Auckland on 15 Aug 1981 when New Zealand beat Fiji 13–0. The highest score during the final stages is 10, scored by Hungary in a 10–1 win over El Salvador at Elche, Spain on 15 Jun 1982. The highest match aggregate in the finals tournament is 12, when Austria beat Switzerland, 7–5, at Lausanne, Switzerland on 26 Jun 1954.

Tournament The greatest number in a single finals tournament is 27 (five games) by Hungary in 1954. Not suprisingly, Brazil have scored the most overall, 148 in 66 matches.

Individual records

Appearances Antonio Carbajal (Mexico) (b. 7 Jun 1929) is the only player to have appeared in five World Cup finals tournaments, keeping goal for Mexico in 1950, 1954, 1958, 1962 and 1966, playing 11 games in all. The most games in finals tournaments is 21 by Uwe Seeler (West Germany) (b. 5 Nov 1936), 1958–70; and by Wladyslaw Zmuda (Poland) (b. 6 Jun 1954), 1974–86.

Pelé (Brazil) is the only player to have been with three World Cup–winning teams, in 1958, 1962 and 1970.

The youngest ever to play in a finals match is Norman Whiteside, who played for Northern Ireland v. Yugoslavia aged 17yr 41days on 17 Jun 1982. The oldest is Pat Jennings (b. 12 Jun 1945) for Northern Ireland v. Brazil on 12 Jun 1986, his 41st birthday.

Most goals *Game* Nine players have scored four goals in a single match. Of these, three have also scored one of the 33 hat-tricks to have occurred in finals matches; Sándor Kocsis (Hungary) (b. 1929), Just Fontaine (France) (b. Marrakech, Morocco, 18 Aug 1933) and Gerd Müller (West Germany) (b. 3 Nov 1945).

Tournament Just Fontaine scored 13 goals in six matches in the final stages of the 1958 competition in Sweden. Fontaine, Jaïrzinho (Brazil) (b. 25 Dec 1944) and Alcide Ghiggia (Uruguay) are the only three players to have scored in every match in a final series. Jaïrzinho scored seven in six games in 1970 and Ghiggia, four in four games in 1950.

Overall Gerd Müller scored ten goals in 1970 and four in 1974 for the highest aggregate of 14 goals.

Final The most goals scored in a final is three by Geoffrey Charles Hurst (b. 8 Dec 1941) for England v. West Germany on 30 Jul 1966. Three players have scored in two finals: Vava (real name Edevaldo Izito Neto) (Brazil) (b. 12 Nov 1934) in 1958 and 1962, Pelé in 1958 and 1970; and Paul Breitner (West Germany) (b. 5 Sep 1951) in 1974 and 1982.

Sports and Games

First-class Team Records

Goal scoring

Match The highest score recorded in a first-class match is 36. This occurred in the Scottish Cup match between Arbroath and Bon Accord on 5 Sep 1885, when Arbroath won 36–0 on their home ground. But for the lack of nets and the consequent waste of retrieval time the score must have been even higher. Seven further goals were disallowed for offside.

The highest margin recorded in an international match is 17, when England beat Australia 17–0 at Sydney on 30 Jun 1951. This match is not listed by England as a *full* international. The highest in the British Isles was when England beat Ireland 13–0 at Belfast on 18 Feb 1882.

The highest score between English clubs in any major competition is 26, when Preston North End beat Hyde 26–0 in an FA Cup tie at Deepdale, Lancs on 15 Oct 1887. The highest score by one side in a Football League (First Division) match is 12 goals when West Bromwich Albion beat Darwen 12–0 at West Bromwich, W Mids on 4 Apr 1892; when Nottingham Forest beat Leicester Fosse by the same score at Nottingham on 21 Apr 1909; and when Aston Villa beat Accrington 12–2 at Perry Barr, W Mids on 12 Mar 1892.

The highest aggregate in League Football was 17 goals when Tranmere Rovers beat Oldham Athletic 13–4 in a Third Division (North) match at Prenton Park, Merseyside, on Boxing Day, 1935. The record margin in a League match has been 13 in the Newcastle United 13, Newport County 0 (Second Division) match on 5 Oct 1946 and in the Stockport County 13, Halifax 0 (Third Division (North)) match on 6 Jan 1934.

Season The highest number of goals by any British team in a professional league in a season is 142 in 34 matches by Raith Rovers (Scottish Second Division) in the 1937/8 season. The English League record is 134 in 46 matches by Peterborough United (Fourth Division) in 1960/61.

League Championships

The record number of successive national league championships is nine by: Celtic (Scotland) 1966–74; CSKA, Sofia (Bulgaria) 1954–62; and MTK Budapest (Hungary) 1917–25. The Sofia club holds a European post-war record of 26 league titles, including two under the name CFKA Sredets (re-named CSKA).

English The greatest number of League Championships (First Division) is 18 by Liverpool in 1901, 1906, 1922–3, 1947, 1964, 1966, 1973, 1976–7, 1979–80, 1982–4, 1986, 1988 and 1990. The record number of wins in a season is 33 from 42 matches by Doncaster Rovers in Third Division (North) in 1946/7. The First Division record is 31 wins from 42 matches by Tottenham Hotspur in 1960/1. In 1893/4 Liverpool won 22 and drew 6 in 28 Second Division games. They also won the promotion match. The most points in a season under the current scoring system is 102 from 46 matches by Swindon in the Fourth Division in 1985/6. Under the new system the First Division record would have been Liverpool's

98 in 1978/9, when they won 30 and drew 8 of their 42 matches.

'Double' The only FA Cup and League Championship 'doubles' are those of Preston North End in 1889, Aston Villa in 1897, Tottenham Hotspur in 1961, Arsenal in 1971, Liverpool in 1986 and Manchester United in 1994. Preston won the League without losing a match and the Cup without having a goal scored against them throughout the whole competition.

Scottish Glasgow Rangers have won the Scottish League Championship 43 times (one shared 1891) between 1891 and 1994. Their 76 points in the Scottish First Division in 1920/1 (from a possible 84) represents a record in any division. However a better percentage was achieved by Rangers in 1898/9 when they gained the maximum of 36 by winning all their 18 matches.

Cup Competitions

FA Cup The greatest number of wins is eight by: Tottenham Hotspur, 1901, 1921, 1961, 1962, 1967, 1981, 1982 and 1991; and Manchester United, 1909, 1948, 1963, 1977, 1983, 1985, 1990 and 1994. The most appearances in the final is 12 by Manchester United and Arsenal (six wins). The most goals in a final is seven; when Blackburn Rovers beat Sheffield Wednesday 6–1 in 1890 and when Blackpool beat Bolton Wanderers 4–3 in 1953. The biggest victory is six when Bury beat Derby County 6–0 in 1903, in which year Bury did not concede a single goal in their five Cup matches.

Scottish FA Cup The greatest number of wins is 29 by Celtic in 1892, 1899, 1900, 1904, 1907–8, 1911–12, 1914, 1923, 1925, 1927, 1931, 1933, 1937, 1951, 1954, 1965, 1967, 1969, 1971–2, 1974–5, 1977, 1980, 1985 and 1988–9.

Football League Cup Instituted in 1960/1, the most wins is four by; Liverpool 1981–4; Nottingham Forest 1978–9, 1989–90; and Aston Villa 1961, 1975, 1977, 1994.

Scottish League Cup Instituted in 1946/7, the most wins is 19 by Rangers between 1947 and 1993. Derek Johnstone (Rangers) (b. 4 Nov 1953) was 16 yr 11 months old when he played in the Scottish League Cup final against Celtic on 24 Oct 1970.

Manchester United won the FA Cup for a record-equalling eighth time in 1994, beating Chelsea 4–0 and thereby became the sixth side to complete the 'Double'. Here the international stars of United celebrate their first goal (from left to right); Andrey Kanchelskis (Ukraine), Paul Ince (England), Roy Keane (Republic of Ireland), Eric Cantona (France, scorer) and Ryan Giggs (Wales). Cantona and Kanchelskis (also Chelsea's Russian 'keeper Dmitry Kharin) were the first players from their respective countries to play in the FA Cup final.
(Photo: Allsport)

GUESS WHAT?

Q Where is the world's largest stadium?
A See Page 91

Nottingham Forest were undefeated in 42 consecutive First Division matches from 20 Nov 1977 to 9 Dec 1978. In Scottish Football Glasgow Celtic were undefeated in 62 matches (49 won, 13 drawn), 13 Nov 1915–21 April 1917.

Individual Records

Goal scoring

Match The most scored by one player in a first-class match is 16 by Stephan Stanis (*né* Stanikowski, b. Poland, 15 Jul 1913) for Racing Club de Lens v. Aubry-Asturies, in Lens, France, in a wartime French Cup game on 13 Dec 1942.

The record number of goals scored by one player in an international match is ten by Sofus Nielsen (1888–1963) for Denmark *v.* France (17–1) in the 1908 Olympic Games and by Gottfried Fuchs (1889–1972) for Germany who beat Russia 16–0 in the 1912 Olympic tournament (consolation event) in Sweden.

Season The most goals in a League season is 60 in 39 games by William Ralph 'Dixie' Dean (1907–80) for Everton (First Division) in 1927/8 and 66 in 38 games by James Smith (1902–76) for Ayr United (Scottish Second Division) in the same season. With three more in Cup ties and 19 in representative matches Dean's total was 82.

Career Artur Friedenreich (Brazil) (1892–1969) scored an undocumented 1329 goals in a 26 year first-class football career, 1909–35. The most goals scored in a specified period is 1279 by Edson Arantes do Nascimento (Brazil) (b. 23 Oct 1940), known as Pelé, from 7 Sep 1956 to 1 Oct 1977 in 1363 games. His best year was 1959 with 126, and the *Milesimo* (1000th) came from a penalty for his club Santos in the Maracaña Stadium, Rio de Janeiro on 19 Nov 1969 when playing his 909th first-class match. He later added two more goals in special appearances. Franz 'Bimbo' Binder (b. 1 Dec 1911) scored 1006 goals in 756 games in Austria and Germany between 1930 and 1950.

The international career record for England is 49 goals by Robert 'Bobby' Charlton (b. 11 Oct 1937). His first was *v.* Scotland on 19 Apr 1958 and his last on 20 May 1970 *v.* Colombia.

The greatest number of goals scored in British first-class football is 550 (410 in Scottish League matches) by James McGrory of Glasgow Celtic (1922–38). The most scored in League matches is 434, for West Bromwich Albion, Fulham, Leicester City and Shrewsbury Town, by George Arthur Rowley (b. 21 Apr 1926) between 1946 and April 1965. Rowley also scored 32 goals in the F.A. Cup and one for England 'B'.

Fastest goals The fastest Football League goals on record were scored in 6 sec by Albert E. Mundy (b. 12 May 1926) (Aldershot) in a Fourth Division match *v.* Hartlepool United at Victoria Ground, Hartlepool, Cleveland on 25 Oct 1958, by Barrie Jones (b. 31 Oct 1938) (Notts County) in a Third Division match *v.* Torquay United on 31 Mar 1962, and by Keith Smith (b. 15 Sep 1940) (Crystal Palace) in a Second Division match *v.* Derby County at the Baseball Ground, Derby on 12 Dec 1964.

The fastest confirmed hat-trick is in 2½ minutes by Ephraim 'Jock' Dodds (b. 7 Sep 1915) for Blackpool *v.* Tranmere Rovers on 28 Feb 1942,

British Goal-Scoring Records

Scottish Cup 13
John Petrie, Arbroath *v.* Bon Accord, 5 Sep 1885.

Football League 10
Joe Payne (1914–77), Luton Town *v.* Bristol Rovers (Div 3S) at Luton on 13 Apr 1936.

Football League Division One 7
Ted Drake (b. 16 Aug 1912), Arsenal *v.* Aston Villa at Birmingham on 14 Dec 1935
James David Ross, Preston North End *v.* Stoke at Preston on 6 Oct 1888.

Football League Cup 6
Frankie Bunn (b. 6 Oct 1962), Oldham Athletic *v.* Scarborough at Oldham on 25 Oct 1989.

FA Cup (Preliminary Round) 10
Chris Marron for South Shields *v.* Radcliffe at South Shields on 20 Sep 1947.

FA Cup 9
Edward 'Ted' MacDougall (b. 8 Jan 1947) for Bournemouth *v.* Margate (first round) at Bournemouth on 20 Nov 1971.

Scottish League 8
James Edward McGrory (1904–82) for Celtic *v.* Dunfermline (Div 1) at Celtic Park, Glasgow on 14 Jan 1928.

Home International 6
Joe Bambrick (b. 3 Nov 1905) for Ireland *v.* Wales at Belfast on 1 Feb 1930.

> Torquay United's Pat Kruse (b. 30 Nov 1953) equalled the fastest goal on record when he headed the ball into his own net only 6 sec after kick-off *v.* Cambridge United on 3 Jan 1977.

and Jimmy Scarth (b. 26 Aug 1920) for Gillingham *v.* Leyton Orient in Third Division (Southern) on 1 Nov 1952. A hat-trick in 1 min 50 sec is claimed for Maglioni of Independiente *v.* Gimnasia y Escrima de la Plata in Argentina on 18 Mar 1973. John McIntyre (Blackburn Rovers) scored four goals in 5 min *v.* Everton at Ewood Park, Blackburn, Lancs on 16 Sep 1922. William 'Ginger' Richardson (West Bromwich Albion) scored four goals in 5 min from the kick-off against West Ham United at Upton Park on 7 Nov 1931. Frank Keetley scored six goals in 21 min in the second half of the Lincoln City *v.* Halifax Town league match on 16 Jan 1932. The international record is three goals in 3½ min by George William Hall (Tottenham Hotspur) for England against Ireland on 16 Nov 1938 at Old Trafford, Greater Manchester.

Goalkeeping

The longest that any goalkeeper has succeeded in preventing any goals being scored past him in top-class competition is 1275 mins by Abel Resino of Athletico Madrid to 17 Mar 1991. The record in international matches is 1142 min for Dino Zoff (Italy) (b. 22 Feb 1942), from September 1972 to June 1974.

The British club record in all competitive matches is 1196 min by Chris Woods (b. 14 Nov 1959) for Glasgow Rangers from 26 Nov 1986 to 31 Jan 1987.

International Caps

Oldest The oldest international has been William Henry 'Billy' Meredith (1874–1958) (Manchester City and United) who played outside right for Wales *v.* England at Highbury, London on 15 Mar 1920 when aged 45 yr 229 days. He played internationally for a record span of 26 years (1895–1920).

Youngest The youngest British international was Norman Whiteside, who played for Northern Ireland *v.* Yugoslavia at 17 yr 41 days on 17 Jun 1982.

England's youngest international was James Frederick McLeod Prinsep (1861–95) (Clapham Rovers) *v.* Scotland at Kennington Oval, London on 5 Apr 1879, at 17 yr 252 days. The youngest Welsh cap was Ryan Giggs (b. 29 Nov 1973) (Manchester United), *v.* Germany at

Neville Southall has made a record 73 appearances for Wales and had a clean sheet on his début against Northern Ireland on 27 May 1982.
(Photo: Allsport/Ben Radford)

British International Appearances

ENGLAND 125, Peter Leslie Shilton (b. 18 Sep 1949) (Leicester City, Stoke City, Nottingham Forest, Southampton, Derby County) 1970–90.

NORTHERN IRELAND 119, Patrick Anthony Jennings (b. 12 Jun 1945) (Watford, Tottenham Hotspur, Arsenal) 1964–86.

SCOTLAND 102, Kenneth Mathieson Dalglish (b. 4 Mar 1951) (Celtic, Liverpool) 1971–86.

REPUBLIC OF IRELAND 73, Pat Bonner (b. 25 May 1960) (Celtic) 1981–94.

WALES 73, Peter Nicholas (b. 10 Nov 1959) (Crystal Palace, Arsenal, Luton Town, Aberdeen, Chelsea, Watford) 1979–91; Neville Southall (b. 16 Sep 1958) (Everton) 1981–94.

Nuremburg, Germany on 16 Oct 1991, aged 17 yr 321 days. Scotland's youngest international has been John Alexander Lambie (1868–1923) (Queen's Park), at 17 yr 92 days *v.* Ireland on 20 Mar 1886. The youngest for the Republic of Ireland was James Holmes (b. 11 Nov 1953) (Coventry City), at 17 yr 200 days *v.* Austria in Dublin on 30 May 1971.

Most international appearances The greatest number of appearances for a national team is 150 by Héctor Chumpitaz (Peru) (b. 12 Apr 1943) from 1963 to 1982. This includes all matches played by the national team. The record for full internationals against other national teams is 125 by Peter Shilton of England.

The most international appearances by a woman is 59 by Linda Curl (b. 1962) for England, 1977–90.

GUESS WHAT?

Q Who has made the most Test appearances at cricket?

A see Page 245

THEN & NOW

Progression of Transfer Fees *for British Players*

The following are notable landmarks of transfer fees between two British Clubs or, in italics, those between a British club and an overseas club. It should be noted, however, that there is no accepted way of quantifying the actual value of transfer fees. They are private contracts and there is no published register of the fees paid. The figures stated are those quoted at the time and generally accepted as fact (or fiction!).

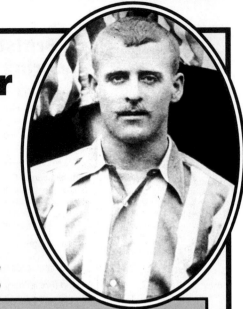

Alf Common, seen here in Sheffield United colours, was the player to be involved in both the first £500 and £1000 transfer deals. (Photo: Colorsport)

£s	Player	Club, from	Club, sold to	Date
500+	Alf Common	Sheffield United	Sunderland	1902
1000+	Alf Common	Sunderland	Middlesbrough	February 1905
10,000+	David Jack	Arsenal	Bolton Wanderers	October 1928
50,000+	*John Charles*	*Leeds United*	*Juventus (Italy)*	*June 1957*
	Denis Law	Huddersfield Town	Manchester City	March 1960
100,000+	*Denis Law*	*Manchester City*	*Torino (Italy)*	*July 1961*
	Alan Ball	Blackpool	Everton	August 1966
250,000+	Denis Tueart	Sunderland	Manchester City	March 1974
500,000+	*Kevin Keegan*	*Liverpool*	*Hamburg (Germany)*	*June 1977*
	David Mills	Middlesbrough	West Bromwich Albion	January 1979
1,000,000+	*Laurie Cunningham*	*West Bromwich Albion*	*Real Madrid (Spain)*	*January 1979*
	Trevor Francis	Birmingham City	Nottingham Forest	February 1979
1,500,000+	Bryan Robson	West Bromwich Albion	Manchester United	October 1981
2,000,000+	Paul Gascoigne	Newcastle United	Tottenham Hotspur	July 1988
3,000,000+	*Ian Rush*	*Liverpool*	*Juventus (Italy)*	*June 1986*
	Alan Shearer	Southampton	Blackburn Rovers	July 1992
4,000,000+	*Chris Waddle*	*Tottenham Hotspur*	*Marseille (France)*	*July 1989*
	Duncan Ferguson	Dundee United	Rangers	July 1993
5,000,000+	*David Platt*	*Aston Villa*	*Bari (Italy)*	*July 1991*

Finally between two overseas clubs:

£s	Player	Club, from	Club, sold to	Date
6,000,000+	*David Platt*	*Bari (Italy)*	*Juventus (Italy)*	*July 1992*

David Platt (far left) has been involved in a number of record deals. In a career which began at Manchester United but for whom he never played, he has been transferred three times for fees in excess of £5 million in three successive years (1991–3); Aston Villa to Bari, Bari to Juventus, Juventus to Sampdoria. (Photo: Allsport)

Duncan Ferguson (left), seen here in action in his first Rangers-Celtic derby match in August 1993, will become the first £4 million player between two British clubs. He was sold for £3.7 million but this will increase to £4.1 million based on his international appearances for Scotland. (Photo: Allsport)

Cup competitions

Youngest player The youngest player in an FA Cup final was James Prinsep (1861–95) for Clapham Rovers *v.* Old Etonians on 29 Mar 1879, aged 17 yr 245 days. The youngest goal scorer in the FA Cup final was Norman Whiteside (b. 7 May 1965) for Manchester United *v.* Brighton at 18 yr 19 days on 26 May 1983. The youngest player ever in the FA Cup competition was full back Andrew Awford (b. 14 Jul 1972) at 15 yr 88 days for Worcester City in a qualifying round tie at Borehamwood, Herts on 10 Oct 1987.

Most medals Three players have won five FA Cupwinners' medals: James Henry Forrest (1864–1925) with Blackburn Rovers (1884–6, 1890–1); the Hon. Sir Arthur Fitzgerald Kinnaird (1847–1923) with Wanderers (1873, 1877–8) and Old Etonians (1879, 1882); and Charles Harold Reynolds Wollaston (1849–1926) with Wanderers (1872–3, 1876–8).

The most Scottish Cupwinners' medals won is eight by Charles Campbell (d. 1927) (Queen's Park) in 1874–6, 1880–82, 1884 and 1886.

Players

Most durable Peter Leslie Shilton (b. 18 Sep 1949) made a record 1374 senior UK appearances, including a record 991 League appearances, 286 for Leicester City (1966–74), 110 for Stoke City (1974–7), 202 for Nottingham Forest (1977–82), 188 for Southampton (1982–7), 175 for Derby County (1987–92) and 30 for Plymouth Argyle (1992), 86 FA Cup, 102 League Cup, 125 internationals, 13 Under-23, 4 Football League XI and 53 various European and other club competitons. Norman John Trollope (b. 14 Jun 1943) made 770 League appearances for one club, Swindon Town, between 1960 and 1980.

Transfer fees The highest transfer fee quoted for a player is a reported £13 million for Gianluigi Lentini (Italy), from Torino to AC Milan in June 1992.

The highest transfer fee for a British player is a reported £6.5 million paid by Juventus to Bari for David Platt (b. 10 Jun 1966) in July 1992. The record fee between two British clubs is a reported £3.75 million paid by Manchester United to Nottingham Forest for Roy Keane (b. 10 Aug 1971) on 21 Jul 1993, however, this may be surpassed by that paid by Rangers to Dundee United for Duncan Ferguson (b. 27 Dec 1971). The fee of £3.7 million for his transfer on 15 Jul 1993 could be augmented up to a total of £4.1 million, depending on Ferguson's international appearances for Scotland.

Attendances

Greatest crowds The greatest recorded crowd at any football match was 199,589 for the Brazil v. Uruguay World Cup match in the Maracaña Municipal Stadium, Rio de Janeiro, Brazil on 16 Jul 1950. The record attendance for a European Cup match is 136,505 at the semi-final between Glasgow Celtic and Leeds United at Hampden Park, Glasgow on 15 Apr 1970.

The British record paid attendance is 149,547 at the Scotland v. England international at Hampden Park, Glasgow on 17 Apr 1937. It is, however, probable that this total was exceeded (estimated 160,000) at the FA Cup final between Bolton Wanderers and West Ham United at Wembley Stadium on 28 Apr 1923, when the crowd spilled onto the pitch and the start was delayed 40 min until it was cleared. The counted admissions were 126,047.

The Scottish Cup record attendance is 146,433 when Celtic played Aberdeen at Hampden Park on 24 Apr 1937. The record attendance for a League match in Britain is 118,567 for Rangers v. Celtic at Ibrox Park, Glasgow on 2 Jan 1939.

The highest attendance at an amateur match has been 120,000 in Senayan Stadium, Jakarta, Indonesia on 26 Feb 1976 for the Pre-Olympic Group II final, North Korea v. Indonesia.

Smallest crowd The smallest crowd at a full home international was 2315 for Wales v. Northern Ireland on 27 May 1982 at the Racecourse Ground, Wrexham, Clwyd. The smallest paying attendance at a Football League fixture was for the Stockport County v. Leicester City match at Old Trafford, Manchester on 7 May 1921. Stockport's own ground was under suspension and the 'crowd' numbered 13 but an estimated 2000 gained free admission. When West Ham beat Castilla of Spain (5–1) in the European Cup Winners Cup at Upton Park, Greater London on 1 Oct 1980 and when Aston Villa beat Besiktas of Turkey (3–1) in the European Cup at Villa Park, Birmingham on 15 Sep 1982, there were no paying spectators due to disciplinary action by the European Football Union.

Other Records (Non first-class games)

Highest scores *Teams* Drayton Grange Colts beat Eldon Sports Reserves 49–0 in a Daventry and District Sunday League match at Grange Estate, Northants on 13 Nov 1988. Every member of the side including the goalkeeper scored at least one goal.

In an Under-14 League match between Midas FC and Courage Colts, in Kent, on 11 Apr 1976, the full-time score after 70 minutes play was 59–1. Top scorer for Midas was Kevin Graham with 17 goals. Courage had scored the first goal.

Needing to improve their goal 'difference' to gain promotion in 1979, Ilinden FC of Yugoslavia, with the collusion of the opposition, Mladost, and the referee, won their final game of the season 134–1. Their rivals for promotion won their match, under similar circumstances, 88–0.

Individual Dean Goodliff scored 26 goals for Deleford Colts v. Iver Minors in the Slough Boys Soccer Combination Under–14 League at Iver, Bucks in his team's 33–0 win on 22 Dec 1985. The women's record is 22 goals by Linda Curl of Norwich Ladies in a 40–0 league victory over Milton Keynes Reserves at Norwich on 25 Sep 1983.

Season The greatest number of goals in a season reported for an individual player in junior professional league football is 96 by Tom Duffy (b. 7 Jan 1937), for Ardeer Thistle FC, Strathclyde in 1960/61. Paul Anthony Moulden (b. 6 Sep 1967) scored 289 goals in 40 games for Bolton Lads Club in Bolton Boys Federation intermediate league and cup matches in 1981/2. An additional 51 goals scored in other tournaments brought his total to 340, the highest season figure reported in any class of competitive football for an individual. He made his Football League debut for Manchester City on 1 Jan 1986 and has played for the England Youth team.

Fastest goals *Individual* Goals scored in 3 seconds and under after the kick-off have been achieved by a number of players. Damian Corcoran (b. 25 Nov 1976) scored three goals within a minute for 7th Fulwood Cubs v. 4th Fulwood Cubs on 1 Feb 1987.

Own goal The fastest own goal on record has been in 4 sec 'scored' by Richard Nash of Newick v. Burgess Hill Reserves at Newick, E Sussex on 8 Feb 1992.

Team The shortest time for a semi-professional team to score three goals from the start of a game is 122 sec by Burton Albion v. Redditch United in a Beazer Homes League Premier Division match on 2 Jan 1989.

Goalkeeping Craig Manktelow (b. 5 Mar 1967) of Kawerau Electrical Services in New Zealand played 15 matches without conceding a goal, a total of 1350 min, from 6 May–19 Aug 1989.

Largest tournament The Metropolitan Police 5-a-side Youth Competition in 1981 attracted an entry of 7008 teams, a record for an FA sanctioned competition.

Most and least successful teams Winlaton West End FC, Tyne & Wear, completed a run of 95 league games without defeat between 1976 and 1980. Penlake Junior Football Club remained unbeaten for 153 games (winning 152 including 85 in succession) in the Warrington Hilden Friendly League from 1981 until defeated in 1986. Stockport United FC, of the Stockport Football League, lost 39 consecutive League and Cup matches, September 1976 to 18 Feb 1978.

Most indisciplined In the local cup match between Tongham Youth Club, Surrey and Hawley, Hants, on 3 Nov 1969, the referee booked all 22 players including one who went to hospital, and one of the linesmen. The match, won by Tongham 2–0, was described by a player as 'a good, hard game'.

In a Gancia Cup match at Waltham Abbey, Essex on 23 Dec 1973, the referee, Michael J. Woodhams, sent off the entire Juventus-Cross team and some club officials. Glencraig United, Faifley, near Clydebank, had all 11 team members and two substitutes for their 2–2 draw against Goldenhill Boys' Club on 2 Feb 1975 booked in the dressing room before a ball was kicked. The referee, Mr Tarbet of Bearsden, took exception to the chant which greeted his arrival. It was not his first meeting with Glencraig.

It was reported on 1 Jun 1993 that in a league match between Sportivo Ameliano and General Caballero in Paraguay, referee William Weiler sent off 20 players. Trouble flared after two Sportivo players were sent off, a ten-minute fight ensued and Weiler then dismissed a further 18 players, including the rest of the Sportivo team. Not suprisingly the match was abandonded.

Heaviest!

The biggest goalkeeper in representative football was the England international Willie Henry 'Fatty' Foulke (1874–1916), who stood 1.90 m *6 ft 3 in* and weighed 141 kg *22 st 3 lb*. His last games were for Bradford City, by which time he was 165 kg *26 st*. He once stopped a game by snapping the cross bar.

Control!

Volkhart Caro (Canada) juggled a regulation soccer ball for 18 hours non-stop with feet, legs and head without the ball ever touching the ground at the St Dominic Catholic Elementary School, Edmonton, Canada on 26–27 Jun 1993. The heading record is 7 hr 5 min 5 sec by Tomas Lundman (Sweden) at Nöjeskällan, Märsta, Sweden on 5 Sep 1992.

Jan Skorkovsky of Prague, Czechoslovakia kept a football up while he travelled a distance of 42.195 km *26.219 miles* for the Prague City Marathon in 7 hr 18 min 55 sec on 8 Jul 1990.

GUESS WHAT?

Q Which teams have won the FA Cup most often?

A See Page 252

Gaelic Football

All-Ireland Championships The greatest number of All–Ireland Championships won by one team is 30 by Ciarraidhe (Kerry) between 1903 and 1986. The greatest number of successive wins is four by Wexford (1915–18) and Kerry twice (1929–32, 1978–81).

The most finals contested by an individual is ten, including eight wins by the Kerry players Pat Spillane, Paudie O'Shea and Denis Moran, 1975–76, 1978–82, 1984–86.

The highest team score in a final was when Dublin, 27 (5 goals, 12 points) beat Armagh, 15 (3 goals, 6 points) on 25 Sep 1977. The highest combined score was 45 points when Cork (26) beat Galway (19) in 1973. A goal equals three points.

The highest individual score in an All-Ireland final has been 2 goals, 6 points by Jimmy Keaveney (Dublin) *v.* Armagh in 1977, and by Michael Sheehy (Kerry) *v.* Dublin in 1979.

Largest crowd The record crowd is 90,556 for the Down *v.* Offaly final at Croke Park, Dublin in 1961.

Gambling

Biggest win The biggest individual gambling win is $111,240,463.10 by Leslie Robbins and Colleen DeVries of Fond du Lac, Wisconsin for the Powerball lottery drawn on 7 Jul 1993.

Bingo

Largest house The largest 'house' in Bingo sessions was 15,756 at the Canadian National Exhibition, Toronto on 19 Aug 1983. Staged by the Variety Club of Ontario Tent Number 28, there was total prize money of $C250,000 with a record one-game payout of $C100,000.

Earliest and latest Full House A 'Full House' call occurred on the 15th number by Norman A. Wilson at Guide Post Working Men's Club, Bedlington, Northumberland on 22 Jun 1978, by Anne Wintle of Bryncethin, Mid Glam, on a coach trip to Bath on 17 Aug 1982 and by Shirley Lord at Kahibah Bowling Club, New South Wales, Australia on 24 Oct 1983.

'House' was not called until the 86th number at the Hillsborough Working Men's Club, Sheffield, S Yorks on 11 Jan 1982. There were 32 winners.

Football Pools

The winning dividend paid out by Littlewoods Pools in their first week in February 1923 was £212s0d. In 1992/3 the three British Pools companies which comprise the Pool Promoters Association (Littlewoods, Vernons and Zetters) had a total record turnover of £869,332,000, of which Littlewoods contributed over 70 per cent.

Biggest win!

British The record individual payout, which is also the biggest ever individual prize paid in any British competition, is **£2,255,387.40** paid by **Littlewoods Pools** to **Barry Mallett of Harwich, Essex** for matches played on **12 Feb 1994.**

Gaelic football action from Croke Park
(Photo: Allsport/Billy Stickland)

Horse Racing

Highest ever odds The highest secured odds were 1,670,759 to 1 by George Rhodes of Aldershot, Hants. For a 5p bet, with a 10 per cent bonus for the ITV Seven, less tax, he was paid £86,024.42 by the William Hill Organization on 30 Sep 1984.

Edward Hodson of Wolverhampton, W Mids landed a 3,956,748 to 1 bet for a 55p stake on 11 Feb 1984, but his bookmaker had a £3000 payout limit.

The world record odds on a 'double' are 31,793 to 1 paid by the New Zealand Totalisator Agency Board on a five shilling tote ticket on *Red Emperor* and *Maida Dillon* at Addington, Christchurch in 1951.

Greatest payout Anthony A. Speelman and Nicholas John Cowan (both Great Britain) won $1,627,084.40, after federal income tax of $406,768.00 was withheld, on a $64 nine-horse accumulator at Santa Anita racecourse, California, USA on 19 Apr 1987. Their first seven selections won and the payout was for a jackpot, accumulated over 24 days.

The largest payout by a British bookmaker is £567,066.25 by Ladbrokes, paid to Dick Mussell of Havant, Hants for a combination of an accumulator, trebles, doubles and singles on five horses at Cheltenham on 12 Mar 1992.

Biggest tote win The best recorded tote win was one of £341 2s 6d to 2s representing odds of 3410¼ to 1, by Catharine Unsworth of Blundellsands, Liverpool, Merseyside at Haydock Park on a race won by *Coole* on 30 Nov 1929. The highest

> The biggest beating handed to a 'one-armed bandit' was $9,357,489.41 by Delores Adams, 60, at the Harrah's Reno Casino-Hotel, Nevada, USA on 30 May 1992.

odds in Irish tote history were £289.64 for a 10p unit on *Gene's Rogue* at Limerick on 28 Dec 1981.

Largest bookmaker The world's largest bookmaker is Ladbrokes with a peak turnover from gambling in 1988 of £2107 million and the largest chain of betting shops, over 1900 in Great Britain and the Republic of Ireland at 1 Jul 1993, as well as outlets in Germany and Belgium.

Topmost tipster The only recorded instance of a racing correspondent forecasting ten out of ten winners on a race card was at Delaware Park, Wilmington, Delaware, USA on 28 Jul 1974 by Charles Lamb of the *Baltimore News American.*

The best performance by a British correspondent is seven out of seven winners for a meeting at Wolverhampton on 22 Mar 1982 by Bob Butchers of the *Daily Mirror.* This was repeated by Fred Shawcross of the *Today* newspaper at York on 12 May 1988. In greyhound racing the best performance is 12 out of 12 by Mark Sullivan of the *Sporting Life* for a meeting at Wimbledon on 21 Dec 1990.

Gliding

Most titles The most World Individual Championships (instituted 1937) won is four by Ingo Renner (Australia) in 1976 (Standard class), 1983, 1985 and 1987 (Open).

British The British National Championship (instituted 1939) has been won eight times by Ralph Jones (b. 29 Mar 1936).

The first woman to win this title was Anne Burns (b. 23 Nov. 1915) of Farnham, Surrey on 30 May 1966.

Women's altitude records The women's single-seater world record for absolute altitude is 12,637m *41,460ft* by Sabrina Jackintell (USA) in an Astir GS on 14 Feb 1979.

The height gain record is 10,212m *33,504ft* by Yvonne Loader (New Zealand) at Omarama, New Zealand on 12 Jan 1988.

The British single-seater absolute altitude record is 10,550m *34,612ft* by Anne Burns in a Skylark 3B over South Africa on 13 Jan 1961, when she set a then world record and still a British record for height gain of 9119m *29,918ft*.

GUESS WHAT?
Q who is the oldest person to fly?
A See Page 129

World & British Gliding Single-Seater Records

Category	Distance	Name	Location	Date
Straight Distance	1460.8km *907.7miles*	Hans-Werner Grosse (West Germany)	Lübeck, Germany to Biarritz, France	25 Apr 1972
(British)	949.70km *590.1miles*	Karla Karel	Australia	20 Jan 1980
Declared Goal Distance	1254.26km *779.36miles*	Bruce Lindsay Drake (New Zealand)	Te Anau to Te Araroa, New Zealand	14 Jan 1978
		David Napier Speight (New Zealand)	Te Anau to Te Araroa, New Zealand	14 Jan 1978
		Sholto Hamilton 'Dick' Georgeson (New Zealand)	Te Anau to Te Araroa, New Zealand	14 Jan 1978
(British)	859.2km *534miles*	M. T. Alan Sands	Ridge soaring to Chilhowee, Va, USA	23 Apr 1986
Goal and Return	1646.68km *1023.20miles*	Thomas L. Knauff (USA)	Gliderport to Williamsport, Pa, USA	25 Apr 1983
(British)	1127.68km *700.72miles*	M. T. Alan Sands	Lock Haven, Pa to Bluefield, Va, USA	7 May 1985
Absolute Altitude	14,938m *49,009ft*	Robert R. Harris (USA)	California, USA	17 Feb 1986
(British)	11,500m *37,729ft*	H. C. Nicholas Goodhart	California, USA	12 May 1955
Height Gain	12,894m *42,303ft*	Paul F. Bikle (USA)	Mojave, Lancaster, California, USA	25 Feb 1961
(British)	10,065m *33,022ft*	David Benton	Portmoak, Scotland	18 Apr 1980

SPEED OVER TRIANGULAR COURSE

Distance	km/h	mph			
100km	195.3	*121.35*	Ingo Renner (Australia)	Tocumwal, Australia	14 Dec 1982
(British)	166.38	*103.38*	Bruce Cooper	Australia	4 Jan 1991
300km	169.50	*105.32*	Jean-Paul Castel (France)	Bitterwasser, Namibia	15 Nov 1986
(British)	146.8	*91.2*	Edward Pearson	South West Africa (now Namibia)	30 Nov 1976
500km	170.06	*105.67*	Beat Bunzli (Switzerland)	Bitterwasser, Namibia	9 Jan 1988
(British)	141.3	*87.8*	Bradley James Grant Pearson	South Africa	28 Dec 1982
750km	158.41	*98.43*	Hans-Werner Grosse (West Germany)	Alice Springs, Australia	8 Jan 1985
(British)	109.8	*68.2*	Michael R. Carlton	South Africa	5 Jan 1975
1000km	145.33	*90.30*	Hans-Werner Grosse (West Germany)	Alice Springs, Australia	3 Jan 1979
(British)	112.15	*69.68*	George Lee	Australia	25 Jan 1989
1250km	133.24	*82.79*	Hans-Werner Grosse (West Germany)	Alice Springs, Australia	9 Dec 1980
(British)	109.01	*67.73*	Robert L. Robertson	USA	2 May 1986

Hang Gliding

World Championships The World Team Championships (officially instituted 1976) have been won most often by Great Britain (1981, 1985, 1989 and 1991).

World records The *Fédération Aéronautique Internationale* recognizes world records for rigid-wing, flexwing and multiplace flexwing. These records are the greatest in each category.

Men Greatest distance in straight line and declared goal distance: 488.2km *303.3 miles* Larry Tudor (USA), Hobbs Airpark, New Mexico to Elkhart, Kansas, 3 Jul 1990. Height gain: 4343m *14,250ft* Larry Tudor (USA), Owens Valley, California, 4 Aug 1985.

Out and return distance: 310.3km *192.8 miles* Larry Tudor (USA) and Geoffrey Loyns (GB), Owens Valley, 26 Jun 1988. Triangular course distance: 196km *121.79 miles* James Lee (USA), Wild Horse Mesa, Colorado, 4 Jul 1991.

Women Greatest distance: 335.8km *208.6 miles* Kari Castle (USA), Owens Valley, 22 Jul 1991. Height gain: 3970m *13,025ft* Judy Leden (GB) Kuruman, South Africa, 1 Dec 1992.

Out and return distance via single turn: 292.1km *181.5 miles* Kari Castle (USA), Hobbs Airpark, 1 Jul 1990. Declared goal distance: 212.50km *132.04 miles* Liavan Mallin (Ireland), Owens Valley, 13 Jul 1989.

Triangular course distance: Judy Leden (GB), 114.1km *70.9 miles*, Kössen, Austria, 22 Jun 1991.

British The British record for distance is held by Geoffrey Loyns, 312.864km *194.41miles*, in Flagstaff, Arizona, USA on 11 Jun 1988. The best in Britain is 244km *151.62miles* by Gordon Rigg from Lords Seat to Witham Friary, Somerset on 4 Jun 1989.

Club!

A Scottish iron golf club of *c.* 1700 sold for £92,400 at Sotheby's sale of golfing memorabilia at Loretto School, Musselburgh, Lothian, held on 13 Jul 1992 to coincide with the 121st Open Championship. It was bought by Titus Kendall on behalf of the Valderamma Golf Club, Sotte Grande, Spain.

Golf

Oldest club The oldest club of which there is written evidence is the Gentlemen Golfers (now the Honourable Company of Edinburgh Golfers) formed in March 1744–ten years prior to the institution of the Royal and Ancient Club of St Andrews, Fife. However, the Royal Burgess Golfing Society of Edinburgh claims to have been founded in 1735.

Largest green Probably the largest green in the world is that of the par-6 635m *695yd* fifth hole at International GC, Bolton, Massachusetts, USA, with an area greater than 2600m² *28,000ft²*.

Highest shot on Earth Gerald Williams (USA) played a shot from the summit of Mt Aconcagua (6960m *22,834ft*), Argentina on 22 Jan 1989.

Biggest bunker The world's biggest bunker (called a trap in the USA) is Hell's Half Acre on the 535m *585yd* seventh hole of the Pine Valley course, Clementon, New Jersey, USA, built in 1912 and generally regarded as the world's most trying course.

The longest hole in the world is the 7th hole (par-7) of the Satsuki GC, Sano, Japan, which measures 964yd *881m*.

The longest hole in Great Britain is the second at Gedney Hill, Lincs, which stretches 613m *671yd*.

On 14 Jul 1992 Titus Kendall also paid a record £19,250 at Phillips, Edinburgh for a gutta (latex-type) golf ball made by Scot Allan Robertson in 1849.

Drive!

The greatest recorded drive on an ordinary course is one of 471m *515yd* by Michael Hoke Austin (b. 17 Feb 1910) of Los Angeles, California, USA, in the US National Seniors Open Championship at Las Vegas, Nevada on 25 Sep 1974. Austin, 1.88m *6ft 2in* tall and weighing 92kg *203lb* drove the ball to within a yard of the green on the par-4 412m *450yd* fifth hole of the Winterwood Course and it rolled 59m *65yd* past the flagstick. He was aided by an estimated 56km/h *35mph* tailwind.

Longest course The world's longest course is the par-77 7612m *8325yd* International GC, Bolton, Massachussetts, USA, from the 'Tiger' tees, remodelled in 1969 by Robert Trent Jones.

Floyd Satterlee Rood used the United States as a course, when he played from the Pacific surf to the Atlantic surf from 14 Sep 1963 to 3 Oct 1964 in 114,737 strokes. He lost 3511 balls on the 5468km *3397.7 mile* trail.

GUESS WHAT? Q On which course is horse racing's Grand National run? A See Page 266

Longest drive A drive of 2414m *2640 yd (1½ miles)* across ice was achieved by an Australian meteorologist named Nils Lied at Mawson Base, Antarctica in 1962.

Longest putt The longest recorded holed putt in a major tournament is 110ft by; Jack Nicklaus (b. 21 Jan 1940) in the 1964 Tournament of Champions; and Nick Price in the 1992 United States PGA.

Robert Tyre 'Bobby' Jones Jr, (1902–71) was reputed to have holed a putt in excess of 30m *100ft* at the fifth green in the first round of the 1927 Open at St Andrews.

Bob Cook (USA) sank a putt measured at 42.74m *140ft 2¾ in* on the 18th at St Andrews in the International Fourball Pro Am Tournament on 1 Oct 1976.

Scores

Lowest 9 holes Nine holes in 25 (4, 3, 3, 2, 3, 3, 1, 4, 2) was recorded by A. J. 'Bill' Burke in a round of 57 (32+25) on the 5842m *6389 yd* par-71 Normandie course at St Louis, Missouri, USA on 20 May 1970.

The tournament record is 27 by Mike Souchak (USA) (b. 10 May 1927) for the second nine (par-35), first round of the 1955 Texas Open (⇨ 72 holes); Andy North (USA) (b. 9 Mar 1950) second nine (par-34), first round, 1975 BC Open at En-Joie GC, Endicott, New York; José Maria Canizares (Spain) (b. 18 Feb 1947), first nine, third round, in the 1978 Swiss Open on the 6228m *6811 yd* Crans GC, Crans-sur-Seine; and Robert Lee (GB) (b. 12 Oct 1961) first nine, first round, in the Monte Carlo Open on the 5714m *6249 yd* Mont Agel course on 28 Jun 1985.

Lowest 18 holes *Men* At least four players have played a long course (over 6000m *6561 yd*) in a score of 58, most recently Monte Carlo Money (USA) (b. 3 Dec 1954) at the par-72, 6041m *6607 yd* Las Vegas Municipal GC, Nevada, USA on 11 Mar 1981.

Alfred Edward Smith (1903–85) achieved an 18-hole score of 55 (15 under par 70) on his home course of 3884m *4248 yd*, scoring 4, 2, 3, 4, 2, 4, 3, 4, 3=29 out, and 2, 3, 3, 3, 3, 2, 5, 4, 1=26 in, on 1 Jan 1936.

The United States PGA Tournament record for 18 holes is 59 by Al Geiberger (b. 1 Sep 1937) (30+29) in the second round of the Danny Thomas Classic, on the 72-par 6628m *7249 yd* Colonial GC course, Memphis, Tennessee on 10 Jun 1977; and by Chip Beck in the third round of the Las Vegas Invitational, on the 72-par 6381m *6979 yd* Sunrise GC course, Las Vegas, Nevada on 11 Oct 1991.

Other golfers to have recorded 59 over 18 holes in major non-PGA tournaments include: Samuel Jackson 'Sam' Snead (b. 27 May 1912) in the third round of the Sam Snead Festival at White Sulphur Springs, West Virginia, USA on 16 May 1959; Gary Player (South Africa) (b. 1 Nov 1935) in the second round of the Brazilian Open in Rio de Janeiro on 29 Nov 1974; and David Jagger (GB) (b. 9 Jun 1949) in a Pro-Am tournament prior to

the 1973 Nigerian Open at Ikoyi GC, Lagos; and Miguel Martin (Spain) in the Argentine Southern Championship at Mar de Plata on 27 Feb 1987.

Women The lowest recorded score on an 18-hole course (over 5120m *5600 yd*) for a woman is 62 (30+32) by Mary 'Mickey' Kathryn Wright (USA) (b. 14 Feb 1935) on the Hogan Park Course (par-71, 5747m *6286 yd*) at Midland, Texas, USA, in November 1964, Janice Arnold (New Zealand) (31+31) at the Coventry Golf Club, W Mids (5317m *5815 yd*) on 24 Sep 1990, Laura Davies (GB) (b. 5 Oct 1963) (32+30) at the Rail Golf Club, Springfield, Illinois, USA on 31 Aug 1991, and Hollis Stacy (b. 16 Mar 1954) in the second round of the 1992 Safeco Classic.

Wanda Morgan (b. 22 Mar 1910) recorded a score of 60 (31+29) on the Westgate and Birchington GC course, Kent, over 18 holes (4573m *5002 yd*) on 11 Jul 1929.

Great Britain The lowest score recorded in a first-class professional tournament on a course of more than 5490m *6000 yd* in Great Britain is 60 (30+30), by Paul Curry in the second round of the Bell's Scottish Open on the King's course (5899m *6452 yd*), Gleneagles, Tayside on 9 Jul 1992.

Lowest 36 holes The record for 36 holes is 122 (59+63) by Sam Snead in the 1959 Sam Snead Festival on 16–17 May 1959.

Horton Smith (1908–63), twice US Masters Champion, scored 121 (63+58) on a short course on 21 Dec 1928 (⇨ 72 holes).

The lowest score by a British golfer has been 124 (61+63) by Alexander Walter Barr 'Sandy' Lyle (b. 9 Feb 1958) in the Nigerian Open at the 5508m *6024 yd* (par-71) Ikoyi GC, Lagos in 1978.

Lowest 72 holes The lowest recorded score on a first-class course is 255 (29 under par) by Leonard Peter Tupling (GB) (b. 6 Apr 1950) in the Nigerian Open at Ikoyi GC, Lagos in February 1981, made up of 63, 66, 62 and 64 (average 63.75 per round).

The lowest 72 holes in a US professional event is 257 (60, 68, 64, 65) by Mike Souchak in the 1955 Texas Open at San Antonio.

The 72 holes record on the European tour is 258 (64, 69, 60, 65) by David Llewellyn (b. 18 Nov 1951) in the Biarritz Open on 1–3 Apr 1988. This was equalled by Ian Woosnam (Wales) (b. 2 Mar 1958) (66, 67, 65, 60) in the Monte Carlo Open on 4–7 Jul 1990.

The lowest 72 holes in an open championship in Europe is 262 (67, 66, 66, 63) by Percy Alliss (GB) (1897–1975) in the 1932 Italian Open at San Remo, and by Lu Liang Huan (Taiwan) (b. 10 Dec 1935) in the 1971 French Open at Biarritz.

The lowest for four rounds in a British first-class tournament is 262 (66, 63, 66, 67) by Bernard Hunt in the Piccadilly Tournament on the par-68 5655m *6184 yd* Wentworth East course, Virginia Water, Surrey on 4–5 Oct 1966.

The lowest four round total in a US LPGA Championship event is 267 (68, 66, 67, 66) by Betsy King (USA) (b. 13 Aug 1955) in the Mazda LPGA Championship on the par-71 5735m *6272 yd* Bethesda Contry Club course, Bethesda, Maryland, USA on 14–17 May 1992. She won by 11 strokes and was 17 under-par, both LPGA Championship records.

Trish Johnson scored 242 (64, 60, 60, 58) (21 under par) in the Bloor Homes Eastleigh Classic at the Fleming Park Course (4025m *4402 yd*) at Eastleigh, Hants on 22–25 Jul 1987.

Horton Smith scored 245 (63, 58, 61 and 63) for 72 holes on the 4297m *4700 yd* course (par-64) at Catalina Country Club, California, USA, to win the Catalina Open on 21–23 Dec 1928.

GUESS WHAT?

Q Where would you find the longest hole in the world?

A See Page 257

Throwing!

The lowest recorded score for throwing a golf ball round 18 holes (over 5490m *6000 yd*) is 82 by Joe Flynn (USA), 21, at the 5695m *6228 yd* Port Royal course, Bermuda on 27 Mar 1975.

The longest throw is 120.24m *394ft 6in* by Stefan Uhr (Sweden) at Prästholmen, Mora, Sweden on 20 Aug 1992.

THE GUINNESS NEWS

14 June 1912

IT WENT STRAIGHT DOWN THE RIVER....

163 over par!

Shawnee-on-Delaware, PA - A lady player competing in the qualifying round of the Shawnee Invitational for Ladies took an amazing 166 strokes for the short 130 yd 16th hole.

Statistically-minded

The player, who not surprisingly wishes to remain anonymous, said, 'Everything had gone exceptionally well until the tee shot from the sixteenth. I didn't think one could hook the ball that far.' But hook it she did, straight into the Binniekill River, where the ball floated. With no relief available, she put out in a boat in pursuit of the ball, with her loyal but statistically-minded husband at the oars.

'Huffing and puffing'

'My wife really did give it a go,' he recalls. 'There was a lot of huffing and puffing and splashing going on. Indeed a couple of times, an over-zealous swing which failed to connect with ball or water, nearly turned the boat over. She did eventually beach the ball 1½ miles downstream but was not yet out of the wood. She had to play through one on the way back. Sadly a number of ricochets sent the ball further from the hole than nearer. However, the icing on the cake was when she three putted from three feet.'

Historic

Unfortunately, Mrs X failed to qualify for the competition, but was presented with a framed copy of her historic score-card as a consolation.

World one-club record Thad Daber (USA), with a 6-iron, played the 5520m *6037yd* Lochmore GC, Cary, North Carolina, USA in 70 to win the 1987 World One-club Championship.

Most shots for one hole The highest score for a single hole in the British Open is 21 by a player in the inaugural meeting at Prestwick in 1860.

Double figures have been recorded on the card of the winner only once, when Willie Fernie (1851–1924) scored a ten at Musselburgh, Lothian in 1883.

Fastest rounds *Individual* With such variations in lengths of courses, speed records, even for rounds under par, are of little comparative value. The fastest round played when the golf ball comes to rest before each new stroke is 27min 9sec by James Carvill (b. 13 Oct 1965) at Warrenpoint Golf Course, Co. Down (18 holes, 5628m *6154 yd*) on 18 Jun 1987.

Team The 35 members of the Team Balls Out Diving completed the 18-hole 5516m *6033yd* John E. Clark course at Point Micu, California, USA in 9 min 39 sec on 16 Nov 1992. They scored 71!

Most holes in 24 hours *On foot* Ian Colston, 35, played 22 rounds and five holes (401 holes) at Bendigo GC, Victoria, Australia (par-73, 5542m *6061yd*) on 27–28 Nov 1971.

GUESS WHAT?

Q What is the fastest knockout recorded in boxing?

A See Page 238

The British record is 360 holes by Antony J. Clark at Childwall GC, Liverpool on 18 Jul 1983.

David Brett of Stockport played 218 holes in 12 hours at Didsbury GC, Greater Manchester (par-70, 5696m *6230yd*) on 22 Jun 1990.

Using golf carts David Cavalier played 846 holes at Arrowhead Country Club, North Canton, Ohio, USA (9-hole course, 2755m *3013yd*) on 6–7 Aug 1990.

Doug Wert played 440 holes in 12 hours on the 5526m *6044yd* course at the Tournament Players Club, Coral Springs, Florida, USA on 7 Jun 1993.

Most holes played in a week Steve Hylton played 1128 holes at the Mason Rudolph GC (5541m *6060yd*), Clarksville, Tennessee, USA from 25–31 Aug 1980. Using a buggy for transport, Colin Young completed 1260 holes at Patshull Park GC (5863m *6412yd*), Pattingham, Shropshire from 2–9 Jul 1988.

The most balls driven in one hour, over 100 yards and into a target area, is 1536 by Noel Hunt at Shrigley Hall, Pott Shrigley, Cheshire on 2 May 1990.

Championship Records

The Open (inaugurated 1860, Prestwick, Strathclyde) *Any round* 63 by: Mark Stephen Hayes (USA) (b. 12 Jul 1949) at Turnberry, Strathclyde on 7 Jul 1977; Isao Aoki (Japan) (b. 31 Aug 1942) at Muirfield, Lothian on 19 Jul 1980; Gregory John Norman (Australia) (b. 10 Feb 1955) at Turnberry on 18 Jul 1986; Paul Broadhurst (GB) (b. 14 Aug 1965) at St Andrews, Fife on 21 Jul 1990; Joseph Martin 'Jodie' Mudd (USA) (b. 23 Apr 1960) at Royal Birkdale on 21 Jul 1991; Nicholas Alexander 'Nick' Faldo (GB) (b. 18 Jul 1957) on 16 July and William Payne Stewart (USA) (b. 30 Jan 1957) on 18 July, both at Royal St George's, Sandwich, Kent in 1993.

First 36 holes Nick Faldo completed the first 36 holes at Muirfield, Lothian in 130 strokes (66, 64) on 16–17 Jul 1992. (Faldo added a third round of 69 to equal the 54–hole record of 199 which he had set at St Andrews in 1990 (67, 65, 67)).

Total aggregate 267 (66, 68, 69, 64) by Greg Norman (Australia) at Royal St George's, 15–18 Jul 1993.

US Open (inaugurated in 1895) *Any round* 63 by: Johnny Miller (b. 29 Apr 1947) on the 6328m *6921yd* par-71 Oakmont Country Club course, Pennsylvania on 17 Jun 1973; by Jack Nicklaus and Tom Weiskopf (USA) (b. 9 Nov 1942) at Baltusrol Country Club (6414m *7015yd*), Springfield, New Jersey, both on 12 Jun 1980.

First 36 holes 134 by: Jack Nicklaus (63, 71) at Baltusrol, 12–13 Jun 1980; Chen Tze-Chung (Taiwan) (65, 69) at Oakland Hills, Birmingham, Michigan in 1985; and Lee Janzen (USA) (b. 28 Aug 1964) (67, 67) at Baltusrol, 17–18 Jun 1993.

Total aggregate 272 by: Jack Nicklaus (63, 71, 70, 68) at Baltusrol, 12–15 Jun 1980; and by Lee Janzen (67, 67, 69, 69) at Baltusrol, 17–20 Jun 1993.

US Masters (played on the 6382m *6980yd* Augusta National Golf Course, Georgia, first in 1934) *Any round* 63 by Nicholas Raymond Leige Price (Zimbabwe) (b. 28 Jan 1957) in 1986.

First 36 holes 131 (65, 66) by Raymond Loran Floyd (b. 4 Sep 1942) in 1976.

Total aggregate 271 by: Jack Nicklaus (67, 71, 64, 69) in 1965 and Raymond Floyd (65, 66, 70, 70) in 1976.

Team Competitons

World Cup (formerly Canada Cup) The World Cup (instituted as the Canada Cup in 1953) has been won most often by the USA with 19 victories between 1955 and 1993.

The only men to have been on six winning teams have been Arnold Palmer (b. 10 Sep 1929) (1960,

Payne Stewart celebrates equalling the lowest ever score in a round of the British Open, 63, during the final round of the 1993 event.
(Photo: Allsport/David Cannon)

1962–4, 1966–7) and Jack Nicklaus (1963–4, 1966–7, 1971 and 1973). Only Nicklaus has taken the individual title three times (1963–4, 1971).

The lowest aggregate score for 144 holes is 544 by Australia, Bruce Devlin (b. 10 Oct 1937) and Anthony David Graham (b. 23 May 1946), at San Isidro, Buenos Aires, Argentina from 12–15 Nov 1970.

The lowest individual score has been 269 by Roberto de Vicenzo (Argentina) (b. 14 Apr 1923), also in 1970.

Ryder Cup The biennial Ryder Cup professional match between the USA and Europe (British Isles or Great Britain prior to 1979) was instituted in 1927. The USA has won 23 to 5 (with 2 draws) to 1993.

Arnold Palmer has the record of winning most Ryder Cup matches with 22 from 32 played, with two halved and 8 lost. Christy O'Connor Sr (Ireland) (b. 21 Dec 1924) played in ten contests, 1955–73.

Walker Cup The series was instituted in 1921 (for the Walker Cup since 1922 and now held biennially). The USA have won 30, Great Britain & Ireland 3 (in 1938, 1971 and 1989) and the 1965 match was tied.

Jay Sigel (USA) (b. 13 Nov 1943) has won a record 18 matches, with five halved and ten lost, 1977–93. Joseph Boynton Carr (GB & I) (b. 18 Feb 1922) played in ten contests, 1947–67.

Curtis Cup The biennial ladies' Curtis Cup match between the USA and Great Britain and Ireland was first held in 1932. The USA have won 20 to 1992, GB & I five (1952, 1956, 1986, 1988 and 1992) and two matches have been tied.

Mary McKenna (GB & I) (b. 29 Apr 1949) played in a record ninth match in 1986, when for the first time she was on the winning team. Carole Semple Thompson (USA) has won a record 12 matches in 7 contests, 1974–92.

Individual Records

Richest prize The greatest first place prize money ever won is $1,000,000 awarded annually from 1987 to 1991 to the winners of the Sun City Challenge, Bophuthatswana, South Africa; Ian Woosnam (Wales) was the first winner in 1987.

The greatest total prize money is $2,700,000 (including $550,000 first prize) for the Johnnie Walker World Championship at Tryall GC, Montego Bay, Jamaica in both 1992 and 1993.

Highest earnings *US PGA and LPGA circuits* The all-time career earnings record on the US PGA circuit is held by Tom Kite (USA) (b. 9 Dec 1949) with $8,963,803, 1982 to 12 Jun 1994. Nick Price (Zimbabwe) won a season's record $1,478,557 in 1993.

The record career earnings for a woman is by Pat Bradley (b. 24 Mar 1951) with $4,641,047 to 7 Jun 1994. The season's record is $863,578 by Beth Daniel in 1990.

European circuit Nick Faldo (GB) won a season's record £708,522 in European Order of Merit tournaments in 1992 (worldwide, he won a record £1,558,978). He also holds the tour career earnings record with £4,413,151 (27 tour victories), 1976–30 Jun 1994.

Most tournament wins John Byron Nelson (USA) (b. 4 Feb 1912) won a record 18 tournaments (plus one unofficial) in one year, including a record 11 consecutively from 8 Mar to 4 Aug 1945.

Sam Snead from turning professional in 1934 won 84 official US PGA tour events, 1936–65. The ladies' PGA record is 88 by Kathy Whitworth (b. 27 Sep 1939) from 1962 to 1985. The most career victories in European Order of Merit tournaments is 52 by Severiano Ballesteros (Spain), 1974–94.

Biggest winning margin The greatest margin of victory in a major tournament is 21 strokes by Jerry Pate (USA) (b. 16 Sep 1953), who won the Colombian Open with 262 from 10–13 Dec 1981.

Cecilia Leitch won the Canadian Ladies' Open Championship in 1921 by the biggest margin for a major title, 17 up and 15 to play.

Youngest and oldest champions The youngest winner of The Open was Tom Morris Jr (1851–75) at Prestwick, Strathclyde in 1868 aged 17 yr 249 days.

The oldest Open champion was 'Old Tom' Morris (1821–1908), aged 46 yr 99 days when he won at Prestwick in 1867. Oldest this century has been the 1967 champion, Roberto de Vincenzo, at 44 yr 93 days.

The oldest US Open champion was Hale Irwin (USA) (b. 3 Jun 1945) at 45 yr 15 days on 18 Jun 1990.

Youngest and oldest national champions Thuashni Selvaratnam (b. 9 Jun 1976) won the 1989 Sri Lankan Ladies Amateur Open Golf Championship, aged 12 yr 324 days, at Nuwara Eliya GC on 29 Apr 1989. Maria Teresa 'Isa' Goldschmid (*née* Bevione) (b. 15 Oct 1925) won the Italian Women's Championship,

aged 50 yr 200 days, at Oligata, Rome on 2 May 1976.

Most club championships Helen Gray has been ladies champion at Todmorden GC, Lancs 38 times between 1952 and 1993.

The men's record is 36 (consecutive) by Richard John Fewster (b. 5 Jul 1935) at Bandee Golf Club, Merredin, Australia, 1956–92.

Patricia Shepherd (b. 7 Jan 1940) won 30 consecutive championships at Turriff GC, Grampian, 1959–88.

Largest tournament The Volkswagen Grand Prix Open Amateur Championship in the United Kingdom attracted a record 321,778 (206,820 men and 114,958 women) competitors in 1984.

Holes-in-One

Longest The longest straight hole ever holed in one shot was, appropriately, the tenth (408 m *447 yd*) at Miracle Hills GC, Omaha, Nebraska, USA by Robert Mitera (b. 1944) on 7 Oct 1965. Mitera stood 1.68 m *5 ft 6 in* tall and weighed 75 kg *165 lb* (11 st 11 lb). He was a two handicap player who normally drove 224 m *245 yd*. A 80 km/h *50 mph* gust carried his shot over a 265 m *290 yd* drop-off.

The longest 'dog-leg' hole achieved in one is the 439 m *480 yd* fifth at Hope Country Club, Arkansas, USA by L. Bruce on 15 Nov 1962.

The women's record is 359 m *393 yd* by Marie Robie on the first hole of the Furnace Brook GC, Wollaston, Massachusetts, USA on 4 Sep 1949.

The longest hole in one performed in the British Isles is the seventh (par-4, 359 m *393 yd*) at West Lancashire GC by Peter Richard Parkinson (b. 26 Aug 1947) on 6 Jun 1972.

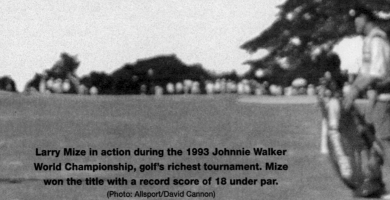

Larry Mize in action during the 1993 Johnnie Walker World Championship, golf's richest tournament. Mize won the title with a record score of 18 under par.
(Photo: Allsport/David Cannon)

Consecutive

There are at least 19 cases of 'aces' being achieved in two consecutive holes, of which the greatest was Norman L. Manley's unique 'double albatross' on the par-4 301m *330yd* seventh and par-4 265m *290yd* eighth holes on the Del Valle Country Club course, Saugus, California, USA on 2 Sep 1964.

The first woman to record consecutive 'aces' was Sue Prell, on the 13th and 14th holes at Chatswood GC, Sydney, Australia on 29 May 1977.

The closest to achieving three consecutive holes in one were Dr Joseph Boydstone on the 3rd, 4th and 9th at Bakersfield GC, California, USA, on 10 Oct 1962 and Rev. Harold Snider (b. 4 Jul 1900) who aced the 8th, 13th and 14th holes of the par-3 Ironwood course, Arizona, USA on 9 Jun 1976.

Youngest and oldest

The youngest golfer recorded to have shot a hole-in-one is Coby Orr (5 years) of Littleton, Colorado on the 94m *103yd* fifth at the Riverside Golf Course, San Antonio, Texas, USA in 1975. The youngest girl is Nicola Mylonas, aged 10yr 64days, on the 122m *133yd* 1st at South Course, Nudgee, Australia on 18 Sep 1993.

The British record was set by Mark Alexander, aged 6yr 251days, on the 99m *109yd* sixth at the Chessington Golf Centre, Greater London on 17 Sep 1989. The youngest girl to score an ace is Nicola Hammond, aged 10yr 204days on the 98m *107yd* third at Dereham GC, Norfolk on 17 June 1990.

The oldest golfers to have performed this feat are: (men) 99yr 244days Otto Bucher (Switzerland) (b. 12 May 1885) on the 119m *130 yd* 12th at La Manga GC, Spain on 13 Jan 1985; (women) 95yr 257days Erna Ross (b. 9 Sep 1890) on the 102m *112 yd* 17th at The Everglades Club, Palm Beach, Florida, USA on 23 Apr 1986.

The British records: (men) 92yr 169days Samuel Richard Walker (b. 6 Jan 1892) at the 143m *156yd* 8th at West Hove GC, E Sussex on 23 Jun 1984; (women) 90yr 236days Dorothy Huntley-Flindt (b. 19 Jun 1898) at the 102m *112yd* 13th at Barton-on-Sea GC, Hants on 10 Feb 1989.

The oldest player to score his age is C. Arthur Thompson (1869–1975) of Victoria, British Columbia, Canada, who scored 103 on the Uplands course of 5682m *6215yd* in 1973.

Lang Martin balanced seven golf balls vertically without adhesive at Charlotte, North Carolina, USA on 9 Feb 1980.

Greyhound Racing

Derby

Two greyhounds have won the English Greyhound Derby (instituted 1927 at White City, London over 525yd, now over 480m at Wimbledon) twice: *Mick the Miller* on 25 Jul 1929, when owned by Albert H. Williams, and on 28 Jun 1930 when owned by Mrs Arundel H. Kempton, and *Patricia's Hope* on 24 Jun 1972 when owned by Gordon and Basil Marks and Brian Stanley and 23 Jun 1973 when owned by G. & B. Marks and J. O'Connor.

The highest prize was £40,000 to *Slippy Blue* for the Derby on 23 Jun 1990.

Grand National

The only greyhound to have won the Grand National (instituted 1927 over 525yd then 500m at White City, now 474m at Hall Green, Brimingham) three times is *Sherry's Prince* (1967–78) owned by Mrs Joyce Mathews of Sanderstead, Surrey, in 1970–72.

Fastest greyhound

The highest speed at which any greyhound has been timed is 67.32km/h *41.83mph* (366m *400yd* in 19.57sec) by *Star Title* on the straightaway track at Wyong, New South Wales, Australia on 5 Mar 1994.

The only greyhounds to win the English, Scottish and Welsh Derby 'triple' are *Trev's Perfection*, owned by Fred Trevillion, in 1947, *Mile Bush Pride*, owned by Noel W. Purvis, in 1959, and *Patricia's Hope* in 1972.

Mush! Mush!

The oldest established sled dog trail is the 1688 km *1049 mile* Iditarod Trail from Anchorage to Nome, Alaska, USA, which has existed since 1910 and has been the course of an annual race since 1967. The fastest time was set by Martin Buser (Switzerland), 10 days 13 hr 2 min 39 sec on 5–16 Mar 1994.

The longest race is the 2000 km *1243 miles* Berengia Trail from Esso to Markovo, Russia, which started as a 250 km *155 miles* route in April 1990. Now established as an annual event, the 1991 race was won by Pavel Lazarev in 10 days 18 hr 17 min 56 sec.

The highest speed recorded for a greyhound in Great Britain is 62.97km/h *39.13 mph* by *Beef Cutlet*, when covering a straight course of 457m *500yd* in 26.13sec at Blackpool, Lancs, on 13 May 1933.

The fastest automatically timed speed recorded for a full four-bend race is 62.59km/h *38.89mph* at Brighton, E Sussex by *Glen Miner* on 4 May 1982 with a time of 29.62sec for 515m *563yd*. The fastest over hurdles is 60.58km/h *37.64mph* at Brighton by *Wotchit Buster* on 22 Aug 1978.

Most wins

The most career wins is 143 by the American greyhound, *JR's Ripper* in 1982–6.

The most consecutive victories is 36 by *Pat C Rendezvous*, owned by Pat Collins from 29 Dec 1993 to 25 Jun 1994, all at Palm Beach Kennel Club, Florida, USA.

Highest earnings

The career earnings record is held by *Homespun Rowdy* with $297,000 in the USA, 1984–7.

The richest first prize for a greyhound race is $125,000 won by *Ben G Speedboat* in the Great Greyhound Race of Champions at Seabrook, New Hampshire, USA on 23 Aug 1986.

Gymnastics

World Championships *Women* The greatest number of titles won in the World Championships (including Olympic Games) is 12 individual wins and six team by Larisa Semyonovna Latynina (*née* Diriy) (b. 27 Dec 1934) of the USSR, between 1954 and 1964.

In the space of just two years, Belarussian Vitaliy Scherbo has won a record 12 individual world titles.
(Photo: Allsport/Bob Martin)

The USSR won the team title on 21 occasions (11 world and 10 Olympics).

Men The most individual titles is 11 by Vitaliy Scherbo (Belarus) (b. 13 Jan 1972) between 1992 and 1994; he also won a team gold in 1992. Boris Anfiyanovich Shakhlin (USSR) (b. 27 Jan 1932) won ten individual titles between 1954 and 1964 but also had three team wins.

Neil Thomas became the first British gymnast to win a medal at the World Championships when he won silver in the floor exercises in 1993, an achievement he repeated at the 1994 championships.
(Photo: Allsport/Chris Cole)

The USSR won the team title a record 13 times (eight World Championships, five Olympics) between 1952 and 1992.

Youngest champions Aurelia Dobre (Romania) (b. 6 Nov 1972) won the women's overall world title at 14yr 352days at Rotterdam, Netherlands on 23 Oct 1987. Daniela Silivas (Romania) revealed in 1990 that she was born on 9 May 1971, a year later than previously claimed, so that she was 14yr 185days when she won the gold medal for balance beam on 10 Nov 1985.

The youngest male world champion was Dmitriy Bilozerchev (USSR) (b. 17 Dec 1966) at 16yr 315days at Budapest, Hungary on 28 Oct 1983.

Olympics The men's team title has been won a record five times by Japan (1960, 1964, 1968, 1972 and 1976) and the USSR (1952, 1956, 1980, 1988 and 1992). The USSR won the women's title ten times (1952–80, 1988 and 1992). Note the successes in 1992 were by the Unified team from the republics of the former USSR.

The most men's individual gold medals is six by: Boris Shakhlin (USSR), one in 1956, four (two shared) in 1960 and one in 1964; and Nikolay Yefimovich Andrianov (USSR) (b. 14 Oct 1952), one in 1972, four in 1976 and one in 1980.

Vera Caslavska-Odlozil (b. 3 May 1942) (Czechoslovakia) has won most individual gold medals with seven, three in 1964 and four (one shared) in 1968.

Larisa Latynina won six individual gold medals and was in three winning teams from 1956–64, making nine gold medals. She also won five silver and four bronze making 18 in all—an Olympic record.

The most medals for a male gymnast is 15 by Nikolay Andrianov (USSR), seven gold, five silver and three bronze from 1972–80.

Aleksandr Nikolayevich Dityatin (USSR) (b. 7 Aug 1957) is the only man to win a medal in all eight categories in the same Games, with three gold, four silver and one bronze at Moscow in 1980.

Highest score Hans Eugster (Switzerland) (b. 27 Mar 1929) scored a perfect 10.00 in the compulsory parallel bars at the 1950 World Championships. Nadia Comaneci (Romania) (b. 12 Nov 1961) was the first to achieve a perfect score (10.00) in the Olympics, and achieved seven in all at Montreal, Canada in July 1976.

British Championships The British Gymnastic Championship was won ten times by Arthur John Whitford (b. 2 Jul 1908) in 1928–36 and 1939. He was also in four winning teams. Wray 'Nik' Stuart (b. 20 Jul 1927) equalled the record of nine successive wins, 1956–64.

The women's record is eight by Mary Patricia Hirst (b. 18 Nov 1918) (1947, 1949–50 and 1952–6). Jackie Brady (b. 12 Dec 1975) uniquely won all apparatus titles and overall title in the same year, 1993.

The most overall titles in Modern Rhythmic Gymnastics is by Sharon Taylor with five successive, 1977–81.

World Cup Gymnasts who have won two World Cup (instituted 1975) overall titles are three men: Nikolay Andrianov (USSR), Aleksandr Dityatin (USSR) and Li Ning (China) (b. 8 Sep 1963), and one woman: Maria Yevgenyevna Filatova (USSR) (b. 19 Jul 1961).

Modern Rhythmic Gymnastics The most overall individual world titles in Modern Rhythmic Gymnastics is three by Maria Gigova (Bulgaria) in 1969, 1971 and 1973 (shared).

Bulgaria has a record seven team titles 1969, 1971, 1981, 1983, 1985, 1987 and 1989 (shared). Bianka Panova (Bulgaria) (b. 27 May 1960) won all four apparatus gold medals all with

Pasakevi 'Voula' Kouna (b. 6 Dec 1971) was aged 9yr 299days at the start of the Balkan Games at Serres, Greece on 1 Oct 1981, when she represented Greece.

maximum scores, and won a team gold in 1987.

At the 1988 Olympic Games Marina Lobach (USSR) (b. 26 Jun 1970) won the rhythmic gymnastic title with perfect scores in all six disciplines.

Somersaults Shigeru Iwasaki (b. 1960) backwards somersaulted 50m *54.68yd* in 10.8sec at Tokyo, Japan on 30 Mar 1980.

The largest number of participants for a gymnastics/aerobic display is 26,017 for the Great Singapore Workout 93 at Padang Field, Singapore on 3 Oct 1993.

Handball

Most championships *Olympic* The USSR won five titles—men 1976, 1988 and 1992 (by the Unified Team from the republics of the ex-USSR), women 1976 and 1980. South Korea has also won two women's titles, in 1988 and 1992.

World Championships (instituted 1938) For the now predominant version of the game, indoors, the most men's titles is three by: Romania, 1961, 1964 and 1970; and Sweden, 1954, 1958 and 1990. However, Germany/West Germany won the outdoor title five times, 1938–66 and have won the indoor title twice, 1938 and 1978. Three women's titles have been won by (all indoor unless stated): Romania, 1956, 1960 (both outdoor) and 1962; the GDR 1971, 1975 and 1978; and the USSR 1982, 1986 and 1990.

European Champions' Cup Spartak of Kiev, USSR won 13 women's titles between 1970 and 1988.

Vfl Gummersbach, West Germany have won a record five men's titles, 1967, 1970–71, 1974, 1983. They are also the only club team to win all three European trophies; European Champions' Cup, European Cup Winners' Cup and IHF Cup.

Highest score The highest score in an international match was recorded when the USSR beat Afghanistan 86–2 in the 'Friendly Army Tournament' at Miskolc, Hungary in August 1981.

Britain *Most titles* The most men's national championship titles is seven by Brentwood '72 (British Championship, 1974; English National League, 1979–83; British League, 1985).

The most women's titles is eight by Wakefield Metros (English National League, 1982–87; British League, 1988, 1990).

Highest score The highest score in a men's league match is by Glasgow University, who beat Claremont, 69–5 at Glasgow, Strathclyde in March 1984.

The women's record is Wakefield Metros 47–13 defeat

GUESS WHAT?

Q What is the largest muscle in the human body?

A See Page 61

Paul Lynch, holder of the one-finger press-up record.
(Photo: Neil Fenwick)

of Ruslip Eagles at Featherstone, W Yorks on 25 Feb 1990.

Highest score by an individual Graham Hammond scored 29 for Wakefield (39) against Hull Universty (13) at Eccles Recreation Centre in November 1990.

The women's record is 15 by Donna Hankinson (b. 24 Mar 1972) for Manchester United SSS (26) against Arcton (9) at Kirkby on 12 Nov 1989, Julie Wells (b. 9 Jan 1963) for Wakefield Metros (47) against Ruislip Eagles (13) at Featherstone, W Yorks on 25 Feb 1990, and by Catherine Densmore for Halewood Town (23) against Ruislip Eagles (17) at Bristol, Avon on 25 May 1991.

Harness Racing

Most successful driver In North American harness racing history has been Hervé Filion (b. 1 Feb 1940) of Québec, Canada, who had achieved 14,194 wins to 21 Apr 1994 including a then record 814 wins in a year (1989). The most wins in a year is 843 by Walter Case (USA) in 1992.

John D. Campbell (USA) (b. 8 Apr 1955) has the highest career earnings of $120,581,538 to 21 Apr 1994. This includes a year record of $11,620,878 in 1990 when he won 543 races.

Greatest winnings For any harness horse is $4,907,307 by the trotter *Peace Corps*, 1988–92. The greatest amount won by a pacer is $3,225,653 by *Nihilator*, who won 35 of 38 races in 1984–5.

Highest!

The most expensive pacer is *Nihilator* who was syndicated by Wall Street Stable and Almahurst Stud Farm for $19.2 million in 1984.

The highest for a trotter is $6 million for *Mack Lobell* by John Erik Magnusson of Vislanda, Sweden in 1988.

The single season records are $2,217,222 by pacer *Precious Bunny* in 1991 and $1,610,608 by trotter *Prakas* in 1985.

The largest ever purse was $2,161,000 for the Woodrow Wilson two-year-old race over 1 mile at the Meadowlands, New Jersey, USA on 16 Aug 1984. Of this sum a record $1,080,500 went to the winner *Nihilator*, driven by William O'Donnell (b. 4 May 1948).

Hockey

Most Olympic medals India was Olympic champion from the re-introduction of Olympic hockey in 1928 until 1960, when Pakistan beat them 1–0 at Rome. They had their eighth win in 1980. Of the six Indians who have won three Olympic team gold medals, two have also won a silver medal—Leslie Walter Claudius (b. 25 Mar 1927), in 1948, 1952, 1956 and 1960 (silver), and Udham Singh (b. 4 Aug 1928), in 1952, 1956, 1964 and 1960 (silver).

A women's tournament was added in 1980, and there have been four separate winners.

Champions!

First held in 1978 and contested annually since 1980 by the top six men's teams in the world; the most wins is six, by Australia, 1983–5, 1989–90 and 1993. The first women's Champions' Trophy was held in 1987, Australia has won twice, 1991 and 1993.

World Cup The FIH World Cup for men was first held in 1971, and for women in 1974. The most wins are, (men) three by Pakistan, 1971, 1978 and 1982; (women) five by the Netherlands, 1974, 1978, 1983, 1986 and 1990.

Men

Highest international score The highest score was when India defeated the USA 24–1 at Los Angeles, California, USA in the 1932 Olympic Games.

The greatest number of goals in an international in Britain was when England defeated France 16–0 at Beckenham, Kent on 25 Mar 1922.

Most international appearances Heiner Dopp (b. 27 Jun 1956) represented West Germany 286 times between 1975 and 1989, indoors and out.

The most by a player from the British Isles is 228 by Richard Leman (b. 13 Jul 1959), 158 (106 outdoor, 52 indoor) for England and 70 for Great Britain, 1980–90. The most for Ireland is 135 by William David Robert McConnell (b. 19 Apr 1956) 1979–93, and Stephen Alexander Martin (b. 13 Apr 1959) 1980–93. The most indoor caps for England is 85 by Richard Clarke (b. 3 Apr 1952), 1976–87.

Greatest scoring feats The greatest number of goals scored in international hockey is 267 by Paul Litjens (Netherlands) (b. 9 Nov 1947) in 177 games.

M. C. Marckx (Bowdon 2nd XI) scored 19 goals against Brooklands 2nd XI (score 23–0) on 31 Dec 1910. He was selected for England in March 1912 but declined due to business priorities. David Ashman has scored a record 2079 goals having played for Hampshire, Southampton, Southampton Kestrals and Hamble Old Boys (for whom he has scored 1920 goals, a record for one club), 1958–94.

Greatest goalkeeping Richard James Allen (India) (b. 4 Jun 1902) did not concede a goal during the 1928 Olympic tournament and a total of only three in 1936.

Women

Most international appearances Alison Ramsay has made a record 234 international

John French scored 7 seconds after the bully-off for England v. West Germany at Nottingham on 25 Apr 1971.

Graham Dennis Nash (b. 15 Mar 1943) umpired in five successive Olympics, 1976–92, and retired after Barcelona having officiated in a record 144 international matches.

appearances, 127 for Scotland and 107 for Great Britain, 1982–94.

Highest scores The highest score in an international match was when England beat France 23–0 at Merton, Greater London on 3 Feb 1923.

In club hockey, Ross Ladies beat Wyeside, at Ross-on-Wye, Herefordshire 40–0 on 24 Jan 1929, when Edna Mary Blakelock (1904–89) scored a record 21 goals.

Highest attendance The highest attendance was 65,165 for the match between England and the USA at Wembley, London on 11 Mar 1978.

Horse Racing

Largest prizes The highest prize money for a day's racing is $10 million for the Breeders' Cup series of seven races staged annually in the USA since 1984. Included each year is a record $3 million for the Breeders' Cup Classic.

Most runners The most horses in a race has been 66 in the Grand National on 22 Mar 1929. The record for the Flat is 58 in the Lincolnshire Handicap at Lincoln on 13 Mar 1948.

Horses

Most successful The horse with the best win-loss record was *Kincsem*, a Hungarian mare foaled in 1874, who was unbeaten in 54 races (1876–79) throughout Europe, including the Goodwood Cup of 1878.

Longest winning sequence Camarero, foaled in 1951, was undefeated in 56 races in Puerto Rico from 19 Apr 1953 to his first defeat on 17 Aug 1955 (in his career to 1956, he won 73 of 77 races).

Career Chorisbar (foaled 1935) won 197 of her 324 races in Puerto Rico, 1937–47. *Lenoxbar* (foaled 1935) won 46 races in one year, 1940, in Puerto Rico from 56 starts.

Same race Doctor Syntax (foaled 1811) won the Preston Gold Cup on seven successive occasions, 1815–21.

Triple Crown winners The English Triple Crown (2000 Guineas, Derby, St Leger) has been won 15 times, most recently by *Nijinsky* in 1970. The fillies' equivalent (1000 Guineas, Oaks, St Leger) has been won nine times, most recently by *Oh So Sharp* in 1985. Two of these fillies also won the 2000 Guineas: *Formosa* (in a dead-heat) in 1868 and *Sceptre* in 1902. The American Triple Crown (Kentucky Derby, Preakness Stakes, Belmont Stakes) has been achieved 11 times, most recently by *Affirmed* in 1978.

Highest price Enormous valuations placed on potential stallions may be determined from sales of a minority holding, but such valuations would, perhaps, not be reached on the open market. The most paid for a yearling is $13.1m on 23 Jul 1985 at Keeneland, Kentucky, USA by Robert Sangster and partners for *Seattle Dancer*.

Greatest winnings The career earnings record is $6,679,242 by the 1987 Kentucky Derby winner *Alysheba* (foaled 1984) from 1986–8. The most prize money earned in a year

GUESS WHAT?

Q What is the greatest number of finishers in a marathon?

A See Page 230

Major Race Records

FLAT

Race (Instituted)	Record Time	Most Wins Jockey	Trainer	Owner	Largest Field
Derby (1780) 1 m 4f 10yd *2423m* Epsom, Surrey	2 min 33.8 sec *Mahmoud* 1936 2 min 33.84 sec *Kahyasi* 1988*	9–Lester Piggott 1954, 57, 60, 68, 70, 72, 76, 77, 83	7–Robert Robson 1793, 1802, 09, 10, 15, 17, 23 7–John Porter 1868, 82, 83, 86, 90, 91, 99 7–Fred Darling 1922, 25, 26, 31, 38, 40, 41	5–3rd Earl of Egremont 1782, 1804, 05, 07, 26 5–HH Aga Khan III 1930, 35, 36, 48, 52	34 (1862)
2000 Guineas (1809) 1 mile *1609m* Newmarket, Suffolk	1 min 35.08 sec *Mister Baileys* 1994	9–Jem Robinson 1825, 28, 31, 33, 34, 35, 36, 47, 48	7–John Scott 1842, 43, 49, 53, 56, 60, 62	5–4th Duke of Grafton 1820, 21, 22, 26, 27 5–5th Earl of Jersey 1831, 34, 35, 36, 37	28 (1930)
1000 Guineas (1814) 1 mile *1609m* Newmarket	1 min 36.85 sec *Oh So Sharp* 1985	7–George Fordham 1859, 61, 65, 68, 69, 81, 83	9–Robert Robson 1818, 19, 20, 21, 22, 23, 25, 26, 27	8–4th Duke of Grafton 1819, 20, 21, 22, 23, 25, 26, 27	29 (1926)
Oaks (1779) 1 m 4f 10yd *2423m* Epsom	2 min 34.19 sec *Intrepidity* 1993	9–Frank Buckle 1797, 98, 99, 1802, 03, 05, 17, 18, 23	12–Robert Robson 1802, 04, 05, 07, 08, 09, 13, 15, 18, 22, 23, 25	6–4th Duke of Grafton 1813, 15, 22, 23, 28, 31	26 (1848)
St Leger (1776) 1 m 6f 132yd *2937m* Doncaster, South Yorkshire	3 min 01.6 sec *Coronach* 1926 *Windsor Lad* 1934	9–Bill Scott 1821, 25, 28, 29, 38, 39, 40, 41, 46	16–John Scott 1827, 28, 29, 32, 34, 38, 39, 40, 41, 45, 51, 53, 56, 57, 59, 62	7–9th Duke of Hamilton 1786, 87, 88, 92, 1808, 09, 14	30 (1825)
King George VI and Queen Elizabeth Diamond Stakes (1951) 1½ miles *2414m* Ascot, Berkshire	2 min 26.98 sec *Grundy* 1975	7–Lester Piggott 1965, 66, 69, 70, 74, 77, 84	5–Dick Hern 1972, 79, 80, 85, 89	2–Nelson Bunker Hunt 1973, 74 2–Sheikh Mohammed 1990, 93	19 (1951)
Prix de l'Arc de Triomphe (1920) 2400 metres *1 mile 864yd* Longchamp, Paris, France	2 min 26.3 sec *Trempolino* 1987	4–Jacques Doyasbère 1942, 44, 50, 51 4–Frédéric 'Freddy' Head 1966, 72, 76, 79 4–Yves Saint-Martin 1970, 74, 82, 84 4–Pat Eddery 1980, 85, 86, 87	4–Charles Semblat 1942, 44, 46, 49 4–Alec Head 1952, 59, 76, 81 4–François Mathet 1950, 51, 70, 82	6–Marcel Boussac 1936, 37, 42, 44, 46, 49	30 (1967)
VRC Melbourne Cup (1861) 3200 metres *1 mile 1739yd* Flemington, Victoria, Australia	3 min 16.3 sec *Kingston Rule* 1990	4–Bobby Lewis 1902, 15, 19, 27 4–Harry White 1974, 75, 78, 79	9–Bart Cummings 1965, 66, 67, 74, 75, 77, 79, 90, 91	4–Etienne de Mestre 1861, 62, 67, 78	39 (1890)
Kentucky Derby (1875) 1¼ miles *2012m* Churchill Downs, Louisville, USA	1 min 59.4 sec *Secretariat* 1973	5–Eddie Arcaro 1938, 41, 45, 48, 52 5–Bill Hartack 1957, 60, 62, 64, 69	6–Ben Jones 1938, 41, 44, 48, 49, 52	8–Calumet Farm 1941, 44, 48, 49, 52, 57, 58, 68	23 (1974)
Irish Derby (1866) 1½ miles *2414m* The Curragh, Co. Kildare	2 min 25.60 sec *St Jovite* 1992	6–Morny Wing 1921, 23, 30, 38, 42, 46	6–Vincent O'Brien 1953, 57, 70, 77, 84, 85	5–HH Aga Khan III 1925, 32, 40, 48, 49	24 (1962)
JUMPING **Grand National (1839)** 4½ miles *7242m* Aintree, Liverpool, Merseyside	8 min 47.8 sec *Mr Frisk* 1990	5–George Stevens 1856, 63, 64, 69, 70	4–Fred Rimell 1956, 61, 70, 76	3–James Machell 1873, 74, 76 3–Sir Charles Assheton-Smith 1893, 1912, 13 3–Noel Le Mare 1973, 74, 77	66 (1929)
Cheltenham Gold Cup (1924) 3m 2f 110yd *5230m* Cheltenham, Gloucestershire	6 min 23.4 sec *Silver Fame* 1951	4–Pat Taaffe 1964, 65, 66, 68	5–Tom Dreaper 1946, 64, 65, 66, 68	7–Dorothy Paget 1932, 33, 34, 35, 36, 40, 52	22 (1982)
Champion Hurdle (1927) 2m 110yd *3218m* Cheltenham	3 min 50.7 sec *Kribensis* 1990	4–Tim Molony 1951, 52, 53, 54	5–Peter Easterby 1967, 76, 77, 80, 81	4–Dorothy Paget 1932, 33, 40, 46	24 (1964) 24 (1991)

*Electronically timed

is $4,578,454 by *Sunday Silence* (foaled 1986) in the USA in 1989. His total included $1,350,000 from the Breeders' Cup Classic and a $1 million bonus for the best record in the Triple Crown races: he won the Kentucky Derby and Preakness Stakes and was second in the Belmont Stakes. The leading money-winning filly or mare is *Dance Smartly* (foaled 1988) with $3,263,346 in North America, 1990–92. The one-race record is $2.6 million by *Spend A Buck* (foaled 1982) for the Jersey Derby, Garden State Park, New Jersey, USA on 27 May 1985, of which $2 million was a bonus for having previously won the Kentucky Derby and two preparatory races at Garden State Park.

World speed records The highest race speed recorded is 69.62km/h *43.26 mph* by *Big Racket*, 20.8sec for ¼ mile *402m*, at Mexico City, Mexico on 5 Feb 1945. The 4-year-old carried 51.7kg *114 lb*. The record for 1½ miles *2414m* is 60.86km/h *37.82 mph* by 3-year-old *Hawkster* (carrying 54.9kg *121 lb*) at Santa Anita Park,

Arcadia, California, USA on 14 Oct 1989 with a time of 2min 22.8sec.

Jockeys

Most successful Billie Lee 'Bill' Shoemaker (USA) (b. weighing 1.1kg *2½lb*, 19 Aug 1931), whose racing weight was 44kg *97lb* at 1.50m *4ft 11in*, rode a record 8833 winners from 40,350 mounts from his first ride on 19 Mar 1949 and first winner on 20 Apr 1949 to his retirement on 3 Feb 1990.

> The biggest weight ever carried is 190.5kg *30 stone* by both Mr Maynard's mare and Mr Baker's horse in a match won by the former over a mile at York on 21 May 1788.

Oldest!

The oldest horses to win on the Flat have been the 18-year-olds *Revenge* at Shrewsbury on 23 Sep 1790, *Marksman* at Ashford, Kent on 4 Sep 1826 and *Jorrocks* at Bathurst, Australia on 28 Feb 1851. At the same age *Wild Aster* won three hurdle races in six days in March 1919 and *Sonny Somers* won two steeplechases in February 1980.

Laffit Pincay (b. 29 Dec 1946, Panama City) has earned a career record $177,697,315 from 1964 to the start of 1994.

The most races won by a jockey in a year is 598 from 2312 rides by Kent Jason Desormeaux (b. 27 Feb 1970) in 1989. The greatest amount won in a year is 2,356,280,400 yen (*c*. $16,250,000 or a little less than £10 million) by Yutaka Take (b. 1969) in Japan in 1990.

Wins The most winners ridden in one day is nine by Chris Wiley Antley (USA) (b. 6 Jan 1966) on 31 Oct 1987. They consisted of four in the afternoon at Aqueduct, New York, USA and five in the evening at The Meadowlands, New Jersey, USA.

One card The most winners ridden on one card is eight by six riders, most recently (and from fewest rides) by Patrick Alan Day (b. 13 Oct 1953) from nine rides at Arlington International, Illinois, USA on 13 Sep 1989.

Consecutive The longest winning streak is 12 by: Sir Gordon Richards (1904–86) (one race at Nottingham on 3 Oct, six out of six at Chepstow on 4 Oct and the first five races next day at Chepstow) in 1933; and by Pieter Stroebel at Bulawayo, Southern Rhodesia (now Zimbabwe), 7 Jun–7 Jul 1958.

Trainers

Jack Charles Van Berg (USA) (b. 7 Jun 1936) has the greatest number of wins in a year, 496 in 1976. The career record is 6362 by Dale Baird (USA) (b. 17 Apr 1935) from 1962 to end of 1993. The greatest amount won in a year is $17,842,358 by Darrell Wayne Lukas (USA) (b. 2 Sep 1935) in 1988 and he has won a record $140,024,750 in his career.

The only trainer to saddle the first five finishers in a championship race is Michael William Dickinson (b. 3 Feb 1950) of Dunkeswick, W Yorks, in the Cheltenham Gold Cup on 17 Mar 1983; he won a record 12 races in one day, 27 Dec 1982.

Owners

The most lifetime wins by an owner is 4775 by Marion H. Van Berg (1895–1971) in North America in 35 years. The most wins in a year is 494 by Dan R. Lasater (USA) in 1974. The greatest amount won in a year is $6,881,902 by Sam-Son Farm in North America in 1991.

British Turf Records:

Flat Racing

Most successful horses *Eclipse* (foaled 1764) still has the best win-loss record, being unbeaten in a career of 18 races between May 1769 and October 1770. The longest winning sequence is 21 races by *Meteor* (foaled 1783) between 1786 and 1788. The most races won in a season is 23 (from 34 starts) by three-year-old *Fisherman* in 1856. *Catherina* (foaled 1830) won a career record 79 out of 176 races, 1832–41. The most successful sire was *Stockwell* (foaled 1849) whose progeny won 1153 races (1858–76) and who in 1866 set a record of 132 races won.

The greatest amount ever won by an British-trained horse is £1,185,491 by *Snurge* (foaled 1987) as at June 1994. In 1985 the 4-year-old filly *Pebbles* won a record £1,012,611 in one season, including the Breeders' Cup Turf at Aqueduct, New York, USA.

The biggest winning margin in a Classic is 20 lengths by *Mayonaise* in the 1000 Guineas on 12 May 1859.

Since the introduction of the Pattern-race system in 1971, the most prolific British-trained winner of such races has been *Brigadier Gerard* (foaled 1968) with 13 wins, 1971–2.

Since the introduction in 1977 of official ratings in the International Classifications, the highest-rated horse has been *Dancing Brave* (foaled 1983) on 141 in 1986.

The only horse to win two Horse of the Year awards (instituted 1959) is the filly *Dahlia* (foaled 1970) in 1973–4.

Most successful jockeys Sir Gordon Richards won 4870 races from 21,815 mounts from his first mount at Lingfield Park, Surrey on 16 Oct 1920 to his last at Sandown Park, Surrey on 10 Jul 1954. His first win was on 31 Mar 1921. In 1953, at his 28th and final attempt, he won the Derby, six days after his knighthood. He was champion jockey 26 times between 1925 and 1953 and won a record 269 races (from 835 rides) in 1947. Lester Keith Piggott (b. 5 Nov 1935) won 4475 races in Great Britain, 1948 to June 1994, but his global total exceeds 5300. The most prize-money won in a year is £2,903,976 by William Fisher Hunter Carson (b. 16 Nov 1942) in 1990. The most wins in a day is seven by Patrick James John Eddery (b. 18 Mar 1952) at Newmarket and Newcastle on 26 Jun 1992.

The most Classic races won by a jockey is 30 by Lester Piggott from his first on *Never Say Die* in the 1954 Derby to the 1992 2000 Guineas on *Rodrigo de Triano*. (Derby—9, St Leger—8, Oaks—6, 2000 Guineas—5, 1000 Guineas—2.)

Most successful trainers The most wins in a season is 182 (fron 1215 starts) by Richard Michael Hannon (b. 3 May 1945) of East Everleigh, Wilts in 1993. The record prize money earned in a season is £2,000,330 by Michael Ronald Stoute (b. 22 Oct 1945) of Newmarket in 1989; he set a record for world-wide earnings of £2,778,405 in 1986. The most Classics won is 40 by John Scott (1794–1871) of Malton, Yorkshire between 1827 and 1863. James Croft (1787–1828) of Middleham, Yorkshire trained the first four horses in the St Leger on 16 Sep 1822. Alexander Taylor (1862–1943) of Manton, Wiltshire, was champion trainer in money won a record 12 times between 1907 and 1925. Henry Richard Amherst Cecil (b. 11 Jan 1943) of Newmarket has been champion in races won a record nine times since 1978.

Most successful owners H H Aga Khan III (1877–1957) was leading owner a record 13 times between 1924 and 1952. The record prize money won in a season is £2,603,693 by Sheikh Mohammed bin Rashid al Maktoum of Dubai (b. 1949) in 1993. His horses won a record 185 races in 1992. The most Classics won is 20 by George Fitzroy, 4th Duke of Grafton (1760–1844) between 1813 and 1831 and by Edward Stanley, 17th Earl of Derby (1865–1948) between 1910 and 1945.

The Derby The greatest of England's five Classics is the Derby Stakes, inaugurated on 4 May 1780, and named after Edward Stanley, 12th Earl of Derby (1752–1834). The distance was increased in 1784 from a mile to 1½ miles *2.414km* (now officially described as 1mile 4furlongs 10yd). The race has been run at Epsom Downs, Surrey, except for the two war periods, when it was run at Newmarket, Cambs, and is for three-year-olds only. Since 1884 the weights have been: colts 57.2kg *9st*, fillies 54.9kg *8st 9lb*. Geldings were eligible until 1906.

Largest and smallest winning margins Shergar won the Derby by a record 10 lengths in 1981. There have been two dead-heats: in 1828 when *Cadland* beat *The Colonel* in the run-off, and in 1884 between *St Gatien* and *Harvester* (stakes divided).

Longest!

The longest winning odds recorded in British horse racing is 250–1 when *Equinoctial* won at Kelso on 21 Nov 1990. Owner-trainer Norman Miller was not surprised by his horse's success despite being beaten in his previous race by 62 lengths.

Mister Baileys, winner of the 2000 Guineas in the fastest ever time, leading the 1994 Derby field around Tattenham Corner. The eventual winner of the richest prize in British racing, Erhaab, is back in the pack on the rails (blue and white striped hat).
(Photo: Allsport/Shaun Botterill)

Stephenson (1920–92) of Leasingthorne, Co. Durham, won a record 2644 races over jumps, plus 344 on the Flat in Britain, 1946–92. He was champion trainer in races won a record ten times between 1966 and 1977.

Largest prize The richest prize on the British Turf is £473,080 for the Derby won by *Erhaab* on 1 Jun 1994.

Longest and shortest odds in the Derby Three winners have been returned at odds of 100–1: *Jeddah* (1898), *Signorinetta* (1908) and *Aboyeur* (1913). The shortest-priced winner was *Ladas* (1894) at 2–9 and the hottest losing favourite was *Surefoot*, fourth at 40–95 in 1890.

Jumping

Most successful horses *Sir Ken* (foaled 1947), who won the Champion Hurdle in 1952–4, won a record 16 hurdle races in succession, April 1951 to March 1953. Three other horses have also won a record three Champion Hurdles; *Hatton's Grace* (foaled 1940) 1949–51; *Persian War* (foaled 1963) 1968–70; *See You Then* (foaled 1980) 1985–7. The greatest number of Cheltenham Gold Cup wins is five by *Golden Miller* (foaled 1927), 1932–6. The mare *Dawn Run* (foaled 1978), uniquely won both the Champion Hurdle (1984) and Cheltenham Gold Cup (1986).

The greatest number of Horse of the Year awards (instituted 1959) is four by *Desert Orchid* (foaled 1979), 1987–90. The greatest amount earned by a British jumper is £652,802 by *Desert Orchid*, 1983–91.

The richest prize won over jumps in Britain is £118,770 by *The Fellow* in the Cheltenham Gold Cup on 17 Mar 1994.

Most successful jockeys Peter Michael Scudamore (b. 13 Jun 1958) won a career record 1678 races over jumps (from 7521 mounts) from 1978 to 7 Apr 1993.

The most wins in a season is 221 (from 663 rides) by Peter Scudamore in 1988/9. The greatest prize money won in a season is £1,193,917 by Adrian Maguire (b. 29 Apr 1971) in 1993/4. The most wins in a day is six by amateur Charles James Cunningham (1849–1906) at Rugby, Warks on 29 Mar 1881. The record number of successive wins is ten by: John Alnham Gilbert (1920–93), 8–30 Sep 1959; and by Philip Charles Tuck (b. 10 Jul 1956), 23 Aug–3 Sep 1986. The record number of championships is eight (one shared) by Peter Scudamore in 1982, 1986–92.

Most successful trainers Martin Charles Pipe (b. 29 May 1945) won £1,203,014 in prize money in 1990/91, when his horses won a record 230 races from 782 starts. Frederick Thomas Winter (b. 20 Sep 1926) of Lambourn, Berks, was champion trainer in money won a record eight times between 1971 and 1985. William Arthur

Grand National The first Grand National Steeple Chase may be regarded as the Grand Liverpool Steeple Chase of 26 Feb 1839 though the race was not given its present name until 1847. It became a handicap in 1843. Except for 1916–18 and 1941–5, the race has been run at Aintree, near Liverpool, over 30 fences.

> The highest weight ever carried to victory in the Grand National is 79.4 kg *12st 7lb* by *Cloister* (1893), *Manifesto* (1899), *Jerry M.* (1912) and *Poethlyn* (1919).

Most wins The only horse to win three times is *Red Rum* (foaled 1965) in 1973, 1974 and 1977, from five runs. He came second in 1975 and 1976. *Manifesto* (foaled 1888) ran a record eight times (1895–1904). He won in 1897 and 1899, came third three times and fourth once.

Hurling

Most titles *All-Ireland* The greatest number of All-Ireland Championships won by one team is 27 by Cork between 1890 and 1990. The greatest number of successive wins is four by Cork (1941–44).

Most appearances The most appearances in All-Ireland finals is ten shared by Christy Ring (Cork and Munster) and John Doyle (Tipperary). They also share the record of All-Ireland medals won with eight each. Ring's appearances on the winning side were in 1941–4, 1946 and 1952–4, while Doyle's were in 1949–51, 1958, 1961–2 and 1964–5. Ring also played in a record 22 inter-provincial finals (1942–63) and was on the winning side 18 times.

Highest and lowest scores The highest score in an All-Ireland final (60 min) was in 1989 when Tipperary 41 (4 goals, 29 points) beat Antrim (3 goals, 9 points). The record aggregate score was when Cork 39 (6 goals, 21 points) defeated Wexford 25 (5 goals, 10 points) in the 80-minute final of 1970. A goal equals three points. The highest recorded individual score was

by Nick Rackard (Wexford), who scored 7 goals and 7 points against Antrim in the 1954 All-Ireland semi-final. The lowest score in an All-Ireland final was when Tipperary (1 goal, 1 point) beat Galway (nil) in the first championship at Birr in 1887.

Largest crowd The largest crowd was 84,865 for the All-Ireland final between Cork and Wexford at Croke Park, Dublin in 1954.

> The greatest distance for a 'lift and stroke' is one of 118 m *129 yd* credited to Tom Murphy of Three Castles, Kilkenny, in a 'long puck' contest in 1906.

Ice Hockey

World Championships and Olympic Games World Championships were first held for amateurs in 1920 in conjunction with the Olympic Games, which were also considered as world championships up to 1968. From 1976 World Championships have been open to professionals. The USSR won 22 world titles between 1954 and 1990, including the Olympic titles of 1956, 1964 and 1968. They have a record eight Olympic titles with a further five, 1972, 1976, 1984, 1988 and 1992 (as the CIS, with all players Russians). The longest Olympic career is that of Richard Torriani (Switzerland) (1911–88) from 1928 to 1948. The most gold medals won by any player is three, achieved by Soviet players Vitaliy Semyenovich Davydov, Anatoliy Vasilyevich Firsov, Viktor Grigoryevich Kuzkin and Aleksandr Pavlovich Ragulin in 1964, 1968 and 1972, and by Vladislav Aleksandrovich Tretyak in 1972, 1976 and 1984.

Women The first two world championships for women were won by Canada in 1990 and 1992.

NHL Records

Stanley Cup The Stanley Cup was first presented in 1893 (original cost $48.67) by Lord Stanley of Preston, then Governor-General of Canada. From 1894 it was contested by amateur teams for the Canadian Championship. From 1910 it became the award for the winners of the professional league play-offs. It has been won most often by the Montreal Canadiens with 24 wins in 1916, 1924, 1930–31, 1944, 1946, 1953, 1956–60, 1965–6, 1968–9, 1971, 1973, 1976–9, 1986, 1993, from a record 32 finals. Joseph Henri Richard (b. 29 Feb 1936) played on a record 11 winning teams for the Canadiens between 1956 and 1973.

Scoring records Wayne Gretzky (Edmonton and Los Angeles) has scored 346 points in Stanley Cup games, 110 goals and 236 assists, all are records. Gretzky scored a season's record 47 points (16 goals and a record 31 assists) in 1985. The most goals in a season is 19 by Reginald Joseph Leach (b. 23 Apr 1950) for Philadelphia in 1976 and Jari Kurri (Finland) (b. 18 May 1960) for Edmonton in 1985.

Five goals in a Stanley Cup game were scored by Maurice Richard (b. 4 Aug 1921) in Montreal's 5–1 win over Toronto on 23 Mar 1944, by Darryl Glen Sittler for Toronto (8) v. Philadelphia (5) on 22 Apr 1976, by Reggie Leach for Philadelphia (6) v. Boston (3) on 6

GUESS WHAT?

Q Stanley Wood was the oldest person to do what?

A See Page 129

GUESS WHAT?

Q What connects Wayne Gretzky and the most expensive cigarette card?

A See Page 233

May 1976, and by Mario Lemieux (b. 5 Oct 1965) for Pittsburgh (10) *v.* Philadelphia (7) on 25 Apr 1989. A record six assists in a game were achieved by Mikko Leinonen (b. 15 Jul 1955) for New York Rangers (7) *v.* Philadelphia (3) on 8 Apr 1982 and by Wayne Gretzky for Edmonton (13) *v.* Los Angeles (3) on 9 Apr 1987, when his team set a Stanley Cup game record of 13 goals. The most points in a game is eight by Patrik Sundström (Sweden) (b. 14 Dec 1961), three goals and five assists, for New Jersey (10) *v.* Washington (4) on 22 Apr 1988 and by Mario Lemieux, five goals and three assists, for Pittsburgh *v.* Philadelphia.

Most games played Gordon 'Gordie' Howe (Canada) (b. 31 Mar 1928) played in a record 1767 regular season games (and 157 play-off games) over a record 26 seasons, from 1946 to 1971 for the Detroit Red Wings and in 1979/80 for the Hartford Whalers. He also played 419 games (and 78 play-off games) for the Houston

Wayne Gretzky takes a breather during the 1993/4 season. Once again Gretzky continued to set NHL records and it was during this season that he broke Gordie Howe's long-standing record of most goals.
(Photo: Allsport USA/Harry Scull)

Aeros and for the New England Whalers in the World Hockey Association (WHA) from 1973 to 1979, and a grand total of 2421 major league games.

Most goals and points *Career & season* Wayne Gretzky (Edmonton Oilers/Los Angeles Kings) holds the NHL scoring records for the regular season as well as for play-off games (▷ above). He has scored 803 goals, 1655 assists for a record 2458 points from 1125 games. He has scored the most goals in a season, 92 for the Edmonton Oilers, 1981/2. He scored a record 215 points, including a record 163 assists in 1985/6. In 1981/2 in all games, adding Stanley Cup play-offs and for Canada in the World Championship, he scored 238 points (103 goals, 135 assists).

The North American career record for goals is 1071 by Gordie Howe in 32 seasons, 1946–80. He took 2204 games to achieve the 1000th goal, but Robert Marvin 'Bobby' Hull (b. 3 Jan 1939) (Chicago Black Hawks and Winnipeg Jets) scored his 1000th in his 1600th game on 12 Mar 1978.

Game The North American major league record for most points scored in one game is ten by Jim Harrison (b. 9 Jul 1947) (three goals, seven assists) for Alberta, later Edmonton Oilers in a WHA match at Edmonton on 30 Jan 1973, and by Darryl Sittler (b. 18 Sep 1950) (six goals, four assists) for Toronto Maple Leafs *v.* Boston Bruins in an NHL match at Toronto on 7 Feb 1976.

The most goals in a game is seven by Joe Malone in Québec's 10–6 win over Toronto St. Patricks at Québec City on 31 Jan 1920. The most assists is seven by Billy Taylor for Detroit *v.* Chicago on 16 Mar 1947 and three times by Wayne Gretzky for Edmonton, *v.* Washington on 15 Feb 1980, *v.* Chicago on 11 Dec 1985, and *v.* Québec on 14 Feb 1986.

Fastest goal From the opening whistle, the fastest is 5 sec by Doug Smail (b. 2 Sep 1957) (Winnipeg Jets) *v.* St Louis Blues at Winnipeg on 20 Dec 1981, and by Bryan John Trottier (b. 17 Jul 1956) (New York Islanders) *v.* Boston Bruins at Boston on 22 Mar 1984. Bill Mosienko (b. 2 Nov 1921) (Chicago Black Hawks) scored three goals in 21 sec *v.* New York Rangers on 23 Mar 1952.

Goaltending Terry Sawchuk (1929–70) played a record 971 games as a goaltender, for Detroit, Boston, Toronto, Los Angeles and New York Rangers from 1950 to 1970. He achieved a record 435 wins (to 337 losses, and 188 ties) and had a record 103 career shutouts. Jacques Plante (1929–86), with 434 NHL wins surpassed Sawchuk's figure by adding 15 wins in his one season in the WHA for a senior league total of 449 from 868 games. Bernie Parent (b. 3 Apr 1945) achieved a record 47 wins in a season, with 13 losses and 12 ties, for Philadelphia in 1973/4.

Gerry Cheevers (b. 2 Dec 1940) (Boston Bruins)

went a record 32 successive games without a defeat in 1971–2.

Team records Montreal Canadiens won a record 60 games and 132 points (with 12 ties) from 80 games played in 1976/7; their eight losses was also the least ever in a season of 70 or more games. The highest percentage of wins in a season was .875% achieved by the Boston Bruins with 30 wins in 44 games in 1929/30. The longest undefeated run during a season, 35 games (25 wins and ten ties), was established by the Philadelphia Flyers from 14 Oct 1979 to 6 Jan 1980. The most goals scored in a season is 446 by the Edmonton Oilers in 1983/4, when they also achieved a record 1182 scoring points.

Game The highest aggregate score is 21 when Montreal Canadiens beat Toronto St Patrick's, 14–7, at Montreal on 10 Jan 1920, and Edmonton Oilers beat Chicago Black Hawks, 12–9, at Chicago on 11 Dec 1985. The single team record is 16 by Montreal Canadiens *v.* Québec Bulldogs (3), at Québec City on 3 Nov 1920.

The longest match was 2 hr 56 min 30 sec (playing time) when Detroit Red Wings beat Montreal Maroons 1–0 in the sixth period of overtime at the Forum, Montreal, at 2:25 a.m. on 25 Mar 1936. Norm Smith, the Red Wings goaltender, turned aside 92 shots for the NHL's longest single shutout.

Other Records

British competitions The English (later British) League Championship (instituted 1934) has been won by Streatham (later Redskins) five times, 1935, 1950, 1953, 1960 and 1982. Murrayfield Racers have won the Northern League (instituted 1966) seven times, 1970–72, 1976, 1979–80 and 1985. The Icy Smith Cup (first held 1966), the premier British club competition until 1981, was won by Murrayfield Racers nine times, 1966, 1969–72, 1975 and 1979–81. The British Championship (instituted 1982) (Heineken Championship until 1993) has been won a record four times by Durham Wasps, 1987–8 and 1991–2. The Heineken League title has been won five times by Durham Wasps, 1985, 1988–9 and 1991–2. The 'Grand Slam' of Autumn Cup (now Benson & Hedges Cup), Heineken League and Heineken Championships has been won by Dundee Rockets (1983/4), Durham Wasps (1990/91) and Cardiff Devils (1992/3).

The greatest number of goals recorded in a world championship match was when Australia beat New Zealand 58–0 at Perth on 15 Mar 1987.

Most goals *British* The highest score and aggregate in a British League match was set when Medway Bears beat Richmond Raiders 48–1 at Gillingham in a Second Division fixture on 1 Dec 1985, when Kevin MacNaught (Canada) (b. 23 Jul 1960) scored a record 25 points from seven goals and 18 assists.

The most individual goals scored in a senior game is 18 by Rick Smith (Canada) (b. 28 Aug 1964) in a 27–2 win for Chelmsford Chieftains against Sheffield Sabres in an English League match on 3 Mar 1991. Steve Moria (Canada) (b. 1960) achieved the highest number of assists, 13, for Fife Flyers at Cleveland on 28 Mar 1987. Rick Fera (Canada) (b. 1964) set British season's records of 165 goals and 318 points for Murrayfield Racers in 48 games in 1986/7. Tim Salmon (Canada) (b. 27 Nov 1964) achieved a

Jayne Torvill and Christopher Dean returned to the international stage of ice dance in 1994 in an attempt to regain the Olympic title they had won in 1984. However, despite winning the British title (for a record 7th time) and European championship, they had to settle for bronze.
(Photo: Allsport/Chris Cole)

season's record 183 assists in 47 games for Ayr Bruins in 1985/6. The highest career points for the Heineken League is 1668 (714 goals, 954 assists) by Tony Hand (GB) (b. 15 Aug 1967) in 341 games to end of the 1992/3 season.

Fastest scoring In minor leagues, Per Olsen scored 2 seconds after the start of the match for Rungsted against Odense in the Danish First Division at Hørsholm, Denmark on 14 Jan 1990. Three goals in 10 seconds was achieved by Jørgen Palmgren Erichsen for Frisk *v.* Holmen in a junior league match in Norway on 17 Mar 1991. The Vernon Cougars scored five goals in 56 seconds against Salmon Arm Aces at Vernon, BC, Canada on 6 Aug 1982. The Kamloops Knights of Columbus scored seven goals in 2 min 22 sec *v.* Prince George Vikings on 25 Jan 1980.

Great Britain The fastest goal in the Heineken League was scored by Stephen Johnson for Durham Wasps after four seconds *v.* Ayr Bruins at Ayr, Strathclyde on 6 Nov 1983. Mark Salisbury (GB) (b. 4 Dec 1970) scored a hat-trick in 19 seconds for Basingstoke Beavers *v.* Telford Tigers on 26 Jan 1991.

In an English Junior League (under-16) game Jonathan Lumbis scored a hat-trick in 13 seconds for Nottingham Cougars *v.* Peterborough Jets on 4 Nov 1984.

GUESS WHAT?

Q How thin is the thinnest glass?

A See Page 71

Ice Skating

Figure Skating

Most titles *Olympic* The most Olympic gold medals won by a figure skater is three by: Gillis Grafström (Sweden) (1893–1938) in 1920, 1924 and 1928 (also silver medal in 1932); Sonja Henie (Norway) (1912–69) in 1928, 1932 and 1936; and Irina Konstantinovna Rodnina (USSR) (b. 12 Sep 1949) with two different partners in the Pairs in 1972, 1976 and 1980.

Robin John Cousins (GB) (b. 17 Aug 1957) achieved 5.81 m *19 ft 1 in* in an axel jump and 5.48 m *18 ft* with a back flip at Richmond Ice Rink, Surrey on 16 Nov 1983.

World The greatest number of men's individual world figure skating titles (instituted 1896) is ten by Ulrich Salchow (Sweden) (1877–1949) in 1901–5 and 1907–11. The women's record (instituted 1906) is also ten individual titles by Sonja Henie between 1927 and 1936. Irina Rodnina won ten pairs titles (instituted 1908), four with Aleksey Nikolayevich Ulanov (b. 4 Nov 1947), 1969–72, and six with her husband Aleksandr Gennadyevich Zaitsev (b. 16 Jun 1952), 1973–8. The most ice dance titles (instituted 1952) won is six by Lyudmila Alekseyevna Pakhomova (1946–86) and her husband Aleksandr Georgiyevich Gorshkov (USSR) (b. 8 Oct 1946), 1970–74 and 1976. They also won the first ever Olympic ice dance title in 1976.

British The most individual British titles are: (men) 11 by Jack Ferguson Page (1900–47) (Manchester SC) in 1922–31 and 1933; and (women) six by Magdalena Cecilia Colledge (b. 28 Nov 1920) (Park Lane FSC, London) in 1935–6, 1937 (two), 1938 and 1946, and by Joanne Conway (b. 11 Mar 1971) between 1985 and 1991. Page and Ethel Muckelt (1885–1953) won nine pairs titles, 1923–31. The most by an ice dance couple is seven by Jayne Torvill (b. 7 Oct 1957) and Christopher Colin Dean (b. 27 Jul 1958), 1978–83, 1994.

Triple Crown Karl Schäfer (Austria) (1909–76) and Sonja Henie achieved double 'Grand Slams', both in the years 1932 and 1936. This feat was repeated by Katarina Witt (GDR) (b. 3 Dec 1965) in 1984 and 1988. The only British skaters to win the 'Grand Slam' of World, Olympic and European titles in the same year are John Anthony Curry (1949–94) in 1976 and the ice dancers Jayne Torvill and Christopher Dean in 1984.

Highest marks The highest tally of maximum six marks awarded in an international championship was 29 to Jayne Torvill and Christopher Dean (GB) in the World Ice Dance Championships at Ottawa, Canada on 22–24 Mar 1984. This comprised seven in the compulsory dances, a perfect set of nine for presentation in the set pattern dance and 13 in the free dance, including another perfect set from all nine judges for artistic presentation. They previously gained a perfect set of nine sixes for artistic presentation in the free dance at the 1983 World Championships in Helsinki, Finland and at the 1984 Winter Olympic Games in Sarajevo, Yugoslavia.

The most by a soloist is seven: by Donald George Jackson (Canada) (b. 2 Apr 1940) in the World Men's Championship at Prague, Czechoslovakia in 1962; and by Midori Ito (Japan) (b. 13 Aug 1969) in the World Women's Championships at Paris, France in 1989.

Largest rink The world's largest indoor ice rink is in the Moscow Olympic arena which has an ice area of 8064 m² *86,800 ft²*. The five rinks at Fujikyu Highland Skating Centre, Japan total 26,500 m² *285,243 ft²*.

Speed Skating

Most titles *Olympic* The most Olympic gold medals won in speed skating is six by Lidiya Pavlovna Skoblikova (USSR) (b. 8 Mar 1939) in 1960 (two) and 1964 (four). The male record is five by: Clas Thunberg (Finland) (1893–1973) (including one tied) in 1924 and 1928; and Eric Arthur Heiden (USA) (b. 14 Jun 1958), uniquely at one Games at Lake Placid, New York, USA in 1980. The most medals is seven by: Clas

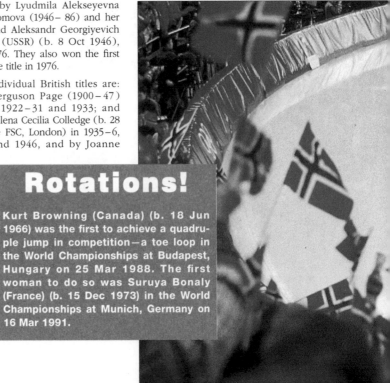

Rotations!

Kurt Browning (Canada) (b. 18 Jun 1966) was the first to achieve a quadruple jump in competition—a toe loop in the World Championships at Budapest, Hungary on 25 Mar 1988. The first woman to do so was Suruya Bonaly (France) (b. 15 Dec 1973) in the World Championships at Munich, Germany on 16 Mar 1991.

Speed Skating

WORLD RECORDS

MEN

Distance (m)min:sec	Name (Country)	Venue	Date
500 ....35.76	Dan Jansen (USA)	Calgary, Canada	30 Jan 1994
1000 ....1:12.43	Dan Jansen (USA)	Hamar, Norway	18 Feb 1994
1:12.05Au	Nick Thometz (USA)	Medeo, USSR	26 Mar 1987
1500 .... 1:51.29	Johann Olav Koss (Norway)	Hamar, Norway	16 Feb 1994
3000 .... 3:56.16	Thomas Bos (Netherlands)	Calgary, Canada	3 Mar 1992
5000 .... 6:34.96	Johann Olav Koss (Norway)	Hamar, Norway	13 Feb 1994
10,000 ....13:30.55	Johann Olav Koss (Norway)	Hamar, Norway	20 Feb 1994

u unofficial. A set at high altitude.

WOMEN

500 ....38.99	Bonnie Blair (USA)	Calgary, Canada	26 Mar 1994
1000 ....1:17.65	Christa Rothenburger (now Luding) (GDR)	Calgary, Canada	26 Feb 1988
1500 ....1:59.30A	Karin Kania (née Enke) (GDR)	Medeo, USSR	22 Mar 1986
3000 ....4:09.32	Gunda Niemann (née Kleeman) (Germany)	Calgary, Canada	25 Mar 1994
5000 ....7:03.26	Gunda Niemann (née Kleeman) (Germany)	Calgary, Canada	26 Mar 1994
10,000* 15:25.25	Yvonne van Gennip (Netherlands)	Heerenveen, Netherlands	19 Mar 1988

* Record not officially recognized for this distance.

WORLD RECORDS - SHORT TRACK

MEN

500 ....43.08	Mirko Vuillermin (Italy)	Beijing, China	27 Mar 1993
1000 ....1:28.47	Michael McMillen (New Zealand)	Denver, Colorado, USA	4 Apr 1992
1500 ....2:22.36	Eric Flaim (USA)	Beijing, China	21 Mar 1993
3000 ....5:00.83	Chae Ji-hoon (South Korea)	Lake Placid, USA	16 Jan 1993
5000 relay 7:10.95	New Zealand	Beijing, China	28 Mar 1993
	(Michael McMillen, Chris Nicholson, Andrew Nicholson, Matthew Briggs)		

WOMEN

500 ....45.60	Zhang Yanmei (China)	Beijing, China	27 Mar 1993
1000 ....1:35.83	Chun Lee-kyung (South Korea)	Asahikawa, Japan	6 Dec 1993
1500 ....2:28.26	Eden Donatelli (Canada)	Seoul, South Korea	31 Mar 1991
3000 ....5:17.59	Won Hye-kyung (South Korea)	Asahikawa, Japan	6 Dec 1993
3000 relay 4:26.56	Canada	Beijing, China	28 Mar 1993
	(Nathalie Lambert, Angela Cutrone, Isabelle Charest, Christine Boudrias)		

BRITISH RECORDS - SHORT TRACK

MEN

500 ....43.68	Nicholas Gooch	Hamar, Norway	26 Feb 1994
1000 ....1:31.65	Wilfred O'Reilly	Denver, Colorado, USA	4 Apr 1992
1500 ....2:21.28	Nicholas Gooch	Nottingham	10 Oct 1993
3000 ....4:59.01	Nicholas Gooch	Humberside	6 Mar 1994
5000 relay 7:18.78	Great Britain	Hamar, Norway	7 Nov 1993
	(Wilfred O'Reilly, Matthew Jasper, Nicholas Gooch, Jamie Fearn)		

WOMEN

500 ....47.93	Debbie Palmer	Hamar, Norway	24 Feb 1994
1000 ....1:43.29	Debbie Palmer	Budapest, Hungary	13 Nov 1993
1500 ....2:38.13	Debbie Palmer	Brugge, Belgium	15 Jan 1994
3000 ....5:59.08	Amanda Worth	Richmond, London	1 Mar 1985
3000 relay 5:05.04	Great Britain	Budapest, Hungary	17 Jan 1988
	(Caron New, Alyson Birch, Nicky Bell, Alea Hopcroft)		

Dan Jansen, one of the world's top sprinters in speed skating, had failed to win any Olympic medal in 1988 and 1992, and the jinx seemed to be continuing in 1994 when he was only 8th at his favoured event, the 500 m. However, in the 1000 m despite a stumble, he clinched gold and set a world record
(Photo: Allsport/Clive Brunskill)

Karin Kania (*née* Enke) (GDR) (b. 20 Jun 1961) in 1982, 1984, 1986–8. Kania also won a record six overall titles at the World Sprint Championships 1980–81, 1983–4, 1986–7. A record six men's sprint overall titles have been won by Igor Zhelezovskiy (USSR/Belarus), 1985–6, 1989 and 1991–3.

The record score achieved for the world overall title is 156.201 points by Rintje Ritsma (Netherlands) at Hamar, Norway on 7–9 Jan 1994. The record low women's score is 164.658 points by Emese Hunyady (Austria) at Calgary, Canada on 26–27 Mar 1994.

World Short-track Championships The most successful skater in these championships (instituted 1978) has been Sylvia Daigle (Canada) (b. 1 Dec 1962) women's overall champion in 1979, 1983 and 1989–90.

The first British skater to win the world title was Wilfred O'Reilly (b. 22 Aug 1964) at Sydney, Australia on 24 Mar 1991.

Longest race The 'Elfstedentocht' ('Tour of the Eleven Towns'), which originated in the 17th century, was held in the Netherlands from 1909–63, and again in 1985 and 1986, covering 200 km *124 miles 483 yd.* As the weather does not permit an annual race in the Netherlands, alternative 'Elfstedentocht' take place at suitable venues. These venues have included Lake Vesijärvi, near Lahti, Finland; Ottawa River, Canada and Lake Weissensee, Austria. The record time for 200 km is: men, 5 hr 40 min 37 sec by Dries van Wijhe (Netherlands); and women, 5 hr 48 min 8 sec by Alida Pasveer (Netherlands), both at Lake

The 1994 Olympics were staged in and around Lillehammer, Norway and it was Norway who won most medals, 26 in all. The most successful individual was speedskater Johann Olav Koss, who won three golds (1500, 5000 and 10,000 m) and set world records in each event.
(Photo: Allsport/Simon Bruty)

Thunberg, who additionally won one silver and one tied bronze; and Ivar Ballangrud (1904–69) (Norway), four gold, two silver and a bronze, 1928–36.

World The greatest number of world overall titles (instituted 1893) won by any skater is five; by Oscar Mathisen (Norway) (1888–1954) in 1908–9 and 1912–14; and by Clas Thunberg in 1923, 1925, 1928–9 and 1931. The most titles won in the women's events (instituted 1936) is five by

Jumping!

The official distance record for jumping on ice skates is 8.97 m *29 ft 5 in* over 18 barrels, by Yvon Jolin at Terrebonne, Québec, Canada on 25 Jan 1981. The women's record is 6.84 m *22 ft 5¼ in* over 13 barrels, by Marie-Josée Houle at Lasalle, Québec on 1 Mar 1987.

Weissensee (altitude 1100 m *3609 ft*), Austria on 11 Feb 1989. Jan-Roelof Kruithof (Netherlands) won the race nine times, 1974, 1976–7, 1979–84. An estimated 16,000 skaters took part in 1986.

24 hours Martinus Kuiper (Netherlands) skated 546.65 km *339.67 miles* at Alkmaar, Netherlands on 12–13 Dec 1988.

Ice and Sand Yachting

Highest speeds The highest speed officially recorded is 230 km/h *143 mph* by John D. Buckstaff in a Class A stern-steerer on Lake Winnebago, Wisconsin, USA in 1938. Such a speed is possible in a wind of 115 km/h *72 mph*.

Sand The official world record for a sand yacht is 107 km/h *66.48 mph* set by Christian-Yves Nau (France) (b. 1944) in *Mobil* at Le Touquet, France on 22 Mar 1981, when the wind speed reached 120 km/h *75 mph*. A speed of 142.26 km/h *88.4 mph* was attained by Nord Embroden (USA) in *Midnight at the Oasis* at Superior Dry Lake, California, USA on 15 Apr 1976.

> The largest ice yacht was *Icicle*, built for Commodore John E. Roosevelt for racing on the Hudson River, New York in 1869. It was 21 m *68 ft 11 in* long and carried 99 m² *1070 ft²* of canvas.

Judo

Most titles *World and Olympic* World Championships were inaugurated in Tokyo, Japan in 1956. Women's championships were first held in 1980 in New York, USA. Yasuhiro Yamashita (b. 1 Jun 1957), who won nine consecutive Japanese titles 1977–85, won five world and Olympic titles; Over 95 kg 1979, 1981 and 1983, Open 1981, and the Olympic Open category in 1984. He retired undefeated after 203 successive wins, 1977–85. Two other men have won four world titles, Shozo Fujii (Japan) (b. 12 May 1950), Under 80 kg 1971, 1973 and 1975, Under 78 kg 1979, and Naoya Ogawa (Japan), Open 1987, 1989, 1991 and Over 95 kg 1989. The only men to have won two Olympic gold medals are Wilhelm Ruska (Netherlands) (b. 29 Aug 1940), Over 93 kg and

> **GUESS WHAT?**
> Q What is the world's largest sailing ship?
> A See Page 109

Open in 1972; Peter Seisenbacher (Austria) (b. 25 Mar 1960), 86 kg 1984 and 1988; Hitoshi Saito (Japan) (b. 2 Jan 1961), Over 95 kg 1984 and 1988; and Waldemar Legien (Poland), 78 kg 1988 and 86 kg 1992. Ingrid Berghmans (Belgium) (b. 24 Aug 1961) has won a record six women's world titles (first held 1980): Open 1980, 1982, 1984 and 1986 and Under 72 kg in 1984 and 1989. She has also won four silver medals and a bronze. She won the Olympic 72 kg title in 1988, when women's judo was introduced as a demonstration sport.

Karen Briggs (b. 11 Apr 1963) is the most successful British player, with four women's world titles, Under 48 kg in 1982, 1984, 1986 and 1989.

British The greatest number of titles (instituted 1966) won is nine by David Colin Starbrook (b. 9 Aug 1945) (6th dan): Middleweight 1969–70, Light-heavyweight 1971–5 and the Open division 1970–71. A record six titles in the women's events (instituted 1971) were won by Christine Gallie (*née* Child) (b. 1946) (6th dan): Heavyweight in 1971–5 and the Open division in 1973. Adrian Neil Adams (b. 27 Sep 1958) has the most successful international record of any British male player. He won two junior (1974 and 1977) and five senior (1979–80, 1983–5) European titles; four World Championships medals (one gold, one silver, two bronze) and two Olympic silver medals. He also won eight British senior titles.

Highest grades The efficiency grades in judo are divided into pupil (*kyu*) and master (*dan*) grades. The highest awarded is the extremely rare red belt *Judan* (10th dan), given to only 13 men so far. The Judo protocol provides for an 11th dan (*Juichidan*) who also would wear a red belt, a 12th dan (*Junidan*) who would wear a white belt twice as wide as an ordinary belt, and the highest of all, *Shihan* (ductor), but these have never been bestowed, save for the 12th dan to the founder of the sport Dr Jigoro Kano (1860–1938).

The highest British native Judo grade is 9th dan by Alfred Bates awarded in 1992. Christine Gallie was awarded her 6th dan in 1983.

> The World Council of Jiu-Jitsu Organization has staged World Championships biennially since 1984. The Canadian team has been the team winners on each occasion.

> Greg Foster and Lee Finney completed 27,083 judo throwing techniques in a ten-hour period at the Forest Judo Club, Leicester on 25 Sep 1993.

Karate

World Championships Great Britain have won a record six world titles (instituted 1970) at the Kumite team event, 1975, 1982, 1984, 1986, 1988 and 1990. Two men's individual kumite titles have been won by: Pat McKay (GB) at Under 80 kg, 1982 and 1984; Emmanuel Pinda (France) at Open, 1984 and Over 80 kg, 1988; Theirry Masci (France) at Under 70 kg, 1986 and 1988 and José Manuel Egea (Spain) at Under 80 kg, 1990 and 1992. Four women's kumite titles have been won by Guus van Mourik (Netherlands) at Over 60 kg, 1982, 1984, 1986 and 1988. Three individual kata titles have been won by men: Tsuguo Sakumoto (Japan) 1984, 1986 and 1988; women: Mie Nakayama (Japan) 1982, 1984 and 1986.

Top exponents The leading exponents among karateka are a number of 10th dans in Japan. The leading exponents in the United Kingdom are 8th dans: Tatsuo Suzuki (*Wado-ryu*) (b. 27 Apr 1928), Steve Arneil (*Kyokushinkai*), Keinosuke Enoeda and Shiro Asano (both *Shotokan*).

Lacrosse

Men

Most titles *World* The USA has won five of the six World Championships, in 1967, 1974, 1982, 1986 and 1990. Canada won the other world title in 1978 beating the USA 17–16 after extra time—this was the first drawn international match.

English The English Club Championship (Iroquois Cup instituted 1890), has been won most often by Stockport with 17 wins between 1897 and 1989. The record score in a final is 33 by Stockport *v.* London University (4) on 9 May 1987.

Most international appearances The record number of international representations is 42 by Peter Daniel Roden (Mellor) (b. 8 Nov 1954) from 1976–90.

Highest scores The highest score in an international match is the USA's 32–8 win over England at Toronto, Canada in 1986.

England's highest score was their 19–11 win over Canada at Melbourne, Australia in August 1974.

Women

World Championships/World Cup The first World Cup was held in 1982, replacing the World Championships which had been held three times since 1969. The USA have won four times, 1974, 1982, 1989 and 1993.

Most international appearances Vivien Jones played in 64 internationals (52 for Wales, 9 for the Celts and 3 for Great Britain), 1977–90. Caro Macintosh (b. 18 Feb 1932) played in 56 internationals (52 for Scotland and four for Great Britain).

Highest score The highest score by an international team was by Great Britain and Ireland with their 40–0 defeat of Long Island during their 1967 tour of the USA.

Marbles

Most championships The British Championship (established 1926) has been won most often by the Toucan Terribles with 20 consecutive titles (1956–75). Three founder members, Len Smith, Jack and Charlie Dempsey, played in every title win. They were finally beaten in 1976 by the Pernod Rams, captained by Len Smith's son, Paul. Len Smith (1917–90) won the individual title 15 times (1957–64, 1966, 1968–73) but lost in 1974 to his son Alan.

Fastest!

The record for clearing the ring (between 1.75 and 1.9 m *5¾–6¼ ft* in diameter) of 49 marbles is 2 min 56 sec by the Black Dog Boozers of Crawley, W Sussex at BBC Television Centre, London for *Record Breakers* on 14 Sep 1987.

Microlighting over Africa.
(Photo: Vandystadt/Y. Arthus-Bertrand)

Microlighting

The *Fédération Aéronautique Internationale* has established two classes of aircraft for which records are accepted, C1 a/o and R 1-2-3, and the following are the overall best of the two classes (all in the C1 a/o class).

World records Distance in a straight line: 1627.78 km *1011.45 miles* Wilhelm Lischak (Austria), Volsau, Austria to Brest, France, 8 Jun 1988.

Distance in a closed circuit: 2702.16 km *1679.04 miles* Wilhelm Lischak (Austria), Wels, Austria, 18 Jun 1988.

Altitude: 9189 m *30,147 ft* Eric S. Winton (Australia), Tyagarah Aerodrome, NSW, Australia, 8 Apr 1989.

Speed over a 500km closed circuit: 293.04 km/h *182 mph* C. T. Andrews (USA), 3 Aug 1982.

David Cook set a British altitude record of 8249 m *27,064 ft* on 28 Apr 1990 at Aldeburgh, Suffolk.

Endurance Eve Jackson flew from Biggin Hill, Kent to Sydney, Australia from 26 Apr 1986 to 1 Aug 1987. The flight took 279 hr 55 min and covered 21,950 km *13,639 miles*. From 1 Dec 1987 to 29 Jan 1988, Brian Milton (GB) flew from London to Sydney with a flying time of 241 hr 20 min and covered 21,968 km *13,650 miles*. Vijaypat Singhania (India) flew from Biggin Hill to Delhi, India, a distance of 8724 km *5420 miles* in 87 hr 55 min, from 18 Aug to 10 Sep 1988.

Modern Pentathlon & Biathlon

Points scored in riding, fencing, cross country and hence overall scores have no comparative value between one competition and another. In shooting and swimming (300 m) the scores are of record significance.

Modern Pentathlon

Most titles *World* András Balczó (Hungary) (b. 16 Aug 1938) won a record number of world titles (instituted 1949), six individual and seven team. He won the world individual title in 1963, 1965–7 and 1969 and the Olympic title in 1972. His seven team titles (1960–70) comprised five world and two Olympic. The USSR has won a record 14 world and four Olympic team titles. Hungary has also won a record four Olympic team titles (and ten world titles).

Women's World Championships were first held in 1981, replacing the World Cup which began in 1978. Poland have won a record five women's world team titles: 1985, 1988–91; Great Britain won three world titles, 1981–3, and three World Cups, 1978–80. Eva Fjellerup (Denmark) has won the individual title three times, 1990–91, 1993.

Olympic (first held 1912) The greatest number of Olympic gold medals won is three, by András Balczó, a member of the winning team in 1960 and 1968 and the 1972 individual champion. Lars Hall (Sweden) (b. 30 Apr 1927) has uniquely won two individual championships (1952 and 1956). Pavel Serafimovich Lednyev (USSR) (b. 25 Mar 1943) won a record seven medals (two team gold, one team silver, one individual silver, three individual bronze), 1968–80.

The best British performance is the team gold medal in 1976 by Jim Fox, Adrian Philip Parker and Daniel Nightingale. The best individual

The 1992 British Olympic team illustrating the five disciplines of the modern pentathlon.

(Photo: Allsport/Howard Boylan)

GUESS WHAT?

Q How many events are there in the heptathlon in athletics?

A See Page 225

placing is fourth by Jeremy Robert 'Jim' Fox (b. 19 Sep 1941) in 1972 and Richard Lawson Phelps (b. 19 Apr 1961) in 1984.

Probably the greatest margin of victory was by William Oscar Guernsey Grut (Sweden) (b. 17 Sep 1914) in the 1948 Games, when he won three events and was placed fifth and eighth in the other two.

British Both Jim Fox (1963, 1965–8, 1970–74) and Richard Phelps have won a record ten titles. Wendy Norman won a record seven women's titles, 1978–80, 1982, 1986–8.

Biathlon

Most titles *Olympic (first held 1960)* Two men's Olympic individual titles have been won by: Magnar Solberg (Norway) (b. 4 Feb 1937), in 1968 and 1972; and by Frank-Peter Rötsch (GDR) (b. 19 Apr 1964) at both 10km and 20km in 1988. Aleksandr Ivanovich Tikhonov (b. 2 Jan 1947) won four relay golds, 1968–80 and also won a silver in the 1968 20km. A women's competition was introduced in 1992. The most titles is two by: Anfissa Restzova (Russia) (b. 16 Dec 1964), 7.5km 1992, 4×7.5km 1994; and Myriam Bédard (Canada) (b. 22 Dec 1969), 7.5km, 15km 1994.

World (instituted 1958) Frank Ullrich (GDR) (b. 24 Jan 1958) has won a record six individual world titles, four at 10km, 1978–81, including the 1980 Olympics, and two at 20km, 1982–3. Aleksandr Tikhonov was in ten winning Soviet relay teams, 1968–80 and won four individual titles.

The Biathlon World Cup (instituted 1979) was won four times by Frank Ullrich, 1978 and 1980–82; and Franz Peter Rötsch (GDR), 1984–5 and 1987–8.

Women The first World Championships were held in 1984. The most individual titles is three by Anne-Elinor Elvebakk (Norway), 10km 1988, 7.5km 1989–90. Kaya Parve (USSR) has won six titles, two individual and four relay, 1984–6, 1988. A women's World Cup began in 1988.

Myriam Bédard celebrates winning her second biathlon gold of the 1994 Olympics. She had easily won gold in the 15km event and repeated her success in the 7.5km although only 1.2 seconds covered the medal positions.
(Photo: Allsport/Clive Brunskill)

Motorcycle Racing

Oldest!

The oldest annually contested motorcycle races in the world are the Auto-Cycle Union Tourist Trophy (TT) series, first held on the 25.44km *15.81 mile* 'Peel' (St John's) course in the Isle of Man on 28 May 1907, and still run in the island on the 'Mountain' circuit.

Fastest circuits The highest average lap speed attained on any closed circuit is 257.958 km/h *160.288mph* by Yvon du Hamel (Canada) (b. 1941) on a modified 903 cc four-cylinder Kawasaki Z1 at the 31-degree banked 4.02km *2.5 mile* Daytona International Speedway, Florida, USA in March 1973. His lap time was 56.149sec.

The fastest road circuit used to be Francorchamps circuit near Spa, Belgium, then 14.12km *8.77 miles* in length. It was lapped in 3 min 50.3 sec (average speed 220.721 km/h *137.150 mph*) by Barry Stephen Frank Sheene (GB) (b. 11 Sep 1950) on a 495 cc 4-cylinder Suzuki during the Belgian Grand Prix on 3 Jul 1977. On that occasion he set a record time for this ten-lap (141.20km *87.74 mile*) race of

38 min 58.5 sec (average speed 217.370 km/h *135.068mph*).

United Kingdom The lap record for the outer circuit (4.453km *2.767 miles*) at the Brooklands Motor Course, near Weybridge, Surrey (open between 1907 and 1939) was 80sec (average speed 200.37km/h *124.51mph*) by Noel Baddow 'Bill' Pope (later Major) (GB) (1909–71) on a Brough Superior powered by a supercharged 996 cc V-twin '8-80' JAP engine developing 110bhp, on 4 Jul 1939.

The fastest circuit in current use is that over public roads at Dundrod, Co. Antrim for the Ulster Grand Prix. Steve Hislop (Scotland) (b. 11 Jan 1962) set a lap record of 199.10 km/h *123.72 mph* and overall average speed of 195.48km/h *121.46 mph* for the 'King of the Road' race on 11 Aug 1990.

Rolf Biland has won 72 World Championship races at side-car, a record for a single class, and for the majority of them Kurt Waltisperg, his Swiss compatriot, has been passenger.
(Photo: Allsport/Mike Hewitt)

Most successful riders *World Championships* The most World Championship titles (instituted by the *Fédération Internationale Motocycliste* in 1949) won is 15 by Giacomo Agostini (Italy) (b. 16 Jun 1942), seven at 350cc, 1968–74, and eight at 500cc in 1966–72, 1975. He is the only man to win two World Championships in five consecutive years (350cc and 500cc titles 1968–72).

Angel Roldan Nieto (Spain) (b. 25 Jan 1947) won a record seven 125cc titles, 1971–2, 1979, 1981–4 and he also won a record six titles at 50cc, 1969–70, 1972, 1975–7. Phil Read (GB) (b. 1 Jan 1934) won a record four 250cc titles, 1964–5, 1968, 1971. Klaus Enders (West Germany) (b. 1937) won six world side-car titles, 1967, 1969–70, 1972–4. This was equalled by Rolf Biland (Switzerland) (b. 1 Apr 1951) in 1993, having previously won in 1978–9, 1981, 1983 and 1992.

The 60.72km *37.73 mile* 'Mountain' circuit on the Isle of Man, over which the principal TT races have been run since 1911 (with minor amendments in 1920), has 264 curves and corners and is the longest used for any motorcycle race.

Agostini won 122 races (68 at 500cc, 54 at 350cc) in the World Championship series between 24 Apr 1965 and 25 Sep 1977, including a record 19 in 1970, a season's total also achieved by Mike Hailwood in

Motor Racing

1966. The record number of career wins for any one class is 72 by Rolf Biland at side-car.

Tourist Trophy The record number of victories in the Isle of Man TT races is 17 by William Joseph Dunlop (Ireland) (b. 25 Feb 1952), 1977–94. The first man to win three consecutive TT titles in two events was James A. Redman (Rhodesia) (b. 8 Nov 1931). He won the 250cc and 350cc events in 1963–5. Stanley Michael Bailey Hailwood (1940–81) won three events in one year, in 1961 and 1967, and this feat was repeated by Joey Dunlop in 1985 and 1988; and by Steve Hislop in 1989 and 1991.

The Isle of Man TT circuit speed record is 198.92km/h *123.61mph* by Carl George Fogarty (b. 1 Jul 1965) on 12 Jun 1992. On the same occasion Steve Hislop set the race speed record, 1hr 51min 59.6sec for an average speed of 195.17km/h *121.28mph* to win the 1992 Senior TT on a Norton. The fastest woman around the 'Mountain' circuit is Gloria Clark (GB) (b. 31 Aug 1961) who achieved a speed of 155.02km/h *96.33mph* on her 600cc Yamaha on 31 Aug 1991.

Trials A record five World Trials Championships have been won by Jordi Tarrès (Spain) (b. 10 Sep 1966), 1987, 1989–91 and 1993.

Moto-cross Joël Robert (Belgium) (b. 11 Nov 1943) won six 250cc Moto-cross World Championships (1964, 1968–72). Between 25 Apr 1964 and 18 Jun 1972 he won a record fifty 250cc Grand Prix. The youngest moto-cross world champion was Dave Strijbos (Netherlands) (b. 9 Nov 1968), who won the 125cc title aged 18yr 296days on 31 Aug 1986. Eric Geboers (Belgium) has uniquely won all three categories of the Moto-Cross World Championships, at 125cc in 1982 and 1983, 250cc in 1987 and 500cc in 1988 and 1990.

Oldest race!

The oldest race in the world still regularly run, is the RAC Tourist Trophy, first staged on 14 Sep 1905, in the Isle of Man. The oldest continental race is the French Grand Prix, first held on 26–27 Jun 1906. The Coppa Florio, in Sicily, has been held irregularly since 1906.

Fastest circuits The highest average lap speed attained on any closed circuit is 403.878km/h *250.958 mph* in a trial by Dr Hans Liebold (Germany) (b. 12 Oct 1926) who lapped the 12.64km *7.85 mile* high-speed track at Nardo, Italy in 1min 52.67sec in a Mercedes-Benz C111-IV experimental coupé on 5 May 1979. It was powered by a V8 engine with two KKK turbochargers, with an output of 500hp at 6200rpm.

Fastest pit stop Robert William 'Bobby' Unser (USA) (b. 20 Feb 1934) took 4seconds to take

Jordi Tarrés, winner of five World trials titles, in action.
(Photo: Vandystadt/Y. Guichaqua)

The 1994 Formula One season saw the sad loss of one of the greatest drivers of the modern era, Ayrton Senna. In a career spanning ten seasons, Senna achieved pole position in over 40 per cent of the races he entered and won one in every four.
(Photos: Allsport/Pascal Rondeau & Mike Hewitt)

on fuel on lap 10 of the Indianapolis 500 on 30 May 1976.

Fastest race The fastest race is the Busch Clash at Daytona, Florida, USA over 50miles *80.5km* on a 2½mile *4km* 31-degree banked track. In 1987 Bill Elliott (b. 8 Oct 1955) averaged 197.802mph *318.331km/h* in a Ford Thunderbird. Al Unser Jr (b. 19 Apr 1962) set the world record for a 500mile *805km* race on 9 Aug 1990 when he won the Michigan 500A at an average speed of 189.7mph *305.2km/h*.

World Championship Grand

Prix Motor Racing

Most successful drivers The World Drivers' Championship, inaugurated in 1950, has been won a record five times by Juan-Manuel Fangio (Argentina) (b. 24 Jun 1911) in 1951 and 1954–57. He retired in 1958, after having won 24 Grand Prix races (two shared) from 51 starts.

Alain Prost (France) (b. 24 Feb 1955) holds the records for both the most Grand Prix points in a career, 798.5 and the most Grand Prix victories, 51 from 200 races, 1980–93. The most Grand Prix victories in a year is nine by Nigel Mansell (GB) (b. 8 Aug 1953) in 1992. The most Grand Prix starts is 255 by Ricardo Patrese (Italy) (b. 17 Apr 1954) from 1977–93. The greatest number of pole positions is 65 by Ayrton Senna (Brazil) (1960–94) from 161 races (41 wins), 1985–94.

Champions!

Loris Capirossi (Italy) (b. 4 Apr 1973) is the youngest rider to win a World Championship. He was 17yr 165 days when he won the 125cc title on 16 Sep 1990. The oldest was Hermann-Peter Müller (1909–76) of West Germany, who won the 250cc title in 1955 aged 46.

Oldest and youngest The youngest world champion was Emerson Fittipaldi (Brazil) (b. 12 Dec 1946) who won his first World Championship on 10 Sep 1972 aged 25 yr 273 days. The oldest world champion was Juan-Manuel Fangio who won his last World Championship on 4 Aug 1957, aged 46 yr 41 days.

The youngest Grand Prix winner was Bruce Leslie McLaren (1937–70) of New Zealand, who won the United States Grand Prix at Sebring, Florida on 12 Dec 1959, aged 22 yr 104 days. Troy Ruttman (USA) was 22 yr 80 days when he won the Indianapolis 500 on 30 May 1952, which was part of the World Championships at the time. The oldest Grand Prix winner (in pre-World Championship days) was Tazio Giorgio Nuvolari (Italy) (1892–1953), who won the Albi Grand Prix at Albi, France on 14 Jul 1946, aged 53 yr 240 days. The oldest Grand Prix driver was Louis Alexandre Chiron (Monaco) (1899–1979), who finished sixth in the Monaco Grand Prix on 22 May 1955, aged 55 yr 292 days. The youngest driver to qualify for a Grand Prix was Michael Christopher Thackwell (New Zealand) (b. 30 Mar 1961) at the Canadian GP on 28 Sep 1980, aged 19 yr 182 days.

GUESS WHAT?

Q Who is the youngest motorcycling world champion?

A See Page 273

apolis 500 race, then included in the World Drivers' Championship, Ferrari won all seven races in 1952 and the first eight (of nine) in 1953.

Fastest race The fastest overall average speed for a Grand Prix race on a circuit in current use is 235.421 km/h *146.284 mph* by Nigel Mansell (GB) in a Williams-Honda at Zeltweg in the Austrian Grand Prix on 16 Aug 1987. The qualifying lap record was set by Keke Rosberg (Finland) at 1 min 05.59 sec, an average speed of 258.802 km/h *160.817 mph*, in a Williams-Honda at Silverstone in the British Grand Prix on 20 Jul 1985.

British Grand Prix

First held in 1926 as the RAC Grand Prix, and held annually with the above name since 1949. The venues have been Aintree, Merseyside; Brands Hatch, Kent; Brooklands, Surrey; Donington, Leics and Silverstone, Northants.

Bobby Rahal is one of the most successful drivers in the Indy Car Championship, having the highest career earnings of Indy drivers with $12,024,828 to end of 1993.

(Photo: Allsport/Pascal Rondeau)

Manufacturers Ferrari have won a record eight manufacturers' World Championships, 1961, 1964, 1975–77, 1979, 1982–83. McLaren have 104 race wins in 394 Grands Prix, 1966–93.

The greatest dominance by one team since the Constructor's Championship was instituted in 1958 was by McLaren in 1988 when they won 15 of the 16 Grands Prix. Ayrton Senna had eight wins and three seconds, Alain Prost had seven wins and seven seconds. The McLarens, powered by Honda engines, amassed over three times the points of their nearest rivals, Ferrari. Excluding the Indian-

Fastest speed The fastest race time is 1 hr 18 min 10.436 sec, average speed 235.405 km/h *146.274 mph*, when Alain Prost won in a McLaren at Silverstone on 21 Jul 1985.

Most wins The most wins by a driver is five by Jim Clark, 1962–5 and 1967, all in Lotus cars. Jim Clark and Jack Brabham (Australia) (b. 2 Apr 1926) have both won the race on three different circuits; Brands Hatch, Silverstone and Aintree. The most wins by a manufacturer is ten by Ferrari, 1951–4, 1956, 1958, 1961, 1976, 1978 and 1990.

Closest!

The closest finish to a World Championship race was when Ayrton Senna (Brazil) in a Lotus beat Nigel Mansell (GB) in a Williams by 0.014 sec in the Spanish Grand Prix at Jerez de la Frontera on 13 Apr 1986. In the Italian Grand Prix at Monza on 5 Sep 1971, 0.61 sec separated winner Peter Gethin (GB) from the fifth placed driver.

Le Mans

The greatest distance ever covered in the 24-hour *Grand Prix d'End-urance* (first held on 26–27 May 1923) on the old Sarthe circuit at Le Mans, France is 5335.302 km *3315.203 miles* by Dr Helmut Marko (Austria) (b. 27 Apr

1943) and Gijs van Lennep (Netherlands) (b. 16 Mar 1942) in a 4907-cc flat-12 Porsche 917K Group 5 sports car, on 12–13 Jun 1971. The record for the greatest distance ever covered for the current circuit is 5331.998 km *3313.150 miles* (average speed 222.166 km/h *138.047 mph*) by Jan Lammers (Holland), Johnny Dumfries and Andy Wallace (both GB) in a Jaguar XJR9 on 11–12 Jun 1988.

The race lap record (now 13.536 km *8.411 mile* lap) is 3 min 21.27 sec (average speed 242.093 km/h *150.429 mph*) by Alain Ferté (France) in a Jaguar XRJ-9 on 10 Jun 1989. Hans Stück (West Germany) set the practice lap speed record of 251.664 km/h *156.377 mph*) on 14 Jun 1985.

Most wins The race has been won by Porsche cars 13 times, in 1970–71, 1976–7, 1979, 1981–7, 1993. The most wins by one man is six by Jacques Bernard 'Jacky' Ickx (Belgium) (b. 1 Jan 1945), 1969, 1975–7 and 1981–2.

Indianapolis 500

The Indianapolis 500 mile *804 km* race (200 laps) was inaugurated in the USA on 30 May 1911. Three drivers have four wins: Anthony Joseph 'A.J.' Foyt Jr (USA) (b. 16 Jan 1935) in 1961, 1964, 1967 and 1977; Al Unser Sr (USA) (b. 29 May 1939) in 1970–71, 1978 and 1987; and Rick Ravon Mears (USA) (b. 3 Dec 1951) in 1979, 1984, 1988 and 1991. The record time is 2 hr 41 min 18.404 sec (299.307 km/h *185.981 mph*) by Arie Luyendyk (Netherlands) driving a Lola-Chevrolet on 27 May 1990. The record average speed for four-laps qualifying is 374.143 km/h *232.482 mph* by Roberto Guerrero (Colombia) in a Lola-Buick (including a one-lap record of 374.362 km/h *232.618 mph*) on 9 May 1992. The track record is 375.673 km/h *233.433 mph* by Jim Crawford (GB) on 4 May 1992. A. J. Foyt Jr started in a record 35 races, 1958–92 and Rick Mears has started from pole position a record six times, 1979, 1982, 1986, 1988–89 and 1991. The record prize fund is $7,681,300 in 1993, and the individual prize record is $1,373,713 by Al Unser Jr in 1994.

Rallying

The earliest long rally was promoted by the Parisian daily *Le Matin* in 1907 from Peking (now Beijing), China to Paris over about 12,000 km *7500 miles* on 10 June. The winner, Prince Scipione Borghese (1872–1927) of Italy, arrived in Paris on 10 Aug 1907 in his 40-hp Itala accompanied by his chauffeur, Ettore, and Luigi Barzini.

Longest The longest ever rally was the *Singapore Airlines* London–Sydney Rally over 31,107 km *19,329 miles* from Covent Garden, London on 14 Aug 1977 to Sydney Opera House, won on 28 Sep 1977 by Andrew Cowan, Colin Malkin and Michael Broad in a Mercedes 280E. The longest held annually is the Safari Rally (first run in 1953 as the Coronation Rally, through Kenya, Tanzania and Uganda, but now restricted to Kenya). The race has covered up to 6234 km *3874 miles*, as in the 17th Safari held from 8–12 Apr 1971. It has been won a record five times by Shekhar Mehta (b. Kenya, 20 Jun 1945) in 1973, 1979–82.

The flying Finn Juha Kankkunen, the most successful driver ever in rallying's World Championship, in action during the 1993 Network Q/RAC Rally which he won. It was his 20th race win in a career which has brought him four World titles.

(Photo: Allsport/Chris Cole)

Monte Carlo The Monte Carlo Rally (first run 1911) has been won a record four times by: Sandro Munari (Italy) (b. 27 Mar 1940) in 1972, 1975, 1976 and 1977; and Walter Röhrl (West Germany) (b. 7 Mar 1947) (with co-driver Christian Geistdorfer) in 1980, 1982–4, each time in a different car. The smallest car to win was an 851-cc Saab driven by Erik Carlsson (Sweden) (b. 5 Mar 1929) and Gunnar Häggbom (Sweden) (b. 7 Dec 1935) on 25 Jan 1962, and by Carlsson and Gunnar Palm on 24 Jan 1963.

Britain The RAC Rally (first held 1932) has been recognized by the FIA since 1957. Hannu Mikkola (Finland) (b. 24 May 1942) (with co-driver Arne Hertz) has a record four wins, in a Ford Escort, 1978–9 and an Audi Quattro, 1981–2.

World Championship The World Drivers' Championships (instituted 1979) has been won by Juha Kankkunen (Finland) (b. 2 Apr 1959) on a record four occasions, 1986–7, 1991 and 1993. The most wins in World Championship races is 21 by Juha Kankkunen (Finland). The most wins in a season is six by Didier Auriol (France) (b. 18 Aug 1958) in 1992. Lancia have won a record eleven manufacturers' World Championships between 1972 and 1992.

Drag Racing

Piston engined The lowest elapsed time recorded by a piston-engined dragster from a standing start for 440 yd *402 m* is 4.726 sec by Scott Kalitta (USA) at Houston, Texas on 6 Mar 1994, and the highest terminal velocity at the end of a 440 yd run is 308.64 mph *496.70 km/h* by Connie Kalitta (USA) at Topeka, Kansas on 3 Oct 1993. For a petrol-driven piston-engined car the lowest elapsed time is 7.027 sec by Warren Johnson (USA) at Houston on 5 Mar 1993, and the highest terminal velocity is 196.59 mph *316.38 km/h* by Scott Geoffrion (USA) at Houston on 5 Mar 1994. The lowest elapsed time for a petrol-driven piston-engined motorcycle is 7.598 sec and the highest terminal velocity is 292.66 km/h *181.85 mph* by David Schultz (USA) at Reading, Pennsylvania on 19 Sep 1993.

Mountaineering

Mt Everest Everest (8848 m *29,029 ft*) was first climbed at 11:30 a.m. on 29 May 1953, when the summit was reached by Edmund Percival Hillary (b. 20 Jul 1919), of New Zealand, and Sherpa Tenzing Norgay (1914–86, formerly called Tenzing Khumjung Bhutia). The successful expedition was led by Col. (later Hon. Brigadier) Henry Cecil John Hunt (b. 22 Jun 1910).

Most conquests Ang Rita Sherpa (b. 1947), with ascents in 1983, 1984, 1985, 1987, 1988, 1990, 1992 and 1993 has scaled Everest eight times and all without the use of bottled oxygen.

Solo Reinhold Messner (Italy) (b. 17 Sep 1944) was the first to make the entire climb solo on 20 Aug 1980. Also Messner, with Peter Habeler (Austria) (b. 22 Jul 1942), made the first entirely oxygen-less ascent on 8 May 1978.

First Britons Douglas Scott (b. 29 May 1941) and Dougal Haston (1940–77) successfully completed the climb on 24 Sep 1975. The first British woman was Rebecca Stephens (b. 3 Oct 1961) on 17 May 1993.

First woman Junko Tabei (Japan) (b. 22 Sep 1939) reached the summit on 16 May 1975.

Oldest Ramon Blanco (Spain) (b. 30 Apr 1933) was aged 60 yr 160 days when he reached the summit on 7 Oct 1993.

Most successful expedition The Mount Everest International Peace Climb, a team of American, Soviet and Chinese climbers, led by James W. Whittaker (USA), in 1990 succeeded in putting the greatest number of people on the summit, 20, from 7–10 May 1990.

Mountaineer Reinhold Messner was the first person to successfully scale all 14 of the world's mountains of over 8000 m *26,250 ft*, all without oxygen. With his ascent of Kanchenjunga in 1982, he was the first to climb the world's three highest mountains, having earlier reached the summits of Everest and K2.

Greatest walls The highest final stage in any wall climb is that on the south face of Annapurna I (8091 m *26,545 ft*). It was climbed by the British expedition led by Christian John Storey Bonington (b. 6 Aug 1934) when from 2 Apr to 27 May 1970, using 5500 m *18,000 ft* of rope, Donald Whillans (1933–85) and Dougal Haston scaled to the summit. The longest wall climb is on the Rupal-Flank from the base camp at 3560 m *11,680 ft* to the South Point 8042 m *26,384 ft* of Nanga Parbat, a vertical ascent of 4482 m *14,704 ft*. This was scaled by the Austro-German-Italian expedition led by Dr Karl Maria Herrligkoffer (b. 13 Jun 1916) in April 1970.

The most demanding free climbs in the world are those rated at 5.13, the premier location for these being in the Yosemite Valley, California, USA.

The top routes in Britain are graded E7.7b, which relates closely to 5.13.

Highest bivouac Mark Whetu (New Zealand) (b. 27 Oct 1959) and Michael Anthony Rheinberger (Australia) (1940–94) reached the summit of Everest on 26 May 1994 and bivouacked just 20 m below the summit that night. Sadly a very weak Rheinberger died the next day during the descent.

Mountain Racing

Mount Cameroon Reginald Esuke (Cameroon) descended from the summit 4095 m *13,435 ft* to Buea Stadium at 915 m *3002 ft* in 1 hr 2 min 15 sec on 24 Jan 1988, achieving a vertical rate of 51 m *167.5 ft* per min. Timothy Leku Lekunze (Cameroon) set the record for the race to the summit and back of 3 hr 46 min 34 sec on 25 Jan 1987, when the temperature varied from 35°C at the start to 0°C at the summit. The record time for the ascent is 2 hr 25 min 20 sec by Jack Maitland (GB) in 1988. The women's record for the race is 4 hr 42 min 31 sec by Fabiola Rueda (Colombia) (b. 26 Mar 1963) in 1989.

GUESS WHAT?

Q What is the highest mountain in the United Kingdom?

A see Page 15

Mountain Endurance Running

Lakeland 24-hour The record is 76 peaks (approximately 11,900 m *39,000 ft* of ascents and descents) from Braithwaite achieved by Mark McDermott (Macclesfield Harriers) on 19–20 Jun 1988.

Scottish 24-hour The record is 28 Munros (mountains over 3000 ft *914 m*) from Cluanie Inn, with 35,000 ft *10,668 m* of ascents and descents achieved by Jon Broxap on 30–31 Jul 1988.

Bob Graham The record for the round of 42 lakeland peaks covering a total distance of 62 miles *99 km* and 26,000 ft *7900 m* of ascent and descent, is 13 hr 54 min by William Bland, 34, on 19 Jun 1982. Ernest Roger Baumeister (b. 17 Dec 1941) (Dark Peak Fell Runners

On 10 May 1993, 40 climbers (32 men and 8 women) from the USA, Canada, Australia, Great Britain, Russia, New Zealand, Finland, Lithuania, India and Nepal, from nine separate expeditions, reached the summit.

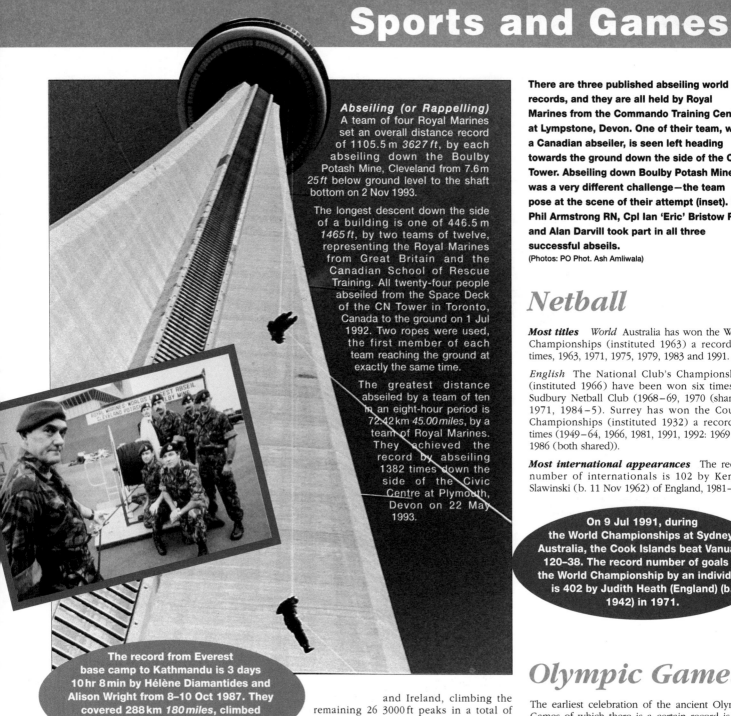

Abseiling (or Rappelling)
A team of four Royal Marines set an overall distance record of 1105.5 m *3627 ft*, by each abseiling down the Boulby Potash Mine, Cleveland from 7.6 m *25 ft* below ground level to the shaft bottom on 2 Nov 1993.

The longest descent down the side of a building is one of 446.5 m *1465 ft*, by two teams of twelve, representing the Royal Marines from Great Britain and the Canadian School of Rescue Training. All twenty-four people abseiled from the Space Deck of the CN Tower in Toronto, Canada to the ground on 1 Jul 1992. Two ropes were used, the first member of each team reaching the ground at exactly the same time.

The greatest distance abseiled by a team of ten in an eight-hour period is 72.42 km *45.00 miles*, by a team of Royal Marines. They achieved the record by abseiling 1382 times down the side of the Civic Centre at Plymouth, Devon on 22 May 1993.

There are three published abseiling world records, and they are all held by Royal Marines from the Commando Training Centre at Lympstone, Devon. One of their team, with a Canadian abseiler, is seen left heading towards the ground down the side of the CN Tower. Abseiling down Boulby Potash Mine was a very different challenge—the team pose at the scene of their attempt (inset). Lt Phil Armstrong RN, Cpl Ian 'Eric' Bristow RM and Alan Darvill took part in all three successful abseils.
(Photos: PO Phot. Ash Amliwala)

Netball

Most titles *World* Australia has won the World Championships (instituted 1963) a record six times, 1963, 1971, 1975, 1979, 1983 and 1991.

English The National Club's Championships (instituted 1966) have been won six times by Sudbury Netball Club (1968–69, 1970 (shared), 1971, 1984–5). Surrey has won the County Championships (instituted 1932) a record 21 times (1949–64, 1966, 1981, 1991, 1992: 1969 and 1986 (both shared)).

Most international appearances The record number of internationals is 102 by Kendra Slawinski (b. 11 Nov 1962) of England, 1981–93.

> On 9 Jul 1991, during the World Championships at Sydney, Australia, the Cook Islands beat Vanuatu 120–38. The record number of goals in the World Championship by an individual is 402 by Judith Heath (England) (b. 1942) in 1971.

> The record from Everest base camp to Kathmandu is 3 days 10 hr 8 min by Hélène Diamantides and Alison Wright from 8–10 Oct 1987. They covered 288 km *180 miles*, climbed 9800 m *32,000 ft* and descended 14,000 m *46,000 ft*.

Club) ran the double Bob Graham Round in 46 hr 34½ min on 30 Jun–1 Jul 1979. The women's single round record is 18 hr 49 min by Anne Stentiford (Macclesfield Harriers) on 21 Sep 1991.

Scottish 4000 ft peaks The record for traversing all eight 4000 ft *1219 m* peaks, a 85 mile *136 km* cross-country route from Glen Nevis to Glen More is 21 hr 39 min by Martin Stone on 4 Jul 1987.

Scottish 3000 ft peaks The Munros record for climbing and linking the 277 peaks (over 3000 ft *914 m*) entirely on foot is 66 days 22 hr by Hugh Symonds (b. 1 Feb 1953). He covered 1374 miles *2211 km* and climbed 422,000 ft *128,600 m* between Ben Hope and Ben Lomond, 19 Apr–25 Jun 1990. He rowed to Skye, sailed to Mull and ran between all the other peaks. He continued on foot through England, Wales

> The longest climb achieved on the vertical face of a building occurred on 25 May 1981 when Daniel Goodwin, 25, of California, USA climbed a record 443.2 m *1454 ft* up the outside of the Sears Tower in Chicago, USA, using suction cups and metal clips for support.

and Ireland, climbing the remaining 26 3000 ft peaks in a total of 97 days.

Welsh 3000 ft peaks The record for traversing the 15 Welsh peaks is 4 hr 19 min 56 sec, from Snowdon Summit to Foel Fras by Colin Donnelly on 11 Jun 1988. The women's record is 5 hr 28 min 41 sec by Angela Carson on 5 Aug 1989.

English 3000 ft peaks The record for a circuit of the four English peaks is 7 hr 35 min by William Bland on 15 Jun 1979.

British Three Peaks record The Three Peaks route from sea level at Fort William, Highland, to sea level at Caernarvon, via the summits of Ben Nevis, Scafell Pike and Snowdon, was walked by Arthur Eddleston (1939–84) (Cambridge H) in 5 days 23 hr 37 min from 11–17 May 1980. The women's walking record is 7 days 31 min by Ann Sayer from 8–15 Sep 1979. Peter and David Ford, David Robinson, Kevin Duggan and John O'Callaghan, of Luton and Dunstable, ran the distance in relay in 54 hr 39 min 14 sec from 7–9 Aug 1981.

Olympic Games

The earliest celebration of the ancient Olympic Games of which there is a certain record is that of July 776 BC, when Coroibos, a cook from Elis, won the foot race, though their origin dates from perhaps as early as c. 1370 BC. The ancient Games were terminated by an order issued in Milan in AD 393 by Theodosius I, 'the Great' (c. 346–95), Emperor of Rome. At the instigation of Pierre de Fredi, Baron de Coubertin (1863–1937), the Olympic Games of the modern era were inaugurated in Athens on 6 Apr 1896.

Ever present Five countries have never failed to be represented at the 23 Summer Games that have been held (1896–1992): Australia, France,

Olympians!

The greatest number of competitors at a Summer Games celebration is 9369 (6659 men, 2710 women), who represented a record 169 nations, at Barcelona, Spain in 1992. The greatest number at the Winter Games is 1737 (1216 men, 521 women) representing 67 countries, at Lillehammer, Norway in 1994.

Most Medals

The total medals, for leading nations, for all Olympic events (including those now discontinued).

SUMMER GAMES (1896–92)

	Gold	Silver	Bronze	Total
USA	789	603	518	1910
USSR[1]	442	361	333	1136
Germany[2]	186	227	236	649
Great Britain	177	224	218	619
France	161	175	191	527
Sweden	133	149	171	453
GDR[3]	154	131	126	411
Italy	153	126	131	410
Hungary	136	124	144	404
Finland	98	77	112	287
Japan	90	83	93	266
Australia	78	76	98	252
Romania	59	70	90	219
Poland	43	62	105	210
Canada	46	66	80	192
Netherlands	45	52	72	169
Switzerland	42	63	58	163
Bulgaria	38	69	55	162
Czechoslovakia[4]	49	50	50	149
Denmark	26	51	53	130

Excludes medals won in Official Art competitions in 1912–48.

WINTER GAMES (1924–94)

	Gold	Silver	Bronze	Total
USSR[1]	99	71	71	241
Norway	73	77	64	214
USA	53	55	39	147
Austria	36	48	44	128
Germany[2]	45	43	37	125
Finland	36	45	42	123
GDR[3]	39	36	35	110
Sweden	39	26	34	99
Switzerland	27	29	29	85
Italy	25	21	21	67
Canada	19	21	24	64
France	16	16	21	53
Netherlands	14	19	17	50
Czechoslovakia[4]	2	8	16	26
Great Britain	7	4	12	23

[1] *Includes Czarist Russia to 1912, CIS 1992, Russia 1994*
[2] *Germany 1896–1964 and 1992, West Germany 1968–88*
[3] *GDR (East Germany) 1968–88*
[4] *Includes Bohemia*

Most medals In ancient Olympic Games victors were given a chaplet of wild olive leaves. Leonidas of Rhodos won 12 running titles 164–152 BC. The most individual gold medals won by a male competitor in the modern Games is ten by Raymond Clarence Ewry (USA) (1873–1937) (⇨ Athletics). The female record is seven by Vera Caslavska-Odlozil (Czechoslovakia) (⇨ Gymnastics).

The most gold medals won by a British competitor is four by: Paul Radmilovic (1886–1968) in water polo, 1908, 1912 and 1920 and 4 × 200m freestyle relay in 1908; and swimmer Henry Taylor (1885–1951) in 1906 and 1908. The Australian swimmer Iain Murray Rose, who won four gold medals, was born in Birmingham, W Mids on 6 Jan 1939.

The only Olympian to win four consecutive individual titles in the same event has been Alfred Adolph Oerter (USA) (b. 19 Sep 1936), who won the discus, in 1956–68. However, Raymond Clarence Ewry (USA) won both the standing long jump and the standing high jump at four games in succession, 1900, 1904, 1906 and 1908. This is if the Intercalated Games of 1906, which were staged officially by the International Olympic Committee, are included. Also Paul B. Elvstrom (Denmark) (b. 25 Feb 1928) won four successive gold medals at monotype yachting events, 1948–60, but there was a class change (1948 Firefly class, 1952–60 Finn class).

Swimmer Mark Andrew Spitz (USA) (b. 10 Feb 1950) won a record seven golds at one celebration, at Munich in 1972, including three in relays. The most won in individual events at one celebration is five by speed skater, Eric Arthur Heiden (USA) (b. 14 Jun 1958) at Lake Placid, New York, USA in 1980.

The only man to win a gold medal in both the Summer and Winter Games is Edward Patrick Francis Eagan (USA) (1898–1967) who won the 1920 light-heavyweight boxing title and was a member of the winning four-man bob in 1932. Christa Luding (*née* Rothenburger) (GDR) (b. 4 Dec 1959) became the first woman to win a medal at both the Summer and Winter Games when she won a silver in the cycling sprint event in 1988. She had previously won medals for speed skating, 500m gold in 1984, and 1000m gold and 500m silver in 1988.

Gymnast Larisa Latynina (USSR) (b. 27 Dec 1934) won a record 18 medals and the men's record is 15 by Nikolay Andrianov (⇨ Gymnastics). The record at one celebration is eight by gymnast Aleksandr Dityatin (USSR) (b. 7 Aug 1957) in 1980.

Youngest and oldest gold medallist The youngest ever winner was a French boy (whose name is not recorded) who coxed the Netherlands pair in 1900. He was 7–10 years old and he substituted for Dr Hermanus Brockmann, who coxed in the heats but proved too heavy. The youngest ever female champion was Kim Yoon-mi (South Korea) (b. 1 Dec 1980), aged 13yr 83days, in the 1994 women's 3000m short-track speedskating relay event. Oscar Swahn was in the winning Running Deer shooting team in 1912 aged 64 yr 258 days and in this event was the oldest medallist, silver, at 72 yr 280 days in 1920.

Youngest and oldest British competitor The youngest competitor to represent Britain in the Olympic Games was Magdalena Cecilia Colledge (b. 28 Nov 1920), aged 11 yr 73 days when she skated in the 1932 Games. The oldest was Hilda Lorna Johnstone (1902–90), aged 70yr 5days, in the equestrian dressage in the 1972 Games.

Longest span The longest span of an Olympic competitor is 40 years by: Dr Ivan Osiier (Denmark) (1888–1965) in fencing, 1908–32 and 1948; Magnus Konow (Norway) (1887–1972) in yachting, 1908–20, 1928 and 1936–48; Paul Elvström (Denmark) in yachting, 1948–60,

GUESS WHAT?

Q Who is the oldest winner of a world title in sport?

A See Page 220

Greece, Great Britain and Switzerland (only contested the Equestrian events, held in Stockholm, Sweden, in 1956 and did not attend the Games in Melbourne). Of these only France, Great Britain and Switzerland have been present at all Winter celebrations (1924–94) as well.

Largest crowd The largest crowd at any Olympic site was 104,102 at the 1952 ski-jumping at the Holmenkøllen, outside Oslo, Norway. Estimates of the number of spectators of the marathon race at Tokyo, Japan on 21 Oct 1964 ranged from 500,000 to 1,500,000. The total spectator attendance at Los Angeles in 1984 was given as 5,797,923 (⇨ General Records).

Olympic Torch relay The longest journey of the torch within one country, was for the XV Olympic Winter Games in Canada in 1988. The torch arrived from Greece at St John's, Newfoundland on 17 Nov 1987 and was transported 18,060 km *11,222 miles* (8188 km *5088 miles* by foot, 7111 km *4419 miles* by aircraft/ferry, 2756 km *1712 miles* by snowmobile and 5 km *3 miles* by dogsled) until its arrival at Calgary on 13 Feb 1988.

The opening ceremony from the 1994 Winter Games at Lillehammer, Norway, the largest Games ever.

(Photo: Allsport/Mike Powell)

1968–72 and 1984–88; and Durward Randolph Knowles (Great Britain 1948, then Bahamas) (b. 2 Nov 1917) in yachting, 1948–72 and 1988. Brothers Piero (b. 4 Mar 1923) and Raimondo d'Inzeo (b. 8 Feb 1925) competed for Italy at a record eight celebrations from 1948–76. Raimondo won one gold, two silver and three bronze medals in equestrian events and Piero won two silver and four bronze medals at show jumping. This feat was equalled by Paul Elvström and Durward Knowles in 1988 and yachtsman Hubert Raudaschl (Austria) (b. 26 Aug 1942), 1964–92 (went to Rome, 1960 but did not compete). The longest feminine span is 28 years by Anne Jessica Ransehousen (*née* Newberry) (USA) (b. 14 Oct 1938) in dressage, 1960, 1964 and 1988. Fencer Kerstin Palm (Sweden) (b. 5 Feb 1946) competed in a women's record seven celebrations, 1964–88.

The longest span of any British competitor is 32 years by Enoch Jenkins (1892–1984) who competed in clay pigeon shooting in 1920, 1924 and 1952. The record number of appearances is six by swimmer and water polo player Paul Radmilovic, 1906–28 and fencer Bill Hoskyns, 1956–76. David Broome, who competed in show jumping in 1960, 1964, 1968, 1972 and 1988, was a member of the British team that travelled to Barcelona in 1992. He was, however, not selected to compete.

The greatest number of appearances for Great Britain by a woman is five by javelin thrower Tessa Ione Sanderson (b. 14 Mar 1956), 1976–92. The longest feminine span is 20 years by Dorothy Jennifer Beatrice Tyler (*née* Odam) (b. 14 Mar 1920) who high-jumped from 1936–56. However, Davina Mary Galica (b. 13 Aug 1944) who competed in alpine skiing, 1964–72, took part in speed skiing which was a demonstration sport in 1992, therefore completing a span of 28 years.

Orienteering

Most titles *World* The men's relay has been won a record seven times by Norway, 1970, 1978, 1981, 1983, 1985, 1987 and 1989. Sweden have won the women's relay ten times, 1966, 1970, 1974, 1976, 1981, 1983, 1985, 1989, 1991 and 1993. Three women's individual titles have been won by Annichen Kringstad (Sweden) (b. 15 Jul 1960), 1981, 1983 and 1985. The men's title has been won twice by: Åge Hadler (Norway) (b. 14 Aug 1944), in 1966 and 1972; Egil Johansen (Norway) (b. 18 Aug 1954), 1976 and 1978; and Øyvin Thon (Norway) (b. 25 Mar 1958), in 1979 and 1981.

Ski (instituted 1975) Sweden have won the men's relay title five times, 1977, 1980, 1982, 1984 and 1990. Finland have won the women's relay five times, 1975, 1977, 1980, 1988 and 1990. The most individual titles is four by Ragnhild Bratberg (Norway), Classic 1986, 1990, Sprint 1988, 1990. The men's record is three by Anssi Juutilainen (Finland) Classic 1984, 1988, Sprint 1992.

British Carol McNeill (b. 20 Feb 1944) won the women's title six times, 1967, 1969, 1972–6. Geoffrey Peck (b. 27 Sep 1949) won the men's individual title a record five times, 1971, 1973, 1976–7 and 1979.

Terry Dooris (b. 22 Sep 1926) of Southern Navigators has competed in all 28 British individual championships, 1967–94.

Most competitors The most competitors at an event in one day is 38,000 for the Ruf des Herbstes at Sibiu, Romania in 1982. The largest event is the five-day Swedish O-Ringen at Småland, which attracted 120,000 in July 1983.

GUESS WHAT?

Q In which sport is the Leonard Trophy awarded?

A See Page 238

Paragliding

The greatest distance flown is 283.9 km *176.4 miles* by Alex François Louw (South Africa) from Kuruman, South Africa on 31 Dec 1992. The women's record is 128.5 km *79.8 miles* by Judy Leden (GB) from Vryburg, South Africa on 9 Dec 1992. The height gain record is 4526 m *14,849 ft*

by Robby Whittal (GB) at Brandvlei, South Africa on 6 Jan 1993 and the women's best is 2971 m *9747 ft* by Verena Muhr (Germany) at Bitterwasser, Namibia on 13 Dec 1991. All these records were tow launched.

British The greatest distance flown is 253 km *157 miles* by Robby Whittal at Kuruman on 22 Jan 1993. The greatest distance flown within Britain is 98.56 km *61.2 miles* from Wetherfell to Stamford Bridge, Humberside by Ross Somerville on 30 Jul 1992 (footlaunched).

Pelota Vasca (Jaï Alaï)

World Championships The *Federación Internacional de Pelota Vasca* stage World Championships every four years (first in 1952). The most successful pair have been Roberto Elias (Argentina) (b. 15 Dec 1918) and Juan Labat (Argentina) (b. 10 Jan 1912), who won the *Trinquete Share* four times, 1952, 1958, 1962 and 1966. Labat won a record seven world titles in all between 1952 and 1966. Riccardo Bizzozero (Argentina) (b. 25 Nov 1948) also won seven world titles in various *Trinquete* and *Frontón corto* events, 1970–82. The most wins in the long court game *Cesta Punta* is three by José Hamuy (Mexico) (1934–83), with two different partners, 1958, 1962 and 1966.

Pétanque

World Championships Winner of the most World Championships (instituted 1959) has been France with 13 titles to 1993. The women's World Championships (instituted 1988) have been won twice by Thailand, 1988 and 1990.

The highest score in 24 hours is by Chris Walker (b. 16 Jan 1942) and his son Richard (b. 26 Dec 1966) who scored a record 2109 points in 24 hours (172 games) at the Gin Trap, Ringstead, Norfolk on 24–25 Jun 1988.

Pigeon Racing

Longest flights The official British duration record (into Great Britain) is 1887 km *1173 miles* in 15 days by *C.S.O.*, owned by Rosie and Bruce of Wick, in the 1976 Palamos Race. In the 1975 Palamos Race, *The Conqueror*, owned by Alan Raeside, homed to Irvine, Strathclyde, 1625 km *1010 miles*, in 43 hr 56 min. The greatest number of flights over 1000 miles flown by one pigeon is that of *Dunning Independence*, owned by D. Smith, which annually flew from Palamos to Dunning, Perthshire, 1672 km *1039 miles*, between 1978 and 1981.

The greatest claimed homing flight by a pigeon was for one owned by the 1st Duke of Wellington (1769–1852). Released from a sailing ship off the Ichabo Islands, West Africa on 8

April, it dropped dead a mile from its loft at Nine Elms, Wandsworth, Greater London on 1 Jun 1845, 55 days later, having apparently flown an airline route of 8700km *5400 miles*, but possibly a distance of 11,250km *7000 miles* to avoid the Sahara Desert. In 1990 it was reported that a pigeon, owned by David Lloyd and George Workman of Nantyffyllon, Mid Glam, had completed a flight of 10,860km *6750 miles* from its release at Lerwick, Shetland to Shanghai, China, possibly the longest non-homing flight ever. In both cases, however, the lack of constant surveillance makes it difficult to confirm that the pigeons completed the distances unaided.

Highest speeds In level flight in windless conditions it is very doubtful if any pigeon can exceed 96km/h *60 mph*. The highest race speed recorded is one of 2952m *3229 yd* per min (177.14km/h *110.07 mph*) in the East Anglian Federation race from East Croydon, Surrey on 8 May 1965 when the 1428 birds were backed by a powerful south-south-west wind. The winner was owned by A. Vigeon & Son, Wickford, Essex.

The highest race speed recorded over a distance of more than 1000km *621.37 miles* is 2224.5m *2432.7 yd* per min (133.46km/h *82.93 mph*) by a hen in the Central Cumberland Combine race over 1099.316km *683 miles 147 yd* from Murray Bridge, South Australia to North Ryde, Sydney on 2 Oct 1971.

Career records The greatest competitive distance flown is 32,318km *20,082 miles* by *Nunnies*, a chequer cock owned by Terry Haley of Abbot's Langley, Herts.

Mass release The largest ever simultaneous release of pigeons was at Orleans, France in August 1988 when over 215,000 pigeons were released for a Dutch National race. In Great Britain the largest liberation was at Beachy Head near Eastbourne, E Sussex on 11 May 1991 when 42,500 birds were released for the Save The Children Fund Eastbourne Classic.

Cheep!

The highest sum paid is £110,800 to Jan Herman of Waalre, Netherlands in July 1992 by Louella Pigeon World of Markfield, Leics for a four-year old cock bird, winner of the 1992 Barcelona International race, and subsequently named *Invincible Spirit*.

Polo

Most titles The British Open Championship for the Cowdray Park Gold Cup (instituted 1956) has been won five times by, Stowell Park, 1973–4, 1976, 1978 and 1980, and Tramontana, 1986–9, 1991.

Highest handicap The highest handicap based on six 7½ min 'chukkas' is ten goals introduced in the USA in 1891 and in the UK and in Argentina in 1910. A total of 56 players have received ten-goal handicaps and there are ten currently playing in Britain, two Mexican and eight Argentinians. The last (of six) ten-goal handicap players from the UK was Gerald Balding in 1939.

The highest handicaps of current UK players is eight by Howard Hipwood (b. 24 Mar 1950) who, however had a handicap of nine in 1992. Claire J. Tomlinson of Gloucestershire attained a handicap of five, the highest ever by a woman, in 1986.

A match of two 40-goal teams has been staged on three occasions at Palermo, Buenos Aires, Argentina in 1975, in the USA in 1990 and Australia in 1991.

Polo is played on the largest playing area of any sport.
(Photo: Allsport/Simon Bruty)

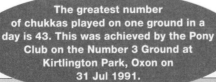

The greatest number of chukkas played on one ground in a day is 43. This was achieved by the Pony Club on the Number 3 Ground at Kirtlington Park, Oxon on 31 Jul 1991.

GUESS WHAT?

Q Where is the world's largest swimming pool?
A See Page 292

Highest score The highest aggregate number of goals scored in an international match is 30, when Argentina beat the USA 21–9 at Meadowbrook, Long Island, New York, USA in September 1936.

Pool

Pool or championship pocket billiards with numbered balls began to become standardized *c.* 1890. The greatest exponents were Ralph Greenleaf (USA) (1899–1950), who won the 'world' professional title 19 times (1919–37), and William Mosconi (USA) (1913–93), who dominated the game from 1941 to 1956.

The longest consecutive run in an American straight pool match is 625 balls by Michael Eufemia at Logan's Billiard Academy, Brooklyn, New York, USA on 2 Feb 1960, although this was not officially recognized. The official best is 526 by Willie Mosconi at Springfield, Ohio, USA in March 1954. The greatest number of balls pocketed in 24 hours is 16,125 by James Abel at White Plains, New York, USA on 17–18 Dec 1991.

The record times for potting all 15 balls in a speed competition are: (men) 37.9 sec by Rob McKenna at Blackpool, Lancs on 7 Nov 1987 and (women) 44.5 sec by Susan Thompson at Shrublands Community Centre, Gorleston, Norfolk on 20 Apr 1990.

Powerboat Racing

APBA Gold Cup The American Power Boat Association (APBA) was formed in 1903 and held its first Gold Cup on the Hudson River, New York, USA in 1904. The most wins is nine Chip Hanauer (USA), 1982–8, 1992–3. The highest average speed for the race is 143.176 mph *230.413 km/h* by Tom D'Eath (USA), piloting *Miss Budweiser* in 1990.

Cowes to Torquay This race was instituted in 1961 and at first was run from Cowes to Torquay, but from 1968 included the return journey, for a distance of 320.4km *199 miles*. The most wins is four by Renato della Valle (Italy), 1982–5. The highest average speed is 138.24km/h *85.89 mph* by Fabio Fuzzi (Italy), piloting *Cesa* in 1988.

Longest races The longest offshore race has been the Port Richborough London to Monte Carlo Marathon Offshore international event. The race extended over 4742km *2947 miles* in 14 stages from 10–25 Jun 1972. It was won by *H.T.S.* (GB) driven by Mike Bellamy, Eddie Chater and Jim Brooker in 71hr 35min 56sec for an average of 66.24km/h *41.15 mph*. The longest circuit race is the 24-hour race held annually since 1962 on the River Seine at Rouen, France.

The fastest crossing from Ambrose Light Tower, New Jersey/New York, USA to Bishop Rock Light, Isles of Scilly, Cornwall is 2 days 14 hr 7 min 47 seconds by *Gentry Eagle*, skippered by Tom Gentry (USA) on 24–27 Jul 1989.

Projectiles

Throwing The greatest distance that any object has been propelled by human power is 1871.84m *6141ft 2in*, in the case of an arrow shot by Harry Drake (USA) (b. 7 May 1915), using a crossbow at the 'Smith Creek' Flight Range near Austin, Nevada, USA on 30 Jul 1988.

The longest independently authenticated throw of any inert object heavier than air is 383.13m *1257ft*, for a flying ring, by Scott Zimmerman on 8 Jul 1986 at Fort Funston, California, USA.

Boomerang throwing The greatest number of consecutive two-handed catches is 801, by Stéphane Marguerite (France, now Canada) on 26 Nov 1989 at Lyon, France.

The longest out-and-return distance is one of 149.12m *489ft 3in*, by Michel Dufayard (France) on 5 Jul 1992 at Shrewsbury, Shrops.

Greatest distances achieved with other miscellaneous objects:

Brick 44.54m *146ft 1in*
(standard 2.27kg *5lb* building brick)
Geoff Capes at Braybrook School, Orton Goldhay, Cambs on 19 Jul 1978.

Egg (fresh hen's)............98.51m *323ft 2½in*
(without breaking it)
Johnny Dell Foley to Keith Thomas at Jewett, Texas, USA on 12 Nov 1978.

Gumboot ('Wellie wanging', using a size 8 Challenger Dunlop boot)
Men 56.70m *186ft 0in*
Olav Jensen at Fagernes, Norway on 10 Jul 1988.
Women...............................40.70m *133ft 6in*
Mette Bergmann at Fagernes, Norway on 10 Jul 1988.
UK Men..............................52.73m *173ft 0in*
Tony Rodgers at London on 9 Sep 1978.
UK Women 39.60m *129ft 11in*
Rosemary Payne at Birmingham, W Mids on 21 Jun 1975.

Haggis 55.11m *180ft 10in*
(minimum weight 680g *1lb 8oz*)
Alan Pettigrew at Inchmurrin, Loch Lomond, Strathclyde on 24 May 1984.

Rolling pin 53.47m *175ft 5in*
(907g *2lb*)
Lori La Deane Adams at Iowa State Fair, Iowa, USA on 21 Aug 1979.

Slinging 477.10m *1565ft 4in*
(using a 127cm *50in* long sling and a 62g *2¼oz* dart)
David P. Engvall at Baldwin Lake, California, USA on 13 Sep 1992.

Spear throwing.............194.67m *638ft 8in*
(using an atlatl or hand-held device which fits onto a short spear)
Wayne Brian at Fairplay, Colorado, USA on 11 Jul 1992.

The longest flight duration (with self-catch) is one of 2min 59.94sec by Dennis Joyce (USA) at Bethlehem, Pennsylvania, USA on 25 Jun 1987.

Robert Parkins (USA) caught 75 boomerang throws in 5 min at Amherst, Massachusetts, USA on 9 Aug 1992.

The juggling record—the number of consecutive catches with two boomerangs, keeping at least one boomerang aloft at all times—is 502, by Chet Snouffer (USA) at Geneva, Switzerland on 22 Aug 1992.

Flying disc throwing (formerly Frisbee) The World Flying Disc Federation distance records are: (men) 197.38 m *647ft 7in*, by Niclas Bergehamn (Sweden) on 11 Aug 1993 at Linköping, Sweden; (women) 130.09 m *426ft 10in*, by Amy Bekken (US) on 25 Jun 1990 at La Habra, California, USA.

The throw, run and catch records are: (men) 92.64m *303ft 11in*, by Hiroshi Oshima (Japan) on 20 Jul 1988 at San Francisco, California, USA; (women) 60.02 m *196ft 11in*, by Judy Horowitz (US) on 29 Jun 1985 at La Mirada, California, USA.

The 24-hour distance records for a pair are: (men) 592.15km *367.94miles*, by Conrad Damon and Pete Fust (US) on 24–25 Apr 1993 at San Marino, California, USA; (women) 186.12km *115.65miles*, by Jo Cahow and Amy Berard (US) on 30–31 Dec 1979 at Pasadena, California, USA.

The records for maximum time aloft are: (men) 16.72sec, by Don Cain (US) on 26 May 1984 at Philadelphia, Pennsylvania, USA; (women) 11.81sec, by Amy Bekken (US) on 1 Aug 1991 at Santa Cruz, California, USA.

Racketball

World Championships Instituted in 1981, held biennially since 1984 and based on the US version of the game (racquetball), the USA has won all six team titles, 1981, 1984, 1986 (tie with Canada), 1988, 1990 and 1992. The most singles titles won is two by: (men) Egan Inoue (USA), 1986 and 1990, and; (women) Cindy Baxter (USA), 1981 and 1986, and Heather Stupp (Canada), 1988 and 1990.

Britain The British Racketball Association was formed and staged inaugural British National Championships in 1984. Five titles have been won in the women's event by Elizabeth 'Bett' Dryhurst (b. 26 Nov 1945), 1985–7, 1989 and 1991.

Cow pat!

The record distances in the country sport of throwing dried cow pats or 'chips' depend on whether or not the projectile may be 'moulded into a spherical shape'. The greatest distance achieved under the 'non-sphericalisation and 100 per cent organic' rule (established in 1970) is 81.1m *266ft*, by Steve Urner at the Mountain Festival, Tehachapi, California, USA on 14 Aug 1981.

Rackets

World Championships Of the 22 world champions since 1820, the longest reign is by Geoffrey Willoughby Thomas Atkins (b. 20 Jan 1927) who gained the title by beating the professional James Dear (1910–81) in 1954, and held it until retiring, after defending it four times, in April 1972.

Most Amateur titles Since the Amateur Singles Championship was instituted in 1888 the most titles won by an individual is nine by: Edgar Maximilian Baerlein (1879–1971) between 1903 and 1923; and William Robin Boone (b. 12 Jul 1950) between 1976 and 1993.

Since the institution of the Amateur Doubles Championship in 1890 the most shares in titles has been eleven by: David Sumner Milford (1905–84), between 1938 and 1959; and John Ross Thompson (b. 10 May 1918), between 1948 and 1966; they won ten titles together. Milford also won seven Amateur Singles titles (1930–51), an Open title (1936) and held the World title from 1937 to 1946. Thompson additionally won an Open Singles title and five Amateur Singles titles.

Real/Royal Tennis

Most titles *World* The first recorded world tennis champion was Clergé (France) *c.*1740. Jacques Edmond Barre (France) (1802–73) held the title for a record 33years from 1829 to 1862. Pierre Etchebaster (1893–1980), a Basque, holds the record for the greatest number of successful defences of the title with eight between 1928 and 1952.

The Women's World Championships (instituted 1985) has been won twice by: Judith Anne Clarke (Australia) (b. 28 Dec 1954), 1985 and 1987; and Penny Lumley (*née* Fellows) (GB), 1989 and 1991.

British The Amateur Championship of the British Isles (instituted 1888) has been won 16 times by Howard Rea Angus (b. 25 Jun 1944) 1966–80 and 1982. He also won eight Amateur Doubles Championships with David Warburg (1923–1987), 1967–70, 1972–4 and 1976, and was world champion 1976–81.

The oldest of the surviving active courts in Great Britain is that at Falkland Palace, Fife built by King James V of Scotland in 1539. It is the only known example of a *jeu quarre* court.

Rodeo

The largest rodeo in the world is the National Finals Rodeo, organized by the Professional Rodeo Cowboys Association (PRCA) and the Women's Professional Rodeo Association (WPRA). The 1990 Finals had a paid attendance of 171,368 for ten performances. In 1990 a record $2.3million in prize money was offered for the event, staged in Las Vegas.

GUESS WHAT?
Q How old is the oldest horse?
A See Page 31

Cervi Rodeo Company, received a record six PRCA saddle bronc of the year awards, 1966–9, 1971–2.

Bareback riding Joe Alexander of Cora, Wyoming, scored 93 out of a possible 100 on *Marlboro* at Cheyenne, Wyoming in 1974. *Sippin' Velvet*, owned by Bernis Johnson, has been awarded a record five PRCA bareback horse of the year titles between 1978 and 1987.

Roller Skating

Most titles *Speed* The most world speed titles won is 18 by two women: Alberta Vianello (Italy), eight track and ten road 1953–65; and Annie Lambrechts (Belgium), one track and 17 road 1964–81, at distances from 500m to 10,000m.

The most British national individual men's titles have been won by Michael Colin McGeogh (b. 30 Mar 1946) with 19 in 1966–85. Chloe Ronaldson (b. 30 Nov 1939) won 40 individual and 14 team women's senior titles from 1958 to 1985.

Figure The records for figure titles are: (men) five by Karl Heinz Losch (West Germany), 1958–9, 1961–2 and 1966; and Sandro Guerra (Italy), 1987–9 and 1991–2; (women) five by Rafaella del Vinaccio (Italy), 1988–92. The most world pair titles is six by Tammy Jeru (USA), 1983–6 (with John Arishita), 1990–91 (with Larry McGrew).

Speed skating The fastest speed put up in an official world record is 44.20 km/h *27.46 mph* when Luca Antoniel (Italy) (b. 12 Feb 1968) recorded 24.678 sec for 300m on a road at Bello, Colombia on 15 Nov 1990. The women's record is 40.30 km/h *25.04 mph* by Marisa Canofoglia (Italy) (b. 30 Sep 1965) for 300m on the road at Grenoble, France on 27 Aug 1987. The world records for 10,000m on a road or track are: (men) 14 min 55.64 sec, Giuseppe de Persio (Italy) (b. 3 Jun 1959) at Gujan-Mestras, France on 1 Aug 1988; (women) 15 min 58.022 sec, Marisa Canofoglia (Italy) at Grenoble, France on 30 Aug 1987.

Largest rink The greatest indoor rink ever to operate was located in the Grand Hall, Olympia, London. Opened in 1890 and closed in 1912, it had an actual skating area of 6300m² *68,000 ft²*. The current largest is the main arena of 3250m² *34,981 ft²* at Guptill Roll-Arena, Boght Corner, New York, USA. The total rink area is 3844m² *41,380 ft²*.

Skateboarding The highest speed recorded on a skateboard is 126.12 km/h *78.37 mph* in a prone position by Roger Hickey, 32, on a course near Los Angeles, California, USA on 15 Mar 1990.

The stand-up record is 89.20 km/h *55.43 mph*, also achieved by Roger Hickey, at San Demas, California, USA on 3 Jul 1990.

Tony Alva, 19, set a long jump record of 5.18m *17 ft* in clearing 17 barrels at the World Professional Skateboard Championships held at Long Beach, also in California, on 25 Sep 1977.

The high-jump record is 1.67m *5 ft 5¾ in* by Trevor Baxter (b. 1 Oct 1962) of Burgess Hill, E Sussex at Grenoble, France on 14 Sep 1982.

Roller Hockey

England won the first World Championships, 1936–9, since when Portugal has won most titles with 14 between 1947 and 1993. Portugal also won a record 17 European (instituted 1926) titles between 1947 and 1992.

Rowing

The earliest established sculling race is the Doggett's Coat and Badge, which was first rowed on 1 Aug 1716 from London Bridge to Chelsea as a race for apprentices, and is still contested annually.

Most Olympic medals Seven oarsmen have won three gold medals: John Brenden Kelly (USA) (1889–1960), father of the late HSH Princess Grace of Monaco, single sculls (1920) and double sculls (1920 and 1924); his cousin Paul Vincent Costello (USA) (1894–1986), double sculls (1920, 1924 and 1928); Jack Beresford Jr (GB) (1899–1977), single sculls (1924), coxless fours (1932) and double sculls (1936), Vyacheslav

---

Ty Murray, the youngest winner of the All-around world rodeo title, showing the poise and balance of a champion bull rider.
(Photo: Allsport USA/Ken Levine)

Most world titles The record number of all-around titles (awarded to the leading money winner in a single season in two or more events) in the PRCA World Championships is six by Larry Mahan (USA) (b. 21 Nov 1943) in 1966–70 and 1973 and, consecutively, 1974–9 by Tom Ferguson (b. 20 Dec 1950). Roy Cooper (b. 13 Nov 1955) has record career earnings of $1,476,108, 1975–93. Jim Shoulders (b. 13 May 1928) of Henrietta, Texas won a record 16 World Championships at four events between 1949 and 1959.

The youngest winner of a world title is Anne Lewis (b. 1 Sep 1958), who won the WPRA barrel racing title in 1968, at 10 years old. Ty Murray is the youngest cowboy to win the PRCA All-Around Champion title, aged 20, in 1989.

The record figure for prize money in a single season is $297,896 by Ty Murray (b. 11 Oct 1969) in 1993. He also holds the record for a single rodeo, $101,243 ($34,227 saddle bronc riding, $43,659 bareback riding, $23,357 bull riding) at the 1991 National Finals Rodeo.

Damian Magee roller skated from Land's End to John o' Groats in 9 days 5 hr 23 min from 19–28 Jun 1992. The fastest time by a woman was 12 days 4 hr 15 min by Cheryl Fisher, 17, from 19 Sep–1 Oct 1987.

Bull riding Jim Sharp (b. 6 Oct 1965) of Kermit, Texas became the first rider to ride all ten bulls at a National Finals Rodeo at Las Vegas in December 1988. This feat was repeated by Norm Curry of Deberry, Texas at the 1990 National Finals. The highest score in bull riding was 100 points out of a possible 100 by Wade Leslie on Wolfman Skoal at Central Point, Oregon, USA in 1991.

The top bucking bull *Red Rock* dislodged 312 riders, 1980–88, and was finally ridden to the eight-second bell by Lane Frost (1963–89) (world champion bull rider 1987) on 20 May 1988. *Red Rock* had retired at the end of the 1987 season but still continued to make guest appearances.

Saddle bronc riding The highest scored saddle bronc ride is 95 out of a possible 100 by Doug Vold on *Transport* at Meadow Lake, Saskatchewan, Canada in 1979. *Descent*, a saddle bronc owned by Beutler Brothers and

Eleftherios Argiropoulos covered a record 436.6 km *271.3 miles* on a skateboard in 36 hr 33 min 17 sec at Ekali, Greece on 4–5 Nov 1993.

Steven Redgrave has won a British record seven World titles, including a world record-equalling three Olympic golds.
(Photo: Allsport/Bob Martin)

Nikolayevich Ivanov (USSR) (b. 30 Jul 1938), single sculls (1956, 1960 and 1964); Siegfried Brietzke (GDR) (b. 12 Jun 1952), coxless pairs (1972) and coxless fours (1976, 1980); Pertti Karppinen (Finland) (b. 17 Feb 1953), single sculls (1976, 1980 and 1984); and Steven Redgrave (GB) (b. 23 Mar 1962), coxed fours (1984), coxless pairs (1988 and 1992).

World Championships
World rowing championships distinct from the Olympic Games were first held in 1962, at first four yearly, but from 1974 annually, except in Olympic years.

The most gold medals won at World Championships and Olympic Games is nine at coxed pairs by the Italian brothers Giuseppe (b. 24 Jul 1959) and Carmine (b. 5 Jan 1962) Abbagnale, World 1981–2, 1985, 1987, 1989–91, Olympics 1984 and 1988. At women's events Yelena Tereshina (b. 6 Feb 1959) has won a record seven golds, all eights for the USSR, 1978–9, 1981–3 and 1985–6.

The most wins at single sculls is five by: Peter-Michael Kolbe (West Germany) (b. 2 Aug 1953), 1975, 1978, 1981, 1983 and 1986; Pertti Karppinen, 1979 and 1985 with his three Olympic wins (above); Thomas Lange, 1987, 1989 and 1991 and two Olympics 1988 and 1992; and in the women's events by Christine Hahn (*née* Scheiblich) (GDR) (b. 31 Dec 1954), 1974–5, 1977–8 (and the 1976 Olympic title).

Longest!

The longest annual rowing race is the annual Tour du Lac Leman, Geneva, Switzerland for coxed fours (the five-man crew taking turns as cox) over 160 km *99 miles*. The record winning time is 12 hr 52 min by LAGA Delft, Netherlands on 3 Oct 1982.

Boat Race The earliest University Boat Race, which Oxford won, was from Hambledon Lock to Henley Bridge on 10 Jun 1829. Outrigged eights were first used in 1846. In the 140 races to 1994, Cambridge won 71 times, Oxford 68 times and there was a dead heat on 24 Mar 1877.

The race record time for the course of 6.779 km *4 miles 374 yd* (Putney to Mortlake) is 16 min 45 sec by Oxford on 18 Mar 1984. This represents an average speed of 24.28 km/h *15.09 mph*. The smallest winning margin has been by a canvas by Oxford in 1952 and 1980. The greatest margin (apart from sinking) was Cambridge's win by 20 lengths in 1900.

Boris Rankov (Oxford, 1978–83) rowed in a record six winning boats. Susan Brown (b. 29 Jun 1958), the first woman to take part, coxed the winning Oxford boats in 1981 and 1982. Daniel Topolski coached Oxford to ten successive victories, 1976–85.

The tallest man ever to row in a University boat has been Gavin Stewart (Wadham, Oxford) (b. 25

Walking!

Rémy Bricka of Paris, France 'walked' across the Atlantic Ocean on skis 4.2 m *13 ft 9 in* long in 1988. Leaving Tenerife, Canary Islands on 2 Apr 1988, he covered 5636 km *3502 miles*, arriving at Trinidad on 31 May 1988.

He also set a speed record of 7 min 7.41 sec for 1 km *1094 yd* on the Olympic pool in Montréal, Canada on 2 Aug 1989. He 'walks on water' by having ski-floats attached to his feet and by moving in the same way as in cross-country skiing, using a double-headed paddle instead of ski-poles.

Feb 1963) at 2.04 m *6 ft 8½ in* in 1987–8. The heaviest was Christopher Heathcote (b. March 1963), the Oxford No. 6, who weighed 110 kg *243 lb* in 1990. The lightest oarsman was the 1882 Oxford Stroke, Alfred Herbert Higgins, at 60 kg *9 st 6½ lb*.

The lightest coxes, Francis Henry Archer (Cambridge) (1843–89) in 1862 and Hart Parker Vincent Massey (Oxford) (b. Canada, 30 Mar 1918) in 1939, were both 32.6 kg *5 st 2 lb*.

The youngest 'blue' ever was Matthew John Brittin (Cambridge) (b. 1 Sep 1968) at 18 yr 208 days, in 1986.

Head of the River A processional race for eights instituted in 1926, the Head has an entry limit of 420 crews (3780 competitors). The record for the course Mortlake–Putney (the reverse of the Boat Race) is 16 min 37 sec by the ARA National Squad in 1987.

Henley Royal Regatta The annual regatta at Henley-on-Thames, Oxon was inaugurated on 26 Mar 1839. Since then the course, except in 1923, has been about 2112 m *1 mile 550 yd*, varying slightly according to the length of boat. In 1967 the shorter craft were 'drawn up' so all bows start level.

The most wins in the Diamond Challenge Sculls (instituted 1844) is six by Guy Nickalls (GB) (1866–1935), 1888–91, 1893–4 and consecutively by Stuart Alexander Mackenzie (Australia and GB) (b. 5 Apr 1937), 1957–62. The record time is 7 min 23 sec by Vaclav Chalupa (Czechoslovakia) (b. 7 Dec 1967) on 2 Jul 1989. The record time for the Grand Challenge Cup (instituted 1839) event is 5 min 58 sec by Hansa Dortmund, West Germany on 2 Jul 1989.

24 hours The greatest distance rowed in 24 hours (upstream and downstream) is 227.33 km *141.26 miles* by six members of Dittons Skiff and Punting Club on the River Thames between Hampton Court and Teddington, Greater London on 3–4 Jun 1994.

Cross-Channel Ivor Lloyd sculled across the English Channel in a record 3 hr 35 min 1 sec on 4 May 1983.

River Thames Five members of the Lower Thames Rowing Club, Gravesend rowed the navigable length of the Thames, 299.14 km *185.88 miles*, from Lechlade Bridge, Glos to Southend Pier, Essex in 38 hr 43 min 20 sec from 8–9 May 1993. The fastest time from Folly Bridge, Oxford to Westminster Bridge, London (180 km *112 miles*) is 14 hr 25 min 15 sec by an eight from Kingston Rowing Club on 1 Feb 1986.

International Dragon Boat Races Instituted in 1975 and held annually in Hong Kong, the fastest time achieved for the 640 m *700 yd* course is 2 min 27.45 sec by the Chinese Shun De team on 30 Jun 1985. The best time for a British team was 2 min

36.40 sec by the Kingston Royals crew on 3 Jun 1990. Teams have 28 members—26 rowers, one steersman and one drummer.

Rugby League

There have been four different scoring systems in Rugby League football. For the purpose of these records all points totals remain as they were under the system in operation at the time they were made.

World Cup There have been nine World Cup Competitions. Australia have the most wins, with six, 1957, 1968, 1970, 1977, 1988 and 1992 as well as a win in the International Championship of 1975.

Most titles The Northern Rugby League was formed in 1901. The word 'Northern' was dropped in 1980. Wigan have won the League Championship a record 15 times (1909, 1922, 1926, 1934, 1946–7, 1950, 1952, 1960, 1987, 1990–94).

The Rugby League Challenge Cup (inaugurated 1896/7 season) has been won a record 15 times by Wigan, 1924, 1929, 1948, 1951, 1958–9, 1965, 1985, 1988–94.

There are four major competitions for RL clubs: Challenge Cup, League Championship, Premiership and Regal Trophy (formerly John Player Special Trophy). In 1990 these were officially called the 'Grand Slam' and as yet no club has achieved this.

Three clubs have won all possible major Rugby League trophies in one season: Hunslet, 1907/8 season, Huddersfield, 1914/15 and Swinton, 1927/8, all won the Challenge Cup, League Championship, County Cup and County League (last two now defunct).

Francis Cummins is the youngest player to have appeared in a Challenge Cup final. Despite being on the losing side, he had the pleasure of scoring a consolation try towards the end of the match.

(Photo: Allsport/David Rodgers)

Highest Scores

Senior match The highest aggregate score in a game where a senior club has been concerned was 121 points, when Huddersfield beat Swinton Park Rangers by 119 (19 goals, 27 tries) to 2 (one goal) in the first round of the Northern Union Cup on 28 Feb 1914. The highest score in League football is 102 points by Leeds *v.* Coventry (nil) on 12 Apr 1913. St Helens beat Carlisle 112–0 in the Lancashire Cup on 14 Sep 1986. In the Yorkshire Cup Hull Kingston Rovers beat Nottingham City 100–6 on 19 Aug 1990. The highest score in the First Division is 90 points by Leeds *v.* Barrow (nil) on 11 Feb 1990. The highest scoring draw is 46–46 between Sheffield Eagles and Leeds on 10 Apr 1994

> Leigh scored a record 1436 points (258 tries, 199 goals, 6 drop goals) in the 1985/6 season, playing in 43 Cup and League games.

Challenge Cup Final The highest score in a Challenge Cup final is 38 points (8 tries, 7 goals) by Wakefield Trinity *v.* Hull (5) at Wembley, London on 14 May 1960. The record aggregate is 52 points when Wigan beat Hull 28–24 at Wembley on 4 May 1985. The greatest winning margin was 34 points when Huddersfield beat St Helens 37–3 at Oldham, Greater Manchester on 1 May 1915.

International match The highest score in an international match is Great Britain's 72–6 defeat of France in a Test match at Headingley, Leeds, W Yorks on 2 Apr 1993.

Touring teams The record score for a British team touring Australasia is 101 points by England *v.* South Australia (nil) at Adelaide in May 1914. The record for a touring team in Britain is 92 (10 goals, 24 tries) by Australia against Bramley 7 (2 goals and 1 try) at the Barley Mow Ground, Bramley, near Leeds on 9 Nov 1921.

Highest Individual Scores

Most points, goals and tries in a game George Henry 'Tich' West (1882–1927) scored 53 points (10 goals and a record 11 tries) for Hull Kingston Rovers (73) in a Challenge Cup tie *v.* Brookland Rovers (5) on 4 Mar 1905.

The record for a League match is 42 (4 tries, 13 goals) by Dean John Marwood (b. 22 Feb 1970) in Workington Town's 78–0 win over Highfield on 1 Nov 1992.

The most goals in a Cup match is 22 kicked by James 'Jim' Sullivan (1903–77) for Wigan *v.* Flimby and Fothergill on 14 Feb 1925. The most goals in a League match is 15 by Michael Stacey (b. 9 Feb 1953) for Leigh *v.* Doncaster on 28 Mar 1976. The most tries in a League match is ten by Lionel Cooper (b. Australia, 1922–87) for Huddersfield *v.* Keighley on 17 Nov 1951.

Most points *Season and career* The record number of points in a season was 496 by

Benjamin Lewis Jones (Leeds) (b. 11 Apr 1931), 194 goals, 36 tries, in 1956/7.

Neil Fox (b. 4 May 1939) scored 6220 points (2575 goals including 4 drop goals, 358 tries) in a senior Rugby League career from 10 Apr 1956 to 19 Aug 1979, consisting of 4488 for Wakefield Trinity, 1089 for five other clubs, 228 for Great Britain, 147 for Yorkshire and 268 in other representative games.

Most tries *Season and career* Albert Aaron Rosenfeld (1885– 1970) (Huddersfield), an Australian-born wing-threequarter, scored 80 tries in 42 matches in the 1913/14 season.

Brian Bevan (Australia) (1924–91), a wing-threequarter, scored 796 tries in 18 seasons (16 with Warrington, two with Blackpool Borough) from 1945 to 1964. He scored 740 for Warrington, 17 for Blackpool and 39 in representative matches.

Most goals *Season and career* The record number of goals in a season is 221, in 47 matches, by David Watkins (b. 5 Mar 1942) (Salford) in the 1972/3 season.

Jim Sullivan (Wigan) kicked 2867 goals in his club and representative career, 1921– 46.

Most consecutive scores David Watkins (Salford) played and scored in every club game during seasons 1972/3 and 1973/4, contributing 41 tries and 403 goals—a total of 929 points, in 92 games.

Individual international records Jim Sullivan (Wigan) played in most internationals (60 for Wales and Great Britain, 1921–39), kicked most goals (160) and scored most points (329).

Michael Sullivan (no kin) (b. 12 Jan 1934) of Huddersfield, Wigan, St Helens, York and Dewsbury played in 51 international games for England and Great Britain and scored a record 45 tries, 1954–63.

Michael O'Connor (b. 30 Nov 1960) scored a record 30 points (4 tries, 7 goals) for Australia *v.* Papua New Guinea at Wagga Wagga, Australia on 20 Jul 1988.

Most Challenge Cup finals The most appearances is nine by Shaun Edwards (b. 17 Oct 1966), Wigan, 1984–5, 1988–94. He was on the winning side eight times (all but 1984). During his career at Wigan, 1983–94, Edwards received 33 winners' or runners-up medals in major competitions.

Youngest and oldest players Harold Spencer Edmondson (1903–82) played his first League game for Bramley at 15yr 81days. The youngest representative player was Harold Wagstaff (1891–1939) who played for Yorkshire at 17yr 141days, and for England at 17yr 228days.

The youngest player in a Cup final was Francis Cummins (b. 12 Oct 1976) at 17yr 200days for Leeds when they lost 16–26 to Wigan at Wembley on 30 Apr 1994.

Shaun Edwards is the most successful player in British rugby league history, winning 33 winners or runners-up medals in his career.
(Photo: Allsport/Mike Hewitt)

> Martin Offiah (b. 29 Dec 1966) became the costliest transferred player on 3 Jan 1992 when Wigan paid Widnes a fee of £440,000.

The youngest Great Britain international is Paul Newlove (b. 10 Aug 1971) who played in the first Test *v.* New Zealand on 21 Oct 1989 at Old Trafford, Greater Manchester, aged 18yr 72days. The oldest player for Great Britain was Jeffrey Grayshon (b. 4 Mar 1949) at 36yr 250days *v.* New Zealand at Elland Road, Leeds on 9 Nov 1985.

Most durable player The most appearances for one club is 774 by Jim Sullivan for Wigan, 1921– 46. He played a record 928 first-class games in all. The longest continuous playing career is that of Augustus John 'Gus' Risman (b. 21 Mar 1911), who played his first game for Salford on 31 Aug 1929 and his last for Batley on 27 Dec 1954.

Keith Elwell (b. 12 Feb 1950) played in 239 consecutive games for Widnes from 5 May 1977 to 5 Sep 1982.

Most and least successful teams Wigan won 31 consecutive league games from February 1970 to February 1971. Huddersfield were undefeated for 40 league and cup games in 1913/14. Hull is the only club to win all League games in a season, 26 in Division II 1978/9. Runcorn Highfield holds the record of losing 55 consecutive League games from 29 Jan 1989 to 27 Jan

---

Kicks!

Arthur Atkinson (1908–63) (Castleford) kicked a penalty from his own 25-yard line, a distance of 75yd *68m* in a League game at St Helens on 26 Oct 1929.

The longest drop goal is 61yd *56m* by Joseph Paul 'Joe' Lydon (b. 22 Nov 1963) for Wigan against Warrington in a Challenge Cup semi-final at Maine Road, Manchester on 25 Mar 1989.

Tries!

Simon Haughton (b. 10 Nov 1975) scored 130 tries, including nine in one game, from the prop-forward position for the Bingley under-14 side, W Yorks in the 1989/90 season.

1991. The run was ended with a 12–12 draw with Carlisle on 3 Feb 1991.

Greatest crowds The greatest attendance at any Rugby League match is 102,569 for the Warrington *v.* Halifax Challenge Cup final replay at Odsal Stadium, Bradford on 5 May 1954.

The record attendance for any international match is 73,631 for the World Cup Final between Australia and Great Britain at Wembley Stadium, London on 24 Oct 1992.

Amateur Rugby League

National Cup Pilkington Recreation (St Helens, Merseyside) have won the National Cup four times (1975, 1979, 1980, 1982). John McCabe (b. 26 Jan 1952) has played in a record five National Cup finals, winning on each occasion. He played for Pilkington Recreation in each of their four successes and captained Thatto Heath (St Helens, Merseyside) to victory in 1987.

Highest score *Major competitions* Humberside beat Carlisle by 138 points to nil in the second round of the National Inter-league Competition on 20 Oct 1984.

GUESS WHAT?

Q What is the highest individual score in first-class cricket?

A See Page 241

Rugby Union

Records are based on the scoring system in use at the time.

World Cup

The World Cup has been held on two occasions, 1987 and 1991, with the winners being New Zealand and Australia respectively. The highest team score is New Zealand's 74–13 victory over Fiji at Christchurch on 27 May 1987 when they scored ten goals, two tries and two penalty goals. The individual match record is 30 (3 tries, 9 conversions) by Didier Camberabero (France) (b. 9 Jan 1961) *v.* Zimbabwe at Auckland on 2 Jun 1987. The leading scorer in the tournament is Grant James Fox (New Zealand) (b. 6 Jun 1962), with 170 points (including a record 126 in 1987).

International Championship

The International Championship was first contested by England, Ireland, Scotland and Wales in 1884. France first played in 1910.

Wales has won a record 21 times outright and tied for first a further 11 times to 1988. The most Grand Slams, winning all four matches, is ten by England 1913–14, 1921, 1923–4, 1928, 1957, 1980 and 1991–2.

Highest team score The highest score in an International Championship match was set at Swansea on 1 Jan 1910 when Wales beat France 49–14 (8 goals, 1 penalty goal, 2 tries, to 1 goal, 2 penalty goals, 1 try).

Season's scoring Jonathon Webb scored a record 67 points (3 tries, 11 penalty goals, 11 conversions) in the four games of an International Championship series in 1992.

Will Carling has captained England a world record 42 times, 1988–94, and in that time England have won 31 games.
(Photo: Allsport/David Rogers)

During this series, England scored a record 118 points in their four games

Individual match records John 'Jack' Bancroft (1879–1942) kicked a record nine goals (8 conversions and 1 penalty goal) for Wales *v.* France at Swansea on 1 Jan 1910. Simon Hodgkinson kicked a Championship record seven penalty goals for England *v.* Wales at Cardiff on 19 Jan 1991.

Highest Team Scores

Internationals The highest score in any full international is when Japan beat Singapore by 120–3 in the Asian Championships at Seoul, South Korea on 20 Sep 1992.

The highest aggregate score for any international match between the Four Home Unions is 82 when England beat Wales by 82 points (7 goals, 1 drop goal and 6 tries) to nil at Blackheath, London on 19 Feb 1881. (Note: there was no point scoring in 1881.) The highest aggregate score under the modern points system between IRFB members is 79, when Australia beat France 48–31 at Ballymore, Brisbane, Australia on 24 Jun 1990.

The highest score by any overseas side in an international in the British Isles is 51 points by New Zealand against Scotland (15) at Murrayfield, Edinburgh on 20 Nov 1993.

Match In Denmark, Comet beat Lindo by 194–0 on 17 Nov 1973. The highest British score is 174–0 by 7th Signal Regiment *v.* 4th Armoured Workshop, REME, on 5 Nov 1980 at Herford,

Germany. Scores of over 200 points have been recorded in school matches. The highest score in the Courage Clubs Championship is 146–0 by Billingham against Hartlepool Athletic in a Durham/Northumberland Division 3 match at Billingham, Co. Durham on 3 Oct 1987.

Season The highest number of points accumulated in a season by a club is 1917 points (including a record 345 tries) in 47 games by Neath, West Glamorgan in 1988/9.

Highest Individual Scores

Internationals Phil Bennett (Wales) (b. 24 Oct 1948) scored 34 points (2 tries, 10 conversions, 2 penalty goals) for Wales v. Japan at Tokyo on 24 Sep 1975, when Wales won 82–6. The highest individual points score in any match between members of the International Board is 27 by Christopher Robert Andrew (b. 18 Feb 1963) (1 try, 2 conversions, 5 penalty goals and a drop goal) for England against South Africa at Pretoria on 4 Jun 1994.

Patrice Lagisquet (b. 4 Sep 1962) scored seven tries for France v. Paraguay on 28 Jun 1988. The most tries in an international match between IRFB members is five by George Campbell Lindsay (1863–1905) for Scotland v. Wales on 26 Feb 1887, and by Douglas 'Daniel' Lambert (1883–1915) for England v. France on 5 Jan 1907. Ian Scott Smith (Scotland) (1903–72) scored a record six consecutive international tries in 1925, comprising the last three v. France and two weeks later, the first three v. Wales. The most penalty goals kicked in a match is eight by: Mark Andrew Wyatt (b. 12 Apr 1961) when scoring all Canada's points in their 24–19 defeat of Scotland at St John, New Brunswick, Canada on 25 May 1991, and Neil Roger Jenkins (b. 8 Jul 1971) who also scored all Wales' points in their 26–24 defeat by Canada at Cardiff, S Glam on 10 Nov 1993.

Career In all internationals Michael Patrick Lynagh (b. 25 Oct 1963) scored a record 821 points in 67 matches for Australia, 1984–94. The most by a British player is 532 by Andrew Gavin Hastings (b. 3 Jan 1962), 466 for Scotland and 66 for the British Isles, 1986–94. The most tries is 59 by David Campese (b. 21 Oct 1962) in 84 internationals for Australia, 1982–94.

Season The first-class season scoring record is 581 points by Samuel Arthur Doble (1944–77) of Moseley, in 52 matches in 1971/2. He also scored 47 points for England in South Africa out of season.

Andy Higgin (b. 4 Mar 1963) scored a record 28 drop goals in a season in first-class rugby, for the Vale of Lune in 1986/7.

Career William Henry 'Dusty' Hare (b. 29 Nov 1952) scored 7337 points in first-class games from 1971–89, comprising 1800 for Nottingham, 4427 for Leicester, 240 for England, 88 for the British Isles and 782 in other representative matches.

Most tries Alan John Morley (b. 25 Jun 1950) scored 473 tries in senior rugby in 1968–86 including 378 for Bristol, a record for one club. John Huins scored 85 tries in 1953–4, 73 for St Luke's College, Exeter and 12 more for Neath and in trial games.

Match Jannie van der Westhuizen scored 80 points (14 tries, 9 conversions, 1 dropped goal, 1 penalty goal) for Carnarvon (88) v. Williston (12) at North West Cape, South Africa on 11 March 1972.

In a junior house match in February 1967 at William Ellis School, Edgware, Greater London, between Cumberland and Nunn, 12-year-old Thanos Morphitis (b. 5 Mar 1954) contributed 90 points (13 tries and 19 conversions) (77) to Cumberland's winning score.

Most international appearances Cameron Michael Henderson Gibson (b. 3 Dec 1942) played in 69 internationals for Ireland, 1964–79, a record for matches between the seven member countries of the International Rugby Football Board and France. Including 12 appearances for the British Isles, he played in a total of 81 international matches. William James 'Willie John' McBride (b. 6 Jun 1940) made a record 17 appearances for the British Isles, as well as 63 for Ireland.

Youngest international Edinburgh Academy pupils Ninian Jamieson Finlay (1858–1936) and Charles Reid (1864–1909) were both 17yr 36days old when they played for Scotland v. England in 1875 and 1881 respectively. However, as Finlay had one less leap year in his lifetime up to his first cap, the outright record must be credited to him. Semi Hekasilau Spec Taupeaafe played in a Test for Tonga against Western Samoa in 1989, aged 16.

County Championships The County Championships (instituted 1889) have been won a record 16 times by Lancashire (between 1891 and 1993). The most individual appearances is 104 by Richard Trickey (Sale) (b. 6 Mar 1945) for Lancashire between 1964 and 1978.

Club Championships The most outright wins in the RFU Club Competition (John Player Cup, 1971–87, now Pilkington Cup) is eight by Bath, 1984–7, 1989–90, 1992, 1994. The highest team score (and aggregate) in the final is for Bath's 48–6 win over Gloucester in 1990. The Courage Clubs Championship (formerly the National Merit Tables and founded in 1985) has been won six times by Bath, 1987, 1989, 1991–4.

The most wins in the Welsh Rugby Union Challenge Cup (Schweppes Welsh Cup, instituted 1971/2) is nine by Llanelli, 1973–6, 1985, 1988 and 1991–3. The highest team score in the

---

Most International Appearances

Country	Apps	Player	Years
FRANCE	101	Philippe Sella (b. 14 Feb 1962)	1982–94
AUSTRALIA	84	David Ian Campese (b. 21 Oct 1962)	1982–94
IRELAND	69	Cameron Michael Henderson Gibson (b. 3 Dec 1942)	1964–79
ENGLAND	67	Rory Underwood (b. 19 Jun 1963)	1984–94
NEW ZEALAND	60	John James Kirwan (b. 16 Dec 1964)	1984–94
WALES	55*	John Peter Rhys 'JPR' Williams (b. 2 Mar 1949)	1969–81
SCOTLAND	52	James Menzies 'Jim' Renwick (b. 12 Feb 1952)	1972–84
	52	Colin Thomas Deans (b. 3 May 1955)	1978–87
SOUTH AFRICA	38	Frederick Christoffel Hendrick Du Preez (b. 28 Nov 1935)	1960–71
	38	Jan Hendrik Ellis (b. 5 Jan 1943)	1965–76

* Gareth Owen Edwards (b. 12 Jul 1947) made a record 53 consecutive international appearances, never missing a match throughout his career for Wales, 1967–78. Willie John McBride (b. 6 Jun 1960) also had 53 consecutive appearances during his 63 games for Ireland.

Note: The criteria used to decide which games are classed as full internationals vary between countries.

The world's most prestigious international tournament for seven-a-side teams is the Hong Kong Sevens, first held in 1976. The record of seven wins is held by Fiji, 1977–8, 1980, 1984, 1990–92.

Neil Jenkins (Wales) kicking one of his record-equalling eight penalties against Canada at Cardiff on 10 Nov 1993.
(Photo: Allsport/David Rogers)

The women's World Cup has been contested twice (1991 and 1994) and the USA and England have reached the final on both occasions. The USA won in 1991 and England in 1994. Here England's scrum-half Emma Mitchell feeds the ball to the backs during the 1994 final.

(Photo: Allsport/Gary Prior)

final is 30 by Llanelli against Cardiff (7) in 1973. The highest aggregate is when Cardiff beat Newport 28–21 in 1986. Llanelli achieved the first league and cup double in Wales in 1993.

The most wins in the Scottish League Division One (instituted 1973/4) is ten by Hawick between 1973 and 1986.

Seven-a-sides Seven-a-side rugby dates from 28 Apr 1883 when Melrose RFC Borders, in order to alleviate the poverty of a club in such a small town, staged a seven-a-side tournament. The idea was that of Ned Haig, the town's butcher.

Middlesex Seven-a-sides The Middlesex Seven-a-sides were inaugurated in 1926 and have been won a record 12 times by Harlequins, 1926–9, 1933, 1935, 1967, 1978, 1986–90.

Greatest crowd The record paying attendance is 104,000 for Scotland's 12–10 win over Wales at Murrayfield, Edinburgh on 1 Mar 1975.

Longest kicks The longest recorded successful drop goal is 82m *90yd* by Gerald Hamilton

> Canadian international Barrie Burnham scored all possible ways—try, conversion, penalty goal, drop goal, goal from mark—for Meralomas v. Georgians (20–11) at Vancouver, BC on 26 Feb 1966.

'Gerry' Brand (b. 8 Oct 1906) for South Africa *v.* England at Twickenham, Greater London, on 2 Jan 1932. This was taken 6m *7yd* inside the England 'half', 50m *55yd* from the posts, and dropped over the dead ball line.

The place kick record is reputed to be 91m *100yd* at Richmond Athletic Ground, London, by Douglas Francis Theodore Morkel (1886–1950) in an unsuccessful penalty for South Africa *v.* Surrey on 19 Dec 1906. This was not measured until 1932. In the match Bridlington School 1st XV *v.* an Army XV at Bridlington, Humberside on 29 Jan 1944, Ernie Cooper (b. 21 May 1926), captaining the school, landed a penalty from a measured 74m *81yd* from the post with a kick which carried over the dead ball line. The record in an international was set at 64.22m *70yd 8½in* by Paul Huw Thorburn (b. 24 Nov 1962) for Wales *v.* Scotland on 1 Feb 1986.

Fastest try The fastest try in an international game was when Herbert Leo 'Bart' Price (1899–1943) scored for England *v.* Wales at Twickenham on 20 Jan 1923 less than 10 sec after kick-off. The fastest try in any game was scored in 8 sec by Andrew Brown for Widden Old Boys *v.* Old Ashtonians at Gloucester on 22 Nov 1990.

> The world's highest rugby union goal posts are 33.54m *110ft ½in* high at the Roan Antelope Rugby Union Club, Luanshya, Zambia. The posts at Old Halesonines RFC, Stourbridge, W Mids are 22.16m *72ft 8½in.*

> Roy Evans of Banbury played a record 1193 games of rugby union all of which were played in the front row at tight head prop. His total includes 1007 played for Osterley from 12 Sep 1950–29 Apr 1989, a record for one club.

Most successful team The Feilding senior 4ths of New Zealand played 108 successive games without defeat from 1984–9. The Chiltern mini rugby side, from their formation as an Under-8 side, played 213 games without defeat, 29 Sep 1985–8 Apr 1990.

Women's Rugby

The women's World Cup has been contested twice (1991 and 1994) and the USA and England have reached the final on both occasions. The USA won in 1991 and England in 1994.

Shinty

Most titles Newtonmore, Highland has won the Camanachd Association Challenge Cup (instituted 1896) a record 28 times, 1907–86. David Ritchie (b. 9 Jun 1944) and Hugh Chisholm (b. 14 Oct 1949) of Newtonmore, have won a record 12 winners' medals. In 1923 the Furnace Club, Argyll won the cup without conceding a goal throughout the competition.

In 1984 Kingussie Camanachd Club won all five senior competitions, including the Camanachd Cup final. This feat was equalled by Newtonmore in 1985.

Highest scores The highest Scottish Cup final score was in 1909 when Newtonmore beat Furnace 11–3 at Glasgow, Dr Johnnie Cattanach scoring eight hails or goals. In 1938 John Macmillan Mactaggart scored ten hails for Mid-Argyll in a Camanachd Cup match.

Shooting–Individual World Records

In 1986, the International Shooting Union (UIT) introduced new regulations for determining major championships and world records. Now the leading competitors undertake an additional round with a target sub-divided to tenths of a point for rifle and pistol shooting, and an extra 25 shots for trap and skeet. Harder targets have since been introduced and the table below shows the world records, as recognised by the UIT at the beginning of 1994, for the 13 Olympic shooting disciplines, giving in brackets the score for the number of shots specified plus the score in the additional round.

MEN

EVENT	Score		Name and Country	Venue	Date
FREE RIFLE 50m 3×40 shots	1287.9	(1186+101.9)	Rajmond Debevec (Slovenia)	Munich, Germany	29 Aug 1992
FREE RIFLE 50m 60 Shots Prone	703.5	(599+104.5)	Jens Harskov (Denmark)	Zürich, Switzerland	6 Jun 1991
AIR RIFLE 10m 60 shots	699.4	(596+103.4)	Rajmond Debevec (Yugoslavia)	Zürich, Switzerland	7 Jun 1990
FREE PISTOL 50m 60 shots	672.5	(575+97.5)	Sergey Pyzhyanov (Russia)	Milan, Italy	15 Jun 1993
RAPID-FIRE PISTOL 25m 60 shots	698.7	(596+102.7)	Ralf Schumann (Germany)	Munich, Germany	29 Aug 1993
AIR PISTOL 10m 60 shots	695.1	(593+102.1)	Sergey Pyzhyanov (USSR)	Munich, Germany	13 Oct 1989
RUNNING TARGET 10m 30/30 shots	679	(582+97)	Lubos Racansky (Czechoslovakia)	Munich, Germany	30 May 1991

WOMEN

EVENT	Score		Name and Country	Venue	Date
STANDARD RIFLE 50m 3×20 shots	689.3	(590+99.3)	Vessela Letcheva (Bulgaria)	Munich, Germany	28 Aug 1992
AIR RIFLE 10m 40 shots	500.8	(399+101.8)	Valentina Cherkasova (USSR)	Los Angeles, USA	23 Mar 1991
SPORT PISTOL 25m 60 shots	693	(593+100)	Nino Salukvadze (USSR)	Zagreb, Yugoslavia	13 Jul 1989
AIR PISTOL 10m 40 shots	492.4	(392+100.4)	Lieselotte Breker (West Germany)	Zagreb, Yugoslavia	18 May 1989

OPEN

EVENT	Score		Name and Country	Venue	Date
TRAP 125 targets	148	(124+24)	Giovanni Pellielo (Italy)	Fagnano, Italy	5 Jun 1993
	148	(123+25)	Marco Venturini (Netherlands)	Barcelona, Spain	15 Jun 1993
SKEET 125 targets	149	(124+25)	Dean Clark (USA)	Barcelona, Spain	20 Jun 1993

Shooting

Most Olympic medals Carl Townsend Osburn (USA) (1884–1966), in 1912, 1920 and 1924, won a record 11, five gold, four silver and two bronze. Six other marksmen have won five gold medals. The only marksman to win three individual gold medals has been Gudbrand Gudbrandsönn Skatteboe (Norway) (1875–1965) in 1906. Separate events for women were first held in 1984.

Bisley The National Rifle Association was instituted in 1859. The Queen's (King's) Prize has been shot since 1860 and has only once been won by a woman, Marjorie Elaine Foster (1894–1974) (score 280) on 19 Jul 1930. Arthur George Fulton (1887–1972) won three times (1912, 1926, 1931). Both his father and his son also won the Prize.

The highest score (possible 300) for the final of the Queen's Prize is 295. This was achieved by Lindsay Peden (Scotland) on 24 Jul 1982 and also, but on targets with a smaller bullseye, by Colin Brook (London & Middlesex RA) on 24 Jul 1993. The record for the Silver Medals is 150 (possible 150) by Martin John Brister (City Rifle Club) (b. 1951) and (Lord) John Swansea (South Wales Rifle Club) (b. 1 Jan 1925) on 24 Jul 1971. This was equalled by John Henry Carmichael (WRA Bromsgrove RC) on 28 Jul 1979 and Robert Stafford (London & Middlesex RA) on 26 Jul 1980, with the size of the bullseye reduced; and by Colin Brook on 23 Jul 1993, with the size of the bullseye reduced further.

Small Bang!

The smallest group on record at 1000yd *914m* is 4.076in *10.353cm* by Robert Frey (USA) with a .308 Baer Magnum at Williamsport, Pennsylvania, USA on 25 Jul 1993. The smallest at 500m *546yd* is 1.5in *3.81cm* by Ross Hicks (Australia) using a rifle of his own design at Canberra, Australia on 12 Mar 1994.

Small-bore The British individual small-bore rifle record for 60 shots prone is 597/600, held jointly by Philip Scanlon (b. 4 Feb 1951), Alister Allan (b. 28 Jan 1944) and John Booker (b. 19 Jul 1940).

Clay pigeon Most world titles have been won by Susan Nattrass (Canada) (b. 5 Nov 1950) with six, 1974–5, 1977–9, 1981.

Colin Brook celebrates winning the Queen's Prize at Bisley in 1993, with a record-equalling score of 295, in the tradtional manner.
(Photo: Allsport/Mike Cooper)

Lyubov Yegorova celebrates anchoring the Russian team to success in the 4 × 5km relay at the 1994 Olympics. It was her third gold of the Games and her sixth overall, a record for any skier.
(Photo: Allsport/Shaun Botterill)

Skiing

Most titles *World/Olympic Championships—Alpine* The World Alpine Championships were inaugurated at Mürren, Switzerland, in 1931. The greatest number of titles won has been by Christl Cranz (b. 1 Jul 1914) of Germany, with seven individual—four slalom (1934, 1937–9) and three downhill (1935, 1937, 1939), and five combined (1934–5, 1937–9). She also won the gold medal for the Combined in the 1936 Olympics. The most won by a man is seven by Anton 'Toni' Sailer (Austria) (b. 17 Nov 1935), who won all

Most Olympic Skiing Titles

MEN
ALPINE.....3 Anton 'Toni' Sailer (Austria) (b. 17 Nov 1935) .....Downhill, slalom, giant slalom, 1956
3 Jean-Claude Killy (France) (b. 30 Aug 1943) ......Downhill, slalom, giant slalom 1968
3 Alberto Tomba (Italy) (b. 19 Dec 1966) * ....Slalom, giant slalom, 1988; giant slalom, 1992
NORDIC ...5 Bjørn Dæhlie (Norway) (b. 19 Jun 1967) ....15km, 50km, 4×10km 1992; 10km, 15km 1994
Jumping ...4 Matti Nykänen (Finland) (b. 17 Jul 1963) ....70m hill 1988; 90m hill 1984, 1988; Team 1988

WOMEN
ALPINE.....3 Vreni Schneider (Switzerland) (b. 26 Nov 1964)* .Giant slalom, slalom 1988; slalom 1994
NORDIC ...6 Lyubov Yegerova (Russia) (b. 5 May 1966) ....10km, 15km 4×5km 1992; 5km, 10km, 4×5km 1994

Most medals
10 (women), Raisa Smetanina (USSR/CIS) (b. 29 Feb 1952), four gold, five silver and one bronze in Nordic events, 1976-92.
9 (men), Sixten Jernberg (Sweden) (b. 6 Feb 1929), four golds, three silver and two bronze in Nordic events, 1956-64.
In Alpine skiing, the record is five: Alberto Tomba won silver in the 1992 and 1994 slalom; Vreni Schneider won silver in the combined and bronze in the giant slalom in 1994; and Kjetil André Aamodt (Norway) (b. 2 Sep 1971) won one gold (super giant slalom 1992), two silver (downhill, combined 1994) and two bronze (giant slalom 1992, super giant slalom 1994).

Alberto Tomba has won an Olympic medal in the slalom in each of the last three Games and has won five medals overall, a record for Alpine skiing.
(Photo: Allsport/Steve Powell)

GUESS WHAT?

Q A bonspiel is associated with which winter sport?

A See Page 247

four in 1956 (giant slalom, slalom, downhill and the non-Olympic Alpine combination) and the downhill, giant slalom and combined in 1958.

World/Olympic Championships — Nordic The first World Nordic Championships were those of the 1924 Winter Olympics in Chamonix, France. The greatest number of titles won is 11 by Gunde Svan (Sweden) (b. 12 Jan 1962), seven individual; 15km 1989, 30km 1985 and 1991, 50km 1985 and 1989, and Olympics, 15km 1984, 50km 1988: and four relays; 4×10km, 1987 and 1989, and Olympics, 1984 and 1988. The most titles won by a woman is nine by Galina Alekseyevna Kulakova (USSR) (b. 29 Apr 1942), five individual and four relay in 1970–78. The most medals is 23 by Raisa Petrovna Smetanina (USSR) (b. 29 Feb 1952) including seven gold, 1974–92. Ulrich Wehling (GDR) (b. 8 Jul 1952) with the Nordic combined in 1972, 1976 and 1980, is the only skier to win the same event at three successive Olympics. The most titles won by a jumper is five by Birger Ruud (b. 23 Aug 1911) of Norway, in 1931–2 and 1935–7. Ruud is the only person to win Olympic events in each of the dissimilar Alpine and Nordic disciplines. In 1936 he won the Ski-jumping and the Alpine downhill (which was not then a separate event, but only a segment of the Combined event).

World Cup The World Cup was introduced for Alpine events in 1967. The most individual event wins is 86 (46 giant slalom, 40 slalom from a total of 287 races) by Ingemar Stenmark (Sweden) (b. 18 Mar 1956) in 1974–89, including a men's record 13 in one season in 1978/9, of which 10 were part of a record 14 successive giant slalom wins from 18 Mar 1978, his 22nd birthday, to 21 Jan 1980. Franz Klammer (Austria) (b. 3 Dec 1953) won a record 25 downhill races, 1974–84. Annemarie Moser (*née* Pröll) (Austria) (b. 27 Mar 1953) won a women's record 62 individual event wins, 1970–79. She had a record 11 consecutive downhill wins from Dec 1972 to Jan 1974. Vreni Schneider (Switzerland) (b. 26 Nov 1964) won a record 13 events (and a combined) including all seven slalom events in the 1988/9 season.

The longest all-downhill ski run in the world is the Weissfluhjoch-Küblis Parsenn course, near Davos, Switzerland, which measures 12.23km 7.6 miles.

The Nations' Cup, awarded on the combined results of the men and women in the World Cup, has been won a record 15 times by Austria 1969, 1973–80, 1982, 1990–94.

Ski-jumping The longest ski-jump ever recorded is one of 194m *636ft* by Piotr Fijas (Poland) at Planica, Yugoslavia on 14 Mar 1987. The women's record is 112m *367ft* by Eva Ganster (Austria) at Bischofshofen, Austria on 7 Jan 1994. The longest dry ski-jump is 92m *302ft* by Hubert Schwarz (West Germany) at Berchtesgarten, Germany on 30 Jun 1981.

Highest speed The official world record, as recognized by the International Ski Federation for a skier, is 233.615km/h *145.161mph* by Philippe Goitschel (France) on 21 Apr 1993 and the fastest by a woman is 219.245 km/h *136.232mph* by Tarja Mulari (Finland) on 22 Feb 1992, both at Les Arcs, France. On 16 Apr 1988 Graham Wilkie (GB) (b. 21 Sep 1959) set a British men's record of 219.914km/h *136.648 mph* and Patrick Knaff (France) set a one-legged record of 185.567 km/h *115.306 mph*. On 21 Apr 1993, a British women's record was set by Divina Galica (b. 13 Aug 1944) at 200.667 km/h *124.689 mph*, also at Les Arcs, France.

The highest average speed in the Olympic downhill race was 104.53km/h *64.95 mph* by William D. Johnson (USA) (b. 30 Mar 1960) at Sarajevo, Yugoslavia on 16 Feb 1984. The fastest in a World Cup downhill is 112.4km/h *69.8mph* by Armin Assinger (Austria) at Sierra Nevada, Spain on 15 Mar 1993.

Highest speed — cross-country The record time for a 50km race in a major championship is 1hr 54min 46sec by Aleksey Prokurorov (Russia) at Thunder Bay, Canada on 19 Mar 1994, an average speed of 26.14 km/h *16.24mph*.

Longest races The world's greatest Nordic ski race is the Vasaloppet, which commemorates an event of 1521 when Gustav Vasa (1496–1560), later King Gustavus Eriksson, fled 85.8km *53.3 miles* from Mora to Sälen, Sweden. He was overtaken by loyal, speedy scouts on skis, who persuaded him to return eastwards to Mora to lead a rebellion and become the king of Sweden. The re-enactment of this return journey is now an annual event at 89km *55.3 miles*. There were a record 10,934 starters on 6 Mar 1977 and a record 10,650 finishers on 4 Mar 1979. The fastest time is 3hr 48min 55sec, by Bengt Hassis (Sweden) on 2 Mar 1986.

The Finlandia Ski Race, 75km *46.6 miles* from Hämeenlinna to Lahti, on 26 Feb 1984 had a record 13,226 starters and 12,909 finishers.

The longest downhill race is the *Inferno* in Switzerland, 15.8km *9.8 miles* from the top of the Schilthorn to Lauterbrunnen. The record entry was 1401 in 1981 and the record time 13min 53.40sec by Urs von Allmen (Switzerland) in 1991.

Long-distance *Nordic* In 24 hours Seppo-Juhani Savolainen covered 415.5km *258.2 miles* at Saariselkä, Finland on 8–9 Apr 1988. The women's record is 330km *205.05 miles*

Snow shoe!

The IASSRF (International Amateur SnowShoe Racing Federation) record for covering 1 mile *1.6 km* is 5 min 56.7 sec by Nick Akers of Edmonton, Alberta, Canada on 3 Feb 1991. The 100 m record is 14.07 sec by Jeremy Badeau at Canaseraga, New York, USA on 31 May 1991.

by Sisko Kainulaisen at Jyväskylä, Finland on 23–24 Mar 1985.

In 48 hours Bjørn Løkken (Norway) (b. 27 Nov 1937) covered 513.568 km *319 miles 205 yd* on 11–13 Mar 1982.

Freestyle The first World Championships were held at Tignes, France in 1986, titles being awarded in ballet, moguls, aerials and combined. Of several skiers to have won two titles, Edgar Grospiron (France) (b. 17 Mar 1969), who won moguls in 1989 and 1991, has also won an Olympic title, 1992. The most Overall titles in the World Cup (instituted 1980) is ten by Connie Kissling (Switzerland) (b. 18 Jul 1961), 1983–92. The men's record is five by Eric Laboureix (France) (b. 12 Apr 1962), 1986–7, 1989–91.

Longest lift The longest gondola ski lift is 6239 m *3.88 miles* long at Grindelwald-Männlichen, Switzerland (in two sections, but one gondola). The longest chair lift in the world was the Alpine Way to Kosciusko Chalet lift above Thredbo, near the Snowy Mountains, New South Wales, Australia. It took from 45 to 75 min to ascend the 5.6 km *3.5 miles*, according to the weather. It has now collapsed. The highest is at Chacaltaya, Bolivia, rising to 5029 m *16,500 ft*.

Ski-bob Origins The ski-bob was the invention of J. C. Stevenson of Hartford, Connecticut, USA in 1891, and patented (No. 47334) on 19 Apr 1892 as a 'bicycle with ski-runners'. The *Fédération Internationale de Skibob* was founded on 14 Jan 1961 in Innsbruck, Austria and the first World Championships were held at Bad Hofgastein, Austria in 1967.

The highest speed attained is 166 km/h *103.1 mph* by Erich Brenter (Austria) (b. 1940) at Cervinia, Italy in 1964.

World Championships The only ski-bobbers to retain a world championship are: men—Alois Fischbauer (Austria) (b. 6 Oct 1951), 1973 and 1975, Robert Mühlberger (West Germany), 1979 and 1981; women—Gerhilde Schiffkorn (Austria) (b. 22 Mar 1950), 1967 and 1969, Gertrude Geberth (Austria) (b. 18 Oct 1951), 1971 and 1973.

Grass Skiing

World Championships (now awarded for Super-G, giant slalom, slalom and combined) were first held in 1979. The most titles won is 14 by Ingrid Hirschhofer (Austria) 1979–93. The most by a man is seven by: Erwin Gansner (Switzerland), 1981–7; and Rainer Grossmann, 1985–93. The feat of winning all four titles in one year has been achieved by: (men) Erwin Gansner, 1987 and Rainer Grossmann, 1991; and (women) Katja Krey (West Germany), 1989 and Ingrid Hirschhofer, 1993.

The speed record is 86.88 km/h *53.99 mph* by Erwin Gansner at

Owen, Germany on 5 Sep 1982. At the same venue Laurence Beck set a British record of 79.49 km/h *49.39 mph* on 8 Sep 1985.

Skipping

10 Mile skip-run Vadivelu Karunakaren (India) skipped 10 miles *16 km* in 58 min at Madras, India, 1 Feb 1990.

Most turns One hour 14,628 by Park Bong-tae (South Korea) at Pusan, South Korea, 2 Jul 1989.

On a single rope, team of 90 160 by students from the Nishigoshi Higashi Elementary School, Kumamoto, Japan, 27 Feb 1987.

On a tightrope 358 (consecutive) by Julian Albulet (USA) at Las Vegas, Nevada, USA, 2 Jul 1990.

Most on a rope (minimum 12 turns obligatory) 220 by a team at the International Rope Skipping Competition, Greeley, Colorado, USA, 28 Jun 1990.

Skittles

The highest score at West Country skittles by a team of eight is 99,051 by the 'Alkies' Skittles team at Courtlands Holiday Inn, Torquay, Devon on 4–5 Apr 1987; they reset the skittles after every ball. The highest hood skittle score in

Most World Cup Titles

ALPINE SKIING (instituted 1967)

MEN

OVERALL	5	Marc Girardelli (Luxembourg) (b. 18 Jul 1963)	1985–6, 1989, 1991, 1993
DOWNHILL	5	Franz Klammer (Austria) (b. 3 Oct 1953)	1975–8, 1983
SLALOM	8	Ingemar Stenmark (Sweden) (b. 18 Mar 1956)	1975–81, 1983
GIANT SLALOM	7	Ingemar Stenmark (Sweden)	1975–6, 1978–81, 1984
SUPER GIANT SLALOM	4	Pirmin Zurbriggen (Switzerland) (b. 4 Feb 1963)	1987–90

Two men have won four titles in one year: Jean-Claude Killy (France) (b. 30 Aug 1943) won all four possible disciplines (downhill, slalom, giant slalom and overall) in 1967; and Pirmin Zurbriggen (Switzerland) (b. 4 Feb 1963) won four of the five possible disciplines (downhill, giant slalom, super giant slalom (added 1986) and overall) in 1987.

WOMEN

OVERALL	6	Annemarie Moser-Pröll (Austria) (b. 27 Mar 1953)	1971–5, 1979
DOWNHILL	7	Annemarie Moser-Pröll	1971–5, 1978–9
SLALOM	5	Vreni Schneider (Switzerland) (b. 26 Nov 1964)	1989–90, 1992–4
GIANT SLALOM	4	Vreni Schneider (Switzerland)	1986–7, 1989, 1991
SUPER GIANT SLALOM	4	Carole Merle (France) (b. 24 Jan 1964)	1989–92

NORDIC SKIING (instituted 1981)

MEN

JUMPING	4	Matti Nykänen (Finland) (b. 17 Jul 1963)	1983, 1985–6, 1988
CROSS-COUNTRY	5	Gunde Svan (Sweden) (b. 12 Jan 1962)	1984–6, 1988–9

WOMEN

CROSS-COUNTRY	3	Marjo Matikainen (Finland) (b. 3 Feb 1965)	1986–8
	3	Yelena Välbe (USSR/Russia) (b. 24 Feb 1968)	1989, 1991–2

Vreni Schneider had a very successful 1994 winning her fifth World Cup slalom title, a record. She also won the Olympic slalom title, her third gold which is also a record.
(Photo: Allsport/Chris Cole)

GUESS WHAT?

Q What is the 'Big Green Machine'?

A See Page 119

break is 155. The only '16 red' clearance ever completed in a tournament was by Steve James (b. 2 May 1961) who made 135 against Alex Higgins (b. 18 Mar 1949) in the World Professional Championships at Sheffield, S Yorks on 14 Apr 1990.

The world amateur record break is 147 by Geet Sethi (India) in the Indian Amateur Championships on 21 Feb 1988.

The highest break by a woman is 137 by Stacey Hillyard in the General Portfolio Women's Classic at Aylesbury, Bucks on 23 Feb 1992.

Three consecutive century breaks were first compiled in a major tournament by Steve Davis: 108, 101 and 104 at Stoke-on-Trent, Staffs on 10 Sep 1988. Doug Mountjoy (b. 8 Jun 1942) equalled the feat: 131, 106 and 124 at Preston, Lancs on 27 Nov 1988. Peter Ebdon made four century breaks in five frames in the European Open qualifying competition at Blackpool on 6 Sep 1992.

Longest unbeaten run From 17 Mar 1990 to his defeat by Jimmy White (b. 2 May 1962) on 13 Jan 1991, Stephen Hendry won five successive titles and 36 consecutive matches in ranking tournaments. During the summer of 1992, Ronnie O'Sullivan won 38 consecutive matches but these were in qualifying competitions.

24 hours is 136,080 pins by 12 players from the Yardley Gobion Sport and Social Club at the Yardley Gobion Recreation Centre, Northants on 15–16 May 1992. The highest long alley score is 82,767 by a team from the White Hart, Headless Cross, Worcs on 25–26 Apr 1992. The highest table skittle score in 24 hours is 116,047 skittles by 12 players at the Castle Mona, Newcastle, Staffs on 15–16 Apr 1990.

Snooker

Most world titles The World Professional Championship (instituted 1927) was won a record 15 times by Joe Davis, on the first 15 occasions it was contested, 1927–40 and 1946. The most wins in the Amateur Championships (instituted 1963) have been two by: Gary Owen (England) in 1963 and 1966; Ray Edmonds (England) 1972 and 1974; and Paul Mifsud (Malta) 1985–6. Allison Fisher (b. 24 Feb 1968) has won seven women's World Championships, 1985–6, 1988–9, 1991, 1993–4.

Maureen Baynton (*née* Barrett) won a record eight Women's Amateur Championships between 1954 and 1968, as well as seven at billiards.

World Championships *Youngest* The youngest man to win a world title is Stephen O'Connor (Ireland) (b. 16 Oct 1972), who was 18 yr 40 days when he won the World Amateur Snooker Championship in Colombo, Sri Lanka on 25 Nov 1990. Stephen Hendry (Scotland) (b. 13 Jan 1969) became the youngest World Professional champion, at 21 yr 106 days on 29 Apr 1990.

Stacey Hillyard (GB) (b. 5 Sep 1969) won the Women's World Amateur Championship in October 1984 at the age of 15.

Highest breaks The first to achieve the 'maximum' break of 147 was E. J. 'Murt' O'Donoghue (New Zealand) (1901–94) at Griffiths, New South

Ronnie O'Sullivan is the youngest winner of a major title, winning the United Kingdom Championship on 28 Nov 1993, aged 17 years 358 days.
(Photo: Allsport/Mike Cooper)

Wales, Australia on 26 Sep 1934. The first officially ratified 147 was by Joe Davis against Willie Smith at Leicester Square Hall, London on 22 Jan 1955. The first achieved in a major tournament were by John Spencer (b. 18 Sep 1935) at Slough, Berks on 13 Jan 1979, but the table had oversized pockets, and by Steve Davis (b. 22 Aug 1957), who had a ratified break of 147 against John Spencer in the Lada Classic at Oldham, Greater Manchester on 11 Jan 1982. The youngest to score a competitive maximum was Ronnie O'Sullivan (b. 5 Dec 1975) at 15 yr 98 days during the English Amateur Championship (Southern Area) at Aldershot, Hants on 13 Mar 1991. Cliff Thorburn (Canada) (b. 16 Jan 1948) was first to make two tournament 147 breaks on 23 Apr 1983 (the first in the World Professional Championships) and 8 Mar 1989. Peter Ebdon (b. 27 Aug 1970) and James Wattana (Thailand) (b. 17 Jan 1970) have also achieved this feat.

Steve Duggan (b. 10 Apr 1958) made a break of 148 in a witnessed practice frame in Doncaster, S Yorks on 27 Apr 1988. The break involved a free ball, which therefore created an 'extra' red, when all 15 reds were still on the table. In these very exceptional circumstances, the maximum

GUESS WHAT?

Q Where is the world's longest breakwater?

A See Page 99

Softball

Most titles The USA has won the men's world championship (instituted 1966) five times, 1966, 1968, 1976 (shared), 1980 and 1988, and the women's title (instituted 1965) three times in 1974, 1978 and 1986. The world's first slow-pitch championships for men's teams was held in Oklahoma City, USA in 1987, when the winners were the USA.

Speedway

World Championships The World Speedway Championship was inaugurated at Wembley, London on 10 Sep 1936. The most wins has been six by Ivan Gerald Mauger (New Zealand) (b. 4 Oct 1939) in 1968–70, 1972, 1977 and 1979. Barry Briggs (New Zealand) (b. 30 Dec 1934) made a record 18 appearances in the finals (1954–70, 1972), won the world title in 1957–8, 1964 and 1966 and scored a record 201 points from 87 races.

Simon Wigg won a record-equalling fourth world Long Track speedway title in 1993, equalling the achievement of the German Karl Maier. Wigg had previously won in 1985 and 1989–90.
(Photo: Allsport/Mike Powell)

Ivan Mauger also won four World Team Cups (three for GB), two World Pairs (including one unofficial) and three world long track titles. Ove Fundin (Sweden) (b. 23 May 1933) won 12 world titles: five individual, one Pairs, and six World Team Cup medals in 1956–70. In 1985 Erik Gundersen (Denmark) became the first man to hold world titles at individual, pairs, team and long-track events simultaneously.

The World Pairs Championships (instituted unofficially 1968, officially 1970) have been won a record eight times by Denmark, 1979, 1985–91. The most successful individual in the World Pairs has been Hans Hollen Nielsen (b. 26 Dec 1959) with seven wins for Denmark. His partners were Ole Olsen, 1979, Erik Gundersen, 1986–9, and Jan O. Pedersen, 1990–91. Maximum points (then 30) were scored in the World Pairs Championship by: Jerzy Szczakiel (b. 28 Jan 1949) and Andrzej Wyglenda (Poland) at Rybnik, Poland in 1971; and Arthur Dennis Sigalos (b. 16 Aug 1959) and Robert Benjamin 'Bobby' Schwartz (USA) (b. 10 Aug 1956) at Liverpool, New South Wales, Australia on 11 Dec 1982. The World Team Cup (instituted 1960) has been won a record nine times by: England/Great Britain (Great Britain 1968, 1971–3; England 1974–5, 1977, 1980, 1989); and Denmark 1978, 1981, 1983–8, 1991. Hans Nielsen (Denmark) has ridden in a record eight Team wins.

British championships League racing was introduced to British speedway in 1929 and consisted of a Southern League and Northern Dirt Track League, the National League was formulated in 1932 and continued to 1964. The Wembley Lions who won in 1932, 1946–7, 1949–53, had a record eight victories. In 1965 it was replaced by the British League which Belle Vue (who had six National League wins, 1933–6, 1939 and 1963) have won five times, including three times in succession (1970–72).

In league racing the highest score recorded was when Berwick beat Exeter 78–18 in the 16-heat formula for the National League on 27 May 1989. A maximum possible score was achieved by Bristol when they defeated Glasgow (White City) 70–14 on 7 Oct 1949 in the National League Division Two. Oxford set a record of 28 successive wins in the British League in 1986. The highest number of League points scored by an individual in a season was 563 by Hans Nielsen for Oxford in the British League in 1988. The League career record is 6471 points by Nigel Boocock (b. 17 Sep 1937), 1955–80.

Belle Vue (Manchester) had a record nine victories (1933–7, 1946–7, 1949 and 1958) in the National Trophy Knock-out Competition (held 1931–64). This was replaced in 1965 by the Knock–Out Cup, which has been won eight times (one shared) by Cradley Heath.

The highest recorded score in this competition is 81–25, when Hull beat Sheffield in 1979.

The British League Riders' Championship was instituted in 1965 and is an annual event contested by the top scorers from each team. Ivan Mauger holds the records for appearances, 15 and points scored, 146, 1965–79. The most wins is six by Barry Briggs, 1965–70.

Leicester are the only team to have used the same seven riders in a complete League programme. This was in 1969 when the same seven riders rode in all of the 36 matches.

Squash Rackets

World Championships Jahangir Khan (Pakistan) (b. 10 Dec 1963) won six World Open (instituted 1976) titles, 1981–5 and 1988, and the International Squash Rackets Federation world individual title (formerly World Amateur, instituted 1967) in 1979, 1983 and 1985. Geoffrey B. Hunt (Australia) (b. 11 Mar 1947) won four World Open titles, 1976–7 and 1979–80 and three World Amateur, 1967, 1969 and 1971.

Jansher Khan has won five World squash titles. He defeated Australian Chris Dittmar on each of the first four occasions and in the fifth, in 1993, he beat the remarkable Jahangir Khan. It was Jahangir's ninth final of which he had won six. Jansher has continued the success of the Khan dynasty from the Peshawar region of Pakistan, following men such as Jahangir, Hashim, Azam and Roshan.

(Photo: Allsport/Gray Mortimore)

The most women's World Open titles is five by Susan Devoy (New Zealand) (b. 4 Jan 1964), 1985, 1987, 1990–92.

The most men's world team titles is six by: Australia 1967, 1969, 1971, 1973, 1989 and 1991; and Pakistan 1977, 1981, 1983, 1985, 1987 and 1993. England won the women's title in 1985, 1987, 1989 and 1990, following Great Britain's win in 1979.

Most titles *Open Championship* The most wins in the Open Championship held annually in Britain, is ten by Jahangir Khan, in successive years, 1982–91. Hashim Khan (Pakistan) (b. 1915) won seven times, 1950–55 and 1957, and also won the Vintage title six times in 1978–83.

The most British Open women's titles is 16 by Heather Pamela McKay (*née* Blundell) (Australia) (b. 31 Jul 1941) from 1961 to 1977. She also won the World Open title in 1976 and 1979.

Amateur Championship The most wins in the Amateur Championship is six by Abdelfattah Amr Bey (Egypt) (b. 14 Feb 1910), who won in 1931–3 and 1935–7. Norman Francis Borrett (b. 1 Oct 1917) of England won in 1946–50.

Longest and shortest championship matches The longest recorded competitive match was one of 2hr 45min when Jahangir Khan beat Gamal Awad (Egypt) (b. 8 Sep 1955) 9–10, 9–5, 9–7, 9–2, the first game lasting a record 1hr 11min, in the final of the Patrick International Festival at Chichester, W Sussex on 30 Mar 1983. Philip Kenyon (England) (b. 9 May 1956) beat Salah Nadi (Egypt) (b. 11 Jan 1956) in just 6min 37sec (9–0, 9–0, 9–0) in the British Open at Lamb's Squash Club, London on 9 Apr 1992.

Most international appearances The men's record is 122 by David Gotto (b. 25 Dec 1948) for Ireland. The women's record is 113 by Rebecca O'Callaghan (*née* Best) for Ireland.

Largest crowd and tournament The finals of the ICI World Team Championships at the Royal Albert Hall, London had a record attendance for squash of 3526 on 30 Oct 1987.

The InterCity National Squash Challenge was contested by 9588 players in 1988, a knock-out tournament record.

Swimming World Records (set in 50m pools)

MEN

Event	min:sec	Name and Country	Venue	Date
FREESTYLE				
50 m	21.81	Tom Jager (USA) (b. 6 Oct 1964)	Nashville, TN, USA	24 Mar 1990
100 m	48.21	Aleksandr Popov (Russia) (b. 16 Nov 1971)	Monte Carlo	18 Jun 1994
200 m	1:46.69	Giorgio Lamberti (Italy) (b. 28 Jan 1969)	Bonn, Germany	15 Aug 1989
400 m	3:45.00	Yevgeniy Sadovyi (Russia) (b. 19 Jan 1973)	Barcelona, Spain	29 Jul 1992
800 m	7:46.60	Kieren John Perkins (Australia) (b. 14 Aug 1973)	Sydney, Australia	15 Feb 1992
1500 m	14:43.48	Kieren John Perkins (Australia)	Barcelona, Spain	31 Jul 1992
4×100 m	3:16.53	USA (Christopher Jacobs, Troy Dalbey, Tom Jager, Matthew Nicholas Biondi)	Seoul, South Korea	23 Sep 1988
4×200 m	7:11.95	CIS (Dmitriy Lepikov, Vladimir Pyechenko, Venyamin Tayanovich, Yevgeniy Sadovyi)	Barcelona, Spain	27 Jul 1992
BREASTSTROKE				
100 m	1:00.95	Károly Güttler (Hungary) (b. 15 Jun 1968)	Sheffield, S Yorks	3 Aug 1993
200 m	2:10.16	Michael Ray Barrowman (USA) (b. 4 Dec 1968)	Barcelona, Spain	29 Jul 1992
BUTTERFLY				
100 m	52.84	Pedro Pablo Morales (USA) (b. 5 Dec 1964)	Orlando, FL, USA	23 Jun 1986
200 m	1:55.69	Melvin Stewart (USA) (b. 18 Nov 1968)	Perth, Australia	12 Jan 1991
BACKSTROKE				
100 m	53.86	Jeff Rouse (USA) (b. 6 Feb 1970) (relay leg)	Barcelona, Spain	31 Jul 1992
200 m	1:56.57	Martin López-Zubero (Spain) (b. 23 Apr 1964)	Tuscaloosa, AL, USA	23 Nov 1991
MEDLEY				
200 m	1:59.36	Tamás Darnyi (Hungary) (b. 3 Jun 1967)	Perth, Australia	13 Jan 1991
400 m	4:12.36	Tamás Darnyi (Hungary)	Perth, Australia	8 Jan 1991
4×100 m	3:36.93	USA (David Berkoff, Richard Schroeder, Matthew Nicholas Biondi, Christopher Jacobs)	Seoul, South Korea	25 Sep 1988
	3:36.93	USA (Jeff Rouse, Nelson Diebel, Pablo Morales, Jon Olsen)	Barcelona, Spain	31 Jul 1992

WOMEN

Event	min:sec	Name and Country	Venue	Date
FREESTYLE				
50 m	24.79	Yang Wenyi (China) (b. 11 Jan 1972)	Barcelona, Spain	31 Jul 1992
100 m	54.48	Jenny Thompson (USA) (b. 26 Feb 1973)	Indianapolis, IN, USA	1 Mar 1992
200 m	1:57.55	Heike Friedrich (GDR) (b. 18 Apr 1970)	East Berlin, Germany	18 Jun 1986
400 m	4:03.85	Janet B Evans (USA) (b. 28 Aug 1971)	Seoul, South Korea	22 Sep 1988
800 m	8:16.22	Janet Evans (USA)	Tokyo, Japan	20 Aug 1989
1500 m	15:52.10	Janet Evans (USA)	Orlando, FL, USA	26 Mar 1988
4×100 m	3:39.46	USA (Nicole Haislett, Dara Torres, Angel Martino, Jenny Thompson)	Barcelona, Spain	28 Jul 1992
4×200 m	7:55.47	GDR (Manuela Stellmach, Astrid Strauss, Anke Möhring, Heike Friedrich)	Strasbourg, France	18 Aug 1987
BREASTSTROKE				
100 m	1:07.91	Silke Hörner (GDR) (b. 12 Sep 1965)	Strasbourg, France	21 Aug 1987
200 m	2:24.76	Rebecca Brown (Australia) (b. 8 May 1977)	Brisbane, Australia	16 Mar 1994
BUTTERFLY				
100 m	57.93	Mary Terstegge Meagher (USA) (b. 27 Oct 1964)	Brown Deer, WI, USA	16 Aug 1981
200 m	2:05.96	Mary Terstegge Meagher (USA)	Brown Deer, WI, USA	13 Aug 1981
BACKSTROKE				
100 m	1:00.31	Krizstina Egerszegi (Hungary) (b. 16 Aug 1974)	Athens, Greece	22 Aug 1991
200 m	2:06.62	Krizstina Egerszegi (Hungary)	Athens, Greece	25 Aug 1991
MEDLEY				
200 m	2:11.65	Li Lin (China) (b. 9 Oct 1976)	Barcelona, Spain	30 Jul 1992
400 m	4:36.10	Petra Schneider (GDR) (b. 11 Jan 1963)	Guayaquil, Ecuador	1 Aug 1982
4×100 m	4:02.54	USA (Lea Loveless, Anita Nall, Chrissy Ahmann-Leighton, Jenny Thompson)	Barcelona, Spain	30 Jul 1992

Surfing

Most titles World Amateur Championships were inaugurated in May 1964 at Sydney, Australia. The most titles is three by Michael Novakov (Australia) who won the Kneeboard event in 1982, 1984 and 1986. A World Professional series was started in 1975. The men's title has been won five times by Mark Richards (Australia), 1975 and 1979–82 and the women's title (instituted 1979) four times by: Frieda Zamba (USA), 1984–6, 1988; and Wendy Botha (Australia, formerly South Africa), 1987, 1989, 1991–2.

Highest waves ridden Waimea Bay, Hawaii reputedly provides the most consistently high waves, often reaching the ridable limit of 9–11m *30–35ft*. The highest wave ever ridden was the *tsunami* of 'perhaps 50ft', which struck Minole, Hawaii on 3 Apr 1868, and was ridden to save his life by a Hawaiian named Holua.

> About four to six times each year rideable surfing waves break in Matanchen Bay near San Blas, Nayarit, Mexico which makes rides of c. 1700m *5700ft* possible.

Longest ride *River bore* The longest recorded rides on a river bore have been set on the Severn bore, England. The official British Surfing Association record for riding a surfboard in a standing position is 4km *2.5 mile* by David Lawson from Lower Rea to Lower Parting on 27 Sep 1988. The longest ride on a surfboard standing or lying down is 4.73km *2.94 miles* by Colin Kerr Wilson (b. 23 Jun 1954) on 23 May 1982.

Swimming

Largest pools The largest swimming pool in the world is the seawater Orthlieb Pool in Casablanca, Morocco. It is 480m *1574ft* long and 75m *246ft* wide, and has an area of 3.6ha *8.9 acres*. The largest land-locked swimming pool with heated water was the Fleishhacker Pool on Sloat Boulevard, near Great Highway, San Francisco, California, USA. It measured 305× 46m *1000×150ft* and up to 4.26m *14ft* deep and contained 28,390 hectolitres *6,245,050 US gal* of heated water. It was opened on 2 May 1925 but has now been abandoned. The largest land-locked pool in current use is Willow Lake at Warren, Ohio, USA. It measures 183m ×46m *600×150ft*. The greatest spectator accommodation is 13,614 at Osaka, Japan. The largest in use in the United Kingdom is the Royal Commonwealth Pool, Edinburgh, completed in 1970 with 2000 permanent seats, but the covered over and unused pool at Earls Court, London (opened 1937) could seat some 12,000 spectators.

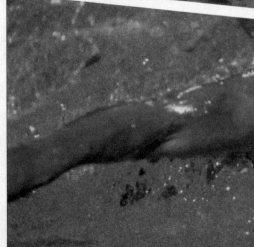

Fastest swimmer In a 25-yd pool, Tom Jager (USA) (b. 6 Oct 1964) achieved an average speed of 8.64 km/h *5.37 mph* for 50 yards in 19.05 sec at Nashville, Tennessee, USA on 23 Mar 1990. The women's fastest is 7.21 km/h *4.48 mph* by Yang Wenyi (China) in her 50 m world record (⟨⟩ World Record table).

Most world records Men: 32, Arne Borg (Sweden) (1901–87), 1921–9. Women: 42, Ragnhild Hveger (Denmark) (b. 10 Dec 1920), 1936–42. For currently recognized events (only metric distances in 50 m pools) the most is 26 by Mark Andrew Spitz (USA) (b. 10 Feb 1950), 1967–72, and 23 by Kornelia Ender (GDR) (b. 25 Oct 1958), 1973–6.

The most world records set in a single pool is 86 in the North Sydney pool, Australia between 1955 and 1978. This total includes 48 imperial distance records which ceased to be recognized in 1969. The pool, which was built in 1936, was originally 55 yards long but was shortened to 50 metres in 1964.

Most world titles In the World Championships (instituted 1973) the most medals won is 13 by Michael Gross (West Germany) (b. 17 Jun 1964), five gold, five silver and three bronze, 1982–90.

Mark Foster (below) holder of the 50 m butterfly short course world record.
(Photo: Allsport/Vandystadt/Richard Martin)

Russian Aleksandr Popov (left) is one of only two swimmers to have broken the 49-second barrier for 100 m freestyle. The other is American Matt Biondi and between them, they hold the ten best times for the distance. Popov surpassed Biondi's 1988 world record of 48.42 by 0.21 at Monte Carlo on 18 Jun 1994, and it is felt he will be the first to break the 48-second threshold. Indeed he shattered that time in 25 m short-course pools—his four world records from January to March 1994 lowered the time from 47.83 to 46.74.
(Photo: Allsport/Vandystadt/Richard Martin)

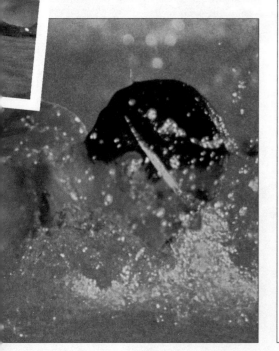

The most by a woman is ten by Kornelia Ender with eight gold and two silver in 1973 and 1975. The most gold medals is six (two individual and four relay) by James Paul Montgomery (USA) (b. 24 Jan 1955) in 1973 and 1975. The most medals at a single championship is seven by Matthew Nicholas Biondi (USA) (b. 8 Oct 1965), three gold, one silver, three bronze, in 1986.

Olympic Records

Most medals *Men* The greatest number of Olympic gold medals won is nine by Mark Spitz (USA): 100 m and 200 m freestyle 1972; 100 m and 200 m butterfly 1972; 4×100 m freestyle 1968 and 1972; 4×200 m freestyle 1968 and 1972; 4×100 m medley 1972. *All but one of these performances*

Short-Course Swimming World Bests (set in 25 m pools)

MEN

Event	min:sec	Name and country	Venue	Date
FREESTYLE				
50 m	21.50	Aleksandr Popov (Russia) (b. 16 Nov 1971)	Desenzano, Italy	13 Mar 1994
100 m	46.74	Aleksandr Popov (Russia)	Gelsenkirchen, Germany	19 Mar 1994
200 m	1:43.64	Giorgio Lamberti (Italy) (b. 28 Jan 1969)	Bonn, Germany	11 Feb 1990
400 m	3:40.81	Anders Holmertz (Sweden) (b. 1 Dec 1968)	Paris, France	4 Feb 1990
800 m	7:34.90	Kieren Perkins (Australia) (b. 14 Aug 1973)	Sydney, Australia	25 Jul 1993
1500 m	14:26.52	Kieren Perkins (Australia)	Auckland, New Zealand	15 Jul 1993
4×50 m	1:27.94	Sweden	Espoo, Finland	21 Nov 1992
4×100 m	3:12.11	Brazil	Palma de Mallorca, Spain	5 Dec 1993
4×200 m	7:05.17	West Germany	Bonn, Germany	9 Feb 1986
BACKSTROKE				
50 m	24.60	Franck Schott (France)	Paris, France	27 Mar 1994
100 m	51.43	Jeff Rouse (USA) (b. 6 Feb 1970)	Sheffield, S Yorks	12 Apr 1993
200 m	1:52.51	Martin Lopez-Zubero (Spain)	Gainesville, FL, USA	11 Apr 1991
BREASTSTROKE				
50 m	27.15	Dmitriy Volkov (USSR) (b. 3 Mar 1966)	Saint-Paul de la Réunion	30 Dec 1989
100 m	59.07	Philip John Rogers (Australia) (b. 24 Apr 1971)	Melbourne, Australia	29 Aug 1993
200 m	2:07.80	Philip John Rogers (Australia)	Melbourne, Australia	28 Aug 1993
BUTTERFLY				
50 m	23.68	Mark Andrew Foster (GB)(b. 12 May 1970)	Sheffield, S Yorks	22 Mar 1994
100 m	52.07	Marcel Gery (Canada) (b. 15 Mar 1965)	Leicester	23 Feb 1990
200 m	1:53.05	Franck Esposito (France) (b. 13 Apr 1971)	Paris, France	26 Mar 1994
MEDLEY				
100 m	53.78	Jani Nikanor Sievinen (Finland) (b. 31 Nov 1974)	Espoo, Finland	21 Nov 1992
200 m	1:54.65	Jani Sievinen (Finland)	Kuopio, Finland	21 Jan 1994
400 m	4:07.10	Jani Sievinen (Finland)	Malmö, Sweden	9 Feb 1993
4×50 m	1:38.10	Finland	Espoo, Finland	22 Nov 1992
4×100 m	3:32.57	USA	Palma de Mallorca, Spain	2 Dec 1993

WOMEN

Event	min:sec	Name and country	Venue	Date
FREESTYLE				
50 m	24.23	Le Jingyi (China) (b. 19 Mar 1975)	Palma de Mallorca, Spain	3 Dec 1993
100 m	53.01	Le Jingyi (China)	Palma de Mallorca, Spain	2 Dec 1993
200 m	1:55.84	Franziska van Almsick (Germany) (b. 5 Apr 1978)	Beijing, China	9 Jan 1993
400 m	4:02.05	Astrid Strauss (GDR) (b. 24 Dec 1968)	Bonn, Germany	8 Feb 1987
800 m	8:15.34	Astrid Strauss (GDR)	Bonn, Germany	6 Feb 1987
1500 m	15:43.31	Petra Schneider (GDR) (b. 11 Jan 1963)	Gainesville, FL, USA	10 Jan 1982
4×50 m	1:40.63	Germany	Espoo, Finland	22 Nov 1992
4×100 m	3:35.97	China	Palma de Mallorca, Spain	4 Dec 1993
4×200 m	7:52.45	China	Palma de Mallorca, Spain	2 Dec 1993
BACKSTROKE				
50 m	27.62	Bai Xiuyu (China)	Malmö, Sweden	15 Mar 1994
100 m	58.50	Angel Martino (USA) (b. 27 Apr 1967)	Palma de Mallorca, Spain	3 Dec 1993
200 m	2:06.09	He Cihong (China)	Palma de Mallorca, Spain	5 Dec 1993
BREASTSTROKE				
50 m	31.19	Louise Karlsson (Sweden)	Espoo, Finland	21 Nov 1992
100 m	1:06.58	Dai Guohong (China)	Palma de Mallorca, Spain	4 Dec 1993
200 m	2:21.99	Dai Guohong (China)	Palma de Mallorca, Spain	3 Dec 1993
BUTTERFLY				
50 m	26.93	Angela Kennedy (Australia) (b. 28 Feb 1976)	Canberra, Australia	22 Jul 1993
100 m**	58.91	Mary Terstegge Meagher (USA) (b. 27 Aug 1964)	Gainesville, FL, USA	3 Jan 1981
200 m	2:05.65	Mary Meagher (USA)	Gainesville, FL, USA	2 Jan 1981
MEDLEY				
100 m	1:01.03	Louise Karlsson (Sweden) (b. 26 Apr 1974)	Espoo, Finland	22 Nov 1992
200 m	2:07.79	Allison Wagner (USA)	Palma de Mallorca, Spain	5 Dec 1993
400 m	4:29.00	Dai Gouhong (China)	Palma de Mallorca, Spain	2 Dec 1993
4×50 m	1:52.44	Germany	Espoo, Finland	21 Nov 1992
4×100 m	3:57.73	China	Palma de Mallorca, Spain	5 Dec 1993

* hand timed for first leg. ** slower than long-course best.

(the 4×200m freestyle of 1968) were also new world records. He also won a silver (100 m butterfly) and a bronze (100m freestyle) in 1968 for a record 11 medals. His record seven medals at one Games in 1972 was equalled by Matt Biondi (USA) who took five gold, one silver and one bronze in 1988. Biondi has also won a record 11 medals in total, winning a gold in 1984, and two golds and a silver in 1992.

Women The record number of gold medals won by a woman is six by Kristin Otto (GDR) (b. 7 Feb 1966) at Seoul in 1988: 100m freestyle, backstroke and butterfly, 50m freestyle, 4×100m freestyle and 4×100m medley. Dawn Fraser (Australia) (b. 4 Sep 1937) is the only swimmer to win the same event, the 100m freestyle, on three successive occasions (1956, 1960 and 1964).

The most medals won by a woman is eight by: Dawn Fraser, four golds and four silvers 1956–64; Kornelia Ender, four golds and four silvers 1972–6; and Shirley Babashoff (USA) (b. 3 Jan 1957), two golds and six silvers 1972–6.

Most individual gold medals
The record number of individual gold medals won is four by: Charles Meldrum Daniels (USA) (1884–1973) (100m freestyle 1906 and 1908, 220yd freestyle 1904, 440yd freestyle 1904); Roland Matthes (GDR) (b. 17 Nov 1950) with 100m and 200m backstroke 1968 and 1972; Mark Spitz and Kristin Otto, and the divers Pat McCormick and Greg Louganis (⇨ Diving).

GUESS WHAT?

Q What is the greatest number of Olympic golds won by an individual?

A See Page 277

Most medals British The record number of gold medals won by a British swimmer (excluding water polo, *q.v.*) is four by Henry Taylor (1885–1951) in the mile freestyle (1906), 400m freestyle (1908), 1500m freestyle (1908) and 4×200m freestyle (1908).

Henry Taylor won a record eight medals in all, with a further silver and three bronzes, 1906–20. The most medals by a British woman is four by Margaret Joyce Cooper (now Badcock) (b. 18 Apr 1909) with one silver and three bronze, 1928–32.

Swimming (British National Records)

MEN

Event	min:sec	Name	Venue	Date
FREESTYLE				
50 m	22.43	Mark Andrew Foster (b. 12 May 1970)	Sheffield, S Yorks	24 May 1992
100 m	50.24	Michael Wenham Fibbens (b. 31 May 1968)	Sheffield, S Yorks	22 May 1992
200 m	1:48.84	Paul Rory Palmer (b. 18 Oct 1974)	Sheffield, S Yorks	3 Aug 1993
400 m	3:48.14	Paul Palmer	Sheffield, S Yorks	6 Aug 1993
800 m	8:00.63	Ian Wilson (b. 19 Dec 1970)	Athens, Greece	25 Aug 1991
1500 m	15:03.72	Ian Wilson	Athens, Greece	25 Aug 1991
4×100 m	3:21.41	GB (Michael Wenham Fibbens, Mark Andrew Foster, Paul Howe, Roland Lee)	Barcelona, Spain	29 Jul 1992
4×200 m	7:22.57	GB (Paul Palmer, Steven Mellor, Stephen Akers, Paul Howe)	Barcelona, Spain	27 Jul 1992
BREASTSTROKE				
100 m	1:01.33	Nicholas Gillingham (b. 22 Jan 1967)	Sheffield, S Yorks	21 May 1992
200 m	2:11.29	Nicholas Gillingham	Barcelona, Spain	29 Jul 1992
BUTTERFLY				
100 m	53.30	Andrew David Jameson (b. 19 Feb 1965)	Seoul, South Korea	21 Sep 1988
200 m	2:00.21	Philip Hubble (b. 19 Jul 1960)	Split, Yugoslavia	11 Sep 1981
BACKSTROKE				
100 m	55.75	Martin Clifford Harris (b. 21 May 1969)	Sheffield, S Yorks	7 Aug 1993
200 m	2:01.13	Adam Ruckwood (b. 13 Sep 1974)	Edinburgh, Lothian	2 Apr 1994
MEDLEY				
200 m	2:03.20	Neil Cochran (b. 12 Apr 1965)	Orlando, FL, USA	25 Mar 1988
400 m	4:24.20	John Philip Davey (b. 29 Dec 1964)	Crystal Palace, London	1 Aug 1987
4×100 m	3:41.66	GB (Martin Harris, Nick Gillingham, Mike Fibbens, Mark Foster)	Sheffield, S Yorks	8 Aug 1993

WOMEN

Event	min:sec	Name	Venue	Date
FREESTYLE				
50 m	26.01	Caroline Woodcock (b. 23 Aug 1972)	Bonn, Germany	20 Aug 1989
100 m	56.11	Karen Pickering (b. 19 Dec 1971)	Sheffield, S Yorks	14 Jun 1992
200 m	1:59.74	June Alexandra Croft (b. 17 Jun 1963)	Brisbane, Australia	4 Oct 1982
400 m	4:07.68	Sarah Hardcastle (b. 9 April 1969)	Edinburgh, Lothian	27 Jul 1986
800 m	8:24.77	Sarah Hardcastle	Edinburgh, Lothian	29 Jul 1986
1500 m	16:39.46	Sarah Hardcastle	Edinburgh, Lothian	31 Mar 1994
4×100 m	3:48.87	GB (Karen Pickering, Sharron Davies, Caroline Woodcock, Joanne Coull)	Bonn, Germany	17 Aug 1989
4×200 m	8:11.11	England (Sarah Hardcastle, Debbie Armitage, Claire Huddart, Karen Pickering)	Sheffield, S Yorks	3 Aug 1993
BREASTSTROKE				
100 m	1:10.39	Susannah 'Suki' Brownsdon (b. 16 Oct 1965)	Strasbourg, France	21 Aug 1987
200 m	2:31.51	Jean Cameron Hill (b. 15 Jul 1964)	Strasbourg, France	19 Aug 1987
BUTTERFLY				
100 m	1:01.33	Madeleine Scarborough (b. 18 Aug 1964)	Auckland, New Zealand	28 Jan 1990
200 m	2:11.97	Samantha Paula Purvis (b. 24 Jun 1967)	Los Angeles, CA, USA	4 Aug 1984
BACKSTROKE				
100 m	1:03.49	Katharine Read (b. 30 Jun 1969)	Sheffield, S Yorks	14 Jun 1992
200 m	2:13.91	Joanne Deakins (b. 20 Nov 1972)	Barcelona, Spain	31 Jul 1992
MEDLEY				
200 m	2:17.21	Jean Cameron Hill	Edinburgh, Lothian	28 Jul 1986
400 m	4:46.83	Sharron Davies (b. 1 Nov 1962)	Moscow, USSR	26 Jul 1980
4×100 m	4:11.88	England (Joanne Deakins, Susannah 'Suki' Brownsdon, Madeleine Scarborough, Karen Pickering)	Auckland, New Zealand	29 Jan 1990

Diving

Most Olympic medals The most medals won by a diver is five by: Klaus Dibiasi (b. Austria, 6 Oct 1947) (Italy) (three gold, two silver), 1964–76; and Gregory Efthimios Louganis (USA) (b. 29 Jan 1960) (four golds, one silver), 1976, 1984, 1988. Dibiasi is the only diver to win the same event (highboard) at three successive Games (1968, 1972 and 1976). Two divers have won the highboard and springboard doubles at two Games: Patricia Joan McCormick (*née* Keller) (USA) (b. 12 May 1930), 1952 and 1956 and Louganis, 1984 and 1988.

British The highest placing by a Briton has been the silver medal by Beatrice Eileen Armstrong (later Purdy) (1894–1981) in the 1920 highboard event. The best placings by male divers are the bronze medals by Harold Clarke (b. 1888) (plain high diving, 1924) and Brian Eric Phelps (b. 21 Apr 1944) (highboard, 1960).

Most world titles Greg Louganis (USA) won a record five world titles, highboard in 1978, and both highboard and springboard in 1982 and 1986, as well as four Olympic gold medals in 1984 and 1988. Three gold medals at one event have also been won by Philip George Boggs (USA) (1949–90), springboard 1973, 1975 and 1978.

Highest scores Greg Louganis achieved record scores at the 1984 Olympic Games in Los Angeles, California, USA with 754.41 points for the 11-dive springboard event and 710.91 for the highboard. At the world championships in Guayaquil, Ecuador in 1984 he was awarded a

High diving!

The highest regularly performed head-first dives are those of professional divers from La Quebrada ('the break in the rocks') at Acapulco, Mexico, a height of 26.7m *87½ft*. The base rocks, 6.4m *21ft* out from the take-off, necessitate a leap of 8.22m *27ft* out. The water is 3.65m *12ft* deep.

The world record high dive from a diving board is 53.9m *176ft 10in* by Olivier Favre (Switzerland) at Villers-le-Lac, France on 30 Aug 1987. The women's record is 36.80m *120ft 9in*, by Lucy Wardle (US) at Ocean Park, Hong Kong on 6 Apr 1985. The highest witnessed in Britain is one of 32.9m *108ft* into 2.43m *8ft* of water at the Aqua Show at Earl's Court, London on 22 Feb 1948 by Roy Fransen (1915–85).

perfect score of 10.0 by all seven judges for his highboard inward 1½ somersault in the pike position.

The first diver to be awarded a score of 10.0 by all seven judges was Michael Holman Finneran (b. 21 Sep 1948) in the 1972 US Olympic Trials, in Chicago, Illinois, for a backward 1½ somersault, 2½ twist, from the 10m board.

Channel Swimming

The first to swim the English Channel from shore to shore (without a life jacket) was the Merchant Navy captain Matthew Webb (1848–83) who swam an estimated 61km *38 miles* to make the 33 km *21 mile* crossing from Dover, England to Calais Sands, France, in 21hr 45min from 12:56p.m. to 10:41a.m., 24–25 Aug 1875. Paul Boyton (USA) had swum from Cap Gris-Nez to the South Foreland in his patent life-saving suit in 23hr 30min on 28–29 May 1875. There is good evidence that Jean-Marie Saletti, a French soldier, escaped from a British prison hulk off Dover by swimming to Boulogne in July or August 1815.

The first crossing from France to England was made by Enrico Tiraboschi, a wealthy Italian living in Argentina, in 16hr 33min on 12 Aug 1923, to win the *Daily Sketch* prize of £1000.

As of May 1994, there had been 6281 attempts to swim the Channel by 4338 people. Of these, 439 individuals (295 men and 144 women) from 47 countries have made 692 successful crossings; 645 solo, 19 double and 3 triple.

The first woman to succeed was Gertrude Caroline Ederle (USA) (b. 23 Oct 1906) who swam from Cap Gris-Nez, France to Deal, England on 6 Aug 1926, in the then overall record time of 14hr 39min.

The first woman to swim from England to France was Florence Chadwick (USA) (b. 1918) in 16hr 19min on 11 Sep 1951. The first Englishwoman to succeed was Mercedes Gleitze (later Carey) (1900–81) who swam from France to England in 15hr 15min on 7 Oct 1927. The first twins to complete the crossing were Carole and Sarah Hunt (b. 23 Aug 1962) who swam from England and landed together in France after 9hr 29min on 6 Aug 1988.

Fastest The official Channel Swimming Association (founded 1927) record is 7hr 40min by Penny Dean (b. 21 Mar 1955) of California, USA, from Shakespeare Beach, Dover to Cap Gris-Nez, France on 29 Jul 1978.

The fastest France–England time is 8hr 5min by Richard Davey (b. 23 Jun 1965) in 1988.

The fastest crossing by a relay team is 6hr 52min (England to France) by the US National Swim Team on 1 Aug 1990. They went on to complete the fastest two-way relay in 14hr 18min.

Earliest and latest The earliest date in the year on which the Channel has been swum is 30 May by Kevin Murphy (GB) (b. 1949) in 1990 in a time of 13hr 16min and with the water at a temperature of 12°C *54°F*. The latest is 28 October by Michael Peter Read (GB) (b. 9 Jun 1941) in 1979 in 17hr 55min.

Double crossing The first double crossing was by Antonio Abertondo (Argentina) (b. 1919), in 43hr 10min on 20–22 Sep 1961. Kevin Murphy completed the first double crossing by a Briton in 35hr 10min on 6 Aug 1970. The first swimmer to achieve a crossing both ways was Edward Harry Temme (1904–78) on 5 Aug 1927 and 19 Aug 1934.

The fastest double crossing was in 16hr 10min by Philip Rush (New Zealand) (b. 6 Nov 1963) on

17 Aug 1987. In setting this record, he completed the fastest ever crossing by a man, 7hr 55min (England to France), and went on to complete the fastest ever triple crossing in 28hr 21min on 17–18 Aug 1987. The women's double crossing record is 17hr 14min by Susie Maroney (Australia) (b. 15 Nov 1974) on 23 Jul 1991. The first British woman to achieve the double crossing was Alison Streeter (b. 29 Aug 1964) in 21hr 16min on 4 Aug 1983.

Triple crossing The first triple crossing was by Jon Erikson (USA) (b. 6 Sep 1954) in 38hr 27min on 11–12 Aug 1981. The first by a woman was by Alison Streeter in 34hr 40min on 2–3 Aug 1990. For the fastest by an individual, ⇨Double crossing.

Most conquests The greatest number of Channel conquests is 31 by Michael Read (GB) from 24 Aug 1969 to 19 Aug 1984. The most by a woman is 23 by Alison Streeter from 1982 to 25 Sep 1993 (including a record seven in one year, 1992).

Oldest swimmer The oldest conqueror has been Bertram Clifford Batt (b. 22 Dec 1919), of Australia at 67 years 241 days when he swam from Cap Gris-Nez to Dover in 18hr 37min from 19–20 Aug 1987. The oldest woman was Stella Ada Rosina Taylor (b. 20 Dec 1929) aged 45 years 250 days when she did the swim in 18hr 15min on 26 Aug 1975.

Long-Distance Swimming

Longest swims The greatest recorded distance ever swum is 2938km *1826 miles* down the Mississippi River, USA between Ford Dam near Minneapolis, Minnesota and Carrollton Ave, New Orleans, Louisiana, by Fred P. Newton, (b. 1903) of Clinton, Oklahoma from 6 Jul to 29 Dec 1930. He was 742hr in the water.

In 1966 Mihir Sen of Calcutta, India uniquely swam the Palk Strait from Sri Lanka to India (in 25hr 36min on 5–6 April); the Straits of Gibraltar (in 8hr 1min on 24 August); the length of the Dardanelles (in 13hr 55min on 12 September); the Bosphorus (in 4hr on 21 September), and the length of the Panama Canal (in 34hr 15min on 29–31 October).

Irish Channel The swimming of the 37km *23 mile* wide North Channel from Donaghadee, Northern Ireland to Portpatrick, Scotland was first accomplished by Tom Blower of Nottingham in 15hr 26min in 1947. A record time of 9hr 53min 42sec was set by Alison Streeter on 22 Aug 1988. She was also the first person to complete the crossing from Scotland to Northern Ireland, in 10hr 4min on 25 Aug 1989.

Lake swims The fastest time for swimming the 36.5km *22.7 mile* long Loch Ness is 9hr 57min by David Trevor Morgan (b. 25 Sep 1963) on 31 Jul 1983. David Morgan achieved a double crossing of Loch Ness in 23hr 4min on 1 Aug 1983. In 1988 he also uniquely swam Loch Ness in 11hr 9min on 16 Jul, Loch Lomond 34.6km *21.5 miles* in 11hr 48min on 18 Jul and the English Channel in 11hr 35min on 20–21 Jul. The fastest time for swimming Lake Windermere, 16.9km *10.5 miles* from Fellfoot to Waterhead, is 3hr 49min 12sec by Justin Palfrey (b. 16 Jul 1971) on 7 Sep 1991.

24 hours Anders Forvass (Sweden) swam 101.9km *63.3 miles* at the 25-metre Linköping public swimming pool, Sweden on 28–29 Oct 1989. In a 50metre pool, Evan Barry (Australia)

swam 96.7km *60.08 miles*, at the Valley Pool, Brisbane, Australia on 19–20 Dec 1987.

The women's record is 93km *57.78 miles* by Melissa Cunningham (Australia) at Chandler Aquatic Centre, Brisbane, Australia on 2–3 July 1993.

Long-distance relays The New Zealand national relay team of 20 swimmers swam a record 182.807km *113.59 miles* in Lower Hutt, New Zealand in 24 hours, passing 160km *100 miles* in 20hr 47min 13sec on 9–10 Dec 1983. The 24 hours club record by a team of five is 162.52km *100.99 miles* by the Portsmouth Northsea SC at the Victoria Swimming Centre, Portsmouth, Hants on 4–5 Mar 1993. The women's record is 143.11km *88.93 miles* by the City of Newcastle ASC on 16–17 Dec 1986. The most participants in a one-day swim relay is 2305, each swimming a length, organized by Auburn YMCA-WEIU at Auburn, New York, USA on 5–6 Mar 1993.

Underwater swimming Paul Cryne (GB) and Samir Sawan al Awami of Qatar swam 78.92km *49.04 miles* in a 24hr period from Doha, Qatar to Umm Said and back on 21–22 Feb 1985 using sub-aqua equipment. They were swimming underwater for 95.5 per cent of the time. A relay team of six swam 151.987km *94.44 miles* in a swimming pool at Olomouc, Czechoslovakia on 17–18 Oct 1987.

Table Tennis

Most titles *World (instituted 1926)* G. Viktor Barna (1911–72) (b. Hungary, Győző Braun) won a record five singles, 1930, 1932–5 and eight men's doubles, 1929–35, 1939. Angelica Rozeanu (Romania) (b. 15 Oct 1921) won a record six women's singles, 1950–55, and Mária Mednyánszky (Hungary) (1901–79) won seven women's doubles, 1928, 1930–35. With two more at mixed doubles and seven team, Viktor Barna had 22 world titles in all, while 18 were won by Mária Mednyánszky. With the staging of the

championships now biennial, the breaking of the above records would be very difficult.

The most men's team titles (Swaythling Cup) is 12 by Hungary, 1927–31, 1933–5, 1938, 1949, 1952 and 1979. The women's record (Marcel Corbillon Cup) is ten by China, 1965, eight successive 1975–89 (biennially) and 1993.

English Open (instituted 1921) Richard Bergmann (Austria, then GB) (1918–70) won a record six singles, 1939–40, 1948, 1950, 1952, 1954 and Viktor Barna won seven men's doubles, 1931, 1933–5, 1938–9, 1949. The women's singles record is six by Maria Alexandru (Romania) (b. 1941), 1963–4, 1970–72, 1974 and Diane Rowe (now Scholer) (b. 14 Apr 1933), won 12 women's doubles titles, 1950–56, 1960, 1962–5. Viktor Barna won 20 titles in all, and Diane Rowe 17.

English Closed The most titles won is 26 by Desmond Hugh Douglas (b. 20 Jul 1955), a record 11 men's singles, 1976, 1979–87 and 1990, 11 men's doubles and 4 mixed doubles. A record seven women's singles were won by Jill Patricia Hammersley (now Parker, *née* Shirley) (b. 6 Dec 1951) in 1973–6, 1978–9, 1981.

Internationals Joy Foster was aged 8 when she represented Jamaica in the West Indies Championships at Port of Spain, Trinidad in August 1958. The youngest ever to play for England was Nicola Deaton (b. 29 Oct 1976), aged 13yr 336days, against Sweden at Burton on Trent, Staffs on 30 Sep 1990.

Jill Parker played for England on a record 413 occasions, 1967–83.

Taekwondo

The first World Taekwondo Championships were organized by the Korean Taekwondo Association and were held at Seoul in 1973. The World Taekwondo Federation was then formed and has organized biennial championships and women's events were first contested in 1987.

Most titles The most world titles won is four by Chung Kook-hyun (South Korea), light-middleweight 1982–3, welterweight 1985, 1987. Taekwondo was included as a demonstration sport at the 1988 Olympic Games.

Tennis (Lawn)

Grand Slam The first man to have won all four of the world's major championship singles: Wimbledon, US, Australian and French Open championships was Frederick John Perry (GB) (b. 18 May 1909) when he won the French title in 1935. The first man to hold all four championships simultaneously was John Donald

Pete Sampras celebrates winning the 1993 US Open. Having already won Wimbledon, he completed a hat-trick of grand slam tournament wins by taking the Australian Open early in 1994. He, however, failed to become the first men's player since Rod Laver to complete the grand slam as he lost to Jim Courier in the quarter-finals of the French Open.
(Photos: Allsport/Chris Cole & Simon Bruty)

Budge (USA) (b. 13 Jun 1915) in 1938, and with Wimbledon and US in 1937, he won six successive grand slam tournaments. The first man to achieve the grand slam twice was Rodney George Laver (Australia) (b. 9 Aug 1938) as an amateur in 1962 and again in 1969 when the titles were open to professionals.

Four women have achieved the grand slam and the first three won six successive grand slam tournaments: Maureen Catherine Connolly (USA) (1934–69), in 1953; Margaret Jean Court (*née* Smith) (Australia) (b. 16 Jul 1942) in 1970; and Martina Navrátilová (USA) (b. 18 Oct 1956) in 1983–4. The fourth was Stefanie Maria 'Steffi' Graf (West Germany) (b. 14 Jun 1969) in 1988, when she also won the women's singles Olympic gold medal. Pamela Howard Shriver (USA) (b. 4 Jul 1962) with Navrátilová won a record eight successive grand slam tournament women's doubles titles and 109 successive matches in all events from April 1983 to July 1985.

GUESS WHAT?

Q Where is the oldest active Real tennis court in Great Britain?

A See Page 280

The first doubles pair to win the grand slam were the Australians Frank Allan Sedgeman (b. 29 Oct 1927) and Kenneth Bruce McGregor (b. 2 Jun 1929) in 1951.

The most singles championships won in grand slam tournaments is 24 by Margaret Court (11 Australian, 5 USA, 5 French, 3 Wimbledon), 1960–73. She also won the US Amateur in 1969 and 1970 when this was held as well as the US Open. The men's record is 12 by Roy Stanley Emerson (Australia) (b. 3 Nov 1936) (6 Australian, 2 each French, USA, Wimbledon), 1961–7.

The most grand slam tournament wins by a doubles partnership is 20 by Althea Louise Brough (USA) (b. 11 Mar 1923) and Margaret Evelyn Du Pont (*née* Osborne) (USA) (b. 4 Mar 1918), (12 US, 5 Wimbledon, 3 French), 1942–57; and by Martina Navrátilová and Pam Shriver, (7 Australian, 5 Wimbledon, 4 French, 4 USA), 1981–9.

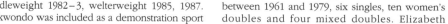
Wimbledon Championships

Most wins *Women* Billie-Jean King (USA) (*née* Moffitt) (b. 22 Nov 1943) won a record 20 titles between 1961 and 1979, six singles, ten women's doubles and four mixed doubles. Elizabeth Montague Ryan (USA) (1892–1979) won a record 19 doubles (12 women's, 7 mixed) titles from 1914 to 1934.

Men The greatest number of titles by a man has been 13 by Hugh Laurence Doherty (GB) (1875–1919) with five singles titles (1902–6) and a record eight men's doubles (1897–1901, 1903–5) partnered by his brother Reginald Frank (1872–1910).

Singles Martina Navrátilová has won a record nine titles, 1978–9, 1982–7 and 1990. The most men's singles wins since the Challenge Round was abolished in 1922 is five consecutively, by Björn Rune Borg (Sweden) (b. 6 Jun 1956) in 1976–80. William Charles Renshaw (GB) (1861–1904) won seven singles in 1881–6 and 1889.

Mixed doubles The male record is four titles shared by: Elias Victor Seixas (USA) (b. 30 Aug 1923) in 1953–6; Kenneth Norman Fletcher (Australia) (b. 15 Jun 1940) in 1963, 1965–6, 1968; and Owen Keir Davidson (Australia) (b. 4 Oct 1943) in 1967, 1971, 1973–4. The female record is seven by Elizabeth Ryan (USA) from 1919 to 1932.

Most appearances Arthur William Charles 'Wentworth' Gore (1868–1928) (GB) made a record 36 appearances at Wimbledon between 1888 and 1927. In 1964, Jean Borotra (France) (b. 13 Aug 1898) made 35 appearances in the men's singles, 1922–64 and then played in the Veterans' Doubles to 1977 when he was 78.

Youngest champions The youngest champion was Charlotte 'Lottie' Dod (1871–1960), who was 15 yr 285 days when she won in 1887. The youngest male champion was Boris Becker (West Germany) (b. 22 Nov 1967) who won the men's singles title in 1985 at 17 yr 227 days. The youngest ever player at Wimbledon was reputedly Mita Klima (Austria) who was 13 yr in the 1907 singles competition. The youngest seed was Jennifer Capriati (USA) (b. 29 Mar 1976) at 14 yr 89 days for her first match on 26 Jun 1990. She won this match, making her the youngest ever winner at Wimbledon.

Oldest champions The oldest champion was Margaret Evelyn du Pont (*née* Osborne) at 44 yr 125 days when she won the mixed doubles in 1962 with Neale Fraser (Australia). The oldest singles champion was Arthur Gore (GB) in 1909 at 41 yr 182 days.

Greatest crowd The record crowd for one day was 39,813 on 26 Jun 1986. The record for the whole championship was 403,706 in 1989.

United States Championships

Most wins Margaret Evelyn du Pont (*née* Osborne) won a record 25 titles between 1941 and 1960. She won a record 13 women's doubles (12 with Althea Louise Brough), nine mixed doubles and three singles. The men's record is 16 by William Tatem Tilden, including seven men's singles, 1920–25, 1929—a record for singles shared with: Richard Dudley Sears (1861–1943), 1881–7; William A. Larned (1872–1926), 1901–2, 1907–11, and at women's singles by: Molla Mallory (*née* Bjurstedt) (1884–1959), 1915–16, 1918, 1920–22, 1926; and Helen Newington Moody (*née* Wills) (USA) (b. 6 Oct 1905), 1923–5, 1927–9, 1931.

Youngest and oldest The youngest champion was Vincent Richards (1903–59), who was 15 yr 139 days when he won the men's doubles with Bill Tilden in 1918. The youngest singles champion was Tracy Ann Austin (b. 12 Dec 1962) who was 16 yr 271 days when she won the women's singles in 1979. The youngest men's champion was Pete Sampras (b. 12 Aug 1971) who was 19 yr 28 days when he won in 1990. The oldest champion was Margaret du Pont who won the mixed doubles at 42 yr 166 days in 1960. The oldest singles champion was William Larned at 38 yr 242 days in 1911.

French Championships

Most wins (from international status 1925) Margaret Court won a record 13 titles, five singles, four women's doubles and four mixed doubles, 1962–73. The men's record is nine by Henri Cochet (France) (1901–87), four singles, three men's doubles and two mixed doubles, 1926–30. The singles record is seven by Chris Evert, 1974–5, 1979–80, 1983, 1985–6. Björn Borg won a record six men's singles, 1974–5, 1978–81.

Youngest and oldest The youngest doubles champions were the 1981 mixed doubles winners, Andrea Jaeger (b. 4 Jun 1965) at 15 yr 339 days and Jimmy Arias (b. 16 Aug 1964) at 16 yr 296 days. The youngest singles winners have been: Monica Seles (Yugoslavia) (b. 2 Dec 1973)

Lawn Tennis' *Grand Slam*

To have achieved what is known as a Grand Slam in tennis is to be the holder of all four major titles (Australian, French, Wimbledon, United States) at the same time although not neccessarily the same year as was originally required. Fourteen players have achieved this feat in singles or doubles, and two, Margaret Court and Martina Navratilova, have performed a Grand Slam in both singles and doubles. The notable performance is that of Navratilova who achieved her 'Slams' at the same time. As can be seen from the following table, the dominance of these players usually extends beyond four consecutive titles.

SINGLES

Men

Donald Budge (USA)	1937 ●●	1938 ○●●●
Rod Laver (Australia)	1962 ○●●●	
	1969 ○●●●	

Women

Maureen Connolly (USA)	1952 ●●	1953 ○●●●
Margaret Court (USA)	1969 ●	1970 ○●●● 1971 ○
Martina Navratilova (USA)	1983 ●●	1984 ○●●●
Steffi Graf (Germany)	1988 ○●●●	1989 ○
	1993 ●●●	1994 ○

DOUBLES

Men

| Frank Sedgeman (Australia) | 1950 ● | 1951 ○●●● 1952 ○●● |
| Ken McGregor (Australia) | 1951 ○●●● | 1952 ○●● |

Women

Louise Brough (USA)	1949 ○●●	1950 ○
Maria Bueno (Brazil)	1960 ○●●●	
Martina Navratilova (USA)	1983 ●●○ 1984 ●●●○ 1985 ●	
	1985 ○ 1986 ●●● 1987 ○○	
Pam Shriver (USA)	1983 ●●○ 1984 ●●●○ 1985 ●	
	1986 ●● 1987 ○○	

Mixed

Margaret Smith (Australia)	1962 ● 1963 ○●●● 1964 ○○
Ken Fletcher (Australia)	1963 ○●●● 1964 ●○○
Owen Davidson (Australia)	1966 ● 1967 ○●●●
Billie Jean King (USA)	1967 ○●● 1968 ○

| ○ Australian | ● French | ● Wimbledon | ● United States |

The term 'Grand Slam' has been borrowed from the card game, bridge. Allison Danzig, tennis correspondent of the *New York Times*, compared Donald Budge's achievement of being holder of all four major championships at the same time, after having won the French title in 1938, to that of a bridge player winning all 13 tricks and scoring a *grand slam*.

who won the 1990 women's title at 16yr 169days and Michael Chang (USA) (b. 22 Feb 1972) the men's at 17yr 109days in 1989. The oldest champion was Elizabeth Ryan who won the 1934 women's doubles with Simone Mathieu (France) at 42yr 88days. The oldest singles champion was Andrés Gimeno (Spain) (b. 3 Aug 1937) in 1972 at 34yr 301days.

Australian Championships

Most wins Margaret Jean Court (*née* Smith) (b. 16 Jul 1942) won the women's singles 11 times (1960–66, 1969–71 and 1973) as well as eight women's doubles and two mixed doubles, for a record total of 21 titles. A record six men's singles were won by Roy Stanley Emerson (Qld)

(b. 3 Nov 1936), 1961 and 1963–7. Thelma Dorothy Long (*née* Coyne) (b. 30 May 1918) won a record 12 women's doubles and four mixed doubles for a record total of 16 doubles titles. Adrian Karl Quist (b. 4 Aug 1913) won ten consecutive men's doubles from 1936 to 1950 (the last eight with John Bromwich) and three men's singles.

Longest span, oldest and youngest Thelma Long won her first (1936) and last (1958) titles 22 years apart. Kenneth Robert Rosewall (b. 2 Nov 1934) won the singles in 1953 and in 1972 was, 19 years later, at 37yr 62days, the oldest singles winner. The oldest champion was (Sir) Norman Everard Brookes (1877–1968), who was 46yr 2months when he won the 1924 men's doubles. The youngest champions were Rodney W. Heath, aged 17, when he won the men's singles in 1905, and Monica Seles, who won the women's singles at 17yr 55days in 1991.

Grand Prix Masters

The first Grand Prix Masters Championships were staged in Tokyo, Japan in 1970. They were held in New York, USA annually, 1977–1989 with qualification by success in the preceding year's Grand Prix tournaments. The event was replaced from 1990 by the ATP Tour Championship, held in Frankfurt, Germany. A record five titles have been won by Ivan Lendl, 1982–3, two in 1986 (January and December) and 1987. James Scott Connors (USA) (b. 2 Sep 1952) uniquely qualified for 14 consecutive years, 1972–85 but chose not to play in 1975, 1976 and 1985. He won in 1977 and qualified again in 1987 and 1988, but did not play in 1988.

A record seven doubles titles were won by John Patrick McEnroe (b. 16 Feb 1959) and Peter Fleming (b. 21 Jan 1955) (both USA), 1978–84.

Virginia Slims Championship
The women's tour finishes with the Virginia Slims Championship, first contested in 1971. The Virginia Slims final is the one women's match played over the best of five sets (since 1983). Martina Navrátilová has a record six singles wins, between 1978 and 1986. She also has a record nine doubles wins, one with Billie-Jean King in 1980, and eight with Pam Shriver to 1991.

International Team

Davis Cup (instituted 1900) The most wins in the Davis Cup, the men's international team championship, has been 30 by the USA between 1900 and 1992. The most appearances for Cup winners is eight by Roy Emerson (Australia), 1959–62, 1964–7. Bill Tilden (USA) played in a record 28 matches in the final, winning a record 21, 17 out of 22 singles and 4 out of 6 doubles. He was in seven winning sides, 1920–26 and then four losing sides, 1927–30.

The British Isles/Great Britain have won nine times, in 1903–6, 1912, 1933–6.

Nicola Pietrangeli (Italy) (b. 11 Sep 1933) played a record 163 rubbers (66 ties), 1954 to 1972, winning 120. He played 109 singles (winning 78) and 54 doubles (winning 42).

The record number of rubbers by a British player is 65 (winning 43) by Michael J. Sangster (b. 9 Sep 1940), 1960–68; the most wins is 45 from 52 rubbers by Fred Perry, including 34 of 38 singles, 1931–6.

Wightman Cup (instituted 1923)
The annual women's match was won 51 times by the United States and 10 times by Great Britain. The contest was suspended from 1990 after a series of whitewashes by the US team. Virginia Wade (GB) (b. 10 Jul 1945) played in a record 21 ties and 56 rubbers, 1965–85, with a British record 19 wins. Christine Marie Evert (USA) (b. 21 Dec 1954) won all 26 of her singles matches, 1971 to 1985 and including doubles achieved a record 34 wins from 38 rubbers played. Jennifer Capriati became, at 13yr 168days, the youngest ever Wightman Cup player when she beat Clare Wood (GB) 6–0, 6–0 at Williamsburg, Virginia, USA on 14 Sep 1989.

Federation Cup (instituted 1963) The most wins in the Federation Cup, the women's international team championship, is 14 by the USA between 1963 and 1990. Virginia Wade (GB) played each year from 1967 to 1983, in a record 57 ties, playing 100 rubbers, including 56 singles (winning 36) and 44 doubles (winning 30). Chris Evert won her first 29 singles matches, 1977–86. Her overall record, 1977–89 was 40 wins in 42 singles and 16 wins in 18 doubles matches.

Longest span as national champion Keith Gledhill (b. 17 Feb 1911) won the US National Boys' Doubles Championship with Sidney Wood in August 1926. Sixty-one years later he won the US National 75 and over Men's Doubles Championship with Elbert Lewis at Goleta, California, USA in August 1987.

Dorothy May Bundy-Cheney (USA) (b. September 1916) won 180 US titles at various age groups from 1941 to March 1988.

International contest *Longest span* Jean Borotra played in every one of the twice yearly contests between the International Club of France and the I.C. of Great Britain from the first in 1929 to his 100th match at Wimbledon on 1–3 Nov 1985. On that occasion he played a mixed doubles against Kitty Godfree (GB). Both were former Wimbledon singles champions, and aged 87 and 88 respectively.

Highest earnings Pete Sampras (USA) won a men's season's record of $3,648,075 and Steffi Graf (Germany) a women's record of $2,622,352, both in 1993. The career earnings records are: (men) $20,400,410 by Ivan Lendl (Czechoslovakia, now USA) (b. 7 Mar 1960); (women) $19,645,645 by Martina Navrátilová,

---

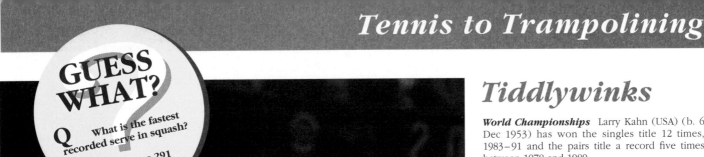

Jana Novotna has recorded the fastest serve, using modern equipment, in women's tennis with a speed of 185 km/h *115 mph*.
(Photo: Allsport/Chris Cole)

Tiddlywinks

World Championships Larry Kahn (USA) (b. 6 Dec 1953) has won the singles title 12 times, 1983–91 and the pairs title a record five times between 1978 and 1989.

National Championships Alan Dean (b. 22 Jul 1949) won the singles title six times, 1971–3, 1976, 1978 and 1986, and the pairs title six times. Jonathan Mapley (b. 1947) won the pairs title seven times, 1972, 1975, 1977, 1980, 1983–4 and 1987.

Potting records The record for potting 24 winks from 18in *45 cm* is 21.8 sec by Stephen Williams (Altrincham Grammar School) in May 1966. Allen R. Astles (University of Wales) potted 10,000 winks in 3 hr 51 min 46 sec at Aberystwyth, Dyfed in February 1966.

On 21 Oct 1989 several records were set by members of the Cambridge University Tiddlywinks Club at Queens' College, Cambridge and these included: 41 winks potted in relay in three minutes by Patrick Barrie, Nick Inglis, Geoff Myers and Andy Purvis, a long jump of 9.17m *30 ft 1 in* by Andy Purvis and a high jump 3.49m *11 ft 5 in* by Adrian Jones, David Smith and Ed Wynn.

Trampolining

Most titles World Championships were instituted in 1964 and held biennially since 1968. The most titles won is nine by Judy Wills (USA) (b. 1948), a record five individual 1964–8, two pairs 1966–7 and two tumbling 1965–6. The men's record is four by: Yevgeniy Yanes (USSR), two individual 1976 (shared), 1978 and two pairs 1976–8; and Vadim Krasnochapaka (USSR), three pairs 1984–8 and individual 1988. Brett Austine (Australia) won three individual titles at double mini, 1982–6.

A record nine United Kingdom titles have been won by Sue Challis (*née Shotton*) (b. 18 Oct 1965) (1980–82, 1984–5, 1987 (shared), 1990, 1992–3). The most by a man has been five by Stewart Matthews (b. 19 Feb 1962) (1976–80).

Youngest international British Andrea Holmes (b. 2 Jan 1970) competed for Britain at 12 yr 131 days in the World Championships at Montana, USA on 13 May 1982.

Blasted!

The fastest service timed with modern equipment is 222 km/h *138 mph* by Steve Denton (USA) (b. 5 Sep 1956) at Beaver Creek, Colorado, USA on 29 Jul 1984. The women's best is 185 km/h *115 mph* by Brenda Schultz (Netherlands) (b. 28 Dec 1970) and Jana Novotna (Czechoslovakia) (b. 2 Oct 1968), both at the 1993 Wimbledon Championships, on 25 June and 1 July respectively.

The longest match in a grand slam tournament is 5 hr 26 min between Stefan Edberg (Sweden) and Michael Chang (USA) for the semi-final of the US Championships on 12–13 Sep 1992. Edberg won 6–7, 7–5, 7–6, 5–7, 6–4.

both to mid-April 1994. Navrátilová won a world record 167 singles tournaments and 164 doubles titles. Earnings from special restricted events and team tennis are not included.

The greatest first-place prize money ever won is $2 million by Pete Sampras when he won the Grand Slam Cup at Munich, Germany on 16 Dec 1990. In the final he beat Brad Gilbert (USA) (b. 9 Aug 1961) 6–3, 6–4, 6–2. Gilbert received $1 million, also well in excess of the previous record figure. The highest total prize money is $9,022,000 for the 1993 US Open Championships.

Greatest crowd A record 30,472 people were at the Astrodome, Houston, Texas, USA for the 'Battle of the Sexes' on 20 Sep 1973, when Billie-Jean King beat Robert Larimore Riggs (USA) (b. 25 Feb 1918). The record for an orthodox tennis match is 25,578 at Sydney, New South Wales,

Australia on 27 Dec 1954 in the Davis Cup Challenge Round (first day) Australia *v.* USA.

Longest game The longest known singles game was one of 37 deuces (80 points) between Anthony Fawcett (Rhodesia) and Keith Glass (GB) in the first round of the Surrey Championships at Surbiton on 26 May 1975. It lasted 31 min. Noëlle van Lottum and Sandra Begijn played a game lasting 52 min in the semi-finals of the Dutch Indoor Championships at Ede, Gelderland on 12 Feb 1984.

The longest tiebreak was 26–24 for the fourth and decisive set of a first round men's doubles at the Wimbledon Championships on 1 Jul 1985. Jan Gunnarsson (Sweden) and Michael Mortensen (Denmark) defeated John Frawley (Australia) and Victor Pecci (Paraguay) 6–3, 6–4, 3–6, 7–6.

Somersaults!

Christopher Gibson performed 3025 consecutive somersaults at Shipley Park, Derbys on 17 Nov 1989.

The most complete somersaults in one minute is 75 by Richard Cobbing of Lightwater, Surrey, at BBC Television Centre, London for *Record Breakers* on 8 Nov 1989. The most baranis in a minute is 78 by Zoe Finn of Chatham, Kent at BBC Television Centre, London for *Blue Peter* on 25 Jan 1988.

Triathlon

The triathlon combines long-distance swimming, cycling and running. Distances for each of the phases can vary, but for the best established event, the Hawaii Ironman (instituted 1978), competitors first swim 3.8km *2.4 miles*, then cycle 180km *112 miles*, and finally run a full marathon of 42.195km *26 miles 385 yards*. Record times for the Hawaii Ironman are: (men) 8hr 7min 45sec Mark Allen (USA) in 1993; (women) 8hr 55min 28sec Paula Newby-Fraser (Zimbabwe) (b. 2 Jun 1962) in 1992. Dave Scott (USA) (b. 4 Jan 1959) has won a record six races, 1980, 1982–84 and 1986–87. Paula Newby-Fraser has won the women's race six times, 1986, 1988–9 and 1991–3. The fastest time recorded over the Ironman distances is 8hr 1min 32sec by Dave Scott at Lake Biwa, Japan on 30 Jul 1989. The women's record is 8hr 55min by Paula Newby-Fraser at Roth, Germany on 12 Jul 1992.

The fastest time recorded by a Briton for the Ironman distances is 8hr 37min 19sec by Alan Ingarfield at Roth, Germany on 11 Jul 1992.

World Championships After earlier abortive efforts a world governing body *L'Union Internationale de Triathlon* (UIT) was founded at Avignon, France on 1 Apr 1989, staging the first official World Championships over the internationally recognised distances (1500m swim, 40km cycle, 10km run) in August 1989.

A 'World Championship' race has been held annually in Nice, France from 1982; the distances 3200m, 120km and 32km respectively, with the swim increased to 4000m from 1988. Mark Allen (USA) has won ten times, 1982–86, 1989–93. Paula Newby-Fraser has a record four women's wins, 1989–92. Record times: men, Mark Allen 5hr 46min 10sec in 1986; women, Erin Baker (New Zealand) (b. 23 May 1961) 6hr 27min 6sec in 1988.

Tug of War

Most titles World Championships were held annually 1975–86 and biennially since, with a women's event introduced in 1986. The most successful team at the World Championships has been England, who have won 16 titles in all categories, 1975–93. Sweden have won the 520kg category twice and the 560kg three times at the women's World Championships.

> The longest tug of war (in distance) is the 2.6km *1.616 miles* Supertug across the Little Traverse Bay, Lake Michigan, USA. It has been contested annually since 1980 between two teams of 20 from Bay View Inn and Harbor Inn.

The Wood Treatment team (formerly the Bosley Farmers) of Cheshire won 20 consecutive AAA Catchweight Championships 1959–78, two world titles (1975–6) and ten European titles at 720kg. Hilary Brown (b. 13 Apr 1934) was in every team. Trevor Brian Thomas (b. 1943) of British Aircraft Corporation Club is the only holder of three winners' medals in the European Open club competitions and added a world gold medal in 1988.

Longest pulls *Duration* The longest recorded pull (prior to the introduction of AAA rules) is one of 2hr 41min when 'H' Company beat 'E'

Company of the 2nd Battalion of the Sherwood Foresters (Derbyshire Regiment) at Jubbulpore, India on 12 Aug 1889. The longest recorded pull under AAA rules (in which lying on the ground or entrenching the feet is not permitted) is one of 24min 45sec for the first pull between the Republic of Ireland and England during the world championships (640kg class) at Malmö, Sweden on 18 Sep 1988.

Volleyball

Most world titles World Championships were instituted in 1949 for men and 1952 for women. The USSR won six men's titles (1949, 1952, 1960, 1962, 1978 and 1982) and five women's (1952, 1956, 1960, 1970 and 1990)

Most Olympic titles The sport was introduced to the Olympic Games for both men and women in 1964. The USSR has won a record three men's (1964, 1968 and 1980) and four women's (1968, 1972, 1980 and 1988) titles. The only player to win four medals is Inna Valeryevna Ryskal (USSR) (b. 15 Jun 1944), who won women's silver medals in 1964 and 1976 and golds in 1968 and 1972. The record for men is held by Yuriy Mikhailovich Poyarkov (USSR) (b. 10 Feb 1937) who won gold medals in 1964 and 1968 and a bronze in 1972, and by Katsutoshi Nekoda (Japan) (b. 1 Feb 1944) who won gold in 1972, silver in 1968 and bronze in 1964.

Most internationals *Great Britain* Ucal Ashman (b. 10 Nov 1957) made a record 153 men's international appearances for England, 1976– 86. The women's record is 171 by Ann Jarvis (b. 3 Jun 1955) for England, 1974–87.

Water Polo

Most Olympic titles Hungary has won the Olympic tournament most often with six wins in 1932, 1936, 1952, 1956, 1964 and 1976. Great Britain won in 1900, 1908, 1912 and 1920.

Five players share the record of three gold medals; Britons George Wilkinson (1879–1946) in 1900, 1908, 1912; Paulo 'Paul' Radmilovic (1886–1968), and Charles Sidney Smith (1879–1951) in 1908, 1912, 1920; and Hungarians Deszö Gyarmati (b. 23 Oct 1927) and György

Kárpáti (b. 23 Jun 1935) in 1952, 1956, 1964. Paul Radmilovic also won a gold medal for the 4×200m freestyle swimming in 1908.

World Championships First held at the World Swimming Championships in 1973. The most wins is two by the USSR, 1975 and 1982, and Yugoslavia, 1986 and 1991. A women's competition was introduced in 1986, when it was won by Australia. The Netherlands won the second women's world title in 1991.

> **GUESS WHAT?**
>
> **Q** What are the three disciplines of freestyle skiing?
>
> **A** See Page 289

Most goals The greatest number of goals scored by an individual in an international is 13 by Debbie Handley for Australia (16) *v.* Canada (10) at the World Championship in Guayaquil, Ecuador in 1982.

Most international appearances The greatest number of international appearances is 412 by Aleksey Stepanovich Barkalov (USSR) (b. 18 Feb 1946), 1965–80. The British record is 126 by Martyn Thomas, of Cheltenham, Glos, 1964–78.

Water Skiing

Most titles World Overall Championships (instituted 1949) have been won four times by Samuel E. 'Sammy' Duvall III (USA) (b. 9 Aug 1962) in 1981, 1983, 1985 and 1987 and three times by two women, Willa McGuire (*née* Worthington) (USA) (b. 1928) in 1949–50 and 1955 and Elizabeth 'Liz' Allan-Shetter (USA) (b. 12 Jul 1947) in 1965, 1969 and 1975. Liz Allan-Shetter has won a record eight individual championship events and is the only person to win all four titles—slalom, jumping, tricks and overall in one year, at Copenhagen, Denmark in 1969. Patrice Martin (France) (b. 24 May 1964) has won a men's record seven titles. The USA have won the team championship on 17 successive occasions, 1957–89.

The most British Overall titles (instituted 1953) won by a man is seven by Michael Hazelwood (b. 14 Apr 1958) in 1974, 1976–9, 1981, 1983; the most by a woman is ten by Philippa Mary

Patrice Martin has won a men's record seven water skiing world titles. He won the tricks title in 1985, 1987 and 1991, slalom 1993 and overall 1989, 1991 and 1993.

(Photo: Allsport/Vandystadt/Jean Marc Barey)

This spectacular shot shows the record 100 water skiers being towed over a nautical mile by the cruiser *Reef Cat* at Cairns, Queensland, Australia on 18 Oct 1986. This feat, organized by the Cairns and District Powerboat and Ski Club, was first performed on double skis and then replicated by the 100 skiers on single skis.

(Photo: Yon Ivanovic, Studio One)

Elizabeth Roberts (b. 11 Apr 1960), 1977, 1982, 1985–92.

Highest speed The fastest water skiing speed recorded is 230.26 km/h *143.08 mph* by Christopher Michael Massey (Australia) on the Hawkesbury River, Windsor, New South Wales, Australia on 6 Mar 1983. His drag boat driver was Stanley Charles Sainty. Donna Patterson Brice (b. 1953) set a feminine record of 178.8 km/h *111.11 mph* at Long Beach, California, USA on 21 Aug 1977.

The fastest recorded speed by a British skier over a measured kilometre is 154.38 km/h *95.93 mph* (average) on Lake Windermere, Cumbria on 16 Oct 1989 by Darren Kirkland. The fastest speed recorded by a British woman is 141.050 km/h *87.647 mph* by Nikki Carpenter on Lake Windermere, Cumbria on 18 Oct 1988.

Water Skiing Records

WORLD

Slalom
MEN: 3.5 buoys on a 10.25 m line, Andrew Mapple (GB) (b. 3 Nov 1958) at Miami, Florida, USA on 6 Oct 1991.
WOMEN: 2 buoys on a 10.75 m line, Susi Graham (Canada) in September 1993.

Tricks
MEN: 11,150 points, Cory Pickos (USA) at Mulberry, Florida, USA on 27 Sep 1992.
WOMEN: 8580 points, Tawn Larsen (USA) at Groveland, Florida, USA on 4 Jul 1992.

Jumping
MEN: 67.1 m *220 ft*, Sammy Duvall (USA) at Santa Rosa Beach, Florida, USA on 10 Sep 1993.
WOMEN: 47.5 m *156 ft*, Deena Mapple (USA) (b. 2 Mar 1960) at Charlotte, North Carolina, USA on 9 Jul 1988.

BRITISH

Slalom
MEN: (see World Listing)
WOMEN: 2 buoys at 11.25 m, Philippa Roberts, Cirencester, Glos, 1990.

Tricks
MEN: 8650 points, John Battleday (b. 1 Feb 1957) at Lyon, France on 5 Aug 1984.
WOMEN: 6820 points, Nicola Rasey (b. 6 Jun 1966) at Martigues, France on 27 Oct 1984.

Jumping
MEN: 61.9 m *203 ft* Michael Hazelwood at Birmingham, Alabama, USA on 30 Jun 1986.
WOMEN: 44.9 m *147 ft*, Kathy Hulme (b. 11 Feb 1959) at Kirtons Farm, Reading, Berkshire on 1 Aug 1982.

Barefoot

World Championships (instituted 1978) The most Over-all titles is four by Kim Lampard (Australia) 1980, 1982, 1985, 1986 and the men's record is three by Brett Wing (Australia) 1978, 1980, 1982. The team title has been won five times by Australia, 1978, 1980, 1982, 1985 and 1986.

Highest speed The official barefoot speed record is 218.44km/h *135.74mph* by Scott Michael Pellaton (b. 8 Oct 1956) over a quarter-mile course at Chandler, Arizona, California, USA in November 1989. The fastest by a woman is 118.56km/h *73.67mph* by Karen Toms (Australia) on the Hawkesbury River, Windsor, New South Wales on 31 Mar 1984.

The British records are: (men) 114.86km/h *71.37mph* by Richard Mainwaring (b. 4 Jun 1953) at Holme Pierrepont, Notts on 2 Dec 1978; (women) 80.25km/h *49.86 mph* by Michele Doherty (b. 28 May 1964) (also 71.54km/h *44.45mph* backwards), both at Witney, Oxon on 18 Oct 1986.

Jumping The records are: men 27.0m *88ft 6in* by Dodd Dwyer (Australia) in 1993; women 16.6m *54ft 5in* by Sharon Stekelenberg (Australia) in 1991.

The British records are: men 24.5m *80ft 4in* by Benjamin Goggin at White Rose, Yorks in September 1993; and women 15.1m *49ft 6in* by Kim Harding at Cirencester, Glos in August 1992.

GUESS WHAT?

Q Who has the world's largest feet?

A See Page 60

Weightlifting

The first championships entitled 'world' were staged at the Café Monico, Piccadilly, London on 28 Mar 1891 and then in Vienna, Austria on 19–20 Jul 1898, subsequently recognized by the IWF. The *Fédération Internationale Haltérophile et Culturiste*, now the International Weightlifting Federation (IWF), was established in 1905, and its first official championships were held in Tallinn, Estonia on 29–30 Apr 1922.

Most titles *World* The most world title wins, including Olympic Games, is eight by: John Henry Davis (USA) (1921–84) in 1938, 1946–52; Tommy Kono (USA) (b. 27 Jun 1930) in 1952–9; and by Vasiliy Alekseyev (USSR) (b. 7 Jan 1942), 1970–77.

Most Olympic medals Norbert Schemansky (USA) (b. 30 May 1924) won a record four Olympic medals: gold, middle-heavyweight 1952; silver, heavyweight 1948; bronze, heavyweight 1960 and 1964.

Youngest and oldest world record holder Naim Suleimanov (later Neum Shalamanov) (Bulgaria) (b. 23 Jan 1967) (now Naim Suleymanoğlü of Turkey) set 56kg world records for clean and jerk (160 kg) and total (285kg) at 16yr 62days at Allentown, New Jersey, USA on 26 Mar 1983. The oldest is Norbert Schemansky (USA) who snatched 362lb 164.2kg in the then unlimited heavyweight class, aged 37yr 333days, at Detroit, Michigan, USA on 28 Apr 1962.

Most successful British lifter The only British lifter to win an Olympic title has been Launceston Elliot (1874–1930), the open one-handed lift champion in 1896 at Athens. Louis George Martin (b. Jamaica, 11 Nov 1936) won four world and European mid-heavyweight titles in 1959, 1962–3, 1965. He won an Olympic silver medal in 1964 and a bronze in 1960 and three Commonwealth gold medals in 1962, 1966, 1970. His total of British titles was 12.

World Weightlifting Records

From 1 Jan 1993, the International Weightlifting Federation (IWF) introduced modified weight categories thereby making the then world records redundant. In February they announced that 'the results of major IWF-controlled competitions and championships will be collected until 30 Sep 1993 and the best results be declared as basic performances, with world records to be broken for the first time at the Melbourne World Championships (12–21 November)'. This is the current list with world standards yet to be set and records set as of 1 Jun 1994 for men and 1 Apr 1994 for women.

Bodyweight	Lift	kg	lb	Name and Country	Place	Date
54 kg *119 lb*	Snatch	125	*275½*	Sevdalin Minchev (Bulgaria)	Sokolov, Czech Republic	4 May 1994
	Jerk	157.5	*347½*	*World Standard*		
	Total	277.5	*611¾*	Ivan Ivanov (Bulgaria)	Melbourne, Australia	12 Nov 1993
59 kg *130 lb*	Snatch	137.5	*303*	*World Standard*		
	Jerk	167.5	*369¼*	Nikolai Pershalov (Bulgaria)	Melbourne, Australia	13 Nov 1993
	Total	305	*672¼*	Nikolai Pershalov (Bulgaria)	Melbourne, Australia	13 Nov 1993
64 kg *141 lb*	Snatch	145	*319¾*	Naim Suleymanoğlü (Turkey)*	Sokolov, Czech Republic	5 May 1994
	Jerk	180	*396¾*	Naim Suleymanoğlü (Turkey)*	Sokolov, Czech Republic	5 May 1994
	Total	325	*716½*	Naim Suleymanoğlü (Turkey)*	Sokolov, Czech Republic	5 May 1994
70 kg *154¼lb*	Snatch	157.5	*347¼*	Israil Militosyan (Armenia)	Sokolov, Czech Republic	5 May 1994
	Jerk	192.5	*424¼*	Yotov Yoto (Bulgaria)	Sokolov, Czech Republic	5 May 1994
	Total	345	*760½*	Yotov Yoto (Bulgaria)	Sokolov, Czech Republic	5 May 1994
76 kg *167½ lb*	Snatch	170	*374¾*	Ruslan Savchenko (Ukriane)	Melbourne, Australia	16 Nov 1993
	Jerk	205	*452*	Pablo Lara (Cuba)	Ponce, Puerto Rico	25 Nov 1993
	Total	370	*815¾*	Ruslan Savchenko (Ukriane)	Melbourne, Australia	16 Nov 1993
83kg *183lb*	Snatch	175	*385¾*	*World Standard*		
	Jerk	210	*463*	Marc Huster (Germany)	Melbourne, Australia	17 Nov 1993
	Total	380	*837¾*	*World Standard*		
91 kg *200½ lb*	Snatch	185	*407¾*	Ivan Chakarov (Australia)	Melbourne, Australia	18 Nov 1993
	Jerk	227.5	*501½*	Alexey Petrov (Russia)	Sokolov, Czech Republic	7 May 1994
	Total	412.5	*909¼*	Alexey Petrov (Russia)	Sokolov, Czech Republic	7 May 1994
99 kg *218½ lb*	Snatch	190.5	*420*	Sergey Syrtsov (Russia)	Sokolov, Czech Republic	7 May 1994
	Jerk	225	*496*	Sergey Syrtsov (Russia)	Sokolov, Czech Republic	7 May 1994
	Total	415	*915*	Sergey Syrtsov (Russia)	Sokolov, Czech Republic	7 May 1994
108 kg *238lb*	Snatch	197.5	*435¼*	*World Standard*		
	Jerk	235	*518*	Timour Taimazov (Ukraine)	Sokolov, Czech Republic	8 May 1994
	Total	430	*948*	Timour Taimazov (Ukraine)	Sokolov, Czech Republic	8 May 1994
Over 108 kg	Snatch	200.5	*442*	Andrey Chermkin (Russia)	Sokolov, Czech Republic	8 May 1994
	Jerk	250	*551*	Andrey Chermkin (Russia)	Sokolov, Czech Republic	8 May 1994
	Total	450	*992*	Andrey Chermkin (Russia)	Sokolov, Czech Republic	8 May 1994

** Formerly Naim Suleimanov or Neum Shalamanov of Bulgaria*

Women's Weightlifting Records

46 kg *101¼ lb*	Snatch	72.5	*159¾*	Luo Hongwei (China)	Shilong, China	15 Dec 1993
	Jerk	92.5	*204*	Luo Hongwei (China)	Shilong, China	15 Dec 1993
	Total	165	*363¾*	Luo Hongwei (China)	Shilong, China	15 Dec 1993
50 kg *110¼ lb*	Snatch	77.5	*170¾*	Liu Xiuhia (China)	Melbourne, Australia	13 Nov 1993
	Jerk	110	*242½*	Liu Xiuhia (China)	Melbourne, Australia	13 Nov 1993
	Total	187.5	*413¼*	Liu Xiuhia (China)	Melbourne, Australia	13 Nov 1993
54 kg *119 lb*	Snatch	90	*198¼*	Chen Xiaoming (China)	Melbourne, Australia	14 Nov 1993
	Jerk	112.5	*248*	Long Yuiling (China)	Shilong, China	16 Dec 1993
	Total	200	*441*	Chen Xiaoming (China)	Melbourne, Australia	14 Nov 1993
59 kg *130 lb*	Snatch	97.5	*215*	Sun Caiyan (China)	Melbourne, Australia	15 Nov 1993
	Jerk	120.5	*265½*	Zuo Feie (China)	Shilong, China	16 Dec 1993
	Total	217.5	*479½*	Sun Caiyan (China)	Melbourne, Australia	15 Nov 1993
64 kg *141 lb*	Snatch	103	*227*	Li Hongyun (China)	Shilong, China	17 Dec 1993
	Jerk	125	*275½*	Lei Li (China)	Shilong, China	17 Dec 1993
	Total	227.5	*501½*	Lei Li (China)	Shilong, China	17 Dec 1993
70 kg *154¼ lb*	Snatch	100	*220½*	Milena Trendafilova (Bulgaria)	Melbourne, Australia	17 Nov 1993
	Jerk	120	*264½*	Milena Trendafilova (Bulgaria)	Melbourne, Australia	17 Nov 1993
	Total	220	*485*	Milena Trendafilova (Bulgaria)	Melbourne, Australia	17 Nov 1993
76 kg *167¼ lb*	Snatch	105	*231½*	Hua Ju (China)	Melbourne, Australia	18 Nov 1993
	Jerk	140	*308½*	Zhang Guimei (China)	Shilong, China	18 Dec 1993
	Total	235	*518*	Zhang Guimei (China)	Shilong, China	18 Dec 1993
83kg *183 lb*	Snatch	107.5	*237*	Xing Shiwen (China)	Melbourne, Australia	19 Nov 1993
	Jerk	127.5	*281*	Chen Shu-chih (Taipei)	Melbourne, Australia	19 Nov 1993
	Total	230	*507*	Chen Shu-chih (Taipei)	Melbourne, Australia	19 Nov 1993
+83 kg	Snatch	105	*231½*	Li Yajuan (China)	Melbourne, Australia	20 Nov 1993
	Jerk	155	*341½*	Li Yajuan (China)	Melbourne, Australia	20 Nov 1993
	Total	260	*573*	Li Yajuan (China)	Melbourne, Australia	20 Nov 1993

World Powerlifting Records (All weights in kilograms)

MEN

Class	Squat		Bench Press		Deadlift		Total	
52 kg	252.5	Andrzej Stanashek (Pol) 1992	172.5	Andrzej Stanashek 1993	256	E S Bhaskaran (Ind) 1993	587.5	Hideaki Inaba (Jap) 1987
56 kg	257.5	Magnus Karlsson (Swe) 1993	175	Magnus Karlsson 1993	289.5	Lamar Gant (USA) 1982	625	Lamar Gant 1982
60 kg	295	Joe Bradley (USA) 1980	180.5	Magnus Karlsson 1993	310	Lamar Gant 1988	707.5	Joe Bradley 1982
67.5 kg	300	Jessie Jackson (USA) 1987	200	Kristoffer Hulecki (Swe) 1985	316	Daniel Austin (USA) 1991	762.5	Daniel Austin 1989
75 kg	328	Ausby Alexander (USA) 1989	217.5	James Rouse (USA) 1980	333	Jarmo Virtanen (Finland) 1988	850	Rick Gaugler (USA) 1982
82.5 kg	379.5	Mike Bridges (USA) 1982	240	Mike Bridges 1981	357.5	Veli Kumpuniemi (Fin) 1980	952.5	Mike Bridges 1982
90 kg	375	Fred Hatfield (USA) 1980	255	Mike MacDonald (USA) 1980	372.5	Walter Thomas (USA) 1982	937.5	Mike Bridges 1980
100 kg	422.5	Ed Coan (USA) 1989	261.5	Mike MacDonald 1977	378	Ed Coan 1989	1032.5	Ed Coan 1989
110 kg	393.5	Dan Wohleber (USA) 1981	270	Jeffrey Magruder (USA) 1982	395	John Kuc (USA) 1980	1000	John Kuc 1980
125 kg	440	Kirk Karwoski (USA) 1993	278.5	Tom Hardman (USA) 1982	387.5	Lars Norén (Swe) 1987	1005	Ernie Hackett (USA) 1982
125+ kg	445	Dwayne Fely (USA) 1982	300	Bill Kazmaier (USA) 1981	406	Lars Norén 1988	1100	Bill Kazmaier 1981

WOMEN

Class	Squat		Bench Press		Deadlift		Total	
44 kg	155.5	Raija Koskinen (Fin) 1993	82.5	Irina Krylova (Rus) 1993	165	Nancy Belliveau (USA) 1985	365	Jacquline Janot (Fra) 1993
48 kg	160	Raija Koskinen 1993	92.5	Svetlana Stepanova (Rus) 1993	182.5	Majik Jones (USA) 1984	390	Majik Jones 1984
52 kg	175.5	Mary Jeffrey (USA) (née Ryan) 1991	105	Mary Jeffrey 1991	197.5	Diana Rowell (USA) 1984	452.5	Mary Jeffrey 1991
56 kg	191	Mary Jeffrey 1989	115	Mary Jeffrey 1988	210	Carrie Boudreau (USA) 1993	500	Carrie Boudreau 1993
60 kg	210	Beate Amdahl (Nor) 1993	107.5	Irmgar Wohlhöfler (Ger) 1993	213	Ruthi Shafer 1983	502.5	Vicki Steenrod (USA) 1985
67.5 kg	230	Ruthi Shafer 1984	120	Vicki Steenrod 1990	244	Ruthi Shafer 1984	565	Ruthi Shafer 1984
75 kg	235	Cathy Millen (NZ) 1991	142.5	Liz Odendaal (Neth) 1989	240	Cathy Millen 1991	602.5	Cathy Millen 1991
82.5 kg	240	Cathy Millen 1991	150.5	Cathy Millen 1993	257.5	Cathy Millen 1993	637.5	Cathy Millen 1993
90 kg	255	Cathy Millen 1993	157.5	Cathy Millen 1993	250	Cathy Millen 1992	655	Cathy Millen 1993
90+kg	272.5	Juanita Trujillo (USA) 1993	150	Ulrike Herchenhein (Ger) 1993	238	Ulrike Herchenhein 1993	622.5	Lorraine Constanzo 1987

British Powerlifting Records (All weights in kilograms)

MEN

Class	Squat		Bench Press		Deadlift		Total	
52 kg	218	Peter Kemp 1993	130	Phil Stringer 1981	225	John Maxwell 1988	530	Phil Stringer 1982
56 kg	235	Phil Stringer 1982	137.5	Phil Stringer 1983	229	Precious McKenzie 1973	577.5	Gary Simes 1991
60 kg	247.5	Tony Galvez 1981	142.5	Clint Lewis 1985	275	Eddy Pengelly 1977	645	Eddy Pengelly 1979
67.5 kg	275	Eddy Pengelly 1981	165	Hassan Salih 1979	295	Eddy Pengelly 1982	710	Eddy Pengelly 1982
75 kg	302.5	John Howells 1979	185	Peter Fiore 1981	310	Robert Limerick 1984	760	Steve Alexander 1983
82.5 kg	337.5	Mike Duffy 1984	210	Mike Duffy 1981	355	Ron Collins 1980	855	Ron Collins 1980
90 kg	347.5	David Caldwell 1985	227.5	Jeff Chandler 1985	350.5	Ron Collins 1980	870	David Caldwell 1985
100 kg	380	Tony Stevens 1984	225.5	Brian Reynolds 1992	362.5	Tony Stevens 1984	955	Tony Stevens 1984
110 kg	372.5	Tony Stevens 1984	250	John Neighbour 1990	380	Arthur White 1982	940	John Neighbour 1987
125 kg	390	John Neighbour 1990	250	John Neighbour 1990	373	David Cullen 1992	957.5	Steven Zetolofsky 1984
125+kg	380	Steven Zetolofsky 1979	258	Terry Purdoe 1971	377.5	Andy Kerr 1982	982.5	Andy Kerr 1983

WOMEN

Class	Squat		Bench Press		Deadlift		Total	
44 kg	130	Helen Wolsey 1991	68	Helen Wolsey 1991	152.5	Helen Wolsey 1990	350	Helen Wolsey 1991
48 kg	132.5	Helen Wolsey 1990	75	Suzanne Smith 1985	155	Helen Wolsey 1990	355	Helen Wolsey 1990
52 kg	143	Jenny Hunter 1988	82	Jenny Hunter 1988	173.5	Jenny Hunter 1988	395	Jenny Hunter 1988
56 kg	158	Jenny Hunter 1988	88	Jenny Hunter 1988	182.5	Jenny Hunter 1988	420	Jenny Hunter 1988
60 kg	163	Rita Bass 1988	92.5	Mandy Wadsworth 1992	190	Jackie Blasbery 1993	422.5	Rita Bass 1989
67.5 kg	175	Debbie Thomas 1988	102.5	Sandra Berry 1992	198	Sandra Berry 1992	460	Sandra Berry 1992
75 kg	202.5	Judith Oakes 1989	115	Judith Oakes 1989	215	Judith Oakes 1989	532.5	Judith Oakes 1989
82.5 kg	215	Judith Oakes 1988	122.5	Joanne Williams 1990	217.5	Judith Oakes 1989	542.5	Judith Oakes 1988
90 kg	200	Beverley Martin 1989	115	Joanne Williams 1989	215	Beverley Martin 1990	495	Beverley Martin 1989
90+kg	220.5	Myrtle Augee 1991	137.5	Myrtle Augee 1989	230	Myrtle Augee 1989	587.5	Myrtle Augee 1989

Heaviest lift to bodyweight The first man to clean and jerk more than three times his bodyweight was Stefan Topurov (Bulgaria) (b. 11 Aug 1964), who lifted 180kg *396¾ lb* at Moscow, USSR on 24 Oct 1983. The first man to snatch two-and-a-half times his own bodyweight was Naim Suleymanoğlü (Turkey), who lifted 150kg *330½ lb* at Cardiff, S Glam on 27 Apr 1988. The first woman to clean and jerk more than two times her own bodyweight was Cheng Jinling (China), who lifted 90kg *198 lb* in the 44kg class of the World Championships at Jakarta, Indonesia in December 1988.

Women's World Championships These are held annually, first at Daytona Beach, Florida in October 1987. Women's world records have been ratified for the best marks at these championships. Peng Liping (China) won a record 12 gold medals with snatch, jerk and total in the 52kg-class each year, 1988–9 and 1991–2.

Powerlifting

The sport of powerlifting was first contested at national level in Great Britain in 1958. The first US Championships were held in 1964. The International Power-lifting Federation was founded in 1972, a year after the first, unofficial world championships were held. Official championships have been held annually for men from 1973 and for women from 1980. The three standard lifts are squat, bench press and dead lift, the totals from the three lifts determining results.

Most titles *World* The winner of the most world titles is Hideaki Inaba (Japan) with 17, at 52kg 1974–83, 1985–91. The most by a women is six by Beverley Francis (Australia) (b. 15 Feb 1955) at 75kg 1980, 1982; 82.5kg 1981, 1983–5; and Sisi Dolman (Netherlands) at 52kg 1985–6, 1988–91. The most by a British lifter is seven by Ron Collins: 75kg 1972–4, 82kg 1975–7 and 1979.

British Edward John Pengelly (b. 8 Dec 1949) has won a record 14 consecutive national titles, 60kg 1976–9, 67½kg 1980–89. He has also won four world titles, 60kg 1976–7, 1979, 67½kg 1985, and a record ten European titles, 60kg 1978–9, 67½kg 1981, 1983–9.

Power!

Cathy Millen (New Zealand) currently holds 11 world records spread over three bodyweight categories, 16 British Commonwealth and 20 New Zealand records spread over five bodyweight categories. She has also won five world championships and her 1994 total (682.5kg) is the highest ever recorded by a woman.

Strandpull!

The International Steel Strandpullers' Association was founded by Gavin Pearson (Scotland) in 1940. The greatest ratified poundage to date is a super-heavyweight right-arm push of 815 lb *369.5 kg* by Malcolm Bartlett (b. 9 Jun 1955) of Oldham, Greater Manchester. The record for the back press anyhow is 650 lb *295 kg* by Paul Anderson, at Hull, Humberside on 29 Mar 1992. A record 22 British Open titles have been won by Ian Storton (b. 2 Feb 1951) of Morecambe, Lancs, 1974–88.

Powerlifting feats Lamar Gant (USA) was the first man to deadlift five times his own bodyweight, lifting 299.5 kg *661 lb* when 59.5 kg *131 lb* in 1985. Cammie Lynn Lusko (USA) (b. 5 Apr 1958) became the first woman to lift more than her bodyweight with one arm, with 59.5 kg *131 lb* at a bodyweight of 58.3 kg *128.5 lb*, at Milwaukee, Wisconsin, USA on 21 May 1983.

Timed lifts *24 hours* A deadlifting record of 2,620,800 kg *5,777,868 lb* was set by a team of ten from HM Prison Long Lartin, Evesham, Worcs on 17–18 Jan 1991. The deadlift record by an individual is 371,094 kg *818,121 lb* by Anthony Wright at HM Prison Featherstone, Wolverhampton, W Mids on 31 Aug–1 Sep 1990. A bench press record of 4,025,120 kg *8,873,860 lb* was set by a nine-man team from the Forum Health Club, Chelmsleywood, W Mids on 19–20 Mar 1994. A squat record of 2,168,625 kg *4,780,994 lb* was set by a ten-man team from St Albans Weightlifting Club and Ware Boys Club, Herts on 20–21 Jul 1986. A record 133,380 arm-curling repetitions using three 22 kg *48½ lb* weightlifting bars and dumb-bells was achieved by a team of nine from Intrim Health and Fitness Club at Gosport, Hants on 4–5 Aug 1989.

12 hours An individual bench press record of 514,750 kg *1,134,828 lb* was set by John 'Jack' Atherton at HMP Featherstone, W Mids on 27 May 1990.

Wrestling

Most titles *Olympic* Three Olympic titles have been won by: Carl Westergren (Sweden) (1895–1958) in 1920, 1924 and 1932; Ivar Johansson (Sweden) (1903–79) in 1932 (two) and 1936; and Aleksandr Vasilyevich Medved (USSR) (b. 16 Sep 1937) in 1964, 1968 and 1972. Four Olympic medals were won by: Eino Leino (Finland) (1891–1986) at freestyle 1920–32; and by Imre Polyák (Hungary) (b. 16 Apr 1932) at Greco-Roman in 1952–64.

World The freestyler Aleksandr Medved (USSR) won a record ten World Championships, 1962–4, 1966–72 at three weight categories. The only wrestler to win the same title in seven successive years has been Valeriy Grigoryevich Rezantsev (USSR) (b. 2 Feb 1947) in the Greco-Roman 90 kg class in 1970–76, including the Olympic Games of 1972 and 1976.

The longest recorded bout was one of 11 hr 40 min when Martin Klein (Estonia representing Russia) (1885–1947) beat Alfred Asikáinen (Finland) (1888–1942) for the Greco-Roman 75 kg 'A' event silver medal in the 1912 Olympic Games in Stockholm, Sweden.

Most titles and longest span *British* The most British titles won in one weight class is 14 by welterweight Fitzlloyd Walker (b. 7 Mar 1957), 1979–92. The longest span for BAWA titles is 24 years by George Mackenzie (1890–1957) between 1909 and 1933. He represented Great Britain in five successive Olympiads, 1908 to 1928.

Most wins In international competition, Osamu Watanabe (b. 21 Oct 1940), of Japan, the 1964 Olympic freestyle 63 kg champion, was unbeaten and did not concede a score in 189 consecutive matches. Outside of FILA sanctioned competition, Wade Schalles (USA) won 821 bouts from 1964 to 1984, with 530 of these victories by pin.

Heaviest heavyweight The heaviest wrestler in Olympic history is Chris Taylor (1950–79), bronze medallist in the super-heavyweight class in 1972, who stood 1.96 m *6 ft 5 in* tall and weighed over 190 kg *420 lb*. FILA introduced an upper weight limit of 130 kg *286 lb* for international competition in 1985.

Sumo Wrestling

The sport's origins in Japan date from *c.* 23 BC. The most successful wrestlers have been *yokozuna* Sadji Akiyoshi (b. 1912), alias Futabayama who set the all-time record of 69 consecutive wins (1937–9), *yokozuna* Koki Naya (b. 1940), alias Taiho ('Great Bird'), who won the Emperor's Cup 32 times up to his retirement in 1971 and the *ozeki* Tameemon Torokichi, alias Raiden (1767–1825), who in 21 years (1789–1810) won 254 bouts and lost only ten for the highest ever winning percentage of 96.2.

Yokozuna Mitsugu Akimoto (b. 1 Jun 1955), alias Chiyonofuji, set a record for domination of one of the six annual tournaments by winning the Kyushu Basho for eight successive years, 1981–88. He also holds the record for the most career wins, 1045 and *Makunouchi* (top division) wins, 807. Toshimitsu Ogata (b. 16 May 1953), alias Kitanoumi, set a record in 1978 winning 82 of the 90 bouts that top *rikishi* fight annually. He is youngest of the 64 men to have attained the rank of *yokozuna* (grand champion), aged 21 years and two months in July 1974.

Hawaiian-born Jesse Kuhaulua (b. 16 Jun 1944), alias Takamiyama, was the first non-Japanese to win an official top-division tournament, in July 1972 and in September 1981 he set a record of 1231 consecutive top-division bouts. In all six divisions, the most consecutive bouts is 1631 by Yukio Shoji (b. 14 Nov 1948), alias Aobajo, 1964–86. The most bouts in a career is 1891 by Kenji Hatano (b. 4 Jan 1948), alias Oshio, 1962–88.

Hawaiian-born Chad Rowan (b. 8 May 1969), alias Akebono, became the first foreign *rikishi* to be promoted to the top rank of *yokozuna* in January 1993. He is the tallest (204 cm *6 ft 8 in*) and heaviest (227 kg *501 lb*) *yokozuna* in sumo history. The heaviest ever *rikishi* is Samoan-American Salevaa Fuali Atisanoe alias Konishiki, of Hawaii, who weighed in at 267 kg *589 lb* at Tokyo's Ryogoku Kokugikan on 3 Jan 1994. Weight is amassed by over-alimentation with a high-protein stew called *chankonabe*.

Yachting

Olympic titles The first sportsman ever to win individual gold medals in four successive Olympic Games was Paul B. Elvström (Denmark) (b. 25 Feb 1928) in the Firefly class in 1948 and the Finn class in 1952, 1956 and 1960. He also won eight other world titles in a total of six classes. The lowest number of penalty points by the winner of any class in an Olympic regatta is three points (five wins, one disqualified and one second in seven starts) by *Superdocious* of the Flying Dutchman class (Lt Rodney Stuart Pattisson, RN (b.

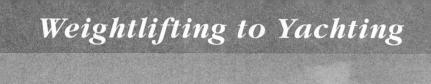

Enza New Zealand, skippered by Peter Blake (New Zealand) and Robin Knox-Johnston (GB), completed the fastest non-stop circumnavigation at Ushant, France on 1 Apr 1994. Inset, the skippers (Blake, left) celebrate their record time of 74 days 22 hours 17 minutes

(Photo: Allsport/Stephen Munday)

GUESS WHAT?

Q What percentage of the Earth is covered by oceans and seas?

A See Page 12

Sports and Games

5 Aug 1943) and Iain Somerled Macdonald-Smith (b. 3 Jul 1945)) at Acapulco Bay, Mexico in October 1968.

British The only British yachtsman to win in two Olympic regattas is Rodney Pattisson in 1968 and again with *Superdoso* crewed by Christopher Davies (b. 29 Jun 1946) at Kiel, Germany in 1972. He gained a silver medal in 1976 with Julian Brooke Houghton (b. 16 Dec 1946).

Admiral's Cup and ocean racing The ocean racing team series which has had the most participating nations (three boats allowed to each nation) is the Admiral's Cup organized by the Royal Ocean Racing Club. A record 19 nations competed in 1975, 1977 and 1979. Britain has a record nine wins.

Modern ocean racing (in moderate or small sailing yachts, rather than professionally manned sailing ships) began with a race from Brooklyn, New York, USA to Bermuda, 630 nautical miles *1166 km* organized by Thomas Fleming Day, editor of the magazine *The Rudder* in June 1906. The race is still held today in every even numbered year, though the course is now Newport, Rhode Island, USA to Bermuda.

The race still regularly run with the earliest foundation, for any type of craft and either kind of water (fresh or salt), is the Chicago to Mackinac race on Lakes Michigan and Huron, first sailed in 1898. It was held again in 1904, then annually until the present day, except for 1917–20. The record for the course (333 nautical miles *616 km*) is 1 day 1 hr 50 min (average speed 12.89 knots *23.84 km/h*) by the sloop *Pied Piper*, owned by Dick Jennings (USA) in 1987.

The current record holder of the elapsed time records for both the premier American and British ocean races (the Newport, Rhode Island, to Bermuda race and the Fastnet race) is the sloop *Nirvana*, owned by Marvin Green (USA). The record for the Bermuda race, 635 nautical miles *1176 km*, is 2 days 14 hr 29 min in 1982 and for the Fastnet race, 605 nautical miles *1120 km*, is 2 days 12 hr 41 min in 1985, an average speed of 10.16 knots *18.81 km/h* and 9.97 knots *18.45 km/h* respectively.

Longest race The world's longest sailing race is the Vendée Globe Challenge, the first of which started from Les Sables d'Olonne, France on 26 Nov 1989. The distance circumnavigated without stopping was 22,500 nautical miles *41,652 km*. The race is for boats between 50 and 60 ft, sailed single-handed. The record time on the course is 109 days 8 hr 48 min 50 sec by Titouan Lamazou (France) (b. 1955) in the sloop *Ecureuil d'Aquitaine* which finished at Les Sables on 19 Mar 1990.

The oldest regular sailing race around the world is the quadrennial Whitbread Round the World race (instituted August 1973) originally organized by the Royal Naval Sailing Association. It starts in England and the course around the world and the number of legs with stops at specified ports is varied from race to race. The distance for 1993–4 was set at 32,000 nautical miles *59,239 km* from

Southampton and return, with stops and re-starts at Punta del Este, Uruguay; Fremantle, Australia; Auckland, New Zealand; Punta del Este, Uruguay and Fort Lauderdale, Florida, USA.

The record time for this race is 120 days 5 hr 9 min by *New Zealand Endeavour*, skippered by Grant Dalton (New Zealand), which finished at Southampton on 3 Jun 1994.

America's Cup The Cup was originally won as an outright prize (with no special name) by the schooner *America* from 14 British yachts at Cowes on 22 Aug 1851. It was offered in 1857 by the winners, John C. Stevens, commodore of the New York Yacht Club and syndicate, as a perpetual challenge trophy 'for friendly competiton between countries'.

> The largest yacht to have competed in the America's Cup was the 1903 defender, the gaff rigged cutter *Reliance*, with an overall length of 43.89 m *144 ft*, a record sail area of 1501 m² *16,160 ft²* and a rig 53.3 m *175 ft* high.

There have been 28 challenges since 8 Aug 1870, with the USA winning on every occasion except 1983. In that year at Newport, Rhode Island *Australia II*, skippered by John Bertrand and owned by a Perth syndicate headed by Alan Bond, beat *Liberty* of the New York Yacht Club 4–3, the narrowest ever series victory. In individual races sailed, American boats have won 81 races and foreign challengers have won just nine. Since 1983, the only race won by a non-American was on 10 May 1992 when, in the first series to be sailed in the specially devised IACC (International America's Cup Class), *Il Moro di Venezia* (Italy), owned by Raul Gardini, crossed the line 3 seconds ahead of *America³*, owned by Bill Koch. This is the closest result ever recorded in a race for the Cup, but not the closest finish. On 4 Oct 1901 *Shamrock II* finished 2 seconds ahead of the American *Columbia*, though the American boat won by 41 seconds on the then handicapping system.

Dennis Walter Conner (USA) (b. 16 Sep 1942) has been helmsman of American boats four times in succession: in 1980, when he successfully defended; in 1983, when he steered the defender, but lost; in 1987 when the American challenger regained the trophy, and in 1988, when he again successfully defended. He was also starting helmsman in 1974 with Ted Hood as skipper. Charlie Barr (USA) (1864–1911) who defended in 1899, 1901 and 1903 and Harold S. Vanderbilt (USA) (1884–1970) in 1930, 1934 and 1937, each steered the successful cup defender three times in succession.

Yacht and dinghy classes The oldest racing class still sailing is the Water Wag class of Dublin, formed in 1887. The design of the boat was changed in 1900 to that which is still used today. The oldest classes in Britain, both established in 1898 and both still racing in the same design of boat are the Seabird Half Rater, centreboard sailing dinghy of Abersoch and other north-west ports, and the Yorkshire One-design keel boat. The latter races from the Royal Yorkshire Yacht Club at Bridlington, Humberside.

The first international class for racing dinghies was the 14-foot International, whose principal trophy in Britain is the Prince of Wales Cup which has been contested annually since 1927

GUESS WHAT?

Q The *Silja Europa* is the world's largest what?

A See Page 108

GUESS WHAT?

Q Where is the world's busiest port?

A See Page 110

(except 1940–45). The most wins is 12 by Stewart Harold Morris between 1932 and 1965.

Highest speeds The highest speed reached under sail on water by any craft over a 500-metre timed run is 46.52 knots *86.21 km/h* by trifoiler *Yellow Pages Endeavour* piloted by Simon McKeon and Tim Daddo, both of Australia, at Sandy Point near Melbourne, Australia on 26 Oct 1993. The women's record is by boardsailer Babethe Coquelle (France) who achieved 40.05 knots *74.22 km/h* at Tarifa, Spain in July 1993.

The record for a boardsail is 45.34 knots *83.95 km/h* by Thierry Bielak (France) at Saintes Maries de-la-Mer canal, Camargue, France on 24 Apr 1993.

British (boardsails) The records are (men) 41.22 knots *76.33 km/h* by Nick Luget and (women) 34.61 knots *64.09 km/h* by Samantha Harrison, both at Saintes Maries de-la-Mer on 22 Mar 1991.

Most competitors The most boats ever to start in a single race was 2072 in the Round Zeeland (Denmark) race on 21 Jun 1984, over a course of 235 nautical miles *435 km*. The greatest number to start in a race in Britain was 1781 keeled yachts and multihulls on 17 Jun 1989 from Cowes in the Annual Round-the-Island Race. The fastest time achieved in this annual event is 3 hr 55 min 28 sec by the trimaran *Paragon*, owned and sailed by Michael Whipp on 31 May 1986.

The largest trans-oceanic race was the ARC (Atlantic Rally for Cruisers), when 204 boats of the 209 starters from 24 nations completed the race from Las Palmas de Gran Canaria (Canary Islands) to Barbados in 1989.

Oldest club The oldest club in the world is the Royal Cork Yacht Club which claims descent from the Cork Harbour Water Club, established in Ireland by 1720.

The oldest active club in Britain is the Starcross Yacht Club at Powderham Point, Devon. Its first regatta was held in 1772. The oldest existing club to have been truly formed as a yacht club is the Royal Yacht Squadron, Cowes, Isle of Wight, instituted as 'The Yacht Club' at a meeting at the Thatched House Tavern, St James's Street, London on 1 Jun 1815.

Boardsailing

World Championships were first held in 1973 and the sport was added to the Olympic Games in 1984 when the winner was Stephan van den Berg (Netherlands) (b. 20 Feb 1962), who also won five world titles 1979–83.

SSSSnake!

The longest 'snake' of boardsails was set by 70 windsurfers in tandem at the 'Sailboard Show '89' event at Narrabeen Lakes, Manly, Australia on 21 Oct 1989.

The world's longest sail board, 50.2 m *165 ft*, was constructed at Fredrikstad, Norway, and first sailed on 28 Jun 1986.

Stop Press

Dear Guinness Book of Records...

Index

Stop Press

Picture overleaf: a group of drillers and scientists celebrating the greatest amount of core to have been recovered during a simple leg of the Ocean Drilling Program.

(Photo: Ocean Drilling Program)

Note—where no page number is indicated the entry concerned is new to the book.

Earth and Space

Meteorites (p. 11) Ann Hodges is no longer the only person to have been hit by a meteorite and survive, as it was reported in May 1994 that the same thing had happened to a boy from Uganda.

Longest-lasting rainbow (p. 23) A rainbow was visible for six hours continuously, from 9 a.m. to 3 p.m., over Sheffield, S Yorks on 14 Mar 1994.

Animal Kingdom

Guide dogs, hearing Donna, a hearing guide dog owned by John Hogan of Pyrmont Point, Australia has completed nine years of active service in Australia to 1994 and eight years of service prior to that in New Zealand. Donna was also the first hearing dog to be licensed under Australian Dog Law in 1985.

'Best-talking bird' (p. 33) Prudle, who won the 'Best-talking parrot-like bird' title at the National Cage and Aviary Bird Show in London for 12 consecutive years (1965–76), died on 13 Jul 1994. She was still talking two days before her death.

Heaviest insect, UK (p. 40) On 2 Jun 1994 10-year-old Ryan Morris and friends James Simpson, Scott Cowan and Ross Cowan found a stag beetle near their homes in Sheppey, Kent which, at 8.9 cm *3.5 in* long was larger than the stag beetle in the British Museum. It was later identified as *Odontolabis delessertii*, a strain of stag beetle that does not naturally occur in Britain—although the Museum knew of no larger specimen.

Tallest Flowering Plants table (p. 44) Bernard Lavery's world record petunia plant now measures 18 ft 6 in *5.6 m* and is still growing.

Fruits and Vegetables table (p. 46) Bill Rogerson of Robersonville, North Carolina, USA, grew a green bean measuring 48 in *121.9 cm* in 1994—a new world record.

Hedge laying (p. 50) Steven Forsyth and Lewis Stephens of Sennybridge, Brecon, hedged by the 'stake and pleach' method a total of 280.7 m *920 ft 11 in* in 11 hr on 23 Apr 1994.

Human Being

Oldest mother (p. 57) It was reported that Rossanna Della Corte (b. February 1931) of Canino, Italy gave birth to a baby boy on 18 Jul 1994, aged 63.

Most premature twins (p. 58) Joanna and Alexander Bagwell were born on 2 Jun 1993 at the John Radcliffe Hospital, Oxford, 114 days premature.

Largest biceps (p. 62) The right bicep of Denis Sester of Bloomington, Minnesota, USA measures 30⅝ in *77.8 cm* cold.

Longest surviving heart transplantee (p. 65) Dirk van Zyl of Cape Town, South Africa (1926–1994) survived 23 yr 57 days having received an unnamed person's heart at the Groote Schuur Hospital, University of Cape Town on 10 May 1971. He died on 6 July.

Right: Peter Bird on his trans-Pacific row.

Haemodialysis patient (p. 66) Brian Wilson (b. 1940) of Edinburgh, Lothian, has suffered from kidney failure since 1964, and began dialysis at the Royal Infirmary of Edinburgh on 30 May 1964. He averages three visits per week to the hospital.

Science and Technology

Quarks (p. 68) The top quark was tentatively identified in April 1994 at Fermilab, Batavia, Illinois, USA.

Lowest friction (p. 71) The lowest coefficient of static and dynamic friction of any solid is 0.03 by Hi-T-Lube, manufactured by General Magnaplate Corporation of Linden, New Jersey, USA. The result was achieved by sliding the material on itself.

Magnetic fields (p. 71) The strongest continuous field strength achieved was a total of 38.7 ± 0.3 teslas at the Francis Bitter National Magnet Laboratory, Massachusetts Institute of Technology, USA on 25 May 1994 by a hybrid magnet with holmium pole pieces. These had the effect of enhancing the central magnetic field of 35.2 ± 0.2 teslas generated by the hybrid magnet.

Largest barometer (p. 72) An oil-filled barometer, of overall height 16.8 m *53.1 ft*, was constructed by Benny Dierckx, Jan Geerts and Marc Gommé of Stedelijk Lyceum Borgerhout in Belgium on 26 Mar 1994. It attained a *standard* height of 13.58 m *44.5 ft* (at which pressure mercury would stand at 0.76 m *2½ ft*). The barometer at Leicester University is still the world's largest permanently-installed barometer.

Fastest chip (p. 73) The world's fastest microprocessor is the DECchip 21064A, developed by Digital Equipment Corporation of Maynard, Massachusetts, USA, and unveiled in October 1993. It can run at speeds of 275 MHz (compared to 66 MHz for a modern personal computer).

Ocean drilling (p. 77) The deepest recorded drilling into the sea bed is 2111 m *6926 ft* by the Ocean Drilling Program's vessel *JOIDES Resolution*, in the eastern equatorial Pacific in 1993. The greatest amount of core recovered during a single leg of the Ocean Drilling Program was 5808 m *19,055 ft* in 1994. The sediment cores, composed of calcareous ooze and chalk, were recovered from the Ceara Rise in the western equatorial Atlantic on ODP Leg 154.

Buildings and Structures

House of cards (p. 89) The greatest number of storeys achieved in building free-standing houses of standard playing cards is 81, to a height of 4.78 m *15 ft 8 in*, built by Bryan Berg of Spirit Lake, Iowa, USA between 20–26 May 1994. No adhesives are allowed in such houses.

Lego tower (p. 91) The world's tallest Lego tower was 21.91 m *70 ft* high and built by The East Asiatic Company (Hong Kong) Limited at Time Square, Causeway Bay, Hong Kong on 4 Apr 1994.

Most durable resident Virginia Hopkins Phillips of Onancock, Virginia, USA resided in the same house from the time of her birth in 1891 until shortly after her 102nd birthday in 1993.

Tallest roller coaster (p. 93) *Pepsi Max—The Big One* at Blackpool Pleasure Beach, Lancs, officially opened on 27 May 1994. It can reach speeds of 82 mph *132 km/h*. The highest point, which is over an artificial lake, rises 222 ft *67.6 m* from the surface of the water to the top of the car rail.

Restaurateurs (p. 93) By 31 Dec 1993 McDonald's licensed and owned 13,993 restaurants in 70 countries. Worldwide sales in 1993 were $23.6 billion.

Tunnels, rail (p. 98) The Channel Tunnel was officially opened by HM the Queen and President François Mitterrand of France on 6 May 1994.

Snow and ice constructions (p. 103) A snow palace with a volume of 103,591.8 m³ *3,658,310.2 ft³* and 30.29 m *99 ft 5 in* in height was unveiled on 8 Feb 1994 at Asahikawa, Hokkaido, Japan. It was made to resemble Suwon castle in South Korea.

The world's largest ice construction was the ice palace completed in January 1992, using 18,000 blocks of ice, at St Paul, Minnesota, USA during the Winter Carnival. Built by TMK Construction Specialties Inc., it was 50.8 m *166 ft 8 in* high and contained 4900 tonnes *10.8 million lb* of ice.

Transport

Smallest submarine William G. Smith of Bognor Regis, West Sussex, constructed a fully-functional submarine only 2.95 m *9 ft 8 in* long, 1.15 m *3 ft 9 in* wide and 1.42 m *4 ft 8 in* high. It can reach depths of around 100 ft *30.5 m* and can remain underwater for at least four hours using 3 hp air cylinders (or more with the use of two additional external cyls). The submarine is now on show at the Aviation Museum in Shoreham, and will eventually be used for locating aircraft wreckage off the Sussex coast.

Longest solo ocean row Peter Bird spent a record 304 days 14 hours non-stop rowing at sea during his trans-Pacific voyage, which began on 12 May 1993 and was prematurely terminated on 12 Mar 1994.

Transatlantic rowing and sailing records table (p. 112) The vessel *Primagaz*, an 18.3 m *60 ft* trimaran, set two new records in 1994, one

Right: we received two claimants for the world's smallest saxophone within three weeks in May/June 1994. The one on the left is the smallest, at 9.8 cm *3.85 in*. It is a miniature alto saxophone designed and created by Paul Gentile of Scarborough, Ontario, Canada. The keys are functional and the mouthpiece actually emits a sound.

On the right is a miniature tenor saxophone, 10 cm *3.9 in* long, made by Erick Paquette of Montréal, Québec, Canada. Once again, it is handmade and playable.

Both instruments took over a year to make.

for the fastest transatlantic sail E–W non-solo and the other for a record transatlantic sail W–E. The record transatlantic sail E–W non-solo, at 9 days 8 hr 58 min 20 sec (12.49 knots), started at Plymouth, Devon (2-star event) on 5 Jun 1994 and finished at Newport, Rhode Island on 14 Jun 1994. It was crewed by Laurent Bourgnon (France) & Cam Lewis (USA). *Primagaz's* transatlantic sail W–E started at Ambrose Light Tower, New York, USA on 27 Jun 1994 and finished at Lizard Point, Cornwall on 4 Jul 1994, and lasted 7 days 2 hr 34 min 42 sec (17.14 knots). The skipper was also Laurent Bourgnon.

Road cars (p. 117) The highest road-tested acceleration reported (0–60 mph) for a street legal car is 3.07 sec for a Ford RS200 Evolution, driven by Graham Hathaway at the Boreham Proving Ground, Essex on 25 May 1994.

Highest mileage (p. 117) Albert Klein's 'Beetle' has clocked up 1,531,125 miles *2,464,107 km* as of 7 Jul 1994.

Largest bus fleet (p. 119) The bus fleet of São Paulo, Brazil has 10,895 single-decker buses.

Model railway (p. 124) The greatest distance covered by a model steam locomotive in 24 hours is 269.9 km *167.7 miles* by the 18.4 cm 7¼ in gauge 'Peggy', with ten drivers working in shifts, at Weston Park Railway, Weston Park, Shrops on 17–18 Jun 1994.

Air-launched records (p. 128) Under the FAI regulations for aerospacecraft, *Columbia* is holder of the current absolute world record for duration — 14 days 17 hr 55 min to main gear touchdown. It was launched on its 17th mission, STS 65, with a crew of seven (six men and one woman) on 8 Jul 1994.

Paper aircraft, duration (p. 132) The level flight duration record for a hand-launched paper aircraft is 18.80 sec by Ken Blackburn in a hangar at JFK airport, New York, USA on 17 Feb 1994.

Paper aircraft, largest (p. 132) The largest flying paper aeroplane, with a wing span of 12.34 m *40 ft 6 in*, was constructed by a team of engineers from BP Chemicals Ltd and flown at Filton, Avon on 24 Jun 1994. It was launched indoors and was flown for a distance of 23.57 m *77 ft 4 in*.

Parachuting, oldest tandem (p. 132) Edward Royds-Jones made a tandem parachute jump at the age of 95 years 170 days at Dunkeswell, Devon on 2 Jul 1994.

Arts and Entertainment

Carpets, highest price (p. 135) On 9 Jun 1994 a Louis XV Savonnerie carpet 18 ft × 19 ft *5.4 m × 5.8 m*, probably made for Louis XV's Chateau de la Mouette in the 1740s, fetched a record £1,321,000 at Christie's, London. The buyer was M Djanhanguir Riahi, a Paris-based Iranian owner of a notable collection of 18th century French art.

Guitar marathon On 7 May 1994 a gathering of 1322 guitarists played *Taking Care of Business* in unison for 68 min 40 sec, in an event organized by Music West of Vancouver, Canada.

Rock concert attendance (p. 149) An estimated 195,000 people attended A-ha's show at the Rock In Rio festival, at the Maracaña Stadium in Brazil in April 1990.

Oldest opera singer (p. 149) The tenor Hugues Cuénod (b. 26 Jun 1902) sang the part of Emperor Altoum in *Turandot* at the Metropolitan Opera House, New York, USA on 10 Mar 1988 at the age of 85.

Dancing dragon (p. 153) The longest dancing dragon measured 1559 m *5114 ft 10 in* from the end of its nose to the tip of its tail. A total of 2180 people brought the dragon to life on 17 Apr 1994, making it dance for 30 min on a newly-opened bridge which links Macau on the southern coast of China with the island of Taipa.

Largest and longest dances (p. 153) Rosie Radiator led an ensemble of 12 tap dancers through the streets of San Francisco, California, USA in a choreographed routine, covering a distance of 15.47 km *9.61 miles* on 11 Jul 1994.

Business World

Jumble sale (p. 162) The greatest amount of money raised at a one-day sale is $214,085.99 at the 62nd one-day rummage sale organized by the Winnetka Congregational Church, Illinois, USA on 12 May 1994.

Highest salary (p. 166) Fund manager George Soros earned at least $1.1 billion in 1993, according to *Financial World's* list of the highest-paid individuals on Wall Street.

Greatest return of cash (p. 168) In May 1994 Howard Jenkins of Tampa, Florida, USA, a 31-year-old roofing company employee, discovered that $88 million had been transferred mistakenly into his bank account. Although he initially succumbed to temptation and withdrew $4 million, his conscience got the better of him shortly afterwards and he returned the $88 million in full.

Cattle birthweights, lightest (p. 172) The lowest live birthweight accurately recorded for a calf is 4.1 kg *9 lb* for a Holstein heifer called Christmas born on 25 Dec 1993 on the farm of Mark and Wendy Theuringer in Hutchinson, Minnesota, USA. The calf died of scours at five weeks.

Most prolific sheep (p. 174) On 4 Sep 1991 a Finnish Landrace ewe owned by the D.M.C. Partnership (comprising Trevor and Diane Cooke, Stephen and Mary Moss and Ken and Carole Mihaere) of Fielding, Manawatu, New Zealand, gave birth to eight healthy lambs. On 19 Apr 1994 the record was equalled by 6-year-old Ewe 835 Ylva, owned by Birgitta and Kent Mossby of Halsarp Farm, Falköping, Sweden.

Shearing, UK (p. 174) The solo record is 654 sheep by Wyn Jones of Welshpool, Powys on 9 Jul 1994 at Canon Farm, near Carno, Powys.

Human World

Longest term of office (p. 184) Marshal Kim Il Sung died on 8 Jul 1994.

Youngest undergraduate and graduate (p. 199) Michael Kearney became the youngest graduate in June 1994, at the age of 10 years 4 months, when he obtained his BA in anthropology from the University of South Alabama.

10-year-old Michael Kearney, looking suitably attired on graduation day.

(Photo: Daniel Vaughn/Rosa Vaughn Photography)

Stop Press

Human Achievements

Most marriages (p. 205) Glynn 'Scotty' Wolfe married for the 28th time on 27 Jun 1994.

Bubble-gum blowing (p. 207) The greatest reported diameter for a bubble-gum bubble is 58.4cm *23in*, by Susan Montgomery Williams of Fresno, California, USA at the ABC-TV studios in New York City, USA on 19 Jul 1994.

Beer keg lifting (p. 208) George Olesen raised a keg of beer weighing 62.9kg *138lb 11oz* above his head 737 times in the space of six hours at Horsens, Denmark on 1 May 1994.

Ladder climbing (p. 209) A team of ten firefighters from Frome Fire Station climbed a vertical height of 54.31km *33.75 miles* up a standard fire-service ladder in 24hours at Frome, Somerset on 24–25 Jun 1994.

Spitting (p. 210) David O'Dell of Apple Valley, California, USA spat a tobacco wad 15.07m *49ft 5½in* at the 19th World Tobacco Spitting Championships held at Calico Ghost Town, California on 26 Mar 1994.

Hop-scotch (p. 211) The greatest number of games of hop-scotch successfully completed in 24hr is 312, by Ian McKewan of Whiston, S Yorks on 25–26 Feb 1994.

Basketball spinning (p. 212) Bruce Crevier span 18 basketballs at the ABC-TV studios in New York City, USA on 18 Jul 1994.

Cocktail (p. 213) The largest cocktail on record was a Finlandia Sea Breeze of 11,102.6 litres *2442.2gal* made at Maui Entertainment Center in Philadelphia, Pennsylvania, USA on 5 Aug 1994. It consisted of Finlandia vodka, cranberry juice, grapefruit juice and ice.

Kebab (p. 213) The longest kebab ever was one 880.6m *2889ft 3in* long, made by the West Yorkshire Family Service Units, Trade Association of Asian Restaurant Owners and National Power at Bradford, W Yorks on 19 Jun 1994.

Milk shake (p. 214) The largest milk shake was a chocolate one of 7400.4 litres *1627.9gal*, made by the Nelspruit and District Child Welfare Society and the Fundraising Five at Nelspruit, South Africa on 5 Mar 1994.

Catherine wheel (p.216) A wheel 19.3 m *63 ft 6 in* wide was built by Essex Pyrotechnics Ltd in July 1994.

Can pyramid (p. 217) Five adults and five children from Dunhurst School in Petersfield, Hants, built a record-breaking pyramid of 4900 cans in 25 min 54 sec (time limit—30 min) on 13 May 1994.

Parking meter collection Lotta Sjölin of Solna, Sweden, has a collection of 269 different parking meters as of May 1994.

Sports and Games

Athletics (p. 224) World records: 100m 9.85 sec Leroy Burrell (USA) (b. 21 Feb 1967) at Lausanne, Switzerland on 6 Jul 1994.

3000 m 7 min 25.11 sec Noureddine Morceli (Algeria) at Monte Carlo, Monaco on 2 Aug 1994.

10,000m 26 min 52.23 sec William Sigei (Kenya) (b. 14 Oct 1969) at Oslo, Norway on 22 Jul 1994.

Pole vault 6.14 m *20 ft 1¾ in* Sergey Bubka (Ukraine) at Sestriere, Italy (high altitude) on 31 Jul 1994.

(p. 225) Women's world record: 2000m 5 min 25.36 sec Sonia O'Sullivan (Ireland) (b. 28 Nov 1969) at Edinburgh, Lothian on 8 Jul 1994.

Leroy Burrell, the fastest man over 100 metres. (Photo: Allsport)

(p. 227) British men's record: 200m 19.87 sec John Regis at Sestriere, Italy (high altitude) on 31 Jul 1994.

(p. 228) British women's record: 2000m 5 min 26.93 sec Yvonne Murray at Edinburgh on 8 Jul 1994.

Board Games, Scrabble (p. 236) The winners of both the 1993 World and British National Championships were the youngest ever. Mark Nyman (GB) (b. 14 Oct 1966) won the world title aged 26yr 320days and Allan Saldanha (b. 31 Oct 1977) the British, aged 15yr 239days.

Cricket (p. 245) Alec Stewart took a record seven catches for Surrey in the NatWest Trophy match *v.* Glamorgan at Swansea on 27 Jul 1994.

(p. 246) Alex Kelly took 10–0 from 27 balls for Bishop Auckland *v.* Newton Aycliffe in the Milburngate Durham County Junior League at Bishop Auckland, Durham in June 1994.

Cycling (p. 248) Miguel Induráin (Spain) won the Tour de France for a fourth successive time in 1994, equalling the achievements of Jacques Anquetil and Eddie Merckx.

Darts (p. 249) A team at the George Inn, Morden, Surrey scored 526,750 using just bulls and 25s in 24hours on 1–2 Jul 1994.

Equestrian sports (p. 250) At the 1994 World Equestrian Games at the Hague, Netherlands, Germany won the dressage team title for a seventh time. Great Britain won the three-day event team title for a fourth time, having previously won in 1970, 1982 and 1986.

Football (p. 253) Pat Bonner played in four matches during the 1994 World Cup bringing his total appearances for the Republic of Ireland to 77.

(p. 254) The highest fee between two British clubs is £5million paid by Blackburn Rovers to Norwich City for Chris Sutton (b. 10 Mar 1973) on 15 Jul 1994.

Gambling, football pools (p. 256) The Remington family from Wigston, Leics won a record £2,281,399.10, paid by Littlewoods Pools, for matches played on 23 Jul 1994.

Golf (p. 259) The Curtis Cup was drawn for a third time, in 1994. Carole Semple Thompson (USA) won a further three matches during the contest to take her total of matches won to 15.

Judo (p. 270) Brian Woodward and David Norman completed 33,681 judo throwing techniques in a ten-hour period at the Whybridge Parent's Association Children Club, Rainham, Essex on 10 Apr 1994.

Lacrosse (p. 270) The USA won a sixth men's world title beating Australia 21–7 at Bury, Greater Manchester on 31 Jul 1994. Scotland scored a record 34 goals against Germany (3) on 25 Jul 1994.

Motorcycle racing (p. 273) Rolf Biland (Switzerland) won his 73rd side-car Grand Prix at Donington Park on 23 Jul 1994.

Motor racing (p. 274) Ferrari equalled the record race wins of McLaren, 104, when Gerhard Berger won the German Grand Prix on 31 Jul 1994.

Drag racing (p. 275) For a piston-engined car, the lowest elapsed time is 6.988 sec and highest terminal velocity is 197.15mph *317.28km/h* by Warren Johnson (USA) at Englishtown, New Jersey on 21 May 1994 and Commerce, Georgia on 22 Apr 1994, respectively. The lowest elapsed time for a motorcycle is 7.542 sec by David Schultz (USA) at Englishtown on 20 May 1994.

Throwing (p. 280) David Engvall threw a weight with a piece of string attached a distance of 385.80m *1265ft 9in* at El Mirage, California, USA on 17 Oct 1993.

Rugby union (p. 285) John Kirwan played his 62nd international for New Zealand on 23 Jul 1994 against South Africa.

Skittles (p. 290) The highest hood skittle score in 24hours is 144,648 pins by 12 players from the Semilong Working Men's Club, Northampton on 13–14 Jun 1992.

Swimming (p. 294) British records (men) 100m backstroke 55.73 sec Martin Harris; (women) 200 m breaststroke 2 min 30.63 sec Marie Hardiman, both at Crystal Palace, Greater London on 31 Jul 1994.

Tennis (p. 298) Jean Borotra died on 17 Jul 1994. He played in every one of the twice yearly contests between the International Club of France and the I.C. of Great Britain from the first in 1929 until October 1993, a total of 116 consecutive matches. He missed his first match, through ill health, at the beginning of 1994.

Tug of war (p. 300) The record distance for a tug of war contest is 3623m *3962yd*, between Freedom Square and Independence Square at Lodz, Poland on 28 May 1994.

Water skiing (p. 301) Philippa Roberts won an 11th British Overall title in July 1994.

Weightlifting (p. 302) World records (men): 99kg class; Snatch 191kg *421lb*, Jerk 227.5kg *501½lb*, Total 417.5kg *920¼lb* by Sergey Syrtsov (Russia) at St Petersburg, Russia on 23 Jul 1994.

108kg class; Snatch 201kg *443lb* by Andrey Chemerkin (Russia) at St Petersburg on 23 Jul 1994.

(p. 304) Chris Lawton bench pressed 535,835kg *1,181,312lb* in 12hours at the Waterside Wine Bar, Solihull, W Mids on 3 Jun 1994.

World Cup *1994*

Brazil won their record fourth title in 1994, capping what had been a superlative event in all aspects.

The tournament itself was watched by more people than ever before. The aggregate **attendance** for the 52 matches was a record 3,567,415, an average of 68,604 per game. It was also the second-highest scoring competition with 141 goals, just five short of the record of 146 in 1982. On the negative side, the tournament had the highest number of **cautions** ever with 227, an average of over four a game, and there were also 15 sendings-off, the record being 16 in 1990.

Brazil won the Cup for the first time ever by way of a penalty shoot-out after the final had finished scoreless. They added to all of their **overall records**, increasing their **total goals** in finals tournaments to 159 and **wins** to 49.

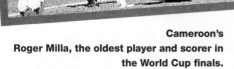

Cameroon's Roger Milla, the oldest player and scorer in the World Cup finals.

During the competition Brazil conceded only three goals in seven games, **the best defensive record of any winning side**, beating England's achievements of 1966 with three goals in six games.

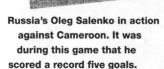

Russia's Oleg Salenko in action against Cameroon. It was during this game that he scored a record five goals.

Of other teams, Mexico added another **defeat** to their record total which now stands at 18 and Germany battled to a record 16th **draw**. The longest running **winless streak** was eventually ended but not before Bulgaria had managed to lose their 17th World Cup finals match against Nigeria. However, in the next match against Greece they won 4–0 and followed this by getting to the semi-finals, beating former champions Argentina and Germany along the way. The batôn that Bulgaria had held for so long now passes to South Korea who extended their winless run to 11 games. The three débutante nations at the 1994 Finals, Greece, Nigeria and Saudi Arabia, all lost at least one game, therefore, maintaining the fact that no qualifiers for the finals are **undefeated**.

Brazilian captain Dunga celebrates his team's success as the world's number one footballing nation after their penalty shoot-out victory over Italy.

Lothar Matthäus

It was also a successful competition for the individual. Both Diego Armando Maradona (Argentina) (b. 30 Oct 1960) and Lothar Matthäus (Germany) (b. 21 Mar 1961) equalled the record of Uwe Seeler and Wladislaw Zmuda by playing their **21st finals match**. They had both made their first appearances during the 1982 tournament. Both were denied the overall record, however, by differing circumstances. Matthäus when Germany was beaten by Bulgaria in the quarter-finals and Maradona having been banned from the tournament for failing a drugs test. On a happier note, the tournament had the **oldest ever player** in a finals competition, Albert Roger Milla (b. 20 May 1952), who came on as a substitute in Cameroon's final group match against Russia on 28 June, aged 42 yr 39 days. He also became the **oldest ever scorer**, with his team's only goal in their 6–1 defeat. It was during this game that Oleg Salenko scored a record **five goals in a single game**. The Brazilian forward Romario de Souza Faria (b. 29 Jan 1966) was voted the FIFA/Adidas Golden Ball Award as the top player at the World Cup.

(Photos: Allsport USA)

Dear Guinness Book of Records.

Photo: Richard Bloomfield/Flinstone Photography

In 1993 our correspondence editor, Amanda Brooks (above), dealt with around 10,000 claims from potential Guinness record-holders. That's more than twice the number that passed through our office three years ago. But while our postbag expands ceaselessly, one cruel factor remains the same: we simply do not have the space in *The Guinness Book of Records* to mention all the extraordinary talents, stupendous stunts, and fascinating feats about which we are informed. The result is that we have to disappoint thousands of correspondents each year.

For this edition, by way of a tribute to those whose achievements dwell silently in the cavernous drawers of our filing cabinets, we are putting the spotlight on a handful of would-bes, whose charms we could not resist for another year.

Dear ma'am or sir,
My name is Ethan Whittet and I am eleven years old.
In October of 1992 I stretched three pieces of Bubble Yum gum 31 feet and three inches. Please let me know if this is a world record, or if you need more information.
You can write to me

Thank you,
Ethan Whittet

TOP 5 FIVE

Five steps to follow when making a record attempt.

1. Choose to beat a record that is in the current edition.

2. If the record you want to try is not in the book, your chances of it being introduced are slim. You might improve those chances by ensuring that your record activity is a measurable one, with plenty of popular appeal. We also prefer those records that can provide a basis for future attempts.

3. Check with us around *two months* before you proceed. The record you have in mind could easily have changed since publication. Even if your record is not published, we may still be able to give you a target to beat.

4. Follow the general or specific guidelines that we can provide for your record attempt.

5. Produce documentation at all stages. It is not possible to send out invigilators, so we need all the proof you can gather.

Below: the 18-ft 5.5-m monument in memory of a rooster called Come On, owned by Guy Valentini of Ontario, Canada. The Valentinis introduced Come On to their household under the erroneous assumption that the little chick would grow up to provide eggs for the family. Imagine their surprise when it grew red wattles and a comb instead! During his lifetime Come On became somewhat of a local celebrity and his death in 1993 was much mourned.

Right: self-proclaimed 'Lava Man' Matthias Wendt of Paris, France is surely the first to hold and sculpt molten rock in his hands for 38 seconds. He always ensures conditions are as favourable as possible before producing what he describes as 'probably the most dramatic art form there is'.

Dear Sir,
My Mummy can give me 130 kisses in 30 secs. Is this a record?
Love from
Edward ✶ (age 6)

Dominique McGarry of Worcester Park, Surrey, displaying the 14 healthy baby hamsters born to her pet Nibbles in January 1994. Unfortunately Nibbles' valiant efforts were not destined to beat the world or the UK record, although it was the largest claim we had received for some time.

These tiny cowboy boots, around 3 in *7.6 cm* high, were constructed by retired bootmaker Gus Mavrakis of Billings, Montana, USA.

Indian Shri Rajendra K. Tiwari, also known as Dukanji of Allahabad, presents a striking pose while demonstrating moustache dancing—a technique he dreamt up and developed himself. The plastic tubes emphasise the movement of the facial muscles.

Raymond Saker of Miami, Florida, USA whose stack of video-tapes towered for 11 ft *3.3 m*, as high as the ceiling would allow.

This 17-ft *5.2-m* tea cosy was knitted by the Rainbows, Brownies, Guides and Rangers of Staffordshire, some 11,000 youngsters in all, in 1991. It was used to raise money for the Building Blocks Appeal in Stoke-on-Trent, and was then dismantled to re-form blankets which were sent to charities in Romania.

Dear Guinness Book:
    My name is Robert Lemke-Oliver. I am six years old and am in the first grade. At school yesterday I burped 844 times in a row while my friends watched and counted. I would like to get in the Guinness Book of Records. I read in the September 1993 issue of 3-2-1 Contact that I can write to you to get information on setting a record.

Sincerely,

Robert Lemke Oliver

Cecep, a 42-year-old cloth vendor from West Java, Indonesia, lived and slept with scorpions for an astonishing 15 days from 24 Dec 1993 to 7 Jan 1994. There were around 4000 altogether.

Index

Index

Index

Acknowledgments

The Editor of *The Guinness Book of Records* wishes to thank: Amanda Brooks, Debbie Collings, Ann Collins, Sallie Collins, Nicholas Heath-Brown, Christine Heilman, Muriel Ling, Sarah Llewellyn-Jones, Michelle D. McCarthy, Maria Morgan, Stewart Newport, Alex Reid, David Roberts, Sarah Silvé, Amanda Ward.

PICTURE RESEARCH James Clift, Alex Goldberg
PHOTOGRAPHIC AND DUPING SERVICES Avart Design Consultants
ARTWORK, MAPS AND DIAGRAMS Ad Vantage Studios, Frances Button, Pat Gibbon, Peter Harper, Sarah Silvé
COVER DESIGN David Roberts/Ad Vantage Studios
COVER PICTURES Allsport, Alton Telegraph, BMG Records, Bruce Coleman, Mary Evans, Matthew Hillier, Telegraph Colour Library
PRESS AND PUBLIC RELATIONS Cathy Brooks

CONTRIBUTORS Andrew Adams, John Arblaster, Brian Bailey, Howard Bass, Robert G. Bednarik, Michael Benton, Dennis Bird, Gerald Blake, Richard Braddish, Peter Brierley, Robert Brooke, Ian Buchanan, Bob Burton, Henry Button, Clive Carpenter, Roger Cass, Chris Cavey, Andy Chipling, Graham Coombs, Brian W Davies, Alan Dawson, Ciaran Deane, Andrew Duncan, Graham Dymott, Colin Dyson, Keith Escott, Clive Everton, Gordon Farr, David Feldman, John Flynn, Brian Ford, Paulette Foyle, Peter Francis, Andrew Frankel, Bill Frindall, Tim Furniss, Steven Goldberg, Ian Goold, Stan Greenberg, Bill Gunston, Mark Ham, Liz Hawley, Robert Headland, Ron Hildebrant, David Hofmann, Rick Hogben, Jeff Howell, Cecil Humphery-Smith, Sir Peter Johnson, Ove Karlsson, Richard Kidd, Bernard Lavery, Peter Lunn, Tessa McWhirter, John Marshall, Charles Melville, Carol Michaelson, Andy Milroy, Michael Minges, Alan Mitchell, Ray Mitchell, David Mondey, John Moody, Patrick Moore, Bill Morris, Ron Moulton, Barry Norman, Guy Oliver, Enzo Paci, Greg Parkinson, Geoff Pearse, Janice Potten, John Randall, Elfan ap Rees, Chris Rhys, Patrick Robertson, Dan Roddick, Adrian Room, Peter Rowan, Joshua Rozenberg, Steven Salberg, Irvin Saxton, Victoria Schilling, Christopher Shores, Colin Smith, Ian Smith, Graham Snowdon, Edwin C. Stern, Martin Stone, Juhani Virola, Tony Waltham, Ray Waterman, David Wells, Rick Wilson, Jackie Woollam, Mark Young.

Grateful acknowledgment is also made to the governing bodies and organizations who have helped in our researches.

Are you eligible to join the Guinness Gold Club?

All you need is 30 or more editions of the Guinness Book of Records (UK editions). We are particularly interested in all those individuals with a complete set of all 41 editions.

Already Guinness has accepted 167 collectors into the Gold Club, not only from the UK but also enthusiasts from Austria, Australia, Germany, New Zealand and South Africa.

When you join this truly superlative club you will receive a regular newsletter, opportunities to contact and meet fellow club members, a chance to swop your spare books and your own personal Gold Club membership credit card.

GUINNESS BOOK OF RECORDS
GOLD CLUB MEMBER
Membership Number HON. MEMBER
Name **NORRIS McWHIRTER**

If you think you qualify for membership please contact Cathy Brooks, Press & PR Manager, Guinness Publishing, 33 London Road, Enfield, Middx, EN2 6DJ. Don't forget to include a photograph clearly showing each of your copies of the Guinness Book of Records. Please also provide us with a complete written list.

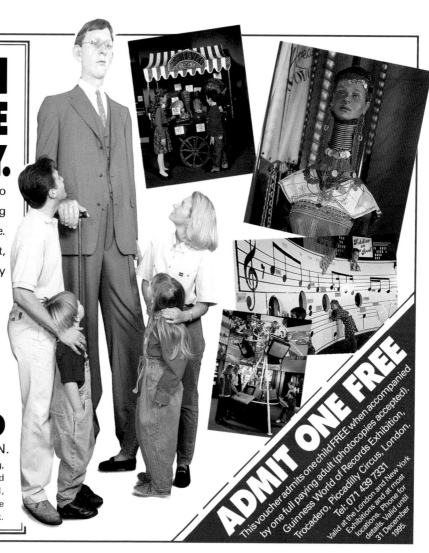

EVERYTHING U

GUINNESS PUBLISHING